CONTENTS

THE NATIONWIDE FOOTBALL ANNUAL 2016–2017

Published by SportsBooks Limited, 9 St Aubyns Place, York, YO24 1EQ
First published in 1887

www.sportsbooks.ltd.uk

A CIP catalogue record for this book is available from the British Library.

Editorial compilation by Stuart Barnes

ISBN-13 9781907524523

Front cover photograph shows Jamie Vardy kissing a trophy he could hardly have expected to win when the season started. Back cover: Sir Bobby Charlton presents Wayne Rooney with a gold boot after Rooney topped his England scoring record.

Printed and bound in the UK by CPI Group (UK) Ltd, Croydon CR0 4YY

COMMENT

By Stuart Barnes

ENGLISH FOOTBALL has never seen a season quite like it; in the corridors of power, the tremors have reverberated around the world; on the European stage, the summer brought the most unlikely of heroes. In years to come, the events of 2015-16 will be treasured by many and treated with bitterness by others. Leicester City began the campaign with a single goal – to avoid another scramble for Premier League safety. They ended it as champions against all the odds under a manager who bought pizzas for his players and recited silly ditties in between transforming a modest looking team into a formidable force. All the big clubs were left in their wake and the upshot was unprecedented managerial change for four of them – Manchester United, Manchester City, Chelsea and Liverpool. It meant that the prospect of Jose Mourinho and Pep Guardiola in direct opposition a few miles across the city, Antonio Conte taking over the reins at Chelsea and Jurgen Klopp trying to revive Liverpool's fortunes is a mouth-watering one for the months ahead. Not to mention Tottenham's bid to cement a place among the elite and Arsene Wenger's latest attempt to put Arsenal back on top.

Further down the ladder there were some exceptional performances. Winning promotion once from the ultra-competitive Championship is tough enough. Repeating that success at the first attempt after being relegated represented a huge achievement for Burnley under Sean Dyche and Hull with Steve Bruce still at the helm. Who would have expected Burton to win a place in the Championship, particularly after having to change managers midway through? There was no bigger transformation in fortunes than that of Barnsley, who went from relegation candidates to League One promotion winners – with a Johnstone's Paint Trophy success at Wembley for good measure – after also losing their manager. Then there was Northampton, who against a background of financial turmoil and the threat of going out of existence, won the League Two title by 13 points.

While all this was unfolding, alleged corruption exposed at FIFA was taking its toll of senior figures at the world governing body, none more so than president Sepp Blatter. The head of UEFA, Michel Platini, was also thrown out for abusing his position. Greg Dyke, outgoing chairman of the FA, called it 'a new day, a new dawn.' For Platini, it was an end to his ambitions to succeed Blatter, along with the humiliation of being absent from the finals of Euro 2016, where the expansion from 16 to 24 teams, had been his brainchild. For Roy Hodgson, it was also the end of the line, after the defeat by Iceland in the first knock-out round – an embarrassment accentuated by the performance of Wales in reaching the semi-finals with the sort of organised, progressive football so lacking by England. Wayne Rooney had taken his side to France on the back of a 100 per cent record in qualifying – and with the captain having overtaken Sir Bobby Charlton as his country's leading scorer. But another failure at a major tournament meant another search for a manager capable of putting some pride back into the national team. Sam Allardyce, Glenn Hoddle, Eddie Howe and Jurgen Klinsmann were some of the names being put forward as we went to press. Whoever takes the job will be expected to ensure a comfortable passage through World Cup qualifying – then to ensure he knows his best side before the finals start, unlike Hodgson who dithered over selection and formation, with predictable results. The saddest thing about our latest failing is that it no longer came as a surprise. England's early elimination has become as predictable as the vast numbers of foreign signings made by clubs during this summer transfer window.

No reflection on 2015–16, would be complete without highlighting the biggest achievement of all. The 27-year campaign by families of the 96 victims of the Hillsborough disaster was finally vindicated when an inquest jury found that the fans were unlawfully killed. The behaviour of Liverpool supporters was exonerated and the jury ruled they did not contribute to what happened at the Leppings Lane of Sheffield Wednesday's ground on that fateful day of April 15, 1989.

WONDER OF WALES – ENGLAND ON ICE

By no stretch of the imagination could Euro 2016 be regarded as a stellar tournament. There were too many teams, too many matches and not enough quality. England will certainly want to forget all about it after a performance in keeping with those delivered by so many of their predecessors over the years. The harsh reality is that we have now become a postscript at major tournaments, the optimism generated in qualifying overtaken by confused, clueless displays when the serious business gets under way. Normally, England's failings are shown up by foreign teams of superior skills and organisation. This time, they were judged, even more harshly, against one of the other home nations. What Wales achieved under Chris Coleman was an embarrassment for Roy Hodgson and his side packed with players from the upper reaches of the Premier League.

When Gareth Bale cheekily suggested that no England player would make it into his own team, it was clearly aimed at sowing a seed of doubt in the minds of their opponent before the group meeting in Lens. It didn't work, with substitutes Jamie Vardy and Daniel Sturridge overturning Bale's first-half free-kick. Yet the longer the tournament went on, the greater the feeling there might have been some substance in what he said. Wales scored a comprehensive victory over Russia to top the group, beat Northern Ireland, albeit with a fortuitous own goal by Gareth McAuley, then reached the semi-finals by overcoming Belgium in a manner which removed any doubts about their qualities. Coleman described the defeat by Portugal as 'a match too far.' Yet although the eventual champions went through deservedly on the back of Cristiano Ronaldo's match-winning display, there was a lingering feeling that it could have been so different had Aaron Ramsey not been suspended. The Arsenal midfielder had proved an influential figure and his link-up play was sorely missed. Some consolation came with a place in UEFA's team of the tournament. The impressive Joe Allen joined him, although surprisingly there was no place for Bale. Wales flew home to a massive reception in Cardiff, while England's return was barely noticed. Not surprising, really, after the way they were knocked out, a goalless draw with Slovakia in the final group game followed by a 2-1 defeat by Iceland after Wayne Rooney's penalty gave them the perfect start. The mind went back to a goalless draw against Algeria in the second group game of the 2010 World Cup in South Africa. That was described in some quarters as England's worst showing of modern times. This was something else and Hodgson admitted he and his players had work to do repairing their reputations – the manager in whatever he decides to do next after stepping down from the job minutes afterwards.

Northern Ireland let no-one down, Michael O'Neill claiming with some justification that they were unlucky to lose to Wales. They went through to the last 16 by beating Ukraine, a match sandwiched between single goal defeats against Poland and Germany. Martin O'Neill also had a case to put on behalf of the Republic of Ireland, who had three fewer days rest than France before their first knockout round match. Robbie Brady, whose late winner against Italy sent them through, converted a second-minute penalty, but his side fell to two goals by Antoine Griezmann, who went on to win the tournament's golden boot. A seventh goal, and probably a championship medal, beckoned in the final. But he miscued the header and it was Portugal defeating the hosts with a goal from substitute Eder, whose own Welsh connection had proved rather less successful – 15 appearances for Swansea and not a goal to show for them. After hobbling off with a knee injury midway through the first-half, Ronaldo lifted the trophy for a team who would not have won any awards for enterprising football, but who went into the tournament with a strategy of containment and countering and stuck to it throughout – **STUART BARNES**

● UEFA's team of the tournament (4-2-3-1): Rui Patricio (Portugal), Kimmich (Germany), Boateng (Germany), Pepe (Portugal), Raphael Guerreiro (Portugal), Kroos (Germany), Allen (Wales), Griezmann (France), Ramsey (Wales), Payet (France), Ronaldo (Portugal)

EUROPEAN CHAMPIONSHIP FINALS – FRANCE 2016

GROUP A

FRANCE 2 ROMANIA 1
Stade de France (75,113); Friday, June 10

France (4-3-3): Lloris, Sagna, Rami, Koscielny, Evra, Pogba (Martial 77), Kante, Matuidi, Griezmann (Coman 66), Giroud, Payet (Sissoko 90). **Scorers**: Giroud (57), Payet (89). **Booked**: Giroud

Romania (4-2-3-1): Tatarusanu, Sapunaru, Chiriches, Grigore, Rat, Hoban, Pintilii, Stanciu (Chipciu 72), Popa, Stancu, Andone (Alibec 61). **Scorer**: Stancu (65 pen). **Booked**: Chiriches, Rat, Popa

Referee: V Kassai (Hungary). **Half-time**: 0-0

ALBANIA 0 SWITZERLAND 1
Lens (33,805); Saturday, June 11

Albania (4-3-3): Berisha, Hysaj, Cana, Mavraj, Agolli, Abrashi, Kukeli, T Xhaka (Kace 61), Roshi (Cikalleshi 73), Sadiku (Gashi 81), Lenjani. **Booked**: Cana, Kace, Kukeli, Mavraj. **Sent off**: Cana (36)

Switzerland (4-2-3-1): Sommer, Lichtsteiner, Schar, Djourou, Rodriguez, Behrami, G Xhaka, Shaqiri (Fernandes 87), Dzemaili (Frei 75), Mehmedi (Embolo 61), Seferovic. **Scorer**: Schar (5). **Booked**: Schar, Behrami

Referee: C Velasco Carballo (Spain). **Half-time**: 0-1

ROMANIA 1 SWITZERLAND 1
Parc des Princes (43,576); Wednesday, June 15

Romania (4-2-3-1): Tatarusanu, Sapunaru, Chiriches, Grigore, Rat (Filip 62), Prepelita, Pintilii (Hoban 46), Torje, Stancu (Andone 83), Chipciu, Keseru. **Scorer**: Stancu (18 pen). **Booked**: Prepelita, Chipciu, Keseru, Grigore

Switzerland (4-2-3-1): Sommer, Lichtsteiner, Schar, Djourou, Rodriguez, Behrami, Xhaka, Shaqiri (Tarashaj 90), Dzemaili (Lang 83), Mehmedi, Seferovic (Embolo 64). **Scorer**: Mehmedi (58). **Booked**: Xhaka, Embolo

Referee: S Karasev (Russia). **Half-time**: 1-0

FRANCE 2 ALBANIA 0
Marseille (63,670); Wednesday, June 15

France (4-2-3-1): Lloris, Sagna, Rami, Koscielny, Evra, Kante, Matuidi, Coman (Griezmann 68), Payet, Martial (Pogba 46), Groud (Gignac 77). **Scorers**: Griezmann (90), Payet (90). **Booked**: Kante

Albania (4-5-1): Berisha, Hysaj, Ajeti (Veseli 85), Mavraj, Agolli, Lila (Roshi 71), Abrashi, Kukeli (Xhaka 74), Memushaj, Lenjani, Sadiku. **Booked**: Kukeli, Abrashi

Referee: W Collum (Scotland). **Half-time**: 0-0

ROMANIA 0 ALBANIA 1
Lyon (49,752); Sunday, June 19

Romania (4-2-3-1): Tatarusanu, Sapunaru, Chiriches, Grigore, Matel, Prepelita (Sanmartean 46), Hoban, Popa (Andone 68), Stanciu, Stancu, Alibec (Torje 57). **Booked**: Matel, Sapunaru, Torje

Albania (4-1-4-1): Berisha, Hysaj, Ajeti, Mavraj, Agolli, Basha, Lila, Abrashi, Memushaj, Lenjani, Sadiku (Balaj 58). **Scorer**: Sadiku (43). **Booked**: Basha, Memushaj, Hysaj

Referee: P Kralovec (Czech Republic). **Half-time**: 0-1

SWITZERLAND 0 FRANCE 0
Lille (45,616); Sunday, June 19

Switzerland (4-2-3-1): Sommer, Lichtsteiner, Schar, Djourou, Rodriguez, Behrami, Xhaka,

Shaqiri (Fernandes 79), Dzemaili, Mehmedi (Lang 86), Embolo (Seferovic 74)
France (4-3-3): Lloris, Sagna, Rami, Koscielny, Evra, Sissoko, Cabaye, Pogba, Griezmann (Matuidi 78), Gignac, Coman (Payet 63). **Booked**: Rami, Koscielny
Referee:D Skomina (Slovenia)

	P	W	D	L	F	A	Pts
France Q	3	2	1	0	4	1	7
Switzerland Q	3	1	2	0	2	1	5
Albania	3	1	0	2	1	3	3
Romania	3	0	1	2	2	4	1

GROUP B

WALES 2 SLOVAKIA 1
Bordeaux (37,831); Saturday, June 11

Wales (3-5-1-1): Ward, Chester, A Williams, Davies, Gunter, Allen, Edwards (Ledley 69), J Williams (Robson-Kanu 71), Taylor, Ramsey (Richards 88), Bale. **Scorers**: Bale (10), Robson-Kanu (81)
Slovakia (4-2-3-1): Kozacik, Pekarik, Skrtel, Durica, Svento, Kucka, Hrosovsky (Duda 69), Weiss (Stoch 83), Hamsik, Mak, Duris (Nemec 60). **Scorer**: Duda (61). **Booked**: Hrosovsky, Mak, Weiss, Kucka, Skrtel
Referee: S Moen (Norway). **Half-time**: 1-0

ENGLAND 1 RUSSIA 1
Marseille (62,343); Saturday, June 11

England (4-3-3): Hart, Walker, Cahill, Smalling, Rose, Alli, Dier, Rooney (Wilshere 78), Lallana, Kane, Sterling (Milner 87). **Scorer**: Dier (73). **Booked**: Cahill
Russia (4-2-3-1): Akinfeev, Smolnikov, V Berezutski, Ignashevich, Shchennikov, Neustadter (Glushakov 80), Golovin, Kokorin, Shatov, Smolov (Mamaev 85), Dzyuba. **Scorer**: V Berezutski (90). **Booked**: Shchennikov
Referee: N Rizzoli (Italy). **Half-time**: 0-0

RUSSIA 1 SLOVAKIA 2
Lille (38,989); Wednesday, June 15

Russia (4-2-3-1): Akinfeev, Smolnikov, V Berezutski, Ignashevich, Shchennikov, Neustadter (Glushakov 46), Golovin (Mamaev 46), Kokorin (Shirokov 75), Shatov, Smolov, Dzyuba. **Scorer**: Glushakov (80)
Slovakia (4-3-2-1): Kozacik, Pekarik, Skrtel, Durica, Hubocan, Kucka, Pecovsky, Hamsik, Mak (Duris 80), Weiss (Svento 75), Duda (Nemec 67). **Scorers**: Weiss (32), Hamsik (45). **Booked**: Durica
Referee: D Skomina (Slovenia). **Half-time**: 0-2

ENGLAND 2 WALES 1
Lens (34,033); Thursday, June 16

England (4-3-3): Hart, Walker, Cahill, Smalling, Rose, Alli, Dier, Rooney, Lallana (Rashford 71), Kane (Vardy 46), Sterling (Sturridge 46). **Scorers**: Vardy (56), Sturridge (90)
Wales (3-5-1-1): Hennessey, Chester, A Williams, Davies, Gunter, Allen, Ledley (Edwards 67), Ramsey, Taylor, Bale, Robson-Kanu (J Williams 72). **Scorer**: Bale (42). **Booked**: Davies
Referee: F Brych (Germany). **Half-time**: 0-1

SLOVAKIA 0 ENGLAND 0
Saint Etienne (39,051); Monday, June 20

Slovakia (4-5-1): Kozacik, Pekarik, Skrtel, Durica, Hubocan, Mak, Kucka, Pecovsky (Gyomber 67), Hamsik, Weiss (Skriniar 79), Duda (Svento 58). **Booked**: Pecovsky
England (4-3-3): Hart, Clyne, Cahill, Smalling, Bertrand, Henderson, Dier, Wilshere (Rooney 59), Sturridge (Kane 76), Vardy, Lallana (Alli 60). **Booked**: Bertrand
Referee: C Velasco Carballo (Spain)

RUSSIA 0 WALES 3
Toulouse (28,840); Monday, June 20

Russia (4-4-1-1): Akinfeev, Smolnikov, V Berezutski (A Berezutski 46), Ignashevich, Kombarov, Kokorin, Mamaev, Glushakov, Smolov (Samedov 70), Shirokov (Golovin 52), Dzyuba. **Booked**: Mamaev

Wales (3-4-2-1): Hennessey, Chester, A Williams, Davies, Gunter, Allen (Edwards 74), Ledley (King 76), Taylor, Bale (Church 83), Ramsey, Vokes. **Scorers**: Ramsey (11), Taylor (20), Bale (67). **Booked**: Vokes

Referee: J Eriksson (Sweden). **Half-time**: 0-2

	P	W	D	L	F	A	Pts
Wales Q	3	2	0	1	6	3	6
England Q	3	1	2	0	3	2	5
Skovakia Q	3	1	1	1	3	3	4
Russia	3	0	1	2	2	6	1

GROUP C

GERMANY 2 UKRAINE 0
Lille (43,035); Sunday, June 12

Germany (4-2-3-1): Neuer, Howedes, Boateng, Mustafi, Hector, Khedria, Kroos, Muller, Ozil, Draxler (Schurrle 78), Gotze (Schweinsteiger 90). **Scorers**: Mustafi (19), Schweinsteiger (90)

Ukraine (4-2-3-1): Pyatov, Fedetskiy, Khacheridi, Rakitskiy, Shevchuk, Sydorchuk, Stepanenko, Yarmolenko, Kovalenko (Zinchenko 73), Konoplyanka, Zozulya (Seleznyov 67). **Booked**: Konoplyanka

Referee: M Atkinson (England). **Half-time**: 1-0

POLAND 1 NORTHERN IRELAND 0
Nice (33,742); Sunday, June 12

Poland (4-4-1-1): Szczesny, Piszczek, Glik, Pazdan, Jedrzejczyk, Blaszczykowski (Grosicki 80), Krychowiak, Maczynski (Jodlowiec 78), Kapustka (Peszko 88), Milik, Lewandowski. **Scorer**: Milik (51). **Booked**: Piszczek, Kapustka

Northern Ireland (3-4-2-1): McGovern, McAuley, Cathcart, J Evans, McLaughlin, McNair (Dallas 46), Baird (Ward 76), Norwood, Ferguson (Washington 66), Davis, Lafferty. **Booked**: Cathcart

Referee: O Hategan (Romania). **Half-time**: 0-0

UKRAINE 0 NORTHERN IRELAND 2
Lyon (51,043): Thursday, June 16

Ukraine (4-2-3-1): Pyatov, Fedetskiy, Khacheridi, Rakitskiy, Shevchuk, Sydorchuk (Garmash 75), Stepanenko, Yarmolenko, Kovalenko (Zinchenko 83), Konoplyanka, Seleznyov (Zozuyla 72). **Booked**: Seleznyov, Sydorchuk

Northern Ireland (4-5-1): McGovern, Hughes, McAuley, Cathcart, J Evans, Ward (McGinn 69), C Evans (McNair 90), Davis, Norwood, Dallas, Washington (Magennis 84). **Scorers**: McAuley (49), McGinn (90). **Booked**: Ward, Dallas, J Evans

Referee: P Kralovec (Czech Republic). **Half-time**: 0-0

GERMANY 0 POLAND 0
Stade de France (73,648); Thursday, June 16

Germany (4-2-3-1): Neuer, Howedes, Boateng, Hummels, Hector, Khedria, Kroos, Muller, Ozil, Draxler (Gomez 71), Gotze (Schurrle 66). **Booked**: Khedira, Ozil, Boateng

Poland (4-4-2): Fabianski, Piszczek, Glik, Pazdan, Jedrzejczyk, Blaszczykowski (Kapustka 80), Krychowiak, Maczynski (Jodlowiec 76), Grosicki (Peszko 87), Milik, Lewandowski. **Booked**: Maczynski, Grosicki, Peszko

Referee: B Kuipers (Holland)

UKRAINE 0 POLAND 1
Marseille (58,874); Tuesday, June 21

Ukraine (4-2-3-1): Pyatov, Fedetskiy, Khacheridi, Kucher, Butko, Stepanenko, Rotan, Yarmolenko, Zinchenko (Kovalenko 73), Konoplyanka, Zozulya (Tymoschuk 90). **Booked**: Rotan, Kucher
Poland (4-4-2): Fabianski, Cionek, Glik, Pazdan, Jedrzejczyk, Zielinski (Blaszczykowski 46), Krychowiak, Jodlowiec, Kapustka (Grosicki 71), Milik (Starzynski 90), Lewandowski. **Scorer**: Blaszczykowski (54). **Booked**: Kapustka
Referee: S Moen (Norway). **Half-time**: 0-0

NORTHERN IRELAND 0 GERMANY 1
Parc des Princes (44,125): Tuesday, June 21

Northern Ireland (4-5-1): McGovern, Hughes, Cathcart, McAuley, J Evans, Ward (Magennis 70), C Evans (McGinn 84), Davis, Norwood, Dallas, Washington (Lafferty 59)
Germany (4-2-3-1): Neuer, Kimmich, Boateng (Howedes 76), Hummels, Hector, Khedira (Schweinsteiger 69), Kroos, Muller, Ozil, Gotze (Schurrle 56), Gomez. **Scorer**: Gomez (30)
Referee: C Turpin (France). **Half-time**: 0-1

	P	W	D	L	F	A	Pts
Germany Q	3	2	1	0	3	0	7
Poland Q	3	2	1	0	2	0	7
Northern Ireland Q	3	1	0	2	2	2	3
Ukraine	3	0	0	3	0	5	0

GROUP D

TURKEY 0 CROATIA 1
Parc des Princes (43.842); Sunday, June 12

Turkey (4-2-3-1): Babacan, Gonul, Topal, Balta, Erkin, Tufan, Inan, Ozyakup (Sen 46), Calhanoglu, Tosun (Mor 69), Turan (Yilmaz 65). **Booked**: Balta
Croatia (4-2-3-1): Subasic, Srna, Corluka, Vida, Strinic, Badelj, Modric, Brozovic. Rakitic (Schildenfeld 87), Perisic (Kramaric 86), Mandzukic (Pjaca 90). **Scorer**: Modric (41). **Booked**: Strinic
Referee: J Eriksson (Sweden). **Half-time**: 0-1

SPAIN 1 CZECH REPUBLIC 0
Toulouse (29,400); Monday, June 13

Spain (4-3-2-1): De Gea, Juanfran, Pique, Sergio Ramos, Jordi Alba, Fabregas (Thiago Alcantara 69), Busquets, Iniesta, Nolito (Pedro 81), Silva, Alvaro Morata (Aduriz 61). **Scorer**: Pique (87)
Czech Republic (4-2-3-1): Cech, Kaderabek, Sivok, Hubnik, Limbersky, Darida, Plasil, Gebre Selassie (Sural 85), Rosicky (Pavelka 88), Krejci, Necid (Lafata 75). **Booked**: Limbersky
Referee: S Marchiniak (Poland). **Half-time**: 0-0

SPAIN 3 TURKEY 0
Nice (33,409); Friday, June 17

Spain (4-3-2-1): De Gea, Juanfran, Pique, Sergio Ramos, Jordi Alba (Azpilicueta 81), Fabregas (Koke 71), Busquets, Iniesta, Nolito, Silva (Soriano 64), Alvaro Morata. **Scorers**: Alvaro Morata (34, 48), Nolito (37). **Booked**: Sergio Ramos
Turkey (4-2-3-1): Babacan, Gonul, Topal, Balta, Erkin, Tufan, Inan (Malli 71), Ozyakup (Sahan 62), Calhanoglu (Sahin 46), Yilmaz, Turan. **Booked**: Yilmaz, Tufan
Referee: M Mazic (Serbia). **Half-time**: 2-0

CZECH REPUBLIC 2 CROATIA 2
Saint Etienne (29,600); Friday, June 17

Czech Republic (4-2-3-1): Cech, Kaderabek, Sivok, Hubnik, Limbersky, Darida, Plasil (Necid 86), Skalak (Sural 67), Rosicky, Krejci, Lafata (Skoda 67). **Scorers**: Skoda (76), Necid (90 pen). **Booked**: Sivok

Croatia (4-2-3-1): Subasic, Srna, Corluka, Vida, Strinic (Vrsaljko 90), Badelj, Modric (Kovacic 62), Brozovic. Rakitic (Schildenfeld 90), Perisic, Mandzukic. **Scorers**: Perisic (37), Rakitic (59). **Booked**: Badelj, Brozovic, Vida
Referee: M Clattenburg (England). **Half-time**: 0-1

CROATIA 2 SPAIN 1
Bordeaux (37,245); Tuesday, June 21

Croatia (4-2-3-1): Subasic, Srna, Corluka, Jedvaj, Vrsaljko, Rog (Kovacic 81), Badelj, Perisic (Kramaric 90), Rakitic, Pjaca (Cop 90), Kalinic. **Scorers**: Kalinic (25), Perisic (87). **Booked**: Rog, Vrsaljko, Srna, Perisic
Spain (4-3-2-1): De Gea, Juanfran, Pique, Sergio Ramos, Jordi Alba, Fabregas (Thiago Alcantara 84), Busquets, Iniesta, Nolito (Soriano 59), Silva, Alvaro Morata (Aduriz 66). **Scorer**: Alvaro Morata (7)
Referee: B Kuipers (Holland). **Half-time**: 1-1

CZECH REPUBLIC 0 TURKEY 2
Lens (32,836); Tuesday, June 21

Czech Republic (4-3-3): Cech, Kaderabek, Sivok, Hubnik, Pudil, Pavelka (Skoda 56), Darida, Plasil (Kolar 90), Dockal (Sural 71), Necid, Krejci. **Booked**: Plasil, Pavelka, Sural
Turkey (4-2-3-1): Babacan, Gonul, Topal, Balta, Koybasi, Tufan, Inan, Mor (Sahan 89), Sen (Ozyakup 61)), Turan, Yilmaz (Tosun 90). **Scorers**: Yilmaz (10), Tufan (65). **Booked**: Koybasi, Balta
Referee: W Collum (Scotland). **Half-time**: 0-1

	P	W	D	L	F	A	Pts
Croatia Q	3	2	1	0	5	3	7
Spain Q	3	2	0	1	5	2	6
Turkey	3	1	0	2	2	4	3
Czech Republic	3	0	1	2	2	5	1

GROUP E

BELGIUM 0 ITALY 2
Lyon (55,408); Monday, June 13

Belgium (4-2-3-1): Courtois, Ciman (Carrasco 75), Alderweireld, Vermaelen, Vertonghen, Witsel, Nainggolan (Mertens 61), De Bruyne, Fellaini, Hazard, Lukaku (Origi 73). **Booked**: Vertonghen
Italy (3-5-2): Buffon, Barzagli, Bonucci, Chiellini, Candreva, Parolo, De Rossi (Motta 78), Giaccherini, Darmian (De Sciglio 58), Pelle, Eder (Immobile 75). **Scorers**: Giaccherini (32), Pelle (90). **Booked**: Chiellini, Eder, Bonucci, Motta
Referee: M Clattenburg (England). **Half-time**: 0-1

REPUBLIC OF IRELAND 1 SWEDEN 1
Stade de France (73,419); Monday, June 13

Republic of Ireland (4-3-1-2): Randolph, Coleman, O'Shea, Clark, Brady, McCarthy (McGeady 85), Whelan, Hendrick, Hoolahan (Keane 78), Walters (McClean 64), Long. **Scorer**: Hoolahan (48). **Booked**: McCarthy, Whelan
Sweden (4-4-2): Isaksson, Lustig (Johansson 46), Lindelof, Granqvist, Olsson, Larsson, Lewicki (Ekdal 86), Kallstrom, Forsberg, Berg (Guidetti 59), Ibrahimovic. **Scorer**: Clark (71 og). **Booked**: Lindelof
Referee: M Mazic (Serbia). **Half-time**: 0-0

ITALY 1 SWEDEN 0
Toulouse (29,600); Friday, June 17

Italy (3-5-2): Buffon, Barzagli, Bonucci, Chiellini, Candreva, Parolo, De Rossi (Motta 74), Giaccherini, Florenzi (Sturaro 85), Pelle (Zaza 60), Eder. **Scorer**: Eder (88). **Booked**: De Rossi, Buffon

Sweden (4-4-2): Isaksson, Lindelof, Johansson, Granqvist, Olsson, Larsson, Ekdal (Lewicki 79), Kallstrom, Forsberg (Durmaz 79), Guidetti (Berg 85), Ibrahimovic. **Booked**: Olsson
Referee: V Kassai (Hungary). **Half-time: 0-0**

BELGIUM 3 REPUBLIC OF IRELAND 0
Bordeaux (39,493); Saturday, June 18

Belgium (4-2-3-1): Courtois, Meunier, Alderweireld, Vermaelen, Vertonghen, Witsel, Dembele (Nainggolan 57), Carrasco (Mertens 64), De Bruyne, Hazard, Lukaku (Benteke 82). **Scorers**: Lukaku (48, 70), Witsel (61). **Booked**: Vermaelen
Republic of Ireland (4-4-1-1): Randolph, Coleman, O'Shea, Clark, Ward, Hendrick, Whelan, McCarthy (McClean 62), Brady, Hoolahan (McGeady 71), Long (Keane 79). **Booked**: Hendrick
Referee: C Cakir (Turkey). **Half-time**: 0-0

ITALY 0 REPUBLIC OF IRELAND 1
Lille (44,268): Wednesday, June 22

Italy (3-5-2): Sirigu, Barzagli, Bonucci, Ogbonna, Bernardeschi (Darmian 60), Sturaro, Motta, Florenzi, De Sciglio (El Shaarawy 81), Zaza, Immobile (Insigne 74).**Booked**: Sirigu, Barzagli, Zaza, Insigne
Republic of Ireland (4-4-2): Randolph, Coleman, Duffy, Keogh, Ward, Hendrick, McCarthy (Hoolahan 77), Brady, McClean, Murphy (McGeady 70), Long (Quinn 90). **Scorer**: Brady (84). **Booked**: Long, Ward
Referee: O Hategan (Romania). **Half-time**: 0-0

SWEDEN 0 BELGIUM 1
Nice (34,011); Wednesday, June 22

Sweden (4-4-2): Isaksson, Lindelof, Johansson, Granqvist, Olsson, Larsson (Durmaz 70), Ekdal, Kallstrom, Forsberg (Zengin 82), Berg (Guidetti 63), Ibrahimovic. **Booked**: Ekdal, Johansson
Belgium (4-2-3-1): Courtois, Meunier, Alderweireld, Vermaelen, Vertonghen, Nainggolan, Witsel, Carrasco (Mertens 71), De Bruyne, Hazard (Origi 90), Lukaku (Benteke 87). **Scorer**: Nainggolan (84). **Booked**: Meunier, Witsel
Referee: F Brych (Germany). **Half-time**: 0-0

	P	W	D	L	F	A	Pts
Italy Q	3	2	0	1	3	1	6
Belgium Q	3	2	0	1	4	2	6
Republic of Ireland Q	3	1	1	1	2	4	4
Sweden	3	0	1	2	1	3	1

GROUP F

AUSTRIA 0 HUNGARY 2
Bordeaux (34,424); Tuesday, June 14

Austria (4-2-3-1): Almer, Klein, Dragovic, Hinteregger, Fuchs, Baumgartlinger, Alaba, Harnick (Schopf 78), Junuzovic (Sabitzer 60), Arnautovic, Janko (Okotie 65). **Booked**: Dragovic. **Sent off**: Dragovic (66)
Hungary (4-1-4-1): Kiraly, Fiola, Guzmics, Lang, Kadar, Gera, Nemeth (Pinter 89), Nagy, Kleinheisler (Stieber 79), Dzsudzsak, Szalai (Priskin 69). **Scorers**: Szalai (63), Stieber (86). **Booked**: Nemeth
Referee: C Turpin (France). **Half-time**: 0-0

PORTUGAL 1 ICELAND 1
Saint Etienne (38,742); Tuesday, June 14

Portugal (4-3-1-2): Rui Patricio, Vieirinha, Pepe, Ricardo Carvalho, Raphael Guerreiro, Andre Gomes (Eder 84), Danilo, Joao Mario (Ricardo Quaresma 75), Joao Moutinho (Renato Sanches 70), Nani, Ronaldo. **Scorer**: Nani (31)
Iceland (4-4-2): Halldorsson, Saevarsson, R Sigurdsson, Arnason, Skulason, Gudmundsson

(E Bjarnason 90), Gunnarsson, G Sigurdsson, B Bjarnason, Sigthorsson (Finnbogason 81), Bodvarsson. **Scorer**: B Bjarnson (50). **Booked**: B Bjarnason, Finnbogason
Referee: C Cakir (Turkey). **Half-time**: 1-0

ICELAND 1 HUNGARY 1
Marseille (60,842); Saturday, June 18

Iceland (4-4-2): Halldorsson, Saevarsson, R Sigurdsson, Arnason, Skulason, Gudmundsson, Gunnarsson (Hallfredsson 65), G Sigurdsson, B Bjarnason, Sigthorsson (Gudjohnsen 83), Bodvarsson (Finnbogason 68). **Scorer**: G Sigurdsson (39 pen). **Booked**: Gudmundsson, Finnbogason, Saevarsson
Hungary (4-3-3): Kiraly, Lang, Juhasz (Szalai 84), Guzmics, Kadar, Kleinheisler, Gera, Nagy, Dzsudzsak, Priskin (Bode 65), Stieber (Nikolic 65). **Scorer**: Saevarsson (88 og). **Booked**: Kadar, Kleinheisler, Nagy
Referee: S Karasev (Russia). **Half-time**: 1-0

PORTUGAL 0 AUSTRIA 0
Parc des Princes (44,291): Saturday, June 18

Portugal (4-4-2): Rui Patricio, Vieirinha, Pepe, Ricardo Carvalho, Raphael Guerreiro, Ricardo Quaresma (Joao Mario 70), William Carvalho, Joao Moutinho, Andre Gomes (Eder 82), Nani (Rafa Silva 88), Ronaldo. **Booked**: Ricardo Quaresma, Pepe
Austria (4-2-3-1): Almer, Klein, Prodl, Hinteregger, Fuchs, Ilsanker (Wimmer 86), Baumgartlinger, Sabitzer (Hinterseer 84), Alaba (Schopf 64), Arnautovic, Harnick. **Booked**: Harnick, Fuchs, Hinteregger, Schopf
Referee: N Rizzoli (Italy)

HUNGARY 3 PORTUGAL 3
Lyon (55,514); Wednesday, June 22

Hungary (4-2-3-1): Kiraly, Lang, Juhasz, Guzmics, Korhut, Gera (Bese 46), Pinter, Lovrencsics (Stieber 83), Elek, Dzsudzsak, Szalai (Nemeth 71). **Scorers**: Gera (19), Dzsudzsak (46, 54). **Booked**: Guzmics, Juhasz, Gera, Dzsudzsak
Portugal (4-4-2): Rui Patricio, Vieirinha, Pepe, Ricardo Carvalho, Eliseu, Joao Mario, William Carvalho, Joao Moutinho, Andre Gomes (Ricardo Quaresma 61), Nani (Danilo 81), Ronaldo. **Scorers**: Nani (42), Ronaldo (49, 61)
Referee: M Atkinson (England). **Half-time**: 1-1

ICELAND 2 AUSTRIA 1
Stade de France (68,714); Wednesday, June 22

Iceland (4-4-2): Halldorsson, Saevarsson, R Sigurdsson, Arnason, Skulason, Gudmundsson (Ingason 86), Gunnarsson G Sigurdsson, B Bjarnason, Sigthorsson (Traustason 80), Bodvarsson (E Bjarnason 71. **Scorers**: Bodvarsson (18), Traustason (90). **Booked**: Skulason, Sigthorsson, Arnason, Halldorsson
Austria (4-2-3-1): Almer, Dragovic, Prodl (Schopf 46), Hinteregger, Fuchs, Ilsanker (Janko 46), Baumgartlinger, Klein, Alaba, Arnautovic, Sabitzer (Jantscher 78). **Scorer**: Schopf (60). **Booked**: Janko
Referee: S Marciniak (Poland). **Half-time**: 1-0

	P	W	D	L	F	A	Pts
Hungary Q	3	1	2	0	6	4	5
Iceland Q	3	1	2	0	4	3	5
Portugal Q	3	0	3	0	4	4	3
Austria	3	0	1	2	1	4	1

ROUND OF 16

SWITZERLAND 1 POLAND 1 (aet, Poland won 5-4 on pens)
Saint Etienne (38,842); Saturday, June 25

Switzerland (4-2-3-1): Sommer, Lichsteiner, Shar, Djourou, Rodriguez, Behrami (Fernandes

78), Xhaka, Shaqiri, Dzemaili (Embolo 58), Mehmedi (Derdiyok 70), Seferovic. **Scorer**: Shaqiri (82). **Booked**: Schar, Djourou
Poland (4-4-2): Fabianski, Piszczek, Glik, Pazdan, Jedrzejczyk, Blaszczykowski, Krychowiak, Maczynski (Jodlowiec 101), Grosicki (Peszko 102), Milik, Lewandowski. **Scorer**: Blaszczykowski (39). **Booked**: Jedrzejczyk, Pazdan
Referee: M Clattenburg (England). **Half-time**: 0-1

WALES 1 NORTHERN IRELAND 0
Parc des Princes (44,342); Saturday, June 25

Wales (3-4-2-1): Hennessey, Chester, A Williams, Davies, Gunter, Allen, Ledley (J Williams 62), Taylor, Bale, Ramsey, Vokes (Robson-Kanu 55). **Scorer**: McAuley (75 og). **Booked**: Taylor, Ramsey
Northern Ireland (4-5-1): McGovern, Hughes, McAuley (Magennis 83), Cathcart, J Evans, Ward (Washington 68), C Evans, Davis, Norwood (McGinn 79), Dallas, Lafferty. **Booked**: Dallas, Davis
Referee: M Atkinson (England). **Half-time**: 0-0

CROATIA 0 PORTUGAL 1 (aet)
Lens (33,523): Saturday, June 25

Croatia (4-2-3-1): Subasic, Srna, Corluka (Kramaric 120), Vida, Strinic, Badelj, Modric, Brozovic, Rakitic (Pjaca 110), Perisic, Mandzukic (Kalinic 88)
Portugal (4-4-2): Rui Patricio, Soares, Pepe, Fonte, Raphael Guerreiro, Joao Mario (Ricardo Quaresma 87), Adrien Silva (Danilo 108), William Carvalho, Andre Gomes (Renato Sanches 50), Nani, Ronaldo. **Scorer**: Ricardo Quaresma (117). **Booked**: William Carvalho
Referee: C Velasco Carballo (Spain). **Half-time**: 0-0

FRANCE 2 REPUBLIC OF IRELAND 1
Lyon (56,279); Sunday, June 26

France (4-3-3): Lloris, Sagna, Rami, Koscielny, Evra, Matuidi, Kante (Coman 46) (Sissoko 90), Pogba, Griezmann, Giroud (Gignac 74), Payet. **Scorer**: Griezmann (57, 61). **Booked**: Kante, Rami
Republic of Ireland (4-4-2): Randolph, Coleman, Duffy, Keogh, Ward, Hendrick, McCarthy (Hoolahan 72), Brady, McClean (O'Shea 69), Murphy (Walters 65), Long (Quinn 90). **Scorer**: Brady (2 pen). **Booked**: Coleman, Hendrick, Long. **Sent off**: Duffy (66)
Referee: N Rizzoli (Italy). **Half-time**: 0-1

GERMANY 3 SLOVAKIA 0
Lille (44,312); Sunday, June 26

Germany (4-2-3-1): Neuer, Kimmich, Boateng (Howedes 72), Hummels, Hector, Khedira (Schweinsteiger 76), Kroos, Muller, Ozil, Draxler (Podolski 72), Gomez. **Scorers**: Boateng (8), Gomez (43), Draxler (63). **Booked**: Kimmich, Hummels
Slovakia (4-3-3): Kozacik, Pekarik, Skrtel, Durica, Gyomber (Salata 84), Hrosovsky, Skriniar, Hamsik, Kucka, Duris (Sestak 64), Weiss (Gregus 46). **Booked**: Skrtel, Kucka
Referee: S Marciniak (Poland). **Half-time**: 2-0

HUNGARY 0 BELGIUM 4
Toulouse (38,921); Sunday, June 26

Hungary (4-2-3-1): Kiraly, Lang, Juhasz (Bode 80), Guzmics, Kadar, Gera (Elek 46), Nagy, Lovrenscics, Pinter (Nikolics 75), Dzsudzsak, Szalai. **Booked**: Kadar, Lang, Elek, Szalai
Belgium (4-2-3-1): Courtois, Meunier, Alderweireld, Vermaelen, Vertonghen, Nainggolan, Witsel, Mertens (Carrasco 70), De Bruyne, Hazard (Fellaini 81)), Lukaku (Batshuayi 76). **Scorers**: Alderweireld (10), Batshuayi (79), Hazard (80), Carrasco (90). **Booked**: Vermaelen, Batshuayi, Fellaini
Referee: M Mazic (Serbia). **Half-time**: 0-1

ITALY 2 SPAIN 0
Stade de France (76,165); Monday, June 27

Italy (3-5-2): Buffon, Barzagli, Bonucci, Chiellini, Florenzi (Darmian 84), Parolo, De Rossi (Motta 54), Giaccherini, De Sciglio, Pelle, Eder (Insigne 81). **Scorers**: Chiellini (33), Pelle

(90). **Booked**: De Sciglio, Pelle, Motta
Spain (4-3-3): De Gea, Juanfran, Pique, Sergio Ramos, Jordi Alba, Fabregas, Busquets, Iniesta, Silva, Alvaro Morata (Lucas Vazquez 70), Nolito (Aduriz 46) (Pedro (81). **Booked**: Nolito, Jordi Alba, Busquets, Silva
Referee: C Cakir (Turkey). **Half-time**: 1-0

ENGLAND 1 ICELAND 2
Nice (33,901); Monday, June 27

England (4-3-3): Hart, Walker, Cahill, Smalling, Rose, Alli, Dier (Wilshere 46), Rooney (Rashford 86), Sturridge, Kane, Sterling (Vardy 60). **Scorer**: Rooney (4 pen). **Booked**: Sturridge
Iceland (4-4-2): Halldorsson, Saevarsson, Arnason, R Sigurdsson, Skulason, Gudmundsson, Gunnarsson, G Sigurdsson, B Bjarnason, Sigthorsson (E Bjarnason 77), Bodvarsson (Traustason 89). **Scorers**: R Sigurdsson (6), Sigthorsson (18). **Booked**: G Sigurdsson, Gunnarsson
Referee: D Skomina (Slovenia). **Half-time**: 1-2

QUARTER-FINALS

POLAND 1 PORTUGAL 1 (aet, Portugal won 5-3 on pens)
Marseille (62,940); Thursday, June 30

Poland (4-4-2): Fabianski, Piszczek, Glik, Pazdan, Jedrzejczyk, Blaszczykowski, Krychowiak, Maczynski (Jodlowiec 97), Grosicki (Kapustka 81), Milik, Lewandowski. **Scorer**: Lewandowski (2). **Booked**: Jedrzejczyk, Glik, Kapustka
Portugal (4-1-3-2): Rui Patricio, Soares, Pepe, Fonte, Eliseu, William Carvalho (Danilo 96), Joao Mario (Ricardo Quaresma 79), Renato Sanches, Adrien Silva (Joao Moutinho 72), Nani, Ronaldo. **Scorer**: Renato Sanches (33). **Booked**: Adrien Silva, William Carvalho
Referee: F Brych (Germany). **Half-time**: 1-1

WALES 3 BELGIUM 1
Lille (45,936); Friday, July 1

Wales (3-4-2-1): Hennessey, Chester, A Williams, Davies, Gunter, Allen, Ledley (King 78), Taylor, Bale, Ramsey (Collins 90), Robson-Kanu (Vokes 80). **Scorers**: A Williams (30), Robson-Kanu (55), Vokes (85). **Booked**: Davies, Chester, Gunter, Ramsey
Belgium (4-2-3-1): Courtois, Meunier, Alderweireld, Denayer, J Lukaku (Mertens 75), Nainggolan, Witsel, Carrasco (Fellaini 46), De Bruyne, Hazard, R Lukaku (Batshuayi 83). **Scorer**: Nainggolan (13). **Booked**: Fellaini, Alderweireld
Referee: D Skomina (Slovenia). **Half-time**: 1-1

GERMANY 1 ITALY 1 (aet Germany won 6-5 on pens)
Bordeaux (38,764); Saturday, July 2

Germany (3-4-2-1): Neuer, Howedes, Boateng, Hummels, Kimmich, Khedira (Schweinsteiger 16), Kroos, Hector, Ozil, Muller, Gomez (Draxler 72). **Scorer**: Ozil (65). **Booked**: Hummels, Schweinsteiger
Italy (3-5-2): Buffon, Barzagli, Bonucci, Chiellini (Zaza 120), Florenzi (Darmian 86), Sturaro, Parolo, Giaccherini, De Sciglio, Pelle, Eder (Insigne 108). **Scorer**: Bonucci (78 pen) **Booked**: Sturaro, De Sciglio, Parolo, Pelle, Giaccherini
Referee: V Kassai (Hungary). **Half-time**: 0-0

FRANCE 5 ICELAND 2
Stade de France (76,833); Sunday, July 3

France (4-2-3-1): Lloris, Sagna, Umtiti, Koscielny (Mangala 72), Evra, Pogba, Matuidi, Sissoko, Griezmann, Payet (Coman 80), Giroud (Gignac 60). **Scorers**: Giroud (12, 59), Pogba (19), Payet (42), Griezmann (45). **Booked**: Umtiti
Iceland (4-4-2): Halldorsson, Saevarsson, Arnason (Ingason 46), R Sigurdsson, Skulason, Gudmundsson, Gunnarsson, G Sigurdsson, B Bjarnason, Sigthorsson (Gudjohnsen 83), Bodvarsson (Finnbogason 46). **Scorers**: Sigthorsson (56), B Bjarnason (84) **Booked**: B Bjarnason
Referee: B Kuipers (Holland). **Half-time**: 4-0

SEMI-FINALS

PORTUGAL 2 WALES 0
Lyon (55,679); Wednesday, July 6

Portugal (4-1-3-2): Rui Patricio, Soares, Bruno Alves, Fonte, Raphael Guerreiro, Danilo, Renato Sanches (Andre Gomes 74), Adrien Silva (Joao Moutinho 79), Joao Mario, Nani (Ricardo Quaresma 87), Ronaldo. **Scorers**: Ronaldo (50), Nani (53). **Booked**: Bruno Alves, Ronaldo
Wales (3-4-2-1): Hennessey, Collins (J Williams 66), A Williams Chester, Gunter, Allen, Ledley (Vokes 58), Taylor, King, Bale, Robson-Kanu (Church 63). **Booked**: Allen, Chester, Bale
Referee: J Eriksson (Sweden). **Half-time**: 0-0

GERMANY 0 FRANCE 2
Marseille (64,078); Thursday, July 7

Germany (4-2-3-1): Neuer, Kimmich, Boateng (Mustafi 61), Howedes, Hector, Emre Can (Gotze 67), Schweinsteiger (Sane 79), Kroos, Ozil, Draxler, Muller. **Booked**: Emre Can, Schweinsteiger, Ozil, Draxler
France (4-2-3-1): Lloris, Sagna, Umtiti, Koscielny, Evra, Pogba, Matuidi, Sissoko, Griezmann (Cabaye 90), Payet (Kante 71), Giroud (Gignac 78). **Scorer**: Griezmann (45 pen, 72). **Booked**: Evra, Kante
Referee: N Rizzoli (Italy). **Half-time**: 0-1

FINAL

PORTUGAL 1 FRANCE 0 (aet)
Stade de France (75,868); Sunday, July 10 2016

Portugal (4-1-3-2): Rui Patricio, Soares, Pepe, Fonte, Raphael Guerreiro, William Carvalho, Renato Sanches (Eder 109), Adrien Silva (Joao Moutinho 66), Joao Mario, Nani, Ronaldo (capt) (Ricardo Quaresma 25). **Subs not used**: Eduardo, Lopes, Bruno Alves, Ricardo Carvalho, Vieirinha, Danilo, Rafa Silva, Eliseu, Andre Gomes. **Scorer**: Eder (109). **Booked**: Soares, Joao Mario, Raphael Guerreiro, William Carvalho, Fonte, Rui Patricio. **Coach**: Fernando Santos
France (4-2-3-1): Lloris (capt), Sagna, Umtiti, Koscielny, Evra, Pogba, Matuidi, Sissoko (Martial 110), Griezmann, Payet (Coman 58), Giroud (Gignac 78). **Subs not used**: Mandanda, Costil, Jallet, Rami, Kante, Cabaye, Schneiderlin, Mangala, Digne **Booked**: Umtiti, Matuidi, Koscielny, Pogba
Referee: M Clattenburg (England). **Half-time**: 0-0

FRANCE 2016 FACTS AND FIGURES

- Portugal had lost all ten of their previous ten internationals to France, stretching back 40 years.
- They became the first team in the same European Championship to go to extra-time on three occasions.
- Portugal's 2-0 win over Wales in the semi-finals was their only victory inside 90 minutes at these finals.
- Cristiano Ronaldo and Pepe completed a European double after helping Real Madrid defeat Atletico Madrid in the final of the Champions League.
- Antoine Griezmann was a two-time loser, having been in that Atletico team. But he had the consolation of winning the tournament's Golden Boot.
- Leading scorers: 6 Griezmann, 3 Ronaldo, Giroud (France), Payet (France), Bale (Wales), Nani (Portugal), Alvaro Morata (Spain).
- Premier League referee Mark Clattenburg completed a notable hat-trick, having taken charge of the finals of the Champions League and FA Cup in May.

England squad: Forster (Southampton), Hart (Manchester City), Heaton (Burnley); Bertrand (Southampton), Cahill (Chelsea), Clyne (Liverpool), Rose (Tottenham), Smalling (Manchester Utd), Stones (Everton), Walker (Tottenham); Alli (Tottenham), Barkley (Everton), Dier (Tottenham), Henderson (Liverpool), Lallana (Liverpool), Milner (Liverpool), Sterling (Manchester City), Wilshere (Arsenal); Kane (Tottenham), Rashford (Manchester Utd), Rooney (Manchester Utd), Sturridge (Liverpool), Vardy (Leicester).

Wales squad: Fon Williams (Inverness), Hennessey (Crystal Palace), Ward (Liverpool); Chester (WBA), Collins (West Ham), Davies (Tottenham), Gunter (Reading), Richards (Fulham), Taylor (Swansea), A Williams (Swansea); Allen (Liverpool), Cotterill (Birmingham), Edwards (Wolves), King (Leicester), Ledley (Crystal Palace), Ramsey (Arsenal), Vaughan (Nottm Forest), G Williams (Fulham), J Williams (Crystal Palace); Bale (Real Madrid), Church (MK Dons), Robson-Kanu (unatt), Vokes (Burnley).

Northern Ireland squad: Carroll (Linfield), Mannus (St Johnstone), McGovern (Hamilton); Baird (Derby), Cathcart (Watford), J Evans (WBA), Hodson (MK Dons), Hughes (unatt), McAuley (WBA), McCullough (Doncaster), McLaughlin (Fleetwood); Dallas (Leeds), Davis (Southampton), C Evans (Blackburn), Ferguson (Millwall), McGinn (Aberdeen), McNair (Manchester Utd), Norwood (Reading); Grigg (Wigan), Lafferty (Norwich), Magennis (Kilmarnock), Ward (Nottm Forest), Washington (QPR).

Republic of Ireland squad: Given (Stoke), Randolph (West Ham), Westwood (Sheffield Wed); Coleman (Everton), Christie (Derby), Clark (Aston Villa), Dufy (Blackburn), Keogh (Derby), O'Shea (Sunderland), Ward (Burnley); Brady (Norwich), Hendrick (Derby), Hoolahan (Norwich), McCarthy (Everton), McClean (WBA), McGeady (Everton), Meyler (Hull), Quinn (Reading), Walters (Stoke), Whelan (Stoke), Keane (LA Galaxy), Long (Southampton), Murphy (Ipswich).

THE THINGS THEY SAY ...

'I'm immensely proud of the players. It's incredible what they've done and how they've performed. I told them this is not the end. Some of them will be here a lot longer than me. Now, they have to go into the next campaign with the same hunger and desire' – **Chris Coleman**, Wales manager, who will step down after the 2018 World Cup.

'The end of the tournament, but the beginning of Wales as a force in world football' – **Ryan Giggs**, former Wales winger, after they went out in the semi-finals.

'Nothing in the three group games gave me any indication that we would play as poorly. One bad game has caused a lot of damage to me personally and the team going forward, because they have major bridges to repair. I'm sorry it ended this way, but these things happen' – **Roy Hodgson**, England manager, after the defeat by Iceland.

'That was the worst performance I've ever seen from an England team. We were out-fought, out-thought, out-battled and totally hopeless for 90 minutes. It looked to me as if Roy was making it up as he was going along' – **Alan Shearer**, former England captain.

'It's devastating. We were the better team on the day. I couldn't ask any more of the players. Gareth knows he has to make one of those decisions on the cross. He had to judge whether there was someone behind him or not' – **Michael O'Neill**, Northern Ireland manager, after Gareth McAuley's own goal against Wales put his side out.

'We definitely got the short straw. I know we knew about it before, but it is an incredible amount of time one side could have as an advantage over another. Reaching the last 16 is still an achievement, but it's not something we want to rest on. The players committed themselves in a major fashion' – **Martin O'Neill**, Republic of Ireland manager, after his team had three fewer days rest than France before their match.

PREVIOUS FINALS

1960 USSR 2 Yugoslavia 1 (aet) (Paris)
1964 Spain 2 USSR 1 (Madrid)
1968 Italy 2 Yugoslavia 0 (replay after 1-1) (Rome)
1972 West Germany 3 USSR 0 (Brussels)
1976 Czechoslovakia 2 West Germany 2 (Czechoslovakia won 5-3 on pens) (Belgrade)
1980 West Germany 2 Belgium 1 (Rome)
1984 France 2 Spain 0 (Paris)
1988 Holland 2 USSR 0 (Munich)
1992 Denmark 2 Germany 0 (Gothenburg)
1996 Germany 2 Czech Republic 1 (golden goal winner) (Wembley)
2000 France 2 Italy 1 (golden goal winner) (Rotterdam)
2004 Greece 1 Portugal 0 (Lisbon)
2008 Spain 1 Germany 0 (Vienna)
2012 Spain 4 Italy 0 (Kiev)

HOW THEY QUALIFIED FOR THE FINALS

GROUP A

	P	W	D	L	F	A	Pts
Czech Rep Q	10	7	1	2	19	14	22
Iceland Q	10	6	2	2	17	6	20
Turkey Q	10	5	3	2	14	9	18
Holland	10	4	1	5	17	14	13
Kazakhstan	10	1	2	7	7	18	5
Latvia	10	0	5	5	6	19	5

GROUP B

	P	W	D	L	F	A	Pts
Belgium Q	10	7	2	1	24	5	23
Wales Q	10	6	3	1	11	4	21
Bosnia-Herz	10	5	2	3	17	12	17
Israel	10	4	1	5	16	14	13
Cyprus	10	4	0	6	16	17	12
Andorra	10	0	0	10	4	36	0

GROUP C

	P	W	D	L	F	A	Pts
Spain Q	10	9	0	1	23	3	27
Slovakia Q	10	7	1	2	17	8	22
Ukraine Q	10	6	1	3	14	4	19
Belarus	10	3	2	5	8	14	11
Luxembourg	10	1	1	8	6	27	4
Macedonia	10	1	1	8	6	18	4

GROUP D

	P	W	D	L	F	A	Pts
Germany Q	10	7	1	2	24	9	22
Poland Q	10	6	3	1	33	10	21
Rep of Ireland Q	10	5	3	2	19	7	18
Scotland	10	4	3	3	22	12	15
Georgia	10	3	0	7	10	16	9
Gibraltar	10	0	0	10	2	56	0

GROUP E

	P	W	D	L	F	A	Pts
England Q	10	10	0	0	31	3	30
Switzerland Q	10	7	0	3	24	8	21
Slovenia	10	5	1	4	18	11	16
Estonia	10	3	1	6	4	9	10
Lithuania	10	3	1	6	7	18	10
San Marino	10	0	1	9	1	36	1

GROUP F

	P	W	D	L	F	A	Pts
Northern Ireland Q	10	6	3	1	16	8	21
Romania Q	10	5	5	0	11	2	20
Hungary Q	10	4	4	2	11	9	16
Finland	10	3	3	4	9	10	12
Faroe Is	10	2	0	8	6	17	6
Greece	10	1	3	6	7	14	6

GROUP G

	P	W	D	L	F	A	Pts
Austria Q	10	9	1	0	22	5	28
Russia Q	10	6	2	2	21	5	20
Sweden Q	10	5	3	2	15	9	18
Montenegro	10	3	2	5	10	13	11
Liechtenstein	10	1	2	7	2	26	5
Moldova	10	0	2	8	4	16	2

GROUP H

	P	W	D	L	F	A	Pts
Italy Q	10	7	3	0	16	7	24
Croatia Q*	10	6	3	1	20	5	20
Norway	10	6	1	3	13	10	19
Bulgaria	10	3	2	5	9	12	11
Azerbaijan	10	1	3	6	7	18	6
Malta	10	0	2	8	3	16	2

*1 pt deducted for racist behaviour

GROUP I

	P	W	D	L	F	A	Pts
Portugal Q	8	7	0	1	11	5	21
Albania Q	8	4	2	2	10	5	14
Denmark	8	3	3	2	8	5	12
Serbia*	8	2	1	5	8	13	4
Armenia	8	0	2	6	5	14	2

*3 pts deducted for crowd trouble

PLAY-OFFS

First leg: Bosnia-Herz 1 **Rep of Ireland** 1; Norway 0 Hungary 1; Sweden 2 Denmark 1; Ukraine 2 Slovenia 0

Second leg: Denmark 2 Sweden 2 (Sweden won 4-3 on agg); Hungry 2 Norway 1 (Hungary won 3-1 on agg); **Rep of Ireland** 2 Bosnia-Herz 0- (Rep of Ireland won 3-1 on agg); Slovenia 1 Ukraine 1 (Ukraine won 3-1 on agg)

DAY BY DAY DIARY 2015–16

JULY 2015

10 Crystal Palace pay a club-record £10m for Paris Saint-Germain's former Newcastle midfielder Yohan Cabaye. Swansea manager Garry Monk signs a contract extension through to 2018.

11 Hull City's second attempt to change their name to Hull Tigers is rejected by the FA. Fabian Delph, the Aston Villa captain, turns down a move to Manchester City.

12 Manchester United sign Germany captain Bastian Schweinsteiger from Bayern Munich for £15m and Southampton's Morgan Schneiderlin for £25m.

13 Claudio Ranieri, manager of Chelsea from 2000-2004 and most recently coach to the Greece national team, is appointed Leicester's new manager.

14 Raheem Sterling becomes the most expensive English player when joining Manchester City from Liverpool for £44m, a fee that could rise to £49m.

15 Former Cardiff manager Malky Mackay and head of recruitment Iain Moody are cleared by the FA after an 11-month investigation into racist and sexist text messages allegedly sent to each other.

17 Fabian Delph changes his mind and joins Manchester City for £8m, declaring the opportunity is too good to resist.

18 Steven Gerrard scores on his Major League Soccer debut and has a hand in two of Robbie Keane's three goals as LA Galaxy beat San Jose 5-2.

20 Nadir Ciftci, Celtic's new signing from Dundee United, is banned for the opening six matches of the season by the Scottish FA for biting Dundee's Jim McAlister.

21 Manager Tony Pulis reminds West Bromwich Albion's James McClean of his 'responsibilities' to the club after the Irish winger turns his back on the English national anthem before a match in Charleston on their tour of the United States.

22 Liverpool pay £32.5m for Aston Villa's Christian Benteke – a record fee for Villa.

23 West Ham require a penalty shoot-out victory against the Maltese club Birkirkara to reach the third qualifying round of the Europa League.

24 Kirk Broadfoot, Rotherham's former Rangers defender, is banned for ten matches and fined £7,500 by the FA for sectarian abuse towards West Bromwich Albion's James McClean – English football's longest suspension for a verbal offence.

25 England are drawn in the same qualifying group as Scotland for the 2018 World Cup. Wales and the Republic of Ireland are paired in another group. Northern Ireland have to play defending champions Germany.

27 UEFA president Michel Platini announces he will be a candidate to succeed Sepp Blatter as president of FIFA.

28 The FA give their backing to Michel Platini's bid to lead football's world governing body.

29 Leading scorer Callum Wilson signs a new four-year contract with newly-promoted Bournemouth.

30 Blackpool are fined £50,000 by the FA for the pitch invasion which caused their final match of last season against Huddersfield to be abandoned.

31 Gillingham and club chairman Paul Scally are each fined £75,000 by the FA after an employment tribunal ruling that striker Mark McCammon's unfair dismissal in January 2011 was an act of racial victimisation. The club's fine is later reduced on appeal to £50,000. Scally's fine stands. Theo Walcott signs a new four-year contract and Santi Cazorla a new two-year deal with Arsenal.

AUGUST 2015

1 Celtic begin their defence of the Scottish Premiership title by beating Ross County 2-0. Chelsea defeat Notts County 1-0 in the first Women's FA Cup Final to be played at Wembley, watched by a crowd of 30,710.

2 A goal by Alex Oxlade-Chamberlain gives Arsenal a 1-0 win over Chelsea in the Community Shield – curtain-raiser to the new English season.

3 Accrington's Crown Ground is renamed the Wham Stadium in a £200,000 sponsorship deal with plastics company What More.

4 The FA introduce a code of conduct for managers and coaches in technical areas, with fines or bans for misbehaviour.

5 Less than a year after signing for Manchester United for £59.7m, Angel di Maria joins Paris Saint-Germain for £44.3m. Ciaran Clark signs a new five-year contract with Aston Villa. Leicester's Riyad Mahrez and Stoke's Marc Muniesa pen new four-year deals.

6 West Ham and Aberdeen are knocked out of the Europa League in the third qualifying round by Astra Giurgiu (Romania) and Kairat Almaty (Kazakhstan) respectively. Newcastle captain Fabricio Coloccini extends his contract for another year. Reading are fined £100,000 by the FA for a pitch invasion by supporters after their FA Cup quarter-final replay win against Bradford. The fine is reduced to £40,000 on appeal.

7 Chelsea manager Jose Mourinho signs a new four-year contract with the club. Manchester City extend Manuel Pellegrini's contract through to 2017. Southampton's Ronald Koeman has an operation on a ruptured achilles and misses the start of the season.

8 Goalkeeper Thibaut Courtois is sent off as Chelsea begin their defence of the Premier League title with a 2-2 draw against Swansea. Barnet and Bristol Rovers, back in the Football League, start with defeats, against Leyton Orient and Northampton respectively. Doncaster manager Paul Dickov orders his players to let Bury walk in an equaliser after Harry Forrester scores while attempting to give the ball back following an injury.

9 Gareth Southgate is relieved of his duties overseeing all England's development teams to concentrate on the Under-21 side.

10 Two clubs make £12m record signings – West Bromwich Albion buying Venezuela striker Salomon Rondon from Zenit St Petersburg and Stoke acquiring Inter Milan's Switzerland midfielder Xherdan Shaqiri.

11 Seven Championship teams lose to lower-division opposition in the Capital One Cup first round, including Brentford who are beaten 4-0 at home by Oxford.

12 Chelsea manager Jose Mourinho's criticism of club doctor Eva Carneiro for treating Eden Hazard on the pitch during the match against Swansea against his wishes escalates into a public fall-out, with doctors' groups defending her action.

13 Jamie Vardy is given a 'substantial' fine by Leicester and ordered to undertake diversity awareness training after being filmed using racist language in a casino.

14 Jose Mourinho refuses to back down over his decision to relieve Eva Carneiro of her first-team duties.

16 Chelsea sign Ghana left-back Baba Rahman from Augsburg for an undisclosed fee, reported to be £21.7m.

18 Sebastien Bassong signs a new two-year contract with Norwich.

19 Chelsea beat Manchester United to the signing of Barcelona forward Pedro, paying £21m for the Spain World Cup winner.

20 Nicolas Otamendi, Valencia's Argentina central defender, joins Manchester City for a £28.5m fee.

21 Burnley sign Andre Gray from Brentford for £6m – a record for both Championship clubs.

22 In a rare move, the Premier League admit that referee Craig Pawson erred by allowing Christian Benteke's match-winning goal for Liverpool against Bournemouth to stand when it should have been disallowed for offside.

24 The Football League call a minute's silence before Capital One Cup second-round ties for those who died in the Shoreham air crash, including Worthing United players Matthew Grimstone and Jacob Schilt.

25 Celtic lose 4-3 on aggregate to Malmo in the play-off round for the Champions League group stage.

26 Wayne Rooney ends a run of ten matches without a goal by scoring a hat-trick as Manchester United beat Club Bruges 4-0 to win their play-off tie 7-1 on aggregate.

27 Southampton are beaten 2-1 on aggregate by the Danish champions Midtjylland in the play-off round for the Europa League group stage.
28 Tottenham sign South Korea forward Son Heung-min from Bayer Leverkusen for £21.9m.
30 Manchester City break their transfer record for the second time in less than two months, paying £52m for Wolfsburg's former Chelsea midfielder Kevin De Bruyne.
31 Manchester United make Anthony Martial the world's most expensive teenager when signing the 19-year-old forward from Monaco for £36m. Victor Moses signs a new four-year contract with Chelsea before joining West Ham on a season-long loan.

SEPTEMBER 2015

1 The summer transfer window closes with Premier League clubs having splashed out a record £898m. Manchester City (£154m) and Manchester United (£115m) are the biggest spenders. United and Real Madrid blame each other for one deal falling through – goalkeeper David de Gea's proposed move to the Bernabeu.
2 Derby chairman Mel Morris becomes sole owner of the club after burying out American Partners LLP. Bournemouth's Max Gradel is ruled out for up to six months with a knee ligament injury .
3 Wales win 1-0 in Cyprus with a header from Gareth Bale to move to the brink of qualifying for Euro 2016. Bournemouth suffer another blow – the loss of record-signing Tyrone Mings for the rest of the season with knee ligament damage sustained six minutes into his debut for the club.
4 Northern Ireland close in on a place in the finals as central defender Gareth McAuley scores twice in a 3-1 victory over the Faroe Islands. Robbie Keane is on the mark twice and Cyrus Christie opens his account for the Republic of Ireland, who keep their hopes alive by beating Gibraltar 4-0. Scotland's chances are take a blow with a 1-0 defeat by Georgia.
5 Wayne Rooney equals Sir Bobby Charlton's all-time record of 49 England goals with a penalty in a 6-0 away over San Marino which confirms his side's place in the finals in France. Ross Barkley nets his first at senior international level.
6 Wales are made to wait for confirmation of their place after being held to a goalless draw by Israel. Dave Robertson becomes the season's first managerial casualty, sacked by Peterborough after a single victory in the first six league games.
7 Kyle Lafferty scores his seventh goal in eight qualifying games – this time in stoppage-time – to give Northern Ireland a 1-1 draw with Hungary after Chris Baird is sent off for a second yellow card. Scotland go down 3-2 to Germany after twice equalising. The Republic of Ireland stay on track for a play-off place by beating Georgia 1-0 with a goal by Jon Walters.
8 Wayne Rooney becomes England's leading scorer on 50 goals with another penalty in a 2-0 victory over Switzerland. Doncaster manager Paul Dickov is dismissed after a single win in the opening six matches.
9 Former England stars David Beckham and Gary Lineker predict that Rooney could go on to put the record out of sight.
10 Hull midfielder Jake Livermore escapes an FA ban for testing positive for cocaine because of depression suffered after the death of his new-born baby. Tottenham's Eric Dier signs a new five-year contract.
11 West Ham are fined £50,000 by the FA for misconduct by their players following the dismissal of Mark Noble against Liverpool – a red card later rescinded.
12 David de Gea signs a new four-year contract with Manchester United following the collapse of his move to Real Madrid.
13 Darren Kelly, manager of Oldham for four months, is sacked following a 5-1 home defeat by Peterborough.
15 Luke Shaw is ruled out for the season with a broken leg sustained in Manchester United's Champions League game against PSV Eindhoven.
16 Liverpool winger Jordon Ibe commits his international future to England following an approach from Nigeria.
18 Jerome Valcke, FIFA's secretary-general, is suspended over allegations of selling World Cup

tickets above face value.

19 Manchester City's starting line-up against West Ham, costing £308.8m, is the most expensive in Premier League history.

20 Graham Westley, formerly in charge at Stevenage and Preston, is named Peterborough's new manager.

21 Bolton chairman Phil Gartside, coach Sammy Lee and agent Jerome Anderson are among ten people cleared by a court of all charges relating to the transfer of Gavin McCann from Aston Villa to Bolton in 2007.

22 Chelsea's Diego Costa receives a three-match FA ban for violent conduct after his clash with Arsenal's Laurent Koscielny is considered retrospectively by the governing body. Poland striker Robert Lewandowski comes off the bench and scores five goals in nine second-half minutes for Bayern Munich in a Bundesliga match against Wolfsburg – a record for a major European league.

23 Eva Carneiro, the Chelsea doctor who had her job downgraded after a row with manager Jose Mourinho, leaves the club.

24 Motherwell manager Ian Baraclough is sacked after his side's defeat by Championship side Morton in the Scottish League Cup.

25 FIFA president Sepp Blatter is placed under criminal investigation by Swiss investigators as the scandal engulfing the world governing body deepens.

26 FIFA confirm the dates for the 2022 World Cup in Qatar – November 21-December 18. Yannick Bolasie signs a new contract with Crystal Palace through to 2019.

27 Brentford dismiss manager Marinus Dijkhuizen after two wins in his nine matches in charge and appoint former Blackburn and Everton midfielder Lee Carsley until the end of the season.

28 Rotherham's Steve Evans, second longest-serving manager in the Championship, leaves after three-and-a-half-years following a difference of opinion on how to take the club forward. Jackie McNamara is sacked as Dundee United manager with his side second from bottom. Aston Villa's Jack Grealish pledges his senior international future to England after four appearances for the Republic of Ireland Under-21 team.

29 Leading scorer Callum Wilson becomes the third Bournemouth to sustain knee ligament damage, ruling him out for at least six months.

30 The FA decide to take no action against Jose Mourinho over his dispute with Eva Carneiro. But chairman Greg Dyke accuses the Chelsea manager of 'a failure of personal judgement and public behaviour.' Fleetwood manager Graham Alexander is sacked following a 5-1 defeat by Gillingham.

OCTOBER 2015

1 Terry Butcher, manager of Newport for five months, is dismissed after a single win in 12 games in charge.

2 Major FIFA sponsors call on Sepp Blatter to resign immediately, instead of waiting until February 2016 before stepping down as president. Hartlepool defender Carl Magnay is banned for six matches and fined £750 by the FA for spitting at a spectator after being sent off against Wycombe. John Sheridan, former Plymouth, Chesterfield and Oldham manager, takes over at Newport.

3 Sergio Aguero joins an elite club of Premier League players – Andy Cole, Alan Shearer, Jermain Defoe and Dimitar Berbatov – by scoring five goals in Manchester City's 6-1 win over Newcastle.

4 Brendan Rodgers, manager of Liverpool for three years, is sacked after the team's indifferent start to the season. Dick Advocaat, in charge at Sunderland for seven months, resigns with his side second from bottom. Chelsea become FA Women's Super League champions, completing the double after their FA Cup success.

5 Owner Roman Abramovich gives manager Jose Mourinho a vote of confidence after Chelsea's poor start to the season – four defeats in the first eight Premier League games. Former Coventry manager Steven Pressley takes over at Fleetwood.

7 Sepp Blatter and Michel Platini, the two most powerful figures in world football, are suspended for 90 days by FIFA's ethics committee over a payment of £1.35m by Blatter to the UEFA president. Jurgen Klopp, former Borussia Dortmund coach, is appointed Liverpool's new manager. Caretaker David Dunn is given the Oldham job on a permanent basis.

8 Northern Ireland reach the European Championship Finals for the first time – and qualify for a major tournament for the first time since the 1986 World Cup – with a 3-1 win over Greece. Captain Steven Davis scores two of the goals and Josh Magennis his first at senior international level. The Republic of Ireland beat Germany 1-0 with a goal from substitute Shane Long, a result which ends Scotland's chances. Gordon Strachan's side draw 2-2 against Poland, conceding a second goal seconds from the end to Robert Lewandowski, scorer of 12 in his previous four games for Bayern Munich. The FA fine Chelsea £40,000 and Arsenal £30,000 for the behavior of their players in a stormy Premier League game.

9 England record a ninth straight win in their group – 2-0 against Estonia. Sam Allardyce succeeds Dick Advocaat at the Stadium of Light – his seventh managerial job. Neil Redfearn, formerly in charge of Leeds, is appointed Rotherham's new manager. Bolton manager Neil Lennon is fined £3,500 by the FA for accusing referee Darren Drysdale of bias after the defeat by Queens Park Rangers.

10 Wales qualify for a major tournament for the first time since the 1958 World Cup in Sweden. They go down 2-0 to Bosnia-Herzegovina, but go through after Israel lose to Cyprus, whose winner is scored by Walsall's Jason Demetriou.

11 Craig Cathcart scores his first goal for Northern Ireland, who finish top of their qualifying group with a 1-1 draw against Finland. The Republic of Ireland have to settle for the play-offs after losing 2-1 to Poland, whose match-winner is the prolific Robert Lewandowski with his 13th goal of the campaign – equaling the 2008 record of Northern Ireland's David Healy. The Irish have John O'Shea sent off in stoppage-time for a second yellow card. Scotland complete their programme with a 6-0 victory over Gibraltar, Steven Fletcher netting his second hat-trick against the international newcomers and Chris Martin scoring his first for the team.

12 England complete a perfect ten by beating Lithuania 3-0. Newcastle goalkeeper Tim Krul is ruled out for the rest of the season with a knee ligament injury sustained while playing for Holland.

13 Gareth Bale scores his seventh goal of the campaign as Wales finish runners-up to Belgium after beating Andorra 2-0 in a game of ten bookings, seven of them for Andorra players. Mark McGhee returns for a second spell as Motherwell manager, having previously been in charge from 2007-09.

14 Former Dundee United striker Mixu Paatelainen is appointed the club's new manager.

15 Jose Mourinho is fined £50,000 and given a suspended one-match stadium ban by the FA for accusing referees of being afraid to award Chelsea penalties. Manchester City announce their first annual profit – £10.7m – since Sheik Mansour took over the club in 2008. Bournemouth extend manager Eddie Howe's contract by two years.

16 Scotland manager Gordon Strachan signs a two-year extension to his contract. Southampton's Jose Fonte signs a new three-year deal. Former Peterborough manager Darren Ferguson takes over at Doncaster.

17 Stevenage goalkeeper Jesse Joronen scores with a clearance over the head of Wycombe's Matt Ingram.

18 Uwe Rosler, manager of Leeds for five months, is sacked after two victories in his 12 games in charge. Swindon, second from bottom, dismiss their manager Mark Cooper.

19 Three weeks after leaving Rotherham, Steve Evans becomes the sixth manager at Elland Road since Massimo Cellino took over the club in April, 2014. Cellino, himself, is banned for the second time by the Football League, this time for a tax offence.

20 Gareth Bale is named on the shortlist for FIFA's Player of the Year award – the only British player.

22 UEFA fine the Scottish FA £14,000 and the Polish FA £28,000 for crowd disturbance at the Euro 2016 qualifier at Hampden Park. The Irish FA are fined £5,000 for pitch invasions at Northern Ireland's qualifier against Greece at Windsor Park.

24 Guy Luzon, Charlton's manager for nine months, is dismissed after a 3-0 home defeat by

Brentford leaves his side third from bottom.

25 Tim Sherwood pays the price for six successive Premier League defeats, dismissed after eight months in the job with Aston Villa second from bottom.

26 Arsenal are fined £60,000 by the FA for breaching rules on agents over the transfer of Calum Chambers from Southampton. Agent Alan Middleton is fined £30,000. The spate of managerial sackings continues, with Russ Wilcox ousted at fourth-from-bottom York.

27 Holders Chelsea are knocked out of the Capital One Cup by Stoke on penalties, adding to the pressure on manager Jose Mourinho after five defeats in the opening ten Premier League games.

28 The FA promise to investigate their legal position after suspended FIFA president Sepp Blatter claims that the venue for the 2018 World Cup – for which England made an unsuccessful bid – was fixed for Russia before voting.

29 Ramires signs a new contract to stay at Chelsea until 2019.

30 Local businessman Andy Holt takes over Accrington, clearing the club's £1.2m of debt and providing working capital.

31 Former Sunderland and Brighton manager Gus Poyet is appointed coach to AEK Athens.

NOVEMBER 2015

1 Remi Garde, the coach of Lyon and a former Arsenal midfielder, succeeds Tim Sherwood at Villa Park.

2 Jose Mourinho is given a one-match stadium ban and £40,000 fine by the FA for abusive behaviour towards Jon Moss in the referee's room at half-time of Chelsea's defeat at West Ham. Aston Villa's Micah Richards is banned for one game and fined £10,000 for a tunnel incident with Swansea's Federico Fernandez. Cambridge, 18th in League Two, sack manager Richard Money.

3 Manchester City win 3-1 away to Sevilla to reach the knockout stage of the Champions League with two matches to spare in a difficult qualifying group. Martin Ling, a member of Swindon's Premiership side in the 1993-94 season, is appointed the club's new manager.

4 Two managers are sacked with their teams in the bottom half of the Championship – Chris Ramsey at Queens Park Rangers and Huddersfield's Chris Powell. Former Scotland defender and Dundee United manager Jackie McNamara takes over at York.

5 David Wagner, Borussia Dortmund's former Under-23 coach, succeeds Chris Powell – Huddersfield's first Continental coach. Tony Pulis, West Bromwich Albion manager, admits 'having a go' at referee Anthony Taylor after losing to Leicester and is fined £8,000 by the FA for improper conduct.

6 The Football League increase parachute payments to clubs relegated to the National League from the 2016-17 season. Preston are fined £10,000 by the FA for crowd trouble at their League One play-off semi-final against Chesterfield.

7 Jon Walters signs a new two-and-a-half-year contract with Stoke.

8 Fulham manager Kit Symons is sacked following a 5-2 home defeat by Birmingham.

9 David Moyes, former Manchester United and Everton manager, is dismissed as Real Sociedad coach after four defeats in five matches. Patrick Vieira, head coach of Manchester City's elite development squad, is appointed head coach of New York City, the Major League Soccer club.

10 Gary Bowyer becomes the season's eighth managerial casualty in the Championship, sacked with Blackburn 16th in the table.

11 The FA fine Chelsea £50,000 and West Ham £40,000 for misconduct by their players who surrounded referee Jon Moss with protests in two separate incidents at Upton Park.

12 The Football League announce a change of name to the English Football League (EFL) ahead of the 2016-17 season. Shaun Derry, formerly in charge at Notts County, is appointed the new Cambridge manager.

13 The Stade de France, where France are playing Germany in a friendly international, is among the targets of terrorist attacks in Paris, with three people killed outside the stadium. Police allow the match to continue, fearing a stampede for the exits if it is abandoned. At

the final whistle, thousands of fans are evacuated on to the pitch before being allowed to leave. Germany's players spend the night in the stadium. The Republic of Ireland draw 1-1 with Bosnia-Herzegovina in the away leg of their Euro 2016 qualifying play-off. In friendly internationals, England lose 2-0 to Spain, Northern Ireland defeat Latvia 1-0, while Wales are beaten 3-2 by Holland after Emyr Huws scores for the first time for his country.

14 The FA and the French Federation agree that the England-France friendly at Wembley should go ahead in three days' time.

15 Paul Lambert, former Aston Villa manager, takes over at Blackburn. Leyton Orient owner Francesco Becchetti orders 18 players and six staff members, including manager Ian Hendon, to spend a week in a hotel after two wins in 12 League Two games.

16 The Republic of Ireland join England, Wales and Northern Ireland at Euro 2016 when two goals by Jon Walters, the first a penalty, deliver a 2-0 win over Bosnia-Herzegovina in the play-off second leg.

17 On an emotional night at Wembley, the stadium's giant arch is illuminated in the red, white and blue of the French national flag, England supporters in a 71,000 crowd sing *La Marseillaise* and the players observe a minute's silence. Amid tightened security, armed police are on duty at the game which England win 2-0, with Dele Alli scoring his first senior international goal on his full debut.

18 The Premier League decide that the French national anthem will be played before all the weekend's matches. The Football League and Scottish League leave the choice up to individual clubs. Sepp Blatter and Michel Platini appeal unsuccessfully against their 90-day suspensions.

19 Reading's Steve Clarke turns down the chance to take the vacant manager's job at Fulham.

20 UEFA decide not to punish Manchester City over their fans booing the Champions League anthem.

21 England Under-21 winger Duncan Watmore signs a new four-and-a-half-year contract with Sunderland.

22 Dinamo Zagreb player Arijan Ademi is banned for four years for failing a drugs test after playing the full 90 minutes of his side's Championships League win over Arsenal. According to UEFA rules, the result stands.

23 Former Oxford United chairman Kelvin Thomas agrees to buy David Cardoza's controlling stake in debt-ridden Northampton, a club trying to avoid administration.

24 Aston Villa's Jack Grealish is ordered to train with the club's Under-21 squad for partying after the team's 4-0 defeat by Everton.

25 Colchester's Tony Humes becomes the 20th managerial departure of the season, sacked after a single victory in nine league matches.

26 Liverpool and Tottenham reach the knockout stage of the Europa League. Celtic go out after finishing bottom of their group.

27 Jamie Vardy, Leicester's record-breaking scorer in the Premier League, launches an academy to give non-league players the chance he had when joining the club from Fleetwood.

28 Dean Saunders, manager of Chesterfield for six months, is sacked after four successive defeats and 12 goals conceded.

29 Dean Smith, longest-serving manager in League One, leaves Walsall after nearly five years to take charge at Brentford.

30 Premier League clubs are shown to have paid a record £130m to agents in the past year – up £15m on 2014 – with Liverpool (£14.3m), Manchester United (£13.9m) and Manchester City (£12.4m) the biggest spenders.

DECEMBER 2015

1 Manchester City owner Sheik Mansour sells a 13 per cent stake in the club to a Chinese consortium for £265m. Paul Sturrock is sacked by Yeovil after eight months as manager, with his team bottom of League Two. Nottingham Forest are fined £12,500 by the FA for misconduct by their players against Brentford. Inverness manager John Hughes signs a new contract through to 2018.

2 Gary Neville, former Manchester United and England full-back, is appointed Valencia's new head coach until the end of the season, joining brother Phil at the Spanish club. He continues to be involved in England's preparations for Euro 2016, but gives up his job as a *Sky Sports* analyst.

3 Gary Cahill signs a new four-year contract with Chelsea. Blackburn have a transfer ban, imposed for breaching Financial Fair Play rules, lifted by the Football League. Celtic suspend Republic of Ireland striker Anthony Stokes for two weeks following his complaints about being left out of the squad.

4 A fortnight after turning down an approach from Fulham, Reading manager Steve Clarke is sacked following a single win in eight matches.

5 Burton's Jimmy Floyd Hasselbaink becomes the new Queens Park Rangers manager.

6 Nigel Clough returns as Burton manager, nearly seven years after leaving the club to take over at Derby.

7 A two-week winter break for Scottish Premiership clubs in January 2017 is announced. Plans for a revamped League Cup, with a summer group stage, and a new television deal with BT Sport, worth around £8m over four years, are also unveiled.

8 Manchester United go out of the Champions League, beaten 3-2 by Wolfsburg in their final group game. Manchester City top their group by scoring three times in the final 11 minutes to defeat Borussia Monchengladbach 4-2.

9 A hat-trick by Olivier Giroud enables Arsenal to qualify for the knockout stage for the 16th successive season. In danger of going out, they win 3-0 away to Olympiacos. Chelsea overcome Porto 2-0 to head their group. Swansea manager Garry Monk, five months into a three-year contract, is sacked after a single win in 11 Premier League matches. The Premier League announce a new three-year deal, reported to be £3.2bn, for global TV rights – on top of the domestic package worth £5.13bn.

10 Liverpool and Tottenham finish top of their respective Europa League qualifying groups. Bolton are served with a winding-up petition by Revenue and Customs over unpaid tax.

11 Bastian Schweinsteiger is banned for three matches by the FA for violent conduct after an incident with Winston Reid is caught on camera during Manchester United's game against West Ham.

12 England and Wales are drawn in the same group at Euro 2016. Northern Ireland face Germany, while the Republic of Ireland draw the toughest group, alongside Italy and Belgium.

13 Sunderland manager Sam Allardyce calls on the Premier League to introduce a winter break to ease the 'relentless' Christmas and New Year programme.

14 Jose Mourinho accuses his players of 'betrayal' after a 2-1 defeat at Leicester leaves Chelsea a single point above the relegation zone.

15 England's Martin Atkinson and Mark Clattenburg and Scotland's Willie Callum are included on UEFA's list of referees for Euro 2016. Pep Guardiola, one of Europe's most admired coaches, is earmarked for a Premier League manager's job after deciding to leave Bayern Munich at the end of the season.

16 Tottenham receive planning approval from the local council for their planned new 60,000-seater stadium at White Hart Lane.

17 Jose Mourinho pays the price for Chelsea's poor title defence, sacked for the second time by owner Roman Abramovich after nine defeats in the first 16 matches. Also dismissed is Luton's John Still following four successive league and cup defeats. Brian McDermott, fired by Reading in March 2013, returns for a second spell as manager.

18 American investors Josh Harris and David Blitzer take a £50m stake in Crystal Palace. The FA fine West Bromwich Albion £25,000 and Tottenham £20,000 for a players' melee. Sean O'Driscoll, former Bristol City, Nottingham Forest, Doncaster and Bournemouth manager, takes over at Walsall.

19 Jimmy Hill, one of the most influential figures in English football as player, manager, chairman, union leader and broadcaster, dies aged 87. Former Holland coach Guus Hiddink is appointed Chelsea's interim manager until the end of the season – his second spell at the club, having been in temporary charge for three months in 2009, during which time they won the FA Cup.

20 Michael O'Neill is named Coach of the Year at the BBC Sports Personality of the Year awards for guiding Northern Ireland to the finals of Euro 2016. Brighton, the only unbeaten side in the four divisions, lose 3-0 at home to Middlesbrough in their 22nd Championship game. Two goals by Luis Suarez and one from Lionel Messi give Barcelona a 3-0 win over River Plate in the Club World Cup Final in Yokohama, Japan.

21 Sepp Blatter and Michel Platini are banned from involvement in football for eight years by FIFA's ethics committee for conflict of interest and disloyalty over the undocumented £1.35m payment FIFA president Blatter paid to the UEFA president in 2011. Blatter is also fined £33,700 and Platini £54,000. Former West Ham midfielder Kevin Keen takes charge of Colchester. Dagenham manager Wayne Burnett is sacked with his side bottom of League Two.

22 The Football League agree a new three-year title sponsorship deal with Sky Bet. James Collins signs a new two-year contract extension with West Ham.

23 Louis van Gaal walks out of a press conference in protest at media speculation that he may be sacked as Manchester United manager after six games without a win.

24 Bolton, Fulham and Nottingham Forest are placed under a transfer embargo for the rest of the season for breaching Football League Financial Fair Play rules. Danny Wilson takes charge at Chesterfield, his ninth managerial appointment.

26 Erik Pieters signs a new contract with Stoke through to the summer of 2020.

27 Former Watford manager Slavisa Jokanovic takes over at Fulham. Ed Balls, former shadow chancellor and lifelong Norwich fan, is appointed the club's chairman.

28 Ricardo Moniz, manager of Notts County for nine months, is sacked after his side concede 19 goals in eight games.

29 Martin Ling, in charge of Swindon for 56 days, resigns for health reasons – the 30th managerial departure of the season.

30 John Still is appointed Dagenham manager for the third time, having previously been in charge from 1992–94 and from 2004–13. Coventry manager Tony Mowbray is given a one-match touchline ban and fined £1,000 by the FA for misconduct during the game at Chesterfield.

31 Yeovil appoint Darren Way, a former midfielder at the club, on a permanent basis after six games as interim manager.

JANUARY 2016

1 Former Manchester United legend Denis Law and ex-Manchester City star Francis Lee are both awarded a CBE in the New Year's Honours. Two of England's successful women's World Cup team, captain Steph Houghton and Fara Williams, receive the MBE. Heather Rabbatts, the FA's first female board member, is made a Dame.

3 Wayne Rooney is named England Player of the Year for the second successive time, having become his country's leading scorer in 2015.

4 One of the most controversial goals in the history of the game – Geoff Hurst's second in England's 1966 World Cup Final win over West Germany – DID cross the line, according to new technology shown by *Sky*.

5 Sunderland manager Sam Allardyce accuses the Premier League of showing disrespect to the FA Cup by scheduling midweek fixtures following the weekend's third round ties.

6 Former Queens Park Rangers manager Chris Ramsey is appointed technical director of the club.

7 Nathan Jones, Brighton's first-team coach, becomes the new manager of Luton, where he started his playing career.

8 Caretaker Alan Curtis is given the Swansea's manager's job until the end of the season.

9 Bournemouth pay £9m, a club record, for Benik Afobe from Wolves and agree a £7m fee to bring Lewis Grabban back to the club from Norwich.

10 Oxford deliver the one major upset of the FA Cup third round, defeating Swansea 3-2. Jamie Fullarton, former Crystal Palace midfielder and Nottingham Forest coach, is appointed Notts County's new manager.

11 Lionel Messi wins the Ballon d'Or World Player of the Year award for the fifth time, with

Cristiano Ronaldo second in the voting and Messi's Barcelona team-mate, Neymar, third.

12 Dele Alli signs a new contract with Tottenham through to 2021. David Dunn, manager of Oldham for four months, is sacked after seven league games without a win. Head coach Mark Sampson, who led England to the semi-finals of the women's World Cup, has his contract extended to beyond the next tournament in France in 2019.

13 Newcastle sign Swansea's Jonjo Shelvey for £12m. FIFA dismiss suspended secretary-general Jerome Valcke after an investigation into the sale of World Cup tickets. Karel Fraeye, Charlton's interim manager for two months, is sacked after a 5-0 defeat by Huddersfield leaves the team second from bottom. John Sheridan, in charge at Newport for three months, leaves the club for a second spell as Oldham manager.

14 Nine months after leading Bristol City to promotion – and to victory in the Johnstone's Paint Trophy – Steve Cotterill is sacked with his side third from bottom of the Championship. Jose Riga takes charge of Charlton for the second time, having led them away from the threat of relegation in 2014. Aston Villa owner Randy Lerner steps down as chairman of the club and appoints businessman Steven Hollis in his place.

15 The FA give Francesco Becchetti a six-match stadium ban and fine him £40,000 for violent conduct after viewing pictures of the Italian owner of Leyton Orient aiming a kick at assistant manager Andy Hessenthaler at the Boxing Day home win over Portsmouth. Warren Feeney, John Sheridan's assistant at Newport, is given the manager's job. Cardiff have a January transfer embargo imposed for breaching financial fair play rules.

17 Francesco Becchetti sacks Ian Hendon, Orient manager for eight months, after a single win in ten league and cup matches.

18 Swansea have a change of heart about their manager's job, appointing former Udinese coach Francesco Guidolin, with Alan Curtis working alongside him. Scunthorpe manager Mark Robins is dismissed following a 5-0 defeat at Blackpool.

19 Liverpool's Simon Mignolet signs a new five-year contract. Arsenal's Nacho Monreal pens a new three-year deal.

20 Kevin Nolan, former West Ham, Newcastle and Bolton captain, becomes Leyton Orient's player-manager.

21 UEFA's executive committee approve the use of goal-line technology at Euro 2016 and in the Champions League from the 2016-17 season.

22 Roy Hodgson is awarded an honorary degree from York University in recognition of 40 years of management.

23 Cardiff's Anthony Pilkington scores a hat-trick of a different kind against Rotherham – two goals for his own side and one deflected into his own net from a corner.

25 The FA fine Chelsea £65,000 and West Bromwich Albion £35,000 for a players' melee at Stamford Bridge. Sunderland's Jordan Pickford signs a contract extension through to 2020.

26 Liverpool beat Stoke 6-5 in a penalty shoot-out after a 1-1 aggregate scoreline to reach the Capital One Cup Final.

27 Manchester City defeat Everton 3-2 over two legs of the second semi-final. Chelsea midfielder Ramires joins Chinese Super League club Jiangsu Suning for £25m - £7m more than the club paid Benfica for him in 2010.

28 Newcastle, the Premier League's biggest spenders in the winter transfer window, pay another £12m for Tottenham's Andros Townsend. Greg Dyke decides not to seek re-election as FA chairman because of opposition to change from factions within the governing body. Former Wales striker Robert Earnshaw, the only player to have scored a hat-trick in the Premier League, all three divisions of the Football League, the FA Cup, League Cup and for his country, announces his retirement at 34.

29 Connor Wickham, of Crystal Palace, is banned for three games by the FA for elbowing Tottenham's Jan Vertonghen – an incident caught on camera. Mousa Dembele signs a new three-year contract with Tottenham. Former Manchester United captain Nemanja Vidic, 34, announces his retirement.

30 Singer Rod Stewart donates £10,000 to Carlisle to help the club recover from flood damage which forced three matches to be played away from Brunton Park. Kilmarnock manager Gary

Locke resigns after a home defeat by Hamilton leaves his side second from bottom of the Scottish Premiership. Hibernian defeat St Johnstone 2-1 to reach the Scottish League Cup Final.

31 Ross County, a goal down after 26 seconds, upset the odds by beating Celtic 3-1 in the second semi-final.

FEBRUARY 2016

1 Pep Guardiola is named as Manchester City's next manager, replacing Manuel Pellegrini at the end of the season. The appointment, reported to carry a record £300,000 a week salary, overshadows transfer deadline day, during which Stoke are the biggest spenders. They pay a club-record £18.3m for Porto midfielder Giannelli Imbula, while Everton sign Lokomotiv Moscow striker Oumar Niasse for £13.5m. Spending of £175m by Premier League clubs in the winter window takes their total outlay for the season to a record £1.04bn. Former England striker Teddy Sheringham, whose own transfers fees in the 1990s totalled £7.6m, is sacked after eight months as Stevenage manager, with his side sixth from bottom.

2 Goalkeeper Barry Roche heads in a 94th minute corner to earn Morecambe a 1-1 draw against Portsmouth.

3 Gary Neville says he will not resign after Valencia's 7-0 defeat by Barcelona in the first leg of their Copa del Ray semi-final.

4 The financial muscle of Chinese clubs is again evident when their transfer record is broken for the third time in nine days. Colombian Jackson Martinez joins Guangzhou Evergrande from Atletico Madrid for £31m. Brazilian Alex Teixeira, linked with Liverpool, moves from Shakhtar Donesk to Jiangsu Suning for £38.4m.

5 Jamie Vardy, Leicester's record-breaking striker, signs a new three-year contract with the club. Manager Lee Johnson leaves Barnsley to take charge at Bristol City, where he was a player from 2006-12 and where his father Gary was manager from 2005-10. Two managers are given one-match touchline bans by the FA for abusive language towards match officials. Doncaster's Darren Ferguson is also fined £1,000 and Newport's Warren Feeney £500.

6 Former Liverpool stalwart Jamie Carragher joins thousands of fans walking out of Anfield during the game against Sunderland in protest at increased season ticket prices.

7 Chelsea's Kurt Zouma sustains a knee injury against Manchester United, misses the rest of the season and is ruled out of contention for a place in the France squad for Euro 2016.

8 Two Championship managers are dismissed. Neil Redfearn, in charge at Rotherham for four months, leaves with his side third from bottom. Paul Clement is sacked after eight months in the job, with Derby's bid for automatic promotion having stalled. They are the 40th and 41st managerial departures of the season.

9 Ronnie Moore, who led Hartlepool to safety against the odds in 2015, is sacked with his team facing another relegation struggle.

10 Liverpool's owners, stung by the mass walk-out, reverse their decision on ticket prices. Craig Hignett, who ended his playing career at Hartlepool, succeeds Ronnie Moore as manager.

11 Adam Johnson is sacked by Sunderland after pleading guilty at Bradford Crown Court to two child sex offences. Neil Warnock is appointed Rotherham's manager until the end of the season – his 12th league club. Two players sign new long-term contracts – West Ham's Dimitri Payet to 2021 and Stoke's Bojan Krkic to 2020. The FA give Mansfield manager Adam Murray a one-match touchline ban and £500 fine for comments towards match officials.

12 Sacked FIFA secretary-general Jerome Valcke is banned from football for 12 years by the governing body's ethics committee.

13 Jack Collison, former West Ham and Wales midfielder, announces his retirement because of persistent knee problems.

14 Lee Clark, former Blackpool, Birmingham and Huddersfield manager, takes charge at Kilmarnock.

15 The FA respond to mounting protests about ticket prices by cutting the cost to supporters of the FA Cup semi-finals and final. Manchester United announce the renaming of the south stand at Old Trafford after Sir Bobby Charlton.

16 The FA back the candidacy of UEFA general-secretary Gianni Infantino to succeed Sepp Blatter as president of FIFA. Derby and Preston are both fined £7,500 by the FA for a players' melee.

17 Franz Beckenbauer, winner of the World Cup with West Germany as a player and manager, is warned and fined £5,000 by FIFA's ethics committee for failing to cooperate with an investigation into the bidding process for the 2018 and 2022 tournaments. The FA fine Birmingham £8,500 and Sheffield Wednesday £10,000 for misconduct by their players at St Andrew's. Craig Dawson extends his contract with West Bromwich Albion until 2018.

18 Bristol Rovers are taken over by the Jordanian Al-Qadi family. Stoke's Andy Wilkinson, out of action since suffering concussion in an FA Cup tie against Blackburn in February 2015, announces his retirement.

19 Sheffield United suspend Jose Baxter for the second time in nine months. The club give no reason for the decision over the striker, whose first suspension was for failing a drugs test.

20 West Bromwich Albion's Chris Brunt escapes serious injury when a coin thrown from the crowd hits him under the left eye during his side's FA Cup fifth round defeat at Reading.

22 A consortium headed by the club's former record-signing, Dean Holdsworth, agrees to take over Bolton from businessman Eddie Davies for an initial £7.5m.

23 The Football League fine Cambridge £7,000, with £5,000 suspended, for fielding an ineligible player, Ryan Ledson, in the 1-0 defeat by Crawley.

24 Sepp Blatter and Michel Platini have their eight-year bans cut to six years by FIFA's appeals committee.

25 Marcus Rashford, 18, scores twice on his debut as Manchester United defeat Midtjylland 5-1 to reach the last 16 of the Europa League 6-3 on aggregate. Tottenham beat Fiorentina 4-1 over the two legs and Liverpool overcome Augsburg 1-0. Gary Neville's Valencia score a record 10-0 aggregate win over Rapid Vienna. Gillingham are given a suspended £4,000 fine for fielding an ineligible player, Emmanuel Osadebe, in their 4-0 win over Sheffield United on the opening day of the season. The Football League decide against a points deduction because of extenuating factors.

26 Gianni Infantino pledges to restore FIFA's battered image after being elected the world governing body's new president. He defeats the favourite, Bahrain's Sheik Salman.

27 After selling his stake in Arsenal, Iranian billionaire Farhad Moshiri becomes Everton's majority shareholder in a deal reported be worth nearly £200m.

28 Reserve goalkeeper Willy Caballero saves three penalties to give Manchester City a 3-1 shoot-out victory over Liverpool after the League Cup Final ends 1-1.

29 Ruben Loftus-Cheek signs a new five-year contract with Chelsea.

MARCH 2016

1 Premier League referee Kevin Friend spends the night in hospital after banging his head against the dug-out while on duty as fourth official for the Bournemouth-Southampton game.

2 Leicester, leaders of the Premier League, post record annual profits of £26.4m.

3 Chris Brunt, a key figure in Northern Ireland reaching Euro 2016, is ruled out of the finals after knee surgery.

5 Newcastle's players release a statement in support of under-pressure manager Steve McClaren.

6 The International FA Board, meeting in Cardiff, pave the way for video assistance for referees faced with difficult decisions on goals, red cards and penalties.

7 Sean O'Driscoll, in charge of Walsall for three months, is sacked after a run of six matches without a win.

8 Margaret Byrne, Sunderland's chief executive, resigns after admitting the club erred by allowing Adam Johnson to continue playing after his arrest.

9 Chelsea are knocked out of the Champions League by Paris Saint-Germain for the second successive season, losing 4-2 on aggregate in the last 16. Premier League clubs agree to cap the price of away tickers for supporters at £30 for the next three seasons. Luke Williams, Swindon's caretaker-manager, is given the job on a permanent basis after a run of four successive victories. Turkish businessman Ziya Eren completes a takeover of League Two Crawley.

10 Steve McClaren is sacked after nine months in charge of Newcastle, with his side second from bottom. Rafael Benitez, former Real Madrid, Chelsea and Liverpool manager, replaces him.

11 Mansfield striker Adi Yussuf is banned for five matches and fined £700 by the FA for urinating at the back of a stand while warming up to come on at Plymouth.

12 Dougie Freedman, Nottingham Forest's manager, is dismissed after a run of five defeats in six matches.

13 Ross County win their first major trophy, beating Hibernian 2-1 in the Scottish League Cup Final with a 90th minute goal from Alex Schalk.

14 Neil Lennon, manager of relegation-bound Bolton, becomes another Championship casualty, with the club's new owners announcing his departure by mutual consent.

15 Manchester City reach the quarter-finals of the Champions League for the first time by defeating Dynamo Kiev 3-1 on aggregate.

16 Arsenal are knocked out in the round of 16 for the sixth successive season, beaten 5-1 on aggregate by Barcelona. Northern Ireland manager Michael O'Neill signs a new four-year contract. Harry Redknapp joins Derby as an advisor until the end of the season. Samir Carruthers (MK Dons) and James Collins (Northampton) are fined two weeks' wages by their clubs for 'unacceptable' behavior at the Cheltenham Festival race meeting.

17 Liverpool defeat Manchester United 3-1 on aggregate in the clubs' first-ever European tie to reach the quarter-finals of the Europa League. Tottenham lose 5-1 to Borussia Dortmund over the two legs. Bolton settle an unpaid tax bill threatening the club's future.

18 Three players sign new contracts – Stoke's Jack Butland and West Ham's Cheikhou Kouyate through to 2021 and Liverpool's Jon Flanagan for another three years.

19 Jamie Fullarton manager of Notts County for 69 days, is sacked after a 4-1 home defeat by Exeter.

20 Mark Cooper, former Swindon manager, takes over at Meadow Lane until the end of the season, with the promise of a permanent appointment if he hits an agreed points total. A winding-up order against Bolton is lifted following payment of a £2.2m tax bill.

21 Harry Redknapp begins a second appointment, working with the Jordan national team for two World Cup qualifying matches.

22 Graham Alexander, former Fleetwood manager, takes charge at Scunthorpe, where he began his playing career.

23 West Ham increase the capacity of the Olympic Stadium from 54,000 to 60,000 following the demand for season tickets ahead of their summer move to Stratford. The FA fine Queens Park Rangers £7,500 and Brentford £10,000 for a players' melee.

24 Johan Cruyff, three times European Footballer of the Year, three times a European Cup winner with Ajax and one of the finest players of all-time, dies of cancer aged 68. Wales and Northern Ireland draw 1-1 in the first of their warm-up matches for Euro 2016. Scotland, the only team from the British Isles not to qualify, defeat one of the group winners, the Czech Republic, 1-0 in Prague. Adam Johnson is jailed for six years at Bradford Crown Court.

25 The Republic of Ireland begin their build-up to the tournament in France by beating Switzerland 1-0.

26 England give their finest performance for several years, transforming a 2-0 deficit into a 3-2 win over Germany in Berlin. Harry Kane's strike is followed by first international goals for Jamie Vardy and, in extra-time, for Eric Dier. League One Dunfermline become the season's first Scottish champions, with five matches to spare.

27 Stoke's Jack Butland is ruled out of the finals with a broken ankle sustained in England's victory.

28 Conor Washington scores his first international goal to give Northern Ireland a 1-0 win over Slovenia and a record-breaking tenth successive unbeaten game, surpassing the mark set by Billy Bingham's team when reaching the 1986 World Cup. Wales lose 1-0 to Ukraine.

29 England are brought down to earth, losing 2-1 to Holland at Wembley. Scotland defeat Denmark 1-0. The Republic of Ireland draw 2-2 with Slovakia, group opponents for England

and Wales in France. Remi Garde leaves relegation-bound Aston Villa after two wins in his 20 Premier League matches.

30 Gary Neville is sacked by Valencia after four troubled months as head coach. Another goalkeeper is ruled out of Euro 2016 – the Republic of Ireland's Rob Elliot with a knee injury sustained in the game against Slovakia. The FA ban Leeds striker Souleymane Doukara for eight matchers and fine him £5,000 for biting Fulham's Fernando Amorebieta in an off-the-ball incident.

31 Sunderland terminate Emmanuel Eboue's contract after the Ivory Coast defender is banned from all football for a year by FIFA for failing to pay money owed to his former agent.

APRIL 2016

1 Chelsea's Diego Costa is given an extra one-match ban, on top of his original two-game suspension, and fined £20,000 by the FA for his reaction to being sent off against Everton.

3 Barnsley beat Oxford United 3-2 in the Johnstone's Paint Trophy Final at Wembley.

4 Italy coach Antonio Conte is named Chelsea's permanent successor to Jose Mourinho, taking over after Euro 2016.

5 Rangers, demoted to the Scottish League's bottom tier in 2012 after the club's financial collapse, complete their rise back to the top division by sealing the Championship title with four games to spare.

6 The former offices of new FIFA president Gianni Infantino at UEFA are raided by Swiss police investigating the sale of TV rights.

7 Northern Ireland achieve their highest-ever FIFA world ranking of 26th after qualifying for Euro 2016.

8 MK Dons are fined £10,000 by the FA for the behavior of their players against Brighton.

9 League Two Northampton become the first Football League club to be promoted. Bolton, from the Championship, and League One Crewe are the first to be relegated. Brentford's Alan Judge sustains a broken leg against Ipswich and is ruled out of contention for a place in the Republic of Ireland's squad for Euro 2016.

10 Rangers complete a league and cup double by beating Peterhead 4-0 in the Scottish Challenge Cup Final.

11 With Leicester and Tottenham disputing the title, the Premier League remove Leicester-based referee Kevin Friend from Tottenham's game at Stoke and replace him with Neil Swarbrick.

12 Manchester City reach the Champions League semi-finals, Kevin De Bruyne scoring the decisive second leg goal for a 3-2 aggregate win over Paris Saint-Germain. Middlesbrough's Cristhian Stuani is banned for three games by the FA for violent conduct, caught on camera, against Preston.

13 Holders Barcelona are knocked out by Atletico Madrid. Kevin Nolan is removed as Leyton Orient manager, after three months in the job, with his side's challenge for a play-off place faltering.

14 Liverpool deliver one of their greatest performances in Europe, overturning a 3-1 deficit in the second leg of their Europa League quarter-final against Jurgen Klopp's former side Borussia Dortmund. They win 4-3 with a stoppage-time goal by Dejan Lovren and go through 5-4 on aggregate. Ian Lenagan, a member of the Football League board, is appointed to succeed Greg Clarke as chairman at the end of the season.

15 Reading team-mates Paul McShane and Danny Williams are banned for three matches by the FA following an on-field row, caught on camera, during the defeat by Middlesbrough.

16 Aston Villa are relegated after 28 years of top-flight football with four Premier League games still to play. Dagenham are demoted from League Two. Cheltenham regain their Football League place at the first attempt, clinching the National League title. Northampton are crowned champions. Hibernian defeat Dundee United on penalties to reach the Scottish Cup Final. Fulham have a transfer embargo lifted by the Football League

17 Rangers win the second semi-final, also on penalties, against Celtic. Burnley's Andre Gray is named Championship Player of the Year. Bradley Dack (Gillingham) and Kemar Roofe (Oxford) receive the League One and League Two awards.

18 David Bernstein, former FA chairman, and Lord Mervyn King, former governor of the Bank of England, resign from the Aston Villa board.

19 Three Leicester players, Riyad Mahrez, Jamie Vardy and N'Golo Kante, along with Arsenal's Mesut Ozil, Tottenham's Harry Kane and West Ham's Dimitri Payet, are shortlisted for the PFA Player of the Year award.

20 Leeds director Edoardo Cellino, son of the club's owner, is suspended from all football-related activity for three matches and fined £5,000 by the FA over an abusive argument with a supporter on social media.

21 Celtic announce that manager Ronny Deila will leave the club at the end of the season. Stoke rename the Britannia Stadium the bet365 Stadium in a deal with the club's owners.

22 Figures show Premier League clubs paying nearly £47m to agents in the first half of the season, with Manchester United (£10m), Liverpool (£6.6m) and Manchester City (£5.8m) spending the most.

23 Manchester United beat Everton 2-1 in the first FA Cup semi-final. York are relegated from League Two. Graham Westley, manager of Peterborough for seven months, is sacked after a fourth defeat in five matches.

24 Crystal Palace defeat Watford 2-1 in the second semi-final. Riyad Mahrez is named PFA Player of the Year and is flown by helicopter to London after Leicester's win over Swansea to receive the trophy. Tottenham's Dele Alli wins the Young Player of the Year award.

25 Jamie Vardy, sent off in Leicester's game against West Ham, has a one-match ban doubled by the FA for his angry reaction to the second yellow card. He is also fined £10,000. Crawley manager Mark Yates is sacked after a run of six successive defeats.

26 An inquest jury rules that the 96 Liverpool fans who died in the Hillsborough disaster of 1989 were unlawfully killed. Norwich and Sunderland are both fined £30,000 by the FA for a touchline scuffle between players. Kevin Keen, manager of Colchester for four months, resigns after his side are relegated.

27 Manchester City's request for their match against Southampton to be brought forward 24 hours to provide more time to prepare for the Champions League semi-final, second leg against Real Madrid is turned down by the Premier League.

28 Dele Alli is banned by the FA from Tottenham's final three matches of the season after being caught on camera punching West Bromwich Albion's Claudio Yacob in the stomach. Paul Lambert announces he will leave Blackburn at the end of the season after six months as manager. Mark Clattenburg is named as referee for the FA Cup Final between Crystal Palace and Manchester United. Liverpool are ordered to pay Burnley £6.5m for Danny Ings, a record fee for a transfer tribunal.

29 Tottenham manager Mauricio Pochettino agrees a two-year extension to his contract, taking it through to 2021.

MAY 2016

1 Celtic's Leigh Griffiths wins the PFA Scotland Player of the Year award. Mark Warburton (Rangers) is named Scottish Manager of the Year.

2 Leicester, 5,000-1 no-hopers at the start of the season, become Premier League champions – a feat described in some quarters as the biggest in English sporting history. The team celebrate at leading scorer Jamie Vardy's house after watching Tottenham's challenge end in a stormy 2-2 draw against Chelsea at Stamford Bridge. Tottenham receive a record nine bookings and players on both sides are involved in brawls. Vardy is named the Football Writers' Association Footballer of the Year. Dundee United are relegated from the Scottish Premiership

3 Bournemouth are fined £7.6m by the Football League for breaching Financial Fair Play rules during the club's promotion season.

4 Manchester City lose to Real Madrid in the Champions League semi-finals, a deflected strike by Gareth Bale the only goal of the two-leg tie. Mixu Paatelainen manager for seven months, is sacked after Dundee United's relegation. John McGreal, in charge of the club's Under-21 side, is appointed Colchester's new manager.

5 Liverpool reach the Europa League Cup Final by beating Villarreal 3-0 at Anfield for a 3-1

aggregate victory. Robert Huth is banned from Leicester's final two games of the season and the first one of the new campaign for pulling Marouane Fellaini's hair in the match against Manchester United. Fellaini also receives a three-match suspension from the FA for elbowing Huth, missing United's last three league games ahead of the FA Cup Final against Crystal Palace.

6 Tottenham's Mousa Dembele is banned for six matches for eye-gouging Chelsea's Diego Costa in another case of the FA acting on video evidence. Arsenal's Alex Oxlade-Chamberlain is ruled out of contention for a place in England's squad for Euro 2016 with a knee injury.

7 Burnley win the Championship title and return to the Premier League at the first attempt. Middlesbrough also go up. Charlton manager Jose Riga resigns after his relegated side's final match of the season.

8 Vincent Kompany, the Manchester City and Belgium captain, is ruled out of Euro 2016 with a groin injury. Celtic are crowned Scottish champions for the fifth successive year. Leigh Griffiths completes a double by winning the Scottish Football Writers' Footballer of the Year award. Wigan go straight back up to the Championship as League One title winners

9 West Ham announce season ticket sales of 52,000 for their first season in the Olympic Stadium. Michel Platini has his six-year ban reduced to four years by the Court of Arbitration for Sport in Lausanne. Mark Clattenburg is given another major match to referee – the Champions League Final.

10 England's Danny Welbeck is ruled out of Euro 2016 after knee surgery which may keep him out of action for nine months. Hooligans attack Manchester United's team bus arriving for West Ham's final match at Upton Park and the kick-off is delayed for 45 minutes. Darren Sarll, Stevenage's caretaker-manager, is given the job on a permanent basis.

11 Sunderland's 3-0 win over Everton preserves their Premier League states and relegates Newcastle and Norwich. Francesco Guidolin signs a two-year contract to stay at Swansea after leading the club away from the threat of going down. Tottenham manager Mauricio Pochettino signs a two-year contract extension through to 2021. Dundee United are deducted three points and fined £30,000 – part of which is suspended – by the Scottish League for fielding two ineligible players in their victory over Inverness.

12 Everton sack manager Roberto Martinez after the club's poorest Premier League finish for 12 years. Nigel Adkins is dismissed by Sheffield United for not reaching the play-offs and replaced by Northampton's Chris Wilder. Ray McKinnon leaves Raith to become Dundee United's new manager. The FA ban Huddersfield's Dean Whitehead for three matches for violent conduct on video evidence of his clash with Brentford's Nico Yennaris.

13 Watford sack manager Quique Sanchez Flores, despite comfortably preserving their Premier League status and reaching the FA Cup semi-finals. West Ham's Slaven Bilic calls the decision 'sick.'

14 Edinburgh City become the first club to be promoted to Scottish League Two through the pyramid system with a 2-1 play-off aggregate win over East Stirling, whose 61 years in senior football comes to an end. Arsenal beat Chelsea 1-0 in the Women's FA Cup Final in front of a crowd of nearly 33,000 at Wembley.

15 A dummy bomb, left in the stadium by mistake after a security exercise, causes the evacuation of 75,000 fans shortly before kick-off of the Manchester United-Bournemouth game at Old Trafford. The match is called off and rescheduled. Grimsby return to the Football League after a six-year absence, beating Forest Green 3-1 in the National League Play-off Final.

16 The FA hand out record fines for the mass confrontations at Stamford Bridge earlier in the month. Chelsea are ordered to pay £375,000 for failing to control their players for the fifth time in 14 months. Tottenham are fined £225,000 for a third offence. An estimated 200,000 people watch Leicester's open-top bus parade through the city. Peterborough appoint coach Grant McCann their new manager after a spell as caretaker.

17 Leicester's Claudio Ranieri is named League Managers' Association Manager of the Year, adding to his Premier League and Italian Coach of the Year awards. Manchester City's Martin Demichelis is fined £22,000 by the FA for breaking betting rules.

18 Liverpool are beaten 3-1 by Sevilla in the Europa League Final, the Spanish club's third successive victory in the competition. Aston Villa owner Randy Lerner agrees to sell the club to Chinese businessman Dr Tony Xia. John Terry agrees a pay cut to stay at Chelsea for another season. Neil Warnock leaves Rotherham, unable to agree new terms after saving the club from relegation. Coach Paul Trollope takes over from Russell Slade as Cardiff manager, with Slade becoming the club's head of football. Relegated Blackpool sack their manager, Neil McDonald.

19 The Football League unveil proposals for an extra division from the 2019-20 season. Port Vale's Robert Page is appointed Northampton's new manager.

20 Former Liverpool and Swansea manager Brendan Rodgers takes charge at Celtic. Former Inter Milan coach Walter Mazzarri is appointed Watford's new manager. John Hughes leaves Inverness after a disagreement on how to take the club forward.

21 Manchester United, down to ten men after Chris Smalling is sent off for a second yellow card, beat Crystal Palace 2-1 in the FA Cup Final with an extra-time goal from substitute Jesse Lingard. The victory comes amid reports that manager Lous van Gaal is being replaced by Jose Mourinho. Hibernian lift the Scottish Cup for the first time since 1902, defeating Rangers 3-2 with a stoppage-time header by captain David Gray. Police horses have to restore order after thousands of fans invade the pitch at the final whistle and the Scottish FA order an inquiry.

22 Wales manager Chris Coleman signs a two-year contract extension to beyond the 2018 World Cup. England defeat Turkey 2-1 at the Etihad in their first warm-up game for Euro 2016. Kilmarnock retain their Scottish Premiership status, beating Falkirk 4-1 on aggregate in the play-offs.

23 Manchester United confirm the dismissal of Luis van Gaal with a reported £5.4m compensation package.

24 UEFA fine Manchester United £44,342 and Liverpool £43,577 for 'illicit chants' and other crowd disturbances at their Europa League tie, with part of the fines suspended. League One Bradford are taken over by German investors Edin Rahic and Stefan Rupp.

25 Rafael Benitez signs a three-year contract to stay at Newcaste. Arsenal make the first big signing of the summer transfer window, paying Borussia Monchengladbach £35m for Switzerland midfielder Granit Xhaka. Liverpool are fined £8,384 by UEFA for fans setting off fireworks during the tie against Borussia Dortmund

26 Jose Mourinho is confirmed as Manchester United's new manager, on a three-year-contract. Manchester City's Fabian Delph is ruled out of contention for a place in England's squad for Euro 2016 with a groin injury. The FA scrap FA Cup quarter-final replays.

27 Manchester United's Marcus Rashford, aged 18 years and 208 days, becomes the youngest player to score on his England debut. His goal comes after 138 seconds of a 2-1 win over Australia at the Stadium of Light. Will Grigg gets his first for Northern Ireland, who beat Belarus 3-0 for a record 11th game without defeat. The Republic of Ireland draw 1-1 against Holland. Brian McDermott is sacked for the second time by Reading, after they finish 17th. Former Leicester manager Nigel Pearson takes over at Derby. John Sheridan leaves Oldham after four months to become Notts County's new manager.

28 Hull return to the Premier League at the first attempt by beating Sheffield Wednesday 1-0 in the Championship Play-off Final with a goal from Mohamed Diame. Real Madrid defeat Atletico Madrid on penalties after the Champions League Final ends 1-1. Brentford's Alan Judge is given a warning by the FA for a breach of doping regulations over the contents of his asthma inhaler.

29 Barnsley defeat Millwall 3-1 in the League One Play-off Final. Scotland lose 1-0 to Italy in a friendly. England's Under-21 side win the ten-nation Toulon Tournament for the first time since 1994, beating France 2-1 in the final in Avignon.

30 AFC Wimbledon beat Plymouth 2-0 in the League Two Play-off Final. Marcus Rashford signs a new contract with Manchester United through to 2020, along with 19-year-old defender Cameron Borthwick-Jackson. Richie Foran, long-serving Inverness player, is appointed the club's new manager.

31 Marcus Rashford is included in England's squad for Euro 2016, just three months after making his Premier League debut. A thigh injury sustained in training costs Bournemouth's

Harry Arter a place in the Republic of Ireland squad for the tournament. The Republic are beaten 2-1 by Belarus in their final warm-up match.

JUNE 2016

1 Leeds manager Steve Evans is sacked after a 13th place finish in the Championship. Walsall caretaker-manager Jon Whitney is given the job on a permanent basis.

2 Chris Smalling scores his first England goal for a 1-0 win over ten-man Portugal in their final warm-up game. Eleven days after celebrating Hibernian's Scottish Cup win, manager Alan Stubbs leaves the club to take over at Rotherham. Pep Guardiola makes his first Manchester City signing – Borussia Dortmund and Germany midfielder Ilkay Gundogan for £21m. Blackpool appoint former Blackburn manager Gary Bowyer. Kyle Storer is banned for eight matches by the FA for biting Bradley Wood in Cheltenham's National League game against Lincoln.

3 Three Championship clubs bring in new managers. Roberto di Matteo, formerly in charge of Chelsea and West Bromwich Albion, takes over at Aston Villa. Garry Monk, sacked by Swansea, becomes the seventh Leeds manager in two years. Owen Coyle, formerly with Bolton and Burnley is given the Blackburn job. Leyton Orient appoint former Gillingham manager Andy Hessenthaler.

4 Northern Ireland complete their competitive build-up to Euro 2016 with a goalless draw in Slovakia. Scotland lose 3-0 to one of the favourites, France, in a friendly.

5 Wales, keeping Gareth Bale on the bench until the last half-hour, are beaten 3-0 in Sweden in their final game before the tournament. An American investment group pays around £100m to take over Swansea.

6 Russell Slade leaves Cardiff after less than a month as head of football to become Charlton's new manager.

7 Former team doctor Eva Carneiro settles her constructive dismissal claim against Chelsea, who apologise 'unreservedly.' She also reaches a discrimination settlement, again confidential, against former manager Jose Mourinho. Notts County have a transfer embargo lifted after clearing debts.

8 Jose Mourinho makes his first Manchester United signing – Villarreal's Ivory Coast defender Eric Bailly for £30m. Former Bolton and Celtic manager Neil Lennon takes over at Hibernian. The Scottish League announce a new format for their Challenge Cup, with all Premiership under-20 teams, clubs from the Highland and Lowland Leagues, the Welsh Premier and Northern Ireland Premier joining the competition.

9 Jermain Defoe signs a contract extension through to 2019 with Sunderland. Southend manager Phil Brown is given a four-match touchline ban and fined £3,000 by the FA for abusive behaviour after the game against Bury. Quique Sanchez Flores, sacked by Watford, is appointed head coach at Espanyol.

10 A spectacular 89th minute goal from 25 yards by West Ham's Dimitri Payet gives hosts France a 2-1 win over Romania in the opening match of Euro 2016. Phil Parkinson leaves Bradford to become Bolton's new manager. Premier League academy teams are given the go-ahead to compete in the Football League Trophy, formerly the Johnstone's Paint Trophy, for League One and League Two clubs. Former England captain Alan Shearer receives a CBE in the Queen's Birthday Honours. Middlesbrough chairman Steve Gibson is awarded an OBE and Emma Hayes, manager of Chelsea's women's team, is made an MBE.

11 England concede a stoppage-time equaliser and are held 1-1 by Russia in their opening match. The game in Marseille is marred by clashes between rival supporters. Wales, playing in their first major tournament for 58 years defeat Slovakia 2-1 with an 81st minute goal by substitute Hal Robson-Kanu.

12 Northern Ireland, in their first finals for 30 years, lose 1-0 to Poland. England and Russia are threatened by UEFA with expulsion from the tournament if there is further crowd trouble.

13 The Republic of Ireland open with a 1-1 draw against Sweden. Reading appoint former Manchester United defender Jaap Stam as their new manager.

14 Ronald Koeman leaves Southampton to become Everton's new manager. UEFA give the Russian Federation a suspended disqualification and fine of 150,000 euros (£119,000).

15 Caretaker-manager Paul Heckingbotton, who led Barnsley to promotion, is appointed on a permanent basis.

16 A stoppage-time goal by substitute Daniel Sturridge gives England a 2-1 victory over Wales Northern Ireland open their account by beating Ukraine 2-0.

18 The Republic of Ireland concede three second-half goals, two of them to Everton's Romelu Lukaku, and go down 3-0 to Belgium.

19 Ched Evans, facing a retrial after having his conviction quashed by the Court of Appeal, signs a one-year contract with Chesterfield.

20 Neil Taylor scores his first goal for Wales, who overcome Russia 3-0 to top their group. England, with six changes, are held 0-0 by Slovakia and finish runners-up. Stuart McCall is appointed Bradford manager for the second time, having been in charge at Valley Parade from 2007-10. Former Leeds and Sheffield United midfielder Bruno Ribeiro is given the Port Vale job.

21 Northern Ireland lose their final group game 1-0 to Germany, but reach the knock-out phase as one of the third-place teams.

22 An 85th minute winner by Robbie Brady against Italy sends the Republic of Ireland through.

23 Jamie Vardy turns down the chance of a move to Arsenal and signs a new four-year contract with Leicester.

24 Norwich receive a club record £11m fee from Southampton for Nathan Redmond.

25 An own goal by Gareth McAuley gives Wales a 1-0 win over Northern Ireland and a place in the quarter-finals.

26 The Republic of Ireland lead France through a second minute Robbie Brady penalty, but concede twice in a four-minute second-half spell, lose 2-1 and have Shane Duffy sent off.

27 Roy Hodgson resigns immediately after England suffer their most embarrassing defeat since losing to the United States in the 1950 World Cup. They are knocked out 2-1 by Iceland after leading lead through Wayne Rooney's penalty. Assistant-manager Ray Lewington and coach Gary Neville also leave their positions. Former Rennes and Real Socieded coach Philippe Montanier takes over at Nottingham Forest.

28 Liverpool pay £34m for Southampton's Sadio Mane, the fifth player to leave St Mary's for Anfield in two years. The fee is a record for Southampton.

30 Frenchman Claude Puel, formerly in charge of Nice, is named Southampton's new manager.

JULY 2016

1 Wales reach the semi-finals of a major tournament for the first time, coming from behind to beat Belgium 3-1. Watford sign Nigerian striker Isaac Success from Granada for £12.5m, a club record. Captain Troy Deeney agrees a new five-year contract.

2 Ryan Giggs ends a 29-year association with Manchester United to pursue his managerial ambitions with another club. Bury are deducted three points for fielding an ineligible player.

3 Michy Batshuayi, Belgium's Euro 2016 striker, becomes Antonio Conte's Chelsea first signing, at £33m from Marseille. Leicester pay £13m for Nice midfielder Nampalys Mendy, a club record.

4 Record fines imposed by the FA following the stormy match at Stamford Bridge at the end of the season are reduced on appeal. Chelsea's penalty of £375,000 is reduced to £290,000, Tottenham's from £225,000 to £175,000.

5 Manchester United pay £26m for the Borussia Dortmund striker Henrikh Mkhitaryan.

6 Wales's great run comes to an end as Cristiano Ronaldo inspires Portugal to a 2-0 victory.

7 France defeat Germany 2-0 in the second semi-final with two goals from Antoine Griezmann, the first a penalty.

8 Chris Coleman says the 2018 World Cup campaign will be his last as Wales manager. Leicester break their transfer record for a second time, paying CSKA Moscow £16.6m for Nigeria striker Ahmed Musa. Liverpool's Mamadou Sakho is cleared of a doping charge by UEFA.

9 Stephen Robinson, No 2 to Northern Ireland's Michael O'Neill at Euro 2016, is appointed Oldham's new manager.

10 Portugal overcome the loss of Cristiano Ronaldo with a knee injury midway through the first half to become European champions with an extra-time goal by Eder.

ENGLISH TABLES 2015–2016

ARCLAYS PREMIER LEAGUE

			Home					Away						
		P	W	D	L	F	A	W	D	L	F	A	GD	Pts
	Leicester	38	12	6	1	35	18	11	6	2	33	18	32	81
	Arsenal	38	12	4	3	31	11	8	7	4	34	25	29	71
	Tottenham	38	10	6	3	35	15	9	7	3	34	20	34	70
	Manchester City	38	12	2	5	47	21	7	7	5	24	20	30	66
	Manchester Utd	38	12	5	2	27	9	7	4	8	22	26	14	66
	Southampton	38	11	3	5	39	22	7	6	6	20	19	18	63
	West Ham	38	9	7	3	34	26	7	7	5	31	25	14	62
	Liverpool	38	8	8	3	33	22	8	4	7	30	28	13	60
	Stoke City	38	8	4	7	22	24	6	5	8	19	31	-14	51
0	Chelsea	38	5	9	5	32	30	7	5	7	27	23	6	50
1	Everton	38	6	5	8	35	30	5	9	5	24	25	4	47
2	Swansea City	38	8	6	5	20	20	4	5	10	22	32	-10	47
3	Watford	38	6	6	7	20	19	6	3	10	20	31	-10	45
4	WBA	38	6	5	8	20	26	4	8	7	14	22	-14	43
5	Crystal Palace	38	6	3	10	19	23	5	6	8	20	28	-12	42
6	Bournemouth	38	5	5	9	23	34	6	4	9	22	33	-22	42
7	Sunderland	38	6	6	7	23	20	3	6	10	25	42	-14	39
8	Newcastle	38	7	7	5	32	24	2	3	14	12	41	-21	37
9	Norwich	38	6	5	8	26	30	3	2	14	13	37	-28	34
0	Aston Villa	38	2	5	12	14	35	1	3	15	13	41	-49	17

eicester, Arsenal and Tottenham into Champions League group stage, Manchester City into ay-off round; Manchester Utd and Southampton into Europa League group stage, West Ham to third qualifying round

rize money (league position = amount received): 1 £93.2m, 2 £100.9m, 3 £95.2m, 4 96.9m, 5 £96.4m, 6 £84.7m, 7 £85.7m, 8 £90.5m, 9 £79.5m, 10 £87.2m, 11 £83.1m, 2 £75.8m, 13 £74.5m, 14 £73.3m, 15 £72.1m, 16 £70.8m, 17 £71.8m, 18 £72.8m, 19 57.1m, 20 £66.6m

ggest win: Aston Villa 0 Liverpool 6

ighest aggregate score: Norwich 4 Liverpool 5

ighest attendance: 75,415 (Manchester Utd v Swansea)

owest attendance: 10,863 (Bournemouth v Stoke)

layer of Year: Jamie Vardy (Leicester)

anager of Year: Claudio Ranieri (Leicester)

olden Boot: 25 Harry Kane (Tottenham)

olden Glove: 16 clean sheets Petr Cech (Arsenal)

FA Team of Year: De Gea (Manchester Utd), Bellerin (Arsenal), Morgan (Leicester), derweireld (Tottenham), Rose (Tottenham), Mahrez (Leicester), Alli (Tottenham), Kante eicester), Payet (West Ham), Vardy (Leicester), Kane (Tottenham)

eading scorers (all competitions): 29 Aguero (Manchester City); 28 Kane (Tottenham), 25 ukaku (Everton); 24 Giroud (Arsenal), Vardy (Leicester); 18 Defoe (Sunderland), Mahrez eicester); 17 Ighalo (Watford), Martial (Manchester Utd); Sanchez (Arsenal); 16 Diego osta (Chelsea); 15 Deeney (Watford), Mane (Southampton), Rooney (Manchester Utd); 4 Iheanacho (Manchester City), Pelle (Southampton); 13 Long (Southampton), Sturridge iverpool); 12 Arnautovic (Stoke), Ayew (Swansea), Barkley (Everton), Coutinho (Liverpool), ayet (West Ham)

lso: 14 Afobe (Bournemouth – 10 for Wolves)

SKY BET CHAMPIONSHIP

			Home					Away						
		P	W	D	L	F	A	W	D	L	F	A	GD	Pts
1	Burnley	46	15	6	2	38	14	11	9	3	34	21	37	93
2	Middlesbrough	46	16	5	2	34	8	10	6	7	29	23	32	89
3	Brighton	46	15	5	3	40	18	9	12	2	32	24	30	89
4	Hull*	46	15	7	1	47	12	9	4	10	22	23	34	83
5	Derby	46	12	7	4	37	16	9	8	6	29	27	23	78
6	Sheffield Wed	46	13	8	2	42	17	6	9	8	24	28	21	74
7	Ipswich	46	9	8	6	28	24	9	7	7	25	27	2	69
8	Cardiff	46	12	9	2	33	20	5	8	10	23	31	5	68
9	Brentford	46	10	4	9	33	30	9	4	10	39	37	5	65
10	Birmingham	46	9	5	9	27	27	7	10	6	26	22	4	63
11	Preston	46	7	10	6	21	21	8	7	8	24	24	0	62
12	QPR	46	10	9	4	37	25	4	9	10	17	29	0	60
13	Leeds	46	7	8	8	23	28	7	9	7	27	30	-8	59
14	Wolves	46	7	10	6	26	26	7	6	10	27	32	-5	58
15	Blackburn	46	8	8	7	29	23	5	8	10	17	23	0	55
16	Nott'm Forest	46	7	8	8	25	26	6	8	9	18	21	-4	55
17	Reading	46	8	9	6	25	20	5	4	14	27	39	-7	52
18	Bristol City	46	7	7	9	34	34	6	6	11	20	37	-17	52
19	Huddersfield	46	7	6	10	33	33	6	6	11	26	37	-11	51
20	Fulham	46	8	5	10	36	36	4	10	9	30	43	-13	51
21	Rotherham	46	8	6	9	31	34	5	4	14	22	37	-18	49
22	Charlton	46	5	8	10	23	35	4	5	14	17	45	-40	40
23	MK Dons	46	7	3	13	21	37	2	9	12	18	32	-30	39
24	Bolton	46	5	11	7	24	26	0	4	19	17	55	-40	30

*Also promoted

Biggest win: Bristol City 6 Bolton 0, Hull 6 Charlton 0
Highest aggregate score: Fulham 2 Birmingham 5, QPR 4 Bolton 3, Rotherham 2 Ipswich 5
Highest attendance: 33,806 (Middlesbrough v Brighton)
Lowest attendance: 8,363 (Brentford v Cardiff)
Player of Year: Andre Gray (Burnley)
Manager of Year: Chris Hughton (Brighton)
Top league scorer: 25 Andre Gray (Burnley – 2 for Brentford)
PFA Team of Year: Heaton (Burnley), Bruno (Brighton), Ayala (Middlesbrough)/Dawson (Hull), Keane (Burnley), Friend (Middlesbrough), Clayton (Middlesbrough), Judge (Brentford), Barton (Burnley), Bannan (Sheffield Wed), Gray (Burnley), McCormack (Fulham)
Leading scorers (all competitions): 25 Gray (Burnley – 2 for Brentford); 23 McCormack (Fulham); 22 Hernandez (Hull); 20 Kodija (Bristol City); 18 Wells (Huddersfield); 17 Dembele (Fulham), Hemed (Brighton), Rhodes (Middlesbrough – 11 for Blackburn); 16 Vokes (Burnley); 15 Forestieri (Sheffield Wed), Martin (Derby); 14 Judge (Brentford), Vibe (Brentford); 13 Blackman (Derby – 13 for Reading); Hooper (Sheffield Wed), Wood (Leeds); 12 Ince (Derby) Also: 15 Washington (QPR – 15 for Peterborough)

SKY BET LEAGUE ONE

			Home					Away						
		P	W	D	L	F	A	W	D	L	F	A	GD	Pts
1	Wigan	46	14	6	3	39	17	10	9	4	43	28	37	87
2	Burton	46	13	8	2	32	16	12	2	9	25	21	20	85
3	Walsall	46	11	6	6	31	26	13	6	4	40	23	22	84
4	Millwall	46	13	3	7	34	22	11	6	6	39	27	24	81
5	Bradford City	46	14	5	4	32	16	9	6	8	23	24	15	80
6	Barnsley*	46	11	4	8	35	24	11	4	8	35	30	16	74
7	Scunthorpe	46	12	6	5	28	15	9	5	9	32	32	13	74
8	Coventry	46	12	6	5	41	24	7	6	10	26	25	18	69
9	Gillingham	46	13	4	6	41	24	6	8	9	30	32	15	69
10	Rochdale	46	12	6	5	41	25	7	6	10	27	36	7	69
11	Sheffield Utd	46	11	4	8	37	29	7	8	8	27	30	5	66
12	Port Vale	46	12	7	4	35	25	6	4	13	21	33	-2	65
13	Peterborough	46	9	4	10	42	37	10	2	11	40	36	9	63
14	Southend	46	10	5	8	30	26	6	6	11	28	38	-6	59
15	Swindon	46	10	4	9	39	36	6	7	10	25	35	-7	59
16	Bury **	46	10	8	5	36	29	6	4	13	20	44	-17	57
17	Oldham	46	7	5	11	25	35	5	13	5	19	23	-14	54
18	Chesterfield	46	6	6	11	36	39	9	2	12	22	31	-12	53
19	Fleetwood	46	9	8	6	33	20	3	7	13	19	36	-4	51
20	Shrewsbury	46	5	5	13	29	39	8	6	9	29	40	-21	50
21	Doncaster	46	7	7	9	27	24	4	6	13	21	40	-16	46
22	Blackpool	46	8	5	10	22	24	4	5	14	18	39	-23	46
23	Colchester	46	4	9	10	32	43	5	4	14	25	56	-42	40
24	Crewe	46	4	7	12	25	40	3	6	14	21	43	-37	34

*Also promoted. ** Deducted 3pts for ineligible player

Biggest win: Chesterfield 7 Shrewsbury 1, Coventry 6 Bury 0, Scunthorpe 6 Swindon 0
Highest aggregate score: Chesterfield 7 Shrewsbury 1, Colchester 4 Walsall 4, Peterborough 5 Millwall 3
Highest attendance: 24,777 (Sheffield Utd v Bradford)
Lowest attendance: 1,767 (Rochdale v Fleetwood)
Player of Year: Bradley Dack (Gillingham)
Manager of Year: Gary Caldwell (Wigan)
Top league scorer: 25 Will Grigg (Wigan)
PFA Team of Year: McLaughlin (Bradford), Wabara (Wigan), Egan (Gillingham), Morgan (Wigan), Henry (Walsall), Wildschut (Wigan), Dack (Gillingham), Sawyers (Walsall), Duffy (Burton), Grigg (Wigan), Armstrong (Coventry)
Leading scorers (all competitions): 28 Grigg (Wigan); 27 Gregory (Millwall); 25 Ajose (Swindon); 24 Winnall (Barnsley); 23 Madden (Scunthorpe); 21 Sharp (Sheffield Utd); 20 Armstrong (Coventry), Bradshaw (Walsall); 19 Morison (Millwall); 18 Clarke (Bury); 16 Williams (Doncaster); 15 Dack (Gillingham), Novak (Chesterfield); 14 Moncur (Colchester); 13 Hanson (Bradford); Henderson (Rochdale), Maddison (Peterborough), Taylor (Peterborough)
Also 13 Nichols (Peterborough – 12 for Exeter)

SKY BET LEAGUE TWO

			Home					Away						
		P	W	D	L	F	A	W	D	L	F	A	GD	Pts
1	Northampton	46	15	5	3	38	19	14	7	2	44	27	36	99
2	Oxford	46	10	7	6	37	20	14	7	2	47	21	43	86
3	Bristol Rov	46	15	2	6	41	21	11	5	7	36	25	31	85
4	Accrington	46	11	9	3	43	30	13	4	6	31	18	26	85
5	Plymouth	46	12	3	8	39	26	12	6	5	33	20	26	81
6	Portsmouth	46	10	7	6	38	19	11	8	4	37	25	31	78
7	AFC Wimbledon*	46	11	4	8	30	25	10	8	5	34	25	14	75
8	Leyton Orient	46	11	4	8	33	31	8	8	7	27	30	-1	69
9	Cambridge	46	10	6	7	37	28	8	8	7	29	27	11	68
10	Carlisle	46	10	6	7	38	35	7	10	6	29	27	5	67
11	Luton	46	7	6	10	27	29	12	3	8	36	32	2	66
12	Mansfield	46	7	10	6	34	26	10	3	10	27	27	8	64
13	Wycombe	46	9	6	8	25	24	8	7	8	20	20	1	64
14	Exeter	46	6	11	6	32	33	11	2	10	31	32	-2	64
15	Barnet	46	13	3	7	37	27	4	8	11	30	41	-1	62
16	Hartlepool	46	9	3	11	27	32	6	3	14	22	40	-23	51
17	Notts Co	46	9	4	10	30	38	5	5	13	24	45	-29	51
18	Stevenage	46	6	8	9	23	32	5	7	11	29	35	-15	48
19	Yeovil	46	6	9	8	23	27	5	6	12	20	32	-16	48
20	Crawley	46	8	5	10	21	30	5	3	15	24	48	-33	47
21	Morecambe	46	7	3	13	36	47	5	7	11	33	44	-22	46
22	Newport	46	4	8	11	21	35	6	5	12	22	29	-21	43
23	Dagenham	46	3	5	15	17	37	5	5	13	29	44	-35	34
24	York	46	6	7	10	33	41	1	6	16	18	46	-36	34

*Also promoted

Biggest win: Cambridge 7 Morecambe 0
Highest aggregate: Carlisle 4 Cambridge 4
Biggest attendance: 18,746 (Portsmouth v Northampton)
Lowest attendance: 1,027 (Morecambe v Dagenham)
Player of Year: Kemar Roofe (Oxford)
Manager of Year: Chris Wilder (Northampton)
Top league scorer: 27 Matt Taylor (Bristol Rov)
PFA Team of Year: Smith (Northampton), Baldock (Oxford), Nelson (Plymouth), Pierre (Wycombe), Jacobson (Wycombe), Holmes (Northampton), O'Toole (Northampton), Crooks (Accrington), Roofe (Oxford), Simpson (Leyton Orient), Taylor (Bristol Rov)
Leading scorers (all competitions): 28 M Taylor (Bristol Rov); 26 Roofe (Oxford); 25 Simpson (Leyton Orient); 24 Akinde (Barnet); 23 L Taylor (AFC Wimbledon); 18 Richards (Northampton); 17 Kee (Accrington), Ibehre (Carlisle), Sercombe (Oxford), Windass (Accrington); 16 Green (Mansfield), Marriott (Luton), Miller (Morecambe); 15 Boden (Newport), Paynter (Hartlepool), Wyke (Carlisle); 14 Hylton (Oxford), Jervis (Plymouth), McGeehan (Luton), Stead (Notts Co)

BARCLAYS PREMIER LEAGUE RESULTS 2015–2016

	Arsenal	Aston Villa	Bournemouth	Chelsea	Crystal Palace	Everton	Leicester	Liverpool	Manchester City	Manchester Utd	Newcastle	Norwich	Southampton	Stoke	Sunderland	Swansea	Tottenham	Watford	WBA	West Ham
Arsenal	–	4-0	2-0	0-1	1-1	2-1	2-1	0-0	2-1	3-0	1-0	1-0	0-0	2-0	3-1	1-2	1-1	4-0	2-0	0-2
Aston Villa	0-2	–	1-2	0-4	1-0	1-3	1-1	0-6	0-0	0-1	0-0	2-0	2-4	0-1	2-2	1-2	0-2	2-3	0-1	1-1
Bournemouth	0-2	0-1	–	1-4	0-0	3-3	1-1	1-2	0-4	2-1	0-1	3-0	2-0	1-3	2-0	3-2	1-5	1-1	1-1	1-3
Chelsea	2-0	2-0	0-1	–	1-2	3-3	1-1	1-3	0-3	1-1	5-1	1-0	1-3	1-1	3-1	2-2	2-2	2-2	2-2	2-2
Crystal Palace	1-2	2-1	1-2	0-3	–	0-0	0-1	1-2	0-1	0-0	5-1	1-0	1-0	2-1	0-1	0-0	1-3	1-2	2-0	1-3
Everton	0-2	4-0	2-1	3-1	1-1	–	2-3	1-1	0-2	0-3	3-0	3-0	1-1	3-4	6-2	1-2	1-1	2-2	0-1	2-3
Leicester	2-5	3-2	0-0	2-1	1-0	3-1	–	2-0	0-0	1-1	1-0	1-0	1-0	3-0	4-2	4-0	1-1	2-1	2-2	2-2
Liverpool	3-3	3-2	1-0	1-1	1-2	4-0	1-0	–	3-0	0-1	2-2	1-1	1-1	4-1	2-2	1-0	1-1	2-0	2-2	0-3
Manchester City	2-2	4-0	5-1	3-0	4-0	0-0	1-3	1-4	–	0-1	6-1	2-1	3-1	4-0	4-1	2-1	1-2	2-0	2-1	1-2
Manchester Utd	3-2	1-0	3-1	0-0	2-0	1-0	1-1	3-1	0-0	–	0-0	1-2	0-1	3-0	3-0	2-1	1-0	1-0	2-0	0-0
Newcastle	0-1	1-1	1-3	2-2	1-0	0-1	0-3	2-0	1-1	3-3	–	6-2	2-2	0-0	1-1	3-0	5-1	1-2	1-0	2-1
Norwich	1-1	2-0	3-1	1-2	1-3	1-1	1-2	4-5	0-0	0-1	3-2	–	1-0	1-1	0-3	1-0	0-3	4-2	0-1	2-2
Southampton	4-0	1-1	2-0	1-2	4-1	0-3	2-2	3-2	4-2	2-3	3-1	3-0	–	0-1	1-1	3-1	0-2	2-0	3-0	1-0
Stoke	0-0	2-1	2-1	1-0	1-2	0-3	2-2	0-1	2-0	2-0	1-0	3-1	1-2	–	1-1	2-2	0-4	0-2	0-1	2-1
Sunderland	0-0	3-1	1-1	3-2	2-2	3-0	0-2	0-1	0-1	2-1	3-0	1-3	0-1	2-0	–	1-1	0-1	0-1	0-0	2-2
Swansea	0-3	1-0	2-2	1-0	1-1	0-0	0-3	3-1	1-1	2-1	2-0	1-0	0-1	0-1	2-4	–	2-2	1-0	1-0	0-0
Tottenham	2-2	3-1	3-0	0-0	1-0	0-0	0-1	0-0	4-1	3-0	1-2	3-0	1-2	2-2	4-1	2-1	–	1-0	1-1	4-1
Watford	0-3	3-2	0-0	0-0	0-1	1-1	0-1	3-0	1-2	1-2	2-1	2-0	0-0	1-2	2-2	1-0	1-2	–	0-0	2-0
WBA	2-1	0-0	1-2	2-3	3-2	2-3	2-3	1-1	0-3	1-0	1-0	0-1	0-0	2-1	1-0	1-1	1-1	0-1	–	0-3
West Ham	3-3	2-0	3-4	2-1	2-2	1-1	1-2	2-0	2-2	3-2	2-0	2-2	2-1	0-0	1-0	1-4	1-0	3-1	1-1	–

SKY BET CHAMPIONSHIP RESULTS 2015–2016

	Birmingham	Blackburn	Bolton	Brentford	Brighton	Bristol City	Burnley	Cardiff	Charlton	Derby Co	Fulham	Huddersfield	Hull	Ipswich	Leeds	Middlesbrough	MK Dons	Nottm Forest	Preston	QPR	Reading	Rotherham	Shffield Wed	Wolves
Birmingham.	–	0-0	1-0	2-1	1-2	4-2	1-2	1-0	0-1	1-1	1-1	0-2	1-0	3-0	1-2	2-2	1-0	0-1	2-2	2-1	2-1	0-2	1-2	0-2
Blackburn	2-0	–	0-0	1-1	0-1	2-2	0-1	1-1	3-0	0-0	3-0	0-2	0-2	2-0	1-2	2-1	3-2	0-0	1-2	1-1	3-1	1-0	2-2	1-2
Bolton	0-1	1-0	–	1-1	2-2	0-0	1-2	2-3	0-0	0-0	2-2	0-2	1-0	2-2	1-1	1-2	3-1	1-1	1-2	1-1	0-1	2-1	0-0	2-1
Brentford	0-2	0-1	3-1	–	0-0	1-1	1-3	2-1	1-2	1-3	3-0	4-2	0-2	2-2	1-1	0-1	2-0	2-1	2-1	1-0	1-3	2-1	1-2	3-0
Brighton	2-1	1-0	3-2	3-0	–	2-1	2-2	1-1	3-2	1-1	5-0	2-1	1-0	0-1	4-0	0-3	2-1	1-0	0-0	4-0	1-0	2-1	0-0	0-1
Bristol City	0-0	0-2	6-0	2-4	0-4	–	1-2	0-2	1-1	2-3	1-4	4-0	1-1	2-1	2-2	1-0	1-1	2-0	1-2	1-1	0-2	1-1	4-1	1-0
Burnley	2-2	1-0	2-0	1-0	1-1	4-0	–	0-0	4-0	4-1	3-1	2-1	1-0	0-0	1-0	1-1	2-1	1-0	0-2	1-0	1-2	2-0	3-1	1-1
Cardiff	1-1	1-0	2-1	3-2	4-1	0-0	2-2	–	2-1	2-1	1-1	2-0	0-2	1-0	0-2	1-0	0-0	1-1	2-1	0-0	2-0	2-2	2-2	2-0
Charlton	2-1	1-1	2-2	0-3	1-3	0-1	0-3	0-0	–	0-1	2-2	1-2	2-1	0-3	0-0	2-0	0-0	1-1	0-3	2-0	3-4	1-1	3-1	0-2
Derby Co	0-3	1-0	4-1	2-0	2-2	4-0	0-0	2-0	1-1	–	2-0	2-0	4-0	0-1	1-2	1-1	0-1	1-0	0-0	1-0	1-1	3-0	1-1	4-2
Fulham	2-5	2-1	1-0	2-2	1-2	1-2	2-3	2-1	3-0	1-1	–	1-1	0-1	1-2	1-1	0-2	2-1	1-3	1-1	4-0	4-2	4-1	0-1	0-3
Huddersfield	1-1	1-1	4-1	1-5	1-1	1-2	1-3	2-3	5-0	1-2	1-1	–	2-2	0-1	0-3	0-2	2-0	1-1	3-1	0-1	3-1	2-0	0-1	1-0
Hull	2-0	1-1	1-0	2-0	0-0	4-0	3-0	2-0	6-0	0-2	2-1	2-0	–	3-0	2-2	3-0	1-1	1-1	2-0	1-1	2-1	5-1	0-0	2-1
Ipswich	1-1	2-0	2-0	1-3	2-3	2-2	2-0	0-0	0-0	0-1	1-1	0-0	0-1	–	2-1	0-2	3-2	1-0	1-1	2-1	2-1	0-1	2-1	2-2
Leeds	0-2	0-2	2-1	1-1	1-2	1-0	1-1	1-0	1-2	2-2	1-1	1-4	2-1	0-1	–	0-0	1-1	0-1	1-0	1-1	3-2	0-1	1-1	2-1
Middlesbrough	0-0	1-1	3-0	3-1	1-1	0-1	1-0	3-1	3-0	2-0	0-0	3-0	1-0	0-0	3-0	–	2-0	0-1	1-0	1-0	2-1	1-0	1-0	2-1
MK Dons	0-2	3-0	1-0	1-4	1-2	0-2	0-5	2-1	1-0	1-3	1-1	1-1	0-2	0-1	1-2	1-1	–	1-2	0-1	2-0	1-0	0-4	2-1	1-2
Nottm Forest	1-1	1-1	3-0	0-3	1-2	1-2	1-1	1-2	0-0	1-0	3-0	0-2	0-1	1-1	1-1	1-2	2-1	–	1-0	0-0	3-1	2-1	0-3	1-1
Preston	1-1	1-2	0-0	1-3	0-0	1-1	0-1	0-0	2-1	1-2	1-2	2-1	1-0	1-2	1-1	0-0	1-1	1-0	–	1-1	1-0	2-1	1-0	1-1
QPR	2-0	2-2	4-3	3-0	2-2	1-0	0-0	2-2	2-1	2-0	1-3	1-1	1-2	1-0	1-0	2-3	3-0	1-2	0-0	–	1-1	4-2	0-0	1-1
Reading	0-2	1-0	2-1	1-2	1-1	1-0	0-0	1-1	1-0	0-1	2-2	2-2	1-2	5-1	0-0	2-0	0-0	2-1	1-2	0-1	–	1-0	1-1	0-0
Rotherham	0-0	0-1	4-0	2-1	2-0	3-0	1-2	2-1	1-4	3-3	1-3	1-1	2-0	2-5	2-1	1-0	1-4	0-0	0-0	0-3	1-1	–	1-2	1-2
Sheffield Wed	3-0	2-1	3-2	4-0	0-0	2-0	1-1	3-0	3-0	0-0	3-2	3-1	1-1	1-1	2-0	1-3	0-0	1-0	3-1	1-1	1-1	0-1	–	4-1
Wolves	0-0	0-0	2-2	0-2	0-0	2-1	0-0	1-3	2-1	2-1	3-2	3-0	1-1	0-0	2-3	1-3	0-0	1-1	1-2	2-3	1-0	0-0	2-1	–

SKY BET LEAGUE ONE RESULTS 2015–2016

	Barnsley	Blackpool	Bradford	Burton	Bury	Chesterfield	Colchester	Coventry	Crewe	Doncaster	Fleetwood	Gillingham	Millwall	Oldham	Peterborough	Port Vale	Rochdale	Scunthorpe	Sheffield Utd	Shrewsbury	Southend	Swindon	Walsall	Wigan
Barnsley	–	4-2	0-0	1-0	3-0	1-2	2-2	2-0	1-2	1-0	0-1	2-0	2-1	2-1	1-0	1-2	6-1	0-0	1-1	1-2	0-2	4-1	0-2	0-2
Blackpool	1-1	–	0-1	1-2	1-1	2-0	0-1	0-1	2-0	0-2	1-0	1-0	1-1	0-0	2-0	0-1	0-2	5-0	0-0	2-3	2-0	1-0	0-4	0-4
Bradford	0-1	1-0	–	2-0	2-1	2-0	1-2	0-0	2-0	2-1	2-1	1-2	1-0	1-0	0-2	1-0	2-2	1-0	2-2	1-1	2-0	1-0	4-0	1-1
Burton	0-0	1-0	3-1	–	1-1	1-0	5-1	1-2	0-0	3-3	2-1	2-1	2-1	0-0	2-1	2-0	1-0	2-1	0-0	1-2	1-0	1-0	0-0	1-1
Bury	0-0	4-3	0-0	1-0	–	1-0	5-2	2-1	0-0	1-0	3-4	0-1	1-3	1-1	3-1	1-0	0-0	1-2	1-0	2-2	3-2	2-2	2-3	2-2
Chesterfield	3-1	1-1	0-1	1-2	3-0	–	3-3	1-1	3-1	1-1	0-0	1-3	1-2	1-2	0-1	4-2	0-0	0-3	0-3	7-1	3-0	0-4	1-4	2-3
Colchester	2-3	2-2	2-0	0-3	0-1	1-1	–	1-3	2-3	4-1	1-1	2-1	0-0	0-0	1-4	2-1	1-2	2-2	1-2	0-0	0-2	1-4	4-4	3-3
Coventry	4-3	0-0	1-0	0-2	6-0	1-0	0-1	–	3-2	2-2	1-2	4-1	2-1	1-1	3-2	1-0	0-1	1-2	3-1	3-0	2-2	0-0	1-1	2-0
Crewe	1-2	1-2	0-1	1-1	3-3	1-2	1-1	0-5	–	3-1	1-1	0-1	1-3	1-0	1-5	0-0	2-0	2-3	1-0	1-2	1-2	1-3	1-1	1-1
Doncaster	2-1	0-1	0-1	0-0	1-1	3-0	2-0	2-0	3-2	–	2-0	2-2	1-1	1-1	1-2	1-2	0-2	0-1	0-1	0-1	0-0	2-2	1-2	3-1
Fleetwood	0-2	0-0	1-1	4-0	2-0	0-1	4-0	0-1	2-0	0-0	–	2-1	2-1	1-1	2-0	1-2	1-1	2-1	2-2	0-0	1-1	5-1	0-1	1-3
Gillingham	2-1	2-1	3-0	0-3	3-1	1-2	1-0	0-0	3-0	1-0	5-1	–	1-2	3-3	2-1	0-2	2-0	2-1	4-0	2-3	1-1	0-0	1-2	2-0
Millwall	2-3	3-0	0-0	2-0	1-0	0-2	4-1	0-4	1-1	2-0	1-0	0-3	–	3-0	3-0	3-1	3-1	0-2	1-0	3-1	0-2	2-0	0-1	0-0
Oldham	1-2	1-0	1-2	0-1	0-1	1-0	1-1	0-2	1-0	1-2	1-0	2-1	1-2	–	1-5	1-1	2-3	2-4	1-1	1-1	2-5	2-0	1-0	1-1
Peterborough	3-2	5-1	0-4	0-1	2-3	2-0	2-1	3-1	3-0	4-0	2-1	1-1	5-3	1-2	–	2-3	1-2	0-2	1-3	1-1	0-0	1-2	1-1	2-3
Port Vale	0-1	2-0	1-1	0-4	1-0	3-2	2-0	1-1	3-0	3-0	0-0	1-1	0-2	1-1	1-1	–	4-1	1-1	2-1	2-0	3-1	1-0	0-5	3-2
Rochdale	3-0	3-0	1-3	2-1	3-0	2-3	3-1	0-0	2-2	2-2	1-0	1-1	0-1	0-0	2-0	2-1	–	2-1	2-0	3-2	4-1	2-2	1-2	0-2
Scunthorpe	2-0	0-1	0-2	1-0	2-1	1-1	3-0	1-0	2-0	2-0	1-0	0-0	0-0	1-1	0-4	1-0	1-1	–	0-1	2-1	1-0	6-0	0-1	1-1
Sheffield Utd	0-0	2-0	3-1	0-1	1-3	2-0	2-3	1-0	3-2	3-1	3-0	0-0	1-2	3-0	2-3	1-0	3-2	0-2	–	2-4	2-2	1-1	2-0	0-2
Shrewsbury	0-3	2-0	1-1	0-1	2-0	1-2	4-2	2-1	0-1	1-2	1-1	2-2	1-2	0-1	3-4	1-1	2-0	2-2	1-2	–	1-2	0-1	1-3	1-5
Southend	2-1	1-0	0-1	3-1	4-1	0-1	3-0	3-0	1-1	0-3	2-2	1-1	0-4	0-1	2-1	1-0	2-2	2-1	3-1	0-1	–	0-1	0-2	0-0
Swindon	0-1	3-2	4-1	0-1	0-1	1-0	1-2	2-2	4-3	2-0	1-1	1-3	2-2	1-2	1-2	2-2	2-1	2-1	0-2	3-0	4-2	–	2-1	1-4
Walsall	1-3	1-1	2-1	2-0	0-1	1-2	2-1	2-1	1-1	2-0	3-1	3-2	0-3	1-1	2-0	2-0	0-3	0-0	1-1	2-1	1-0	1-1	–	1-2
Wigan	1-4	0-1	1-0	0-1	3-0	3-1	5-0	1-0	1-0	0-0	2-1	3-2	2-2	0-0	1-1	3-0	1-0	3-0	3-3	1-0	4-1	1-0	0-0	–

SKY BET LEAGUE TWO RESULTS 2015–2016

	Accrington	Bafnet	Bristol Rov	Cambridge	Carlisle	Crawley	Dag & Red	Exeter	Hartlepool	Leyton Orient	Luton	Mansfield	Morecambe	Newport	Northampton	Notts Co	Oxford	Plymouth	Portsmouth	Stevenage	Wimbledon	Wycombe	Yeovil	York
Accrington	–	2-2	1-0	1-1	1-1	4-1	3-1	4-2	3-1	1-0	1-1	1-0	2-2	2-2	1-1	3-2	1-3	2-1	1-3	0-0	3-4	1-1	2-1	3-0
Barnet	1-2	–	1-0	0-0	0-0	4-2	3-1	2-0	1-3	3-0	2-1	1-3	0-0	2-0	2-0	3-1	0-3	1-0	1-0	3-2	1-2	0-2	3-4	3-1
Bristol Rov	0-1	3-1	–	3-0	2-0	3-0	2-1	3-1	4-1	2-1	2-0	1-0	2-1	1-4	0-1	0-0	0-1	1-1	1-2	1-2	3-1	3-0	2-1	2-1
Cambridge	2-3	2-1	1-2	–	0-0	0-3	1-0	0-1	1-1	1-1	1-3	1-1	7-0	3-0	2-1	3-1	0-0	2-2	1-3	1-0	1-4	1-0	3-0	3-1
Carlisle	2-0	3-2	3-2	4-4	–	3-1	2-1	1-0	1-0	2-2	1-2	1-2	2-3	0-1	1-4	3-0	0-2	0-2	2-2	1-0	1-1	1-1	3-2	1-1
Crawley	0-3	0-3	2-1	1-0	0-1	–	3-2	0-2	0-0	3-2	2-1	0-1	1-1	2-0	1-2	0-1	1-5	1-1	0-0	2-1	1-2	0-0	0-1	1-0
Dag & Red	0-1	0-2	0-3	0-3	0-0	3-0	–	1-2	0-1	1-3	0-2	3-4	2-1	0-0	1-2	1-1	0-1	1-1	1-4	1-1	0-2	1-2	0-1	1-0
Exeter	2-1	1-1	1-1	1-0	2-2	2-2	1-2	–	1-0	4-0	2-3	2-3	1-1	1-1	0-0	1-1	1-4	2-1	1-1	3-3	0-2	0-2	3-2	0-0
Hartlepool	1-2	1-1	0-3	0-0	2-3	1-2	3-1	0-2	–	3-1	1-4	2-1	2-0	1-0	0-0	2-3	0-1	1-2	0-2	1-2	1-0	1-0	2-1	2-1
Leyton Orient	0-1	2-0	2-0	1-3	1-2	2-0	3-2	1-3	0-2	–	0-1	1-0	1-0	1-0	0-4	3-1	2-2	1-3	3-2	3-0	1-1	1-1	1-1	3-2
Luton	0-2	2-0	0-1	0-0	3-4	0-1	1-0	4-1	2-1	1-1	–	1-0	1-0	1-1	3-4	0-2	2-2	1-2	1-2	0-1	2-0	0-2	1-1	1-1
Mansfield	2-3	1-1	1-2	0-0	1-1	4-0	3-2	0-2	3-1	1-1	0-2	–	2-1	3-0	2-2	5-0	1-1	0-0	1-1	2-1	1-1	0-2	0-1	1-1
Morecambe	1-0	4-2	3-4	2-4	1-2	3-1	1-0	1-1	2-5	0-1	1-3	1-2	–	1-2	2-4	4-1	2-4	0-2	1-1	1-4	2-1	0-1	2-1	1-1
Newport	0-2	0-3	1-4	0-1	1-0	0-3	2-2	1-1	0-0	2-3	3-0	1-0	1-2	–	2-2	0-1	1-1	1-2	0-1	2-2	2-2	1-0	0-0	0-3
Northampton	1-0	3-0	2-2	1-1	3-2	2-1	1-2	3-0	2-1	1-1	2-0	1-0	3-1	1-0	–	2-2	1-0	0-2	1-2	2-1	1-1	1-0	2-0	2-0
Notts Co	1-1	4-2	0-2	1-2	0-5	4-1	0-0	1-4	1-0	0-1	3-2	0-2	2-2	4-3	1-2	–	2-4	0-2	2-1	1-0	0-2	0-0	2-0	1-0
Oxford	1-2	2-3	1-2	1-0	1-1	1-1	4-0	3-0	2-0	0-1	2-3	2-2	0-0	1-1	0-1	3-1	–	1-0	1-1	1-1	1-0	3-0	2-0	4-0
Plymouth	1-0	2-1	1-1	1-2	4-1	2-1	2-3	1-2	5-0	1-1	0-1	3-0	2-0	1-0	1-2	1-0	2-2	–	1-2	3-2	1-2	0-1	1-0	3-2
Portsmouth	0-0	3-1	3-1	2-1	1-0	3-0	3-0	1-2	4-0	0-1	0-0	0-0	3-3	0-3	1-2	4-0	0-1	1-2	–	1-1	0-0	2-1	0-0	6-0
Stevenage	1-1	0-0	0-0	2-0	0-1	0-1	1-3	0-2	2-0	2-2	0-0	0-2	4-3	2-1	2-3	0-2	1-5	2-1	0-2	–	0-0	2-1	0-0	2-2
Wimbledon	0-0	2-0	0-0	1-2	1-0	1-0	0-1	2-1	2-0	1-0	4-1	3-1	2-5	1-0	1-1	2-1	1-2	0-2	0-1	1-2	–	1-1	2-3	2-1
Wycombe	0-1	1-1	1-0	1-0	1-1	2-0	1-1	1-0	2-1	0-2	0-1	1-0	0-2	0-2	2-3	2-2	2-1	1-2	2-2	1-0	1-2	–	0-0	3-0
Yeovil	1-0	2-2	0-1	2-3	0-0	2-1	2-2	0-2	1-2	0-1	3-2	0-1	2-4	1-0	1-1	1-0	0-0	0-0	1-1	2-2	1-1	0-1	–	1-0
York	1-5	1-1	1-4	2-2	2-2	2-2	2-2	2-0	1-2	1-1	2-3	1-2	2-1	0-1	1-2	2-1	1-2	1-2	3-1	2-1	1-3	1-1	1-0	–

HIGHLIGHTS OF THE PREMIER LEAGUE SEASON 2015–16

AUGUST 2015

8 Thibaut Courtois is sent off as Chelsea open their defence of the title with a 2-2 draw against Swansea at Stamford Bridge. The goalkeeper brings down Bafetimbi Gomis, who converts the resulting penalty, and new-signing Andre Ayew is also on the mark for Garry Monk's side. Two others players score on their debuts. Rudy Gestede heads the only goal of the game for Aston Villa at Bournemouth, while record-buy Yohan Cabaye rounds off a 3-1 victory for Crystal Palace at Norwich, who have a Cameron Jerome equaliser controversially disallowed for a high boot by new Premier League referee Simon Hooper. Watford, under new manager Quique Flores, are the only one of the three promoted sides to gain a point, Miguel Layun opening his account for the club in a 2-2 draw at Everton. Riyad Mahrez celebrates a new four-year contract with a brace, one a penalty, for Leicester, who pick up the threads of the previous season's great escape by beating Sunderland 4-2 in Claudio Ranieri's first match in charge.

9 Slaven Bilic has a memorable Premier League introduction as manager of West Ham, who deliver the first shock of the season with a 2-0 away win over Arsenal, courtesy of goals by Cheikhou Kouyate and Mauro Zarate, alongside an assured debut by 16-year-old midfielder Reece Oxford, the club's youngest-ever player at this level. Steve McClaren begins life at Newcastle with a 2-2 draw against Southampton, Georginio Wijnaldum scoring one of their goals on his debut. Liverpool go some way to erasing a 6-1 defeat by Stoke at the end of the previous season with a 1-0 success at the Britannia Stadium earned by a trademark long-range drive from Philippe Coutinho.

10 Manchester City begin impressively as Yaya Toure strikes twice in a 3-0 away win over West Bromwich Albion. One is later accredited to David Silva by the dubious goals panel.

14 In a rare Friday night game, brought forward because of a large police presence needed for an English Defence League march on the Saturday, Adnan Januzaj scores his first goal for 16 months to give Manchester United a 1-0 victory at Villa Park.

15 Defenders Russell Martin and Steven Whittaker are on the mark as Norwich open their account with a 3-1 win at Sunderland, for whom Duncan Watmore replies on his Premier League debut. Shinji Okazaki scores his first goal for Leicester, who prevail 2-1 at Upton Park. Dimitri Payet nets his first for West Ham, who have goalkeeper Adrian shown a straight red card for dangerous play when joining the attack for a stoppage-time corner. Everton are also away winners, 3-0 against Southampton, with Romelu Lukaku scoring twice. Substitute Stephen Ireland inspires a Stoke comeback at Tottenham, where they transform a 2-0 deficit into a point with goals from Marko Arnautovic (penalty) and Mame Biram Diouf. With his seventh goal in eight Premier League games, Bafetimbi Gomis puts Swansea on the way to a 2-0 success against Newcastle, who have Daryl Janmaat dismissed for two yellow cards.

16 Chelsea manager Jose Mourinho, involved all week in a public row with club doctor Eva Carneiro, sees his side swept aside by Manchester City, who win 3-0 with goals by Sergio Aguero, Vincent Kompany and Fernandinho. With the south stand extension complete, the attendance of 54,331 is a record for the Etihad.

17 Christian Benteke delivers the only goal of the game on his Anfield debut to give Liverpool the verdict against Bournemouth, whose claim for an offside decision is backed by TV replays.

22 Callum Wilson, leading marksman in Bournemouth's promotion-winning campaign, fires a hat-trick in their first Premier League success – 4-3 at Upton Park. He completes it with a penalty, conceded by Carl Jenkinson, whose straight red card is West Ham's fifth dismissal in the first nine matches in all competitions. Bakary Sako marks his Crystal Palace debut with an 87th minute winner for 2-1 against Aston Villa. Substitute Dele Alli's first goal for Tottenham earns a 1-1 draw at Leicester, whose reply from Riyad Mahrez is his fourth of the season, matching his total for the whole of the previous campaign.

23 Manchester City are installed as early season favourites for the title after beating Everton 2-0 away from home. Former Barcelona star Pedro makes an impressive debut for Chelsea in an eventful 3-2 win at The Hawthorns, opening the scoring and setting up Diego Costa for the second goal. But his new side have John Terry shown a straight red card for pulling back West Bromwich Albion's record-signing Salomon Rondon and come under further pressure from James Morrison's second strike of the match. Morrison also has a penalty saved by Thibaut Courtois with the scoresheet blank.

29 Chelsea suffer a first home defeat by Crystal Palace since 1982. Alan Pardew's side win 2-1 and he becomes the first manager to score a hat-trick of victories over Jose Mourinho. Bakary Sako puts Palace ahead and lays on their winner for Joel Ward after on-loan Falcao nets his first for Chelsea. Manchester City extend their lead over the defending champions to eight points after four matches with a club-record tenth straight victory, six of them at the end of the previous season. Raheem Sterling scores his first goal for City, who see off Watford 2-0. Sunderland's Yann M'Vila and Jeremain Lens are on the mark for the first time in a 2-2 draw against Aston Villa, for whom Scott Sinclair's two goals – one a penalty – follow his midweek hat-trick against Notts County in the League Cup. Salomon Rondon's first for West Bromwich Albion secures a 1-0 success at Stoke, who have two players shown straight red cards by Michael Oliver – Ibrahim Afellay for slapping Craig Gardner and Charlie Adam six minutes later for treading on Craig Dawson. Afellay's ban is reduced on appeal from three to two matches. There are also two dismissals, by Kevin Friend, at Anfield, where West Ham win for the first time since 1963. Mark Noble, one of their marksmen in a 3-0 scoreline, is dismissed for lunging at Danny Ings, while the home side's Philippe Coutinho commits two yellow-card offences. Noble's sending-off is later rescinded. Another straight red is shown to Newcastle's Aleksandar Mitrovic for his challenge on Francis Coquelin in a 1-0 home defeat by Arsenal.

30 Steven Whittaker is the sixth player to be dismissed, his two yellow cards coming in a 3-0 defeat for Norwich at Southampton, where Dusan Tadic scores twice. Swansea record a third successive 2-1 victory over Manchester United, Andre Ayew heading their first goal, then sending in Bafetimbi Gomis for the second with one of the passes of the season.

SEPTEMBER 2015

12 A hat-trick by Steven Naismith, a ninth minute substitute for the injured Muhamed Besic, gives Everton a 3-1 victory over Chelsea, who are left fourth from bottom with three defeats already – as many as in the whole of the previous season. Two more substitutes make the headlines. Kelechi Iheanacho, an 18-year-old Nigerian, comes on after 89 minutes to score the only goal of the game in stoppage-time for Manchester City at Crystal Palace. Anthony Martial, 19 and the world's most expensive teenager after joining Manchester United from Monaco for an initial £36m, rounds off their 3-1 success against Liverpool on his debut. On-loan Matt Jarvis is also on the mark on his first appearance as Norwich beat Bournemouth 3-1. Watford's first win, 1-0 against Swansea, is soured by a straight red card for Valon Behrami for stamping on Andre Ayew.

13 Another loanee, Nathan Dyer, completes Leicester's comeback from 2-0 down with an 89th minute winner on his debut off the bench against Aston Villa, for whom Jack Grealish scores for the first time.

14 Dimitri Payet delivers both goals as West Ham continue their encouraging start by overcoming Newcastle 2-0.

19 West Ham, victors at Arsenal and Liverpool, complete a notable hat-trick by ending Manchester City's 11-match winning streak with a 2-1 success at the Etihad. On-loan Victor Moses scores his first goal for the club, Diafra Sakho adds to it, while record-signing Kevin De Bruyne nets his first for City, whose starting line-up costing £308m is the most expensive in Premier League history. Arsenal have two players sent off in a 2-0 defeat at Chelsea, Santi Cazorla for two yellow cards and Gabriel, whose red for retaliating against Diego Costa is later overturned. Kevin Mirallas is dismissed in stoppage-time for a studs-up challenge on Modou Barrow two minutes after coming off the Everton bench in a goalless draw at Swansea. And Sunderland's Younes Kaboul receives a second yellow in a 2-0 defeat at

Bournemouth, where Matt Ritchie scores one of the goals of the season with a 25-yard volley. More problems, too, for Newcastle, beaten 2-1 at home by two Odion Ighalo goals for Watford.

20 Norwich captain Russell Martin returns home overnight from the team's Merseyside hotel for the birth of his third child, flies back to play at Anfield and scores the equaliser in a 1-1 draw. Danny Ings is on the mark for Liverpool for the first time. Anthony Martial continues his eye-catching start for Manchester United with a brace in their 3-2 win at Southampton. So does Asian football's most expensive player, South Korean Son Heung-min. Tottenham's £21.9m signing from Bayer Leverkusen follows up his two midweek Europa League goals with the only one of the game against Crystal Palace.

26 A second successive defeat for Manchester City results in the first change of leadership. They lose 4-1 at Tottenham, where Harry Kane brings a smile to the face of watching England manager Roy Hodgson with his first goal of the season and Toby Alderweireld nets his first for the club. City are replaced at the top by Manchester United, who defeat Sunderland 3-0, helped by Wayne Rooney's first of the campaign in the league. Alexis Sanchez also gets off the mark, his hat-trick highlighting Arsenal's 5-2 victory away to Leicester, whose goals come from Jamie Vardy. Chelsea, heading for a fourth successive defeat at St James' Park when trailing Newcastle 2-0 with 11 minutes of normal time remaining, salvage a point through substitutes Ramires and Willian. Former Celtic defender Virgil van Dijk scores for the first time in English football as Southampton overcome Swansea 3-1, while two other players, James Milner and Robbie Brady, celebrate first goals for new clubs. Milner opens the scoring after 66 seconds and injury-dogged Daniel Sturridge is back on track for the first time for six months with a brace as Liverpool are 3-2 winners over Aston Villa, who reply with two from Rudy Gestede. Brady's strike for Norwich comes in a 2-2 draw at West Ham. Bournemouth suffer another blow in a 2-1 defeat at Stoke, Callum Wilson joining Max Gradel and Tyrone Mings on the long-term casualty list with knee ligament damage.

28 Romelu Lukaku's brace helps Everton retrieve a two-goal deficit and win 3-2 away to West Bromwich Albion.

OCTOBER 2015

3 Sergio Aguero scores five times in the space of 23 minutes for Manchester City, who come from behind to overwhelm Newcastle 6-1. Steve McClaren's side, level at half-time after Aleksandar Mitrovic's first goal for the club, are left without a win in eight games – their worst start to a Premier League season. Southampton also hit back in style after trailing Chelsea, Graziano Pelle providing assists for Steven Davis and Sadio Mane, then scoring himself to complete a 3-1 success at Stamford Bridge. Delight for Glenn Murray, with his first for Bournemouth, turns to despair when his late penalty is saved by Heurelho Gomes, resulting in Watford securing a 1-1 draw. Carl Jenkinson nets his first for West Ham, who draw 2-2 at Sunderland in what proves to be Dick Advocaat's last match in charge of the home side. They lead 2-0, with Jeremain Lens scoring the second goal, but lose the advantage after Lens receives a second yellow card. Substitute Dieumerci Mbokani, a Congolese striker on loan from Dynamo Kiev, records his first for Norwich, but it's not enough to prevent a 2-1 home defeat by Leicester.

4 Arsenal, beaten at home by Olympiacos in a midweek Champions League game, run Manchester United ragged in the opening 20 minutes, scoring three times for a 3-0 victory. Alexis Sanchez is on the mark twice and has a hand in one for Mesut Ozil. Everton and Liverpool finish 1-1, but for once the Merseyside derby is overshadowed by events off the field – the dismissal of Liverpool manager Brendan Rodgers. Harry Kane slices a cross into his own net, but two Christian Eriksen free-kicks earn Tottenham a 2-2 draw at Swansea.

17 Jamie Vardy and Alexis Sanchez maintain impressive scoring runs. Vardy's two goals take his tally to eight in six matches, enabling Leicester to retrieve a 2-0 deficit for a point at Southampton. Sanchez puts Arsenal on the way to a 3-0 success at Watford with his seventh strike in four games. Raheem Sterling is also celebrating after a first-half hat-trick, the first of his career, in Manchester City's 5-1 victory over Bournemouth. Wilfried Bony claims the other two. Morgan Schneiderlin opens his account for Manchester United in a 3-0 win at Everton, while two new managers have mixed fortunes. Jurgen Klopp sees Liverpool share a goalless draw at Tottenham; Sunderland, under Sam Allaydyce, go down 1-0 away to West Bromwich Albion. West Ham continue their eye-catching away form with a 3-1 win over ten-man Crystal Palace, who lose Dwight Gayle to a second yellow card.

18 Georginio Wijnaldum fires Newcastle to a spectacular first win of the season – 6-2 over Norwich. The Dutchman scores four times and also makes a goalline clearance with the game poised at 3-2.

24 A nightmare start to the season for Jose Mourinho and his team continues at Upton Park. Chelsea lose for the fifth time in ten matches and their manager is sent to the stands for a half-time confrontation with referee Jon Moss following the sending-off of Nemanja Matic. Coach Silvino Louro is also dismissed, while the club incur a mandatory £25,000 fine for seven bookings – two of them for Matic. West Ham, making their best start to a Premier League campaign, win the match 2-1 with a header from the injury-dogged Andy Carroll, his first goal since January. Tim Sherwood's eight months as Aston Villa manager come to an end when a sixth successive defeat is followed by the sack. His side lead through Jordan Ayew, but fail to sustain it and Ayew's brother Andre gives Swansea a 2-1 away victory with an 87th minute goal. Troy Deeney, a key figure in Watford's promotion, also has a day to remember. His first goal in the top flight comes in a 2-0 victory at Stoke which spoils the 100th game in charge for the home side's manager Mark Hughes. Arsenal go top for a day with a 2-1 win over Everton, who have Gareth Barry sent off for a second yellow card.

25 Sunderland extend their record run of victories over Newcastle to six. They are second best until Fabricio Coloccini is shown a straight red card – later rescinded – for barging Steven Fletcher to the ground. Adam Johnson converts the resulting penalty, Billy Jones scores for the club for the first time and they go on to prevail 3-0. By contrast, the Manchester derby is a tepid affair and ends goalless. Also dismissed is Southampton's Sadio Mane, who receives a second yellow in stoppage-time after earning his side a 1-1 draw at Liverpool with an 86th minute equaliser. Harry Kane, with a single goal in the opening nine matches, nets a hat-trick as Tottenham recover from falling behind after 49 seconds to win 5-1 at Bournemouth.

31 Any prospect of Chelsea retaining the title is effectively ended as Liverpool give Jurgen Klopp his first victory by 3-1 at Stamford Bridge, with Philippe Coutinho on the mark twice. The result leaves Chelsea 14 points behind Manchester City, who need an 89th minute penalty by Yaya Toure to overcome Norwich 2-1 after Russell Martin handles and is shown a straight red card. City's opener from Nicolas Otamendi is his first for the club. They are level on 25 points with Arsenal, who win 3-0 at Swansea as Olivier Giroud scores the club's 2,000th goal in all competitions under Arsene Wenger and Joel Campbell records his first. Leicester are three points behind after Jamie Vardy overtakes Arthur Rowley's 1957 club record by scoring for the eighth successive Premier League game. Riyad Mahrez nets twice in a 3-2 success away to West Bromwich Albion, for whom Rickie Lambert registers his first from the penalty spot. Watford's Odion Ighalo also scores twice for a 2-0 success against West Ham, who have James Collins shown a straight red for a late challenge on the Nigerian striker.

NOVEMBER 2015

1 A hat-trick by Arouna Kone highlights Everton's 6-2 victory over Sunderland. Southampton's 2-0 win against Bournemouth in the first meeting of the teams in the top flight is marred by the dismissal of Victor Wanyama for a second yellow card.

2 New manager Remi Garde sees Aston Villa suffer a club record-equalling seventh successive Premier League defeat – 3-1 at Tottenham.

7 Jose Mourinho and Jamie Vardy again make the headlines. The Chelsea manager, serving a one-match stadium ban, watches on TV in a hotel room as Chelsea lose 1-0 at Stoke. Vardy maintains his remarkable run by winning a penalty and scoring from the spot as Leicester defeat Watford 2-1, with N'Golo Kante earlier netting his first goal for the club. Jesse Lingard opens his account in Manchester United's 2-0 win over West Bromwich Albion, who have Gareth McAuley shown a straight red card for tripping Anthony Martial in the penalty area.

8 Kieran Gibbs scores three minutes after coming off the bench to earn Arsenal a point in a 1-1 draw with Tottenham. Another defender, Scott Dann, heads the winner at Anfield as Crystal Palace inflict Jurgen Klopp's first defeat as Liverpool manager by 2-1. Aston Villa end their run of defeats by holding Manchester City to a goalless draw.

21 On the day the French national anthem is played before all Premier League games as a mark of respect to victims of the terrorist attacks in Paris, Jamie Vardy scores for the tenth successive match, equalling Ruud van Nistelrooy's Premier League record, as Leicester win 3-0 at Newcastle to go top. They move above Manchester City and Arsenal, who both lose. City suffer their worst defeat at the Etihad, 4-1 to Liverpool, for whom Roberto Firmino scores for the first time and has a hand in two other goals. Arsenal are beaten 2-1 by West Bromwich Albion after Santi Cazorla slips on his run-up and puts a penalty over the crossbar. Watford's Troy Deeney makes no mistake with his spot-kick, then concedes an own goal in stoppage-time to give Manchester United the verdict by 2-1. Also on the mark with a penalty is Jonjo Shelvey, who completes Swansea's comeback from 2-0 down for a point against Bournemouth, who have Josh King on the mark for the first time. Ross Barkley and Romelu Lukaku share the goals as Everton crush Aston Villa 4-0.

22 Harry Kane makes it seven goals in four league games with a brace in Tottenham's 4-1 success against West Ham.

28 Jamie Vardy makes the record his own by putting Leicester ahead against Manchester United – his 13th goal of the sequence. Bastian Schweinsteiger heads his first for United for a point, while three other players open their accounts. Ramiro Funes Mori puts Everton ahead at Bournemouth in one of the season's most dramatic matches. His side surrender a 2-0 advantage, regain the lead through Ross Barkley in the 95th minutes and are then pegged back again when Junior Stanislas scores his second goal for the home side in the eighth minute of stoppage-time for a 3-3 scoreline. Fabian Delph scores on his full debut for Manchester City in a 3-1 victory over Southampton, while Micah Richards nets his first for Aston Villa in a 3-2 home defeat by Watford. Another struggling side, Newcastle, are beaten 5-1 after taking the lead at Selhurst Park. James McArthur and Yannick Bolasie share four of the goals for Crystal Palace, who score five for the first time in the Premier League. Ryan Shawcross is sent off for a second yellow card in Stoke's 2-0 defeat at Sunderland.

29 An injury-hit season for Arsenal continues, with Alexis Sanchez and Santi Cazorla the latest casualties in a 1-1 draw at Norwich. Manchester City end the month back on top on goal difference from Leicester.

DECEMBER 2015

5 Eddie Howe hails Bournemouth's 1-0 victory at Stamford Bridge as 'the biggest result in the club's history.' Glenn Murray scores 99 seconds after coming off the bench to leave Chelsea 14 points adrift of fourth place and Jose Mourinho effectively writing off their chances of a Champions League spot. Stoke also rise to the occasion to defeat Manchester City 2-0 with two Marko Arnautovic goals. Jamie Vardy misses two chances to match Jimmy Dunne's top-flight record of scoring in 12 successive matches for Sheffield United in the 1931-32 season. But Vardy still has a hand in Leicester's 3-0 win at Swansea, setting up Riyad Mahrez for his hat-trick goal. Three players score for the first time for their clubs – Southampton substitute Oriol Romeu and Aston Villa's Joleon Lescott at St Mary's; James McClean for West Bromwich Albion in another 1-1 draw, against Tottenham. Olivier Giroud concedes an own goal against Sunderland, but makes amends with Arsenal's second in a 3-1 success.

6 Georginio Wijnaldum has a major say in Newcastle's much-needed 2-0 win over Liverpool, forcing an own goal from Martin Skrtel and scoring the second himself.

12 Junior Stanislas scores direct from a corner after one minute and 40 seconds to put Bournemouth on the way to another major success. With midfielder Harry Arter insisting on playing just days after he and his partner lost their baby at birth, they defeat Manchester United 2-1. Swansea, with coach Alan Curtis in charge following the dismissal of manager Garry Monk, look to have secured a point away to Manchester City when Bafetimbi Gomis equalises in the 90th minute. Instead, the home side win it in stoppage-time as Yaya Toure's shot is deflected in by Kelechi Iheanacho. Romelu Lukaku becomes the first Everton player to score in six straight Premier League games, but despite their dominance his side have to be satisfied with a 1-1 draw at Norwich.

13 Olivier Giroud, hat-trick hero of Arsenal's crucial Champions League victory over Olympiacos, completes a week to remember by putting them on the way to a 2-0 win at Villa Park from the penalty spot. Tottenham, unbeaten in 14 league games, surrender the chance to move into the top four when a goal by Ayoze Perez gives Newcastle a 2-1 win at White Hart Lane. Liverpool's Divock Origi also strikes in added time for a 2-2 draw with West Bromwich Albion in a fractious Anfield encounter during which managers Jurgen Klopp and Tony Pulis are involved in heated exchanges on the touchline.

14 Leicester establish a nine-point cushion for a Champions League place when goals by Jamie Vardy and Riyad Mahrez deliver a 2-1 win over Chelsea, who are left a single point above the relegation zone. Three days later, Jose Mourinho is sacked.

19 Two penalties by Riyad Mahrez enable Leicester to make history by beating Everton 3-2 away. They become the first side to be top at Christmas 12 months after languishing in bottom place. Chelsea fans chant Jose Mourinho's name and single out Cesc Fabregas and Diego Costa for criticism, despite a 3-1 victory over Sunderland. At Old Trafford, supporters give Louis van Gaal a hard time as Norwich win there for the first time since 1989. Cameron Jerome and Alex Tettey are on the mark in a 2-1 scoreline to spoil Wayne Rooney's 500th appearance for United. Connor Wickham, from the penalty spot, and substitute Lee Chung-Yong, with a spectacular 25-yard drive, record their first goals for Crystal Palace, who prevail 2-1 at Stoke. Also successful from the spot is Charlie Daniels, who gives Bournemouth victory by the same scoreline at The Hawthorns, where West Bromwich Albion have two players shown straight red cards – James McClean for scything down Adam Smith and Salomon Rondon for thrusting his forehead at Dan Gosling.

20 On-loan Nathan Ake's first goal for the club and two by the prolific Odion Ighalo give Watford a 3-0 victory over Liverpool.

22 In the biggest game of the season so far, Arsenal overcome Manchester City 2-1 with goals by Theo Walcott and Olivier Giroud. Both are set up by Mesut Ozil, taking his total of assists to 15 in his 15 league games.

26 Boxing Day brings setbacks for the top two. Leicester's run of ten unbeaten matches is ended by the only goal of the game against Liverpool, scored by substitute Christian Benteke. Arsenal suffer their biggest defeat of the campaign – 4-0 against Southampton, for whom Shane Long scores twice and Dutch full-back Cuco Martina provides a contender for goal of the season with a 30-yard half-volley. Manchester City take advantage by beating Sunderland 4-1, Kevin De Bruyne rounding off the scoring and providing crosses for two other goals. The win is marred when Vincent Kompany's comeback is halted after nine minutes by a recurrence of a calf injury. Manchester United, with Wayne Rooney left out of the startling line-up, slip further behind after a fourth straight defeat – 2-0 against Stoke – for the first time in one season since 1961. New interim manager Guus Hiddink sees Chelsea draw level at 2-2 against Watford with Diego Costa's second goal and have a golden opportunity to take all three points. But Oscar slips on his run-up and fires a penalty over the crossbar. Harry Kane makes no mistake with his spot-kick, then overtakes Teddy Sheringham's club record with his 27th goal of the calendar year as Tottenham see off Norwich 3-0. Tom Cleverley also has a moment to remember, heading his first for Everton with a goalless draw against Newcastle seconds away.

28 Petr Cech overtakes David James's record of 169 Premier League clean sheets and Gabriel Paulista scores his first goal for the club as Arsenal defeat Bournemouth 2-0 to end the year on top. Xherdan Shaqiri, with a brace, and substitute Joselu are on the mark for the first time for Stoke in a Goodison Park thriller which they win 4-3 with a stoppage-time penalty by Marko Arnautovic. Romelu Lukaku's two goals for Everton take his tally to 11 in ten league and cup games. By contrast, Manchester United and Chelsea play out a goalless draw, after which under-pressure Louis van Gaal insist he will not resign as United manager. Michail

Antonio records his first for West Ham, who beat Southampton 2-1, while Tottenham come out on top by the same scoreline at Watford, who have on-loan Nathan Ake shown a straight red card for a dangerous tackle on Erik Lamela.

29 A goalless draw between Leicester and Manchester City leaves Arsenal and Leicester both on 39 points, City with 36 and Tottenham on 35.

JANUARY 2016

2 Two goals by Jermain Defoe point Sunderland to a 3-1 victory over Aston Villa in the meeting of the bottom two. Newcastle's performance at the Emirates belies their 18th position and Arsenal owe much to goalkeeper Petr Cech for a 1-0 win. Leicester are held to a goalless draw by ten-man Bournemouth after Artur Borac keeps out a Riyad Mahrez penalty, awarded when Jamie Vardy is brought down by Simon Francis, who receives a straight red card. Manchester City also find it hard going at Watford before two goals in the final ten minutes deliver a 2-1 scoreline after Aleksandar Kolarov's own goal gives the home side the lead. Sadio Mane is left out of Southampton's starting line-up at Norwich for disciplinary reasons. And there are more problems for his side when Victor Wanyama is shown a second yellow card in a 1-0 defeat. A stoppage-time goal by Jonny Evans, his first for the club, gives West Bromwich Albion a 2-1 success against Stoke, who have Geoff Cameron shown a straight red for pushing Claudio Yacob. The dismissal is rescinded on appeal. Manchester United's first win in nine games in all competitions – 2-1 against Swansea – is sealed by Wayne Rooney's 188th Premier League goal, which takes him above Andy Cole and into second place in the all-time list behind Alan Shearer (260).

3 Chelsea regain some of their old style and swagger to provide Guus Hiddink with his first win – 3-0 away to Crystal Palace.

12 Aston Villa secure three points for the first time since the opening day of the season. Joleon Lescott is initially credited with the 1-0 scoreline against Crystal Palace, but the dubious goals panel rule it goes down as an own goal by goalkeeper Wayne Hennessey. Wayne Rooney's second at St James' Park looks to have given Manchester United victory, but Paul Dummett salvages a 3-3 draw for Newcastle in the 90th minute. Enner Valencia, out for most of the season with injury, is also on the mark twice as West Ham come from behind to win 3-1 at Bournemouth – a performance marred when injury-dogged Andy Carroll limps off with a hamstring problem.

13 Late goals, controversial refereeing decisions and the season's most senseless sending-off make for an eventful night at the top and bottom of the table. Joe Allen's 90th minute strike earns Liverpool a 3-3 draw with Arsenal in a game of fluctuating fortunes in which Roberto Firmino's first Anfield goals are matched by a brace from Olivier Giroud. Four days after conceding an 89th minute equaliser to Tottenham in the FA Cup, Leicester return to White Hart Lane and score the only goal through Robert Huth seven minutes from the end of normal time. For Manchester City, there is more frustration against Everton, a goalless draw at the Etihad coming a week after defeat at Goodison Park in the first leg of the teams' Capital One Cup semi-final. Referee Graham Scott is at the heart of the controversy in a relegation battle at Swansea, where Jermain Defoe's hat-trick gives Sunderland a 4-2 success. The home side, who have Leon Britton making his 500th appearance, claim two of Defoe's goals are clearly offside and question the official's decision to show a straight red card to Kyle Naughton for his challenge on Yann M'Vila. This is later rescinded on appeal. In contrast, Gary O'Neil's straight red for launching himself into the back of Stoke's Ibrahim Afellay on the touchline receives widespread condemnation, not least from his Norwich manager Alex Neil after the 3-1 defeat.

16 John Terry's 700th appearance for Chelsea is an eventful one. The captain concedes an own goal to give Everton the lead, then makes it 3-3 in the eighth minute of stoppage-time, an equaliser which even his own manager Guus Hiddink admits is offside. Everton's Roberto Martinez protests vigorously after watching his side concede this late for the second time in two months. Three players are on the mark twice, including Southampton's James Ward-Prowse, whose free-kick and penalty in a 3-0 win over West Bromwich Albion come after a single goal in his previous 92 Premier League appearances. Sergio Aguero has the chance to complete a hat-trick against Crystal Palace, but unselfishly lays on the opening for David Silva to complete Manchester City's 4-0 victory. Tottenham come from behind to beat Sunderland 4-1 with two from Christian Eriksen. Record-buy Benik Afobe opens his account for Bournemouth, who defeat Norwich 3-0, while Newcastle's new signing, Jonjo Shelvey, makes an immediate impact by setting up both goals which account for West Ham 2-1. For once, Riyad Mahrez lets Leicester down, having a penalty saved by Mark Bunn in a 1-1 draw with Aston Villa.

17 Wayne Rooney overtakes Thierry Henry's record with Arsenal to become the highest scoring player for one Premier League club, his 176th for Manchester United delivering a 1-0 win at Liverpool. Goalkeepers Jack Butland and Petr Cech take the honours in Stoke's goalless draw with Arsenal.

23 Carrow Road and Selhurst Park witness strong contenders for match of the season and goal of the season. Liverpool recover from 3-1 down to lead Norwich 4-3, concede again going into stoppage-time, then prevail 5-4 thanks to substitute Adam Lallana's volley. Robert Firmino scores twice for the winners, while Steven Naismith is on the mark on his Norwich debut. England manager Roy Hodgson sees Dele Alli's spectacular strike in Tottenham's 3-1 victory over Crystal Palace, achieved by close control, overhead flick and a 20-yard volley. Jamie Vardy ends a run of six matches without a goal as Leicester defeat Stoke 3-0 to end the month on top, three points clear of Manchester City, who are held 2-2 at West Ham, with Sergio Aguero and Enner Valencia sharing the goals. Manchester United's title chances look to have gone after Charlie Austin comes off the bench to head the only goal at Old Trafford on his Southampton debut. Jamaal Lascelles opens his account on his first start for Newcastle, but his side remain in trouble after a 2-1 defeat at Watford.

24 Arsenal miss the chance to go top after Per Mertesacker is shown a straight red card for bringing down Chelsea's Diego Costa. The Brazilian scores the only goal at the Emirates five minutes later to stretch his side's unbeaten Premier League run against Arsenal to nine games. Francesco Guidolin makes a winning start in charge of Swansea, who beat Everton for the first time in the league – 2-1 – with goals from Gylfi Sigurdsson (penalty) and Andre Ayew at Goodison Park. At the end of the month, Leicester lead with 47 points, followed by Manchester City and Arsenal on 44 and Tottenham with 42.

FEBRUARY 2016

2 Jamie Vardy delivers another contender for goal of the season – a 30-yard volley against Liverpool. Vardy is on the mark again ten minutes later for a 2-0 Leicester victory. Harry Kane takes his tally to 14 in 15 games as Tottenham underline their title threat with a 3-0 success at Norwich. But Manchester City and Arsenal find it hard going. City, with Manuel Pellegrini in charge of his 100th game the day after announcing he is making way at the end of the season for Pep Guardiola, are fortunate to prevail 1-0 at Sunderland. Arsenal, frustrated by goalkeeper Fraser Forster, are held to a goalless draw by Southampton. At the bottom, Jordan Ayew undermines Aston Villa's fight for survival with a straight red card for elbowing Aaron Cresswell in the 17th minute against West Ham, who take advantage to win 2-0.

3 Ross Barkley marks his 100th Premier League appearance with penalties in the 88th and 90th minutes to seal Everton's 3-0 victory over Newcastle. Jamaal Lascelles trips Barkley for the second and is dismissed for a second yellow card.

6 Leicester dispel any doubts about their right to be challenging for the title with an emphatic victory at the Etihad. They overcome Manchester City 3-1 with two goals from central defender Robert Huth and a beauty from Riyad Mahrez to move six points ahead of their rivals. Kieran Trippier's first for Tottenham earns a 1-0 win at Watford to keep their momentum going. Sunderland again show the character needed to stay up, retrieving a 2-0 deficit for a point at Anfield with goals by Adam Johnson (82) and Jermain Defoe (89). They come after thousands of Liverpool fans stage a walk-out in the 77th minute in protest at a £77 increase for some season tickets. Southampton overcome Victor Wanyama's third dismissal of the season, this time a straight red for lunging in at Dimitri Payet, to defeat

West Ham 1-0, while Everton record back-to-back wins for the first time, inflicting a third successive 3-0 scoreline on faltering Stoke.

7 Alex Oxlade-Chamberlain scores for the first time away from home in the Premier League as Arsenal win 2-0 at Bournemouth. Diego Costa's stoppage-time goal gives Chelsea a 1-1 draw against Manchester United.

13 Sunderland and Newcastle experience contrasting fortunes in their struggle against relegation. Sam Allardyce's side master Manchester United for the first time in a Premier League match at the Stadium of Light, with new signings Wahbi Khazri and Lamine Kone playing key roles in a 2-1 success. Khazri scores his first goal for the club with a 35-yard free-kick and delivers the corner for Kone's header which David de Gea fumbles into his own net. Andros Townsend's first for Newcastle is no consolation for a 5-1 defeat by Chelsea, who have Pedro on the mark twice. Two other winter acquisitions open their accounts. Giannelli Imbula, Stoke's record buy, sets them on the way to a 3-1 victory at Bournemouth. Emmanuel Adebayor's header boosts Crystal Palace, but they go down 2-1 at home to two Troy Deeney goals for Watford – the second a penalty – and finish with ten men after a straight red card for Pape Souare for a two-footed challenge on Valon Behrami. West Ham, FA Cup winners against Liverpool, complete a successful week by retrieving a 2-0 deficit for a point at Norwich.

14 Arsenal and Tottenham win with late goals in top-of-the-table matches. Leicester lead at the Emirates through Jamie Vardy's penalty. But they have Danny Simpson sent off for a second yellow card, concede an equaliser to Theo Walcott, then pay the price for more indiscipline when Marcin Wasilewski recklessly concedes a free-kick in the 95th minute and substitute Danny Welbeck heads Arsenal's winner on his first appearance of the season. At the Etihad, Tottenham defeat Manchester City by the same scoreline with an 83rd minute goal from Christian Eriksen on his 24th birthday. Aston Villa, giving every impression of being resigned to relegation, crash 6-0 to Liverpool, the club's worst home result for 81 years. Kolo Toure rounds off the scoring with his first goal for the club.

27 An 89th minute goal by substitute Leonardo Ulloa, the only one of the game, gives Leicester victory over Norwich. Fraser Forster sets a Southampton goalkeeping record in the home match against Chelsea, reaching 708 minutes without conceding a Premier League goal. But the run is ended by Cesc Fabregas and Branislav Ivanovic who inflict a 2-1 defeat on his side. Two goals by Marko Arnautovic, one a penalty, give Stoke victory by the same scoreline against Aston Villa. Connor Wickham is also on the mark twice in a Crystal Palace comeback, but West Bromwich Albion hold on for victory after scoring three times in the first 32 minutes.

28 Marcus Rashford, 18, completes a remarkable week to undermine Arsenal's title chances. Three days after scoring two goals on his Manchester United debut in the Europa League against Midtjylland, he becomes the youngest player to net twice in his first Premier League match. Rashford also sets up United's third goal for Ander Herrera in a 3-2 victory. Tottenham come from behind for a 2-1 win over Swansea, who have Alberto Paloschi on the mark for the first time. Mauricio Pochettino's team end the month on 54 points, two behind leaders Leicester, with Arsenal on 51 and League Cup winners Manchester City on 47.

MARCH 2016

1 Leicester are held 2-2 by West Bromwich Albion, but manager Claudio Ranieri insists he is 'more confident' they can become champions. Brazilian winger Kenedy scores the fastest goal of the season, after 39 seconds, to set Chelsea on the way to a 2-1 victory at Norwich. Connor Wickham nets two more for Crystal Palace, but Sunderland substitute Fabio Borini strikes in stoppage-time to earn his side a point.

2 All three of Leicester's rivals are beaten. Tottenham lose away from home in the league for the first time since the opening day of the season, Michail Antonio scoring the only goal of the game for West Ham. Arsenal are beaten by Swansea at the Emirates for the third time in four seasons, this time after leading through Joel Campell and hitting the woodwork three times. Captain Ashley Williams boosts his side's survival chances with the winner for 2-1 – a tonic also for manager Francesco Guidolin, in hospital with a chest infection. Manchester City go down 3-0 at Anfield, three days after beating Liverpool in the League Cup Final.

5 Arsenal overcome the sending-off of Francis Coquelin for a second yellow card to hold Tottenham 2-2 at White Hart Lane in one of the most important north London derbies for years. The result enables Leicester to stretch their lead over both rivals after Riyad Mahrez scores the only goal of their game at Watford. Manchester City see off Aston Villa 4-0, Sergio Aguero scoring twice, then spurning the chance of a hat-trick by firing a penalty against the post. Romelu Lukaku also fails from the spot with Everton poised to extend their lead over West Ham to 3-0 at Goodison Park, despite the dismissal previously of Kevin Mirallas for two yellows. Adrian saves the kick, giving his side the impetus for one of the winning recoveries of the season which delivers goals from Michail Antonio, Diafra Sakho and Dimitri Payet in the final 12 minutes. Southampton's Jose Fonte is shown a straight red for bringing down Fabio Borini, but they too come back, equalising in stoppage-time through Virgil van Dijk to deprive Sunderland of a badly-needed three points. Bournemouth move 11 points clear of the bottom three by winning 3-1 at Newcastle in what proves to be Steve McClaren's last match in charge at St James' Park. Swansea's 1-0 victory over Norwich takes them nine points away from trouble. That effectively leaves Sunderland, Newcastle and Norwich fighting to avoid two places alongside Villa in the Championship. At Stamford Bridge, Chelsea's 1-1 draw with Stoke takes Gus Hiddink's unbeaten record since taking charge to 12 games – a Premier League record for an incoming manager.

6 Two more players are sent off for second yellows. Juan Mata walks for the first time in his career as Manchester United lose a league match – 1-0 – to West Bromwich Albion at the Hawthorns for the first time since 1984. James Milner is dismissed in Liverpool's 2-1 victory at Crystal Palace.

12 Manchester City are left nine points adrift after a goalless draw at Norwich and seemingly out of the title race. Max Gradel sets Bournemouth on the way to a 3-2 win over Swansea with his first goal for the club since he was on loan from Leicester in 2008. Graziano Pelle ends a near four-month drought for Southampton with a brace in their 2-1 victory at Stoke. Team-mate Sadio Mane's straight red card for a clash with Erik Pieters is rescinded on appeal.

13 Harry Kane is on the mark twice in a 2-0 win at Villa Park, enabling Tottenham to keep the pressure on Leicester.

14 Shinji Okazaki scores the only one of the night as Claudio Ranieri's side respond by beating Newcastle, who have Rafael Benitez making his debut as manager.

19 Another 1-0 victory for Leicester, courtesy of Riyad Mahrez at Crystal Palace, keeps them clear at the top. Alex Iwobi scores his first goal for Arsenal, who make light of their midweek Champions League exit by winning 2-0 at Everton, and Federico Fernandez opens his account with the only one of the game for Swansea against Aston Villa. Norwich also prevail 1-0, Robbie Brady's strike at West Bromwich Albion ending his side's ten-match run without a win. West Ham are denied a top-four place by Cesc Fabregas, who follows up his earlier free-kick with an 89th minute penalty to give Chelsea a 2-2 draw.

20 With big games elsewhere at both ends of the table, Southampton seem to be out of the limelight when trailing Liverpool 2-0 at St Mary's. Instead, they take the day's main honours with a thrilling second-half performance for a 3-2 victory, courtesy of two goals by Sadio Mane – who also has a penalty saved by Simon Mignolet – and one from Graziano Pelle. Harry Kane is also on the mark twice in Tottenham's 3-0 victory over Bournemouth, as well as setting up Christian Eriksen for the third. At the Etihad, Manchester United's Marcus Rashford scores the only goal against Manchester City and at 18 becomes the youngest player in Premier League history to score in this derby match. At St James' Park, Newcastle are heading for a seventh successive defeat by Sunderland until Aleksandar Mitrovic, in the 83rd minute, cancels out Jermain Defoe's goal for a 1-1 scoreline.

APRIL 2016

2 Harry Kane becomes Tottenham's highest scorer in a single Premier League season, but his 22nd goal of this campaign is not enough to prevent them losing ground in a 1-1 draw with

Liverpool. At the bottom, Timm Klose opens his account for Norwich and Martin Olsson strikes in stoppage time for a 3-2 victory after substitute Aleksandar Mitrovic's second of the game looks to have earned Newcastle a point. Sunderland, keeping a clean sheet for the first time in 18 games, are also left frustrated as West Bromwich Albion goalkeeper Ben Foster denies them in a goalless draw. So, too, are West Ham, held 2-2 by Crystal Palace after having Cheikhou Kouyate shown a straight red card, which is later rescinded. Chelsea loanee Alexandre Pato enjoys a successful debut, winning and converting a penalty, as well as providing two assists in the 4-0 victory over Aston Villa, who have Alan Hutton sent off for a second yellow card. Arsenal and Manchester City win by the same scoreline, against Watford and Bournemouth respectively.

3 Captain Wes Morgan heads his first goal of the season to give Leicester their fourth successive 1-0 win, this time against Southampton. It stretches their lead over Tottenham to seven points, with Arsenal a further four points back.

9 Andy Carroll's hat-trick effectively ends Arsenal's title chances. It comes in the space of seven minutes either side of half-time and earns West Ham a 3-3 draw. Newcastle slip deeper into trouble when losing 3-1 at Southampton, while Norwich are beaten 1-0 at Crystal Palace, who win in the league for the first time in 2016 with Jason Puncheon's first goal of the season. Chelsea's 1-0 defeat at Swansea, inflicted by Gylfi Sigurdsson's ninth goal in 14 games, is Guus Hiddink's first in 15 league matches as interim manager.

10 Jamie Vardy scores his 20th and 21st goals of the season to give Leicester a 2-0 win at Sunderland, a ten-point lead and a guaranteed Champions League place. Later in the day, Tottenham cut it back to seven by beating Manchester United with three second-half goals in seven minutes. Divock Origi follows up his midweek goal in Liverpool's Europa League quarter-final against Borussia Dortmund with a brace in the 4-1 defeat of Stoke.

13 Everton's James McCarthy is sent off for a second yellow card in a goalless draw at Crystal palace.

16 On the day Aston Villa's relegation is confirmed by a 1-0 defeat by Manchester United, there are 3-0 victories for two sides battling to avoid joining them in the Championship. In a 'six-pointer' at Carrow Road, Sunderland overcome Norwich, with Jermain Defoe scoring his tenth goal in 14 away matches. At St James' Park, Newcastle give Rafael Benitez a first win in charge, on his 56th birthday, against Swansea. Goalkeepers Heurelho Gomes and Thibault Courtois have sharply-contrasting fortunes. Gomes becomes the first in the Premier League to save two penalties in a game on two occasions. He denies Saido Berahino in Watford's 1-0 away win over West Bromwich Albion, having achieved the feat for Tottenham against Sunderland's Darren Bent six years previously. Chelsea's Courtois is shown a straight red card for bringing down Fernandinho, enabling Sergio Aguero to complete a hat-trick and a 3-0 success for Manchester City.

17 Jamie Vardy is sent off for a second yellow card, but Leicester earn a 2-2 draw against West Ham with a stoppage-time penalty from substitute Leonardo Ulloa.

18 Tottenham close the gap at the top to five points with a 4-0 win at Stoke, Harry Kane and Dele Alli sharing the goals.

19 Sergio Aguero scores his 100th Premier League goal on his 147th appearance for Manchester City, who draw 1-1 at Newcastle.

20 Liverpool record one of the most one-sided Merseyside derby victories – 4-0 against Everton, who have Ramiro Funes Mori shown a straight red card for stamping on Divock Origi. Heurelho Gomes faces two more penalties and is beaten both times by Mark Noble in West Ham's 3-1 success against Watford. Matteo Darmian scores his first goal for the club as Manchester United defeat Crystal Palace 2-0.

21 Arsenal beat West Bromwich Albion 2-0 with two goals from Alexis Sanchez.

23 Newcastle retrieve a two-goal deficit to draw 2-2 with Liverpool and end a run of nine successive away defeats. Eden Hazard scores his first Premier League goals of the season for Chelsea, who win 4-1 at Bournemouth. Also on the mark twice are Kelechi Iheanacho, in Manchester City's 4-0 victory over Stoke, and Dusan Tadic as Southampton are 4-2 winners over Aston Villa, for whom Ashley Westwood nets both goals.

24 Leicester make light of the absence of the suspended Jamie Vardy to defeat Swansea 4-0, with Vardy's replacement, Leonardo Ulloa, on the mark twice. Sunderland move out of the bottom three with a goalless draw against Arsenal.

25 Tottenham's chances of closing the gap are hit when Craig Dawson makes amends for an own goal by heading in a corner to give West Bromwich Albion a 1-1 draw at White Hart Lane.

30 Two penalties add to the tension at the foot of the table. Karl Darlow, Newcastle's third-choice goalkeeper saves one from Yohan Cabaye to preserve his side's 1-0 victory over Crystal Palace, delivered by Andros Townsend's 30-yard free-kick. Sunderland's Jermain Defoe makes no mistake with his stoppage-time spot-kick which earns a 1-1 draw at Stoke. Norwich lose to the only goal against Arsenal, leaving them with 31 points, Sunderland on 32 and Newcastle on 33. Mark Noble scores twice for the second successive match as West Ham beat West Bromwich Albion 3-0 away from home to reach a club-record 59 points. Troy Deeney also gets two, one in the 90th minute, the second in added time, to give Watford a 3-2 victory over Aston Villa, who have Aly Cissokho shown a straight red card for a professional foul on Ikechi Anya.

MAY 2016

1 Wes Morgan's header earns Leicester a 1-1 draw at Old Trafford, but they again finish with ten men after a second yellow card for Danny Drinkwater. Sadio Mane's hat-trick points Southampton to a 4-2 victory over a Manchester City side with their sights set on the Champions League second semi-final against Real Madrid. Kelechi Iheanacho nets both City goals. Liverpool, preparing for a Europa League semi-final return tie with Villarreal, field the club's youngest line-up of the Premier League era – 23 years and 218 days – against Swansea. One of the fringe players, Brad Smith, is sent off for a second yellow card as Swansea win 3-1, with Andre Ayew on the mark twice.

2 Leicester are crowned champions – without kicking a ball. Tottenham lead 2-0 against Chelsea at Stamford Bridge through Harry Kane and Son Heung-min, but are pegged back by goals from Gary Cahill and Eden Hazard. In a stormy match, on and off the pitch, Tottenham have nine players booked and receive an automatic £25,000 fine, while both clubs face disciplinary action from the FA.

7 Jamie Vardy scores twice on his return from suspension – and misses a hat-trick by firing a second penalty over the bar – as Leicester celebrate their momentous achievement with a 3-1 victory over Everton. Sunderland twice come from behind, then score the winner through Jermain Defoe for a priceless 3-2 success against Chelsea, who have John Terry sent off for a second yellow card. Newcastle miss the chance to keep pace in a goalless draw at Aston Villa, who end a run of 11 successive defeats. Norwich's chances of staying up look bleak after a 1-0 home defeat by Manchester United. Dwight Gayle stakes a claim for a place in Crystal Palace's FA Cup Final team with both goals in a 2-1 win over Stoke.

8 Steven Davis doubles his tally for the season with both goals in Southampton's 2-1 win at Tottenham.

10 West Ham's final game at Upton Park before a move to the Olympic Stadium is marred when hooligans attack Manchester United's team bus and the kick-off is delayed by 45 minutes. An 81st minute Winston Reid header gives his side a 3-2 win, with two goals from Anthony Martial not enough to take United up into a Champions League position.

11 Sunderland survive by beating Everton 3-0 – a result which sends Newcastle and Norwich down. Lamine Kone scores twice against a side who have Roberto Martinez in charge for the final time before his dismissal. Norwich, ironically, give one of their best performances of the season to defeat Watford 4-2, with Dieumerci Mbokani on the mark twice.

15 On a bizarre afternoon, Manchester United's match against Bournemouth is called off because of a security alert, Manchester City deny them the final Champions League place and Newcastle play more like champions than chumps. As Old Trafford empties after the discovery of a suspicious package, Kelechi Iheanacho gives City the lead at Swansea. The home side equalise through Andre Ayew, but a point is enough for Manuel Pellegrini to bequeath fourth place to the incoming Pep Guardiola. Newcastle fans, meanwhile, call for

Rafael Benitez to stay and lead their side back to the Premier League after a miserable season at St James' Park ends with a 5-1 win over Tottenham, whose manager Mauricio Pochettino publicly apologises for a shambolic performance. Georgino Wijnaldum scores two of the goals, one a penalty, as Newcastle make light of losing Aleksandar Mitrovic to a straight red card for planning his studs into Kyle Walker's shin. The defeat costs Tottenham second place, Arsenal overtaking their arch-rivals by beating Aston Villa 4-0 with a hat-trick from Olivier Giroud. Leicester wrap up a memorable season with a point at Stamford Bridge, courtesy of a 25-yard equaliser from Danny Drinkwater. Sadio Mane's eighth goal in eight games sets Southampton on the way to a 4-1 victory over Crystal Palace – and the club's highest top-flight finish for 31 years, sixth, together with a record Premier League points tally of 63.

17 Marcus Rashford celebrates his inclusion in England's provisional squad for Euro 2016 with his eighth goal in 17 appearances in all competitions as Manchester United defeat Bournemouth 3-1 in their rearranged fixture which closes the Premier League season.

THE IMPOSSIBLE DREAM THAT CAME TRUE

The manager was sacked from his previous job for losing to the Faroe Islands; the top scorer was playing for a steelworks team well into his 20s; the midfield master cost less than some League One players. Their team had struggled against the threat of relegation for much of the previous season, so it was no surprise that Leicester City were among the favourites to go down this time. Almost as an aside, their chances of winning the title were put at 5,000-1, which seemed just about right. Instead, Claudio Ranieri, Jamie Vardy and Riyad Mahrez, together with team-mates making just as much a mockery of their modest standing in the game, defied not just the odds but also footballing logic which demanded that one of the big clubs must finish on top.

For all the splendid achievements of Nottingham Forest and Derby County in the 1970s and Blackburn Rovers in the early years of the Premier League, this was on a different level, considering the intensity and financial implications of the modern-day game. Ranieri had two advantages over his rival managers – one the absence of major injuries which enabled him to field a settled side; the other no distractions in the shape of lengthy Cup runs or European involvement. Yet the overriding factor in their triumph was the way he organised his side, extracted the maximum from each player and kept the pressures off for much of the season, until even he himself had to admit that the impossible was becoming reality. Ranieri made one crucial change early on, introducing Danny Simpson and Christian Fuchs to the full-back positions and giving his defence an extra dimension. For the rest of the campaign, the 'tinkerman' tag was almost forgotten. Eight of his players, Vardy, Mahrez, Kasper Schmeichel, Wes Morgan, Robert Huth, Danny Drinkwater, Marc Albrighton and N'Golo Kante featured in more than 30 matches. When that consistency was rewarded on the night their only rivals Tottenham dropped points against Chelsea, it was less than eight months since the manager was dismissed by Greece after that Euro 2016 qualifying humiliation.

There was one further example of the resolve which put Leicester on top. They trailed 1-0 in the final match to the deposed champions at Stamford Bridge and would have been forgiven for settling for that. Not a bit of it as Drinkwater drove an 82nd minute equaliser from 30 yards to maintain a ten-point led. From start to finish, they played like champions.

WHAT THEY SAID BEFORE THE SEASON ...

'For Ranieri to get this job was quite incredible. I hope he does well, because he is a nice guy, but he's fortunate' – **Phil Thompson**.

I think it could be a massive struggle this season. I think he might struggle with the spirit there' – **Matt Le Tissier**.

'Claudio Ranieri is clearly experienced, but this is an uninspired choice by Leicester. It's amazing how the same old names keep getting a go on the managerial merry-go-round' – **Gary Lineker**.

'He's done well to get the job. After what happened with Greece, I'm surprised he can walk back into the Premier League' – **Harry Redknapp**.

'I'd have gone back to (Martin) O'Neill or (Neil) Lennon. It will be a relegation battle whoever was manager. Big name, bad choice in my opinion' – **Robbie Savage**.

WHAT THEY SAID AFTER IT ...

'I've followed them since I was a little kid and I just can't get my head round it. You could have given me ten million to one and I'd have said "Nah, it's a waste of a quid." Extraordinary' – **Gary Lineker**.

'There's no doubt it is the greatest achievement in the history of our game. Leicester have given inspiration to every football club, every manager, player, supporter all across the land that one day it could be them' – **Jamie Carragher**.

'It hurts passing the Premier League title to Leicester but credit to them. They've been superb. Claudio Ranieri is different class' – **John Terry.**

'It's made mugs of all of us and that is just the most fantastic feeling' – **Richard Scudamore**, executive chairman of the Premier League.

AND THE MANAGER HIMSELF ...

'I never expected this when I arrived. I'm a pragmatic man – I just wanted to win match after match and help my players to improve week after week. I did not think about where it would take us. The players have been fantastic. Their focus, their determination, their spirit has made this possible. Every game they fight for each other. They deserve to be champions.' – **Claudio Ranieri**.

HOW LEICESTER CITY WON THE PREMIER LEAGUE TITLE

AUGUST 2015

8 Leicester 4 (Vardy 11, Mahrez 18, 25 pen, Albrighton 66) Sunderland 2 (Defoe 60, Fletcher 71). Att: 32,242

15 West Ham 1 (Payet 55) Leicester 2 (Okazaki 27, Mahrez 38). Att: 34,857

22 Leicester 1 (Mahrez 82) Tottenham 1 (Alli 82). Att: 31,971

29 Bournemouth 1 (Wilson 24) Leicester 1 (Vardy 86 pen). Att: 11,155

SEPTEMBER 2015

13 Leicester 3 (De Laet 72, Vardy 82, Dyer 89) Aston Villa 2 (Grealish 39, Gil 63). Att: 31,733

19 Stoke 2 (Krkic 13, Walters 20) Leicester 2 (Mahrez 51 pen, Vardy 69). Att: 27,642

26 Leicester 2 (Vardy 13, 89) Arsenal 5 (Walcott 18, Sanchez 33, 57, 81, Giroud 90). Att: 32,047

OCTOBER 2015

3 Norwich 1 (Mbokani 68) Leicester 2 (Vardy 28 pen, Schlupp 47). Att: 27,067

17 Southampton 2 (Fonte 21, Van Dijk 37) Leicester 2 (Vardy 66, 90). Att: 30,966
24 Leicester 1 (Vardy 59) Crystal Palace 0. Att: 31,752
31 WBA 2 (Rondon 30, Lambert 84 pen) Leicester 3 (Mahrez 57, 64, Vardy 77). Att: 24,150

NOVEMBER 2015

7 Leicester 2 (Kante 52, Vardy 65 pen) Watford 1 (Deeney 75 pen). Att: 32,029
21 Newcastle 0 Leicester 3 (Vardy 45, Ulloa 62, Okazaki 83). Att: 50,151
28 Leicester 1 (Vardy 24) Manchester Utd 1 (Schweinsteiger 45). Att: 32,115

DECEMBER 2015

5 Swansea 0 Leicester 3 (Mahrez 5, 22, 67). Att: 20,836
14 Leicester 2 (Vardy 34, Mahrez 48) Chelsea 1 (Remy 77). Att: 32,054
19 Everton 2 (Lukaku 32, Mirallas 89) Leicester 3 (Mahrez 27 pen, 65 pen, Okazaki 69). Att: 39,570
26 Liverpool 1 (Benteke 63) Leicester 0. Att: 44,123
29 Leicester 0 Manchester City 0. Att: 32,072

JANUARY 2016

2 Leicester 0 Bournemouth 0. Att: 32,006
13 Tottenham 0 Leicester 1 (Huth 83). Att: 35,850
16 Aston Villa 1 (Gestede 75) Leicester 1 (Okazaki 28). Att: 32,763
23 Leicester 3 (Drinkwater 42, Vardy 66, Ulloa 87) Stoke 0. Att: 32,018

FEBRUARY 2016

2 Leicester 2 (Vardy 60, 71) Liverpool 0. Att: 32,121
6 Manchester City 1 (Aguero 87) Leicester 3 (Huth 3, 60, Mahrez 48). Att: 54,693
14 Arsenal 2 (Walcott 70, Welbeck 90) Leicester 1 (Vardy 45 pen). Att: 60,009
27 Leicester 1 (Ulloa 89) Norwich 0. Att: 32,114

MARCH 2016

1 Leicester 2 (Olsson 30 og, King 45) WBA 2 (Rondon 11, Gardner 50). Att: 32,018
5 Watford 0 Leicester 1 (Mahrez 56). Att: 20,884
14 Leicester 1 (Okazaki 25) Newcastle 0. Att: 31,824
19 Crystal Palace 0 Leicester 1 (Mahrez 34). Att: 25,041

APRIL 2016

3 Leicester 1 (Morgan 38) Southampton 0. Att: 32,071
10 Sunderland 0 Leicester 2 (Vardy 66, 90). Att: 46,531
17 Leicester 2 (Vardy 18, Ulloa 90 pen) West Ham 2 (Carroll 84 pen, Cresswell 86). Att: 32,104
24 Leicester 4 (Mahrez 10, Ulloa 30, 60, Albrighton 85) Swansea 0. Att: 31,962

MAY 2016

1 Manchester Utd 1 (Martial 8) Leicester 1 (Morgan 17). Att: 75,275
2 (Clinched title when Tottenham draw 2-2 with Chelsea)
7 Leicester 3 (Vardy 5, 65 pen, King 33) Everton 1 (Mirallas 88). Att: 32,140
15 Chelsea 1 (Fabregas 66 pen) Leicester 1 (Drinkwater 82). Att: 41,494

FOOTBALL LEAGUE PLAY-OFFS 2015–16

A goal worthy of winning any game, certainly one with an estimated £200m price tag attached to it, took Hull back to the big time at the first attempt. It was scored by Mohamed Diame against Sheffield Wednesday in the 72nd minute of a match notable for the number of chances his side had created and wasted. From 25 yards, the French-born, Senegal international midfielder curled a superb shot into the top corner which even the excellent Keiren Westwood had no chance of stopping. Hull protected the lead – surviving one strong penalty appeal for hands – to land football's richest-ever prize and join Championship winners Burnley in returning to the top flight a year after being relegated. It was the fourth time that manager Steve Bruce had won promotion to the Premier League, twice with Hull and twice with Birmingham. Diame, who previously hit a post, was his driving force and the player who did most to block Wednesday's bid to end 16 years in the game's second tier. They had an estimated 40,000 fans at Wembley, but were unable to produce the form which took them to Wembley in Portuguese manager Carlos Carvalhal's first season in charge. Another spectacular goal put Wednesday's neighbours, Barnsley, on the way to a league and cup double. They returned to Wembley after winning the Johnstone's Paint Trophy to score twice in the first 19 minutes of the League One Final against Millwall. Adam Hammill bent his shot into the far corner from similar distance to Diame's strike after Manchester United loanee Ashley Fletcher's second minute opener. Lloyd Isgrove made it 3-1 after Mark Beevers pulled one back for Millwall, who lost central defender Byron Webster in the warm-up and had to reorganise. AFC Wimbledon recorded their sixth promotion since being formed by supporters in 2002 and setting out in the Combined Counties League after the original club 'moved' to Milton Keynes. A 2-0 win over favourites Plymouth in the League Two Final meant they would face relegated MK Dons in the new season. Leading marksman Lyle Taylor and 16st, out-of-contract Adebayo Akinfenwa, with a penalty in the 11th minute of stoppage-time, scored the goals. Grimsby ended a six-year absence from the Football League by beating Forest Green 3-1 in the Conference Final, Omar Bogle scoring twice.

SEMI-FINALS, FIRST LEG

CHAMPIONSHIP

Derby 0 **Hull** 3 (Hernandez 30, Shackell 40 og, Robertson 90). Att: 29,969. **Sheffield Wed** 2 (Wallace 45, Lee 73) **Brighton** 0. Att: 34,260

LEAGUE ONE

Barnsley 3 (Demetriou 45 og, Winnall 54, 55) **Walsall** 0. Att: 16,051. **Bradford** 1 (McMahon 13 pen) **Millwall** 3 (Gregory 15, Morison 34, Martin 45). Att: 19,241

LEAGUE TWO

AFC Wimbledon 1 (Beere 90) **Accrington** 0. Att: 4,870. **Portsmouth** 2 (McNulty 3, Roberts 51 pen) **Plymouth** 2 (Matt 9, 19). Att: 17,622

NATIONAL LEAGUE

Dover 0 **Forest Green** 1 (Williams 35). Att: 2,071. **Grimsby** 0 **Braintree** 1 (Davis 53 pen). Att: 5,271

SEMI-FINALS, SECOND LEG

CHAMPIONSHIP

Brighton 1 (Dunk 19) **Sheffield Wed** 1 (Wallace 28). Att: 27,272 (Sheffield Wed won 3-1 on agg). **Hull** 0 **Derby** 2 (Russell 7, Robertson 36 og). Att: 20,470 (Hull won 3-2 on agg)

LEAGUE ONE

Millwall 1 (Gregory 34) **Bradford** 1 (Proctor 44). Att: 16,301 (Millwall won 4-2 on agg). **Walsall** 1 (Cook 85) **Barnsley** 3 (Hammill 18, Fletcher 66, Brownhill 90). Att: 8,022 (Barnsley won 6-1 on agg)

LEAGUE TWO
Accrington 2 (Windass 39 pen, Mingoia 59) **AFC Wimbledon** 2 (Akinfenwa 68, Taylor 104). Att: 4,634 (aet, AFC Wimbledon won 3-2 on agg). **Plymouth** 1 (Hartley 90) **Portsmouth** 0. Att: 15,011 (Plymouth won 3-2 on agg)

NATIONAL LEAGUE
Forest Green 1 (Marsh-Brown 54) **Dover** 1 (Miller 49). Att: 2,755 (Forest Green won 2-1 on agg). **Braintree** 0 **Grimsby** 2 (Amond 75 pen, Bogle 110). Att: 3,102 (aet, Grimsby won 2-1 on agg)

FINALS

CHAMPIONSHIP – SATURDAY, MAY 28, 2016

Hull City 1 (Diame 72) **Sheffield Wednesday** 0. Att: 70,189 (Wembley)
Hull City (4-2-3-1): Jakupovic, Odubajo, Dawson (capt), Davies, Robertson, Livermore, Huddlestone, Elmohamady, Diame (Maguire 89), Snodgrass (Clucas 82), Hernandez (Meyler 85). **Subs not used**: Kuciak, Alex Bruce, Maloney, Akpom. **Booked**: Dawson. **Manager**: Steve Bruce
Sheffield Wednesday (4-4-1-1): Westwood, Hunt, Lees, Loovens (capt), Pudil (Lucas Joao 86), Wallace (Helan 63), Hutchinson (Nuhiu 76), Lee, Bannan, Forestieri, Hooper. **Subs not used**: Wildsmith, Matias, Lopez, Sasso. **Manager**: Carlos Carvalhal
Referee: R Madley (Yorks). **Half-time**: 0-0

LEAGUE ONE – SUNDAY, MAY 29, 2016

Barnsley 3 (Fletcher 2, Hammill 19, Isgrove 74) **Millwall** 1 (Beevers 34). Att: 51,277 (Wembley)
Barnsley (4-4-2): Davies, Scowen, Roberts, Mawson, G Williams, Isgrove (Watkins 85), Brownhill, Hourihane (capt), Hammill, Winnall, Fletcher (Toney 81). **Subs not used**: Townsend, Nyatanga, McCourt, Chapman, White. **Booked**: G Williams, Roberts. **Manager**: Paul Heckingbottom
Millwall (4-4-2): Archer, Edwards (S Williams 82), Craig (capt), Beevers, Martin (O'Brien 43), Taylor, Thompson (Onyedinma 76), Abdou, Ferguson, Gregory, Morison. **Subs not used**: Forde, Upson, Nelson, Philpot. **Manager**: Neil Harris
Referee: S Attwell (Warwicks). **Half-time**: 2-1

LEAGUE TWO – MONDAY, MAY 30, 2016

AFC Wimbledon 2 (Taylor 78, Akinfenwa 90 pen) **Plymouth Argyle** 0. Att: 57,956 (Wembley)
AFC Wimbledon (4-4-2): Roos, Fuller (capt), Robinson, Charles, Kennedy, Smith (Meades 69), Bulman, Reeves, Barcham, Taylor (Azeez 90), Elliott (Akinfenwa 77). **Subs not used**: Shea, Rigg, Sweeney, Murphy. **Booked**: Charles, Taylor, Akinfenwa. **Manager**: Neal Ardley
Plymouth Argyle (4-2-3-1): McCormick, Mellor, Nelson (capt), Hartley (Forster 86), Sawyer, Boateng, McHugh, Jervis (Tanner 67), Carey, Wylde (Reid 81), Matt. **Subs not used**: Dorel, Harvey, Purrington, Houghton. **Booked**: Wylde, Sawyer. **Manager**: Derek Adams
Referee: I Williamson (Berks). **Half-time**: 0-0

NATIONAL LEAGUE – SUNDAY, MAY 15, 2016

Forest Green Rovers 1 (Marsh-Brown 60) **Grimsby Town** 3 (Bogle 42, 44, Arnold 90). Att: 17,198 (Wembley)
Forest Green Rovers (4-4-2): S Arnold, Bennett, Clough, Racine (capt), Jefford (Jennings 71), Marsh-Brown, Pipe, Carter, Frear, Guthrie (Jeffrey 78), Williams (Parkin 46). **Subs not used**: Maxted, Kamdjo. **Booked**: Carter. **Manager**: Scott Bartlett
Grimsby Town (4-4-2): McKeown, Tait, Nsiala, Gowling, Robertson, N Arnold (Pearson 90), Disley (capt), Clay, Nolan, Bogle (Hoban 89), Amond (Pittman 90). **Subs not used**: East, Marshall. **Manager**: Paul Hurst
Referee: R Jones (Cheshire). **Half-time**: 0-2

PLAY-OFF FINALS – HOME & AWAY

1987: Divs 1/2: Charlton beat Leeds 2-1 in replay (Birmingham) after 1-1 agg (1-0h, 0-1a).

Charlton remained in Div 1 Losing semi-finalists: Ipswich and Oldham. **Divs 2/3: Swindon** beat Gillingham 2-0 in replay (Crystal Palace) after 2-2 agg (0-1a, 2-1h). Swindon promoted to Div 2. Losing semi-finalists: Sunderland and Wigan; Sunderland relegated to Div 3. **Divs 3/4: Aldershot** beat Wolves 3-0 on agg (2-0h, 1-0a) and promoted to Div 3. Losing semi-finalists: Bolton and Colchester; Bolton relegated to Div 4

1988: Divs 1/2: Middlesbrough beat Chelsea 2-1 on agg (2-0h, 0-1a) and promoted to Div 1; Chelsea relegated to Div 2. Losing semi-finalists: Blackburn and Bradford City. **Divs 2/3: Walsall** beat Bristol City 4-0 in replay (h) after 3-3 agg (3-1a, 0-2h) and promoted to Div 2. Losing semi-finalists: Sheffield Utd and Notts County; Sheffield Utd relegated to Div 3. **Divs 3/4: Swansea** beat Torquay 5-4 on agg (2-1h, 3-3a) and promoted to Div 3. Losing semi-finalists: Rotherham and Scunthorpe.; Rotherham relegated to Div 4

1989: Div 2: Crystal Palace beat Blackburn 4-3 on agg (1-3a, 3-0h). Losing semi-finalists: Watford and Swindon. **Div 3: Port Vale** beat Bristol Rovers 2-1 on agg (1-1a, 1-0h). Losing semi-finalists: Fulham and Preston **Div.4: Leyton Orient** beat Wrexham 2-1 on agg (0-0a, 2-1h). Losing semi-finalists: Scarborough and Scunthorpe

PLAY-OFF FINALS AT WEMBLEY

1990: Div 2: Swindon 1 Sunderland 0 (att: 72,873). Swindon promoted, then demoted for financial irregularities; Sunderland promoted. Losing semi-finalists: Blackburn and Newcastle Utd **Div 3: Notts County** 2 Tranmere 0 (att: 29,252). Losing semi-finalists: Bolton and Bury. **Div 4: Cambridge Utd** 1 Chesterfield 0 (att: 26,404). Losing semi-finalists: Maidstone and Stockport County

1991: Div 2: Notts County 3 Brighton 1 (att: 59,940). Losing semi-finalists: Middlesbrough and Millwall. **Div 3: Tranmere** 1 Bolton 0 (att: 30,217). Losing semi-finalists: Brentford and Bury. **Div 4: Torquay 2** Blackpool 2 – Torquay won 5-4 on pens (att: 21,615). Losing semi-finalists: Burnley and Scunthorpe

1992: Div 2: Blackburn 1 Leicester 0 (att: 68,147). Losing semi-finalists: Derby and Cambridge Utd. **Div 3: Peterborough** 2 Stockport 1 (att: 35,087). Losing semi-finalists: Huddersfield and Stoke. **Div 4: Blackpool** 1 Scunthorpe 1 aet, Blackpool won 4-3 on pens (att: 22,741). Losing semi-finalists: Barnet and Crewe

1993: Div 1: Swindon 4 Leicester 3 (att: 73,802). Losing semi-finalists: Portsmouth and Tranmere. **Div 2: WBA** 3 Port Vale 0 (att: 53,471). Losing semi-finalists: Stockport and Swansea. **Div 3: York** 1 Crewe 1 aet, York won 5-3 on pens (att: 22,416). Losing semi-finalists: Bury and Walsall

1994: Div 1: Leicester 2 Derby 1 (att: 73,671). Losing semi-finalists: Millwall and Tranmere. **Div 2: Burnley** 2 Stockport 1 (att: 44,806). Losing semi-finalists: Plymouth Argyle and York. **Div 3: Wycombe** 4 Preston 2 (att: 40,109). Losing semi-finalists: Carlisle and Torquay

1995: Div 1: Bolton 4 Reading 3 (att: 64,107). Losing semi-finalists: Tranmere and Wolves. **Div 2: Huddersfield** 2 Bristol Rov 1 (att: 59,175). Losing semi-finalists: Brentford and Crewe. **Div 3: Chesterfield** 2 Bury 0 (att: 22,814). Losing semi-finalists: Mansfield and Preston

1996: Div 1: Leicester 2 Crystal Palace 1 aet (att: 73,573). Losing semi-finalists: Charlton and Stoke. **Div 2: Bradford City** 2 Notts Co 0 (att: 39,972). Losing semi-finalists: Blackpool and Crewe. **Div 3: Plymouth Argyle** 1 Darlington 0 (att: 43,431). Losing semi-finalists: Colchester and Hereford

1997: Div 1: Crystal Palace 1 Sheffield Utd 0 (att: 64,383). Losing semi-finalists: Ipswich and Wolves. **Div 2: Crewe** 1 Brentford 0 (att: 34,149). Losing semi-finalists: Bristol City and Luton. **Div 3: Northampton** 1 Swansea 0 (att: 46,804). Losing semi-finalists: Cardiff and Chester

1998: Div 1: Charlton 4 Sunderland 4 aet, Charlton won 7-6 on pens (att: 77, 739). Losing semi-finalists: Ipswich and Sheffield Utd. **Div 2: Grimsby** 1 Northampton 0 (att: 62,988). Losing semi-finalists: Bristol Rov and Fulham. **Div 3: Colchester** 1 Torquay 0 (att: 19,486). Losing semi-finalists: Barnet and Scarborough

1999: Div 1: Watford 2 Bolton 0 (att: 70,343). Losing semi-finalists: Ipswich and Birmingham. **Div 2: Manchester City** 2 Gillingham 2 aet, Manchester City won 3-1 on pens (att: 76,935). Losing semi-finalists: Preston and Wigan. **Div 3: Scunthorpe** 1 Leyton Orient 0 (att: 36,985). Losing semi-finalists: Rotherham and Swansea

2000: Div 1: Ipswich 4 Barnsley 2 (att: 73,427). Losing semi-finalists: Birmingham and Bolton. **Div 2: Gillingham** 3 Wigan 2 aet (att: 53,764). Losing semi-finalists: Millwall and Stoke. **Div 3: Peterborough** 1 Darlington 0 (att: 33,383). Losing semi-finalists: Barnet and Hartlepool

PLAY-OFF FINALS AT MILLENNIUM STADIUM

2001: Div 1: Bolton 3 Preston 0 (att: 54,328). Losing semi-finalists: Birmingham and WBA. **Div 2: Walsall** 3 Reading 2 aet (att: 50,496). Losing semi-finalists: Stoke and Wigan. **Div 3: Blackpool** 4 Leyton Orient 2 (att: 23,600). Losing semi-finalists: Hartlepool and Hull.

2002: Div 1: Birmingham 1 Norwich 1 aet, Birmingham won 4-2 on pens, (att: 71,597). Losing semi-finalists: Millwall and Wolves. **Div 2: Stoke** 2 Brentford 0 (att: 42,523). Losing semi-finalists: Cardiff and Huddersfield. **Div 3: Cheltenham** 3 Rushden & Diamonds 1 (att: 24,368). Losing semi-finalists: Hartlepool and Rochdale

2003: Div 1: Wolves 3 Sheffield Utd 0 (att: 69,473). Losing semi-finalists: Nott'm Forest and Reading. **Div 2: Cardiff** 1 QPR. 0 aet (att: 66,096). Losing semi-finalists: Bristol City and Oldham. **Div 3: Bournemouth** 5 Lincoln 2 (att: 32,148). Losing semi-finalists: Bury and Scunthorpe

2004: Div 1: Crystal Palace 1 West Ham 0 (att: 72,523). Losing semi-finalists: Ipswich and Sunderland. **Div 2: Brighton** 1 Bristol City 0 (att: 65,167). Losing semi-finalists: Hartlepool and Swindon. **Div 3: Huddersfield** 0 Mansfield 0 aet, Huddersfield won 4-1 on pens (att: 37,298). Losing semi-finalists: Lincoln and Northampton

2005: Championship: West Ham 1 Preston 0 (att: 70,275). Losing semifinalists: Derby Co and Ipswich. **League 1: Sheffield Wed** 4 Hartlepool 2 aet (att: 59,808). Losing semi-finalists: Brentford and Tranmere **League 2: Southend** 2 Lincoln 0 aet (att: 19532). Losing semi-finalists: Macclesfield and Northampton

2006: Championship: Watford 3 Leeds 0 (att: 64,736). Losing semi-finalists: Crystal Palace and Preston. **League 1: Barnsley** 2 Swansea 2 aet (att: 55,419), Barnsley won 4-3 on pens. Losing semi-finalists: Huddersfield and Brentford. **League 2: Cheltenham** 1 Grimsby 0 (att: 29,196). Losing semi-finalists: Wycombe and Lincoln

PLAY-OFF FINALS AT WEMBLEY

2007: Championship: Derby 1 WBA 0 (att: 74,993). Losing semi-finalists: Southampton and Wolves. **League 1: Blackpool** 2 Yeovil 0 (att: 59,313). Losing semi-finalists: Nottm Forest and Oldham. **League 2: Bristol Rov** 3 Shrewsbury 1 (att: 61,589). Losing semi-finalists: Lincoln and MK Dons

2008: Championship: Hull 1 Bristol City 0 (att: 86,703). Losing semi-finalists: Crystal Palace and Watford. **League 1: Doncaster** 1 Leeds 0 (att: 75,132). Losing semi-finalists: Carlisle and Southend. **League 2: Stockport** 3 Rochdale 2 (att: 35,715). Losing semi-finalists: Darlington and Wycombe

2009: Championship: Burnley 1 Sheffield Utd 0 (att: 80,518). Losing semi-finalists: Preston and Reading. **League 1: Scunthorpe** 3 Millwall 2 (att: 59,661). Losing semi-finalists: Leeds and MK Dons. **League 2: Gillingham** 1 Shrewsbury 0 (att: 53,706). Losing semi-finalists: Bury and Rochdale

2010: Championship: Blackpool 3 Cardiff 2 (att: 82,244). Losing semi-finalists: Leicester and Nottm Forest. **League 1: Millwall** 1 Swindon 0 (att:73,108). Losing semi-finalists: Charlton and Huddersfield. **League 2: Dagenham & Redbridge** 3 Rotherham 2 (att: 32,054). Losing semi-finalists: Aldershot and Morecambe

2011: Championship: Swansea 4 Reading 2 (att: 86,581). Losing semi-finalists: Cardiff and Nottm Forest. **League 1: Peterborough** 3 Huddersfield 0 (Old Trafford, att:48,410). Losing semi-finalists: Bournemouth and MK Dons. **League 2: Stevenage** 1 Torquay 0 (Old Trafford, att: 11,484. Losing semi-finalists: Accrington and Shrewsbury

2012: Championship: West Ham 2 Blackpool 1 (att: 78,523). Losing semi-finalists: Birmingham and Cardiff. **League 1: Huddersfield** 0 Sheffield Utd 0 aet, Huddersfield won 8-7 on pens (att: 52,100). Losing semi-finalists: MK Dons and Stevenage. **League 2: Crewe** 2 Cheltenham 0 (att: 24,029). Losing semi-finalists: Southend and Torquay

2013: Championship: Crystal Palace 1 Watford 0 (att: 82,025). Losing semi-finalists: Brighton and Leicester. **League 1: Yeovil** 2 Brentford 1 (att: 41,955). Losing semi-finalists: Sheffield Utd and Swindon. **League 2: Bradford** 3 Northampton 0 (att: 47,127). Losing semi-finalists: Burton and Cheltenham

2014: Championship: QPR 1 Derby 0 (att: 87,348). Losing semi-finalists: Brighton and Wigan. **League 1: Rotherham** 2 Leyton Orient 2 aet, Rotherham won 4-3 on pens (att: 43,401). Losing semi-finalists: Peterborough and Preston. **League 2: Fleetwood** 1 Burton 0 (att: 14,007). Losing semi-finalists: Southend and York)

2015: Championship: Norwich 2 Middlesbrough 0 (att: 85,656). Losing semi-finalists: Brentford and Ipswich. **League 1: Preston** 4 Swindon 0 (att: 48,236). Losing semi-finalists: Chesterfield and Sheffield Utd. **League 2: Southend** 1 Wycombe 1 aet, Southend won 7-6 on pens (att: 38,252). Losing semi-finalists: Stevenage and Plymouth

HISTORY OF THE PLAY-OFFS

Play-off matches were introduced by the Football League to decide final promotion and relegation issues at the end of season 1986-87. A similar series styled 'Test Matches' had operated between Divisions One and Two for six seasons from 1893-98, and was abolished when both divisions were increased from 16 to 18 clubs.

Eighty-eight years later, the play-offs were back in vogue. In the first three seasons (1987-88-89), the Finals were played home-and-away, and since they were made one-off matches in 1990, they have featured regularly in Wembley's spring calendar, until the old stadium closed its doors and the action switched to the Millennium Stadium in Cardiff in 2001.

Through the years, these have been the ups and downs of the play-offs:

1987: Initially, the 12 clubs involved comprised the one that finished directly above those relegated in Divisions One, Two and Three and the three who followed the sides automatically promoted in each section. Two of the home-and-away Finals went to neutral-ground replays, in which **Charlton** clung to First Division status by denying Leeds promotion while **Swindon** beat Gillingham to complete their climb from Fourth Division to Second in successive seasons, via the play-offs, Sunderland fell into the Third and Bolton into Division Four, both for the first time. **Aldershot** went up after finishing only sixth in Division Four; in their Final, they beat Wolves, who had finished nine points higher and missed automatic promotion by one point.

1988: Chelsea were relegated from the First Division after losing on aggregate to **Middlesbrough**, who had finished third in Division Two. So Middlesbrough, managed by Bruce Rioch, completed the rise from Third Division to First in successive seasons, only two years after their very existence had been threatened by the bailiffs. Also promoted via the play-offs: **Walsall** from Division Three and **Swansea** from the Fourth. Relegated, besides Chelsea: Sheffield Utd (to Division Three) and Rotherham (to Division Four).

1989: After two seasons of promotion-relegation play-offs, the system was changed to involve the four clubs who had just missed automatic promotion. That format has remained. Steve Coppell's **Crystal Palace**, third in Division Two, returned to the top flight after eight years, beating Blackburn 4-3 on aggregate after extra time. Similarly, **Port Vale** confirmed third place in

Division Three with promotion via the play-offs. For **Leyton Orient**, promotion seemed out of the question in Division Four when they stood 15th on March 1. But eight wins and a draw in the last nine home games swept them to sixth in the final table, and two more home victories in the play-offs completed their season in triumph.

1990: The play-off Finals now moved to Wembley over three days of the Spring Holiday weekend. On successive afternoons, **Cambridge Utd** won promotion from Division Four and **Notts Co** from the Third. Then, on Bank Holiday Monday, the biggest crowd for years at a Football League fixture (72,873) saw Ossie Ardiles' **Swindon** beat Sunderland 1-0 to reach the First Division for the first time. A few weeks later, however, Wembley losers **Sunderland** were promoted instead, by default; Swindon were found guilty of "financial irregularities" and stayed in Division Two.

1991: Again, the season's biggest League crowd (59,940) gathered at Wembley for the First Division Final in which **Notts Co** (having missed promotion by one point) still fulfilled their ambition, beating Brighton 3-1. In successive years, County had climbed from Third Division to First via the play-offs – the first club to achieve double promotion by this route. Bolton were denied automatic promotion in Division Three on goal difference, and lost at Wembley to an extra-time goal by **Tranmere**. The Fourth Division Final made history, with Blackpool beaten 5-4 on penalties by **Torquay** – first instance of promotion being decided by a shoot-out. In the table, Blackpool had finished seven points ahead of Torquay.

1992: Wembley that Spring Bank Holiday was the turning point in the history of **Blackburn.** Bolstered by Kenny Dalglish's return to management and owner Jack Walker's millions, they beat Leicester 1-0 by Mike Newell's 45th-minute penalty to achieve their objective – a place in the new Premier League. Newell, who also missed a second-half penalty, had recovered from a broken leg just in time for the play-offs. In the Fourth Division Final **Blackpool** (denied by penalties the previous year) this time won a shoot-out 4-3 against Scunthorpe., who were unlucky in the play-offs for the fourth time in five years. **Peterborough** climbed out of the Third Division for the first time, beating Stockport County 2-1 at Wembley.

1993: The crowd of 73,802 at Wembley to see **Swindon** beat Leicester 4-3 in the First Division Final was 11,000 bigger than that for the FA Cup Final replay between Arsenal and Sheffield Wed Leicester rallied from three down to 3-3 before Paul Bodin's late penalty wiped away **Swindon**'s bitter memories of three years earlier, when they were denied promotion after winning at Wembley. In the Third Division Final, **York** beat Crewe 5-3 in a shoot-out after a 1-1 draw, and in the Second Division decider, **WBA** beat Port Vale 3-0. That was tough on Vale, who had finished third in the table with 89 points – the highest total never to earn promotion in any division. They had beaten Albion twice in the League, too.

1994: Wembley's record turn-out of 158,586 spectators at the three Finals started with a crowd of 40,109 to see Martin O'Neill's **Wycombe** beat Preston 4-2. They thus climbed from Conference to Second Division with successive promotions. **Burnley**'s 2-1 victory in the Second Division Final was marred by the sending-off of two Stockport players, and in the First Division decider **Leicester** came from behind to beat Derby Co and end the worst Wembley record of any club. They had lost on all six previous appearances there – four times in the FA Cup Final and in the play-offs of 1992 and 1993.

1995: Two months after losing the Coca-Cola Cup Final to Liverpool, Bruce Rioch's **Bolton** were back at Wembley for the First Division play-off Final. From two goals down to Reading in front of a crowd of 64,107, they returned to the top company after 15 years, winning 4-3 with two extra-time goals. **Huddersfield** ended the first season at their new £15m. home with promotion to the First Division via a 2-1 victory against Bristol Rov – manager Neil Warnock's third play-off success (after two with Notts Co). Of the three clubs who missed automatic promotion by one place, only **Chesterfield** achieved it in the play-offs, comfortably beating Bury 2-0.

1996: Under new manager Martin O'Neill (a Wembley play-off winner with Wycombe in 1994), **Leicester** returned to the Premiership a year after leaving it. They had finished fifth in the table, but in the Final came from behind to beat third-placed Crystal Palace by Steve Claridge's shot in the last seconds of extra time. In the Second Division **Bradford City** came sixth, nine points behind Blackpool (3rd), but beat them (from two down in the semi-final first leg) and then clinched promotion by 2-0 v Notts County at Wembley. It was City's greatest day since they won the Cup in 1911. **Plymouth Argyle** beat Darlington in the Third Division Final to earn promotion a year after being relegated. It was manager Neil Warnock's fourth play-off triumph in seven seasons after two with Notts County (1990 and 1991) and a third with Huddersfield in 1995.

1997: High drama at Wembley as **Crystal Palace** left it late against Sheffield Utd in the First Division play-off final. The match was scoreless until the last 10 seconds when David Hopkin lobbed Blades' keeper Simon Tracey from 25 yards to send the Eagles back to the Premiership after two seasons of Nationwide action. In the Second Division play-off final, **Crewe** beat Brentford 1-0 courtesy of a Shaun Smith goal. **Northampton** celebrated their first Wembley appearance with a 1-0 victory over Swansea thanks to John Frain's injury-time free-kick in the Third Division play-off final.

1998: In one of the finest games ever seen at Wembley, **Charlton** eventually triumphed 7-6 on penalties over Sunderland. For Charlton, Wearside-born Clive Mendonca scored a hat-trick and Richard Rufus his first career goal in a match that lurched between joy and despair for both sides as it ended 4-4. Sunderland defender Michael Gray's superb performance ill deserved to end with his weakly struck spot kick being saved by Sasa Ilic. In the Third Division, the penalty spot also had a role to play, as **Colchester**'s David Gregory scored the only goal to defeat Torquay, while in the Second Division a Kevin Donovan goal gave **Grimsby** victory over Northampton.

1999: Elton John, watching via a personal satellite link in Seattle, saw his **Watford** side overcome Bolton 2-0 to reach the Premiership. Against technically superior opponents, Watford prevailed with application and teamwork. They also gave Bolton a lesson in finishing through match-winners by Nick Wright and Allan Smart. **Manchester City** staged a remarkable comeback to win the Second Division Final after trailing to goals by Carl Asaba and Robert Taylor for Gillingham. Kevin Horlock and Paul Dickov scored in stoppage time and City went on to win on penalties. A goal by Spaniard Alex Calvo-Garcia earned **Scunthorpe** a 1-0 success against Leyton Orient in the Third Division Final.

2000: After three successive play-off failures, **Ipswich** finally secured a place in the Premiership. They overcame the injury loss of leading scorer David Johnson to beat Barnsley 4-2 with goals by 36-year-old Tony Mowbray, Marcus Stewart and substitutes Richard Naylor and Martijn Reuser. With six minutes left of extra-time in the Second Division Final, **Gillingham** trailed Wigan 2-1. But headers by 38-year-old player-coach Steve Butler and fellow substitute Andy Thomson gave them a 3-2 victory. Andy Clarke, approaching his 33rd birthday, scored the only goal of the Third Division decider for **Peterborough** against Darlington.

2001: Bolton, unsuccessful play-off contenders in the two previous seasons, made no mistake at the third attempt. They flourished in the new surroundings of the Millennium Stadium to beat Preston 3-0 with goals by Gareth Farrelly, Michael Ricketts – his 24th of the season – and Ricardo Gardner to reach the Premiership. **Walsall**, relegated 12 months earlier, scored twice in a three-minute spell of extra time to win 3-2 against Reading in the Second Division Final, while **Blackpool** capped a marked improvement in the second half of the season by overcoming Leyton Orient 4-2 in the Third Division Final.

2002: Holding their nerve to win a penalty shoot-out 4-2, **Birmingham** wiped away the memory of three successive defeats in the semi-finals of the play-offs to return to the top division after an absence of 16 years. Substitute Darren Carter completed a fairy-tale first season as a professional by scoring the fourth spot-kick against Norwich. **Stoke** became the first successful team to come from the south dressing room in 12 finals since football was adopted by the home of Welsh rugby, beating Brentford 2-0 in the Second Division Final with Deon Burton's strike and a Ben Burgess own goal. Julian Alsop's 26th goal of the season helped **Cheltenham** defeat League newcomers Rushden & Diamonds 3-1 in the Third Division decider.

2003: Wolves benefactor Sir Jack Hayward finally saw his £60m investment pay dividends when the club he first supported as a boy returned to the top flight after an absence of 19 years by beating Sheffield Utd 3-0. It was also a moment to savour for manager Dave Jones, who was forced to leave his previous club Southampton because of child abuse allegations, which were later found to be groundless. **Cardiff**, away from the game's second tier for 18 years, returned with an extra-time winner from substitute Andy Campbell against QPR after a goalless 90 minutes in the Division Two Final. **Bournemouth**, relegated 12 months earlier, became the first team to score five in the end-of-season deciders, beating Lincoln 5-2 in the Division Three Final.

2004: Three tight, tense Finals produced only two goals, the lowest number since the Play-offs were introduced. One of them, scored by Neil Shipperley, gave **Crystal Palace** victory over West Ham, the much-travelled striker tapping in a rebound after Stephen Bywater parried Andy Johnson's shot. It completed a remarkable transformation for Crystal Palace, who were 19th in the table when Iain Dowie left Oldham to become their manager. **Brighton** made an immediate return to Division One in a poor game against Bristol City which looked set for extra-time until Leon Knight netted his 27th goal of the campaign from the penalty spot after 84 minutes. **Huddersfield** also went back up at the first attempt, winning the Division Three Final in a penalty shoot-out after a goalless 120 minutes against Mansfield.

2005: Goals were few and far between for Bobby Zamora during **West Ham**'s Championship season – but what a difference in the Play-offs. The former Brighton and Tottenham striker scored three times in the 4-2 aggregate win over Ipswich in the semi-finals and was on the mark again with the only goal against Preston at the Millennium Stadium. **Sheffield Wed** were eight minute away from defeat against Hartlepool in the League One decider when Steven MacLean made it 2-2 from the penalty spot and they went on to win 4-2 in extra-time. **Southend**, edged out of an automatic promotion place, won the League Two Final 2-0 against Lincoln, Freddy Eastwood scoring their first in extra-time and making the second for Duncan Jupp. **Carlisle** beat Stevenage 1-0 with a goal by Peter Murphy in the Conference Final to regain their League place 12 months after being relegated.

2006: From the moment Marlon King scored his 22nd goal of the season to set up a 3-0 win over Crystal Palace in the semi-final first leg, **Watford** had the conviction of a team going places. Sure enough, they went on to beat Leeds just as comfortably in the final. Jay DeMerit, who was playing non-league football 18 months earlier, headed his side in front. James Chambers fired in a shot that hit a post and went in off goalkeeper Neil Sullivan. Then Darius Henderson put away a penalty after King was brought down by Shaun Derry, the man whose tackle had ended Boothroyd's playing career at the age of 26. **Barnsley** beat Swansea on penalties in the League One Final, Nick Colgan making the vital save from Alan Tate, while Steve Guinan's goal earned **Cheltenham** a 1-0 win over Grimsby in the League Two Final. **Hereford** returned to the Football League after a nine-year absence with Ryan Green's extra-time winner against Halifax in the Conference Final.

2007: Record crowds, plenty of goals and a return to Wembley for the finals made for some eventful and entertaining matches. Stephen Pearson, signed from Celtic for £650,000 in the January transfer window, took **Derby** back to the Premier League after an absence of five seasons with a 61st minute winner, his first goal for the club, against accounted for West Bromwich Albion. It was third time lucky for manager Billy Davies, who had led Preston into the play-offs, without success, in the two previous seasons. **Blackpool** claimed a place in the game's second tier for the first time for 30 years by beating Yeovil 2-0 – their tenth successive victory in a remarkable end-of-season run. Richard Walker took his tally for the season to 23 with two goals for **Bristol Rov**, who beat Shrewsbury 3-1 in the League Two Final. Sammy McIlroy, who led Macclesfield into the league in 1997, saw his Morecambe side fall behind in the Conference Final against Exeter, but they recovered to win 2-1.

2008: Wembley has produced some unlikely heroes down the years, but rarely one to match 39-year-old Dean Windass. The **Hull** striker took his home-town club into the top-flight for the first time with the only goal of the Championship Final against Bristol City – and it was a goal fit to grace any game. In front of a record crowd for the final of 86,703, Fraizer Campbell, his 20-year-old partner up front, picked out Windass on the edge of the penalty box and a sweetly-struck volley flew into the net. **Doncaster**, who like Hull faced an uncertain future a few years earlier, beat

Leeds 1-0 in the League One Final with a header by James Hayer from Brian Stock's corner. Jim Gannon had lost four Wembley finals with **Stockport** as a player, but his first as manager brought a 3-2 win against Rochdale in the League Two Final with goals by Anthony Pilkington and Liam Dickinson and a Nathan Stanton own goal. Exeter's 1-0 win over Cambridge United in the Conference Final took them back into the Football League after an absence of five years.

2009: Delight for Burnley, back in the big time after 33 years thanks to a fine goal from 20 yards by Wade Elliott, and for their town which became the smallest to host Premier League football. Despair for Sheffield Utd, whose bid to regain a top-flight place ended with two players, Jamie Ward and Lee Hendrie, sent off by referee Mike Dean. Martyn Woolford capped a man-of-the match performance with an 85th minute winner for Scunthorpe, who beat Millwall 3-2 to make an immediate return to the Championship, Matt Sparrow having scored their first two goals. Gillingham also went back up at the first attempt, beating Shrewsbury with Simeon Jackson's header seconds from the end of normal time in the League Two Final. Torquay returned to the Football League after a two-year absence by beating Cambridge United 2-0 in the Conference Final.

2010: Blackpool, under the eccentric yet shrewd Ian Holloway, claimed the big prize two years almost to the day after the manager was sacked from his previous job at Leicester. On a scorching afternoon, with temperatures reaching 106 degrees, they twice came back from a goal down to draw level against Cardiff through Charlie Adam and Gary Taylor-Fletcher, then scored what proved to be the winner through Brett Ormerod at the end of a pulsating first half. **Millwall**, beaten in five previous play-offs, reached the Championship with the only goal of the game against Swindon from captain Paul Robinson. **Dagenham & Redbridge** defeated Rotherham 3-2 in the League Two Final, Jon Nurse scoring the winner 20 minutes from the end. **Oxford** returned to the Football League after an absence of four years with a 3-1 over York in the Conference Final.

2011: Scott Sinclair scored a hat-trick as **Swansea** reached the top flight, just eight years after almost going out of the Football League. Two of his goals came from the penalty spot as Reading were beaten 4-2 in the Championship Final, with Stephen Dobbie netting their other goal. The day after his father's side lost to Barcelona in the Champions League Final, Darren Ferguson led **Peterborough** back to the Championship at the first attempt with goals by Tommy Rowe, Craig Mackail-Smith and Grant McCann in the final 12 minutes against Huddersfield. John Mousinho scored the only one of the League Two Final for **Stevenage**, who won a second successive promotion by beating Torquay. **AFC Wimbledon**, formed by supporters in 2002 after the former FA Cup-winning club relocated to Milton Keynes, completed their rise from the Combined Counties to the Football League by winning a penalty shoot-out against Luton after a goalless draw in the Conference Final.

2012: **West Ham** were third in the Championship and second best to Blackpool in the final. But they passed the post first at Wembley, thanks to an 87th minute goal from Ricardo Vaz Te which gave Sam Allardyce's side a 2-1 victory. Allardyce brought the Portuguese striker to Upton Park from Barnsley for £500,000 – a fee dwarfed by the millions his goal was worth to the club. Goalkeepers took centre stage in the League One Final, with **Huddersfield** and Sheffield United still locked in a marathon shoot-out after a goalless 120 minutes. Alex Smithies put the 21st penalty past his opposite number Steve Simonsen, who then drove over the crossbar to give Huddersfield victory by 8-7. Nick Powell, 18, lit up the League Two Final with a spectacular volley as **Crewe** beat Cheltenham 2-0. **York** regained a Football League place after an absence of eight years by beating Luton 2-1 in the Conference decider.

2013: Veteran Kevin Phillips, a loser in three previous finals, came off the bench to fire **Crystal Palace** into the Premier League with an extra-time penalty. Wilfried Zaha was brought down by Marco Cassetti and 39-year-old Phillips showed nerves of steel to convert the spot-kick. A goalline clearance by Joel Ward then denied Fernando Forestieri as Watford sought an equaliser. **Yeovil** upset the odds by reaching the Championship for the first time. They defeated Brentford 2-1, Paddy Madden scoring his 23rd goal of the season and on-loan Dan Burn adding the second. **Bradford**, back at Wembley three months after their Capital One Cup adventure, swept aside Northampton 3-0 in the League Two Final with goals from James Hanson, Rory McArdle and Nahki Wells. **Newport** returned to the Football League after a 25-year absence by defeating Wrexham 2-0 in the Conference Final.

2014: An immediate return to the Premier League for **Queens Park Rangers** seemed unlikely when Gary O'Neil was sent off for bringing down Derby's Johnny Russell. There was still more than half-an-hour to go of a match Derby had dominated. But Rangers held on and with 90 minutes nearly up Bobby Zamora punished a mistake by captain Richard Keogh to score the only goal. **Rotherham** retrieved a 2-0 deficit against Leyton Orient with two goals by Alex Revell in the League One Final and won the eventual penalty shoot-out 4-3 for a second successive promotion. **Fleetwood** achieved their sixth promotion in ten seasons with a 1-0 victory over Burton, courtesy of a free-kick from Antoni Sarcevic in the League Two Final. Liam Hughes and Ryan Donaldson were on the mark as **Cambridge United** returned to the Football League after a nine-year absence by beating Gateshead 2-1 in the Conference Final, two months after winning the FA Trophy at Wembley

2015: **Norwich** were rewarded for a flying start with a return to the Premier League at the first attempt. Cameron Jerome put them ahead against Middlesbrough after 12 minutes of the Championship Final and Nathan Redmond made it 2-0 three minutes later, a scoreline they maintained without too many problems. Jermaine Beckford's hat-trick put **Preston** on the way to a record 4-0 victory over Swindon in the League One Final. **Southend**, who like Preston were denied automatic promotion on the final day of the regular season, beat Wycombe 7-6 on penalties after the League Two Final ended 1-1. **Bristol Rovers** were also penalty winners, by 5-3 against Grimsby in the Conference decider, so making an immediate return to the Football League.

1987	20	310,000	2002	15	327,894
1988	19	305,817	2003	15	374,461
1989	18	234,393	2004	15	388,675
1990	15	291,428	2005	15	353,330
1991	15	266,442	2006	15	340,804
1992	15	277,684	2007	15	405,278 (record)
1993	15	319,907	2008	15	382,032
1994	15	314,817	2009	15	380,329
1995	15	295,317	2010	15	370,055
1996	15	308,515	2011	15	310,998
1997	15	309,085	2012	15	332,930
1998	15	320,795	2013	15	346,062
1999	15	372,969	2014	15	307,011
2000	15	333,999	2015	15	367,374
2001	15	317,745	2016	15	393,145

THE THINGS THEY SAY ...

'We can look at our club now in two perspectives. One is the past three years, another is the club's history. I prefer to forget the last three years' – **Jose Mourinho**, Manchester United's new manager, draws a veil over the time Louis van Gaal and David Moyes spent in charge.

'I show you the FA Cup and I don't discuss it with my friends of the media who have already sacked me for six months. Which manager can do what I have done? I don't want to talk about leaving the club' – **Louis van Gaal**, bitter about his treatment by the media, presents the trophy at his final United press conference after victory at Wembley.

ENGLISH HONOURS LIST

PREMIER LEAGUE

	First	*Pts*	*Second*	*Pts*	*Third*	*Pts*
1992–3*a*	Manchester Utd	84	Aston Villa	74	Norwich	72
1993–4*a*	Manchester Utd	92	Blackburn	84	Newcastle	77
1994–5*a*	Blackburn	89	Manchester Utd	88	Nottm Forest	77
1995–6*b*	Manchester Utd	82	Newcastle	78	Liverpool	71
1996–7*b*	Manchester Utd	75	Newcastle	68	Arsenal	68
1997–8*b*	Arsenal	78	Manchester Utd	77	Liverpool	65
1998–9*b*	Manchester Utd	79	Arsenal	78	Chelsea	75
1999–00*b*	Manchester Utd	91	Arsenal	73	Leeds	69
2000–01*b*	Manchester Utd	80	Arsenal	70	Liverpool	69
2001–02*b*	Arsenal	87	Liverpool	80	Manchester Utd	77
2002–03*b*	Manchester Utd	83	Arsenal	78	Newcastle	69
2003–04*b*	Arsenal	90	Chelsea	79	Manchester Utd	75
2004–05*b*	Chelsea	95	Arsenal	83	Manchester Utd	77
2005–06*b*	Chelsea	91	Manchester Utd	83	Liverpool	82
2006–07*b*	Manchester Utd	89	Chelsea	83	Liverpool	68
2007–08*b*	Manchester Utd	87	Chelsea	85	Arsenal	83
2008-09*b*	Manchester Utd	90	Liverpool	86	Chelsea	83
2009–10*b*	Chelsea	86	Manchester Utd	85	Arsenal	75
2010–11*b*	Manchester Utd	80	Chelsea	71	Manchester City	71
2011–12*b*	*Manchester City	89	Manchester Ud	89	Arsenal	70
2012–13*b*	Manchester Utd	89	Manchester City	78	Chelsea	75
2013-14*b*	Manchester City	86	Liverpool	84	Chelsea	82
2014-15*b*	Chelsea	87	Manchester City	79	Arsenal	75
2015-16*b*	Leicester	81	Arsenal	71	Tottenham	70

* won on goal difference. Maximum points: *a*, 126; *b*, 114

FOOTBALL LEAGUE

FIRST DIVISION

1992–3	Newcastle	96	West Ham	88	††Portsmouth	88
1993–4	Crystal Palace	90	Nottm Forest	83	††Millwall	74
1994–5	Middlesbrough	82	††Reading	79	Bolton	77
1995–6	Sunderland	83	Derby	79	††Crystal Palace	75
1996–7	Bolton	98	Barnsley	80	††Wolves	76
1997–8	Nottm Forest	94	Middlesbrough	91	††Sunderland	90
1998–9	Sunderland	105	Bradford City	87	††Ipswich	86
1999–00	Charlton	91	Manchester City	89	Ipswich	87
2000–01	Fulham	101	Blackburn	91	Bolton	87
2001–02	Manchester City	99	WBA	89	††Wolves	86
2002–03	Portsmouth	98	Leicester	92	††Sheffield Utd	80
2003–04	Norwich	94	WBA	86	††Sunderland	79

CHAMPIONSHIP

2004–05	Sunderland	94	Wigan	87	††Ipswich	85
2005–06	Reading	106	Sheffield Utd	90	Watford	81
2006–07	Sunderland	88	Birmingham	86	Derby	84
2007–08	WBA	81	Stoke	79	Hull	75
2008–09	Wolves	90	Birmingham	83	††Sheffield Utd	80
2009–10	Newcastle	102	WBA	91	††Nottm Forest	79
2010–11	QPR	88	Norwich	84	Swansea	80
2011–12	Reading	89	Southampton	88	West Ham	86
2012–13	Cardiff	87	Hull	79	††Watford	77

2013-14	Leicester	102	Burnley	93	††Derby	85
2014-15	Bournemouth	90	Watford	89	Norwich	86
2015-16	Burnley	93	Middlesbrough	89	††Brighton	89

Maximum points: 138 ††Not promoted after play–offs

SECOND DIVISION

1992–3	Stoke	93	Bolton	90	††Port Vale	89
1993–4	Reading	89	Port Vale	88	††Plymouth Argyle	85
1994–5	Birmingham	89	††Brentford	85	††Crewe	83
1995–6	Swindon	92	Oxford Utd	83	††Blackpool	82
1996–7	Bury	84	Stockport	82	††Luton	78
1997–8	Watford	88	Bristol City	85	Grimsby	72
1998–9	Fulham	101	Walsall	87	Manchester City	82
1999–00	Preston	95	Burnley	88	Gillingham	85
2000–01	Millwall	93	Rotherham	91	††Reading	86
2001–02	Brighton	90	Reading	84	††Brentford	83
2002–03	Wigan	100	Crewe	86	††Bristol City	83
2003–04	Plymouth Argyle	90	QPR	83	††Bristol City	82

LEAGUE ONE

2004–05	Luton	98	Hull	86	††Tranmere	79
2005–06	Southend	82	Colchester	79	††Brentford	76
2006–07	Scunthorpe	91	Bristol City	85	Blackpool	83
2007-08	Swansea	92	Nottm Forest	82	Doncaster	80
2008-09	Leicester	96	Peterborough	89	††MK Dons	87
2009–10	Norwich	95	Leeds	86	Millwall	85
2010–11	Brighton	95	Southampton	92	††Huddersfield	87
2011–12	Charlton	101	Sheffield Wed	93	††Sheffield Utd	90
2012–13	Doncaster	84	Bournemouth	83	††Brentford	79
2013–14	Wolves	103	Brentford	94	††Leyton Orient	86
2014–15	Bristol City	99	MK Dons	91	Preston	89
2015-16	Wigan	87	Burton	85	††Walsall	84

Maximum points: 138 †† Not promoted after play–offs

THIRD DIVISION

1992–3*a*	Cardiff	83	Wrexham	80	Barnet	79
1993–4*a*	Shrewsbury	79	Chester	74	Crewe	73
1994–5*a*	Carlisle	91	Walsall	83	Chesterfield	81
1995–6*b*	Preston	86	Gillingham	83	Bury	79
1996–7*b*	Wigan	87	Fulham	87	Carlisle	84
1997–8*b*	Notts Co	99	Macclesfield	82	Lincoln	75
1998–9*b*	Brentford	85	Cambridge Utd	81	Cardiff	80
1999–00*b*	Swansea	85	Rotherham	84	Northampton	82
2000–01*b*	Brighton	92	Cardiff	82	*Chesterfield	80
2001–02*b*	Plymouth Argyle	102	Luton	97	Mansfield	79
2002–03*b*	Rushden & D	87	Hartlepool Utd	85	Wrexham	84
2003–04*b*	Doncaster	92	Hull	88	Torquay	81

* Deducted 9 points for financial irregularities

LEAGUE TWO

2004–05*b*	Yeovil	83	Scunthorpe	80	Swansea	80
2005–06*b*	Carlisle	86	Northampton	83	Leyton Orient	81
2006–07*b*	Walsall	89	Hartlepool	88	Swindon	85
2007-08*b*	MK Dons	97	Peterborough	92	Hereford	88
2008-09*b*	Brentford	85	Exeter	79	Wycombe	78
2009–10*b*	Notts Co	93	Bournemouth	83	Rochdale	82
2010–11*b*	Chesterfield	86	Bury	81	Wycombe	80

2011–12*b*	Swindon	93	Shrewsbury	88	Crawley	84
2012–13*b*	Gillingham	83	Rotherham	79	Port Vale	78
2013–14*b*	Chesterfield	84	Scunthorpe	81	Rochdale	81
2014–15*b*	Burton	94	Shrewsbury	89	Bury	85
2015-16*b*	Northampton	99	Oxford	86	Bristol Rov	85

Maximum points: *a*, 126; *b*, 138;

FOOTBALL LEAGUE 1888–1992

1888–89*a*	Preston	40	Aston Villa	29	Wolves	28
1889–90*a*	Preston	33	Everton	31	Blackburn	27
1890–1*a*	Everton	29	Preston	27	Notts Co	26
1891–2*b*	Sunderland	42	Preston	37	Bolton	36

OLD FIRST DIVISION

1892–3*c*	Sunderland	48	Preston	37	Everton	36
1893–4*c*	Aston Villa	44	Sunderland	38	Derby	36
1894–5*c*	Sunderland	47	Everton	42	Aston Villa	39
1895–6*c*	Aston Villa	45	Derby	41	Everton	39
1896–7*c*	Aston Villa	47	Sheffield Utd	36	Derby	36
1897–8*c*	Sheffield Utd	42	Sunderland	39	Wolves	35
1898–9*d*	Aston Villa	45	Liverpool	43	Burnley	39
1899–1900*d*	Aston Villa	50	Sheffield Utd	48	Sunderland	41
1900–1*d*	Liverpool	45	Sunderland	43	Notts Co	40
1901–2*d*	Sunderland	44	Everton	41	Newcastle	37
1902–3*d*	The Wednesday	42	Aston Villa	41	Sunderland	41
1903–4*d*	The Wednesday	47	Manchester City	44	Everton	43
1904–5*d*	Newcastle	48	Everton	47	Manchester City	46
1905–6*e*	Liverpool	51	Preston	47	The Wednesday	44
1906–7*e*	Newcastle	51	Bristol City	48	Everton	45
1907–8*e*	Manchester Utd	52	Aston Villa	43	Manchester City	43
1908–9*e*	Newcastle	53	Everton	46	Sunderland	44
1909–10*e*	Aston Villa	53	Liverpool	48	Blackburn	45
1910–11*e*	Manchester Utd	52	Aston Villa	51	Sunderland	45
1911–12*e*	Blackburn	49	Everton	46	Newcastle	44
1912–13*e*	Sunderland	54	Aston Villa	50	Sheffield Wed	49
1913–14*e*	Blackburn	51	Aston Villa	44	Middlesbrough	43
1914–15*e*	Everton	46	Oldham	45	Blackburn	43
1919–20*f*	WBA	60	Burnley	51	Chelsea	49
1920–1*f*	Burnley	59	Manchester City	54	Bolton	52
1921–2*f*	Liverpool	57	Tottenham	51	Burnley	49
1922–3*f*	Liverpool	60	Sunderland	54	Huddersfield	53
1923–4*f*	*Huddersfield	57	Cardiff	57	Sunderland	53
1924–5*f*	Huddersfield	58	WBA	56	Bolton	55
1925–6*f*	Huddersfield	57	Arsenal	52	Sunderland	48
1926–7*f*	Newcastle	56	Huddersfield	51	Sunderland	49
1927–8*f*	Everton	53	Huddersfield	51	Leicester	48
1928–9*f*	Sheffield Wed	52	Leicester	51	Aston Villa	50
1929–30*f*	Sheffield Wed	60	Derby	50	Manchester City	47
1930–1*f*	Arsenal	66	Aston Villa	59	Sheffield Wed	52
1931–2*f*	Everton	56	Arsenal	54	Sheffield Wed	50
1932–3*f*	Arsenal	58	Aston Villa	54	Sheffield Wed	51
1933–4*f*	Arsenal	59	Huddersfield	56	Tottenham	49
1934–5*f*	Arsenal	58	Sunderland	54	Sheffield Wed	49
1935–6*f*	Sunderland	56	Derby	48	Huddersfield	48
1936–7*f*	Manchester City	57	Charlton	54	Arsenal	52

1937–8*f*	Arsenal	52	Wolves	51	Preston	49
1938–9*f*	Everton	59	Wolves	55	Charlton	50
1946–7*f*	Liverpool	57	Manchester Utd	56	Wolves	56
1947–8*f*	Arsenal	59	Manchester Utd	52	Burnley	52
1948–9*f*	Portsmouth	58	Manchester Utd	53	Derby	53
1949–50*f*	*Portsmouth	53	Wolves	53	Sunderland	52
1950–1*f*	Tottenham	60	Manchester Utd	56	Blackpool	50
1951–2*f*	Manchester Utd	57	Tottenham	53	Arsenal	53
1952–3*f*	*Arsenal	54	Preston	54	Wolves	51
1953–4*f*	Wolves	57	WBA	53	Huddersfield	51
1954–5*f*	Chelsea	52	Wolves	48	Portsmouth	48
1955–6*f*	Manchester Utd	60	Blackpool	49	Wolves	49
1956–7*f*	Manchester Utd	64	Tottenham	56	Preston	56
1957–8*f*	Wolves	64	Preston	59	Tottenham	51
1958–9*f*	Wolves	61	Manchester Utd	55	Arsenal	50
1959–60*f*	Burnley	55	Wolves	54	Tottenham	53
1960–1*f*	Tottenham	66	Sheffield Wed	58	Wolves	57
1961–2*f*	Ipswich	56	Burnley	53	Tottenham	52
1962–3*f*	Everton	61	Tottenham	55	Burnley	54
1963–4*f*	Liverpool	57	Manchester Utd	53	Everton	52
1964–5*f*	*Manchester Utd	61	Leeds	61	Chelsea	56
1965–6*f*	Liverpool	61	Leeds	55	Burnley	55
1966–7*f*	Manchester Utd	60	Nottm Forest	56	Tottenham	56
1967–8*f*	Manchester City	58	Manchester Utd	56	Liverpool	55
1968–9*f*	Leeds	67	Liverpool	61	Everton	57
1969–70*f*	Everton	66	Leeds	57	Chelsea	55
1970–1*f*	Arsenal	65	Leeds	64	Tottenham	52
1971–2*f*	Derby	58	Leeds	57	Liverpool	57
1972–3*f*	Liverpool	60	Arsenal	57	Leeds	53
1973–4*f*	Leeds	62	Liverpool	57	Derby	48
1974–5*f*	Derby	53	Liverpool	51	Ipswich	51
1975–6*f*	Liverpool	60	QPR	59	Manchester Utd	56
1976–7*f*	Liverpool	57	Manchester City	56	Ipswich	52
1977–8*f*	Nottm Forest	64	Liverpool	57	Everton	55
1978–9*f*	Liverpool	68	Nottm Forest	60	WBA	59
1979–80*f*	Liverpool	60	Manchester Utd	58	Ipswich	53
1980–1*f*	Aston Villa	60	Ipswich	56	Arsenal	53
1981–2*g*	Liverpool	87	Ipswich	83	Manchester Utd	78
1982–3*g*	Liverpool	82	Watford	71	Manchester Utd	70
1983–4*g*	Liverpool	80	Southampton	77	Nottm Forest	74
1984–5*g*	Everton	90	Liverpool	77	Tottenham	77
1985–6*g*	Liverpool	88	Everton	86	West Ham	84
1986–7*g*	Everton	86	Liverpool	77	Tottenham	71
1987–8*h*	Liverpool	90	Manchester Utd	81	Nottm Forest	73
1988–9*j*	††Arsenal	76	Liverpool	76	Nottm Forest	64
1989–90*j*	Liverpool	79	Aston Villa	70	Tottenham	63
1990–1*j*	Arsenal	83	Liverpool	76	Crystal Palace	69
1991–2*g*	Leeds	82	Manchester Utd	78	Sheffield Wed	75

Maximum points: *a*, 44; *b*, 52; *c*, 60; *d*, 68; *e*, 76; *f*, 84; *g*, 126; *h*, 120; *j*, 114
*Won on goal average †Won on goal diff ††Won on goals scored No comp 1915–19 –1939–46

OLD SECOND DIVISION 1892–1992

1892–3*a*	Small Heath	36	Sheffield Utd	35	Darwen	30
1893–4*b*	Liverpool	50	Small Heath	42	Notts Co	39
1894–5*c*	Bury	48	Notts Co	39	Newton Heath	38

1895–6*c*	*Liverpool	46	Manchester City	46	Grimsby	42
1896–7*c*	Notts Co	42	Newton Heath	39	Grimsby	38
1897–8*c*	Burnley	48	Newcastle	45	Manchester City	39
1898–9*d*	Manchester City	52	Glossop	46	Leicester Fosse	45
1899–1900*d*	The Wednesday	54	Bolton	52	Small Heath	46
1900–1*d*	Grimsby	49	Small Heath	48	Burnley	44
1901–2*d*	WBA	55	Middlesbrough	51	Preston	42
1902–3*d*	Manchester City	54	Small Heath	51	Woolwich Arsenal	48
1903–4*d*	Preston	50	Woolwich Arsenal	49	Manchester Utd	48
1904–5*d*	Liverpool	58	Bolton	56	Manchester Utd	53
1905–6*e*	Bristol City	66	Manchester Utd	62	Chelsea	53
1906–7*e*	Nottm Forest	60	Chelsea	57	Leicester Fosse	48
1907–8*e*	Bradford City	54	Leicester Fosse	52	Oldham	50
1908–9*e*	Bolton	52	Tottenham	51	WBA	51
1909–10*e*	Manchester City	54	Oldham	53	Hull	53
1910–11*e*	WBA	53	Bolton	51	Chelsea	49
1911–12*e*	*Derby	54	Chelsea	54	Burnley	52
1912–13*e*	Preston	53	Burnley	50	Birmingham	46
1913–14*e*	Notts Co	53	Bradford PA	49	Woolwich Arsenal	49
1914–15*e*	Derby	53	Preston	50	Barnsley	47
1919–20*f*	Tottenham	70	Huddersfield	64	Birmingham	56
1920–1*f*	*Birmingham	58	Cardiff	58	Bristol City	51
1921–2*f*	Nottm Forest	56	Stoke	52	Barnsley	52
1922–3*f*	Notts Co	53	West Ham	51	Leicester	51
1923–4*f*	Leeds	54	Bury	51	Derby	51
1924–5*f*	Leicester	59	Manchester Utd	57	Derby	55
1925–6*f*	Sheffield Wed	60	Derby	57	Chelsea	52
1926–7*f*	Middlesbrough	62	Portsmouth	54	Manchester City	54
1927–8*f*	Manchester City	59	Leeds	57	Chelsea	54
1928–9*f*	Middlesbrough	55	Grimsby	53	Bradford City	48
1929–30*f*	Blackpool	58	Chelsea	55	Oldham	53
1930–1*f*	Everton	61	WBA	54	Tottenham	51
1931–2*f*	Wolves	56	Leeds	54	Stoke	52
1932–3*f*	Stoke	56	Tottenham	55	Fulham	50
1933–4*f*	Grimsby	59	Preston	52	Bolton	51
1934–5*f*	Brentford	61	Bolton	56	West Ham	56
1935–6*f*	Manchester Utd	56	Charlton	55	Sheffield Utd	52
1936–7*f*	Leicester	56	Blackpool	55	Bury	52
1937–8*f*	Aston Villa	57	Manchester Utd	53	Sheffield Utd	53
1938–9*f*	Blackburn	55	Sheffield Utd	54	Sheffield Wed	53
1946–7*f*	Manchester City	62	Burnley	58	Birmingham	55
1947–8*f*	Birmingham	59	Newcastle	56	Southampton	52
1948–9*f*	Fulham	57	WBA	56	Southampton	55
1949–50*f*	Tottenham	61	Sheffield Wed	52	Sheffield Utd	52
1950–1*f*	Preston	57	Manchester City	52	Cardiff	50
1951–2*f*	Sheffield Wed	53	Cardiff	51	Birmingham	51
1952–3*f*	Sheffield Utd	60	Huddersfield	58	Luton	52
1953–4*f*	*Leicester	56	Everton	56	Blackburn	55
1954–5*f*	*Birmingham	54	Luton	54	Rotherham	54
1955–6*f*	Sheffield Wed	55	Leeds	52	Liverpool	48
1956–7*f*	Leicester	61	Nottm Forest	54	Liverpool	53
1957–8*f*	West Ham	57	Blackburn	56	Charlton	55
1958–9*f*	Sheffield Wed	62	Fulham	60	Sheffield Utd	53
1959–60*f*	Aston Villa	59	Cardiff	58	Liverpool	50

1960–1*f*	Ipswich	59	Sheffield Utd	58	Liverpool	52
1961–2*f*	Liverpool	62	Leyton Orient	54	Sunderland	53
1962–3*f*	Stoke	53	Chelsea	52	Sunderland	52
1963–4*f*	Leeds	63	Sunderland	61	Preston	56
1964–5*f*	Newcastle	57	Northampton	56	Bolton	50
1965–6*f*	Manchester City	59	Southampton	54	Coventry	53
1966–7*f*	Coventry	59	Wolves	58	Carlisle	52
1967–8*f*	Ipswich	59	QPR	58	Blackpool	58
1968–9*f*	Derby	63	Crystal Palace	56	Charlton	50
1969–70*f*	Huddersfield	60	Blackpool	53	Leicester	51
1970–1*f*	Leicester	59	Sheffield Utd	56	Cardiff	53
1971–2*f*	Norwich	57	Birmingham	56	Millwall	55
1972–3*f*	Burnley	62	QPR	61	Aston Villa	50
1973–4*f*	Middlesbrough	65	Luton	50	Carlisle	49
1974–5*f*	Manchester Utd	61	Aston Villa	58	Norwich	53
1975–6*f*	Sunderland	56	Bristol City	53	WBA	53
1976–7*f*	Wolves	57	Chelsea	55	Nottm Forest	52
1977–8*f*	Bolton	58	Southampton	57	Tottenham	56
1978–9*f*	Crystal Palace	57	Brighton	56	Stoke	56
1979–80*f*	Leicester	55	Sunderland	54	Birmingham	53
1980–1*f*	West Ham	66	Notts Co	53	Swansea	50
1981–2*g*	Luton	88	Watford	80	Norwich	71
1982–3*g*	QPR	85	Wolves	75	Leicester	70
1983–4*g*	†Chelsea	88	Sheffield Wed	88	Newcastle	80
1984–5*g*	Oxford Utd	84	Birmingham	82	Manchester City	74
1985–6*g*	Norwich	84	Charlton	77	Wimbledon	76
1986–7*g*	Derby	84	Portsmouth	78	††Oldham	75
1987–8*h*	Millwall	82	Aston Villa	78	Middlesbrough	78
1988–9*j*	Chelsea	99	Manchester City	82	Crystal Palace	81
1989–90j	†Leeds	85	Sheffield Utd	85	†† Newcastle	80
1990–1*j*	Oldham	88	West Ham	87	Sheffield Wed	82
1991–2*j*	Ipswich	84	Middlesbrough	80	†† Derby	78

Maximum points: *a*, 44; *b*, 56; *c*, 60; *d*, 68; *e*, 76; *f*, 84; *g*, 126; *h*, 132; *j*, 138 * Won on goal average † Won on goal difference †† Not promoted after play–offs

THIRD DIVISION 1958–92

1958–9	Plymouth Argyle	62	Hull	61	Brentford	57
1959–60	Southampton	61	Norwich	59	Shrewsbury	52
1960–1	Bury	68	Walsall	62	QPR	60
1961–2	Portsmouth	65	Grimsby	62	Bournemouth	59
1962–3	Northampton	62	Swindon	58	Port Vale	54
1963–4	*Coventry	60	Crystal Palace	60	Watford	58
1964–5	Carlisle	60	Bristol City	59	Mansfield	59
1965–6	Hull	69	Millwall	65	QPR	57
1966–7	QPR	67	Middlesbrough	55	Watford	54
1967–8	Oxford Utd	57	Bury	56	Shrewsbury	55
1968–9	*Watford	64	Swindon	64	Luton	61
1969–70	Orient	62	Luton	60	Bristol Rov	56
1970–1	Preston	61	Fulham	60	Halifax	56
1971–2	Aston Villa	70	Brighton	65	Bournemouth	62
1972–3	Bolton	61	Notts Co	57	Blackburn	55
1973–4	Oldham	62	Bristol Rov	61	York	61
1974–5	Blackburn	60	Plymouth Argyle	59	Charlton	55
1975–6	Hereford	63	Cardiff	57	Millwall	56
1976–7	Mansfield	64	Brighton	61	Crystal Palace	59
1977–8	Wrexham	61	Cambridge Utd	58	Preston	56
1978–9	Shrewsbury	61	Watford	60	Swansea	60

1979–80	Grimsby	62	Blackburn	59	Sheffield Wed	58
1980–1	Rotherham	61	Barnsley	59	Charlton	59
†1981–2	**Burnley	80	Carlisle	80	Fulham	78
†1982–3	Portsmouth	91	Cardiff	86	Huddersfield	82
†1983–4	Oxford Utd	95	Wimbledon	87	Sheffield Utd	83
†1984–5	Bradford City	94	Millwall	90	Hull	87
†1985–6	Reading	94	Plymouth Argyle	87	Derby	84
†1986–7	Bournemouth	97	Middlesbrough	94	Swindon	87
†1987–8	Sunderland	93	Brighton	84	Walsall	82
†1988–9	Wolves	92	Sheffield Utd	84	Port Vale	84
†1989–90	Bristol Rov	93	Bristol City	91	Notts Co	87
†1990–1	Cambridge Utd	86	Southend	85	Grimsby	83
†1991–2	Brentford	82	Birmingham	81	††Huddersfield	78

* Won on goal average ** Won on goal difference † Maximum points 138 (previously 92) †† Not promoted after play–offs

FOURTH DIVISION 1958–92

1958–9	Port Vale	64	Coventry	60	York	60	Shrewsbury	58
1959–60	Walsall	65	Notts Co	60	Torquay	60	Watford	57
1960–1	Peterborough	66	Crystal Palace	64	Northampton	60	Bradford PA	60
1961–2	Millwall	56	Colchester	55	Wrexham	53	Carlisle	52
1962–3	Brentford	62	Oldham	59	Crewe	59	Mansfield	57
1963–4	*Gillingham	60	Carlisle	60	Workington	59	Exeter	58
1964–5	Brighton	63	Millwall	62	York	62	Oxford Utd	61
1965–6	*Doncaster	59	Darlington	59	Torquay	58	Colchester	56
1966–7	Stockport	64	Southport	59	Barrow	59	Tranmere	58
1967–8	Luton	66	Barnsley	61	Hartlepool Utd	60	Crewe	58
1968–9	Doncaster	59	Halifax	57	Rochdale	56	Bradford City	56
1969–70	Chesterfield	64	Wrexham	61	Swansea	60	Port Vale	59
1970–1	Notts Co	69	Bournemouth	60	Oldham	59	York	56
1971–2	Grimsby	63	Southend	60	Brentford	59	Scunthorpe	57
1972–3	Southport	62	Hereford	58	Cambridge Utd	57	Aldershot	56
1973–4	Peterborough	65	Gillingham	62	Colchester	60	Bury	59
1974–5	Mansfield	68	Shrewsbury	62	Rotherham	58	Chester	57
1975–6	Lincoln	74	Northampton	68	Reading	60	Tranmere	58
1976–7	Cambridge Utd	65	Exeter	62	Colchester	59	Bradford City	59
1977–8	Watford	71	Southend	60	Swansea	56	Brentford	59
1978–9	Reading	65	Grimsby	61	Wimbledon	61	Barnsley	61
1979–80	Huddersfield	66	Walsall	64	Newport	61	Portsmouth	60
1980–1	Southend	67	Lincoln	65	Doncaster	56	Wimbledon	55
†1981–2	Sheffield Utd	96	Bradford City	91	Wigan	91	Bournemouth	88
†1982–3	Wimbledon	98	Hull	90	Port Vale	88	Scunthorpe	83
†1983–4	York	101	Doncaster	85	Reading	82	Bristol City	82
†1984–5	Chesterfield	91	Blackpool	86	Darlington	85	Bury	84
†1985–6	Swindon	102	Chester	84	Mansfield	81	Port Vale	79
†1986–7	Northampton	99	Preston	90	Southend	80	††Wolves	79
†1987–8	Wolves	90	Cardiff	85	Bolton	78	††Scunthorpe	77
†1988–9	Rotherham	82	Tranmere	80	Crewe	78	††Scunthorpe	77
†1989–90	Exeter	89	Grimsby	79	Southend	75	††Stockport	74
†1990–1	Darlington	83	Stockport	82	Hartlepool Utd	82	Peterborough	80
1991–2*a*	Burnley	83	Rotherham	77	Mansfield	77	Blackpool	76

* Won on goal average Maximum points: †, 138; *a*, 126; previously 92 †† Not promoted after play–offs

THIRD DIVISION – SOUTH 1920–58

1920–1*a*	Crystal Palace	59	Southampton	54	QPR	53
1921–2*a*	*Southampton	61	Plymouth Argyle	61	Portsmouth	53
1922–3*a*	Bristol City	59	Plymouth Argyle	53	Swansea	53
1923–4*a*	Portsmouth	59	Plymouth Argyle	55	Millwall	54
1924–5*a*	Swansea	57	Plymouth Argyle	56	Bristol City	53

1925–6*a*	Reading	57	Plymouth Argyle	56	Millwall	53
1926–7*a*	Bristol City	62	Plymouth Argyle	60	Millwall	56
1927–8*a*	Millwall	65	Northampton	55	Plymouth Argyle	53
1928–9*a*	*Charlton	54	Crystal Palace	54	Northampton	52
1929–30*a*	Plymouth Argyle	68	Brentford	61	QPR	51
1930–31*a*	Notts Co	59	Crystal Palace	51	Brentford	50
1931–2*a*	Fulham	57	Reading	55	Southend	53
1932–3*a*	Brentford	62	Exeter	58	Norwich	57
1933–4*a*	Norwich	61	Coventry	54	Reading	54
1934–5*a*	Charlton	61	Reading	53	Coventry	51
1935–6*a*	Coventry	57	Luton	56	Reading	54
1936–7*a*	Luton	58	Notts Co	56	Brighton	53
1937–8*a*	Millwall	56	Bristol City	55	QPR	53
1938–9*a*	Newport	55	Crystal Palace	52	Brighton	49
1946–7*a*	Cardiff	66	QPR	57	Bristol City	51
1947–8*a*	QPR	61	Bournemouth	57	Walsall	51
1948–9*a*	Swansea	62	Reading	55	Bournemouth	52
1949–50*a*	Notts Co	58	Northampton	51	Southend	51
1950–1*d*	Nottm Forest	70	Norwich	64	Reading	57
1951–2*d*	Plymouth Argyle	66	Reading	61	Norwich	61
1952–3*d*	Bristol Rov	64	Millwall	62	Northampton	62
1953–4*d*	Ipswich	64	Brighton	61	Bristol City	56
1954–5*d*	Bristol City	70	Leyton Orient	61	Southampton	59
1955–6*d*	Leyton Orient	66	Brighton	65	Ipswich	64
1956–7*d*	*Ipswich	59	Torquay	59	Colchester	58
1957–8*d*	Brighton	60	Brentford	58	Plymouth Argyle	58

THIRD DIVISION – NORTH 1921–58

1921–2*b*	Stockport	56	Darlington	50	Grimsby	50
1922–3*b*	Nelson	51	Bradford PA	47	Walsall	46
1923–4*a*	Wolves	63	Rochdale	62	Chesterfield	54
1924–5*a*	Darlington	58	Nelson	53	New Brighton	53
1925–6*a*	Grimsby	61	Bradford PA	60	Rochdale	59
1926–7*a*	Stoke	63	Rochdale	58	Bradford PA	57
1927–8*a*	Bradford PA	63	Lincoln	55	Stockport	54
1928–9*a*	Bradford City	63	Stockport	62	Wrexham	52
1929–30*a*	Port Vale	67	Stockport	63	Darlington	50
1930–1*a*	Chesterfield	58	Lincoln	57	Wrexham	54
1931–2*c*	*Lincoln	57	Gateshead	57	Chester	50
1932–3*a*	Hull	59	Wrexham	57	Stockport	54
1933–4*a*	Barnsley	62	Chesterfield	61	Stockport	59
1934–5*a*	Doncaster	57	Halifax	55	Chester	54
1935–6*a*	Chesterfield	60	Chester	55	Tranmere	54
1936–7*a*	Stockport	60	Lincoln	57	Chester	53
1937–8*a*	Tranmere	56	Doncaster	54	Hull	53
1938–9*a*	Barnsley	67	Doncaster	56	Bradford City	52
1946–7*a*	Doncaster	72	Rotherham	64	Chester	56
1947–8*a*	Lincoln	60	Rotherham	59	Wrexham	50
1948–9*a*	Hull	65	Rotherham	62	Doncaster	50
1949–50*a*	Doncaster	55	Gateshead	53	Rochdale	51
1950–1*d*	Rotherham	71	Mansfield	64	Carlisle	62
1951–2*d*	Lincoln	69	Grimsby	66	Stockport	59
1952–3*d*	Oldham	59	Port Vale	58	Wrexham	56
1953–4*d*	Port Vale	69	Barnsley	58	Scunthorpe	57
1954–5*d*	Barnsley	65	Accrington	61	Scunthorpe	58
1955–6*d*	Grimsby	68	Derby	63	Accrington	59
1956–7*d*	Derby	63	Hartlepool Utd	59	Accrington	58
1957–8*d*	Scunthorpe	66	Accrington	59	Bradford City	57

Maximum points: *a*, 84; *b*, 76; *c*, 80; *d*, 92 * Won on goal average

TITLE WINNERS

PREMIER LEAGUE

Manchester Utd 13
Chelsea 4
Arsenal 3
Manchester City 2
Blackburn 1
Leicester 1

FOOTBALL LEAGUE CHAMPIONSHIP

Reading 2
Sunderland 2
Bournemouth 1
Burnley 1
Cardiff 1
Leicester 1
Newcastle 1
QPR 1
WBA 1
Wolves 1

DIV 1 (NEW)

Sunderland 2
Bolton 1
Brighton 1
Charlton 1
Crystal Palace 1
Fulham 1
Manchester City 1
Middlesbrough 1
Newcastle 1
Norwich 1
Nottm Forest 1
Portsmouth 1

DIV 1 (ORIGINAL)

Liverpool 18
Arsenal 10
Everton 9
Aston Villa 7
Manchester Utd 7
Sunderland 6
Newcastle 4
Sheffield Wed 4
Huddersfield 3
Leeds 3
Wolves 3
Blackburn 2
Burnley 2
Derby 2
Manchester City 2
Portsmouth 2
Preston 2
Tottenham 2
Chelsea 1
Ipswich 1
Nottm Forest 1
Sheffield Utd 1
WBA 1

LEAGUE ONE

Brighton 1
Bristol City 1
Charlton 1
Doncaster 1
Leicester 1
Luton 1
Norwich 1
Scunthorpe 1
Southend 1
Swansea 1
Wigan 1
Wolves 1

DIV 2 (NEW)

Birmingham 1
Brighton 1
Bury 1
Chesterfield 1
Fulham 1
Millwall 1
Plymouth Argyle 1
Preston 1
Reading 1
Stoke 1
Swindon 1
Watford 1
Wigan 1
Notts Co 1

DIV 2 (ORIGINAL)

Leicester 6
Manchester City 6
Sheffield Wed 5
Birmingham 4
Derby 4
Liverpool 4
Ipswich 3
Leeds 3
Middlesbrough 3
Notts County 3
Preston 3
Aston Villa 2
Bolton 2
Burnley 2
Chelsea 2
Grimsby 2
Manchester Utd 2
Norwich 2
Nottm Forest 2
Stoke 2
Tottenham 2
WBA 2
West Ham 2
Wolves 2
Blackburn 1
Blackpool 1
Bradford City 1
Brentford 1
Bristol City 1
Bury 1
Coventry 1
Crystal Palace 1
Everton 1
Fulham 1
Huddersfield 1
Luton 1
Millwall 1
Newcastle 1
Oldham 1
Oxford Utd 1
QPR 1
Sheffield Utd 1
Sunderland 1

LEAGUE TWO

Chesterfield 2
Brentford 1
Burton 1
Carlisle 1
Gillingham 1
MK Dons 1
Northampton 1
Notts County 1
Swindon 1
Walsall 1
Yeovil 1

APPLICATIONS FOR RE–ELECTION (System discontinued 1987)

14	Hartlepool
12	Halifax
11	Barrow
11	Southport
10	Crewe
10	Newport
10	Rochdale
8	Darlington
8	Exeter
7	Chester
7	Walsall
7	Workington
7	York
6	Stockport
5	Accrington
5	Gillingham
5	Lincoln
5	New Brighton
4	Bradford PA
4	Northampton
4	Norwich
3	Aldershot
3	Bradford City
3	Crystal Palace
3	Doncaster
3	Hereford
3	Merthyr

3	Swindon	2	Millwall	1	Cambridge Utd
3	Torquay	2	Nelson	1	Cardiff
3	Tranmere	2	Oldham	1	Carlisle
2	Aberdare	2	QPR	1	Charlton
2	Ashington	2	Rotherham	1	Mansfield
2	Bournemouth	2	Scunthorpe	1	Port Vale
2	Brentford	2	Southend	1	Preston
2	Colchester	2	Watford	1	Shrewsbury
2	Durham	1	Blackpool	1	Swansea
2	Gateshead	1	Brighton	1	Thames
2	Grimsby	1	Bristol Rov	1	Wrexham

RELEGATED CLUBS (TO 1992)

1892–3 In Test matches, Darwen and Sheffield Utd won promotion in place of Accrington and Notts Co
1893–4 Tests, Liverpool and Small Heath won promotion Darwen and Newton Heath relegated
1894–5 After Tests, Bury promoted, Liverpool relegated
1895–6 After Tests, Liverpool promoted, Small Heath relegated
1896–7 After Tests, Notts Co promoted, Burnley relegated
1897–8 Test system abolished after success of Burnley and Stoke, League extended Blackburn and Newcastle elected to First Division
Automatic promotion and relegation introduced

FIRST DIVISION TO SECOND DIVISION

1898–9 Bolton, Sheffield Wed
1899–00 Burnley, Glossop
1900–1 Preston, WBA
1901–2 Small Heath, Manchester City
1902–3 Grimsby, Bolton
1903–4 Liverpool, WBA
1904–5 League extended Bury and Notts Co, two bottom clubs in First Division, re–elected
1905–6 Nottm Forest, Wolves
1906–7 Derby, Stoke
1907–8 Bolton, Birmingham
1908–9 Manchester City, Leicester Fosse
1909–10 Bolton, Chelsea
1910–11 Bristol City, Nottm Forest
1911–12 Preston, Bury
1912–13 Notts Co, Woolwich Arsenal
1913–14 Preston, Derby
1914–15 Tottenham, *Chelsea
1919–20 Notts Co, Sheffield Wed
1920–1 Derby, Bradford PA
1921–2 Bradford City, Manchester Utd
1922–3 Stoke, Oldham
1923–4 Chelsea, Middlesbrough
1924–5 Preston, Nottm Forest
1925–6 Manchester City, Notts Co
1926–7 Leeds, WBA
1927–8 Tottenham, Middlesbrough
1928–9 Bury, Cardiff
1929–30 Burnley, Everton
1930–1 Leeds, Manchester Utd
1931–2 Grimsby, West Ham
1932–3 Bolton, Blackpool
1933–4 Newcastle, Sheffield Utd
1934–5 Leicester, Tottenham
1935–6 Aston Villa, Blackburn
1936–7 Manchester Utd, Sheffield Wed

1937–8	Manchester City, WBA
1938–9	Birmingham, Leicester
1946–7	Brentford, Leeds
1947–8	Blackburn, Grimsby
1948–9	Preston, Sheffield Utd
1949–50	Manchester City, Birmingham
1950–1	Sheffield Wed, Everton
1951–2	Huddersfield, Fulham
1952–3	Stoke, Derby
1953–4	Middlesbrough, Liverpool
1954–5	Leicester, Sheffield Wed
1955–6	Huddersfield, Sheffield Utd
1956–7	Charlton, Cardiff
1957–8	Sheffield Wed, Sunderland
1958–9	Portsmouth, Aston Villa
1959–60	Luton, Leeds
1960–61	Preston, Newcastle
1961–2	Chelsea, Cardiff
1962–3	Manchester City, Leyton Orient
1963–4	Bolton, Ipswich
1964–5	Wolves, Birmingham
1965–6	Northampton, Blackburn
1966–7	Aston Villa, Blackpool
1967–8	Fulham, Sheffield Utd
1968–9	Leicester, QPR
1969–70	Sheffield Wed, Sunderland
1970–1	Burnley, Blackpool
1971–2	Nottm Forest, Huddersfield
1972–3	WBA, Crystal Palace
1973–4	Norwich, Manchester Utd, Southampton
1974–5	Chelsea, Luton, Carlisle
1975–6	Sheffield Utd, Burnley, Wolves
1976–7	Tottenham, Stoke, Sunderland
1977–8	Leicester, West Ham, Newcastle
1978–9	QPR, Birmingham, Chelsea
1979–80	Bristol City, Derby, Bolton
1980–1	Norwich, Leicester, Crystal Palace
1981–2	Leeds, Wolves, Middlesbrough
1982–3	Manchester City, Swansea, Brighton
1983–4	Birmingham, Notts Co, Wolves
1984–5	Norwich, Sunderland, Stoke
1985–6	Ipswich, Birmingham, WBA
1986–7	Leicester, Manchester City, Aston Villa
1987–8	Chelsea**, Portsmouth, Watford, Oxford Utd
1988–9	Middlesbrough, West Ham, Newcastle
1989–90	Sheffield Wed, Charlton, Millwall
1990–1	Sunderland, Derby
1991–2	Luton, Notts Co, West Ham

* Subsequently re–elected to First Division when League extended after the war

** Relegated after play–offs

SECOND DIVISION TO THIRD DIVISION

1920–1	Stockport
1921–2	Bradford City, Bristol City
1922–3	Rotherham, Wolves
1923–4	Nelson, Bristol City
1924–5	Crystal Palace, Coventry
1925–6	Stoke, Stockport
1926–7	Darlington, Bradford City
1927–8	Fulham, South Shields
1928–9	Port Vale, Clapton Orient

1929–30 Hull, Notts County
1930–1 Reading, Cardiff
1931–2 Barnsley, Bristol City
1932–3 Chesterfield, Charlton
1933–4 Millwall, Lincoln
1934–5 Oldham, Notts Co
1935–6 Port Vale, Hull
1936–7 Doncaster, Bradford City
1937–8 Barnsley, Stockport
1938–9 Norwich, Tranmere
1946–7 Swansea, Newport
1947–8 Doncaster, Millwall
1948–9 Nottm Forest, Lincoln
1949–50 Plymouth Argyle, Bradford PA
1950–1 Grimsby, Chesterfield
1951–2 Coventry, QPR
1952–3 Southampton, Barnsley
1953–4 Brentford, Oldham
1954–5 Ipswich, Derby
1955–6 Plymouth Argyle, Hull
1956–7 Port Vale, Bury
1957–8 Doncaster, Notts Co
1958–9 Barnsley, Grimsby
1959–60 Bristol City, Hull
1960–1 Lincoln, Portsmouth
1961–2 Brighton, Bristol Rov
1962–3 Walsall, Luton
1963–4 Grimsby, Scunthorpe
1964–5 Swindon, Swansea
1965–6 Middlesbrough, Leyton Orient
1966–7 Northampton, Bury
1967–8 Plymouth Argyle, Rotherham
1968–9 Fulham, Bury
1969–70 Preston, Aston Villa
1970–1 Blackburn, Bolton
1971–2 Charlton, Watford
1972–3 Huddersfield, Brighton
1973–4 Crystal Palace, Preston, Swindon
1974–5 Millwall, Cardiff, Sheffield Wed
1975–6 Portsmouth, Oxford Utd, York
1976–7 Carlisle, Plymouth Argyle, Hereford
1977–8 Hull, Mansfield, Blackpool
1978–9 Sheffield Utd, Millwall, Blackburn
1979–80 Fulham, Burnley, Charlton
1980–1 Preston, Bristol City, Bristol Rov
1981–2 Cardiff, Wrexham, Orient
1982–3 Rotherham, Burnley, Bolton
1983–4 Derby, Swansea, Cambridge Utd
1984–5 Notts Co, Cardiff, Wolves
1985–6 Carlisle, Middlesbrough, Fulham
1986–7 Sunderland**, Grimsby, Brighton
1987–8 Sheffield Utd**, Reading, Huddersfield
1988–9 Shrewsbury, Birmingham, Walsall
1989–90 Bournemouth, Bradford City, Stoke
1990–1 WBA, Hull
1991–2 Plymouth Argyle, Brighton, Port Vale

** Relegated after play–offs

THIRD DIVISION TO FOURTH DIVISION

1958–9 Rochdale, Notts Co, Doncaster, Stockport
1959–60 Accrington, Wrexham, Mansfield, York

1960–1	Chesterfield, Colchester, Bradford City, Tranmere
1961–2	Newport, Brentford, Lincoln, Torquay
1962–3	Bradford PA, Brighton, Carlisle, Halifax
1963–4	Millwall, Crewe, Wrexham, Notts Co
1964–5	Luton, Port Vale, Colchester, Barnsley
1965–6	Southend, Exeter, Brentford, York
1966–7	Doncaster, Workington, Darlington, Swansea
1967–8	Scunthorpe, Colchester, Grimsby, Peterborough (demoted)
1968–9	Oldham, Crewe, Hartlepool Utd, Northampton
1969–70	Bournemouth, Southport, Barrow, Stockport
1970–1	Gillingham, Doncaster, Bury, Reading
1971–2	Mansfield, Barnsley, Torquay, Bradford City
1972–3	Scunthorpe, Swansea, Brentford, Rotherham
1973–4	Cambridge Utd, Shrewsbury, Rochdale, Southport
1974–5	Bournemouth, Watford, Tranmere, Huddersfield
1975–6	Aldershot, Colchester, Southend, Halifax
1976–7	Reading, Northampton, Grimsby, York
1977–8	Port Vale, Bradford City, Hereford, Portsmouth
1978–9	Peterborough, Walsall, Tranmere, Lincoln
1979–80	Bury, Southend, Mansfield, Wimbledon
1980–1	Sheffield Utd, Colchester, Blackpool, Hull
1981–2	Wimbledon, Swindon, Bristol City, Chester
1982–3	Reading, Wrexham, Doncaster, Chesterfield
1983–4	Scunthorpe, Southend, Port Vale, Exeter
1984–5	Burnley, Orient, Preston, Cambridge Utd
1985–6	Lincoln, Cardiff, Wolves, Swansea
1986–7	Bolton**, Carlisle, Darlington, Newport
1987–8	Doncaster, York, Grimsby, Rotherham**
1988–9	Southend, Chesterfield, Gillingham, Aldershot
1989–90	Cardiff, Northampton, Blackpool, Walsall
1990–1	Crewe, Rotherham, Mansfield
1991–2	Bury, Shrewsbury, Torquay, Darlington

** Relegated after plays–offs

DEMOTED FROM FOURTH DIVISION TO CONFERENCE

1987	Lincoln
1988	Newport
1989	Darlington
1990	Colchester
1991	No demotion
1992	No demotion

DEMOTED FROM THIRD DIVISION TO CONFERENCE

1993	Halifax
1994–6	No demotion
1997	Hereford
1998	Doncaster
1999	Scarborough
2000	Chester
2001	Barnet
2002	Halifax
2003	Exeter, Shrewsbury
2004	Carlisle, York

DEMOTED FROM LEAGUE TWO TO CONFERENCE

2005	Kidderminster, Cambridge Utd
2006	Oxford Utd, Rushden & Diamonds
2007	Boston, Torquay

2008 Mansfield, Wrexham
2009 Chester Luton
2010 Grimsby, Darlington
2011 Lincoln, Stockport
2012 Hereford, Macclesfield
2013 Barnet, Aldershot
2014 Bristol Rov, Torquay
2015 Cheltenham, Tranmere
2016 Dagenham, York

RELEGATED CLUBS (SINCE 1993)

1993
Premier League to Div 1: Crystal Palace, Middlesbrough, Nottm Forest
Div 1 to Div 2: Brentford, Cambridge Utd, Bristol Rov
Div 2 to Div 3: Preston, Mansfield, Wigan, Chester

1994
Premier League to Div 1: Sheffield Utd, Oldham, Swindon
Div 1 to Div 2: Birmingham, Oxford Utd, Peterborough
Div 2 to Div 3: Fulham, Exeter, Hartlepool Utd, Barnet

1995
Premier League to Div 1: Crystal Palace, Norwich, Leicester, Ipswich
Div 1 to Div 2: Swindon, Burnley, Bristol City, Notts Co
Div 2 to Div 3: Cambridge Utd, Plymouth Argyle, Cardiff, Chester, Leyton Orient

1996
Premier League to Div 1: Manchester City, QPR, Bolton
Div 1 to Div 2: Millwall, Watford, Luton
Div 2 to Div 3: Carlisle, Swansea, Brighton, Hull

1997
Premier League to Div 1: Sunderland, Middlesbrough, Nottm Forest
Div 1 to Div 2: Grimsby, Oldham, Southend
Div 2 to Div 3: Peterborough, Shrewsbury, Rotherham, Notts Co

1998
Premier League to Div 1: Bolton, Barnsley, Crystal Palace
Div 1 to Div 2: Manchester City, Stoke, Reading
Div 2 to Div 3: Brentford, Plymouth Argyle, Carlisle, Southend

1999
Premier League to Div 1: Charlton, Blackburn, Nottm Forest
Div 1 to Div 2: Bury, Oxford Utd, Bristol City
Div 2 to Div 3: York, Northampton, Lincoln, Macclesfield

2000
Premier League to Div 1: Wimbledon, Sheffield Wed, Watford
Div 1 to Div 2: Walsall, Port Vale, Swindon
Div 2 to Div 3: Cardiff, Blackpool, Scunthorpe, Chesterfield

2001
Premier League to Div 1: Manchester City, Coventry, Bradford City
Div 1 to Div 2: Huddersfield, QPR, Tranmere
Div 2 to Div 3: Bristol Rov, Luton, Swansea, Oxford Utd

2002
Premier League to Div 1: Ipswich, Derby, Leicester
Div 1 to Div 2: Crewe, Barnsley, Stockport
Div 2 to Div 3: Bournemouth, Bury, Wrexham, Cambridge Utd

2003
Premier League to Div 1: West Ham, WBA, Sunderland
Div 1 to Div 2: Sheffield Wed, Brighton, Grimsby
Div 2 to Div 3: Cheltenham, Huddersfield, Mansfield, Northampton

2004
Premier League to Div 1: Leicester, Leeds, Wolves
Div 1 to Div 2: Walsall, Bradford City, Wimbledon
Div 2 to Div 3: Grimsby, Rushden & Diamonds, Notts Co, Wycombe

2005
Premier League to Championship: Crystal Palace, Norwich, Southampton
Championship to League 1: Gillingham, Nottm Forest, Rotherham
League 1 to League 2: Torquay, Wrexham, Peterborough, Stockport

2006
Premier League to Championship: Birmingham, WBA, Sunderland
Championship to League 1: Crewe, Millwall, Brighton
League 1 to League 2: Hartlepool Utd, MK Dons, Swindon, Walsall

2007
Premier League to Championship: Sheffield Utd, Charlton, Watford
Championship to League 1: Southend, Luton, Leeds
League 1 to League 2: Chesterfield, Bradford City, Rotherham, Brentford

2008
Premier League to Championship: Reading, Birmingham, Derby
Championship to League 1: Leicester, Scunthorpe, Colchester
League 1 to League 2: Bournemouth, Gillingham, Port Vale, Luton

2009
Premier League to Championship: Newcastle, Middlesbrough, WBA
Championship to League 1: Norwich, Southampton, Charlton
League 1 to League 2: Northampton, Crewe, Cheltenham, Hereford

2010
Premier League to Championship: Burnley, Hull, Portsmouth
Championship to League 1: Sheffield Wed, Plymouth, Peterborough
League 1 to League 2: Gillingham, Wycombe, Southend, Stockport

2011
Premier League to Championship: Birmingham, Blackpool, West Ham
Championship to League 1: Preston, Sheffield Utd, Scunthorpe
League 1 to League 2: Dagenham & Redbridge, Bristol Rov, Plymouth, Swindon

2012
Premier League to Championship: Bolton, Blackburn, Wolves
Championship to League 1: Portsmouth, Coventry, Doncaster
League 1 to League 2: Wycombe, Chesterfield, Exeter, Rochdale

2013
Premier League to Championship: Wigan, Reading, QPR
Championship to League 1: Peterborough, Wolves, Bristol City
League 1 to League 2: Scunthorpe, Bury, Hartlepool, Portsmouth

2014
Premier League to Championship: Norwich, Fulham, Cardiff
Championship to League 1: Doncaster, Barnsley, Yeovil
League 1 to League 2: Tranmere, Carlisle, Shrewsbury, Stevenage

2015
Premier League to Championship: Hull, Burnley QPR
Championship to League 1: Millwall, Wigan, Blackpool
League 1 to League 2: Notts Co, Crawley, Leyton Orient, Yeovil

2016
Premier League to Championship: Newcastle, Norwich, Aston Villa
Championship to League 1: Charlton, MK Dons, Bolton
League 1 to League 2: Doncaster, Blackpool, Colchester, Crewe

ANNUAL AWARDS

OOTBALL WRITERS' ASSOCIATION

otballer of the Year: 1948 Stanley Matthews (Blackpool); **1949** Johnny Carey (Manchester Utd); **50** Joe Mercer (Arsenal); **1951** Harry Johnston (Blackpool); **1952** Billy Wright (Wolves); **1953** ıt Lofthouse (Bolton); **1954** Tom Finney (Preston); **1955** Don Revie (Manchester City); **1956** Bert autmann (Manchester City); **1957** Tom Finney (Preston); **1958** Danny Blanchflower (Tottenham); **59** Syd Owen (Luton); **1960** Bill Slater (Wolves); **1961** Danny Blanchflower (Tottenham); **62** Jimmy Adamson (Burnley); **1963** Stanley Matthews (Stoke); **1964** Bobby Moore (West ım); **1965** Bobby Collins (Leeds); **1966** Bobby Charlton (Manchester Utd); **1967** Jack Charlton eeds); **1968** George Best (Manchester Utd); **1969** Tony Book (Manchester City) & Dave Mackay erby) – shared; **1970** Billy Bremner (Leeds); **1971** Frank McLintock (Arsenal); **1972** Gordon ınks (Stoke); **1973** Pat Jennings (Tottenham); **1974** Ian Callaghan (Liverpool); **1975** Alan Mullery ulham); **1976** Kevin Keegan (Liverpool); **1977** Emlyn Hughes (Liverpool); **1978** Kenny Burns ott'm Forest); **1979** Kenny Dalglish (Liverpool); **1980** Terry McDermott (Liverpool); **1981** Frans ıijssen (Ipswich); **1982** Steve Perryman (Tottenham); **1983** Kenny Dalglish (Liverpool); **1984** Ian ısh (Liverpool); **1985** Neville Southall (Everton); **1986** Gary Lineker (Everton); **1987** Clive Allen ottenham); **1988** John Barnes (Liverpool); **1989** Steve Nicol (Liverpool); Special award to the verpool players for the compassion shown to bereaved families after the Hillsborough Disaster; **90** John Barnes (Liverpool); **1991** Gordon Strachan (Leeds); **1992** Gary Lineker (Tottenham); **93** Chris Waddle (Sheffield Wed); **1994** Alan Shearer (Blackburn); **1995** Jurgen Klinsmann ottenham); **1996** Eric Cantona (Manchester Utd); **1997** Gianfranco Zola (Chelsea); **1998** Dennis ergkamp (Arsenal); **1999** David Ginola (Tottenham); **2000** Roy Keane (Manchester Utd); **2001** ddy Sheringham (Manchester Utd); **2002** Robert Pires (Arsenal); **2003** Thierry Henry (Arsenal); **04** Thierry Henry (Arsenal); **2005** Frank Lampard (Chelsea); **2006** Thierry Henry (Arsenal); **07** Cristiano Ronaldo (Manchester Utd); **2008** Cristiano Ronaldo (Manchester Utd), **2009** even Gerrard (Liverpool), **2010** Wayne Rooney (Manchester Utd), **2011** Scott Parker (West Ham), **12** Robin van Persie (Arsenal), **2013** Gareth Bale (Tottenham), **2014** Luis Suarez (Liverpool), **15** Eden Hazard (Chelsea), **2016** Jamie Vardy (Leicester)

ROFESSIONAL FOOTBALLERS' ASSOCIATION

ayer of the Year: 1974 Norman Hunter (Leeds); **1975** Colin Todd (Derby); **1976** Pat Jennings ottenham); **1977** Andy Gray (Aston Villa); **1978** Peter Shilton (Nott'm Forest); **1979** Liam ady (Arsenal); **1980** Terry McDermott (Liverpool); **1981** John Wark (Ipswich); **1982** Kevin eegan (Southampton); **1983** Kenny Dalglish (Liverpool); **1984** Ian Rush (Liverpool); **1985** eter Reid (Everton); **1986** Gary Lineker (Everton); **1987** Clive Allen (Tottenham); **1988** John ırnes (Liverpool); **1989** Mark Hughes (Manchester Utd); **1990** David Platt (Aston Villa); **1991** ark Hughes (Manchester Utd); **1992** Gary Pallister (Manchester Utd); **1993** Paul McGrath ston Villa); **1994** Eric Cantona (Manchester Utd); **1995** Alan Shearer (Blackburn); **1996** Les rdinand (Newcastle); **1997** Alan Shearer (Newcastle); **1998** Dennis Bergkamp (Arsenal); **99** David Ginola (Tottenham); **2000** Roy Keane (Manchester Utd); **2001** Teddy Sheringham anchester Utd); **2002** Ruud van Nistelrooy (Manchester Utd); **2003** Thierry Henry (Arsenal); **04** Thierry Henry (Arsenal); **2005** John Terry (Chelsea); **2006** Steven Gerrard (Liverpool); **07** Cristiano Ronaldo (Manchester Utd); **2008** Cristiano Ronaldo (Manchester Utd), **2009** yan Giggs (Manchester Utd), **2010** Wayne Rooney (Manchester Utd), **2011** Gareth Bale ottenham), **2012** Robin van Persie (Arsenal), **2013** Gareth Bale (Tottenham), **2014** Luis Suarez iverpool), **2015** Eden Hazard (Chelsea), **2016** Riyad Mahrez (Leicester)

ung Player of the Year: 1974 Kevin Beattie (Ipswich); **1975** Mervyn Day (West Ham); **1976** eter Barnes (Manchester City); **1977** Andy Gray (Aston Villa); **1978** Tony Woodcock (Nott'm rest); **1979** Cyrille Regis (WBA); **1980** Glenn Hoddle (Tottenham); **1981** Gary Shaw (Aston lla); **1982** Steve Moran (Southampton); **1983** Ian Rush (Liverpool); **1984** Paul Walsh uton); **1985** Mark Hughes (Manchester Utd); **1986** Tony Cottee (West Ham); **1987** Tony lams (Arsenal); **1988** Paul Gascoigne (Newcastle); **1989** Paul Merson (Arsenal); **1990**

Matthew Le Tissier (Southampton); **1991** Lee Sharpe (Manchester Utd); **1992** Ryan Gigg (Manchester Utd); **1993** Ryan Giggs (Manchester Utd); **1994** Andy Cole (Newcastle); **199** Robbie Fowler (Liverpool); **1996** Robbie Fowler (Liverpool); **1997** David Beckham (Manchest Utd); **1998** Michael Owen (Liverpool); **1999** Nicolas Anelka (Arsenal); **2000** Harry Kewe (Leeds); **2001** Steven Gerrard (Liverpool); **2002** Craig Bellamy (Newcastle); **2003** Jermai Jenas (Newcastle); **2004** Scott Parker (Chelsea); **2005** Wayne Rooney (Manchester Utd **2006** Wayne Rooney (Manchester Utd); **2007** Cristiano Ronaldo (Manchester Utd); **2008** Ces Fabregas (Arsenal), **2009** Ashley Young (Aston Villa), **2010** James Milner (Aston Villa), **201** Jack Wilshere (Arsenal), **2012** Kyle Walker (Tottenham), **2013** Gareth Bale (Tottenham), **201** Eden Hazard (Chelsea), **2015** Harry Kane (Tottenham), **2016** Dele Alli (Tottenham)

Merit Awards: 1974 Bobby Charlton & Cliff Lloyd; **1975** Denis Law; **1976** George Easthar **1977** Jack Taylor; **1978** Bill Shankly; **1979** Tom Finney; **1980** Sir Matt Busby; **1981** Joh Trollope; **1982** Joe Mercer; **1983** Bob Paisley; **1984** Bill Nicholson; **1985** Ron Greenwoo **1986** England 1966 World Cup-winning team; **1987** Sir Stanley Matthews; **1988** Billy Bond **1989** Nat Lofthouse; **1990** Peter Shilton; **1991** Tommy Hutchison; **1992** Brian Clough; **199** Manchester Utd, 1968 European Champions; Eusebio; **1994** Billy Bingham; **1995** Gord Strachan; **1996** Pele; **1997** Peter Beardsley; **1998** Steve Ogrizovic; **1999** Tony Ford; **200** Gary Mabbutt; **2001** Jimmy Hill; **2002** Niall Quinn; **2003** Sir Bobby Robson; **2004** Dario Grac **2005** Shaka Hislop; **2006** George Best; **2007** Sir Alex Ferguson; **2008** Jimmy Armfield; **200** John McDermott, **2010** Lucas Radebe, **2011** Howard Webb, **2012** Graham Alexander, **2013** E Harrison/Manchester Utd Class of '92, **2014** Donald Bell (posthumously; only footballer to w Victoria Cross, World War 1), **2015** Steven Gerrard & Frank Lampard, **2016** Ryan Giggs

MANAGER OF THE YEAR 1 (chosen by media and sponsors)

1966 Jock Stein (Celtic); **1967** Jock Stein (Celtic); **1968** Matt Busby (Manchester Utc **1969** Don Revie (Leeds); **1970** Don Revie (Leeds); **1971** Bertie Mee (Arsenal); **1972** D Revie (Leeds); **1973** Bill Shankly (Liverpool); **1974** Jack Charlton (Middlesbrough); **1975** R Saunders (Aston Villa); **1976** Bob Paisley (Liverpool); **1977** Bob Paisley (Liverpool); **1978** Bri Clough (Nott'm Forest); **1979** Bob Paisley (Liverpool); **1980** Bob Paisley (Liverpool); **1981** R Saunders (Aston Villa); **1982** Bob Paisley (Liverpool); **1983** Bob Paisley (Liverpool); **1984** J Fagan (Liverpool); **1985** Howard Kendall (Everton); **1986** Kenny Dalglish (Liverpool); **198** Howard Kendall (Everton); **1988** Kenny Dalglish (Liverpool); **1989** George Graham (Arsena **1990** Kenny Dalglish (Liverpool); **1991** George Graham (Arsenal); **1992** Howard Wilkins (Leeds); **1993** Alex Ferguson (Manchester Utd); **1994** Alex Ferguson (Manchester Utd); **199** Kenny Dalglish (Blackburn); **1996** Alex Ferguson (Manchester Utd); **1997** Alex Fergus (Manchester Utd); **1998** Arsene Wenger (Arsenal); **1999** Alex Ferguson (Manchester Utc **2000** Sir Alex Ferguson (Manchester Utd); **2001** George Burley (Ipswich); **2002** Arsene Weng (Arsenal); **2003** Sir Alex Ferguson (Manchester Utd); **2004** Arsene Wenger (Arsenal); **2005** Jo Mourinho (Chelsea); **2006** Jose Mourinho (Chelsea); **2007** Sir Alex Ferguson (Manchester Utc **2008** Sir Alex Ferguson (Manchester Utd); **2009** Sir Alex Ferguson (Manchester Utd), **201** Harry Redknapp (Tottenham), **2011** Sir Alex Ferguson (Manchester Utd), **2012**: Alan Parde (Newcastle), **2013** Sir Alex Ferguson (Manchester Utd), **2014** Tony Pulis (Crystal Palace), **201** Jose Mourinho (Chelsea), **2016** Claudio Ranieri (Leicester)

MANAGER OF THE YEAR 2 (Chosen by the League Managers' Association)

1993 Dave Bassett (Sheffield Utd); **1994** Joe Kinnear (Wimbledon); **1995** Frank Clark (Nott' Forest); **1996** Peter Reid (Sunderland); **1997** Danny Wilson (Barnsley); **1998** David Jon (Southampton); **1999** Alex Ferguson (Manchester Utd); **2000** Alan Curbishley (Charlt Athletic); **2001** George Burley (Ipswich); **2002** Arsene Wenger (Arsenal); **2003** David Moy (Everton); **2004** Arsene Wenger (Arsenal); **2005** David Moyes (Everton); **2006** Steve Copp (Reading); **2007** Steve Coppell (Reading); **2008** Sir Alex Ferguson (Manchester Utd); **200** David Moyes (Everton), **2010** Roy Hodgson (Fulham), **2011** Sir Alex Ferguson (Manchester Utc **2012**: Alan Pardew (Newcastle), **2013** Sir Alex Ferguson (Manchester Utd), **2014** Brend Rodgers (Liverpool), **2015** Eddie Howe (Bournemouth), **2016** Claudio Ranieri (Leicester)

SCOTTISH FOOTBALL WRITERS' ASSOCIATION

Footballer of the Year: 1965 Billy McNeill (Celtic); **1966** John Greig (Rangers); **1967** Ronnie Simpson (Celtic); **1968** Gordon Wallace (Raith); **1969** Bobby Murdoch (Celtic); **1970** Pat Stanton (Hibernian); **1971** Martin Buchan (Aberdeen); **1972** David Smith (Rangers); **1973** George Connelly (Celtic); **1974** World Cup Squad; **1975** Sandy Jardine (Rangers); **1976** John Greig (Rangers); **1977** Danny McGrain (Celtic); **1978** Derek Johnstone (Rangers); **1979** Andy Ritchie (Morton); **1980** Gordon Strachan (Aberdeen); **1981** Alan Rough (Partick Thistle); **1982** Paul Sturrock (Dundee Utd); **1983** Charlie Nicholas (Celtic); **1984** Willie Miller (Aberdeen); **1985** Hamish McAlpine (Dundee Utd); **1986** Sandy Jardine (Hearts); **1987** Brian McClair (Celtic); **1988** Paul McStay (Celtic); **1989** Richard Gough (Rangers); **1990** Alex McLeish (Aberdeen); **1991** Maurice Malpas (Dundee Utd); **1992** Ally McCoist (Rangers); **1993** Andy Goram (Rangers); **1994** Mark Hateley (Rangers); **1995** Brian Laudrup (Rangers); **1996** Paul Gascoigne (Rangers); **1997** Brian Laudrup (Rangers); **1998** Craig Burley (Celtic); **1999** Henrik Larsson (Celtic); **2000** Barry Ferguson (Rangers); **2001** Henrik Larsson (Celtic); **2002** Paul Lambert (Celtic); **2003** Barry Ferguson (Rangers); **2004** Jackie McNamara (Celtic); **2005** John Hartson (Celtic); **2006** Craig Gordon (Hearts); **2007** Shunsuke Nakamura (Celtic); **2008** Carlos Cuellar (Rangers); **2009** Gary Caldwell (Celtic), **2010** David Weir (Rangers), **2011** Emilio Izaguirre (Celtic), **2012** Charlie Mulgrew (Celtic), **2013** Leigh Griffiths (Hibernian), **2014** Kris Commons (Celtic), **2015** Craig Gordon (Celtic), **2016** Leigh Griffiths (Celtic)

PROFESSIONAL FOOTBALLERS' ASSOCIATION SCOTLAND

Player of the Year: 1978 Derek Johnstone (Rangers); **1979** Paul Hegarty (Dundee Utd); **1980** Davie Provan (Celtic); **1981** Mark McGhee (Aberdeen); **1982** Sandy Clarke (Airdrieonians); **1983** Charlie Nicholas (Celtic); **1984** Willie Miller (Aberdeen); **1985** Jim Duffy (Morton); **1986** Richard Gough (Dundee Utd); **1987** Brian McClair (Celtic); **1988** Paul McStay (Celtic); **1989** Theo Snelders (Aberdeen); **1990** Jim Bett (Aberdeen); **1991** Paul Elliott (Celtic); **1992** Ally McCoist (Rangers); **1993** Andy Goram (Rangers); **1994** Mark Hateley (Rangers); **1995** Brian Laudrup (Rangers); **1996** Paul Gascoigne (Rangers); **1997** Paolo Di Canio (Celtic) **1998** Jackie McNamara (Celtic); **1999** Henrik Larsson (Celtic); **2000** Mark Viduka (Celtic); **2001** Henrik Larsson (Celtic); **2002** Lorenzo Amoruso (Rangers); **2003** Barry Ferguson (Rangers); **2004** Chris Sutton (Celtic); **2005** John Hartson (Celtic) and Fernando Ricksen (Rangers); **2006** Shaun Maloney (Celtic); **2007** Shunsuke Nakamura (Celtic); **2008** Aiden McGeady (Celtic); **2009** Scott Brown (Celtic), **2010** Steven Davis (Rangers), **2011** Emilio Izaguirre (Celtic), **2012** Charlie Mulgrew (Celtic), **2013** Michael Higdon (Motherwell), **2014** Kris Commons (Celtic), **2015** Stefan Johansen (Celtic), **2016** Leigh Griffiths (Celtic)

Young Player of the Year: 1978 Graeme Payne (Dundee Utd); **1979** Ray Stewart (Dundee Utd); **1980** John McDonald (Rangers); **1981** Charlie Nicholas (Celtic); **1982** Frank McAvennie (St Mirren); **1983** Paul McStay (Celtic); **1984** John Robertson (Hearts); **1985** Craig Levein (Hearts); **1986** Craig Levein (Hearts); **1987** Robert Fleck (Rangers); **1988** John Collins (Hibernian); **1989** Billy McKinlay (Dundee Utd); **1990** Scott Crabbe (Hearts); **1991** Eoin Jess (Aberdeen); **1992** Phil O'Donnell (Motherwell); **1993** Eoin Jess (Aberdeen); **1994** Phil O'Donnell (Motherwell); **1995** Charlie Miller (Rangers); **1996** Jackie McNamara (Celtic); **1997** Robbie Winters (Dundee Utd); **1998** Gary Naysmith (Hearts); **1999** Barry Ferguson (Rangers); **2000** Kenny Miller (Hibernian); **2001** Stilian Petrov (Celtic); **2002** Kevin McNaughton (Aberdeen); **2003** James McFadden (Motherwell); **2004** Stephen Pearson (Celtic); **2005** Derek Riordan (Hibernian); **2006** Shaun Maloney (Celtic); **2007** Steven Naismith (Kilmarnock); **2008** Aiden McGeady (Celtic); **2009** James McCarthy (Hamilton), **2010** Danny Wilson (Rangers), **2011:** David Goodwillie (Dundee Utd), **2012** James Forrest (Celtic), **2013** Leigh Griffiths (Hibernian), **2014** Andy Robertson (Dundee Utd), **2015** Jason Denayer (Celtic), **2016** Kieran Tierney (Celtic)

SCOTTISH MANAGER OF THE YEAR

1987 Jim McLean (Dundee Utd); **1988** Billy McNeill (Celtic); **1989** Graeme Souness (Rangers); **1990** Andy Roxburgh (Scotland); **1991** Alex Totten (St Johnstone); **1992** Walter Smith (Rangers);

1993 Walter Smith (Rangers); **1994** Walter Smith (Rangers); **1995** Jimmy Nicholl (Raith); **199** Walter Smith (Rangers); **1997** Walter Smith (Rangers); **1998** Wim Jansen (Celtic); **1999** Dic Advocaat (Rangers); **2000** Dick Advocaat (Rangers); **2001** Martin O'Neill (Celtic); **2002** Joh Lambie (Partick Thistle); **2003** Alex McLeish (Rangers); **2004** Martin O'Neill (Celtic); **200** Alex McLeish (Rangers); **2006** Gordon Strachan (Celtic); **2007** Gordon Strachan (Celtic); **200** Billy Reid (Hamilton); **2009** Csaba Laszlo (Hearts), **2010** Walter Smith (Rangers), **2011:** Mix Paatelainen (Kilmarnock), **2012** Neil Lennon (Celtic), **2013** Neil Lennon (Celtic), **2014** Dere McInnes (Aberdeen), **2015** John Hughes (Inverness), **2016** Mark Warburton (Rangers)

EUROPEAN FOOTBALLER OF THE YEAR

1956 Stanley Matthews (Blackpool); **1957** Alfredo di Stefano (Real Madrid); **1958** Raymon Kopa (Real Madrid); **1959** Alfredo di Stefano (Real Madrid); **1960** Luis Suarez (Barcelona) **1961** Omar Sivori (Juventus); **1962** Josef Masopust (Dukla Prague); **1963** Lev Yashin (Mosco Dynamo); **1964** Denis Law (Manchester Utd); **1965** Eusebio (Benfica); **1966** Bobby Charlto (Manchester Utd); **1967** Florian Albert (Ferencvaros); **1968** George Best (Manchester Utd) **1969** Gianni Rivera (AC Milan); **1970** Gerd Muller (Bayern Munich); **1971** Johan Cruyff (Ajax) **1972** Franz Beckenbauer (Bayern Munich); **1973** Johan Cruyff (Barcelona); **1974** Johan Cruyf (Barcelona); **1975** Oleg Blokhin (Dynamo Kiev); **1976** Franz Beckenbauer (Bayern Munich) **1977** Allan Simonsen (Borussia Moenchengladbach); **1978** Kevin Keegan (SV Hamburg) **1979** Kevin Keegan (SV Hamburg); **1980** Karl-Heinz Rummenigge (Bayern Munich); **198** Karl-Heinz Rummenigge (Bayern Munich); **1982** Paolo Rossi (Juventus); **1983** Michel Platin (Juventus); **1984** Michel Platini (Juventus); **1985** Michel Platini (Juventus); **1986** Igor Belano (Dynamo Kiev); **1987** Ruud Gullit (AC Milan); **1988** Marco van Basten (AC Milan); **198** Marco van Basten (AC Milan); **1990** Lothar Matthaus (Inter Milan); **1991** Jean-Pierre Papi (Marseille); **1992** Marco van Basten (AC Milan); **1993** Roberto Baggio (Juventus); **1994** Hrist Stoichkov (Barcelona); **1995** George Weah (AC Milan); **1996** Matthias Sammer (Borussi Dortmund); **1997** Ronaldo (Inter Milan); **1998** Zinedine Zidane (Juventus); **1999** Rivald (Barcelona); **2000** Luis Figo (Real Madrid); **2001** Michael Owen (Liverpool); **2002** Ronald (Real Madrid); **2003** Pavel Nedved (Juventus); **2004** Andriy Shevchenko (AC Milan); **200** Ronaldinho (Barcelona); **2006** Fabio Cannavaro (Real Madrid); **2007** Kaka (AC Milan); **200** Cristiano Ronaldo (Manchester United), **2009** Lionel Messi (Barcelona)

WORLD FOOTBALLER OF YEAR

1991 Lothar Matthaus (Inter Milan and Germany); **1992** Marco van Basten (AC Milan an Holland); **1993** Roberto Baggio (Juventus and Italy); **1994** Romario (Barcelona and Brazil) **1995** George Weah (AC Milan and Liberia); **1996** Ronaldo (Barcelona and Brazil); **1997** Ronald (Inter Milan and Brazil); **1998** Zinedine Zidane (Juventus and France); **1999** Rivaldo (Barcelon and Brazil); **2000** Zinedine Zidane (Juventus and France); **2001** Luis Figo (Real Madrid an Portugal); **2002** Ronaldo (Real Madrid and Brazil); **2003** Zinedine Zidane (Real Madrid an France); **2004** Ronaldinho (Barcelona and Brazil); **2005** Ronaldinho (Barcelona and Brazil) **2006** Fabio Cannavaro (Real Madrid and Italy); **2007** Kaka (AC Milan and Brazil); **2008** Cristian Ronaldo (Manchester United and Portugal), **2009** Lionel Messi (Barcelona and Argentina)

FIFA BALLON D'OR

(replaces European and World Footballer of the Year)

2010: Lionel Messi (Barcelona). **2011** Lionel Messi (Barcelona), **2012** Lionel Messi (Barcelona), **2013** Cristiano Ronaldo (Real Madrid), **2014**: Cristiano Ronaldo (Real Madrid), **2015** Lionel Messi (Barcelona)

FIFA WORLD COACH OF THE YEAR

2010: Jose Mourinho (Inter Milan). **2011** Pep Guardiola (Barcelona), **2012** Vicente del Bosque (Spain), **2013** Jupp Heynckes (Bayern Munich), **2014** Joachim Low (Germany), **2015** Luis Enrique (Barcelona)

PREMIER LEAGUE 2015–16

REVIEWS, APPEARANCES, SCORERS

(Figures in brackets denote appearances as substitute)

ARSENAL

Another Premier League season rich in promise got away from Arsene Wenger, who faced calls from some sections of the Emirates crowd to step down at the end of it. This time, they were riding high at the start of the New Year, overtaking Leicester and seemingly coping with the loss of Santi Cazorla and Alexis Sanchez. But a last-minute equaliser conceded to Liverpool at Anfield proved the start of a costly run of eight matches yielding only two victories and culminating in a home defeat by Swansea. By then, Arsenal trailed Leicester by six points, with Sanchez having taken time to regain his influence after returning from a hamstring injury. Tottenham had moved in as the main title challengers and when the Chilean eventually recaptured some of his earlier form it was too late. His team had also been knocked out of the Champions League – by Barcelona – at the last 16 stage for the sixth successive season, while a quarter-final home defeat by Watford meant there would be no third successive FA Cup triumph. A 4-0 league win over the same opponents three weeks later at least kept them on course for a 19th successive season in Europe's premier club competition. And the campaign ended on a satisfying note when a hat-trick by Olivier Giroud delivered a 4-0 victory over Aston Villa, one which enabled them to overtake faltering Spurs for the runners-up spot, the club's highest position since 2005.

Arteta M .... - (9)
Bellerin H 36
Campbell J 11 (8)
Cazorla S 15
Cech P 34
Chambers C 2 (10)
Coquelin F 21 (5)
Debuchy M 2
Elneny M 9 (2)
Flamini M 12 (4)
Gabriel 18 (3)
Gibbs K 3 (12)
Giroud O 26 (12)
Iwobi A 8 (5)
Koscielny L 33
Mertesacker P 24
Monreal N 36 (1)
Ospina D 4
Oxlade-Chamberlain A .. 9 (13)
Ozil M 35
Ramsey A 29 (2)
Sanchez A 28 (2)
Walcott T 15 (13)
Welbeck D 7 (4)
Wilshere J 1 (2)

League goals (65): Giroud 16, Sanchez 13, Ozil 6, Ramsey 5, Walcott 5, Koscielny 4, Welbeck 4, Campbell 3, Iwobi 2, Bellerin 1, Gabriel 1, Gibbs 1, Oxlade-Chamberlain 1, Opponents 3
FA Cup goals (10): Giroud 3, Walcott 2, Campbell 1, Chambers 1, Ramsey 1, Sanchez 1, Welbeck 1. **League Cup goals** (2): Flamini 2. **Community Shield goals** (1): Oxlade-Chamberlain 1
Champions League goals (13): Giroud 5, Sanchez 3, Ozil 2, Walcott 2, Elneny 1
Average home league attendance: 59,944. **Player of Year**: Mesut Ozil

ASTON VILLA

The writing was on the wall when they finished fourth from bottom in 2015, suffered an embarrassing 4-0 FA Cup Final defeat by Arsenal and lost Christian Benteke, Fabian Delph and Tom Cleverley during the summer. An outlay of £52.5m on new players offered some hope, but it quickly became apparent that many were ill equipped for the Premier League. Tim Sherwood admitted it would be a long, hard season – and so it proved. The manager paid the price after six successive defeats, dismissed eight months into the job with his team second from the foot of the table. They hit rock bottom soon afterwards and stayed there, with Sherwood's replacement, Lyon coach Remi Garde, unable to do anything about it. Villa's record run without a league win extended to 19 matches and the failure to sign anyone in the winter transfer window was followed by the worst home defeat for 81 years – 6-0 by Liverpool. When former Arsenal defender Garde left, supposedly by mutual agreement, after five months, his side were 12 points from safety with seven games remaining and angry supporters long having given up on the chance of survival. Confirmation of an end to 28 years of top-flight football came three matches later in a 1-0 defeat by Manchester United, ironically after one of their better performances under caretaker

Eric Black. By then, changes to the whole structure of the club were under way. And, at least, Villa avoided a club record 12th straight defeat with a goalless draw against Newcastle. Former Chelsea manager Roberto di Matteo was given the job of restoring lost pride.

Agbonlahor G 13 (2)
Amavi J 9 (1)
Ayew J..................... 27 (3)
Bacuna L................. 27 (4)
Bunn M 10
Gil C........................ 17 (6)
Cissokho A......................18
Clark C 16 (2)
Crespo J A 1
Gestede R............. 14 (18)
Grealish J................... 9 (7)
Green A...................... - (2)
Gueye I 35
Guzan B.........................28
Hepburn-Murphy R....... - (1)
Hutton A 26 (2)
Kozak L..................... 3 (1)
Lescott J 30
Lyden J 2 (2)
N'Zogbia C .... - (2)
Okore J 12
Richards M...............23 (1)
Richardson K.............8 (3)
Sanchez C...............16 (4)
Sinclair S 19 (8)
Toner K 3 (1)
Traore A ....- (10)
Veretout J................21 (4)
Westwood A.............31 (1)

League goals (27): Ayew 7, Gestede 5, Gil 2, Sinclair 2, Westwood 2, Agbonlahor 1, Bacuna 1, Clark 1, Grealish 1, Lescott 1, Richards 1, Opponents 3
FA Cup goals (3): Clark 1, Gueye 1, Richards 1. **League Cup goals** (7): Sinclair 4, Bennett J 1, Gestede 1, Traore 1,
Average home league attendance: 34,479. **Player of Year**: No award

BOURNEMOUTH

Eddie Howe's team upset all the odds to reach the Premier League – and they did it again to retain their status in the face of a nightmare run of injuries. With the season little more than a month old, Howe had lost four key players, three of them to knee ligament damage. Record-signing Tyrone Mings was ruled out for the rest of the campaign after just six minutes of his debut. Leading scorer Callum Wilson and winger Max Gradel were sidelined for six months. So, too, was captain Tommy Elphick with an ankle injury. Their loss was compounded by 5-1 defeats by Manchester City and Tottenham in successive weeks, followed by reversals against Southampton and Newcastle. But Glenn Murray's winner, 99 seconds after coming off the bench, delivered a victory at Stamford Bridge which the manager described as 'the biggest result in the club's history.' Bournemouth defeated Manchester United for another lift, while the January signing of Wolves striker Benik Afobe for a new record fee proved a significant investment. He scored goals immediately, one against Southampton in the first of three victories in March taking them clear of the bottom three with eight matches still to play. It was a massive achievement for a side containing six players from their League One days, even allowing for a poor finish which brought a single victory from those final fixtures.

Afobe B 12 (3)
Allsop R...................... - (1)
Arter H 21
Boruc A 32
Cook S...........................36
Daniels C 37
Distin S 9 (3)
Elphick T................ 11 (1)
Federici A.........................6
Francis S 38
Gosling D 28 (6)
Grabban L............... 4 (11)
Gradel M................. 11 (3)
Iturbe J M .... - (2)
Kermorgant Y.............. - (7)
King J 24 (7)
MacDonald S.............. - (3)
Mings T...................... - (1)
Murray G................. 6 (13)
O'Kane E................. 6 (10)
Pugh M 15 (11)
Rantie T.....................- (3)
Ritchie M.................33 (4)
Smith A 22 (9)
Stanislas J...............17 (4)
Surman A.......................38
Tomlin L....................3 (3)
Wilson C.....................9 (4)

League goals (45): King 6, Wilson 5, Afobe 4, Cook 4, Ritchie 4, Daniels 3, Gosling 3, Murray 3, Pugh 3, Stanislas 3, Smith 2, Arter 1, Elphick 1, Gradel 1, Opponents 2
FA Cup goals (4): King 1, Murray 1, Pugh 1 Tomlin 1. **League Cup goals** (6): Stanislas 2, Gosling 1 Kermorgant 1, MacDonald 1, Pugh 1
Average home league attendance: 11,189. **Player of Year**: Simon Francis

CHELSEA

Who would have thought it? The strongest of favourites for another title win mounted the poorest of all defences, which was virtually over with little more than a month of the season gone. They suffered three defeats – as many as in the whole of the previous campaign – fell 11 points adrift and never looked like getting back into contention. A 2-0 win over Arsenal proved a false dawn. Even Jose Mourinho wrote off their chances following a home defeat by Bournemouth, accusing the players of 'betrayal.' With his side a single point off the relegation zone, and Eden Hazard a pale shadow of the player who had previously influenced so much, Mourinho was sacked for the second time by Roman Abramovich, the club admitting he has 'lost' the dressing room. Guus Hiddink came back as interim manager to deliver a measure of respectability. He supervised an unbeaten league run of 14 matches to take Chelsea into the top half of the table, before a 3-0 home defeat by Manchester City proved a sharp reminder of how far they had fallen. There was no success either in the knock-out competitions – beaten by Paris Saint-Germain for the second successive year in the Champions League and defeated by Everton in the FA Cup. Job done, Hiddink made way at the end of the season for Italy coach Antonio Conte, who became the club's 12th manager in Abramovich's 13 years as owner.

Abraham T.................. - (2)
Azpilicueta C............ 36 (1)
Begovic A 15 (2)
Cahill G 21 (2)
Clarke-Salter J............ - (1)
Courtois T 23
Cuadrado J.................. - (1)
Diego Costa.............. 27 (1)
Fabregas C............... 33 (4)
Falcao R 1 (9)
Hazard E................. 25 (6)
Ivanovic B 33
Kenedy 4 (10)
Loftus-Cheek R........... 4 (9)
Matic N.................... 28 (5)
Miazga M 2
Mikel J O................. 19 (6)
Oscar..........................20 (7
Pato A........................ 1 (1)
Pedro....................... 24 (5)
Rahman B................11 (4)
Ramires 7 (5)
Remy L....................3 (10)
Terry J..........................24
Tomori R ....- (1)
Traore B 4 (6)
Willian 32 (3)
Zouma K 21 (2)

League goals (59): Diego Costa 12, Pedro 7, Fabregas 5, Willian 5, Hazard 4, Oscar 3, Azpilicueta 2, Cahill 2, Ivanovic 2, Matic 2, Ramires 2, Traore 2, Falcao 1, Kenedy 1, Loftus-Cheek 1, Pato 1, Remy 1, Terry 1, Zouma 1, Opponents 4

FA Cup goals (12): Oscar 3, Diego Costa 2, Hazard 2, Traore 2, Cahill 1, Loftus-Cheek 1, Willian 1. **League Cup goals** (5): Remy 2, Kenedy 1, Pedro 1, Ramires 1. **Community Shield goals**: None

Champions League goals (15): Willian 5, Diego Costa 2, Oscar 2, Cahill 1, Fabregas 1, Mikel 1, Zouma 1, Opponents 2

Average home league attendance: 41,500. **Player of Year**: Willian

CRYSTAL PALACE

With Yohan Cabaye one of the signings of the summer and Yannick Bolasie a force alongside him in midfield, Palace exceeded Premier League expectations throughout the first half of the season. They won at Chelsea and Liverpool, defeated Alan Pardew's former side Newcastle 5-1 and at the half-way stage were up to fifth. A £50m stake in the club, taken by American investors Josh Harris and David Blitzer, added to the sense of wellbeing. After that, it was a different story. Bolasie missed two months with a hip injury and took time to regain full power on his return. Cabaye's influence began to wane, while an acute shortage of goals, which the signing of Emmanuel Adebayor failed to solve, sent them sliding. Palace won just two more league games, against Norwich and Stoke, and while sufficient points had been accumulated to insure against being sucked into a relegation struggle, a 15th place finish proved disappointing. The saving grace was an impressive FA Cup run which took them past Southampton, Stoke, Tottenham, Reading and Watford on the way to the final. They led at Wembley through substitute Jason Puncheon, but conceded three minutes later and lost 2-1 after failing to punish ten-man Manchester United in extra-time.

Player	Apps
Adebayor E	7 (5)
Bamford P	- (6)
Boateng H	- (1)
Bolasie Y	23 (3)
Cabaye Y	32 (1)
Campbell F	4 (7)
Chamakh M	1 (9)
Dann S	35
Delaney D	32
Gayle D	8 (8)
Hangeland B	7
Hennessey W	29
Jedinak M	16 (11)
Kaikai S	- (1)
Kelly M	11 (2)
Ledley J	11 (8)
Lee Chung-Yong	4 (9)
Mariappa A	3
McArthur J	26 (2)
McCarthy A	7
Murray G	2
Mutch J	7 (13)
Souare P	34
Puncheon J	31
Sako B	11 (9)
Speroni J	2
Ward J	30
Wickham C	15 (6)
Williams J	- (1)
Zaha W	30 (4)

League goals (39): Bolasie 5, Cabaye 5, Dann 5, Wickham 5, Gayle 3, Delaney 2, McArthur 2, Puncheon 2, Sako 2, Ward 2, Zaha 2, Adebayor 1, Ledley 1, Lee Chung-Yong 1, Opponents 1
FA Cup goals (9): Zaha 2, Bolasie 1, Cabaye 1, Campbell 1, Kelly 1, Puncheon 1, Ward 1, Wickham 1. **League Cup goals** (9): Gayle 4, Campbell 1, Delaney 1, Lee Chung-Yong 1, Murray 1, Zaha 1
Average home league attendance: 24,825. **Player of Year**: Wilfried Zaha

EVERTON

Two semi-final places did nothing to camouflage a poor Premier League season. Neither did a sackful of goals for Romelu Lukaku. A strong-looking squad failed to match expectations, particularly at Goodison Park, where the points tally was the lowest since the introduction of three for a win in 1981. The club's new majority shareholder, Iranian billionaire Farhad Moshiri, was not impressed and the position of Roberto Martinez came under even greater scrutiny after a 4-0 beating by Liverpool in one of the most one-sided Merseyside derbies in living memory. Another heavy defeat, 3-0 by Sunderland, was followed by the manager's sacking after three years in charge. Only once had his side scored back-to-back wins – 3-0 against Newcastle and Stoke. Surrendering winning positions proved costly, a tendency underlined when West Ham transformed a two-goal deficit into a 3-2 victory in the final 12 minutes. Everton dropped into the bottom half of the table, but at least finished on a brighter note by beating Norwich 3-0, with academy graduates Kieran Dowell, Tom Davies, Matthew Pennington and Jonjoe Kenny offering a glimpse of the future and goalkeeper Tim Howard a reminder of the past on his 414th and final appearance. Lukaku became the club's first player since Gary Lineker in 1985-6 to score 25 goals in a season. Ironically, he had enough chances to have changed the course of the FA Cup semi-final against Manchester United, including one from the penalty spot which David de Gea saved in United's 2-1 win. Everton also reached the last four of the League Cup, losing 4-3 on aggregate to Manchester City. Southampton's Ronald Koeman succeeded Martinez.

Player	Apps
Baines L	16 (2)
Barkley R	36 (2)
Barry G	32 (1)
Besic M	7 (5)
Browning T	3 (2)
Cleverley T	17 (5)
Coleman S	27 (1)
Connolly C	- (1)
Davies T	1 (1)
Deulofeu G	16 (10)
Dowell K	1 (1)
Funes Mori R	24 (4)
Galloway B	14 (1)
Gibson D	2 (5)
Hibbert T	- (1)
Howard T	25
Jagielka P	21
Kenny J	- (1)
Kone A	16 (9)
Lennon A	17 (8)
Lukaku R	36 (1)
McCarthy J	29
Mirallas K	10 (13)
Naismith S	4 (6)
Niasse O	2 (3)
Osman L	2 (7)
Oviedo B	12 (2)
Pennington M	4
Pienaar S	- (4)
Robles J	13
Stones J	31 (2)

League goals (59): Lukaku 18, Barkley 8, Kone 5, Lennon 5, Funes Mori 4, Mirallas 4, Naismit 3, Baines 2, Cleverley 2, Deulofeu 2, McCarthy 2, Coleman 1, Opponents 3
FA Cup goals (10): Lukaku 3, Barkley 2, Kone 2, Lennon 1, Mirallas 1, Opponents 1. **Leagu Cup goals** (13): Lukaku 4, Barkley 2, Deulofeu 2, Funes Mori 1, Mirallas 1, Naismith 1, Osma 1, Opponents 1
Average home league attendance: 38,124. **Player of Year**: Gareth Barry

LEICESTER CITY

In the end, they didn't just deliver a magical, monumental, triumph; they became champions by a ten-point margin. While every other side failed to last the pace, Claudio Ranieri's players never weakened, or stopped believing. After each of their three defeats, two inflicted by Arsenal, one by Liverpool, they came back strongly. And by the time Tottenham's challenge fell apart in the final four matches, Leicester were out on their own. If there was a defining period during a remarkable season, it came in the first fortnight of February with a demanding three-match run which many felt might derail them. Instead, Jamie Vardy scored both goals in a 2-0 win in the return fixture with Liverpool, followed by Robert Huth's brace in a 3-1 victory over Manchester City at the Etihad. The return at the Emirates was settled by Danny Welbeck's 95th minute header on his first appearance of the campaign. But, if anything, Leicester's performance in that game strengthened the belief that nothing was going to stop them. From then on they were relentless, just as Chelsea were the previous season, with a string of single-goal successes. Vardy's two-match suspension proved no handicap as Swansea were beaten 4-0 and Manchester United matched at Old Trafford. The players gathered at the home of their leading scorer to see the title clinched as Tottenham were held by Chelsea. They celebrated on the pitch by beating Everton 3-1. Then, in the final game at Stamford Bridge with nothing at stake, came a timely reminder of the team's battling qualities with a late equaliser from Danny Drinkwater.

Albrighton M 34 (4)
Amartey D 1 (4)
Benalouane Y .... - (4)
De Laet R 7 (5)
Dodoo J .... - (1)
Drinkwater D 35
Dyer N .... - (12)
Fuchs C 30 (2)
Gray D 1 (11)
Huth R 35
Inler G 3 (2)
Kante N 33 (4)
King A 9 (16)
Kramaric A .... - (2)
Mahrez R 36 (1)
Morgan W 38
Okazaki S 28 (8)
Schlupp J 14 (10)
Schmeichel K 38
Simpson D 30
Ulloa L 7 (22)
Vardy J 36
Wasilewski M 3 (1)

League goals (68): Vardy 24, Mahrez 17, Ulloa 6, Okazaki 5, Huth 3, Albrighton 2, Drinkwater 2, King 2, Morgan 2, De Laet 1, Dyer 1, Kante 1, Schlupp 1, Opponents 1
FA Cup goals (2): Okazaki 1, Wasilewski 1. **League Cup goals** (7): Dodoo 4, King 1, Kramaric 1, Mahrez 1
Average home league attendance: 32,021. **Player of Year**: Riyad Mahrez

LIVERPOOL

Jurgen Klopp brought a new sense of excitement and optimism to Anfield after replacing Brendan Rodgers two months into the season. He went some way to meeting expectations by delivering domestic and European finals. Against that was a modest eighth place finish in the league, along with the acknowledgement that his squad needing boosting during the summer months. Liverpool looked like top-four contenders when winning 3-1 at Chelsea and 4-1 at Manchester City. There was also the 4-0 defeat of Everton in one of the most one-sided Merseyside derbies in living memory. That victory kept hopes alive until a 2-0 lead was surrendered to Newcastle, followed by a 3-1 defeat at Swansea, leaving them out of range. Overall, his side were prone to conceding goals from set pieces, lost too many points from leading positions and consequently lacked genuine consistency. Liverpool enjoyed some great nights at Anfield in the knock-out stages of the Europa League, notably against Manchester United and Klopp's former club, Borussia Dortmund. But defeat by Sevilla in the final underlined the need to strengthen. In the League Cup, an 83rd minute goal by Philippe Coutinho took the final into extra-time, after which Manchester City won it 3-1 on penalties.

Allen J 8 (11)
Benteke C 14 (15)
Bogdan A 2
Brannagan C 1 (2)
Canos S .... - (1)
Caulker S .... - (3)
Chirivella P 1
Clyne N 33
Coutinho P 24 (2)
Emre Can 28 (2)
Firmino R 24 (7)
Flanagan J 5
Gomez J 5
Henderson J 15 (2)
Ibe J 12 (15)

Ings D 3 (3)
Lallana A 23 (7)
Lovren D 22 (2)
Lucas Leiva 21 (6)
Mignolet S 34
Milner J 28
Moreno A 28 (4)
Ojo S 5 (3)
Origi D 7 (9)
Randall C 2 (1)
Rossiter J .... - (1)
Sakho M 21 (1)
Skrtel M 21 (1)
Smith B 3 (1)
Stewart K 6 (1)
Sturridge D 11 (3)
Teixeira J .... - (1)
Toure K 9 (5)
Ward D 2

League goals (63): Firmino 10, Benteke 9, Coutinho 8, Sturridge 8, Milner 5, Origi 5, Lallana 4, Allen 2, Henderson 2, Ings 2, Clyne 1, Emre Can 1, Ibe 1, Moreno 1, Sakho 1, Skrtel 1, Toure 1, Opponents 1

FA Cup goals (6): Allen 1, Coutinho 1, Ojo 1, Sinclair 1, Smith 1, Teixeira 1. **League Cup goals** (10): Origi 3, Ibe 2, Sturridge 2, Clyne 1, Coutinho 1, Ings 1

Europa League goals (19): Lallana 3, Sturridge 3, Coutinho 2, Milner 2, Origi 2, Benteke 1, Emre Can 1, Firmino 1, Ibe 1, Lovren 1, Sakho 1, Opponents 1

Average home league attendance: 43,910. **Player of Year**: Philippe Coutinho

MANCHESTER CITY

Manuel Pellegrini delivered the club's best performance in the Champions League and another League Cup in his final season at the Etihad. The manager came up well short in the Premier League, so overall it proved a mixed campaign. Pellegrini, however, earned plenty of praise for the dignified way he handled being told he would be replaced at the end of it by Pep Guardiola. After a flying start of five straight wins, his side were disrupted by captain Vincent Kompany's recurring calf problem, Kevin De Bruyne's ankle injury and the loss of Samir Nasri. There was also a significant lack of success against the other leading sides, as demonstrated by straight defeats by Leicester, Tottenham and Liverpool at a time when they held down second place. Those put City ten points adrift. Losing at home to Manchester United left a top-four place as the only remaining domestic target and they achieved it with a point at Swansea in the final fixture to deny their neighbours on goal difference. Pellegrini sacrificed the FA Cup in order to confirm continued progress in Europe against Dynamo Kiev and ahead of the Capital One Cup Final, which they won on penalties against Liverpool. De Bruyne returned to score the winner against Paris Saint-Germain to earn a semi-final place against Real Madrid, who went through with the only goal of the tie. Sergio Aguero reached 100 Premier League goals in 147 appearances for the club, having netted five against Newcastle and a hat-trick against Chelsea.

Aguero S 29 (1)
Bony W 13 (13)
Caballero W 3 (1)
Celina B .... - (1)
Clichy G 12 (2)
De Bruyne K 22 (3)
Delph F 8 (9)
Demichelis M 10 (10)
Fernandinho 31 (2)
Fernando 17 (7)
Garcia M .... - (1)
Hart J 35
Iheanacho K 7 (19)
Jesus Navas 24 (10)
Kolarov A 25 (4)
Kompany V 13 (1)
Mangala E 23
Nasri S 4 (8)
Otamendi N 30
Roberts P ....- (1)
Sagna B 27 (1)
Silva D 22 (2)
Sterling R 23 (8)
Toure Y 28 (4)
Zabaleta P 12 (1)

League goals (71): Aguero 24, Iheanacho 8, De Bruyne 7, Sterling 6, Toure 6, Bony 4, Kolarov 3, Delph 2, Fernandinho 2, Fernando 2, Kompany 2, Nasri 2, Silva 2, Otamendi 1

FA Cup goals (8): Iheanacho 4, Aguero 1, De Bruyne 1, Faupala 1, Sterling 1. **League Cup goals** (18): De Bruyne 5, Aguero 2, Bony 2, Fernandinho 2, Iheanacho 2, Garcia 1, Jesus Navas 1, Sterling 1, Toure 1, Opponents 1

Champions League goals (18): De Bruyne 3, Sterling 3, Aguero 2, Bony 2, Fernandinho 2, Silva 2, Demichelis 1, Toure 1, Opponents 2

Average home league attendance: 54,041. **Player of Year**: Kevin De Bruyne

MANCHESTER UNITED

What now for Manchester United under Jose Mourinho? A return to the stability and success delivered by Sir Alex Ferguson – or more of the uncertainty and indecision under David Moyes and Louis van Gaal? Whatever the outcome, life at Old Trafford will certainly be eventful, particularly with Pep Guardiola a few miles down the road at Manchester City. United had a single week on top of the table after five wins in the opening seven matches. They retained a place in the top four for the next three months, until a home defeat by Norwich followed the failure to progress from a modest Champions League group. After that, Van Gaal came under increasing pressure to retrieve the situation, in the face of a mounting injury list which, at one time or another, left 14 players on the treatment table. The failure to do so, despite the emergence of the exciting 18-year-old Marcus Rashford, was compounded by City denying them on goal difference. Also hard to swallow was a Europa League defeat by Liverpool. That left the FA Cup as the only target and here United delivered, courtesy of Jesse Lingard's eye-catching extra-time winner against Crystal Palace at Wembley. By then, however, the club had decided on a change of manager, although the circumstances of how it was handled – with reports of his sacking circulating just as Van Gaal was hoisting the trophy – left much to be desired.

Blind D..........................35
Borthwick-Jackson C... 6 (4)
Carrick M................ 22 (6)
Darmian M............... 24 (4)
De Gea D.......................34
Depay M................ 16 (13)
Fellaini M 12 (6)
Fosu-Mensah T........... 2 (6)
Hernandez J................- (1)
Herrera A............... 17 (10)
Januzaj A................... 2 (3)
Jones P...................... 6 (4)
Keane W .... - (1)
Lingard J................. 19 (6)
Love D .... - (1)
Martial A................. 29 (2)
Mata J 34 (4)
McNair P.................... 3 (5)
Pereira A..................... - (4)
Powell N .... - (1)
Rashford M.....................11
Rojo M..................... 15 (1)
Romero S 4
Rooney W.................27 (1)
Schneiderlin M 25 (4)
Schweinsteiger B 13 (5)
Shaw L............................ 5
Smalling C 35
Valencia A 8 (6)
Varela G 3 (1)
Weir J ....- (1)
Wilson J ....- (1)
Young A 11 (6)

League goals (49): Martial 11, Rooney 8, Mata 6, Rashford 5. Lingard 4, Herrera 3, Depay 2, Blind 1, Darmian 1, Fellaini 1, Januzaj 1, Schneiderlin 1, Schweinsteiger 1, Young 1, Opponents 3
FA Cup goals (14): Mata 3, Fellaini 2, Lingard 2, Martial 2, Rooney 2, Blind 1, Smalling 1, Rashford 1. **League Cup goals** (3): Martial 1, Rooney 1, Pereira 1
Champions League goals (14): Rooney 4, Depay 3, Martial 2, Fellaini 1, Herrera 1, Mata 1, Smalling 1, Opponents 1. **Europa League goals** (7): Depay 2, Rashford 2, Hererra 1, Martial 1, Opponents 1
Average home league attendance: 75,286. **Player of Year**: David de Gea

NEWCASTLE UNITED

Relegation was bad enough. What made it worse was Sunderland surviving – and their arch-rivals condemning them to the Championship by beating Everton in the penultimate fixture. Rafael Benitez, brought in when Steve McClaren was sacked, did his best to turn things round, but it was asking a lot to reverse the club's decline in ten matches. There were wins over Swansea and Crystal Palace, the latter delivered by Andros Townsend's 30-yard free-kick and Karl Darlow's penalty save from Yohan Cabaye. Newcastle also retrieved a two-goal deficit to draw 2-2 with Liverpool to end a run of nine successive away defeats. But missed chances proved costly in a goalless draw with relegated Aston Villa and over the course of the season they could not argue with finishing third from bottom. It was a poor return on the £52m spent in the summer transfer window and the £24m invested in Townsend and Jonjo Shelvey in January. The writing was soon on the wall – the club's worst start of three points from eight matches since 1898. One of the new players, Georginio Wijnaldum, scored four goals in a 6-2 win over Norwich, but his side's tendency to drop points from winning positions proved costly. McClaren was dismissed after Bournemouth won 3-1 at St James' Park and Benitez installed hours later on a three-year contract with a relegation get-out clause. Bizarrely, Newcastle closed by overwhelming Tottenham 5-1, prompting supporters to call on Benitez to stay and lead their bid for an immediate return to the Premier League, which he agreed to do.

Aarons R.................... 3 (7)
Anita V.................... 24 (4)
Perez A.................. 22 (12)
Cisse P.................... 14 (7)
Colback J................. 28 (1)
Coloccini F.....................26
Darlow K..........................9
De Jong S............... 3 (15)
Doumbia S................. - (3)
Dummett P....................23
Elliot R.........................21
Gouffran Y................. 2 (6)
Haidara M................. 6 (1)
Janmaat D.....................32
Krul T.............................8
Lascelles J.............. 10 (8)
Mbabu K................... 2 (1)
Mbemba C.....................33
Mitrovic A.............. 22 (12)
Obertan G.................. 3 (2)
Riviere E.................... 1 (2)
Saivet H.................... 2 (2)
Shelvey J.................11 (4)
Sissoko M.....................37
Sterry J......................- (1)
Taylor S......................9 (1)
Thauvin T................3 (10)
Tiote C....................16 (4)
Toney I........................- (2)
Townsend A.............12 (1)
Wijnaldum G............36 (2)

League goals (44): Wijnaldum 11, Mitrovic 9, Perez 6, Townsend 4, Cisse 3, Janmaat 2, Lascelles 2, Anita 1, Arrons 1, Colback 1, Coloccini 1, Dummett 1, Sissoko 1, Opponents 1
FA Cup goals: None. **League Cup goals** (4): Janmaat 1, De Jong 1, Thauvin 1, Williamson M 1
Average home league attendance: 49,754

NORWICH CITY

If ever a single 90 minutes defined a team's relegation season, it was the home defeat by Manchester United. Sufficient chances were created to have kept slim survival hopes alive. All were wasted and an equally familiar defensive error presented United with the only goal of the game. Manager Alex Neil admitted afterwards that all too often his side's efforts had been undermined by lapses of concentration. It was a fourth successive defeat at a crucial point of the campaign. Four days later they got it right, beating Watford 4-2. But the victory came too late, Sunderland's win over Everton condemning them to an immediate return to the Championship. Norwich had climbed out of the bottom three by beating West Bromwich Albion and Newcastle to open up a four-point cushion and suggest they might have turned the corner. The loss of Switzerland defender Timm Klose, one of six signings in the winter transfer window, was a blow. So too was the most significant of the four defeats, 3-0 at home to Sunderland, who delivered an object lesson in ruthless finishing. Previously, Norwich suggested better times lay ahead when winning at Old Trafford for the first time since 1989, then defeating Aston Villa and Southampton. They moved six points clear of the bottom three as a result, but a run of eight matches yielding a single point put them back in trouble.

Bamford P................ 2 (5)
Bassong S................ 30 (2)
Bennett R................ 20 (2)
Brady R.................. 34 (2)
Mbokani D............ 15 (14)
Dorrans G................ 14 (7)
Grabban L................. 3 (3)
Hoolahan W............ 25 (5)
Hooper G.................... - (2)
Howson J................ 33 (3)
Jarvis M.................. 13 (6)
Jerome C.............. 19 (15)
Johnson B................. 1 (3)
Klose T..........................10
Lafferty K.................... - (1)
Martin R.........................30
Mulumbu Y................ 5 (2)
Naismith S.............. 11 (2)
O'Neil G.................. 19 (8)
Odjidja-Ofoe V........... 3 (7)
Olsson M.................20 (4)
Pinto I.......................9 (1)
Redmond N............24 (11)
Rudd D.........................11
Ruddy J.........................27
Tettey A.........................23
Whittaker S.....................8
Wisdom A..................9 (1)

League goals (39): Mbokani 7, Redmond 6, Hoolahan 4, Brady 3, Howson 3, Jerome 3, Martin 3, Tettey 2, Bassong 1, Grabban 1, Jarvis 1, Klose 1, Naismith 1, Olsson 1, Whittaker 1, Opponents 1
FA Cup goals: None. **League Cup goals** (6): Bassong 1, Howson 1, Jarvis 1, Lafferty 1, Van Wolfswinkel 1, Opponents 1
Average home league attendance: 26,972. **Player of Year**: Jonny Howson

SOUTHAMPTON

Onwards and upwards went Southampton. Eighth in 2014 under Mauricio Pochettino, seventh a year later with Ronald Koeman at the helm and this time a Premier League best of sixth, with Koeman leading them nearer to a place among the division's elite. They did it by turning what looked like being a solid season's work into a record tally of 63 points with a storming finish. The final nine matches yielded seven wins, 23 goals and the chance to make a bigger impact in the Europa League, where defeat by the Danish club Midtjlland in the play-offs proved something of an anti-climax. Koeman lost two more senior players – Nathaniel Clyne and Morgan Schneiderlin – in the summer, having seen five leave St Mary's 12 months earlier. Southampton made a decent start, fell back after a single win in eight games – albeit 4-0 against Arsenal – then drew renewed impetus from the return of Fraser Forster from ten months out with a knee injury. The 6ft 7in goalkeeper kept a clean sheet for six successive matches, during which his side gathered 16 points, and went on to complete a club-record 708 minutes without conceding before he was beaten by Chelsea's Cesc Fabregas. Defeat at Bournemouth followed, then the goals started to flow. Sadio Mane netted a hat-trick against Manchester City, Steven Davis doubled his tally for the campaign with a brace against Tottenham and with Long, Pelle and Tadic all on the mark, Southampton flourished. They moved above West Ham in the final fixture by beating Crystal Palace 4-1, Mane scoring his eighth goal in eight games. But success again came at a price for the club, this time with Koeman leaving to take charge at Everton. All of which came at a cost – yet again. Koeman left for Everton, to be replaced by Frenchman Claude Puel, Mane moved to Liverpool and Victor Wanyama joined Tottenham.

Austin C 2 (5)
Bertrand R 32
Caulker S 1 (2)
Clasie J 20 (2)
Davis K 1
Davis S 31 (3)
Fonte J 37
Forster F 18
Gazzaniga P 2
Juanmi .... - (12)
Long S 23 (5)
Mane S 30 (7)
Martina C 11 (4)
Pelle G 23 (7)
Ramirez G .... - (3)
Reed H .... - (1)
Rodriguez J 3 (9)
Romeu O 17 (12)
Soares C 23 (1)
Stekelenburg M 17
Tadic D 27 (7)
Targett M 13 (1)
Wanyama V 29 (1)
Ward-Prowse J 14 (19)
Yoshida M 10 (10)
Van Dijk V 34

League goals (59): Mane 11, Pelle 11, Long 10, Tadic 7, Davis 5, Van Dijk 3, Fonte 2, Ward-Prowse 2, Austin 1, Bertrand 1, Martina 1, Romeu 1, Wanyama 1, Yoshida 1, Opponents 2
FA Cup goals (1): Romeu 1. **League Cup goals** (9): Mane 3, Long 2, Rodriguez 2, Pelle 1, Yoshida 1. **Europa League goals** (6): Pelle 2, Long 1, Mane 1, Rodriguez 1, Tadic 1
Average home league attendance: 30,751. **Player of Year**: Virgil van Dijk

STOKE CITY

Record signings in both transfer windows reflected the club's aim to build on a breakthrough into the Premier League's top ten in the two previous seasons. They paid £12m in the summer for Xherdan Shaqiri and £18.3m for another midfielder, Giannelli Imbula, in January. The investment looked as if it might be rewarded with a record high – and a place in Europe – when Stoke climbed to eighth going into April's fixtures. Instead, they lost England goalkeeper Jack Butland with a broken ankle, which also ruled him out of the European Championship finals, and lost a two-goal lead at home to Swansea, who came back to draw 2-2. Then, four goals were conceded to Liverpool, Tottenham and Manchester City in quick succession, pushing them down with little or no chance of regaining lost ground in the remaining matches. There was also a second serious injury, sustained by the influential Ibrahim Afellay, whose knee ligament damage could rule him out until Christmas. All round, it looked like a disappointing finish for a side who had overcome a poor start – three points from the opening six games – to build real momentum. But an 88th minute winner from Mame Biram Diouf brought victory over West Ham on the final day and a move above Chelsea into a third successive ninth place.

Adam C 12 (10)
Afellay I 24 (7)
Arnautovic M 33 (1)
Bardsley P 9 (2)
Biram Diouf M 12 (14)
Butland J 31
Cameron G 27 (3)
Crouch P 4 (7)
Given S 3
Haugaard J 4 (1)
Imbula G 14
Ireland S .... - (13)
Johnson G 25
Joselu 10 (12)
Krkic B 22 (5)

Muniesa M.............. 12 (3)	Shawcross R 20	Whelan G.......................37
Odemwingie P............. - (5)	Sidwell S .... - (1)	Wilson M 1 (3)
Pieters E........................35	Teixeira D..................... - (1)	Wollscheid P 30 (1)
Shaqiri X........................27	Walters J................. 18 (9)	Van Ginkel M............. 8 (9)

League goals (41): Arnautovic 11, Krkic 7, Biram Diouf 5, Walters 5, Joselu 4, Shaqiri 3, Afellay 2, Imbula 2, Adam 1, Opponents 1

FA Cup goals (2): Crouch 1, Walters 1. **League Cup goals** (6): Walters 2, Afellay 1, Arnautovic 1, Bardsley 1, Crouch 1,

Average home league attendance: 27,534. **Player of Year**: Jack Butland

SUNDERLAND

First it was Paolo Di Canio, then Gus Poyet and Dick Advocaat, this time Sam Allardyce. For the fourth successive season Sunderland won the battle to stay up, led to safety by their latest manager's shrewd work in the transfer market, Jermain Defoe's goals and a collective will to survive. When Allardyce took over after Advocaat's resignation two months into the season, he warned it would take time for his impact to be felt. His new side were second from bottom and were still there when the January window opened. In came German Jan Kirchhoff, French-born Ivorian Lamine Kone and Tunisian international Wahbi Khazri, at a cost of £15m, to stiffen the defence and add authority in the midfield. It was money well spent. After a 1-1 draw with Newcastle with two months of the campaign remaining, Allardyce predicted four wins were needed to survive. In fact, it was three, starting with a 'six-pointer' at Norwich. Then, in front of a packed Stadium of Light, came the victories which took them clear, sent Newcastle and Norwich down and maintained the manager's record of never have been relegated from the top division. Sunderland twice come from behind against Chelsea and scored the winner through Defoe for a 3-2 success. Their other saviour was goalkeeper Vito Mannone who, at 2-1 for Chelsea, made two crucial saves from Diego Costa. Four days later, Kone scored twice, his first goals for the club, in 3-0 win over Everton. By then, Defoe had 15 goals to his credit and Allardyce was admitting he 'dreaded to think' what would have happened without them.

Borini F.................. 22 (4)	Jones B.................. 23 (1)	O'Shea J 23 (5)
Brown W..........................6	Kaboul Y................ 22 (1)	Pantillimon C................17
Cattermole L........... 27 (4)	Khazri W................ 13 (1)	Pickford J........................2
Coates S................. 14 (2)	Kirchhoff J.............. 14 (1)	Robson T.........................1
Defoe J................... 28 (5)	Kone L...........................15	Rodwell J.................9 (13)
Fletcher S............... 11 (5)	Larsson S................ 6 (12)	Toivonen O 9 (3)
Gomez J 5 (1)	Lens J..................... 14 (6)	Watmore D 7 (16)
Graham D................. 4 (6)	M'Vila Y 36 (1)	Yedlin D...................21 (2)
Greenwood R....................1	Mannone V.....................19	Van Aanholt P...............33
Honeyman G .... - (1)	Matthews A .... - (1)	
Johnson A............... 11 (8)	N'Doye D................... 5 (6)	

League goals (48): Defoe 15, Borini 5, Fletcher 4, Van Aanholt 4, Lens 3, Watmore 3, Johnson 2, Khazri 2, Kone 2, Jones 1, M'Vila 1, N'Doye 1, Rodwell 1, Opponents 4

FA Cup goals (1): Lens 1. **League Cup goals** (7): Defoe 3, Rodwell 2, Toivonen 1, Watmore 1

Average home league attendance: 43,071. **Player of Year**: Jermain Defoe

SWANSEA CITY

The Italian manager, the Icelandic midfielder and the Welsh club stalwart joined forces to remove the threat of relegation. They came together after Garry Monk was sacked five months into a three-year contract, awarded for achieving Swansea's highest Premier League position of eighth in 2015. His side had stumbled after a bright start, with a single win in 11 matches approaching the half-way point of the season. Long-serving coach and former Wales international Alan Curtis was initially given the job until the end of the season. Then, in a change of heart, the club brought in former Udinese coach Francesco Guidolin who, with

Curtis alongside him, turned the tide, starting with the club's first league win over Everton at Goodison Park. Another important 2-1 away victory, this time against Arsenal, was followed three days later by a single-goal success against Norwich – results which gave Swansea breathing space. When Gylfi Sigurdsson scored his ninth goal in 14 matches for another 1-0 win over Chelsea, it took his side to the notional safety mark of 40 points with five matches still to play. The manner of a 4-0 defeat at Leicester led to speculation about whether Guidolin would stay beyond the end of his short-term contract. But seven goals against Liverpool and West Ham convinced the club to give him a new two-year deal.

Amat J........................ 5 (3)	Fabianksi L.....................37	Naughton K.............19 (8)
Ayew A 34	Fer L.......................... 9 (2)	Nordfeldt K 1
Barrow M................. 6 (16)	Fernandez F 32	Paloschi A..................7 (3)
Bartley K 3 (2)	Fulton J .... - (2)	Rangel A 20 (3)
Britton L.................. 19 (6)	Gomis B................ 18 (15)	Routledge W.............22 (6)
Cork J...................... 28 (7)	Grimes M 1	Shelvey J..................14 (2)
Dyer N........................ - (1)	Ki Sung-Yueng.......... 21 (7)	Sigurdson G.............32 (4)
Eder........................ 2 (11)	Kingsley S 4	Taylor N 33 (1)
Emnes M 1 (1)	Montero J................ 14 (9)	Williams A......................36

League goals (42): Ayew 12, Sigurdsson 11, Gomis 6, Ki Sung-Yueng 2, Paloschi 2, Routledge 2, Williams 2, Barrow 1, Cork 1, Fernandez 1, Shelvey 1, Opponents 1
FA Cup goals (2): Gomis 1, Montero 1. **League Cup goals** (3): Dyer 1, Emnes 1, Grimes 1
Average home league attendance: 20,711. **Player of Year**: Gylfi Sigurdsson

TOTTENHAM HOTSPUR

Tottenham finally blossomed as a Premier League power after years of knocking on the door. It wasn't enough to match Leicester's extraordinary run to the title, or hold on to the runners-up spot in a disappointing finish to the season. But the division's youngest squad, under Mauricio Pochettino, gave every impression of being here to stay and of developing further in the new campaign. They started slowly, built momentum as the goals started flowing again for Harry Kane and broke into the top four in mid-December. Pochettino sacrificed their chances of Europa League success by resting key players for the last 16 tie against Borussia Dortmund and his side responded by keeping the pressure on Leicester with seven goals in successive matches against Manchester United and Stoke. But with no margin for error, they faltered at home to West Bromwich Albion, as well as losing the influential Dele Alli, banned for punching Claudio Yacob. Then, a two-goal lead was surrendered to Chelsea, who came back for a point in a stormy encounter at Stamford Bridge in which nine Spurs players were booked. After that, they had nothing left, losing to Southampton and humbled 5-1 at Newcastle. Pochettino publicly apologised for the manner of that defeat, which enabled Arsenal to overtake them for second place by winning their final match. Some consolation came with Kane's 25 goals earning him the Golden Boot, while Pochettino pledged his future to the club by agreeing a two-year extension to his contract, taking it through to 2021.

Alderweireld T................38	Eriksen C 33 (2)	Rose D............................ 24
Alli D....................... 28 (5)	Kane H 38	Son Heung-Min.......13 (15)
Bentaleb N 2 (3)	Lamela E................. 28 (6)	Townsend A ....- (3)
Carroll T 4 (15)	Lloris H...........................37	Trippier K 5 (1)
Chadli N 10 (19)	Mason R.................. 8 (14)	Vertonghen J.................. 29
Davies B 14 (3)	N'Jie C......................... - (8)	Vorm M 1
Dembele M 27 (2)	Onomah J..................... - (8)	Walker K 33
Dier E.............................37	Pritchard A................. - (1)	Wimmer K.................9 (1)

League goals (69): Kane 25, Alli 10, Eriksen 6, Lamela 5, Alderweireld 4, Son Heung-Min 4, Chadli 3, Dembele 3, Dier 3, Carroll 1, Mason 1, Rose 1, Trippier 1, Walker 1, Opponents 1
FA Cup goals (8): Chadli 3, Carroll 1, Dier 1, Eriksen 1, Kane 1, Son Heung-Min 1. **League Cup goals** (1): Opponents 1

Europa League goals (17): Lamela 6, Son Heung-Min 3, Kane 2, Carroll 1, Chadli 1, Dembele 1, Eriksen 1, Mason 1, Opponents 1
Average home league attendance: 35,776. **Player of Year**: Toby Alderweireld

WATFORD

Skipper Troy Deeney described the decision as 'crazy.' West Ham manager Slaven Bilic called it 'sick.' Strong words, but they echoed the depth of feeling in many quarters at the sacking of Quique Sanchez Flores after leading his side to safety with a month of the season remaining – and reaching the semi-finals of the FA Cup. Outside of Vicarage Road, Watford were most people's favourites to go straight back down. At best, they faced having to fight every inch of the way for survival. Instead, enough points were harvested in the first half of the campaign to compensate for a difficult time from the New Year onwards. Indeed, with Deeney and Odion Ighalo scoring almost as freely as they did in the Championship, their side rose as high as seventh. Ighalo had 13 to his name, made it 14 in late Januaery, but did not add to that tally until the penultimate match against Norwich. Deeney fared better, with a brace against both Crystal Palace and Aston Villa to keep the points total moving. Watford reached the 40-point 'safety' mark courtesy of Ben Watson's match-winner, and two penalty saves by Heurelho Gomes from Saido Berahino, against West Bromwich Albion. A week later they were beaten 2-1 by Palace at Wembley, having reached the last four of the Cup by defeating Arsenal by the same scoreline at the Emirates.

Abdi A	25 (7)	Cathcart C	34 (1)	Layun M	2 (1)
Ake N	20 (4)	Deeney T	36 (2)	Nyom A-R	29 (3)
Amrabat N	4 (8)	Diamanti A	- (3)	Oulare O	- (2)
Anya I	17 (11)	Gomes H	38	Paredes J C	7 (10)
Arlauskis G	- (1)	Guedioura A	3 (15)	Prodl S	19 (2)
Behrami V	14 (7)	Holebas J	11	Suarez M	8 (7)
Berghuis S	- (9)	Ibarbo V	- (4)	Watson B	31 (4)
Britos M	24	Ighalo O	36 (1)		
Capoue E	33	Jurado J M	27		

League goals (40): Ighalo 15, Deeney 13, Abdi 2, Prodl 2, Watson 2, Ake 1, Cathcart 1, Layun 1, Opponents 3
FA Cup goals (6): Deeney 2, Ighalo 2, Gudioura 1, Opponents 1. **League Cup goals**: None
Average home league attendance: 20,594. **Player of Year**: Heurelho Gomes

WEST BROMWICH ALBION

Tony Pulis maintained his record of never having been relegated as a manager as Saido Berahino's return to the starting line-up helped Albion ease their way to safety. The England Under-21 striker was in dispute with the club for much of the season after having a summer transfer deadline-day move to Tottenham blocked. He was confined to a substitute's role before settling his differences and partnering record-signing Salomon Rondon for a crucial four-match run which yielded ten points. Rondon scored the winner against Everton, delivered Albion's first league victory over Manchester United at the Hawthorns since 1984 and was on the mark again in a 2-2 draw with Leicester. Berahino netted their third goal against Crystal Palace and Pulis felt that had he been able to pair them more regularly, the safety mark would have been achieved much sooner. Albion reached 40 points in a goalless draw at Sunderland and a better finish would have had them pushing towards mid-table. But they failed to win any of the final nine matches, one of them a 1-0 defeat by Watford in which Berahino had two penalties saved by Heurelho Gomes. There was a silver lining in the rich promise shown by 17-year-old forward Jonathan Leko, the club's Young Player of the Season, who became the first born in 1999 to start a Premier League game.

Anichebe V	3 (7)	Chester J	9 (4)	Field S	- (1)
Berahino S	17 (14)	Dawson C	38	Fletcher D	38
Brunt C	20 (2)	Evans J	30	Foster B	15

Gamboa C - (1)
Gardner C 20 (14)
Gnabry S - (1)
Lambert R 5 (14)
Leko J 3 (2)
Lescott J 2
McAuley G 34
McClean J 28 (7)
McManaman C 2 (10)
Morrison J 17 (1)
Myhill B 23
Olsoon J 25 (3)
Pocognoli S - (1)
Pritchard A - (2)
Roberts T - (1)
Rondon S 30 (4)
Sandro 5 (7)
Sessegnon S 21 (4)
Yacob C 33 (1)

League goals (34): Rondon 9, Berahino 4, Dawson 4, Gardner 3, Morrison 3, McClean 2, Sessegnon 2, Evans 1, Fletcher 1, Lambert 1, McAuley 1, Olsson 1, Opponents 2
FA Cup goals (7): Berahino 3, Fletcher 2, Morrison 1, Rondon 1. **League Cup goals**: None
Average home league attendance: 24,631. **Player of Year**: Jonny Evans

WEST HAM UNITED

It was somewhat ironic that West Ham should set the pace for their final season at Upton Park with eye-catching away victories over Arsenal (2-0), Liverpool (3-0) and Manchester City (2-1); even more so because in between there were home defeats by Leicester and Bournemouth. Nevertheless, 20 points from the opening 10 fixtures represented the club's best start to a Premier League campaign and put them on the way to a record points total. Slaven Bilic had to contend with a succession of injuries to key players, including the influential Dimitri Payet, which contributed to a run of seven games without a victory, accompanied by a drop into mid-table. It proved the only prolonged lean spell. His side restored momentum, helped by another tremendous performance on their travels – a 3-2 success at Everton after trailing 2-0 with 12 minutes remaining. Payet got the winner in the last minute, decorated his displays in midfield with some stunning free-kicks and was shortlisted for the PFA's Player of the Year award. There was disappointment with a 2-1 defeat by Manchester United in an FA Cup sixth round replay. And the end to 112 years at the Boleyn Ground, in a rearranged league fixture, was marred when United's team bus was attacked by hooligans, causing the kick-off to be delayed by 45 minutes. But a thrilling 3-2 win pushed West Ham towards 62 points, together with Europa League football for their new home at the Olympic Stadium.

Adrian 32
Antonio M 23 (3)
Byram S 2 (2)
Carroll A 13 (14)
Collins J 16 (3)
Cresswell A 37
Cullen J - (1)
Emenike E 5 (8)
Jarvis M - (3)
Jelavic N 1 (12)
Jenkinson C 13 (7)
Kouyate C 34
Lanzini M 23 (3)
Maiga M - (3)
Moses V 13 (8)
Noble M 37
Nolan K 1 (1)
Obiang P 11 (13)
Ogbonna A 27 (1)
Oxford R 3 (4)
Payet D 29 (1)
Randolph D 6
Reid W 24
Sakho D 18 (3)
Song A 8 (4)
Tomkins J 23 (2)
Valencia E 10 (9)
Zarate M 9 (6)

League goals (65): Carroll 9, Payet 9, Antonio 8, Noble 7, Lanzini 6, Kouyate 5, Sakho 5, Valencia 4, Zarate 3, Cresswell 2, Jenkinson 2, Jelavic 1, Maiga 1, Moses 1, Reid 1, Opponents 1
FA Cup goals (10): Payet 3, Emenike 2, Antonio 1, Jelavic 1, Moses 1, Ogbonna 1, Tomkins 1.
League Cup goals (1): Zarate.
Europa League goals (8): Sakho 2, Tomkins 2, Lanzini 1, Lee E 1, Valencia 1, Zarate 1
Average home league attendance: 34,910. **Player of Year**: Dmitri Payet

CHAMPIONSHIP

BIRMINGHAM CITY

A see-saw season ended with Gary Rowett's side some way short of the play-offs. They were up to second after 12 games, slipped back with a single win in the next nine, then surged again in the New Year. Successive 3-0 victories over Derby and Ipswich put them within goal difference of sixth-place Sheffield Wednesday and gave every indication of more to come. Instead, Birmingham were unable to make the breakthrough, largely as a result of a string of home defeats against tough opposition. After losing to Wednesday and Brighton, they regained a glimmer of hope by beating Reading. But 2-1 reversals against Leeds and Burnley in the space of five days meant another season of Championship football. That win proved the only one in the final 12 matches, resulting in a repeat of the tenth-place finish of 2015. One of their better performances at St Andrew's, in the final fixture, tested promotion-chasing Middlesbrough to the limit, with Stephen Gleeson firing a belated contender for goal of the season and David Davis almost matching him for a 2-2 draw in front of the campaign's biggest crowd of 21,380.

Adams C.................... 1 (1)
Brock-Madsen N......... 3 (3)
Brown R .... - (1)
Buckley W.................. 5 (5)
Caddis P.................. 37 (2)
Cotterill D 24 (5)
Davis D.................. 23 (12)
Donaldson C............ 38 (2)
Eardley N.........................5
Fabbrini D.................. 7 (7)
Gleeson S................ 42 (2)
Gray D 22 (2)
Grounds J.......................45
Halford G .... - (3)
Kieftenbeld M........... 41 (1)
Kuszczak T.....................41
Lafferty K.................. 4 (2)
Legzdins A 5
Lowry S...........................1
Maghoma J............ 25 (15)
Morrison M......................46
Robinson P...............20 (5)
Shinnie A...................5 (9)
Shotton R..........................9
Solomon-Otabor-V 2 (20)
Spector J..................22 (3)
Toral J-M..................28 (8)
Vaughan J 5 (10)

League goals (53): Donaldson 11, Toral 8, Gleeson 5, Maghoma 5, Caddis 4, Cotterill 4, Kieftenbeld 3, Morrison 3, Robinson 3, Buckley 1, Davis 1, Gray 1, Grounds 1, Lafferty 1, Shotton 1, Solomon-Otabor 1

FA Cup goals (1): Morrison 1. **League Cup goals** (4): Thomas 2, Maghoma 1, Shinnie 1

Average home league attendance: 17,603. **Player of Year**: Jon Toral

BLACKBURN ROVERS

The season never got out of second gear for Blackburn, who started poorly, gained no impetus from a change of manager and spent little more than a week in the top half of the table. They were second from bottom after failing to win any of the opening seven fixtures. A flurry of goals from Jordan Rhodes finally broke the ice, but there was no sustained improvement and Gary Bowyer became the season's eighth managerial casualty in the Championship, three months into the campaign. He was replaced by former Aston Villa manager Paul Lambert, who started with a derby win over Preston, followed by victories over Bristol City and Rotherham which took Rovers beyond mid-table for the first time. Again they slipped back and Lambert lost Rhodes to Middlesbrough in the winter transfer window. There was some satisfaction in beating his leading scorer's new team, with on-loan Danny Graham on the mark, That win helped avoid the threat of being sucked into a relegation struggle and Rovers finished 15th after closing with maximum points gained against Rotherham and Reading. Lambert then activated a release clause in his contract and left the club. He was replaced by former Bolton and Burnley manager Owen Coyle.

Akpan H 29 (6)
Barrow M 1 (3)
Bennett E 16 (5)
Brown C.................. 4 (13)
Conway C................. 29 (6)
Delfouneso N 7 (8)
Duffy S.........................41
Evans C 26 (4)
Gomez J 17 (2)
Graham D 18
Grimes M.................. 9 (4)
Guthrie D................ 10 (6)
Hanley G........................44
Henley A................. 20 (4)
Henry D...................... - (1)
Jackson S 3 (14)
Kilgallon M 7 (3)
Koita B-F 8 (6)

Lawrence T 14 (7)
Lenihan D 18 (5)
Lowe J 9 (1)
Mahoney C 2
Marshall B 44
O'Sullivan J .... - (2)
Olsson M 19 (1)
Raya D 5
Rhodes J 25
Spurr T 20 (3)
Steele J 41
Taylor C 6 (6)
Ward E 6 (1)
Watt T 6 (3)
Williamson L 2 (8)

League goals (46): Rhodes 10, Graham 7, Duffy 4, Akpan 3, Conway 3, Gomez 3, Bennett 2, Hanley 2, Jackson 2, Lawrence 2, Marshall 2, Delfouneso 1, Evans 1, Ward 1, Watt 1, Opponents 2
FA Cup goals (6): Marshall 4, Rhodes 1, Watt 1. **League Cup goals** (1): Delfouneso 1
Average home league attendance: 14,131. **Player of Year**: Grant Hanley

BOLTON WANDERERS

Bolton, the epitome of a club in crisis, continued their fall from grace and will play in the third tier of English football for the first time since 1993. From the first month of the season, when the opening six league and cup games yielded a single goal, the team looked relegation candidates. What few expected, however, was the extent of their failings. After a first victory, over Wolves, they went 17 matches without another and were seven points from safety. The players were not paid for November and the club had a transfer ban imposed for breaching Financial Fair Platy rules. There were brief signs of life with seven points gained against MK Dons, Wolves and Rotherham. And Bolton's future was assured when a consortium headed by former record-signing Dean Holdsworth, took over from owner Eddie Davies, who agreed to write off most of the £185m owed to him. But with no significant improvement on the pitch, manager Neil Lennon departed by mutual agreement. Caretaker Jimmy Phillips started with a 6-0 defeat at Bristol City and three matches later a 4-1 defeat at Derby brought the inevitable, with five games still remaining. Bolton finished bottom, 19 points adrift. Bradford's Phil Parkinson came in as the new manager.

Ameobi S 6 (2)
Amos B 40
Clayton M 5 (3)
Clough Z 25 (3)
Danns N 21 (11)
Davies M 34 (2)
Derik 22 (1)
Dervite D 21 (1)
Dobbie S 3 (21)
Feeney L 36 (1)
Finney A 1 (1)
Garrett T 2 (1)
Gouano P-D 19
Heskey E 14 (15)
Holding R 26
Jose Casado 9
Madine G 22 (10)
Maher N 5
Moxey D 33
Newell G .... - (2)
Pisano F 2 (1)
Pratley D 36
Rachubka P 6 (1)
Samizadeh A .... - (1)
Spearing J 18 (4)
Threlkeld O 3
Trotter L 8 (5)
Twardzik F ....- (2)
Vela J 30 (1)
Walker T 3 (4)
Wellington Silva 14 (8)
Wheater D 26 (2)
Wilson L 11 (1)
Woolery K 5 (12)

League goals (41): Clough 7, Feeney 5, Madine 5, Dobbie 4, Ameobi 2, Danns 2, Heskey 2, Spearing 2, Vela 2, Wellington Silva 2, Woolery 2, Dervite 1, Holding 1, Pratley 1, Trotter 1, Wheater 1, Wilson 1
FA Cup goals (5): Pratley 3, Madine 1, Moxey 1. **League Cup goals**: None
Average home league attendance: 15,056. **Player of Year**: Rob Holding

BRENTFORD

Early problems following the departure of Mark Warburton, gave way to a more settled season which ended in rousing style. While Warburton set out to take Rangers back to the Scottish Premiership after being shown the door at Griffin Park, despite reaching the 2015 play-offs, his replacement Marinus Dijkhuizen struggled. The Dutch manager lost leading scorer Andre Gray to Burnley, saw record-signing Andreas Bjelland ruled out for the season with a knee injury sustained on his debut and had Josh McEachran and Spanish midfielder Jota also sidelined. He was sacked after two wins in his nine matches in charge, making way for former Everton midfielder Lee Carsley, who won October's Manager of the Month award for four wins out of five after an appointment supposedly until the end of the season. Instead, Walsall's Dean Smith, longest-serving manager in League One, came in on a permanent deal, which itself came into question when Brentford slipped to the fringes of the relegation zone after seven defeats in eight games. But they responded with nine goals against Nottingham Forest, Bolton and Ipswich – five of them from Danish international Lasse Vibe – to go clear. Scott Hogan, back after two cruciate knee ligament injuries, also enjoyed himself, netting seven times as Brentford won seven of their final nine games, accumulating 24 goals to finish joint top scorers in the division.

Barbet Y........................18
Bidwell J........................45
Button D.......................46
Canos S................. 18 (20)
Clarke J..................... 4 (7)
Colin M.................... 20 (1)
Dean H..........................42
Diagouraga T............ 26 (1)
Djuricin M................ 17 (5)
Field T.............................1
Gogia A...................... 5 (8)
Gray A........................ 1 (1)
Hofmann P.............. 5 (16)
Hogan S..................... 2 (5)
Jota 1 (4)
Judge A..........................38
Kerschbaumer K..... 18 (12)
MacLeod L................. - (1)
McCormack A........... 25 (2)
McEachran J............ 10 (4)
O'Connell J................ 9 (7)
Rodriguez L.....................2
Saunders S............ 12 (13)
Swift J...................... 23 (4)
Tarkowski J....................23
Udumaga J.................- (3)
Vibe L..................... 29 (12)
Woods R.................. 38 (3)
Yennaris N................ 28 (3)

League goals (72): Judge 14, Vibe 14, Canos 7, Hogan 7, Swift 6, Djuricin 4, Hofmann 4, Bidwell 3, Saunders 3, Gray 2, Woods 2, Yennaris 2, Barbet 1, O'Connell 1, Swift 1, Tarkowski 1
FA Cup goals: None. **League Cup goals**: None
Average home league attendance: 10,310. **Player of Year**: Alan Judge

BRIGHTON AND HOVE ALBION

Brighton flourished, faded, then found their touch again to reach the play-offs for the third time in four years. But once again they fell at the semi-final hurdle, beaten by Sheffield Wednesday who had finished 15 points behind them. Chris Hughton's side went down 2-0 in the first leg at Hillsborough after losing four players to injuries – Tomer Hemed, Connor Goldson, Steve Sidwell and Anthony Knockaert. Leading scorer Hemed and Goldson were ruled out of the return leg in which Lewis Dunk cut the deficit and Knockaert hit a post before Wednesday replied for a 1-1 draw. It was the same scoreline Brighton had recorded in the final match of the regular season at Middlesbrough, where a win would have meant automatic promotion alongside Burnley. There was some consolation for Hughton with the Championship Manager of the Year award. He also received a new four-year contract for his season's work, which started with a club-record run of 22 undefeated matches before a 3-0 home defeat by Middlesbrough. That was the first of five goalless matches which pushed Brighton down to sixth. But they restored momentum, ran neck-and-neck with their rivals for the top two places and finished as joint highest scorers on 72 goals. There were just five defeats – the fewest number by any team not to win go up from the division.

Baldock S................ 25 (3)
Bong G.................... 13 (3)
Bruno............................46
Calderon I................ 10 (7)
Chicksen A.................. - (1)
Crofts A................... 5 (12)
Dunk L.................... 37 (1)
Forster-Caskey J.......... - (2)
Goldson C................ 22 (2)
Greer G..........................20
Hemed T.................. 40 (4)
Holla D....................... - (1)
Hunemeier U............ 13 (2)
Ince R...................... 1 (11)
Kayal B..........................43
Knockaert A............. 18 (1)
LuaLua K.................. 9 (9)
Manu E....................... - (8)
March S................... 13 (3)
Murphy J.................. 31 (6)
O'Grady C.................. - (3)
Ridgewell L......................5
Rosenior L............... 27 (4)
Sidwell S................. 4 (12)
Skalak J..................... 8 (4)
Stephens D....................45
Stockdale D....................46
Wilson J................. 11 (14)
Zamora R............... 10 (16)
Van La Parra R............ 4 (2)

Play-offs – appearances: Baldock 2, Bong 2, Bruno 2, Greer 2, Kayal 2, Knockaert 2, Sidwell 2, Skalak 2, Stockdale 2, Wilson 1 (1), Dunk 1, Goldson 1, Hemed 1, Rosenior – (2), LuaLua – (1), Towell – (1)
League goals (72): Hemed 17, Zamora 7, Stephens 7, Murphy 6, Knockaert 5, Wilson 5, Baldock 4, Dunk 3, Lua Lua 3, March 3, Goldson 2, Kayal 2, Skalak 2, Van La Parra 2, Bruno 1, Sidwell

1, Opponents 2. **Play-offs – goals**: Dunk 1
FA Cup goals: None. **League Cup goals** (2): Forster-Caskey 1, LuaLua 1
Average home league attendance: 25,583. **Player of Year**: Beram Kayal

BRISTOL CITY

Lee Johnson led City away from the threat of an immediate return to League One after renewing the family ties with Ashton Gate. He left a developing promotion challenge at Barnsley to replace Steve Cotterill, sacked nine months after taking the club up – and winning the Johnstone's Paint Trophy. City had slipped to third from bottom after a single win in 11 matches. Johnson, who spent five years as a City player and whose father Gary had five years as manager, watched from the stands as his new team won 1-0 away to fellow-strugglers Charlton to move out of the relegation zone. His first game in charge was a 2-1 victory over Ipswich, delivered with two identical headed goals from corners by central defender Aden Flint, whose 14 goals had helped secure promotion. Further wins over MK Dons and Nottingham Forest confirmed their improvement, while a 6-0 win over Bolton left them six points clear. City then overcame promotion-contenders Sheffield Wednesday 4-1 to effectively secure another season of Championship football. Another four came in the final home fixture against Huddersfield, with two for Jonathan Kodija taking him to 19 for the season.

Agard K 7 (18)
Ayling L 29 (4)
Baker N 36
Bennett E 15
Bryan J 34 (5)
Burns W 2 (12)
Cox S .... - (4)
Dowling G .... - (2)
Fielding F 21
Flint A...........................44
Fredericks R.............. 3 (1)
Freeman L............... 36 (5)
Gladwin B 1
Golbourne S 16
Hamer B 4
Kodija J 42 (3)
Little M................. 10 (13)
Matthews A 9
Moore L 5 (5)
O'Donnell R.....................21
Odemwingie P............ 3 (4)
Pack M 45
Pearce A 3 (4)
Reid B 16 (12)
Robinson C.................1 (5)
Smith K 36
Tomlin L........................18
Vyner Z 2 (2)
Wagstaff S.................1 (8)
Wilbraham A...........25 (18)
Williams D................21 (3)

League goals (54): Kodija 19, Wilbraham 8, Flint 6, Tomlin 6, Agard 2, Bryan 2, Odemwingie 2, Reid 2, Baker 1, Burns 1, Freeman 1, Pack 1, Wagstaff 1, Williams 1, Opponents 1
FA Cup goals (2): Agard 1, Kodja 1. **League Cup goals** (1): Robinson 1
Average home league attendance: 15,292. **Player of Year**: Aden Flint

BURNLEY

Winning promotion once from the ultra-competitive Championship is tough enough. Repeating that success after the bitter disappointment of relegation from the Premier League represented a huge achievement for Sean Dyche and his side. A 22nd successive unbeaten match – 1-0 against Queens Park Rangers courtesy of a goal by Sam Vokes – took them beyond the reach of both Middlesbrough and Brighton. A 23rd by a 3-0 margin in the final fixture at Charlton delivered the title. Burnley did it with the majority of the squad that went down in 2015. Dyche lost his leading scorer Danny Ings, but in club-record signing Andre Gray had the perfect replacement, while Joey Barton came in to prove an influential midfield presence. At the mid-way point of the season they were nine points adrift of top spot after losing 3-0 to Hull on Boxing Day. A 5-0 win over MK Dons, the club's biggest away from home since 1947, was followed by a 4-1 success over much-fancied Derby. Now in full flow, Burnley went top with six successive victories. The undefeated run was preserved by Michael Keane's stoppage-time equaliser against Middlesbrough and his team continued to hold their nerve in the tense run-in. Individual recognition followed. Gray won the division's Player of the Year award and was joined in the PFA Team of the Year by Keane, Barton and goalkeeper Tom Heaton.

Arfield S 46
Barnes A.................... 1 (7)
Barton J.................. 37 (1)
Boyd G 42 (2)
Darikwa T 21
Duff M..................... 23 (1)

Dyer L .... - (3)
Gray A 41
Heaton T........................46
Hennings R............. 3 (23)
Jones D 39 (2)
Jutkiewicz L............... 3 (2)
Keane M........................44
Kightly M................ 12 (6)
Long C....................... 1 (9)
Lowton M................ 25 (2)
Marney D.................. 7 (5)
Mee B 46
Sordell M.................... - (3)
Tarkowski J 2 (2)
Taylor M.................. 1 (26)
Ulvestad F 1 (4)
Vokes S 39 (4)
Vossen J 3 (1)
Ward S 23 (1)

League goals (72): Gray 23, Vokes 15, Arfield 8, Boyd 5, Keane 5, Taylor 4, Barton 3, Mee 2, Darikwa 1, Hennings 1, Jones 1, Lowton 1, Ward 1, Opponents 2
FA Cup goals (3): Hennings 1, Vokes 1, Ward 1. **League Cup goals**: None
Average home league attendance: 16,709. **Player of Year**: Joey Barton

CARDIFF CITY

Cardiff's promotion push survived two setbacks in the January transfer window – a ban on signings for breaching Financial Fair Play rules and the loss of leading scorer Joe Mason to Wolves. They remained on the fringe of the top six and closed to within two points by beating Derby 2-1 in front of a record crowd for a club match of 28,680. What Russell Slade's team could not survive, however, was conceding late goals in the final month of the season. They lost 2-1 in stoppage-time to Fulham on the day that Sheffield Wednesday, their rivals for the final play-off spot, went down 4-1 to Bristol City. A goalless draw with Queens Park Rangers was followed by another 2-1 reversal against Brentford, whose goals came in the final ten minutes. Cardiff themselves got a late one of their own, Peter Whittingham's penalty, to defeat relegated Bolton by the same scoreline, leaving a crucial visit to Hillsborough in the final away fixture. It brought a 3-0 defeat, with Wednesday making sure of sixth place at the expense of their rivals. Slade became the club's head of football and was replaced as manager by coach Paul Trollope at the end of the campaign. Slade then left after less than a month to become Charlton's new manager.

Ameobi S................. 8 (28)
Connolly M.....................42
Dikgacoi K 16 (7)
Ecuele Manga B 20 (4)
Da Silva F............... 18 (5)
Gunnarsson A......... 16 (12)
Harris K...................... - (3)
Immers L................ 14 (1)
John D........................ - (1)
Jones K 15 (4)
Kennedy M.................. - (1)
Lawrence T.............. 11 (3)
Macheda F .... - (6)
Malone S................. 36 (5)
Marshall D......................40
Mason J 21 (2)
Moore S 6 (1)
Morrison S............... 29 (1)
Noone C................ 24 (14)
O'Keefe S................ 19 (5)
Peltier L...................38 (3)
Pilkington A.............38 (3)
Ralls J 42 (1)
Revell A 7 (3)
Saadi I ....- (2)
Turner B.......................... 1
Watt T.............................9
Whittingham P..........34 (2)
Zohore K 2 (10)

League goals (56): Pilkington 9, Mason 6, Whittingham 6, Immers 5, Jones 5, Noone 5, Morrison 3, Ecuele Manga 2, Gunnarsson 2, Malone 2, O'Keefe 2, Watt 2, Zohore 2, Ameobi 1, Connolly 1, Da Silva 1, Ralls 1, Opponents 1
FA Cup goals: None. **League Cup goals** (2): Noone 1, Revell 1
Average home league attendance: 16,463. **Player of Year**: Matthew Connolly

CHARLTON ATHLETIC

Two years after a successful 'troubleshooting' job at The Valley, Jose Riga was invited back and asked to save Charlton once again from the threat of relegation. This time, the task was a much sterner one and proved beyond him in a turbulent season which, ironically, had started so well with wins over two of the relegated clubs, Queens Park Rangers and Hull. Just two points from the next nine games resulted in the dismissal of Guy Luzon and the interim appointment of Karel Fraeye. It lasted two months before he paid the penalty for an FA Cup defeat by Colchester, followed three days later by a 5-0 Championship loss to Huddersfield. Riga's first match, a 6-0 defeat in the return with Hull, underlined the size of the assignment. In a run of 17 games, Charlton won just once, leading to supporters' protests against the club's owners coming to a head, inside and outside the ground, for the visit of second-place Middlesbrough. A 2-0 success took some of the heat out of the situation, while a stoppage-time winner by Jorge Teixeira against Birmingham offered another lifeline. Those wins, however, were not enough to match Rotherham's resurgence under Neil Warnock, which took them clear of trouble and left Charlton rooted in the bottom three. The drop was confirmed in a goalless draw against an already doomed Bolton, with three games remaining, and after a 3-0 defeat in the final game against Burnley Riga resigned. He was replaced by former Cardiff manager Russell Slade.

Ahearne-Grant K........ 7(10)
Hadji Ba E............ 13 (12)
Bauer P........................19
Bergdich Z............ 11 (12)
Ceballos C................ 3 (2)
Charles-Cook R........... - (1)
Cousins J.......................39
Diarra A.................. 31 (1)
Fanni R.................. 13 (1)
Fox M..................... 40 (2)
Ghoochanneijhad R. 10 (13)
Gudmundsson J B..... 39 (1)
Harriott C................ 15 (5)
Henderson S..................22
Holmes-Dennis T......... 5 (6)
Jackson J............... 21 (8)
Johnson R.......................4
Kashi A.........................11
Kennedy M......................2
Lennon H............... 16 (3)
Lookman A............. 17 (7)
Makienok S.......... 22 (14)
McAleny C................ 3 (5)
Motta M................... 9 (3)
Moussa F................. 2 (4)
Pope N.........................24
Poyet D.....................4 (2)
Sanogo Y...................4 (4)
Sarr M-N...................9 (3)
Solly C....................33 (1)
Teixeira J...................... 19
Umerah J....................- (1)
Vaz Te R...................8 (3)
Vetokele I................11 (5)
Watt T.....................11 (3)
Williams R.................2 (1)
Yun Suk-Young...........7 (2)

League goals (40): Gudmundsson 6, Lookman 5, Makienok 5, Harriott 3, Jackson 3, Sanogo 3, Cousins 2, Ghoochanneijhad 2, Lennon 2, Teixeira 2, Watt 2, Ahearne-Grant 1, Bauer 1, Fox 1, Sarr 1, Vetokele 1

FA Cup goals (1): Ghoochanneijhad 1. **League Cup goals** (9): Ahearne-Grant 2, Bergdich 1, Ghoochanneijhad 1, Kashi 1, Kennedy 1, Sarr 1, Vetokele 1, Watt 1

Average home league attendance: 15,632. **Player of Year**: Jordan Cousins

DERBY COUNTY

For the third successive season, Derby experienced bitter disappointment, their bid for a return to the Premier League again crushed under the weight of expectancy. It came in the first leg of a play-off semi-final against Hull, a side they had beaten 4-0 a month earlier. This time, a 3-0 defeat on a day when everything that could go wrong did go wrong, left them with little chance of going through. At least they made a fight of it in the second leg, winning 2-0 with a strike by Johnny Russell followed by an own goal, but a third proved out of reach. Under new manager Paul Clement, a former Real Madrid assistant coach, Derby had started poorly, failing to win any of the first five games, then gradually built some momentum to climb the table and move into an automatic promotion place when Tom Ince scored a hat-trick in a 4-0 win over Bristol City. Ince then got the winner at Ipswich and his side went top after beating Fulham on Boxing Day. But they faltered in the New Year, failing to win in six games and Clement was dismissed after eight months in the job. Darren Wassall, the academy director, took over for the remainder of the campaign, with Harry Redknapp alongside him in an advisory role, and Derby qualifed for the knock-out stage with something to spare. Former Leicester manager Nigel Pearson was appointment in a permanent position.

Baird C...................... 8 (6)
Bent D.................... 4 (17)
Blackman N.............. 5 (9)
Bryson C................. 14 (7)
Butterfield J............ 29 (8)
Buxton J.................... - (3)
Camara A................... - (4)
Carson S.......................36
Christie C................ 40 (2)
Forsyth C................ 10 (2)
Grant L.........................10
Hanson J................. 10 (8)
Hendrick J............ 21 (11)
Hughes W................. 4 (2)
Ince T..................... 37 (5)
Johnson B............... 30 (1)
Keogh R........................46
Martin C.................. 42 (3)
Olsson M......................16
Russell J...............35 (10)
Shackell J.....................46
Shotton R...................- (6)
Thorne G.................32 (2)
Warnock S...............19 (1)
Weimann A............12 (18)

Play-offs – appearances: Bryson 2, Carson 2, Christie 2, Hughes 2, Keogh 2, Martin 2, Olsson 2, Russell 2, Shackell 2, Ince 1 (1), Hendrick 1, Johnson 1, Weimann 1, Bent – (2), Blackman – (1), Butterfield – (1), Camara – (1)
League goals (66): Martin 15, Ince 12, Russell 9, Butterfield 7, Johnson 5, Weimann 4, Bryson 3, Bent 2, Hendrick 2, Thorne 2, Christie 1, Keogh 1, Olsson 1, Shackell 1, Opponents 1. **Play-offs** – goals (2): Russell 1, Opponents 1
FA Cup goals (3): Bent 1, Butterfield 1, Thorne 1. **League Cup goals** (1): Shackell 1
Average home league attendance: 29,663. **Player of Year**: Richard Keogh

FULHAM

The prolific partnership of Ross McCormack and Moussa Dembele was not nearly enough to prevent a poor season in west London. Neither was a change of manager, with Kit Symons sacked after a 5-2 home defeat by Birmingham in early November. It was not until late December that he was replaced by Slavisa Jokanovic, who took Watford into the Premier League, then left the club when failing to agree new terms. By then, Fulham had gone nine matches without a win and were sliding. The club also had a transfer ban imposed by Football League for breaching Financial Fair Play rules. Jokanovic watched from the stands as his new team defeated Rotherham 4-1. His first game in charge was a home defeat by Sheffield Wednesday and it was not until six games later that he secured his first win – 3-1 against Queens Park Rangers. A failure to sustain winning leads led to more inconsistency and a fall to fourth from bottom, a single point away from the relegation zone. They escaped with an April rally which delivered 2-1 victories over MK Dons, Preston and Cardiff in the space of eight days. But a 5-0 defeat by Brighton and a 3-0 reversal against neighbours Brentford again exposed failings. Fulham finished 20th, despite 21 goals for McCormack and 15 for Dembele.

Amorebieta F....................14
Baird C....................... 3 (4)
Bettinelli M.....................11
Bodurov N.................. 2 (1)
Burn D 28 (4)
Cairney T 37 (2)
Christensen L V 17 (10)
Dembele M 37 (6)
Fredericks R............. 23 (9)
Garbutt L................. 19 (6)
Husband J 12
Hutchinson S 8 (1)
Hyndman E............... 9 (7)
Ince R 8 (2)
Kacaniklic A........... 10 (13)
Kavanagh S.......................2
Labyad Z...................... - (2)
Lewis J 7 (1)
Lonergan A 28 (1)
Madl M.................... 12 (1)
Mattila S.................... 2 (4)
McCormack R.................45
O'Hara J 32 (5)
Parker S 20 (4)
Pringle B 12 (3)
Ream T.................... 27 (2)
Richards A.............. 21 (1)
Smith M 5 (15)
Stearman R.............. 27 (2)
Tunnicliffe R 23 (4)
Voser K...................... 4 (3)
Williams G .... - (1)
Woodrow C.............. 1 (13)

League goals (66): McCormack 21, Dembele 15, Cairney 8, Woodrow 4, Kacaniklic 3, Pringle 2, Smith 2, Tunnicliffe 2, Christensen 1, Garbutt 1, Hyndman 1, Ince 1, Madl 1, O'Hara 1, Parker 1, Opponents 2
FA Cup goals (1): Dembele 1. **League Cup goals** (4): McCormack 2, Dembele 1, Kacaniklic 1
Average home league attendance: 17,566. **Player of Year**: Moussa Dembele

HUDDERSFIELD TOWN

David Wagner had a sobering introduction to the competitive nature of the Championship after becoming the club's first Continental manager. Borussia Dortmund's former Under-23 coach, watched from the stands as his new team lost 3-0 at home to Leeds. His first two games in charge brought further defeats by Sheffield Wednesday and Middlesbrough, leaving them in the bottom three. Wagner, appointed when Chris Powell was sacked, had his first success next time out – 2-0 at Birminghm approaching the midway point of the season. Huddersfield went on to make a good start to the New Year, defeating Bolton and Charlton, but the threat of being dragged back into the relegation zone remained until the return fixture with Leeds provided breathing space. After falling behind, and despite Nahki Wells missing a penalty, they won 4-1 with goals by Harry Bunn, Karim Matmour and Wells in eight second-half minutes. Then, with Wells delivering his 17th goal of the season, they were 2-0 winners at Blackburn to go comfortably clear of trouble. There was still a sting in the tail, with nine goals conceded in the final two fixtures against Bristol City and Brentford.

Allinson L .... (1)
Billing P 8 (5)
Bojaj F .... - (8)
Boyle W...................... - (1)
Bunn H.................... 34 (8)
Butterfield J.....................5
Carayol M 9 (6)
Chilwell B.................. 7 (1)
Cranie M................. 28 (9)
Davidson J 26 (1)
Dempsey K 10 (11)
Hammill A .... - (1)
Hogg J 19 (3)
Holmes D.................. 2 (4)
Hudson M 39
Husband J.............. 10 (1)
Huws E.................. 27 (3)
Lolley J 25 (7)
Lynch J 34 (3)
Manu E....................... - (5)
Matmour K................ 7 (9)
Miller I.................... 12 (6)
Murphy J.........................7
Paterson J 22 (12)
Scannell S................20 (9)
Smith T....................33 (3)
Smithies A 1
Steer J 38
Vaughan J ....- (4)
Wallace M 1 (1)
Ward E............................5
Wells N 39 (5)
Whitehead D............31 (3)
Van La Parra R...........7 (1)

League goals (59): Wells 17, Bunn 6, Paterson 6, Huws 5, Lolley 4, Carayol 3, Hudson 3, Lynch 2, Billing 1, Butterfield 1, Davidson 1, Dempsey 1, Bojaj 1, Holmes 1, Matmour 1, Miller 1, Scannell 1, Opponents 4
FA Cup goals (4): Paterson 2, Smith 1, Wells 1. **League Cup goals** (1): Wallace 1
Average home league attendance: 12,631. **Player of Year**: Nahki Wells

HULL CITY

Steve Bruce led his side straight back to the Premier League in a season which had its fair share of ups and downs before a goal by Mohamed Diame made everything worthwhile. Two spells at the top of the table suggested they might be on course for automatic promotion, first after a 3-0 win over Middlesbrough in early November, then in the wake of a 6-0 victory over Charlton in mid-January. Each time, Hull faltered and lost their footing, enabling Middlesbrough, Burnley and Brighton to take up the running. It meant they spent the last month of the campaign effectively in limbo, too far away from a top-two place, while at the same time having a play-off spot protected. That was reflected by their last two results – defeat by relegated Bolton, followed by a 5-1 win over Rotherham. When Derby were beaten 3-0 on their own ground in the first leg of the semi-final, Abel Hernandez scoring his 20th goal, Hull should have been riding high again. Instead, two first-half goals were conceded in a nervy return match and it needed backs-to-the-wall defending to prevent a third. There was more cause for concern in the final when Hull missed several chances to translate their superiority into goals. In the end, though, it all came right as Diame curled a shot into the top corner from 25 yards with 18 minutes of normal time remaining against Sheffield Wednesday at Wembley.

Akpom C............... 19 (16)
Aluko S.................... 8 (17)
Bruce A..................... 9 (2)
Clucas S.................. 39 (5)
Davies C 37 (2)
Dawson M.......................32
Diame M................. 31 (7)
Diomande A.............. 3 (8)
Elmohamady A....... 31 (10)
Hayden I 9 (9)
Hernandez A............ 34 (5)
Huddlestone T........ 24 (13)
Jahraldo-Martin C......... - (1)
Jakupovic E.......................2
Jelavic N.................... 3 (1)
Lenihan B 1
Livermore J.............. 33 (1)
Luer G .... - (2)
Maguire H 17 (5)
Maloney S 8 (12)
McGregord A..................44
Meyler D 20 (6)
Odubajo M 42
Powell N ....- (3)
Robertson A.............41 (1)
Snodgrass R 18 (6)
Taylor R......................1 (3)

Play-offs – appearances: Davies 3, Dawson 3, Diame 3, Elmohamady 3, Hernandez 3, Huddlestone 3, Jakupovic 3, Livermore 3, Odubajo 3, Robertson 3, Snodgrass 3, Clucas – (3), Maguire – (2), Meyler – (2), Akpom – (1), Bruce 1
League goals (69): Hernandez 20, Diame 9, Clucas 6, Livermore 4, Akpom 3, Aluko 3, Diomande 3, Elmohamady 3, Snodgrass 3, Davies 2, Huddlestone 2, Meyler 2, Robertson 2, Bruce 1, Dawson 1, Hayden 1, Jelavic 1, Maloney 1, Opponents 2. **Play-offs – goals** (4): Diame 1, Hernandez 1, Robertson 1, Opponents 1

FA Cup goals (4): Akpom 3, Snodgrass 1. **League Cup goals** (6): Luer 2, Akpom 1, Hernandez 1, Meyler 1, Robertson 1
Average home league attendance: 17,199. **Player of Year**: Abel Hernandez

IPSWICH TOWN

A season petering out with the play-offs beyond reach delivered a special goal to remember. Andre Dozzell, aged 16 years and 350 days, came off the bench for his debut and headed the equaliser for a 1-1 draw against Sheffield Wednesday. Remarkably, he repeated the achievement of his father Jason, who scored on his first senior appearance, aged 16 years and 57 days, against Burnley in 1984. Dozzell senior, who remains the youngest scorer in English top-flight football, was at Hillsborough to see his son's big moment, which came after Ipswich were unable to sustain a challenge for a second successive top-six place.. They were handily placed a point away after two goals by Daryl Murphy secured victory over Blackburn. But home defeats by Rotherham and Brentford, accompanied by a goalless Portman Road draw against Charlton, cast them adrift. It was also a frustrating time for Murphy, top scorer in the four divisions with 27 in the previous campaign. He had a purple patch during November, scoring six times, including a first career hat-trick, and helping the Republic of Ireland reach Euro 2016. But there were also lengthy spells without a goal. His team finished strongly, beating MK Dons and Derby, to finish seventh.

Berra C..........................43
Bialkowski B..................20
Bishop E.................... 2 (2)
Bru K...................... 20 (8)
Chambers L....................45
Coke G...................... 1 (9)
Digby P...................... 1 (3)
Douglas J................ 32 (6)
Dozzell A.................. 1 (1)
Emmanuel J.............. 3 (1)
Feeney L.................... 7 (2)
Foley K...................... 6 (2)
Fraser R.................. 15 (3)
Gerken D.......................26
Hyam L...................... 9 (6)
Kenlock M.........................2
Knudsen J......................42
Maitland-Niles A....... 21 (9)
Malarczyk P................ - (3)
McDonnell A....................1
McGoldrick D........... 9 (15)
Murphy D................. 30 (4)
Oar T.......................... 1 (5)
Parr J.......................... 3 (6)
Pitman B............... 24 (18)
Pringle B.................... 9 (1)
Sears F.................... 44 (1)
Skuse C 39
Smith T.........................45
Toure L...................... 3 (4)
Varney L.................. 2 (16)

League goals (53): Murphy 10, Pitman 10, Sears 6, Fraser 4, McGoldrick 4, Chambers 3, Douglas 3, Bru 2, Pringle 2, Smith 2, Berra 1, Dozzell 1, Feeney 1, Knudsen 1, Maitland-Niles 1, Parr 1, Varney 1
FA Cup goals (3): Fraser 1, Maitland-Niles 1, Oar 1. **League Cup goals** (6): Alabi J 1, Fraser 1, McGoldrick 1, Pitman 1, Tabb J 1, Yorwerth J 1
Average home league attendance: 18,989. **Player of Year**: Bartosz Bialkowski

LEEDS UNITED

Protesting fans, managerial upheaval, disciplinary action against the Cellino family – and another season of under-achievement. Nothing seems to change at Elland Road, where the football, at times, tends to be something of an irrelevancy alongside the actions of the owners of the club. This time, protests came to a head when supporters assembled in the city square for a march to the stadium ahead of the game against Reading. A few days later, director Edoardo Cellini was banned from football-related activity for three games and fined £5,000 by the FA following an abusive row with a fan on social media. His father, Massimo, received a second ban, from the Football League, the previous season. Earlier in this campaign, he agreed in principle to sell to a supporters' group, but changed his mind a week later. On the pitch, two wins in his 12 games in charge led to Uwe Rosler's dismissal and the appointment of Steve Evans – three weeks after he left Rotherham. Evans became the sixth manager since the takeover of the club in April, 2014 and like, his predecessors, struggled to make Leeds a force in the Championship. His side finished 13th, an improvement of two places on 2015. Evans was sacked and in came Garry Monk, who had been dismissed by Swansea during the season.

Adeyemi T............... 17 (6)	Carayol M.................. 6 (6)	Murphy L 25 (11)
Antenucci M 21 (18)	Cook L..................... 41 (2)	Peacock-Farrell B............1
Bamba S................. 28 (2)	Cooper L.........................39	Phillips K...................3 (7)
Bellusci G............... 25 (2)	Coyle L...................... 6 (5)	Silvestri M...................45
Berardi G................ 25 (3)	Dallas S.................. 38 (7)	Taylor C.........................39
Botaka J................. 3 (10)	Diagouraga T........... 13 (4)	Vieira R.......................- (1)
Bridcutt L............... 23 (1)	Doukara S............. 13 (10)	Wood C....................33 (3)
Buckley W.................. 1 (3)	Erwin L...................... 2 (9)	Wootton S................21 (2)
Byram S.................. 16 (6)	Mowatt A............... 22 (12)	

League goals (50): Wood 13, Antenucci 9, Dallas 5, Bamba 4, Byram 3, Doukara 3, Adeyemi 2, Diagouraga 2, Mowatt 2, Carayol 1, Cook 1, Cooper 1, Murphy 1, Taylor 1, Opponents 2
FA Cup goals (4): Doukara 2, Carayol 1, Diagouraga 1. **League Cup goals** (1): Cook 1
Average home league attendance: 22,446. **Player of Year**: Charlie Taylor

MIDDLESBROUGH

Middlesbrough negotiated a New Year wobble, Aitor Karanka's fallout with his players and a tense finish to the season to return to the Premier League after a seven-year absence. They claimed the runners-up spot behind Burnley with the meanest defence in the Championship – 22 clean sheets in their 46 matches, including a club record nine in succession spread over two months from late November. The end of that unbeaten run was followed immediately by a spell of five games without a win and the loss of the leadership. Then, just as momentum was being restored, Karanka criticised his players after a defeat by struggling Rotherham and walked out of a training session. The Spaniard was missing from the next game at Charlton, raising doubts about his future, but returned to supervise six successive victories in which Jordan Rhodes started paying back some of his £9m transfer fee. Of the three top teams, Burnley showed the greater consistency during the run-in to take the title, leaving Middlesbrough and Brighton, level on 88 points, to contest a last-day decider for second place in front of a crowd of nearly 34,000 at the Riverside. The home side, with a superior goal difference, went ahead through Cristhian Stuani, were pegged back by Dale Stephens, then had to negotiate eight minutes of stoppage-time as ten-man Brighton pressed for the winner despite having Stephens sent off for a foul on Gaston Ramirez.

Adomah A............... 36 (7)	Forshaw A............... 9 (20)	Nugent D 24 (14)
Amorebieta F........... 11 (2)	Friend G.................. 39 (1)	Ramirez G................15 (3)
Ayala D................... 34 (1)	Fry D.............................7	Reach A....................3 (1)
Clayton A................ 41 (2)	Gibson B................ 32 (1)	Rhodes J..................13 (5)
De Laet R.................. 9 (1)	Kalas T................... 19 (7)	Sola E........................1 (1)
De Pena C................. 3 (3)	Kike....................... 10 (9)	Stephens J.................- (1)
De Sart J.................... - (2)	Konstantopoulos D..........46	Stuani C.................20 (16)
Downing S............... 40 (5)	Leadbitter G............ 39 (2)	Wildschut Y.....................1
Fabbrini D.............. 14 (8)	Nsue E.................... 37 (3)	Zuculini B.................3 (2)

League goals (63): Nugent 8, Ramirez 7, Stuani 7, Adomah 6, Rhodes 6, Fabbrini 4, Kike 4, Leadbitter 4, Ayala 3, Downing 3, Nsue 3, Forshaw 2, Clayton 1, Friend 1, Gibson 1, Reach 1, Opponents 2
FA Cup goals (1): Fabbrini 1. **League Cup goals** (8): Stuani 4, Adomah 2, Fabbrini 1, Wildschut 1
Average home league attendance: 24,627. **Player of Year**: Daniel Ayala

MILTON KEYNES DONS

Karl Robinson's side managed to keep their heads above water for much of the season – despite a lack of goals. But they began sinking towards the end, felt the full force of a crushing home defeat at a crucial time and went straight back to League One. The step up was always going to be a challenge, particularly after the loss of their three leading promotion marksmen – Will Grigg, Dele Alli and Benik Afobe. It was no coincidence that Dons became the division's lowest scorers after starting off in some style with a 4-1 away win over Rotherham. Ironically, it was the Yorkshire side's resurgence under Neil Warnock which dealt a hammer blow to their survival hopes in the return fixture. Victory would have closed the gap between the teams to three points. Instead, they went two down in 17 minutes and were crushed 4-0. It was a sixth successive game without a win and left them with little chance of retrieving what had become a nine-point deficit. That sequence had extended to nine when a 4-1 defeat by Brentford in the penultimate home fixture sealed their fate. Further losses against Ipswich and Nottingham Forest completed a bleak campaign.

Baker C 18 (16)
Baldock G......................15
Benavente C............... 1 (1)
Bowditch D........... 26 (11)
Burns C 3 (1)
Carruthers S............. 33 (6)
Church S 9 (10)
Cropper C 8 (1)
Emmanuel-Thomas J... 2 (2)
Forster-Caskey J 19 (1)
Furlong C.................... - (1)
Gallagher S................ 6 (7)
Hall R 18 (9)
Hodson L .... - (3)
Jackson O.................... - (1)
Jennings D .... - (1)
Kay A...................... 33 (1)
Lewington D 46
Long K.............................2
Martin D..........................35
Maynard N 23 (12)
McFadzean K..................39
Murphy J..................33 (9)
Potter D 36 (1)
Powell D..................7 (15)
Poyet D 17 (1)
Rasulo G ....- (1)
Reeves B....................9 (9)
Revell A 8 (9)
Spence J 31 (2)
Upson M 1 (2)
Walsh J 17 (1)
Williams J 11 (2)

League goals (39): Maynard 6, Murphy 5, Bowditch 4, Revell 4, Baker 3, Reeves 3, Church 2, Hall 2, Kay 2, Powell 2, Carruthers 1, Forster-Caskey 1, Lewington 1, Walsh 1, Opponents 2
FA Cup goals (6): Church 1, Maynard 1, Murphy 1, Potter 1, Reeves 1, Opponents 1. **League Cup goals** (4): Baker 2, Murphy 1, Opponents 1
Average home league attendance: 13,158. **Player of Year**: David Martin

NOTTINGHAM FOREST

Forest seemed to have turned the corner under Dougie Freedman after a run of eight games without a victory put the manager under pressure with a third of the season gone. Successive home wins against Derby, Reading and Fulham took them up the table. And despite a transfer ban imposed on Christmas Eve by the Football League for breaching Financial Fair Play rules, they stretched an unbeaten run to 13 games. But a home defeat by Huddersfield proved the start of another lean spell, with five defeats in six matches resulting in Freedman's dismissal. First-team coach Paul Williams, appointed until the end of the season, started with a point at Hull, but had to wait eight matches for a win – 3-1 at Fulham with two goals by Henri Lansbury, one from the penalty spot. Forest closed by beating MK Dons 2-1, despite the sending-off of Danny Fox, with Britt Assombalonga scoring his first goal since a 14-month lay-off with a knee injury for the winner. His side finished a disappointing 16th. Former Rennes and Real Socieded coach Philippe Montanier took over in the summer.

Antonio M 4
Assombalonga B .... - (4)
Blackstock D.......... 12 (17)
Burke C 7 (2)
Burke O................... 6 (12)
Cohen C.................. 11 (4)
De Vries D......................45
Ebecilio K.................. 3 (2)
Evtimov D 1
Fox D 8 (2)
Gardner G 18 (2)
Grant J 2 (8)
Hobbs J 18 (2)
Jokic B..................... 19 (1)
Lansbury H............... 26 (2)
Lichaj E 43
Machedo F 3
Mancienne M............ 29 (2)
McDonagh G............... - (1)
Mendes R................. 26 (6)
Mills M 42
Oliveira N................ 24 (4)
O'Grady C................ 15 (6)
Osborn B.................. 32 (4)
Paterson J ....- (1)
Petravicius D ....- (1)
Pinillos D 19
Tesche R 17 (7)
Trotter L 5 (4)
Vaughan D................31 (4)
Walker T.....................5 (9)
Ward J 20 (11)
Williams J 4 (6)
Wilson K 11 (3)

League goals (43): Oliveira 9, Mills 5, Blackstock 4, Lansbury 4, Osborn 3, Antonio 2, Burke O 2, Gardner 2, Mendes 2, O'Grady 2, Ward 2, Assombalonga 1, Cohen 1, Lichaj 1, Tesche 1, Trotter 1, Vaughan 1
FA Cup goals (1): Ward 1. **League Cup goals** (3): Antonio 2, Walker 1
Average home league attendance: 19,676. **Player of Year**: Dorus de Vries

PRESTON NORTH END

Simon Grayson's side initially found it hard going on their return to the Championship. They recorded only one victory in the opening 11 matches and a demanding season looked to be on the cards. Goals were hard to come by, particularly for Joe Garner who netted 25 in that promotion campaign. It took him 17 matches to open his account this time, although by then his side were coming to terms with the demands of the division and starting to climb the table. They ended 2015 having beaten Burnley and Hull and consolidated in the New Year. The most productive spell brought successive victories over Huddersfield, Wolves, Sheffield Wednesday and Charlton in February and pushed them up to ninth. Later, successive away wins over Bolton and Blackburn consolidated a place in the top half of the table. There was also a welcome return to the side for Jermaine Beckford, scorer of a hat-trick in the Play-off Final win over Swindon. Beckford, back alongside Garner, was on the mark against MK Dons and Reading, his first goals after a seven-month lay-off with a knee injury as Preston finished 11th.

Beckford J 4 (6)	Humphrey C 5 (5)	Pearson B 13 (2)
Browne A 27 (9)	Huntington P 30 (8)	Pickford J 24
Brownhill J .... - (3)	Johnson D 40 (3)	Reach A 35
Clarke T 34 (1)	Johnstone S 4	Reid K .... - (1)
Cunningham G 43	Keane W 12 (8)	Robinson C 4 (10)
Doyle E 15 (13)	Kilkenny N 6 (7)	Vermijl M 20 (8)
Gallagher P 41	Kirkland C 4 (1)	Welsh J 13 (11)
Garner J 39 (2)	Lindegaard A 14	Woods C 28 (4)
Hudson M .... - (1)	May S 4 (3)	Wright B 38
Hugill J 8 (21)	McCarthy P 1	

League goals (45): Johnson 8, Garner 6, Gallagher 5, Doyle 4, Reach 4, Browne 3, Hugill 3, Beckford 2, Cunningham 2, Robinson 2, Keane 1, Kilkenny 1, Vermijl 1, Opponents 3
FA Cup goals: None. **League Cup goals** (6): Hugill 2 Brownhill 1, Johnson 1, Keane 1, Vermijl 1
Average home league attendance: 13,035. **Player of Year**: Greg Cunningham

QUEENS PARK RANGERS

A bright start to the season suggested Rangers might be capable of mounting a challenge for a return to the Premier League at the first attempt. Charlie Austin, the previous season's leading scorer, was soon back among the goals, with successive wins over Wolves, Rotherham and Huddersfield putting his side among the early leaders. But the promise faded, inconsistency took over and Chris Ramsey was sacked after they slipped into the bottom half of the table after 15 games, losing touch with the leading group. Neil Warnock had a spell as interim manager before former Chelsea striker Jimmy Floyd Hasselbaink was given the job after making his mark while in charge of Burton. Hasselbaink had to wait until his ninth league and cup game for a victory – 3-0 at Rotherham on the day Austin joined Southampton. The win failed to spark any sustained improvement until Birmingham, Derby and Brentford were overcome in the space of four games in the run-up to Easter. Even then, Rangers were nine points short of a play-off place with little prospect of closing the gap during a tough run-in against some of the leading teams. They finished in mid-table.

Angella G 16 (1)	Hall G 37 (2)	Perch J 34 (1)
Austin C 12 (4)	Henry K 36 (2)	Petrasso M 3 (5)
Blackwood T .... - (1)	Hill C 13	Phillips M 43 (1)
Chery T 25 (14)	Hoilett J 24 (5)	Polter S 18 (13)
Doughty M 1 (4)	Ingram M 4	Robinson J 1
El Khayati A 3 (13)	Konchesky P 33 (1)	Sandro 9 (2)
Emmanuel-Thomas J... 5 (7)	Kpekawa C 3 (2)	Smithies A 17 (1)
Faurlin A 28 (2)	Lumley J 1	Tozser D 11 (5)
Fer L 14 (5)	Luongo M 26 (4)	Washington C 7 (8)
Gladwin B 3 (4)	Mackie J 6 (9)	Yun Suk-Young 3
Green R 24	Onuoha N 46	

League goals (54): Austin 10, Chery 10, Phillips 8, Hoilett 6, Polter 6, Emmanuel-Thomas 3, Fer 2, Onuoha 2, Angella 1, El Khayati 1, Hall 1, Henry 1, Hill 1, Mackie 1, Tozser 1
FA Cup goals: None. **League Cup goals** (4): Emmanuel-Thomas 2, Onuoha 1, Polter 1
Average home league attendance: 15,994. **Player of Year**: Grant Hall

READING

In an echo of the 2014-15 season, a poor league showing was offset to some degree by a good FA Cup run. Reading also changed their manager again, this time after early season promise turned sour for Steve Clarke. A spell of six wins in seven matches, which took his side up to second, gave way to a single victory in the next eight games, with Clarke sacked a fortnight after turning down an approach from Fulham. He was replaced by Brian McDermott, who took the club into the Premier League in 2012 before he was dismissed as they headed straight back to the Championship. Reading never looked like regaining that earlier sparkle, having to make do with a run to the quarter-finals of the Cup. They defeated Huddersfield, in a replay, Walsall and West Bromwich Albion before conceding two late goals to Crystal Palace in the quarter-finals after Jake Cooper was sent off for a second yellow card. After that, there were only two wins in the remaining 11 league matches, sending them down to a 17th, an improvement of two places on the previous campaign. McDermott was dismissed for a second time and replaced by former Manchester United defender Jaap Stam.

Al Habsi A 32
Fernandez A.............. 2 (6)
Barrett J 1 (2)
Blackman N............ 23 (2)
Bond J...........................14
Cooper J 21 (3)
Cox S 6 (7)
Evans G.................... 5 (1)
Ferdinand A............ 18 (1)
Gunter C................. 43 (1)
Hector M 26 (4)
Hurtado P.................. - (5)
John O.................... 8 (20)
Kermorgant Y.......... 15 (2)
Liburd R.................... - (3)
Piazon L................. 19 (4)
McCleary G 20 (14)
McShane P...................35
Norwood O...................43
Obita J 24 (2)
Quinn S........................27
Rakels D................... 5 (7)
Dickie R .... - (1)
Robson-Kanu H........ 21 (7)
Sa O....................... 16 (3)
Samuel D................... - (1)
Taylor A 17 (2)
Tshibola A................. 6 (6)
Vydra M 24 (7)
Williams D 35 (4)

League goals (52): Blackman 11, Sa 5, Williams 5, John 4, McCleary 4, Kermorgant 3, Piazon 3, Norwood 3, Rakels 3, Robson-Kanu 3, Vydra 3, Cooper 2, Cox 1, Hector 1, Quinn 1
FA Cup goals (14): Vydra 6, Piazon 2, Robson-Kanu 2, Fernandez 1, Hector 1, McShane 1, Williams 1. **League Cup goals** (4): Blackman 2, Gunter 1, McCleary 1
Average home league attendance: 17,285. **Player of Year**: Ali Al Habsi

ROTHERHAM UNITED

When Neil Warnock calls time on a long managerial career and looks back on events at a dozen or so league clubs, there will be nothing more satisfying that having led Rotherham away from relegation against all the odds. He was handed a 'troubleshooting' role until the end of the season after the departure of Steve Evans, over a difference of opinion on how to take the club forward, and the dismissal of Neil Redfearn four months into the job. Warnock's first game was a goalless draw against Birmingham, achieved with nine men after the dismissals of Richard Wood and Joe Mattock. Defeat in the next two left them six points from safety. Then came the recovery – victory over Brentford, followed by maximum points against promotion-chasing Sheffield Wednesday and Middlesbrough. Next was a remarkable comeback against Derby when a 3-0 deficit with seven minutes of normal time remaining was cancelled out by goals from Danny Ward and substitute Leon Best (2). Leeds were beaten by Greg Halford's 90th minute penalty, after which a 4-0 away win over MK Dons, which opened up a nine-point gap between the two sides, effectively ensured safety. The final five fixtures, culminating in a 5-1 defeat at Hull, proved something of an anti-climax. So, too, did Warnock's subsequent departure after failing to agree terms to stay on. In came Hibernian's Alan Stubbs.

Andreu A 10 (1)
Bailey-King D.............. - (1)
Barker B.................... 1 (3)
Becchio L................... - (2)
Belaid A 3
Best L 10 (6)

Bowery J 2 (5)
Broadfoot K 31 (1)
Burke C 5
Buxton L 18 (2)
Camp L 41
Clarke-Harris J 19 (16)
Collin A 1
Collins D 21 (3)
Derbyshire M 28 (7)
Doyley L 3
Facey S 5
Frecklington L 26 (1)
Green P 14 (10)
Halford G 19 (2)
Hyam L 2 (3)
Kelly S 13 (2)
Ledesma E 1 (4)
Maguire C 6 (8)
Mattock J 35
Newell J 28 (7)
Odjidja-Ofoe V 4
Rawson F 15 (1)
Richardson F 13 (4)
Roos K 4
Shinnie A 1 (2)
Smallwood R 42 (1)
Thomas J 3 (3)
Thorpe T 5 (2)
Toffolo H 6 (1)
Ward G 33 (7)
Ward D 22 (12)
White A 3 (5)
Wood R 13

League goals (53): Derbyshire 8, Clarke-Harris 6, Frecklington 5, Newell 5, Best 4, Ward D 4, Andreu 2, Burke 2, Collins 2, Halford 2, Rawson 2, Thorpe 2, Ward G 2, Barker 1, Broadfoot 1, Mattock 1, Odjidja-Ofoe 1, Smallwood 1, Opponents 2
FA Cup goals: None. **League Cup goals** (2): Bowery 1, Green 1
Average home league attendance: 10,025. **Player of Year**: Lee Camp

SHEFFIELD WEDNESDAY

Wednesday fell at the final hurdle at the end of a season in which their fortunes were transformed under Carlos Carvalhal. A 1-0 defeat by Hull in the Play-off-Final ended the hopes of nearly 40,000 supporters of a return to Premier League after an absence of 16 years. But there was consolation in the way the Portuguese manager assembled a team who were competitive, free-scoring and provided good value for money. These qualities were in sharp contrast to the previous campaign which delivered just five wins and 16 goals in 23 games at Hillsborough. This time, only one side – ironically Hull – bettered their tally of 42 goals at home. Carvalhal made 11 summer signings and more during the January window, notably Gary Hooper after a spell on loan. The former Norwich striker scored 13 goals, including seven in five matches which powered his new side into the top six. They comfortably stayed there, progressing to a 3-1 aggregate win over Brighton in the semi-finals, with Ross Wallace on the mark in both legs. Carvalhal, who signed a new three-year-contract ahead of the final, admitted that Hull were the better side at Wembley and deserved to win. He looked forward to leading a fresh challenge in the new season with a continuation of Wednesday's attacking football, rated among the most eye-catching in the division.

Bannan B 35
Bennett J 3
Bus S - (2)
Forestieri F 35 (1)
Helan J 6 (14)
Hooper G 22 (7)
Hunt J 33 (1)
Hutchinson S 25
Lee K 40 (3)
Lees T 34
Loovens G 31
Lopez A 14 (8)
Lucas Joao 15 (25)
Matias M 9 (8)
McGeady A 10 (3)
McGugan L 5 (8)
Nuhiu A 22 (19)
Palmer L 13 (2)
Price L 4 (1)
Pudil D 35 (1)
Sasso V 11 (4)
Semedo J 7 (3)
Sougou M 5 (4)
Stobbs J - (1)
Turner M 11
Wallace R 34 (6)
Westwood K 34
Wiggins R 5 (1)
Wildsmith J 8 (1)

Play-offs – appearances: Bannan 3, Forestieri 3, Hooper 3, Hunt 3, Lee 3, Lees 3, Loovens 3, Pudil 3, Wallace 3, Westwood 3, Lopez 2, Hutchinson 1 (1), Nuhiu – (3), Helan – (2), Lucas Joao – (2), Matias – (1)
League goals (66): Forestieri 15, Hooper 13, Lucas Joao 6, Lee 5, Lees 3, Matias 3, McGugan 3, Nuhiu 3, Wallace 3, Bannan 2, Pudil 2, Sougou 2, McGeady 1, Turner 1, Opponents 4. **Play-offs – goals** (3): Wallace 2, Lee 1
FA Cup goals (4): McGugan 2, Bannan 1, Nuhiu 1. **League Cup goals** (9): Lucas Joao 2, Hutchinson 1, Lee 1, McGugan 1, Nuhiu 1, Semedo 1, Sougou 1, Wallace 1
Average home league attendance: 22,641. **Player of Year**: Fernando Forestieri

WOLVERHAMPTON WANDERERS

After missing out on a play-off place on goal difference the previous season, Wolves were among the favourites to go up this time. Instead, they meandered through the middle reaches of the table for much of the time – setting an unwanted club record in the process. For the first time, supporters had to sit through seven goalless draws at Molineux, four of them in succession at the tail end of the campaign. Even when that run ended on the final afternoon, it was an own goal that set them on the way to a 2-1 win over Sheffield Wednesday, Michael Turner turning a cross from Matt Doherty past his own goalkeeper before George Saville made sure of the points with a second. Only once did Wolves show the consistency needed to make the breakthrough. That came around the turn of the year when successive victories over Reading, Charlton, Brighton and Fulham took them into the top half of the table and to within seven points of a top-six place. The Championship, however, is an unforgiving place for those teams unable to go the extra step. Within a month, Wolves had slipped back, with a 2-1 win over Derby earned by two goals from Saville not enough to spark another charge. They finished in the bottom half.

Afobe B 23 (2)
Batth D 38
Byrne N 10 (14)
Coady C 33 (4)
Deslandes S 3
Dicko N 4 (1)
Doherty M 28 (6)
Ebanks-Landell E 21
Edwards D 26 (3)
Enobakhare B 1 (6)
Goulbourne S 20
Graham J 11
Hause K 23 (2)
Helan J 8
Henry J 33 (6)
Holt G .... - (4)
Hunte C .... - (2)
Ikeme C 33 (1)
Iorfa D 42
Le Fondre A 10 (16)
Martinez E 13
Mason J 9 (7)
McDonald K 32 (1)
Ojo S 5 (12)
Price J 20 (4)
Rowe T 2 (1)
Saville G 16 (3)
Sigurdarson B 11 (3)
Stearman R 4
Wallace J 6 (3)
Williamson M 5
Van La Parra R 11 (2)
Zyro M 5 (2)

League goals (53): Afobe 9, Henry 7, Edwards 5, Saville 5, Le Fondre 3, Mason 3, McDonald 3, Zyro 3, Batth 2, Byrne 2, Doherty 2, Ojo 2, Ebanks-Landell 1, Graham 1, Price 1, Opponents 4
FA Cup goals: None. **League Cup goals** (4): Afobe 1 Dicko 1, Enobakhare 1, Ojo 1
Average home league attendance: 20,157. **Player of Year**: Matt Doherty

LEAGUE ONE

BARNSLEY

There was no bigger transformation in fortunes than the one achieved by Barnsley, who went from relegation candidates to promotion winners – with a second Wembley success for good measure. What made the feat even more remarkable was that they did it after losing manager Gary Johnson, who took over at Bristol City two days after his side beat Fleetwood on penalties to reach the final of the Johnstone's Paint Trophy. Caretaker Paul Heckingbottom supervised a 3-2 victory over Oxford United with goals from Adam Hammill, Manchester United loanee Ashley Fletcher and an own goal. Heckingbottom also sustained his side's surge up the table after eight successive defeats had left them second from bottom with nearly half the season gone. Debutant Kevin Long brought the sequence to an end with an 89th minute winner against Oldham. Then, Sam Winnall scored ten goals in seven straight victories. They included the 'perfect' hat-trick in a 6-1 victory over Rochdale – left foot, right foot, header. Barnsley went on to clinch the last play-off place on the last day of the regular campaign, winning 4-1 away to champions Wigan to deny Scunthorpe sixth place on goal difference. They overcame Walsall 6-1 on aggregate in the two-leg semi-final, Winnall taking his tally to 24 in all competitions, and beat Millwall 3-1 in the final, a performance highlighted by spectacular 25-yard drive by man-of-the-match Hammill for the second goal. Heckingbottom was rewarded with the job on a permanent basis.

Bree J 17 (2)
Brownhill J 21 (1)
Chapman H 3 (8)
Connolly C 3
Crowley D 6 (5)
Davies A 38

Digby P......1	Mawson A......45	Toney I......10 (5)
Fletcher A......12 (9)	McCourt J......- (1)	Townsend N......8
Hammill A......25	Nyatanga L......19 (2)	Tuton S......- (7)
Harris K......7 (4)	Pearson B......23	Wabara R......18 (1)
Hourihane C......40 (1)	Roberts M......27 (5)	Watkins M......32 (2)
Isgrove L......27	Rothwell J......2 (2)	White A......14
Jackson S......1 (8)	Scowen J......23 (11)	Wilkinson C......2 (6)
Khan O......- (3)	Smith G......14 (5)	Williams G......16 (3)
Long K......11	Smith M......4 (9)	Williams R......1 (4)
Maris G......- (1)	Templeton M......- (2)	Winnall S......36 (7)

Play-offs – appearances: Brownhill 3, Davies 3, Fletcher 3, Hammill 3, Hourihane 3, Isgrove 3, Mawson 3, Roberts 3, Scowen 3, Williams G 3, Winnall 3, Toney – (3), Chapman – (2), McCourt – (1), Watkins – (1), White – (1)

League goals (70): Winnall 21, Hourihane 10, Mawson 6, Fletcher 5, Watkins 5, Hammill 4, Scowen 4, Brownhill 2, Long 2, Nyatanga 2, Chapman 1, Pearson 1, Roberts 1, Templeton 1, Toney 1, Wabara 1, Wilkinson 1, Williams G 1, Opponents 1. **Play-offs – goals** (9): Fletcher 2, Hammill 2, Winnall 2, Brownhill 1, Isgrove 1, Opponents 1

FA Cup goals: None. **League Cup goals** (4): Crowley 1, Scowen 1, Watkins 1, Winnall 1. **Johnstone's Paint Trophy goals** (13): Hammill 3, Fletcher 2, Watkins 2, Hourihane 1, Mawson 1, Nyatanga 1, Pearson 1, Toney 1, Opponents 1

Average home league attendance: 9,499. **Player of Year**: Adam Hammill

BLACKPOOL

The continued decline of this once-proud club was played out against a familiar backdrop of prolonged protests against the club's owners – and accompanied by bitter irony. Blackpool kicked off their Premier League adventure in 2010 with a 4-0 win over Wigan. Now they are in League Two after losing by an identical scoreline inflicted by the same opponents in the final home game of this latest miserable season. A second-half collapse in which all four goals were conceded still left them a slim chance of surviving. But it depended on victory at Peterborough and Fleetwood losing to bottom team Crewe in the final round of fixtures. Neither materialised, with Neil McDonald's side crushed 5-1 after leading through Jacob Blyth. Blackpool had previously given long-suffering supporters some hope by climbing out of the bottom four on the back of ten points accumulated against Crewe, Bury, Doncaster and Southend. But they slipped back into trouble by failing to score in the next three matches and another blank scoresheet against champions-elect Wigan made it 21 for the season. McDonald was sacked after 11 months in the job. He was replaced by former Blackburn manager Gary Bowyer.

Aimson W......14 (1)	Higham L......11	Osavi-Samuel B......10 (13)
Aldred T......42	Ikpeazu U......3 (9)	Paterson M......- (17)
Blyth J......6 (2)	Jones L......10	Philliskirk D......22
Boyce E......17 (9)	Lee E......3 (1)	Potts B......45
Cameron H......12 (2)	Letheren K......4 (1)	Redshaw J......27 (9)
Cubero J......4 (3)	Smith L......4 (4)	Rivers J......2 (8)
Cullen M......37 (4)	Little A......3 (2)	Robertson C......35 (3)
Doyle C......33	Lyness D......9	Thomas K......2 (16)
Dunne C......2 (2)	McAlister J......43 (1)	White H......29
Ferguson D......29 (1)	Norris D......34 (4)	Yeates M......8 (3)
Herron J......5 (10)	Oliver C......1 (3)	

League goals (40): Cullen 9, Redshaw 7, Potts 6, Aldred 5, Philliskirk 5, Blyth 2, Little 1, Norris 1, Robertson 1, White 1, Opponents 2

FA Cup goals: None. **League Cup goals**: None. **Johnstone's Paint Trophy goals** (2): Rivers 1, Robertson 1

Average home league attendance: 7,052

BRADFORD CITY

Bradford went into the play-offs with the second best defensive record in the division. They kept a clean sheet in 22 of their 46 matches – nine of them in the last two months of the season when Phil Parkinson's side broke into the top six on the back of nine victories. But in front of a crowd of more than 19,000 for the first leg against Millwall at Valley Parade, uncharacteristic errors proved costly and they were beaten 3-1 after taking the lead through Tony McMahon's penalty. It left them with a huge task in the return at The Den, one of the most intimidating of grounds, where they had not won in seven previous visits. And despite a more resolute performance, it was Millwall who went through after a 1-1 draw, having proved the better team over the two matches. Bradford had recovered from a sticky start to the season – losing 4-1 at Swindon in the opening fixture, winning only one of the first five home matches and lying sixth from bottom after ten games. They were up into the top half of the table by the midway point and launched the decisive run, ironically, by beating Millwall 1-0, courtesy of a header from substitute Steve Davies. Parkinson ended five years at the club by becoming Bolton's new manager in the summer. He was replaced by Stuart McCall, previously manager at Valley Parade from 2007–10.

Anderson P 5 (6)	Hanson J 30 (11)	Morais F 2 (5)
Bowery J 1 (2)	James L 1 (8)	Morris J 8 (5)
Burke R 34	Jones B 3	Mottley Henry D .... - (1)
Clarke N 19 (6)	Knott B 17 (7)	Proctor J 13 (5)
Clarke B 21 (8)	Leigh G 6	Reid K 32 (2)
Cole D 12 (7)	Liddle G 17 (3)	Routis C 9 (2)
Cullen J 15	Marshall M 8 (23)	Sheehan A 2
Darby S 46	McArdle R 35	Thomas W 6 (4)
Davies S 7 (18)	McMahon T 39 (1)	Thorpe T 2 (1)
Evans L 34 (1)	Meredith J 39 (3)	Williams B 43

Play-offs – appearances: Clarke N 2, Cullen 2, Darby 2, Evans 2, Reid 2, McArdle 2, McMahon 2, Meredith 2, Proctor 2, Williams 2, Clarke B 1, Morais 1, Anderson – (2), Davies – (2), Thorpe 1
League goals (55): Hanson 11, Cole 5, Davies 5, Proctor 5, Clarke 4, Evans 4, McMahon 4, McArdle 3, Reid 3, Burke 2, Liddle 2, Leigh 1, Meredith 1, Morais 1, Morris 1, Thomas 1, Opponents 2. **Play-offs – goals** (2): McMahon 1, Proctor 1
FA Cup goals (6): Cole 1, Hanson 1, Leigh 1, Liddle 1, McMahon 1, Reid 1. **League Cup goals** (2): Hanson 1, Routis 1. **Johnstone's Paint Trophy goals** (1): Knott 1
Average home league attendance: 18,090. **Player of Year**: Reece Burke

BURTON ALBION

Just when it seemed as if their bid for a second successive promotion might be derailed by a goal drought, a hat-trick by Lucas Akins took Burton to within touching distance of a place in the Championship. It delivered a 3-0 victory at Colchester and coupled with a defeat for rivals Walsall at Bradford, left everything in their own hands. Nigel Clough's side still had to negotiate a nerve-shredding afternoon at Doncaster before clinching the runners-up spot in the final round of fixtures. A goalless draw proved enough. Yet anything less would have meant Walsall going up automatically with a superior goal difference established by a 5-0 win at Port Vale. A month earlier, Burton had seemed unstoppable after Akins put them on the way to a 4-0 victory at Vale Park to cement a six-point advantage. Instead, the next six games produced just two goals, the lead was halved and the play-offs suddenly beckoned. It was one of the Football League's most outstanding achievements of the season. The loss of Jimmy Floyd Hasselbaink, who took the club up from League Two, to Queens Park Rangers threatened to undermine progress approaching the midway point of the campaign. But there was a seamless transfer of the manager's job to Clough, who returned nearly seven years after leaving for Derby to maintain momentum from the moment his first game back brought a 3-0 win at Gillingham.

Akins L 31 (13)	Bennett M 6 (10)	Butcher C 29 (10)
Beavon S 41 (2)	Binnom-Williams J 8 (7)	Cansdell-Sherriff S 29

Choudhury H............ 9 (4)
Duffy M.................. 44 (1)
Edwards P.....................46
El Khayati A............ 23 (1)
Flanagan T............. 13 (5)
Harness M .... - (5)
Ismail Z..................... - (3)
Joachim A.................. - (7)
Matthews R.............. 1 (1)
McCrory D.............. 37 (1)
McLaughlin J 45
Mousinho J 46
Naylor T.................. 35 (6)
O'Connor A 12 (9)
Palmer M.................. 7 (7)
Reilly C................... 4 (10)
Thiele T.................. 7 (15)
Walker T 1 (5)
Weir R.................... 32 (4)

League goals (57): Akins 12, Duffy 8, El Khayati 8, Beavon 7, Naylor 6, Butcher 5, McCrory 3, Bennett 1, Binnom-Williams 1, O'Connor 1, Thiele 1, Walker 1, Opponents 3
FA Cup goals: None. **League Cup goals** (2): Palmer 1, Opponents 1. **Johnstone's Paint Trophy goals**: None
Average home league attendance: 4,089. **Player of Year**: Stuart Beavon

BURY

Any doubts about the ability of David Flitcroft's side to hold their own after winning promotion were quickly dispelled. Five successive wins, three away from home, lifted them to fourth in the table and would have given Flitcroft September's Manager of the Month award had Jimmy Floyd Hasselbaink not taken Burton to the top of League One. While unable to maintain this level of performance, Bury were just a point away from a play-off place approaching the midway point of season. Then, a single win in eight games, including a 6-0 beating at Coventry, pinned them in the bottom half. Craig Jones delivered the only goal of the game to complete a double over Sheffield United and that victory was followed by a splendid recovery against Colchester, Andrew Tutte scoring a hat-trick in 11 minutes as his side came from 2-0 down to win 5-2. Bury went on to finish just below halfway. At the end, there was a big moment for Ryan Lowe on his farewell appearance for the club, the 37-year-old converting a stoppage-time penalty for a 3-2 win over Southend. But that victory proved costly with the club deducted three points for fielding an ineligible player. They dropped from 14th to 16th.

Bachmann D...................8
Bolger C.........................9
Bourne R.................. - (1)
Brown R 15 (13)
Burgess S 1 (2)
Cameron N...................28
Clare S...................... - (4)
Clarke L.......................32
Clarke P.................. 44 (1)
Delfouneso N 3 (1)
Dodoo J..........................4
Dudley A................... 2 (1)
Eagles C.................. 1 (3)
Erwin L..................... 1 (2)
Etuhu K 16 (2)
Gardner D.................. 4 (2)
Hope H..................... 1 (5)
Hussey C................. 39 (2)
Jones C................... 28 (8)
Lainton R.....................10
Lawlor I.........................12
Lowe R.................... 12 (7)
Mayor D 43 (1)
McCarey A.......................1
Mellis J................... 14 (9)
Miller G...................... - (1)
Mohammed K .... - (1)
Nardiello D................ - (1)
Neal C 10
O'Sullivan J.............12 (7)
Pope T..................21 (15)
Pugh D..................28 (11)
Riley J 32 (1)
Rose D.....................7 (21)
Ruddy J 1
Sedgwick C.................- (1)
Soares T.......................42
Styles C ....- (1)
Tutte A....................21 (1)
Walton C 4

League goals (56): Clarke L 15, Lowe 6, Pope 6, Mayor 5, Rose 5, Soares 4, Tutte 4, Cameron 3, Jones 3, Clarke P 1, Dodoo 1, Hussey 1, Riley 1, Opponents 1
FA Cup goals (6): Cameron 1, Clarke L 1, Jones 1, Mayor 1, Pope 1, Rose 1. **League Cup goals** (3): Clarke L 2, Mayor 1. **Johnstone's Paint Trophy goals** (2): Hope 1, Tutte 1
Average home league attendance: 3,751. **Player of Year**: Peter Clarke

CHESTERFIELD

Danny Wilson led Chesterfield away from the threat of relegation in his ninth managerial job. They were wobbling from four successive defeats and 12 goals conceded, a run which cost Dean Saunders his job after six months in charge. Wilson watched from the stands on Boxing Day as his new side were beaten 2-0 at Peterborough, the club's seventh straight league defeat for the first time since 1988. Two days later, in his first home game, an 89th minute equaliser was conceded to Coventry. His second brought a 7-1 victory over Shrewsbury – the first time the club had scored that many since 1979. Lee Novak led the way with a hat-trick and he went on play an important role in efforts to avoid being sucked into the bottom four. Novak was on the mark in six more matches which netted maximum points – one of them a 2-1 success at Barnsley earned with ten men after the dismissal of Jamal Campbell-Ryce. The last, 3-0 against Bury in the final home match, confirmed Chesterfield's League One status for another season and took Novak's tally to 14.

Anderson T 18
Angel..............................3
Ariyibi G 27 (11)
Banks O.................. 24 (8)
Campbell-Ryce J......... 6 (3)
Daly D 1
Dieseruvwe E............ 3 (13)
Dimaio C................... 9 (2)
Donohue D............... 15 (2)
Ebanks-Blake S 29 (4)
Evatt I 23
Fitzwater J................... - (1)
Gardner D................ 22 (8)
Gnanduillet A .... - (9)
Harrison B.................. - (3)
Herd C 20 (3)
Hird S..................... 39 (1)
Humphreys R.............. - (3)
John D 5 (1)
Jones D.........................19
Lee T 46
Liddle G........................15
Morsy S........................26
Novak L 32 (3)
O'Neil L 24 (2)
O'Shea J 39 (7)
Orrell J........................- (2)
Raglan C 22 (5)
Simons R 6 (14)
Slew J..........................- (7)
Talbot D 29 (5)
Wood R 4 (1)

League goals (58): Novak 14, Ebanks-Blake 10, O'Shea 9, Gardner 4, Morsy 4, Simons 4, Ariyibi 2, Banks 2, Campbell-Ryce 2, Hird 2, Dimaio 1, Evatt 1, Jones 1, Opponents 2
FA Cup goals (5): Ariyibi 1, Banks 1, Morsy 1, Novak 1, Simons 1. **League Cup goals** (1): Dieseruvwe 1. **Johnstone's Paint Trophy goals** (1): Opponents 1
Average home league attendance: 6,676. **Player of Year**: Sam Hird

COLCHESTER UNITED

Colchester survived on the final day of the previous season, but this time their fate was settled long before. A club-record run of 19 matches without a win in a single season sent them down, a subsequent mini-revival unable to repair the damage. It came after a solid start, which lifted them into the top of the table after ten matches with successive wins over Sheffield United, Gillingham, Swindon and Bradford, and hinted at a decent campaign. The run started, ironically, in a thrilling 4-4 draw against Walsall, whose equaliser came in stoppage-time. It spanned four months in which 50 goals were conceded. Manager Tony Humes was sacked after a 3-2 home defeat by bottom team Crewe and replaced a month later by the former West Ham and Stoke midfielder Kevin Keen, who finally saw two goals by Darren Ambrose against Bradford deliver a victory. By then, however, his side were ten points from safety and although further wins followed against fellow-strugglers Doncaster and Blackpool, relegation was confirmed with two games remaining. Keen resigned after four months in charge and was replaced by John McGreal, manager of the club's Under-21 team.

Akinwande F 1 (1)
Ambrose D............ 13 (12)
Bonne M............... 13 (20)
Bransgrove J 1
Briggs M................. 25 (1)
Brindley R................ 17 (4)
Chambers L............... 5 (1)
Dunne L 1 (1)
Eastman T 43
Edwards J 40 (2)
Elokobi G................ 15 (2)
Garvan O................. 28 (4)
Gilbey A.................. 31 (6)
Harney J.................... 1 (3)
Harriott C 19 (1)
James C...................... - (1)
Jones J...........................17
Kean J 3
Kent F 23 (3)
Lapslie T................... 7 (3)
Lee E...................... 11 (4)
Massey G 37 (5)
Moncur G................ 40 (5)
Oduwa N..................... - (2)
Olufemi T.....................10
Parish E........................25
Porter C 26 (6)
Sembie-Ferris D..........1 (7)
Shorey N 13 (2)
Sordell M 19 (2)
Szmodics S 1 (4)
Vincent-Young K 10 (4)
Wright D..................1 (10)
Wynter A 9 (3)

League goals (57): Moncur 12, Porter 7, Gilbey 5, Harriott 5, Ambrose 4, Massey 4, Sordell 4, Bonne 3, Eastman 2, Edwards 2, Elokobi 2, Lee 2, Brindley 1, Garvan 1, Lapslie 1, Opponents 2
FA Cup goals (12): Bonne 4, Harriott 2, Moncur 2, Sordell 2, Lapslie 1, Opponents 1. **League Cup goals**: None. **Johnstone's Paint Trophy goals** (2): Bonne 2
Average home league attendance: 4,136. **Player of Year**: Alex Gilbey

COVENTRY CITY

Coventry, among the pre-season favourites for promotion, made the club's best start since 1963 and for six months were prime candidates to go up. They had two spells as leaders, were out of the top six for only a week and had one of the division's leading marksmen. When Alan Armstrong took his tally to 19 with two goals in a 6-0 win over Bury on the weekend of the city's celebrations of the life of former manager Jimmy Hill, who took the club from the third to the first division, Tony Mowbray's side seemed to be going places. Instead, Newcastle loanee Armstrong's goals dried up and they won only one of the next ten games, scoring just four times. It meant a slide from fifth to mid-table, 11 points off a play-off place and out of the reckoning. Ironically, a 2-1 win over Millwall was followed by further success against two more promotion-minded teams, Bradford and Sheffield United. When Armstrong finally netted his 20th goal on the final day at Oldham, Coventry had moved back up to eighth, having accumulated 12 points from their final five matches. Mowbray acknowledged the need to need to beef up his squad, complementing skill with greater strength in order to stay the course next time.

Armstrong A............ 38 (2)
Bigirimana G............. 9 (4)
Burge L..........................9
Cargill B..........................5
Charles-Cook R..............37
Cole J...................... 18 (4)
Fleck J.........................40
Fortune M-A........... 14 (10)
Gadzhev V.................. - (2)
Harries C........................1
Haynes R.................. 4 (5)
Henderson D.............. - (5)
Hunt S............................5
Johnson R......................12
Jones J...................... 4 (2)
Kelly-Evans D............. - (1)
Kent R.................... 10 (7)
Lameiras R............ 18 (11)
Lorentzson M............. 5 (2)
Maddison J.............. 14 (9)
Martin A........................29
Morris B.................... 1 (5)
Murphy J............... 29 (11)
O'Brien J................ 20 (6)
Phillips A................17 (6)
Ramage P..................3 (1)
Ricketts S.....................43
Rose A.......................7 (6)
Stephens J....................16
Stokes C........................36
Thomas C....................- (3)
Thomas G...................2 (5)
Tudgay M 6 (19)
Turner B..........................5
Vincelot R 45
Willis J............................4

League goals (67): Armstrong 20, Murphy 9, Fleck 4, Fortune 4, Tuday 4, Vincelot 4, Maddison 3, Cole 2, Johnson 2, Lameiras 2, Martin 2, O'Brien 2, Rose 2, Stokes 2, Cargill 1, Kent 1, Ricketts 1, Turner 1, Opponents 1
FA Cup goals (1): Murphy 1. **League Cup goals** (1): Tudgay 1. **Johnstone's Paint Trophy goals**: None
Average home league attendance: 12,570. **Player of Year**: John Fleck

CREWE ALEXANDRA

League One status was preserved in the final round of matches of 2014 and 2015. This time there was no escape. Neither could any consolation be found in stretching another season-long struggle to the wire. Crewe were relegated with five matches still to play and finished up rock bottom. Compounding a campaign to forget was a home defeat by non-league Eastleigh in the first round of the FA Cup. They were again up against from the start, failing to win any of the first seven matches, and spending almost every week in the bottom four. Back-to-back victories over Colchester and Oldham kept them in touch with the teams above them approaching the midway point. But a 5-0 home defeat by Coventry opened up a gap and despite a run of six goals in as many games by Brad Inman, his side continued to fall behind. A sixth straight defeat, 3-0 against Port Vale, sealed their fate and they finished 16 points adrift of the 20th placed team Shrewsbury. There were only two wins in the second half of the season – 2-0 against Rochdale and 3-1 over Doncaster in the penultimate match.

Ainley C................... 6 (10)
Ajayi S..........................13
Atkinson C 7 (9)
Baillie J...................... 1 (3)
Bakayogo Z 16 (6)
Bingham B............... 17 (4)
Colclough R 23 (4)
Cooper G............... 13 (14)
Dalla Valle L............. 10 (4)
Davis H.................... 10 (1)
Fox D 39
Garratt B........................46
Guthrie J................. 38 (1)
Haber M 36 (4)
Hitchcock T 6 91)
Howell J .... - (2)
Inman B 33 (6)
James J 29 (2)
King A...................22m (2)
Kingsley S................. 9 (3)
Kirk C........................ 9 (5)
Lowe R 5 (10
Ng P.......................... 1 (5)
Nugent B 39 (1)
Ray G 19 (3)
Saunders C 6 (12)
Seager R.................... 3 (1)
Turton O 46
Udoh D...................... 1 (5)
Wilson H................... 3 (4)
Wintle R .... - (3)

League goals (46): Inman 10, Haber 9, Colclough 7, King 4, Dalla Valle 2, Fox 2, Lowe 2, Saunders 2, Ainley 1, Bakayogo 1, Cooper 1, Davis 1, Guthrie 1, Nugent 1, Seager 1, Turton 1
FA Cup goals: None. **League Cup goals** (1): King 1. **Johnstone's Paint Trophy goals** (2): Colclough 1, Haber 1
Average home league attendance: 4,551. **Player of Year**: Brad Inman

DONCASTER ROVERS

When Darren Ferguson led his side into the top of the table early in the New Year with a handsome 3-0 victory at Southend, the prospect of further progress – and perhaps a genuine challenge for a play-off place – did not seem out of place. That belief strengthened a week later when a battling performance against Stoke in the FA Cup could easily have brought a replay, rather than a 2-1 defeat. But from then on it all went wrong. Doncaster declined to such an extent that three months later they were heading for a second relegation in the space of three seasons, the penalty for 16 matches without another win. Crucially, there were successive defeats by rivals in distress – 4-1 at Colchester and 1-0 at home to Blackpool. Victory over eventual champions-elect Wigan and Coventry, kept hopes alive, but a 3-1 defeat by bottom-of-the-table Crewe in the penultimate match effectively sent them down. Ferguson had taken over when Paul Dickov was sacked after a single win in the opening six fixtures. Midfielder James Coppinger made a club record 469th appearance in the Cup win over Stalybridge.

Alcock C................. 24 (3)
Anderson K 5 (2)
Butler A.........................40
Calder R 7 (5)
Chaplow R 20 (7)
Coppinger J.............. 38 (1)
Evina C................... 38 (4)
Forrester H................ 3 (4)
Gobern O 4 (1)
Gooch L.................... 7 (3)
Grant C.................... 18 (1)
Horsfield J 2
Jones R...........................2
Keegan P 11 (4)
Lecygne E .... - (1)
Longbottom W .... - (1)
Lund M.................... 25 (5)
MacKenzie G 11 (4)
Main C...................... 6 (4)
Mandeville L.............. 2 (6)
Marosi M.................... - (1)
Matthews R 9
Mattioni F 5
McCullough L 28 (4)
McSheffrey G..................7
Middleton H 24 (10)
N'Guessan D..............1 (7)
Neal C 2
Rowe T.......................9 (1)
Sinclair A 38 (5)
Stewart C 11 (15)
Stuckmann T...........35 (1)
Tyson N.................22 (10)
Wellens R................11 (1)
Whitehouse B ....- (2)
Williams A................41 (5)

League goals (48): Williams 12, Tyson 6, Butler 4, Stewart 4, Anderson 3, Coppinger 3, Rowe 3, Chaplow 2, Grant 2, Sinclair 2, Evina 1, Forrester 1, Keegan 1, Lund 1, Main 1, Mandeville 1, McSheffrey 1
FA Cup goals (6): Grant 2, Williams 2, Lund 1, Tyson 1. **League Cup goals** (2): Williams 2. **Johnstone's Paint Trophy goals**: None
Average home league attendance: 6,553. **Player of Year**: Craig Alcock

FLEETWOOD TOWN

Events on and off the field were in sharp contrast for Steven Pressley and his players as the end of the season approached. They watched as a new £8m training facility, opened by Sir Alex Ferguson, offered a bright, long-term future for the club. At the same time, there was the threat of returning to League Two and setting back their remarkable rise from non-league obscurity. Fleetwood had looked to be edging away from trouble when beating Scunthorpe, Coventry and Gillingham in a productive spell of five matches yielding ten points. But a single victory in the next ten left them vulnerable. A 3-1 defeat at Walsall, in which captain Nathan Bond made a club-record 422nd appearance, meant they could still be overhauled by Blackpool on the final day of the season. Bobby Grant and Devante Cole did their bit with the goals that delivered a home win over Crewe, although in the end it proved unnecessary with their neighbours losing at Peterborough and remaining in the drop zone. Pressley took over when Graham Alexander was sacked following a 5-1 defeat by Gillingham in the tenth game of a season in which Fleetwood spent most of the time on the edge of trouble.

Kiwomya A................ 2 (2)
Ameobi S.................. 7 (3)
Andrew D.................. 8 (1)
Ball D.................. 26 (11)
Bell A..........................44
Burns W 11 (3)
Cole D 3 (11)
Davis J 17 (2)
Deacon K.................... - (1)
Della-Verde L 6 (1)
Fosu-Henry T............. 4 (2)
Grant R................. 25 (13)
Grant T...........................3
Harris R..........................1
Haughton N 7 (11)
Henen D.................... 9 (2)
Hornby-Forbes T....... 11 (5)
Hunter A............... 12 (12)
Jonsson E 36 (3)
Jordan S 20 (1)
Matt J...................... 7 (10)
Maxwell C......................46
McLaughlin C................37
McManus D.............. 3 (4)
Nilsson M 11 (2)
Nirennold V............. 11 (6)
Pond N................... 20 (1)
Proctor J............... 13 (10)
Ryan J..........................43
Sanogo V .... - (1)
Sarcevic A............... 37 (2)
Scougall S 9 (1)
Sowerby J 3 (5)
Teixeira D.........................8
Wood R...........................6

League goals (52): Grant 10, Burns 5, Hunter 5, Ball 4, Proctor 4, Jonsson 3, Matt 3, Sarcevic 3, Cole 2, Hornby-Forbes 2, McLaughlin 2, Ryan 2, Ameobi 1, Fosu-Henry 1, Henen 1, McManus 1, Nilsson 1, Scougall 1, Opponents 1
FA Cup goals: None. **League Cup goals**: None. **Johnstone's Paint Trophy goals** (6): Hunter 2, Ball 1, Grant 1, Ryan 1, Opponents 1
Average home league attendance: 3,308. **Player of Year**: Chris Maxwell

GILLINGHAM

A season which started in some style and continued to hold plenty of promise, lost its momentum in the final month. A run of eight matches without a win, which included successive home defeats by Walsall, Port Vale and Shrewsbury knocked Gillingham out of the play-off places for the first time. It meant they had to win their final fixture against Millwall, already guaranteed a top-six place, and hope the teams directly above them faltererd. In the event, another loss was rendered irrelevant with both Barnsley and Scunthorpe winning their matches. There was some consolation for the club when Bradley Dack was named League One's Player of the Year for 13 goals and numerous assists from midfield. His side could not have wished for a better start – a 4-0 victory over title favourites Sheffield United, followed by wins over two more fancied sides, Bradford and Wigan. The leadership was shared with Coventry, Walsall and Burton well into the New Year and although Burton, along with Wigan, eventually broke away from the pack, Gillingham looked to be doing enough to reach the knock-out phase.

Chicksen A................ 5 (1)
Crofts A..........................6
Dack B 39 (1)
Dickenson B........... 21 (12)
Donnelly R 24 (14)
Egan J..................... 35 (1)
Ehmer M.......................30
El-Abd A..........................8
Garmston B........... 23 (10)
Hessenthaler J........ 26 (12)
Houghton J.............. 10 (1)
Jackson R................ 34 (3)
Lennon H.........................6
List E......................... - (6)
Loft D................... 16 (10)
McDonald C............. 13 (9)
McGlashan J............ 6 (11)
Morris A.................. 31 (4)
Nelson S.......................46
Norris L...................25 (8)
Osadebe E...............10 (8)
Oshilaja A................21 (1)
Samuel D.................24 (1)
Williams G..................3 (7)
Williamson B..............4 (5)
Wright J..................40 (1)

League goals (71): Dack 13, Donnelly 10, Norris 8, Samuel 7, Egan 6, McDonald 5, Hessenthaler 4, Loft 4, Oshilaja 3, Jackson 2, Lennon 2, Osadebe 2, Dickenson 1, Houghton 1, Wright 1, Opponents 2
FA Cup goals: None. **League Cup goals** (2): Dack 1, Hessenthaler 1. **Johnstone's Paint Trophy goals** (3): Dack 1, Ehmer 1, Garmston 1
Average home league attendance: 6,316. **Player of Year**: Bradley Dack

MILLWALL

Millwall went into the play-offs in good heart after three successive wins rounded off the regular season. When the productive strike partnership of Lee Gregory and Steve Morison paved the way for a 4-2 aggregate victory over Bradford with first-half goals in the first leg of the semi-final at Valley Parade, they looked a decent bet for an immediate return to the Championship. But they were forced into a defensive reshuffle when losing the influential Byron Webster in the warm-up for the final, conceded a goal to Barnsley after two minutes and a second with 19 minutes gone. Neil Harris had to make another change when Joe Martin limped off after Mark Beevers pulled one back before half-time. A third goal sealed Barnsley's victory, which Harris admitted they merited, while at the same arguing that the injuries had been a factor in the outcome. Defeat was compounded by hooligan supporters, whose behaviour during the game was condemned in a statement issued later by the club. Millwall overcame an indifferent start to the season to climb the table, breaking into the top six on the back of a New Year run of 16 points from six matches in which Gregory scored eight goals.

Abdou N 27 (2)
Archer J.........................39
Beevers M......................42
Chesmain N .... - (1)
Cowan-Hall P .... - (3)
Craig T 16 (2)
Cummings S 15 (1)
Edwards C......................15
Ferguson S............ 28 (11)
Forde D 7 (1)
Gregory L 32 (9)
Martin L.................... 2 (6)
Martin J 27 (2)
Morison S................ 44 (2)
Nelson S 9
O'Brien A 31 (12)
Onyedinma F 18 (16)
Pavey A...................... - (4)
Philpot J .... - (6)
Powell J 1
Romeo M 18
Saville G 12
Taylor C......................9 (1)
Thompson B 19 (9)
Upson E.................16 (16)
Wallace J.......................12
Webster B 35 (5)
Williams S...............32 (1)

Play-offs – appearances: Abdou 3, Archer 3, Beevers 3, Edwards 3, Ferguson 3, Gregory 3, Martin 3, Morison 3, Taylor 3, Thompson 3, Webster 2, Craig 1 (2), Williams – (3), O'Brien – (2), Onyedinma – (1)
League goals (73): Gregory 18, Morison 15, O'Brien 10, Webster 6, Beevers 4, Onyedinma 4, Ferguson 3, Taylor 3, Martin 2, Williams 2, Abdou 1, Craig 1, Cummings 1, Romeo 1, Thompson 1, Wallace 1. **Play-offs – goals** (5): Gregory 2, Beevers 1, Martin 1, Morison 1
FA Cup goals (4): Morison 1, Gregory 1, O'Brien 1, Thompson 1. **League Cup goals** (1): Morison 1. **Johnstone's Paint Trophy goals** (11): Gregory 6, O'Brien 2, Williams 2, Morison 1
Average home league attendance: 9,108. **Player of Year**: Jordan Archer

OLDHAM ATHLETIC

John Sheridan promised to address what he called 'unfinished business' after being appointed manager for the second time. He was as good as his word, leading Oldham away from the threat of relegation which had been present for much of the season. Sheridan, a former player with the club whose first spell in charge ended with the sack in 2009, left Newport after three months in charge to take over a side third from bottom. Two months later, they were in the same position and unable to win in front of their own supporters. But a run of 16 points from seven matches lifted them clear, with on-loan Curtis Main's goals proving invaluable. It was third time lucky for the club, with first Darren Kelly then David Dunn unable to improve their fortunes. Kelly, manager for four months, was sacked following a 5-1 defeat by Peterborough. Dunn, former long-serving Blackburn midfielder who got the job after a spell as caretaker, lasted three months before paying the price for a continuation of failings at home stretching to a club record 12 matches. There was one more after Sheridan came in, before goals by Tim Dieng and Jonathan Forte earned a 2-1 victory over Gillingham. His stay also proved a short one – a move to Notts County leaving the club looking again for a new man.

Brown C 10 (3)
Burn J 12
Cassidy J 8 (13)
Coleman J 32
Cornell D 14
Croft L 13 (8)
Dieng T 34 (4)
Dummigan C 25 (1)
Dunn D 4 (4)
Eckersley R 3 (1)
Edmundson S 2
Forte J 20 (6)
Fuller R 1 (4)
Fulton J 9 (2)
Gerrard A 18
Green G - (3)
Higdon M 9 (2)
Holloway A 9 (1)
Holmes-Dennis T 10
Jones M 29 (6)
Kelly L 41
Lafferty D 15
Main C 16 (2)
Mills J 14 (1)
Murphy R 7 (6)
O'Connell E 2
Palmer M 14
Philliskirk D 21 (2)
Poleon D 14 (11)
Rasulo G 1 (2)
Stankevicius S 1 (3)
Thiele T - (4)
Tuohy J - (1)
Turner R 2 (4)
Wellens R 2 (1)
Wilson B 22 (4)
Wilson J 42 (1)
Winchester C 22 (9)
Yeates M 8 (8)

League goals (44): Kelly 6, Higdon 5, Philliskirk 5, Main 4, Poleon 4, Forte 3, Jones 3, Murphy 3, Holloway 2, Burn 1, Croft 1, Dieng 1, Dummigan 1, Lafferty 1, Mills 1, Palmer 1, Winchester 1, Yeates 1
FA Cup goals (2): Philliskirk 1, Poleon 1. **League Cup goals** (1): Philliskirk 1. **Johnstone's Paint Trophy goals**: None
Average home league attendance: 4,361. **Player of Year**: Liam Kelly

PETERBOROUGH UNITED

An FA Cup hangover cost Peterborough the chance of sustaining a promotion challenge. A week after holding West Bromwich Albion 2-2 in a fourth round tie at The Hawthorns, they moved to within three points of a play-off place by winning at Chesterfield, despite having Michael Smith and Ricardo Santos sent off. But a penalty shoot-out defeat in the replay was followed by a fall into the bottom half of the table when the next seven games yielded a single point. The sequence included a 3-2 home defeat by Port Vale when a 2-0 lead was surrendered and two goals conceded in the final four minutes of normal time. Graham Westley's side stopped the rot with successive victories over Doncaster, Coventry and Crewe. But by then they were 12 points adrift and another slump – four defeats in five – led to Westley's dismissal. Westley, formerly in charge of Stevenage and Preston, had replaced Dave Robertson, who became the season's first managerial casualty, sacked four months into a three-year contract after a single win in the first six league games. Coach Grant McCann became the club's 11th manager since Darragh MacAthony took control in 2006.

Addison M 2 (1)
Adebayo-Rowling T 3 (1)
Alnwick B 39
Anderson H 3 (2)
Anderson J 13 (1)
Angol L 24 (9)
Baldwin J 17 (1)
Beautyman H 19 (3)
Bostwick M 35 (1)
Brisley S - (2)
Chettie C - (5)
Collison J 2 (8)
Coulibaly S 13 (14)
Coulthirst S 11 (8)
Da Silva-Lopes L 4 (4)
Davey A 6 (1)
Elder C 18
Forrester C 33 (2)
Fox A 9 (9)
Gillett S 3 (2)
Gormley J 4
Henry D - (1)
Maddison M 31 (8)
Moore S 4
Nabi A 4 (2)
Nichols T 5 (2)
Nicholson J - (2)
Ntlhe K 6 (1)
Oztumer E 28 (2)
Payne J 1 (1)
Samuelson M 7 (10)
Santos R 33 (4)
Smith M 37 (1)
Taylor J 32 (12)
Toffolo H 6 (1)
Tyler M 3
Vassell K 1 (4)
Washington C 21 (4)
Williams A 6 (4)
Wilson L 1 (1)
Zakuani G 22 (2)

League goals (82): Angol 11, Maddison 11, Taylor 11, Washington 10, Oztumer 6, Coulibaly 5, Anderson J 4, Bostwick 4, Beautyman 3, Zakuani 3, Coulthirst 2, Forrester 2, Williams 2, Addison 1, Baldwin 1, Elder 1, Fox 1, Nichols 1, Samuelson 1, Santos 1, Smith 1
FA Cup goals (10): Washington 4, Taylor 2, Anderson J 1, Coulthirst 1, Maddison 1, Samuelson 1. **League Cup goals** (3): Anderson J 1, Maddison 1, Washington 1. **Johnstone's Paint Trophy goals**: None
Average home league attendance: 5,481. **Player of Year**: Marcus Maddison

PORT VALE

Just when it looked as if their bid for a place in the play-offs was gathering real momentum, Vale fell away and slipped out of contention. They were three points off a place in the top six after a spirited comeback at Peterborough, where a 2-0 deficit was transformed into a 3-2 victory. Byron Moore sparked the recovery after half-time and late goals from JJ Hooper (86) and Louis Dodds (89) lifted confidence sky-high. But it was followed by successive lapses in front of their own supporters, who had seen just one defeat all season. Vale were beaten 4-0 by Burton and went down to the only goal of the game against Barnsley. Then, four goals were conceded in the second-half at Chesterfield, resulting in the gap extending to ten points. Vale cut that in half by scoring nine goals against Crewe, Gillingham and Rochdale, but the rally came too late and a see-saw season ended on a low with a 5-0 home defeat by promotion-chasing Walsall. It also brought the departure of manager Robert Page, who took over at Northampton after Chris Wilder's move to Sheffield United. In came former Leeds and Sheffield United midfielder Bruno Ribeiro.

Alnwick J.......................41	Grant A.........................38	McGivern R.............26 (2)
Birchall C.................. 4 (7)	Hooper JJ................ 9 (19)	Moore B..................27 (9)
Brown M.................... 7 (6)	Ikpeazu U................ 14 (7)	Neal C.......................5 (1)
Daniel C.................. 11 (9)	Inniss R..................12 93)	O'Connor M.............25 (1)
Dickinson C....................44	Kelly S.................... 9 (19)	Purkiss B.....................39
Dodds L.................. 31 (6)	Kennedy M................ 9 (3)	Robinson T.................8 (6)
Duffy R..........................45	Leitch-Smith AJ...... 27 (10)	Streete R.................12 (1)
Andoh E................. 11 (1)	Lloyd R...................... - (5)	Turner D......................- (1)
Foley S.................... 42 (3)	McCourt J.................... - (2)	Yates A.....................10 (1)

League goals (56): Leitch-Smith 10, Dodds 8, Foley 6, Hooper 5, Ikpeazu 5, O'Connor 4, Dickinson 3, Kelly 3, Moore 3, Birchall 2, Daniel 2, Robinson 2, Andoh 1, Grant 1, Opponents 1
FA Cup goals (4): Leitch-Smith 2, Moore 1, O'Connor 1. **League Cup goals** (1): Moore 1.
Johnstone's Paint Trophy goals (2): Grant 1, Ikpeazu 1
Average home league attendance: 4,993. **Player of Year**: Anthony Grant

ROCHDALE

Rochdale's chances of getting anywhere near the previous season's highest-ever league placing of eighth looked slim after a lean run beginning early in the New Year. Seven matches delivered a single victory, with a 6-1 defeat at Barnsley contributing to a fall into the bottom half of the table. A return to form brought six wins in the next seven fixtures, accompanied by a climb back to within four points of a play-off place. And they were still in contention when Callum Camps put them ahead against Gillingham – shortly after the stadium announcer read out the number plate of a car with its lights left on outside the ground, not realising it belonged to the midfielder. His side conceded an equaliser, then next time out gave away two penalties to go down 4-1 at Port Vale and lose touch. But they still finished tenth with 69 points, the same as the teams immediately above them, Gillingham and Coventry but with an inferior goal difference.

Alessandra L.............. 3 (5)	Eastham A............... 19 (1)	Mendez-Laing N..... 18 (15)
Allen J.................... 35 93)	Henderson I............. 36 (3)	Noble-Lazarus R......... 2 (8)
Andrew C............... 14 (16)	Holt G.................... 3 (11)	O'Sullivan J..................... 2
Barry-Murphy B.......... - ()1)	Hooper J.................... 1 (1)	Rafferty J................ 29 (2)
Bennett R.................. 7 (9)	Kennedy T............... 17 (1)	Rose M.................... 23 (7)
Bunney J............... 19 (13)	Lancashire O..................34	Syers D...................... 2 (4)
Camps C.................. 28 (4)	Lillis J...........................40	Tanser S.................... 6 (1)
Canavan N.....................11	Lund M.................... 25 (4)	Vincenti P............. 26 (12)
Cannon A................. 22 (3)	McDermott D............ 32 (5)	
Pereira J C.......................6	McNulty J.......................46	

League goals (68): Henderson 13, Bunney 9, Vincenti 8, Mendez-Laing 7, Andrew 6, Camps 5, Allen 3, Bennett 2, Eastham 2, Holt 2, Lancashire 2, McDermott 2, Alessandra 1, Canavan 1,

Lund 1, Noble-Lazarus 1, Rafferty 1, Rose 1, Opponents 1
FA Cup goals (3): Mendez-Laing 3. **League Cup goals** (1): McDermott 1. **Johnstone's Paint Trophy goals** (2): Alessandra 1, Tanser 1
Average home league attendance: 3,098. **Player of Year**: Josh Lillis

SCUNTHORPE UNITED

A season that seemed to be drifting towards a comfortable, middle-of-the-table conclusion suddenly took on a new dimension with the appointment of Graham Alexander as manager of the club where he started his playing career. His first home game delivered a 6-0 win over Swindon, followed by a 1-0 defeat at Bradford. After that, Scunthorpe reeled off five successive victories to go into the final game against Sheffield United level on 71 points with Barnsley for the final play-off place. Paddy Madden scored his 20th goal in a 2-0 victory at Bramall Lane, but his side lost out on goal difference as Barnsley came through 4-1 away to the champions Wigan. Alexander, sacked by Fleetwood replaced Mark Robins, himself dismissed after a see-saw first half of the season which brought a struggling start, the Manager of the Month award for October, a commendable performance in a 2-0 FA Cup defeat by Chelsea at Stamford Bridge, then a 5-0 defeat at Blackpool. Joint-caretakers Nick Daws and Andy Dawson immediately supervised four successive wins and Daws was installed as interim manager until the end of the season, before chairman Peter Swann decided on a permanent appointment.

Adelakun H	9 (12)	King J	25 (11)	Sutton L	- (1)
Anyon J	7 (1)	Laird S	25 (7)	Syers D	- (3)
Bishop N	42	Lolley J	3 (3)	Townsend C	20
Canavan N	10	Luer G	1 (3)	Vose D	- (2)
Goode C	6 (4)	Madden P	46	Wallace M	33
Clarke J	29 (4)	McAllister S	15 (11)	Williams L	21 (7)
Daniels L	39	Mirfin D	35	Wiseman S	21 (3)
Dawson S	22 (1)	Ness J	24 (3)	Wootton K	3 (17)
Henderson D	5 (8)	O'Brien J	7 (2)	Van Veen K	10 (10)
Hopper T	29 (5)	Rowe T	14		

League goals (60): Madden 20, Hopper 8, McSheffrey 5, Williams 5, Wootton 3, Adelakun 2, Clarke 2, Laird 2, Mirfin 2, Wallace 2, Van Veen 2, Bishop 1, Goode 1, King 1, O'Brien 1, Rowe 1, Townsend 1, Opponents 1
FA Cup goals (5): Madden 2, Adelakun 1, King 1, Opponents 1. **League Cup goals** (1): Madden 1. **Johnstone's Paint Trophy goals** (1): Goode 1
Average home league attendance: 3,907. **Player of Year**: Paddy Madden

SHEFFIELD UNITED

Once again United started as favourites to go up; once again they failed to live up to the billing. This time it was Nigel Adkins charged with delivering the Championship status the club's profile and support demanded, having replaced Nigel Clough at the end of the previous season after a play-off semi-final defeat. Adkins twice took Scunthorpe – a club with fewer resources and expectations – into the game's second tier. And for a third of the season his new side held down a play-off place. Then, a run of six matches without a victory pushed them into mid-table and they never regained lost ground, despite the impetus offered by a widely-praised performance in the FA Cup. Manchester United were restricted to two shots on target and needed a stoppage-time penalty from Wayne Rooney to go through to the fourth round. Three days later, United came from 3-0 down to draw 3-3 at Wigan with goals from Matt Done (2) and Billy Sharp. There was still a slim chance after successive victories over Chesterfield and Shrewsbury. But a goalless draw in a local derby with Barnsley, watched by a crowd of more than 23,000, was not enough and defeats by Coventry and Scunthorpe to finish with were followed by Atkins's dismissal. He was replaced by Chris Wilder, fresh from winning League Two with Northampton.

Adams C 29 (7)
Alcock C 1 (2)
Baptiste A 10 (1)
Basham C 43 (1)
Baxter J 18 (6)
Brayford J 19
Calvert-Lewin D 3 (6)
Campbell-Ryce J 13 (5)
Collins N 30
Coutts P 26 (6)
Cuvelier F 4 (5)
Done M 25 (6)
Edgar D 35 (1)
Flynn R 18 (9)
Freeman K 17 (2)
Hammond D 30
Harris R 5
Higdon M - (2)
Howard M 15
Kelly G - (1)
Kennedy T - (1)
Long G 31
McEveley J 33 (3)
McFadzean C 1
McGahey H 5 (2)
McNulty M 1 (4)
Murphy J 1
Reed L 9 (10)
Sammon C 15 (12)
Scougall S 4 (7)
Sharp B 42 (2)
Wallace K 7 (4)
Wallace J - (4)
Whiteman B 3 (3)
Woolford M 13 (15)

League goals (64): Sharp 21, Adams 11, Sammon 5, Baxter 4, Basham 4, Done 4, Collins 3, Edgar 2, Flynn 2, Hammond 2, Baptiste 1, Brayford 1, McNulty 1, Woolford 1, Opponents 2
FA Cup goals (4): Baxter 1, Done 1 Freeman 1, Sammon 1. **League Cup goals** (1): Collins 1.
Johnstone's Paint Trophy goals (6): Baxter 2, Adams 1, Done 1, Flynn 1, Scougall 1
Average home league attendance: 19,803. **Player of Year**: Billy Sharp

SHREWSBURY TOWN

Shrewsbury survived a potentially costly setback in their final home match to avoid returning to League Two. After retrieving a three-goal deficit against Peterborough with goals by Jean-Louis Akpa Akpro, Andy Mangan and Jack Grimmer, they were beaten in stoppage time. It was a club-record 13th defeat in front of their own supporters. But they were spared a nail-biting last day of the season at Swindon by defeats for two of the teams below them, Doncaster and Blackpool. A week earlier, a late winner of their own proved crucial to staying up, Akpa Akpro's deflected strike after 81 minutes earning the points at promotion-chasing Gillingham. Four successive defeats at Greenhous Meadow to start with had pointed to difficult times ahead. So it proved, with Shrewsbury on the fringes of the bottom four for much of the time. Some relief came through an FA Cup run, which brought wins over Cardiff and Sheffield Wednesday, the latter with goals from Shaun Whalley and Grimmer in the final five minutes, earning a fifth round home tie against Manchester United, who won it 3-0.

Akpa Akpro J-L 16 (22)
Barnett T 11 (10)
Black I 26 (4)
Brown J 29 (2)
Burton C 1
Clark J 13 (7)
Cole L 24 (5)
Collins J 18 (5)
Demetriou M 1
Ellis M 9
Gerrard A 10 (1)
Goldson C 2
Grandison J 19
Grimmer J 21
Halstead M 16
Hendry J 6
Jones E - (1)
Kaikai S 23 (3)
Knight-Percival N 33 (2)
Lawrence L 10 (8)
Leutwiler J 29
Mangan A 15 (4)
McAlinden L 2 (6)
Ogogo A 42
Sadler M 19 (5)
Smith D 17 (4)
Tootle M 16
Vassell K 11 (2)
Vernon S 9 (4)
Wallace J 3 (4)
Wellens R 7 (5)
Wesolowski J 5
Whalley S 13 (11)
Whitbread Z 21 (1)
Woods M 4
Woods R 5

League goals (58): Kaikai 12, Akpa Akpro 6, Whalley 6, Collins 5, Knight-Percival 5, Mangan 5, Barnett 4, Cole 3, Clark 2, Ogogo 2, Sadler 2, Black 1, Ellis 1, Grimmer 1, Vernon 1, Whitbread 1, Opponents 1
FA Cup goals (6): Akpa Akpro 1, Collins 1, Grimmer 1, Mangan 1, Ogogo 1, Whalley 1. **League Cup goals** (3): Barnett 1, Collins 1, Tootle 1. **Johnstone's Paint Trophy goals** (3): Barnett 1, Brown 1, McAlinden 1
Average home league attendance: 5,407. **Player of Year**: Abu Ogogo

SOUTHEND UNITED

Phil Brown's promoted side experienced spells on the fringes of the top six and bottom four in an up-and-down season. But there was no real breakthrough, or any great course for concern, and they finished just below mid-table. Southend started slowly, with goals hard to come by and no wins in five. They were up and running at Peterborough's expense, the first of six victories in eight games which held out plenty of promise. A 5-2 win at Oldham also caught the eye and approaching half-way only goal difference separated them from a play-off place. Then, seven goals were conceded in successive home matches against Millwall and Doncaster, followed immediately by a 4-2 defeat at Swindon, where a two-goal lead was surrendered. Again, the team displayed commendable powers of recovery and again the play-offs came into view after victories over Burton, Barnsley and Sheffield United. They offered the opportunity to go for it in the busy April programme. Instead, six matches brought a single point and another defeat by Bury in the final game compounded a limp finish.

Atkinson W 29 (7)
Barnett T 20
Barrett A........................37
Bentley D.......................43
Bolger C 22
Bridge J..................... 1 (1)
Coker B 40
Deegan G................. 23 (2)
Hendrie S 5
Hunt N.................... 13 (8)
Hurst K...................... 9 (5)
Kamara G...................5 (1)
Leonard R 35 (2)
Loza J........................ 1 (9)
Malarczyk P.......................2
McLaughlin S 9 (8)
McQueen S.............. 4 (14)
Mooney D................ 27 (6)
Moussa F 1
O'Neill L 13 (1)
Payne J.................... 25 (7)
Pigott J 10 (13)
Prosser L.................11 (2)
Rea G 5 (9)
Smith T.......................... 3
Thompson A 24 (1)
Timlin M 17 (4)
Weston M................6 (11)
White J 27 (2)
Williams J ....- (2)
Wordsworth A...........15 (6)
Worrall D...............24 (11)

League goals (58): Payne 9, Mooney 8, Barnett 5, Barrett 4, Hunt 4, Wordsworth 4, Pigott 3, Worrall 3, Atkinson 2, Leonard 2, McQueen 2, Prosser 2, Thompson 2, Timlin 2, Coker 1, Hendrie 1, McLaughlin 1, Moussa 1, White 1, Opponents 1

FA Cup goals (1): Leonard 1. **League Cup goals**: None. **Johnstone's Paint Trophy goals** (4): Pigott 2, Weston 1, White 1

Average home league attendance: 7,001. **Player of Year**: Ryan Leonard

SWINDON TOWN

A productive start raised hopes of another good season for Swindon, who twice reached the play-offs in the three previous years. They kicked off with a 4-1 win over Bradford and accumulated 11 points from the opening six games. But the early promise was not maintained amid major managerial upheaval at the club. Mark Cooper was sacked after his team took a single point from the next eight matches and slipped to second from bottom. He was replaced by Martin Ling, a member of Swindon's Premiership side in the 1993-94 season, who resigned for health reasons after 56 days in charge. Luke Williams was then was given the job after winning six out of ten games as caretaker. On their day, Swindon were a free-scoring force, netting four more against Chesterfield, Southend, Crewe and Colchester, with Nicky Ajose on the mark twice each time. Ajose also scored a hat-trick against Blackpool on the way to 24 for the campaign. Some heavy defeats, notably 6-0 at Scunthorpe and 5-1 at Fleetwood, contributed to a bottom half of the table finish, although there were encouraging performances from young players, including 16-year-old Jordan Young, who netted his first senior goal in the final game against Shrewsbury.

Ajose N.........................38
Balmy J 1 (11)
Bangoura M 1
Barry B.........................35
Belford T 8
Brophy J 16 (12)
Byrne N...........................5
Cooke J....................... - (2)
Doughty M 20
El-Abd A........................13
Evans J....................... - (1)
Gladwin B.....................13
Henry W 2
Hylton J..................... 8 (8)
Iandolo E.................. 6 (6)

Kasim Y.................. 24 (3)	Rodgers A............... 29 (7)	Thomas W................. 5 (1)
Kean J.............................3	Branco R.......................36	Thompson L............ 23 (5)
Marshall L.................. - (2)	Sendles-White J.......... 8 (2)	Thompson N 21 (2)
Obika J.................... 27 (5)	Smith M 4 (1)	Traore D................. 15 (9)
Ojamaa H 7 (2)	Smith T .... - (1)	Turnbull J 42
Ormonde-Ottewill B 28	Stewart K.................. 3 (2)	Vigouroux L...................33
Randall W.................. - (4)	Stewart J .... - (1)	Williams J.........................9
Robert F 23 (12)	Storey M..................... - (2)	Young J...................... - (3)

League goals (64): Ajose 24, Obika 11, Doughty 5, Robert 4, Byrne 3, Gladwin 2, Rodgers 2, Thomas 2, Thompson L 2, Kasim 1, Ormonde-Ottewill 1, Branco 1, Smith T 1, Thompson N 1, Young 1, Opponents 3

FA Cup goals (1): Ajose 1. **League Cup goals** (1): Obika 1. **Johnstone's Paint Trophy goals** (1): Rodgers 1

Averge home league attendance: 7,409. **Player of Year**: Nicky Ajose

WALSALL

A five-star performance on the final day of the regular season was not enough to take Walsall up. Needing a three-goal swing in goal difference to stand a chance of dislodging Burton from the runners-up spot, they achieved it with something to spare, winning 5-0 at Port Vale. But their rivals held on for a goalless draw at Doncaster to finish a point ahead. Six days later Walsall's hopes of making it through the play-offs were effectively killed off by a 3-0 defeat at Barnsley in their semi-final first leg. Despite an improved performance in the return, a 3-1 loss left them with nothing to show for their efforts throughout the campaign. They had overcome two managerial upheavals to spent most of the time in the top six, including sharing the leadership with Burton and Gillingham before Wigan took a grip on the title. Dean Smith, longest-serving manager in League One, left after nearly five years to take over at Brentford. Sean O'Driscoll, former Bristol City, Nottingham Forest, Doncaster and Bournemouth manager, replaced him, but was sacked three months into the job after a run of six games without a win. Jon Whitney put them back on course after his interim appointment. He was then given the job on a permanent basis.

Baxendale J .... - (3)	Flanagan R................ 8 (6)	Morris K................12 (21)
Bradshaw T............. 38 (3)	Forde A................. 26 (15)	Morris B......................- (1)
Chambers A...................45	Henry R 30 (5)	O'Connor J 37
Cook J..................... 5 (29)	Hiwula J.................... 8 (5)	Pennington M 5
Demetriou J 42 (1)	Kinsella L.................. 4 (3)	Preston M..................4 (6)
Downing P.....................46	Lalkovic M............. 27 (13)	Roberts L 1
Etheridge N....................40	MacGillivray C..................5	Sawyers R 45 (1)
Evans G........................12	Mantom S 33 (4)	Taylor A..................33 (1)

Play-offs – appearances: Bradshaw 2, Chambers 2, Demetriou 2, Downing 2, Etheridge 2, Henry 2, O'Connor 2, Sawyers 2, Forde 1 (1), Hiwula 1 (1), Lalkovic 1 (1), Mantom 1 (1), Morris K 1 Taylor 1, Cook – (2),

League goals (71): Bradshaw 17, Mantom 8, Lalkovic 7, Sawyers 6, Forde 4, Cook 3, Demetriou 3, Downing 3, Evans 3, Hiwula 3, Morris 3, Henry 2, Preston 2, Taylor 2, Kinsella 1, O'Connor 1, Opponents 3. **Play-offs – goals** (1): Cook 1

FA Cup goals (4): Demetriou 1, Evans 1, Forde 1, Mantom 1. **League Cup goals** (7): Bradshaw 3 Henry 1, Lalkovic 1, O'Connor 1, Sawyers 1. **Johnstone's Paint Trophy goals**: None

Average home league attendance: 5,382. **Player of Year**: Adam Chambers

WIGAN ATHLETIC

Gary Caldwell followed a notable playing career for club and country with a successful start in management. The former Celtic and Scotland defender, who finished his playing days with 'igan, led the club back to the Championship at the first attempt during an unbeaten run of 20 ·atches which enabled them to outstrip every promotion rival. It began a week before Christmas, athered momentum with new signings in the January transfer window and continued until a 3-1 efeat at Doncaster in mid-April. By then, the run had yielded 46 points and 42 goals, with a 5-1 ctory at Shrewsbury having brought the top spot, held at various times by Gillingham, Walsall ıd Burton. The prolific Will Grigg, whose goals the previous season had been instrumental in ·omotion for MK Dons, scored twice in that match. Two more came in a 4-1 win over Southend ·hich effectively made sure Wigan went up, while a 4-0 victory against Blackpool sealed the tle. Grigg's final tally was 25 and he was joined in the PFA's League One Team of the Season y defenders Reece Wabara and Craig Morgan and winger Yanic Wildschut. Caldwell received the 'visional Manager of the Year accolade for starting to reverse the club's slide from the Premier eague.

arnett L................ 16 (4)
how T...................... 3 (8)
olclough R............... 7 (3)
oulthirst S................. - (2)
owie D...................... 2 (3)
aniels D................ 40 (2)
avies C.................. 7 (19)
lores J...................... 2 (1)
'ancisco Junior......... 5 (5)
rigg W.................. 35 (5)
iwula J.................... 7 (7)
olt G........................ - (4)
Jaaskelainen J...............35
Jacobs M................. 30 (5)
James R.................. 25 (1)
Kellett A..................... 4 (5)
Kenny J...................... 6 (1)
Love D....................... 4 (3)
McAleny C.................. 9 (4)
McCann C............... 31 (7)
McKay B..................... - (1)
McNaughton K........... 1 (1)
Morgan C.......................36
Morsy S.................. 13 (3)
Murray S.................... 2 (5)
Nicholls L................... 1 (1)
O'Donnell R.................... 10
Odelusi S...................... - (3)
Pearce J.................. 29 (2)
Perkins D................ 44 (1)
Power M.................. 43 (1)
Revell A...................... 4 (2)
Vuckic H................. 5 (10)
Wabara R................ 14 (5)
Warnock S...................... 11
Wildschut Y............. 25 (9)

eague goals (82): Grigg 25, Jacobs 10, Wildschut 7, Power 6, McAleny 4, McCann 4, Daniels , Colclough 2, Davies 2, Hiwula 2, Kellett 2, Morgan 2, Pearce 2, Vuckic 2, Barnett 1, Flores , Francisco Junior 1, James 1, Morsy 1, Revell 1, Wabara 1, Opponents 2

A Cup goals: None. **League Cup goals** (1): Grigg 1. **Johnstone's Paint Trophy goals** (9): iwula 4, Grigg 2, Wildschut 2, Murray 1

verage home league attendance: 9,465. **Player of Yea**: David Perkins

LEAGUE TWO

.CCRINGTON STANLEY

ɔ near, yet so far. John Coleman's side went into the final match of the regular season in an ɹtomatic promotion place, needing to win their home game against Stevenage to guarantee :aying there. They were frustrated in a goalless draw, with Shay McCartan, twice, and Matty earson striking the woodwork. But it still looked enough to take them up until Bristol Rovers :ored in the second minute of stoppage-time to defeat relegated Dagenham and Redbridge and ·ertake them with a superior goal difference. Accrington went into the play-offs against AFC 'imbledon and there was more disappointment. They overturned a one-goal deficit from the rst leg with goals by Josh Windass, from the penalty spot, and Piero Mingoia. But Wimbledon velled the tie on aggregate and won it with a goal in extra-time. Coleman rated his squad the :rongest in his 16-year association with the club, despite having the smallest budget in the vision. Accrington were knocking on the door of a top-three place throughout the second-half the season and finally broke through with a 2-0 win at Luton, delivered by goals from Scott rown and Terry Gornell.

arry A...................... 2 (6)
oco R...................... 6 (5)
rown S.................... 8 (5)
runa G...................... - (3)
ɹxton A................. 25 (3)
Carver M.................... - (2)
Conneely S.....................46
Crooks M.......................32
Davies T................ 31 (1)
Etheridge R...................21
Fosu-Henry T............. 4 (4)
Gornell T................. 8 (12)
Halliday B............... 31 (1)
Hughes M.....................15
Kee B.................... 39 (6)

McCartan S............ 10 (17)
McConville S............ 40 (2)
Mingoia P......................46
Mohamed K................- (3)
Mooney J................. 25 (1)
Morgan A.....................- (2)
Pearson M......................46
Procter A 1 (10)
Shaw B.........................- (4)
Wakefield L............... 7 (5)
Windass J 30
Winnard D............... 14 (1)
Wright J.................. 19 (1)

Play-offs – appearances: Brown 2, Buxton 2, Conneely 2, Davies 2, Etheridge 2, Hughes 2, Ke 2, Mingoia 2, Pearson 2, Windass 2, McCartan 1 (1), McConville 1, Gornell – (2), Boco – (1 Fosu-Henry – (1), Halliday – (1)
League goals (74): Kee 17, Windass 15, McCartan 7, Crooks 6, McConville 5, Brown 3, Conneel 3, Fosu-Henry 3, Gornell 3, Mingoia 3, Pearson 3, Boco 2, Buxton 1, Davies 1, Hughes 1 Opponents 1. **Play-offs – goals** (2): Mingoia 1, Windass 1
FA Cup goals (3): Crooks 1, McConville 1, Windass 1. **League Cup goals** (2): Crooks 1, Gornell 1
Johnstone's Paint Trophy goals (1): Bruna 1
Average home league attendance: 1,834.

AFC WIMBLEDON

No wonder Neal Ardley and his players celebrated wildly after beating Plymouth 2-0 in the Leagu Two Play-off Final. Not only had Wimbledon recorded a sixth promotion since being formed b supporters and setting out in the Combined Counties League in 2002. More significantly, th one brought them alongside MK Dons, the controversial reincarnation of the old Plough Lan club, who were relegated from the Championship. The teams now meet in League One aft Wembley goals from leading scorer Lyle Taylor and 16st, out-of-contract Adebayo Akinfenw whose penalty clincher came in the 11th minute of stoppage-time. This unlikely double-act we also on the mark to carry Wimbledon through their semi-final against Accrington in extra-tim Ardley, who spent a decade as a player with the former Wimbledon, led his side from the botto half of the table into a challenging position with a New Year surge of seven wins out of eigh Then, after a loss of momentum, they regained a place in the top seven with five successi victories, one of which came at Plymouth. Taylor was on the mark six times in that sequence t take his tally for the season to 20.

Ajayi S............................5
Akinfenwa A........... 20 (18)
Azeez A 9 (33)
Barcham A............... 31 (2)
Beere T...................... 1 (1)
Bulman D............... 39 (3)
Charles D........................9
Elliott T................ 25 (14)
Fitzpatrick D 2 (3)
Francomb G............ 36 (4)
Fuller B.........................45
Kaja E.........................- (2)
Kennedy C............... 10 (9)
Meades J................. 40 (1)
Murphy R 6 (1)
Nightingale W............ 3 (1)
Oakley G ....- (1)
Olusanya T ....- (1)
Osborne K 21 (2)
Reeves J.................. 39 (1)
Rigg S................... 18 (21
Robinson P..................44
Roos K..........................17
Shea J 21
Smith C 7 (3
Sweeney R 10
Taylor L....................38 (4
Toonga C....................2 (2
Wilson B 8

Play-offs – appearances: Barcham 3, Bulman 3, Charles 3, Elliott 3, Fuller 3, Kennedy 3, Reeves 3 Robinson 3, Roos 3, Taylor 3, Rigg 2, Smith 1, Akinfenwa – (3), Azeez – (3), Beere – (2), Meades – (
League goals (64): Taylor 20, Azeez 7, Akinfenwa 6, Elliott 6, Barcham 5, Bulman 3, Francom 3, Meades 3, Robinson 3, Rigg 2, Fitzpatrick 1, Kennedy 1, Murphy 1, Olusanya 1, Reeves 1 Opponents 1. **Play-offs – goals** (5): Akinfenwa 2, Taylor 2, Beere 1
FA Cup goals (1): Kennedy 1. **League Cup goals**: None. **Johnstone's Paint Trophy goals** (2 Azeez 1, Taylor 1
Average home league attendance: 4,138. **Player of Year**: Paul Robinson

BARNET

Back in the Football League after a two-year absence, this time with a new ground at The Hiv Barnet consolidated successfully. Martin Allen packed plenty of experience into his side, whi blooding some promising youngsters with an eye to the future. They were good value from a ntertainment point of view, scoring three or more goals in ten matches, while also conceding enty. The outcome was a finish just below halfway after an indifferent opening which left them cond from bottom after five defeats in seven games. Successive home wins over Stevenage -2) and Dagenham and Redbridge (3-1) proved the turning point, backed up by a 3-2 victory Oxford, with one of the best performances of the campaign rewarded by goals from Curtis eston, John Akinde and Josh Clark in the space of five minutes. Akinde, whose 31 goals the evious season fired Barnet to the Conference title, netted 23 this time, nine of them coming the final eight matches.

kinde J 41 (2)	Johnson E 41	Roberts J.................... 1 (1)
ailey N 1 (1)	Lawlor I...........................5	Sesay A....................10 (3)
att S...................... 4 (12)	Lisbie K .... - (3)	Shomotun F................3 (7)
hampion T 19 (7)	McKenzie L .... - (1)	Stacey J 2
arke J 10	Mclean A................. 13 (7)	Stack G..........................7
ocombe M....................5	Muggleton S 8 (15)	Stephens J 29
ay T .... - (1)	Nana Kyei 1	Stevens M 2 (8)
embele B.............. 25 (1)	Nelson M 22 (5)	Taylor H 4 (4)
onguck W ....– (1)	N'Gala B 39 (3)	Togwell S..................34 (5)
ambin L.............. 30 (14)	Nwogu J..................... 2 (2)	Tomlinson B 1 (2)
ash M................. 20 (14)	Odofin H .... - (1)	Vilhete M....................8 (7)
ackett C 5 (1)	Pearson J 14 (1)	Weston C..................36 (1)
oyte G 16 (3)	Randall M 8 (4)	Yiadom A.......................40

eague goals (67): Akinde 23, Gash 9, Yiadom 6, Mclean 5, Gambin 4, Clarke 3, Dembele 3, eston 3, Randall 2, Hoyte 1, Johnson 1, N'Gala 1, Nelson 1, Shomotun 1, Stevens 1, Togwell , Opponents 2

A Cup goals (2): Champion 1, Gash 1. **League Cup goals** (3): Akinde 1, Dembele 1, Yiadom 1.

ohnstone's Paint Trophy goals: None

verage home league attendance: 2,358. **Player of Year**: Jamie Stephens

RISTOL ROVERS

nother dramatic final day of the season at the Memorial Stadium – and this time Darrell Clarke nd his players were celebrating. Two years previously, Rovers were relegated from the Football eague on goal difference after losing to Mansfield. They bounced straight back in 2015 and arned a second successive promotion with a goal from Lee Brown in the second minute of oppage-time It brought a 2-1 victory over relegated Dagenham and Redbridge just as Rovers oked to be heading for the play-offs. Clarke's side went up automatically, overtaking Accrington, ho were held to a goalless draw by Stevenage in their final game. Again, it all boiled down to oal difference, with Matt Taylor's prolific campaign proving a crucial factor in their favour. The ading marksman netted 27 goals, including hat-tricks against Wycombe and Hartlepool, the rmer in the space of 12 minutes. The latter came shortly after a takeover of the club by the rdanian Al-Qadi family. The new owners saw their team regain a play-off place by beating orecambe, then go on to reach the fringes of a top-three place. During that spell, Taylor netted 3 of his goals in 12 matches.

issett N .... - (2)	Gaffney R................ 23 (1)	McBurnie O.................- (5)
odin B................ 26 (12)	Gosling J................. 8 (10)	McChrystal M 20 (1)
room R .... - (1)	Harrison E............. 10 (20)	Mildenhall S.............25 (1)
rown L........................46	Lawrence L................ 8 (4)	Monakana J ....- (3)
hapman A......................5	Leadbitter D 28 (5)	Montano C.............12 (16)
larke J 36 (1)	Lines C 30 (3)	Nicholls L...................... 15
arke O 22 (11)	Lockyer T 42 (1)	Parkes T...................29 (2)
owan-Hall P 2 (1)	Lucas J .... - (1)	Puddy W 1
aster J 21 (21)	Lyttle T 1	Sinclair S 30
allon R..................... - (3)	Mansell L......................28	Taylor M..................38 (8)

League goals (77): Taylor 27, Bodin 13, Gaffney 8, Easter 7, Harrison 7, Brown 6, Clarke O Mansell 2, Montano 2, Sinclair 2, Lawrence 1
FA Cup goals: None. **League Cup goals** (1): Harrison 1. **Johnstone's Paint Trophy goals** (2 Easter 1, Taylor 1
Average home league attendance: 8,096. **Player of Year**: Matt Taylor

CAMBRIDGE UNITED

A club-record performance kept Shaun Derry's side in with an outside chance of reaching tl play-offs. Three days after a frustrating goalless draw against Carlisle, Cambridge trounc Morecambe 7-0, scoring five times in the first-half for the club's biggest Football League victo A 2-1 away win over Notts County followed and hopes were still alive when Ben Williams (84) and Jimmy Spencer (86) put them ahead with late goals against Plymouth. Instea their opponents equalised in stoppage-time, so the final game against Mansfield was render irrelevant, with the team immediately above them, AFC Wimbledon, now five points clear. Der had replaced Richard Money, who was sacked as manager with his side down in 18th plac After starting with two defeats, he led them up into the top half with a run of 16 points frc six matches. The loss of leading scorer Barry Corr, who had knee surgery and was ruled out f the rest of the season, was a blow, although the signing of Williamson, after a loan spell, we some way to compensating, Cambridge remaining within striking distance of a top-seven spot.

Ahearne-Grant K......... 1 (2)
Beasant S............... 14 (1)
Berry L.................... 41 (5)
Blyth J....................... 2 (3)
Carr D........................ 1 (3)
Chiedozie J................. - (2)
Clark M...................... 7 (2)
Corr B...................... 19 (3)
Coulson J................. 22 (1)
Demetriou M............ 12 (3)
Donaldson R 18 (12)
Dunk H.................... 41 (4)
Dunn C..........................11
Dunne J.........................19
Furlong D.......................21
Gaffney R 3 (3)
Gayle C............................4
Haynes R.......................10
Hughes J 7 (2)
Hughes L................ 11 (5)
Ismail Z..................... 8 (3)
Jones J.............................1
Keane K 3 (1)
Kennedy T 2
Ledson R.......................27
Legge L.........................39
Morrissey G................ - (2)
Newton C................ 16 (6)
Norris W 2
O'Neill S..................... 1 (1
Omozusi E 9 (5
Page L.............................(
Roberts M................ 26 (4
Sesay A ....
Simpson R............ 14 (18
Slew J 4 (6
Spencer J 11 (7
Taft G...................... 10 (1
Taylor G.................. 12 (4
Williams D .... - (1
Williamson B........... 27 (1

League goals (66): Berry 12, Corr 12, Williamson 12, Spencer 6, Dunk 4, Simpson 4, Legg 3, Donaldson 2, Gaffney 2, Roberts 2, Blyth 1, Coulsen 1, Dunne 1, Gayle 1, Ismail 1, Taft Opponents 1
FA Cup goals (2): Berry 1, Hughes J 1. **League Cup goals**: None. **Johnstone's Paint Trophy goal** None
Average home league attendance: 5,262. **Player of Year**: Leon Legge

CARLISLE UNITED

A season that will always be remembered for the floods which forced the club to play thr home matches away from Brunton Park could also have brought the chance of promotion. Aft spending much of the campaign on the fringes of a play-off place, Keith Curle's side closed within two points after beating Bristol Rovers and Hartlepool. A home game against Mansfiel whose own challenge had faltered through seven without a win, presented the opportunity make the breakthrough. Instead, Carlisle were beaten 2-1 and Curle's challenge to his players win their five remaining fixtures proved an unrealistic one. In a tightly packed division, they f back before finishing with a 5-0 win over Notts County. With their ground under water, supporte travelled to Preston for a 3-0 win over Notts County, to Blackburn for a 2-0 defeat by Plymou and to Blackpool, where a 2-2 FA Cup draw with Yeovil was followed by victory on penalties the replay. That earned a fourth round tie against Everton, which drew the club's biggest crowd, more than 17,000, since 1989 for a 3-0 defeat by the Premier League side.

Archibald-Henville T ... 6 (6)
Asamoah D 13 (30)
Atkinson D 23 (2)
Balanta A.................. 4 (3)
Brough P 6 (1)
Comley B 12
Dicker G 13 (6)
Ellis M...........................30
Gillesphey M 18 (5)
Gillespie M 45
Gillieard A 23 (12)
Grainger D......................36
Hanford D 1 (1)
Hery B 16 (4)
Hope H 16 (5)
Ibehre J 29 (7)
Joyce L 34 (3)
Kennedy J 44
McQueen A.............. 15 (6)
Miller T 28 (1)
Osei K........................1 (7)
Pedro L........................- (1)
Raynes M 39 (1)
Rigg S.........................2 (6)
Smith M......................1 (1)
Stacey J 7 (2)
Sweeney A................11 (8)
Thompson J.............4 (11)
Wyke C......................29 (5)

League goals (67): Ibehre 15, Wyke 12, Asamoah 6, Grainger 6, Gillieard 5, Miller 5, Hope 4, Raynes 3, Archibald-Henville 2, Gillesphey 2, Kennedy 2, Stacey 2, Balanta 1, Sweeney 1, Thompson 1

FA Cup goals (10): Sweeney 3, Wyke 3, Grainger 2, Ellis 1, Hope 1. **League Cup** goals (6): Asamoah 2, Ibehre 2, Kennedy 1, Osei 1. **Johnstone's Paint Trophy goals**: None

Average home league attendance: 4,838. **Player of Year**: Danny Grainger

CRAWLEY TOWN

A takeover of the club by Turkish businessman Ziya Eren was the main talking point of a season which proved another poor one on the pitch. He set an ambitious long-term target of reaching the Championship over the next decade. In the short-term, his plans were to increase the playing budget, beef up the commercial side and look at establishing an academy. The new owner also said he would also be 'assessing' the performance manager of Mark Yates. Eren attended his first match, against Oxford, and saw a promising start when Joe McNerney gave Crawley the lead. But they collapsed in the second-half, conceding four goals and losing 5-1. Yates was sacked after a sixth successive defeat and replaced by former Chelsea and Arsenal coach Dermot Drummy – his first managerial appointment. Drummy took charge for the final two games, 3-0 beatings by relegated Dagenham and Redbridge, then Barnet. They left Crawley, relegated the previous season, fifth from bottom and the new man looking to make wholesale changes to the squad.

Ashton J 26 (4)
Atkinson C 5 (2)
Barnard L 14 (14)
Bawling B 7 (8)
Bond A.................... 11 (1)
Bradley S.......................46
Dallison T 1
Deacon R............... 21 (16)
Della-Verde L 10 (2)
Donnelly L 9 (1)
Dunne C 12
Edwards G 40 (2)
Emmanuel J.............. 1 (1)
Fenelon S................ 9 (21)
Flahavan D.....................13
Hancox M.......................15
Harrold M................ 33 (4)
Henderson C.............. 2 (1)
Jenkins R 7 (7)
Jones P 8
McAlinden L............... 5 (1)
McNerney J 10 (1)
Murphy R.......................15
Oyebanjo L 7
Preston C 9
Rooney L................. 9 (10)
Rose J............................5
Scales C.....................7 (1)
Smith G 4
Smith J....................29 (2)
Sutherland F.............10 (1)
Tomlin G 11 (5)
Van Den Bogaert B 1
Walton S 31 (6)
Woodman F 11
Yorwerth J 23 (1)
Young L....................29 (9)

League goals (45): Murphy 9, Edwards 8, Harrold 8, Deacon 5, Walton 4, Fenelon 2, Hancox 2, Barnard 1, Bradley 1, McAlinden 1, McNerney 1, Rooney 1, Smith J 1, Opponents 1

FA Cup goals (1): Harrold 1. **League Cup goals**: None. **Johnstone's Paint Trophy goals**: None

Average home league attendance: 2,405. **Player of Year**: Gwion Edwards

DAGENHAM AND REDBRIDGE

Dagenham had overcome modest crowds and limited resources to retain their Football League place since being promoted in 2007. What they couldn't survive in a ninth season of membership was a run of 16 home games without a win – a sequence which not even the experienced John Still, in his third spell as manager, could counter. Still, who took the club up from the Conference, returned to his roots from an unsuccessful spell at Luton after Wayne Burnett was sacked four days before Christmas with just two away wins to show from 22 matches. His first game delivered a 2-1 victory at Exeter. The second, a gritty defensive performance in the FA Cup, which frustrated Everton for long periods, also held out the promise of better things. Instead, Dagenham had to wait another two months for that elusive first success at Victoria Road – 1-0 against fellow-strugglers York earned by a first senior goal for Josh Passley. By then, they were seven points adrift at the bottom of the table, a gap which had grown to 11 points when a second home win was forthcoming against Morecambe. A 4-1 defeat by Portsmouth effectively sealed their fate, confirmation coming in a 3-2 defeat at Leyton Orient with four matches to play.

Boucaud A............... 21 (4)
Cash M..........................12
Chambers A 22 (9)
Connors J................... 7 (2)
Cousins M............... 22 (1)
Cureton J............... 21 (17)
Dikamona C 23 (4)
Doidge C.................. 29 (6)
Dunne J..........................9
Ferdinand K............ 14 (1)
Guttridge L 2 (1)
Hamalainen N..................1
Hawkins O 4 (14)
Hemmings A............ 37 (2)
Hines Z...................... 1 (5)
Hoyte J 22 (4)
Hyam D..........................16
Jones J.................. 12 (15)
Labadie J 26 (2)
McClure M 11 (9)
Muldoon O 18
Mulraney J 3 (3)
Nosworthy N............ 16 (1)
O'Brien L 24
Obileye A 15 (1)
Partridge M 2
Pask J.............................5
Passley J..................36 (2)
Pennell L 4 (1)
Raymond F.................8 (2)
Richards M.................9 (1)
Shephard J.....................2
Sutherland F...............2 (2)
Taylor Q......................1 (1)
Vassell K 4 (4)
Widdowson J.................31
Worrall J........................14
Yusuff A......................- (1)

League goals (46): Doidge 8, Cureton 7, Chambers 4, Hemmings 4, Labadie 4, McClure 4, Cash 3, Jones 3, Dikamona 2, Ferdinand 1, Guttridge 1, Hawkins 1, Nosworthy 1, Passley 1, Raymond 1, Worrall 1

FA Cup goals (8): Vassell 3, Cureton 1, Dunne 1, Labadie 1, Obileye 1, Pashley 1. **League Cup goals** (1): Doidge 1. **Johnstone's Paint Trophy goals** (4): Chambers 1, Cureton 1, Hemmings 1, McClure 1

Average home league attendance: 1,979. **Player of Year**: Joss Labadie

EXETER CITY

With a month of the season remaining, Exeter were one of six clubs contesting the last play-off place up for grabs. Paul Tisdale's side had worked their way up from the bottom half of the table with a run of 21 points from nine matchers, sparked by seven goals from Ollie Watkins, winner of the Football League's Young Player of the Month award for March. They included two in the 2-1 win over Plymouth which completed a satisfying league double over their local rivals. Watkins was also on the mark, along with Christian Ribeiro, against Mansfield as Exeter retrieved a two-goal deficit. But they conceded another eight minutes from the end for a 3-2 defeat. That was followed by a 3-0 reversal against Bristol Rovers which ruled them out of contention. Earlier in the season, Tisdale, in charge since June 2006 and the second longest-serving manager behind Arsenal's Arsene Wenger, took charge of his 500th game. Ironically, he rated the 4-1 home defeat by Oxford one of the poorest of his long tenure. Exeter had a taste of the FA Cup limelight, holding Liverpool to 2-2 at St James Park before losing the third round replay 3-0.

rown T.................. 39 (1)
utterfield D.............. 8 (2)
avies A................ 18 (10)
rant J.................... 19 (7)
iamon J.........................1
'arley R.................. 26 (2)
iolmes L................. 30 (7)
loskins W.................. 2 (7)
1cAllister J.............. 25 (3)
McCready T................ 8 (2)
Moore-Taylor J................32
Morrison C................ 4 (16)
Nichols T................ 19 (4)
Nicholls A............... 26 (9)
Noble D.................. 24 (6)
Oakley M................. 24 (5)
Olejnik B........................45
Oyeleke E.................. 4 (4)
Reid J.........................8 (6)
Ribeiro C..................31 (4)
Stockley J..................21 (1)
Taylor J.......................7 (9)
Tillson J...................22 (4)
Watkins O.................15 (5)
Wheeler D.................26 (5)
Woodman C..............22 (3)

eague goals (63): Nichols 10, Stockley 10, Watkins 8, Wheeler 6, Nicholls 5, Grant 4, Harley , Ribeiro 4, Taylor 4, Holmes 2, Brown 1, Davies 1, Hoskins 1, Morrison 1, Reid 1, Tillson 1
A Cup goals (7): Nichols 2, Holmes 1, Morrison 1, Nicholls 1, Tillson 1, Watkins 1. **League up goals** (5): Wheeler 2, McCready 1, Nicholls 1, Oyeleke 1. **Johnstone's Paint Trophy goals** 2): Harley 1, Nicholls 1
verage home league attendance: 4,008. **Player of Year**: Lee Holmes

IARTLEPOOL UNITED

:onnie Moore made ten signings after engineering a great escape from relegation the previous eason – and his reshaped side made a promising start to the new one. They scored successive ictories over Morecambe, York and Newport which suggested brighter times ahead. Instead, ptimism faded as Hartlepool hit familiar hard times. They managed to keep their distance from ne teams at the bottom until a single win in eight matches around the halfway point left them hird from the foot of the table, albeit with fixtures in hand. Moore was sacked and replaced nmediately by former Middlesbrough midfielder Craig Hignett, who finished his playing career at ne club. Hignett won his first match, against Yeovil, but a single point from the next four resulted 1 a slide to within two points of the drop zone. Hartlepool responded with six goals in the next wo games, against Barnet and Dagenham, and went on to move well clear of trouble with a run f five victories in seven games, including a 5-2 success at Morecambe. A tough run-in against our promotion-chasing sides, all ending in defeat, left them in 16th place.

:anton J..................... - (4)
:artlett A.......................12
:ates M.................. 30 (2)
ingham R............ 18 (13)
:lackford J................ - (1)
:oyce A..................... 7 (1)
:arroll J.........................41
:arson T.........................34
)uckworth M........... 11 (2)
eatherstone N......... 40 (5)
'enwick S............. 11 (12)
iray J..................... 26 (3)
Halliday B..........................6
Harrison E..........................2
Harrison S............... 21 (1)
Hawkins L............... 18 (4)
Hendrie L..........................3
Jackson A............... 28 (1)
James L.................. 19 (1)
Jones D.................. 10 (1)
Jones R..................... 5 (2)
Laurent J................... 1 (2)
Magnay C................ 30 (3)
Mandron M............... 3 (2)
Naismith K.......................4
Nelson-Addy E............ - (2)
Oates R................ 21 (17)
Okuonghae M..................4
Oyenuga K................ 2 (6)
Paynter B................ 31 (1)
Richards J................. 8 (3)
Smith C.................... 2 (3)
Thomas N............... 21 (1)
Walker B................ 8 (15)
Woods M................. 26 (7)
Worley H.........................3

eague goals (49): Paynter 14, Gray 5, Thomas 5, Bingham 4, Fenwick 4, Jackson 3, Woods 3, **l**awkins 2, Oates 2, Carroll 1, Harrison 1, James 1, Magnay 1, Oyenuga 1, Walker 1, Opponents 1
A Cup goals (5): Fenwick 1, Gray 1, Mandron 1, Oates 1, Oyenuga 1. **League Cup goals** (1): 'aynter 1. **Johnstone's Paint Trophy goals** (1): Fenwick 1
verage home league attendance: 3,890. **Player of Year**: Trevor Carson

.EYTON ORIENT

ın eventful season, on and off the field, looked as if it might bring the chance of an immediate return ɔ League One. With nine matches remaining, Orient were in a play-off position under Kevin Nolan. :ut as their challenge faltered, Nolan was removed as manager after three months in the job and his assistant Andy Hessenthaler given the chance to get them back on track. The move failed as his side slid out of contention and finished six points short. Nolan, former West Ham, Newcastle and Bolton captain, took over after the dismissal of Ian Hendon, whose spell in charge included five successive wins to start the season, a run of one victory in ten league and cup matches and a week in a hotel along with 18 players and other staff members, ordered by owner Francesco Becchetti. Later, the FA give Becchetti a six-match stadium ban and fined him £40,000 for violent conduct after watching TV pictures of the Italian aiming a kick at Hessenthaler at the Boxing Day home win over Portsmouth. The season's one consistent factor was the prolific form of Jay Simpson, who became club's first player to score 25 goals in a season since Tommy Johnston more than 50 years previously.

Adeboyejo V - (1)	Grainger C 2	Nolan K 12 (2)
Atangana N 16	Hunt N 16	Palmer O 25 (20)
Baudry M 33 (1)	Jahraldo-Martin C 8 (7)	Payne J 26 (3)
Binnom-Williams J 12 (1)	James L 17 (8)	Pollock A 2
Brisley S 16	Kashket S 1 (14)	Pritchard B 24 (5)
Chicksen A 6	Koroma J - (3)	Ramage P 8
Cisak A 43	Kpekawa C 8 (1)	Sargeant S 1
Clohessy S 41 (1)	Marquis J 9 (4)	Semedo S 2 (1)
Cox D 12 (2)	McAnuff J 14 (3)	Shaw F 20 (5)
Dunne A 3 (5)	McCallum P 8 (2)	Simpson J 45
Essam C 23 (1)	Moore S 27 (3)	Turgott B 10 (21)
Gnanduillet A 8 (9)	Mvoto J-Y 8	

League goals (60): Simpson 25, Palmer 7, Gnanduillet 4, James 4, Cox 3, McAnuff 3, McCallum 3, Baudry 2, Moore 2, Brisley 1, Jahraldo-Martin 1, Kashket 1, Payne 1, Pritchard 1, Turgott 1, Opponents 1
FA Cup goals (6): Cox 2, Palmer 2, Clohessy 1, Marquis 1. **League Cup goals** (1): Opponents 1
Johnstone's Paint Trophy goals (1): James 1
Average home league attendance: 5,332. **Player of Year**: Jay Simpson

LUTON TOWN

One of the teams strongly fancied for promotion fell some way short. They were let down by poor home form which resulted in ten defeats at Kenilworth Road and cost manager John Still his job. Luton failed to win any of their first five matches of the season, home or away, looked to be getting into their stride with four successive victories, along with ten goals, then suffered 4-3 defeats by Carlisle and Northampton in consecutive home games. Still was sacked and replaced by Nathan Jones, Brighton's first-team coach, who started his career at the club. He, too, found no cure for this inconsistency, having to rely on the greater freedom and confidence which Luton displayed on their travels to stay alive. It brought them to within three points of a top-six place before further home lapses against Stevenage and Accrington effectively ended their chances and they finished nine points away from the play-offs. At least there was a strong finish as Jack Marriott capped a promising first full league season with his 13th and 14th goals in a 4-1 success against Exeter.

Bakinson T - (1)	Lawless A 21 (7)	O'Donnell S 30
Banton Z - (4)	Lee O 31 (3)	Okuonghae M 7 (4)
Benson P 13 (7)	Long S 7 (2)	Pigott J 10 (5)
Cuthbert S 36	Mackail-Smith C 27 (6)	Potts D 14
Doyle N 6 (5)	Marriott J 21 (19)	Rea G 10
Green D 19 (6)	McCourt P 15 (9)	Ruddock P 12 (9)
Griffiths S 17 (1)	McGeehan C 35 (6)	Sheehan A 20
Guttridge L 6 (2)	McNulty S 9 (1)	Smith J 33 (4)
Hall R 5 (5)	McQuoid J 20 (9)	Tyler M 27
Howells J 14 (3)	Mitchell J 5	Wilkinson L 20
Justham E 14 (1)	Musonda F - (3)	
Justin J - (1)	O'Brien M 2 (4)	

eague goals (63): Marriott 14, McGeehan 12, Green 5, Benson 4, Mackail-Smith 4, Pigott , Smith 4, Lee 3, McQuoid 3, Wilkinson 3, Guttridge 2, Ruddock 2, Lawless 1, McCourt 1, heehan 1

A Cup goals (2): McQuoid 2. **League Cup goals** (4): Marriott 2, Benson 1, McGeehan 1.
ohnstone's Paint Trophy goals (3): Green 1, McGeehan 1, O'Donnell 1
verage home league attendance: 8,226. **Player of Year**: Jack Marriott

IANSFIELD TOWN

late surge was not enough to resurrect a promotion challenge, leaving Mansfield with the feeling f what might have been. They spent much of the season in or just outside the play-off zone, rising fifth after a 2-1 victory over Morecambe in which Scott Shearer saved two penalties. But a failure beat any of the leading teams held them back, while a run of seven matches without any win esulted in a fall to mid-table with a month of the season remaining. That sequence was ended by 2-1 success at Carlisle. It was followed by the club's biggest local derby win over Notts County – -0. And when Ryan Tafazolli scored his second goal of the game for a 3-2 scoreline at Exeter, his ide were still in with an outside chance. It went begging in a 1-1 home draw against Barnet and lansfield finished well adrift of the leading group. Even so, a place in the top half represented a ig improvement on the previous season's fourth-from-bottom finish.

dams B........................13
lfei D....................... 8 (4)
axendale J 11 (4)
eardsley C............... 6 (8)
enning M.............. 30 (1)
lair M.................. 20 (12)
hapman A............. 36 (1)
lements C............. 32 (6)
ollins L................. 29 (6)
Daniel C 5 (4)
Dieseruvwe E............. 9 (1)
Green M 44
Hakeem Z .... - (1)
Hunt N 19
Jensen B........................25
Kavanagh S............... 2 (5)
Lambe R.................. 30 (7)
McGuire J 15 (5)
Pearce K.................. 36 (2)
Rose M.................... 26 (8)
Shearer S.......................21
Tafazolli R......................44
Thomas J.............. 15 (18)
Thomas N 9 (8)
Westcarr C 21 (3)
Yussuf A .... - (26)

eague goals (61): Green 16, Clements 5, Lambe 5, Tafazolli 5, Yussuf 5, Benning 4, Pearce , Westcarr 3, Blair 2, Chapman 2, Daniel 2, Rose 2, Thomas 2, Baxendale 1, Beardsley 1, ieseruvwe 1, Thomas N 1, Opponents 1

A Cup goals: None. **League Cup goals** (1): Tafazolli 1. **Johnstone's Paint Trophy goals** (1): estcarr 1

verage home league attendance: 3,439. **Player of Year**: Ryan Tafazolli

IORECAMBE

lo team in the four divisions came close to matching Morecambe's aggregate of goals scored nd conceded. No goalkeeper experienced a more eventful season than Barry Roche. From start finish, his team provided rousing entertainment. But they were glad to see the back of it after club-record 7-0 hammering by Cambridge in the penultimate away game sent them on the way own to 21st place in the table, their lowest in nine seasons in the Football League. A total of 91 oals were conceded. On the plus side, 69 were scored, including five against AFC Wimbledon nd four against Notts County, Yeovil and Barnet. There never seemed to be a dull moment. A -0 lead was surrendered at Portsmouth, whose equaliser came in stoppage-time. Morecambe, hemselves, trailed 2-0 at Yeovil, but won 4-2 with goals by Aaron Wildig, Andrew Fleming, Lee lolyneux and Kevin Ellison. Roche had moments to remember when heading a 94th minute qualiser in the return fixture against Portsmouth and saving two penalties against Stevenage. hose to forget were two red cards in the space of five matches for conceding spot-kicks gainst Leyton Orient and Hartlepool. At least, suspension spared him more embarrassment t Cambridge.

arkhuizen T............ 36 (4)
eeley S........................39
Conlan L................. 14 (2)
Devitt J.................. 34 (5)
Doyle C..........................8
Dugdale A......................24

Edwards R 35 (2)
Ellison K................. 36 (8)
Fleming A................ 29 (4)
Forrester A................. 1 (2)
Goodall A................ 32 (5)
Kelleher J .... - (1)
Kenyon A................. 21 (8)
McGowan A............. 14 (7)
Miller S 32 (5)
Molyneux L 18 (16)
Mullin P 11 (29)
Murphy P.................. 5 (2)
O'Hara K................... 4 (1)
Oliver C 1 (4)
Parrish A................. 31 (1
Roche B 42
Ryan J........................ - (3)
Stockton C................ 2 (5)
Thompson T................ - (1)
Wildig A................. 22 (10)
Wilson L 15 (13)

League goals (69): Miller 15, Bakhuizen 10, Ellison 9, Mullin 9, Devitt 6, Goodall 4, Flemin 3, Kenyon 3, Molyneux 3, Wildig 2, Doyle 1, Murphy 1, Roche 1, Stockton 1, Opponents 1
FA Cup goals (2): Barkhuizen 1, Wildig 1. **League Cup goals**: None. **Johnstone's Paint Troph goals** (4): Barkhuizen 1, Devitt 1, Miller 1, Mullin 1
Average home league attendance: 1,572. **Player of Year**: Jamie Devitt

NEWPORT COUNTY

Scott Boden struck a purple patch to banish the threat of relegation under Newport's thir manager of the season. He scored seven goals in eight games as Warren Feeney's side eased ou of trouble after slipping to within four points of the bottom two. One came in a 3-0 away wi over promotion-chasing Portsmouth. Newport then looked capable of climbing further. Insteac they went sliding on the back of a miserable run through to the end of the season. The final 1 matches failed to deliver another win, they failed to score in seven of them and finished third fror bottom, albeit nine points better off than the two relegated teams, Dagenham and Redbridg and York. Assistant manager Feeney took over early in the New Year when John Sheridan le after three months in the job for a second spell as Oldham manager. Sheridan, himself, ha replaced former England captain Terry Butcher, sacked after a single win in 12 games in charge His team were then bottom. But the pressure eased during a seven-match unbeaten run durin which 19-year-old Oliver McBurnie, on a one-month youth loan from Swansea, scored all thre goals in a 3-0 win over Luton.

Ansah Z..................... 9 (4)
Ayina....................... 10 (4)
Bamford L.................. - (1)
Barnum-Bobb J 11 (1)
Barrow S.................. 27 (7)
Beeney M 4
Bennett S 12
Blackwood T 1 (2)
Boden S 30 (15)
Byrne M.................. 45 (1)
Collins A................. 8 (10)
Coulibaly S 2 (4)
Davies B 16 (3)
Day J............................41
Donacien J 24 (5)
Dymond C 1
Elito M..................... 36 (2)
Feely K 3
Gosling J................... 2 (4)
Hayden A................... 4 (1)
Holmes D................ 33 (2)
Hughes A 24 (1)
John-Lewis L 26 (2)
Jones D.........................17
Klukowski Y........... 17 (11)
Laurent J..................... - (3)
McBurnie O............... 2 (1)
Meechan T .... - (3)
Morgan D 2 (7
O'Sullivan T............. 14 (6
Ofori-Twumasi N 9 (1
Owen-Evans T............6 (9
Parselle K........................ 7
Partridge M 19 (1
Poole R......................3 (1
Rodman A 25 (4
Smalley D........................ 3
Taylor M 2 (2
Taylor R.......................... 1
Wilkinson C 10 (2

League goals (43): Boden 13, Rodman 4, John-Lewis 3, McBurnie 3, Ansah 2, Barrow 2, Byrn 2, Collins 2, Ayina 1, Blackwood 1, Coulibaly 1, Elito 1, Jones 1, Klukowski 1, Morgan 1 O'Sullivan 1, Wilkinson 1, Opponents 3
FA Cup goals (8): John-Lewis 2, Bennett 1, Boden 1, Byrne 1, Klukowski 1, Rodman 1 Opponents 1. **League Cup goals** (1): Boden 1. **Johnstone's Paint Trophy goals** (1): Collins 1
Average home league attendance: 2,731. **Player of Year**: Mark Byrne

NORTHAMPTON TOWN

Against a background of financial turmoil, Chris Wilder and his team exceeded all expectations They played through the threat to the club of a winding-up petition, the possibility of enterin administration and worries about when the next pay packet would arrive to keep pace with the leaders. When the pressures eased, following a takeover by former Oxford United chairman Kelvin Thomas, Wilder's players dislodged Plymouth from top spot early in the New Year – and never looked back. Ten successive league wins delivered a club record. Northampton then became the first Football League side to clinch promotion – with five matches still to play – against Bristol Rovers. A week later, a goalless draw at Exeter was good enough to make them champions and they finished off with a lead of 13 points. There was more success when Wilder was named League Two Manager of the Year and winger Ricky Holmes was shortlisted for the division's Player of the Year award. It was all a far cry from the problems Thomas had to sort out when he took over – notably the unpaid £10.25m council loan for the redevelopment at Sixfields and the £166,000 owed to Revenue and Customs. But success also came at a price, with Wilder leaving to replace the sacked Nigel Adkins at Sheffield United. Port Vale's Robert Page succeeded him.

Adams N.................. 34 (5)
Brisley S..........................9
Buchanan D...................46
Byrom J................... 33 (2)
Calvert-Lewin D........ 7 (13)
Collins J.................. 16 (5)
Corry P....................... - (3)
Cresswell R............... 18 6)
D'Ath L.................. 25 (14)
Diamond Z............... 37 (2)
Furlong D.......................10
Hackett C.................. 2 (4)
Holmes R................ 20 (8)
Hoskins S.............. 16 (18)
Lelan J..................... 10 (1)
Marquis J................ 13 (2)
Martin L..................... 9 (1)
McDonald R 21 (2)
Moloney B......................25
O'Toole J-J............... 36 (2)
Potter A 12 (9)
Prosser L...................7 (1)
Richards M..............28 (3)
Rose D.....................13 (2)
Smith A 46
Taylor J 8 (22)
Watson R...................4 (7)
Yates A........................... 1

League goals (82): Richards 15, O'Toole 12, Holmes 9, Collins 8, Hoskins 6, Marquis 6, Calvert-Lewin 5, D'Ath 4, Adams 3, McDonald 3, Byrom 2, Cresswell 2, Brisley 1, Diamond 1, Moloney 1, Potter 1, Rose 1, Taylor 1, Opponents 1

FA Cup goals (7): Holmes 2, Calvert-Lewin 1, Diamond 1, Hoskins 1, Richards 1, Taylor 1. **League Cup goals** (4): Calvert-Lewin 1, Hackett 1, Hoskins 1, Richards 1. **Johnstone's Paint Trophy goals** (3): Calvert-Lewin 1, Richards 1, Watson 1

Average home league attendance: 5,279. **Player of Year**: John-Joe O'Toole

NOTTS COUNTY

More managerial upheaval, an embarrassing FA Cup defeat and a poor league finish represented another troubled season at Meadow Lane. A squad reshaped with 18 signings following relegation experienced defensive failings from an early stage, with Ricardo Moniz eventually sacked after a run of 19 goals conceded in eight games. They included a 2-0 first round defeat by Salford. Jamie Fullarton, former Crystal Palace midfielder and Nottingham Forest coach, replaced him, winning three of his first five matches. But the next seven yielded a single point and he was dismissed after 69 days in charge. In came Mark Cooper, former Swindon manager, with the promise of an appointment beyond the end of the season if he hit an agreed points total. Cooper's first match was a 4-0 defeat at Portsmouth, followed by the first home wins of 2016, against Stevenage and Hartlepool. Then came two 5-0 defeats by Mansfield and Carlisle which left County down in 17th. They also left the club looking for another manager after Cooper departed for National League Forest Green. He was replaced by Oldham's John Sheridan.

Aborah S.................. 25 (1)
Adams B........................15
Amevor M 6 (5)
Atkinson W 15 (2)
Audel T.................... 25 (3)
Banton J..........................9
Barmby J 3 (2)
Bennett S 5 (1)
Bishop C..................... - (1)
Boyce A...........................3
Burke G................ 21 (10)
Campbell A........... 29 (15)
Carroll R........................32
De Silva K................. 2 (2)
Edwards M.............. 21 (1)
Gibson M.................... - (4)
Hewitt E 35 (3)
Hollis H.................. 27 (2)
Jenner J..................... 4 (7)
Sarpong L................... - (1)
Loach S..........................14
MacKenzie G..,..................4
McLeod I 30 (7)
Milsom R................. 12 (2)

Murray R.................3 (13)
Noble L...................31 (6)
Sharpe R....................- (5)
Sheehan A....................14
Smith A..................25 (3)
Snijders G.................8 (6)
Spencer J.................1 (6)
Sprockel C.......................5
Stead J...................40 (3)
Swerts G.......................12
Thompson C.............23 (3)
Valencic F.................7 (2)

League goals (54): Stead 11, McLeod 9, Noble 8, Campbell 4, Edwards 4, Audel 2, Burke 2, Hollis 2, Sheehan 2, Snijders 2, Thompson 2, Aborah 1, Amevor 1, Murray 1, Valencic 1, Opponents 2
FA Cup goals: None. **League Cup goals** (5): Noble 2, Burke 1, Snijders 1, Stead 1. **Johnstone's Paint Trophy goals** (4): Stead 2, Edwards 1, McLeod 1
Average home league attendance: 4,860

OXFORD UNITED

Oxford finally fulfilled their potential with the runners-up spot and a Wembley appearance, along with individual honours for Kemar Roofe. They did it in some style, with 84 goals making Michael Appleton's side the top scorers in the four divisions. After a modest start, they climbed into the top three in early October and remained there for the remainder of the season in the face of strong competition for two of the automatic promotion places. Who would go up with Northampton remained in doubt until the final round of matches. Oxford made sure by beating Wycombe 3-0 with goals from Cheyenne Dunkley, Chris Maguire from the penalty spot and Callum O'Dowda to overtake Accrington for second place. They had also made a mark in two of the knock-out competitions, Roofe scoring twice in the one major upset of the FA Cup third round – a 3-2 win over Swansea. Four days later, the former West Bromwich Albion trainee netted two more against Millwall in the semi-finals of the Johnstone's Paint Trophy on the way to 26 for the campaign in all competitions. The final brought a 3-2 defeat by Barnsley, but Roofe was a winner when named League Two's Player of the Year. Appleton was also rewarded, with a new rolling contract.

Ashby J......................– (3)
Baldock G.....................27
Bowery J...................9 (8)
Buchel B.......................23
Dunkley C...............26 (3)
Evans J.....................4 (5)
George AJ...................- (2)
Graham J..................3 (2)
Hoban P.................2 (21)
Hylton D.................34 (7)
Ismail Z......................- (5)
Kenny J.........................17
Long S........................- (1)
Lundstram J.............33 (4)
MacDonald A...........35 (5)
Maguire C.......................21
Mullins J.................39 (1)
O'Dowda C............18 (20)
Roberts J...................1 (3)
Roofe K....................39 (1)
Rose D....................11 (2)
Ruffles J.....................8 (8)
Sercombe L..................45
Skarz J..........................41
Slocombe S..................23
Taylor R...................15 (7)
Waring G..................3 (11)
Wright J.......................29

League goals: (84): Roofe 18, Sercombe 14, Hylton 12, O'Dowda 8, Bowery 7, MacDonald 5, Dunkley 4, Maguire 4, Lundstram 3, Taylor 3, Baldock 2, Hoban 2, Waring 1, Opponents 1
FA Cup goals (8): Roofe 3, Hoban 2, Sercombe 2, Taylor 1. **League Cup goals** (4): Hylton 1, Mullins 1, Roofe 1, Sercombe 1. **Johnstone's Paint Trophy goals** (11): Roofe 4, O'Dowda 2, Evans 1, Hoban 1, Hylton 1, MacDonald 1, Maguire 1
Average home league attendance: 7,211. **Player of Year**: Kemar Roofe

PLYMOUTH ARGYLE

A stoppage-time goal by Peter Hartley enabled Plymouth to go one better than the previous season's progress to the semi-finals of the play-offs. It delivered victory over Portsmouth and his side went to Wembley, with nearly 35,000 supporters behind them, as firm favourites to beat AFC Wimbledon. Instead, they fell behind after 78 minutes and conceded again in added time after being caught on the counter throwing everything at an equaliser. Derek Adams and his players were left to regret a shock defeat in the penultimate home game which cost them the chance of automatic promotion. Relegated Dagenham and Redbridge scored three times in the first-half and replies from Hartley and Graham Carey were not enough to repair the damage.

Neither was a 2-2 draw at Cambridge, earned by Carey's stoppage-time goal. Plymouth were 5-0 winners of the final fixture against Hartlepool, but finished four points adrift. They had made the club's best start to a season since 1958 and went on to spend three months at the top of the table before faltering with a run of just two wins in ten matches.

Bentley J .... - (1)
Bittner J 1
Boateng H............... 22 (2)
Brunt R 17 (17)
Carey G.................... 34 (5)
Cox L.......................... - (4)
Croll L 3
Dorel V 1
Forster J 8 (4)
Hartley P 42
Harvey T.................... 1 (5)
Houghton J....................10
Jervis J.................... 38 (4)
Matt J 9 (2)
McCormick L 40
McHugh C............... 34 (3)
Mellor K.................. 37 (4)
Nardiello D................. - (4)
Nelson C.......................46
Purrington B.............. 6 (7)
Reid R 22 (7)
Rooney L......................... 1
Sawyer G........................ 43
Simpson J 14 (10)
Smalley D.....................- (1)
Tanner C 22 (20)
Threlkeld O.............. 18 (7)
Walton C 4
Wylde G 33 (10)

Play-offs – appearances: Boateng 3, Carey 3, Hartley 3, Jervis 3, Matt 3, McCormick 3, McHugh 3, Mellor 3, Nelson 3, Sawyer 3, Wylde 3, Tanner – (3), Forster – (1), Purrington – (1), Reid – (1), **League goals** (72): Carey 11, Jervis 11, Brunt 9, Reid 7, Wylde 7, Matt 5, Tanner 4, McHugh 3, Nelson 3, Hartley 2, Harvey 2, Rooney 2, Boateng 1, Houghton 1, Mellor 1, Simpson 1, Threlkeld 1, Opponents 1. **Play-offs – goals** (3): Matt 2, Hartley 1

FA Cup goals: None. **League Cup goals** (1): Tanner 1. **Johnstone's Paint Trophy goals** (8): Jervis 3, Boateng 1, Brunt 1, Carey 1, McHugh 1, Tanner 1

Average home league attendance: 8,798. **Player of Year**: Carl McHugh

PORTSMOUTH

Portsmouth carried a considerable weight of expectation into the season. With a new manager and crowds dwarfing every other team, they were odds-on favourites to begin redressing the club's plunge through the divisions. They were also backed heavily to go up as champions. In the event, Paul Cook's side were unable to deliver, losing to Plymouth in the semi-finals of the play-offs. The first leg at Fratton Park ended 2-2 and the teams were still locked going into stoppage time in return at Home Park. Then, a goal by Peter Hartley sent Plymouth through to face AFC Wimbledon at Wembley, leaving Cook to start preparing for another promotion bid. Portsmouth had been unable to keep up with the pace set first by Plymouth, then ultimately by Northampton at the head of the table. They also faced strong competition for the play-off positions and were briefly out of the top seven after a run of six matches yielding a single victory. Wins over Cambridge, Stevenage and Accrington put them back on track and Michael Smith's winner at Wimbledon secured their place with two games remaining.

Allsop..............................
Atangana N............... 8 (5)
Barton A.................. 11 (5)
Bennett K............... 40 (2)
Boco R 2 (2)
Burgess C 37
Chaplin C................ 6 (24)
Clarke M................. 26 (3)
Close B...................... 6 (1)
Davies B.......................43
Doyle M.................. 43 (1)
Evans G.................. 32 (8)
Freeman K................ 4 (3)
Fulton R 12
Haunstrup B 1
Hollands D............. 27 (5)
Jones P...................... 8 (1)
Lavery C 11 (2)
May A........................ - (1)
McCarey A 6
McGurk A 12 (15)
McNulty M.............. 19 (8)
Murphy B................ 20 (1)
Naismith K 10 (9)
Roberts G 27 (6)
Smith M 13 (3)
Stevens E 45
Stockley J 4 (5)
Tollitt B .... - (12)
Tubbs M 8 (8)
Webster A 24 (3)
Whatmough J 1 (1)
Wilkinson C................ - (1)

Play-offs – appearances: Allsop 2, Barton 2, Bennett 2, Burgess 2, Davies 2, Doyle 2, Evans 2, Hollands 2, McNulty 2, Roberts 2, Stevens 2, McGurk – (2), Chaplin – (1), Close – (1), Naismith – (1)

League goals (75): Evans 10, McNulty 10, Chaplin 8, Roberts 7, Bennett 6, Tubbs 5, Lavery 4,

Smith 4, Naismith 3, Burgess 2, Doyle 2, McGurk 2, Stockley 2, Webster 2, Clarke 1, Davies 1, Tollitt 1, Opponents 5. **Play-offs – goals** (2): McNulty 1, Roberts 1

FA Cup goals (8): McGurk 3, Roberts 2, Bennett 1, Chaplin 1, McNulty 1. **League Cup goals** (3): Chaplin 2, McGurk 1. **Johnstone's Paint Trophy goals**: None

Average home league attendance: 16,399. **Player of Year**: Ben Davies

STEVENAGE

Teddy Sheringham had his first managerial job cut short eight months into a three-year contract. The high-profile appointment by chairman Phil Wallace was intended to take the club on a 'different route' after their 2015 defeat in the play-offs under Graham Westley. But he was sacked two days after losing to bottom team York, with his side sixth from the foot of the table. The former England striker had it tough from the start, operating on a reduced budget and forced to bring in a succession of loanees. He was also handicapped by injuries to senior players, managing just six wins in 29 matches. Chris Whelpdale scored a hat-trick – as well as having a penalty saved – in one of them against Morecambe. In another, goalkeeper Jesse Joronen scored with a clearance over the head of Wycombe's Matt Ingram. Caretaker Darren Sarll also found it hard going, Stevenage finishing 18th, their lowest finish in six seasons in the Football League. But the last nine games brought a single defeat and Sarll was given the job on a permanent basis.

Adams C .... - (2)
Akinyemi D 6 (9)
Conlon T................ 15 (17)
Cox L........................... 9 (3)
Day C 19
Franks F 37 (1)
Gnanduillet A............. 9 (5)
Gordon R 3 (1)
Gorman D 6 (7)
Harrison B 6 (3)
Hedges R.................... 5 (1)
Henry R................... 30 (1)
Hitchcock T 5 (5)
Hoban P 1
Hughes M 19 (1)
Jebb J 3 (2)
Johnson R 4 (3)
Jones J...........................17
Joronen J 10
Keane K..................... 5 (1)
Kennedy B 13 (9)
Lee C....................... 21 (9)
Loza J 1
Luer G 9 (1)
Marriott A.................. 1 (5)
Matt J......................... 6 (2)
McAllister D .... - (1)
McCombe J 13 (1)
McEvoy K.................... - (1)
McFadzean C...................6
Mulraney J 5 (1)
O'Connor A................ 9 (4)
Ogilvie C 21
Okimo J 13
Parrett D 22 (5)
Petravicius D 1 (1)
Pett T 34 (6)
Pritchard B......................4
Schumacher S 15
Smith C 3 (1)
Storer J........................- (1)
Tonge M 29
Wells D 28
Whelpdale C 18 (3)
Wilkinson L 17 (2)
Williams B..................7 (8)
Zanzala O...................1 (1)

League goals (52): Whelpdale 8, Gnanduillet 5, Franks 3, Harrison 3, Lee 3, Parrett 3, Conlon 2, Hitchcock 2, Kennedy 2, Schumacher 2, Tonge 2, Wells 2, Wilkinson 2, Williams 2, Akinyemi 1, Hughes 1, Joronen 1, Keane 1, Matt 1, Mulraney 1, O'Connor 1, Ogilvie 1, Okimo 1, Pett 1, Opponents 1

FA Cup goals (3): Gnanduillet 1, Schumacher 1, Whelpdale 1. **League Cup goals** (1): Opponents 1. **Johnstone's Paint Trophy goals** (1): Kennedy 1

Average home league attendance: 3,349. **Player of Year**: Michael Tonge

WYCOMBE WANDERERS

Wycombe's two previous seasons had been decided right at the death – a penalty shoot-out defeat by Southend in the Play-off Final and before that survival on the final day of the regular campaign. This time, the outcome was not so finely balanced, their promotion bid petering out through an acute shortage of goals and a catalogue of injuries. Wycombe scored reasonably well in the first-half of the campaign – 32 goals in 23 games. The second- half brought just 13, with a 2-1 win over Dagenham and Redbridge the only match in which they scored more than once. Even so, they managed to stay within reach of seventh-place AFC Wimbledon until a run of four draws and two defeats in six matches, culminating in a 2-1 loss to Portsmouth, left them too far adrift. Two more defeats against promotion-chasing teams, Accrington and Oxford, pushed Wycombe down to just below mid-table. It was a disappointing finish to a season which started on a high with three successive victories and Wycombe on top after ten matches.

Allsop R........................18
Banton J.................... 3 (2)
Bean M.................... 27 (3)
Bloomfield M........... 20 (7)
Cowan-Hall P 4 (1)
Donacien J.......................2
Harriman M............. 42 (3)
Hayes P.................. 34 (3)
Holloway A.............. 8 (15)
Ingram M......................24
Jacobson J 34
Jombati S................ 32 (2)
Kretzschmar M 8 (14)
Liburd R.................... 4 (6)
Lynch A..........................3
McCarthy J....................35
McGinn S............... 21 (5)
O'Nien L 33 (2)
Pierre A.........................40
Richardson B.............. - (1)
Rowe D......................8 (4)
Sellars J.....................5 (3)
Sellers R ....- (15)
Siegrist B 1
Stewart A 27
Thompson G.............35 (8)
Udumaga J..................- (4)
Ugwu G..................13 (16)
Wood S 25 (4)

League goals (45): Harriman 7, Thompson 7, O'Nien 5, Hayes 4, Holloway 3, Kretzschmar 2, McCarthy 2, Pierre 2, Ugwu 2, Wood 2, Banton 1, Bloomfield 1, Cowan-Hall 1, Jacobson 1, Jombati 1, McGinn 1, Rowe 1, Stewart 1, Opponents 1
FA Cup goals (7): Harriman 1, Hayes 1, Holloway 1, Jacobson 1, Jombati 1, Kretzschmar 1, Thompson 1. **League Cup goals**: None. **Johnstone's Paint Trophy goals**: None
Average home league attendance: 3,984. **Player of Year**: Jason McCarthy

YEOVIL TOWN

Darren Way won plenty of midfield battles during eight years as a player at the club, before injuries sustained in a car crash forced him to retire. But few would have been as important as the one he successfully fought after being charged with saving Yeovil from a third successive relegation and a return to non-league football. They were bottom of the table, approaching the midway point of the season, when he took over from Paul Sturrock, sacked after 12 matches without a victory. Way had a spell as caretaker before taking over on a permanent basis and making a winning start against fellow-strugglers York, courtesy of Matt Dolan's penalty. Successive victories over Crawley and Wimbledon lifted his side out of the bottom two. Then, after they slipped back into trouble, four straight 1-0 wins over Dagenham and Redbridge, Accrington, Mansfield and Notts County, opened up a nine-point gap. It was not all plain sailing. A single goal in the next five matches offered York and Dagenham the opportunity to close the gap. But neither took advantage and Way was rewarded with a new three-year contract.

Allen I 2 (10)
Arthurworrey S...............14
Bassett O........................2
Beck M..................... 3 (5)
Bird R 19 (17)
Burrows J.................. - (1)
Campbell T 8 (9)
Compton J 14 (6)
Cornick H 28 (8)
Dawson K 4 (6)
Dickson R 34 (3)
Dolan M................. 38 (1)
Fogden W 13
Gibbons J 1 (2)
Gillett S..................... - (6)
Goodship B............... 6 (4)
Howells J.................. 5 (1)
Jeffers S.............. 13 (12)
Krysiak A......................38
Lacey A.................. 16 (4)
Laird M.................. 14 (6)
Lita L....................... 4 (4)
Norris D..................... - (1)
Roberts C......................45
Sheehan J......................13
Shephard L......................6
Smith N................. 38 (2)
Sokolik J................. 32 (2)
Sowunmi O 3 (2)
Thomas G 3 (2)
Tozer B 22 (4)
Wakefield J 5
Walsh L 15
Ward D 18
Weale C 8 (1)
Zoko F 22 (3)

League goals (43): Bird 8, Cornick 7, Zoko 7, Compton 4, Dolan 3, Dickson 2, Sheehan 2, Arthurworrey 1, Campbell 1, Goodship 1, Jeffers 1, Lita 1, Smith 1, Sokolik 1, Sowunmi 1, Walsh 1, Ward 1
FA Cup goals (5): Compton 1, Fogden 1, Jeffers 1, Tozer 1, Zoko 1. **League Cup goals**: None.
Johnstone's Paint Trophy goals (1): Opponents 1
Average home league attendance: 3,936. **Player of Year**: Connor Roberts

YORK CITY

One long run without a victory is usually the most a team can absorb without being relegated. Two can mean only one thing – and York were no exception, returning to non-league football after four seasons in League Two. Russ Wilcox, who led them out of trouble the previous season, was sacked with his side on the way to a club-record nine successive defeats in league and cup matches. They included a 6-0 beating at Portsmouth, followed by a 5-1 home defeat by Accrington, prompting the new manager, former Scotland defender and Dundee United manager Jackie McNamara, to sign six players – five on loan. One of them, Bradley Fewster from Middlesbrough, won the division's Player of the Month award for February when he scored five goals in five games and York recorded back-to-back wins over Notts County and Exeter. They were then out of the bottom two, before another slump, coupled to Yeovil's revival, proved decisive. McNamara insisted they could still stay up by overhauling faltering Stevenage. But despite a 3-1 win over Portsmouth with their best performance of the season, their fate was sealed by defeat at Accrington in the penultimate away match.

Alessandra L.................11
Bennett S......................11
Berrett J................. 33 (3)
Boyle W.........................12
Cameron K.....................18
Carson J................. 6 (16)
Collins M.........................7
Coulson M............... 20 (2)
Dixon M..................... 6 (1)
Fewster B............... 18 (6)
Flinders S......................43
Galbraith D............. 14 (7)
Godfrey B................. 5 (7)
Greening J................ 2 (1)
Hendrie L.......................18
Hyde J...................... 4 (7)
Ilesanmi F............... 35 (2)
Ingham M.........................3
Kitching M.......................1
Lowe K.................... 15 (1)
Lussey J...........................1
Massanka N............... 1 (2)
McCombe J......................5
McCoy M........................14
McEvoy K................ 10 (9)
Morris B...........................3
Nolan E................... 11 (4)
O'Connor S.......................4
Oliver V...................31 (6)
Penn R.....................32 (2)
Riordan D...................1 (3)
Rzonca C.....................- (1)
Satka L......................5 (1)
Sinclair E...................3 (9)
Straker A....................6 (5)
Summerfield L..........33 (1)
Swan G......................3 (1)
Thompson R..............9 (4)
Turner R.....................5 (4)
Tutonda D..................7 (5)
Winfield D...............36 (1)
Zubar S..........................4

League goals (51): Fewster 8, Oliver 7, Summerfeld 7, Coulson 5, Berrett 4, Penn 3, Thompson 3, Alessandra 2, McEvoy 2, Winfield 2, Cameron 1, Carson 1, Galbraith 1, Godfrey 1, Lowe 1, McCombe 1, Nolan 1, Turner 1

FA Cup goals (2): Coulson 1, Oliver 1. **League Cup goals** (2): Berrett 1, Summerfield 1. **Johnstone's Paint Trophy goals** (3): Oliver 2, Coulson 1

Average home league attendance: 3,218. **Player of Year**: Dave Winfield

LEAGUE CLUB MANAGERS 2016–17

Figure in brackets = number of managerial changes at club since the War. †Second spell at club

PREMIER LEAGUE

Arsenal (11)	Arsene Wenger	October 1996
Bournemouth (24)	Eddie Howe†	October 2012
Burnley (24)	Sean Dyche	October 2012
Chelsea (29)	Antonio Conte	July 2016
Crystal Palace (40)	Alan Pardew	January 2015
Everton (18)	Ronald Koeman	June 2016
Hull (26)	Steve Bruce	June 2012
Leicester (28)	Claudio Ranieri	July 2015
Liverpool (14)	Jurgen Klopp	October 2015
Manchester City (30)	Pep Guardiola	May 2016
Manchester Utd (11)	Jose Mourinho	May 2016
Middlesbrough (20)	Aitor Karanka	November 2013
Southampton (26)	Claude Puel	June 2016
Stoke (23)	Mark Hughes	May 2013
Sunderland (28)	Sam Allardyce	October 2015
Swansea (33)	Francesco Guidolin	January 2016
Tottenham (23)	Mauricio Pochettino	May 2014
Watford (34)	Walter Mazzarri	May 2016
WBA (32)	Tony Pulis	January 2015
West Ham (14)	Slaven Bliic	June 2015

CHAMPIONSHIP

Aston Villa (25)	Roberto di Matteo	June 2016
Barnsley (25)	Paul Heckingbottom	June 2016
Birmingham (25)	Gary Rowett	October 2014
Blackburn (30)	Owen Coyle	June 2016
Brentford (33)	Dean Smith	November 2015
Brighton (33)	Chris Hughton	December 2014
Bristol City (26)	Lee Johnson	February 2016
Burton (3)	Nigel Clough	December 2015
Cardiff (30)	Paul Trollope	May 2016
Derby (24)	Nigel Pearson	May 2016
Fulham (32)	Slavisa Jokanovic	December 2015
Huddersfield (28)	David Wagner	November 2015
Newcastle (27)	Rafael Benitez	March 2016
Ipswich (13)	Mick McCarthy	November 2012
Leeds (30)	Garry Monk	June 2016
Norwich (28)	Alex Neil	January 2015
Nottm Forest (23)	Philippe Montanier	June 2016
Preston (28)	Simon Grayson	February 2013
QPR (33)	Jimmy Floyd Hasselbaink	December 2015
Reading (22)	Jaap Stam	June 2016
Rotherham (26)	Alan Stubbs	June 2016
Sheffield Wed (29)	Carlos Carvalhal	June 2015
Wigan (22)	Gary Caldwell	April 2015
Wolves (23)	Kenny Jackett	May 2013

Number of changes since elected to Football League: Wigan 1978, Burton 2009

LEAGUE ONE

AFC Wimbledon (1)	Neal Ardley	October 2012
Bolton (23)	Phil Parkinson	June 2016
Bradford (34)	Stuart McCall †	June 2016

Bristol Rov (-)	Darrell Clarke	March 2014
Bury (25)	David Flitcroft	December 2013
Charlton (23)	Russell Slade	June 2016
Chesterfield (21)	Danny Wilson	December 2015
Coventry (33)	Tony Mowbray	March 2015
Fleetwood (2)	Steven Pressley	October 2015
Gillingham (24)	Justin Edinburgh	February 2015
Millwall (31)	Neil Harris	April 2015
MK Dons (15)	Karl Robinson	April 2010
Northampton (32)	Robert Page	May 2016
Oldham (30)	Stephen Robinson	July 2016
Oxford (2)	Michael Appleton	July 2014
Peterborough (30)	Grant McCann	May 2016
Port Vale (25)	Bruno Ribeiro	June 2016
Rochdale (32)	Keith Hill†	January 2013
Scunthorpe (28)	Graham Alexander	March 2016
Sheffield Utd (38)	Chris Wilder	May 2016
Shrewsbury (4)	Micky Mellon	May 2014
Southend (28)	Phil Brown	March 2013
Swindon (30)	Luke Williams	March 2016
Walsall (35)	Jon Whitney	June 2016

Number of changes since elected to Football League: Peterborough 1960, AFC Wimbledon 2011, Fleetwood 2012. Since returning: Shrewsbury 2004, Oxford 2010

LEAGUE TWO

Accrington (4)	John Coleman†	September 2014
Barnet (-)	Martin Allen	March 2014
Blackpool (31)	Gary Bowyer	June 2016
Cambridge (1)	Shaun Derrty	November 2015
Carlisle (5)	Keith Curle	September 2014
Cheltenham (-)	Gary Johnson	March 2015
Colchester (28)	John McGreal	May 2016
Crawley (6)	Dermot Drummy	April 2016
Crewe (21)	Steve Davis	November 2011
Doncaster (3)	Darren Ferguson	October 2015
Exeter (-)	Paul Tisdale	June 2006
Grimsby (-)	Paul Hurst	March 2011
Hartlepool (37)	Craig Hignett	February 2016
Leyton Orient (27)	Andy Hessenthaler	June 2016
Luton (1)	Nathan Jones	January 2016
Mansfield (1)	Adam Murray	December 2014
Morecambe (1)	Jim Bentley	May 2011
Newport (3)	Warren Feeney	January 2016
Notts Co (42)	John Sheridan	May 2016
Plymouth (34)	Derek Adams	June 2015
Portsmouth (33)	Paul Cook	May 2015
Stevenage (4)	Darren Sarll	May 2016
Wycombe (10)	Gareth Ainsworth	November 2012
Yeovil (6)	Darren Way	December 2015

Number of changes since elected to Football League: Wycombe 1993, Morecambe 2007, Stevenage 2010, Crawley 2011. Since returning: Carlisle 2005, Accrington 2006, Exeter 2008, Mansfield 2013, Newport 2013, Cambridge 2014, Luton 2014, Barnet 2015, Bristol Rov 2015, Cheltenham 2016, Grimsby 2016

MANAGERIAL INS AND OUTS 2015–16

REMIER LEAGUE

ston Villa: Out – Tim Sherwood (Oct 2015); In – Remi Garde; Out (Mar 2016); In – Roberto di Matteo
helsea: Out – Jose Mourinho (Dec 2015); In – Guus Hiddink; Out (May 2016); In – Antonio Conte
erton: Out – Roberto Martinez (May 2016); In – Ronald Koeman
verpool: Out – Brendan Rodgers (Oct 2015); In – Jurgen Klopp
anchester City: Out – Manuel Pellegrini (May 2016); In – Pep Guardiola
anchester Utd: Out – Louis van Gaal (May 2016); In – Jose Mourinho
ewcastle: Out – Steve McClaren (Mar 2016); In – Rafael Benitez
outhampton: Out – Ronald Koeman (June 2016); In – Claude Puel
underland: Out – Dick Advocaat (Oct 2015); In – Sam Allardyce
wansea: Out – Garry Monk (Dec 2015); In – Francesco Guidolin
atford: Out – Quique Sanchez Flores (May 2016); In – Walter Mazzarri

HAMPIONSHIP

ackburn: Out – Gary Bowyer (Nov 2015); In – Paul Lambert; Out (May2016); In – Owen Coyle
olton: Out – Neil Lennon (Mar 2016); In – Phil Parkinson
entford: Out – Marinus Dijkhuisen (Sep 2015); In – Dean Smith
istol City: Out – Steve Cotterill (Jan 2016); In – Lee Johnson
ardiff: Out – Russell Slade (May 2016); In – Paul Trollope
harlton: Out – Guy Luzon (Oct 2015); In – Karel Fraeye; Out (Jan 2016); In – Jose Riga; Out (May 2016); In – Russell Slade
erby: Out – Paul Clement (Feb 2016); In – Nigel Pearson
ulham: Out – Kit Symons (Nov 2015); In – Slavisa Jokanovic
uddersfield: Out – Chris Powell (Nov 2015); In – David Wagner
eeds: Out – Uwe Rosler (Oct 2015); In – Steve Evans; Out (May 2016); In – Garry Monk
ottm Forest: Out – Dougie Freedman (Mar 2016); In – Philippe Montanier
PR: Out – Chris Ramsey (Nov 2015); In – Jimmy Floyd Hasselbaink
eading: Out – Steve Clarke (Dec 2015); In – Brian McDermott; Out (May 2016); In Jaap Stam
otherham: Out – Steve Evans (Sep 2015); In – Neil Redfearn; Out (Feb 2016); In – Neil Warnock; Out (May 2016); In – Alan Stubbs

EAGUE ONE

arnsley: Out – Lee Johnson (Feb 2016); In – Paul Heckingbottom
ackpool: Out – Neil McDonald (May 2016); In – Gary Bowyer
adford: Out – Phil Parkinson (June 2016); In – Stuart McCall
urton: Out – Jimmy Floyd Hasselbaink (Dec 2015); In – Nigel Clough
hesterfield: Out – Dean Saunders (Nov 2015); In – Danny Wilson
olchester: Out – Tony Humes (Nov 2015); In – Kevin Keen; Out (Apr 2016); In – John McGreal
oncaster: Out – Paul Dickov (Sep 2015); In – Darren Ferguson
eetwood: Out – Graham Alexander (Sep 2015); In – Steven Pressley
dham: Out – Darren Kelly (Sep 2015); In – David Dunn; Out (Jan 2016); In – John Sheridan; Out (May 2016); In – Stephen Robinson
eterborough: Out – Dave Robertson (Sep 2015); In – Graham Westley; Out (Apr 2016); In – Grant McCann
ort Vale: Out - Robert Page (May 2016); In – Bruno Ribeiro
cunthorpe: Out – Mark Robins (Jan 2016); In – Graham Alexander
heffield Utd: Out – Nigel Adkins (May 2016); In – Chris Wilder
windon: Out – Mark Cooper (Oct 2015); In – Martin Ling; Out (Dec 2015); In – Luke Williams
alsall: Out – Dean Smith (Nov 2015); In – Sean O'Driscoll; Out (Mar 2016); In – Jon Whitney

LEAGUE TWO

Cambridge: Out – Richard Money (Nov 2015); In – Shaun Derry
Crawley: Out – Mark Yates (Apr 2016); In – Dermot Drummy
Dagenham: Out – Wayne Burnett (Dec 2015); In – John Still
Hartlepool: Out – Ronnie Moore (Feb 2016); In – Craig Hignett
Leyton Orient: Out – Ian Hendon (Jan 2016); In – Kevin Nolan; Out (April 2016);
In – Andy Hessenthaler
Luton: Out – John Still (Dec 2015); In – Nathan Jones
Newport: Out – Terry Butcher (Oct 2015); In – John Sheridan; Out (Jan 2016); In – Warren Feene
Northampton: Out – Chris Wilder (May 2016); In – Robert Page
Notts Co: Out – Ricardo Moniz (Dec 2015); In – Jamie Fullarton; Out (Mar 2016);
In – Mark Cooper; Out (May 2016); In – John Sheridan
Stevenage: Out – Teddy Sheringham (Jan 2016); In – Darren Sarll
Yeovil: Out – Paul Sturrock (Dec 2015); In – Darren Way
York: Out – Russ Wilcox (Oct 2015); In – Jackie McNamara

THE THINGS THEY SAY ...

'It's sick. They had a season to be proud of, the place was buzzing. It's common in England, bu completely wrong' – **Slaven Bilic**, West Ham manager, on Watford's decision to replace Quiqu Sanchez Flores.

'The club and me don't have the same point of view about the season' – **Quique Sanchez Flores**

'It was clear they were going to take him when he became free. If I had won two Champion Leagues and two Premier Leagues, he would still have come here' – **Manuel Pellegrini** on leavin Manchester City to make way for Pep Guardiola as the club's new manager.

'He has shown great dignity and great human qualities. I believe he is respected by everybody i the Premier League' – **Arsene Wenger**, Arsenal manager, praising Pellegrini.

'Whoever was responsible for the last 15 minutes, an utter shambles, should go away now and lock themselves in a darkened room' – **Alan Green**, BBC commentator, on the pre-match entertainment at the FA Cup Final which caused the kick-off to be delayed.

'To stand here in front of people who 14 years ago had their club ripped away from them, to stand here as one of their own – it doesn't get any better than that' – **Neal Ardley**, manager of AFC Wimbledon and a player with the old club, after his side's League Two Play-off Final win over Plymouth.

'All good things come to an end, I know that. But I was dreading the day I had to leave becaus it's been my home' – **Tim Howard,** Everton goalkeeper, says farewell to the club, after a decade at Goodison Park, to return to the United States.

'We will restore the image and the respect of FIFA and everyone will applaud us. FIFA has gone through sad times, moments of crisis, but those times are over. We will implement good governance and transparency' – **Gianni Infantino** after being voted Sepp Blatter's successor as president of the world governing body.

'We've got a reform package and a president we can trust. This is a new day, a new dawn' – **Greg Dyke** reaffirming the FA's support.

EMIRATES FA CUP 2015–16

FIRST ROUND

Salford, the club partly owned by Manchester's United's 'Class of 92', deliver the first upset of the tournament by beating Notts County 2-0 with goals by former United striker Danny Webber and Richie Allen. Gary Neville, Paul Scholes and Nicky Butt are in the crowd, with Phil Neville and Ryan Giggs absent on duty with their clubs. Salford are among five teams overcoming Football League opposition. Darren Carter, former West Bromwich Albion midfielder, puts Forest Green ahead against AFC Wimbledon and Elliott Frear is on the mark in stoppage-time for a 2-1 victory. Winners by the only goal of the game are Altrincham (Damian Reeves) against Barnsley, Chesham (Ryan Blake) against Bristol Rovers and Eastleigh, who see off Crewe with a Ben Strevens penalty. Macauley Bonne scores four times as Colchester beat Wealdstone 6-2, while a hat-trick by Nathaniel Mendez-Laing gives Rochdale a 3-1 success against Swindon.

Accrington 3 York 2
AFC Wimbledon 1 Forest Green 2
Aldershot 0 Bradford 0
Altrincham 1 Barnsley 0
Barnet 2 Blackpool 0
Barwell 0 Welling 2
Brackley 2 Newport 2
Braintree 1 Oxford 1
Bristol Rov 0 Chesham 1
Burton 0 Peterborough 3
Bury 4 Wigan 0
Cambridge 1 Basingstoke 0
Coventry 1 Northampton 2
Crawley 1 Luton 2
Crewe 0 Eastleigh 1
Dagenham 0 Morecambe 0
Didcot 0 Exeter 3
Doncaster 2 Stalybridge 0
Dover 1 Stourbridge 2
FC United 1 Chesterfield 4
Gainsborough 0 Shrewsbury 1
Grimsby 5 St Albans 1
Halifax 0 Wycombe 4
Hartlepool 1 Cheltenham 0
Leyton Orient 6 Staines 1
Maidstone 0 Yeovil 1
Mansfield 0 Oldham 0
Millwall 3 Fylde 1
Northwich 1 Boreham Wood 1
Plymouth 0 Carlisle 2
Portsmouth 2 Macclesfield 1
Port Vale 1 Maidenhead 1
Rochdale 3 Swindon 1
Salford 2 Notts Co 0
Scunthorpe 2 Southend 1
Sheffield Utd 3 Worcester 0
Stevenage 3 Gillingham 0
Walsall 2 Fleetwood 0
Wealdstone 2 Colchester 6
Whitehawk 5 Lincoln 3

Replays

Boreham Wood 1 Northwich 2
Bradford 2 Aldershot 0
Maidenhead 1 Port Vale 3
Morecambe 2 Dagenham 4
Newport 4 Brackley 1
Oldham 2 Mansfield 0
Oxford 3 Braintree 1

SECOND ROUND

Missed chances cost Salford the chance of further progress at Hartlepool, who take advantage by scoring twice in extra-time for a 2-0 victory after the teams' first meeting ends 1-1. Eastleigh are the only non-leaguers to go through, with James Constable and Josh Payne on the mark in a 2-0 win over Stourbridge. Northwich, lead 2-0 at Northampton, then concede three goals in the final seven minutes of normal down and go down 3-2. Altrincham twice go ahead at Colchester, but lose by the same scoreline to Callum Harriott's stoppage-time strike. Charlie Wyke scores a hat-trick as Carlisle beat ten-man Welling 5-0.

Barnet 0 Newport 1
Bradford 4 Chesham 0
Cambridge 1 Doncaster 3
Chesterfield 1 Walsall 1
Colchester 3 Altrincham 2
Dagenham 1 Whitehawk 1
Exeter 2 Port Vale 0
Grimsby 0 Shrewsbury 0
Leyton Orient 0 Scunthorpe 0
Millwall 1 Wycombe 2

Northampton 3 Northwich 2
Oxford 1 Forest Green 0
Peterborough 2 Luton 0
Portsmouth 1 Accrington 0
Rochdale 0 Bury 1
Salford 1 Hartlepool 1
Sheffield Utd 1 Oldham 0
Stourbridge 0 Eastleigh 2
Welling 0 Carlisle 5
Yeovil 1 Stevenage 0

Replays

Hartlepool 2 Salford 0 (aet)
Scunthorpe 3 Leyton Orient 0
Shrewsbury 1 Grimsby 0
Walsall 0 Chesterfield 0
(aet, Walsall won 5-3 on pens)
Whitehawk 2 Dagenham 3 (aet)

THIRD ROUND

Oxford deliver the one major upset, with two goals by former West Bromwich Albion trainee Kemar Roofe and a Liam Sercombe penalty accounting for Swansea 3-2. Two other League Two sides earn replays against top division clubs. Liverpool twice have to come from behind to take Exeter back to Anfield, where they prevail 3-0. Four of Liverpool's five scorers in the tie are on the mark for the first time for the club – Jerome Sinclair, Brad Smith, Sheyi Ojo and Joao Teixeira. Wycombe hold Aston Villa to 1-1 and resist for 75 minutes at the second attempt before conceding the first of two goals. Ryan Fraser saves Ipswich from a home defeat by Portsmouth with an 88th minute equaliser, but they lose the replay 2-1 to a Gary Roberts penalty and Marc McNulty's header for the 2008 winners of the competition. Wayne Rooney and Harry Kane also convert important spot-kicks. Rooney's, in stoppage-time, gives Manchester United a 1-0 victory over Sheffield United. Kane's, in the 89th minute against Leicester, earns Tottenham a second chance which they translate into a 2-0 win. West Bromwich Albion need a 94th minute equaliser from James Morrison to deny Bristol City and they, too, prevail in the replay by 1-0. Eastleigh's run comes to an end, but not before they stretch Bolton all the way. The Championship side need Darren Pratley's 87th strike to stay alive and Pratley again comes to their rescue with the winner for a 3-2 scoreline in the teams' second meeting. Reading mount the comeback of the round, Matej Vydra firing a hat-trick as they retrieve a two-goal deficit to defeat Huddersfield 5-2 in a replay, while Brentford's new manager, Dean Smith, is a victim of his old team Walsall, who go through 1-0 with a goal from Sam Mantom.

Arsenal 3 Sunderland 1
Birmingham 1 Bournemouth 2
Brentford 0 Walsall 1
Bury 0 Bradford 0
Cardiff 0 Shrewsbury 1
Carlisle 2 Yeovil 2
Chelsea 2 Scunthorpe 0
Colchester 2 Charlton 1
Doncaster 1 Stoke 2
Eastleigh 1 Bolton 1
Everton 2 Dagenham 0
Exeter 2 Liverpool 2
Hartlepool 1 Derby 2
Huddersfield 2 Reading 2
Hull 1 Brighton 0
Ipswich 2 Portsmouth 2
Leeds 2 Rotherham 0
Manchester Utd 1 Sheffield Utd 0
Middlesbrough 1 Burnley 2
Newport 1 Blackburn 2
Northampton 2 MK Dons 2
Norwich 0 Manchester City 3
Nottm Forest 1 QPR 0
Oxford 3 Swansea 2
Peterborough 2 Preston 0
Sheffield Wed 2 Fulham 1
Southampton 1 **Crystal Palace 2**
Tottenham 2 Leicester 2
Watford 1 Newcastle 0
WBA 2 Bristol City 2
West Ham 1 Wolves 0
Wycombe 1 Aston Villa 1

Replays

Aston Villa 2 Wycombe 0
Bolton 3 Eastleigh 2
Bradford 0 Bury 0
(aet, Bury won 4-2 on pens)
Bristol City 0 WBA1
Leicester 0 Tottenham 2
Liverpool 3 Exeter 0
MK Dons 3 Northampton 0
Portsmouth 2 Ipswich 1
Reading 5 Hudderfield 2
Yeovil 1 Carlisle 1
(aet Carlisle won 5-4 on pens)

FOURTH ROUND

Oxford's run ends with a 3-0 home defeat by Blackburn. Peterborough lose on penalties after holding West Bromwich Albion to 2-2 at The Hawthorns and to 1-1 after extra-time in the replay. But Shrewsbury keep the flag flying for the lower divisions, coming from behind to beat Sheffield Wednesday 3-2 with goals by Shaun Whalley in the 87th minute and on-loan Jack Grimmer in the seventh minute of time added on. There is also late drama at Upton Park, where Angelo Ogbonna's header in the dying seconds of extra-time, his first goal for the club, gives West Ham a 2-1 victory over Liverpool. There are hat-tricks for three players, including Oscar for Chelsea, who are 5-1 winners over MK Dons in front of a record crowd of 28,127 for the Championship club. Kelechi Iheanacho, a 19-year-old academy graduate, gets the headlines for Manchester City's 4-0 stroll at Villa Park, while Chuba Akpom nets all three in Hull's 3-1 success at Bury.

Arsenal 2 Burnley 1
Aston Villa 0 Manchester City 4
Bolton 1 Leeds 2
Bury 1 Hull 3
Carlisle 0 Everton 3
Colchester 1 Tottenham 4
Crystal Palace 1 Stoke 0
Derby 1 **Manchester Utd** 3
Liverpool 0 West Ham 0
MK Dons 1 Chelsea 5
Nottm Forest 0 Watford 1
Oxford 0 Blackburn 3
Portsmouth 1 Bournemouth 2
Reading 4 Walsall 0
Shrewsbury 3 Sheffield Wed 2
WBA 2 Peterborough 2
Replays
Peterborough 1 WBA 1
(aet, WBA won 4-3 on pens)
West Ham 2 Liverpool 1 (aet)

FIFTH ROUND

Manuel Pellegrini sacrifices Manchester City's chances of progress by fielding a makeshift side against Chelsea, preferring to keep key players fresh for the Champions League and the League Cup Final against Liverpool. City, with five teenagers making their full debuts are beaten 5-1. Two Chelsea players on loan at Reading, Michael Hector and Lucas Piazon, are on the mark in a 3-1 victory over West Bromwich Albion, whose winger Chris Brunt escapes serious injury when hit under the left eye by a coin thrown from the crowd. Martin Kelly scores his first goal since November 2011 to give Crystal Palace a 1-0 success over Tottenham at White Hart Lane. Arsene Wenger's 100th FA Cup tie is a frustrating one as goalkeeper Eldin Jakupovic's outstanding display earns Hull a goalless draw at the Emirates. But the holders make no mistake in the replay, winning 4-0 with two goals each from Olivier Giroud and Theo Walcott.

Arsenal 0 Hull 0
Blackburn 1 West Ham 5
Bournemouth 0 Everton 2
Chelsea 5 Manchester City 1
Reading 3 WBA 1
Shrewsbury 0 **Manchester Utd** 3
Tottenham 0 **Crystal Palace** 1
Watford 1 Leeds 0
Replay
Hull 0 Arsenal 4

SIXTH ROUND

Arsenal's bid for a third successive victory in the competition is ended by Watford, who win 2-1 at the Emirates with goals by Odion Ighalo and Adlene Guedioura. Two goals in the final 13 minutes of normal time by Romelu Lukaku give Everton a 2-0 victory over Chelsea. Crystal Palace and Reading are deadlocked until Yohan Cabaye's 86th minute penalty for Alan Pardew's side, conceded by Jake Cooper, who is sent off for a second yellow card. Fraizer Campbell, in stoppage-time, makes sure. A superb finish by 18-year-old Marcus Rashford, followed by Marouane Fellaini's goal, put Manchester United through 2-1 against West Ham in a replay at Upton Park.

Arsenal 1 Watford 2
Everton 2 Chelsea 0
Manchester Utd 1 West Ham 1
Reading 0 **Crystal Palace** 2
Replay
West Ham 1 **Manchester Utd** 2

SEMI-FINALS (both at Wembley)

A goal by Anthony Martial in the third minute of stoppage-time goal gives Manchester United a 2-1 win over Everton, who rue a succession of chances missed by Romelu Lukaku, particularly a penalty saved by David de Gea. Crystal Palace defeat Watford by the same scoreline with goals from Yannick Bolasie and Connor Wickham.

Crystal Palace 2 Watford 1

Everton 1 **Manchester Utd** 2

FINAL

CRYSTAL PALACE 1 MANCHESTER UNITED 2 (aet)
Wembley (88,619); Saturday, May 21 2016

Crystal Palace (4-2-3-1): Hennessey, Ward, Dann (Mariappa 90), Delaney, Souare, Cabaye (Puncheon 72), Jedinak (capt), Zaha, McArthur, Bolasie, Wickham (Gayle 85). **Subs not used**: Speroni, Adebayor, Sako, Kelly. **Scorer**: Puncheon (78). **Booked**: Dann, Delaney, McArthur. **Manager**: Alan Pardew

Manchester United (4-3-2-1): De Gea, Valencia, Smalling, Blind, Rojo (Darmian 65), Carrick, Rooney (capt), Fellaini, Mata (Lingard 90), Martial, Rashford (Young 71). **Subs not used**: Romero, Jones, Herrera, Schneiderlin. **Scorers**: Mata (81), Lingard (110). **Booked**: Smalling, Rojo, Mata, Rooney, Fellaini, Lingard. **Sent off**: Smalling (105). **Manager**: Louis van Gaal

Referee: M Clattenburg (Co Durham). **Half-time**: 0-0

At least the winning goal, scored by substitute Jesse Lingard, was in keeping with the romance and tradition of the FA Cup. So much else at Wembley was not. Shambolic pre-match entertainment meant a late kick-off. The game itself was largely a pedestrian affair, blighted by a flood of cards brandished by Mark Clattenburg. Then, the whole occasion was overshadowed by the final episode of the Louis van Gaal soap opera, which had been running for much of the season. When the Dutch manager brought the trophy into the post-match press conference and planted it on the dais, he had already been told of reports circulating that he was about to be sacked. A reference to 'friends in the media' dripped with contempt over the way he had been written off long before. It was a thoroughly unpleasant moment and certainly not what the FA would have chosen for the first final under the title sponsorship of Emirates. Van Gaal, at least, had the satisfaction of bowing out with some silverware, which his team merited, if only for the way they way they coped with the extra-time dismissal of Chris Smalling and continued carrying the game to Palace. Lingard's sumptuous volley deserved to win any match. So, too, in a different way did Wayne Rooney's crossfield run and pin-point cross for Juan Mata's first United goal. Alan Pardew felt that was the decisive moment, followed closely by Clattenburg's decision to haul back Connor Wickham, instead of playing the advantage and allowing the Palace striker to continue his run on goal.

HOW THEY REACHED THE FINAL

Crystal Palace
Round 3: 2-1 away to Southampton (Ward, Zaha)
Round 4: 1-0 home to Stoke (Zaha)
Round 5: 1-0 away to Tottenham (Kelly)
Round 6: 2-0 away to Reading (Cabaye pen, Campbell)
Semi-finals: 2-1 v Watford (Bolasie, Wickham)
Manchester United
Round 3: 1-0 home to Sheffield Utd (Rooney pen)
Round 4: 3-1 away to Derby (Rooney, Blind, Mata)
Round 5: 3-0 away to Shrewsbury (Smalling, Mata, Lingard
Round 6: 1-1 home to West Ham (Martial); 2-1 away to West Ham (Rashford, Fellaini)
Semi-finals: 2-1 v Everton (Fellaini, Martial)
Leading scorers: 6 Vydra (Reading); 4 Bonne (Colchester), Iheanacho (Manchester City), Marshall (Blackburn), Washington (Peterborough)

FINAL FACTS AND FIGURES

● Manchester United joined Arsenal on a record 12 FA Cup wins with their first triumph since 2004

● Wayne Rooney and Michael Carrick completed a full set of domestic league and cup honours

● Chris Smalling became the fourth player to be sent off in the final after United's Kevin Moran in 1985, Arsenal's Jose Reyes (2005) and Manchester City's Pablo Zabaleta (2013)
Louis van Gaal is the third Dutch manager to lift the trophy after Ruud Gullit (1997) and Guus Hiddink (2009), both with Chelsea.

● Alan Pardew, a player with Crystal Palace against Manchester United in 1990, and manager of West Ham against Liverpool in 2006, suffered his third defeat in the final

● Harry Redknapp remains the only English manager in the last 20 years to have been successful in the competition, winning the 2008 final with Portsmouth. ; Mark Clattenburg was refereeing the first of three major finals, ahead of the Champions League decider between Real Madrid and Atletico Madrid and the final of Euro 2016

● Clattenburg showed yellow cards to six Manchester United players and three from Crystal Palace – the most in an FA Cup Final

FA CUP FINAL SCORES & TEAMS

1872 **Wanderers 1** (Betts) Bowen, Alcock, Bonsor, Welch; Betts, Crake, Hooman, Lubbock, Thompson, Vidal, Wollaston. Note: Betts played under the pseudonym 'AH Chequer' on the day of the match **Royal Engineers 0** Capt Merriman; Capt Marindin; Lieut Addison, Lieut Cresswell, Lieut Mitchell, Lieut Renny-Tailyour, Lieut Rich, Lieut George Goodwyn, Lieut Muirhead, Lieut Cotter, Lieut Bogle

1873 **Wanderers 2** (Wollaston, Kinnaird) Bowen; Thompson, Welch, Kinnaird, Howell, Wollaston, Sturgis, Rev Stewart, Kenyon-Slaney, Kingsford, Bonsor **Oxford University 0** Kirke-Smith; Leach, Mackarness, Birley, Longman, Chappell-Maddison, Dixon, Paton, Vidal, Sumner, Ottaway. March 29; 3,000; A Stair

1874 **Oxford University 2** (Mackarness, Patton) Neapean; Mackarness, Birley, Green, Vidal, Ottaway, Benson, Patton, Rawson, Chappell-Maddison, Rev Johnson **Royal Engineers 0** Capt Merriman; Major Marindin, Lieut W Addison, Gerald Onslow, Lieut Oliver, Lieut Digby, Lieut Renny-Tailyour, Lieut Rawson, Lieut Blackman Lieut Wood, Lieut von Donop. March 14; 2,000; A Stair

1875 **Royal Engineers 1** (Renny-Tailyour) Capt Merriman; Lieut Sim, Lieut Onslow, Lieut (later Sir) Ruck, Lieut Von Donop, Lieut Wood, Lieut Rawson, Lieut Stafford, Capt Renny-Tailyour, Lieut Mein, Lieut Wingfield-Stratford **Old Etonians 1** (Bonsor) Thompson; Benson, Lubbock, Wilson, Kinnaird, (Sir) Stronge, Patton, Farmer, Bonsor, Ottaway, Kenyon-Slaney. March 13; 2,000; CW Alcock. aet **Replay – Royal Engineers 2** (Renny-Tailyour, Stafford) Capt Merriman; Lieut Sim, Lieut Onslow, Lieut (later Sir) Ruck, Lieut Von Donop, Lieut Wood, Lieut Rawson, Lieut Stafford, Capt Renny-Tailyour, Lieut Mein, Lieut Wingfield-Stratford **Old Etonians 0** Capt Drummond-Moray; Kinnaird, (Sir) Stronge, Hammond, Lubbock, Patton, Farrer, Bonsor, Lubbock, Wilson, Farmer. March 16; 3,000; CW Alcock

1876 **Wanderers 1** (Edwards) Greig; Stratford, Lindsay, Chappell-Maddison, Birley, Wollaston, C Heron, G Heron, Edwards, Kenrick, Hughes **Old Etonians 1** (Bonsor) Hogg; Rev Welldon, Lyttleton, Thompson, Kinnaird, Meysey, Kenyon-Slaney, Lyttleton, Sturgis, Bonsor, Allene. March 11; 3,500; WS Rawson aet **Replay – Wanderers 3** (Wollaston, Hughes 2) Greig, Stratford, Lindsay, Chappel-Maddison, Birley, Wollaston, C Heron, G Heron, Edwards, Kenrick, Hughes **Old Etonians 0** Hogg, Lubbock, Lyttleton, Farrer, Kinnaird, (Sir) Stronge, Kenyon-Slaney, Lyttleton, Sturgis, Bonsor, Allene. March 18; 1,500; WS Rawson

1877 **Wanderers 2** (Kenrick, Lindsay) Kinnaird; Birley, Denton, Green, Heron, Hughes, Kenrick, Lindsay, Stratford, Wace, Wollaston **Oxford University 1** (Kinnaird og) Allington; Bain, Dunnell, Rev Savory, Todd, Waddington, Rev Fernandez, Otter, Parry, Rawson. March 24; 3,000; SH Wright, aet

1878 **Wanderers 3** (Kinnaird, Kenrick 2) (Sir) Kirkpatrick; Stratford, Lindsay, Kinnaird, Green, Wollaston, Heron, Wylie, Wace, Denton, Kenrick **Royal Engineers 1** (Morris) Friend; Cowan, (Sir) Morris, Mayne,

Heath, Haynes, Lindsay, Hedley, (Sir) Bond, Barnet, Ruck. March 23; 4,500; SR Bastard

1879 Old Etonians 1 (Clerke) Hawtrey; Edward, Bury, Kinnaird, Lubbock, Clerke, Pares, Goodhart, Whitfield, Chevalier, Beaufoy **Clapham Rovers 0** Birkett; Ogilvie, Field, Bailey, Prinsep, Rawson, Stanley, Scott, Bevington, Growse, Keith-Falconer. March 29; 5,000; CW Alcock

1880 Clapham Rovers 1 (Lloyd-Jones) Birkett; Ogilvie, Field, Weston, Bailey, Stanley, Brougham, Sparkes, Barry, Ram, Lloyd-Jones **Oxford University 0** Parr; Wilson, King, Phillips, Rogers, Heygate, Rev Childs, Eyre, (Dr) Crowdy, Hill, Lubbock. April 10; 6,000; Major Marindin

1881 Old Carthusians 3 (Page, Wynyard, Parry) Gillett; Norris, (Sir) Colvin, Prinsep, (Sir) Vintcent, Hansell, Richards, Page, Wynyard, Parry, Todd **Old Etonians 0** Rawlinson; Foley, French, Kinnaird, Farrer, Macauley, Goodhart, Whitfield, Novelli, Anderson, Chevallier. April 9; 4,000; W Pierce-Dix

1882 Old Etonians 1 (Macauley) Rawlinson; French, de Paravicini, Kinnaird, Foley, Novelli, Dunn, Macauley, Goodhart, Chevallier, Anderson **Blackburn Rov 0** Howarth; McIntyre, Suter, Hargreaves, Sharples, Hargreaves, Avery, Brown, Strachan, Douglas, Duckworth. March 25; 6,500; JC Clegg

1883 Blackburn Olympic 2 (Matthews, Costley) Hacking; Ward, Warburton, Gibson, Astley, Hunter, Dewhurst, Matthews, Wilson, Costley, Yates **Old Etonians 1** (Goodhart) Rawlinson; French, de Paravicini, Kinnaird, Foley, Dunn, Bainbridge, Chevallier, Anderson, Goodhart, Macauley. March 31; 8,000; Major Marindin, aet

1884 Blackburn Rov 2 (Sowerbutts, Forrest) Arthur; Suter, Beverley, McIntyre, Forrest, Hargreaves, Brown, Inglis Sowerbutts, Douglas, Lofthouse **Queen's Park 1** (Christie) Gillespie; MacDonald, Arnott, Gow, Campbell, Allan, Harrower, (Dr) Smith, Anderson, Watt, Christie. March 29; 4,000; Major Marindin

1885 Blackburn Rov 2 (Forrest, Brown) Arthur; Turner, Suter, Haworth, McIntyre, Forrest, Sowerbutts, Lofthouse, Douglas, Brown, Fecitt **Queen's Park 0** Gillespie; Arnott, MacLeod, MacDonald, Campbell, Sellar, Anderson, McWhammel, Hamilton, Allan, Gray. April 4; 12,500; Major Marindin

1886 Blackburn Rov 0 Arthur; Turner, Suter, Heyes, Forrest, McIntyre, Douglas, Strachan, Sowerbutts, Fecitt, Brown **WBA 0** Roberts; Green, Bell, Horton, Perry, Timmins, Woodhall, Green, Bayliss, Loach, Bell. April 3; 15,000; Major Marindin **Replay – Blackburn Rov 2** (Sowerbutts, Brown) Arthur; Turner, Suter, Walton, Forrest, McIntyre, Douglas, Strachan, Sowerbutts, Fecitt, Brown **WBA 0** Roberts; Green, Bell, Horton, Perry, Timmins, Woodhall, Green, Bayliss, Loach, Bell. April 10; 12,000; Major Marindin

1887 Aston Villa 2 (Hodgetts, Hunter) Warner; Coulton, Simmonds, Yates, Dawson, Burton, Davis, Albert Brown, Hunter, Vaughton, Hodgetts **WBA 0** Roberts; Green, Aldridge, Horton, Perry, Timmins, Woodhall, Green, Bayliss, Paddock, Pearson. April 2; 15,500; Major Marindin

1888 WBA 2 (Bayliss), Woodhall) Roberts; Aldridge, Green, Horton, Perry, Timmins, Woodhall, Bassett, Bayliss, Wilson, Pearson **Preston 1** (Dewhurst) Mills-Roberts; Howarth, Holmes, Ross, Russell, Gordon, Ross, Goodall, Dewhurst, Drummond, Graham. March 24; 19,000; Major Marindin

1889 Preston 3 (Dewhurst, Ross, Thomson) Mills-Roberts; Howarth, Holmes, Drummond, Russell, Graham, Gordon, Goodall, Dewhurst, Thompson, Ross **Wolves 0** Baynton; Baugh, Mason, Fletcher, Allen, Lowder, Hunter, Wykes, Brodie, Wood, Knight. March 30; 22,000; Major Marindin

1890 Blackburn Rov 6 (Lofthouse, Jack Southworth, Walton, Townley 3) Horne; James Southworth, Forbes, Barton, Dewar, Forrest, Lofthouse, Campbell, Jack Southworth, Walton, Townley **Sheffield Wed 1** (Bennett) Smith; Morley, Brayshaw, Dungworth, Betts, Waller, Ingram, Woolhouse, Bennett, Mumford, Cawley. March 29; 20,000; Major Marindin

1891 Blackburn Rov 3 (Dewar, Jack Southworth, Townley) Pennington; Brandon, Forbes, Barton, Dewar, Forrest, Lofthouse, Walton, Southworth, Hall, Townley **Notts Co 1** (Oswald) Thraves; Ferguson, Hendry, Osborne, Calderhead, Shelton, McGregror, McInnes Oswald, Locker, Daft. March 21; 23,000; CJ Hughes

1892 WBA 3 (Geddes, Nicholls, Reynolds) Reader; Nicholson, McCulloch, Reynolds, Perry, Groves, Bassett, McLeod, Nicholls, Pearson, Geddes **Aston Villa 0** Warner; Evans, Cox, Devey, Cowan, Baird, Athersmith, Devey, Dickson, Hodgetts, Campbell. March 19; 32,810; JC Clegg

1893 Wolves 1 (Allen) Rose; Baugh, Swift, Malpass, Allen, Kinsey, Topham, Wykes, Butcher, Griffin, Wood **Everton 0** Williams; Kelso, Howarth, Boyle, Holt, Stewart, Latta, Gordon, Maxwell, Chadwick, Milward. March 25; 45,000; CJ Hughes

1894 Notts Co 4 (Watson, Logan 3) Toone; Harper, Hendry, Bramley, Calderhead, Shelton, Watson, Donnelly, Logan Bruce, Daft **Bolton 1** (Cassidy) Sutcliffe; Somerville, Jones , Gardiner, Paton, Hughes, Tannahill, Wilson, Cassidy, Bentley, Dickenson. March 31; 37,000; CJ Hughes

1895 Aston Villa 1 (Chatt) Wilkes; Spencer, Welford, Reynolds, Cowan, Russell, Athersmith Chatt, Devey, Hodgetts, Smith **WBA 0** Reader; Williams, Horton, Perry, Higgins, Taggart, Bassett, McLeod, Richards, Hutchinson, Banks. April 20; 42,560; J Lewis

1896 Sheffield Wed 2 (Spikesley 2) Massey; Earp, Langley, Brandon, Crawshaw, Petrie, Brash, Brady, Bell, Davis, Spikesley **Wolves 1** (Black) Tennant; Baugh, Dunn, Owen, Malpass, Griffiths, Tonks, Henderson, Beats, Wood, Black. April 18; 48,836; Lieut Simpson

1897 Aston Villa 3 (Campbell, Wheldon, Crabtree) Whitehouse; Spencer, Reynolds, Evans, Cowan, Crabtree, Athersmith, Devey, Campbell, Wheldon, Cowan **Everton 2** (Bell, Boyle) Menham; Meechan, Storrier, Boyle, Holt, Stewart, Taylor, Bell, Hartley, Chadwick, Milward. April 10; 65,891; J Lewis

1898 Nottm Forest 3 (Capes 2, McPherson) Allsop; Ritchie, Scott, Forman, McPherson, Wragg, McInnes, Richards, Benbow, Capes, Spouncer **Derby 1** (Bloomer) Fryer; Methven, Leiper, Cox, Goodall, Bloomer, Boag, Stevenson, McQueen. April 16; 62,017; J Lewis

1899 Sheffield Utd 4 (Bennett, Beers, Almond, Priest) Foulke; Thickett, Boyle, Johnson, Morren, Needham, Bennett, Beers, Hedley, Almond, Priest **Derby 1** (Boag) Fryer; Methven, Staley, Cox, Paterson, May, Arkesden, Bloomer, Boag, McDonald, Allen. April 15; 73,833; A Scragg

1900 Bury 4 (McLuckie 2, Wood, Plant) Thompson; Darroch, Davidson, Pray, Leeming, Ross, Richards, Wood, McLuckie, Sagar, Plant **Southampton 0** Robinson; Meechan, Durber, Meston, Chadwick, Petrie, Turner, Yates, Farrell, Wood, Milward. April 21; 68,945; A Kingscott

1901 Tottenham 2 (Brown 2) Clawley; Erentz, Tait, Morris, Hughes, Jones, Smith, Cameron, Brown, Copeland, Kirwan **Sheffield Utd 2** (Priest, Bennett) Foulke; Thickett, Boyle, Johnson, Morren, Needham, Bennett, Field, Hedley, Priest, Lipsham. April 20; 110,820; A Kingscott **Replay – Tottenham 3** (Cameron, Smith, Brown) Clawley; Erentz, Tait, Morris, Hughes, Jones, Smith, Cameron, Brown, Copeland, Kirwan. **Sheffield Utd 1** (Priest) Foulke; Thickett, Boyle, Johnson, Morren, Needham, Bennett, Field, Hedley, Priest, Lipsham. April 27; 20,470; A Kingscott

1902 Sheffield Utd 1 (Common) Foulke; Thickett, Boyle, Needham, Wilkinson, Johnson, Bennett, Common, Hedley, Priest, Lipsham **Southampton 1** (Wood) Robinson; Fry, Molyneux, Meston, Bowman, Lee, Turner, Wood Brown, Chadwick, Turner. April 19; 76,914; T Kirkham. **Replay – Sheffield Utd 2** (Hedley, Barnes) Foulke; Thickett, Boyle, Needham, Wilkinson, Johnson, Barnes, Common, Hedley, Priest, Lipsham **Southampton 1** (Brown) Robinson; Fry, Molyneux, Meston, Bowman, Lee, Turner, Wood, Brown, Chadwick, Turner. April 26; 33,068; T Kirkham

1903 Bury 6 (Leeming 2, Ross, Sagar, Wood, Plant) Monteith; Lindsey, McEwen, Johnston, Thorpe, Ross, Richards, Wood, Sagar Leeming, Plant **Derby 0** Fryer; Methven, Morris, Warren, Goodall, May, Warrington, York, Boag, Richards, Davis. April 18; 63,102; J Adams

1904 Manchester City 1 (Meredith) Hillman; McMahon, Burgess, Frost, Hynds, Ashworth, Meredith, Livingstone, Gillespie, Turnbull, Booth **Bolton 0** Davies; Brown, Struthers, Clifford, Greenhalgh, Freebairn, Stokes, Marsh, Yenson, White, Taylor. April 23; 61,374; AJ Barker

1905 Aston Villa 2 (Hampton 2) George; Spencer, Miles, Pearson, Leake, Windmill, Brawn, Garratty, Hampton, Bache, Hall **Newcastle 0** Lawrence; McCombie, Carr, Gardner, Aitken, McWilliam, Rutherford, Howie, Appleyard, Veitch, Gosnell. April 15; 101,117; PR Harrower

1906 Everton 1 (Young) Scott; Crelley, W Balmer, Makepeace, Taylor, Abbott, Sharp, Bolton, Young, Settle, Hardman **Newcastle 0** Lawrence; McCombie, Carr, Gardner, Aitken, McWilliam, Rutherford, Howie, Orr, Veitch, Gosnell. April 21; 75,609; F Kirkham

1907 Sheffield Wed 2 (Stewart, Simpson) Lyall; Layton, Burton, Brittleton, Crawshaw, Bartlett, Chapman, Bradshaw, Wilson, Stewart, Simpson **Everton 1** (Sharp) Scott; W Balmer, B Balmer, Makepeace, Taylor, Abbott, Sharp, Bolton, Young, Settle, Hardman. April 20; 84,594; N Whittaker

1908 Wolves 3 (Hunt, Hedley, Harrison) Lunn; Jones, Collins, Rev Hunt, Wooldridge, Bishop, Harrison, Shelton, Hedley, Radford, Pedley **Newcastle 1** (Howie) Lawrence; McCracken, Pudan, Gardner, Veitch, McWilliam, Rutherford, Howie, Appleyard, Speedie, Wilson. April 25; 74,697; TP Campbell

1909 Manchester Utd 1 (Sandy Turnbull) Moger; Stacey, Hayes, Duckworth, Roberts, Bell, Meredith, Halse, J Turnbull, S Turnbull, Wall **Bristol City 0** Clay; Annan, Cottle, Hanlin, Wedlock, Spear, Staniforth, Hardy, Gilligan, Burton, Hilton. April 24; 71,401; J Mason

1910 Newcastle 1 (Rutherford) Lawrence; McCracken, Whitson, Veitch, Low, McWilliam, Rutherford, Howie, Higgins, Shepherd, Wilson **Barnsley 1** (Tufnell) Mearns; Downs, Ness, Glendinning, Boyle, Utley, Tufnell, Lillycrop, Gadsby, Forman, Bartrop. April 23; 77,747; JT Ibbotson **Replay – Newcastle 2** (Shepherd 2, 1pen) Lawrence; McCracken, Carr, Veitch, Low, McWilliam, Rutherford, Howie, Higgins, Shepherd, Wilson **Barnsley 0** Mearns; Downs, Ness, Glendinning, Boyle, Utley, Tufnell, Lillycrop, Gadsby, Forman, Bartrop. April 28; 69,000; JT Ibbotson.

1911 Bradford City 0 Mellors; Campbell, Taylor, Robinson, Gildea, McDonald, Logan, Speirs, O'Rourke, Devine, Thompson **Newcastle 0** Lawrence; McCracken, Whitson, Veitch, Low, Willis, Rutherford, Jobey, Stewart, Higgins, Wilson. April 22; 69,068; JH Pearson **Replay – Bradford City 1** (Speirs) Mellors; Campbell, Taylor, Robinson, Torrance, McDonald, Logan, Speirs, O'Rourke, Devine, Thompson **Newcastle 0** Lawrence; McCracken, Whitson, Veitch, Low, Willis, Rutherford, Jobey, Stewart, Higgins, Wilson. April 26; 58,000; JH Pearson

1912 Barnsley 0 Cooper; Downs, Taylor, Glendinning, Bratley, Utley, Bartrop, Tufnell, Lillycrop, Travers, Moore **WBA 0** Pearson; Cook, Pennington, Baddeley, Buck, McNeal, Jephcott, Wright, Pailor, Bowser, Shearman. April 20; 54,556; JR Shumacher **Replay – Barnsley 1** (Tufnell) Cooper; Downs, Taylor, Glendinning, Bratley, Utley, Bartrop, Harry, Lillycrop, Travers, Jimmy Moore **WBA 0** Pearson; Cook, Pennington, Baddeley, Buck, McNeal, Jephcott, Wright, Pailor, Bowser, Shearman. April 24; 38,555; JR Schumacher. aet

1913 Aston Villa 1 (Barber) Hardy; Lyons, Weston, Barber, Harrop, Leach, Wallace, Halse, Hampton, Stephenson, Bache **Sunderland 0** Butler; Gladwin, Ness, Cuggy, Thomson, Low, Mordue, Buchan, Richardson, Holley, Martin. April 19; 120,081; A Adams

1914 Burnley 1 (Freeman) Sewell; Bamford, Taylor, Halley, Boyle, Watson, Nesbit, Lindley, Freeman, Hodgson, Mosscrop **Liverpool 0** Campbell; Longworth, Pursell, Fairfoul, Ferguson, McKinley, Sheldon, Metcalfe, Miller, Lacey, Nicholl. April 25; 72,778; HS Bamlett

1915 Sheffield Utd 3 (Simmons, Fazackerly, Kitchen) Gough; Cook, English, Sturgess, Brelsford, Utley, Simmons, Fazackerly, Kitchen, Masterman, Evans **Chelsea 0** Molyneux; Bettridge, Harrow, Taylor, Logan, Walker, Ford, Halse, Thomson, Croal, McNeil. April 24; 49,557; HH Taylor

1920 Aston Villa 1 (Kirton) Hardy; Smart, Weston, Ducat, Barson, Moss, Wallace, Kirton, Walker, Stephenson, Dorrell **Huddersfield 0** Mutch; Wood, Bullock, Slade, Wilson, Watson, Richardson, Mann, Taylor, Swann, Islip. April 24; 50,018; JT Howcroft. aet

1921 Tottenham 1 (Dimmock) Hunter; Clay, McDonald, Smith, Walters, Grimsdell, Banks, Seed, Cantrell, Bliss, Dimmock **Wolves 0** George; Woodward, Marshall, Gregory, Hodnett, Riley, Lea, Burrill, Edmonds, Potts, Brooks. April 23; 72,805; S Davies

1922 Huddersfield 1 (Smith pen) Mutch; Wood, Wadsworth, Slade, Wilson, Watson, Richardson, Mann, Islip, Stephenson, Billy Smith **Preston 0** Mitchell; Hamilton, Doolan, Duxbury, McCall, Williamson, Rawlings, Jefferis, Roberts, Woodhouse, Quinn. April 29; 53,000; JWP Fowler

1923 Bolton 2 (Jack, JR Smith) Pym; Haworth, Finney, Nuttall, Seddon, Jennings, Butler, Jack, JR Smith, Joe Smith, Vizard **West Ham 0** Hufton; Henderson, Young, Bishop, Kay, Tresadern, Richards, Brown, Watson, Moore, Ruffell. April 28; 126,047; DH Asson

1924 Newcastle 2 (Harris, Seymour) Bradley; Hampson, Hudspeth, Mooney, Spencer, Gibson, Low, Cowan, Harris, McDonald, Seymour **Aston Villa 0** Jackson; Smart, Mort, Moss, Milne, Blackburn, York, Kirton, Capewell, Walker, Dorrell. April 26; 91,695; WE Russell

1925 Sheffield Utd 1 (Tunstall) Sutcliffe; Cook, Milton, Pantling, King, Green, Mercer, Boyle, Johnson, Gillespie, Tunstall **Cardiff 0** Farquharson; Nelson, Blair, Wake, Keenor, Hardy, Davies, Gill, Nicholson, Beadles, Evans. April 25; 91,763; GN Watson

1926 Bolton 1 (Jack) Pym; Haworth, Greenhalgh, Nuttall, Seddon, Jennings, Butler, JR Smith, Jack, Joe Smith, Vizard **Manchester City 0** Goodchild; Cookson, McCloy, Pringle, Cowan, McMullan, Austin, Browell, Roberts, Johnson, Hicks. April 24; 91,447; I Baker

1927 Cardiff 1 (Ferguson) Farquharson; Nelson, Watson, Keenor, Sloan, Hardy, Curtis, Irving, Ferguson, Davies, McLachlan **Arsenal 0** Lewis; Parker, Kennedy, Baker, Butler, John, Hulme, Buchan, Brain, Blythe, Hoar. April 23; 91,206; WF Bunnell

1928 Blackburn 3 (Roscamp 2, McLean) Crawford; Hutton, Jones, Healless, Rankin, Campbell, Thornewell, Puddefoot, Roscamp, McLean, Rigby **Huddersfield 1** (Jackson) Mercer; Goodall, Barkas, Redfern, Wilson, Steele, Jackson, Kelly, Brown, Stephenson, Smith. April 21; 92,041; TG Bryan

1929 Bolton 2 (Butler, Blackmore) Pym; Haworth, Finney, Kean, Seddon, Nuttall, Butler, McClelland, Blackmore, Gibson, Cook **Portsmouth 0** Gilfillan; Mackie, Bell, Nichol, McIlwaine, Thackeray, Forward, Smith, Weddle, Watson, Cook. April 27; 92,576; A Josephs

1930 Arsenal 2 (James, Lambert) Preedy; Parker, Hapgood, Baker, Seddon, John, Hulme, Jack, Lambert, James, Bastin **Huddersfield 0** Turner; Goodall, Spence, Naylor, Wilson, Campbell, Jackson, Kelly, Davies, Raw, Smith. April 26; 92,488; T Crew

1931 WBA 2 (WG Richardson 2) Pearson; Shaw, Trentham, Magee, Bill Richardson, Edwards, Glidden, Carter, WG Richardson, Sandford, Wood **Birmingham 1** (Bradford) Hibbs; Liddell, Barkas, Cringan, Morrall, Leslie, Briggs, Crosbie, Bradford, Gregg, Curtis. April 25; 92,406; AH Kingscott

1932 Newcastle 2 (Allen 2) McInroy; Nelson, Fairhurst, McKenzie, Davidson, Weaver, Boyd, Richardson, Allen, McMenemy, Lang **Arsenal 1** (John) Moss; Parker, Hapgood, Jones, Roberts, Male, Hulme, Jack, Lambert, Bastin, John. April 23; 92,298; WP Harper

1933 Everton 3 (Stein, Dean, Dunn) Sagar; Cook, Cresswell, Britton, White, Thomson, Geldard, Dunn, Dean, Johnson, Stein **Manchester City 0** Langford; Cann, Dale, Busby, Cowan, Bray, Toseland, Marshall, Herd, McMullan, Eric Brook. April 29; 92,950; E Wood

1934 Manchester City 2 (Tilson 2) Swift; Barnett, Dale, Busby, Cowan, Bray, Toseland, Marshall, Tilson, Herd, Brook **Portsmouth 1** (Rutherford) Gilfillan; Mackie, Smith, Nichol, Allen, Thackeray, Worrall, Smith, Weddle, Easson, Rutherford. April 28; 93,258; Stanley Rous

1935 Sheffield Wed 4 (Rimmer 2, Palethorpe, Hooper) Brown; Nibloe, Catlin, Sharp, Millership, Burrows, Hooper, Surtees, Palethorpe, Starling, Rimmer **WBA 2** (Boyes, Sandford) Pearson; Shaw, Trentham, Murphy, Bill Richardson, Edwards, Glidden, Carter, WG Richardson, Sandford, Wally. April 27; 93,204; AE Fogg

1936 Arsenal 1 (Drake) Wilson; Male, Hapgood, Crayston, Roberts, Copping, Hulme, Bowden, Drake, James, Bastin **Sheffield Utd 0** Smith; Hooper, Wilkinson, Jackson, Johnson, McPherson, Barton, Barclay, Dodds, Pickering, Williams. April 25; 93,384; H Nattrass

1937 Sunderland 3 (Gurney, Carter, Burbanks) Mapson; Gorman, Hall, Thomson, Johnston, McNab, Duns, Carter, Gurney, Gallacher, Burbanks **Preston 1** (Frank O'Donnell) Burns; Gallimore, Beattie, Shankly, Tremelling, Milne, Dougal, Beresford, O'Donnell, Fagan, O'Donnell. May 1; 93,495; RG Rudd

1938 Preston 1 (Mutch pen) Holdcroft; Gallimore, Beattie, Shankly, Smith, Batey, Watmough, Mutch, Maxwell, Beattie, O'Donnell **Huddersfield 0** Hesford; Craig, Mountford, Willingham, Young, Boot, Hulme, Issac, MacFadyen, Barclay, Beasley. April 30; 93,497; AJ Jewell. aet

1939 Portsmouth 4 (Parker 2, Barlow, Anderson) Walker; Morgan, Rochford, Guthrie, Rowe, Wharton, Worrall, McAlinden, Anderson, Barlow, Parker **Wolves 1** (Dorsett) Scott; Morris, Taylor, Galley, Cullis, Gardiner, Burton, McIntosh, Westcott, Dorsett, Maguire. April 29; 99,370; T Thompson

1946 Derby 4 (Stamps 2. Doherty, B Turner og) Woodley; Nicholas, Howe, Bullions, Leuty, Musson, Harrison, Carter, Stamps, Doherty, Duncan **Charlton Athletic 1** (B Turner) Bartram; Phipps, Shreeve, Turner, Oakes, Johnson, Fell, Brown, Turner, Welsh, Duffy. April 27; 98,000; ED Smith. aet

1947 Charlton Athletic 1 (Duffy) Bartram; Croker, Shreeve, Johnson, Phipps, Whittaker, Hurst, Dawson, Robinson, Welsh, Duffy **Burnley 0** Strong; Woodruff, Mather, Attwell, Brown, Bray, Chew, Morris, Harrison, Potts, Kippax. April 26; 99,000; JM Wiltshire. aet

1948 Manchester Utd 4 (Rowley 2, Pearson, Anderson) Crompton; Carey, Aston, Anderson, Chilton, Cockburn, Delaney, Morris, Rowley, Pearson, Mitten **Blackpool 2** (Shimwell pen, Mortensen) Robinson; Shimwell, Crosland, Johnston, Hayward, Kelly, Matthews, Munro, Mortensen, Dick, Rickett. April 24; 99,000; CJ Barrick

1949 Wolves 3 (Pye 2, Smyth) Williams; Pritchard, Springthorpe Crook, Shorthouse, Wright, Hancocks,

Smyth, Pye, Dunn, Mullen **Leicester 1** (Griffiths) Bradley; Jelly, Scott, Harrison, Plummer, King, Griffiths, Lee, Harrison, Chisholm, Adam. April 30; 99,500; RA Mortimer

1950 **Arsenal 2** (Lewis 2) Swindin; Scott, Barnes, Forbes, L Compton, Mercer, Cox, Logie, Goring, Lewis, D Compton **Liverpool 0** Sidlow; Lambert, Spicer, Taylor, Hughes, Jones, Payne, Baron, Stubbins, Fagan, Liddell. April 29; 100,000; H Pearce

1951 **Newcastle 2** (Milburn 2) Fairbrother; Cowell, Corbett, Harvey, Brennan, Crowe, Walker, Taylor, Milburn, Jorge Robledo, Mitchell **Blackpool 0** Farm; Shimwell, Garrett, Johnston, Hayward, Kelly, Matthews, Mudie, Mortensen, Slater, Perry. April 28; 100,000; W Ling

1952 **Newcastle 1** (G Robledo) Simpson; Cowell, McMichael, Harvey, Brennan, Eduardo Robledo, Walker, Foulkes, Milburn, Jorge Robledo, Mitchell **Arsenal 0** Swindin; Barnes, Smith, Forbes, Daniel Mercer, Cox, Logie, Holton, Lishman, Roper. May 3; 100,000; A Ellis

1953 **Blackpool 4** (Mortensen 3, Perry) Farm; Shimwell, Garrett, Fenton, Johnston, Robinson, Matthews, Taylor, Mortensen, Mudie, Perry **Bolton 3** (Lofthouse, Moir, Bell) Hanson; Ball, Banks, Wheeler, Barrass, Bell, Holden, Moir, Lofthouse, Hassall, Langton. May 2; 100,000; M Griffiths

1954 **WBA 3** (Allen 2 [1pen], Griffin) Sanders; Kennedy, Millard, Dudley, Dugdale, Barlow, Griffin, Ryan, Allen, Nicholls, Lee **Preston 2** (Morrison, Wayman) Thompson; Cunningham, Walton, Docherty, Marston, Forbes, Finney, Foster, Wayman, Baxter, Morrison. May 1; 100,000; A Luty

1955 **Newcastle 3** (Milburn, Mitchell, Hannah) Simpson; Cowell, Batty, Scoular, Stokoe, Casey, White, Milburn, Keeble, Hannah, Mitchell **Manchester City 1** (Johnstone) Trautmann; Meadows, Little, Barnes, Ewing, Paul, Spurdle, Hayes, Revie, Johnstone, Fagan. May 7; 100,000; R Leafe

1956 **Manchester City 3** (Hayes, Dyson, Johnstone) Trautmann; Leivers, Little, Barnes, Ewing, Paul, Johnstone, Hayes, Revie, Dyson, Clarke **Birmingham 1** (Kinsey) Merrick; Hall, Green, Newman, Smith, Boyd, Astall, Kinsey, Brown, Murphy, Govan. May 5; 100,000; A Bond

1957 **Aston Villa 2** (McParland 2) Sims; Lynn, Aldis, Crowther, Dugdale, Saward, Smith, Sewell, Myerscough, Dixon, McParland **Manchester Utd 1** (Taylor) Wood; Foulkes, Byrne, Colman, Blanchflower, Edwards, Berry, Whelan, Taylor, Charlton, Pegg. May 4; 100,000; F Coultas

1958 **Bolton 2** (Lofthouse 2) Hopkinson; Hartle, Banks, Hennin, Higgins, Edwards, Birch, Stevens, Lofthouse, Parry, Holden **Manchester Utd 0** Gregg; Foulkes, Greaves, Goodwin, Cope, Crowther, Dawson, Taylor, Charlton, Viollet, Webster. May 3; 100,000; J Sherlock

1959 **Nottingham Forest 2** (Dwight, Wilson) Thomson; Whare, McDonald, Whitefoot, McKinlay, Burkitt, Dwight, Quigley, Wilson, Gray, Imlach **Luton Town 1** (Pacey) Baynham; McNally, Hawkes, Groves, Owen, Pacey, Bingham, Brown, Morton, Cummins, Gregory. May 2; 100,000; J Clough

1960 **Wolves 3** (McGrath og, Deeley 2) Finlayson; Showell, Harris, Clamp, Slater, Flowers, Deeley, Stobart, Murray, Broadbent, Horne **Blackburn 0** Leyland; Bray, Whelan, Clayton, Woods, McGrath, Bimpson, Dobing, Dougan, Douglas, McLeod. May 7; 100,000; K Howley

1961 **Tottenham 2** (Smith, Dyson) Brown; Baker, Henry, Blanchflower, Norman, Mackay, Jones, White, Smith, Allen, Dyson **Leicester 0** Banks; Chalmers, Norman, McLintock, King, Appleton, Riley, Walsh, McIlmoyle, Keyworth, Cheesebrough. May 6; 100,000; J Kelly

1962 **Tottenham 3** (Greaves, Smith, Blanchflower pen) Brown; Baker, Henry, Blanchflower, Norman, Mackay, Medwin, White, Smith, Greaves, Jones **Burnley 1** (Robson) Blacklaw; Angus, Elder, Adamson, Cummings, Miller, Connelly, McIlroy, Pointer, Robson, Harris. May 5; 100,000; J Finney

1963 **Manchester Utd 3** (Law, Herd 2) Gaskell; Dunne, Cantwell, Crerand, Foulkes, Setters, Giles, Quixall, Herd, Law, Charlton **Leicester 1** (Keyworth) Banks; Sjoberg, Norman, McLintock, King, Appleton, Riley, Cross, Keyworth, Gibson, Stringfellow. May 25; 100,000; K Aston

1964 **West Ham 3** (Sissons, Hurst, Boyce) Standen; Bond, Burkett, Bovington, Brown, Moore, Brabrook, Boyce, Byrne, Hurst, Sissons **Preston 2** (Holden, Dawson) Kelly; Ross, Lawton, Smith, Singleton, Kendall, Wilson, Ashworth, Dawson, Spavin, Holden. May 2; 100,000; A Holland

1965 **Liverpool 2** (Hunt, St John) Lawrence; Lawler, Byrne, Strong, Yeats, Stevenson, Callaghan, Hunt, St John, Smith, Thompson **Leeds 1** (Bremner) Sprake; Reaney, Bell, Bremner, Charlton, Hunter, Giles,

Storrie, Peacock, Collins, Johanneson. May 1; 100,000; W Clements. aet

1966 **Everton 3** (Trebilcock 2, Temple) West; Wright, Wilson, Gabriel, Labone, Harris, Scott, Trebilcock, Young, Harvey, Temple **Sheffield Wed 2** (McCalliog, Ford) Springett; Smith, Megson, Eustace, Ellis, Young, Pugh, Fantham, McCalliog, Ford, Quinn. May 14; 100,000; JK Taylor

1967 **Tottenham 2** (Robertson, Saul) Jennings; Kinnear, Knowles, Mullery, England, Mackay, Robertson, Greaves, Gilzean, Venables, Saul. Unused sub: Jones **Chelsea 1** (Tambling) Bonetti; Allan Harris, McCreadie, Hollins, Hinton, Ron Harris, Cooke, Baldwin, Hateley, Tambling, Boyle. Unused sub: Kirkup. May 20; 100,000; K Dagnall

1968 **WBA 1** (Astle) John Osborne; Fraser, Williams, Brown, Talbut, Kaye, Lovett, Collard, Astle Hope, Clark Sub: Clarke rep Kaye 91 **Everton 0** West; Wright, Wilson, Kendall, Labone, Harvey, Husband, Ball, Royle, Hurst, Morrissey. Unused sub: Kenyon. May 18; 100,000; L Callaghan. aet

1969 **Manchester City 1** (Young) Dowd: Book, Pardoe, Doyle, Booth, Oakes, Summerbee, Bell, Lee, Young, Coleman. Unused sub: Connor **Leicester 0** Shilton; Rodrigues, Nish, Roberts, Woollett, Cross, Fern, Gibson, Lochhead, Clarke, Glover. Sub: Manley rep Glover 70. April 26; 100,000; G McCabe

1970 **Chelsea 2** (Houseman, Hutchinson) Bonetti; Webb, McCreadie, Hollins, Dempsey, R Harris, Baldwin, Houseman, Osgood, Hutchinson, Cooke. Sub: Hinton rep Harris 91 **Leeds 2** (Charlton, Jones) Sprake; Madeley, Cooper, Bremner, Charlton, Hunter, Lorimer, Clarke, Jones, Giles, Gray Unusued sub: Bates. April 11; 100,000; E Jennings. aet **Replay – Chelsea 2** (Osgood, Webb) Bonetti, Webb, McCreadie, Hollins, Dempsey, R Harris, Baldwin, Houseman, Osgood, Hutchinson, Cooke. Sub: Hinton rep Osgood 105 **Leeds 1** (Jones) Harvey; Madeley, Cooper, Bremner, Charlton, Hunter, Lorimer, Clarke, Jones, Giles, Gray Unusued sub: Bates. April 29; 62,078; E Jennings. aet

1971 **Arsenal 2** (Kelly, George) Wilson; Rice, McNab, Storey, McLintock Simpson, Armstrong, Graham, Radford, Kennedy, George. Sub: Kelly rep Storey 70 **Liverpool 1** (Heighway) Clemence; Lawler, Lindsay, Smith, Lloyd, Hughes, Callaghan, Evans, Heighway, Toshack, Hall. Sub: Thompson rep Evans 70. May 8; 100,000; N Burtenshaw. aet

1972 **Leeds 1** (Clarke) Harvey; Reaney, Madeley, Bremner, Charlton, Hunter, Lorimer, Clarke, Jones, Giles, Gray. Unused sub: Bates **Arsenal 0** Barnett; Rice, McNab, Storey, McLintock, Simpson, Armstrong, Ball, George, Radford, Graham. Sub: Kennedy rep Radford 80. May 6; 100,000; DW Smith

1973 **Sunderland 1** (Porterfield) Montgomery; Malone, Guthrie, Horswill, Watson, Pitt, Kerr, Hughes, Halom, Porterfield, Tueart. Unused sub: Young **Leeds 0** Harvey; Reaney, Cherry, Bremner, Madeley, Hunter, Lorimer, Clarke, Jones, Giles, Gray. Sub: Yorath rep Gray 75. May 5; 100,000; K Burns

1974 **Liverpool 3** (Keegan 2, Heighway) Clemence; Smith, Lindsay, Thompson, Cormack, Hughes, Keegan, Hall, Heighway, Toshack, Callaghan. Unused sub: Lawler **Newcastle 0** McFaul; Clark, Kennedy, McDermott, Howard, Moncur, Smith, Cassidy, Macdonald, Tudor, Hibbitt. Sub: Gibb rep Smith 70. May 4; 100,000; GC Kew

1975 **West Ham 2** (Taylor 2) Day; McDowell, Taylor, Lock, Lampard, Bonds, Paddon, Brooking, Jennings, Taylor, Holland. Unused sub: Gould **Fulham 0** Mellor; Cutbush, Lacy, Moore, Fraser, Mullery, Conway, Slough, Mitchell, Busby, Barrett. Unused sub: Lloyd. May 3; 100,000; P Partridge

1976 **Southampton 1** (Stokes) Turner; Rodrigues, Peach, Holmes, Blyth, Steele, Gilchrist, Channon, Osgood, McCalliog, Stokes. Unused sub: Fisher **Manchester Utd 0** Stepney; Forsyth, Houston, Daly, Greenhoff, Buchan, Coppell, McIlroy, Pearson, Macari, Hill. Sub: McCreery rep Hill 66. May 1; 100,000; C Thomas

1977 **Manchester Utd 2** (Pearson, J Greenhoff) Stepney; Nicholl, Albiston, McIlroy, B Greenhoff, Buchan, Coppell, J Greenhoff, Pearson, Macari, Hill. Sub: McCreery rep Hill 81 **Liverpool 1** (Case) Clemence; Neal, Jones, Smith, Kennedy, Hughes, Keegan, Case, Heighway, Johnson, McDermott. Sub: Callaghan rep Johnson 64. May 21; 100,000; R Matthewson

1978 **Ipswich Town 1** (Osborne) Cooper; Burley, Mills, Talbot, Hunter, Beattie, Osborne, Wark, Mariner, Geddis, Woods. Sub: Lambert rep Osborne 79 **Arsenal 0** Jennings; Rice, Nelson, Price, Young, O'Leary, Brady, Hudson, Macdonald, Stapleton, Sunderland. Sub: Rix rep Brady 65. May 6; 100,000; D Nippard

1979 **Arsenal 3** (Talbot, Stapleton, Sunderland) Jennings; Rice, Nelson, Talbot, O'Leary, Young, Brady,

Sunderland, Stapleton, Price, Rix. Sub: Walford rep Rix 83 **Manchester Utd 2** (McQueen, McIlroy) Bailey; Nicholl, Albiston, McIlroy, McQueen, Buchan, Coppell, J Greenhoff, Jordan, Macari, Thomas. Unused sub: Greenhoff. May 12; 100,000; R Challis

1980 West Ham 1 (Brooking) Parkes; Stewart, Lampard, Bonds, Martin, Devonshire, Allen, Pearson, Cross, Brooking, Pike. Unused sub: Brush **Arsenal 0** Jennings; Rice, Devine, Talbot, O'Leary, Young, Brady, Sunderland, Stapleton, Price, Rix. Sub: Nelson rep Devine 61. May 10; 100,000; G Courtney

1981 Tottenham 1 (Hutchinson og) Aleksic; Hughton, Miller, Roberts, Perryman, Villa, Ardiles, Archibald, Galvin, Hoddle, Crooks. Sub: Brooke rep Villa 68. **Manchester City 1** (Hutchinson) Corrigan; Ranson, McDonald, Reid, Power, Caton, Bennett, Gow, Mackenzie, Hutchison Reeves. Sub: Henry rep Hutchison 82. May 9; 100,000; K Hackett. aet **Replay – Tottenham 3** (Villa 2, Crooks) Aleksic; Hughton, Miller, Roberts, Perryman, Villa, Ardiles, Archibald, Galvin, Hoddle, Crooks. Unused sub: Brooke **Manchester City 2** (Mackenzie, Reeves pen) Corrigan; Ranson, McDonald, Reid, Power, Caton, Bennett, Gow, Mackenzie, Hutchison Reeves. Sub: Tueart rep McDonald 79. May 14; 92,000; K Hackett

1982 Tottenham 1 (Hoddle) Clemence; Hughton, Miller, Price, Hazard, Perryman, Roberts, Archibald, Galvin, Hoddle, Crooks. Sub: Brooke rep Hazard 104 **Queens Park Rangers 1** (Fenwick) Hucker; Fenwick, Gillard, Waddock, Hazell, Roeder, Currie, Flanagan, Allen, Stainrod, Gregory. Sub: Micklewhite rep Allen 50. May 22; 100,000; C White. aet **Replay – Tottenham 1** (Hoddle pen) Clemence; Hughton, Miller, Price, Hazard, Perryman, Roberts, Archibald, Galvin, Hoddle, Crooks. Sub: Brooke rep Hazard 67 **Queens Park Rangers 0** Hucker; Fenwick, Gillard, Waddock, Hazell, Neill, Currie, Flanagan, Micklewhite, Stainrod, Gregory. Sub: Burke rep Micklewhite 84. May 27; 90,000; C White

1983 Manchester Utd 2 (Stapleton, Wilkins) Bailey; Duxbury, Moran, McQueen, Albiston, Davies, Wilkins, Robson, Muhren, Stapleton, Whiteside. Unused sub: Grimes **Brighton 2** (Smith, Stevens) Moseley; Ramsey, Gary A Stevens, Pearce, Gatting, Smillie, Case, Grealish, Howlett, Robinson, Smith. Sub: Ryan rep Ramsey 56. May 21; 100,000; AW Grey, aet **Replay – Manchester Utd 4** (Robson 2, Whiteside, Muhren pen) Bailey; Duxbury, Moran, McQueen, Albiston, Davies, Wilkins, Robson, Muhren, Stapleton, Whiteside. Unused sub: Grimes **Brighton 0** Moseley; Gary A Stevens, Pearce, Foster, Gatting, Smillie, Case, Grealish, Howlett, Robinson, Smith. Sub: Ryan rep Howlett 74. May 26; 100,000; AW Grey

1984 Everton 2 (Sharp, Gray) Southall; Gary M Stevens, Bailey, Ratcliffe, Mountfield, Reid, Steven, Heath, Sharp, Gray, Richardson. Unused sub: Harper **Watford 0** Sherwood; Bardsley, Price, Taylor, Terry, Sinnott, Callaghan, Johnston, Reilly, Jackett, Barnes. Sub: Atkinson rep Price 58. May 19; 100,000; J Hunting

1985 Manchester Utd 1 (Whiteside) Bailey; Gidman, Albiston, Whiteside, McGrath, Moran, Robson, Strachan, Hughes, Stapleton, Olsen. Sub: Duxbury rep Albiston 91. Moran sent off 77. **Everton 0** Southall; Gary M Stevens, Van den Hauwe, Ratcliffe, Mountfield, Reid, Steven, Sharp, Gray, Bracewell, Sheedy. Unused sub: Harper. May 18; 100,000; P Willis. aet

1986 Liverpool 3 (Rush 2, Johnston) Grobbelaar; Lawrenson, Beglin, Nicol, Whelan, Hansen, Dalglish, Johnston, Rush, Molby, MacDonald. Unused sub: McMahon **Everton 1** (Lineker) Mimms; Gary M Stevens, Van den Hauwe, Ratcliffe, Mountfield, Reid, Steven, Lineker, Sharp, Bracewell, Sheedy. Sub: Heath rep Stevens 65. May 10; 98,000; A Robinson

1987 Coventry City 3 (Bennett, Houchen, Mabbutt og) Ogrizovic; Phillips, Downs, McGrath, Kilcline, Peake, Bennett, Gynn, Regis, Houchen, Pickering. Sub: Rodger rep Kilcline 88. Unused sub: Sedgley **Tottenham 2** (Allen, Mabbutt) Clemence; Hughton Thomas, Hodge, Gough, Mabbutt, C Allen, P Allen, Waddle, Hoddle, Ardiles. Subs: Gary A Stevens rep Ardiles 91; Claesen rep Hughton 97. May 16; 98,000; N Midgley. aet

1988 Wimbledon 1 (Sanchez) Beasant; Goodyear, Phelan, Jones, Young, Thorn, Gibson Cork, Fashanu, Sanchez, Wise. Subs: Cunningham rep Cork 56; Scales rep Gibson 63 **Liverpool 0** Grobbelaar; Gillespie, Ablett, Nicol, Spackman, Hansen, Beardsley, Aldridge, Houghton, Barnes, McMahon. Subs: Johnston rep Aldridge 63; Molby rep Spackman 72. May 14; 98,203; B Hill

1989 Liverpool 3 (Aldridge, Rush 2) Grobbelaar; Ablett, Staunton, Nichol, Whelan, Hansen, Beardsley, Aldridge Houghton, Barnes, McMahon. Subs: Rush rep Aldridge 72; Venison rep Staunton 91 **Everton 2** (McCall 2) Southall; McDonald, Van den Hauwe, Ratcliffe, Watson, Bracewell, Nevin, Trevor Steven, Cottee, Sharp, Sheedy. Subs: McCall rep Bracewell 58; Wilson rep Sheedy 77. May 20; 82,500; J Worrall. aet

1990 **Manchester Utd 3** (Robson, Hughes 2) Leighton; Ince, Martin, Bruce, Phelan, Pallister, Robson, Webb, McClair, Hughes, Wallace. Subs: Blackmore rep Martin 88; Robins rep Pallister 93. **Crystal Palace 3** (O'Reilly, Wright 2) Martyn; Pemberton, Shaw, Gray, O'Reilly, Thorn, Barber, Thomas, Bright, Salako, Pardew. Subs: Wright rep Barber 69; Madden rep Gray 117. May 12; 80,000; A Gunn. aet **Replay – Manchester Utd 1** (Martin) Sealey; Ince, Martin, Bruce, Phelan, Pallister, Robson, Webb, McClair, Hughes, Wallace. Unused subs: Robins, Blackmore **Crystal Palace 0** Martyn; Pemberton, Shaw, Gray, O'Reilly, Thorn, Barber, Thomas, Bright, Salako, Pardew. Subs: Wright rep Barber 64; Madden rep Salako 79. May 17; 80,000; A Gunn

1991 **Tottenham 2** (Stewart, Walker og) Thorstvedt; Edinburgh, Van den Hauwe, Sedgley, Howells, Mabbutt, Stewart, Gascoigne, Samways, Lineker, Allen. Subs: Nayim rep Gascoigne 18; Walsh rep Samways 82. **Nottingham Forest 1** (Pearce) Crossley; Charles, Pearce, Walker, Chettle, Keane, Crosby, Parker, Clough, Glover, Woan. Subs: Hodge rep Woan 62; Laws rep Glover 108. May 18; 80,000; R Milford. aet

1992 **Liverpool 2** (Thomas, Rush) Grobbelaar; Jones, Burrows, Nicol, Molby, Wright, Saunders, Houghton, Rush, McManaman, Thomas. Unused subs: Marsh, Walters **Sunderland 0** Norman; Owers, Ball, Bennett, Rogan, Rush, Bracewell, Davenport, Armstrong, Byrne, Atkinson. Subs: Hardyman rep Rush 69; Hawke rep Armstrong 77. May 9; 80,000; P Don

1993 **Arsenal 1** (Wright) Seaman; Dixon, Winterburn, Linighan, Adams, Jensen, Davis, Parlour, Merson, Campbell, Wright. Subs: Smith rep Parlour 66; O'Leary rep Wright 90. **Sheffield Wed 1** (Hirst) Woods; Nilsson Worthington, Palmer, Hirst, Anderson, Waddle, Warhurst, Bright, Sheridan, Harkes. Subs: Hyde rep Anderson 85; Bart-Williams rep Waddle 112. May 15; 79,347; K Barratt. aet **Replay – Arsenal 2** (Wright, Linighan) Seaman; Dixon, Winterburn, Linighan, Adams, Jensen, Davis, Smith, Merson, Campbell, Wright. Sub: O'Leary rep Wright 81. Unused sub: Selley **Sheffield Wed 1** (Waddle) Woods; Nilsson, Worthington, Palmer, Hirst, Wilson, Waddle, Warhurst, Bright, Sheridan, Harkes. Subs: Hyde rep Wilson 62; Bart-Williams rep Nilsson 118. May 20; 62,267; K Barratt. aet

1994 **Manchester Utd 4** (Cantona 2 [2pens], Hughes, McClair) Schmeichel; Parker, Bruce, Pallister, Irwin, Kanchelskis, Keane, Ince, Giggs, Cantona, Hughes. Subs: Sharpe rep Irwin 84; McClair rep Kanchelskis 84. Unused sub: Walsh (gk) **Chelsea 0** Kharine; Clarke, Sinclair, Kjeldberg, Johnsen, Burley, Spencer, Newton, Stein, Peacock, Wise Substitutions Hoddle rep Burley 65; Cascarino rep Stein 78. Unused sub: Kevin Hitchcock (gk) May 14; 79,634; D Elleray

1995 **Everton 1** (Rideout) Southall; Jackson, Hinchcliffe, Ablett, Watson, Parkinson, Unsworth, Horne, Stuart, Rideout, Limpar. Subs: Ferguson rep Rideout 51; Amokachi rep Limpar 69. Unused sub: Kearton (gk) **Manchester Utd 0** Schmeichel; Neville, Irwin, Bruce, Sharpe, Pallister, Keane, Ince, Brian McClair, Hughes, Butt. Subs: Giggs rep Bruce 46; Scholes rep Sharpe 72. Unused sub: Gary Walsh (gk) May 20; 79,592; G Ashby

1996 **Manchester Utd 1** (Cantona) Schmeichel; Irwin, P Neville, May, Keane, Pallister, Cantona, Beckham, Cole, Butt, Giggs. Subs: Scholes rep Cole 65; G Neville rep Beckham 89. Unused sub: Sharpe **Liverpool 0** James; McAteer, Scales, Wright, Babb, Jones, McManaman, Barnes, Redknapp, Collymore, Fowler. Subs: Rush rep Collymore 74; Thomas rep Jones 85. Unused sub: Warner (gk) May 11; 79,007; D Gallagher

1997 **Chelsea 2** (Di Matteo, Newton) Grodas; Petrescu, Minto, Sinclair, Lebouef, Clarke, Zola, Di Matteo, Newton, Hughes, Wise. Sub: Vialli rep Zola 89. Unused subs: Hitchcock (gk), Myers **Middlesbrough 0** Roberts; Blackmore, Fleming, Stamp, Pearson, Festa, Emerson, Mustoe, Ravanelli, Juninho, Hignett. Subs: Beck rep Ravanelli 24; Vickers rep Mustoe 29; Kinder, rep Hignett 74. May 17; 79,160; S Lodge

1998 **Arsenal 2** (Overmars, Anelka) Seaman; Dixon, Winterburn, Vieira, Keown, Adams, Parlour, Anelka, Petit, Wreh, Overmars. Sub: Platt rep Wreh 63. Unused subs: Manninger (gk); Bould, Wright, Grimandi **Newcastle 0** Given; Pistone, Pearce, Batty, Dabizas, Howey, Lee, Barton, Shearer, Ketsbaia, Speed. Subs: Andersson rep Pearce 72; Watson rep Barton 77; Barnes rep Ketsbaia 85. Unused subs: Hislop (gk); Albert. May 16; 79,183; P Durkin

1999 **Manchester Utd 2** (Sheringham, Scholes) Schmeichel; G Neville, Johnsen, May, P Neville, Beckham, Scholes, Keane, Giggs, Cole, Solskjaer. Subs: Sheringham rep Keane 9; Yorke rep Cole 61; Stam rep Scholes 77. Unused subs: Blomqvist, Van Der Gouw **Newcastle 0** Harper; Griffin, Charvet, Dabizas, Domi, Lee, Hamann, Speed, Solano, Ketsbaia, Shearer. Subs: Ferguson rep Hamann 46; Maric rep Solano 68; Glass rep Ketsbaia 79. Unused subs: Given (gk); Barton. May 22; 79,101; P Jones

2000 **Chelsea 1** (Di Matteo) de Goey; Melchiot Desailly, Lebouef, Babayaro, Di Matteo, Wise, Deschamps, Poyet, Weah, Zola. Subs: Flo rep Weah 87; Morris rep Zola 90. Unused subs: Cudicini (gk), Terry , Harley **Aston Villa 0** James; Ehiogu, Southgate, Barry, Delaney, Taylor, Boateng, Merson, Wright, Dublin, Carbone. Subs: Stone rep Taylor 79; Joachim rep Carbone 79; Hendrie rep Wright 88. Unused subs: Enckelman (gk); Samuel May 20; 78,217; G Poll

2001 **Liverpool 2** (Owen 2) Westerveld; Babbel, Henchoz, Hyypia, Carragher, Murphy, Hamann, Gerrard, Smicer, Heskey, Owen. Subs: McAllister rep Hamann 60; Fowler rep Smicer 77; Berger rep Murphy 77. Unused subs: Arphexad (gk); Vignal **Arsenal 1** (Ljungberg) Seaman; Dixon, Keown, Adams, Cole, Ljungberg, Grimandi, Vieira, Pires, Henry, Wiltord Subs: Parlour rep Wiltord 76; Kanu rep Ljungberg 85; Bergkamp rep Dixon 90. Unused subs: Manninger (gk); Lauren. May 12; 72,500; S Dunn

2002 **Arsenal 2** (Parlour, Ljungberg) Seaman; Lauren, Campbell, Adams, Cole, Parlour, Wiltord, Vieira, Ljungberg, Bergkamp, Henry Subs: Edu rep Bergkamp 72; Kanu rep Henry 81; Keown rep Wiltord 90. Unused subs: Wright (gk); Dixon **Chelsea 0** Cudicini; Melchiot, Desailly, Gallas, Babayaro, Gronkjaer, Lampard, Petit, Le Saux, Floyd Hasselbaink, Gudjohnsen. Subs: Terry rep Babayaro 46; Zola rep Hasselbaink 68; Zenden rep Melchiot 77. Unused subs: de Goey (gk); Jokanovic. May 4; 73,963; M Riley

2003 **Arsenal 1** (Pires) Seaman; Lauren, Luzhny, Keown, Cole, Ljungberg, Parlour, Gilberto, Pires, Bergkamp, Henry. Sub: Wiltord rep Bergkamp 77. Unused subs: Taylor (gk); Kanu, Toure, van Bronckhorst **Southampton 0** Niemi; Baird, Svensson, Lundekvam, Bridge, Telfer, Svensson, Oakley, Marsden, Beattie, Ormerod. Subs: Jones rep Niemi 66; Fernandes rep Baird 87; Tessem rep Svensson 75. Unused subs: Williams, Higginbotham. May 17; 73,726; G Barber

2004 **Manchester Utd 3** (Van Nistelrooy [2, 1 pen], Ronaldo) Howard; G Neville, Brown, Silvestre, O'Shea, Fletcher, Keane, Ronaldo, Scholes, Giggs, Van Nistelrooy. Subs: Carroll rep Howard, Butt rep Fletcher, Solskjaer rep Ronaldo 84. Unused subs: P Neville, Djemba-Djemba **Millwall 0** Marshall; Elliott, Lawrence, Ward, Ryan, Wise, Ifill, Cahill, Livermore, Sweeney, Harris. Subs: Cogan rep Ryan, McCammon rep Harris 74 Weston rep Wise 88. Unused subs: Gueret (gk); Dunne. May 22; 71,350; J Winter

2005 **Arsenal 0** Lehmann; Lauren, Toure, Senderos, Cole, Fabregas, Gilberto, Vieira, Pires, Reyes, Bergkamp Subs: Ljungberg rep Bergkamp 65, Van Persie rep Fabregas 86, Edu rep Pires 105. Unused subs: Almunia (gk); Campbell. Reyes sent off 90. **Manchester Utd 0** Carroll; Brown, Ferdinand, Silvestre, O'Shea, Fletcher, Keane, Scholes, Rooney, Van Nistelrooy, Ronaldo. Subs: Fortune rep O'Shea 77, Giggs rep Fletcher 91. Unused subs: Howard (gk); G Neville, Smith. **Arsenal** (Lauren, Ljungberg, van Persie, Cole, Vieira) beat Manchester Utd (van Nistelrooy, Scholes [missed], Ronaldo, Rooney, Keane) 5-4 on penalties

2006 **Liverpool 3** (Gerrard 2, Cisse) Reina; Finnan, Carragher, Hyypiä, Riise, Gerrard, Xabi, Sissoko, Kewell, Cisse, Crouch. Subs: Morientes rep Kewell 48, Kromkamp rep Alonso 67, Hamman rep Crouch 71. Unused subs: Dudek (gk); Traoré **West Ham 3** (Ashton, Konchesky, Carragher (og)) Hislop; Scaloni, Ferdinand, Gabbidon, Konchesky, Benayoun, Fletcher, Reo-Coker, Etherington, Ashton, Harewood. Subs: Zamora rep Ashton 71, Dailly rep Fletcher, Sheringham rep Etherington 85. Unused subs: Walker (gk); Collins. **Liverpool** (Hamann, Hyypiä [missed], Gerrard, Riise) beat **West Ham** (Zamora [missed], Sheringham, Konchesky [missed], Ferdinand [missed]) 3-1 on penalties. May 13; 71,140; A Wiley

2007 **Chelsea 1** (Drogba) Cech, Ferreira, Essien, Terry, Bridge, Mikel, Makelele, Lampard, Wright-Phillips, Drogba, J Cole Subs: Robben rep J Cole 45, Kalou rep Wright-Phillips 93, A Cole rep Robben 108. Unused subs: Cudicini (gk); Diarra. **Manchester Utd 0** Van der Sar, Brown, Ferdinand, Vidic, Heinze, Fletcher, Scholes, Carrick, Ronaldo, Rooney, Giggs Subs: Smith rep Fletcher 92, O'Shea rep Carrick, Solskjaer rep Giggs 112. Unused subs: Kuszczak (gk); Evra. May 19; 89,826; S Bennett

2008 **Portsmouth 1** (Kanu) James; Johnson, Campbell, Distin, Hreidarsson, Utaka, Muntari, Mendes, Diarra, Kranjcar, Kanu. Subs: Nugent rep Utaka 69, Diop rep Mendes 78, Baros rep Kanu 87. Unused subs: Ashdown (gk); Pamarot. **Cardiff 0** Enckelman; McNaughton, Johnson, Loovens, Capaldi, Whittingham, Rae, McPhail, Ledley, Hasselbaink, Parry. Subs: Ramsey rep Whittingham 62, Thompson rep Hasselbaink 70, Sinclair rep Rae 87. Unused subs: Oakes (gk); Purse. May 17; 89,874; M Dean

2009 Chelsea 2 (Drogba, Lampard), Cech; Bosingwa, Alex, Terry, A Cole, Essien, Mikel, Lampard, Drogba, Anelka, Malouda. Subs: Ballack rep Essien 61. Unused subs: Hilario (gk), Ivanovic, Di Santo, Kalou, Belletti, Mancienne. **Everton** 1 (Saha) Howard; Hibbert, Yobo, Lescott, Baines, Osman, Neville, Cahill, Pienaar, Fellaini, Saha. Subs: Jacobsen rep Hibbert 46, Vaughan rep Saha 77, Gosling rep Osman 83. Unused subs: Nash, Castillo, Rodwell, Baxter. May 30; 89,391; H Webb

2010 Chelsea 1 (Drogba) Cech; Ivanovic, Alex, Terry, A Cole, Lampard, Ballack, Malouda, Kalou, Drogba, Anelka. Subs: Belletti rep Ballack 44, J Cole rep Kalou 71, Sturridge rep Anelka 90. Unused subs: Hilario (gk), Zhirkov, Paulo Ferreira, Matic. **Portsmouth 0** James; Finnan, Mokoena, Rocha, Mullins, Dindane, Brown, Diop, Boateng, O'Hara, Piquionne. Subs: Utaka rep Boateng 73, Belhadj rep Mullins 81, Kanu rep Diop 81. Unused subs: Ashdown (gk), Vanden Borre, Hughes, Ben Haim. May 15; 88,335; C Foy

2011 Manchester City 1 (Y Toure) Hart; Richards, Kompany, Lescott, Kolarov, De Jong, Barry, Silva, Y Toure, Balotelli, Tevez. Subs: Johnson rep Barry73, Zabaleta rep Tevez 87, Vieira rep Silva 90. Unused subs: Given (gk), Boyata, Milner, Dzeko. **Stoke 0** Sorensen; Wilkinson, Shawcross, Huth, Wilson, Pennant, Whelan, Delap, Etherington, Walters, Jones. Subs: Whitehead rep Etherington 62, Carew rep Delap 80, Pugh rep Whelan 84. Unused subs: Nash (gk), Collins, Faye, Diao. May 14; 88,643; M Atkinson

2012 Chelsea 2 (Ramires, Drogba) Cech; Bosingwa, Ivanovic, Terry, Cole, Mikel, Lampard, Ramires, Mata, Kalou, Drogba. Subs: Meireles rep Ramires76, Malouda rep Mata 90. Unused subs: Turnbull (gk), Paulo Ferreira, Essien, Torres, Sturridge. **Liverpool 1** (Carroll) Reina; Johnson, Skrtel, Agger, Luis Enrique, Spearing, Bellamy, Henderson, Gerrard, Downing, Suarez. Subs Carroll rep Spearing 55, Kuyt rep Bellamy 78. Unused subs: Doni (gk), Carragher, Kelly, Shelvey, Rodriguez. May 5; 89,102; P Dowd

2013 Wigan 1 (Watson) Robles; Boyce, Alcaraz, Scharner, McCarthy, McArthur, McManaman, Maloney, Gomez, Espinoza, Kone. Subs: Watson rep Gomez 81. Unused subs: Al Habsi (gk), Caldwell, Golobart, Fyvie, Henriquez, Di Santo. **Manchester City 0** Hart, Zabaleta, Kompany, Nastasic, Clichy, Toure, Barry, Silva, Tevez, Nasri, Aguero. Subs: Milner rep Nasri 54, Rodwell rep Tevez 69, Dzeko rep Barry 90. Unused subs: Pantilimon (gk), Lescott, Kolarov, Garcia. Sent off Zabaleta (84). May 11; 86,254; A Marriner

2014 Arsenal 3 (Cazorla, Koscielny, Ramsey) Fabianski; Sagna, Koscielny, Mertesacker, Gibbs, Arteta, Ramsey, Cazorla, Ozil, Podolski, Giroud. Subs: Sanogo rep Podolski 61, Rosicky rep Cazorla 106, Wilshire rep Ozil 106. Unused subs: Szczesny (gk), Vermaelen, Monreal, Flamini. **Hull** 2 (Chester, Davies) McGregor; Davies, Bruce, Chester, Elmohamady, Livermore, Huddlestone, Meyler, Rosenior, Quinn, Fryatt. Subs: McShane rep Bruce 67, Aluko rep Quinn 71, Boyd rep Rosenior 102. Unused subs: Harper (gk), Figueroa, Koren, Sagbo. May 17; 89,345; L Probert. aet

2015 Arsenal 4 (Walcott, Sanchez, Mertesacker, Giroud) Szczesny; Bellerin, Koscielny, Mertesacker, Monreal, Coquelin, Cazorla, Ramsey, Ozil, A Sanchez, Walcott. Subs: Wilshere rep Ozil 77, Giroud rep Walcott 77, Oxlade-Chamberlain rep A Sanchez 90. Unused subs: Ospina (gk), Gibbs, Gabriel, Flamini. **Aston Villa** 0 Given; Hutton, Okore, Vlaar, Richardson, Cleverley, Westwood, Delph, N'Zogbia, Benteke, Grealish. Subs: Agbonlahor rep N'Zogbia 53, Bacuna rep Richardson 68, C Sanchez rep Westwood 71. Unused subs: Guzan (gk), Baker, Sinclair, Cole. May 30; 89,283; J Moss

VENUES

Kennington Oval 1872; **Lillie Bridge** 1873; **Kennington Oval** 1874 – 1892 (1886 replay at the **Racecourse Ground, Derby**); **Fallowfield**, Manchester, 1893; **Goodison Park** 1894; **Crystal Palace** 1895 – 1915 (1901 replay at **Burnden Park**; 1910 replay at **Goodison Park**; 1912 replay at **Bramall Lane**); **Old Trafford** 1915; **Stamford Bridge** 1920 – 1922; **Wembley** 1923 – 2000 (1970 replay at **Old Trafford**; all replays after 1981 at **Wembley**); **Millennium Stadium** 2001 – 2006; **Wembley** 2007 – 2016

SUMMARY OF FA CUP WINS

Arsenal	12
Manchester Utd	12
Tottenham	8
Aston Villa	7
Liverpool	7
Chelsea	7
Blackburn Rov	6
Newcastle	6
Everton	5
Manchester City	5
The Wanderers	5
WBA	5
Bolton	4
Sheffield Utd	4
Wolves	4
Sheffield Wed	3
West Ham	3
Bury	2
Nottm Forest	2
Old Etonians	2
Portsmouth	2
Preston	2
Sunderland	2
Barnsley	1
Blackburn Olympic	1
Blackpool	1
Bradford City	1
Burnley	1
Cardiff	1
Charlton	1
Clapham Rov	1
Coventry	1
Derby	1
Huddersfield	1
Ipswich	1
Leeds	1
Notts Co	1
Old Carthusians	1
Oxford University	1
Royal Engineers	1
Southampton	1
Wigan	1
Wimbledon	1

APPEARANCES IN FINALS

(Figures do not include replays)

Arsenal	19
Manchester Utd	19
Liverpool	14
Everton	13
Newcastle	13
Aston Villa	11
Chelsea	11
Manchester City	10
WBA	10
Tottenham	9
Blackburn Rov	8
Wolves	8
Bolton	7
Preston	7
Old Etonians	6
Sheffield Utd	6
Sheffield Wed	6
Huddersfield	5
Portsmouth	5
The Wanderers*	5
West Ham	5
Derby	4
Leeds	4
Leicester	4
Oxford University	4
Royal Engineers	4
Southampton	4
Sunderland	4
Blackpool	3
Burnley	3
Cardiff	3
Nottm Forest	3
Barnsley	2
Birmingham	2
Bury*	2
Charlton	2
Clapham Rov	2
Crystal Palace	2
Notts Co	2
Queen's Park (Glasgow)	2
Blackburn Olympic*	1
Bradford City*	1
Brighton	1
Bristol City	1
Coventry*	1
Fulham	1
Hull	1
Ipswich*	1
Luton	1
Middlesbrough	1
Millwall	1
Old Carthusians*	1
QPR	1
Stoke	1
Watford	1
Wigan	1
Wimbledon*	1

(* Denotes undefeated)

APPEARANCES IN SEMI-FINALS

(Figures do not include replays)

28 Arsenal, Manchester Utd; **26** Everton; **24** Liverpool; **21** Aston Villa, Chelsea; **20** WBA; **19** Tottenham; **18** Blackburn; **17** Newcastle; **16** Sheffield Wed; **14** Bolton, Sheffield Utd, Wolves; **13** Derby; **12** Manchester City, Nottm Forest, Sunderland; **11** Southampton; **10** Preston; **9** Birmingham; **8** Burnley, Leeds; **7** Huddersfield, Leicester, Portsmouth, West Ham; **6** Fulham, Old Etonians, Oxford University, Watford; **5** Millwall, Notts Co, The Wanderers; **4** Cardiff, *Crystal Palace, Luton, Queen's Park (Glasgow), Royal Engineers, Stoke; **3** Barnsley, Blackpool, Clapham Rov, Ipswich, Middlesbrough, Norwich, Old Carthusians, Oldham, The Swifts; **2** Blackburn Olympic, Bristol City, Bury, Charlton, Grimsby, Hull, Reading, Swansea, Swindon, Wigan, Wimbledon; **1** Bradford City, Brighton, Cambridge University, Chesterfield, Coventry, Crewe, Darwen, Derby Junction, Marlow, Old Harrovians, Orient, Plymouth Argyle, Port Vale, QPR, Rangers (Glasgow), Shropshire Wand, Wycombe, York

(*A previous and different Crystal Palace club also reached the semi-final in season 1871–72)

LEAGUE CUP 2015–16

FIRST ROUND

Accrington 2 Hull 2
(aet, Hull won 4- 3 on pens)
Blackburn 1 Shrewsbury 2
Bolton 0 Burton 1
Brentford 0 Oxford 4
Bristol Rov 1 Birmingham 2
Cardiff 1 AFC Wimbledon 0
Carlisle 3 Chesterfield 1 aet)
Charlton 4 Dagenham 1
Colchester 0 Reading 1 (aet)
Crewe 1 Preston 3
Doncaster 1 Leeds 1
(aet, Doncaster won 4- 2 on pens)
Fleetwood 0 Hartlepool 1
Huddersfield 1 Notts Co 2
Ipswich 2 Stevenage 1
Luton 3 Bristol City 1
Millwall 1 Barnet 2 (aet)
MK Dons 2 Leyton Orient 1
Morecambe 0 Sheffield Utd 1
Northampton 3 Blackpool 0
Nottm Forest 3 Walsall 4
Oldham 1 Middlesbrough 3
Peterborough 2 Crawley 0
Plymouth 1 Gillingham 2
Port Vale 1 Burnley 0
Portsmouth 2 Derby 1
Rochdale 1 Coventry 1
(aet, Rochdale won 5- 3 on pens)
Rotherham 1 Cambridge 0
Scunthorpe 1 Barnsley 1
(aet, Barnsley won 7-6 on pens)
Sheffield Wed 4 Mansfield 1
Southend 0 Brighton 1
Swindon 1 Exeter 2
Wigan 1 Bury 2
Wolves 2 Newport 1
Wycombe 0 Fulham 1
Yeovil 0 QPR 3
York 2 Bradford 2
(aet, York won 4- 2 on pens)

SECOND ROUND

Aston Villa 5 Notts Co 3 (aet)
Barnsley 3 Everton 5 (aet)
Birmingham 2 Gillingham 0
Burton 1 Middlesbrough 2 (aet)
Bury 1 Leicester 4
Crystal Palace 4 Shrewsbury 1 (aet)
Doncaster 1 Ipswich 4 (aet)
Fulham 3 Sheffield Utd 0
Hartlepool 0 Bournemouth 4
Hull 1 Rochdale 0
Luton 1 Stoke 1
(aet, Stoke won 8-7 on pens)
MK Dons 2 Cardiff 1 (aet)
Newcastle 4 Northampton 1
Peterborough 1 Charlton 4
Portsmouth 1 Reading 2
Preston 1 Watford 0
QPR 1 Carlisle 2
Rotherham 1 Norwich 2
Sheffield Wed 1 Oxford 0
Sunderland 6 Exeter 3
Swansea 3 York 0
Walsall 2 Brighton 1
WBA 0 Port Vale 0
(aet, WBA won 5- 3 on pens)
Wolves 2 Barnet 1

THIRD ROUND

Aston Villa 1 Birmingham 0
Crystal Palace 4 Charlton 1
Fulham 0 Stoke 1
Hull 1 Swansea 0
Leicester 2 West Ham 1 (aet)
Liverpool 1 Carlisle 1
(aet, Liverpool won 3-2 on pens)
Manchester Utd 3 Ipswich 0
MK Dons 0 Southampton 6
Middlesbrough 3 Wolves 0
Newcastle 0 Sheffield Wed 1
Norwich 3 WBA 0
Preston 2 Bournemouth+B 2
(aet, Bournemouth won 3-2 on pens)
Reading 1 Everton 2
Sunderland 1 **Manchester City 4**
Tottenham 1 Arsenal 2
Walsall 1 Chelsea 4

FOURTH ROUND

Everton 1 Norwich 1
(aet, Everton won 4-3 on pens)
Hull 1 Leicester 1
(aet, Hull won 5-4 on pens)
Liverpool 1 Bournemouth 0
Manchester City 5 Crystal Palace 1
Manchester Utd 0 Middlesbrough 0
(aet, Middlesbrough won 3-1 on pens)
Sheffield Wed 3 Arsenal 0
Southampton 2 Aston Villa 1
Stoke 1 Chelsea 1
(aet, Stoke won 5-4 on pens)

FIFTH ROUND

Manchester City 4 Hull 1
Middlesbrough 0 Everton 2
Southampton 1 **Liverpool** 6
Stoke 2 Sheffield Wed 0

SEMI-FINALS (two legs)

Everton 2 **Manchester City** 1
Manchester City 3 Everton 1
Stoke 0 **Liverpool** 1
Liverpool 0 Stoke 1
(aet, Liverpool won 6-5 on pens)

FINAL

LIVERPOOL 1 MANCHESTER CITY 1
(aet, Manchester City won 3-1 on pens)
Wembley (86,206); Sunday, February 28 2016

Liverpool (4-2-3-1): Mignolet, Clyne, Lucas, Sakho (K Toure 25), Moreno (Lallana 72), Henderson (capt), Emre Can, Milner, Coutinho, Firmino (Origi 80), Sturridge. **Subs not used**: Bogdan, Benteke, Allen, Flanagan. **Scorer**: Coutinho (83). **Booked**: Clyne, Moreno, Coutinho, Emre Can, Lallana. **Manager**: Jurgen Klopp

Manchester City (4-2-3-1): Caballero, Sagna (Zabaleta 90), Kompany (capt), Otamendi, Clichy, Fernando (Jesus Navas 90), Y Toure, Fernandinho, Silva (Bony 110), Sterling, Aguero. **Subs not used**: Hart, Kolarov, Demichelis, Iheanacho. **Scorer**: Fernandinho (49). **Booked**: Fernando, Kompany, Otamendi, Y Toure, Fernandinho. **Manager**: Manuel Pellegrini

Referee: M Oliver (Northumberland). **Half-time**: 0-0

Penalty shoot-out (Liverpool first): Emre Can 1-0, Fernandinho missed, Lucas saved, Jesus Navas 1-1, Coutinho saved, Aguero 1-2, Lallana saved, Y Toure 1-3

Reserve goalkeepers are rarely the toast of Wembley. The most they can usually hope for is a supporting role on the bench, followed by a place at the end of the queue with the other substitutes for a winner's medal. For Willy Caballero, however, there was not just a slot in Manchester City's starting line-up against Liverpool. He ended up capturing all the headlines with three saves in a penalty shoot-out which delivered the Capital One Cup to the manager who kept faith with him. Manuel Pellegrini, who previously coached the 34-year-old at Malaga, promised he would play in all of City's matches in the competition. And although Caballero had a nightmare a week earlier in a 5-1 FA Cup defeat by Chelsea when they fielded a shadow side because of more pressing Champions League and Premier League commitments, Pellegrini kept his word. He preferred not to recall England's Joe Hart and was rewarded for the decision, first when Caballero played solidly throughout 120 minutes, then excelled when it came to sudden death. Liverpool won shoot-outs in earlier rounds against Carlisle and Stoke. This time, Lucas, Philippe Coutinho and Adam Lallana were all denied by the Argentine's instinct and agility, opening the way for Yaya Toure to deliver the decisive spot-kick which gave his club their fourth League Cup success. It also guaranteed Pellegrini a trophy in his final season at the Etihad before stepping aside for Pep Guardiola. Few outside Merseyside, would have begrudged him it. City were superior for much of the game and Jurgen Klopp admitted afterwards that his Liverpool team had not made a strong enough case for victory.

HOW THEY REACHED THE FINAL

Liverpool

Round 3: 1-1 home to Carlisle (Ings) – aet, won 3-2 on pens
Round 4: 1-0 home to Bournemouth (Clyne)
Round 5: 6-1 away to Southampton (Origi 3, Sturridge 2, Ibe)
Semi-finals: v Stoke – first leg, 1-0 away (Ibe); second leg, 0-1 home, aet; agg 1-1, won 6-5 on pens)

Manchester City

Round 3: 4-1 away to Sunderland (Aguero pen, De Bruyne, Mannone og, Sterling)
Round 4: 5-1 home to Crystal Palace (Bony, De Bruyne, Iheanacho, Toure pen, Garcia)
Round 5: 4-1 home to Hull (De Bruyne 2, Iheanacho, Bony)
Semi-finals: v Everton – first leg 1-2 away (Jesus Navas); second leg, 3-1 home (Fernandinho, De Bruyne, Aguero)

LEAGUE CUP – COMPLETE RESULTS

LEAGUE CUP FINALS

1961* Aston Villa beat Rotherham 3-2 on agg (0-2a, 3-0h)
1962 Norwich beat Rochdale 4-0 on agg (3-0a, 1-0h)
1963 Birmingham beat Aston Villa 3-1 o agg (3-1h, 0-0a)
1964 Leicester beat Stoke 4-3 on agg (1-1a, 3-2h)
1965 Chelsea beat Leicester 3-2 on agg (3-2h, 0-0a)
1966 WBA beat West Ham 5-3 on agg (1-2a, 4-1h)

AT WEMBLEY

1967 QPR beat WBA (3-2)
1968 Leeds beat Arsenal (1-0)
1969* Swindon beat Arsenal (3-1)
1970* Man City beat WBA (2-1)
1971 Tottenham beat Aston Villa (2-0)
1972 Stoke beat Chelsea (2-1)
1973 Tottenham beat Norwich (1-0)
1974 Wolves beat Man City (2-1)
1975 Aston Villa beat Norwich (1-0)
1976 Man City beat Newcastle (2-1)
1977†* Aston Villa beat Everton (3-2 after 0-0 and 1-1 draws)
1978†† Nottm Forest beat Liverpool (1-0 after 0-0 draw)
1979 Nottm Forest beat Southampton (3-2)
1980 Wolves beat Nottm Forest (1-0)
1981††† Liverpool beat West Ham (2-1 after 1-1 draw)

MILK CUP

1982* Liverpool beat Tottenham (3-1)
1983* Liverpool beat Man Utd (2-1)
1984** Liverpool beat Everton (1-0 after *0-0 draw)
1985 Norwich beat Sunderland (1-0)
1986 Oxford Utd beat QPR (3-0)

LITTLEWOODS CUP

1987 Arsenal beat Liverpool (2-1)
1988 Luton beat Arsenal (3-2)
1989 Nottm Forest beat Luton (3-1)
1990 Nottm Forest beat Oldham (1-0)

RUMBELOWS CUP

1991 Sheffield Wed beat Man Utd (1-0)
1992 Man Utd beat Nottm Forest (1-0)

COCA-COLA CUP

1993 Arsenal beat Sheffield Wed (2-1)
1994 Aston Villa beat Man Utd (3-1)
1995 Liverpool beat Bolton (2-1)
1996 Aston Villa beat Leeds (3-0)
1997*** Leicester beat Middlesbrough (*1-0 after *1-1 draw)
1998 Chelsea beat Middlesbrough (2-0)

WORTHINGTON CUP (at Millennium Stadium from 2001)

1999 Tottenham beat Leicester (1-0)
2000 Leicester beat Tranmere (2-1)
2001 Liverpool beat Birmingham (5-4 on pens after *1-1 draw)
2002 Blackburn beat Tottenham (2-1)
2003 Liverpool beat Man Utd (2-0)

CARLING CUP (at Wembley from 2008)

2004 Middlesbrough beat Bolton (2-1)
2005* Chelsea beat Liverpool (3-2)
2006 Man Utd beat Wigan (4-0)
2007 Chelsea beat Arsenal (2-1)
2008* Tottenham beat Chelsea (2-1)
2009 Man Utd beat Tottenham
(4-1 on pens after *0-0 draw)
2010 Man Utd beat Aston Villa (2-1)
2011 Birmingham beat Arsenal (2-1)
2012 Liverpool beat Cardiff
(3-2 on pens after *2-2 draw)

CAPITAL ONE CUP (at Wembley from 2013)

2013 Swansea beat Bradford (5-0)
2014 Manchester City beat Sunderland (3-1)
2015 Chelsea beat Tottenham (2-0)
2016 Manchester City beat Liverpool
(3-1 on pens after *1-1 draw)

* After extra time. † First replay at Hillsborough, second replay at Old Trafford. †† Replayed at Old Trafford. ††† Replayed at Villa Park. ** Replayed at Maine Road. *** Replayed at Hillsborough

SUMMARY OF LEAGUE CUP WINNERS

Liverpool 8
Aston Villa 5
Chelsea 5
Nottm Forest 4
Tottenham 4
Manchester City............4
Manchester Utd............3
Leicester......................3
Arsenal.......................2
Birmingham 2
Norwich 2
Wolves 2
Blackburn 1
Leeds. 1
Luton 1
Middlesbrough 1
Oxford Utd 1
QPR............................ 1
Sheffield Wed 1
Stoke.......................... 1
Swansea...................... 1
Swindon 1
WBA 1

LEAGUE CUP FINAL APPEARANCES

12 Liverpool; **8** Aston Villa, Manchester Utd, Tottenham; **7** Arsenal, Chelsea; **6** Nottm Forest; **5** Leicester; Manchester City, Norwich; **3** Birmingham, Middlesbrough, WBA; **2** Bolton, Everton, Leeds, Luton, QPR, Sheffield Wed, Stoke, Sunderland, West Ham, Wolves; **1** Blackburn, Bradford, Cardiff, Newcastle, Oldham, Oxford Utd, Rochdale, Rotherham, Southampton, Swansea, Swindon, Tranmere, Wigan (Figures do not include replays)

LEAGUE CUP SEMI-FINAL APPEARANCES

16 Liverpool, Tottenham; **14** Arsenal, Aston Villa; **13** Manchester Utd; **12** Chelsea; **9** Manchester City, West Ham; **6** Blackburn, Nottm Forest; **5** Birmingham, Everton, Leeds, Leicester, Middlesbrough, Norwich; **4** Bolton, Burnley, Crystal Palace, Ipswich, Sheffield Wed, Sunderland, WBA; **3** QPR, Stoke, Swindon, Wolves; **2** Bristol City, Cardiff, Coventry, Derby, Luton, Oxford Utd, Plymouth, Sheffield Utd, Southampton, Tranmere, Watford, Wimbledon; **1** Blackpool, Bradford, Bury, Carlisle, Chester, Huddersfield, Newcastle, Oldham, Peterborough, Rochdale, Rotherham, Shrewsbury, Stockport, Swansea, Walsall, Wigan, Wycombe
(Figures do not include replays)

OTHER COMPETITIONS 2015–16

FA COMMUNITY SHIELD

ARSENAL 1 CHELSEA 0

Wembley (85,437); Sunday, August 2 2015

Arsenal (4-2-3-1): Cech, Bellerin, Mertesacker, Koscielny, Monreal, Coquelin, Cazorla, Oxlade-Chamberlain (Arteta, capt, 77), Ramsey, Ozil (Gibbs 82), Walcott (Giroud 66). **Subs not used**: Martinez, Gabriel, Debuchy, Iwobi. **Scorer**: Oxlade-Chamberlain (24). **Booked**: Coquelin. **Manager**: Arsene Wenger

Chelsea (4-2-3-1): Courtois, Ivanovic, Terry (capt) (Moses 82), Cahill, Azpilicueta (Zouma 69), Ramires (Oscar 54), Matic, Willian, Fabregas, Hazard, Remy (Falcao 46). **Subs not used**: Begovic, Mikel, Cuadrado. **Booked**: Azpilicueta. **Manager**: Jose Mourinho

Referee: A Taylor (Lancs). **Half-time**: 1-0

JOHNSTONE'S PAINT TROPHY

FIRST ROUND

Northern: Accrington 1 Bury 2; Doncaster 0 Burton 0 (Doncaster won 5-3 on pens); Hartlepool 1 Sheffield Utd 1 (Sheffield Utd won 4-3 on pens); Morecambe 2 Walsall 0; Notts Co 3 Mansfield 1; Port Vale 1 Carlisle 0; Scunthorpe 1 Barnsley 2; Shrewsbury 2 Oldham 0

Southern: AFC Wimbledon 2 Plymouth 3; Cambridge 0 Dagenham 2; Exeter 2 Portsmouth 0; Luton 2 Leyton Orient 1; Millwall 1 Peterborough 0; Newport 1 Swindon 1 (Swindon won 7-6 on pens); Northampton 3 Colchester 2; Yeovil 1 Barnet 0

SECOND ROUND

Northern: Bradford 1 Barnsley 2; Bury 0 Morecambe 1; Crewe 2 Wigan 3; Fleetwood 2 Shrewsbury 1; Port Vale 1 Blackpool 2; Rochdale 2 Chesterfield 1; Sheffield Utd 5 Notts Co 1; York 2 Doncaster 0

Southern: Bristol Rov 2 Wycombe 0; Crawley 0 Southend 3; Gillingham 2 Luton 1; Millwall 2 Northampton 0; Oxford 2 Swindon 0; Plymouth 2 Exeter 0; Stevenage 1 Dagenham 2; Yeovil 0 Coventry 0 (Yeovil won 4-3 on pens)

THIRD ROUND

Northern: Barnsley 2 York 1; Fleetwood 0 Sheffield Utd 0 (Fleetwood won 4-1 on pens); Rochdale 0 Morecambe 1; Wigan 4 Blackpool 0

Southern: Dagenham 0 Oxford 2; Gillingham 1 Yeovil 1 (Yeovil won 5-4 on pens); Plymouth 3 Millwall 5; Southend 1 Bristol Rov 0

SEMI-FINALS

Northern: Fleetwood 2 Morecambe 0; Wigan 2 Barnsley 2 (Barnsley won 4-2 on pens)

Southern: Oxford 3 Yeovil 2; Southend 0 Millwall 2

AREA FINALS

Northern first leg: Barnsley 1 (Fletcher 73) Fleetwood 1 (Davies 61 og). Att: 11,403. **Second leg**: Fleetwood 1 (Hunter 81) Barnsley 1 (Hourihane 67). Att: 3,705 (agg 2-2, Barnsley won 4-2 on pens)

Southern first leg: Millwall 0 Oxford 2 (Roofe 15, 43). Att: 7,275. **Second leg**: Oxford 0 Millwall 1 (Gregory 54). Att: 10,138 (Oxford won 2-1 on agg)

FINAL

BARNSLEY 3 OXFORD UNITED 2

Wembley (59,230); Sunday, April 3 2016

Barnsley (4-4-2): Davies, Williams, Roberts, Mawson, White, Isgrove (Scowen 77), Brownhill, Hourihane (capt), Hammill, Fletcher (Chapman 90), Winnall (Toney 67). **Subs not used**: Townsend, Bree, Nyatanga, Watkins. **Scorers**: Dunkley (52 og), Fletcher (68), Hammill (74). **Booked**: Toney. **Manager**: Paul Heckingbottom

Oxford United (4-4-2): Buchel, Kenny, Mullins (capt), Dunkley, Evans, MacDonald (Maguire 65), Ruffels, Sercombe, O'Dowda (Waring 85), Roofe, Hylton (Bowery 80). **Subs not used:** Slocombe, Wright, Long, Ashby. **Scorers**: O'Dowda (29), Hylton (76). **Booked:** Maguire. **Manager**: Michael Appleton
Referee: A Woolmer (Northants). **Half-time**: 0-1

FA TROPHY

FIRST ROUND: Aldershot 0 Eastleigh 1; Altrincham 1 Leamington 1; Boreham Wood 1 Woking 2; Bradford PA 2 Lincoln 1; Braintree 1 Bromley 0; Burscough 2 Guiseley 2; Bury 1 Dulwich Hamlet 2; Cheltenham 3 Chelmsford 1; Corinthian Cas 1 Hungerford 2; Curzon 3 Nuneaton 1; East Thurrock 1 Maidenhead 4; Eastbourne 7 Hemel Hempstead 4; Fylde 4 Skelmersdale 4; Gateshead 4 Stocksbridge 1; Grimsby 1 Solihull 1; Halifax 5 Tamworth 0; Havant 2 Forest Green 0; Macclesfield 4 Ashton 0; Maidstone 0 Bognor Regis 1; Nantwich 2 Matlock 0; Oxford 3 Ebbsfleet 1; Southport 0 Worcester 0; Stourbridge 2 Kidderminster 1; Sutton Coldfield 0 Barrow 1; Sutton 3 Lowestoft 1; Telford 0 Chester 2; Tilbury 3 Welling 4; Torquay 0 Chesham 0; Tranmere 2 Wrexham 4; Truro 2 Cirencester 2; Weston SM 3 Wealdstone 2; Whitehawk 1 Dover 3. **Replays**: Chesham 0 Torquay 2; Cirencester 0 Truro 1; Guiseley 3 Burscough 2; Leamington 1 Altrincham 2 (aet); Skelmersdale 0 Fylde 4; Solihull 2 Grimsby 3; Worcester 2 Southport 3

SECOND ROUND: Bognor Regis 2 Altrincham 1; Bradford PA 1 Nantwich 1; Braintree 0 Stourbridge 1; Chester 4 Hungerford 0; Dover 2 Southport 1; Dulwich Hamlet 1 Guiseley 2; Eastbourne 1 Fylde 4; Eastleigh 1 Gateshead 2; Grimsby 3 Weston SM 1; Halifax 1 Barrow 0; Havant 2 Welling 1; Oxford 2 Cheltenham 2; Sutton 1 Curzon 0; Torquay 1 Wrexham 0; Truro 2 Macclesfield 2; Woking 6 Maidenhead 1. **Replays**: Cheltenham 0 Oxford 3; Macclesfield 2 Truro 0; Nantwich 5 Bradford PA 0

THIRD ROUND: Dover 2 Guiseley 2; Gateshead 1 Fylde 0; Grimsby 3 Havant 0; Halifax 1 Chester 0; Nantwich 1 Stourbridge 0; Sutton 0 Bognor Regis 0; Torquay 3 Macclesfield 3; Woking 1 Oxford 0. **Replays**: Bognor Regis 2 Sutton 1; Guiseley 0 Dover 3; Macclesfield 0 Torquay 1

FOURTH ROUND: Bognor Regis 1 Torquay 0; Halifax 0 Gateshead 0; Grimsby 2 Woking 0; Nantwich 2 Dover 1. **Replays**: Gateshead 3 Halifax 3 (aet, Halifax won 5-4 on pens)

SEMI-FINALS:
First leg: Bognor Regis 0 Grimsby 1 (Arnold 75). Att: 2,629. Nantwich 2 (Cooke 44, Kosylo 77) Halifax 4 (McManus 3, Fairhurst 21, Burrows 46, 61 pen)
Second leg: Grimsby 2 (Amond 7 pen, 79) Bognor Regis 1 (Beck 30). Att: 2,447 (Grimsby won 3-1 on agg). Halifax 2 (Burrow 4, White 90 og) Nantwich 2 (Shotton 10, Bailey 31). Att: 3,009 (Halifax won 6-4 on agg)

FINAL

FC HALIFAX 1 GRIMSBY TOWN 0
Wembley (46,781); Sunday, May 22 2016

FC Halifax (4-4-2): Johnson, Bolton, Brown, Roberts, Bencherif, Hibbs, Wroe (capt), McManus (James 74), Peniket (Hughes 85), MacDonald (Walker 62), Burrow. **Subs not used**: Porter, McDonald. **Scorer**: McManus (48). **Manager**: Jim Harvey
Grimsby Town (4-4-2): McKeown, Tait (East 81), Pearson, Nsiala, Robertson, Disley (capt), Clay (Arnold 62), Nolan, Monkhouse (Pittman 68), Bogle, Amond. **Subs not used**: Gowling, Venney. **Manager**: Paul Hurst
Referee: L Mason (Lancs). **Half-time**: 0-0

WELSH CUP FINAL

New Saints 2 (Brobbel 33, Quigley 49) Airbus 0 – Racecourse Ground, Werexham. Att: 1,402

FA VASE FINAL

Morpeth 4 (Swailes 34, Carr 47, Taylor 59, Bell 90) Hereford 1 (Purdie 2) – Wembley. Att: 46,718 (combined with FA Trophy Final)

WOMEN'S FA CUP FINAL

Arsenal 1 (Carter 18) Chelsea 0 – Wembley. Att: 32,912

FA SUNDAY CUP FINAL

New Salamis (London) 1 (Georgiou 69) Barnes (London) 1 (Gallagher 7), aet, New Salamis won 4-3 on pens – Selhurst Park

FINALS – RESULTS

Associated Members' Cup

1984 (Hull) Bournemouth 2 Hull 1

Freight Rover Trophy – Wembley

1985 Wigan 3 Brentford 1
1986 Bristol City 3 Bolton 0
1987 Mansfield 1 Bristol City 1 (aet; Mansfield won 5-4 on pens)

Sherpa Van Trophy – Wembley

1988 Wolves 2 Burnley 0
1989 Bolton 4 Torquay 1

Leyland Daf Cup – Wembley

1990 Tranmere 2 Bristol Rov 1
1991 Birmingham 3 Tranmere 2

Autoglass Trophy – Wembley

1992 Stoke 1 Stockport 0
1993 Port Vale 2 Stockport 1
1994 Huddersfield 1 Swansea 1 (aet; Swansea won 3-1 on pens)

Auto Windscreens Shield – Wembley

1995 Birmingham 1 Carlisle 0 (Birmingham won in sudden-death overtime)
1996 Rotherham 2 Shrewsbury 1
1997 Carlisle 0 Colchester 0 (aet; Carlisle won 4-3 on pens)
1998 Grimsby 2 Bournemouth 1 (Grimsby won with golden goal in extra-time)
1999 Wigan 1 Millwall 0
2000 Stoke 2 Bristol City 1

LDV Vans Trophy – Millennium Stadium

2001 Port Vale 2 Brentford 1
2002 Blackpool 4 Cambridge Utd 1
2003 Bristol City 2 Carlisle 0
2004 Blackpool 2 Southend 0
2005 Wrexham 2 Southend 0

Football League Trophy – Millennium Stadium

2006 Swansea 2 Carlisle 1

Johnstone's Paint Trophy – Wembley

2007 Doncaster 3 Bristol Rov 2 (aet) (Millennium Stadium)
2008 MK Dons 2 Grimsby 0
2009 Luton 3 Scunthorpe 2 (aet)
2010 Southampton 4 Carlisle 1
2011 Carlisle 1 Brentford 0
2012 Chesterfield 2 Swindon 0
2013 Crewe 2 Southend 0
2014 Peterborough 3 Chesterfield 1
2015 Bristol City 2 Walsall 0
2016 Barnsley 3 Oxford 2

OTHER LEAGUE CLUBS' CUP COMPETITIONS

FINALS – AT WEMBLEY

Full Members' Cup (Discontinued after 1992)

1985–86 Chelsea 5 Man City 4
1986–87 Blackburn 1 Charlton 0

Simod Cup

1987–88 Reading 4 Luton 1
1988–89 Nottm Forest 4 Everton 3

Zenith Data Systems Cup

1989–90 Chelsea 1 Middlesbrough 0
1990–91 Crystal Palace 4 Everton 1
1991–92 Nottm Forest 3 Southampton 2

Anglo-Italian Cup (Discontinued after 1996 * Home club)

1970 *Napoli 0 Swindon 3
1971 *Bologna 1 Blackpool 2 (aet)
1972 *AS Roma 3 Blackpool 1
1973 *Fiorentina 1 Newcastle 2
1993 Derby 1 Cremonese 3 (at Wembley)
1994 Notts Co 0 Brescia 1 (at Wembley)
1995 Ascoli 1 Notts Co 2 (at Wembley)
1996 Port Vale 2 Genoa 5 (at Wembley)

FA Vase

At Wembley (until 2000 and from 2007)

1975 Hoddesdon 2 Epsom & Ewell 1
1976 Billericay 1 Stamford 0*
1977 Billericay 2 Sheffield 1 (replay Nottingham after a 1-1 at Wembley)
1978 Blue Star 2 Barton Rov 1
1979 Billericay 4 Almondsbury Greenway 1
1980 Stamford 2 Guisborough Town 0
1981 Whickham 3 Willenhall 2*
1982 Forest Green 3 Rainworth MF Welfare 0
1983 VS Rugby 1 Halesowen 0
1984 Stansted 3 Stamford 2
1985 Halesowen 3 Fleetwood 1
1986 Halesowen 3 Southall 0
1987 St Helens 3 Warrington 2
1988 Colne Dynamoes 1 Emley 0*
1989 Tamworth 3 Sudbury 0 (replay Peterborough after a 1-1 at Wembley)
1990 Yeading 1 Bridlington 0 (replay Leeds after 0-0 at Wembley)
1991 Guiseley 3 Gresley Rov 1 (replay Bramall Lane Sheffield after a 4-4 at Wembley)
1992 Wimborne 5 Guiseley 3
1993 Bridlington 1 Tiverton 0
1994 Diss 2 Taunton 1*
1995 Arlesey 2 Oxford City 1
1996 Brigg Town 3 Clitheroe 0
1997 Whitby Town 3 North Ferriby 0
1998 Tiverton 1 Tow Law 0
1999 Tiverton 1 Bedlington 0
2000 Deal 1 Chippenham 0
2001 Taunton 2 Berkhamsted 1 (Villa Park)
2002 Whitley Bay 1 Tiptree 0* (Villa Park)
2003 Brigg 2 AFC Sudbury 1 (Upton Park)
2004 Winchester 2 AFC Sudbury 0 (St Andrews)
2005 Didcot 3 AFC Sudbury 2 (White Hart Lane)
2006 Nantwich 3 Hillingdon 1 (St Andrews)
2007 Truro 3 AFC Totton 1
2008 Kirkham & Wesham (Fylde) 2 Lowestoft 1
2009 Whitley Bay 2 Glossop 0
2010 Whitley Bay 6 Wroxham1
2011 Whitley Bay 3 Coalville 2
2012 Dunston 2 West Auckland 0
2013 Spennymoor 2 Tunbridge Wells 1
2014 Sholing 1 West Auckland 0
2015 North Shields 2 Glossop North End 1*
2016 Morpeth 4 Hereford 1

* After extra-time

FA Trophy Finals

At Wembley

1970 Macclesfield 2 Telford 0
1971 Telford 3 Hillingdon 2
1972 Stafford 3 Barnet 0
1973 Scarborough 2 Wigan 1*
1974 Morecambe 2 Dartford 1
1975 Matlock 4 Scarborough 0
1976 Scarborough 3 Stafford 2*
1977 Scarborough 2 Dag & Red 1
1978 Altrincham 3 Leatherhead 1
1979 Stafford 2 Kettering 0
1980 Dag & Red 2 Mossley 1
1981 Bishop's Stortford 1 Sutton 0
1982 Enfield 1 Altrincham 0*
1983 Telford 2 Northwich 1
1984 Northwich 2 Bangor 1 (replay Stoke after a 1-1 at Wembley)
1985 Wealdstone 2 Boston 1
1986 Altrincham 1 Runcorn 0
1987 Kidderminster 2 Burton 1 (replay WBA after a 0-0 at Wembley)
1988 Enfield 3 Telford 2 (replay WBA afte a 0-0 at Wembley)
1989 Telford 1 Macclesfield 0*
1990 Barrow 3 Leek 0
1991 Wycombe 2 Kidderminster 1
1992 Colchester 3 Witton 1
1993 Wycombe 4 Runcorn 1
1994 Woking 2 Runcorn 1
1995 Woking 2 Kidderminster 1
1996 Macclesfield 3 Northwich 1
1997 Woking 1 Dag & Red & Redbridge 0*
1998 Cheltenham 1 Southport 0
1999 Kingstonian 1 Forest Green 0
2000 Kingstonian 3 Kettering 2

At Villa Park

2001 Canvey 1 Forest Green 0
2002 Yeovil 2 Stevenage 0
2003 Burscough 2 Tamworth 1
2004 Hednesford 3 Canvey 2
2005 Grays 1 Hucknall 1* (Grays won 6-5 on pens)

At Upton Park

2006 Grays 2 Woking 0

At Wembley

2007 Stevenage 3 Kidderminster 2
2008 Ebbsfleet 1 Torquay 0
2009 Stevenage 2 York 0
2010 Barrow 2 Stevenage 1*
2011 Darlington 1 Mansfield 0 *
2012 York 2 Newport 0

2013 Wrexham 1 Grimsby 1 * Wrexham won 4-1 on pens)
2014 Cambridge Utd 4 Gosport 0
2015 North Ferriby 3 Wrexham 3* (North Ferriby won 5-4 on pens)
2016 Halifax 1 Grimsby 0
(*After extra-time)

FA Youth Cup Winners

Year	Winners	Runners-up	Agg
1953	Man Utd	Wolves	9-3
1954	Man Utd	Wolves	5-4
1955	Man Utd	WBA	7-1
1956	Man Utd	Chesterfield	4-3
1957	Man Utd	West Ham	8-2
1958	Wolves	Chelsea	7-6
1959	Blackburn	West Ham	2-1
1960	Chelsea	Preston	5-2
1961	Chelsea	Everton	5-3
1962	Newcastle	Wolves	2-1
1963	West Ham	Liverpool	6-5
1964	Man Utd	Swindon	5-2
1965	Everton	Arsenal	3-2
1966	Arsenal	Sunderland	5-3
1967	Sunderland	Birmingham	2-0
1968	Burnley	Coventry	3-2
1969	Sunderland	WBA	6-3
1970	Tottenham	Coventry	4-3
1971	Arsenal	Cardiff	2-0
1972	Aston Villa	Liverpool	5-2
1973	Ipswich	Bristol City	4-1
1974	Tottenham	Huddersfield	2-1
1975	Ipswich	West Ham	5-1
1976	WBA	Wolves	5-0
1977	Crystal Palace	Everton	1-0
1978	Crystal Palace	Aston Villa	*1-0
1979	Millwall	Man City	2-0
1980	Aston Villa	Man City	3-2
1981	West Ham	Tottenham	2-1
1982	Watford	Man Utd	7-6
1983	Norwich	Everton	6-5
1984	Everton	Stoke	4-2
1985	Newcastle	Watford	4-1
1986	Man City	Man Utd	3-1
1987	Coventry	Charlton	2-1
1988	Arsenal	Doncaster	6-1
1989	Watford	Man City	2-1
1990	Tottenham	Middlesbrough	3-2
1991	Millwall	Sheffield Wed	3-0
1992	Man Utd	Crystal Palace	6-3
1993	Leeds	Man Utd	4-1
1994	Arsenal	Millwall	5-3
1995	Man Utd	Tottenham	†2-2
1996	Liverpool	West Ham	4-1
1997	Leeds	Crystal Palace	3-1
1998	Everton	Blackburn	5-3
1999	West Ham	Coventry	9-0
2000	Arsenal	Coventry	5-1
2001	Arsenal	Blackburn	6-3
2002	Aston Villa	Everton	4-2
2003	Man Utd	Middlesbrough	3-1
2004	Middlesbrough	Aston Villa	4-0
2005	Ipswich	Southampton	3-2
2006	Liverpool	Man City	3-2
2007	Liverpool	Man Utd	††2-2
2008	Man City	Chelsea	4-2
2009	Arsenal	Liverpool	6-2
2010	Chelsea	Aston Villa	3-2
2011	Man Utd	Sheffield Utd	6-3
2012	Chelsea	Blackburn	4-1
2013	Norwich	Chelsea	4-2
2014	Chelsea	Fulham	7-6
2015	Chelsea	Man City	5-2
2016	Chelsea	Man City	4-2

(*One match only; †Manchester Utd won 4-3 on pens, ††Liverpool won 4-3 on pens)

CHARITY/COMMUNITY SHIELD RESULTS (POST WAR)
[CHARITY SHIELD]

Year	**Winners**	**Runners-up**	**Score**
1948	Arsenal	Manchester Utd	4-3
1949	Portsmouth	Wolves	*1-1
1950	England World Cup XI	FA Canadian Tour Team	4-2
1951	Tottenham	Newcastle	2-1
1952	Manchester Utd	Newcastle	4-2
1953	Arsenal	Blackpool	3-1
1954	Wolves	WBA	*4-4
1955	Chelsea	Newcastle	3-0
1956	Manchester Utd	Manchester City	1-0
1957	Manchester Utd	Aston Villa	4-0
1958	Bolton	Wolves	4-1

1959	Wolves	Nottm Forest	3-1
1960	Burnley	Wolves	*2-2
1961	Tottenham	FA XI	3-2
1962	Tottenham	Ipswich Town	5-1
1963	Everton	Manchester Utd	4-0
1964	Liverpool	West Ham	*2-2
1965	Manchester Utd	Liverpool	*2-2
1966	Liverpool	Everton	1-0
1967	Manchester Utd	Tottenham	*3-3
1968	Manchester City	WBA	6-1
1969	Leeds	Manchester City	2-1
1970	Everton	Chelsea	2-1
1971	Leicester	Liverpool	1-0
1972	Manchester City	Aston Villa	1-0
1973	Burnley	Manchester City	1-0
1974	Liverpool	Leeds	1-1
	(Liverpool won 6-5 on penalties)		
1975	Derby Co	West Ham	2-0
1976	Liverpool	Southampton	1-0
1977	Liverpool	Manchester Utd	*0-0
1978	Nottm Forest	Ipswich	5-0
1979	Liverpool	Arsenal	3-1
1980	Liverpool	West Ham	1-0
1981	Aston Villa	Tottenham	*2-2
1982	Liverpool	Tottenham	1-0
1983	Manchester Utd	Liverpool	2-0
1984	Everton	Liverpool	1-0
1985	Everton	Manchester Utd	2-0
1986	Everton	Liverpool	*1-1
1987	Everton	Coventry	1-0
1988	Liverpool	Wimbledon	2-1
1989	Liverpool	Arsenal	1-0
1990	Liverpool	Manchester Utd	*1-1
1991	Arsenal	Tottenham	*0-0
1992	Leeds	Liverpool	4-3
1993	Manchester Utd	Arsenal	1-1
	(Manchester Utd won 5-4 on penalties)		
1994	Manchester Utd	Blackburn	2-0
1995	Everton	Blackburn	1-0
1996	Manchester Utd	Newcastle	4-0
1997	Manchester Utd	Chelsea	1-1
	(Manchester Utd won 4-2 on penalties)		
1998	Arsenal	Manchester Utd	3-0
1999	Arsenal	Manchester Utd	2-1
2000	Chelsea	Manchester Utd	2-0
2001	Liverpool	Manchester Utd	2-1

COMMUNITY SHIELD

Year	Winners	Runners-up	Score
2002	Arsenal	Liverpool	1-0
2003	Manchester Utd	Arsenal	1-1
	(Manchester Utd won 4-3 on penalties)		
2004	Arsenal	Manchester Utd	3-1
2005	Chelsea	Arsenal	2-1

2006	Liverpool	Chelsea	2-1
2007	Manchester Utd	Chelsea	1-1
	(Manchester Utd won 3-0 on penalties)		
2008	Manchester Utd	Portsmouth	0-0
	(Manchester Utd won 3-1 on pens)		
2009	Chelsea	Manchester Utd	2-2
	(Chelsea won 4-1 on pens)		
2010	Manchester Utd	Chelsea	3-1
2011	Manchester Utd	Manchester City	3-2
2012	Manchester City	Chelsea	3-2
2013	Manchester Utd	Wigan	2-0
2014	Arsenal	Manchester City	3-0
2015	Arsenal	Chelsea	1-0

(Fixture played at Wembley 1974–2000 and from 2007); Millennium Stadium 2001–06; Villa Park 2012) * Trophy shared

THE THINGS THEY SAY ...

'Relegation lies at my feet and no-one else's' – **Randy Lerner**, Aston Villa owner, takes the blame for his club's demise before selling the club.

'We live in a bubble. Compared to the rest of society we earn a ridiculous amount. It's unfathomable' – **Juan Mata**, Manchester United midfielder.

'The club is in trouble. The results are not good. There obviously seemed to be a palpable discord between manager and players and we feel it was time to act' – **Michael Emenalo**, Chelsea's sporting director, on the sacking of Jose Mourinho.

'He was one of those great footballers who made you excited whenever he had the ball. There wasn't a negative thought in his head. He loved the game and he loved life' – **Sir Bobby Charlton** paying tribute to the late Johan Cruyff.

'While people grieve in their own way, I found it easier to come in and play and try to do everyone proud' – **Harry Arter**, Bournemouth midfielder, on his decision to play against Manchester United days after he and his partner lost their baby at birth.

'Without him I dread to think where we might have been' – **Sam Allardyce**, Sunderland manager, on Jermain Defoe's goals which helped keep Sunderland up.

'I'll probably grab a coffee at McDonald's like I normally do' – **Sean Dyche**, Burnley manager, planning a low-key promotion celebration.

'Honestly, I must have stopped going to mass' – **Martin O'Neill**, Republic of Ireland manager and a regular churchgoer, after his side were drawn in Euro 2016's toughest group alongside Belgium, Italy and Sweden.

'If I'd turned down this job, I could have said goodbye to my credibility in football. After sitting on (Sky) television talking about coaches for these last few years, the time had come for me to stand up' – **Gary Neville** on becoming Valencia's head coach.

'Results had not been to my standards or those required by the club' – **Gary Neville** after being sacked less than four months into the job.

FOOTBALL'S CHANGING HOMES

West Ham have moved into their new home at the Olympic Stadium – and **Tottenham** will the next Premier League side to have a new stadium after plans were approved by Harin Council and the previous Mayor of London, Boris Johnson. The £400m arena, next to White H Lane, is scheduled to be ready for the 2018-19 season. It increases capacity from 36,000 60,000 and has a retractable pitch for American football games and concerts. The surround complex includes a 180-bedroom hotel, sports and health centre. A nearby listed building become an interactive museum devoted to the club's history. This season, the club are to p their Champions League home matches at Wembley. There is also an option for all home leag and cup games, as well as any European fixtures, at the national stadium in the 2017- campaign. West Ham ended 112 years at Upton Park by beating Manchester United 3-2 watch by a crowd of nearly 35,000. They are guaranteed a huge increase in Stratford, having sold 52,000 season tickets. The target now is to raise capacity for a second time, taking it fr 60,000 to 66,000. **Chelsea** submitted a planning application for a new 60,000-seater are at Stamford Bridge to Hammersmith and Fulham Council at the end of 2015. The club s the planning process would be a lengthy one. **Manchester City**'s owners believe there is sc for further expansion at the Etihad. A new third tier at the north stand would take capacity close to 61,000, the second biggest in the Premier League behind Manchester's Old Traff (75,000). **Liverpool** are also looking at another increase at Anfield, where capacity is rising 54,000 with redevelopment of the main stand. That would go up to 58,000 with expansior the Anfield Road end. **Stoke** announced a change of name and new capacity for the Britan Stadium. It becomes the bet365 Stadium under a naming rights deal with the betting fi Filling in the corner between two stands will create 1,800 new seats and mean a capac approaching 30,000.

AFC Wimbledon have taken another step towards returning to their 'spiritual' home in Plo Lane after exchanging contracts for the sale of their Kingsmeadow ground in Kingston up Thames to Chelsea. The club intend to use the money, reported to be £2m, towards fund the proposed 11,000-seater ground - with the provision of going up to 20,000. Merton Cou granted planning permission and the project is now subject to approval from the present Ma of London, Sadiq Khan. Chelsea plan to use 4,800-capacity Kingsmeadow for their acade and women's team matches. **Luton** unveiled two sites in the town, Power Court and Newla Park, for a new 17,500-capacity home and have asked supporters for their views. **Accring** announced plans for multi-million-pound redevelopment of the Wham Stadium after agree terms on a new 50-year lease. The first phase would be a 1,500-seater, single-tier stand al the Whinney Hill side. **Aberdeen** hope to build a new stadium and training facility to the w of the city at Kingsfordl and move from Pittodrie in the 2019-20 season. A proposed relocat to Loirston, to the south, ran into planning problems. The £25m redevelopment of **Wind Park**, Northern Ireland's national stadium in Belfast, is nearing completion. Two stands h been rebuilt and new seating installed in two more, taking capacity to 18,000. The aim is have everything ready for World Cup qualifiers against San Marino (October 8) and Azerbai (November 11).

SCOTTISH TABLES 2015–2016

ADBROKES PREMIERSHIP

		Home					Away						
	P	W	D	L	F	A	W	D	L	F	A	Gd	Pts
Celtic	38	14	4	1	55	12	12	4	3	38	19	62	86
Aberdeen	38	12	4	3	30	19	10	1	8	32	29	14	71
Hearts	38	11	5	3	37	22	7	6	6	22	18	19	65
St Johnstone	38	8	6	5	27	22	8	2	9	31	33	3	56
Motherwell	38	8	3	8	27	27	7	2	10	20	36	-16	50
Ross Co	38	9	0	10	29	33	5	6	8	26	28	-6	48
Inverness	38	7	5	7	25	20	7	5	7	29	28	6	52
Dundee	38	7	7	5	30	23	4	8	7	23	34	-4	48
Partick	38	6	4	9	21	29	6	6	7	20	21	-9	46
) Hamilton	38	4	6	9	21	28	7	4	8	21	35	-21	43
l Kilmarnock	38	4	4	11	19	37	5	5	9	22	27	-23	36
2 Dundee Utd*	38	3	4	12	22	35	5	3	11	23	35	-25	28*

ague split after 33 games, with teams staying in top six and bottom six regardless of points.
ltic into Champions League second qualifying round. Aberdeen and Hearts into Europa ague first qualifying round

)undee Utd deducted 3 pts for ineligible players

ay-offs (on agg): **Quarter-final**: Hibernian 2 Raith 1. **Semi-final**: Falkirk 5 Hibernian 4. **Final**: lmarnock 4 Falkirk 1

ayer of Year: Leigh Griffiths (Celtic). **Manager of Year:** Tommy Wright (St Johnstone)

FA Team of Year: Bain (Dundee), Logan (Aberdeen), Ozturk (Hearts), Davies (Ross Co), Tierney eltic), Hayes (Aberdeen), McLean (Aberdeen), Shinnie (Aberdeen), Hemmings (Dundee), iffiths (Celtic), Stewart (Dundee)

ading scorers (all competitions): 40 Griffiths (Celtic); 25 Hemmings (Dundee); 20 Boyce oss Co), Rooney (Aberdeen); 18 Moult (Motherwell); 15 MacLean (St Johnstone); 14 oolan (Partick), McDonald (Motherwell); 13 Juanma (Hearts), McKay (Dundee Utd); Storey nverness); 12 Magennis (Kilmarnock), McGinn (Aberdeen)

ADBROKES CHAMPIONSHIP

		Home					Away						
	P	W	D	L	F	A	W	D	L	F	A	Gd	Pts
Rangers	36	16	2	0	48	13	9	4	5	40	21	54	81
Falkirk	36	13	3	2	33	13	6	10	2	28	21	27	70
Hibernian	36	14	3	1	37	15	7	4	7	22	19	25	70
Raith	36	10	4	4	31	19	8	4	6	21	27	6	62
Morton	36	7	4	7	17	17	4	6	8	22	25	-3	43
St Mirren	36	5	6	7	24	28	6	3	9	20	25	-9	42
Queen of South	36	8	4	6	27	26	4	2	12	19	30	-10	42
Dumbarton	36	8	3	7	26	34	2	4	12	9	32	-31	37
Livingston	36	3	6	9	14	19	5	1	12	23	32	-14	31
Alloa	36	1	6	11	12	30	3	3	12	10	37	-45	21

bernian into Europa League second qualifying round as Scottish Cup winners

ay-offs (on agg) – **Semi-finals**: Ayr 6 Peterhead 2. Stranraer 8 Livingston 6. **Final**: Ayr 1 ranraer 1 (aet, agg 1-1, Ayr won 3-1 on pens)

ayer of Year: John McGinn (Hibernian). **Manager of Year**: Peter Houston (Falkirk)

A Team of Year: Rogers (Falkirk), Tavernier (Rangers), McGregor (Hibernian), Grant (Falkirk), allace (Rangers), Holt (Rangers), McGinn (Hibernian), McKay (Rangers), Baird (Falkirk), aghorn (Rangers), Cummings (Hibernian)

ading league scorers: 20 Waghorn (Rangers); 18 Cummings (Hibernian); 17 Baird (Falkirk); 4 Johnstone (Morton), Miller (Rangers); 13 Lyle (Queen of South); 11 Buchanan (Livingston), allan (St Mirren), Russell (Queen of South)

LADBROKES LEAGUE ONE

		Home					Away						
		P	W	D	L	F	A	W	D	L	F	A	Gd	Pts
1	Dunfermline	36	12	4	2	45	15	12	3	3	38	15	53	79
2	Ayr	36	11	2	5	38	22	8	2	8	27	25	18	61
3	Peterhead	36	9	6	3	39	20	7	5	6	33	27	25	59
4	Stranraer	36	8	2	8	21	25	7	4	7	22	24	-6	51
5	Airdrieonians	36	5	5	8	19	21	9	2	7	29	29	-2	49
6	Albion Rov	36	7	5	6	25	21	6	5	7	15	23	-4	49
7	Brechin	36	8	4	6	29	24	4	2	12	18	35	-12	42
8	Stenhousemuir	36	6	3	9	25	42	5	4	9	21	38	-34	40
9	Cowdenbeath	36	7	3	8	27	28	4	3	11	19	44	-26	39
10	Forfar	36	5	3	10	24	28	3	7	8	24	32	-12	34

Play-offs (on agg) – **Semi-finals**: Clyde 5 Elgin 1. Queen's Park 2 Cowdenbeath 1. **Final**: Queen's Park 3 Clyde 2
Player of Year: Faissal El Bakhtaoui (Dunfermline). **Manager of Year**: Ian McCall (Ayr)
PFA Team of Year: Smith (Peterhead), Devlin (Ayr), Dunlop (Albion Rov), Richards-Everton (Dunfermline), Boyle (Ayr), Watt (Airdrieonians), Geggan (Dunfermline), Cardle (Dunfermline), Spence (Cowdenbeath), McAllister (Peterhead), El Bakhtaoui (Dunfermline)
League league scorers: 22 El Bakhtaoui (Dunfermline), McAllister (Peterhead); 17 Spence (Cowdenbeath); 15 Thomson (Brechin); 14 Cardle (Dunfermline), Moore (Ayr); 13 Preston (Ayr), Sutherland (Peterhead)

LADBROKES LEAGUE TWO

		Home					Away						
		P	W	D	L	F	A	W	D	L	F	A	Gd	Pts
1	East Fife	36	10	4	4	30	17	8	4	6	32	24	21	62
2	Elgin	36	12	5	1	36	15	5	3	10	23	31	13	59
3	Clyde	36	9	3	6	29	22	8	3	7	27	23	11	57
4	Queen's Park	36	7	5	6	21	18	8	6	4	25	14	14	56
5	Annan	36	9	6	3	39	29	7	2	9	30	28	12	56
6	Berwick	36	10	4	4	29	22	4	3	11	16	28	-5	49
7	Stirling Alb	36	9	3	6	27	21	4	6	8	20	25	1	48
8	Montrose	36	9	4	5	30	31	2	6	10	20	39	-20	43
9	Arbroath	36	5	4	9	19	21	6	2	10	23	30	-9	39
10	East Stirling	36	6	1	11	21	40	3	4	11	20	39	-38	32

Play-off (on agg) – **Final**: Edinburgh City 2 East Stirling 1
Player of Year: Nathan Austin (East Fife). **Manager of the Year**: Gary Naysmith (East Fife)
PFA Team of Year: Smith (Stirling Alb), Little (Arbroath), Page (East Fife), Naysmith (East Fife Linton (Clyde), Flynn (Annan), Wilkie (East Fife), Linn (Arbroath), Weatherson (Annan), Austin (East Fife), Gunn (Elgin)
Leading league scorers: 22 Austin (East Fife); 21 Gunn (Elgin); 19 Fraser (Montrose); 17 Henderson (Berwick); 16 Weatherson (Annan); 13 Todd (Annan); 12 Flynn (Annan), Osadolor (Annan)

LADBROKES SCOTTISH LEAGUE RESULTS 2016–2016

PREMIERSHIP

	Aberdeen	Celtic	Dundee	Dundee Urd	Hamilton	IHearts	Inverness	Kilmarnock	Motherwell	Partick	Ross Co	St Johnstone
Aberdeen	–	2-1	2-0	2-0	1-0	1-0	2-2	2-0	1-1	0-0	3-1	1-5
		2-1	1-0		3-0	0-1		2-1	4-1		0-4	1-1
Celtic	3-1	–	6-0	5-0	8-1	0-0	4-2	0-0	1-2	1-0	2-0	3-1
	3-2	–	0-0			3-1	3-0		7-0		2-0	3-1
											1-1	
Dundee	0-2	0-0	–	2-1	4-0	1-2	1-1	1-2	2-1	1-1	3-3	2-1
			–	2-1	0-1	0-1	1-1	1-1	2-2		5-2	2-0
Dundee Utd	0-1	1-3	2-2	–	1-2	0-1	1-1	1-2	0-3	0-1	1-0	1-2
	0-1	1-4	2-2	–	1-3	2-1	0-2	5-1		3-3		
Hamilton	1-1	1-2	1-1	4-0	–	3-2	3-4	0-1	1-0	0-0	1-3	2-4
		1-1	2-1	0-0	–	0-0	0-1	0-4	0-1	1-2		
Hearts	1-3	2-2	1-1	3-2	2-0	–	2-0	1-1	2-0	3-0	2-0	4-3
	2-1	1-3				–		1-0	6-0	1-0	1-1	0-3
												2-2
Inverness	2-1	1-3	1-1	2-2	0-2	2-0	–	2-1	0-1	0-0	2-0	0-1
	3-1		4-0	2-3	0-1	0-0	–	3-1	1-2	0-0		
Kilmarnock	0-4	2-2	0-4	1-1	1-2-	2-2	2-0	–	0-1	2-5	0-4	2-1
		0-1	0-0	2-4	0-1		2-1	–	–	0-2	0-2	3-0
Motherwell	1-2	0-1	3-1	0-2	3-3	2-2	1-3	1-0	–	2-1	1-1	2-0
	2-1	1-2		2-1		1-0		0-2		3-1	1-2	1-2
Partick	0-2	0-2	0-1	3-0	1-1	0-4	2-1	2-2	1-0	–	1-0	2-0
	1-2	1-2	2-4	1-0	2-2		1-4	0-0				
			1-2									
Ross Co	2-0	1-4	5-2	2-1	2-0	1-2	1-2	3-2	3-0	1-0	–	2-3
	2-3			0-3	2-1	0-3	0-3		1-3	1-0	–	0-1
St Johnstone	3-4	0-3	1-1	2-1	4-1	0-0	1-1	2-1	2-1	1-2	1-1	–
	3-0	2-1		0-1	0-0		1-0		2-1	1-2	1-1	–

CHAMPIONSHIP

	Alloa	Dumbarton	Falkirk	Hibernian	Livingston	Morton	Queen of South	Raith	Rangers	St Mirren
Alloa	–	0-2	1-1	0-1	0-3	0-1	1-2	0-1	1-5	0-2
	–	1-1	0-1	1-0	1-3	2-2	2-2	1-1	1-1	0-1
Dumbarton	0-2	–	0-5	2-1	2-1	1-2	0-2	3-3	1-2	1-0
	3-1	–	1-1	3-2	1-0	0-0	4-2	2-3	0-6	2-1
Falkirk	5-0	2-1	–	0-1	2-0	1-0	0-0	1-0	2-1	3-0
	2-0	1-0	–	1-1	1-2	1-0	3-1	2-2	3-2	3-2
Hibernian	3-0	4-2	1-1	–	2-1	1-0	1-0	2-0	2-1	1-1
	3-0	4-0	2-2	–	2-1	0-3	2-0	1-0	3-2	3-1
Livingston	0-1	1-1	1-2	0-1	–	2-4	0-1	3-0	1-1	0-1
	0-0	2-0	1-1	0-0	–	0-0	0-2	0-1	1-0	2-3
Morton	1-0	0-0	1-1	0-1	1-0	–	2-0	1-2	0-4	0-0
	4-1	2-0	0-1	0-0	2-1	–	3-2	0-1	0-2	0-1
Queen of South	3-1	1-0	2-2	0-3	1-4	2-2	–	1-1	1-5	0-2
	1-0	6-0	2-2	1-0	3-1	1-0	–	1-2	0-1	1-0
Raith	3-0	1-0	1-2	1-2	3-0	2-1	1-0	–	0-1	1-1
	0-1	0-0-	2-2	2-1	2-0	3-2	2-0	–	3-3	4-3
Rangers	4-0	4-0	3-1	1-0	3-0	2-2	2-1	5-0	–	3-1
	1-1	1-0	1-0	4-2	4-1	3-1	4-3	2-0	–	1-0
St Mirren	1-1	1-2	2-3	1-4	1-1	1-1	1-0	1-2	0-1	–
	3-1	1-0	0-0	2-2	1-4	3-1	2-1	1-2	2-2	–

LEAGUE ONE

	Airdreeonians	Albion Rov	Ayr	Brechin	Cowdenbeath	Dunferline	Forfar	Peterhead	Stenhousemuir	Stranraer
Airdrieonians	–	1-1	1-2	1-0	3-2	0-2	0-1	1-0	0-1	0-1
		1-1	0-1	0-2	2-0	3-0	1-1	3-4	1-1	1-1
Albion Rov	1-3	–	3-0	3-1	2-1	1-1	1-1	1-0	2-0	0-2
	1-2		1-3	4-1	0-0	0-1	3-2	1-1	1-1	0-1
Ayr	3-0	1-0	–	2-1	5-0	1-2	2-2	1-1	5-2	3-1
	0-3	0-1		2-1	4-1	0-2	2-1	1-2	4-1	2-1
Brechin	1-2	0-1	1-1	–	2-0	1-6	0-2	1-1	1-2	2-0
	3-3	2-1	1-0		2-2	1-2	4-0	5-1	1-0	1-0
Cowdenbeath	3-0	1-0	4-2	3-0	–	0-0	2-1	2-2	2-2	1-2
	1-3	1-2	1-0	2-1		0-1	1-4	2-3	1-3	0-2
Dunfermline	1-1	3-0	0-2	3-1	7-1	–	4-0	0-0	1-0	3-1
	0-1	1-1	3-2	3-1	2-1		2-2	1-0	5-0	6-1
Forfar	2-3	4-0	2-2	0-1	0-1	0-4	–	0-2	4-1	1-2
	0-2	1-0	3-1	1-2	1-1	2-4		2-0	0-1	1-1
Peterhead	2-0	1-1	3-0	2-3	7-0	2-1	2-2	–	2-2	1-1
	1-0	5-1	0-4	4-1	0-1	0-0	3-2		4-1	0-0
Stenhousemuir	2-1	0-1	0-1	2-2	4-2	0-5	2-2	4-3	–	1-0
	3-2	1-3	0-4	0-0	2-3	0-3	2-1	1-4		1-5
Stranraer	1-3	0-1	1-2	1-0	0-3	0-3	0-0	0-4	1-2	–
	4-0	0-0	1-0	2-0	1-0	4-1	1-0	1-5	3-1	–

LEAGUE TWO

	Annan	Arbroath	Berwick	Clyde	East Fife	East Stirling	Elgin	Montrose	Queen's Park	Stirling Alb
Annan	–	2-2	1-0	2-3	2-0	3-1	1-1	3-2	3-1	1-1
		4-1	1-0	3-3	2-4	1-3	4-2	3-3	1-0	2-2
Arbroath	0-2	–	3-1	0-1	1-1	0-0	0-3	3-1	1-2	2-0
	2-1		1-2	0-1	0-1	3-0	2-3	0-0	0-1	1-1
Berwick	0-2	2-2	–	0-5	1-1	2-1	2-3	2-1	1-0	1-2
	3-2	3-0		3-0	2-0	2-2	2-0	1-0	1-1	1-0
Clyde	4-2	0-2	1-1	–	2-0	3-1	4-2	3-1	0-2	0-1
	2-1	1-2	2-1		0-0	0-1	1-0	3-3	0-1	3-1
East Fife	0-1	0-1	5-0	1-0	–	5-3	2-1	1-1	0-2	1-1
	4-2	2-1	1-0	2-0		1-1	0-2	3-0	1-1	1-0
East Stirling	3-1	0-4	0-4	0-3	1-0	–	2-0	3-1	2-1	2-3
	0-1	0-3	0-0	2-4	1-3		0-3	2-4	0-3	3-2
Elgin	3-2	2-0	4-1	1-1	4-2	4-0	–	2-0	0-0	1-0
	2-2	4-1	1-0	1-0	1-3	2-0		1-1	1-1	2-1
Montrose	1-1	3-0	4-1	2-0	1-4	2-1	2-0	–	1-6	1-3
	0-5	0-2	1-0	2-1	2-2	3-2	3-1		1-1	1-1
Queen's Park	0-1	1-0	0-1	1-1	0-2	5-1	3-1	0-1	–	1-0
	1-3	2-1	0-0	2-1	3-0	0-3	0-0	1-1		1-1
Stirling Alb	1-0	3-1	1-3	0-1	1-3	0-0	3-1	1-0	1-2	–
	2-1	1-0	2-1	1-2	0-6	3-0	0-0	7-0	0-0	–

HOW CELTIC WON A FIFTH SUCCESSIVE TITLE

AUGUST 2015

1 Celtic 2 (Griffiths 4 pen, Johansen 35) Ross Co 0. Att: 45,197
8 Partick 0 Celtic 2 (Rogic 28, Commons 63). Att: 7,088
12 Kilmarnock 2 (Magennis 44, Higginbotham 88 pen) Celtic 2 (Griffiths 3, Biton 55). Att: 6,090
15 Celtic 4 (Lustig 8, Griffiths 12, Armstrong 55, 69) Inverness 2 (Christie 71, Lopez 78). Att: 42,727
22 Dundee Utd 1 (Erskine 45 pen) Celtic 3 (Griffiths 17, Durnan 44 og, McGregor 74). Att: 10,605
29 Celtic 3 (Griffiths 18, Rogic 45, Mulgrew 67) St Johnstone 1 (Boyata 11 og). Att: 42,507

SEPTEMBER 2015

12 Aberdeen 2 (Rooney 56 pen, Quinn 86) Celtic 1 (Griffiths 35 pen). Att: 20,385
20 Celtic 6 (Rogic 14, Grifiths 16, Izaguirre 54, 61, Brown 87, Ciftci 88) Dundee 0. Att: 48,558
26 Celtic 0 Hearts 0. Att: 46,297

OCTOBER 2015

4 Hamilton 1 (Kurtaj 4) Celtic 2 (Boyata 26, Griffiths 31). Att: 4,910
17 Motherwell 0 Celtic 1 (Ciftci 15). Att: 8,888
25 Celtic 5 (Griffiths 23, Boyata 40, Commons 45 pen, 54, Kuhl 89 og) Dundee Utd 0. Att: 42,718
31 Celtic 3 (Griffiths 44, 53 pen, Forrest 60) Aberdeen 1 (Rooney 89). Att: 48,161

NOVEMBER 2015

8 Ross Co 1 (Dingwall 59) Celtic 4 (Rogic 38, Griffiths 54, 56, Biton 75). Att: 6,042
21 Celtic 0 Kilmarnock 0. Att: 42,770
29 Inverness 1 (Storey 39) Celtic 3 (McGregor 7, Griffiths 59, Devine 85 og). Att: 5,976

DECEMBER 2015

13 St Johnstone 0 Celtic 3 (Ciftci 35, 67, Boyata 49). Att: 6,418
19 Celtic 1 (Biton 49) Motherwell 2 (Moult 53, 59 pen). Att: 42,603
27 Hearts 2 (Nicholson 45, Sow 90) Celtic 2 (Biton 42, Rogic 70). Att: 16,844

JANUARY 2016

2 Celtic 1 (Griffiths 90) Partick 0. Att: 46,067
15 Dundee Utd 1 (Murray 31) Celtic 4 (Griffiths 21, 48, Simunovic 27, Commons 56). Att: 10,848
19 Celtic 8 (Lustig 4, Biton 9, Rogic 10, Griffiths 22, 34, 54, Forrest 53, McGregor 89) Hamilton 1 (Brophy 73). Att: 45,659
23 Celtic 3 (Mackay-Steven 9, 55, Armstrong 43) St Johnstone 1 (MacLean 12). Att: 43,948

FEBRUARY 2016

3 Aberdeen 2 (Hayes 31, Church 38) Celtic 1 (Griffiths 90). Att: 19,003
13 Celtic 2 (Griffiths 34, Boyata 57) Ross Co 0. Att: 42,550
20 Celtic 3 (Mackay-Steven 54, Griffiths 59, 90) Inverness 0. Att: 43,600
26 Hamilton 1 (Brophy 73) Celtic 1 (Griffiths 35 pen). Att: 5,017

MARCH 2016

2 Celtic 0 Dundee 0. Att: 41,451
12 Partick 1 (Welsh 85 pen) Celtic 2 (Griffiths 45, McGregor 54). Att: 7,238
19 Kilmarnock 0 Celtic 1 (Rogic 90). Att: 6,867

APRIL 2016

2 Celtic 3 (Mackay-Steven 15, Roberts 35, 49) Hearts 1 (Walker 5). Att: 49,009
5 Dundee 0 Celtic 0. Att: 9,566
9 Motherwell 1 (McDonald 60) Celtic 2 (Griffiths 44, 75). Att: 9,123
24 Celtic 1 (Griffiths 23) Ross Co 1 (Murdoch 64). Att: 41,396
30 Hearts 1 (Dauda 57) Celtic 3 (Kazim-Richards 17, Roberts 66, Griffiths 85). Att: 16,527

MAY 2016

8 Celtic 3 (Roberts 7, 20, Lustig 49) Aberdeen 2 (McGinn 57, Considine 64). Att: 47,877 (Celtic sealed title)
11 St Johnstone 2 (MacLean 56, Cummins 77) Celtic 1 (Griffiths 53). Att: 5,959
15 Celtic 7 (Tierney 21, Rogic 26, Lustig 28, Armstrong 50, Roberts 54, Christie 59, Aitchison 77) Motherwell 0. Att: 49,050

SCOTTISH HONOURS LIST

PREMIER DIVISION

	First	*Pts*	*Second*	*Pts*	*Third*	*Pts*
1975–6	Rangers	54	Celtic	48	Hibernian	43
1976–7	Celtic	55	Rangers	46	Aberdeen	43
1977–8	Rangers	55	Aberdeen	53	Dundee Utd	40
1978–9	Celtic	48	Rangers	45	Dundee Utd	44
1979–80	Aberdeen	48	Celtic	47	St Mirren	42
1980–81	Celtic	56	Aberdeen	49	Rangers	44
1981–2	Celtic	55	Aberdeen	53	Rangers	43
1982–3	Dundee Utd	56	Celtic	55	Aberdeen	55
1983–4	Aberdeen	57	Celtic	50	Dundee Utd	47
1984–5	Aberdeen	59	Celtic	52	Dundee Utd	47
1985–6	*Celtic	50	Hearts	50	Dundee Utd	47
1986–7	Rangers	69	Celtic	63	Dundee Utd	60
1987–8	Celtic	72	Hearts	62	Rangers	60
1988–9	Rangers	56	Aberdeen	50	Celtic	46
1989–90	Rangers	51	Aberdeen	44	Hearts	44
1990–1	Rangers	55	Aberdeen	53	Celtic	41
1991–2	Rangers	72	Hearts	63	Celtic	62
1992–3	Rangers	73	Aberdeen	64	Celtic	60
1993–4	Rangers	58	Aberdeen	55	Motherwell	54
1994–5	Rangers	69	Motherwell	54	Hibernian	53
1995–6	Rangers	87	Celtic	83	Aberdeen	55
1996–7	Rangers	80	Celtic	75	Dundee Utd	60
1997–8	Celtic	74	Rangers	72	Hearts	67

PREMIER LEAGUE

	First	*Pts*	*Second*	*Pts*	*Third*	*Pts*
1998–99	Rangers	77	Celtic	71	St Johnstone	57
1999–2000	Rangers	90	Celtic	69	Hearts	54
2000–01	Celtic	97	Rangers	82	Hibernian	66

2001–02	Celtic 103	Rangers 85	Livingston 58
2002–03	*Rangers 97	Celtic 97	Hearts 63
2003–04	Celtic 98	Rangers 81	Hearts 68
2004–05	Rangers 93	Celtic 92	Hibernian 61
2005–06	Celtic 91	Hearts 74	Rangers 73
2006–07	Celtic 84	Rangers 72	Aberdeen 65
2007–08	Celtic 89	Rangers 86	Motherwell 60
2008–09	Rangers 86	Celtic 82	Hearts 59
2009–10	Rangers 87	Celtic 81	Dundee Utd 63
2010–11	Rangers 93	Celtic 92	Hearts 63
2011–12	Celtic 93	**Rangers 73	Motherwell 62
2012–13	Celtic 79	Motherwell 63	St Johnstone 56

Maximum points: 72 except 1986–8, 1991–4 (88), 1994–2000 (108), 2001–10 (114)
* Won on goal difference. **Deducted 10 pts for administration

PREMIERSHIP

	First *Pts*	*Second* *Pts*	*Third* *Pts*
2013–14	Celtic 99	Motherwell 70	Aberdeen 68
2014–15	Celtic 92	Aberdeen 75	Inverness 65
2015–16	Celtic 86	Aberden 71	Hearts 65

FIRST DIVISION (Scottish Championship until 1975–76)

	First *Pts*	*Second* *Pts*	*Third* *Pts*
1890–1a	††Dumbarton 29	Rangers 29	Celtic 24
1891–2b	Dumbarton 37	Celtic 35	Hearts 30
1892–3a	Celtic 29	Rangers 28	St Mirren 23
1893–4a	Celtic 29	Hearts 26	St Bernard's 22
1894–5a	Hearts 31	Celtic 26	Rangers 21
1895–6a	Celtic 30	Rangers 26	Hibernian 24
1896–7a	Hearts 28	Hibernian 26	Rangers 25
1897–8a	Celtic 33	Rangers 29	Hibernian 22
1898–9a	Rangers 36	Hearts 26	Celtic 24
1899–1900a	Rangers 32	Celtic 25	Hibernian 24
1900–1c	Rangers 35	Celtic 29	Hibernian 25
1901–2a	Rangers 28	Celtic 26	Hearts 22
1902–3b	Hibernian 37	Dundee 31	Rangers 29
1903–4d	Third Lanark 43	Hearts 39	Rangers 38
1904–5a	†Celtic 41	Rangers 41	Third Lanark 35
1905–6a	Celtic 46	Hearts 39	Rangers 38
1906–7f	Celtic 55	Dundee 48	Rangers 45
1907–8f	Celtic 55	Falkirk 51	Rangers 50
1908–9f	Celtic 51	Dundee 50	Clyde 48
1909–10f	Celtic 54	Falkirk 52	Rangers 49
1910–11f	Rangers 52	Aberdeen 48	Falkirk 44
1911–12f	Rangers 51	Celtic 45	Clyde 42
1912–13f	Rangers 53	Celtic 49	Hearts 41
1913–14g	Celtic 65	Rangers 59	Hearts 54
1914–15g	Celtic 65	Hearts 61	Rangers 50
1915–16g	Celtic 67	Rangers 56	Morton 51
1916–17g	Celtic 64	Morton 54	Rangers 53
1917–18f	Rangers 56	Celtic 55	Kilmarnock 43
1918–19f	Celtic 58	Rangers 57	Morton 47
1919–20h	Rangers 71	Celtic 68	Motherwell 57
1920–1h	Rangers 76	Celtic 66	Hearts 56
1921–2h	Celtic 67	Rangers 66	Raith 56
1922–3g	Rangers 55	Airdrieonians 50	Celtic 40
1923–4g	Rangers 59	Airdrieonians 50	Celtic 41
1924–5g	Rangers 60	Airdrieonians 57	Hibernian 52
1925–6g	Celtic 58	Airdrieonians 50	Hearts 50
1926–7g	Rangers 56	Motherwell 51	Celtic 49

1927–8g	Rangers	60	Celtic	55	Motherwell	55
1928–9g	Rangers	67	Celtic	51	Motherwell	50
1929–30g	Rangers	60	Motherwell	55	Aberdeen	53
1930–1g	Rangers	60	Celtic	58	Motherwell	56
1931–2g	Motherwell	66	Rangers	61	Celtic	48
1932–3g	Rangers	62	Motherwell	59	Hearts	50
1933–4g	Rangers	66	Motherwell	62	Celtic	47
1934–5g	Rangers	55	Celtic	52	Hearts	50
1935–6g	Celtic	68	Rangers	61	Aberdeen	61
1936–7g	Rangers	61	Aberdeen	54	Celtic	52
1937–8g	Celtic	61	Hearts	58	Rangers	49
1938–9f	Rangers	59	Celtic	48	Aberdeen	46
1946–7f	Rangers	46	Hibernian	44	Aberdeen	39
1947–8g	Hibernian	48	Rangers	46	Partick	46
1948–9i	Rangers	46	Dundee	45	Hibernian	39
1949–50i	Rangers	50	Hibernian	49	Hearts	43
1950–1i	Hibernian	48	Rangers	38	Dundee	38
1951–2i	Hibernian	45	Rangers	41	East Fife	37
1952–3i	*Rangers	43	Hibernian	43	East Fife	39
1953–4i	Celtic	43	Hearts	38	Partick	35
1954–5f	Aberdeen	49	Celtic	46	Rangers	41
1955–6f	Rangers	52	Aberdeen	46	Hearts	45
1956–7f	Rangers	55	Hearts	53	Kilmarnock	42
1957–8f	Hearts	62	Rangers	49	Celtic	46
1958–9f	Rangers	50	Hearts	48	Motherwell	44
1959–60f	Hearts	54	Kilmarnock	50	Rangers	42
1960–1f	Rangers	51	Kilmarnock	50	Third Lanark	42
1961–2f	Dundee	54	Rangers	51	Celtic	46
1962–3f	Rangers	57	Kilmarnock	48	Partick	46
1963–4f	Rangers	55	Kilmarnock	49	Celtic	47
1964–5f	*Kilmarnock	50	Hearts	50	Dunfermline	49
1965–6f	Celtic	57	Rangers	55	Kilmarnock	45
1966–7f	Celtic	58	Rangers	55	Clyde	46
1967–8f	Celtic	63	Rangers	61	Hibernian	45
1968–9f	Celtic	54	Rangers	49	Dunfermline	45
1969–70f	Celtic	57	Rangers	45	Hibernian	44
1970–1f	Celtic	56	Aberdeen	54	St Johnstone	44
1971–2f	Celtic	60	Aberdeen	50	Rangers	44
1972–3f	Celtic	57	Rangers	56	Hibernian	45
1973–4f	Celtic	53	Hibernian	49	Rangers	48
1974–5f	Rangers	56	Hibernian	49	Celtic	45

*Won on goal average †Won on deciding match ††Title shared. Competition suspended 1940–46 (Second World War)

SCOTTISH CHAMPIONSHIP WINS

Rangers	*54	Hibernian	4	Kilmarnock	1
Celtic	47	Dumbarton	*2	Motherwell	1
Aberdeen	4	Dundee	1	Third Lanark	1
Hearts	4	Dundee Utd	1	(*Incl 1 shared)	

FIRST DIVISION (Since formation of Premier Division)

	First	*Pts*	*Second*	*Pts*	*Third*	*Pts*
1975–6d	Partick	41	Kilmarnock	35	Montrose	30
1976–7j	St Mirren	62	Clydebank	58	Dundee	51
1977–8j	*Morton	58	Hearts	58	Dundee	57
1978–9j	Dundee	55	Kilmarnock	54	Clydebank	54
1979–80j	Hearts	53	Airdrieonians	51	Ayr	44
1980–1j	Hibernian	57	Dundee	52	St Johnstone	51
1981–2j	Motherwell	61	Kilmarnock	51	Hearts	50
1982–3j	St Johnstone	55	Hearts	54	Clydebank	50

1983–4j	Morton 54	Dumbarton 51	Partick...................... 46
1984–5j	Motherwell............. 50	Clydebank 48	Falkirk 45
1985–6j	Hamilton 56	Falkirk 45	Kilmarnock 44
1986–7k	Morton 57	Dunfermline 56	Dumbarton................ 53
1987–8k	Hamilton 56	Meadowbank 52	Clydebank................. 49
1988–9j	Dunfermline........... 54	Falkirk 52	Clydebank................. 48
1989–90j	St Johnstone.......... 58	Airdrieonians 54	Clydebank................. 44
1990–1j	Falkirk................... 54	Airdrieonians 53	Dundee...................... 52
1991–2k	Dundee 58	Partick.....................57	Hamilton.................... 57
1992–3k	Raith..................... 65	Kilmarnock...............54	Dunfermline 52
1993–4k	Falkirk................... 66	Dunfermline 65	Airdrieonians............. 54
1994–5l	Raith..................... 69	Dunfermline 68	Dundee...................... 68
1995–6l	Dunfermline........... 71	Dundee Utd...............67	Morton....................... 67
1996–7l	St Johnstone.......... 80	Airdrieonians 60	Dundee...................... 58
1997–8l	Dundee 70	Falkirk 65	Raith 60
1998–9l	Hibernian 89	Falkirk 66	Ayr 62
1999–2000l	St Mirren............... 76	Dunfermline 71	Falkirk 68
2000–01l	Livingston.............. 76	Ayr 69	Falkirk 56
2001–02l	Partick 66	Airdie 56	Ayr 52
2002–03l	Falkirk................... 81	Clyde........................72	St Johnstone 67
2003–04l	Inverness............... 70	Clyde........................69	St Johnstone 57
2004–05l	Falkirk................... 75	St Mirren 60	Clyde......................... 60
2005–06l	St Mirren............... 76	St Johnstone 66	Hamilton.................... 59
2006–07l	Gretna................... 66	St Johnstone 65	Dundee...................... 53
2007–08l	Hamilton 76	Dundee.....................69	St Johnstone 58
2008–09l	St Johnstone.......... 65	Partick......................55	Dunfermline 51
2009–10l	Inverness............... 73	Dundee.....................61	Dunfermline 58
2010–11l	Dunfermline........... 70	Raith 60	Falkirk 58
2011–12l	Ross...................... 79	Dundee.....................55	Falkirk 52
2012–13l	Partick 78	Morton......................67	Falkirk 53

CHAMPIONSHIP

	First .... *Pts*	*Second* .... *Pts*	*Third* .... *Pts*
2013–14l	Dundee 69	Hamilton...................67	Falkirk 66
2014–15l	Hearts...................91	Hibernian..................70	Rangers 67
2015–16l	Rangers.................81	Falkirk 70	Hibernian.................. 70

Maximum points: a, 36; b, 44; c,.40; d 52; e, 60; f, 68; g, 76; h, 84; i, 60; j, 78; k, 88; l, 108
*Won on goal difference

SECOND DIVISION

	First .... *Pts*	*Second* ....*Pts*	*Third* .... *Pts*
1921–2a	Alloa 60	Cowdenbeath............47	Armadale 45
1922–3a	Queen's Park.......... 57	Clydebank 52	St Johnstone 50
1923–4a	St Johnstone.......... 56	Cowdenbeath............55	Bathgate.................... 44
1924–5a	Dundee Utd 50	Clydebank 48	Clyde......................... 47
1925–6a	Dunfermline........... 59	Clyde........................53	Ayr 52
1926–7a	Bo'ness 56	Raith 49	Clydebank.................. 45
1927–8a	Ayr........................ 54	Third Lanark.............45	King'sPark.................. 44
1928–9b	Dundee Utd 51	Morton......................50	Arbroath 47
1929–30a	*LeithAthletic 57	East Fife 57	Albion........................ 54
1930–1a	Third Lanark 61	Dundee Utd...............50	Dunfermline 47
1931–2a	*E Stirling 55	St Johnstone 55	Stenhousemuir 46
1932–3c	Hibernian 55	Queen of South.........49	Dunfermline 47
1933–4c	Albion 45	Dunfermline 44	Arbroath 44
1934–5c	Third Lanark 52	Arbroath...................50	St Bernard's 47
1935–6c	Falkirk................... 59	St Mirren 52	Morton....................... 48
1936–7c	Ayr 54	Morton......................51	St Bernard's 48
1937–8c	Raith..................... 59	Albion......................48	Airdrieonians............. 47

1938–9c	Cowdenbeath 60	Alloa 48	East Fife 48
1946–7d	Dundee Utd 45	Airdrieonians 42	East Fife 31
1947–8e	East Fife 53	Albion 42	Hamilton 40
1948–9e	*Raith 42	Stirling 42	Airdrieonians 41
1949–50e	Morton 47	Airdrieonians 44	St Johnstone 36
1950–1e	*Queen of South 45	Stirling 45	Ayr 36
1951–2e	Clyde 44	Falkirk 43	Ayr 39
1952–3	E Stirling 44	Hamilton 43	Queen's Park 37
1953–4e	Motherwell 45	Kilmarnock 42	Third Lanark 36
1954–5e	Airdrieonians 46	Dunfermline 42	Hamilton 39
1955–6b	Queen's Park 54	Ayr 51	St Johnstone 49
1956–7b	Clyde 64	Third Lanark 51	Cowdenbeath 45
1957–8b	Stirling 55	Dunfermline 53	Arbroath 47
1958–9b	Ayr 60	Arbroath 51	Stenhousemuir 46
1959–60b	St Johnstone 53	Dundee Utd 50	Queen of South 49
1960–1b	Stirling 55	Falkirk 54	Stenhousemuir 50
1961–2b	Clyde 54	Queen of South 53	Morton 44
1962–3b	St Johnstone 55	E Stirling 49	Morton 48
1963–4b	Morton 67	Clyde 53	Arbroath 46
1964–5b	Stirling 59	Hamilton 50	Queen of South 45
1965–6b	Ayr 53	Airdrieonians 50	Queen of South 47
1966–7b	Morton 69	Raith 58	Arbroath 57
1967–8b	St Mirren 62	Arbroath 53	East Fife 49
1968–9b	Motherwell 64	Ayr 53	East Fife 48
1969–70b	Falkirk 56	Cowdenbeath 55	Queen of South 50
1970–1b	Partick 56	East Fife 51	Arbroath 46
1971–2b	*Dumbarton 52	Arbroath 52	Stirling 50
1972–3b	Clyde 56	Dunfermline 52	Raith 47
1973–4b	Airdrieonians 60	Kilmarnock 58	Hamilton 55
1974–5b	Falkirk 54	Queen of South 53	Montrose 53

SECOND DIVISION (MODERN)

	First .... *Pts*	*Second* .... *Pts*	*Third* .... *Pts*
1975–6d	*Clydebank 40	Raith 40	Alloa 35
1976–7f	Stirling 55	Alloa 51	Dunfermline 50
1977–8f	*Clyde 53	Raith 53	Dunfermline 48
1978–9f	Berwick 54	Dunfermline 52	Falkirk 50
1979–80f	Falkirk 50	E Stirling 49	Forfar 46
1980–1f	Queen's Park 50	Queen of South 46	Cowdenbeath 45
1981–2f	Clyde 59	Alloa 50	Arbroath 50
1982–3f	Brechin 55	Meadowbank 54	Arbroath 49
1983–4f	Forfar 63	East Fife 47	Berwick 43
1984–5f	Montrose 53	Alloa 50	Dunfermline 49
1985–6f	Dunfermline 57	Queen of South 55	Meadowbank 49
1986–7f	Meadowbank 55	Raith 52	Stirling 52
1987–8f	Ayr 61	St Johnstone 59	Queen's Park 51
1988–9f	Albion 50	Alloa 45	Brechin 43
1989–90f	Brechin 49	Kilmarnock 48	Stirling 47
1990–1f	Stirling 54	Montrose 46	Cowdenbeath 45
1991–2f	Dumbarton 52	Cowdenbeath 51	Alloa 50
1992–3f	Clyde 54	Brechin 53	Stranraer 53
1993–4f	Stranraer 56	Berwick 48	Stenhousemuir 47
1994–5g	Morton 64	Dumbarton 60	Stirling 58
1995–6g	Stirling 81	East Fife 67	Berwick 60
1996–7g	Ayr 77	Hamilton 74	Livingston 64
1997–8g	Stranraer 61	Clydebank 60	Livingston 59
1998–9g	Livingston 77	Inverness 72	Clyde 53
1999–2000g	Clyde 65	Alloa 64	Ross Co 62
2000–01g	Partick 75	Arbroath 58	Berwick 54

2001–02g	Queen of South 67	Alloa........................59	Forfar Athletic 53
2002–03g	Raith 59	Brechin.....................55	Airdrie 54
2003–04g	Airdrie..................... 70	Hamilton...................62	Dumbarton................. 60
2004–05g	Brechin 72	Stranraer...................63	Morton....................... 62
2005–06g	Gretna..................... 88	Morton.......................70	Peterhead 57
2006–07g	Morton 77	Stirling 69	Raith.......................... 62
2007–08g	Ross........................ 73	Airdrie 66	Raith.......................... 60
2008–09g	Raith....................... 76	Ayr 74	Brechin...................... 62
2009–10g	*Stirling 65	Alloa..........................65	Cowdenbeath.............. 59
2010–11g	Livingston............... 82	*Ayr...........................59	Forfar 59
2011–12g	Cowdenbeath 71	Arbroath....................63	Dumbarton................. 58
2012–13g	Queen of South 92	Alloa..........................67	Brechin...................... 61

LEAGUE ONE

	First...................... *Pts*	*Second* .... *Pts*	*Third* .... *Pts*
2013–14g	Rangers................102	Dunfermline 63	Stranraer.................... 51
2014–15g	Morton 69	Stranraer...................67	Forfar 66
2015–16g	Dunfermline............79	Ayr 61	Peterhead 59

Maximum points: a, 76; b, 72; c, 68; d, 52 e, 60; f, 78; g, 108 *Won on goal average/goal difference

THIRD DIVISION (MODERN)

1994–5	Forfar..................... 80	Montrose...................67	Ross Co 60
1995–6	Livingston............... 72	Brechin.....................63	Caledonian Th 57
1996–7	Inverness................ 76	Forfar 67	Ross Co 77
1997–8	Alloa 76	Arbroath....................68	Ross Co 67
1998–9	Ross Co.................. 77	Stenhousemuir 64	Brechin...................... 59
1999–2000	Queen's Park........... 69	Berwick 66	Forfar 61
2000–01	*Hamilton............... 76	Cowdenbeath.............76	Brechin...................... 72
2001–02	Brechin 73	Dumbarton 61	Albion........................ 59
2002–03	Morton 72	East Fife 71	Albion........................ 70
2003–04	Stranraer 79	Stirling 77	Gretna 68
2004–05	Gretna..................... 98	Peterhead 78	Cowdenbeath.............. 51
2005–06	*Cowdenbeath......... 76	Berwick 76	Stenhousemuir 73
2006–07	Berwick 75	Arbroath....................70	Queen's Park 68
2007–08	East Fife................. 88	Stranraer...................65	Montrose.................... 59
2008–09	Dumbarton 67	Cowdenbeath.............63	East Stirling 61
2009–10	Livingston............... 78	Forfar 63	East Stirling 61
2010–11	Arbroath 66	Albion........................61	Queen's Park 59
2011–12	Alloa 77	Queen's Park 63	Stranraer.................... 58
2012–13	Rangers.................. 83	Peterhead 59	Queen's Park 56

LEAGUE TWO

	First...................... *Pts*	*Second* .... *Pts*	*Third* .... *Pts*
2013–14	Peterhead...............76	Annan........................63	Stirling 58
2014–15	Albion 71	Queen's Park 61	Arbroath 56
2015–16	East Fife.................62	Elgin 59	Clyde......................... 57

Maximum points: 108 * Won on goal difference

RELEGATED FROM PREMIER DIVISION/PREMIER LEAGUE/PREMIERSHIP

1975–6	Dundee,	St Johnstone	1982–3	Morton,	Kilmarnock
1976–7	Kilmarnock,	Hearts	1983–4	St Johnstone,	Motherwell
1977–8	Ayr,	Clydebank	1984–5	Dumbarton,	Morton
1978–9	Hearts,	Motherwell	1985–6	No relegation	
1979–80	Dundee,	Hibernian	1986–7	Clydebank, Hamilton	
1980–1	Kilmarnock,	Hearts	1987–8	Falkirk, Dunfermline, Morton	
1981–2	Partick,	Airdrieonians	1988–9	Hamilton	

1989–90 Dundee
1990–1 No relegation
1991–2 St Mirren, Dunfermline
1992–3 Falkirk, Airdrieonians
1993–4 St J'stone, Raith, Dundee
1994–5 Dundee Utd
1995–6 Falkirk, Partick
1996–7 Raith
1997–8 Hibernian
1998–9 Dunfermline
1999–2000 No relegation
2000–01 St Mirren
2001–02 St Johnstone
2002–03 No relegation
2003–04 Partick
2004–05 Dundee
2005–06 Livingston
2006–07 Dunfermline
2007–08 Gretna
2008–09 Inverness
2009–10 Falkirk
2010–11 Hamilton
2011–12 Dunfermline, *Rangers
2012–13 Dundee
2013–14 Hibernian, **Hearts
2014–15 St Mirren
2015–16 Dundee Utd

*Following administration, liquidationand new club formed.

**Deducted 15 points for administration

RELEGATED FROM FIRST DIVISION/CHAMPIONSHIP

1975–6 Dunfermline, Clyde
1976–7 Raith, Falkirk
1977–8 Alloa, East Fife
1978–9 Montrose, Queen of South
1979–80 Arbroath, Clyde
1980–1 Stirling, Berwick
1981–2 E Stirling, Queen of South
1982–3 Dunfermline, Queen's Park
1983–4 Raith, Alloa
1984–5 Meadowbank, St Johnstone
1985–6 Ayr, Alloa
1986–7 Brechin, Montrose
1987–8 East Fife, Dumbarton
1988–9 Kilmarnock, Queen of South
1989–90 Albion, Alloa
1990–1 Clyde, Brechin
1991–2 Montrose, Forfar
1992–3 Meadowbank, Cowdenbeath
1993–4 Dumbarton, Stirling, Clyde, Morton, Brechin
1994–5 Ayr, Stranraer
1995–6 Hamilton, Dumbarton
1996–7 Clydebank, East Fife
1997–8 Partick, Stirling
1998–9 Hamilton, Stranraer
1999–2000 Clydebank
2000–01 Morton, Alloa
2001–02 Raith
2002–03 Alloa Athletic, Arbroath
2003–04 Ayr, Brechin
2004–05 Partick, Raith
2005–06 Brechin, Stranraer
2006–07 Airdrie Utd, Ross Co
2007–08 Stirling
2008–09 *Livingston, Clyde
2009–10 Airdrie, Ayr
2010–11 Cowdenbeath, Stirling
2011–12 Ayr, Queen of South
2012–13 Dunfermline, Airdrie
2013–14 Morton
2014–15 Cowdenbeath
2015–16 Livingston, Alloa

*relegated to Division Three for breaching insolvency rules

RELEGATED FROM SECOND DIVISION/LEAGUE ONE

1993–4 Alloa, Forfar, E Stirling, Montrose, Queen's Park, Arbroath, Albion, Cowdenbeath
1994–5 Meadowbank, Brechin
1995–6 Forfar, Montrose
1996–7 Dumbarton, Berwick
1997–8 Stenhousemuir, Brechin
1998–9 East Fife, Forfar
1999–2000 Hamilton
2000–01 Queen's Park, Stirling
2001–02 Morton
2002–03 Stranraer, Cowdenbeath
2003–04 East Fife, Stenhousemuir
2004–05 Arbroath, Berwick
2005–06 Dumbarton
2006–07 Stranraer, Forfar
2007–08 Cowdenbeath, Berwick
2008–09 Queen's Park, Stranraer
2009–10 Arbroath, Clyde
2010–11 Alloa, Peterhead
2011–12 Stirling
2012–13 Albion
2013–14 East Fife, Arbroath
2014–15 Stirling
2015–16 Cowdenbeath, Forfar

RELEGATED FROM LEAGUE TWO

2015–16 East Stirling

SCOTTISH PREMIERSHIP 2015–2016

(appearances and scorers)

ABERDEEN

Brown S ... 13
Church S ... 13
Collin A ... 3
Considine A ... 26 (6)
Flood W ... 18 (4)
Goodwillie D ... 7 (10)
Harvie D ... - (2)
Hayes J ... 35
Jack R ... 26 (2)
Lennox A ... 1
Logan S ... 35 (2)
McGinn N ... 33 (3)
McKenna S ... 2 (1)
McLaughlin R ... 1 (3)
McLean K ... 38
McLennan C ... - (1)
Nuttall J ... - (2)
Parker J ... 1 (6)
Pawlett P ... 9 (9)
Quinn P ... 9 (4)
Reynolds M ... 19 (3)
Robson B ... 3 (9)
Rooney A ... 22 (5)
Rose M ... 1
Ross F ... - (2)
Shinnie G ... 37
Smith C ... 2 (12)
Storie C ... 6 (4)
Taylor A ... 36 (1)
Ward D ... 21
Wright S ... 1 (3)

League goals (62): Rooney 20, McGinn 10, Church 6, McLean 6, Hayes 5, Logan 4, Taylor 4, Considine 2, Goodwillie 2, Pawlett 1, Quinn 1, Shinnie 1
Scottish Cup goals: None. **League Cup goals**: None. **Europa League goals** (8): McLean 3, McGinn 2, Considine 1, Hayes 1, Pawlett 1
Average home league attendance: 13,094. **Player of Year**: Jonny Hayes

CELTIC

Aitchison J ... - (1)
Allan S ... 2 (11)
Ambrose E ... 15 (6)
Armstrong S ... 19 (6)
Bailly L ... 3
Biton N ... 28 (2)
Blackett T ... 3
Boyata D ... 25 (1)
Brown S ... 22
Christie R ... 2 (3)
Ciftci N ... 5 (6)
Cole C ... - (4)
Commons K ... 16 (5)
Forrest J ... 10 (9)
Gordon C ... 35
Griffiths L ... 32 (2)
Henderson L ... - (1)
Izaguirre E ... 14 (3)
Janko S ... 6 (4)
Johansen S ... 22 (1)
Kazim-Richards C ... 4 (7)
Lustig M ... 29 (1)
Mackay-Steven G ... 15 (10)
McGregor C ... 15 (12)
Mulgrew C ... 8 (5)
O'Connell E ... 1
Ralston A ... (1)
Roberts P ... 9 (2)
Rogic T ... 24 (6)
Scepovic S ... - (1)
Simunovic J ... 11
Stokes A ... 1
Sviatchenko E ... 14
Thompson J ... - (1)
Tierney K ... 23
Van Dijk V ... 5

League goals (93): Griffiths 31, Rogic 8, Roberts 6, Biton 5, Armstrong 4, Boyata 4, Ciftci 4, Commons 4, Lustig 4, Mackay-Steven 4, McGregor 4, Forrest 2, Izaguirre 2, Aitchison 1, Brown 1, Christie 1, Johansen 1, Kazim-Richards 1, Mulgrew 1, Simunovic 1, Tierney 1, Opponents 3,
Scottish Cup goals (10): Griffiths 4, Cole 1, Kazim-Richards 1, Mackay-Steven 1, McGregor 1, Rogic 1, Sviatchenko 1. **League Cup goals** (5): Commons 1, Griffiths 1, Johansen 1, Mackay-Steven 1, Rogic 1
Champions League goals (10): Griffiths 3, Biton 2, Boyata 2, Johansen 2, Mulgrew 1. **Europa League goals** (8): Commons 4, Biton 1, Griffiths 1, Lustig 1, McGregor 1
Average home league attendance: 44,849. **Player of Year**: Leigh Griffiths

DUNDEE

Arturo ... - (3)
Bain S ... 37
Black A ... - (1)
Calder R ... 3 (8)
Carreiro D ... - (2)
Colquhoun C ... 2 (1)
Curran J ... - (3)
Etxabeguren J ... 20 (3)
Ferry S ... - (1)
Gadzhalov K ... 8 (6)
Harkins G ... 22 (8)
Healey R ... 4 (3)
Hemmings K ... 34 (3)
Holt K ... 34
Irvine G ... 6 (1)
Kerr C ... 7 (3)
Konrad T ... 20 (7)
Low N ... 15 (6)
Loy R ... 21 (8)
McGinn P ... 33 (1)
McGowan P ... 27 (3)
McPake J ... 16
Meggatt D ... 2 (4)
Mitchell D ... 1 (1)
O'Dea D ... 16
Ross N ... 36 (1)
Stewart G ... 36 (1)
Tankulic L ... - (1)
Thomson K ... 11 (1)
Wighton C ... 7 (6)

LLeague goals (53): Hemmings 21, Loy 9, Stewart 9, Harkins 4, Holt 2, McPake 2, Wighton 2, Gadzhalov 1, Healey 1, McGowan 1, Ross 1
Scottish Cup goals (8): Hemmings 3, Stewart 2, Harkins 1, Holt 1, McGinn 1. **League Cup goals** (1): Hemmings 1
Average home league attendance: 6,122. **Player of Year**: Kane Hemmings

DUNDEE UNITED

Anier H..................... 5 (2)
Ballantyne C .... - (2)
Bilate M 1 (1)
Bodul D..................... 7 (4)
Connolly A 1 (10)
Coote A...................... - (1)
Demel G 12
Dillon S 22 (4)
Dixon P................... 27 (1)
Donaldson C............ 15 (3)
Dow R 12 (6)
Durnan M 26 (2)
Erskine C.................. 8 (7)
Fraser S.................. 23 (9)
Gunning G 19
Johnson J 1 (2)
Kawashima E 16
Knoyle K................... 8 (1)
Kuhl A............................5
McGlowan R..................22
McKay B................. 28 (1)
Morris C........................13
Muirhead R............... 1 (2)
Murray S................. 9 (13)
Ofere E...................... 6 (7)
Paton P 13 (1)
Rankin J................. 34 (1)
Riski R 1 (2)
Sinama Pongolle F............4
Smith B...................... - (2)
Smith M 2
Sneijder R.................. - (1)
Souttar H.................. 1 (1)
Souttar J................. 17 (3)
Spark E 1
Spittal B................. 27 (6)
Szromnik M......................9
Taggart A 4 (3)
Telfer C..................... 5 (2)
Zwick L M......................13

League goals (45): McKay 12, Murray 7, Spittal 5, Ofere 3, Durnan 2, Dillon 2, Dow 2, Paton 2, Rankin 2, Anier 1, Demel 1, Erskine 1, Fraser 1, Johnson 1, Souttar H 1, Opponents 2
Scottish Cup goals (5): Anier 2, Fraser 1, McKay 1, Spittal 1. **League Cup goals** (3): Fraser 1, Morris 1, Spittal 1
Average home league attendance: 7,969

HAMILTON ACADEMICAL

Agustien K................ 1 (1)
Boyd S 2 (3)
Brophy E.................. 7 (7)
Canning M 1 (2)
Crawford A.............. 32 (1)
Cunningham R .... - (1)
D'Acol A 3 (12)
Devlin M.......................16
Diaby O 1 (5)
Docherty G............ 16 (18)
Gillespie G.............. 28 (2)
Gordon Z.......................38
Hughes R.................... - (2)
Imrie D.................. 34 (1)
Kurakins A....................35
Kurtaj G.................. 28 (6)
Longridge L............... 6 (9)
Tagliapietra L 34
Lyon D...................... 9 (3)
MacKinnon D 30 (1)
Martin A 1
McGovern M..................37
Morris C.................. 27 (5)
Nade C 4 (13)
Redmond D............. 1 (10)
Sendles-White J.......... 4 (3)
Tena J G 20 (3)
Turner C..........................3
Watson C .... - (1)

League goals (42): Morris 8, Imrie 6, Crawford 5, Brophy 4, Tena 4, Kurtaj 3, Tagliapietra 3, Gordon 2, Nade 2, Docherty 1, Gillespie 1, Longridge 1, MacKinnon 1, Opponents 1
Scottish Cup goals (1): Docherty 1. **League Cup goals** (1): Nade 1
Average home league attendance: 3,024. **Player of Year**: Michael McGovern

HEART OF MIDLOTHIAN

Alexander B 35
Augustyn B 21 (1)
Buaben P................ 33 (3)
Cowie D.................... 7 (3)
Dauda A 7 (6)
Djoum A 24 (4)
Gomis M................. 12 (5)
Hamilton J......................3
Juanma 28 (5)
King B...................... 7 (8)
Kitchen P 9 (1)
McGhee J 10 (12)
McHattie K .... - (1)
McKirdy S.................. 1 (1)
Moore L...........................1
Morrison C .... - (1)
Nicholson S 28 (8)
Oliver G .... - (1)
Oshaniwa J 24
Ozturk A 24
Pallardo M 10 (6)
Paterson C 27 (2)
Reilly G 11 (17)
Rossi I..................... 28 (1)
Smith L 5 (5)
Souttar J................. 14 (1)
Sow O..................... 22 (1)
Swanson D................ 4 (4)
Walker J.................. 20 (2)
Zanatta D................ 3 (10)

League goals (59): Juanma 12, Sow 9, Walker 7, Dauda 5, Djoum 5, Paterson 5, Reilly 4, Nicholson 3, Buaben 2, King 2, Rossi 2, Ozturk 1, Opponents 2
Scottish Cup goals (3): Djoum 1, Nicholson 1, Paterson 1. **League Cup goals** (10): Sow 2, Djoum 1, Juanma 1, McGhee 1, McHattie 1, Nicholson 1, Ozturk 1, Paterson 1, Opponents 1
Average home league attendance: 16,423. **Player of Year**: Arnaud Djoum

INVERNESS CALEDONIAN THISTLE

Christie R 12 (1)
Lopez D 5 (2)
Devine D........................37
Draper R................. 31 (1)
Fisher A..................... - (1)
Fon Williams O...............38
Foran R .... - (7)
Horner L................. 11 (5)
Hughes L.................. 4 (5)
Mbuyi-Mutombo A .. 12 (13)
Meekings J.....................21
Polworth L 33 (3)
Raven D.................. 18 (1)
Roberts J 8 (1)
Sho-Silva T .... - (5)
Storey M................. 29 (1)
Sutherland A.............. - (5)
Tansey G........................37
Tremarco C.............. 28 (4)
Vigurs I.................... 24 (6)
Vincent J 14 (2)
Warren G 23 (2)
Wedderburn N............ 8 (7)
Williams D 25 (10)
Williams R .... - (7)

League goals (54): Storey 11, Tansey 8, Polworth 6, Vigurs 6, Draper, 5, Christie 3, Devine 2, Meekings 2, Roberts 2, Tremarco 2, Vincent 2, Lopez 1, Foran 1, Horner 1, Raven 1, Williams 1
Scottish Cup goals (6): Mbuyi-Mutombo 2, Vigurs 2, Roberts 1, Storey 1. **League Cup goals** (3): Devine 1, Storey 1, Tansey 1. **Europa League goals**: None
Average home league attendance: 3,753

KILMARNOCK

Addison M 6
Ashcroft L............... 14 (1)
Balatoni C......................30
Barbour R 1 (1)
Boyd K 15 (14)
Brennan C................. 1 (2)
Carrick D 1 (10)
Clark L .... - (1)
Connolly M.....................10
Dicker G 12
Faubert J 7 (2)
Findlay S 21 (1)
Frizzell A 6 (4)
Hamill J.................. 14 (2)
Henshall A................ 1 (1)
Higginbotham K 23 (4)
Hodson L........................13
Johnston C.......................1
Kiltie G.................... 30 (5)
MacDonald J..................37
Magennis J 32 (2)
McCulloch L.....................1
McHattie K 18 (3)
McKenzie R 23 (5)
McLean S .... - (1)
O'Hara M................ 23 (6)
Obadeyi T 15 (15)
Robinson S 6 (6)
Slater C 23 (3)
Smith S................... 21 (1)
Splaine A................... 1 (6)
Syme D...................... 4 (1)
Taylor G 1
Westlake D................ 7 (1)

League goals (41): Magennis 10, Kiltie 6, Boyd 5, Higginbotham 5, Obadeyi 3, Balatoni 3, Connolly 2, Slater 2, Smith 2, McHattie 1, McKenzie 1, Opponents 1. **Play-offs – goals** (4): Kiltie 2, Addison 1, Boyd 1
Scottish Cup goals (2): McKenzie 1, Slater 1. **League Cup goals** (6): Magennis 2, Boyd 1, Higginbotham 1, McKenzie 1, Slater 1
Average home league attendance: 3,993. **Player of Year**: Greg Kiltie

MOTHERWELL

Ainsworth L............ 17 (12)
Cadden C................ 16 (4)
Chalmers J............... 11 (6)
Clarkson D .... - (7)
Fletcher W 5 (9)
Gomis M.................... 8 (2)
Grimshaw L............. 13 (1)
Hall B...................... 16 (2)
Hammell S.............. 25 (2)
Johnson M 34 (4)
Kennedy K.............. 18 (4)
Laing L................... 13 (2)
Lasley K 30
Law J 28 (1)
Leitch J 3 (8)
Mackin D.................... - (1)
McDonald S 34 (3)
McFadden J 2 (1)
McManus S....................37
Moult L.................... 34 (4)
Pearson S 25 (1)
Ripley C.........................36
Robinson T 2 (8)
Samson C 2
Taylor J..................... 6 (1)
Thomas D 2 (12)
Watt L 1 (1)

League goals (47): Moult 15, McDonald 10, Pearson 7, Johnson 5, Ainsworth 2, Cadden 2,

Fletcher 1, Hall 1, Laing 1, Lasley 1, McManus 1, Opponents 1
Scottish Cup goals (6): McDonald 2, Pearson 2, Johnson 1, Moult 1. **League Cup goals** (5): McDonald 2, Moult 2, Ainsworth 1
Average home league attendance: 4,912. **Player of Year**: Lewis Moult

PARTICK THISTLE

Amoo D 27 (10)
Bannigan S 26
Booth C 34
Cerny T 28
Doolan K 24 (12)
Dumbuya M 19 (2)
Edwards R 10 (7)
Elliott C 5 (7)
Frans F 17 (4)
Fraser G 7 (5)
Gallacher P 1
German A - (2)
Hendry J 1 (2)
Lawless S 36 (1)
Lindsay L 25
McDaid D 1 (3)
Miller G 20 (1)
Muirhead R 4 (4)
Nesbit K - (8)
Nesbitt A 4 (3)
Osman A 32 (1)
Penrice J 2
Pogba M 13 (15)
Scully R 9 (1)
Seaborne D 31 (1)
Stevenson R 6 (4)
Welsh S 32 (2)
Wilson D 4 (7)

League goals (41): Doolan 14, Amoo 5, Lawless 5, Booth 2, Edwards 2, Muirhead 2, Pogba 2, Bannigan 1, Dumbuya 1, Frans 1, Fraser 1, Lindsay 1, Miller 1, Stevenson 1, Welsh 1, Opponents 1
Scottish Cup goals (2): Amoo 1, Seaborne 1. **League Cup goals**: None
Average home league attendance: 3,799. **Player of Year**: Tomas Cerny

ROSS COUNTY

Bachmann D - (1)
Boyce L 29 (6)
Boyd S 12 (3)
Curran C 15 (4)
Davies A 31
De Vita R 8 (11)
Dingwall T 5 (7)
Foster R 28 (4)
Fox S 27
Franks J 18 (11)
Fraser M 29
Gardyne M 34 (1)
Goodwillie D 4 (5)
Graham B 10 (13)
Irvine J 34 (2)
McLaughlin C 2
McShane I 16 (2)
Morrison G - (2)
Murdoch S 14 (15)
Quinn P 14
Quinn R 5 (5)
Reckord J 14 (2)
Robertson C 21 (2)
Schalk A 14 (10)
Woods G 11 (1)
Woods M 23 (3)

League goals (55): Boyce 15, Curran 7, Graham 6, Gardyne 5, Schalk 5, Davies 3, McShane 3, Dingwall 2, Irvine 2, Murdoch 2, Franks 1, Goodwillie 1, Woods M 1, Opponents 2
Scottish Cup goals (9): Graham 4, Schalk 2, Boyce 1, De Vita 1, Quinn 1. **League Cup goals** (16): Boyce 4, Gardyne 3, Schalk 2, De Vita 1, Franks 1, Graham 1, Holden 1, Irvine 1, Quinn 1, Woods M 1
Average home league attendance: 4,033. **Player of Year**: Jackson Irvine

ST JOHNSTONE

Anderson S 23 (1)
Brown S 2 (3)
Caddis L - (5)
Clark Z 5 (1)
Craig L 24 (11)
Cummins G 23 (9)
Davidson M 30
Doyle M - (2)
Easton B 26 (3)
Fisher D 22 (1)
Gordon L 1
Hurst G - (2)
Kane C 10 (19)
Krachunov P 1 (1)
Lappin S 14 (9)
MacKay D 17
MacLean S 29 (4)
Mannus A 33
McKay B 2
Millar C 20
O'Halloran M 19 (1)
Scobbie T 28 (2)
Shaughnessy J 35 (2)
Sutton J 5 (16)
Swanson D 14
Thomson C 2 (8)
Wotherspoon D 32 (3)
Wright F 1

League goals (58): MacLean 14, Wotherspoon 9, Cummins 8, Craig 6, Kane 4, Davidson 3, Lappin 2, O'Halloran 2, Scobbie 2, Anderson 1, Easton 1, Fisher 1, MacKay 1, Shaughnessy 1, Sutton 1, Swanson 1, Opponents 1
Scottish Cup goals: None. **League Cup goals** (7): O'Halloran 2, Davidson 1, Kane 1, Lappin 1, MacLean 1, Shaughnessy 1. **Europa League goals** (2): O'Halloran 1, McKay 1
Average home league attendance: 3,879. **Player of Year**: Murray Davidson

SCOTTISH LEAGUE CUP 2015–16

FIRST ROUND

Annan 3 Queen of South 4 (aet)
Ayr 2 Brechin 0
Berwick 3 Alloa 2 (aet)
Dunfermline 5 Cowdenbeath 1
East Fife 1 Dumbarton 1
(aet, East Fife won 4-3 on pens)
Falkirk 5 East Stirling 0
Hearts 4 Arbroath 2
Hibernian 3 Montrose 0
Livingston 1 Clyde 0 (aet)
Morton 5 Elgin 0
Queen's Park 0 Forfar 2
Rangers 3 Peterhead 0
Raith 3 Albion Rov 0
Stirling Alb 0 Airdrieonians 1
Stranraer 2 Stenhousemuir 0

SECOND ROUND

Airdrieonians 0 Rangers 5
Dunfermline 3 Dundee 1
East Fife 1 Motherwell 3 (aet)
Forfar 1 Hearts 2 (aet)
Hibernian 1 Stranraer 0
Kilmarnock 4 Berwick 1
Partick 0 Falkirk 1
Queen of South 0 Morton 1
Raith 2 Hamilton 1
Ross Co 2 Ayr 0
St Mirren 2 Livingston 3

THIRD ROUND

Celtic 2 Raith 0
Dundee Utd 3 Dunfermline 1 (aet)
Hibernian 2 Aberdeen 0
Kilmarnock 2 Hearts 3
Livingston 0 Inverness 2
Morton 3 Motherwell 2 (aet)
Rangers 1 St Johnstone 3
Ross Co 7 Falkirk 0

FOURTH ROUND

Hearts 1 Celtic 2
Hibernian 3 Dundee Utd 0
Inverness 1 **Ross Co** 2
Morton 1 St Johnstone 3

SEMI-FINALS

Hibernian 2 St Johnstone 1
at Tynecastle
Celtic 1 **Ross Co** 3
at Hampden Park

FINAL

HIBERNIAN 1 ROSS COUNTY 2

Hampden Park (38,796); Sunday, March 13, 2016

Hibernian (4-4-2): Oxley, Gray (capt), McGregor, Fontaine, Stevenson, Henderson, Bartley (Boyle 90), Thomson (Keatings 76), McGinn, Cummings, Stokes. **Subs not used**: Virtanen, El Alagui, Handling, Gunnarson, Dagnall. **Scorer**: Fontaine (45). **Booked**: Bartley, McGinn. **Manager**: Alan Stubbs.

Ross County (4-4-2): G Woods, Fraser, Quinn, Davies (capt), Foster (Franks 85), Gardyne, Irvine, M Woods, McShane (Murdoch 79), Boyce (Graham 59), Schalk. **Subs not used**: Konopka, Boyd, Robertson, De Vita. **Scorers**: Gardyne (25), Schalk (90). **Manager**: Jim McIntyre

Referee: K Clancy. **Half-time**: 1-1

SCOTTISH LEAGUE CUP FINALS

1946 Aberdeen beat Rangers (3-2)
1947 Rangers beat Aberdeen (4-0)
1948 East Fife beat Falkirk (4-1 after 0-0 draw)
1949 Rangers beat Raith Rov (2-0)
1950 East Fife beat Dunfermline Athletic (3-0)
1951 Motherwell beat Hibernian (3-0)
1952 Dundee beat Rangers (3-2)
1953 Dundee beat Kilmarnock (2-0)
1954 East Fife beat Partick (3-2)
1955 Hearts beat Motherwell (4-2)
1956 Aberdeen beat St Mirren (2-1)
1957 Celtic beat Partick (3-0 after 0-0 draw)
1958 Celtic beat Rangers (7-1)
1959 Hearts beat Partick (5-1)
1960 Hearts beat Third Lanark (2-1)
1961 Rangers beat Kilmarnock (2-0)
1962 Rangers beat Hearts (3-1 after 1-1 draw)
1963 Hearts beat Kilmarnock (1-0)
1964 Rangers beat Morton (5-0)
1965 Rangers beat Celtic (2-1)
1966 Celtic beat Rangers (2-1)
1967 Celtic beat Rangers (1-0)
1968 Celtic beat Dundee (5-3)
1969 Celtic beat Hibernian (6-2)
1970 Celtic beat St Johnstone (1-0)
1971 Rangers beat Celtic (1-0)
1972 Partick beat Celtic (4-1)
1973 Hibernian beat Celtic (2-1)
1974 Dundee beat Celtic (1-0)
1975 Celtic beat Hibernian (6-3)
1976 Rangers beat Celtic (1-0)
1977† Aberdeen beat Celtic (2-1)
1978† Rangers beat Celtic (2-1)
1979 Rangers beat Aberdeen (2-1)
1980 Dundee Utd beat Aberdeen (3-0 after 0-0 draw)
1981 Dundee Utd beat Dundee (3-0)
1982 Rangers beat Dundee Utd (2-1)
1983 Celtic beat Rangers (2-1)
1984† Rangers beat Celtic (3-2)
1985 Rangers beat Dundee Utd (1-0)
1986 Aberdeen beat Hibernian (3-0)
1987 Rangers beat Celtic (2-1)
1988† Rangers beat Aberdeen (5-3 on pens after 3-3 draw)
1989 Rangers beat Aberdeen (3-2)
1990† Aberdeen beat Rangers (2-1)
1991† Rangers beat Celtic (2-1)
1992 Hibernian beat Dunfermline Athletic (2-0)
1993† Rangers beat Aberdeen (2-1)
1994 Rangers beat Hibernian (2-1)
1995 Raith Rov beat Celtic (6-5 on pens after 2-2 draw)
1996 Aberdeen beat Dundee (2-0)
1997 Rangers beat Hearts (4-3)
1998 Celtic beat Dundee Utd (3-0)

1999 Rangers beat St Johnstone (2-1)
2000 Celtic beat Aberdeen (2-0)
2001 Celtic beat Kilmarnock (3-0)
2002 Rangers beat Ayr (4-0)
2003 Rangers beat Celtic (2-1)
2004 Livingston beat Hibernian (2-0)
2005 Rangers beat Motherwell (5-1)
2006 Celtic beat Dunfermline Athletic (3-0)
2007 Hibernian beat Kilmarnock (5-1)
2008 Rangers beat Dundee Utd (3-2 on pens after 2-2 draw)
2009† Celtic beat Rangers (2-0)
2010 Rangers beat St Mirren (1-0)
2011† Rangers beat Celtic (2-1)
2012 Kilmarnock beat Celtic (1-0)
2013 St Mirren beat Hearts (3-2)
2014 Aberdeen beat Inverness Caledonian Thistle (4-2 on pens after 0-0 draw)
2015 Celtic beat Dundee Utd (2-0)
2016 Ross Co beat Hibernian (2-1)
(† After extra time; Skol Cup 1985-93, Coca-Cola Cup 1995-97, Co-operative Insurance Cup 1999 onwards)

SUMMARY OF SCOTTISH LEAGUE CUP WINNERS

Rangers	27	East Fife	3	Motherwell	1
Celtic	15	Hibernian	3	Partick	1
Aberdeen	7	Dundee Utd	2	Raith	1
Hearts	4	Kilmarnock	2	Ross Co	1
Dundee	3	Livingston	1	St Mirren	1

PETROFAC TRAINING CUP 2015–16

First round north: Arbroath 1 Dunfermline 4; Brechin 0 Peterhead 3; Brora 0 Alloa 1; Cowdenbeath 0 Raith 1; East Stirling 2 Stenhousemuir 3; Elgin 3 Stirling Alb 2; Falkirk 3 East Fife 1; Forfar 1 Montrose 0

First round south: Annan 3 Airdrie 1; Ayr 3 Albion Rov 1; Edinburgh City 0 Queens's Park 0 (aet, Queen's Park won 3-1 on agg); Hibernian 2 Rangers 6; Livingston 2 Clyde 1; Morton 2 Dumbarton 3; Queen of South 2 Stranraer 0; St Mirren 3 Berwick 1

Second round: Alloa 0 Elgin 2; Annan 1 St Mirren 2; Ayr 0 Rangers 2; Falkirk 3 Peterhead 5; Forfar 0 Dunfermline 3; Queen of South 0 Livingston 1 (aet); Queen's Park 1 Dumbarton 0; Stenhousemuir 2 Raith 0

Third round: Peterhead 3 Stenhousemuir 0; Queen's Park 2 Elgin 1; Rangers 1 Livingston 0; St Mirren 4 Dunfermline 0

Semi-finals: Queen's Park 1 (Woods 22 pen) Peterhead 2 (McAllister 17, McIntosh 27). Att: 917. Rangers 4 (Holt 34, Miller 77, Waghorn 84, Kelly 90 og) St Mirren 0. Att: 22,369

FINAL

RANGERS 4 PETERHEAD 0

Hampden Park (48,133); Sunday, April 10 2016

Rangers (4-4-2): Foderingham, Tavernier, Kiernan, Wilson, Wallace (capt) (O'Halloran 67), Holt, Ball, Halliday, Forrester (King 67), Miller, McKay (Shiels 78). **Subs not used**: Bell, Law, Zelalem, Clark. **Scorers**: Gilchrist (17 og), Tavernier (40), Halliday (85 pen), Miller (89). **Booked**: Wilson. **Manager**: Mark Warburton

Peterhead (4-4-2): Smith, Strachan (Stevenson 26), Ross, Gilchrist, Noble (capt), Redman McIntosh 64), Ferry, Dzierzawski, Brown, Sutherland (Riley 58), McAllister. **Subs not used**: Jarvie, Blockley, Ferries, Rodgers. **Booked**: Ross, Noble, Dzierzawski, Riley. **Manager**: Jim McNally

Referee: G Salmond. **Half-time**: 2-0

WILLIAM HILL SCOTTISH FA CUP 2015–16

FIRST ROUND

Banks O'Dee 2 Cove 3
BSC Glasgow 2 Auchinleck 2
Buckie 7 Rothes 0
Deveronvale 0 Clachnacuddin 5
Formartine 3 Gretna 1
Fraserburgh 3 Dalbeattie 2
Gala 0 Linlithgow 2
Hawick 0 Huntly 3
Keith 1 Inverurie 5
Lossiemouth 1 Forres 4
Lothian 3 Kelty 0
Nairn 5 Selkirk 0
Preston 2 Fort William 3
Spartans 5 Coldstream 1
Strathspey 1 Edinburgh City 2
Threave 1 Stirling Univ 3
Wick 2 Whitehill 2
Cumbernauld 3 Glasgow Univ 0

Replays

Auchinleck 5 BSC Glasgow 0
Whitehill 2 Wick 3

SECOND ROUND

Annan 4 Berwick 1
Brora 1 Arbroath 2
Clachnacuddin 1 Linlithgow 3
Cumbernauld 2 Auchinleck 0
East Fife 0 Stirling Alb 0
East Kilbride 1 Forres 1
Edinburgh City 1 Buckie 2
Elgin 1 Spartans 0
Formartine 2 Clyde 0
Fort William 0 Cove 4
Huntly 2 East Stirling 1
Inverurie 2 Edinburgh Univ 1
Lothian 1 Montrose 1
Nairn 2 Wick 2
Stirling Univ 0 Queen's Park 2.
Turriff 2 Fraserburgh 3

Replays

Forres 2 East Kilbride 3
Montrose 1 Lothian 2 (aet)
Stirling Alb 1 East Fife 0
Wick 5 Nairn 2

THIRD ROUND

Airdrieonians 3 Brechin 1
Albion Rov 0 Morton 2
Ayr 0 Dunfermline 1
Cowdenbeath 1 Arbroath 1
Dumbarton 5 Alloa 0
Elgin 1 Raith 2
Falkirk 4 Fraserburgh 1
Formartine 1 Cove 1
Huntly 1 Lothian 1
Inverurie 4 Annan 4
Peterhead 1 Livingston 3
Queen's Park 1 Forfar 1
Stenhousemuir 2 East Kilbride 2
Stirling Alb 6 Cumbernauld 0
Stranraer 3 Buckie 1
Wick 2 Linlithgow 2

Replays

Annan 1 Inverurie 0
Arbroath 2 Cowdenbeath 4
Cove 4 Formartine 1
East Kilbride 2 Stenhousemuir 1 (aet)
Forfar 2 Queen's Park 1
Linlithgow 5 Wick 1
Lothian 3 Huntly 0

FOURTH ROUND

Airdrieonians 0 Dundee Utd 1
Annan 4 Hamilton 1
Dumbarton 2 Queen of South 1
Dundee 3 Falkirk 1
Dunfermline 2 Ross Co 2
East Kilbride 2 Lothian 0
Hearts 1 Aberdeen 0
Linlithgow 3 Forfar 3
Livingston 0 Morton 1
Motherwell 5 Cove 0
Raith 0 **Hibernian** 2
Rangers 5 Cowdenbeath 1
St Johnstone 0 Kilmarnock 1
St Mirren 1 Partick 2
Stirling Alb 0 Inverness 0
Stranraer 0 Celtic 3

Replays

Inverness 2 Stirling Alb 0
Forfar 0 Linlithgow 1
Ross Co 1 Dumfermline 0

FIFTH ROUND

Annan 1 Morton 4
Dumbarton 0 Dundee 0
Dundee Utd 1 Partick 0
East Kilbride 0 Celtic 2
Hearts 2 **Hibernian** 2
Motherwell 1 Inverness 2
Rangers 0 Kilmarnock 0
Ross Co 4 Linlithgow 2
Replays
Dundee 5 Dumbarton 0
Hibernian 1 Hearts 0
Kilmarnock 1 **Rangers** 2

SIXTH ROUND

Celtic 3 Morton 0
Hibernian 1 Inverness 1
Rangers 4 Dundee 0
Ross Co 2 Dundee Utd 3
Replay
Inverness 1 **Hibernian** 2

SEMI-FINALS (both at Hampden Park)

Dundee Utd 0 **Hibernian** 0
(aet, **Hibernian** won 4-2 on pens)
Rangers 2 Celtic 2
(aet, **Rangers** won 5-4 on pens)

FINAL

RANGERS 2 HIBERNIAN 3
Hampden Park (50,701); Saturday, May 21 2016

Rangers (4-1-4-1): Foderingham, Tavernier, Kiernan, Wilson, Wallace (capt), Zelalem (Shiels 62), Halliday, Holt, Waghorn (Clark 74), Miller, McKay. **Subs not used**: Bell, Law, Burt. **Scorers**: Miller (27), Halliday (63). **Booked:** Tavernier. **Manager**: Mark Warburton

Hibernian (3-5-2): Logan, McGregor, Hanlon (Gunnarsson 82), Fontaine (Henderson 69), Gray (capt), Fyvie, McGeouch, McGinn, Stevenson, Stokes, Cummings (Keatings 64). **Subs not used**: Oxley, Bartley, Boyle, Dagnall. **Scorers**: Stokes (3, 80), Gray (90,). **Booked**: Fyvie. **Manager**: Alan Stubbs

Referee: S McLean. **Half-time**: 1-1

SCOTTISH FA CUP FINALS

1874 Queen's Park beat Clydesdale (2-0)
1875 Queen's Park beat Renton (3-0)
1876 Queen's Park beat Third Lanark (2-0 after 1-1 draw)
1877 Vale of Leven beat Rangers (3-2 after 0-0, 1-1 draws)
1878 Vale of Leven beat Third Lanark (1-0)
1879 Vale of Leven awarded Cup (Rangers withdrew after 1-1 draw)
1880 Queen's Park beat Thornlibank (3-0)
1881 Queen's Park beat Dumbarton (3-1)
1882 Queen's Park beat Dumbarton (4-1 after 2-2 draw)
1883 Dumbarton beat Vale of Leven (2-1 after 2-2 draw)
1884 Queen's Park awarded Cup (Vale of Leven withdrew from Final)
1885 Renton beat Vale of Leven (3-1 after 0-0 draw)
1886 Queen's Park beat Renton (3-1)
1887 Hibernian beat Dumbarton (2-1)
1888 Renton beat Cambuslang (6-1)
1889 Third Lanark beat Celtic (2-1)
1890 Queen's Park beat Vale of Leven (2-1 after 1-1 draw)
1891 Hearts beat Dumbarton (1-0)
1892 Celtic beat Queen's Park (5-1)
1893 Queen's Park beat Celtic (2-1)
1894 Rangers beat Celtic (3-1)
1895 St Bernard's beat Renton (2-1)
1896 Hearts beat Hibernian (3-1)
1897 Rangers beat Dumbarton (5-1)

1898 Rangers beat Kilmarnock (2-0)
1899 Celtic beat Rangers (2-0)
1900 Celtic beat Queen's Park (4-3)
1901 Hearts beat Celtic (4-3)
1902 Hibernian beat Celtic (1-0)
1903 Rangers beat Hearts (2-0 after 0-0, 1-1 draws)
1904 Celtic beat Rangers (3-2)
1905 Third Lanark beat Rangers (3-1 after 0-0 draw)
1906 Hearts beat Third Lanark (1-0)
1907 Celtic beat Hearts (3-0)
1908 Celtic beat St Mirren (5-1)
1909 Cup withheld because of riot after two drawn games in final between Celtic and Rangers (2-2, 1-1)
1910 Dundee beat Clyde (2-1 after 2-2, 0-0 draws)
1911 Celtic beat Hamilton (2-0 after 0-0 draw)
1912 Celtic beat Clyde (2-0)
1913 Falkirk beat Raith (2-0)
1914 Celtic beat Hibernian (4-1 after 0-0 draw)
1915–19 No competition (World War 1)
1920 Kilmarnock beat Albion (3-2)
1921 Partick beat Rangers (1-0)
1922 Morton beat Rangers (1-0)
1923 Celtic beat Hibernian (1-0)
1924 Airdrieonians beat Hibernian (2-0)
1925 Celtic beat Dundee (2-1)
1926 St Mirren beat Celtic (2-0)
1927 Celtic beat East Fife (3-1)
1928 Rangers beat Celtic (4-0)
1929 Kilmarnock beat Rangers (2-0)
1930 Rangers beat Partick (2-1 after 0-0 draw)
1931 Celtic beat Motherwell (4-2 after 2-2 draw)
1932 Rangers beat Kilmarnock (3-0 after 1-1 draw)
1933 Celtic beat Motherwell (1-0)
1934 Rangers beat St Mirren (5-0)
1935 Rangers beat Hamilton (2-1)
1936 Rangers beat Third Lanark (1-0)
1937 Celtic beat Aberdeen (2-1)
1938 East Fife beat Kilmarnock (4-2 after 1-1 draw)
1939 Clyde beat Motherwell (4-0)
1940–6 No competition (World War 2)
1947 Aberdeen beat Hibernian (2-1)
1948† Rangers beat Morton (1-0 after 1-1 draw)
1949 Rangers beat Clyde (4-1)
1950 Rangers beat East Fife (3-0)
1951 Celtic beat Motherwell (1-0)
1952 Motherwell beat Dundee (4-0)
1953 Rangers beat Aberdeen (1-0 after 1-1 draw)
1954 Celtic beat Aberdeen (2-1)
1955 Clyde beat Celtic (1-0 after 1-1 draw)
1956 Hearts beat Celtic (3-1)
1957† Falkirk beat Kilmarnock (2-1 after 1-1 draw)
1958 Clyde beat Hibernian (1-0)
1959 St Mirren beat Aberdeen (3-1)
1960 Rangers beat Kilmarnock (2-0)
1961 Dunfermline beat Celtic (2-0 after 0-0 draw)
1962 Rangers beat St Mirren (2-0)
1963 Rangers beat Celtic (3-0 after 1-1 draw)
1964 Rangers beat Dundee (3-1)
1965 Celtic beat Dunfermline (3-2)

1966 Rangers beat Celtic (1-0 after 0-0 draw)
1967 Celtic beat Aberdeen (2-0)
1968 Dunfermline beat Hearts (3-1)
1969 Celtic beat Rangers (4-0)
1970 Aberdeen beat Celtic (3-1)
1971 Celtic beat Rangers (2-1 after 1-1 draw)
1972 Celtic beat Hibernian (6-1)
1973 Rangers beat Celtic (3-2)
1974 Celtic beat Dundee Utd (3-0)
1975 Celtic beat Airdrieonians (3-1)
1976 Rangers beat Hearts (3-1)
1977 Celtic beat Rangers (1-0)
1978 Rangers beat Aberdeen (2-1)
1979† Rangers beat Hibernian (3-2 after two 0-0 draws)
1980† Celtic beat Rangers (1-0)
1981 Rangers beat Dundee Utd (4-1 after 0-0 draw)
1982† Aberdeen beat Rangers (4-1)
1983† Aberdeen beat Rangers (1-0)
1984† Aberdeen beat Celtic (2-1)
1985 Celtic beat Dundee Utd (2-1)
1986 Aberdeen beat Hearts (3-0)
1987† St Mirren beat Dundee Utd (1-0)
1988 Celtic beat Dundee Utd (2-1)
1989 Celtic beat Rangers (1-0)
1990† Aberdeen beat Celtic (9-8 on pens after 0-0 draw)
1991† Motherwell beat Dundee Utd (4-3)
1992 Rangers beat Airdrieonians (2-1)
1993 Rangers beat Aberdeen (2-1)
1994 Dundee Utd beat Rangers (1-0)
1995 Celtic beat Airdrieonians (1-0)
1996 Rangers beat Hearts (5-1)
1997 Kilmarnock beat Falkirk (1-0)
1998 Hearts beat Rangers (2-1)
1999 Rangers beat Celtic (1-0)
2000 Rangers beat Aberdeen (4-0)
2001 Celtic beat Hibernian (3-0)
2002 Rangers beat Celtic (3-2)
2003 Rangers beat Dundee (1-0)
2004 Celtic beat Dunfermline (3-1)
2005 Celtic beat Dundee Utd (1-0)
2006† Hearts beat Gretna (4-2 on pens after 1-1 draw)
2007 Celtic beat Dunfermline (1-0)
2008 Rangers beat Queen of the South (3-2)
2009 Rangers beat Falkirk (1-0)
2010 Dundee Utd beat Ross Co (3-0)
2011 Celtic beat Motherwell (3-0)
2012 Hearts beat Hibernian (5-1)
2013 Celtic beat Hibernian (3-0)
2014 St Johnstone beat Dundee Utd (2-0)
2015 Inverness beat Falkirk (2-1)
2016 Hibernian beat Rangers (3-2)
† After extra time

SUMMARY OF SCOTTISH CUP WINNERS

Celtic 36, Rangers 33, Queen's Park 10, Hearts 8, Aberdeen 7, Clyde 3, Hibernian 3, Kilmarnock 3, St Mirren 3, Vale of Leven 3, Dundee Utd 2, Dunfermline 2, Falkirk 2, Motherwell 2, Renton 2, Third Lanark 2, Airdrieonians 1, Dumbarton 1, Dundee 1, East Fife 1, Inverness 1, Morton 1, Partick 1, St Bernard's 1, St Johnstone 1

VANARAMA NATIONAL LEAGUE 2015–2016

			Home					Away						
		P	*W*	*D*	*L*	*F*	*A*	*W*	*D*	*L*	*F*	*A*	*GD*	*PTS*
1	Cheltenham	46	17	5	1	49	13	13	6	4	38	17	57	101
2	Forest Green	46	15	3	5	37	17	11	8	4	32	25	27	89
3	Braintree	46	13	6	4	24	12	10	6	7	32	26	18	81
4	Grimsby*	46	13	6	4	44	17	9	8	6	38	28	37	80
5	Dover	46	13	5	5	43	22	10	6	7	32	31	22	80
6	Tranmere	46	12	2	9	31	23	10	10	3	30	21	17	78
7	Eastleigh	46	13	5	5	32	23	8	7	8	32	30	11	75
8	Wrexham	46	13	4	6	48	27	7	5	11	23	29	15	69
9	Gateshead	46	9	4	10	33	39	10	6	7	26	31	-11	67
10	Macclesfield	46	10	5	8	28	21	9	4	10	32	27	12	66
11	Barrow	46	11	8	4	38	26	6	6	11	26	45	-7	65
12	Woking	46	9	7	7	36	29	8	3	12	35	39	3	61
13	Lincoln	46	10	7	6	37	25	6	6	11	32	43	1	61
14	Bromley	46	11	4	8	38	26	6	5	12	29	46	-5	60
15	Aldershot	46	7	4	12	23	31	9	4	10	31	41	-18	56
16	Southport	46	6	7	10	34	44	8	6	9	18	21	-13	55
17	Chester	46	9	8	6	43	29	5	4	14	24	42	-4	54
18	Torquay	46	7	5	11	26	33	6	7	10	28	43	-22	51
19	Boreham Wood	46	5	7	11	18	24	7	7	9	26	25	-5	50
20	Guiseley	46	8	7	8	33	38	3	9	11	14	32	-23	49
21	Halifax	46	6	10	7	35	43	6	2	15	20	39	-27	48
22	Altrincham	46	8	9	6	34	30	2	5	16	14	43	-25	44
23	Kidderminster	46	5	7	11	21	29	4	6	13	28	42	-22	40
24	Welling	46	5	6	12	21	33	3	5	15	14	40	-38	35

*Also promoted

Player of Year: Dan Holman (Cheltenham). **Manager of Year:** Gary Johnson (Cheltenham)
Leading league scorers: 30 Amond (Grimsby), Holman (Cheltenham – 14 for Woking); 24 Cook (Barrow); 22 Dennis (Macclesfield), Hannah (Chester), Wright (Cheltenham); 20 Ademola (Bromley), Miller (Dover), Rhead (Lincoln)
Team of Year: McKeown (Grimsby), Jennings (Forest Green), Habergham (Braintree), Parslow (Cheltenham), Gowling (Grimsby), Storer (Cheltenham), Pell (Cheltenham), Deverdics (Dover), Amond (Grimsby), Holman (Cheltenham), Frear (Forest Green)

CHAMPIONS

1979–80	Altrincham	1993–94	Kidderminster	2007–08*	Aldershot
1980–81	Altrincham	1994–95	Macclesfield	2008–09*	Burton
1981–82	Runcorn	1995–96	Stevenage	2009–10*	Stevenage
1982–83	Enfield	1996–97*	Macclesfield	2010–11*	Crawley
1983–84	Maidstone	1997–98*	Halifax	2011–2012*	Fleetwood
1984–85	Wealdstone	1998–99*	Cheltenham	2012–13*	Mansfield
1985–86	Enfield	1999–2000*	Kidderminster	2013–14*	Luton
1986–87*	Scarborough	2000–01*	Rushden	2014–15*	Barnet
1987–88*	Lincoln	2001–02*	Boston	2015–16*	Cheltenham
1988–89*	Maidstone	2002–03*	Yeovil		
1989–90*	Darlington	2003–04*	Chester		
1990–91*	Barnet	2004–05*	Barnet		
1991–92*	Colchester	2005–06*	Accrington		
1992–93*	Wycombe	2006–07*	Dagenham		

*Promoted to Football League

Conference – Record attendance: 11,085 Bristol Rov v Alfreton, April 25, 2015

VANARAMA NATIONAL LEAGUE RESULTS 2015–2016

	Aldershot	Altrincham	Barrow	Boreham Wood	Braintree	Bromley	Cheltenham	Chester	Dover	Eastleigh	Forest Green	Gateshead	Grimsby	Guiseley	Halifax	K'minster	Lincoln	Macclesfield	Southport	Torquay	Tranmere	Welling	Woking	Wrexham
Aldershot	–	2-0	0-1	1-2	2-1	1-1	0-2	3-1	1-1	1-2	0-3	1-2	3-4	1-0	3-2	1-0	1-2	0-3	1-2	0-0	0-0	1-0	0-1	0-1
Altrincham	4-0	–	1-0	1-0	0-4	0-0	2-1	0-3	1-2	1-1	0-1	2-3	2-1	1-1	1-3	2-2	3-3	0-0	1-1	1-1	2-1	5-0	3-1	1-1
Barrow	1-3	3-2	–	0-0	2-0	1-1	1-2	3-2	2-1	1-0	2-2	0-0	1-3	1-1	4-1	1-1	1-0	1-1	1-0	4-0	3-4	1-1	2-1	2-0
Boreham Wood	0-1	0-1	0-2	–	1-0	2-3	0-0	0-0	3-0	1-1	0-1	2-3	1-3	1-0	3-1	0-2	1-1	0-0	0-2	0-1	0-0	2-0	1-1	0-1
Braintree	1-2	3-0	1-1	0-2	–	1-0	1-0	2-0	1-0	2-0	1-1	0-0	0-0	0-1	2-0	2-1	1-3	1-0	1-0	0-0	0-0	1-0	2-1	1-0
Bromley	1-3	1-3	5-0	1-2	1-2	–	1-2	3-0	1-1	2-2	2-2	3-0	1-2	2-0	1-0	3-2	2-0	1-0	0-0	0-2	0-1	2-0	2-1	3-1
Cheltenham	0-0	1-0	2-1	4-1	1-1	4-1	–	3-1	3-2	1-1	1-1	0-0	3-1	5-0	2-0	2-0	3-1	2-0	3-0	1-0	0-1	2-0	4-0	2-1
Chester	8-2	1-1	1-2	2-2	1-0	1-1	1-1	–	1-1	1-0	1-2	4-2	1-1	1-1	2-1	3-1	2-3	0-2	0-0	4-1	0-1	4-0	1-2	3-2
Dover.	5-2	2-1	3-1	2-1	0-0	2-3	1-2	0-0	–	1-2	0-1	4-0	1-1	0-0	1-0	3-2	4-1	2-1	1-2	5-0	0-0	2-1	2-0	2-1
Eastleigh	1-1	2-0	3-1	1-0	0-2	2-0	1-0	1-0	2-5	–	3-2	1-2	0-1	1-1	2-1	3-1	1-1	1-0	1-0	3-2	0-1	0-0	2-1	1-1
Forest Green	0-0	2-0	4-0	1-0	1-0	2-1	2-2	2-1	3-1	2-1	–	0-1	0-1	3-0	0-1	3-0	3-1	2-1	2-1	3-1	0-2	1-0	1-2	0-0
Gateshead	3-2	2-2	1-1	2-1	2-3	3-1	1-1	1-0	2-3	2-1	0-1	–	1-0	3-0	1-4	1-1	2-0	0-3	0-1	1-2	1-4	1-2	1-5	2-1
Grimsby	4-1	5-0	4-1	0-0	0-1	4-1	0-1	1-2	1-0	0-0	1-1	2-1	–	1-1	7-0	1-0	2-0	0-2	1-0	2-2	1-1	3-1	3-1	1-0
Guiseley	0-4	1-0	3-1	1-1	1-1	2-0	0-2	3-3	0-1	1-4	0-1	0-2	2-2	–	2-1	1-0	0-1	0-3	1-1	4-3	2-2	2-0	4-4	3-1
Halifax	0-2	1-0	3-1	3-2	3-6	2-2	1-7	0-1	4-2	0-0	0-2	1-1	4-2	1-1	–	1-1	2-2	1-1	2-2	2-3	1-1	1-1	0-3	2-0
K'minster	2-0	1-1	0-0	1-1	0-1	0-1	1-2	2-2	1-1	3-2	0-2	0-1	2-2	0-1	1-0	–	0-2	3-1	0-1	2-2	0-2	0-1	1-0	1-3
Lincoln	2-0	1-1	2-2	3-1	2-0	0-1	1-1	2-1	2-3	3-0	0-1	1-1	1-1	1-0	0-1	1-2	–	5-3	3-1	2-0	1-0	1-1	2-3	1-1
Macclesfield	0-2	3-0	1-2	0-0	3-1	2-0	0-1	1-2	0-0	1-2	4-1	1-0	2-1	1-0	0-1	2-1	1-1	–	0-0	1-2	1-2	2-1	2-1	0-0
Southport	1-1	3-0	2-1	0-3	1-1	5-3	0-4	1-2	0-0	0-4	0-1	1-2	0-4	2-0	0-1	3-4	2-2	3-1	–	0-1	2-2	3-3	2-2	3-2
Torquay	0-2	2-0	2-2	1-2	0-0	3-7	0-3	2-0	2-3	0-1	4-1	0-2	1-1	1-1	0-0	3-2	1-3	1-0	1-0	–	0-1	2-0	0-1	0-1
Tranmere	3-1	1-0	0-1	0-2	1-2	4-0	0-1	2-0	0-1	1-2	1-1	3-1	1-0	2-1	1-0	2-2	3-2	0-1	1-0	2-1	–	1-2	1-0	1-2
Welling	0-1	1-1	1-2	0-3	1-2	1-2	1-1	2-1	1-2	2-2	1-1	0-1	0-4	1-0	2-0	1-2	2-1	0-1	0-1	1-1	1-1	–	2-1	0-2
Woking	2-1	2-0	2-2	0-0	1-1	2-0	0-1	5-2	0-1	2-1	2-1	1-1	1-3	0-1	1-1	1-1	3-1	2-5	1-2	2-2	4-1	2-0	–	0-1
Wrexham	3-0	3-1	4-1	1-0	2-3	2-0	2-1	3-0	0-1	2-3	2-2	4-0	0-0	3-3	3-1	2-0	3-1	2-3	0-1	3-1	2-2	1-0	1-3	–

NATIONAL LEAGUE NORTH

			Home					Away						
		P	W	D	L	F	A	W	D	L	F	A	GD	PTS
1	Solihull	42	14	1	6	39	21	11	9	1	45	27	36	85
2	North Ferriby*	42	13	5	3	41	14	9	5	7	41	35	33	76
3	Fylde	42	11	4	6	41	26	11	5	5	35	27	23	75
4	Harrogate	42	11	6	4	42	21	10	3	8	31	25	27	72
5	Boston	42	12	3	6	37	27	10	2	9	36	33	13	71
6	Nuneaton **	42	8	9	4	27	17	12	4	5	44	29	25	70
7	Tamworth	42	9	9	3	28	18	7	6	8	27	27	10	63
8	Chorley	42	11	5	5	36	21	7	4	10	28	34	9	63
9	Stockport	42	6	7	8	24	28	9	7	5	26	21	1	59
10	Alfreton	42	6	6	9	26	29	9	7	5	32	25	4	58
11	Curzon	42	9	6	6	29	25	5	9	7	26	27	3	57
12	Stalybridge	42	7	7	7	35	38	7	4	10	27	37	-13	53
13	FC United	42	8	4	9	38	37	7	4	10	22	38	-15	53
14	Bradford PA	42	10	6	5	37	28	3	5	13	14	31	-8	50
15	Gloucester	42	7	5	9	20	23	5	9	7	19	26	-10	50
16	Gainsborough	42	8	6	7	24	27	6	2	13	22	35	-16	50
17	Worcester	42	7	7	7	34	27	5	5	11	21	34	-6	48
18	Telford	42	9	4	8	28	27	4	4	13	19	33	-13	47
19	Brackley	42	7	6	8	27	27	4	7	10	18	27	-9	46
20	Lowestoft	42	8	6	7	28	27	4	4	13	20	42	-21	46
21	Hednesford	42	5	6	10	26	38	3	8	10	24	39	-27	38
22	Corby	42	4	3	14	27	51	3	8	10	20	42	-46	32

* Also promoted. ** 3pts deduucted for ineligible player. Play-off Final: North Ferriby 2 Fylde 1 (aet)

NATIONAL LEAGUE SOUTH

			Home					Away						
		P	W	D	L	F	A	W	D	L	F	A	GD	PTS
1	Sutton	42	11	8	2	42	19	15	4	2	41	13	51	90
2	Ebbsfleet	42	11	6	4	40	22	13	6	2	33	14	37	84
3	Maidstone *	42	12	2	7	29	22	12	3	6	26	18	15	77
4	Truro	42	10	4	7	34	32	7	10	4	28	23	7	65
5	Whitehawk	42	9	3	9	32	24	9	7	5	43	38	13	64
6	Hemel Hempstead	42	7	7	7	33	30	9	6	6	39	36	6	61
7	Maidenhead	42	11	7	3	36	21	5	4	12	30	41	4	59
8	Dartford	42	8	7	6	35	27	8	4	9	23	29	2	59
9	Gosport	42	8	6	7	31	34	7	5	9	22	29	-10	56
10	Concord	42	6	4	11	29	32	9	6	6	37	36	-2	55
11	Bishop's St	42	10	2	9	30	26	5	8	8	26	37	-7	55
12	Oxford	42	6	9	6	36	30	7	6	8	34	30	10	54
13	Wealdstone	42	6	10	5	37	31	6	7	8	26	33	-1	53
14	Bath	42	8	5	8	25	26	6	6	9	25	35	-11	53
15	Chelmsford	42	9	2	10	42	35	6	5	10	24	29	2	52
16	Weston-S-M	42	8	3	10	31	38	6	6	9	32	38	-13	51
17	Eastbourne	42	7	8	6	32	25	6	3	12	28	38	-3	50
18	St Albans	42	9	5	7	41	26	4	5	12	17	39	-7	49
19	Margate	42	7	4	10	25	34	6	4	11	26	39	-22	47
20	Havant	42	10	4	7	30	25	2	7	12	22	50	-23	47
21	Hayes	42	3	9	9	25	45	8	4	9	26	31	-25	46
22	Basingstoke	42	6	6	9	24	27	3	5	13	22	42	-23	38

* Also promoted. Play-off Final: Maidstone 2 Ebbsfleet 2 (aet, Maidstone won 4-3 on pens)

OTHER LEAGUES 2015–16

DAFABET WELSH PREMIER LEAGUE

	P	W	D	L	F	A	GD	Pts
New Saints	32	18	10	4	72	24	48	64
Bala	32	15	12	5	48	27	21	57
Llandudno	32	15	7	10	53	46	7	52
Connah's Quay	32	15	3	14	50	42	8	48
Newtown	32	11	9	12	46	54	-8	42
Airbus	32	12	6	14	46	55	-9	42
Carmarthen	32	14	5	13	45	52	-7	47
Aberystwyth	32	13	7	12	51	47	4	46
Bangor	32	13	6	13	49	52	-3	45
Port Talbot	32	10	9	13	39	56	-17	39
Rhyl	32	5	12	15	36	50	-14	27
Haverfordwest	32	5	6	21	27	57	-30	21

League split after 22 games, with teams playing ten further games and remaining in top six and bottom six regardless of results

Cup Final: New Saints 2 Denbigh 0

RYMAN PREMIER LEAGUE

	P	W	D	L	F	A	GD	Pts
Hampton & Richmond	46	28	11	7	105	52	53	95
Bognor Regis	46	29	7	10	95	42	53	94
East Thurrock*	46	26	13	7	107	53	54	91
Tonbridge	46	24	13	9	90	49	41	85
Dulwich Hamlet	46	23	12	11	93	58	35	81
Enfield	46	24	8	14	74	47	27	80
Kingstonian	46	21	10	15	78	64	14	73
Leiston	46	20	12	14	72	57	15	72
Billericay	46	18	17	11	76	53	23	71
Merstham	46	18	8	20	74	80	-6	62
Leatherhead	46	18	8	20	67	81	-14	62
Met Police	46	17	10	19	60	79	-19	61
Wingate & Finchley	46	17	9	20	66	70	-4	60
Canvey Is	46	17	9	20	69	89	-20	60
Grays	46	15	12	19	63	74	-11	57
Staines	46	15	10	21	53	74	-21	55
Harrow	46	15	9	22	66	80	-14	54
Farnborough	46	16	5	25	65	88	-23	53
Hendon	46	13	13	20	68	85	-17	52
Needham Market	46	13	12	21	51	76	-25	51
Burgess Hill	46	12	14	20	57	73	-16	50
Brentwood	46	10	10	26	51	80	-29	40
Lewes	46	6	16	24	48	87	-39	34
VCD	46	8	10	28	46	103	-57	34

*Also promoted. Play-off Final: East Thurrock 3 Dulwich Hamlet 1

EVOSTICK NORTH PREMIER LEAGUE

	P	*W*	*D*	*L*	*F*	*A*	*GD*	*PTS*
Darlington	46	33	5	8	106	42	64	104
Blyth	46	32	3	11	89	41	48	99
Salford*	46	27	9	10	94	48	46	90
Ashton	46	26	9	11	90	52	38	87
Workington	46	25	11	10	78	50	28	86
Stourbridge	46	25	9	12	90	63	27	84
Frickley	46	22	11	13	69	46	23	77
Nantwich	46	20	15	11	94	62	32	75
Barwell	46	23	4	19	82	66	16	73
Rushall	46	19	12	15	74	61	13	69
Buxton	46	21	4	21	71	74	-3	67
Sutton Coldfield	46	17	11	18	59	66	-7	62
Halesowen	46	17	11	18	53	63	-10	62
Ilkeston	46	15	9	22	61	79	-18	54
Marine	46	12	17	17	53	61	-8	53
Skelmersdale	46	14	11	21	66	82	-16	53
Matlock	46	14	10	22	59	79	-20	52
Grantham	46	13	12	21	51	85	-34	51
Whitby	46	12	11	23	60	79	-19	47
Mickleover	46	11	13	22	50	74	-24	46
Stamford	46	12	9	25	71	97	-26	45
Hyde	46	11	7	28	53	90	-37	40
Colwyn Bay	46	10	8	28	51	95	-44	38
Ramsbottom	46	5	11	30	43	112	-69	26

*Also promoted. Play-off Final: Salford 3 Workington 2

EVOSTICK SOUTH PREMIER LEAGUE

	P	*W*	*D*	*L*	*F*	*A*	*GD*	*Pts*
Poole	46	27	12	7	86	35	51	93
Redditch**	46	24	15	7	82	37	45	84
Hitchin	46	24	12	10	78	50	28	84
Hungerford*	46	24	11	11	73	43	30	83
Leamington	46	23	12	11	59	38	21	81
Kettering	46	24	8	14	83	53	30	80
Weymouth	46	21	14	11	63	39	24	77
Chippenham	46	21	13	12	76	53	23	76
King's Lynn	46	21	7	18	58	54	4	70
Merthyr	46	19	9	18	69	58	11	66
Chesham	46	18	10	18	72	70	2	64
Dunstable	46	17	11	18	68	68	0	62
Dorchester	46	18	8	20	67	69	-2	62
Biggleswade	46	17	9	20	76	82	-6	60
Cirencester	46	18	6	22	67	76	-9	60
Frome	46	14	16	16	51	73	-22	58
Slough	46	16	9	21	67	77	-10	57
Cambridge	46	15	7	24	63	80	-17	52
Stratford	46	13	11	22	59	68	-9	50
St Neots	46	10	18	18	69	78	-9	48
Bedworth	46	12	8	26	58	107	-49	44
Histon	46	11	7	28	63	98	-35	40
Bideford	46	8	13	25	38	88	-50	37
Paulton	46	8	12	26	38	89	-51	36

*Also promoted. **3 pts deducted for two ineligible players. Play-off Final: Hungerford 2 Leamington 1

PRESS AND JOURNAL HIGHLAND LEAGUE

	P	W	D	L	F	A	GD	Pts
Cove	34	29	2	3	98	28	70	89
Formartine	34	27	4	3	137	35	102	85
Brora	34	27	4	3	128	35	93	85
Turriff	34	20	8	6	88	31	57	68
Wick	34	18	6	10	76	42	34	60
Inverurie	34	18	4	12	71	43	28	58
Buckie	34	18	4	12	80	77	3	58
Nairn	34	17	6	11	75	55	20	57
Fraserburgh	34	15	8	11	63	49	14	53
Keith	34	17	1	16	70	76	-6	52
Forres	34	15	4	15	60	65	-5	49
Lossiemouth	34	12	2	20	46	70	-24	38
Deveronvale	34	8	8	18	46	64	-18	32
Clachnacuddin	34	10	2	22	59	80	-21	32
Huntly	34	7	5	22	49	89	-40	26
Strathspey	34	6	2	26	38	118	-80	20
Fort William	34	5	1	28	38	116	-78	16
Rothes	34	1	1	32	16	165	-149	4

Cup Final: Brora 0 Nairn 0 (aet, Brora won 5-4 on pens)

BARCLAYS UNDER-21 PREMIER LEAGUE

DIVISION ONE

	P	W	D	L	F	A	GD	Pts
Manchester Utd	22	15	3	4	44	19	25	48
Sunderland	22	13	4	5	38	20	18	43
Everton	22	10	7	5	35	27	8	37
Manchester City	22	10	4	8	35	26	9	34
Chelsea	22	9	6	7	34	30	4	33
Southampton	22	8	6	8	39	40	-1	30
Liverpool	22	8	4	10	26	37	-11	28
Tottenham	22	7	6	9	44	43	1	27
Reading	22	7	6	9	34	40	-6	27
Leicester	22	6	3	13	25	48	-23	21
Middlesbrough	22	5	5	12	33	37	-4	20
Norwich	22	5	4	13	30	50	-20	19

DIVISION TWO

	P	W	D	L	F	A	GD	Pts
Derby	22	13	3	6	44	26	18	42
Arsenal	22	12	4	6	40	25	15	40
Swansea	22	12	3	7	42	24	18	39
Aston Villa	22	11	6	5	28	27	1	39
Blackburn	22	10	4	8	29	33	-4	34
WBA	22	8	9	5	24	20	4	33
West Ham	22	9	5	8	37	34	3	32
Stoke	22	10	2	10	24	24	0	32
Fulham	22	8	5	9	26	29	-3	29
Newcastle	22	4	6	12	30	48	-18	18
Brighton	22	2	8	12	17	36	-19	14
Wolves	22	2	7	13	20	35	-15	13

Cup Final (on agg): West Ham 1 Hull 1 (aet, West Ham won 5-3 on pens)

FA WOMEN'S PREMIER LEAGUE

NORTH DIVISION

	P	W	D	L	F	A	GD	Pts
Sporting Club	22	17	2	3	55	22	33	53
Preston	22	15	4	3	71	20	51	49
Blackburn	22	14	4	4	39	20	19	46
Stoke	22	14	2	6	59	28	31	44
Bradford	22	12	2	8	48	31	17	38
Nottm Forest	22	11	4	7	37	27	10	37
Derby	22	9	1	12	37	47	-10	28
Huddersfield	22	7	4	11	47	56	-9	25
Newcastle	22	7	1	14	33	57	-24	22
Nuneaton	22	4	2	16	26	67	-41	14
Guiseley	22	3	4	15	26	71	-45	13
Loughborough	22	3	2	17	26	58	-32	11

SOUTH DIVISION

	P	W	D	L	F	A	GD	Pts
Brighton	22	17	3	2	58	18	40	54
Charlton	22	16	4	2	68	20	48	52
Cardiff	22	15	2	5	66	27	39	47
Coventry	22	13	5	4	64	18	46	44
Portsmouth	22	14	2	6	61	27	34	44
Tottenham	22	11	1	10	34	30	4	34
Lewes	22	8	1	13	30	42	-12	25
Basildon	22	7	4	11	38	55	-17	25
QPR	22	6	3	13	25	45	-20	21
West Ham	22	5	4	13	21	60	-39	19
Forest Green	22	2	2	18	19	76	-57	8
Plymouth	22	1	3	18	23	89	66	6

Play-off Final: Brighton 4 Sporting Club 2. Cup Final: Tottenham 2 Cardiff 1 (aet)

FA WOMEN'S SUPER LEAGUE 2015

	P	W	D	L	F	A	GD	Pts
Chelsea	14	10	2	2	30	10	20	32
Manchester City	14	9	3	2	25	11	14	30
Arsenal	14	8	3	3	21	13	8	27
Sunderland	14	6	2	6	24	20	0	20
Notts Co	14	4	3	7	20	20	0	15
Birmingham	14	3	4	7	7	14	-7	13
Liverpool	14	4	1	9	15	24	-9	13
Bristol Acad	14	2	2	10	12	38	-26	8

Continental Cup Final: Arsenal 3 Notts Co 0

IRISH FOOTBALL 2015–16

SSE AIRTRICITY LEAGUE OF IRELAND

PREMIER DIVISION

	P	W	D	L	F	A	Pts
Dundalk	33	23	9	1	78	23	78
Cork City	33	19	10	4	57	25	67
Shamrock Rov	33	18	11	4	56	27	65
St Patrick's Ath	33	18	4	11	52	34	58
Bohemians	33	15	8	10	49	42	53
Longford Town	33	10	9	14	41	53	39
Derry City	33	9	8	16	32	41	35
Bray Wdrs	33	9	6	18	27	51	33
Sligo Rov	33	7	10	16	39	55	31
Galway Utd	33	9	4	20	39	61	31
Limerick	33	7	8	18	45	72	29
Drogheda Utd	33	7	7	19	32	62	28

Leading scorer: 25 Richie Towell (Dundalk). **Player of Year**: Richie Towell. **Young Player of Year**: Brandon Miele (Shamrock Rov). **Goalkeeper of Year**: Gary Rogers (Dundalk). **Personality of Year**: Richie Towell

FIRST DIVISION

	P	W	D	L	F	A	Pts
Wexford Youths	28	20	1	7	63	32	61
Finn Harps	28	16	7	5	42	23	55
UCD	28	14	7	7	51	27	49
Shelbourne	28	13	6	9	37	34	45
Athlone Town	28	9	6	13	36	42	33
Cobh Ramblers	28	8	6	14	27	45	30
Waterford Utd	28	5	6	17	25	51	21
Cabinteely	28	5	5	18	23	50	20

Leading Scorer: 30 Danny Furlong (Wexford Youths). **Player of Year**: Danny Furlong

DAILY MAIL CUP FINAL

Dundalk 1 (Towell) **Cork City** 0. Aviva Stadium, November 8, 2015
Dundalk: Rogers, Gannon (O'Donnell), Gartland, Boyle, Massey, Shields, Towell, Meenan (Mountney), Finn, Horgan, McMillan (Kilduff)
Cork City: McNulty, Dunleavy, Bennett, D Dennehy, Gaynor, Miller (Healy), O'Connor, B Dennehy, Buckley, Sheppard (Murray), O'Sullivan (Morrissey)
Referee: D. McKeon (Dublin)

EA SPORTS LEAGUE CUP FINAL

Galway Utd 0 **St Patrick's Ath** 0 (aet, St Patrick's won 4-3 on pens). Eamon Deacy Park, Galway, September 19, 2015

DANSKE BANK PREMIERSHIP

	P	W	D	L	F	A	Pts
Crusaders	38	28	7	3	79	28	91
Linfield	38	26	5	7	91	35	83
Glenvavon	38	20	9	9	72	40	69
Cliftonville	38	18	10	10	58	53	64
Coleraine	38	18	4	16	47	46	58
Glentoran	38	15	7	16	46	55	52
Dungannon Swifts	38	12	7	19	51	66	43
Ballymena Utd	38	11	7	20	57	81	40
Portadown	38	11	5	22	43	67	38
Carrick Rgrs	38	8	11	19	43	68	35
Ballinamallard Utd	38	9	7	22	39	59	34
Warrenpoint Town	38	9	7	22	45	73	34

Leading scorer: 22 Paul Heatley Crusaders), Andy Waterworth (Linfield). **Manager of Year**: Stephen Baxter (Crusaders). **Player of Year**: Billy Joe Burns (Crusaders). **Young Player of Year**: Joel Cooper (Glenavon). **Goalkeeper of Year**: Jonny Tuffey(Glenavon)

BELFAST TELEGRAPH CHAMPIONSHIP – DIVISION ONE

	P	W	D	L	F	A	Pts
Ards	26	17	3	6	59	35	54
HW Welders	26	15	6	5	54	28	51
Armagh City	26	13	5	8	64	36	44
Knockbreda	26	12	7	7	48	32	43
Institute	26	12	6	8	40	20	42
Larne	26	12	6	8	64	45	42
Lurgan Celtic	26	11	6	9	40	40	39
Ballyclare Comrades	26	9	10	7	44	40	37
Loughall	26	10	6	10	45	54	36
Bangor	26	10	5	11	44	40	35
Dergview	26	9	8	9	41	40	35
Annagh Utd	26	7	6	13	37	57	27
Donegal Celtic	26	2	4	20	34	80	10
Lisburn Distillery	26	2	4	20	18	85	10

Leading scorer: 18 Stefan Lavery (Armagh City). **Player of Year**: Scott Davidson (HW Welders)

TENNENT'S IRISH CUP FINAL

Glenavon 2 (Braniff, Hall) **Linfield** 0. Windsor Park, May 7, 2016
Glenavon: Tuffey, Kelly, Dillon, Kilmartin, Marshall, Cooper (Kearns), Bradley (Hamilton), Hall, Patton, Braniff, Martyn (Sykes)
Linfield: Deane, Haughey, Callacher (Quinn), Waterworth, Lowry, Burns, Ward, Clarke (Millar), Mulgrew, Gaynor, Smyth
Referee: R Hetherington (Dungannon)

JBE LEAGUE CUP FINAL

Cliftonville 3 (M Donnelly, McDaid, Garrett) **Ards** 0. Solitude, Belfast, February 13, 2016

COUNTY ANTRIM SHIELD FINAL

Ballymena United 3 (McNally, Cushley, Kane) **Linfield** 2 (Bates, Stafford). Windsor Park, Belfast, January 12, 2016

UEFA CHAMPIONS LEAGUE 2015–16

FIRST QUALIFYING ROUND, FIRST LEG

Crusaders 0 Levadia Tallinn 0. Att: 1,748. Torshavn 1 (Samuelsen 7) **New Saints** 2 (Quigley 9, Wilde 90). Att: 1,050

FIRST QUALIFYING ROUND, SECOND LEG

Levadia Tallinn 1 (Luts 22) **Crusaders** 1 (Carvill 4). Att: 1,230 (agg 1-1, Crusaders won on away goal). **New Saints** 4 (Wilde 15, 27, 47, Williams 89) Torshavn 1 (Cieslewicz 90). Att: 1,148 (New Saints won 6-2 on agg)

FIRST QUALIFYING ROUND, ON AGGREGATE

Lincoln Red Imps 2 Santa Coloma 1; Pyunik Yerevan 4 Folgore Falciano 2

SECOND QUALIFYING ROUND, FIRST LEG

Bate Borisov 2 (Karnitskiy 11, Yablonskiy 38) **Dundalk** 1 (McMillan 32). Att: 11,421. **Celtic** 2 (Boyata 44, Johansen 56) Stjarnan 0. Att: 48,185. **New Saints** 0 Videoton 1 (Gyurcso 77). Att: 1,068. Skenderbeu 4 (Nimaja 15, Salihi 34, 83, Berisha 76) **Crusaders** 1 (Owens 48). Att: 5,500

SECOND QUALIFYING ROUND, SECOND LEG

Crusaders 3 (O'Flynn 50, Mitchell 90, Snoddy 90) Skenderbeu 2 (Berisha 69, Litifi 77). Att: 1,548 (Skenderbeu won 6-4 on agg). **Dundalk** 0 Bate Borisov 0. Att: 3,103 (Bate Borisov won 2-1 on agg). Stjarnan 1 (Finsen 7) **Celtic** 4 (Biton 33, Mulgrew 49, Griffiths 88, Johansen 90). Att: 1,022 (Celtic won 6-1 on agg); Videoton 1 (Gyurcso 107) **New Saints** 1 (Williams 78). Att: 3,218 (aet, Videoton won 2-1 on agg)

SECOND QUALIFYING ROUND, ON AGGREGATE

Apoel Nicosia 1 Vardar 1 (Apoel Nicosia won on away goal); Astana 3 Maribor 2; Dinamo Zagreb 4 Fola Esch 1; HJK Helsinki 4 Ventspils 1; Lech Poznan 3 Sarajevo 0; Maccabi Tel Aviv 6 Hibernians 3; Malmo 1 Zalgiris 0; Midtjylland 3 Lincoln Red Imps 0; Milsami 3 Ludogorets 1; Molde 5 Pyunik Yerevan 1; Partizan Belgrade 3 Dila Gori 0; Qarabag 1 Rudar 0; Steaua Bucharest 4 Dukla Trencin 3

THIRD QUALIFYING ROUND, FIRST LEG

Celtic 1 (Boyata 82) Qarabag 0. Att: 43,011

THIRD QUALIFYING ROUND, SECOND LEG

Qarabag 0 **Celtic** 0. Att: 31,850 (Celtic won 1-0 on agg)

THIRD QUALIFYING ROUND, ON AGGREGATE

Apoel Nicosia 2 Midtjylland 2 (Apoel Nicosia won on away goals); Astana 4 HJK Helsinki 3; Bate Borisov 2 Videoton 1; Basle 4 Lech Poznan 1; Club Bruges 4 Panathinaikos 2; CSKA Moscow 5 Sparta Prague 4; Dinamo Zagreb 4 Molde 4 (Dinamo Zagreb won on away goals); Maccabi Tel Aviv 3 Plzen 2; Malmo 3 Salzburg 2; Monaco 7 Young Boys 1; Partizan Belgrade 5 Steaua Bucharest 3; Rapid Vienna 5 Ajax 4; Shakhtar Donetsk 3 Fenerbahce 0; Skenderbeu 4 Milsami 0

PLAY-OFFS, FIRST LEG

Celtic 3 (Griffiths 3, 62, Biton 10) Malmo 2 (Berget 52, 90). Att: 52,412; **Manchester Utd** 3 (Depay 13, 43, Fellaini 90) Club Bruges 1 (Carrick 8 og). Att: 75,312

PLAY-OFFS, SECOND LEG

Club Bruges 0 **Manchester Utd** 4 (Rooney 20, 49, 57, Herrera 63). Att: 28,733 (Manchester Utd won 7-1 on agg); Malmo 2 (Rosenberg 23, Boyata 55 og) **Celtic** 0. Att: 20,500 (Malmo won 4-3 on agg)

PLAY-OFFS, ON AGGREGATE

Astana 2 Apoel Nicosia 1; Bate Borisov 2 Partizan Belgrade 2 (Bate Borisov won on away goal); Bayer Leverkusen 3 Lazio 1; CSKA Moscow 4 Sporting 3; Dinamo Zagreb 6 Skenderbeu 2; Maccabi Tel Aviv 3 Basle 3 (Maccabi Tel Aviv won on away goals); Shakhtar Donestsk 3 Rapid Vienna 2; Valencia 4 Monaco 3

GROUP A

September 15, 2015
Paris SG 2 (Di Maria 4, Cavani 61) **Malmo** 0. Att: 46,612
Real Madrid 4 (Benzema 30, Ronaldo 55 pen, 64 pen, 81) **Shakhtar Donetsk** 0. Att: 66,389

September 30, 2015
Malmo 0 **Real Madrid** 2 (Ronaldo 29, 90). Att: 20,500
Shakhtar Donetsk 0 **Paris SG** 3 (Aurier 7, Luiz 23, Ibrahimovic 90). Att: 32,730

October 21, 2015
Malmo 1 (Rosenberg 17) **Shakhtar Donetsk** 0. Att: 20,500
Paris SG 0 **Real Madrid** 0. At: 46,858

November 3, 2015
Real Madrid 1 (Nacho 35) **Paris SG** 0. Att: 78,300
Shakhtar Donetsk 4 (Gladkyy 29, Srna 48 pen, Eduardo 55, Teixeira 73) **Malmo** 0. Att: 23,721

November 25, 2015
Malmo 0 **Paris SG** 5 (Rabiot 3, Di Maria 14, 68, Ibrahimovic 50, Lucas Moura 82). Att: 20,500
Shakhtar Donetsk 3 (Teixeira 77 pen, 88, Dentinho 83) **Real Madrid** 4 (Ronaldo 18, 70, Modric 50, Carvajal 52). Att: 33,990

December 8, 2015
Paris SG 2 (Lucas Moura 57, Ibrahimovic 86) **Shakhtar Donetsk** 0. Att: 44,408
Real Madrid 8 (Benzema 13, 24, 73, Ronaldo 38, 47, 50, 59, Kovacic 70) **Malmo** 0 Att: 60,663

	P	W	D	L;	F	A	Pts
Real Madrid Q	6	5	1	0	19	3	16
Paris SG Q	6	4	1	1	12	1	13
Shakhtar Donetsk	6	1	0	5	7	14	3
Malmo	6	1	0	5	1	21	3

GROUP B

September 15, 2015
PSV Eindhoven 2 (Moreno 45, Narsingh 57) **Manchester Utd** 1 (Depay 41). Att: 35,292
Manchester Utd (4-2-3-1): De Gea, Darmian, Smalling, Blind, Shaw (Rojo 24), Schweinsteiger, Herrera (Fellaini 75), Young (Valencia 86), Mata, Depay, Martial. **Booked**: Smalling
Wolfsburg 1 (Draxler 40) **CSKA Moscow** 0. Att: 20,126

September 30, 2015
CSKA Moscow 3 (Musa 7, Doumbia 21, 36 pen) **PSV Eindhoven** 2 (Lestienne 60, 68). Att: 16,152
Manchester Utd 2 (Mata 34 pen, Smalling 53) **Wolfsburg** 1 (Caligiuri 4). Att: 74,811
Manchester Utd (4-2-3-1): De Gea, Valencia (Young 46), Smalling, Blind, Darmian,

Schweinsteiger (Jones 72), Schneiderlin, Mata, Rooney, Depay (Pereira 52), Martial. **Booked:** Schneiderlin, Depay, Schweinsteiger, Young

October 21, 2015
CSKA Moscow 1 (Doumbia 15) **Manchester Utd** 1 (Martial 65). Att: 18,456
Manchester Utd (4-2-3-1): De Gea, Valencia, Smalling, Jones, Rojo (Blind 63), Schweinsteiger (Fellaini 46), Schneiderlin, Lingard (Depay 80), Herrera, Martial, Rooney. **Booked**: Martial, Herrera, Fellaini
Wolfsburg 2 (Dost 47, Kruse 57) **PSV Eindhoven** 0. Att: 23,375

November 3, 2015
Manchester Utd 1 (Rooney 79) **CSKA Moscow** 0. Att: 75,165
Manchester Utd (4-2-3-1): De Gea, Young, Smalling, Blind, Rojo, Schweinsteiger (Herrera 89), Carrick, Mata (Depay 76), Rooney, Lingard, Martial (Fellaini 66)
PSV Eindhoven 2 (Locadia 55, De Jong 86) **Wolfsburg** 0. Att: 35,000

November 25, 2015
CSKA Moscow 0 **Wolfsburg** 2 (Akinfeev 67 og, Schurrle 88). Att: 16,450
Manchester Utd 0 **PSV Eindhoven** 0. Att: 75,321
Manchester Utd (4-2-3-1): De Gea, Darmian (Mata 85), Smalling, Blind, Rojo, Schneiderlin, Schweinsteiger (Fellaini 58), Lingard, Rooney, Depay (Young 59), Martial. **Booked**: Lingard

December 8, 2015
PSV Eindhoven 2 (De Jong 78, Propper 85) **CSKA Moscow** 1 (Ignashevich 76 pen)). Att: 34,000
Wolfsburg 3 (Naldo 14, 84, Vieirinha 29) **Manchester Utd** 2 (Martial 10, Guilavogui 82 og). Att: 26.400
Manchester Utd (4-2-3-1): De Dea, Varela, Smalling, Blind, Darmian (Borthwick-Jackson 43, Fellaini, Schweinsteiger (Carrick 69), Lingard, Mata (Powell 69), Depay, Martial. **Booked**: Darmian, Varela

	P	W	D	L	F	A	Pts
Wolfsburg Q	6	4	0	2	9	6	12
PSV Eindhoven Q	6	3	1	2	8	7	10
Manchester Utd	6	2	2	2	7	7	8
CSKA Moscow	6	1	1	4	5	9	4

GROUP C

September 15, 2015
Benfica 2 (Gaitan 51, Mitroglu 62) **Astana** 0. Att: 32,799
Galatasaray 0 **Atletico Madrid** 2 (Griezmann 18, 25). Att: 33,469

September 30, 2015
Astana 2 (Balta 77 og, Canas 89) **Galatasaray** 2 (Kisa 31, Eric 86 og). Att: 27,264
Atletico Madrid 1 (Correa 23) **Benfica** 2 (Gaitan 36, Goncalo Guedes 51). Att: 40,938

October 21, 2015
Atletico Madrid 4 (Saul 23, Martinez 23, Torres 63, Dedechko 89 og) **Astana** 0. Att: 33,853
Galatasaray 2 (Inan 20 pen, Podolski 33) **Benfica** 1 (Gaitan 2). Att: 33,615

November 3, 2015
Astana 0 **Atletico Madrid** 0. Att: 29,231
Benfica 2 (Jonas 52, Luisao 67) **Galatasaray** 1 (Podolski 58). Att: 35,726

November 25, 2015
Astana 2 (Twumasi 19, Anicic 31) **Benfica** 2 (Jimenez 40, 72). Att: 15,089
Atletico Madrid 2 (Griezmann 12, 65) **Galatasaray** 0. Att: 35,753

December 8, 2015
Benfica 1 (Mitroglou 75) **Atletico Madrid** 2 (Saul 33, Vietto 55). Att: 47,630
Galatasaray 1 (Inan 64) **Astana** 1 (Twumasi 62). Att: 26,464

	P	W	D	L	F	A	Pts
Atletico Madrid Q	6	4	1	1	11	3	13
Benfica Q	6	3	1	2	10	8	10
Galatasaray	6	1	2	3	6	10	5
Astana	6	0	4	2	5	11	4

GROUP D

September 15, 2015
Manchester City 1 (Chiellini 57 og) **Juventus** 2 (Mandzukic 70, Morata 81). Att: 50,363
Manchester City (4-2-3-1): Hart, Sagna, Kompany (Otamendi 74), Mangala, Kolarov, Fernandinho, Toure, Nasri (Aguero 83), Silva, Sterling (De Bruyne 71), Bony
Sevilla 3 (Gameiro 47 pen, Banega 66 pen, Konoplyanka 84) **Borussis Monchengladbach** 0. Att: 36,959

September 30, 2015
Borussia Monchengladbach 1 (Stindl 54) **Manchester City** 2 (Demichelis 66, Aguero 90 pen). Att: 46,279
Manchester City (4-2-3-1): Hart, Sagna, Demichelis, Otamendi, Kolarov, Fernandinho, Toure (Fernando 46), De Bruyne, Silva (Jesus Navas 65), Sterling (Zabaleta 90), Aguero. **Booked**: Otamendi
Juventus 2 (Morata 41, Zaza 87) **Sevilla** 0. Att: 36,640

October 21, 2015
Juventus 0 **Borussia Monchengladbach** 0. Att: 40,940
Manchester City 2 (Rami 36 og, De Bruyne 90) **Sevilla** 1 (Konoplyanka 30). Att: 45,595
Manchester City (4-2-3-1): Hart, Zabaleta (Kolarov 60), Otamendi, Mangala, Sagna, Fernandinho, Toure, Jesus Navas, Sterling, De Bruyne (Kompany 90), Bony (Fernando 76). **Booked**: Bony

November 3, 2015
Borussia Monchengladbach 1 (Johnson 18) **Juventus** 1 (Lichtsteiner 44). Att: 46,217
Sevilla 1 (Tremoulinas 25) **Manchester City** 3 (Sterling 8, Fernandinho 11, Bony 36). Att: 39,261
Manchester City (4-2-3-1): Hart, Sagna, Kompany, Otamendi, Kolarov, Fernando, Fernandinho (Demichelis 90), Jesus Navas, Toure, Sterling (De Bruyne 73), Bony (Delph 86)

November 25, 2015
Borussia Monchengladbach 4 (Stindl 29, 83, Johnson 68, Raffael 78) **Sevilla** 2 (Vitolo 82, Banega 90 pen). Att: 45,177
Juventus 1 (Mandzukic 18) **Manchester City** 0. Att: 38,193
Manchester City (4-2-3-1): Hart (Caballero 81), Sagna, Demichelis, Otamendi, Clichy, Fernando, Fernandinho (Delph 60), Jesus Navas, Toure, De Bruyne, Aguero (Sterling 69). **Booked**: Fernandinho, Sagna, Jesus Navas

December 8, 2015
Manchester City 4 (Silva 16, Sterling 79, 81, Bony 85) **Borussia Monchengladbach** 2 (Korb 18, Raffael 42). Att: 41,829
Manchester City (4-3-2-1): Hart, Clichy (Sagna 80), Otamendi, Mangala, Kolarov, Toure, Fernandinho, Delph (Bony 65), Silva, De Bruyne (Jesus Navas 65), Sterling
Sevilla 1 (Llorente 65) **Juventus** 0. Att: 35,583

	P	W	D	L	F	A	Pts
Manchester City Q	6	4	0	2	12	8	12
Juventus Q	6	3	2	1	6	3	11
Sevilla	6	2	0	4	8	11	6
Borussia M'bach	6	1	2	3	8	12	5

GROUP E

September 16, 2015

Bayer Leverkusen 4 (Mehmedi 4, Calhanoglu 47, 75 pen, Hernandez 58) **Bate Borisov** 1 (Milunovic 13). Att: 24,280

Roma 1 (Florenzi 31) **Barcelona** 1 (Suarez 21). Att: 57,836

September 29, 2015

Bate Borisov 3 (Stasevich 8, Mladenovic 12, 31) **Roma** 2 (Gervinho 66, Torosidis 82). Att: 12,767

Barcelona 2 (Sergi Roberto 81, Suarez 82) **Bayer Leverkusen** 1 (Papadopoulos 23). Att: 68,694

October 20, 2015

Bate Borisov 0 **Barcelona** 2 (Rakitic 48, 65). Att: 13,074

Bayer Leverkusen 4 (Hernandez 4 pen, 19, Kampl 84, Mehmedi 86) **Roma** 4 (De Rossi 30, 38, Pjanic 54, Falque 73). Att: 29,412

November 4, 2015

Barcelona 3 (Neymar 31 pen, 83, Suarez 60) **Bate Borisov** 0. Att: 68.502

Roma 3 (Salah 2, Dzeko 29, Pjanic 80 pen) **Bayer Leverlusen** 2 (Mehmedi 46, Hernandez 51). Att: 38,361

November 24, 2015

Barcelona 6 (Suarez 15, 44, Messi 18, 61, Pique 56, Adriano 77) Roma 1 (Dzeko 90). Att: 71,433

Bate Borisov 1 (Gordeichuk 2) **Bayer Leverkusen** 1 (Mehmedi 68). Att: 12,601

December 9, 2015

Bayer Leveerkusen 1 (Hernandez 23) **Barcelona** 1 (Messi 20). Att: 29,412

Roma 0 **Bate Borisov** 0. Att: 29,489

	P	W	D	L	F	A	Pts
Barcelona Q	6	4	2	0	15	4	14
Roma Q	6	1	3	2	11	16	6
Bayer Leverklusen	6	1	3	2	13	12	6
Bate Borisov	6	1	2	3	5	12	5

GROUP F

September 16, 2015

Dinamo Zagreb 2 (Oxlade-Chamberlain 24 og, Fernandes 58) **Arsenal** 1 (Walcott 79). Att: 17,840

Arsenal (4-2-3-1): Ospina, Debuchy, Gabriel, Koscielny, Gibbs (Campbell 65), Cazorla, Arteta (Coquelin 64), Oxlade-Chamberlain (Walcott 64), Ozil, Sanchez, Giroud. **Booked**: Giroud, Campbell. **Sent off**: Giroud (40)

Olympiacos 0 **Bayern Munich** 3 (Muller 52, 90 pen, Gotze 89). Att: 31,688

September 29, 2015

Arsenal 2 (Walcott 35, Sanchez 65) **Olympiacos** 3 (Pardo 32, Ospina 40 og, Finnbogason 66). Att: 59,428

Arsenal (4-2-3-1): Ospina, Bellerin (Campbell 86), Gabriel, Koscielny (Mertesacker 57), Gibbs, Coquelin (Ramsey 60), Cazorla, Oxlade-Chamberlain, Ozil, Sanchez, Walcott. **Booked**: Gabriel, Sanchez, Ozil

Bayern Munich 5 (Douglas Costa 13, Lewandowski 21, 28, 55, Gotze 25) **Dinamo Zagreb** 0. Att: 70,080

October 20, 2015
Arsenal 2 (Giroud 77, Ozil 90) **Bayern Munich** 0. Att: 49,824
Arsenal (4-2-3-1): Cech, Bellerin, Mertesacker, Koscielny, Monreal, Coquelin, Cazorla, Ramsey (Oxlade-Chamberlain 57, Ozil, Sanchez (Gibbs 82), Walcott (Giroud 74)
Dinamo Zagreb 0 **Olympiacos** 1 (Ideye 79). Att: 13,678

November 4, 2015
Bayern Munich 5 (Lewandowski 11, Muller 29, 89, Alaba 44, Robben 55) **Arsenal** 1 (Giroud 69). Att: 70,000
Arsenal (4-2-3-1): Cech, Debuchy, Mertesacker, Gabriel, Monreal, Coquelin, Cazorla (Chambers 87), Sanchez, Ozil, Campbell (Gibbs 59), Giroud (Iwobi 85). **Booked**: Ozil, Campbell
Olympiacos 2 (Pardo 65, 90) **Dinamo Zagreb** 1 (Hodzic 21). Att: 31,473

November 24, 2015
Arsenal 3 (Ozil 29, Sanchez 33, 69) **Dinamo Zagreb** 0. Att: 58,978
Arsenal (4-2-3-1): Cech, Bellerin (Debuchy 82), Mertesaker, Koscielny, Monreal, Flamini, Cazorla (Chambers 82), Campbell, Ozil, Sanchez, Giroud (Ramsey 69). **Booked**: Monreal
Bayern Munich 4 (Douglas Costa 8, Lewandowski 16, Muller 20, Coman 70) **Olympiacos** 0 Att: 70,000

December 9, 2015
Dinamo Zagreb 0 **Bayern Munich** 2 (Lewandowski 61, 64). Att: 19,681
Olympiacos 0 **Arsenal** 3 (Giroud 29, 49, 67 pen), Att: 31,388
Arsenal (4-2-3-1): Cech, Bellerin, Mertesacker, Koscielny, Monreal, Flamini, Ramsey, Walcott (Gibbs 72), Ozil, Campbell (Oxlade-Chamberlain 90), Giroud (Chambers 90). **Booked**: Ramsey, Giroud

	P	W	D	L	F	A	Pts
Bayern Munich Q	6	5	0	1	19	3	15
Arsenal Q	6	3	0	3	12	10	9
Olympiacos	6	3	0	3	6	13	9
Dinamo Zagreb	6	1	0	5	3	14	3

GROUP G

September 16, 2015
Chelsea 4 (Willian 15, Oscar 45 pen, Diego Costa 58, Fabregas 78) **Maccabi Tel Aviv** 0. Att: 40,684
Chelsea (4-2-3-1): Begovic, Azpilicueta, Zouma, Cahill, Rahman, Fabregas, Loftus-Cheek (Traore 77), Willian (Diego Costa 23), Oscar (Ramires 65), Hazard, Remy. **Booked**: Loftus-Cheek
Dynamo Kiev 2 (Gusev 20, Buyalsky 89). **Porto** 2 (Aboubakar 23, 81). Att: 52,369

September 29, 2015
Maccabi Tel Aviv 0 **Dynamo Kiev** 2 (Yarmolenko 4, Junior Moraes 50). Att: 27,100
Porto 2 (Andre 39, Maicon 52) **Chelsea** 1 (Willian 45). Att: 46,120
Chelsea (4-2-3-1): Begovic, Ivanovic, Zouma, Cahill, Azpilicueta, Ramires (Matic 73), Mikel (Hazard 62), Pedro (Kenedy 73), Fabregas, Willian, Diego Costa. **Booked**: Cahill, Azpilicueta, Matic

October 20, 2015
Dynamo Kiev 0 **Chelsea** 0. Att: 60,291
Chelsea (4-3-2-1): Begovic, Zouma, Cahill, Terry, Azpilicueta, Matic, Ramires, Fabregas (Oscar 75), Willian, Hazard, Diego Costa. **Booked**: Zouma
Porto 2 (Aboubakar 37, Brahimi 41) **Maccabi Tel Aviv** 0. Att: 35,209

November 4, 2015
Chelsea 2 (Dragovic 34 og, Willian 83) **Dynamo Kiev** 1 (Dragovic 78). Att: 41,241
Chelsea (4-2-3-1): Begovic, Azpilicueta, Zouma, Terry, Rahman, Ramires, Matic, Willian (Cahill 90), Fabregas (Pedro 79), Oscar (Hazard 79), Diego Costa
Maccabi Tel Aviv 1 (Zahavi 75 pen) **Porto** 3 (Tello 19, Andre 49, Layun 72). Att: 26,646

November 24, 2015
Maccabi Tel Aviv 0 **Chelsea** 4 (Cahill 21, Willian 73, Oscar 77, Zouma 90). Att: 29,121
Chelsea (4-2-3-1): Begovic, Azpilicueta, Cahill, Terry (Zouma 72), Rahman, Matic, Fabregas, Willian (Remy 79), Oscar, Hazard (Pedro 69) Diega Costa. **Booked**: Matic, Fabregas
Porto 0 **Dynamo Kiev** 2 (Yarmolenko 35 pen, Gonzalez 64). Att: 31,220

December 9, 2010
Chelsea 2 (Marcano 12 og, Willian 52) **Porto** 0. Att: 41,096
Chelsea (4-2-3-1): Courtois, Ivanovic, Zouma, Terry, Azpilicueta, Ramires, Matic, Willian, Oscar (Pedro 81), Hazard (Remy 90), Diego Costa (Mikel 86). **Booked**: Matic, Diego Costa, Ivanovic
Dynamo Kiev 1 (Garmash 16) **Maccabi Tel Aviv** 0. Played behind closed doors – previous crowd trouble

	P	W	D	L	F	A	Pts
Chelsea Q	6	4	1	1	13	3	13
Dynamo Kiev Q	6	3	2	1	8	4	11
Porto	6	3	1	2	9	8	10
Maccabi Tel Aviv	6	0	0	6	1	16	0

GROUP H

September 16, 2015
Gent 1 (Milicevic 68) **Lyon** 1 (Jallet 58). Att: 19,601
Valencia 2 (Cancelo 54, Gomes 73) **Zenit St Petersburg** 3 (Hulk 9, 44, Witsel 76). Att: 28,005

September 29, 2015
Lyon 0 **Valencia** 1 (Feghouli 42). Att: 33,534
Zenit St Petersburg 2 (Dzjuba 35, Shatov 67) **Gent** 1 (Matton 56). Att: 18,095

October 20, 2015
Valencia 2 (Feghouli 15 Mitrovic 73 og) **Gent** 1 (Foket 40). Att: 38,207
Zenit St Petersburg 3 (Dzjuba 2, Hulk 56, Danny 82) **Lyon** 1 (Lacazette 49). Att: 17,517

November 4, 2015
Gent 1 (Kums 49 pen) **Valencia** 0. Att: 19,452
Lyon 0 **Zenit St Petersburg** 2 (Dzjuba 25, 57). Att: 30,173

November 24, 2015
Lyon 1 (Ferri 7) **Gent** 2 (Milicevic 32, Coulibaly 90). Att: 30,206
Zenit St Petersburg 2 (Shatov 15, Dzjuba 74) **Valencia** 0. Att: 17,002

December 9, 2015
Gent 2 (Depoitre 18, Milicevic 78) **Zenit St Petersburg 1** (Dzjuba 65). Att: 19,978
Valencia 0 **Lyon** 2 (Cornet 37, Lacazette 76). Att: 32,494

	P	W	D	L	F	A	Pts
Zenit St Petersburg Q	6	5	0	1	13	6	15
Gent Q	6	3	1	2	8	7	10
Valencia	6	2	0	4	5	9	6
Lyon	6	1	1	4	5	9	4

ROUND OF 16, FIRST LEG

February 16, 2016

Benfica 1 (Jonas 90) **Zenit St Petersburg** 0. Att: 48,615

Paris SG 2 (Ibrahimovic 39, Casani 78) **Chelsea** 1 (Mikel 45). Att: 46,505

Chelsea (4-2-3-1): Courtois, Azpilicueta, Cahill, Ivanovic, Rahman, Mikel, Fabregas, Pedro, Willian, Hazard (Oscar 71), Diego Costa. **Booked**: Mikel, Pedro

February 17, 2016

Gent 2 (Kums 80, Coulibaly 89) **Wolfsburg** 3 (Draxler 44, 54, Kruse 60). Att: 19,978

Roma 0 **Real Madrid** 2 (Ronaldo 57, Jese 86). Att: 55,612

February 23, 2016

Arsenal 0 **Barcelona** 2 (Messi 71, 84 pen). Att: 59,889

Arsenal (4-2-3-1): Cech, Bellerin, Mertesacker, Koscielny, Monreal, Ramsey, Coquelin (Flamini 82), Oxlade-Chamberlain (Walcott 50), Ozil, Sanchez, Giroud (Welbeck 72). **Booked** Monreal

Juventus 2 (Dybala 63, Sturaro 76) **Bayern Munich** 2 (Muller 43, Robben 55). Att: 41,332

February 24, 2016

Dynamo Kiev 1 (Buyalsky 58) **Manchester City** 3 (Aguero 15, Silva 40, Toure 89). Att: 53,691

Manchester City (4-2-3-1): Hart, Sagna, Kompany, Otamendi, Clichy, Fernandinho, Fernando, Silva, Toure, Sterling, Aguero (Iheanacho 90)

PSV Eindhoven 0 **Atletico Madrid** 0. Att: 34,948

ROUND OF 16, SECOND LEG

March 8, 2016

Real Madrid 2 (Ronaldo 64, Rodriguez 68) **Roma** 0. Att: 76,654 (Real Madrid won 4-0 on agg)

Wolfsburg 1 (Schurrle 74) **Gent** 0. Att: 23,457 (Wolfsburg won 4-2 on agg)

March 9, 2016

Chelsea 1 (Diego Costa 27) **Paris SG** 2 (Rabiot 16, Ibrahimovic 67). Att: 37,591 (Paris SG won 4-2 on agg)

Chelsea (4-2-3-1): Courtois, Azpilicueta, Ivanovic, Cahill, Kenedy, Mikel, Fabregas, Pedro, Willian, Hazard (Oscar 77), Diego Costa (Traore 60). **Booked**: Fabregas, Mikel, Ivanovic

Zenit St Petersburg 1 (Hulk 69) **Benfica** 2 (Gaitan 86, Anderson Talisca (90). Att: 17,688 (Benfica won 3-1 on agg)

March 15, 2016

Atletico Madrid 0 **PSV Eindhoven** 0. Att: 50,135 (aet, agg 0-0, Atletico Madrid won 8-7 on pens)

Manchester City 0 **Dynamo Kiev** 0. Att: 43,630 (Manchester City won 3-1 on agg)

Manchester City (4-2-3-1): Hart, Zabaleta, Kompany (Mangala 7), Otamendi (Demichelis 24), Clichy, Fernando, Fernandinho, Jesus Navas, Toure, Silva, Aguero (Sterling 79). **Booked**: Otamendi

March 16, 2016

Barcelona 3 (Neymar 18, Suarez 65, Messi 88) **Arsenal** 1 (Elneny 51). Att: 76,092 (Barcelona won 5-1 on agg)

Arsenal (4-2-3-1): Ospina, Bellerin, Koscielny, Gabriel, Monreal, Flamini (Coquelin 44), Elneny, Iwobi, (Giroud 72), Ozil, Sanchez, Welbeck (Walcott 73). **Booked**: Flamini, Gabriel, Sanchez, Giroud

Bayern Munich 4 (Lewandowski 73, Muller 90, Thiago Alcantara 108, Coman 110) Juventus 2 (Pogba 5, Cuadrado 28). Att: 70,000 (aet, Bayern Munich won 6-4 on agg)

QUARTER-FINALS, FIRST LEG

April 5, 2016

Barcelona 2 (Suarez 63, 74) **Atletico Madrid** 1 (Torres 25). Att: 88,534

Bayern Munich 1 (Vidal 2) **Benfica** 0. Att: 70,000

April 6, 2016
Paris SG 2 (Ibrahimovic 41, Rabiot 60) **Manchester City** 2 (De Bruyne 38, Fernandinho 73). Att: 47,228
Manchester City (4-2-3-1): Hart, Sagna, Mangala, Otamendi, Clichy, Fernando, Fernandinho, Jesus Navas, De Bruyne (Delph 77), Silva (Bony 88), Aguero (Kolarov 90). **Booked**: Clichy, Fernando, Mangala, Jesus Navas
Wolfsburg 2 (Rodriguez 18 pen, Arnold 25) **Real Madrid** 0. Att: 26,400

QUARTER-FINALS, SECOND LEG

April 12, 2016
Manchester City 1 (De Bruyne 76) **Paris SG** 0. Att: 53,039 (Manchester City won 3-2 on agg)
Manchester City (4-2-3-1): Hart, Sagna, Mangala, Otamendi, Clichy, Fernando, Fernandinho, Jesus Navas, De Bruyne (Toure 84), Silva (Delph 87), Aguero (Iheanacho 90). **Booked**: Fernandinho
Real Madrid 3 (Ronaldo 16, 17, 77) **Wolfsburg** 0. Att: 76,684 (Real Madrid won 3-2 on agg)

April 13, 2016
Atletico Madrid 2 (Griezmann 36, 88 pen) **Barcelona** 0. Att: 52,851 (Atletico Madrid won 3-2 on agg)
Benfica 2 (Jimenez 27, Anderson Talisca 77) **Bayern Munich** 2 (Vidal 38, Muller 52). Att: 63,235 (Bayern Munich won 3-2 on agg)

SEMI-FINALS, FIRST LEG

April 26, 2016
Manchester City 0 **Real Madrid** 0. Att: 52,221
Manchester City (4-2-3-1): Hart, Sagna, Kompany, Otamendi, Clichy, Fernando, Fernandinho, Jesus Navas (Sterling 77), De Bruyne, Silva (Iheanacho 40), Aguero. **Booked**: Silva
April 27, 2016
Atletico Madrid 1 (Saul 11) **Bayern Munich** 0. Att: 52,127

SEMI-FINALS, SECOND LEG

May 3, 2016
Bayern Munich 2 (Xabi Alonso 31, Lewandowski 74) **Atletico Madrid** 1 (Griezmann 54). Att: 70,000 (agg 2-2, Atletico Madrid won on away goal)
May 4, 2016
Real Madrid 1 (Fernando 20 og) **Manchester City** 0. Att: 78,300 (Real Madrid won 1-0 on agg)
Manchester City (4-2-3-1): Hart, Sagna, Kompany (Mangala 10), Otamendi, Clichy, Fernando, Fernandinho, Jesus Navas (Iheanacho 69), Toure (Sterling 61), De Bruyne, Aguero. **Booked**: Otamendui, Fernando

FINAL

REAL MADRID 1 ATLETICO MADRID 1
(aet, Real Madrid won 5-3 on pens)
San Siro Stadium, Milan (75,000); Saturday, May 28 2016

Real Madrid (4-3-3): Navas, Carvajal (Danilo 51), Pepe, Sergio Ramos (capt), Marcelo, Modric, Casemiro, Kroos (Isco 72), Bale, Benzema (Lucas 76), Ronaldo. **Subs not used**: Casilla, Nacho, Rodriguez, Jese. **Scorer**: Sergio Ramos (15). **Booked**: Carvajal, Navas, Casemiro, Sergio Ramos, Danilo, Pepe. **Coach**: Zinedine Zidane
Atletico Madrid (4-4-2): Oblak, Juanfran, Savic, Godin, Filipe Luis (Hernandez 109), Saul, Gabi (capt), Fernandez (Carrasco 46), Koke (Partey 116), Torres, Griezmann. **Subs not used**: Moya, Mendes, Correa, Gimenez. **Scorer**: Carrasco (79). **Booked**: Gabi, Torres. **Coach**: Diego Simeone
Penalty shoot-out: 1-0 (Lucas), 1-1 (Griezmann), 2-1 (Marcelo), 2-2 (Gabi), 3-2 (Bale), 3-3 (Saul), 4-3 (Sergio Ramos), 4-3 (Juanfran hit post), 5-3 (Ronaldo)
Referee: M Clattenburg (England). **Half-time**: 1-0

Leading scorers: 16 Ronaldo (Real Madrid); 9 Lewandowski (Bayern Munich); 8 Muller (Bayern Munich), Suarez (Barcelona); 7 Griezmann (Atletico Madrid); 6 Dzyuba (Zenit St Petersburg), Messi (Barcelona); 5 Giroud (Arsenal), Hernandez (Bayer Leverkusen), Ibrahimovic (Paris SG), Willian (Chelsea)

FINAL FACTS AND FIGURES

- Real Madrid became champions of Europe for the 11th time.
- They have not lost a final since a 1-0 defeat by Liverpool in 1981.
- Sergio Ramos is the first defender to score in two Champions League Finals, having previously netted in the victory over Atletico in 2014.
- Zinedine Zidane became the first French manager to win the Champions League.
- Zidane is the second man, after Miguel Munoz, to lift the European Cup/Champions/ League trophy with Real as a player and coach.
- Atletico have now lost all three of their finals in the tournament, beaten also by Bayern Munich in 1974.

EUROPEAN CUP/CHAMPIONS LEAGUE FINALS

1956	Real Madrid 4 Reims 3 (Paris)
1957	Real Madrid 2 Fiorentina 0 (Madrid)
1958†	Real Madrid 3 AC Milan 2 (Brussels)
1959	Real Madrid 2 Reims 0 (Stuttgart)
1960	Real Madrid 7 Eintracht Frankfurt 3 (Glasgow)
1961	Benfica 3 Barcelona 2 (Berne)
1962	Benfica 5 Real Madrid 3 (Amsterdam)
1963	AC Milan 2 Benfica 1 (Wembley)
1964	Inter Milan 3 Real Madrid 1 (Vienna)
1965	Inter Milan 1 Benfica 0 (Milan)
1966	Real Madrid 2 Partizan Belgrade 1 (Brussels)
1967	Celtic 2 Inter Milan 1 (Lisbon)
1968†	Manchester Utd 4 Benfica 1 (Wembley)
1969	AC Milan 4 Ajax 1 (Madrid)
1970†	Feyenoord 2 Celtic 1 (Milan)
1971	Ajax 2 Panathinaikos 0 (Wembley)
1972	Ajax 2 Inter Milan 0 (Rotterdam)
1973	Ajax 1 Juventus 0 (Belgrade)
1974	Bayern Munich 4 Atletico Madrid 0 (replay Brussels after a 1-1 draw Brussels)
1975	Bayern Munich 2 Leeds Utd 0 (Paris)
1976	Bayern Munich 1 St. Etienne 0 (Glasgow)
1977	Liverpool 3 Borussia Moenchengladbach 1 (Rome)
1978	Liverpool 1 Brugge 0 (Wembley)
1979	Nottm Forest 1 Malmo 0 (Munich)
1980	Nottm Forest 1 Hamburg 0 (Madrid)
1981	Liverpool 1 Real Madrid 0 (Paris)
1982	Aston Villa 1 Bayern Munich 0 (Rotterdam)
1983	SV Hamburg 1 Juventus 0 (Athens)
1984†	Liverpool 1 AS Roma 1 (Liverpool won 4-2 on penalties) (Rome)
1985	Juventus 1 Liverpool 0 (Brussels)
1986†	Steaua Bucharest 0 Barcelona 0 (Steaua won 2-0 on penalties) (Seville)
1987	Porto 2 Bayern Munich 1 (Vienna)
1988†	PSV Eindhoven 0 Benfica 0 (PSV won 6-5 on penalties) (Stuttgart)
1989	AC Milan 4 Steaua Bucharest 0 (Barcelona)
1990	AC Milan 1 Benfica 0 (Vienna)
1991†	Red Star Belgrade 0 Marseille 0 (Red Star won 5-3 on penalties) (Bari)
1992	Barcelona 1 Sampdoria 0 (Wembley)
1993	Marseille 1 AC Milan 0 (Munich)

1994	AC Milan 4 Barcelona 0 (Athens)
1995	Ajax 1 AC Milan 0 (Vienna)
1996†	Juventus 1 Ajax 1 (Juventus won 4-2 on penalties) (Rome)
1997	Borussia Dortmund 3 Juventus 1 (Munich)
1998	Real Madrid 1 Juventus 0 (Amsterdam)
1999	Manchester Utd 2 Bayern Munich 1 (Barcelona)
2000	Real Madrid 3 Valencia 0 (Paris)
2001	Bayern Munich 1 Valencia 1 (Bayern Munich won 5-4 on penalties) (Milan)
2002	Real Madrid 2 Bayer Leverkusen 1 (Glasgow)
2003†	AC Milan 0 Juventus 0 (AC Milan won 3-2 on penalties) (Manchester)
2004	FC Porto 3 Monaco 0 (Gelsenkirchen)
2005†	Liverpool 3 AC Milan 3 (Liverpool won 3-2 on penalties) (Istanbul)
2006	Barcelona 2 Arsenal 1 (Paris)
2007	AC Milan 2 Liverpool 1 (Athens)
2008†	Manchester Utd 1 Chelsea 1 (Manchester Utd won 6-5 on penalties) (Moscow)
2009	Barcelona 2 Manchester Utd 0 (Rome)
2010	Inter Milan 2 Bayern Munich 0 (Madrid)
2011	Barcelona 3 Manchester Utd 1 (Wembley)
2012†	Chelsea 1 Bayern Munich 1 (Chelsea won 4-3 on pens) (Munich)
2013	Bayern Munich 3 Borussia Dortmund 1 (Wembley)
2014†	Real Madrid 4 Atletico Madrid 1 (Lisbon)
2015	Barcelona 3 Juventus 1 (Berlin)
2016	Real Madrid 1 Atletico Madrid 1 (Real Madrid won 5-3 on pens) (Milan)

† aet
● Champions League since 1993

UEFA EUROPA LEAGUE 2015–16

FIRST QUALIFYING ROUND (selected results)

FIRST LEG

Airbus 1 (Riley 28) Lokomotiva Zagreb 3 (Sovsic 48, Maric 61, Kolar 68). Att: 543. Alashkert 1 (Manasyan 59) **St Johnstone** 0. Att: 2,600. **Cork** 1 (Bennett 19) Reykjavic 1 (Hauksson 28). Att: 4,641. Differdange 3 (Rafik 4, Caron 7, Sinani 26) **Bala** 1 (Sheridan 38). Att: 1,223. **Glenavon** 1 (Patton 86) Shakhter 2 (Afanasyev 2, Komarovski 30). Att: 640. **Glentoran** 1 (McMenamin 66) Zilina 4 (Jelic 13, Paur 20, Cmelik 59, Kane 81 og). Att: 1,676. **Linfield** 2 (Waterworth 57, Bates 73) Runavik 0. Att: 1,824. **Newtown** 2 (Boundford 40, Oswell 90) Valletta 1 (de Conceicao 73). Att: 1,420. Niedercorn 0 **Shamrock** 0. Att: 1,451. Shkendija Tetovo 1 (Kirovski 84) **Aberdeen** 1 (McGinn 79). Att: 7,040. Skonto Riga 2 (Karasausks 30, Gutkovskis 65) **St Patrick's** 1 (Greene 21). Att: 1,780. **UCD** 1 (Swan 45) Dudelange 0. Att: 1,075. **West Ham** 3 (Sakho 40, 45, Tomkins 58) Lusitanos 0. Att: 34,966

SECOND LEG

Aberdeen 0 Shkendija Tetovo 0. Att: 14,112 (agg 1-1, Aberdeen won on away goal). **Bala** 2 (Murtagh 48, Sheridan 83) Differdange 1 (Rafik 90). Att: 1,049 (Differdange won 4-3 on agg). Dudelange 2 (Pedro 43, Nakache 45) **UCD** 1 (Swan 17). Att: 1,245 (agg 2-2, UCD won on away goal). Lokomotiva Zagreb 2 (Fiolic 65, Sovsic 73) **Airbus** 2 (Budrys 45, Jones 75). Att: 650 (Lokokomotiva Zagreb won 5-3 on agg). Lusitanos 0 **West Ham** 1 (Lee 21). Att: 837 (West Ham won 4-0 on agg). Reykjavik 2 (Palmason 75, Schoop 99) **Cork** 1 (O'Sullivan 14). Att: 1,145 (aet, Reykjavik won 3-2 on agg). Runavik 4 (Olsen 17, Justinussen 19, 85, Joensen 45) **Linfield** 3 (Glendinning 14, Bates 33, Waterworth 69). Att: 550 (Linfield won 5-4 on agg). Shakhter 3 (Yurevich 8, Yanush 66, Komarovski 87) **Glenavon** 0. Att: 3,200 (Shakhter won 5-1 on agg). **Shamrock** 3 (Webster 21, Waters 41, 57) Niedercorn 0. Att: 3,250 (Shamrock won 3-0 on agg). **St Johnstone** 2 (O'Halloran 34, McKay 86) Alashkert 1 (Gyozalyan 73). Att: 5,764 (agg 2-2, Alashkert won on away goal). **St Patrick's** 0 Skonto Riga 2 (Sorokins 37, Karasausks 59). Att: 2,354 (Skonto Riga won 4-1 on agg). Valletta 1 (Fidjeu 45) **Newtown** 2 (Oswell 7, Owen 86). Att: 1,914 (Newtown won 4-2 on agg)

SECOND QUALIFYING ROUND (selected results)

FIRST LEG

Copenhagen 2 (Verbic 3, Kuski 75 **Newtown** 0. Att: 8,104. **Inverness** 0 Astra Giurgiu 1 (Budescu 24). Att: 5,534. Rijeka 0 **Aberdeen** 3 (Considine 38, Pawlett 52, McLean 75). Att: 9,000. **Shamrock** 0 Odd Grenland 2 (Occean 53, 67). Att: 2,900. Slovan Bratislava 1 (Zrelak 84) **UCD** 0. Att: 3,050. Spartak Trnava 2 (Sabo 16 pen, Mikovic 34) **Linfield** 1 (Kee 21). Att: 3,220. **West Ham** 1 (Tomkins 90) Birkirkara 0. Att: 33,048

SECOND LEG

Aberdeen 2 (McGinn 64, Hayes 72) Rijeka 2 (Tomasov 58, Kvrzic 63). Att: 15,803 (Aberdeen won 5-2 on agg). Astra Giurgiu 0 **Inverness** 0. Att: 3,067 (Astra Giurgiu won 1-0 on agg). Birkirkara 1 (Miccoli 14) **West Ham** 0. Att: 14,571 (aet, agg 1-1, West Ham won 5-3 on pens). **Linfield** 1 (Lowry 34) Spartak Trnava 3 (Sabo 54, 84, Vojtus 60). Att: 3,001 (Spartak Trnava won 5-2 on agg). **Newtown** 1 (Goodwin 70) Copenhagen 3 (Pourie 28, 51, Jorgensen 40 pen). Att: 1,400 (Copenhagen won 5-1 on agg). Odd Grenland 2 (Halvorsen 72, Hagen 86) **Shamrock** 1 (G Brennan 90). Att: 3,814 (Odd Grenland won 4-1 on agg). **UCD** 1 (Swan 57) Slovan Bratislava 5 (Vittek 41, 90, 90, Milinkovic 49, Salata 81). Att: 1,361 (Slovan Bratislava won 6-1 on agg)

THIRD QUALIFYING ROUND (selected results)

FIRST LEG

Kairat Almaty 2 (Bakaev 13, Islamkhan 22) **Aberdeen** 1 (McLean 68). Att: 23,500. **Southampton** 3 (Pelle 37, Tadic 45 pen, Long 84) Vitesse 0. Att: 30,050. **West Ham** 2 (Valencia 23, Zarate 51) Astra Giurgiu 2 (Boldrin 71, Ogbonna 82 og). Att: 33,858

SECOND LEG

Aberdeen 1 (McLean 84)Kairat Almaty 1 (Gohou 59). Att: 20,317 (Kairat Almaty won 3-2 on agg). Astra Giurgiu 2 (Budescu 32, 36) **West Ham** 1 (Lanzini 3). Att: 6,306 (Astra Giurgiu won 4-3 on agg). Vitesse 0 **Southampton** 2 (Pelle 4, Mane 89). Att: 20,550 (Southampton won 5-0 on agg)

PLAY-OFFS

FIRST LEG

Southampton 1 (Rodriguez 56 pen) Midtjylland 1 (Sparv 45). Att: 28, 890

SECOND LEG

Midtjylland 1 (Rasmussen 28) **Southampton** 0. Att: 9,481 (Midtjylland won 2-1 on agg)

ON AGGREGATE

Ajax 1 Jablonec 0; Athletic Bilbao 3 Zilina 3 (Athletic Bilbao won on away goals); AZ Alkmaar 4 Astra Giurgiu 3; Belenenses 1 Altach 0; Bordeaux 2 Kairat Almaty 2 (Bordeaux won on away goal); Borussia Dortmund 11 Odd Grenland 5; Dinamo Minsk 2 Salzburg 2 (aet, Dinamo Minsk won 3-2 on pens); Fenerbahce 4 Atromitos 0; Krasnodar 5 HJK Helsinki 1; Lech Poznan 4 Videoton 0; Legia Warsaw 4 Zarya Lugansk 2; Molde 3 Standard Liege 3 (Molde won on away goal); PAOK Salonika 6 Brondby 1; Plzen 5 Vojvodina 0; Qabala 2 Panathinaikos 2 (Qabala won on away goals); Qarabag 4 Young Boys 0; Rosenborg 3 Steaua Bucharest 1; Rubin Kazan 2 Rabotnicki 1; Slovan Liberec 2 Hajduk Split 0; Sparta Prague 6 Thun 4; St Etienne 2 Milsami 1

GROUP A

Match-day 1: Ajax 2 (Fischer 24, Schone 84) **Celtic** 2 (Biton 8, Lustig 42). Att: 47,455. Fenerbahce 1 (Nani 42) Molde 3 (Hoiland 36 pen, Elyounoussi 53, Linnes 65). Att: 31,209
Match-day 2: **Celtic** 2 (Griffiths 28, Commons 32) Fenerbahce 2 (De Santana 43, 48). Att: 41,330. Molde 1 (Hestad 7) Ajax 1 (Fischer 18). Att: 7,890
Match-day 3: Fenerbahce 1 (De Santana 89) Ajax 0. Att: 35,292. Molde 3 (Kamara 11, Forren 18, Elyounoussi 56) **Celtic** 1 (Commons). Att: 9,166
Match-day 4: Ajax 0 Fenerbahce 0. Att: 48.990. **Celtic** 1 (Commons 26) Molde 2 (Elyounoussi 21, Hestad 37). Att: 37,071

Match-day 5: **Celtic** 1 (McGregor 4) Ajax 2 (Milik 22, Cerny 87). Att: 44,118. Molde 0 Fenerbahce 2 (De Santana 68, Turfan 84). Att: 8,235
Match-day 6: Ajax 1 (Van de Beek14) Molde 1 (Singh 29). Att: 48,041. Fenerbahce 1 (Markovic 39) **Celtic** 1 (Commons 75). Att: 35,372

	P	W	D	L	F	A	Pts
Molde Q	6	3	2	1	10	7	11
Fenerbahce Q	6	2	3	1	7	6	9
Ajax	6	1	4	1	6	6	7
Celtic	6	0	3	3	8	12	3

GROUP B

Match-day 1: Bordeaux 1 (Jussie 81) **Liverpool** 1 (Lallana 65). Att: 35,328
Sion 2 (Konate 11, 82) Rubin Kazan 1 (Kanunnikov 65). Att: 7,000
Match-day 2: **Liverpool** 1 (Lallana 4) Sion 1 (Assifuah 18). Att: 37,252. Rubin Kazan 0 Bordeaux 0. Att: 17,642
Match-day 3: Bordeaux 0 Sion 1 (Lacroix 21). Att: 18,318. **Liverpool** 1 (Emre Can 37) Rubin Kazan 1 (Devic 15). Att: 42,951
Match-day 4: Rubin Kazan 0 Liverpool 1 (Ibe 52). Att: 41,585. Sion 1 (Chantome 90 og) Bordeaux 1 (Toure 67). Att: 9,000
Match-day 5: Rubin Kazan 2 (Georgiev 72, Devic 90) Sion 0. Att: 15,116. **Liverpool** 2 (Milner 38 pen, Benteke 45) Bordeaux 1 (Saivet 33). Att: 37,254
Match-day 6: Bordeaux 2 (Laborde 58, Rolan 63) Rubin Kazan 2 (Kannunikov 31, Ustinov 76). Att: 13,640. Sion 0 **Liverpool** 0. Att: 10,000

	P	W	D	L	F	A	Pts
Liverpool Q	6	2	4	0	6	4	10
Sion Q	6	2	3	1	5	5	9
Rubin Kazan	6	1	3	2	6	6	6
Bordeaux	6	0	4	2	5	7	4

GROUP C

Match-day 1: Borussia Dortmund 2 (Ginter 45, Park 90) Krasnodar 1 (Mamaev 12). Att: 55,200. Qabala 0 PAOK Salonika 0. Att: 7,500
Match-day 2: Krasnodar 2 (Wanderson 8, Smolov 84) Qabala 1 (Dodo 51). Att: 8,901. PAOK Salonika 1 (Mak 34) Borussia Dortmund 1 (Castro 72). Att: 25,663
Match-day 3: PAOK Salonika 0 Krasnodar 0. Att: 9,325. Qabala 1 (Dodo 90) Borussia Dortmund 3 (Aubameyang 31, 38, 72). Att: 10,500
Match-day 4: Borussia Dortmund 4 (Reus 28, Aubameyang 45, Zenjov 67 og, Mkhitaryan 70) Qabala 0. Att: 57,000. Krasnodar 2 (Ari 33, Joaozinho 67 pen) PAOK Salonika 1 (Mak 90). Att: 15,550
Match-day 5: Krasnodar 1 (Mamaev 2 pen) Borussia Dortmund 0. Att: 30,150. PAOK Salonika 0 Qabala 0. Att: 6,131
Match-day 6: Borussia Dortmund 0 PAOK Salonika 1 (Mak 33). Att: 55,200. Qabala 0 Krasnodar 3 (Sigurdsson 26, Pereyra 40, Wanderson 76). Att: 3,000

	P	W	D	L	F	A	Pts
Krasnodar Q	6	4	1	1	9	4	13
Borussia Dortmund Q	6	3	1	2	10	5	10
PAOK Salonika	6	1	4	1	3	3	7
Qabala	6	0	2	4	2	12	2

GROUP D

Match-day 1: Midtjylland 1 (Kucharczyk 60 og) Legia Warsaw 0. Att: 6,798
Napoli 5 (Callejon 5, 77, Mertens 19, 25, Hamsik 53) Club Bruges 0. Att: 13,043

Match-day 2: Club Bruges 1 (Meunier 79) Midtjylland 3 (Sisto 51, Onuachu 67, Novak 74). Att: 14,126. Legia Warsaw 0 Napoli 2 (Mertens 53, Higuain 84). Att: 26,357
Match-day 3: Legia Warsaw 1 (Kucharczyk 51) Club Bruges 1 (De Fauw 39). Att: 16,230. Midtjylland 1 (Pusic 43) Napoli 4 (Callejon 19, Gabbiadini 31, 40, Higuain 90). Att: 9,210
Match-day 4: Club Bruges 1 (Meunier 38) Legia Warsaw 0. Att: 16,349. Napoli 5 (El Kaddouri 13, Gabbiadini 23, 38, Maggio 54, Callejon 77) Midtjylland 0. Att: 18,475
Match-day 5: Club Bruges 0 Napoli 1 (Chiriches 41). Played behind closed doors – security reasons. Legia Warsaw 1 (Prijovic 35) Midtjylland 0. Att: 9,468
Match-day 6: Midtjylland 1 (Sisto 27) Club Bruges 1 (Vossen 68). Att: 8,624. Napoli 5 (Chalobah 32, Insigne 39, Callejon 57, Mertens 65, 90) Legia Warsaw 2 (Vranjes 62, Prijovic 90). Att: 7,922

	P	W	D	L	F	A	Pts
Napoli Q	6	6	0	0	22	3	18
Midtjylland Q	6	2	1	3	6	12	7
Club Bruges	6	1	2	3	4	11	5
Legia Warsaw	6	1	1	4	4	10	4

GROUP E

Match-day 1: Plzen 2 (Horava 36, Petrzela 75) Dinamo Minsk 0. Att: 10,784
Rapid Vienna 2 (Schwab 50, Hofmann 53 pen) Villarreal 1 (Baptistao 45). Att: 36,200
Match-day 2: Dinamo Minsk 0 Rapid Vienna 1 (Hofmann 54). Att: 4,553. Villarreal 1 (Baptistao 54) Plzen 0. Att: 17,481
Match-day 3: Rapid Vienna 3 (Hofmann 34, Schaub 52, Petsos 67) Plzen 2 (Duris 12, Hrosovsky 76). Att: 39,400. Villarreal 4 (Bakambu 77, 32, Soldado 61, Bailly 70) Dinamo Minsk 0. Att: 14,025
Match-day 4: Dinamo Minsk 1 (Vitus 69) Villarreal 3 (Soldado 72 pen, 86, Politevich 86 og). Att: 4,959. Plzen 1 (Holdenda 71) Rapid Vienna 2 (Schobesberger 13, 77). Att: 11,691
Match-day 5: Dinamo Minsk 1 (Adamovic 90) Plzen 0. Att: 4,250. Villarreal 1 (Bruno 78) Rapid Vienna 0. Att: 14,760
Match-day 6: Plzen 3 (Kolar 8 pen, Kovarik 65, Horava 90) Villarreal 3 (Bakambu 40, Dos Santos 62, Bruno 90). Att: 10,071. Rapid Vienna 2 (Hofmann 29, Jelic 59) Dinamo Minsk 1 (El-Monir 64). Att: 34,800

	P	W	D	L	F	A	Pts
Rapid Vienna Q	6	5	0	1	10	6	15
Villarreal Q	6	4	1	1	12	6	13
Plzen	6	1	1	4	8	10	4
Dinamo Minsk	6	1	0	5	3	11	3

GROUP F

Match-day 1: Groningen 0 Marseille 3 (Nkoudou 25, Ocampos 39, Alessandrini 61). Att: 21,520. Slovan Liberec 0 Braga 1 (Silva 60). Att: 8,132
Match-day 2: Braga 1 (Hassan 5) Groningen 0. Att: 9,150. Marseille 0 Slovan Liberec 1 (Djimsiti 84). Att: 10,040
Match-day 3: Braga 3 (Hassan 61, Eduardo 77, Alan 88) Marseille 2 (Alessandrini 84, Batshuayi 87). Att: 10,495. Slovan Liberec 1 (Luckassen 87) Groningen 1 (Hoesen 90). Att: 8,793
Match-day 4: Groningen 0 Slovan Liberec 2 (Folprecht 81, Padt 81 og). Att: 18,693. Marseille 1 (Nkoudou 39) Braga 0. Att: 12,973
Match-day 5: Braga 2 (Ricardo Ferreira 42, Crislan 90) Slovan Liberec 1 (Efremov 35). Att: 8,144. Marseille 2 (Nkoudou 28, Batshuayi 88) Groningen 1 (Maduro 50). Att: 9,107
Match-day 6: Groningen 0 Braga 0. Att: 15,715. Slovan Liberec 2 (Bakos 75 pen, Sural 76) Marseille 4 (Batshuayi 14, Nkoudou 43, Barrada 48, Ocampos 90). Att: 9,600

	P	W	D	L	F	A	Pts
Braga Q	6	4	1	1	7	4	13
Marseille Q	6	4	0	2	12	7	12
Slovan Liberec	6	2	1	3	6	8	7
Groningen	6	0	2	4	2	8	2

GROUP G

Match-day 1: Dnipro 1 (Seleznyov 90) Lazio 1 (Milinkovic-Savic 34). Played behind closed doors – previous crowd trouble. St Etienne 2 (Beric 4, Roux 87 pen) Rosenborg 2 (Mikkelsen 6, Svensson 79). Att: 22,826

Match-day 2: Lazio 3 (Onazi 22, Hoedt 48, Biglia 80) St Etienne 2 (Bayal Sall 6, Monnet-Paquet 84). Att: 11,039. Rosenborg 0 Dnipro 1 (Seleznyov 79). Att: 13,939

Match-day 3: Dnipro 0 St Etienne 1 (Hamouma 44). Played behind closed doors – previous crowd trouble. Lazio 3 (Matri 28, Anderson 54, Candreva 79) Rosenborg 1 (Porvaldsson 69). Att: 8,630

Match-day 4: Rosenborg 0 Lazio 2 (Djordjevic 9, 29). Att: 16,038. St Etienne 3 (Monnet-Paquet 38, Beric 52, Hamouma 65) Dnipro 0. Att: 24,582

Match-day 5: Lazio 3 (Candreva 4, Mandziuk 68, Djordjevic 90) Dnipro 1 (Gama 65). Att: ,058. Rosenborg 1 (Porvaldsson 40) St Etienne 1 (Roux 80 pen). Att: 15,038

Match-day 6: Dnipro 3 (Matheus 35, 60, Shakhov 79) Rosenborg 0. Att: 4,541. St Etienne 1 (Eysseric 76) Lazio 1 (Matri 52) Att: 28,954

	P	W	D	L	F	A	Pts
Lazio Q	6	4	2	0	13	6	14
St Etienne Q	6	2	3	1	10	7	9
Dnipro	6	2	1	3	6	8	7
Rosenborg	6	0	2	4	4	12	2

GROUP H

Match-day 1: Skenderbeu 0 Besiktas 1 (Sosa 28). Att: 5,482. Sporting Lisbon 1 (Montero 50) Lokomotiv Moscow 3 (Samedov 12, 56, Niasse 65). Att: 25,400

Match-day 2: Besiktas 1 (Tore 61) Sporting Lisbon 1 (Ruiz 16). Att: 25,827. Lokomotiv Moscow 2 (Niasse 35, Samedov 73) Skenderbeu 0. Att: 10,340

Match-day 3: Lokomotiv Moscow 1 (Maicon 54) Besiktas 1 (Gomez 64). Att: 19,124. Sporting Lisbon 5 (Aquilani 38 pen, Montero 41 pen, Pereira 64, 77, Figueiredo 69) Skenderbeu 1 (Mashanica 89). Att: 20,567

Match-day 4: Besiktas 1 (Quaresma 58) Lokomotiv Moscow 1 (Niasse 76). Att: 24,690. . Skenderbeu 3 (Lilaj 15, 19 pen, Nimaga 55) Sporting Lisbon 0. Att: 1,783

Match-day 5: Besiktas 2 (Tosun 35, 78) Skenderbeu 0. Att: 11,155. Lokomotiv Moscow 2 (Maicon 5, Miranchuk 86) Sporting Lisbon 4 (Montero 20, Ruiz 38, Martins 43, Pereira 60. Att: 11,043

Match-day 6: Skenderbeu 0 Lokomotiv Moscow 3 (Tarasov 18, Niassen 88, Samedov 90). Att: ,152. Sporting Lisbon 3 (Slimani 67, Ruiz 72, Gutierrez 77) Besiktas 1 (Gomez 58). Att: 8,211

	P	W	D	L	F	A	Pts
Lokomotiv Moscow Q	6	3	2	1	12	7	11
Sporting Lisbon Q	6	3	1	2	14	11	10
Besiktas	6	2	3	1	7	6	9
Skenderbeu	6	1	0	5	4	13	3

GROUP I

Match-day 1: Fiorentina 1 (Kalinic 3) Basle 2 (Bjarnason 71, El-Nenny 79). Att: 15,212. Lech Poznan 0 Belenenses 0. Att: 7,934

Match-day 2: Basle 2 (Bjarnason 55, Embolo 90) Lech Poznan 0. Att: 17,567. Belenenses 0

Fiorentina 4 (Bernarderschi 18, Babacar 45, Tonel 83 og, Rossi 90). Att: 6,886
Match-day 3: Basle 1 (Lang 15) Belenenses 2 (Leal 27, Alves Miranda 45). Att: 17,275. Fiorentina 1 (Rossi 90) Lech Poznan 2 (Kownacki 65, Gajos 82). Att: 13,792
Match-day 4: Belenenses 0 Basle 2 (Janko 45 pen, Embolo 64). Att: 4,802. Lech Poznan 0 Fiorentina 2 (Ilicic 42, 83). Att: 22,343
Match-day 5: Basle 2 (Suchy 40, El-Nenny 74) Fiorentina 2 (Bernarderschi 23, 36). Att: 22,550. Belenenses 0 Lech Poznan 0. Att: 1,987
Match-day 6: Fiorentina 1 (Babacar 67) Belenenses 0. Att: 12,756. Lech Poznan 0 Basle 1 (Boetius 50). Att: 10,457

	P	W	D	L	F	A	Pts
Basle Q	6	4	1	1	10	5	13
Fiorentina Q	6	3	1	2	11	6	10
Lech Poznan	6	1	2	3	2	6	5
Belenenses	6	1	2	3	2	8	5

GROUP J

Match-day 1: Anderlecht 1 (Gillet 11) Monaco 1 (Traore 85). Att: 15,576. **Tottenham** 3 (Son Heung-min 28, 30, Lamela 86) Qarabag 1 (Richard 7 pen). Att: 26,463
Match-day 2: Monaco 1 (El Shaarawy 81) **Tottenham** 1 (Lamela 35). Att: 7,216. Qarabag 1 (Richard 36) Anderlecht 0. Att: 25,000
Match-day 3: Anderlecht 2 (Gillet 13, Okaka 75) **Tottenham** 1 (Eriksen 4). Att: 18,504. Monaco 1 (Traore 70) Qarabag 0. Att: 6,165
Match-day 4: Qarabag 1 (Armenteros 39) Monaco 1 (Cavaleiro 72). Att: 30,200. **Tottenham** 2 (Kane 29, Dembele 87) Anderlecht 1 (Ezekiel 72). Att: 33,479
Match-day 5: Monaco 0 Anderlecht 2 (Gillet 45, Acheampong 78). Att: 5,913. Qarabag 0 **Tottenham** 1 (Kane 78). Att: 28,000
Match-day 6: Anderlecht 2 (Najar 28, Okaka 31) Qarabag 1 (Quitana Sosa 26). Att: 16,075. **Tottenham** 4 (Lamela 2, 15, 37, Carroll 77) Monaco 1 (El Shaarawy 61). Att: 34,122

	P	W	D	L	F	A	Pts
Tottenham Q	6	4	1	1	12	6	13
Anderlecht Q	6	3	1	2	8	6	10
Monaco	6	1	3	2	5	9	6
Qarabag	6	1	1	4	4	8	4

GROUP K

Match-day 1: Apoel Nicosia 0 Schalke 3 (Matip 28, Huntelaar 35, 71). Att: 13,512. Asteras Triplolis 1 (Mazza 2) Sparta Prague 1 (Lafata 56). Att: 2,984
Match-day 2: Schalke 4 (Di Santo 28, 37, 44 pen, Huntelaar 84) Asteras Tripolis 0. Att: 42,447. Sparta Prague 2 (Fatai 24, Brabec 60) Apoel Nicosia 0. Att: 9,130
Match-day 3: Apoel Nicosia 2 (Cavenaghi 43 pen, Carlao 59) Asteras Tripolis 1 (Lluy 8). Att: 12,783. Schalke 2 (Di Santo 6, Sane 73) Sparta Prague 2 (Fatai 50, Lafata 63). Att: 51,244
Match-day 4: Asteras Tripolis 2 (Bertoglio 2, Giannou 45) Apoel Nicosia 0. Att: 3,624. Sparta Prague 1 (Lafata 6) Schalke 1 (Geis 20 pen). Att: 17,352
Match-day 5: Schalke 1 (Choupo-Moting 86) Apoel Nicosia 0. Att: 43,117. Sparta Prague 1 (Brabec 33) Asteras Tripolis 0. Att: 10,140
Match-day 6: Apoel Nicosia 1 (Cavenaghi 6) Sparta Prague 3 (Julis 63, Lafata 77, 87). Att: 5,940. Asteras Tripolis 0 Schalke 4 (Di Santo 29, Choupo-Moting 37, 78, Meyer 86). Att: 2,50

	P	W	D	L	F	A	Pts
Schalke Q	6	4	2	0	15	3	14
Sparta Prague Q	6	3	3	0	10	5	12
Asteras Tripolis	6	1	1	4	4	12	4
Apoel Nicosia	6	1	0	5	3	12	3

ROUP L

latch-day 1: Athletic Bilbao 3 (Aduriz 55, 66, Del Moral 90) Augsburg 1 (Altintop 15). Att: 7,838. Partizan 3 (Oumarou 11, 39, Zivkovic 89) Alkmaar 2 (Van der Linden 34, Henriksen 0). Att: 7,949

latch-day 2: Alkmaar 2 (Henriksen 55, Boveda 65 og) Athletic Bilbao 1 (Aduriz 75). Att: 1,434. Augsburg 1 (Bobadilla 57) Partizan 3 (Zivkovic 31, 62, Silva Dornellas 54). Att: 2,948

latch-day 3: Alkmaar 0 Augsburg 1 (Trochowski 43). Att: 16,511. Partizan 0 Athletic Bilbao 2 Garcia 32, Benat 85). Att: 11,128

latch-day 4: Athletic Bilbao 5 (Williams 16, 19, Benat 40, Aduriz 71, Elustondo 81) Partizan (Oumarou 17). Att: 39,849. Augsburg 4 (Bobadilla 24, 33, 74, Ji 66) Alkmaar 1 (Janssen 5). Att: 24,241

latch-day 5: Alkmaar 1 (Souza 48) Partizan 2 (Oumarou 65, Zivkovic 89). Att: 12,784. ugsburg 2 (Trochowski 41, Bobadilla 59) Athletic Bilbao 3 (Del Moral 10, Aduriz 83, 86). tt: 23,741

latch-day 6: Athletic Bilbao 2 (Sola 43, San Jose 47) Alkmaar 2 (Van Overeem 26, Janssen 8). Att: 29,483. Partizan 1 (Oumarou 11) Augsburg 3 (Hong 45, Verhaegh 51. Bobadilla 89). tt: 14,132

	P	W	D	L	F	A	Pts
thletic Bilbao Q	6	4	1	1	16	8	13
ugsburg Q	6	3	0	3	12	11	9
artizan	6	3	0	3	10	14	9
lkmaar	6	1	1	4	8	13	4

OUND OF 32, FIRST LEG

nderlecht 1 (Mbodj 67) Olympiacos 0. Att: 15,397. Augsburg 0 **Liverpool** 0. Att: 25,000. orussia Dortmund 2 (Piszczek 6, Reus 71) Porto 0. Att: 65,851; Fenerbahce 2 (Souza 18, 2) Lokomotiv Moscow 0. Att: 36,195

iorentina 1 (Bernarderschi 59) **Tottenham** 1 (Chadli 37 pen). Att: 16,536. Galatasaray 1 Sarioglu 12) Lazio 1 (Milinkovic-Savic 21). Att: 33,353. Marseille 0 Athletic Bilbao 1 (Aduriz 4) Att: 29,727. Midtjylland 2 (Sisto 44, Onuachu 77) **Manchester Utd** 1 (Depay 37). Att: ,182 Sevilla 3 (Llorente 35, 49, Gameiro 72) Molde 0. Att: 28,920. Shakhtar Donetsk 0 chalke 0. 23,615. Sion 1 (Konate 53) Braga 2 (Stojiljkovic 13, Silva 61). Att: 7,776. St tienne 3 (Bayal Sall 9, Monnet-Paquet 39, Bahebeck 77) Basle 2 (Samuel 44, Janko 56 en). Att: 27,013

parta Prague 1 (Julis 64) Krasnodar 0. Att: 14,120. Sporting Lisbon 0 Bayer Leverkusen 1 Bellarabi 26). Att: 26,201. Villarreal 1 (Suarez 82) Napoli 0. Att: 17,686. Valencia 6 (Mina , 25, Parejo 10, Negredo 29, Gomes 35, Rodrigo 89) Rapid Vienna 0. Att: 28,831

OUND OF 32, SECOND LEG

thletic Bilbao 1 (Sabin 81) Marseille 1 (Batshuayi 40). Att: 38,259 (Athletic Bilbao won -1 on agg). Basle 2 (Zuffi 15, 90) St Etienne 1 (Bayal Sall 89). Att: 20,976 (agg 4-4, Basle on on away goals). Bayer Leverkusen 3 (Bellarabi 29, 65, Calhanoglu 87) Sporting Lisbon (Mario 38). Att: 26,585 (Bayer Leverklusen won 4-1 on agg). Braga 2 (Josue 27 pen, tojiljkovic 48) Sion 2 (Gekas 16, 29). Att: 6,759 (Braga won 4-3 on agg)

rasnodar 0 Sparta Prague 3 (Marecek 51, Frydek 57, Fatai 70). Att: 14,850 (Sparta Prague on 4-0 on agg). Lazio 3 (Mandziuk 59, Anderson 61, Klose 72) Galatasaray 1 (Oztekin 62). tt: 14,019 (Lazio won 4-2 on agg). **Liverpool** 1 (Milner 5 pen) Augsburg 0. Att: 43,801 Liverpool won 1-0 on agg). Lokomotiv Moscow 1 (Samedov 45) Fenerbahce 1 (Topal 83). Att: 5,695 (Fenerbahce won 3-1 on agg).

lanchester Utd 5 (Bodurov 32 og, Rashford 63, 75, Herrera 87 pen, Depay 90) Midtjylland (Sisto 27). Att: 58,609 (Manchester Utd won 6-3 on agg). Molde 1 (Hestad 43) Sevilla 0. t: 7,284 (Sevilla won 3-1 on agg). Napoli 1 (Hamsik 17) Villarreal 1 (Pina 59). Att: 23,928

(Villarreal won 2-1 on agg). Olympiacos 1 (Fortounis 29 pen) Anderlecht 2 (Acheampong 103, 111). Att: 31,005 (aet, Anderlecht won 3-1 on agg)

Porto 0 Borussia Dortmund 1 (Casillas 23 og). Att: 32,707 (Borussia Dortmund won 3-0 on agg) Rapid Vienna 0 Valencia 4 (Rodrigo 59, Feghouli 63, Piatti 72, Vezo 88). Att: 39,800 (Valencia won 10-0 on agg – Europa League record); Schalke 0 Shakhtar Donetsk 3 (Marlos 26, Ferreyra 63, Kovalenko 77). Att 45,308 (Shakhtar Donetsk won 3-0 on agg). **Tottenham** 3 (Mason 25, Lamela 63, Gonzalo 81 og) Fiorentina 0. Att: 34,880 (Tottenham won 4-1 on agg)

ROUND OF 16, FIRST LEG

Athletic Bilbao 1 (Garcia 20) Valencia 0. Att: 35,765. Basle 0 Sevilla 0. Att: 22,403. Borussia Dortmund 3 (Aubameyang 30, Reus 61, 70) **Tottenham** 0. Att: 65,848. Fenerbahce 1 (Topal 82) Braga 0. Att: 40,197

Liverpool 2 (Sturridge 20 pen, Firmino 73) **Manchester Utd** 0. Att: 43,228. Shakhtar Donetsk 3 (Taison 21, Kucher 24, Eduardo 79) Anderlecht 1 (Acheampong 68). Att: 23,621. Sparta Prague 1 (Frydek 13) Lazio 1 (Mandziuk 38). Att: 17,482. Villarreal 2 (Bakambu 4, 56) Bayer Leverkusen 0. Att: 16,211

ROUND OF 16, SECOND LEG

Anderlecht 0 Shakhtar Donetsk 1 (Eduardo 90). Att: 13,785 (Shakhtar Donetsko won 4-1 on agg). Bayer Leverkusen 0 Villarreal 0. Att: 23,409 (Villarreal won 2-0 on agg). Braga 4 (Hassan 11, Josue 69 pen, Stojilikovic 74, Silva 83) Fenerbahce 1 (Potuk 45). Att: 16,431 (Braga won 4-2 on agg). Lazio 0 Sparta Prague 3 (Dockal 10, Krejci 12, Julis 44). Att: 18,827 (Sparta Prague won 4-1 on agg)

Manchester Utd 1 (Martial 32 pen) **Liverpool** 1 (Coutinho 45). Att: 75,180 (Liverpool won 3-1 on agg). Sevilla 3 (Rami 35, Gameiro 44, 45) Basle 0. Att: 35,546 (Sevilla won 3-0 on agg) **Tottenham** 1 (Son Heung-Min 73) Borussia Dortmund 2 (Aubameyang 24, 70). Att: 34,943 (Borussia Dortmund won 5-1 on agg). Valencia 2 (Mina 13, Santos 37) Athletic Bilbao 1 (Aduriz 75). Att: 31,681 (agg 2-2, Athletic Bilbao won on away goal)

QUARTER-FINALS, FIRST LEG

Athletic Bilbao 1 (Aduriz 48) Sevilla 2 (Kolodzieczak 56, Iborra 83). Att: 40,856. Borussia Dortmund 1 (Hummels 48) **Liverpool** 1 (Origi 36). Att: 65,848. Braga 1 (Eduardo 89) Shakhtar Donetsk 2 (Rakitskiy 45, Ferreyra 75). Att: 21,645. Villarreal 2 (Bakambu 3, 63) Sparta Prague 1 (Brabec 45). Att: 15,803

QUARTER-FINALS, SECOND LEG

Liverpool 4 (Origi 48, Coutinho 66, Sakho 78, Lovren 90) Borussia Dortmund 3 (Mkhitaryan 5, Aubameyang 9, Reus 57). Att: 42,984 (Liverpool won 5-4 on agg). Sevilla 1 (Gameiro 59) Athletic Bilbao 2 (Aduriz 57, Raul Garcia 80). Att: 38,567 (aet, agg 3-3, Sevilla won 5-4 on pens). Shakhtar Donetsk 4 (Srna 25 pen, Ricardo Ferreira 42 og, 74 og, Kovalenko 50) Braga 0. Att: 33,617 (Shakhtar Donetsk won 6-1 on agg). Sparta Prague 2 (Dockal 65, Krejci 71) Villarreal 4 (Bakambu 5, 49, Castillejo 43, Lafata 45 og). Att: 18,201 (Villarreal won 6-3 on agg)

SEMI-FINALS, FIRST LEG

Shakhtar Donetsk 2 (Marios 23, Stepanenko 36) Sevilla 2 (Vitolo 6, Gameiro 82 pen). Att: 34,267. Villarreal 1 (Adrian 90) **Liverpool** 0. Att: 21,606

SEMI-FINALS, SECOND LEG

Liverpool 3 (Bruno 8 og, Sturridge 63, Lallana 81) Villarreal 0. Att: 43,074 (Liverpool won 3-1 on agg). Sevilla 3 (Gameiro 9, 47, Mariano 59) Shakhtar Donetsk 1 (Eduardo 44). Att: 41,286 (Sevilla won 5-3 on agg)

FINAL

LIVERPOOL 1 SEVILLA 3

St Jakob Park, Basle (34,429); Wednesday, May 18 2016

Liverpool (4-2-3-1): Mignolet, Clyne, Lovren, Toure (Benteke 82), Moreno, Milner (capt), Emre Can, Lallana (Allen 73), Firmino (Origi 69), Coutinho, Sturridge. **Subs not used**: Ward, Henderson, Skrtel, Lucas. **Scorer**: Sturridge (35). **Booked**: Lovren, Origi, Clyne. **Manager**: Jurgen Klopp

Sevilla (4-2-3-1): Soria, Mariano, Rami (Kolodziejczak 78), Carrico, Escudero, Krychowiak, Nzonzi, Coke (capt), Banega (Cristoforo 90), Vitolo, Gameiro (Iborra 89). **Subs not used**: Rico, Pareja, Konoplyanka, Llorente. **Scorers**: Coke (64, 70), Gameiro (46). **Booked**: Vitolo, Banega, Rami, Mariano. **Coach**: Unai Emery

Referee: J Eriksson (Sweden). **Half-time**: 1-0

The manner of the defeat hurt Jurgen Klopp and his players just as much – if not more – than having to finish the season without a trophy, without the Champions League place on offer and, indeed, without any European football to look forward to. A goal to the good at half-time, courtesy of Daniel Sturridge, they conceded 17 seconds after the restart and were simply outplayed throughout the second-half. The fact that Sevilla joined illustrious company in Real Madrid, Bayern Munich and Ajax in winning a third straight European title made their collapse no easier to accept. The Spanish side had become hardened to success in this tournament, yet Liverpool themselves had given every indication in previous rounds of being able to match them. They knocked out Manchester United, served up one of the great nights at Anfield to overcome Klopp's former side Borussia Dortmund and proved too good for Villarreal in the semi-finals. All of which reflected the zest and optimism he had brought to the club in the six months or so since replacing Brendan Rodgers. Defeat on penalties in the League Cup against Manchester City on penalties would have been put aside without too much worry. This one, Klopp's fifth in succession in a cup final, meant he would have to re-examine the way forward and what it might take to make Liverpool a force again.

Leading scorers (from group stage): 10 Aduriz (Athletic Bilbao); 9 Bakambu (Villarreal); 8 Aubameyang (Borussia Dortmund), Gameiro (Sevilla); 6 Bobadilla (Augsburg), Lamela (Tottenham); 5 Callejon (Napoli), Di Santo (Schalke), Lafata (Sparta Prague), Mertens (Napoli), Reus (Borussia Dortmund), Samedov (Lokomotiv)

FIFA CLUB WORLD CUP – JAPAN 2015

QUALIFYING MATCHES

America (Mexico) 1 (Peralta 55) Guangzhou Evergrande (China) 2 (Zheng Long 80, Paulinho 90). Att: 18,772 (Osaka). Mazembe (Dem Rep of Congo) 0 Sanfrecce Hiroshima (Japan) 3 (Shiotani 44, Chiba 56, Asano 78). Att: 23,609 (Osaka)

SEMI-FINALS

Sanfrecce Hiroshima 0 River Plate (Argentina) 1 (Alario 72). Att: 20,133 (Osaka). Barcelona 3 (Suarez 39, 50, 67 pen) Guangzhou Evergrande 0. Att: 63,870 (Yokohama)

FINAL

RIVER PLATE 0 BARCELONA 3

Yokohama (66,853); Sunday, December 20 2015

River Plate (4-1-3-2): Barovero, Mercado, Maidana, Alvarez, Vangioni, Kranevitter, Sanchez, Viudez (Driussi 56), Ponzio (Gonzalez 46), Mora (Martinez 46), Alario. **Subs not used**: Batalla, Chiarini, Vega, Saviola, Pisculichi, Bertolo, Mayada, Casco, Mammana. **Booked**: Kranevitter, Ponzio. **Coach**: Marcelo Gallardo

Barcelona (4-3-3): Bravo, Dani Alves, Pique, Mascherano (Vermaelen 81), Jordi Alba, Rakitic

(Sergi Roberto 67), Busquets, Iniesta, Messi, Suarez, Neymar (Mathieu 89). **Subs not used**: ter Stegen, Masip, Bartra, Munir, Ramirez, Adriano, Sergi Samper, Gumbau. **Scorers**: Messi (36), Suarez (49, 68). **Booked**: Jordi Alba, Rakitic, Neymar, Sergi Roberto. **Coach**: Luis Enrique
Referee: A Faghani (Iran). **Half-time**: 0-1

EUROPEAN SUPER CUP

BARCELONA 5 SEVILLA 4 (aet)
Tbilisi (51,940); Tuesday, August 11 2015

Barcelona (4-3-3): ter Stegen, Dani Alves, Pique, Mascherano (Pedro 93), Mathieu, Rakitic, Busquets, Iniesta (Sergi Roberto 63), Messi, L Suarez, Rafinha (Bartra 78). **Subs not used**: Bravo, Adriano, Ramirez, Munir. **Scorers**: Messi (7, 16), Rafinha (44), L Suarez (52), Pedro (115). **Booked**: Mathieu, Pedro, Busquets, Dani Alves. **Coach**: Luis Enrique
Sevilla (4-2-3-1): Beto, Coke, Rami, Krychowiak, Tremoulinas, Krohn-Dehli, Banega, Reyes (Konoplyanka 68), Iborra (Mariano 80), Vitolo, Gameiro (Immobile 80). **Subs not used**: Rico, Kakuta, Sanchez D Suarez. **Scorers**: Banega (3), Reyes (57), Gameiro (72 pen), Konoplyanka (81). **Booked**: Krychowiak, Coke, Banega, Immobile, Krohn-Dehli. **Coach**: Unai Emery
Referee: W Collum (Scotland). **Half-time**: 3-1

UEFA CUP FINALS

1972 Tottenham beat Wolves 3-2 on agg (2-1a, 1-1h)
1973 Liverpool beat Borussia Moenchengladbach 3-2 on agg (3-0h, 0-2a)
1974 Feyenoord beat Tottenham 4-2 on agg (2-2a, 2-0h)
1975 Borussia Moenchengladbach beat Twente Enschede 5-1 on agg (0-0h, 5-1a)
1976 Liverpool beat Brugge 4-3 on agg (3-2h, 1-1a)
1977 Juventus beat Atletico Bilbao on away goals after 2-2 agg (1-0h, 1-2a)
1978 PSV Eindhoven beat Bastia 3-0 on agg (0-0a, 3-0h)
1979 Borussia Moenchengladbach beat Red Star Belgrade 2-1 on agg (1-1a, 1-0h)
1980 Eintracht Frankfurt beat Borussia Moenchengladbach on away goals after 3-3 agg (2-3a, 1-0h)
1981 Ipswich Town beat AZ 67 Alkmaar 5-4 on agg (3-0h, 2-4a)
1982 IFK Gothenburg beat SV Hamburg 4-0 on agg (1-0h, 3-0a)
1983 Anderlecht beat Benfica 2-1 on agg (1-0h, 1-1a)
1984 Tottenham beat Anderlecht 4-3 on penalties after 2-2 agg (1-1a, 1-1h)
1985 Real Madrid beat Videoton 3-1 on agg (3-0a, 0-1h)
1986 Real Madrid beat Cologne 5-3 on agg (5-1h, 0-2a)
1987 IFK Gothenburg beat Dundee Utd 2-1 on agg (1-0h, 1-1a)
1988 Bayer Leverkusen beat Espanol 3-2 on penalties after 3-3 agg (0-3a, 3-0h)
1989 Napoli beat VfB Stuttgart 5-4 on agg (2-1h, 3-3a)
1990 Juventus beat Fiorentina 3-1 on agg (3-1h, 0-0a)
1991 Inter Milan beat AS Roma 2-1 on agg (2-0h, 0-1a)
1992 Ajax beat Torino on away goals after 2-2 agg (2-2a, 0-0h)
1993 Juventus beat Borussia Dortmund 6-1 on agg (3-1a, 3-0h)
1994 Inter Milan beat Salzburg 2-0 on agg (1-0a, 1-0h)
1995 Parma beat Juventus 2-1 on agg (1-0h, 1-1a)
1996 Bayern Munich beat Bordeaux 5-1 on agg (2-0h, 3-1a)
1997 FC Schalke beat Inter Milan 4-1 on penalties after 1-1 agg (1-0h, 0-1a)
1998 Inter Milan beat Lazio 3-0 (one match) – Paris
1999 Parma beat Marseille 3-0 (one match) – Moscow
2000 Galatasaray beat Arsenal 4-1 on penalties after 0-0 (one match) – Copenhagen
2001 Liverpool beat Alaves 5-4 on golden goal (one match) – Dortmund
2002 Feyenoord beat Borussia Dortmund 3-2 (one match) – Rotterdam
2003 FC Porto beat Celtic 3-2 on silver goal (one match) – Seville

2004 Valencia beat Marseille 2-0 (one match) – Gothenburg
2005 CSKA Moscow beat Sporting Lisbon 3-1 (one match) – Lisbon
2006 Sevilla beat Middlesbrough 4-0 (one match) – Eindhoven
2007 Sevilla beat Espanyol 3-1 on penalties after 2-2 (one match) – Hampden Park
2008 Zenit St Petersburg beat Rangers 2-0 (one match) – City of Manchester Stadium
2009† Shakhtar Donetsk beat Werder Bremen 2-1 (one match) – Istanbul

EUROPA LEAGUE FINALS

2010† Atletico Madrid beat Fulham 2-1 (one match) – Hamburg
2011 Porto beat Braga 1-0 (one match) – Dublin
2012 Atletico Madrid beat Athletic Bilbao 3-0 (one match) – Bucharest
2013 Chelsea beat Benfica 2-1 (one match) – Amsterdam
2014 Sevilla beat Benfica 4-2 on penalties after 0-0 (one match) – Turin
2015 Sevilla beat Dnipro 3-2 (one match) - Warsaw
2016 Sevilla beat Liverpool 3-1 (one match) - Basle
(† After extra-time)

FAIRS CUP FINALS

(As UEFA Cup previously known)
1958 Barcelona beat London 8-2 on agg (2-2a, 6-0h)
1960 Barcelona beat Birmingham 4-1 on agg (0-0a, 4-1h)
1961 AS Roma beat Birmingham City 4-2 on agg (2-2a, 2-0h)
1962 Valencia beat Barcelona 7-3 on agg (6-2h, 1-1a)
1963 Valencia beat Dynamo Zagreb 4-1 on agg (2-1a, 2-0h)
1964 Real Zaragoza beat Valencia 2-1 (Barcelona)
1965 Ferencvaros beat Juventus 1-0 (Turin)
1966 Barcelona beat Real Zaragoza 4-3 on agg (0-1h, 4-2a)
1967 Dinamo Zagreb beat Leeds Utd 2-0 on agg (2-0h, 0-0a)
1968 Leeds Utd beat Ferencvaros 1-0 on agg (1-0h, 0-0a)
1969 Newcastle Utd beat Ujpest Dozsa 6-2 on agg (3-0h, 3-2a)
1970 Arsenal beat Anderlecht 4-3 on agg (1-3a, 3-0h)
1971 Leeds Utd beat Juventus on away goals after 3-3 agg (2-2a, 1-1h)

CUP-WINNERS' CUP FINALS

1961 Fiorentina beat Rangers 4-1 on agg (2-0 Glasgow first leg, 2-1 Florence second leg)
1962 Atletico Madrid beat Fiorentina 3-0 (replay Stuttgart, after a 1-1 draw, Glasgow)
1963 Tottenham beat Atletico Madrid 5-1 (Rotterdam)
1964 Sporting Lisbon beat MTK Budapest 1-0 (replay Antwerp, after a 3-3 draw, Brussels)
1965 West Ham Utd beat Munich 1860 2-0 (Wembley)
1966† Borussia Dortmund beat Liverpool 2-1 (Glasgow)
1967† Bayern Munich beat Rangers 1-0 (Nuremberg)
1968 AC Milan beat SV Hamburg 2-0 (Rotterdam)
1969 Slovan Bratislava beat Barcelona 3-2 (Basle)
1970 Manchester City beat Gornik Zabrze 2-1 (Vienna)
1971† Chelsea beat Real Madrid 2-1 (replay Athens, after a 1-1 draw, Athens)
1972 Rangers beat Moscow Dynamo 3-2 (Barcelona)
1973 AC Milan beat Leeds Utd 1-0 (Salonika)
1974 Magdeburg beat AC Milan 2-0 (Rotterdam)
1975 Dynamo Kiev beat Ferencvaros 3-0 (Basle)
1976 Anderlecht beat West Ham Utd 4-2 (Brussels)
1977 SV Hamburg beat Anderlecht 2-0 (Amsterdam)

1978 Anderlecht beat Austria WAC 4-0 (Paris)
1979† Barcelona beat Fortuna Dusseldorf 4-3 (Basle)
1980† Valencia beat Arsenal 5-4 on penalties after a 0-0 draw (Brussels)
1981 Dinamo Tbilisi beat Carl Zeiss Jena 2-1 (Dusseldorf)
1982 Barcelona beat Standard Liege 2-1 (Barcelona)
1983† Aberdeen beat Real Madrid 2-1 (Gothenburg)
1984 Juventus beat Porto 2-1 (Basle)
1985 Everton beat Rapid Vienna 3-1 (Rotterdam)
1986 Dynamo Kiev beat Atletico Madrid 3-0 (Lyon)
1987 Ajax beat Lokomotiv Leipzig 1-0 (Athens)
1988 Mechelen beat Ajax 1-0 (Strasbourg)
1989 Barcelona beat Sampdoria 2-0 (Berne)
1990 Sampdoria beat Anderlecht 2-0 (Gothenburg)
1991 Manchester Utd beat Barcelona 2-1 (Rotterdam)
1992 Werder Bremen beat Monaco 2-0 (Lisbon)
1993 Parma beat Royal Antwerp 3-1 (Wembley)
1994 Arsenal beat Parma 1-0 (Copenhagen)
1995† Real Zaragoza beat Arsenal 2-1 (Paris)
1996 Paris St Germain beat Rapid Vienna 1-0 (Brussels)
1997 Barcelona beat Paris St Germain 1-0 (Rotterdam)
1998 Chelsea beat VfB Stuttgart 1-0 (Stockholm)
1999 Lazio beat Real Mallorca 2-1 (Villa Park, Birmingham)
(† After extra time)

EUROPEAN SUPER CUP RESULTS

1972* Ajax beat Rangers 6-3 on agg (3-1, 3-2)
1973 Ajax beat AC Milan 6-1 on agg (0-1, 6-0)
1974 Bayern Munich and Magdeburg did not play
1975 Dynamo Kiev beat Bayern Munich 3-0 on agg (1-0, 2-0)
1976 Anderlecht beat Bayern Munich 5-3 on agg (1-2, 4-1)
1977 Liverpool beat Hamburg 7-1 on agg (1-1, 6-0)
1978 Anderlecht beat Liverpool 4-3 on agg (3-1, 1-2)
1979 Nottm Forest beat Barcelona 2-1 on agg (1-0, 1-1)
1980 Valencia beat Nottm Forest on away goal after 2-2 agg (1-2, 1-0)
1981 Liverpool and Dinamo Tbilisi did not play
1982 Aston Villa beat Barcelona 3-1 on agg (0-1, 3-0 aet)
1983 Aberdeen beat Hamburg 2-0 on agg (0-0, 2-0)
1984 Juventus beat Liverpool 2-0 - one match (Turin)
1985 Juventus and Everton did not play
1986 Steaua Bucharest beat Dynamo Kiev 1-0 – one match (Monaco)
1987 Porto beat Ajax 2-0 on agg (1-0, 1-0)
1988 Mechelen beat PSV Eindhoven 3-1 on agg (3-0, 0-1)
1989 AC Milan beat Barcelona 2-1 on agg (1-1, 1-0)
1990 AC Milan beat Sampdoria 3-1 on agg (1-1, 2-0)
1991 Manchester Utd beat Red Star Belgrade 1-0 – one match (Old Trafford)
1992 Barcelona beat Werder Bremen 3-2 on agg (1-1, 2-1)
1993 Parma beat AC Milan 2-1 on agg (0-1, 2-0 aet)
1994 AC Milan beat Arsenal 2-0 on agg (0-0, 2-0)
1995 Ajax beat Real Zaragoza 5-1 on agg (1-1, 4-0)
1996 Juventus beat Paris St Germain 9-2 on agg (6-1, 3-1)
1997 Barcelona beat Borussia Dortmund 3-1 on agg (2-0, 1-1)
1998 Chelsea beat Real Madrid 1-0 (Monaco)
1999 Lazio beat Manchester Utd 1-0 (Monaco)

2000 Galatasaray beat Real Madrid 2-1 – aet, golden goal (Monaco)
2001 Liverpool beat Bayern Munich 3-2 (Monaco)
2002 Real Madrid beat Feyenoord 3-1 (Monaco)
2003 AC Milan beat Porto 1-0 (Monaco)
2004 Valencia beat Porto 2-1 (Monaco)
2005 Liverpool beat CSKA Moscow 3-1 – aet (Monaco)
2006 Sevilla beat Barcelona 3-0 (Monaco)
2007 AC Milan beat Sevilla 3-1 (Monaco)
2008 Zenit St Petersburg beat Manchester Utd 2-1 (Monaco)
2009 Barcelona beat Shakhtar Donetsk 1-0 – aet (Monaco)
2010 Atletico Madrid beat Inter Milan 2-0 (Monaco)
2011 Barcelona beat Porto 2-0 (Monaco)
2012 Atletico Madrid beat Chelsea 4-1 (Monaco)
2013 Bayern Munich beat Chelsea 5-4 on pens, aet – 2-2 (Prague)
2014 Real Madrid beat Sevilla 2-0 (Cardiff)
2015 Barcelona beat Sevilla 5-4 – aet (Tbilisi)

*not recognised by UEFA; from 1998 one match

INTER-CONTINENTAL CUP

Year	*Winners*	*Runners-up*	*Score*
1960	Real Madrid (Spa)	Penarol (Uru)	0-0 5-1
1961	Penarol (Uru)	Benfica (Por)	0-1 2-1 5-0
1962	Santos (Bra)	Benfica (Por)	3-2 5-2
1963	Santos (Bra)	AC Milan (Ita)	2-4 4-2 1-0
1964	Inter Milan (Ita)	Independiente (Arg)	0-1 2-0 1-0
1965	Inter Milan (Ita)	Independiente (Arg)	3-0 0-0
1966	Penarol (Uru)	Real Madrid (Spa)	2-0 2-0
1967	Racing (Arg)	Celtic (Sco)	0-1 2-1 1-0
1968	Estudiantes (Arg)	Manchester Utd (Eng)	1-0 1-1
1969	AC Milan (Ita)	Estudiantes (Arg)	3-0 1-2
1970	Feyenoord (Hol)	Estudiantes (Arg)	2-2 1-0
1971	Nacional (Uru)	Panathanaikos (Gre)	* 1-1 2-1
1972	Ajax (Hol)	Independiente (Arg)	1-1 3-0
1973	Independiente (Arg)	Juventus* (Ita)	1-0 #
1974	Atletico Madrid (Spa)*	Independiente (Arg)	0-1 2-0
1975	Not played		
1976	Bayern Munich (WGer)	Cruzeiro (Bra)	2-0 0-0
1977	Boca Juniors (Arg)	Borussia Mönchengladbach* (WGer)	2-2 3-0
1978	Not played		
1979	Olimpia Asuncion (Par)	Malmö* (Swe)	1-0 2-1
1980	Nacional (Arg)	Nott'm Forest (Eng)	1-0
1981	Flamengo (Bra)	Liverpool (Eng)	3-0
1982	Penarol (Uru)	Aston Villa (Eng)	2-0
1983	Porto Alegre (Bra)	SV Hamburg (WGer)	2-1
1984	Independiente (Arg)	Liverpool (Eng)	1-0
1985	Juventus (Ita)	Argentinos Juniors (Arg)	2-2 (aet)
		(Juventus won 4-2 on penalties)	
1986	River Plate (Arg)	Steaua Bucharest (Rom)	1-0
1987	Porto (Por)	Penarol (Uru)	2-1 (aet)
1988	Nacional (Uru)	PSV Eindhoven (Hol)	1-1 (aet)
		(Nacional won 7-6 on penalties)	

1989	AC Milan (Ita)	Nacional (Col)	1-0 (aet)
1990	AC Milan (Ita)	Olimpia Asuncion (Par)	3-0
1991	Red Star (Yug)	Colo Colo (Chi)	3-0
1992	Sao Paulo (Bra)	Barcelona (Spa)	2-1
1993	Sao Paulo (Bra)	AC Milan (Ita)	3-2
1994	Velez Sarsfield (Arg)	AC Milan (Ita)	2-0
1995	Ajax (Hol)	Gremio (Bra)	0-0 (aet)
		(Ajax won 4-3 on penalties)	
1996	Juventus (Ita)	River Plate (Arg)	1-0
1997	Borussia Dortmund (Ger)	Cruzeiro (Arg)	2-0
1998	Real Madrid (Spa)	Vasco da Gama (Bra)	2-1
1999	Manchester Utd (Eng)	Palmeiras (Bra)	1-0
2000	Boca Juniors (Arg)	Real Madrid (Spa)	2-1
2001	Bayern Munich (Ger)	Boca Juniors (Arg)	1-0
2002	Real Madrid (Spa)	Olimpia Ascuncion (Par)	2-0
2003	Boca Juniors (Arg)	AC Milan (Ita)	1-1
(Boca Juniors won 3-1 on penalties)			
2004	FC Porto (Por)	Caldas (Col)	0-0
(FC Porto won 8-7 on penalties)			

Played as a single match in Japan since 1980

* European Cup runners-up # One match only

Summary: 43 contests; South America 22 wins, Europe 23 wins

CLUB WORLD CHAMPIONSHIP

2005	Sao Paulo beat Liverpool	1-0
2006	Internacional (Bra) beat Barcelona	1-0
2007	AC Milan beat Boca Juniors (Arg)	4-2

CLUB WORLD CUP

2008	Manchester Utd beat Liga de Quito	1-0
2009	Barcelona beat Estudiantes	2-1 (aet)
2010	Inter Milan beat TP Mazembe	3-0
2011	Barcelona beat Santos	4-0
2012	Corinthians beat Chelsea	1-0
2013	Bayern Munich beat Raja Casablanca	2-0
2014	Real Madrid beat San Lorenzo	2-0
2015	Barcelona beat River Plate	3-0

THE THINGS THEY SAY ...

'Usually I have a second pair around, but I couldn't find them. It is really difficult looking for glasses without glasses' – **Jurgen Klopp**, Liverpool manager, whose spectacles were smashed b his players celebrating a 5-4 win against Norwich.

'From cloud nine to ground zero' – **Clive Tyldesley**, ITV commentator, after England's comebac win over Germany is followed by a Wembley defeat by Holland.

EUROPEAN TABLES 2015–2016

FRANCE – LIGUE 1

	P	W	D	L	F	A	GD	Pts
Paris SG	38	30	6	2	102	19	83	96
Lyon	38	19	8	11	67	43	24	65
Monaco	38	17	14	7	57	50	7	65
Nice	38	18	9	11	58	41	17	63
Lille	38	15	15	8	39	27	12	60
St Etienne	38	17	7	14	42	37	5	58
Caen	38	16	6	16	39	52	-13	54
Rennes	38	13	13	12	52	54	-2	52
Angers	38	13	11	14	40	38	2	50
Bastia	38	14	8	16	36	42	-6	50
Bordeaux	38	12	14	12	50	57	-7	50
Montpellier	38	14	7	17	49	47	2	49
Marseille	38	10	18	10	48	42	6	48
Nantes	38	12	12	14	33	44	-11	48
Lorient	38	11	13	14	47	58	-11	46
Guingamp	38	11	11	16	47	56	-9	44
Toulouse	38	9	13	16	45	55	-10	40
Reims	38	10	9	19	44	57	-13	39
Ajaccio	38	8	13	17	37	58	-21	37
Troyes	38	3	9	26	28	83	-55	18

Leading league scorers: 38 Ibrahimovic (Paris SG); 21 Lacazette (Lyon); 19 Cavani (Paris SG); 17 Batshuayi (Marseille), Ben Arfa (Nice), Ben Yedder (Toulouse); 14 Germain (Nice); 13 Moukandjo (Lorient); 12 Dembele (Rennes), Delort (Caen)

Cup Final: Paris SG 4 (Matuidi 2, Ibrahimovic 47 pen, 82, Cavani 57) Marseille 2 (Thauvin 12, Batshuayi 87)

HOLLAND – EREDIVISIE

	P	W	D	L	F	A	GD	Pts
PSV Eindhoven	34	26	6	2	88	32	56	84
Ajax	34	25	7	2	81	21	60	82
Feyenoord	34	19	6	9	62	40	22	63
Alkmaar	34	18	5	11	70	53	17	59
Utrecht	34	15	8	11	57	48	9	53
Heracles	34	14	9	11	47	49	-2	51
Groningen	34	14	8	12	41	48	-7	50
Zwolle	34	14	6	14	56	54	2	48
Vitesse Arnhem	34	12	10	12	55	38	17	46
Nijmegen	34	13	7	14	37	42	-5	46
Den Haag	34	10	13	11	48	49	-1	43
Heerenveen	34	11	9	14	46	61	-15	42
Twente*	34	12	7	15	49	64	-15	40
Roda	34	8	10	16	34	55	-21	34
Excelsior	34	7	9	18	34	60	-26	30
Willem	34	6	11	17	35	53	-18	29
De Graafschap	34	5	8	21	39	66	-27	23
Cambuur	34	3	9	22	33	79	-46	18

*3 pts deducted for financial irregularities

Leading league scorers: 27 Janssen (Alkmaar); 26 De Jong (PSV Eindhoven); 21 Milik (Ajax); 19 Kuyt (Feyenoord); 17 Haller (Utrecht), Ziyech (Twente); 16 Havenaar (Den Haag), Santos (Nijmegen); 14 Kramer (Feyenoord), Veldwijk (Zwoller)

Cup Final: Feyenoord 2 (Kramer 42, Bednarek 75 og) Utrecht 1 (Leeuwin 57)

GERMANY – BUNDESLIGA

	P	W	D	L	F	A	GD	Pts
Bayern Munich	34	28	4	2	80	17	63	88
Borussia Dortmund	34	24	6	4	82	34	48	78
Bayer Leverkusen	34	18	6	10	56	40	16	60
Borussia M'gladbach	34	17	4	13	67	50	17	55
Schalke	34	15	7	12	51	49	2	52
Mainz	34	14	8	12	46	42	4	50
Hertha Berlin	34	14	8	12	42	42	0	50
Wolfsburg	34	12	9	13	47	49	-2	45
Cologne	34	10	13	11	38	42	-4	43
Hamburg	34	11	8	15	40	46	-6	41
Ingolstadt	34	10	10	14	33	42	-9	40
Augsburg	34	9	11	14	42	52	-10	38
Werder Bremen	34	10	8	16	50	65	-15	38
Darmstadt	34	9	11	14	38	53	-15	38
Hoffenheim	34	9	10	15	39	54	-15	37
Eintracht Frankfurt	34	9	9	16	34	52	-18	36
Stuttgart	34	9	6	19	50	75	-25	33
Hannover	34	7	4	23	31	62	-31	25

Leading league scorers: 30 Lewandowski (Bayern Munich); 25 Aubameyang (Borussia Dortmund); 20 Muller (Bayern Munich); 17 Hernandez (Bayer Leverkusen); 15 Modeste (Cologne); 14 Kalou (Hertha Berlin), Pizarro (Werder Bremen), Wagner (Darmstadt); 13 Didavi (Stuttgart), Raffael (Borussia M'gladbach)

Cup Final: Bayern Munich 0 Borussia Dortmund 0 (aet, Bayern Munich won 4-3 on pens)

ITALY – SERIE A

	P	W	D	L	F	A	GD	Pts
Juventus	38	29	4	5	75	20	55	91
Napoli	38	25	7	6	80	32	48	82
Roma	38	23	11	4	83	41	42	80
Inter Milan	38	20	7	11	50	38	12	67
Fiorentina	38	18	10	10	60	42	18	64
Sassuolo	38	16	13	9	49	40	9	61
AC Milan	38	15	12	11	49	43	6	57
Lazio	38	15	9	14	52	52	0	54
Chievo	38	13	11	14	43	45	-2	50
Empoli	38	12	10	16	40	49	-9	46
Genoa	38	13	7	18	45	48	-3	46
Torino	38	12	9	17	52	55	-3	45
Atalanta	38	11	12	15	41	47	-6	45
Bologna	38	11	9	18	33	45	-12	42
Sampdoria	38	10	10	18	48	61	-13	40
Palermo	38	10	9	19	38	65	-27	39
Udinese	38	10	9	19	35	60	-25	39
Carpi	38	9	11	18	37	57	-20	38
Frosinone	38	8	7	23	35	76	-41	31
Verona	38	5	13	20	34	63	-29	28

Leading league scorers: 36 Higuain (Napoli); 19 Dybala (Juventus); 18 Bacca (AC Milan); 16 Icardi (Inter Milan); 14 Pavoletti (Genoa), Salah (Roma); 13 Eder (Inter Milan), Ilicic (Fiorentina), Maccarone (Empoli); 12 Belotti (Palermo), Kalinic (Fiorentina), Insigne (Napoli)

Cup Final: Juventus 1 (Morata 110) AC Milan 0 (aet)

PORTUGAL – PRIMEIRA LIGA

	P	W	D	L	F	A	GD	Pts
Benfica	34	29	1	4	88	22	66	88
Sporting	34	27	5	2	79	21	58	86
Porto	34	23	4	7	67	30	37	73
Braga	34	16	10	8	54	35	19	58
Arouca	34	13	15	6	47	38	9	54
Rio Ave	34	14	8	12	44	44	0	50
Pacos Ferreira	34	13	10	11	43	42	1	49
Estoril	34	13	8	13	40	41	-1	47
Belenenses	34	10	11	13	44	66	-22	41
Guimaraes	34	9	13	12	45	53	-8	40
Nacional	34	10	8	16	40	56	-16	38
Moreirense	34	9	9	16	38	54	-16	36
Maritimo	34	10	5	19	45	63	-18	35
Boavista	34	8	9	17	24	41	-17	33
Setubal	34	6	12	16	40	61	-21	30
Tondela	34	8	6	20	34	54	-20	30
Uniao	34	7	8	19	27	50	-23	29
Academica	34	5	10	19	32	60	-28	25

Leading league scorers: 32 Jonas (Benfica); 27 Slimani (Sporting); 19 Mitroglu (Benfica); 17 Bonatini (Estoril); 16 Martins (Moreirense); 14 Moreira (Pacos Ferreira); 13 Aboubakar (Porto), Junior (Tondela)

Cup Final: Braga 2 (Fonte 12, Josue 58) Porto 2 (Silva 61, 90) – aet (Braga won 4-2 on pens)

SPAIN – LA LIGA

	P	W	D	L	F	A	GD	Pts
Barcelona	38	29	4	5	112	29	83	91
Real Madrid	38	28	6	4	110	34	76	90
Atletico Madrid	38	28	4	6	63	18	45	88
Villarreal	38	18	10	10	44	35	9	64
Athletic Bilbao	38	18	8	12	58	45	13	62
Celta Vigo	38	17	9	12	51	59	-8	60
Sevilla	38	14	10	14	51	50	1	52
Malaga	38	12	12	14	38	35	3	48
Real Sociedad	38	13	9	16	45	48	-3	48
Real Betis	38	11	12	15	34	52	-18	45
Las Palmas	38	12	8	18	45	53	-8	44
Valencia	38	11	11	16	46	48	-2	44
Espanyol	38	12	7	19	40	74	-34	43
Eibar	38	11	10	17	49	61	-12	43
Deportivo	38	8	18	12	45	61	-16	42
Granada	38	10	9	19	46	69	-23	39
Sporting Gijon	38	10	9	19	40	62	-22	39
Rayo Vallecano	38	9	11	18	52	73	-21	38
Getafe	38	9	9	20	37	67	-30	36
Levante	36	8	8	22	37	70	-33	32

Leading league scorers: 40 Suarez (Barcelona); 35 Ronaldo (Real Madrid); 26 Messi (Barcelona); 24 Benzema (Real Madrid), Neymar (Barcelona); 22 Griezmann (Atletico Madrid); 20 Aduriz (Athletic Bilbao); 19 Bale (Real Madrid); Castro (Real Betis); 18 Borja (Eibar); 17 Lucas (Deportivo La Coruna)

Cup Final: Barcelona 2 (Jordi Alba 97, Neymar 120) Sevilla 0 - aet

ROONEY ON THE SPOT FOR ENGLAND

HIS SCORING RECORD

When Italian referee Gianluca Rocchi pointed to the penalty spot after Raheem Sterling was brought down by Timm Klose in the 84th minute of England's Euro 2016 qualifier against Switzerland, a roar of anticipation swept around Wembley. Wayne Rooney had previously been limited to half-chances, but here was a golden opportunity to make history. Calmly he placed the ball on the spot, walked back to the edge of the penalty area, took a deep breath – then fired the ball right-footed towards the top corner of the goal. Goalkeeper Yann Sommer got a hand to it, but there was too much power in Rooney's shot – and the captain had overtaken Sir Bobby Charlton's 45-year-old record to become England's all-time leading scorer with his 50th goal in his 107th international. Here is how he did it.

2003
Sep 6 Macedonia 1 England 2 ECQ (Skopje) – 1 goal
Sep 10 England 2 Liechtenstein 0 ECQ (Old Trafford) – 1 goal
Nov 16 England 2 Denmark 3 Friendly (Old Trafford) – 1 goal

2004
Jun 5 England 6 Iceland 1 FA Tournament (City of Manchester Stadium) – 2 goals
Jun 17 England 3 Switzerland 0 ECF (Coimbra) – 2 goals
Jun 21 England 4 Croatia 2 ECF (Lisbon) – 2 goals

2005
Aug 17 Denmark 4 England 1 Friendly (Copenhagen) – 1 goal
Nov 12 England 3 Argentina 2 Friendly (Geneva) – 1 goal

2006
Nov 15 Holland 1 England 1 Friendly (Amsterdam) – 1 goal

2007
Oct 13 England 3 Estonia 0 ECQ (Wembley) – 1 goal
Oct 17 Russia 2 England 1 ECQ (Moscow) – 1 goal

2008
Sep 10 Croatia 1 England 4 WCQ (Zagreb) – 1 goal
Oct 11 England 5 Kazakhstan 1 WCQ (Wembley) – 2 goals
Oct 15 Belarus 1 England 3 WCQ (Minsk) – 2 goals

2009
Mar 28 England 4 Slovakia 0 Friendly (Wembley) – 2 goals
Jun 6 Kazakhstan 0 England 4 WCQ (Almaty) – 1 goal
Jun 10 England 6 Andorra 0 WCQ (Wembley) – 2 goals
Sep 9 England 5 Croatia 1 WCQ (Wembley) – 1 goal

2010
Sep 7 Switzerland 1 England 3 ECQ (Basle) – 1 goal

2011
Sep 2 Bulgaria 0 England 3 ECQ (Sofia) – 2 goals

2012
Jun 19 Ukraine 0 England 1 ECF (Donetsk) – 1 goal
Oct 12 England 5 San Marino 0 WCQ (Wembley) – 2 goals (1 pen)
Oct 17 Poland 1 England 1 WCQ (Warsaw) – 1 goal

2013
Feb 6 England 2 Brazil 1 Friendly (Wembley) – 1 goal
Mar 22 San Marino 0 England 8 WCQ (Serravalle) – 1 goal
Mar 26 Montenegro 1 England 1 WCQ (Podgorica) – 1 goal

Jun 2 Brazil 2 England 2 Friendly (Rio de Janeiro) – 1 goal
Oct 11 England 4 Montenegro 1 WCQ (Wembley) – 1 goal
Oct 15 England 2 Poland 0 WCQ (Wembley) – 1 goal

2014

Jun 4 England 2 Ecuador 2 Friendly (Miami) – 1 goal
Jun 18 England 1 Uruguay 2 WCF (Sao Paulo) – 1 goal
Sep 3 England 1 Norway 0 Friendly (Wembley) – 1 goal (pen)
Oct 9 England 5 San Marino 0 ECQ (Wembley) – 1 goal (pen)
Oct 12 Estonia 0 England 1 ECQ (Tallinn) – 1 goal
Nov 15 England 3 Slovenia 1 ECQ (Wembley) – 1 goal (pen), Rooney's 100th cap
Nov 18 Scotland 1 England 3 Friendly (Celtic Park) – 2 goals

2015

Mar 27 England 4 Lithuania 0 ECQ (Wembley) – 1 goal
Jun 17 Slovenia 2 England 3 ECQ (Ljubljana) – 1 goal
Sep 5 San Marino 0 England 6 ECQ (Serravalle) – 1 goal (pen)
Sep 8 England 2 Switzerland 0 ECQ (Wembley) – 1 goal (pen)
(50th goal to become England's all-time leading scorer)
Nov 17 England 2 France 0 Friendly (Wembley) – 1 goal

2016

May 27 England 2 Australia 1 Friendly (Sunderland) – 1 goal
Jun 27 England 1 Iceland 2 ECF (Nice) – 1 goal (pen)

FIVE MEMORABLE GOALS

- Aged 17 years and 317 days, he becomes England's youngest-ever scorer – overtaking Michael Owen – in a 2-1 victory over Macedonia in a European Championship qualifier in September 2003. Emile Heskey heads down David Beckham's lofted pass and Rooney fires in from the edge of the penalty box.
- A 25-yard drive gives Rooney the first of his two goals in a 4-2 win over Croatia which confirms England's place in the second round of Euro 2004.
- Owen lays the ball off to Rooney, who chests it down and delivers a spectacular volley in England's 2-1 defeat by Russia in a qualifier for Euro 2008.
- England become the first national team to visit the rebuilt Maracana Stadium in Rio de Janeiro and Rooney scores a goal worthy of the occasion from 25 yards in a 2-2 draw with Brazil in 2013.
- The Manchester United player overtakes Sir Bobby Charlton's record and is presented with a commemorative shirt by England manager Roy Hodgson. Before England's next match at Wembley, he receives a Golden Boot from Sir Bobby.

THE THINGS THEY SAY ...

'It's a dream come true – a huge moment for me and my family. I'd like to thank every one of you, coaches, players, staff who I've worked with for such a long time. Hopefully, for the team and myself, there's a lot more to come' – **Wayne Rooney**.

'I cannot deny that I am disappointed that I no longer hold this record. However, I'm absolutely delighted it is Wayne, as captain of my beloved club and country, who now holds it"
– **Sir Bobby Charlton**.

'I know how much it means to Wayne to play for his country. He can continue with England for another five years and I really hope he does' – **David Beckham**, former England captain.

'You would definitely back him to score plenty more. He could put it into the 60s. When he looks at England's next World Cup qualifying group, his eyes will light up' – **Gary Lineker**, now third on England's all-time list with 48 goals.

BRITISH & IRISH INTERNATIONALS 2015–2016

* denotes new cap

EUROPEAN CHAMPIONSHIP 2016 – QUALIFYING

CYPRUS 0 WALES 1

Group B: Nicosia (14,492); Thursday, September 3 2015

Cyprus (4-4-2): Giorgallides, Demetriou, Dossa Junior, Laifis, Antoniades, Charalambides (Englezou 75), Nikolaou, Economides, Makridis (Sotiriou 84) Mitidis (Kolokoudias 65), Makris
Wales (3-4-2-1): Hennessey, Gunter, A Williams, Davies, Richards, King, Edwards, Taylor, Ramsey (MacDonald 90), Bale (Church 90), Robson-Kanu (Vokes 68). **Scorer**: Bale (81)
Referee: S Marciniak (Poland). **Half-time**: 0-0

GEORGIA 1 SCOTLAND 0

Group D: Tbilisi (23,000); Friday, September 4 2015

Georgia (3-4-2-1): Revishvili, Kverkvelia, Amisulashvile, Kashia, Lobzhanidze, Kankava, Ananidze (Daushvili 82), Navalovski, Kazaishvili, Okriashvili (Merebashvili 71), Mchedlidze (Vatsadze 90). **Scorer**: Kazaishvili (37). **Booked**: Kashia, Ananidze, Navalovski
Scotland (4-2-3-1): Marshall, Hutton, R Martin, Mulgrew, Robertson (Hanley 59), Morrison, Brown, Maloney, Naismith (Forrest 59), Anya (Griffiths 75), S Fletcher
Referee: O Hatergan (Romania). **Half-time**: 1-0

FAROE ISLANDS 1 NORTHERN IRELAND 3

Group F: Torshavn (4,513); Friday, September 4 2015

Faroe Islands (4-5-1): Nielsen, Naes, Nattestadt, Faero, Sorensen, Benjaminsen (Baldvinsson 87), Holst, Hansson, Henriksen (Bartalsstovu 83), Vatnhamar, Edmundsson. **Scorer**: Edmundsson (36). **Booked**: Hansson, Edmundsson. **Sent off**: Edmundsson (64)
Northern Ireland (4-2-3-1): McGovern, McLaughlin (Magennis 69), McAuley, J Evans, Brunt (Ferguson, 83), Baird, Norwood, McGinn, Davis, Dallas, K Lafferty (McNair 78). **Scorers**: McAuley (12, 71), K Lafferty (75). **Booked**: McLaughlin, Magennis
Referee: F Zwayer (Germany). **Half-time**: 1-1

GIBRALTAR 0 REPUBLIC OF IRELAND 4

Group D: Faro, Portugal (5,393); Friday, September 4, 2015

Gibraltar (4-4-2): Perez, Garcia, Barnett, R Chipolina, J Chipolina, Sergeant, Walker, Bardon, K Casciaro (Gosling 61), L Casciaro, Duarte (Yome 73). **Booked**: K Casciaro, Barnett
Republic of Ireland (4-2-3-1): Given, Christie, O'Shea, Clark, Brady, Whelan, McCarthy (Quinn 70), Walters Hendrick, Hoolahan (McGeady 77), Keane (Long 70). **Scorers**: Christie (26), Keane (49, 51 pen), Long (79). **Booked**: Walters
Referee: M Strahonja (Croatia). **Half-time**: 0-1

SAN MARINO 0 ENGLAND 6

Group E: Serravalle (4,378); Saturday, September 5 2015

San Marino (4-5-1): A Simoncini, Bonini (Tosi 72), Brolli, D Simoncini (Della Valle 80), Palazzi, Berardi, Hirsch, Battistini, Chiaruzzi, Vitaioli, Selva (Rinaldi 75). **Booked**: Berardi
England (4-2-3-1): Hart, Clyne, Stones, Jagielka, Shaw, Shelvey, Milner (Delph 58), Oxlade-Chamberlain (Walcott 67), Barkley, Vardy, Rooney (Kane 58). **Scorers**: Rooney (13 pen), Brolli (30 og), Barkley (46), Walcott (68, 78), Kane (77)
Referee: L Trattou (Cyprus). **Half-time**: 0-2

WALES 0 ISRAEL 0

Group B: Cardiff City Stadium (32,653); Sunday, September 6 2015

Wales (3-4-2-1): Hennessey, Gunter, A Williams, Davies, Richards, King (Vokes 86), Edwards, Taylor, Ramsey, Bale, Robson-Kanu (Church 79). **Booked**: Richards
Israel (5-3-2): Marciano, Dasa, Dgani, Ben Haim, Tibi, Haruch, Natcho, Bitton, Kayal (Ben Haim 11 45), Zahavi (Sahar 90), Dabbur (Hemed 46). **Booked**: Dabbur, Dasa, Dgani, Bitton
Referee: I Bebek (Croatia)

SCOTLAND 2 GERMANY 3

Group D: Hampden Park (50,753); Monday, September 7 2015

Scotland (4-2-3-1): Marshall, Hutton, R Martin, Hanley, Mulgrew, McArthur, Brown (C Martin 81), Forrest (Ritchie 81), Morrison, Maloney (Anya 60), S Fletcher. **Scorers**: Hummels (28 og), McArthur (43). **Booked**: Morrison, Maloney

Germany (4-2-3-1): Neuer, Emre Can, Boateng, Hummels, Hector, Schweinsteiger, Kroos, Muller, Gundogan, Ozil (Kramer 90), Gotze (Schurrle 86). **Scorers**: Muller (18, 34), Gundogan (54)

Referee: B Kuipers (Holland). **Half-time**: 2-2

NORTHERN IRELAND 1 HUNGARY 1

Group F: Windsor Park (10,200); Monday, September 7, 2015

Northern Ireland (4-2-3-1): McGovern, McLaughlin, McAuley, J Evans, Brunt, Baird, Norwood (Magennis, 75), C Evans (McGinn 56), Davis, Dallas (Ferguson 84), K Lafferty. **Scorer**: K Lafferty (90). **Booked**: K Lafferty, McLaughlin, Baird. **Sent off**: Baird (81)

Hungary (4-4-2): Kiraly, Fiola, Guzmics, Kadar, Leandro, Nemeth (Vanczak 89), Elek (Nagy 23), Kalmar, Dzsudzsak, Szalai (Priskin 68), Gera. **Scorer**: Guzmics (74). **Booked**: Guzmics, Leandro, Nemeth, Priskin

Referee: C Cakir (Turkey). **Half-time**: 0-0

REPUBLIC OF IRELAND 1 GEORGIA 0

Group D: Aviva Stadium (27,200); Monday, September 7 2015

Republic of Ireland (4-3-1-2): Given, Coleman, O'Shea, Clark, Brady, Whelan, McCarthy, Hendrick, Hoolahan (McClean 75), Walters, Keane (Long 46). **Scorer**: Walters (69). **Booked**: Whelan, McClean

Georgia (3-4-2-1): Revishvili, Kverkvelia, Amisulashvile, Khizanishvili (Kenia 81), Lobzhanidze, Kashia (Tsintadze 76), Kankava, Navalovski, Kazaishvili (Papunashvili 64), Okriashvili, Mchedlidze

Referee: I Vad (Hungary). **Half-time**: 0-0

ENGLAND 2 SWITZERLAND 0

Group E: Wembley (75,751); Tuesday, September 8 2015

England (4-3-3): Hart, Clyne (Stones 68), Cahill, Smalling, Shaw, Delph (Barkley 3), Shelvey, (Kane, 57), Milner, Oxlade-Chamberlain, Rooney, Sterling. **Scorers**: Kane (67), Rooney (84 pen). **Booked**: Milner, Smalling

Switzerland (4-3-3): Sommer, Lichtsteiner, Klose, Schar, Rodriguez, Behrami (Dzemaili 79), Inler, Xhaka, Shaqiri, Drmic (Embolo 63), Stocker (Seferovic 72).

Referee: G Rocchi (Italy). **Half-time**: 0-0

(Wayne Rooney's record 50th England goal)

SCOTLAND 2 POLAND 2

Group D: Hampden Park (49,359); Thursday, October 8 2015

Scotland (4-2-3-1): Marshall, Hutton, R Martin, Hanley, Whittaker, Brown, D Fletcher (McArthur 74), Ritchie, Naismith (Maloney 69), Forrest (Dorrans 84), S Fletcher. **Scorers**: Ritchie (45), S Fletcher (62). **Booked**: Brown, Hutton

Poland (4-2-3-1): Fabianski, Piszczek, Glik, Pazdan, Rybus (Wawrzyniak 71), Krychowiak, Maczynski, Blaszczykowski (Olkowski 83), Milik (Jodlowiec 62), Grosicki, Lewandowski. **Scorer**: Lewandowski (3, 90). **Booked**: Rybus, Krychowiak

Referee: V Kassai (Hungary). **Half-time**: 1-1

NORTHERN IRELAND 3 GREECE 1

Group F: Windsor Park (11,700); Thursday, October 8 2015

Northern Ireland (4-2-3-1): McGovern, McNair (McCullough 85), McAuley, Cathcart, Brunt, C Evans, Norwood, Ward (McGinn 81), Davis, Dallas, Magennis (Boyce 78). **Scorers**: Davis (35, 58), Magennis (50)

Greece (4-1-4-1): Karzenis, Torosidis, Moras, Papastathopoulos, Holebas, Tziolis, Samaris, Karelis (Mantalos 65), Kone (Pelkas 71), Aravidis, Mitroglu (Athanasiadis 76). **Scorer**: Aravidis (87)

Referee: B Nijuis (Holland). **Half-time**: 1-0

REPUBLIC OF IRELAND 1 GERMANY 0
Group D: Aviva Stadium (50,604); Thursday, October 8 2015

Republic of Ireland (4-4-1-1): Given (Randolph 44), Christie, Keogh, O'Shea, Ward (Meyler 69), Walters, Hendrick, McCarthy, Brady, Hoolahan, Murphy (Long 65). **Scorer**: Long (70). **Booked**: Hoolahan
Germany (4-2-3-1): Neuer, Ginter, Hummels, Boateng, Hector, Gundogan, Kroos, Muller, Ozil, Reus, Gotze (Schurrle 35). **Booked**: Hummels
Referee: C Carballo (Spain). **Half-time**: 0-0

ENGLAND 2 ESTONIA 0
Group E: Wembley (75,427); Friday, October 9 2015

England (4-2-3-1): Hart, Clyne, Cahill, Smalling, Bertrand, Milner, Barkley (*Alli 88), Walcott (Vardy 83), Lallana (Oxlade-Chamberlain 73), Sterling, Kane. **Scorers**: Walcott (45), Sterling (85).
Estonia (4-4-2): Aksalu, Teniste, Jaager, Klavan, Pikk, Kallaste (Luts 88), Dmitrijev (Lindpere 70), Mets, Zenjov, Purje (Puri 70), Vassiljev. **Booked**: Pikk
Referee: I Vad (Hungary). **Half-time**: 1-0

BOSNIA-HERZEGOVINA 2 WALES 0
Group B: Zenica (10,250); Saturday, October 10 2015

Bosnia-Herzegovina (4-1-4-1): Begovic, Mujdza, Sunjic, Spahic (Cocalic 46), Zukanovic, Hadzic (Bicakcic 89), Visca (Djuric 61), Pjanic, Lulic, Salihovic, Ibvisevic. **Scorers**: Djuric (71), Ibisevic (90). **Booked**: Spahic, Begovic, Sunjic
Wales (3-4-2-1): Hennessey, Gunter, A Williams, Davies, Richards, Allen (Edwards 84), Ledley (Vokes 75), Taylor, Ramsey, Bale, Robson-Kanu (Church 84). **Booked**: Taylor
Referee: A Undiano (Spain). **Half-time**: 0-0

GIBRALTAR 0 SCOTLAND 6
Group D: Faro, Portugal (12,401); Sunday, October 11 2015

Gibraltar (3-5-1-1): Robba, Barnett, R Chipolina, R Casciaro, Garcia, Walker, D Duarte (Perez 57), Bardon, J Chipolina, L Casciaro (J Duarte 82), K Casciaro (Yome 89)
Scotland (4-2-3-1): McGregor, Hutton, Greer, Berra, Robertson, Brown (D Fletcher 63), Dorrans, Ritchie (Russell 63), C Martin (Naismith 76), Maloney, S Fletcher. **Scorers**: Martin (24), Maloney (39), S Fletcher (52, 56, 85), Naismith (90)
Referee: A Kulbakox (Belarus). **Half-time**: 0-2

FINLAND 1 NORTHERN IRELAND 1
Group F: Helsinki (14,550); Sunday, October 11 2015

Finland (4-4-2): Hradecky, Jalasto, Arajuuri, Ojala, Uronen, Schuller (Hamalainen 79), Mattila, Sparv, Ring (Lod 44), Pohjanpalo, Sadik (Pukki 66). **Scorer**: Arajuuri (87)
Northern Ireland (4-3-3): McGovern, McNair, (McLaughlin 51), McAuley, Cathcart, Brunt, Davis, Baird, Norwood, McGinn (Ferguson 71), K Lafferty (Magennis 79), Dallas
Scorer: Cathcart (31)
Referee: S Karasev (Russia). **Half-time**: 0-1

POLAND 2 REPUBLIC OF IRELAND 1
Group D: Warsaw (57,497); Sunday, October 11 2015

Poland (4-2-3-1): Fabianski, Piszczek, Glik, Pazdan, Wawrzyniak, Linetty, Krychowiak, Olkowski (Blasczykowski 63), Maczynski (Szukala 78), Grosicki (Peszko 85), Lewandowski. **Scorers**: Krychowiak (13), Lewandowski (42). **Booked**: Glik, Peszko
Republic of Ireland (4-2-3-1): Randolph, Coleman, Keogh, O'Shea, Brady, Whelan (McGeady 58), McCarthy, Walters, Hendrick, McClean (Hoolahan 73), Long (Keane 55). **Scorer**: Walters (16 pen). **Booked**: O'Shea, Whelan, Walters. **Sent off**: O'Shea (90)
Referee: C Cakir (Turkey). **Half-time**: 2-1

LITHUANIA 0 ENGLAND 3
Group E: Vilnius (5,051); Monday, October 12 2015

Lithuania (4-2-3-1): Arlauskis, Freidgeimas, Mikuckis, Klimavicius, Andriuskevicius (Vaitkunas

82), Panka, Zulpa, Novikovas (Petravicius 63), Silvka, Cernych, Spalvis (Matulevicius 86). **Booked**: Spalvis, Vaitkunas
England (4-3-3): Butland, Walker, Jones, Jagielka, Gibbs, Lallana (Alli 67), Shelvey, Barkley (Townsend 73), Oxlade-Chamberlain, Kane (*Ings 59), Vardy. **Scorers**: Barkley (29), Arlauskis (35 og), Oxlade-Chamberlain (62). **Booked**: Shelvey, Vardy
Referee: K Hansen (Denmark). **Half-time**: 0-2

WALES 2 ANDORRA 0
Group B: Cardiff City Stadium (33,280); Tuesday, October 13 2015
Wales (4-3-3): Hennessey, Gunter, A Williams, Chester, Davies, J Williams (Church 86), Vaughan, Ramsey, Bale, Vokes, Robson-Kanu (Edwards 23) (*Lawrence 46). **Scorers**: Ramsey (50), Bale (86). **Booked**: Vaughan, Gunter, A Williams
Andorra (4-5-1): Pol, Moises, Rodrigues, Lima, Llovera, Rubio, Lorenzo (Garcia 81), Sonejee (Ayala 70), Vieira, Moreira (Riera 12), Sanchez. **Booked**: Lima, Lorenzo, Vieira, Pol, Rodrigues, Ayala, Sanchez
Referee: K Blom (Holland). **Half-time**: 0-0

BOSNIA-HERZEGOVINA 1 REPUBLIC OF IRELAND 1
Play-off, first leg: Zenica (15,260); Friday, November 13 2015
Bosnia-Herzegovina (4-4-2): Begovic, Mujdza (Vranjes 51), Sunjic, Spahic, Zukanovic, Visca (Djuric 73), Pjanic, Cocalic, Lulic (Hajrovic 88), Dzeko, Ibisevic. **Scorer**: Dzeko (85).
Republic of Ireland (4-2-3-1): Randolph, Coleman, Keogh, Clark, Ward (Wilson, 67), Whelan, McCarthy, Hendrick, Hoolahan (McClean 60), Brady (McGeady 86), Murphy. **Scorer**: Brady (82). **Booked**: Ward
Referee: F Brych (Germany). **Half-time**: 0-0

REPUBLIC OF IRELAND 2 BOSNIA-HERZEGOVINA 0
Play-off, second leg: Aviva Stadium (50,500); Monday, November 16 2015
Republic of Ireland (4-2-3-1): Randolph, Coleman, Keogh, Clark, Brady, Whelan (O'Shea 90), McCarthy, Hendrick, Hoolahan (McClean 55), Walters, Murphy (Long 55). **Scorer**: Walters (24 pen, 70). **Booked**: McClean
Bosnia-Herzegovina (4-2-3-1): Begovic, Vranjes, Kolasinac, Spahic, Zukanovic, Cocalic (Besic 46), Medunjanin (Djuric 69), Visca, Pjanic, Lulic (Ibisevic 80), Dzeko. **Booked**: Spahic, Lulic, Zukanovic, Dzeko, Djuric
Referee: B Kuipers (Holland). **Half-time**: 1-0

INTERNATIONAL FRIENDLIES

SPAIN 2 ENGLAND 0
Alicante (25,300); Friday, November 13 2015
Spain (4-1-3-2): Casillas, Mario, Pique, Bartra (Azpilicueta 78), Jordi Alba, Busquets (Koke 78), Thiago (Cazorla 27), Iniesta (Nolito 46), Fabregas, Diego Costa (Mata 64), Alacer (Pedro 74). **Scorers**: Mario (72), Cazorla (84)
England (4-2-3-1): Hart, Walker, Jones, Smalling (Cahill 84), Bertrand, Delph (*Dier 63), Carrick (Shelvey 90), Lallana (Alli, 63), Barkley (Rooney 73), Sterling, Kane. **Booked**: Hart
Referee: P Mazzoleni (Italy). **Half-time**: 0-0

WALES 2 HOLLAND 3
Cardiff City Stadium (25,669); Friday, November 13 2015
Wales (3-4-2-1): Hennessey (*Fon Williams 74), Chester, A Williams (Collins 46), Davies , Gunter (*Henley 66), Allen, Ledley (Huws 56), Taylor (Dummett 65), J Williams (G Williams 60), King, Lawrence. **Scorers**: Ledley (45), Huws (70)
Holland (5-3-2): Cillessen, Janmaat, Bruma, Van Dijk (Veltman 46), Blind, Kongolo, Clasie (Bazoer 87), Promes (Wijnaldum 90), Sneijder, Robben, Dost. **Scorers**: Dost (32), Robben (54, 81). **Booked**: Bruma, Kongolo
Referee: B Bastien (France). **Half-time**: 1-1

NORTHERN IRELAND 1 LATVIA 0
Windsor Park (11,707); Friday, November 13 2015

Northern Ireland (3-5-2): McGovern (Carroll 46), Cathcart, McAuley, J Evans, McLaughlin, Davis (McCourt 84), Baird, Norwood (C Evans 46), Dallas (Ferguson 69), Ward (Boyce 69), K Lafferty (Magennis 54). **Scorer**: Davis (55)
Latvia (4-1-4-1): Vanins (Steinbors 74), Zukanovic, Jagodinskis, Gorkss, Kurakins, Tarasovs, Rakels (Hasler 85), Laizans (Ikaunieks 78), Salihovic, Visnakovs (Rudnevs 59), Visnjakovs (Sabala 71)
Referee: M Al Hoaish (Saudi Arabia). **Half-time**: 0-0

ENGLAND 2 FRANCE 0
Wembley (71,223); Tuesday, November 17 2015

England (4-3-3): Hart (Butland 46), Clyne, Stones, Cahill, Gibbs, Alli (Jones 88), Dier, Barkley (Shelvey 79), Sterling (Lallana 68), Kane (Bertrand 80), Rooney. **Scorers**: Alli (39), Rooney (48)
France (4-2-3-1): Lloris, Sagna, Varane, Koscielny, Digne, Schneiderlin (Sissoko 83), Matuidi (Pogba 46), Ben Arfa (Coman 46), Cabaye (Diarra 57), Martial (Griezmann 57), Gignac (Giroud 57)
Referee: J Eriksson (Sweden). **Half-time**: 1-0

WALES 1 NORTHERN IRELAND 1
Cardiff City Stadium (21,885); Thursday, March 24 2016

Wales (4-2-3-1): Hennessey (*Ward 46), Gunter, Chester, A Williams, Matthews, Ledley (Crofts 46), Vaughan (Allen 71), G William (*Isgrove 62), Lawrence (J Williams 62), Cotterill, Vokes (Church 76). **Scorer**: Church (89 pen)
Northern Ireland (4-2-3-1): McGovern, McLaughlin (Hughes 81), Cathcart, McAuley, J Evans (D Lafferty 74), Norwood, McNair (Paton 74), Davis, *Washington (Ward 46), Dallas (Ferguson 90), K Lafferty (McKay 81) **Scorer**: Cathcart (60)
Referee: S McLean (Scotland). **Half-time**: 0-0

CZECH REPUBLIC 0 SCOTLAND 1
Prague (14, 580); Thursday, March 24 2016

Czech Republic (4-2-3-1): Koubeck, Kaderabek, Sivok, Kadlec, Limbersky, Vacek (Marecek 78), Frydek (Skalak 46), Dockal (Kolar 65), Darida (Rada 87), Sural (Pudil 78), Necid (Vydra 65). **Booked**: Limbersky, Skalak
Scotland (4-2-3-1): McGregor, Hutton, R Martin, Berra, Robertson (Phillips 58), Snodgrass, *McLean (Bannan 58), Mulgrew, D Fletcher, McCormack (*Watt 77), Anya (*Caddis 88). **Scorer**: Anya (10)
Referee: P McLaughlin (Republic of Ireland). **Half-time**: 0-0

REPUBLIC OF IRELAND 1 SWITZERLAND 0
Aviva Stadium (35,450); Friday, March 25 2016

Republic of Ireland (4-4-2): Randolph, Coleman, Duffy, Clark, Brady, *Judge, Meyler (*O'Kane 61), Quinn (McCarthy 62), McGeady (*Hayes 61), Long (McClean 84), Doyle (Murphy 26) (Hoolahan 79). **Scorer**: Clark (3)
Switzerland (4-3-3): Sommer, Lang (Widmer 82), Schar, Klose, Rodriguez (Moubandje 78), Dzemaili, Xhaka, Behrami (Fernandes 72), Embolo, Seferovic (Steffen 62), Mehmedi (Kasami 71). **Booked**: Dzemaili, Xhaka
Referee: M Zelinka (Czech Republic). **Half-time**: 1-0

GERMANY 2 ENGLAND 3
Berlin (71,413); Saturday, March 26 2016

Germany (4-2-3-1): Neuer, Emre Can, Rudiger, Hummels (Tah 46), Hector, Khedira, Kroos, Muller (Podolski 76), Ozil, Reus (Schurle 64), Gomez (Gotze 79). **Scorers**: Kroos (43), Gomez (57). **Booked**: Emre Can
England (4-2-3-1): Butland (Forster 45), Clyne, Cahill, Smalling, *Rose, Dier, Henderson, Lallana (Barkley 71), Alli, Welbeck (Vardy 71), Kane. **Scorers**: Kane (61), Vardy (74), Dier (90). **Booked**: Dier
Referee: G Rocchi (Italy). **Half-time**: 1-0

UKRAINE 1 WALES 0
Kiev (20,000); Monday, March 28 2016

Ukraine (4-2-2-2-1): Pyatov, Khacheridi, Kucher, Fedetskiy, Shevchuk, Stepanenko, Garmash, Yarmolenko, Zozulya, Rotan (Sydorchuk 59) Kovalenko. **Scorer**: Yarmolenko (28). **Booked**: Garmash, Khacheridi, Fedetskiy
Wales (3-4-2-1): Hennessey, Chester, A Williams (Richards 65), Davies, Gunter, Allen, Huws (Ledley 79), Taylor (Henley 72), J Williams (MacDonald 61), Lawrence (*Bradshaw 73), Church (Vokes 61). **Booked**: Richards
Referee: S Gozubuyuk (Holland). **Half-time**: 1-0

NORTHERN IRELAND 1 SLOVENIA 0
Windsor Park (13,500); Monday, March 28 2016

Northern Ireland (3-1-4-2): Carroll, Cathcart, McAuley (Hughes 46), J Evans, McNair (McGinn 79), *Smith (McLaughlin 71), Davis, Norwood, Ferguson (Dallas 60), Washington (Magennis 70), Ward (K Lafferty 60). **Scorer**: Washington (41). **Booked**: Ward, Washington, J Evans
Slovenia (4-3-1-2): Oblak, Skubic (Stojanovic 61), Samardzic, Cesar (Struna 80), Jokic, Kurtic (Vrhovec 46), Krhin, Verbic (Kirm 62), Birsa, Ilicic (Navakovic 46), Bezjak (Crnic 75). **Booked**: Oblak, Vrhovec
Referee: K Tohver (Estonia). **Half-time**: 1-0

ENGLAND 1 HOLLAND 2
Wembley (82,835); Tuesday, March 29 2016

England (4-1-3-2): Forster, Walker, Smalling (Jagielka 70), Stones, Rose (Clyne 58), *Drinkwater (Dier 85), Milner (Alli 82), Lallana (Kane 70), Barkley, Vardy, Sturridge (Walcott 58). **Scorer**: Vardy (41)
Holland (4-2-3-1): Zoet, Veltman, Bruma, Blind, Willems (Van Aanholt 82), Bazoer (Van Ginkel 79), Wijnaldum, Promes (Narsingh 37), Afellay, Depay, Janssen (Clasie 90). **Scorers**: Janssen (51 pen), Narsingh (77). **Booked**: Bruma
Referee: A Mateu (Spain). **Half-time**: 1-0

SCOTLAND 1 DENMARK 0
Hampden Park (18,385); Tuesday, March 29 2016

Scotland (4-4-2): Gordon, Whittaker, Greer, Hanley,*Tierney (Mulgrew 46), Ritchie (*Burke 82), Brown,*McGinn Maloney (Bridcutt 68), S Fletcher (Anya 46), Griffiths (C Martin 59). **Scorer**: Ritchie (8). **Booked**: McGinn, Bridcutt, Greer
Denmark (3-4-1-2): Schmeichel (Lossi 46), Kjaer, Christensen, Agger (Sviatchenko 64), Dalsgaard, Hojbjerg, Delaney, Durmisi, Eriksen (Schone 81), Poulsen (Bratihwaite 46), Jorgensen
Referee: S Moen (Norway). **Half-time**: 1-0

REPUBLIC OF IRELAND 2 SLOVAKIA 2
Aviva Stadium (30,217); Tuesday, March 29 2016

Republic of Ireland (4-3-1-2): Elliot (Randolph 16), Christie, O'Shea (Pearce 46), McShane, Ward (Hayes 79), O'Kane (Pilkington 66), Whelan, McCarthy, Hoolahan (McGeady 73), McClean, Long (Brady 46). **Scorers**: Long (21 pen), McClean (24 pen). **Booked**: McClean
Slovakia (4-3-3): Kozacik, Pekarik, Skrtel, Salata, Svento (Tesak 88), Sabo (Duda 64), Gregus (Hrosovsky 74), Hamsik, Sestak (Weiss 66), Vittek (Nemec 66), Stoch (Mak 64). **Scorers**: Stoch (14), McShane (45 og). **Booked**: Sabo, Pekarik, Gregus
Referee: O Nilsen (Norway). **Half-time**: 2-2

ENGLAND 2 TURKEY 1
Etihad Stadium (44,866); Sunday, May 22 2016

England (4-2-3-1): Hart, Walker, Cahill, Stones, Rose, Dier, Wilshere (Henderson 66), Sterling (Drinkwater 73), Alli, Vardy, Kane **Scorers**: Kane (3), Vardy (83). **Booked**: Wilshere
Turkey (4-1-4-1): Babacan, Gonul, Balta, Topal, Erkin (Koybasi 70), Inan, Sen (Oztekin 84), Ozyakup (Tekdemir 70), Tufan (Erdinc 87), Calhanoglu (Sahan 78), Tosun. **Scorer**: Calhanoglu (13). **Booked**: Ozyakup, Topal
Referee: D Aytekin (Germany). **Half-time**: 1-1

ENGLAND 2 AUSTRALIA 1

Stadium of Light (46,595); Friday, May 27 2016

England (4-1-2-1-2): Forster (*Heaton 87), Clyne, Smalling (Dier 73), Stones, Bertrand, Wilshere (Milner 46), Henderson, Drinkwater, Lallana (Rooney 46), Sterling (Townsend 76), *Rashford (Barkley 63). **Scorers**: Rashford (3), Rooney (55)

Australia (4-1-2-1-2): Ryan, Risdon (Degenek 74), Milligan, Wright, Smith, Jedinak, Luongo (Ikonomidis 58), Mooy (Irvine 84), Rogic (Juric 73), Kruse (Goodwin 84), MacLaren (McKay 58). **Scorer**: Dier (75 og). **Booked**: Mooy

Referee: D Makkelie (Holland). **Half-time**: 1-0

NORTHERN IRELAND 3 BELARUS 0

Windsor Park (14,229): Friday, May 27, 2016

Northern Ireland (4-3-1-2): Carroll (Mannus 46), McLaughlin, Cathcart, Baird, J Evans, C Evans (Hughes, unatt 73), McNair, Dallas (McGinn 73), Davis (Norwood 46), K Lafferty (Grigg 61), Washington (Ward, 61). **Scorers**: Lafferty (6), Washington (44), Grigg (88). **Booked**: J Evans

Belarus (4-2-3-1): Gorbunov, Shitov (Palitevich 77), Martynovich, Filipenko (Sivakov 38), Volodko, Korzun, Kislyak, Gordeychuk, Krivets (Hleb 60), Stasevich, Yanush (Polyakov 71). **Booked**: Martynovich. Kislyak, Sivakov

Referee: M Atkinson (England). **Half-time**: 2-0

REPUBLIC OF IRELAND 1 HOLLAND 1

Aviva Stadium (42,438); Friday, May 27 2016

Republic of Ireland (4-3-3): Randolph, Coleman, Duffy, O'Shea, Brady, Arter (O'Kane 83), Whelan (Gibson 67), Quinn (Hendrick 67), Long (McClean 67), McGoldrick (Hoolahan 76), Walters. **Scorer**: Long (30). **Booked**: Arter

Holland (4-3-3): Cillessen, Veltman, Bruma, Van Dijk, Willems, Strootman (Van Ginkel 70), Wijnaldum (De Jong 82), Bazoer, Promes, Janssen (Dost 75), Depay (Berghius 61). **Scorer**: De Jong (85)

Referee: A Soares (Portugal). **Half-time**: 1-0

ITALY 1 SCOTLAND 0

Ta'Qali, Malta (12,000); Sunday, May 29 2016

Italy (3-5-2): Buffon, Barzagli, Bonucci, Chiellini, Candreva (Parolo 62), Florenzie, De Rossi (Jorginho 67), Giaccherini (Bonaventura 80), Darmian (Bernardeschi 60), Pelle (Zaza 67), Eder (Insigne 59). **Scorer**: Pelle (57)

Scotland (4-4-2): Marshall, *Paterson (Berra 46), R Martin, Hanley, Mulgrew, Phillips (Burke 71), D Fletcher McArthur (Bryson 83), Anya (Naismith 71), Ritchie, McCormack (S Fletcher 46)

Referee: A Sant (Malta). **Half-time**: 0-0

REPUBLIC OF IRELAND 1 BELARUS 2

Turner's Cross, Cork (7,200); Tuesday, May 31 2016

Republic of Ireland (4-2-3-1): Given (Forde 69), Christie, Keogh, Clark, Ward, Gibson, (Hoolahan, 68), Meyler (O'Kane 75), McGeady (*O'Dowda 75), Hendrick, McClean (McGoldrick 79), Murphy (Long 68). **Scorer**: Ward (72)

Belarus (4-1-4-1): Chernik, Polyakov, Martynovich, Sivakov, Volodko, Korzun, Gordeychuk (Palitevich 76), Hleb (Krivets 90), Kislyak, Stasevich (Nekhajchik 90), Yanush. **Scorers**: Gordeychuk (20), Volodko (63). **Booked**: Sivakov

Referee: D Jakimovski (Macedonia). **Half-time**: 0-1

ENGLAND 1 PORTUGAL 0

Wembley (82,503); Thursday, June 2 2016

England (4-3-3): Hart, Walker, Smalling, Cahill, Rose, Milner (Wilshere 66), Dier, Alli (Henderson 90), Kane (Sturridge 78), Rooney (Lallana 78), Vardy (Sterling 66). **Scorer**: Smalling (86). **Booked**: Cahill

Portugal (4-4-2): Rui Patricio, Vieirinha, Bruno Alves, Ricardo Carvalho (Eder 90), Eliseu, Joao Moutinho (William Carvalho 72), Joao Mario, (Andre Gomes 46), Danilo, Rafa Silva (Fonte 38), Adrien Silva (Renato Sanches 72), Nani (Ricardo Quaresma 61), **Booked**: Danilo. **Sent off** Bruno Alves (35)

Referee: M Guida (Italy). **Half-time**: 0-0

FRANCE 3 SCOTLAND 0

Metz (35,000); Saturday June 4 2016

France (4-3-3): Lloris, Sagna, Rami, Koscielny, Evra (Digne 83), Pogba, Kante (Sissoko 88), Matuidi (Cabaye 69), Coman (Griezmann 46), Giroud (Gignac 63), Payet (Martial 46) **Scorers**: Giroud (8, 35), Koscielny (39)
Scotland (4-2-3-1): Marshall, R Martin, Greer, Hanley, Robertson (Mulgrew 46), McArthur (*McKay 88), D Fletcher, Snodgrass (*Kingsley 66), Maloney (Anya 46), Ritchie, S Fletcher (Naismith 58)
Referee: S Delferiere (Belgium). **Half-time**: 3-0

SLOVAKIA 0 NORTHERN IRELAND 0

Trnava (18,111); Saturday, June 4 2016

Slovakia (4-2-3-1): Kozacik, Pekarik, Skrtel, Durica, Svento, Kucka (Nemec 84), Hrosovsky, Mak (Stoch 65), Hamsik, Weiss, Duris (Duda 65)
Northern Ireland (5-3-2): McGovern, McNair (McLaughlin 90), Cathcart (Hughes 30), McAuley, J Evans, Ferguson (Hodson,86), Norwood (C Evans, 84), Baird, Davis, K Lafferty (Washington 55), Ward (Magennis, 46). **Booked**: McNair
Referee: R Petrescu (Romania)
(Aaron Hughes's 100th Northern Ireland cap)

SWEDEN 3 WALES 0

Stockholm (37,942); Sunday, June 5 2016

Sweden (4-4-2): Isaksson (Olsen 46), Lustig, Johansson, Granqvist, Olsson (Augustinsson 46), Larsson, Kallstrom, Lewicki (Ekdal 61), Forsberg (Durmaz 61), Berg (Guidetti 76), Ibrahimovic (Kujovic 61). **Scorers**: Forsberg (40), Lustig (57), Guidetti (87)
Wales (3-4-2-1): Hennessey (Ward 46), Chester (Collins 65), A Williams, Davies, Gunter, King (Bale 65), Vaughan (Edwards 65), Taylor, J Williams (Huws 73), Ramsey, Vokes (Church 73)
Referee: T Welz (Germany). **Half-time**: 1-0

THE THINGS THEY SAY ...

'If you want us to respect the FA Cup, don't put Premier League fixtures in midweek. It's diabolical and stupid' – **Sam Allardyce**, Sunderland manager, warning of weakened teams in the third round of the competition because of a full league programme a few days later.

'This has got to be the best loss of my life' – **Gareth Bale** after Wales qualify for Euro 2016, despite losing to Bosnia-Herzegovina.

'The English will have to face up to the fact that their young players don't get the minutes for their clubs. That is why the national team haven't set the world alight in major championships' – **Joachim Low**, Germany's World Cup-winning coach,

'Paul put football into a good place' – **David Flitcroft**, Bury manager, applauding Doncaster's Paul Dickov who ordered his players to allow Leon Clarke to walk in an equaliser for Bury after Harry Forrester scored when attempting to give the ball back following an injury.

OTHER BRITISH & IRISH INTERNATIONAL RESULTS

ENGLAND

v ALBANIA

		E	A
1989	Tirana (WC)	2	0
1989	Wembley (WC)	5	0
2001	Tirana (WC)	3	1
2001	Newcastle (WC)	2	0

v ALGERIA

		E	A
2010	Cape Town (WC)	0	0

v ANDORRA

		E	A
2006	Old Trafford (EC)	5	0
2007	Barcelona (EC)	3	0
2008	Barcelona (WC)	2	0
2009	Wembley (WC)	6	0

v ARGENTINA

		E	A
1951	Wembley	2	1
1953*	Buenos Aires	0	0
1962	Rancagua (WC)	3	1
1964	Rio de Janeiro	0	1
1966	Wembley (WC)	1	0
1974	Wembley	2	2
1977	Buenos Aires	1	1
1980	Wembley	3	1
1986	Mexico City (WC)	1	2
1991	Wembley	2	2
1998†	St Etienne (WC)	2	2
2000	Wembley	0	0
2002	Sapporo (WC)	1	0
2005	Geneva	3	2

(*Abandoned after 21 mins – rain)
(† England lost 3-4 on pens)

v AUSTRALIA

		E	A
1980	Sydney	2	1
1983	Sydney	0	0
1983	Brisbane	1	0
1983	Melbourne	1	1
1991	Sydney	1	0
2003	West Ham	1	3
2016	Sunderland	2	1

v AUSTRIA

		E	A
1908	Vienna	6	1
1908	Vienna	11	1
1909	Vienna	8	1
1930	Vienna	0	0
1932	Stamford Bridge	4	3
1936	Vienna	1	2
1951	Wembley	2	2
1952	Vienna	3	2
1958	Boras (WC)	2	2
1961	Vienna	1	3
1962	Wembley	3	1
1965	Wembley	2	3
1967	Vienna	1	0
1973	Wembley	7	0
1979	Vienna	3	4
2004	Vienna (WC)	2	2
2005	Old Trafford (WC)	1	0
2007	Vienna	1	0

v AZERBAIJAN

		E	A
2004	Baku (WC)	1	0
2005	Newcastle (WC)	2	0

v BELARUS

		E	B
2008	Minsk (WC)	3	1
2009	Wembley (WC)	3	0

v BELGIUM

		E	B
1921	Brussels	2	0
1923	Highbury	6	1
1923	Antwerp	2	2
1924	West Bromwich	4	0
1926	Antwerp	5	3
1927	Brussels	9	1
1928	Antwerp	3	1
1929	Brussels	5	1
1931	Brussels	4	1
1936	Brussels	2	3
1947	Brussels	5	2
1950	Brussels	4	1
1952	Wembley	5	0
1954	Basle (WC)	4	4
1964	Wembley	2	2
1970	Brussels	3	1
1980	Turin (EC)	1	1
1990	Bologna (WC)	1	0
1998*	Casablanca	0	0
1999	Sunderland	2	1
2012	Wembley	1	0

(*England lost 3-4 on pens)

v BOHEMIA

		E	B
1908	Prague	4	0

v BRAZIL

		E	B
1956	Wembley	4	2
1958	Gothenburg (WC)	0	0
1959	Rio de Janeiro	0	2
1962	Vina del Mar (WC)	1	3
1963	Wembley	1	1
1964	Rio de Janeiro	1	5
1969	Rio de Janeiro	1	2
1970	Guadalajara (WC)	0	1
1976	Los Angeles	0	1
1977	Rio de Janeiro	0	0
1978	Wembley	1	1
1981	Wembley	0	1
1984	Rio de Janeiro	2	0
1987	Wembley	1	1
1990	Wembley	1	0
1992	Wembley	1	1
1993	Washington	1	1
1995	Wembley	1	3
1997	Paris (TF)	0	1

2000	Wembley	1	1
2002	Shizuoka (WC)	1	2
2007	Wembley	1	1
2009	Doha	0	1
2013	Wembley	2	1
2013	Rio de Janeiro	2	2

v BULGARIA

		E	*B*
1962	Rancagua (WC)	0	0
1968	Wembley	1	1
1974	Sofia	1	0
1979	Sofia (EC)	3	0
1979	Wembley (EC)	2	0
1996	Wembley	1	0
1998	Wembley (EC)	0	0
1999	Sofia (EC)	1	1
2010	Wembley (EC)	4	0
2011	Sofia (EC)	3	0

v CAMEROON

		E	*C*
1990	Naples (WC)	3	2
1991	Wembley	2	0
1997	Wembley	2	0
2002	Kobe (Japan)	2	2

v CANADA

		E	*C*
1986	Vancouver	1	0

v CHILE

		E	*C*
1950	Rio de Janeiro (WC)	2	0
1953	Santiago	2	1
1984	Santiago	0	0
1989	Wembley	0	0
1998	Wembley	0	2
2013	Wembley	0	2

v CHINA

		E	*C*
1996	Beijing	3	0

v CIS
(formerly Soviet Union)

		E	*CIS*
1992	Moscow	2	2

v COLOMBIA

		E	*C*
1970	Bogota	4	0
1988	Wembley	1	1
1995	Wembley	0	0
1998	Lens (WC)	2	0
2005	New York	3	2

v COSTA RICA

		E	*CR*
2014	Belo Horizonte (WC)	0	0

v CROATIA

		E	*C*
1995	Wembley	0	0
2003	Ipswich	3	1
2004	Lisbon (EC)	4	2
2006	Zagreb (EC)	0	2
2007	Wembley (EC)	2	3
2008	Zagreb (WC)	4	1
2009	Wembley (WC)	5	1

v CYPRUS

		E	*C*
1975	Wembley (EC)	5	0
1975	Limassol (EC)	1	0

v CZECH REPUBLIC

		E	*C*
1998	Wembley	2	0
2008	Wembley	2	2

v CZECHOSLOVAKIA

		E	*C*
1934	Prague	1	2
1937	White Hart Lane	5	4
1963	Bratislava	4	2
1966	Wembley	0	0
1970	Guadalajara (WC)	1	0
1973	Prague	1	1
1974	Wembley (EC)	3	0
1975*	Bratislava (EC)	1	2
1978	Wembley (EC)	1	0
1982	Bilbao (WC)	2	0
1990	Wembley	4	2
1992	Prague	2	2

(* Aband 0-0, 17 mins prev day – fog)

v DENMARK

		E	*D*
1948	Copenhagen	0	0
1955	Copenhagen	5	1
1956	W'hampton (WC)	5	2
1957	Copenhagen (WC)	4	1
1966	Copenhagen	2	0
1978	Copenhagen (EC)	4	3
1979	Wembley (EC)	1	0
1982	Copenhagen (EC)	2	2
1983	Wembley (EC)	0	1
1988	Wembley	1	0
1989	Copenhagen	1	1
1990	Wembley	1	0
1992	Malmo (EC)	0	0
1994	Wembley	1	0
2002	Niigata (WC)	3	0
2003	Old Trafford	2	3
2005	Copenhagen	1	4
2011	Copenhagen	2	1
2014	Wembley	1	0

v EAST GERMANY

		E	*EG*
1963	Leipzig	2	1
1970	Wembley	3	1
1974	Leipzig	1	1
1984	Wembley	1	0

v ECUADOR

		E	*Ec*
1970	Quito	2	0
2006	Stuttgart (WC)	1	0
2014	Miami	2	2

v EGYPT

		E	*Eg*
1986	Cairo	4	0
1990	Cagliari (WC)	1	0
2010	Wembley	3	1

v ESTONIA

		E	Est
2007	Tallinn (EC)	3	0
2007	Wembley (EC)	3	0
2014	Tallinn (EC)	1	0
2015	Wembley (EC)	2	0

v FIFA

		E	F
1938	Highbury	3	0
1953	Wembley	4	4
1963	Wembley	2	1

v FINLAND

		E	F
1937	Helsinki	8	0
1956	Helsinki	5	1
1966	Helsinki	3	0
1976	Helsinki (WC)	4	1
1976	Wembley (WC)	2	1
1982	Helsinki	4	1
1984	Wembley (WC)	5	0
1985	Helsinki (WC)	1	1
1992	Helsinki	2	1
2000	Helsinki (WC)	0	0
2001	Liverpool (WC)	2	1

v FRANCE

		E	F
1923	Paris	4	1
1924	Paris	3	1
1925	Paris	3	2
1927	Paris	6	0
1928	Paris	5	1
1929	Paris	4	1
1931	Paris	2	5
1933	White Hart Lane	4	1
1938	Paris	4	2
1947	Highbury	3	0
1949	Paris	3	1
1951	Highbury	2	2
1955	Paris	0	1
1957	Wembley	4	0
1962	Hillsborough (EC)	1	1
1963	Paris (EC)	2	5
1966	Wembley (WC)	2	0
1969	Wembley	5	0
1982	Bilbao (WC)	3	1
1984	Paris	0	2
1992	Wembley	2	0
1992	Malmo (EC)	0	0
1997	Montpellier (TF)	1	0
1999	Wembley	0	2
2000	Paris	1	1
2004	Lisbon (EC)	1	2
2008	Paris	0	1
2010	Wembley	1	2
2012	Donetsk (EC)	1	1
2015	Wembley	2	0

v GEORGIA

		E	G
1996	Tbilisi (WC)	2	0
1997	Wembley (WC)	2	0

v GERMANY/WEST GERMANY

		E	G
1930	Berlin	3	3
1935	White Hart Lane	3	0
1938	Berlin	6	3
1954	Wembley	3	1
1956	Berlin	3	1
1965	Nuremberg	1	0
1966	Wembley	1	0
1966	Wembley (WCF)	4	2
1968	Hanover	0	1
1970	Leon (WC)	2	3
1972	Wembley (EC)	1	3
1972	Berlin (EC)	0	0
1975	Wembley	2	0
1978	Munich	1	2
1982	Madrid (WC)	0	0
1982	Wembley	1	2
1985	Mexico City	3	0
1987	Dusseldorf	1	3
1990*	Turin (WC)	1	1
1991	Wembley	0	1
1993	Detroit	1	2
1996†	Wembley (EC)	1	1
2000	Charleroi (EC)	1	0
2000	Wembley (WC)	0	1
2001	Munich (WC)	5	1
2007	Wembley	1	2
2008	Berlin	2	1
2010	Bloemfontein (WC)	1	4
2012	Donetsk (EC)	1	1
2013	Wembley	0	1
2016	Berlin	3	2

(*England lost 3-4 on pens)
(† England lost 5-6 on pens)

v GHANA

		E	G
2011	Wembley	1	1

v GREECE

		E	G
1971	Wembley (EC)	3	0
1971	Athens (EC)	2	0
1982	Salonika (EC)	3	0
1983	Wembley (EC)	0	0
1989	Athens	2	1
1994	Wembley	5	0
2001	Athens (WC)	2	0
2001	Old Trafford (WC)	2	2
2006	Old Trafford	4	0

v HOLLAND

		E	H
1935	Amsterdam	1	0
1946	Huddersfield	8	2
1964	Amsterdam	1	1
1969	Amsterdam	1	0
1970	Wembley	0	0
1977	Wembley	0	2
1982	Wembley	2	0
1988	Wembley	2	2
1988	Dusseldorf (EC)	1	3
1990	Cagliari (WC)	0	0
1993	Wembley (WC)	2	2
1993	Rotterdam (WC)	0	2
1996	Wembley (EC)	4	1
2001	White Hart Lane	0	2
2002	Amsterdam	1	1

2005	Villa Park	0	0
2006	Amsterdam	1	1
2009	Amsterdam	2	2
2012	Wembley	2	3
2016	Wembley	1	2

v HONDURAS

		E	H
2014	Miami	0	0

v HUNGARY

		E	H
1908	Budapest	7	0
1909	Budapest	4	2
1909	Budapest	8	2
1934	Budapest	1	2
1936	Highbury	6	2
1953	Wembley	3	6
1954	Budapest	1	7
1960	Budapest	0	2
1962	Rancagua (WC)	1	2
1965	Wembley	1	0
1978	Wembley	4	1
1981	Budapest (WC)	3	1
1981	Wembley (WC)	1	0
1983	Wembley (EC)	2	0
1983	Budapest (EC)	3	0
1988	Budapest	0	0
1990	Wembley	1	0
1992	Budapest	1	0
1996	Wembley	3	0
1999	Budapest	1	1
2006	Old Trafford	3	1
2010	Wembley	2	1

v ICELAND

		E	I
1982	Reykjavik	1	1
2004	City of Manchester	6	1
2016	Nice (EC)	1	2

v ISRAEL

		E	I
1986	Tel Aviv	2	1
1988	Tel Aviv	0	0
2006	Tel Aviv (EC)	0	0
2007	Wembley (EC)	3	0

v ITALY

		E	I
1933	Rome	1	1
1934	Highbury	3	2
1939	Milan	2	2
1948	Turin	4	0
1949	White Hart Lane	2	0
1952	Florence	1	1
1959	Wembley	2	2
1961	Rome	3	2
1973	Turin	0	2
1973	Wembley	0	1
1976	New York	3	2
1976	Rome (WC)	0	2
1977	Wembley (WC)	2	0
1980	Turin (EC)	0	1
1985	Mexico City	1	2
1989	Wembley	0	0
1990	Bari (WC)	1	2
1996	Wembley (WC)	0	1
1997	Nantes (TF)	2	0
1997	Rome (WC)	0	0
2000	Turin	0	1
2002	Leeds	1	2
2012*	Kiev (EC)	0	0
2012	Berne	2	1
2014	Manaus (WC)	1	2
2015	Turin	1	1

(*England lost 2-4 on pens)

v JAMAICA

		E	J
2006	Old Trafford	6	0

v JAPAN

		E	J
1995	Wembley	2	1
2004	City of Manchester	1	1
2010	Graz	2	1

v KAZAKHSTAN

		E	K
2008	Wembley (WC)	5	1
2009	Almaty (WC)	4	0

v KUWAIT

		E	K
1982	Bilbao (WC)	1	0

v LIECHTENSTEIN

		E	L
2003	Vaduz (EC)	2	0
2003	Old Trafford (EC)	2	0

v LITHUANIA

		E	L
2015	Wembley (EC)	4	0
2015	Vilnius (EC)	3	0

v LUXEMBOURG

		E	L
1927	Luxembourg	5	2
1960	Luxembourg (WC)	9	0
1961	Highbury (WC)	4	1
1977	Wembley (WC)	5	0
1977	Luxembourg (WC)	2	0
1982	Wembley (EC)	9	0
1983	Luxembourg (EC)	4	0
1998	Luxembourg (EC)	3	0
1999	Wembley (EC)	6	0

v MACEDONIA

		E	M
2002	Southampton (EC)	2	2
2003	Skopje (EC)	2	1
2006	Skopje (EC)	1	0
2006	Old Trafford (EC)	0	0

v MALAYSIA

		E	M
1991	Kuala Lumpur	4	2

v MALTA

		E	M
1971	Valletta (EC)	1	0
1971	Wembley (EC)	5	0
2000	Valletta	2	1

v MEXICO

		E	M
1959	Mexico City	1	2
1961	Wembley	8	0

1966	Wembley (WC)	2	0
1969	Mexico City	0	0
1985	Mexico City	0	1
1986	Los Angeles	3	0
1997	Wembley	2	0
2001	Derby	4	0
2010	Wembley	3	1

v MOLDOVA

		E	*M*
1996	Kishinev	3	0
1997	Wembley (WC)	4	0
2012	Chisinu (WC)	5	0
2013	Wembley (WC)	4	0

v MONTENEGRO

		E	*M*
2010	Wembley (EC)	0	0
2011	Podgorica (EC)	2	2
2013	Podgorica (WC)	1	1
2013	Wembley (WC)	4	1

v MOROCCO

		E	*M*
1986	Monterrey (WC)	0	0
1998	Casablanca	1	0

v NEW ZEALAND

		E	*NZ*
1991	Auckland	1	0
1991	Wellington	2	0

v NIGERIA

		E	*NZ*
1994	Wembley	1	0
2002	Osaka (WC)	0	0

v NORWAY

		E	*NZ*
1937	Oslo	6	0
1938	Newcastle	4	0
1949	Oslo	4	1
1966	Oslo	6	1
1980	Wembley (WC)	4	0
1981	Oslo (WC)	1	2
1992	Wembley (WC)	1	1
1993	Oslo (WC)	0	2
1994	Wembley	0	0
1995	Oslo	0	0
2012	Oslo	1	0
2014	Wembley	1	0

v PARAGUAY

		E	*P*
1986	Mexico City (WC)	3	0
2002	Anfield	4	0
2006	Frankfurt (WC)	1	0

v PERU

		E	*P*
1959	Lima	1	4
1961	Lima	4	0
2014	Wembley	3	0

v POLAND

		E	*P*
1966	Goodison Park	1	1
1966	Chorzow	1	0
1973	Chorzow (WC)	0	2
1973	Wembley (WC)	1	1
1986	Monterrey (WC)	3	0
1989	Wembley (WC)	3	0
1989	Katowice (WC)	0	0
1990	Wembley (EC)	2	0
1991	Poznan (EC)	1	1
1993	Chorzow (WC)	1	1
1993	Wembley (WC)	3	0
1996	Wembley (WC)	2	1
1997	Katowice (WC)	2	0
1999	Wembley (EC)	3	1
1999	Warsaw (EC)	0	0
2004	Katowice (WC)	2	1
2005	Old Trafford (WC)	2	1
2012	Warsaw (WC)	1	1
2013	Wembley (WC)	2	0

v PORTUGAL

		E	*P*
1947	Lisbon	10	0
1950	Lisbon	5	3
1951	Goodison Park	5	2
1955	Oporto	1	3
1958	Wembley	2	1
1961	Lisbon (WC)	1	1
1961	Wembley (WC)	2	0
1964	Lisbon	4	3
1964	Sao Paulo	1	1
1966	Wembley (WC)	2	1
1969	Wembley	1	0
1974	Lisbon	0	0
1974	Wembley (EC)	0	0
1975	Lisbon (EC)	1	1
1986	Monterrey (WC)	0	1
1995	Wembley	1	1
1998	Wembley	3	0
2000	Eindhoven (EC)	2	3
2002	Villa Park	1	1
2004	Faro	1	1
2004*	Lisbon (EC)	2	2
2006†	Gelsenkirchen (WC)	0	0
2016	Wembley	1	0

(† England lost 1–3 on pens)
(*England lost 5–6 on pens)

v REPUBLIC OF IRELAND

		E	*RoI*
1946	Dublin	1	0
1949	Goodison Park	0	2
1957	Wembley (WC)	5	1
1957	Dublin (WC)	1	1
1964	Dublin	3	1
1977	Wembley	1	1
1978	Dublin (EC)	1	1
1980	Wembley (EC)	2	0
1985	Wembley	2	1
1988	Stuttgart (EC)	0	1
1990	Cagliari (WC)	1	1
1990	Dublin (EC)	1	1
1991	Wembley (EC)	1	1
1995*	Dublin	0	1
2013	Wembley	1	1
2015	Dublin	0	0

(*Abandoned 27 mins – crowd riot)

v ROMANIA

		E	R
1939	Bucharest	2	0
1968	Bucharest	0	0
1969	Wembley	1	1
1970	Guadalajara (WC)	1	0
1980	Bucharest (WC)	1	2
1981	Wembley (WC)	0	0
1985	Bucharest (WC)	0	0
1985	Wembley (WC)	1	1
1994	Wembley	1	1
1998	Toulouse (WC)	1	2
2000	Charleroi (EC)	2	3

v RUSSIA

		E	R
2007	Wembley (EC)	3	0
2007	Moscow (EC)	1	2
2016	Marseille (EC)	1	1

v SAN MARINO

		E	SM
1992	Wembley (WC)	6	0
1993	Bologna (WC)	7	1
2012	Wembley (WC)	5	0
2013	Serravalle (WC)	8	0
2014	Wembley (EC)	5	0
2015	Serravalle (EC)	6	0

v SAUDI ARABIA

		E	SA
1988	Riyadh	1	1
1998	Wembley	0	0

v SERBIA-MONTENEGRO

		E	S-M
2003	Leicester	2	1

v SLOVAKIA

		E	S
2002	Bratislava (EC)	2	1
2003	Middlesbrough (EC)	2	1
2009	Wembley	4	0
2016	St Etienne (EC)	0	0

v SLOVENIA

		E	S
2009	Wembley	2	1
2010	Port Elizabeth (WC)	1	0
2014	Wembley (EC)	3	1
2015	Ljubljana (EC)	3	2

v SOUTH AFRICA

		E	SA
1997	Old Trafford	2	1
2003	Durban	2	1

v SOUTH KOREA

		E	SK
2002	Seoguipo	1	1

v SOVIET UNION (see also CIS)

		E	SU
1958	Moscow	1	1
1958	Gothenburg (WC)	2	2
1958	Gothenburg (WC)	0	1
1958	Wembley	5	0
1967	Wembley	2	2
1968	Rome (EC)	2	0
1973	Moscow	2	1
1984	Wembley	0	2
1986	Tbilisi	1	0
1988	Frankfurt (EC)	1	3
1991	Wembley	3	1

v SPAIN

		E	S
1929	Madrid	3	4
1931	Highbury	7	1
1950	Rio de Janeiro (WC)	0	1
1955	Madrid	1	1
1955	Wembley	4	1
1960	Madrid	0	3
1960	Wembley	4	2
1965	Madrid	2	0
1967	Wembley	2	0
1968	Wembley (EC)	1	0
1968	Madrid (EC)	2	1
1980	Barcelona	2	0
1980	Naples (EC)	2	1
1981	Wembley	1	2
1982	Madrid (WC)	0	0
1987	Madrid	4	2
1992	Santander	0	1
1996*	Wembley (EC)	0	0
2001	Villa Park	3	0
2004	Madrid	0	1
2007	Old Trafford	0	1
2009	Seville	0	2
2011	Wembley	1	0
2015	Alicante	0	2

(*England won 4-2 on pens)

v SWEDEN

		E	S
1923	Stockholm	4	2
1923	Stockholm	3	1
1937	Stockholm	4	0
1948	Highbury	4	2
1949	Stockholm	1	3
1956	Stockholm	0	0
1959	Wembley	2	3
1965	Gothenburg	2	1
1968	Wembley	3	1
1979	Stockholm	0	0
1986	Stockholm	0	1
1988	Wembley (WC)	0	0
1989	Stockholm (WC)	0	0
1992	Stockholm (EC)	1	2
1995	Leeds	3	3
1998	Stockholm (EC)	1	2
1999	Wembley (EC)	0	0
2001	Old Trafford	1	1
2002	Saitama (WC)	1	1
2004	Gothenburg	0	1
2006	Cologne (WC)	2	2
2011	Wembley	1	0
2012	Kiev (EC)	3	2
2012	Stockholm	2	4

v SWITZERLAND

		E	S
1933	Berne	4	0
1938	Zurich	1	2
1947	Zurich	0	1
1949	Highbury	6	0

1952	Zurich	3	0
1954	Berne (WC)	2	0
1962	Wembley	3	1
1963	Basle	8	1
1971	Basle (EC)	3	2
1971	Wembley (EC)	1	1
1975	Basle	2	1
1977	Wembley	0	0
1980	Wembley (WC)	2	1
1981	Basle (WC)	1	2
1988	Lausanne	1	0
1995	Wembley	3	1
1996	Wembley (EC)	1	1
1998	Berne	1	1
2004	Coimbra (EC)	3	0
2008	Wembley	2	1
2010	Basle (EC)	3	1
2011	Wembley (EC)	2	2
2014	Basle (EC)	2	0
2015	Wembley (EC)	2	0

v TRINIDAD & TOBAGO

		E	*T*
2006	Nuremberg (WC)	2	0
2008	Port of Spain	3	0

v TUNISIA

		E	*T*
1990	Tunis	1	1
1998	Marseille (WC)	2	0

v TURKEY

		E	*T*
1984	Istanbul (WC)	8	0
1985	Wembley (WC)	5	0
1987	Izmir (EC)	0	0
1987	Wembley (EC)	8	0
1991	Izmir (EC)	1	0
1991	Wembley (EC)	1	0
1992	Wembley (WC)	4	0
1993	Izmir (WC)	2	0
2003	Sunderland (EC)	2	0
2003	Istanbul (EC)	0	0
2016	Etihad Stadium	2	1

v UKRAINE

		E	*U*
2000	Wembley	2	0
2004	Newcastle	3	0
2009	Wembley (WC)	2	1
2009	Dnipropetrovski (WC)	0	1
2012	Donetsk (EC)	1	0
2012	Wembley (WC)	1	1
2013	Kiev (WC)	0	0

v URUGUAY

		E	*U*
1953	Montevideo	1	2
1954	Basle (WC)	2	4
1964	Wembley	2	1
1966	Wembley (WC)	0	0
1969	Montevideo	2	1
1977	Montevideo	0	0
1984	Montevideo	0	2
1990	Wembley	1	2
1995	Wembley	0	0
2006	Anfield	2	1
2014	Sao Paulo (WC)	1	2

v USA

		E	*USA*
1950	Belo Horizonte (WC)	0	1
1953	New York	6	3
1959	Los Angeles	8	1
1964	New York	10	0
1985	Los Angeles	5	0
1993	Boston	0	2
1994	Wembley	2	0
2005	Chicago	2	1
2008	Wembley	2	0
2010	Rustenburg (WC)	1	1

v YUGOSLAVIA

		E	*Y*
1939	Belgrade	1	2
1950	Highbury	2	2
1954	Belgrade	0	1
1956	Wembley	3	0
1958	Belgrade	0	5
1960	Wembley	3	3
1965	Belgrade	1	1
1966	Wembley	2	0
1968	Florence (EC)	0	1
1972	Wembley	1	1
1974	Belgrade	2	2
1986	Wembley (EC)	2	0
1987	Belgrade (EC)	4	1
1989	Wembley	2	1

ENGLAND'S RECORD

England's first international was a 0-0 draw against Scotland in Glasgow, on the West of Scotland cricket ground, Partick, on November 30, 1872 Their complete record at the start of 2016–17 is:

P	*W*	*D*	*L*	*F*	*A*
959	545	233	181	2111	950

ENGLAND'S 'B' TEAM RESULTS

England scores first

1937	Stockholm	4	0
1948	Highbury	4	2
1949	Stockholm	1	3
1956	Stockholm	0	0
1959	Wembley	2	3
1965	Gothenburg	2	1
1968	Wembley	3	1
1979	Stockholm	0	0
1986	Stockholm	0	1
1988	Wembley (WC)	0	0
1989	Stockholm (WC)	0	0
1992	Stockholm (EC)	1	2
1995	Leeds	3	3
1998	Stockholm (EC)	1	2

1999	Wembley (EC)	0	0
2001	Old Trafford	1	1
2002	Saitama (WC)	1	1
2004	Gothenburg	0	1
2006	Cologne (WC)	2	2
1949	Finland (A)	4	0
1949	Holland (A)	4	0
1950	Italy (A)	0	5
1950	Holland (H)	1	0
1950	Holland (A)	0	3
1950	Luxembourg (A)	2	1
1950	Switzerland (H)	5	0
1952	Holland (A)	1	0
1952	France (A)	1	7
1953	Scotland (A)	2	2
1954	Scotland (H)	1	1
1954	Germany (A)	4	0
1954	Yugoslavia (A)	1	2
1954	Switzerland (A)	0	2
1955	Germany (H)	1	1
1955	Yugoslavia (H)	5	1
1956	Switzerland (H)	4	1
1956	Scotland (A)	2	2
1957	Scotland (H)	4	1
1978	W Germany (A)	2	1
1978	Czechoslovakia (A)	1	0
1978	Singapore (A)	8	0
1978	Malaysia (A)	1	1
1978	N Zealand (A)	4	0
1978	N Zealand (A)	3	1
1978	N Zealand (A)	4	0
1979	Austria (A)	1	0
1979	N Zealand (H)	4	1
1980	USA (H)	1	0
1980	Spain (H)	1	0
1980	Australia (H)	1	0
1981	Spain (A)	2	3
1984	N Zealand (H)	2	0
1987	Malta (A)	2	0
1989	Switzerland (A)	2	0
1989	Iceland (A)	2	0
1989	Norway (A)	1	0
1989	Italy (H)	1	1
1989	Yugoslavia (H)	2	1
1990	Rep of Ireland (A)	1	4
1990	Czechoslovakia (H)	2	0
1990	Algeria (A)	0	0
1991	Wales (A)	1	0
1991	Iceland (H)	1	0
1991	Switzerland (H)	2	1
1991	Spanish XI (A)	1	0
1992	France (H)	3	0
1992	Czechoslovakia (A)	1	0
1992	CIS (A)	1	1
1994	N Ireland (H)	4	2
1995	Rep of Ireland (H)	2	0
1998	Chile (H)	1	2
1998	Russia (H)	4	1
2006	Belarus (H)	1	2
2007	Albania	3	1

GREAT BRITAIN v REST OF EUROPE (FIFA)

		GB	RofE
1947	Glasgow	6	1
1955	Belfast	1	4

SCOTLAND

v ARGENTINA

		S	A
1977	Buenos Aires	1	1
1979	Glasgow	1	3
1990	Glasgow	1	0
2008	Glasgow	0	1

v AUSTRALIA

		S	A
1985*	Glasgow (WC)	2	0
1985*	Melbourne (WC)	0	0
1996	Glasgow	1	0
2000	Glasgow	0	2
2012	Edinburgh	3	1

(* World Cup play-off)

v AUSTRIA

		S	A
1931	Vienna	0	5
1933	Glasgow	2	2
1937	Vienna	1	1
1950	Glasgow	0	1
1951	Vienna	0	4
1954	Zurich (WC)	0	1
1955	Vienna	4	1
1956	Glasgow	1	1
1960	Vienna	1	4
1963*	Glasgow	4	1
1968	Glasgow (WC)	2	1
1969	Vienna (WC)	0	2
1978	Vienna (EC)	2	3
1979	Glasgow (EC)	1	1
1994	Vienna	2	1
1996	Vienna (WC)	0	0
1997	Glasgow (WC)	2	0

(* Abandoned after 79 minutes)

		S	A
2003	Glasgow	0	2
2005	Graz	2	2
2007	Vienna	1	0

v BELARUS

		S	B
1997	Minsk (WC)	1	0
1997	Aberdeen (WC)	4	1
2005	Minsk (WC)	0	0
2005	Glasgow (WC)	0	1

v BELGIUM

		S	B
1947	Brussels	1	2

1948	Glasgow	2	0
1951	Brussels	5	0
1971	Liege (EC)	0	3
1971	Aberdeen (EC)	1	0
1974	Brugge	1	2
1979	Brussels (EC)	0	2
1979	Glasgow (EC)	1	3
1982	Brussels (EC)	2	3
1983	Glasgow (EC)	1	1
1987	Brussels (EC)	1	4
1987	Glasgow (EC)	2	0
2001	Glasgow (WC)	2	2
2001	Brussels (WC)	0	2
2012	Brussels (WC)	0	2
2013	Glasgow (WC)	0	2

v BOSNIA

		S	B
1999	Sarajevo (EC)	2	1
1999	Glasgow (EC)	1	0

v BRAZIL

		S	B
1966	Glasgow	1	1
1972	Rio de Janeiro	0	1
1973	Glasgow	0	1
1974	Frankfurt (WC)	0	0
1977	Rio de Janeiro	0	2
1982	Seville (WC)	1	4
1987	Glasgow	0	2
1990	Turin (WC)	0	1
1998	St Denis (WC)	1	2
2011	Arsenal	0	2

v BULGARIA

		S	B
1978	Glasgow	2	1
1986	Glasgow (EC)	0	0
1987	Sofia (EC)	1	0
1990	Sofia (EC)	1	1
1991	Glasgow (EC)	1	1
2006	Kobe	5	1

v CANADA

		S	C
1983	Vancouver	2	0
1983	Edmonton	3	0
1983	Toronto	2	0
1992	Toronto	3	1
2002	Edinburgh	3	1

v CHILE

		S	C
1977	Santiago	4	2
1989	Glasgow	2	0

v CIS (formerly Soviet Union)

		S	C
1992	Norrkoping (EC)	3	0

v COLOMBIA

		S	C
1988	Glasgow	0	0
1996	Miami	0	1
1998	New York	2	2

v COSTA RICA

		S	C
1990	Genoa (WC)	0	1

v CROATIA

		S	C
2000	Zagreb (WC)	1	1
2001	Glasgow (WC)	0	0
2008	Glasgow	1	1
2013	Zagreb (WC)	1	0
2013	Glasgow (WC)	2	0

v CYPRUS

		S	C
1968	Nicosia (WC)	5	0
1969	Glasgow (WC)	8	0
1989	Limassol (WC)	3	2
1989	Glasgow (WC)	2	1
2011	Larnaca	2	1

v CZECH REPUBLIC

		S	C
1999	Glasgow (EC)	1	2
1999	Prague (EC)	2	3
2008	Prague	1	3
2010	Glasgow	1	0
2010	Prague (EC)	0	1
2011	Glasgow (EC)	2	2
2016	Prague	1	0

v CZECHOSLOVAKIA

		S	C
1937	Prague	3	1
1937	Glasgow	5	0
1961	Bratislava (WC)	0	4
1961	Glasgow (WC)	3	2
1961*	Brussels (WC)	2	4
1972	Porto Alegre	0	0
1973	Glasgow (WC)	2	1
1973	Bratislava (WC)	0	1
1976	Prague (WC)	0	2
1977	Glasgow (WC)	3	1

(*World Cup play-off)

v DENMARK

		S	D
1951	Glasgow	3	1
1952	Copenhagen	2	1
1968	Copenhagen	1	0
1970	Glasgow (EC)	1	0
1971	Copenhagen (EC)	0	1
1972	Copenhagen (WC)	4	1
1972	Glasgow (WC)	2	0
1975	Copenhagen (EC)	1	0
1975	Glasgow (EC)	3	1
1986	Neza (WC)	0	1
1996	Copenhagen	0	2
1998	Glasgow	0	1
2002	Glasgow	0	1
2004	Copenhagen	0	1
2011	Glasgow	2	1
2016	Glasgow	1	0

v EAST GERMANY

		S	EG
1974	Glasgow	3	0
1977	East Berlin	0	1
1982	Glasgow (EC)	2	0
1983	Halle (EC)	1	2
1986	Glasgow	0	0
1990	Glasgow	0	1

v ECUADOR

		S	E
1995	Toyama, Japan	2	1

v EGYPT

		S	E
1990	Aberdeen	1	3

v ESTONIA

		S	E
1993	Tallinn (WC)	3	0
1993	Aberdeen	3	1
1996	Tallinn (WC)	*No result	
1997	Monaco (WC)	0	0
1997	Kilmarnock (WC)	2	0
1998	Edinburgh (EC)	3	2
1999	Tallinn (EC)	0	0
(* Estonia absent)			
2004	Tallinn	1	0
2013	Aberdeen	1	0

v FAROE ISLANDS

		S	F
1994	Glasgow (EC)	5	1
1995	Toftir (EC)	2	0
1998	Aberdeen (EC)	2	1
1999	Toftir (EC)	1	1
2002	Toftir (EC)	2	2
2003	Glasgow (EC)	3	1
2006	Glasgow (EC)	6	0
2007	Toftir (EC)	2	0
2010	Aberdeen	3	0

v FINLAND

		S	F
1954	Helsinki	2	1
1964	Glasgow (WC)	3	1
1965	Helsinki (WC)	2	1
1976	Glasgow	6	0
1992	Glasgow	1	1
1994	Helsinki (EC)	2	0
1995	Glasgow (EC)	1	0
1998	Edinburgh	1	1

v FRANCE

		S	F
1930	Paris	2	0
1932	Paris	3	1
1948	Paris	0	3
1949	Glasgow	2	0
1950	Paris	1	0
1951	Glasgow	1	0
1958	Orebro (WC)	1	2
1984	Marseilles	0	2
1989	Glasgow (WC)	2	0
1990	Paris (WC)	0	3
1997	St Etienne	1	2
2000	Glasgow	0	2
2002	Paris	0	5
2006	Glasgow (EC)	1	0
2007	Paris (EC)	1	0
2016	Metz	0	3

v GEORGIA

		S	G
2007	Glasgow (EC)	2	1
2007	Tbilisi (EC)	0	2
2014	Glasgow (EC)	1	0
2015	Tbilisi (EC)	0	1

v GERMANY/WEST GERMANY

		S	G
1929	Berlin	1	1
1936	Glasgow	2	0
1957	Stuttgart	3	1
1959	Glasgow	3	2
1964	Hanover	2	2
1969	Glasgow (WC)	1	1
1969	Hamburg (WC)	2	3
1973	Glasgow	1	1
1974	Frankfurt	1	2
1986	Queretaro (WC)	1	2
1992	Norrkoping (EC)	0	2
1993	Glasgow	0	1
1999	Bremen	1	0
2003	Glasgow (EC)	1	1
2003	Dortmund (EC)	1	2
2014	Dortmund (EC)	1	2
2015	Glasgow (EC)	2	3

v GIBRALTAR

		S	G
2015	Glasgow (EC)	6	1
2015	Faro (EC)	6	0

v GREECE

		S	G
1994	Athens (EC)	0	1
1995	Glasgow	1	0

v HOLLAND

		S	H
1929	Amsterdam	2	0
1938	Amsterdam	3	1
1959	Amsterdam	2	1
1966	Glasgow	0	3
1968	Amsterdam	0	0
1971	Amsterdam	1	2
1978	Mendoza (WC)	3	2
1982	Glasgow	2	1
1986	Eindhoven	0	0
1992	Gothenburg (EC)	0	1
1994	Glasgow	0	1
1994	Utrecht	1	3
1996	Birmingham (EC)	0	0
2000	Arnhem	0	0
2003*	Glasgow (EC)	1	0
2003*	Amsterdam (EC)	0	6
2009	Amsterdam (WC)	0	3
2009	Glasgow (WC)	0	1
(*Qual Round play-off)			

v HUNGARY

		S	H
1938	Glasgow	3	1
1955	Glasgow	2	4
1955	Budapest	1	3
1958	Glasgow	1	1
1960	Budapest	3	3
1980	Budapest	1	3
1987	Glasgow	2	0
2004	Glasgow	0	3

v ICELAND

		S	I
1984	Glasgow (WC)	3	0
1985	Reykjavik (WC)	1	0

2002	Reykjavik (EC)	2	0
2003	Glasgow (EC)	2	1
2008	Reykjavik (WC)	2	1
2009	Glasgow (WC)	2	1

v IRAN

		S	*I*
1978	Cordoba (WC)	1	1

v ISRAEL

		S	*I*
1981	Tel Aviv (WC)	1	0
1981	Glasgow (WC)	3	1
1986	Tel Aviv	1	0

v ITALY

		S	*I*
1931	Rome	0	3
1965	Glasgow (WC)	1	0
1965	Naples (WC)	0	3
1988	Perugia	0	2
1992	Glasgow (WC)	0	0
1993	Rome (WC)	1	3
2005	Milan (WC)	0	2
2005	Glasgow (WC)	1	1
2007	Bari (EC)	0	2
2007	Glasgow (EC)	1	2
2016	Ta'Qali	0	1

v JAPAN

		S	*J*
1995	Hiroshima	0	0
2006	Saitama	0	0
2009	Yokohama	0	2

v LATVIA

		S	*L*
1996	Riga (WC)	2	0
1997	Glasgow (WC)	2	0
2000	Riga (WC)	1	0
2001	Glasgow (WC)	2	1

v LIECHTENSTEIN

		S	*L*
2010	Glasgow (EC)	2	1
2011	Vaduz (EC)	1	0

v LITHUANIA

		S	*L*
1998	Vilnius (EC)	0	0
1999	Glasgow (EC)	3	0
2003	Kaunus (EC)	0	1
2003	Glasgow (EC)	1	0
2006	Kaunas (EC)	2	1
2007	Glasgow (EC)	3	1
2010	Kaunas (EC)	0	0
2011	Glasgow (EC)	1	0

v LUXEMBOURG

		S	*L*
1947	Luxembourg	6	0
1986	Glasgow (EC)	3	0
1987	Esch (EC)	0	0
2012	Josy Barthel	2	1`

v MACEDONIA

		S	*M*
2008	Skopje (WC)	0	1
2009	Glasgow (WC)	2	0
2012	Glasgow (WC)	1	1
2013	Skopje (WC)	2	1

v MALTA

		S	*M*
1988	Valletta	1	1
1990	Valletta	2	1
1993	Glasgow (WC)	3	0
1993	Valletta (WC)	2	0
1997	Valletta	3	2

v MOLDOVA

		S	*M*
2004	Chisinau (WC)	1	1
2005	Glasgow (WC)	2	0

v MOROCCO

		S	*M.*
1998	St Etienne (WC)	0	3

v NEW ZEALAND

		S	*NZ*
1982	Malaga (WC)	5	2
2003	Edinburgh	1	1

v NIGERIA

		S	*N*
2002	Aberdeen	1	2
2014	Fulham	2	2

v NORWAY

		S	*N*
1929	Bergen	7	3
1954	Glasgow	1	0
1954	Oslo	1	1
1963	Bergen	3	4
1963	Glasgow	6	1
1974	Oslo	2	1
1978	Glasgow (EC)	3	2
1979	Oslo (EC)	4	0
1988	Oslo (WC)	2	1
1989	Glasgow (WC)	1	1
1992	Oslo	0	0
1998	Bordeaux (WC)	1	1
2003	Oslo	0	0
2004	Glasgow (WC)	0	1
2005	Oslo (WC)	2	1
2008	Glasgow (WC)	0	0
2009	Oslo (WC)	0	4
2013	Molde	1	0

v PARAGUAY

		S	*P*
1958	Norrkoping (WC)	2	3

v PERU

		S	*P*
1972	Glasgow	2	0
1978	Cordoba (WC)	1	3
1979	Glasgow	1	1

v POLAND

		S	*P*
1958	Warsaw	2	1
1960	Glasgow	2	3
1965	Chorzow (WC)	1	1
1965	Glasgow (WC)	1	2
1980	Poznan	0	1
1990	Glasgow	1	1
2001	Bydgoszcz	1	1
2014	Warsaw	1	0
2014	Warsaw (EC)	2	2
2015	Glasgow (EC)	2	2

v PORTUGAL

		S	P
1950	Lisbon	2	2
1955	Glasgow	3	0
1959	Lisbon	0	1
1966	Glasgow	0	1
1971	Lisbon (EC)	0	2
1971	Glasgow (EC)	2	1
1975	Glasgow	1	0
1978	Lisbon (EC)	0	1
1980	Glasgow (EC)	4	1
1980	Glasgow (WC)	0	0
1981	Lisbon (WC)	1	2
1992	Glasgow (WC)	0	0
1993	Lisbon (WC)	0	5
2002	Braga	0	2

v QATAR

		S	Q
2015	Edinburgh	1	0

v REPUBLIC OF IRELAND

		S	RoI
1961	Glasgow (WC)	4	1
1961	Dublin (WC)	3	0
1963	Dublin	0	1
1969	Dublin	1	1
1986	Dublin (EC)	0	0
1987	Glasgow (EC)	0	1
2000	Dublin	2	1
2003	Glasgow (EC)	0	2
2011	Dublin (CC)	0	1
2014	Glasgow (EC)	1	0
2015	Dublin (EC)	1	1

v ROMANIA

		S	R
1975	Bucharest (EC)	1	1
1975	Glasgow (EC)	1	1
1986	Glasgow	3	0
1990	Glasgow (EC)	2	1
1991	Bucharest (EC)	0	1
2004	Glasgow	1	2

v RUSSIA

		S	R
1994	Glasgow (EC)	1	1
1995	Moscow (EC)	0	0

v SAN MARINO

		S	SM
1991	Serravalle (EC)	2	0
1991	Glasgow (EC)	4	0
1995	Serravalle (EC)	2	0
1995	Glasgow (EC)	5	0
2000	Serravalle (WC)	2	0
2001	Glasgow (WC)	4	0

v SAUDI ARABIA

		S	SA
1988	Riyadh	2	2

v SERBIA

		S	Se
2012	Glasgow (WC)	0	0
2013	Novi Sad (WC)	0	2

v SLOVENIA

		S	SL
2004	Glasgow (WC)	0	0
2005	Celje (WC)	3	0
2012	Koper	1	1

v SOUTH AFRICA

		S	SA
2002	Hong Kong	0	2
2007	Aberdeen	1	0

v SOUTH KOREA

		S	SK
2002	Busan	1	4

v SOVIET UNION (see also CIS and RUSSIA)

		S	SU
1967	Glasgow	0	2
1971	Moscow	0	1
1982	Malaga (WC)	2	2
1991	Glasgow	0	1

v SPAIN

		S	Sp
1957	Glasgow (WC)	4	2
1957	Madrid (WC)	1	4
1963	Madrid	6	2
1965	Glasgow	0	0
1975	Glasgow (EC)	1	2
1975	Valencia (EC)	1	1
1982	Valencia	0	3
1985	Glasgow (WC)	3	1
1985	Seville (WC)	0	1
1988	Madrid	0	0
2004*	Valencia	1	1
(*Abandoned after 59 mins – floodlight failure)			
2010	Glasgow (EC)	2	3
2011	Alicante (EC)	1	3

v SWEDEN

		S	Swe
1952	Stockholm	1	3
1953	Glasgow	1	2
1975	Gothenburg	1	1
1977	Glasgow	3	1
1980	Stockholm (WC)	1	0
1981	Glasgow (WC)	2	0
1990	Genoa (WC)	2	1
1995	Solna	0	2
1996	Glasgow (WC)	1	0
1997	Gothenburg (WC)	1	2
2004	Edinburgh	1	4
2010	Stockholm	0	3

v SWITZERLAND

		S	Sw
1931	Geneva	3	2
1948	Berne	1	2
1950	Glasgow	3	1
1957	Basle (WC)	2	1
1957	Glasgow (WC)	3	2
1973	Berne	0	1
1976	Glasgow	1	0
1982	Berne (EC)	0	2
1983	Glasgow (EC)	2	2
1990	Glasgow (EC)	2	1
1991	Berne (EC)	2	2
1992	Berne (WC)	1	3
1993	Aberdeen (WC)	1	1
1996	Birmingham (EC)	1	0
2006	Glasgow	1	3

v TRINIDAD & TOBAGO

		S	T
2004	Hibernian	4	1

v TURKEY

		S	T
1960	Ankara	2	4

v UKRAINE

		S	U
2006	Kiev (EC)	0	2
2007	Glasgow (EC)	3	1

v USA

		S	USA
1952	Glasgow	6	0
1992	Denver	1	0
1996	New Britain, Conn	1	2
1998	Washington	0	0
2005	Glasgow	1	1
2012	Jacksonville	1	5
2013	Glasgow	0	0

v URUGUAY

		S	U
1954	Basle (WC)	0	7
1962	Glasgow	2	3
1983	Glasgow	2	0
1986	Neza (WC)	0	0

v YUGOSLAVIA

		S	Y
1955	Belgrade	2	2
1956	Glasgow	2	0
1958	Vaasteras (WC)	1	1
1972	Belo Horizonte	2	2
1974	Frankfurt (WC)	1	1
1984	Glasgow	6	1
1988	Glasgow (WC)	1	1
1989	Zagreb (WC)	1	3

v ZAIRE

		S	Z
1974	Dortmund (WC)	2	0

WALES

v ALBANIA

		W	A
1994	Cardiff (EC)	2	0
1995	Tirana (EC)	1	1

v ANDORRA

		W	A
2014	La Vella (EC)	2	1
2015	Cardiff (EC)	2	0

v ARGENTINA

		W	A
1992	Gifu (Japan)	0	1
2002	Cardiff	1	1

v ARMENIA

		W	A
2001	Yerevan (WC)	2	2
2001	Cardiff (WC)	0	0

v AUSTRALIA

		W	A
2011	Cardiff	1	2

v AUSTRIA

		W	A
1954	Vienna	0	2
1955	Wrexham	1	2
1975	Vienna (EC)	1	2
1975	Wrexham (EC)	1	0
1992	Vienna	1	1
2005	Cardiff	0	2
2005	Vienna	0	1
2013	Swansea	2	1

v AZERBAIJAN

		W	A
2002	Baku (EC)	2	0
2003	Cardiff (EC)	4	0
2004	Baku (WC)	1	1
2005	Cardiff (WC)	2	0
2008	Cardiff (WC)	1	0
2009	Baku (WC)	1	0

v BELARUS

		W	B
1998	Cardiff (EC)	3	2
1999	Minsk (EC)	2	1
2000	Minsk (WC)	1	2
2001	Cardiff (WC)	1	0

v BELGIUM

		W	B
1949	Liege	1	3
1949	Cardiff	5	1
1990	Cardiff (EC)	3	1
1991	Brussels (EC)	1	1
1992	Brussels (WC)	0	2
1993	Cardiff (WC)	2	0
1997	Cardiff (WC)	1	2
1997	Brussels (WC)	2	3
2012	Cardiff (WC)	0	2
2013	Brussels (WC)	1	1
2014	Brussels (EC)	0	0
2015	Cardiff (EC)	1	0
2016	Lille (EC)	3	1

v BOSNIA-HERZEGOVINA

		W	B-H
2003	Cardiff	2	2
2012	Llanelli	0	2
2014	Cardiff (EC)	0	0
2015	Zenica (EC)	0	2

v BRAZIL

		W	B
1958	Gothenburg (WC)	0	1
1962	Rio de Janeiro	1	3
1962	Sao Paulo	1	3
1966	Rio de Janeiro	1	3
1966	Belo Horizonte	0	1
1983	Cardiff	1	1
1991	Cardiff	1	0
1997	Brasilia	0	3
2000	Cardiff	0	3
2006	White Hart Lane	0	2

v BULGARIA

		W	B
1983	Wrexham (EC)	1	0
1983	Sofia (EC)	0	1
1994	Cardiff (EC)	0	3
1995	Sofia (EC)	1	3
2006	Swansea	0	0
2007	Bourgas	1	0
2010	Cardiff (EC)	0	1
2011	Sofia (EC)	1	0

v CANADA

		W	C
1986	Toronto	0	2
1986	Vancouver	3	0
2004	Wrexham	1	0

v CHILE

		W	C
1966	Santiago	0	2

v COSTA RICA

		W	C
1990	Cardiff	1	0
2012	Cardiff	0	1

v CROATIA

		W	C
2002	Varazdin	1	1
2010	Osijek	0	2
2012	Osijek (WC)	0	2
2013	Swansea (WC)	1	2

v CYPRUS

		W	C
1992	Limassol (WC)	1	0
1993	Cardiff (WC)	2	0
2005	Limassol	0	1
2006	Cardiff (EC)	3	1
2007	Nicosia (EC)	1	3
2014	Cardiff (EC)	2	1
2015	Nicosia	1	0

v CZECHOSLOVAKIA (see also RCS)

		W	C
1957	Cardiff (WC)	1	0
1957	Prague (WC)	0	2
1971	Swansea (EC)	1	3
1971	Prague (EC)	0	1
1977	Wrexham (WC)	3	0
1977	Prague (WC)	0	1
1980	Cardiff (WC)	1	0
1981	Prague (WC)	0	2
1987	Wrexham (EC)	1	1
1987	Prague (EC)	0	2

v CZECH REPUBLIC

		W	CR
2002	Cardiff	0	0
2006	Teplice (EC)	1	2
2007	Cardiff (EC)	0	0

v DENMARK

		W	D
1964	Copenhagen (WC)	0	1
1965	Wrexham (WC)	4	2
1987	Cardiff (EC)	1	0
1987	Copenhagen (EC)	0	1
1990	Copenhagen	0	1
1998	Copenhagen (EC)	2	1
1999	Anfield (EC)	0	2
2008	Copenhagen	1	0

v EAST GERMANY

		W	EG
1957	Leipzig (WC)	1	2
1957	Cardiff (WC)	4	1
1969	Dresden (WC)	1	2
1969	Cardiff (WC)	1	3

v ESTONIA

		W	E
1994	Tallinn	2	1
2009	Llanelli	1	0

v FAROE ISLANDS

		W	FI
1992	Cardiff (WC)	6	0
1993	Toftir (WC)	3	0

v FINLAND

		W	F
1971	Helsinki (EC)	1	0
1971	Swansea (EC)	3	0
1986	Helsinki (EC)	1	1
1987	Wrexham (EC)	4	0
1988	Swansea (WC)	2	2
1989	Helsinki (WC)	0	1
2000	Cardiff	1	2
2002	Helsinki (EC)	2	0
2003	Cardiff (EC)	1	1
2009	Cardiff (WC)	0	2
2009	Helsinki (WC)	1	2
2013	Cardiff	1	1

v FRANCE

		W	F
1933	Paris	1	1
1939	Paris	1	2
1953	Paris	1	6
1982	Toulouse	1	0

v GEORGIA

		W	G
1994	Tbilisi (EC)	0	5
1995	Cardiff (EC)	0	1
2008	Swansea	1	2

v GERMANY/WEST GERMANY

		W	G
1968	Cardiff	1	1
1969	Frankfurt	1	1
1977	Cardiff	0	2
1977	Dortmund	1	1
1979	Wrexham (EC)	0	2
1979	Cologne (EC)	1	5
1989	Cardiff (WC)	0	0
1989	Cologne (WC)	1	2
1991	Cardiff (EC)	1	0
1991	Nuremberg (EC)	1	4
1995	Dusseldorf (EC)	1	1
1995	Cardiff (EC)	1	2
2002	Cardiff	1	0
2007	Cardiff (EC)	0	2
2007	Frankfurt (EC)	0	0
2008	Moenchengladbach (WC)	0	1
2009	Cardiff (WC)	0	2

v GREECE

		W	G
1964	Athens (WC)	0	2
1965	Cardiff (WC)	4	1

v HOLLAND

		W	H
1988	Amsterdam (WC)	0	1
1989	Wrexham (WC)	1	2
1992	Utrecht	0	4
1996	Cardiff (WC)	1	3
1996	Eindhoven (WC)	1	7
2008	Rotterdam	0	2
2014	Amsterdam	0	2
2015	Cardiff	2	3

v HUNGARY

		W	H
1958	Sanviken (WC)	1	1
1958	Stockholm (WC)	2	1
1961	Budapest	2	3
1963	Budapest (EC)	1	3
1963	Cardiff (EC)	1	1
1974	Cardiff (EC)	2	0
1975	Budapest (EC)	2	1
1986	Cardiff	0	3
2004	Budapest	2	1
2005	Cardiff	2	0

v ICELAND

		W	I
1980	Reykjavik (WC)	4	0
1981	Swansea (WC)	2	2
1984	Reykjavik (WC)	0	1
1984	Cardiff (WC)	2	1
1991	Cardiff	1	0
2008	Reykjavik	1	0
2014	Cardiff	3	1

v IRAN

		W	I
1978	Tehran	1	0

v ISRAEL

		W	I
1958	Tel Aviv (WC)	2	0
1958	Cardiff (WC)	2	0
1984	Tel Aviv	0	0
1989	Tel Aviv	3	3
2015	Haifa (EC)	3	0
2015	Cardiff (EC)	0	0

v ITALY

		W	I
1965	Florence	1	4
1968	Cardiff (WC)	0	1
1969	Rome (WC)	1	4
1988	Brescia	1	0
1996	Terni	0	3
1998	Anfield (EC)	0	2
1999	Bologna (EC)	0	4
2002	Cardiff (EC)	2	1
2003	Milan (EC)	0	4

v JAMAICA

		W	J
1998	Cardiff	0	0

v JAPAN

		W	J
1992	Matsuyama	1	0

v KUWAIT

		W	K
1977	Wrexham	0	0
1977	Kuwait City	0	0

v LATVIA

		W	L
2004	Riga	2	0

v LIECHTENSTEIN

		W	L
2006	Wrexham	4	0
2008	Cardfiff (WC)	2	0
2009	Vaduz (WC)	2	0

v LUXEMBOURG

		W	L
1974	Swansea (EC)	5	0
1975	Luxembourg (EC)	3	1
1990	Luxembourg (EC)	1	0
1991	Luxembourg (EC)	1	0
2008	Luxembourg	2	0
2010	Llanelli	5	1

v MACEDONIA

		W	M
2013	Skopje (WC)	1	2
2013	Cardiff (WC)	1	0

v MALTA

		W	M
1978	Wrexham (EC)	7	0
1979	Valletta (EC)	2	0
1988	Valletta	3	2
1998	Valletta	3	0

v MEXICO

		W	M
1958	Stockholm (WC)	1	1
1962	Mexico City	1	2
2012	New York	0	2

v MOLDOVA

		W	M
1994	Kishinev (EC)	2	3
1995	Cardiff (EC)	1	0

v MONTENEGRO

		W	M
2009	Podgorica	1	2
2010	Podgorica (EC)	0	1
2011	Cardiff (EC)	2	1

v NEW ZEALAND

		W	NZ
2007	Wrexham	2	2

v NORWAY

		W	N
1982	Swansea (EC)	1	0
1983	Oslo (EC)	0	0
1984	Trondheim	0	1
1985	Wrexham	1	1
1985	Bergen	2	4
1994	Cardiff	1	3
2000	Cardiff (WC)	1	1
2001	Oslo (WC)	2	3
2004	Oslo	0	0
2008	Wrexham	3	0
2011	Cardiff	4	1

v PARAGUAY

		W	P
2006	Cardiff	0	0

POLAND

		W	P
973	Cardiff (WC)	2	0
973	Katowice (WC)	0	3
991	Radom	0	0
000	Warsaw (WC)	0	0
001	Cardiff (WC)	1	2
004	Cardiff (WC)	2	3
005	Warsaw (WC)	0	1
009	Vila-Real (Por)	0	1

PORTUGAL

		W	P
949	Lisbon	2	3
951	Cardiff	2	1
000	Chaves	0	3
016	Lyon (EC)	0	2

QATAR

		W	Q
000	Doha	1	0

RCS (formerly Czechoslovakia)

		W	RCS
993	Ostrava (WC)	1	1
993	Cardiff (WC)	2	2

REPUBLIC OF IRELAND

		W	RI
960	Dublin	3	2
979	Swansea	2	1
981	Dublin	3	1
986	Dublin	1	0
990	Dublin	0	1
991	Wrexham	0	3
992	Dublin	1	0
993	Dublin	1	2
997	Cardiff	0	0
007	Dublin (EC)	0	1
007	Cardiff (EC)	2	2
011	Dublin (CC)	0	3
013	Cardiff	0	0

REST OF UNITED KINGDOM

		W	UK
951	Cardiff	3	2
969	Cardiff	0	1

ROMANIA

		W	R
970	Cardiff (EC)	0	0
971	Bucharest (EC)	0	2
983	Wrexham	5	0
992	Bucharest (WC)	1	5
993	Cardiff (WC)	1	2

RUSSIA (See also Soviet Union)

		W	R
003*	Moscow (EC)	0	0
003*	Cardiff (EC)	0	1
008	Moscow (WC)	1	2
009	Cardiff (WC)	1	3
016	Toulouse (EC)	3	0

*Qual Round play-offs)

SAN MARINO

		W	SM
996	Serravalle (WC)	5	0
996	Cardiff (WC)	6	0
007	Cardiff (EC)	3	0
2007	Serravalle (EC)	2	1

v SAUDI ARABIA

		W	SA
1986	Dahran	2	1

v SERBIA

		W	S
2012	Novi Sad (WC)	1	6
2013	Cardiff (WC)	0	3

v SERBIA & MONTENEGRO

		W	S
2003	Belgrade (EC)	0	1
2003	Cardiff (EC)	2	3

v SLOVAKIA

		W	S
2006	Cardiff (EC)	1	5
2007	Trnava (EC)	5	2
2016	Bordeaux (EC)	2	1

v SLOVENIA

		W	S
2005	Swansea	0	0

v SOVIET UNION (See also Russia)

		W	SU
1965	Moscow (WC)	1	2
1965	Cardiff (WC)	2	1
1981	Wrexham (WC)	0	0
1981	Tbilisi (WC)	0	3
1987	Swansea	0	0

v SPAIN

		W	S
1961	Cardiff (WC)	1	2
1961	Madrid (WC)	1	1
1982	Valencia	1	1
1984	Seville (WC)	0	3
1985	Wrexham (WC)	3	0

v SWEDEN

		W	S
1958	Stockholm (WC)	0	0
1988	Stockholm	1	4
1989	Wrexham	0	2
1990	Stockholm	2	4
1994	Wrexham	0	2
2010	Swansea	0	1
2016	Stockholm	0	3

v SWITZERLAND

		W	S
1949	Berne	0	4
1951	Wrexham	3	2
1996	Lugano	0	2
1999	Zurich (EC)	0	2
1999	Wrexham (EC)	0	2
2010	Basle (EC)	1	4
2011	Swansea (EC)	2	0

v TRINIDAD & TOBAGO

		W	T
2006	Graz	2	1

v TUNISIA

		W	T
1998	Tunis	0	4

v TURKEY

		W	T
1978	Wrexham (EC)	1	0
1979	Izmir (EC)	0	1

1980	Cardiff (WC)	4	0
1981	Ankara (WC)	1	0
1996	Cardiff (WC)	0	0
1997	Istanbul (WC)	4	6

v UKRAINE

		W	U
2001	Cardiff (WC)	1	1
2001	Kiev (WC)	1	1
2015	Kiev	0	1

v URUGUAY

		W	U
1986	Wrexham	0	0

v USA

		W	USA
2003	San Jose	0	2

v YUGOSLAVIA

		W	Y
1953	Belgrade	2	5
1954	Cardiff	1	3
1976	Zagreb (EC)	0	2
1976	Cardiff (EC)	1	1
1982	Titograd (EC)	4	4
1983	Cardiff (EC)	1	1
1988	Swansea	1	2

NORTHERN IRELAND

v ALBANIA

		NI	A
1965	Belfast (WC)	4	1
1965	Tirana (WC)	1	1
1983	Tirana (EC)	0	0
1983	Belfast (EC)	1	0
1992	Belfast (WC)	3	0
1993	Tirana (WC)	2	1
1996	Belfast (WC)	2	0
1997	Zurich (WC)	0	1
2010	Tirana	0	1

v ALGERIA

		NI	A
1986	Guadalajara (WC)	1	1

v ARGENTINA

		NI	A
1958	Halmstad (WC)	1	3

v ARMENIA

		NI	A
1996	Belfast (WC)	1	1
1997	Yerevan (WC)	0	0
2003	Yerevan (EC)	0	1
2003	Belfast (EC)	0	1

v AUSTRALIA

		NI	A
1980	Sydney	2	1
1980	Melbourne	1	1
1980	Adelaide	2	1

v AUSTRIA

		NI	A
1982	Madrid (WC)	2	2
1982	Vienna (EC)	0	2
1983	Belfast (EC)	3	1
1990	Vienna (EC)	0	0
1991	Belfast (EC)	2	1
1994	Vienna (EC)	2	1
1995	Belfast (EC)	5	3
2004	Belfast (WC)	3	3
2005	Vienna (WC)	0	2

v AZERBAIJAN

		NI	A
2004	Baku (WC)	0	0
2005	Belfast (WC)	2	0
2012	Belfast (WC)	1	1
2013	Baku (WC)	0	2

v BARBADOS

		NI	B
2004	Bridgetown	1	1

v BELARUS

		NI	B
2016	Belfast	3	0

v BELGIUM

		NI	B
1976	Liege (WC)	0	2
1977	Belfast (WC)	3	0
1997	Belfast	3	0

v BRAZIL

		NI	B
1986	Guadalajara (WC)	0	3

v BULGARIA

		NI	B
1972	Sofia (WC)	0	3
1973	Sheffield (WC)	0	0
1978	Sofia (EC)	2	0
1979	Belfast (EC)	2	0
2001	Sofia (WC)	3	4
2001	Belfast (WC)	0	1
2008	Belfast	0	1

v CANADA

		NI	C
1995	Edmonton	0	2
1999	Belfast	1	1
2005	Belfast	0	1

v CHILE

		NI	C
1989	Belfast	0	1
1995	Edmonton, Canada	0	2
2010	Chillan	0	1
2014	Valparaiso	0	2

v COLOMBIA

		NI	C
1994	Boston, USA	0	2

v CYPRUS

		NI	C
1971	Nicosia (EC)	3	0
1971	Belfast (EC)	5	0
1973	Nicosia (WC)	0	1
1973	Fulham (WC)	3	0
2002	Belfast	0	0

2014	Nicosia	0	0

v CZECHOSLOVAKIA/CZECH REP

		NI	*C*
1958	Halmstad (WC)	1	0
1958	Malmo (WC)	2	1
2001	Belfast (WC)	0	1
2001	Teplice (WC)	1	3
2008	Belfast (WC)	0	0
2009	Prague (WC)	0	0

v DENMARK

		NI	*D*
1978	Belfast (EC)	2	1
1979	Copenhagen (EC)	0	4
1986	Belfast	1	1
1990	Belfast (EC)	1	1
1991	Odense (EC)	1	2
1992	Belfast (WC)	0	1
1993	Copenhagen (WC)	0	1
2000	Belfast (WC)	1	1
2001	Copenhagen (WC)	1	1
2006	Copenhagen (EC)	0	0
2007	Belfast (EC)	2	1

v ESTONIA

		NI	*E*
2004	Tallinn	1	0
2006	Belfast	1	0
2011	Tallinn (EC)	1	4
2011	Belfast (EC)	1	2

v FAROE ISLANDS

		NI	*FI*
1991	Belfast (EC)	1	1
1991	Landskrona, Sw (EC)	5	0
2010	Toftir (EC)	1	1
2011	Belfast (EC)	4	0
2014	Belfast (EC)	2	0
2015	Torshavn (EC)	3	1

v FINLAND

		NI	*F*
1984	Pori (WC)	0	1
1984	Belfast (WC)	2	1
1998	Belfast (EC)	1	0
1999	Helsinki (EC)	1	4
2003	Belfast	0	1
2006	Helsinki	2	1
2012	Belfast	3	3
2015	Belfast (EC)	2	1
2015	Helsinki (EC)	1	1

v FRANCE

		NI	*F*
1951	Belfast	2	2
1952	Paris	1	3
1958	Norrkoping (WC)	0	4
1982	Paris	0	4
1982	Madrid (WC)	1	4
1986	Paris	0	0
1988	Belfast	0	0
1999	Belfast	0	1

v GEORGIA

		NI	*G*
2008	Belfast	4	1

v GERMANY/WEST GERMANY

		NI	*G*
1958	Malmo (WC)	2	2
1960	Belfast (WC)	3	4
1961	Berlin (WC)	1	2
1966	Belfast	0	2
1977	Cologne	0	5
1982	Belfast (EC)	1	0
1983	Hamburg (EC)	1	0
1992	Bremen	1	1
1996	Belfast	1	1
1997	Nuremberg (WC)	1	1
1997	Belfast (WC)	1	3
1999	Belfast (EC)	0	3
1999	Dortmund (EC)	0	4
2005	Belfast	1	4
2016	Paris (EC)	0	1

v GREECE

		NI	*G*
1961	Athens (WC)	1	2
1961	Belfast (WC)	2	0
1988	Athens	2	3
2003	Belfast (EC)	0	2
2003	Athens (EC)	0	1
2014	Piraeus (EC)	2	0
2015	Belfast (EC)	3	1

v HOLLAND

		NI	*H*
1962	Rotterdam	0	4
1965	Belfast (WC)	2	1
1965	Rotterdam (WC)	0	0
1976	Rotterdam (WC)	2	2
1977	Belfast (WC)	0	1
2012	Amsterdam	0	6

v HONDURAS

		NI	*H*
1982	Zaragoza (WC)	1	1

v HUNGARY

		NI	*H*
1988	Budapest (WC)	0	1
1989	Belfast (WC)	1	2
2000	Belfast	0	1
2008	Belfast	0	2
2014	Budapest (EC)	2	1
2015	Belfast (EC)	1	1

v ICELAND

		NI	*I*
1977	Reykjavik (WC)	0	1
1977	Belfast (WC)	2	0
2000	Reykjavik (WC)	0	1
2001	Belfast (WC)	3	0
2006	Belfast (EC)	0	3
2007	Reykjavik (EC)	1	2

v ISRAEL

		NI	*I*
1968	Jaffa	3	2
1976	Tel Aviv	1	1
1980	Tel Aviv (WC)	0	0
1981	Belfast (WC)	1	0
1984	Belfast	3	0
1987	Tel Aviv	1	1
2009	Belfast	1	1

2013	Belfast (WC)	0	2
2013	Ramat Gan (WC)	1	1

v ITALY

		NI	I
1957	Rome (WC)	0	1
1957	Belfast	2	2
1958	Belfast (WC)	2	1
1961	Bologna	2	3
1997	Palermo	0	2
2003	Campobasso	0	2
2009	Pisa	0	3
2010	Belfast (EC)	0	0
2011	Pescara (EC)	0	3

v LATVIA

		NI	L
1993	Riga (WC)	2	1
1993	Belfast (WC)	2	0
1995	Riga (EC)	1	0
1995	Belfast (EC)	1	2
2006	Belfast (EC)	1	0
2007	Riga (EC)	0	1
2015	Belfast	1	0

v LIECHTENSTEIN

		NI	L
1994	Belfast (EC)	4	1
1995	Eschen (EC)	4	0
2002	Vaduz	0	0
2007	Vaduz (EC)	4	1
2007	Belfast (EC)	3	1

v LITHUANIA

		NI	L
1992	Belfast (WC)	2	2

v LUXEMBOURG

		NI	L
2000	Luxembourg	3	1
2012	Belfast (WC)	1	1
2013	Luxembourg (WC)	2	3

v MALTA

		NI	M
1988	Belfast (WC)	3	0
1989	Valletta (WC)	2	0
2000	Ta'Qali	3	0
2000	Belfast (WC)	1	0
2001	Valletta (WC)	1	0
2005	Valletta	1	1
2013	Ta'Qali	0	0

v MEXICO

		NI	M
1966	Belfast	4	1
1994	Miami	0	3

v MOLDOVA

		NI	M
1998	Belfast (EC)	2	2
1999	Kishinev (EC)	0	0

v MONTENEGRO

		W	M
2010	Podgorica	0	2

v MOROCCO

		NI	M
1986	Belfast	2	1
2010	Belfast	1	1

v NORWAY

		NI	N
1974	Oslo (EC)	1	2
1975	Belfast (EC)	3	0
1990	Belfast	2	3
1996	Belfast	0	2
2001	Belfast	0	4
2004	Belfast	1	4
2012	Belfast	0	3

v POLAND

		NI	P
1962	Katowice (EC)	2	0
1962	Belfast (EC)	2	0
1988	Belfast	1	1
1991	Belfast	3	1
2002	Limassol (Cyprus)	1	4
2004	Belfast (WC)	0	3
2005	Warsaw (WC)	0	1
2009	Belfast (WC)	3	2
2009	Chorzow (WC)	1	1
2016	Nice (EC)	0	1

v PORTUGAL

		NI	P
1957	Lisbon (WC)	1	1
1957	Belfast (WC)	3	0
1973	Coventry (WC)	1	1
1973	Lisbon (WC)	1	1
1980	Lisbon (WC)	0	1
1981	Belfast (WC)	1	0
1994	Belfast (EC)	1	2
1995	Oporto (EC)	1	1
1997	Belfast (WC)	0	0
1997	Lisbon (WC)	0	1
2005	Belfast	1	1
2012	Porto (WC)	1	1
2013	Belfast (WC)	2	4

v QATAR

		NI	Q
2015	Crewe	1	1

v REPUBLIC OF IRELAND

		NI	RI
1978	Dublin (EC)	0	0
1979	Belfast (EC)	1	0
1988	Belfast (WC)	0	0
1989	Dublin (WC)	0	3
1993	Dublin (WC)	0	3
1993	Belfast (WC)	1	1
1994	Belfast (EC)	0	4
1995	Dublin (EC)	1	1
1999	Dublin	1	0
2011	Dublin (CC)	0	5

v ROMANIA

		NI	R
1984	Belfast (WC)	3	2
1985	Bucharest (WC)	1	0
1994	Belfast	2	0
2006	Chicago	0	2
2014	Bucharest (EC)	0	2
2015	Belfast (EC)	0	0

v RUSSIA

		NI	R

2012	Moscow (WC)	0	2
2013	Belfast (WC)	1	0

v SAN MARINO

		NI	SM
2008	Belfast (WC)	4	0
2009	Serravalle (WC)	3	0

v SERBIA & MONTENEGRO

		NI	S
2004	Belfast	1	1

v SERBIA

		NI	S
2009	Belfast	0	1
2011	Belgrade (EC)	1	2
2011	Belfast (EC)	0	1

v SLOVAKIA

		NI	S
1998	Belfast	1	0
2008	Bratislava (WC)	1	2
2009	Belfast (WC)	0	2
2016	Trnava	0	0

v SLOVENIA

		NI	S
2008	Maribor (WC)	0	2
2009	Belfast (WC)	1	0
2010	Maribor (EC)	1	0
2011	Belfast (EC)	0	0
2016	Belfast	1	0

v SOVIET UNION

		NI	SU
1969	Belfast (WC)	0	0
1969	Moscow (WC)	0	2
1971	Moscow (EC)	0	1
1971	Belfast (EC)	1	1

v SPAIN

		NI	S
1958	Madrid	2	6
1963	Bilbao	1	1
1963	Belfast	0	1
1970	Seville (EC)	0	3
1972	Hull (EC)	1	1
1982	Valencia (WC)	1	0
1985	Palma, Majorca	0	0
1986	Guadalajara (WC)	1	2
1988	Seville (WC)	0	4
1989	Belfast (WC)	0	2
1992	Belfast (WC)	0	0
1993	Seville (WC)	1	3
1998	Santander	1	4
2002	Belfast	0	5
2002	Albacete (EC)	0	3
2003	Belfast (EC)	0	0
2006	Belfast (EC)	3	2
2007	Las Palmas (EC)	0	1

v ST KITTS & NEVIS

		NI	SK
2004	Basseterre	2	0

v SWEDEN

		NI	S
1974	Solna (EC)	2	0
1975	Belfast (EC)	1	2
1980	Belfast (WC)	3	0
1981	Stockholm (WC)	0	1
1996	Belfast	1	2
2007	Belfast (EC)	2	1
2007	Stockholm (EC)	1	1

v SWITZERLAND

		NI	S
1964	Belfast (WC)	1	0
1964	Lausanne (WC)	1	2
1998	Belfast	1	0
2004	Zurich	0	0
2010	Basle (EC)	1	4

v THAILAND

		NI	T
1997	Bangkok	0	0

v TRINIDAD & TOBAGO

		NI	T
2004	Port of Spain	3	0

v TURKEY

		NI	T
1968	Belfast (WC)	4	1
1968	Istanbul (WC)	3	0
1983	Belfast (EC)	2	1
1983	Ankara (EC)	0	1
1985	Belfast (WC)	2	0
1985	Izmir (WC)	0	0
1986	Izmir (EC)	0	0
1987	Belfast (EC)	1	0
1998	Istanbul (EC)	0	3
1999	Belfast (EC)	0	3
2010	Connecticut	0	2
2013	Adana	0	1

v UKRAINE

		NI	U
1996	Belfast (WC)	0	1
1997	Kiev (WC)	1	2
2002	Belfast (EC)	0	0
2003	Donetsk (EC)	0	0
2016	Lyon (EC)	2	0

v URUGUAY

		NI	U
1964	Belfast	3	0
1990	Belfast	1	0
2006	New Jersey	0	1
2014	Montevideo	0	1

v YUGOSLAVIA

		NI	Y
1975	Belfast (EC)	1	0
1975	Belgrade (EC)	0	1
1982	Zaragoza (WC)	0	0
1987	Belfast (EC)	1	2
1987	Sarajevo (EC)	0	3
1990	Belfast (EC)	0	2
1991	Belgrade (EC)	1	4
2000	Belfast	1	2

v ALBANIA

		RI	A
1992	Dublin (WC)	2	0
1993	Tirana (WC)	2	1
2003	Tirana (EC)	0	0
2003	Dublin (EC)	2	1

REPUBLIC OF IRELAND

v ALGERIA

		RI	A
1982	Algiers	0	2
2010	Dublin	3	0

v ANDORRA

		RI	A
2001	Barcelona (WC)	3	0
2001	Dublin (WC)	3	1
2010	Dublin (EC)	3	1
2011	La Vella (EC)	2	0

v ARGENTINA

		RI	A
1951	Dublin	0	1
1979*	Dublin	0	0
1980	Dublin	0	1
1998	Dublin	0	2
2010	Dublin	0	1

(*Not regarded as full Int)

v ARMENIA

		RI	A
2010	Yerevan (EC)	1	0
2011	Dublin (EC)	2	1

v AUSTRALIA

		RI	A
2003	Dublin	2	1
2009	Limerick	0	3

v AUSTRIA

		RI	A
1952	Vienna	0	6
1953	Dublin	4	0
1958	Vienna	1	3
1962	Dublin	2	3
1963	Vienna (EC)	0	0
1963	Dublin (EC)	3	2
1966	Vienna	0	1
1968	Dublin	2	2
1971	Dublin (EC)	1	4
1971	Linz (EC)	0	6
1995	Dublin (EC)	1	3
1995	Vienna (EC)	1	3
2013	Dublin (WC)	2	2
2013	Vienna (WC)	0	1

v BELARUS

		RI	B
2016	Cork	1	2

v BELGIUM

		RI	B
1928	Liege	4	2
1929	Dublin	4	0
1930	Brussels	3	1
1934	Dublin (WC)	4	4
1949	Dublin	0	2
1950	Brussels	1	5
1965	Dublin	0	2
1966	Liege	3	2
1980	Dublin (WC)	1	1
1981	Brussels (WC)	0	1
1986	Brussels (EC)	2	2
1987	Dublin (EC)	0	0
1997*	Dublin (WC)	1	1
1997*	Brussels (WC)	1	2
2016	Bordeaux (EC)	0	3

(*World Cup play-off)

v BOLIVIA

		RI	B
1994	Dublin	1	0
1996	East Rutherford, NJ	3	0
2007	Boston	1	1

v BOSNIA HERZEGOVINA

		RI	B-H
2012	Dublin	1	0
2015	Zenica (EC)	1	1
2015	Dublin (EC)	2	0

v BRAZIL

		RI	B
1974	Rio de Janeiro	1	2
1982	Uberlandia	0	7
1987	Dublin	1	0
2004	Dublin	0	0
2008	Dublin	0	1
2010	Arsenal	0	2

v BULGARIA

		RI	B
1977	Sofia (WC)	1	2
1977	Dublin (WC)	0	0
1979	Sofia (EC)	0	1
1979	Dublin (EC)	3	0
1987	Sofia (EC)	1	2
1987	Dublin (EC)	2	0
2004	Dublin	1	1
2009	Dublin (WC)	1	1
2009	Sofia (WC)	1	1

v CAMEROON

		RI	C
2002	Niigata (WC)	1	1

v CANADA

		RI	C
2003	Dublin	3	0

v CHILE

		RI	C
1960	Dublin	2	0
1972	Recife	1	2
1974	Santiago	2	1
1982	Santiago	0	1
1991	Dublin	1	1
2006	Dublin	0	1

v CHINA

		RI	C
1984	Sapporo	1	0
2005	Dublin	1	0

v COLOMBIA

		RI	C
2008	Fulham	1	0

v COSTA RICA

		RI	CR
2014	Chester, USA	1	1

v CROATIA

		RI	C
1996	Dublin	2	2
1998	Dublin (EC)	2	0
1999	Zagreb (EC)	0	1
2001	Dublin	2	2
2004	Dublin	1	0
2011	Dublin	0	0
2012	Poznan (EC)	1	3

v CYPRUS

		RI	C
1980	Nicosia (WC)	3	2
1980	Dublin (WC)	6	0
2001	Nicosia (WC)	4	0
2001	Dublin (WC)	4	0
2004	Dublin (WC)	3	0
2005	Nicosia (WC)	1	0
2006	Nicosia (EC)	2	5
2007	Dublin (EC)	1	1
2008	Dublin (WC)	1	0
2009	Nicosia (WC)	2	1

v CZECHOSLOVAKIA/CZECH REP

		RI	C
1938	Prague	2	2
1959	Dublin (EC)	2	0
1959	Bratislava (EC)	0	4
1961	Dublin (WC)	1	3
1961	Prague (WC)	1	7
1967	Dublin (EC)	0	2
1967	Prague (EC)	2	1
1969	Dublin (WC)	1	2
1969	Prague (WC)	0	3
1979	Prague	1	4
1981	Dublin	3	1
1986	Reykjavik	1	0
1994	Dublin	1	3
1996	Prague	0	2
1998	Olomouc	1	2
2000	Dublin	3	2
2004	Dublin	2	1
2006	Dublin (EC)	1	1
2007	Prague (EC)	0	1
2012	Dublin	1	1

v DENMARK

		RI	D
1956	Dublin (WC)	2	1
1957	Copenhagen (WC)	2	0
1968*	Dublin (WC)	1	1
1969	Copenhagen (WC)	0	2
1969	Dublin (WC)	1	1
1978	Copenhagen (EC)	3	3
1979	Dublin (EC)	2	0
1984	Copenhagen (WC)	0	3
1985	Dublin (WC)	1	4
1992	Copenhagen (WC)	0	0
1993	Dublin (WC)	1	1
2002	Dublin	3	0
(*Abandoned after 51 mins – fog)			
2007	Aarhus	4	0

v ECUADOR

		RI	E
1972	Natal	3	2
2007	New York	1	1

v EGYPT

		RI	E
1990	Palermo (WC)	0	0

v ESTONIA

		RI	E
2000	Dublin (WC)	2	0
2001	Tallinn (WC)	2	0
2011	Tallinn (EC)	4	0
2011	Dublin (EC)	1	1

v FAROE ISLANDS

		RI	F
2004	Dublin (WC)	2	0
2005	Torshavn (WC)	2	0
2012	Torshavn (WC)	4	1
2013	Dublin (WC)	3	0

v FINLAND

		RI	F
1949	Dublin (WC)	3	0
1949	Helsinki (WC)	1	1
1990	Dublin	1	1
2000	Dublin	3	0
2002	Helsinki	3	0

v FRANCE

		RI	F
1937	Paris	2	0
1952	Dublin	1	1
1953	Dublin (WC)	3	5
1953	Paris (WC)	0	1
1972	Dublin (WC)	2	1
1973	Paris (WC)	1	1
1976	Paris (WC)	0	2
1977	Dublin (WC)	1	0
1980	Paris (WC)	0	2
1981	Dublin (WC)	3	2
1989	Dublin	0	0
2004	Paris (WC)	0	0
2005	Dublin (WC)	0	1
2009	Dublin (WC)	0	1
2009	Paris (WC)	1	1
2016	Lyon (EC)	1	2

v GEORGIA

		RI	G
2002	Tbilisi (EC)	2	1
2003	Dublin (EC)	2	0
2008	Mainz (WC)	2	1
2009	Dublin (WC)	2	1
2013	Dublin	4	0
2014	Tbilisi (EC)	2	1
2015	Dublin (EC)	1	0

v GERMANY/WEST GERMANY

		RI	G
1935	Dortmund	1	3
1936	Dublin	5	2
1939	Bremen	1	1
1951	Dublin	3	2
1952	Cologne	0	3
1955	Hamburg	1	2
1956	Dublin	3	0
1960	Dusseldorf	1	0
1966	Dublin	0	4
1970	Berlin	1	2

1975*	Dublin	1	0
1979	Dublin	1	3
1981	Bremen	0	3
1989	Dublin	1	1
1994	Hanover	2	0
2002	Ibaraki (WC)	1	1
2006	Stuttgart (EC)	0	1
2007	Dublin (EC)	0	0
2012	Dublin (WC)	1	6
2013	Cologne (WC)	0	3
2014	Gelsenkirchen (EC)	1	1
2015	Dublin (EC)	1	0

(*v W Germany 'B')

v GIBRALTAR

		RI	*G*
2014	Dublin (EC)	7	0
2015	Faro (EC)	4	0

v GREECE

		RI	*G*
2000	Dublin	0	1
2002	Athens	0	0
2012	Dublin	0	1

v HOLLAND

		RI	*H.*
1932	Amsterdam	2	0
1934	Amsterdam	2	5
1935	Dublin	3	5
1955	Dublin	1	0
1956	Rotterdam	4	1
1980	Dublin (WC)	2	1
1981	Rotterdam (WC)	2	2
1982	Rotterdam (EC)	1	2
1983	Dublin (EC)	2	3
1988	Gelsenkirchen (EC)	0	1
1990	Palermo (WC)	1	1
1994	Tilburg	1	0
1994	Orlando (WC)	0	2
1995*	Liverpool (EC)	0	2
1996	Rotterdam	1	3
(*Qual Round play-off)			
2000	Amsterdam (WC)	2	2
2001	Dublin (WC)	1	0
2004	Amsterdam	1	0
2006	Dublin	0	4
2016	Dublin	1	1

v HUNGARY

		RI	*H*
1934	Dublin	2	4
1936	Budapest	3	3
1936	Dublin	2	3
1939	Cork	2	2
1939	Budapest	2	2
1969	Dublin (WC)	1	2
1969	Budapest (WC)	0	4
1989	Budapest (WC)	0	0
1989	Dublin (WC)	2	0
1992	Gyor	2	1
2012	Budapest	0	0

v ICELAND

		RI	*I*
1962	Dublin (EC)	4	2
1962	Reykjavik (EC)	1	1
1982	Dublin (EC)	2	0
1983	Reykjavik (EC)	3	0
1986	Reykjavik	2	1
1996	Dublin (WC)	0	0
1997	Reykjavik (WC)	4	2

v IRAN

		RI	*I*
1972	Recife	2	1
2001*	Dublin (WC)	2	0
2001*	Tehran (WC)	0	1

(*Qual Round play-off)

v ISRAEL

		RI	*I*
1984	Tel Aviv	0	3
1985	Tel Aviv	0	0
1987	Dublin	5	0
2005	Tel Aviv (WC)	1	1
2005	Dublin (WC)	2	2

v ITALY

		RI	*I*
1926	Turin	0	3
1927	Dublin	1	2
1970	Florence (EC)	0	3
1971	Dublin (EC)	1	2
1985	Dublin	1	2
1990	Rome (WC)	0	1
1992	Boston, USA	0	2
1994	New York (WC)	1	0
2005	Dublin	1	2
2009	Bari (WC)	1	1
2009	Dublin (WC)	2	2
2011	Liege	2	0
2012	Poznan (EC)	0	2
2014	Fulham	0	0
2016	Lille (EC)	1	0

v JAMAICA

		RI	*J*
2004	Charlton	1	0

v KAZAKHSTAN

		RI	*K*
2012	Astana (WC)	2	1
2013	Dublin (WC)	3	1

v LATVIA

		RI	*L*
1992	Dublin (WC)	4	0
1993	Riga (WC)	2	0
1994	Riga (EC)	3	0
1995	Dublin (EC)	2	1
2013	Dublin	3	0

v LIECHTENSTEIN

		RI	*L*
1994	Dublin (EC)	4	0
1995	Eschen (EC)	0	0
1996	Eschen (WC)	5	0
1997	Dublin (WC)	5	0

v LITHUANIA

		RI	*L*
1993	Vilnius (WC)	1	0
1993	Dublin (WC)	2	0
1997	Dublin (WC)	0	0
1997	Zalgiris (WC)	2	1

		RI	L
[illegible]	[illegible]	5	1
[illegible]	[illegible]	4	0
[illegible]	[illegible]	1	0
[illegible]	[illegible]	2	0
[illegible]	[illegible]	2	1

		RI	M
[illegible]	[illegible]	3	0
[illegible]	[illegible]	2	3
[illegible]	[illegible]	1	0
[illegible]	[illegible] (EC)	1	1
[illegible]	Dublin (EC)	2	1
[illegible]	Skopje (EC)	2	0

v MALTA

		RI	M
1983	Valletta (EC)	1	0
1983	Dublin (EC)	8	0
1989	Dublin (WC)	2	0
1989	Valletta (WC)	2	0
1990	Valletta	3	0
1998	Dublin (EC)	1	0
1999	Valletta (EC)	3	2

v MEXICO

		RI	M
1984	Dublin	0	0
1994	Orlando (WC)	1	2
1996	New Jersey	2	2
1998	Dublin	0	0
2000	Chicago	2	2

v MONTENEGRO

		RI	M
2008	Podgorica (WC)	0	0
2009	Dublin (WC)	0	0

v MOROCCO

		RI	M
1990	Dublin	1	0

v NIGERIA

		RI	N
2002	Dublin	1	2
2004	Charlton	0	3
2009	Fulham	1	1

v NORWAY

		RI	N
1937	Oslo (WC)	2	3
1937	Dublin (WC)	3	3
1950	Dublin	2	2
1951	Oslo	3	2
1954	Dublin	2	1
1955	Oslo	3	1
1960	Dublin	3	1
1964	Oslo	4	1
1973	Oslo	1	1
1976	Dublin	3	0
1978	Oslo	0	0
1984	Oslo (WC)	0	1
1985	Dublin (WC)	0	0
1988	Oslo	0	0
1994	New York (WC)	0	0
2003	Dublin	1	0
2008	Oslo	1	1
2010	Dublin	1	2

v OMAN

		RI	O
2012	Fulham	4	1
2014	Dublin	2	0

v PARAGUAY

		RI	P
1999	Dublin	2	0
2010	Dublin	2	1

v POLAND

		RI	P
1938	Warsaw	0	6
1938	Dublin	3	2
1958	Katowice	2	2
1958	Dublin	2	2
1964	Cracow	1	3
1964	Dublin	3	2
1968	Dublin	2	2
1968	Katowice	0	1
1970	Dublin	1	2
1970	Poznan	0	2
1973	Wroclaw	0	2
1973	Dublin	1	0
1976	Poznan	2	0
1977	Dublin	0	0
1978	Lodz	0	3
1981	Bydgoszcz	0	3
1984	Dublin	0	0
1986	Warsaw	0	1
1988	Dublin	3	1
1991	Dublin (EC)	0	0
1991	Poznan (EC)	3	3
2004	Bydgoszcz	0	0
2008	Dublin	2	3
2013	Dublin	2	0
2013	Poznan	0	0
2015	Dublin (EC)	1	1
2015	Warsaw (EC)	1	2

v PORTUGAL

		RI	P
1946	Lisbon	1	3
1947	Dublin	0	2
1948	Lisbon	0	2
1949	Dublin	1	0
1972	Recife	1	2
1992	Boston, USA	2	0
1995	Dublin (EC)	1	0
1995	Lisbon (EC)	0	3
1996	Dublin	0	1
2000	Lisbon (WC)	1	1
2001	Dublin (WC)	1	1
2005	Dublin	1	0
2014	East Rutherford, USA	1	5

v ROMANIA

		RI	R
1988	Dublin	2	0
1990*	Genoa	0	0
1997	Bucharest (WC)	0	1
1997	Dublin (WC)	1	1
2004	Dublin	1	0

(*Rep won 5-4 on pens)

v RUSSIA (See also Soviet Union)

		RI	R
1994	Dublin	0	0
1996	Dublin	0	2
2002	Dublin	2	0
2002	Moscow (EC)	2	4
2003	Dublin (EC)	1	1
2010	Dublin (EC)	2	3
2011	Moscow (EC)	0	0

v SAN MARINO

		RI	SM
2006	Dublin (EC)	5	0
2007	Rimini (EC)	2	1

v SAUDI ARABIA

		RI	SA
2002	Yokohama (WC)	3	0

v SERBIA

		RI	S
2008	Dublin	1	1
2012	Belgrade	0	0
2014	Dublin	1	2

v SLOVAKIA

		RI	S
2007	Dublin (EC)	1	0
2007	Bratislava (EC)	2	2
2010	Zilina (EC)	1	1
2011	Dublin (EC)	0	0
2016	Dublin	2	2

v SOUTH AFRICA

		RI	SA
2000	New Jersey	2	1
2009	Limerick	1	0

v SOVIET UNION (See also Russia)

		RI	SU
1972	Dublin (WC)	1	2
1973	Moscow (WC)	0	1
1974	Dublin (EC)	3	0
1975	Kiev (EC)	1	2
1984	Dublin (WC)	1	0
1985	Moscow (WC)	0	2
1988	Hanover (EC)	1	1
1990	Dublin	1	0

v SPAIN

		RI	S
1931	Barcelona	1	1
1931	Dublin	0	5
1946	Madrid	1	0
1947	Dublin	3	2
1948	Barcelona	1	2
1949	Dublin	1	4
1952	Madrid	0	6
1955	Dublin	2	2
1964	Seville (EC)	1	5
1964	Dublin (EC)	0	2
1965	Dublin (WC)	1	0
1965	Seville (WC)	1	4
1965	Paris (WC)	0	1
1966	Dublin (EC)	0	0
1966	Valencia (EC)	0	2
1977	Dublin	0	1
1982	Dublin (EC)	3	3
1983	Zaragoza (EC)	0	2
1985	Cork	[illegible]	[illegible]
1988	Seville (WC)	[illegible]	[illegible]
1989	Dublin (WC)	[illegible]	[illegible]
1992	Seville (WC)	[illegible]	[illegible]
1993	Dublin (WC)	[illegible]	[illegible]
2002*	Suwon (WC)	[illegible]	[illegible]
(*Rep lost 3-2 on pens)			
2012	Gdansk (EC)	[illegible]	[illegible]
2013	New York	[illegible]	[illegible]

v SWEDEN

		RI	S
1949	Stockholm (WC)	[illegible]	[illegible]
1949	Dublin (WC)	[illegible]	[illegible]
1959	Dublin	[illegible]	[illegible]
1960	Malmo	1	[illegible]
1970	Dublin (EC)	1	1
1970	Malmo (EC)	0	1
1999	Dublin	2	0
2006	Dublin	3	0
2013	Stockholm (WC)	0	0
2013	Dublin (WC)	1	2
2016	Paris (EC)	1	1

v SWITZERLAND

		RI	S
1935	Basle	0	1
1936	Dublin	1	0
1937	Berne	1	0
1938	Dublin	4	0
1948	Dublin	0	1
1975	Dublin (EC)	2	1
1975	Berne (EC)	0	1
1980	Dublin	2	0
1985	Dublin (WC)	3	0
1985	Berne (WC)	0	0
1992	Dublin	2	1
2002	Dublin (EC)	1	2
2003	Basle (EC)	0	2
2004	Basle (WC)	1	1
2005	Dublin (WC)	0	0
2016	Dublin	1	0

v TRINIDAD & TOBAGO

		RI	T&T
1982	Port of Spain	1	2

v TUNISIA

		RI	T
1988	Dublin	4	0

v TURKEY

		RI	T
1966	Dublin (EC)	2	1
1967	Ankara (EC)	1	2
1974	Izmir (EC)	1	1
1975	Dublin (EC)	4	0
1976	Ankara	3	3
1978	Dublin	4	2
1990	Izmir	0	0
1990	Dublin (EC)	5	0
1991	Istanbul (EC)	3	1
1999	Dublin (EC)	1	1
1999	Bursa (EC)	0	0
2003	Dublin	2	2
2014	Dublin	1	2

v URUGUAY

		RI	U
1974	Montevideo	0	2
1986	Dublin	1	1
2011	Dublin	2	3

v USA

		RI	USA
1979	Dublin	3	2
1991	Boston	1	1
1992	Dublin	4	1
1992	Washington	1	3
1996	Boston	1	2
2000	Foxboro	1	1
2002	Dublin	2	1
2014	Dublin	4	1

v YUGOSLAVIA

		RI	Y
1955	Dublin	1	4
1988	Dublin	2	0
1998	Belgrade (EC)	0	1
1999	Dublin (EC)	2	1

THE THINGS THEY SAY ...

'We're normally the warm-up act for countries going to the finals' – **Martin O'Neill** as his team prepared with a friendly against Holland.

'We'll all shoot ourselves if we don't get out of the group' – **Greg Dyke**, outgoing FA chairman, refusing to contemplate England failing at the tournament.

'He is just like the Roadrunner .... beep, beep and then whoosh, he's gone' – **Claudio Ranieri**, Leicester manager, on his Algerian midfielder Riyad Mahrez.

'When you have a competition it has to be between the champions. I said it 20 years ago and I say it now. Sport is to win, not to be second or third' – **Louis van Gaal**, former Manchester United manager, insisting the Champions League should be for champions only.

'He's been one of the greatest managers this country has seen. I find it appalling people can criticise someone who has helped build a fantastic club and kept them in the top four for many years' – **Steve Bruce**, Hull manager, defends Arsenal's Arsene Wenger'

'The decision to stay initially was based purely on the emotion and feelings I hold for the club, rather than looking at the football opportunity that had been placed before me' – **Fabian Delph** on why he left Aston Villa for Manchester City after first turning down the move.

BRITISH AND IRISH INTERNATIONAL APPEARANCES SINCE THE WAR (1946–2016)

(As at start of season 2016–17; in year shown 2016 = season 2015–16
*Also a pre-war International player. Totals include appearances as substitute)

ENGLAND

Agbonlahor G (Aston Villa, 2009–10) 3
A'Court A (Liverpool, 1958–59) 5
Adams T (Arsenal, 1987–2001) 66
Alli D (Tottenham, 2016) 12
Allen A (Stoke, 1960) 3
Allen C (QPR, Tottenham, 1984–88) 5
Allen R (WBA, 1952–55) 5
Anderson S (Sunderland, 1962) 2
Anderson V (Nottm Forest, Arsenal, Manchester Utd, 1979–88) 30
Anderton D (Tottenham, 1994–2002) 30
Angus J (Burnley, 1961) 1
Armfield J (Blackpool, 1959–66) 43
Armstrong D (Middlesbrough, Southampton, 1980–4) 3
Armstrong K (Chelsea, 1955) 1
Ashton D (West Ham, 2008) 1
Astall G (Birmingham, 1956) 2
Astle J (WBA, 1969–70) 5
Aston J (Manchester Utd, 1949–51) 17
Atyeo J (Bristol City, 1956–57) 6

Bailey G (Manchester Utd, 1985) 2
Bailey M (Charlton, 1964–5) 2
Baily E (Tottenham, 1950–3) 9
Baines L (Everton, 2010–15) 30
Baker J (Hibernian, Arsenal, 1960–6) 8
Ball A (Blackpool, Everton, Arsenal, 1965–75) 72
Ball M (Everton, 2001) 1
Banks G (Leicester, Stoke, 1963–72) 73
Banks T (Bolton, 1958–59) 6
Bardsley D (QPR, 1993) 2
Barham M (Norwich, 1983) 2
Barkley R (Everton, 2014–16) 22
Barlow R (WBA, 1955) 1
Barmby N (Tottenham, Middlesbrough, Everton, Liverpool, 1995–2002) 23
Barnes J (Watford, Liverpool, 1983–96) 79
Barnes P (Manchester City, WBA, Leeds, 1978–82) 22
Barrass M (Bolton, 1952–53) 3
Barrett E (Oldham, Aston Villa, 1991–93) 3
Barry G (Aston Villa, Manchester City, 2000–12) 53
Barton J (Manchester City, 2007) 1
Barton W (Wimbledon, Newcastle, 1995) 3
Batty D (Leeds, Blackburn, Newcastle, Leeds, 1991–2000) 42
Baynham R (Luton, 1956) 3
Beardsley P (Newcastle, Liverpool, Newcastle, 1986–96) 59
Beasant D (Chelsea, 1990) 2
Beattie J (Southampton, 2003–04) 5
Beattie K (Ipswich, 1975–58) 9
Beckham D (Manchester Utd, Real Madrid, LA Galaxy, AC Milan 1997–2010) 115
Bell C (Manchester City, 1968–76) 48
Bent D (Charlton, Tottenham Sunderland, Aston Villa, 2006–12) 13
Bentley D (Blackburn, 2008–09) 7
Bentley R (Chelsea, 1949–55) 12
Berry J (Manchester Utd, 1953–56) 4
Bertrand R (Chelsea, Southampton, 2013–16) 9
Birtles G (Nottm Forest, 1980–81) 3
Blissett L (Watford, AC Milan, 1983–84) 14
Blockley J (Arsenal, 1973) 1
Blunstone F (Chelsea, 1955–57) 5
Bonetti P (Chelsea, 1966–70) 7
Bothroyd J (Cardiff, 2011) 1
Bould S (Arsenal, 1994) 2
Bowles S (QPR, 1974–77) 5
Bowyer L (Leeds, 2003) 1
Boyer P (Norwich, 1976) 1
Brabrook P (Chelsea, 1958–60) 3
Bracewell P (Everton, 1985–86) 3
Bradford G (Bristol Rov, 1956) 1
Bradley W (Manchester Utd, 1959) 3
Bridge W (Southampton, Chelsea, Manchester City 2002–10) 36
Bridges B (Chelsea, 1965–66) 4
Broadbent P (Wolves, 1958–60) 7
Broadis I (Manchester City, Newcastle, 1952–54) 14
Brooking T (West Ham, 1974–82) 47
Brooks J (Tottenham, 1957) 3
Brown A (WBA, 1971) 1
Brown K (West Ham, 1960) 1
Brown W (Manchester Utd, 1999–2010) 23
Bull S (Wolves, 1989–91) 13
Butcher T (Ipswich, Rangers, 1980–90) 77
Butland J (Birmingham, Stoke, 2013–16) 4
Butt N (Manchester Utd, Newcastle, 1997–2005) 39
Byrne G (Liverpool, 1963–66) 2
Byrne J (Crystal Palace, West Ham, 1962–65) 11
Byrne R (Manchester Utd, 1954–58) 33

Cahill G (Bolton, Chelsea, 2011–16) 47
Callaghan I (Liverpool, 1966–78) 4
Campbell F (Sunderland, 2012) 1
Campbell S (Tottenham, Arsenal, Portsmouth, 1996–2008) 73
Carragher J (Liverpool, 1999–2010) 38
Carrick M (West Ham, Tottenham, Manchester Utd, 2001–16) 34
Carroll A (Newcastle, Liverpool 2011– 13) 9
Carson S (Liverpool, Aston Villa WBA, Bursaspor 2008–12) 4
*Carter H (Derby, 1947) 7

Caulker S (Tottenham, 2013) 1
Chamberlain M (Stoke, 1983–85) 8
Chambers C (Arsenal, 2015) 3
Channon M (Southampton, Manchester City, 1973–78) 46
Charles G (Nottm Forest, 1991) 2
Charlton, J (Leeds, 1965–70) 35
Charlton, R (Manchester Utd, 1958–70) 106
Charnley R (Blackpool, 1963) 1
Cherry T (Leeds, 1976–80) 27
Chilton A (Manchester Utd, 1951–52) 2
Chivers M (Tottenham, 1971–74) 24
Clamp E (Wolves, 1958) 4
Clapton D (Arsenal, 1959) 1
Clarke A (Leeds, 1970–6) 19
Clarke H (Tottenham, 1954) 1
Clayton R (Blackburn, 1956–60) 35
Clemence R (Liverpool, Tottenham, 1973–84) 61
Clement D (QPR, 1976–7) 5
Cleverley T (Manchester Utd, 2013–14) 13
Clough B (Middlesbrough, 1960) 2
Clough N (Nottm Forest, Liverpool, 1989–93) 14
Clyne N (Southampton, Liverpool, 2015–16) 13
Coates R (Burnley, Tottenham, 1970–71) 4
Cockburn H (Manchester Utd, 1947–52) 13
Cohen G (Fulham, 1964–68) 37
Cole Andy (Manchester Utd, 1995–2002) 15
Cole Ashley (Arsenal, Chelsea, 2001–14) 107
Cole C (West Ham, 2009–10) 7
Cole J (West Ham, Chelsea, 2001–10) 56
Collymore S (Nottm Forest, Aston Villa, 1995–97) 3
Compton L (Arsenal, 1951) 2
Connelly J (Burnley, Manchester Utd, 1960–66) 20
Cooper C (Nottm Forest, 1995) 2
Cooper T (Leeds, 1969–75) 20
Coppell S (Manchester Utd, 1978–83) 42
Corrigan J (Manchester City, 1976–82) 9
Cottee T (West Ham, Everton, 1987–89) 7
Cowans G (Aston Villa, Bari, Aston Villa, 1983–91) 10
Crawford R (Ipswich, 1962) 2
Crouch P (Southampton, Liverpool, Portsmouth, Tottenham, 2005–11) 42
Crowe C (Wolves, 1963) 1
Cunningham L (WBA, Real Madrid, 1979–81) 6
Curle K (Manchester City, 1992) 3
Currie A (Sheffield Utd, Leeds, 1972–79) 17

Daley T (Aston Villa, 1992) 7
Davenport P (Nottm Forest, 1985) 1
Davies K (Bolton, 2011) 1
Dawson M (Tottenham 2011) 4
Deane B (Sheffield Utd, 1991–93) 3
Deeley N (Wolves, 1959) 2
Defoe J (Tottenham, Portsmouth, Tottenham, 2004–14) 55
Delph F (Aston Villa, Manchester City, 2015–16) 9
Devonshire A (West Ham, 1980–84) 8
Dickinson J (Portsmouth, 1949–57) 48
Dier E (Tottenham, 2016) 11
Ditchburn E (Tottenham, 1949–57) 6
Dixon K (Chelsea, 1985–87) 8
Dixon L (Arsenal, 1990–99) 22
Dobson M (Burnley, Everton, 1974–75) 5
Dorigo T (Chelsea, Leeds, 1990–94) 15
Douglas B (Blackburn, 1959–63) 36
Downing S (Middlesbrough, Aston Villa, Liverpool, West Ham, 2005–15) 35
Doyle M (Manchester City, 1976–77) 5
Drinkwater D (Leicester, 2016) 3
Dublin D (Coventry, Aston Villa, 1998–99) 4
Dunn D (Blackburn, 2003) 1
Duxbury, M (Manchester Utd, 1984–85) 10
Dyer K (Newcastle, West Ham, 2000–08) 33

Eastham G (Arsenal, 1963–66) 19
Eckersley W (Blackburn, 1950–54) 17
Edwards, D (Manchester Utd, 1955–58) 18
Ehiogu U (Aston Villa, Middlesbrough, 1996–2002) 4
Ellerington W (Southampton, 1949) 2
Elliott W (Burnley, 1952–53) 5

Fantham J (Sheffield Wed, 1962) 1
Fashanu J (Wimbledon, 1989) 2
Fenwick T (QPR, 1984–88) 20
Ferdinand L (QPR, Newcastle, Tottenham, 1993–98) 17
Ferdinand R (West Ham, Leeds, Manchester Utd, 1997–2011) 81
Finney T (Preston, 1947–59) 76
Flanagan J (Liverpool, 2014) 1
Flowers R (Wolves, 1955–66) 49
Flowers T (Southampton, Blackburn, 1993–98) 11
Forster F (Celtic, Southampton, 2014–16) 6
Foster B (Manchester Utd, Birmingham, WBA, 2007–14) 8
Foster S (Brighton, 1982) 3
Foulkes W (Manchester Utd, 1955) 1
Fowler R (Liverpool, Leeds, 1996–2002) 26
Francis G (QPR, 1975–76) 12
Francis T (Birmingham, Nottm Forest, Man City, Sampdoria, 1977–86) 52
Franklin N (Stoke, 1947–50) 27
Froggatt J (Portsmouth, 1950–53) 13
Froggatt R (Sheffield Wed, 1953) 4

Gardner A (Tottenham, 2004) 1
Garrett T (Blackpool, 1952–54) 3
Gascoigne P (Tottenham, Lazio, Rangers, Middlesbrough, 1989–98) 57
Gates E (Ipswich, 1981) 2
George C (Derby, 1977) 1
Gerrard S (Liverpool, 2000–14) 114
Gibbs K (Arsenal, 2011–16) 10
Gidman J (Aston Villa, 1977) 1
Gillard I (QPR, 1975–76) 3
Goddard P (West Ham, 1982) 1
Grainger C (Sheffield Utd, Sunderland, 1956–57) 7
Gray A (Crystal Palace, 1992) 1

Gray M (Sunderland, 1999) 3
Greaves J (Chelsea, Tottenham, 1959–67) 57
Green R (Norwich, West Ham 2005–12) 12
Greenhoff B (Manchester Utd, Leeds, 1976–80) 18
Gregory J (QPR, 1983–84) 6
Guppy S (Leicester, 2000) 1

Hagan J (Sheffield Utd, 1949) 1
Haines J (WBA, 1949) 1
Hall J (Birmingham, 1956–57) 17
Hancocks J (Wolves, 1949–50) 3
Hardwick G (Middlesbrough, 1947–48) 13
Harford M (Luton, 1988–89) 2
Hargreaves O (Bayern Munich, Manchester Utd, 2002–08) 42
Harris G (Burnley, 1966) 1
Harris P (Portsmouth, 1950–54) 2
Hart J (Manchester City, 2010–16) 63
Harvey C (Everton, 1971) 1
Hassall H (Huddersfield, Bolton, 1951–54) 5
Hateley M (Portsmouth, AC Milan, Monaco, Rangers, 1984–92) 32
Haynes J (Fulham, 1955–62) 56
Heaton T (Burnley, 2016) 1
Hector K (Derby, 1974) 2
Hellawell M (Birmingham, 1963) 2
Henderson J (Sunderland, Liverpool, 2011–16) 27
Hendrie L (Aston Villa, 1999) 1
Henry R (Tottenham, 1963) 1
Heskey E (Leicester, Liverpool, Birmingham, Wigan, Aston Villa 1999–2010) 62
Hill F (Bolton, 1963) 2
Hill G (Manchester Utd, 1976–78) 6
Hill R (Luton, 1983–86) 3
Hinchcliffe A (Everton, Sheffield Wed, 1997–99) 7
Hinton A (Wolves, Nottm Forest, 1963–65) 3
Hirst D (Sheffield Wed, 1991–92) 3
Hitchens G (Aston Villa, Inter Milan, 1961–62) 7
Hoddle G (Tottenham, Monaco, 1980–88) 53
Hodge S (Aston Villa, Tottenham, Nottm Forest, 1986–91) 24
Hodgkinson A (Sheffield Utd, 1957–61) 5
Holden D (Bolton, 1959) 5
Holliday E (Middlesbrough, 1960) 3
Hollins J (Chelsea, 1967) 1
Hopkinson E (Bolton, 1958–60) 14
Howe D (WBA, 1958–60) 23
Howe J (Derby, 1948–49) 3
Howey S (Newcastle, 1995–96) 4
Huddlestone T (Tottenham, 2010–13) 4
Hudson A (Stoke, 1975) 2
Hughes E (Liverpool, Wolves, 1970–80) 62
Hughes L (Liverpool, 1950) 3
Hunt R (Liverpool, 1962–69) 34
Hunt S (WBA, 1984) 2
Hunter N (Leeds, 1966–75) 28
Hurst G (West Ham, 1966–72) 49

Ince P (Manchester Utd, Inter Milan, Liverpool, Middlesbrough, 1993–2000) 53
Ings D (Liverpool 2016) 1

Jagielka P (Everton, 2008–16) 39
James D (Liverpool, Aston Villa, West Ham, Manchester City, Portsmouth, 1997–2010) 53
Jarvis M (Wolves, 2011) 1
Jeffers F (Arsenal, 2003) 1
Jenas J (Newcastle, Tottenham, 2003–10) 21
Jenkinson C (Arsenal, 2013) 1
Jezzard B (Fulham, 1954–56) 2
Johnson A (Crystal Palace, Everton, 2005–08) 8
Johnson A (Manchester City, 2010–13) 12
Johnson D (Ipswich, Liverpool, 1975–80) 8
Johnson G (Chelsea, Portsmouth, Liverpool, 2004–14) 54
Johnson S (Derby, 2001) 1
Johnston H (Blackpool, 1947–54) 10
Jones M (Leeds, Sheffield Utd, 1965–70) 3
Jones P (Manchester Utd, 2012–16) 20
Jones R (Liverpool, 1992–95) 8
Jones W H (Liverpool, 1950) 2

Kane H (Tottenham, 2015–16) 16
Kay A (Everton, 1963) 1
Keegan K (Liverpool, Hamburg, Southampton, 1973–82) 63
Kelly, M (Liverpool, 2012) 1
Kennedy A (Liverpool, 1984) 2
Kennedy R (Liverpool, 1976–80) 17
Keown M (Everton, Arsenal, 1992–2002) 43
Kevan D (WBA, 1957–61) 14
Kidd B (Manchester Utd, 1970) 2
King L (Tottenham, 2002–10) 21
Kirkland C (Liverpool, 2007) 1
Knight Z (Fulham, 2005) 2
Knowles C (Tottenham, 1968) 4
Konchesky P (Charlton, 2003–06) 2

Labone B (Everton, 1963–70) 26
Lallana A (Southampton, Liverpool, 2014–16) 26
Lambert R (Southampton, Liverpool, 2014–15) 11
Lampard F Snr (West Ham, 1973–80) 2
Lampard F Jnr (West Ham, Chelsea, 2000–14) 106
Langley J (Fulham, 1958) 3
Langton R (Blackburn, Preston, Bolton, 1947–51) 11
Latchford R (Everton, 1978–9) 12
Lawler C (Liverpool, 1971–72) 4
*Lawton T (Chelsea, Notts Co, 1947–49) 15
Lee F (Manchester City, 1969–72) 27
Lee J (Derby, 1951) 1
Lee R (Newcastle, 1995–99) 21
Lee S (Liverpool, 1983–84) 14
Lennon A (Tottenham, 2006–13) 21
Le Saux G (Blackburn, Chelsea, 1994–2001) 36
Lescott J (Everton, Manchester City, 2008–13) 26
Le Tissier M (Southampton, 1994–97) 8
Lindsay A (Liverpool, 1974) 4
Lineker G (Leicester, Everton, Barcelona, Tottenham, 1985–92) 80
Little B (Aston Villa, 1975) 1
Livermore J (Tottenham, 2013) 1

Lloyd L (Liverpool, Nottm Forest, 1971–80) 4
Lofthouse N (Bolton, 1951–59) 33
Lowe E (Aston Villa, 1947) 3

Mabbutt G (Tottenham, 1983–92) 16
Macdonald M (Newcastle, 1972–76) 14
Madeley P (Leeds, 1971–77) 24
Mannion W (Middlesbrough, 1947–52) 26
Mariner P (Ipswich, Arsenal, 1977–85) 35
Marsh R (QPR, Manchester City, 1972–73) 9
Mason R (Tottenham, 2015) 1
Martin A (West Ham, 1981–87) 17
Martyn N (Crystal Palace, Leeds, 1992–2002) 23
Marwood B (Arsenal, 1989) 1
Matthews R (Coventry, 1956–57) 5
*Matthews S (Stoke, Blackpool, 1947–57) 37
McCann G (Sunderland, 2001) 1
McDermott T (Liverpool, 1978–82) 25
McDonald C (Burnley, 1958–59) 8
McFarland R (Derby, 1971–77) 28
McGarry W (Huddersfield, 1954–56) 4
McGuinness W (Manchester Utd, 1959) 2
McMahon S (Liverpool, 1988–91) 17
McManaman S (Liverpool, Real Madrid, 1995–2002) 37
McNab R (Arsenal, 1969) 4
McNeil M (Middlesbrough, 1961–62) 9
Meadows J (Manchester City, 1955) 1
Medley L (Tottenham, 1951–52) 6
Melia J (Liverpool, 1963) 2
Merrick G (Birmingham, 1952–54) 23
Merson P (Arsenal, Middlesbrough, Aston Villa, 1992–99) 21
Metcalfe V (Huddersfield, 1951) 2
Milburn J (Newcastle, 1949–56) 13
Miller B (Burnley, 1961) 1
Mills D (Leeds, 2001–04) 19
Mills M (Ipswich, 1973–82) 42
Milne G (Liverpool, 1963–65) 14
Milner J (Aston Villa, Manchester City, Liverpool, 2010–16) 61
Milton A (Arsenal, 1952) 1
Moore R (West Ham, 1962–74) 108
Morley A (Aston Villa, 1982–83) 6
Morris J (Derby, 1949–50) 3
Mortensen S (Blackpool, 1947–54) 25
Mozley B (Derby, 1950) 3
Mullen J (Wolves, 1947–54) 12
Mullery A (Tottenham, 1965–72) 35
Murphy D (Liverpool, 2002–04) 9

Neal P (Liverpool, 1976–84) 50
Neville G (Manchester Utd, 1995–2009) 85
Neville P (Manchester Utd, Everton, 1996–2008) 59
Newton K (Blackburn, Everton, 1966–70) 27
Nicholls J (WBA, 1954) 2
Nicholson W (Tottenham, 1951) 1
Nish D (Derby, 1973–74) 5
Norman M (Tottenham, 1962–5) 23
Nugent D (Preston, 2007) 1
O'Grady M (Huddersfield, Leeds, 1963–9) 2
Osgood P (Chelsea, 1970–74) 4
Osman L (Everton, 2013) 2
Osman R (Ipswich, 1980–84) 11
Owen M (Liverpool, Real Madrid, Newcastle, 1998–2008) 89
Owen S (Luton, 1954) 3
Oxlade–Chamberlain A (Arsenal, 2012–16) 24

Paine T (Southampton, 1963–66) 19
Pallister G (Middlesbrough, Manchester Utd 1988–97) 22
Palmer C (Sheffield Wed, 1992–94) 18
Parker P (QPR, Manchester Utd, 1989–94) 19
Parker S (Charlton, Chelsea, Newcastle, West Ham, Tottenham, 2004–13) 18
Parkes P (QPR, 1974) 1
Parlour R (Arsenal, 1999–2001) 10
Parry R (Bolton, 1960) 2
Peacock A (Middlesbrough, Leeds, 1962–66) 6
Pearce S (Nottm Forest, West Ham, 1987–2000) 78
Pearson Stan (Manchester Utd, 1948–52) 8
Pearson Stuart (Manchester Utd, 1976–78) 15
Pegg D (Manchester Utd, 1957) 1
Pejic M (Stoke, 1974) 4
Perry W (Blackpool, 1956) 3
Perryman S (Tottenham, 1982) 1
Peters M (West Ham, Tottenham, 1966–74) 67
Phelan M (Manchester Utd, 1990) 1
Phillips K (Sunderland, 1999–2002) 8
Phillips L (Portsmouth, 1952–55) 3
Pickering F (Everton, 1964–65) 3
Pickering N (Sunderland, 1983) 1
Pilkington B (Burnley, 1955) 1
Platt D (Aston Villa, Bari, Juventus, Sampdoria, Arsenal, 1990–96) 62
Pointer R (Burnley, 1962) 3
Powell C (Charlton, 2001–02) 5
Pye J (Wolves, 1950) 1

Quixall A (Sheffield Wed, 1954–55) 5

Radford J (Arsenal, 1969–72) 2
Ramsey A (Southampton, Tottenham, 1949–54) 32
Rashford M (Manchester Utd, 2016) 3
Reaney P (Leeds, 1969–71) 3
Redknapp J (Liverpool, 1996–2000) 17
Reeves K (Norwich, Manchester City, 1980) 2
Regis C (WBA, Coventry, 1982–88) 5
Reid P (Everton, 1985–88) 13
Revie D (Manchester City, 1955–57) 6
Richards, J (Wolves, 1973) 1
Richards M (Manchester City, 2007–12) 13
Richardson K (Aston Villa, 1994) 1
Richardson K (Manchester Utd, 2005–07) 8
Rickaby S (WBA, 1954) 1
Ricketts M (Bolton, 2002) 1
Rimmer J (Arsenal, 1976) 1
Ripley S (Blackburn, 1994–97) 2

Rix G (Arsenal, 1981–84) 17
Robb G (Tottenham, 1954) 1
Roberts G (Tottenham, 1983–84) 6
Robinson P (Leeds, Tottenham, 2003–08) 41
Robson B (WBA, Manchester Utd, 1980–92) 90
Robson R (WBA, 1958–62) 20
Rocastle D (Arsenal, 1989–92) 14
Rodriguez J (Southampton, 2014) 1
Rodwell J (Everton, Manchester City, 2012–13) 3
Rooney W (Everton, Manchester Utd, 2003–16) 115
Rose D (Tottenham, 2016) 7
Rowley J (Manchester Utd, 1949–52) 6
Royle J (Everton, Manchester City, 1971–77) 6
Ruddock N (Liverpool, 1995) 1
Ruddy J (Norwich, 2013) 1

Sadler D (Manchester Utd, 1968–71) 4
Salako J (Crystal Palace, 1991–92) 5
Sansom K (Crystal Palace, Arsenal, 1979–88) 86
Scales J (Liverpool, 1995) 3
Scholes P (Manchester Utd, 1997–2004) 66
Scott L (Arsenal, 1947–49) 17
Seaman D (QPR, Arsenal, 1989–2003) 75
Sewell J (Sheffield Wed, 1952–54) 6
Shackleton L (Sunderland, 1949–55) 5
Sharpe L (Manchester Utd, 1991–94) 8
Shaw G (Sheffield Utd, 1959–63) 5
Shaw L (Southampton, Manchester Utd, 2014–16) 6
Shawcross, R (Stoke, 2013) 1
Shearer A (Southampton, Blackburn, Newcastle, 1992–2000) 63
Shellito K (Chelsea, 1963) 1
Shelvey J (Liverpool, Swansea, 2013–16) 6
Sheringham E (Tottenham, Manchester Utd, Tottenham, 1993–2002) 51
Sherwood T (Tottenham, 1999) 3
Shilton P (Leicester, Stoke, Nottm Forest, Southampton, Derby, 1971–90) 125
Shimwell E (Blackpool, 1949) 1
Shorey N (Reading, 2007) 2
Sillett P (Chelsea, 1955) 3
Sinclair T (West Ham, Manchester City, 2002–04) 12
Sinton A (QPR, Sheffield Wed, 1992–94) 12
Slater W (Wolves, 1955–60) 12
Smalling C (Manchester Utd, 2012–16) 29
Smith A (Arsenal, 1989–92) 13
Smith A (Leeds, Manchester Utd, Newcastle, 2001–08) 19
Smith L (Arsenal, 1951–53) 6
Smith R (Tottenham, 1961–64) 15
Smith T (Birmingham, 1960) 2
Smith T (Liverpool, 1971) 1
Southgate G (Aston Villa, Middlesbrough, 1996–2004) 57
Spink N (Aston Villa, 1983) 1
Springett R (Sheffield Wed, 1960–66) 33
Staniforth R (Huddersfield, 1954–55) 8
Statham D (WBA, 1983) 3
Stein B (Luton, 1984) 1
Stepney A (Manchester Utd, 1968) 1
Sterland M (Sheffield Wed, 1989) 1
Sterling R (Liverpool, Manchester City, 2013–16) 26
Steven T (Everton, Rangers, Marseille, 1985–92) 36
Stevens G (Everton, Rangers, 1985–92) 46
Stevens G (Tottenham, 1985–86) 7
Stewart P (Tottenham, 1992) 3
Stiles N (Manchester Utd, 1965–70) 28
Stone S (Nottm Forest, 1996) 9
Stones J (Everton, 2014–16) 10
Storey P (Arsenal, 1971–73) 19
Storey-Moore I (Nottm Forest, 1970) 1
Streten B (Luton, 1950) 1
Sturridge D (Chelsea, Liverpool, 2012–16) 21
Summerbee M (Manchester City, 1968–73) 8
Sunderland, A (Arsenal, 1980) 1
Sutton C (Blackburn, 1997) 1
Swan P (Sheffield Wed, 1960–62) 19
Swift F (Manchester City, 1947–79) 19

Talbot B (Ipswich, Arsenal, 1977–80) 6
Tambling R (Chelsea, 1963–66) 3
Taylor E (Blackpool, 1954) 1
Taylor J (Fulham, 1951) 2
Taylor P (Liverpool, 1948) 3
Taylor P (Crystal Palace, 1976) 4
Taylor T (Manchester Utd, 1953–58) 19
Temple D (Everton, 1965) 1
Terry J (Chelsea, 2003–13) 78
Thomas D (QPR, 1975–76) 8
Thomas D (Coventry, 1983) 2
Thomas G (Crystal Palace, 1991–92) 9
Thomas M (Arsenal, 1989–90) 2
Thompson A (Celtic, 2004) 1
Thompson Peter (Liverpool, 1964–70) 16
Thompson Phil (Liverpool, 1976–83) 42
Thompson T (Aston Villa, Preston, 1952–57) 2
Thomson R (Wolves, 1964–65) 8
Todd C (Derby, 1972–77) 27
Towers A (Sunderland, 1978) 3
Townsend A (Tottenham, Newcastle, 2014–16) 11
Tueart D (Manchester City, 1975–77) 6

Ufton D (Charlton, 1954) 1
Unsworth D (Everton, 1995) 1
Upson M (Birmingham, West Ham, 2003–10) 21

Vardy J (Leicester, 2015–16) 11
Vassell D (Aston Villa, 2002–04) 22
Venables T (Chelsea, 1965) 2
Venison B (Newcastle, 1995) 2
Viljoen C (Ipswich, 1975) 2
Viollet D (Manchester Utd, 1960) 2

Waddle C (Newcastle, Tottenham, Marseille, 1985–92) 62
Waiters A (Blackpool, 1964–65) 5

Walcott T (Arsenal, 2006–16) 43
Walker D (Nottm Forest, Sampdoria, Sheffield Wed, 1989–94) 59
Walker I (Tottenham, Leicester, 1996–2004) 4
Walker K (Tottenham, 2012–16) 19
Wallace D (Southampton, 1986) 1
Walsh P (Luton, 1983–4) 5
Walters M (Rangers, 1991) 1
Ward P (Brighton, 1980) 1
Ward T (Derby, 1948) 2
Warnock S (Blackburn, Aston Villa, 2008–11) 2
Watson D (Sunderland, Manchester City, Werder Bremen, Southampton, Stoke, 1974–82) 65
Watson D (Norwich, Everton, 1984–8) 12
Watson W (Sunderland, 1950–1) 4
Webb N (Nottm Forest, Manchester Utd, 1988–92) 26
Welbeck D (Manchester Utd, Arsenal, 2011–16) 34
Weller K (Leicester, 1974) 4
West G (Everton, 1969) 3
Wheeler J (Bolton, 1955) 1
White D (Manchester City, 1993) 1
Whitworth S (Leicester, 1975–76) 7
Whymark T (Ipswich, 1978) 1
Wignall F (Nottm Forest, 1965) 2
Wilcox J (Blackburn, Leeds, 1996–2000) 3
Wilkins R (Chelsea, Manchester Utd, AC Milan, 1976–87) 84
Williams B (Wolves, 1949–56) 24
Williams S (Southampton, 1983–85) 6
Willis A (Tottenham, 1952) 1
Wilshaw D (Wolves, 1954–57) 12
Wilshere J (Arsenal, 2011–16) 34
Wilson R (Huddersfield, Everton, 1960–8) 63
Winterburn N (Arsenal, 1990–93) 2
Wise D (Chelsea, 1991–2001) 21
Withe P (Aston Villa, 1981–85) 11
Wood R (Manchester Utd, 1955–56) 3
Woodcock A (Nottm Forest, Cologne, Arsenal, 1977–86) 42
Woodgate J (Leeds, Newcastle, Middlesbrough, Tottenham, 1999–2008) 8
Woods C (Norwich, Rangers, Sheffield Wed, 1984–93) 43
Worthington F (Leicester, 1974–75) 8
Wright I (Crystal Palace, Arsenal, West Ham, 1991–99) 33
Wright M (Southampton, Derby, Liverpool, 1984–96) 45
Wright R (Ipswich, Arsenal, 2000–02) 2
Wright T (Everton, 1968–70) 11
Wright W (Wolves, 1947–59) 105
Wright-Phillips S (Manchester City, Chelsea, Manchester City, 2005–11) 36

Young A (Aston Villa, Manchester Utd, 2008–14) 30
Young G (Sheffield Wed, 1965) 1
Young L (Charlton, 2005) 7

Zaha W (Manchester Utd, 2013–14) 2
Zamora R (Fulham, 2011–12) 2

SCOTLAND

Adam C (Rangers, Blackpool, Liverpool, Stoke, 2007–15) 26
Aird J (Burnley, 1954) 4
Aitken G (East Fife, 1949–54) 8
Aitken R (Celtic, Newcastle, St Mirren, 1980–92) 57
Albiston A (Manchester Utd, 1982–6) 14
Alexander G (Preston, Burnley, 2002–10) 40
Alexander N (Cardiff, 2006) 2
Allan T (Dundee, 1974) 2
Anderson J (Leicester, 1954) 1
Anderson R (Aberdeen, Sunderland, 2003–08) 11
Anya I (Watford, 2014–16) 21
Archibald S (Aberdeen, Tottenham, Barcelona, 1980–86) 27
Auld B (Celtic, 1959–60) 3

Baird H (Airdrie, 1956) 1
Baird S (Rangers, 1957–58) 7
Bannan B (Aston Villa, Crystal Palace, Sheffield Wed, 2011–16) 21
Bannon E (Dundee Utd, 1980–86) 11
Bardsley P (Sunderland, 2011–14) 13
Barr D (Falkirk, 2009) 1
Bauld W (Hearts, 1950) 3
Baxter J (Rangers, Sunderland, 1961–68) 34
Beattie C (Celtic, WBA, 2006–08) 7
Bell C (Kilmarnock, 2011) 1
Bell W (Leeds, 1966) 2
Bernard P (Oldham, 1995) 2
Berra C (Hearts, Wolves, Ipswich, 2008–16) 33
Bett J (Rangers, Lokeren, Aberdeen, 1982–90) 26
Black E (Metz, 1988) 2
Black I (Southampton, 1948) 1
Black I (Rangers, 2013) 1
Blacklaw A (Burnley, 1963–66) 3
Blackley J (Hibernian, 1974–77) 7
Blair J (Blackpool, 1947) 1
Blyth J (Coventry, 1978) 2
Bone J (Norwich, 1972–73) 2
Booth S (Aberdeen, Borussia Dortmund, Twente Enschede 1993–2002) 22
Bowman D (Dundee Utd, 1992–94) 6
Boyd G (Peterborough, Hull, 2013–14) 2
Boyd K (Rangers, Middlesbrough, 2006–11) 18
Boyd T (Motherwell, Chelsea, Celtic, 1991–2002) 72
Brand R (Rangers, 1961–62) 8
Brazil A (Ipswich, Tottenham, 1980–83) 13
Bremner D (Hibernian, 1976) 1
Bremner W (Leeds, 1965–76) 54
Brennan F (Newcastle, 1947–54) 7
Bridcutt L (Brighton, Sunderland, 2013–16) 2
Broadfoot K (Rangers, 2009–11) 4
Brogan J (Celtic, 1971) 4
Brown A (East Fife, Blackpool, 1950–54) 13

Brown H (Partick, 1947) 3
Brown J (Sheffield Utd, 1975) 1
Brown R (Rangers, 1947–52) 3
Brown S (Hibernian, Celtic, 2007–16) 50
Brown W (Dundee, Tottenham, 1958–66) 28
Brownlie J (Hibernian, 1971–76) 7
Bryson C (Kilmarnock, Derby, 2011–16) 3
Buchan M (Aberdeen, Manchester Utd, 1972–8) 34
Buckley P (Aberdeen, 1954–55) 3
Burchill M (Celtic, 2000) 6
Burke C (Rangers, Birmingham, 2006–14) 7
Burke O (Nottm Forest, 2016) 2
Burley C (Chelsea, Celtic, Derby, 1995–2003) 46
Burley G (Ipswich, 1979–82) 11
Burns F (Manchester Utd, 1970) 1
Burns K (Birmingham, Nottm Forest, 1974–81) 20
Burns T (Celtic, 1981–88) 8

Caddis P (Birmingham, 2016) 1
Calderwood C (Tottenham, Aston Villa, 1995–2000) 36
Caldow E (Rangers, 1957–63) 40
Caldwell G (Newcastle, Sunderland, Hibernian, Wigan, 2002–13) 55
Caldwell S (Newcastle, Sunderland, Celtic, Wigan, 2001–11) 12
Callaghan T (Dunfermline, 1970) 2
Cameron C (Hearts, Wolves, 1999–2005) 28
Campbell R (Falkirk, Chelsea, 1947–50) 5
Campbell W (Morton, 1947–48) 5
Canero P (Leicester, 2004) 1
Carr W (Coventry, 1970–73) 6
Chalmers S (Celtic, 1965–67) 5
Clark J (Celtic, 1966–67) 4
Clark R (Aberdeen, 1968–73) 17
Clarke S (Chelsea, 1988–94) 6
Clarkson D (Motherwell, 2008–09) 2
Collins J (Hibernian, Celtic, Monaco, Everton, 1988–2000) 58
Collins R (Celtic, Everton, Leeds, 1951–65) 31
Colquhoun E (Sheffield Utd, 1972–73) 9
Colquhoun J (Hearts, 1988) 2
Combe J (Hibernian, 1948) 3
Commons K (Derby, Celtic, 2009–13) 12
Conn A (Hearts, 1956) 1
Conn A (Tottenham, 1975) 2
Connachan E (Dunfermline, 1962) 2
Connelly G (Celtic, 1974) 2
Connolly J (Everton, 1973) 1
Connor R (Dundee, Aberdeen, 1986–91) 4
Conway C (Dundee Utd, Cardiff, 2010–14) 7
Cooke C (Dundee, Chelsea, 1966–75) 16
Cooper D (Rangers, Motherwell, 1980–90) 22
Cormack P (Hibernian, 1966–72) 9
Cowan J (Morton, 1948–52) 25
Cowie D (Dundee, 1953–58) 20
Cowie D (Watford, 2010–12) 10
Cox C (Hearts, 1948) 1
Cox S (Rangers, 1948–54) 25
Craig JP (Celtic, 1968) 1
Craig J (Celtic, 1977) 1
Craig T (Newcastle, 1976) 1
Crainey S (Celtic, Southampton, Blackpool, 2002–12) 12
Crawford S (Raith, Dunfermline, Plymouth Argyle, 1995–2005) 25
Crerand P (Celtic, Manchester Utd, 1961–66) 16
Cropley A (Hibernian, 1972) 2
Cruickshank J (Hearts, 1964–76) 6
Cullen M (Luton, 1956) 1
Cumming J (Hearts, 1955–60) 9
Cummings W (Chelsea, 2002) 1
Cunningham W (Preston, 1954–55) 8
Curran H (Wolves, 1970–71) 5

Dailly C (Derby, Blackburn, West Ham, 1997–2008) 67
Dalglish K (Celtic, Liverpool, 1972–87) 102
Davidson C (Blackburn, Leicester, Preston, 1999–2010) 19
Davidson M (St Johnstone, 2013) 1
Davidson J (Partick, 1954–55) 8
Dawson A (Rangers, 1980–83) 5
Deans J (Celtic, 1975) 2
*Delaney J (Manchester Utd, 1947–48) 4
Devlin P (Birmingham, 2003–04) 10
Dick J (West Ham, 1959) 1
Dickov P (Manchester City, Leicester, Blackburn, 2001–05) 10
Dickson W (Kilmarnock, 1970–71) 5
Dixon P (Huddersfield, 2013) 3
Dobie S (WBA, 2002–03) 6
Docherty T (Preston, Arsenal, 1952–59) 25
Dodds D (Dundee Utd, 1984) 2
Dodds W (Aberdeen, Dundee Utd, Rangers, 1997–2002) 26
Donachie W (Manchester City, 1972–79) 35
Donnelly S (Celtic, 1997–99) 10
Dorrans G (WBA, Norwich, 2010–16) 12
Dougall C (Birmingham, 1947) 1
Dougan R (Hearts, 1950) 1
Douglas R (Celtic, Leicester, 2002–06) 19
Doyle J (Ayr, 1976) 1
Duncan A (Hibernian, 1975–76) 6
Duncan D (East Fife, 1948) 3
Duncanson J (Rangers, 1947) 1
Durie G (Chelsea, Tottenham, Rangers, 1988–98) 43
Durrant I (Rangers, Kilmarnock, 1988–2000) 20

Elliott M (Leicester, 1997–2002) 18
Evans A (Aston Villa, 1982) 4
Evans R (Celtic, Chelsea, 1949–60) 48
Ewing T (Partick, 1958) 2

Farm G (Blackpool, 1953–59) 10
Ferguson B (Rangers, Blackburn, Rangers, 1999–2009) 45

Ferguson D (Dundee Utd, Everton, 1992–97) 7
Ferguson D (Rangers, 1988) 2
Ferguson I (Rangers, 1989–97) 9
Ferguson R (Kilmarnock, 1966–67) 7
Fernie W (Celtic, 1954–58) 12
Flavell R (Airdrie, 1947) 2
Fleck R (Norwich, 1990–91) 4
Fleming C (East Fife, 1954) 1
Fletcher D (Manchester Utd, WBA, 2004–16) 73
Fletcher S (Hibernian, Burnley, Wolves, Sunderland, 2008–16) 28
Forbes A (Sheffield Utd, Arsenal, 1947–52) 14
Ford D (Hearts, 1974) 3
Forrest J (Motherwell, 1958) 1
Forrest J (Rangers, Aberdeen, 1966–71) 5
Forrest J (Celtic, 2011–16) 13
Forsyth A (Partick, Manchester Utd, 1972–76) 10
Forsyth C (Kilmarnock, 1964) 4
Forsyth C (Derby, 2014–15) 4
Forsyth T (Motherwell, Rangers, 1971–78) 22
Fox D (Burnley, Southampton, 2010–13) 4
Fraser D (WBA, 1968–69) 2
Fraser W (Sunderland, 1955) 2
Freedman D (Crystal Palace, 2002) 2

Gabriel J (Everton, 1961–64) 2
Gallacher K (Dundee Utd, Coventry, Blackburn, Newcastle, 1988–2001) 53
Gallacher P (Dundee Utd, 2003–04) 8
Gallagher P (Blackburn, 2004) 1
Galloway M (Celtic, 1992) 1
Gardiner I (Motherwell, 1958) 1
Gemmell T (St Mirren, 1955) 2
Gemmell T (Celtic, 1966–71) 18
Gemmill A (Derby, Nottm Forest, Birmingham, 1971–81) 43
Gemmill S (Nottm Forest, Everton, 1995–2003) 26
Gibson D (Leicester, 1963–65) 7
Gilks M (Blackpool, 2013–14) 3
Gillespie G (Liverpool, 1988–91) 13
Gilzean A (Dundee, Tottenham, 1964–71) 22
Glass S (Newcastle Utd 1999) 1
Glavin R (Celtic, 1977) 1
Glen A (Aberdeen, 1956) 2
Goodwillie D (Dundee Utd, Blackburn, 2011–12) 3
Goram A (Oldham, Hibernian, Rangers, 1986–98) 43
Gordon C (Hearts, Sunderland, Celtic, 2004–16) 44
Gough R (Dundee Utd, Tottenham, Rangers, 1983–93) 61
Gould J (Celtic, 2000–01) 2
Govan J (Hibernian, 1948–49) 6
Graham A (Leeds, 1978–81) 10
Graham G (Arsenal, Manchester Utd, 1972–73) 12
Gray A (Aston Villa, Wolves, Everton, 1976–85) 20
Gray A (Bradford City, 2003) 2
Gray E (Leeds, 1969–77) 12
Gray F (Leeds, Nottm Forest, 1976–83) 32
Grant J (Hibernian, 1958) 2
Grant P (Celtic, 1989) 2
Green A (Blackpool, Newcastle, 1971–72) 6
Greer G (Brighton, 2014–16) 11
Greig J (Rangers, 1964–76) 44
Griffiths L (Wolves, Celtic, 2013–16) 7
Gunn B (Norwich, 1990–94) 6

Haddock H (Clyde, 1955–58) 6
Haffey F (Celtic, 1960–61) 2
Hamilton A (Dundee, 1962–66) 24
Hamilton G (Aberdeen, 1947–54) 5
Hamilton W (Hibernian, 1965) 1
Hammell S (Motherwell, 2005) 1
Hanley G (Blackburn, 2011–16) 23
Hansen A (Liverpool, 1979–87) 26
Hansen J (Partick, 1972) 2
Harper J (Aberdeen, Hibernian, 1973–78) 4
Hartford A (WBA, Manchester City, Everton, 1972–82) 50
Hartley P (Hearts, Celtic, Bristol City, 2005–10) 25
Harvey D (Leeds, 1973–77) 16
Haughney M (Celtic, 1954) 1
Hay D (Celtic, 1970–74) 27
Hegarty P (Dundee Utd, 1979–83) 8
Henderson J (Portsmouth, Arsenal, 1953–59) 7
Henderson W (Rangers, 1963–71) 29
Hendry C (Blackburn, Rangers, Coventry, Bolton, 1994–2001) 51
Herd D (Arsenal, 1959–61) 5
Herd G (Clyde, 1958–61) 5
Herriot J (Birmingham, 1969–70) 8
Hewie J (Charlton, 1956–60) 19
Holt D (Hearts, 1963–64) 5
Holt G (Kilmarnock, Norwich, 2001–05) 10
Holton J (Manchester Utd, 1973–75) 15
Hope R (WBA, 1968–69) 2
Hopkin D (Crystal Palace, Leeds, 1997–2000) 7
Houliston W (Queen of the South, 1949) 3
Houston S (Manchester Utd, 1976) 1
Howie H (Hibernian, 1949) 1
Hughes J (Celtic, 1965–70) 8
Hughes R (Portsmouth, 2004–06) 5
Hughes S (Norwich, 2010) 1
Hughes W (Sunderland, 1975) 1
Humphries W (Motherwell, 1952) 1
Hunter A (Kilmarnock, Celtic, 1972–74) 4
Hunter W (Motherwell, 1960–61) 3
Husband J (Partick, 1947) 1
Hutchison D (Everton, Sunderland, West Ham, 1999–2004) 26
Hutchison T (Coventry, 1974–76) 17
Hutton A (Rangers, Tottenham, Aston Villa, 2007–16) 50

Imlach S (Nottm Forest, 1958) 4
Irvine B (Aberdeen, 1991–94) 9

Iwelumo C (Wolves, Burnley, 2009–11) 4

Jackson C (Rangers, 1975–77) 8
Jackson D (Hibernian, Celtic, 1995–99) 28
Jardine A (Rangers, 1971–80) 38
Jarvie A (Airdrie, 1971) 3
Jess E (Aberdeen, Coventry, Aberdeen, 1993–99) 18
Johnston A (Sunderland, Rangers, Middlesbrough, 1999–2003) 18
Johnston L (Clyde, 1948) 2
Johnston M (Watford, Celtic, Nantes, Rangers, 1984–92) 38
Johnston W (Rangers, WBA, 1966–78) 21
Johnstone D (Rangers, 1973–80) 14
Johnstone J (Celtic, 1965–75) 23
Johnstone R (Hibernian, Manchester City, 1951–56) 17
Jordan J (Leeds, Manchester Utd, AC Milan, 1973–82) 52

Kelly H (Blackpool, 1952) 1
Kelly J (Barnsley, 1949) 2
Kelly L (Kilmarnock, 2013) 1
Kennedy J (Celtic, 1964–65) 6
Kennedy J (Celtic, 2004) 1
Kennedy S (Rangers, 1975) 5
Kennedy S (Aberdeen, 1978–82) 8
Kenneth G (Dundee Utd, 2011) 2
Kerr A (Partick, 1955) 2
Kerr B (Newcastle, 2003–04) 3
Kingsley S (Swansea, 2016) 1
Kyle K (Sunderland, Kilmarnock, 2002–10) 10

Lambert P (Motherwell, Borussia Dortmund, Celtic, 1995–2003) 40
Law D (Huddersfield, Manchester City, Torino, Manchester Utd, 1959–74) 55
Lawrence T (Liverpool, 1963–69) 3
Leggat G (Aberdeen, Fulham, 1956–60) 18
Leighton J (Aberdeen, Manchester Utd, Hibernian, Aberdeen, 1983–99) 91
Lennox R (Celtic, 1967–70) 10
Leslie L (Airdrie, 1961) 5
Levein C (Hearts, 1990–95) 16
Liddell W (Liverpool, 1947–55) 28
Linwood A (Clyde, 1950) 1
Little R (Rangers, 1953) 1
Logie J (Arsenal, 1953) 1
Long H (Clyde, 1947) 1
Lorimer P (Leeds, 1970–76) 21

Macari L (Celtic, Manchester Utd, 1972–78) 24
Macaulay A (Brentford, Arsenal, 1947–48) 7
MacDonald A (Rangers, 1976) 1
MacDougall E (Norwich, 1975–76) 7
Mackail-Smith C (Peterborough, Brighton 2011–12) 7
MacKay D (Celtic, 1959–62) 14
Mackay D (Hearts, Tottenham, 1957–66) 22
Mackay G (Hearts, 1988) 4
Mackay M (Norwich, 2004–05) 5
Mackay-Steven G (Dundee Utd, 2014) 1
MacKenzie J (Partick, 1954–56) 9
Mackie J (QPR, 2011–13) 9
MacLeod J (Hibernian, 1961) 4
MacLeod M (Celtic, Borussia Dortmund, Hibernian, 1985–91) 20
Maguire C (Aberdeen, 2011) 2
Maloney S (Celtic, Aston Villa, Celtic, Wigan, Chicago, Hull, 2006–16) 47
Malpas M (Dundee Utd, 1984–93) 55
Marshall D (Celtic, Cardiff, 2005–16) 24
Marshall G (Celtic, 1992) 1
Martin B (Motherwell, 1995) 2
Martin C (Derby, 2014–16) 8
Martin F (Aberdeen, 1954–55) 6
Martin N (Hibernian, Sunderland, 1965–66) 3
Martin R (Norwich, 2011–16) 25
Martis J (Motherwell, 1961) 1
Mason J (Third Lanark 1949–51) 7
Masson D (QPR, Derby, 1976–78) 17
Mathers D (Partick, 1954) 1
Matteo D (Leeds, 2001–02) 6
May S (Sheffield Wed, 2015) 1
McAllister B (Wimbledon, 1997) 3
McAllister G (Leicester, Leeds, Coventry, 1990–99) 57
McAllister J (Livingston, 2004) 1
McArthur J (Wigan, Crystal Palace, 2011–16) 24
McAvennie F (West Ham, Celtic, 1986–88) 5
McBride J (Celtic, 1967) 2
McCall S (Everton, Rangers, 1990–98) 40
McCalliog J (Sheffield Wed, Wolves, 1967–71) 5
McCann N (Hearts, Rangers, Southampton, 1999–2006) 26
McCann R (Motherwell, 1959–61) 5
McClair B (Celtic, Manchester Utd, 1987–93) 30
McCloy P (Rangers, 1973) 4
McCoist A (Rangers, Kilmarnock, 1986–99) 61
McColl I (Rangers, 1950–58) 14
McCormack R (Motherwell, Cardiff, Leeds, Fulham, 2008–16) 13
McCreadie E (Chelsea, 1965–9) 23
McCulloch L (Wigan, Rangers, 2005–11) 18
McDonald J (Sunderland, 1956) 2
McEveley, J (Derby, 2008) 3
McFadden J (Motherwell, Everton, Birmingham, 2002–11) 48
McFarlane W (Hearts, 1947) 1
McGarr E (Aberdeen, 1970) 2
McGarvey F (Liverpool, Celtic, 1979–84) 7
McGhee M (Aberdeen, 1983–84) 4
McGinlay J (Bolton, 1995–97) 13
McGinn J (Hibernian, 2016) 1
McGrain D (Celtic, 1973–82) 62
McGregor A (Rangers, Besiktas, Hull, 2007–16) 35
McGrory J (Kilmarnock, 1965–66) 3
McInally A (Aston Villa, Bayern Munich, 1989–90) 8
McInally J (Dundee Utd, 1987–93) 10

McInnes D (WBA, 2003) 2
McKay B (Rangers, 2016) 1
McKean R (Rangers, 1976) 1
McKimmie S (Aberdeen, 1989–96) 40
McKinlay T (Celtic, 1996–98) 22
McKinlay W (Dundee Utd, Blackburn, 1994–99) 29
McKinnon R (Rangers, 1966–71) 28
McKinnon R (Motherwell, 1994–95) 3
McLaren A (Preston, 1947–48) 4
McLaren A (Hearts, Rangers, 1992–96) 24
McLaren A (Kilmarnock, 2001) 1
McLean G (Dundee, 1968) 1
McLean K (Aberdeen, 2016) 1
McLean T (Kilmarnock, Rangers, 1969–71) 6
McLeish A (Aberdeen, 1980–93) 77
McLintock F (Leicester, Arsenal, 1963–71) 9
McManus S (Celtic, Middlesbrough, 2007–11) 26
McMillan I (Airdrie, 1952–61) 6
McNamara J (Celtic, Wolves, 1997–2006) 33
McNamee D (Livingston, 2004–06) 4
McNaught W (Raith, 1951–55) 5
McNaughton K (Aberdeen, Cardiff, 2002–08) 4
McNeill W (Celtic, 1961–72) 29
McPhail J (Celtic, 1950–54) 5
McPherson D (Hearts, Rangers, 1989–93) 27
McQueen G (Leeds, Manchester Utd, 1974–81) 30
McStay P (Celtic, 1984–97) 76
McSwegan G (Hearts, 2000) 2
Millar J (Rangers, 1963) 2
Miller C (Dundee Utd, 2001) 1
Miller K (Rangers, Wolves, Celtic, Derby, Rangers, Bursaspor, Cardiff, Vancouver, 2001–14) 69
Miller L (Dundee Utd, Aberdeen 2006–10) 3
Miller W (Celtic, 1946–47) 6
Miller W (Aberdeen, 1975–90) 65
Mitchell R (Newcastle, 1951) 2
Mochan N (Celtic, 1954) 3
Moir W (Bolton, 1950) 1
Moncur R (Newcastle, 1968–72) 16
Morgan W (Burnley, Manchester Utd, 1968–74) 21
Morris H (East Fife, 1950) 1
Morrison J (WBA, 2008–16) 41
Mudie J (Blackpool, 1957–58) 17
Mulgrew C (Celtic, 2012–16) 24
Mulhall G (Aberdeen, Sunderland, 1960–64) 3
Munro F (Wolves, 1971–75) 9
Munro I (St Mirren, 1979–80) 7
Murdoch R (Celtic, 1966–70) 12
Murray I (Hibernian, Rangers, 2003–06) 6
Murray J (Hearts, 1958) 5
Murray S (Aberdeen, 1972) 1
Murty G (Reading, 2004–08) 4

Naismith S (Kilmarnock, Rangers, Everton, Norwich, 2007–16) 43
Narey D (Dundee Utd, 1977–89) 35
Naysmith G (Hearts, Everton, Sheffield Utd, 2000–09) 46
Neilson R (Hearts, 2007) 1
Nevin P (Chelsea, Everton, Tranmere, 1987–96) 28
Nicholas C (Celtic, Arsenal, Aberdeen, 1983–89) 20
Nicholson B (Dunfermline, 2001–05) 3
Nicol S (Liverpool, 1985–92) 27
O'Connor G (Hibernian, Lokomotiv Moscow, Birmingham, 2002–10) 16
O'Donnell P (Motherwell, 1994) 1
O'Hare J (Derby, 1970–72) 13
O'Neil B (Celtic, VfL Wolfsburg, Derby, Preston, 1996–2006) 7
O'Neil J (Hibernian, 2001) 1
Ormond W (Hibernian, 1954–59) 6
Orr T (Morton, 1952) 2

Parker A (Falkirk, Everton, 1955–56) 15
Parlane D (Rangers, 1973–77) 12
Paterson C (Hearts. 2016) 1
Paton A (Motherwell, 1952) 2
Pearson S (Motherwell, Celtic, Derby, 2004–07) 10
Pearson T (Newcastle, 1947) 2
Penman A (Dundee, 1966) 1
Pettigrew W (Motherwell, 1976–77) 5
Phillips M (Blackpool, QPR, 2012–16) 4
Plenderleith J (Manchester City, 1961) 1
Pressley S (Hearts, 2000–07) 32
Provan D (Rangers, 1964–66) 5
Provan D (Celtic, 1980–82) 10

Quashie N (Portsmouth, Southampton, WBA, 2004–07) 14
Quinn P (Motherwell, 1961–62) 4

Rae G (Dundee, Rangers, Cardiff, 2001–09) 14
Redpath W (Motherwell, 1949–52) 9
Reilly L (Hibernian, 1949–57) 38
Rhodes J (Huddersfield, Blackburn, 2012–15) 13
Ring T (Clyde, 1953–58) 12
Rioch B (Derby, Everton, 1975–78) 24
Riordan D (Hibernian, 2006–10) 3
Ritchie M (Bournemouth, 2015–16) 10
Ritchie P (Hearts, Bolton, 1999–2000) 7
Ritchie W (Rangers, 1962) 1
Robb D (Aberdeen, 1971) 5
Robertson A (Clyde, 1955) 5
Robertson A (Dundee Utd, Hull, 2014–16) 10
Robertson D (Rangers, 1992–94) 3
Robertson H (Dundee, 1962) 1
Robertson J (Tottenham, 1964) 1
Robertson J (Nottm Forest, Derby, 1978–84) 28
Robertson J (Hearts, 1991–96) 16
Robertson S (Dundee Utd, 2009–11) 2
Robinson R (Dundee, 1974–75) 4

Robson B (Celtic, Middlesbrough, 2008–12) 17
Ross M (Rangers, 2002–04) 13
Rough A (Partick, Hibernian, 1976–86) 53
Rougvie D (Aberdeen, 1984) 1
Russell J (Derby, 2015–16) 4
Rutherford E (Rangers, 1948) 1

Saunders S (Motherwell, 2011) 1
Schaedler E (Hibernian, 1974) 1
Scott A (Rangers, Everton, 1957–66) 16
Scott J (Hibernian, 1966) 1
Scott J (Dundee, 1971) 2
Scoular J (Portsmouth, 1951–53) 9
Severin S (Hearts, Aberdeen, 2002–07) 15
Sharp G (Everton, 1985–88) 12
Shaw D (Hibernian, 1947–49) 8
Shaw J (Rangers, 1947) 4
Shearer D (Aberdeen, 1994–96) 7
Shearer R (Rangers, 1961) 4
Shinnie A (Inverness, 2013) 1
Simpson N (Aberdeen, 1983–88) 5
Simpson R (Celtic, 1967–69) 5
Sinclair J (Leicester, 1966) 1
Smith D (Aberdeen, Rangers, 1966–68) 2
Smith G (Hibernian, 1947–57) 18
Smith H (Hearts, 1988–92) 3
Smith JE (Celtic, 1959) 2
Smith J (Aberdeen, Newcastle, 1968–74) 4
Smith J (Celtic, 2003) 2
Snodgrass R (Leeds, Norwich, 2011–16) 17
Souness G (Middlesbrough, Liverpool, Sampdoria, Rangers, 1975–86) 54
Speedie D (Chelsea, Coventry, 1985–89) 10
Spencer J (Chelsea, QPR, 1995–97) 14
Stanton P (Hibernian, 1966–74) 16
Steel W (Morton, Derby, Dundee, 1947–53) 30
Stein C (Rangers, Coventry, 1969–73) 21
Stephen J (Bradford City, 1947–48) 2
Stewart D (Leeds, 1978) 1
Stewart J (Kilmarnock, Middlesbrough, 1977–79) 2
Stewart M (Manchester Utd, Hearts 2002–09) 4
Stewart R (West Ham, 1981–7) 10
St John I (Motherwell, Liverpool, 1959–65) 21
Stockdale R (Middlesbrough, 2002–03) 5
Strachan G (Aberdeen, Manchester Utd, Leeds, 1980–92) 50
Sturrock P (Dundee Utd, 1981–87) 20
Sullivan N (Wimbledon, Tottenham, 1997–2003) 28

Teale G (Wigan, Derby, 2006–09) 13
Telfer P (Coventry, 2000) 1
Telfer W (St Mirren, 1954) 1
Thomson K (Rangers, Middlesbrough, 2009–11) 3
Thompson S (Dundee Utd, Rangers, 2002–05) 16
Thomson W (St Mirren, 1980–84) 7
Thornton W (Rangers, 1947–52) 7
Tierney K (Celtic, 2016) 1
Toner W (Kilmarnock, 1959) 2
Turnbull E (Hibernian, 1948–58) 8

Ure I (Dundee, Arsenal, 1962–68) 11

Waddell W (Rangers, 1947–55) 17
Walker A (Celtic, 1988–95) 3
Walker N (Hearts, 1993–96) 2
Wallace I (Coventry, 1978–79) 3
Wallace L (Hearts, Rangers, 2010–14) 8
Wallace R (Preston, 2010) 1
Wallace W (Hearts, Celtic, 1965–69) 7
Wardhaugh J (Hearts, 1955–57) 2
Wark J (Ipswich, Liverpool, 1979–85) 29
Watson J (Motherwell, Huddersfield, 1948–54) 2
Watson R (Motherwell, 1971) 1
Watt T (Charlton, 2016) 1
Webster A (Hearts, Rangers, Hearts, 2003–13) 28
Weir A (Motherwell, 1959–60) 6
Weir D (Hearts, Everton, Rangers, 1997–2011) 69
Weir P (St Mirren, Aberdeen, 1980–84) 6
White J (Falkirk, Tottenham, 1959–64) 22
Whittaker S (Rangers, Norwich, 2010–16) 31
Whyte D (Celtic, Middlesbrough, Aberdeen, 1988–99) 12
Wilkie L (Dundee, 2002–03) 11
Williams G (Nottm Forest, 2002–03) 5
Wilson A (Portsmouth, 1954) 1
Wilson D (Liverpool, 2011–12) 5
Wilson D (Rangers, 1961–65) 22
Wilson I (Leicester, Everton, 1987–8) 5
Wilson M (Celtic, 2011) 1
Wilson P (Celtic, 1975) 1
Wilson R (Arsenal, 1972) 2
Wood G (Everton, Arsenal, 1978–82) 4
Woodburn W (Rangers, 1947–52) 24
Wright K (Hibernian, 1992) 1
Wright S (Aberdeen, 1993) 2
Wright T (Sunderland, 1953) 3

Yeats R (Liverpool, 1965–66) 2
Yorston H (Aberdeen, 1955) 1
Young A (Hearts, Everton, 1960–66) 8
Young G (Rangers, 1947–57) 53
Younger T (Hibernian, Liverpool, 1955–58) 24

WALES

Aizlewood M (Charlton, Leeds, Bradford City, Bristol City, Cardiff, 1986–95) 39
Allchurch I (Swansea City, Newcastle, Cardiff, 1951–66) 68
Allchurch L (Swansea City, Sheffield Utd, 1955–64) 11
Allen B (Coventry, 1951) 2
Allen J (Swansea, Liverpool, 2009–16) 31
Allen M (Watford, Norwich, Millwall, Newcastle, 1986–94) 14

Baker C (Cardiff, 1958–62) 7
Baker W (Cardiff, 1948) 1
Bale G (Southampton, Tottenham, Real Madrid, 2006–16) 61
Barnard D (Barnsley, Grimsby, 1998–2004 24
Barnes W (Arsenal, 1948–55) 22
Bellamy C (Norwich, Coventry, Newcastle, Blackburn, Liverpool, West Ham, Manchester City, Liverpool, Cardiff, 1998–2014) 78
Berry G (Wolves, Stoke, 1979–83) 5
Blackmore C (Manchester Utd, Middlesbrough, 1985–97) 39
Blake D (Cardiff, Crystal Palace, 2011–13) 14
Blake N (Sheffield Utd, Bolton, Blackburn, Wolves, 1994–2004) 29
Bodin P (Swindon, Crystal Palace, Swindon, 1990–95) 23
Bowen D (Arsenal, 1955–59) 19
Bowen J (Swansea City, Birmingham, 1994–97) 2
Bowen M (Tottenham, Norwich, West Ham, 1986–97) 41
Boyle T (Crystal Palace, 1981) 2
Bradley M (Walsall, 2010) 1
Bradshaw T (Walsall, 2016) 1
Brown J (Gillingham, Blackburn, Aberdeen, 2006–12) 3
Browning M (Bristol Rov, Huddersfield, 1996–97) 5
Burgess R (Tottenham, 1947–54) 32
Burton A (Norwich, Newcastle, 1963–72) 9

Cartwright L (Coventry, Wrexham, 1974–79) 7
Charles Jeremy (Swansea City, QPR, Oxford Utd, 1981–87) 19
Charles John (Leeds, Juventus, Cardiff, 1950–65) 38
Charles M (Swansea City, Arsenal, Cardiff, 1955–63) 31
Chester J (Hull, WBA, 2014–16) 17
Church S (Reading, Nottm Forest, Charlton, MK Dons 2009–16) 38
Clarke R (Manchester City, 1949–56) 22
Coleman C (Crystal Palace, Blackburn, Fulham, 1992–2002) 32
Collins D (Sunderland, Stoke, 2005–11) 12
Collins J (Cardiff, West Ham, Aston Villa, West Ham, 2004–16) 49
Collison J (West Ham, 2008–14) 17
Cornforth J (Swansea City, 1995) 2
Cotterill D (Bristol City, Wigan, Sheffield Utd, Swansea, Doncaster, Birmingham, 2006–16) 23
Coyne D (Tranmere, Grimsby, Leicester, Burnley, Tranmere, 1996–2008) 16
Crofts A (Gillingham, Brighton, Norwich, Brighton, 2006–16) 28
Crossley M (Nottm Forest, Middlesbrough, Fulham, 1997–2005) 8
Crowe V (Aston Villa, 1959–63) 16
Curtis A (Swansea City, Leeds, Southampton, Cardiff, 1976–87) 35
Daniel R (Arsenal, Sunderland, 1951–57) 21
Davies A (Manchester Utd, Newcastle, Swansea City, Bradford City, 1983–90) 13
Davies A (Yeovil 2006) 1
Davies B (Swansea, Tottenham 2013–16) 25
Davies C (Charlton, 1972) 1
Davies C (Oxford, Verona, Oldham, Barnsley, Bolton, 2006–14) 7
Davies D (Everton, Wrexham, Swansea City 1975–83) 52
Davies ER (Newcastle, 1953–58) 6
Davies G (Fulham, Chelsea, Manchester City, 1980–86) 16
Davies RT (Norwich, Southampton, Portsmouth, 1964–74) 29
Davies RW (Bolton, Newcastle, Man Utd, Man City, Blackpool, 1964–74) 34
Davies S (Manchester Utd, 1996) 1
Davies S (Tottenham, Everton, Fulham, 2001–10) 58
Davis G (Wrexham, 1978) 3
Deacy N (PSV Eindhoven, Beringen, 1977–79) 12
Delaney M (Aston Villa, 2000–07) 36
Derrett S (Cardiff, 1969–71) 4
Dibble A (Luton, Manchester City, 1986–89) 3
Dorman A (St Mirren, Crystal Palace, 2010–11) 3
Dummett P (Newcastle, 2014–16) 2
Duffy R (Portsmouth, 2006–08) 13
Durban A (Derby, 1966–72) 27
Dwyer P (Cardiff, 1978–80) 10

Eardley N (Oldham, Blackpool, 2008–11) 16
Earnshaw R (Cardiff, WBA, Norwich, Derby, Nottm Forest, Cardiff, 2002–13) 59
Easter J (Wycombe, Crystal Palace, Millwall, 2007–14) 12
Eastwood F (Wolves, Coventry, 2008–11) 11
Edwards C (Swansea City, 1996) 1
Edwards D (Luton, Wolves, 2007–16) 35
Edwards, G (Birmingham, Cardiff, 1947–50) 12
Edwards, I (Chester, Wrexham, 1978–80) 4
Edwards, L (Charlton, 1957) 2
Edwards, R (Bristol City, 1997–98) 4
Edwards, R (Aston Villa, Wolves, 2003–07) 15
Emmanuel W (Bristol City, 1973) 2
England M (Blackburn, Tottenham, 1962–75) 44
Evans B (Swansea City, Hereford, 1972–74) 7
Evans C (Manchester City, Sheffield Utd, 2008–11) 13
Evans I (Crystal Palace, 1976–78) 13
Evans P (Brentford, Bradford City, 2002–03) 2
Evans R (Swansea City, 1964) 1
Evans S (Wrexham, 2007–09) 7

Felgate D (Lincoln, 1984) 1
Fletcher C (Bournemouth, West Ham, Crystal Palace, 2004–09) 36

Flynn B (Burnley, Leeds, 1975–84) 66
Fon Williams O (Inverness, 2016) 1
Ford T (Swansea City, Sunderland, Aston Villa, Cardiff, 1947–57) 38
Foulkes W (Newcastle, 1952–54) 11
Freestone R (Swansea City, 2000–03) 1

Gabbidon D (Cardiff, West Ham, QPR, Crystal Palace, 2002–14) 49
Garner G (Leyton Orient, 2006) 1
Giggs R (Manchester Utd, 1992–2007) 64
Giles D (Swansea City, Crystal Palace, 1980–83) 12
Godfrey B (Preston, 1964–65) 3
Goss J (Norwich, 1991–96) 9
Green C (Birmingham, 1965–69) 15
Green R (Wolves, 1998) 2
Griffiths A (Wrexham, 1971–77) 17
Griffiths H (Swansea City, 1953) 1
Griffiths M (Leicester, 1947–54) 11
Gunter C (Cardiff, Tottenham, Nottm Forest, Reading, 2007–16) 73

Hall G (Chelsea, 1988–92) 9
Harrington A (Cardiff, 1956–62) 11
Harris C (Leeds, 1976–82) 24
Harris W (Middlesbrough, 1954–58) 6
Hartson J (Arsenal, West Ham, Wimbledon, Coventry, Celtic, 1995–2006) 51
Haworth S (Cardiff, Coventry, 1997–8) 5
Henley A (Blackburn, 2016) 2
Hennessey T (Birmingham, Nottm Forest, Derby, 1962–73) 39
Hennessey W (Wolves, Crystal Palace, 2007–16) 62
Hewitt R (Cardiff, 1958) 5
Hill M (Ipswich, 1972) 2
Hockey T (Sheffield Utd, Norwich, Aston Villa, 1972–74) 9
Hodges G (Wimbledon, Newcastle, Watford, Sheffield Utd, 1984–96) 18
Holden A (Chester, 1984) 1
Hole B (Cardiff, Blackburn, Aston Villa, Swansea City, 1963–71) 30
Hollins D (Newcastle, 1962–66) 11
Hopkins J (Fulham, Crystal Palace, 1983–90) 16
Hopkins M (Tottenham, 1956–63) 34
Horne B (Portsmouth, Southampton, Everton, Birmingham, 1988–97) 59
Howells R (Cardiff, 1954) 2
Hughes C (Luton, Wimbledon, 1992–97) 8
Hughes I (Luton, 1951) 4
Hughes M (Manchester Utd, Barcelona, Bayern Munich, Manchester Utd, Chelsea, Southampton, 1984–99) 72
*Hughes W (Birmingham, 1947) 3
Hughes WA (Blackburn, 1949) 5
Humphreys J (Everton, 1947) 1
Huws E (Manchester City, Wigan, 2014–16) 7

Isgrove L (Southampton, 2016) 1

Jackett K (Watford, 1983–88) 31
James EG (Blackpool, 1966–71) 9
James L (Burnley, Derby, QPR, Swansea City, Sunderland, 1972–83) 54
James R (Swansea, Stoke, QPR, Leicester, Swansea, 1979–88) 47
Jarvis A (Hull, 1967) 3
Jenkins S (Swansea, Huddersfield, 1996–2002) 16
John D (Cardiff, 2014) 2
Johnson A (Nottm Forest, WBA, 1999–2005) 15
Johnson M (Swansea, 1964) 1
Jones A (Port Vale, Charlton, 1987–90) 6
Jones Barrie (Swansea, Plymouth Argyle, Cardiff, 1963–9) 15
*Jones Bryn (Arsenal, 1947–9) 4
Jones C (Swansea, Tottenham, Fulham, 1954–69) 59
Jones D (Norwich, 1976–80) 8
Jones E (Swansea, Tottenham, 1947–9) 4
Jones J (Liverpool, Wrexham, Chelsea, Huddersfield, 1976–86) 72
Jones K (Aston Villa, 1950) 1
Jones L (Liverpool, Tranmere, 1997) 2
Jones M (Leeds, Leicester, 2000–03) 13
Jones M (Wrexham, 2007–08) 2
Jones P (Stockport, Southampton, Wolves, Millwall, QPR, 1997–2007) 50
Jones R (Sheffield Wed, 1994) 1
*Jones TG (Everton, 1946–49) 13
Jones V (Wimbledon, 1995–97) 9
Jones W (Bristol Rov, 1971) 1

Kelsey J (Arsenal, 1954–62) 41
King A (Leicester, 2009–16) 36
King J (Swansea, 1955) 1
Kinsey N (Norwich, Birmingham, 1951–56) 7
Knill A (Swansea, 1989) 1
Koumas J (Tranmere, WBA, Wigan, 2001–09) 34
Krzywicki R (WBA, Huddersfield, 1970–72) 8

Lambert R (Liverpool, 1947–9) 5
Law B (QPR, 1990) 1
Lawrence T (Leicester, 2016) 4
Ledley J (Cardiff, Celtic, Crystal Palace, 2006–16) 67
Lea C (Ipswich, 1965) 2
Leek K (Leicester, Newcastle, Birmingham, Northampton, 1961–65) 13
Legg A (Birmingham, Cardiff, 1996–2001) 6
Lever A (Leicester, 1953) 1
Lewis D (Swansea, 1983) 1
Llewellyn C (Norwich, Wrexham, 1998–2007) 6
Lloyd B (Wrexham, 1976) 3
Lovell S (Crystal Palace, Millwall, 1982–86) 6
Lowndes S (Newport, Millwall, Brighton, Barnsley, 1983–88) 10

Lowrie G (Coventry, Newcastle, 1948–49) 4
Lucas M (Leyton Orient, 1962–63) 4
Lucas W (Swansea, 1949–51) 7
Lynch J (Huddersfield, 2013) 1

MacDonald S (Swansea, Bournemouth 2011–2015) 2
Maguire G (Portsmouth, 1990–92) 7
Mahoney J (Stoke, Middlesbrough, Swansea, 1968–83) 51
Mardon P (WBA, 1996) 1
Margetson M (Cardiff, 2004) 1
Marriott A (Wrexham, 1996–98) 5
Marustik C (Swansea, 1982–83) 6
Matthews A (Cardiff, Celtic, Sunderland, 2011–16) 13
Medwin T (Swansea, Tottenham, 1953–63) 30
Melville A (Swansea, Oxford Utd, Sunderland, Fulham, West Ham, 1990–2005) 65
Mielczarek R (Rotherham, 1971) 1
Millington A (WBA, Peterborough, Swansea, 1963–72) 21
Moore G (Cardiff, Chelsea, Manchester Utd, Northampton, Charlton, 1960–71) 21
Morgan C (MK Dons, Peterborough, Preston, 2007–11) 23
Morison S (Millwall, Norwich, 2011–13) 20
Morris W (Burnley, 1947–52) 5
Myhill B (Hull, WBA, 2008–14) 20

Nardiello D (Coventry, 1978) 2
Nardiello D (Barnsley, 2007–08) 1
Neilson A (Newcastle, Southampton, 1992–97) 5
Nicholas P (Crystal Palace, Arsenal, Crystal Palace, Luton, Aberdeen, Chelsea, Watford, 1979–92) 73
Niedzwiecki E (Chelsea, 1985–88) 2
Nogan L (Watford, Reading, 1991–96) 2
Norman T (Hull, 1986–88) 5
Nurse M (Swansea, Middlesbrough, 1960–63) 12
Nyatanga L (Derby, Bristol City, 2006–11) 34

O'Sullivan P (Brighton, 1973–78) 3
Oster J (Everton, Sunderland, 1997–2005) 13

Page M (Birmingham, 1971–79) 28
Page R (Watford, Sheffield Utd, Cardiff, Coventry, 1997–2006) 41
Palmer D (Swansea, 1957) 3
Parry J (Swansea, 1951) 1
Parry P (Cardiff, 2004–07) 12
Partridge D (Motherwell, Bristol City, 2005–06) 7
Pascoe C (Swansea, Sunderland, 1984–92) 10
Paul R (Swansea, Manchester City, 1949–56) 33
Pembridge M (Luton, Derby, Sheffield Wed, Benfica, Everton, Fulham, 1992–2005) 54
Perry J (Cardiff, 1994) 1
Phillips D (Plymouth Argyle, Manchester City, Coventry, Norwich, Nottm Forest, 1984–96) 62
Phillips J (Chelsea, 1973–78) 4
Phillips L (Cardiff, Aston Villa, Swansea, Charlton, 1971–82) 58
Pipe D (Coventry, 2003) 1
Pontin K (Cardiff, 1980) 2
Powell A (Leeds, Everton, Birmingham, 1947–51) 8
Powell D (Wrexham, Sheffield Utd, 1968–71) 11
Powell I (QPR, Aston Villa, 1947–51) 8
Price L (Ipswich, Derby, Crystal Palace, 2006–13) 11
Price P (Luton, Tottenham, 1980–84) 25
Pring K (Rotherham, 1966–67) 3
Pritchard H (Bristol City, 1985) 1

Ramsey A (Arsenal, 2009–16) 44
Rankmore F (Peterborough, 1966) 1
Ratcliffe K (Everton, Cardiff, 1981–93) 59
Ready K (QPR, 1997–98) 5
Reece G (Sheffield Utd, Cardiff, 1966–75) 29
Reed W (Ipswich, 1955) 2
Rees A (Birmingham, 1984) 1
Rees J (Luton, 1992) 1
Rees R (Coventry, WBA, Nottm Forest, 1965–72) 39
Rees W (Cardiff, Tottenham, 1949–50) 4
Ribeiro C (Bristol City, 2010–11) 2
Richards A (Swansea, Fulham, 2012–16) 10
Richards, S (Cardiff, 1947) 1
Ricketts S (Swansea, Hull, Bolton, Wolves, 2005–14) 52
Roberts A (QPR, 1993–97) 2
Roberts D (Oxford Utd, Hull, 1973–78) 17
Roberts G (Tranmere 2000–06) 9
Roberts I (Watford, Huddersfield, Leicester, Norwich, 1990–2002) 15
Roberts J (Arsenal, Birmingham, 1971–76) 22
Roberts J (Bolton, 1949) 1
Roberts N (Wrexham, Wigan, 2000–04) 4
Roberts P (Portsmouth, 1974) 4
Roberts S (Wrexham, 2005) 1
Robinson C (Wolves, Portsmouth, Sunderland, Norwich, Toronto 2000–08) 52
Robinson J (Charlton, 1996–2002) 30
Robson-Kanu H (Reading, 2010–15) 35
Rodrigues P (Cardiff, Leicester, City Sheffield Wed, 1965–74) 40
Rogan A (Celtic, Sunderland, Millwall, 1988–97) 18
Rouse V (Crystal Palace, 1959) 1
Rowley T (Tranmere, 1959) 1
Rush I (Liverpool, Juventus, Liverpool, 1980–96) 73

Saunders D (Brighton, Oxford Utd, Derby, Liverpool, Aston Villa, Galatasaray, Nottm Forest, Sheffield Utd, Benfica, Bradford City, 1986–2001) 75

Savage R (Crewe, Leicester, Birmingham, 1996–2005) 39
Sayer P (Cardiff, 1977–8) 7
Scrine F (Swansea, 1950) 2
Sear C (Manchester City, 1963) 1
Sherwood A (Cardiff, Newport, 1947–57) 41
Shortt W (Plymouth Argyle, 1947–53) 12
Showers D (Cardiff, 1975) 2
Sidlow C (Liverpool, 1947–50) 7
Slatter N (Bristol Rov, Oxford Utd, 1983–89) 22
Smallman D (Wrexham, Everton, 1974–6) 7
Southall N (Everton, 1982–97) 92
Speed G (Leeds, Everton, Newcastle, 1990–2004) 85
Sprake G (Leeds, Birmingham, 1964–75) 37
Stansfield F (Cardiff, 1949) 1
Stevenson B (Leeds, Birmingham, 1978–82) 15
Stevenson N (Swansea, 1982–83) 4
Stitfall R (Cardiff, 1953–57) 2
Stock B (Doncaster, 2010–11) 3
Sullivan D (Cardiff, 1953–60) 17
Symons K (Portsmouth, Manchester City, Fulham, Crystal Palace, 1992–2004) 37

Tapscott D (Arsenal, Cardiff, 1954–59) 14
Taylor G (Crystal Palace, Sheffield Utd, Burnley, Nottm Forest, 1996–2005) 15
Taylor J (Reading, 2015) 1
Taylor N (Wrexham, Swansea, 2010–16) 34
Thatcher B (Leicester, Manchester City, 2004–05) 7
Thomas D (Swansea, 1957–58) 2
Thomas M (Wrexham, Manchester Utd, Everton, Brighton, Stoke, Chelsea, WBA, 1977–86) 51
Thomas M (Newcastle, 1987) 1
Thomas R (Swindon, Derby, Cardiff, 1967–78) 50
Thomas S (Fulham, 1948–49) 4
Toshack J (Cardiff, Liverpool, Swansea, 1969–80) 40
Trollope P (Derby, Fulham, Northampton, 1997–2003) 9
Tudur Jones O (Swansea, Norwich, Hibernian, 2008–14) 7

Van den Hauwe P (Everton, 1985–89) 13
Vaughan D (Crewe, Real Sociedad, Blackpool, Sunderland, Nottm Forest, 20013–16) 42
Vaughan N (Newport, Cardiff, 1983–85) 10
Vearncombe G (Cardiff, 1958–61) 2
Vernon R (Blackburn, Everton, Stoke, 1957–68) 32
Villars A (Cardiff, 1974) 3
Vokes S (Wolves, Burnley, 2008–16) 44

Walley T (Watford, 1971) 1
Walsh I (Crystal Palace, 1980–82) 18
Ward D (Bristol Rov, Cardiff, 1959–62) 2
Ward D (Notts Co, Nottm Forest, 2000–04) 5
Ward D (Liverpool, 2016) 3
Webster C (Manchester Utd, 1957–58) 4
Weston R (Arsenal, Cardiff, 2000–05) 7
Williams A (Stockport, Swansea, 2008–16) 65
Williams A (Reading, Wolves, Reading, 1994–2003) 13
Williams A (Southampton, 1997–98) 2
Williams D (Norwich, 1986–87) 5
Williams G (Cardiff, 1951) 1
Williams G (Derby, Ipswich, 1988–96) 13
Williams G (West Ham, 2006) 2
Williams G (Fulham, 2014–16) 7
Williams GE (WBA, 1960–69) 26
Williams GG (Swansea, 1961–62) 5
Williams HJ (Swansea, 1965–72) 3
Williams HT (Newport, Leeds, 1949–50) 4
Williams J (Crystal Palace, 2013–16) 17
Williams S (WBA, Southampton, 1954–66) 43
Wilson H (Liverpool, 2014) 1
Wilson J (Bristol City, 2014) 1
Witcomb D (WBA, Sheffield Wed, 1947) 3
Woosnam P (Leyton Orient, West Ham, Aston Villa, 1959–63) 17
Yorath T (Leeds, Coventry, Tottenham, Vancouver Whitecaps 1970–81) 59
Young E (Wimbledon, Crystal Palace, Wolves, 1990–96) 21

NORTHERN IRELAND

Aherne T (Belfast Celtic, Luton, 1947–50) 4
Anderson T (Manchester Utd, Swindon, Peterborough, 1973–79) 22
Armstrong G (Tottenham, Watford, Real Mallorca, WBA, 1977–86) 63

Baird C (Southampton, Fulham, Burnley, WBA, Derby, 2003–16) 79
Barr H (Linfield, Coventry, 1962–63) 3
Barton A (Preston, 2011) 1
Best G (Manchester Utd, Fulham, 1964–77) 37
Bingham W (Sunderland, Luton, Everton, Port Vale, 1951–64) 56
Black K (Luton, Nottm Forest, 1988–94) 30
Blair R (Oldham, 1975–76) 5
Blanchflower RD (Barnsley, Aston Villa, Tottenham, 1950–63) 56
Blanchflower J (Manchester Utd, 1954–58) 12
Blayney A (Doncaster, Linfield, 2006–11) 5
Bowler G (Hull, 1950) 3
Boyce L (Werder Bremen, Ross Co, 2011–16) 7
Braithwaite R (Linfield, Middlesbrough, 1962–65) 10
Braniff K (Portadown, 2010) 2
Brennan R (Luton, Birmingham, Fulham, 1949–51) 5
Briggs W (Manchester Utd, Swansea, 1962–65) 2

Brotherston N (Blackburn, 1980–85) 27
Bruce A (Hull, 2013–14) 2
Bruce W (Glentoran, 1961–67) 2
Brunt C (Sheffield Wed, WBA, 2005–16) 54
Bryan, M (Watford, 2010) 2

Camp L (Nottm Forest, 2011–13) 9
Campbell D (Nottm Forest, Charlton, 1987–88) 10
Campbell J (Fulham, 1951) 2
Campbell R (Crusaders, 1963–65) 2
Campbell R (Bradford City, 1982) 2
Campbell W (Dundee, 1968–70) 6
Capaldi A (Plymouth Argyle, Cardiff, 2004–08) 22
Carey J (Manchester Utd, 1947–49) 7
Carroll R (Wigan, Manchester Utd, West Ham, Olympiacos, Notts Co, 1997–2016) 44
Carson J (Ipswich, 2011–13) 4
Carson S (Coleraine, 2009) 1
Casey T (Newcastle, Portsmouth, 1955–59) 12
Casement C (Ipswich, 2009) 1
Caskey W (Derby, Tulsa, Roughnecks, 1979–82) 7
Cassidy T (Newcastle, Burnley, 1971–82) 24
Cathcart C (Blackpool, Watford, 2011–16) 32
Caughey M (Linfield, 1986) 2
Clarke C (Bournemouth, Southampton, QPR, Portsmouth, 1986–93) 38
Cleary J (Glentoran, 1982–85) 5
Clements D (Coventry, Sheffield Wed, Everton, New York Cosmos, 1965–76) 48
Clingan S (Nottm Forest, Norwich, Coventry, Kilmarnock, 2006–15) 39
Clyde, M (Wolves, 2005) 3
Coates C (Crusaders, 2009–11) 6
Cochrane A (Coleraine, Burnley, Middlesbrough, Gillingham, 1976–84) 26
Cochrane D (Leeds, 1947–50) 10
Connell T (Coleraine, 1978) 1
Coote A (Norwich, 1999–2000) 6
Cowan J (Newcastle, 1970) 1
Coyle F (Coleraine, Nottm Forest, 1956–58) 4
Coyle L (Derry City, 1989) 1
Coyle R (Sheffield Wed, 1973–74) 5
Craig D (Newcastle, 1967–75) 25
Craigan S (Partick, Motherwell, 2003–11) 54
Crossan E (Blackburn, 1950–55) 3
Crossan J (Sparta Rotterdam, Sunderland, Manchester City, Middlesbrough, 1960–68) 24
Cunningham W (St Mirren, Leicester, Dunfermline, 1951–62) 30
Cush W (Glenavon, Leeds, Portadown, 1951–62) 26

Dallas S (Crusaders, Brentford, Leeds, 2011–16) 17
D'Arcy S (Chelsea, Brentford, 1952–53) 5
Davis S (Aston Villa, Fulham, Rangers, Southampton, 2005–16) 87
Davison A (Bolton, Bradford City, Grimsby, 1996–97) 3
Dennison R (Wolves, 1988–97) 18
Devine J (Glentoran, 1990) 1
Dickson D (Coleraine, 1970–73) 4
Dickson T (Linfield, 1957) 1
Dickson W (Chelsea, Arsenal, 1951–55) 12
Doherty L (Linfield, 1985–88) 2
*Doherty P (Derby, Huddersfield, Doncaster, 1946–50) 6
Doherty T (Bristol City, 2003–05) 9
Donaghy M (Luton, Manchester Utd, Chelsea, 1980–94) 91
Donnelly L (Fulham, 2014) 1
Donnelly M (Crusaders, 2009) 1
Dougan D (Portsmouth, Blackburn, Aston Villa, Leicester, Wolves, 1958–73) 43
Douglas J (Belfast Celtic, 1947) 1
Dowd H (Glenavon, 1974) 3
Dowie I (Luton, Southampton, Crystal Palace, West Ham, QPR, 1990–2000) 59
Duff M (Cheltenham, Burnley, 2002–12) 24
Dunlop G (Linfield, 1985–90) 4

Eglington T (Everton, 1947–49) 6
Elder A (Burnley, Stoke, 1960–70) 40
Elliott S (Motherwell, Hull, 2001–08) 38
Evans C (Manchester Utd, Hull, Blackburn, 2009–16) 37
Evans J (Manchester Utd, WBA, 2007–16) 53

Farrell P (Everton, 1947–49) 7
Feeney J (Linfield, Swansea, 1947–50) 2
Feeney W (Glentoran, 1976) 1
Feeney W (Bournemouth, Luton, Cardiff, Oldham, Plymouth 2002–12) 46
Ferguson G (Linfield, 1999–2001) 5
Ferguson S (Newcastle, Millwall, 2009–16) 26
Ferguson W (Linfield, 1966–67) 2
Ferris R (Birmingham, 1950–52) 3
Fettis A (Hull, Nottm Forest, Blackburn, 1992–99) 25
Finney T (Sunderland, Cambridge Utd, 1975–80) 14
Fleming G (Nottm Forest, Manchester City, Barnsley, 1987–95) 31
Forde J (Ards, 1959–61) 4

Gallogly C (Huddersfield, 1951) 2
Garrett R (Stoke, Linfield, 2009–11) 5
Gaston R (Coleraine, 1969) 1
Gault M (Linfield, 2008) 1
Gillespie K (Manchester Utd, Newcastle, Blackburn, Leicester, Sheffield Utd, 1995–2009) 86
Gorman J (Wolves, 2010–12) 9
Gorman W (Brentford, 1947–48) 4
Graham W (Doncaster, 1951–99) 14
Gray P (Luton, Sunderland, Nancy, Burnley, Oxford Utd, 1993–2001) 25
Gregg H (Doncaster, Manchester Utd, 1954–64) 25

Griffin D (St Johnstone, Dundee Utd, Stockport, 1996–2004) 29
Grigg W (Walsall, Brentford, Wigan, 2012–16) 8

Hamill R (Glentoran, 1999) 1
Hamilton B (Linfield, Ipswich, Everton, Millwall, Swindon, 1969–80) 50
Hamilton G (Glentoran, Portadown, 2003–08) 5
Hamilton W (QPR, Burnley, Oxford Utd, 1978–86) 41
Harkin J (Southport, Shrewsbury, 1968–70) 5
Harvey M (Sunderland, 1961–71) 34
Hatton S (Linfield, 1963) 2
Healy D (Manchester Utd, Preston, Leeds, Fulham, Sunderland, Rangers, Bury, 2000–13) 95
Healy F (Coleraine, Glentoran, 1982–83) 4
Hegan D (WBA, Wolves, 1970–73) 7
Hill C (Sheffield Utd, Leicester, Trelleborg, Northampton, 1990–99) 27
Hill J (Norwich, Everton, 1959–64) 7
Hinton E (Fulham, Millwall, 1947–51) 7
Hodson L (Watford, MK Dons, 2011–16) 16
Holmes S (Wrexham, 2002) 1
Horlock K (Swindon, Manchester City, 1995–2003) 32
Hughes A (Newcastle, Aston Villa, Fulham, QPR, Brighton, Melbourne, 1997–2016) 103
Hughes J (Lincoln, 2006) 2
Hughes M (Oldham, 2006) 2
Hughes M (Manchester City, Strasbourg, West Ham, Wimbledon, Crystal Palace, 1992–2005) 71
Hughes P (Bury, 1987) 3
Hughes W (Bolton, 1951) 1
Humphries W (Ards, Coventry, Swansea, 1962–65) 14
Hunter A (Blackburn, Ipswich, 1970–80) 53
Hunter B (Wrexham, Reading, 1995–2000) 15
Hunter V (Coleraine, 1962) 2
Ingham M (Sunderland, Wrexham, 2005–07) 3
Irvine R (Linfield, Stoke, 1962–5) 8
Irvine W (Burnley, Preston, Brighton, 1963–72) 23

Jackson T (Everton, Nottm Forest, Manchester Utd, 1969–77) 35
Jamison J (Glentoran, 1976) 1
Jenkins I (Chester, Dundee Utd, 1997–2000) 6
Jennings P (Watford, Tottenham, Arsenal, Tottenham, 1964–86) 119
Johnson D (Blackburn, Birmingham, 1999–2010) 56
Johnston W (Glenavon, Oldham, 1962–66) 2
Jones J (Glenavon, 1956–57) 3
Jones S (Crewe, Burnley, 2003–08) 29
Keane T (Swansea, 1949) 1
Kee P (Oxford Utd, Ards, 1990–95) 9
Keith R (Newcastle, 1958–62) 23
Kelly H (Fulham, Southampton, 1950–51) 4
Kelly P (Barnsley, 1950) 1
Kennedy P (Watford, Wigan, 1999–2004) 20
Kirk A (Hearts, Boston, Northampton, Dunfermline, 2000–10) 11

Lafferty D (Burnley, 2012–16) 13
Lafferty K (Burnley, Rangers, Sion, Palermo, Norwich, 2006–16) 54
Lawrie J (Port Vale, 2009–10) 3
Lawther W (Sunderland, Blackburn, 1960–62) 4
Lennon N (Crewe, Leicester, Celtic, 1994–2002) 40
Little A (Rangers, 2009–13) 9
Lockhart N (Linfield, Coventry, Aston Villa, 1947–56) 8
Lomas S (Manchester City, West Ham, 1994–2003) 45
Lutton B (Wolves, West Ham, 1970–4) 6

Magennis J (Cardiff, Aberdeen, Kilmarnock, 2010–16) 22
Magill E (Arsenal, Brighton, 1962–66) 26
Magilton J (Oxford Utd, Southampton, Sheffield Wed, Ipswich, 1991–2002) 52
Mannus A (Linfield, St Johnstone, 2004–16) 8
Martin C (Glentoran, Leeds, Aston Villa, 1947–50) 6
McAdams W (Manchester City, Bolton, Leeds, 1954–62) 15
*McAlinden J (Portsmouth, Southend, 1947–49) 2
McArdle R (Rochdale, Aberdeen, Bradford, 2010–14) 7
McAuley G (Lincoln, Leicester, Ipswich, WBA, 2005–16) 65
McBride S (Glenavon, 1991–92) 4
McCabe J (Leeds, 1949–54) 6
McCann G (West Ham, Cheltenham, Barnsley, Scunthorpe, Peterborough, 2002–12) 39
McCarthy J (Port Vale, Birmingham, 1996–2001) 18
McCartney G (Sunderland, West Ham) Sunderland 2002–10) 34
McCavana T (Coleraine, 1954–55) 3
McCleary J (Cliftonville, 1955) 1
McClelland J (Arsenal, Fulham, 1961–67) 6
McClelland J (Mansfield, Rangers, Watford, Leeds, 1980–90) 53
McCourt F (Manchester City, 1952–53) 6
McCourt P (Rochdale, Celtic, Barnsley, Brighton, Luton, 2002–16) 18
McCoy R (Coleraine, 1987) 1
McCreery D (Manchester Utd, QPR, Tulsa, Newcastle, 1976–90) 67
McCrory S (Southend, 1958) 1
McCullough L (Doncaster, 2014–16) 5
McCullough W (Arsenal, Millwall, 1961–67) 10
McCurdy C (Linfield, 1980) 1
McDonald A (QPR, 1986–96) 52
McElhinney G (Bolton, 1984–85) 6
McEvilly L (Rochdale, 2002) 1
McFaul W (Linfield, Newcastle, 1967–74) 6
McGarry J (Cliftonville, 1951) 3

McGaughey M (Linfield, 1985) 1
McGibbon P (Manchester Utd, Wigan, 1995–2000) 7
McGinn N (Derry, Celtic, Aberdeen, 2009–16) 45
McGivern R (Manchester City, Hibernian, Port Vale, 2009–15) 23
McGovern M (Ross Co, Hamilton, 2010–16) 15
McGrath C (Tottenham, Manchester Utd 1974–79) 21
McIlroy J (Burnley, Stoke, 1952–66) 55
McIlroy S (Manchester Utd, Stoke, Manchester City, 1972–87) 88
McKay W (Inverness, Wigan, 2013–16) 11
McKeag W (Glentoran, 1968) 2
McKenna J (Huddersfield, 1950–52) 7
McKenzie R (Airdrie, 1967) 1
McKinney W (Falkirk, 1966) 1
McKnight A (Celtic, West Ham, 1988–89) 10
McLaughlin C (Preston, Fleetwood, 2012–16) 19
McLaughlin J (Shrewsbury, Swansea, 1962–66) 12
McLaughlin R (Liverpool, 2014–15) 3
McLean B (Motherwell, 2006) 1
McMahon G (Tottenham, Stoke, 1995–98) 17
McMichael A (Newcastle, 1950–60) 40
McMillan S (Manchester Utd, 1963) 2
McMordie A (Middlesbrough, 1969–73) 21
McMorran E (Belfast Celtic, Barnsley, Doncaster, 1947–57) 15
McNair P (Manchester Utd, 2015–16) 11
McNally B (Shrewsbury, 1987–88) 5
McPake J (Coventry, 2012) 1
McParland P (Aston Villa, Wolves, 1954–62) 34
McQuoid J (Millwall, 2011–12) 5
McVeigh P (Tottenham, Norwich, 1999–2005) 20
Montgomery F (Coleraine, 1955) 1
Moore C (Glentoran, 1949) 1
Moreland V (Derby, 1979–80) 6
Morgan S (Port Vale, Aston Villa, Brighton, Sparta Rotterdam, 1972–99) 18
Morrow S (Arsenal, QPR, 1990–2000) 39
Mulgrew J (Linfield, 2010) 2
Mullan G (Glentoran, 1983) 4
Mulryne P (Manchester Utd, Norwich, 1997–2005) 27
Murdock C (Preston, Hibernian, Crewe, Rotherham, 2000–06) 34

Napier R (Bolton, 1966) 1
Neill T (Arsenal, Hull, 1961–73) 59
Nelson S (Arsenal, Brighton, 1970–82) 51
Nicholl C (Aston Villa, Southampton, Grimsby, 1975–83) 51
Nicholl J (Manchester Utd, Toronto, Sunderland, Rangers, WBA, 1976–86) 73
Nicholson J (Manchester Utd, Huddersfield, 1961–72) 41
Nolan I (Sheffield Wed, Bradford City, Wigan, 1997–2002) 18
Norwood O (Manchester Utd, Huddersfield, Reading, 2011–16) 38

O'Boyle G (Dunfermline, St Johnstone, 1994–99) 13
O'Connor M (Crewe, Scunthorpe, Rotherham, 2008–14) 11
O'Doherty A (Coleraine, 1970) 2
O'Driscoll J (Swansea, 1949) 3
O'Kane W (Nottm Forest, 1970–75) 20
O'Neill C (Motherwell, 1989–91) 3
O'Neill J (Sunderland, 1962) 1
O'Neill J (Leicester, 1980–86) 39
O'Neill M (Distillery, Nottm Forest, Norwich, Manchester City, Notts Co, 1972–85) 64
O'Neill M (Newcastle, Dundee Utd, Hibernian, Coventry, 1989–97) 31
Owens J (Crusaders, 2011) 1

Parke J (Linfield, Hibernian, Sunderland, 1964–68)14
Paterson M (Scunthorpe, Burnley, Huddersfield, 2008–14) 22
Paton, P (Dundee Utd, 2014–16) 2
Patterson D (Crystal Palace, Luton, Dundee Utd, 1994–99) 17
Patterson R (Coleraine, Plymouth, 2010–11) 5
Peacock R (Celtic, Coleraine, 1952–62) 31
Penney S (Brighton, 1985–89) 17
Platt J (Middlesbrough, Ballymena, Coleraine, 1976–86) 23

Quinn J (Blackburn, Swindon, Leicester, Bradford City, West Ham, Bournemouth, Reading, 1985–96) 46
Quinn SJ (Blackpool, WBA, Willem 11, Sheffield Wed, Peterborough, Northampton, 1996–2007) 50

Rafferty P (Linfield, 1979) 1
Ramsey P (Leicester, 1984–89) 14
Reeves B (MK Dons, 2015) 2
Rice P (Arsenal, 1969–80) 49
Robinson S (Bournemouth, Luton, 1997–2008) 7
Rogan A (Celtic, Sunderland, Millwall, 1988–97) 18
Ross W (Newcastle, 1969) 1
Rowland K (West Ham, QPR, 1994–99) 19
Russell A (Linfield, 1947) 1
Ryan R (WBA, 1950) 1

Sanchez L (Wimbledon, 1987–89) 3
Scott J (Grimsby, 1958) 2
Scott P (Everton, York, Aldershot, 1976–79) 10
Sharkey P (Ipswich, 1976) 1
Shields J (Southampton, 1957) 1
Shiels D (Hibernian, Doncaster, Kilmarnock, Rangers, 2006–13) 14
Simpson W (Rangers, 1951–59) 12
Sloan D (Oxford Utd, 1969–71) 2
Sloan J (Arsenal, 1947) 1
Sloan T (Manchester Utd, 1979) 3
Smith A (Glentoran, Preston, 2003–05) 18
Smith M (Peterborough, 2016) 1

Smyth S (Wolves, Stoke, 1948–52) 9
Smyth W (Distillery, 1949–54) 4
Sonner D (Ipswich, Sheffield Wed, Birmingham, Nottm Forest, Peterborough, 1997–2005) 13
Spence D (Bury, Blackpool, Southend, 1975–82) 29
Sproule I (Hibernian, 2006–08) 11
*Stevenson A (Everton, 1947–48) 3
Steele J (New York Bulls, 2014) 3
Stewart A (Glentoran, Derby, 1967–69) 7
Stewart D (Hull, 1978) 1
Stewart I (QPR, Newcastle, 1982–87) 31
Stewart T (Linfield, 1961) 1

Taggart G (Barnsley, Bolton, Leicester, 1990–2003) 51
Taylor M (Fulham, Birmingham, 1999–2012) 88
Thompson A (Watford, 2011) 2
Thompson P (Linfield, 2006–08) 8
Todd S (Burnley, Sheffield Wed, 1966–71) 11
Toner C (Leyton Orient, 2003) 2
Trainor D (Crusaders, 1967) 1
Tuffey J (Partick, Inverness, 2009–11) 8
Tully C (Celtic, 1949–59) 10
Uprichard W (Swindon, Portsmouth, 1952–59) 18
Vernon J (Belfast Celtic, WBA, 1947–52) 17

Walker J (Doncaster, 1955) 1
Walsh D (WBA, 1947–50) 9
Walsh W (Manchester City, 1948–49) 5
Ward J (Derby, Nottm Forest, 2012–16) 26
Washington C (QPR, 2016) 8
Watson P (Distillery, 1971) 1
Webb S (Ross Co, 2006–07) 4
Welsh E (Carlisle, 1966–67) 4
Whiteside N (Manchester Utd, Everton, 1982–90) 38
Whitley Jeff (Manchester City, Sunderland, Cardiff, 1997–2006) 20
Whitley Jim (Manchester City, 1998–2000) 3
Williams M (Chesterfield, Watford, Wimbledon, Stoke, Wimbledon, MK Dons, 1999–2005) 36
Williams M (Chesterfield, Watford Wimbledon, Stoke, Wimbledon MK Dons 1999–2005) 36
Williams P (WBA, 1991) 1
Wilson D (Brighton, Luton, Sheffield Wed, 1987–92) 24
Wilson K (Ipswich, Chelsea, Notts Co, Walsall, 1987–95) 42
Wilson S (Glenavon, Falkirk, Dundee, 1962–68) 12
Winchester C (Oldham, 2011) 1
Wood T (Walsall, 1996) 1
Worthington N (Sheffield Wed, Leeds, Stoke, 1984–97) 66
Wright T (Newcastle, Nottm Forest, Reading, Manchester City, 1989–2000) 31

REPUBLIC OF IRELAND

Aherne T (Belfast Celtic, Luton, 1946–54) 16
Aldridge J (Oxford Utd, Liverpool, Real Sociedad, Tranmere, 1986–97) 69
Ambrose P (Shamrock R, 1955–64) 5
Anderson J (Preston, Newcastle, 1980–89) 16
Andrews K (Blackburn, WBA, 2009–13) 35
Arter H (Bournemouth, 2015–16) 2

Babb P (Coventry, Liverpool, Sunderland, 1994–2003) 35
Bailham E (Shamrock R, 1964) 1
Barber E (Bohemians, Birmingham, 1966) 2
Barrett G (Arsenal, Coventry, 2003–05) 6
Beglin J (Liverpool, 1984–87) 15
Bennett A (Reading, 2007) 2
Best L (Coventry, 2009–10) 7
Braddish S (Dundalk, 1978) 2
Branagan K (Bolton, 1997) 1
Bonner P (Celtic, 1981–96) 80
Brady L (Arsenal, Juventus, Sampdoria, Inter-Milan, Ascoli, West Ham, 1975–90) 72
Brady R (QPR, 1964) 6
Brady R (Manchester Utd, Hull, 2013–16) 27
Breen G (Birmingham, Coventry, West Ham, Sunderland, 1996–2006) 63
*Breen T (Shamrock R, 1947) 3
Brennan F (Drumcondra, 1965) 1
Brennan S (Manchester Utd, Waterford, 1965–71) 19
Browne W (Bohemians, 1964) 3
Bruce A (Ipswich, 2007–09) 2
Buckley L (Shamrock R, Waregem, 1984–85) 2
Burke F (Cork Ath, 1952) 1
Butler P (Sunderland, 2000) 1
Butler T (Sunderland, 2003) 2
Byrne A (Southampton, 1970–74) 14
Byrne J (Shelbourne, 2004–06) 2
Byrne J (QPR, Le Havre, Brighton, Sunderland, Millwall, 1985–93) 23
Byrne P (Shamrock R, 1984–86) 8

Campbell A (Santander, 1985) 3
Campbell N (St Patrick's Ath, Fortuna Cologne, 1971–77) 11
Cantwell N (West Ham, Manchester Utd, 1954–67) 36
Carey B (Manchester Utd, Leicester, 1992–94) 3
*Carey J (Manchester Utd, 1946–53) 21
Carolan J (Manchester Utd, 1960) 2
Carr S (Tottenham, Newcastle, 1999–2008) 43
Carroll B (Shelbourne, 1949–50) 2
Carroll T (Ipswich, 1968–73) 17
Carsley L (Derby, Blackburn, Coventry,

Everton, 1997–2008) 39
Cascarino A (Gillingham, Millwall, Aston Villa, Chelsea, Marseille, Nancy, 1986–2000) 88
Chandler J (Leeds, 1980) 2
Christie C (Derby, 2015–16) 5
Clark C (Aston Villa, 2011–16) 19
Clarke C (Stoke, 2004) 2
Clarke J (Drogheda, 1978) 1
Clarke K (Drumcondra, 1948) 2
Clarke M (Shamrock R, 1950) 1
Clinton T (Everton, 1951–54) 3
Coad P (Shamrock R, 1947–52) 11
Coffey T (Drumcondra, 1950) 1
Colfer M (Shelbourne, 1950–51) 2
Coleman S (Everton, 2011–16) 38
Colgan N (Hibernian, 2002–07) 9
Conmy O (Peterborough, 1965–70) 5
Connolly D (Watford, Feyenoord, Excelsior Feyenoord, Wimbledon, West Ham, Wigan, 1996–2006) 41
Conroy G (Stoke, 1970–77) 27
Conway J (Fulham, Manchester City, 1967–77) 20
Corr P (Everton, 1949–50) 4
Courtney E (Cork Utd, 1946) 1
Cox S (WBA, Nottm Forest, 2011–14) 30
Coyle O (Bolton, 1994) 1
Coyne T (Celtic, Tranmere, Motherwell, 1992–98) 22
Crowe G (Bohemians, 2003) 2
Cummins G (Luton, 1954–61) 19
Cuneen T (Limerick, 1951) 1
Cunningham G (Man City, Bristol City, 2010–13) 4
Cunningham K (Wimbledon, Birmingham, 1996–2006) 72
Curtis D (Shelbourne, Bristol City, Ipswich, Exeter, 1956–63) 17
Cusack S (Limerick, 1953) 1

Daish L (Cambridge Utd, Coventry, 1992–96) 5
Daly G (Manchester Utd, Derby, Coventry, Birmingham, Shrewsbury, 1973–87) 48
Daly M (Wolves, 1978) 2
Daly P (Shamrock R, 1950) 1
Deacy E (Aston Villa, 1982) 4
Delaney D (QPR, Ipswich, Crystal Palace, 2008–14) 9
Delap R (Derby, Southampton, 1998–2004) 11
De Mange K (Liverpool, Hull, 1987–89) 2
Dempsey J (Fulham, Chelsea, 1967–72) 19
Dennehy J (Cork Hibernian, Nottm Forest, Walsall, 1972–77) 11
Desmond P (Middlesbrough, 1950) 4
Devine J (Arsenal, 1980–85) 13
Doherty G (Tottenham, Norwich, 2000–06) 34
Donovan D (Everton, 1955–57) 5
Donovan T (Aston Villa, 1980) 2
Douglas J (Blackburn, Leeds, 2004–08) 8
Doyle C (Shelbourne, 1959) 1
Doyle C (Birmingham, 2007) 1
Doyle K (Reading, Wolves, Colorado, 2006–16) 62
Doyle M (Coventry, 2004) 1
Duff D (Blackburn, Chelsea, Newcastle, Fulham, 1998–2012) 100
Duffy B (Shamrock R, 1950) 1
Duffy S (Everton, Blackburn, 2014–16) 5
Dunne A (Manchester Utd, Bolton,1962–76) 33
Dunne J (Fulham, 1971) 1
Dunne P (Manchester Utd, 1965–67) 5
Dunne R (Everton, Manchester City, Aston Villa, 2000–14) 80
Dunne S (Luton, 1953–60) 15
Dunne T (St Patrick's, 1956–57) 3
Dunning P (Shelbourne, 1971) 2
Dunphy E (York, Millwall, 1966–71) 23
Dwyer N (West Ham, Swansea, 1960–65) 14

Eccles P (Shamrock R, 1986) 1
Eglington T (Shamrock R, Everton, 1946–56) 24
Elliot R (Newcastle, 2014–16) 4
Elliott S (Sunderland, 2005–07) 9
Evans M (Southampton, 1997) 1

Fagan E (Shamrock R, 1973) 1
Fagan F (Manchester City, Derby, 1955–61) 8
Fahey K (Birmingham, 2010–13) 16
Fairclough M (Dundalk, 1982) 2
Fallon S (Celtic, 1951–55) 8
Farrell P (Shamrock R, Everton, 1946–57) 28
Farrelly G (Aston Villa, Everton, Bolton, 1996–2000) 6
Finnan S (Fulham, Liverpool, Espanyol 2000–09) 53
Finucane A (Limerick, 1967–72) 11
Fitzgerald F (Waterford, 1955–6) 2
Fitzgerald P (Leeds, 1961–2) 5
Fitzpatrick K (Limerick, 1970) 1
Fitzsimons A (Middlesbrough, Lincoln, 1950–59) 26
Fleming C (Middlesbrough, 1996–8) 10
Fogarty A (Sunderland, Hartlepool Utd, 1960–64) 11
Folan C (Hull, 2009–10) 7
Foley D (Watford, 2000–01) 6
Foley K (Wolves, 2009–11) 8
Foley T (Northampton, 1964–67) 9
Fullam J (Preston, Shamrock R, 1961–70) 11
Forde D (Millwall, 2011–16) 24
Fullam J (Preston, Shamrock, 1961–70) 11

Gallagher C (Celtic, 1967) 2
Gallagher M (Hibernian, 1954) 1
Galvin A (Tottenham, Sheffield Wed, Swindon, 1983–90) 29
Gamble J (Cork City, 2007) 2
Gannon E (Notts Co, Sheffield Wed, Shelbourne, 1949–55) 14
Gannon M (Shelbourne, 1972) 1

Gavin J (Norwich, Tottenham, Norwich, 1950–57) 7
Gibbons A (St Patrick's Ath, 1952–56) 4
Gibson D (Manchester Utd, Everton, 2008–16) 27
Gilbert R (Shamrock R, 1966) 1
Giles C (Doncaster, 1951) 1
Giles J (Manchester Utd, Leeds, WBA, Shamrock R, 1960–79) 59
Given S (Blackburn, Newcastle, Manchester City, Aston Villa, Stoke, 1996–2016) 134
Givens D (Manchester Utd, Luton, QPR, Birmingham, Neuchatel, 1969–82) 56
Gleeson S (Wolves, 2007) 2
Glynn D (Drumcondra, 1952–55) 2
Godwin T (Shamrock R, Leicester, Bournemouth, 1949–58) 13
Goodman J (Wimbledon, 1997) 4
Goodwin J (Stockport, 2003) 1
*Gorman W (Brentford, 1947) 2
Grealish A (Orient Luton, Brighton, WBA, 1976–86) 45
Green P (Derby, Leeds, 2010–14) 22
Gregg E (Bohemians, 1978–80) 8
Grimes A (Manchester Utd, Coventry, Luton, 1978–88) 18

Hale A (Aston Villa, Doncaster, Waterford, 1962–72) 14
Hamilton T (Shamrock R, 1959) 2
Hand E (Portsmouth, 1969–76) 20
Harte I (Leeds, Levante, 1996–2007) 64
Hartnett J (Middlesbrough, 1949–54) 2
Haverty J (Arsenal, Blackburn, Millwall, Celtic, Bristol Rov, Shelbourne, 1956–67) 32
Hayes A (Southampton, 1979) 1
Hayes J (Aberdeen, 2016) 2
*Hayes W (Huddersfield, 1947) 2
Hayes W (Limerick, 1949) 1
Healey R (Cardiff, 1977–80) 2
Healy C (Celtic, Sunderland, 2002–04) 13
Heighway S (Liverpool, Minnesota, 1971–82) 34
Henderson B (Drumcondra, 1948) 2
Henderson W (Brighton, Preston, 2006–08) 6
Hendrick J (Derby, 2013–16) 25
Hennessy J (Shelbourne, St Patrick's Ath, 1956–69) 5
Herrick J (Cork Hibernian, Shamrock R, 1972–73) 3
Higgins J (Birmingham, 1951) 1
Holland M (Ipswich, Charlton, 2000–06) 49
Holmes J (Coventry, Tottenham, Vancouver W'caps, 1971–81) 30
Hoolahan W (Blackpool, Norwich, 2008–16) 34
Houghton R (Oxford Utd, Liverpool, Aston Villa, Crystal Palace, Reading, 1986–97) 73
Howlett G (Brighton, 1984) 1
Hughton C (Tottenham, West Ham, 1980–92) 53
Hunt N (Reading, 2009) 2
Hunt S (Reading, Hull, Wolves, 2007–12) 39
Hurley C (Millwall, Sunderland, Bolton, 1957–69) 40

Ireland S (Manchester City, 2006–08) 6
Irwin D (Manchester Utd, 1991–2000) 56

Judge A (Brentford, 2016) 1

Kavanagh G (Stoke, Cardiff, Wigan, 1998–2007) 16
Keane R (Wolves, Coventry, Inter Milan, Leeds, Tottenham, Liverpool, LA Galaxy, 1998–2016) 145
Keane R (Nottm Forest, Manchester Utd, 1991–2006) 67
Keane T (Swansea, 1949) 4
Kearin M (Shamrock R, 1972) 1
Kearns F (West Ham, 1954) 1
Kearns M (Oxford Utd, Walsall, Wolves, 1970–80) 18
Kelly A (Sheffield Utd, Blackburn, 1993–2002) 34
Kelly D (Walsall, West Ham, Leicester, Newcastle, Wolves, Sunderland, Tranmere, 1988–98) 26
Kelly G (Leeds, 1994–2003) 52
Kelly JA (Drumcondra, Preston, 1957–73) 47
Kelly M (Portsmouth, 1988–91) 4
Kelly N (Nottm Forest, 1954) 1
Kelly P (Wolves, 1961–62) 5
Kelly S (Tottenham, Birmingham, Fulham, Reading, 2006–14) 39
Kenna J (Blackburn, 1995–2000) 27
Kennedy M (Portsmouth, 1986) 2
Kennedy M (Liverpool, Wimbledon, Manchester City, Wolves, 1996–2004) 35
Kenny P (Sheffield Utd, 2004–07) 7
Keogh A (Wolves, Millwall, 2007–14) 30
Keogh J (Shamrock R, 1966) 1
Keogh R (Derby, 2013–16) 14
Keogh S (Shamrock R, 1959) 1
Kernaghan A (Middlesbrough, Manchester City, 1993–96) 22
Kiely D (Charlton, WBA, 2000–09) 11
Kiernan F (Shamrock R, Southampton, 1951–2) 5
Kilbane K (WBA, Sunderland, Everton, Wigan, Hull, 1997–2011) 110
Kinnear J (Tottenham, Brighton, 1967–76) 26
Kinsella M (Charlton, Aston Villa, WBA, 1998–2004) 48

Langan D (Derby, Birmingham, Oxford Utd, 1978–88) 26
Lapira J (Notre Dame, 2007) 1
Lawler R (Fulham, 1953–56) 8
Lawlor J (Drumcondra, Doncaster, 1949–51) 3
Lawlor M (Shamrock R, 1971–73) 5

Lawrence L (Stoke, Portsmouth, 2009–11) 15
Lawrenson M (Preston, Brighton, Liverpool, 1977–88) 39
Lee A (Rotherham, Cardiff, Ipswich, 2003–07) 10
Leech M (Shamrock R, 1969–73) 8
Long S (Reading, WBA Hull, Southampton, 2007–16) 67
Lowry D (St Patrick's Ath, 1962) 1

McAlinden J (Portsmouth, 1946) 2
McAteer J (Bolton, Liverpool, Blackburn, Sunderland, 1994–2004) 52
McCann J (Shamrock R, 1957) 1
McCarthy J (Wigan, Everton, 2011–16) 39
McCarthy M (Manchester City, Celtic, Lyon, Millwall, 1984–92) 57
McClean J (Sunderland, Wigan, WBA, 2012–16) 42
McConville T (Dundalk, Waterford, 1972–73) 6
McDonagh J (Everton, Bolton, Sunderland, Notts Co, 1981–86) 25
McDonagh J (Shamrock R, 1984–85) 3
McEvoy A (Blackburn, 1961–67) 17
McGeady A (Celtic, Spartak Moscow, Everton, 2014–16) 85
McGee P (QPR, Preston, 1978–81) 15
McGoldrick E (Crystal Palace, Arsenal, 1992–95) 15
McGoldrick D (Ipswich, 2015–16) 4
McGowan D (West Ham, 1949) 3
McGowan J (Cork Utd, 1947) 1
McGrath M (Blackburn, Bradford PA, 1958–66) 22
McGrath P (Manchester Utd, Aston Villa, Derby, 1985–97) 83
Macken J (Manchester City, 2005) 1
Mackey G (Shamrock R, 1957) 3
McLoughlin A (Swindon, Southampton, Portsmouth, 1990–2000) 42
McMillan W (Belfast Celtic, 1946) 2
McNally B (Luton, 1959–63) 3
McPhail S (Leeds, 2000–04) 10
McShane P (WBA, Sunderland, Hull, Reading, 2006–16) 33
Macken A (Derby, 1977) 1
Madden P (Yeovil, 2014) 1
Mahon A (Tranmere, 2000) 2
Malone G (Shelbourne, 1949) 1
Mancini T (QPR, Arsenal, 1974–75) 5
Martin C (Glentoran, Leeds, Aston Villa, 1946–56) 30
Martin M (Bohemians, Manchester Utd, 1972–83) 52
Maybury, A (Leeds, Hearts, Leicester, 1998–2005) 10
Meagan M (Everton, Huddersfield, Drogheda, 1961–70) 17
Meyler D (Sunderland, Hull, 2013–16) 16
Miller L (Celtic, Manchester Utd, Sunderland, QPR 2004–10) 21
Milligan M (Oldham, 1992) 1
Mooney J (Shamrock R, 1965) 2
Moore A (Middlesbrough, 1996–97) 8
Moran K (Manchester Utd, Sporting Gijon, Blackburn, 1980–94) 71
Moroney T (West Ham, 1948–54) 12
Morris C (Celtic, Middlesbrough, 1988–93) 35
Morrison C (Crystal Palace, Birmingham, Crystal Palace, 2002–07) 36
Moulson G (Lincoln, 1948–49) 3
Mucklan C (Drogheda, 1978) 1
Mulligan P (Shamrock R, Chelsea, Crystal Palace, WBA, Shamrock R, 1969–80) 50
Munroe L (Shamrock R, 1954) 1
Murphy A (Clyde, 1956) 1
Murphy B (Bohemians, 1986) 1
Murphy D (Sunderland, Ipswich, 2007–16) 23
Murphy J (Crystal Palace, 1980) 3
Murphy J (Scunthorpe, 2009–10) 2
Murphy J (WBA, 2004) 1
Murphy P (Carlisle, 2007) 1
Murray T (Dundalk, 1950) 1

Newman W (Shelbourne, 1969) 1
Nolan E (Preston, 2009–10) 3
Nolan R (Shamrock R, 1957–63) 10

O'Brien Alan (Newcastle, 2007) 5
O'Brien Andy (Newcastle, Portsmouth, 2001–07) 26
O'Brien F (Philadelphia Forest, 1980) 3
O'Brien J (Bolton, West Ham, 2006–13) 5
O'Brien L (Shamrock R, Manchester Utd, Newcastle, Tranmere, 1986–97) 16
O'Brien R (Notts Co, 1976–77) 5
O'Byrne L (Shamrock R, 1949) 1
O'Callaghan B (Stoke, 1979–82) 6
O'Callaghan K (Ipswich, Portsmouth, 1981–87) 21
O'Cearuill J (Arsenal, 2007) 2
O'Connell A (Dundalk, Bohemians, 1967–71) 2
O'Connor T (Shamrock R, 1950) 4
O'Connor T (Fulham, Dundalk, Bohemians, 1968–73) 7
O'Dowda C (Oxford 2016) 1
O'Dea D (Celtic, Toronto, Metalurh Donetsk, 2010–14) 20
O'Driscoll J (Swansea, 1949) 3
O'Driscoll S (Fulham, 1982) 3
O'Farrell F (West Ham, Preston, 1952–59) 9
*O'Flanagan Dr K (Arsenal, 1947) 3
O'Flanagan M (Bohemians, 1947) 1
O'Halloran S (Aston Villa, 2007) 2
O'Hanlon K (Rotherham, 1988) 1
O'Kane E (Bournemouth, 2016) 4
O'Keefe E (Everton, Port Vale, 1981–85) 5
O'Leary D (Arsenal, 1977–93) 68
O'Leary P (Shamrock R, 1980–1) 7
O'Neill F (Shamrock R, 1962–72) 20
O'Neill J (Everton, 1952–59) 17
O'Neill J (Preston, 1961) 1
O'Neill K (Norwich, Middlesbrough, 1996–2000) 13
O'Regan K (Brighton, 1984–85) 4

O'Reilly J (Cork Utd, 1946) 2
O'Shea J (Manchester Utd, Sunderland, 2002–16) 114

Pearce A (Reading, Derby, 2013–16) 7
Peyton G (Fulham, Bournemouth, Everton, 1977–92) 33
Peyton N (Shamrock R, Leeds, 1957–61) 6
Phelan T (Wimbledon, Manchester City, Chelsea, Everton, Fulham, 1992–2000) 42
Pilkington A (Norwich, Cardiff, 2014–16) 9
Potter D (Wolves, 2007–08) 5

Quinn A (Sheffield Wed, Sheffield Utd, 2003–07) 7
Quinn B (Coventry, 2000) 4
Quinn N (Arsenal, Manchester City, Sunderland, 1986–2002) 92
Quinn S (Hull, Reading, 2013–16) 17

Randolph D (Motherwell, West Ham, 2013–16) 13
Reid A (Nottm Forest, Tottenham, Charlton, Sunderland, Nottm Forest, 2004–14) 29
Reid S (Millwall, Blackburn, 2002–09) 23
Richardson D (Shamrock R, Gillingham, 1972–80) 3
Ringstead A (Sheffield Utd, 1951–59) 20
Robinson M (Brighton, Liverpool, QPR, 1981–86) 24
Roche P (Shelbourne, Manchester Utd, 1972–76) 8
Rogers E (Blackburn, Charlton, 1968–73) 19
Rowlands M (QPR, 2004–10) 5
Ryan G (Derby, Brighton, 1978–85) 18
Ryan R (WBA, Derby, 1950–56) 16

Sadlier R (Millwall, 2002) 1
Sammon C (Derby, 2013–14) 9
Savage D (Millwall, 1996) 5
Saward P (Millwall, Aston Villa, Huddersfield, 1954–63) 18
Scannell T (Southend, 1954) 1
Scully P (Arsenal, 1989) 1
Sheedy K (Everton, Newcastle, 1984–93) 46
Sheridan C (Celtic, CSKA Sofia, 2010–11) 3
Sheridan J (Leeds, Sheffield Wed, 1988–96) 34
Slaven B (Middlesbrough, 1990–93) 7
Sloan P (Arsenal, 1946) 2
Smyth M (Shamrock R, 1969) 1
St Ledger S (Preston, Leicester, 2009–14) 37
Stapleton F (Arsenal, Manchester Utd, Ajax Derby, Le Havre, Blackburn, 1977–90) 71
Staunton S (Liverpool, Aston Villa, Liverpool, Crystal Palace, Aston Villa, 1989–2002) 102
*Stevenson A (Everton, 1947–49) 6
Stokes A (Sunderland, Celtic, 2007–15) 9
Strahan F (Shelbourne, 1964–65) 5
Swan M (Drumcondra, 1960) 1
Synnott N (Shamrock R, 1978–79) 3
Taylor T (Waterford, 1959) 1
Thomas P (Waterford, 1974) 2
Thompson J (Nottm Forest, 2004) 1
Townsend A (Norwich, Chelsea, Aston Villa, Middlesbrough, 1989–97) 70
Traynor T (Southampton, 1954–64) 8
Treacy K (Preston, Burnley 2011–12) 6
Treacy R (WBA, Charlton, Swindon, Preston, Shamrock R, 1966–80) 42
Tuohy L (Shamrock R, Newcastle, Shamrock R, 1956–65) 8
Turner A (Celtic, 1963) 2

Vernon J (Belfast Celtic, 1946) 2

Waddock G (QPR, Millwall, 1980–90) 21
Walsh D (WBA, Aston Villa, 1946–54) 20
Walsh J (Limerick, 1982) 1
Walsh M (Blackpool, Everton, QPR, Porto, 1976–85) 21
Walsh M (Everton, Norwich, 1982–83) 4
Walsh W (Manchester City, 1947–50) 9
Walters J (Stoke 2011–16) 41
Ward S (Wolves, Burnley, 2011–16) 36
Waters J (Grimsby, 1977–80) 2
Westwood K (Coventry, Sunderland, Sheffield Wed, 2009–15) 18
Whelan G (Stoke, 2009–16) 73
Whelan R (St Patrick's Ath, 1964) 2
Whelan R (Liverpool, Southend, 1981–95) 53
Whelan L (Manchester Utd, 1956–57) 4
Whittaker R (Chelsea, 1959) 1
Wilson M (Stoke, 2011–16) 24

INTERNATIONAL GOALSCORERS 1946–2016

(start of season 2016–17)

ENGLAND

Rooney 53
Charlton R 49
Lineker 48
Greaves 44
Owen 40
Finney 30
Lofthouse 30
Shearer 30
Lampard Frank jnr 29
Platt 27
Robson B 26
Hurst 24
Mortensen 23
Crouch 22
Channon 21
Gerrard 21
Keegan 21
Peters 20
Defoe 19
Haynes 18
Hunt R 18
Beckham 17
Lawton 16
Taylor T 16
Woodcock 16
Scholes 14
Welbeck 14
Chivers 13
Mariner 13
Smith R 13
Francis T 12
Barnes J 11
Douglas 11
Mannion 11
Sheringham 11
Clarke A 10
Cole J 10
Flowers R 10
Gascoigne 10
Lee F 10
Milburn 10
Wilshaw 10
Beardsley 9
Bell 9
Bentley 9
Hateley 9
Wright I 9
Ball 8
Broadis 8
Byrne J 8
Hoddle 8
Kevan 8
Anderton 7
Connelly 7
Coppell 7
Fowler 7
Heskey 7
Paine 7
Walcott 7
Young A 7
Charlton J 6
Macdonald 6
Mullen 6
Rowley 6
Sturridge 6
Terry 6
Vassell 6
Waddle 6
Wright-Phillips S 6
Adams 5
Atyeo 5
Baily 5
Brooking 5
Carter 5
Edwards 5
Ferdinand L 5
Hitchens 5
Johnson D 5
Kane 5
Latchford 5
Neal 5
Oxlade-Chamberlain 5
Pearce 5
Pearson Stan 5
Pearson Stuart 5
Pickering F 5
Barmby 4
Barnes P 4
Bent 4
Bull 4
Dixon K 4
Hassall 4
Revie 4
Robson R 4
Steven 4
Vardy 4
Watson Dave (Sunderland) 4
Baker 3
Blissett 3
Butcher 3
Cahill 3
Currie 3
Elliott 3
Francis G 3
Grainger 3
Jagielka 3
Kennedy R 3
Lambert 3
McDermott 3
McManaman 3
Matthews S 3
Merson 3
Morris 3
O'Grady 3
Peacock 3
Ramsey 3
Sewell 3
Townsend 3
Webb 3
Wilkins 3
Wright W 3
Allen R 2
Anderson 2
Barkley 2
Barry 2
Bradley 2
Broadbent 2
Brooks 2
Carroll 2
Cowans 2
Dier 2
Eastham 2
Ferdinand R 2
Froggatt J 2
Froggatt R 2
Haines 2
Hancocks 2
Hunter 2
Ince 2
Johnson A 2
Keown 2
Lee R 2
Lee S 2
Moore 2
Perry 2
Pointer 2
Richardson 2
Royle 2
Smith A (1989–92) 2
Southgate 2
Sterling 2
Stone 2
Taylor P 2
Tueart 2
Upson 2
Wignall 2
Wilshere 2
Worthington 2
A'Court 1
Alli 1
Astall 1
Baines 1
Beattie K 1
Bowles 1
Bradford 1
Bridge 1
Bridges 1

Brown.....1
Campbell.....1
Caulker.....1
Chamberlain.....1
Cole Andy.....1
Crawford.....1
Dixon L.....1
Ehiogu.....1
Goddard.....1
Hirst.....1
Hughes E.....1
Jeffers.....1
Jenas.....1
Johnson G.....1
Kay.....1
Kidd.....1
King.....1
Langton.....1
Lawler.....1
Lee J.....1
Lescott.....1
Le Saux.....1
Mabbutt.....1
Marsh.....1
Medley.....1
Melia.....1
Milner.....1
Mullery.....1
Murphy.....1
Nicholls.....1
Nicholson.....1
Nugent.....1
Palmer.....1
Parry.....1
Rashford.....1
Redknapp.....1
Richards.....1
Sansom.....1
Shackleton.....1
Smalling.....1
Smith A (2001–5).....1
Stiles.....1
Summerbee.....1
Tambling.....1
Thompson Phil.....1
Viollet.....1
Wallace.....1
Walsh.....1
Weller.....1
Wise.....1
Withe.....1
Wright M.....1

SCOTLAND

Dalglish.....30
Law.....30
Reilly.....22
McCoist.....19
Miller K.....18
McFadden.....15
Johnston M.....14
Collins J.....12
Gilzean.....12
Steel.....12
Jordan.....11
Collins R.....10
Johnstone R.....10
Wilson D.....10
Gallacher.....9
McStay.....9
Mudie.....9
St John.....9
Stein.....9
Brand.....8
Fletcher S.....8
Gemmill A.....8
Leggat.....8
Robertson J (1978–84).....8
Boyd K.....7
Dodds.....7
Durie.....7
Gray A.....7
Maloney.....7
Wark.....7
Booth.....6
Brown A.....6
Cooper.....6
Dailly.....6
Gough.....6
Hutchison D.....6
Naismith.....6
Liddell.....6
Murdoch.....6
Rioch.....6
Waddell.....6
Fletcher D.....5
Hartford.....5
Henderson W.....5
Macari.....5
Masson.....5
McAllister G.....5
McQueen.....5
Nevin.....5
Nicholas.....5
O'Hare.....5
Scott A.....5
Strachan.....5
Young A.....5
Archibald.....4
Brown S.....4
Caldow.....4
Crawford.....4
Hamilton.....4
Jackson D.....4
Johnstone J.....4
Lorimer.....4
Mackay D.....4
Mason.....4
McGinlay.....4
McKinlay W.....4
McLaren.....4
O'Connor.....4
Smith G.....4
Souness.....4
Anya.....3
Baxter.....3
Berra.....3
Bremner W.....3
Burley C.....3
Chalmers.....3
Ferguson B.....3
Gibson.....3
Graham G.....3
Gray E.....3
Greig.....3
Hendry.....3
Herd D.....3
Lennox.....3
MacDougall.....3
McCann.....3
McInally A.....3
McNeill.....3
McPhail.....3
Morris.....3
Morrison.....3
Rhodes.....3
Ritchie M.....3
Robertson J (1991–5).....3
Snodgrass.....3
Sturrock.....3
Thompson.....3
White.....3
Baird S.....2
Bauld.....2
Burke.....2
Caldwell G.....2
Cameron.....2
Commons.....2
Flavell.....2
Fleming.....2
Graham A.....2
Harper.....2
Hewie.....2
Holton.....2
Hopkin.....2
Houliston.....2
Jess.....2
Johnston A.....2
Johnstone D.....2
Mackie.....2
McArthur.....2
McClair.....2
McCormack.....2
McGhee.....2
McMillan.....2
McManus.....2
Mulgrew.....2

Ormond	2
Pettigrew	2
Ring	2
Robertson A (1955)	2
Shearer D	2
Aitken R	1
Bannon	1
Beattie	1
Bett	1
Bone	1
Boyd T	1
Brazil	1
Broadfoot	1
Buckley	1
Burns	1
Calderwood	1
Campbell R	1
Clarkson	1
Combe	1
Conn A (1956)	1
Craig J	1
Curran	1
Davidson	1
Dickov	1
Dobie	1
Docherty	1
Duncan D	1
Elliott	1
Fernie	1
Freedman	1
Goodwillie	1
Gray F	1
Gemmill S	1
Gemmell T (1966–71)	1
Gemmell T (1955)	1
Hanley	1
Hartley	1
Henderson J	1
Herd G	1
Holt	1
Howie	1
Hughes J	1
Hunter W	1
Hutchison T	1
Goodwillie	1
Jackson C	1
Jardine	1
Johnston L	1
Kyle	1
Lambert	1
Linwood	1
Mackail-Smith	1
Mackay G	1
MacLeod	1
MacKenzie	1
McAvennie	1
McCall	1
McCalliog	1
McCulloch	1
McKimmie	1
McKinnon	1
McLean	1
McLintock	1
McSwegan	1
Miller W	1
Mitchell	1
Morgan	1
Mulhall	1
Murray J	1
Narey	1
Naysmith	1
Orr	1
Parlane	1
Provan D (1980–82)	1
Quashie	1
Ritchie P	1
Robertson A (2014–16)	1
Sharp	1
Stewart R	1
Thornton	1
Wallace I	1
Webster	1
Weir A	1
Weir D	1
Wilkie	1
Wilson Danny	1

WALES

Rush	28
Allchurch I	23
Ford	23
Bale	22
Saunders	22
Bellamy	19
Earnshaw	16
Hughes M	16
Jones C	16
Charles John	15
Hartson	14
Toshack	13
Giggs	12
Ramsey	11
James L	10
Koumas	10
Davies RT	9
Vernon	8
Flynn	7
James R	7
Speed	7
Vokes	7
Walsh I	7
Charles M	6
Curtis A	6
Davies RW	6
Davies S	6
Griffiths A	6
Medwin	6
Pembridge	6
Clarke R	5
Leek	5
Blake	4
Coleman	4
Deacy	4
Eastwood	4
Edwards I	4
England	4
Ledley	4
Tapscott	4
Thomas M	4
Allen M	3
Bodin	3
Bowen M	3
Church	3
Collins J	3
Edwards D	3
Melville	3
Palmer D	3
Rees R	3
Robinson J	3
Robson-Kanu	3
Woosnam	3
Cotterill	2
Davies G	2
Durban A	2
Dwyer	2
Edwards G	2
Evans C	2
Giles D	2
Godfrey	2
Griffiths M	2
Hodges	2
Horne	2
Jones Barrie	2
Jones Bryn	2
King	2
Lowrie	2
Nicholas	2
Phillips D	2
Reece G	2
Savage	2
Slatter	2
Symons	2
Taylor N	2
Williams Ashley	2
Yorath	2
Barnes	1
Blackmore	1
Blake	1
Bowen D	1
Boyle T	1
Burgess R	1
Charles Jeremy	1
Evans I	1
Fletcher	1
Foulkes	1
Harris C	1
Hewitt R	1

Hockey 1
Huws 1
Jones A 1
Jones D 1
Jones J 1
Krzywicki 1
Llewellyn 1
Lovell 1
Mahoney 1
Moore G 1
Morison 1
O'Sullivan 1
Parry 1
Paul 1
Powell A 1
Powell D 1
Price P 1
Roberts P 1
Robinson C 1
Smallman 1
Vaughan 1
Williams Adrian 1
Williams GE 1
Williams GG 1
Young 1

N IRELAND

Healy 36
Lafferty 17
Clarke 13
Armstrong 12
Dowie 12
Quinn JM 12
Bingham 10
Crossan J 10
McIlroy J 10
McParland 10
Best 9
Whiteside 9
Davis 8
Dougan 8
Irvine W 8
McAuley 8
O'Neill M (1972–85) 8
McAdams 7
Taggart G 7
Wilson S 7
Gray 6
McLaughlin 6
Nicholson J 6
Wilson K 6
Cush 5
Feeney (2002–9)) 5
Hamilton W 5
Hughes M 5
Magilton 5
McIlroy S 5
Simpson 5
Smyth S 5
Walsh D 5
Anderson T 4
Elliott 4
Hamilton B 4
McCann 4
McGrath 4
McMorran 4
O'Neill M (1989–96) 4
Quinn SJ 4
Brotherston 3
Harvey M 3
Lockhart 3
Lomas 3
McDonald 3
McGinn 3
McMordie 3
Morgan S 3
Mulryne 3
Nicholl C 3
Paterson 3
Spence D 3
Tully 3
Whitley (1997–2006) 3
Blanchflower D 2
Casey 2
Cathcart 2
Clements 2
Doherty P 2
Finney 2
Gillespie 2
Harkin 2
Lennon 2
McCourt 2
McMahon 2
Neill W 2
O'Neill J 2
Peacock 2
Penney 2
Stewart I 2
Ward 2
Washington 2
Whitley 3
Barr 1
Black 1
Blanchflower J 1
Brennan 1
Brunt 1
Campbell W 1
Caskey 1
Cassidy 1
Cochrane T 1
Crossan E 1
Dallas 1
D'Arcy 1
Doherty L 1
Elder 1
Evans C 1
Evans J 1
Ferguson S 1
Ferguson W 1
Ferris 1
Griffin 1
Grigg 1
Hill C 1
Hughes 1
Humphries 1
Hunter A 1
Hunter B 1
Johnston 1
Jones J 1
Jones, S 1
Magennis 1
McCartney 1
McClelland (1961) 1
McCrory 1
McCurdy 1
McGarry 1
Moreland 1
Morrow 1
Murdock 1
Nelson 1
Nicholl J 1
O'Boyle 1
O'Kane 1
Patterson D 1
Patterson R 1
Rowland 1
Shiels 1
Sproule 1
Stevenson 1
Thompson 1
Walker 1
Welsh 1
Williams 1
Wilson D 1

REP OF IRELAND

Keane Robbie 67
Quinn N 21
Stapleton 20
Aldridge 19
Cascarino 19
Givens 19
Long 16
Cantwell 14
Doyle 14
Daly 13
Harte 12
Walters 10
Brady L 9
Connolly 9
Keane Roy 9
Kelly D 9
Morrison 9
Sheedy 9
Curtis 8
Duff 8
Dunne R 8
Grealish 8
Kilbane 8
McGrath P 8

Staunton	8	Fogarty	3	Christie	1
Breen G	7	Haverty	3	Dempsey	1
Fitzsimons	7	Hoolahan	3	Duffy	1
Ringstead	7	Kennedy Mark	3	Elliott	1
Townsend	7	Kinsella	3	Fitzgerald F	1
Brady R	6	McAteer	3	Fullam	1
Coyne	6	O'Shea	3	Galvin	1
Houghton	6	Ryan R	3	Gibson	1
McEvoy	6	St Ledger S	3	Glynn	1
Martin C	6	Waddock	3	Green	1
Moran	6	Walsh M	3	Grimes	1
Cummins	5	Ward	3	Healy	1
Fagan F	5	Whelan R	3	Holmes	1
Giles	5	Barrett	2	Hughton	1
Holland	5	Clark	2	Hunt S	1
Lawrenson	5	Conroy	2	Gibson	1
McClean	5	Dennehy	2	Kavanagh	1
McGeady	5	Eglington	2	Keogh R	1
Rogers	5	Fallon	2	Kernaghan	1
Sheridan	5	Finnan	2	Mancini	1
Treacy	5	Fitzgerald P	2	McCann	1
Walsh D	5	Foley	2	McPhail	1
Walters	5	Gavin	2	Miller	1
Byrne J	4	Hale	2	Mooney	1
Cox	4	Hand	2	Moroney	1
Doherty	4	Hurley	2	Mulligan	1
Ireland	4	Kelly G	2	O'Brien A	1
Irwin	4	Keogh A	2	O'Dea	1
McGee	4	Lawrence	2	O'Callaghan K	1
Martin M	4	Leech	2	O'Keefe	1
O'Neill K	4	McCarthy	2	O'Leary	1
Reid A	4	McLoughlin	2	O'Neill F	1
Robinson	4	O'Connor (1968–73	2	O'Reilly J	1
Tuohy	4	O'Farrell	2	Pilkington	1
Andrews	3	Pearce	2	Ryan G	1
Carey J	3	Reid S	2	Slaven	1
Coad	3	Whelan G	2	Sloan	1
Conway	3	Ambrose	1	Strahan	1
Fahey	3	Anderson	1	Waters	1
Farrell	3	Carroll	1	Wilson	1

HOME INTERNATIONAL RESULTS

Note: In the results that follow, WC = World Cup, EC = European Championship, CC = Carling Cup
TF = Tournoi de France For Northern Ireland read Ireland before 1921

ENGLAND V SCOTLAND

Played 112; England won 47; Scotland 41; drawn 24 Goals: England 198, Scotland 172

		E	*S*
1872	Glasgow	0	0
1873	The Oval	4	2
1874	Glasgow	1	2
1875	The Oval	2	2
1876	Glasgow	0	3
1877	The Oval	1	3
1878	Glasgow	2	7
1879	The Oval	5	4
1880	Glasgow	4	5
1881	The Oval	1	6
1882	Glasgow	1	5
1883	Sheffield	2	3
1884	Glasgow	0	1
1885	The Oval	1	1
1886	Glasgow	1	1
1887	Blackburn	2	3
1888	Glasgow	5	0
1889	The Oval	2	3
1890	Glasgow	1	1
1891	Blackburn	2	1
1892	Glasgow	4	1
1893	Richmond	5	2
1894	Glasgow	2	2
1895	Goodison Park	3	0
1896	Glasgow	1	2
1897	Crystal Palace	1	2
1898	Glasgow	3	1

1899	Birmingham	2	1
1900	Glasgow	1	4
1901	Crystal Palace	2	2
1902	Birmingham	2	2
1903	Sheffield	1	2
1904	Glasgow	1	0
1905	Crystal Palace	1	0
1906	Glasgow	1	2
1907	Newcastle	1	1
1908	Glasgow	1	1
1909	Crystal Palace	2	0
1910	Glasgow	0	2
1911	Goodison Park	1	1
1912	Glasgow	1	1
1913	Stamford Bridge	1	0
1914	Glasgow	1	3
1920	Sheffield	5	4
1921	Glasgow	0	3
1922	Birmingham	0	1
1923	Glasgow	2	2
1924	Wembley	1	1
1925	Glasgow	0	2
1926	Manchester	0	1
1927	Glasgow	2	1
1928	Wembley	1	5
1929	Glasgow	0	1
1930	Wembley	5	2
1931	Glasgow	0	2
1932	Wembley	3	0
1933	Glasgow	1	2
1934	Wembley	3	0
1935	Glasgow	0	2
1936	Wembley	1	1
1937	Glasgow	1	3
1938	Wembley	0	1
1939	Glasgow	2	1
1947	Wembley	1	1
1948	Glasgow	2	0
1949	Wembley	1	3
1950	Glasgow (WC)	1	0
1951	Wembley	2	3
1952	Glasgow	2	1
1953	Wembley	2	2
1954	Glasgow (WC)	4	2
1955	Wembley	7	2
1956	Glasgow	1	1
1957	Wembley	2	1
1958	Glasgow	4	0
1959	Wembley	1	0
1960	Glasgow	1	1
1961	Wembley	9	3
1962	Glasgow	0	2
1963	Wembley	1	2
1964	Glasgow	0	1
1965	Wembley	2	2
1966	Glasgow	4	3
1967	Wembley (EC)	2	3
1968	Glasgow (EC)	1	1
1969	Wembley	4	1
1970	Glasgow	0	0
1971	Wembley	3	1
1972	Glasgow	1	0
1973	Glasgow	5	0
1973	Wembley	1	0
1974	Glasgow	0	2
1975	Wembley	5	1
1976	Glasgow	1	2
1977	Wembley	1	2
1978	Glasgow	1	0
1979	Wembley	3	1
1980	Glasgow	2	0
1981	Wembley	0	1
1982	Glasgow	1	0
1983	Wembley	2	0
1984	Glasgow	1	1
1985	Glasgow	0	1
1986	Wembley	2	1
1987	Glasgow	0	0
1988	Wembley	1	0
1989	Glasgow	2	0
1996	Wembley (EC)	2	0
1999	Glasgow (EC)	2	0
1999	Wembley (EC)	0	1
2013	Wembley	3	2
2014	Glasgow	3	1

ENGLAND v WALES

Played 102; England won 67; Wales 14; drawn 21; Goals: England 247 Wales 91

		E	W
1879	The Oval	2	1
1880	Wrexham	3	2
1881	Blackburn	0	1
1882	Wrexham	3	5
1883	The Oval	5	0
1884	Wrexham	4	0
1885	Blackburn	1	1
1886	Wrexham	3	1
1887	The Oval	4	0
1888	Crewe	5	1
1889	Stoke	4	1
1890	Wrexham	3	1
1891	Sunderland	4	1
1892	Wrexham	2	0
1893	Stoke	6	0
1894	Wrexham	5	1
1895	Queens Club, London	1	1
1896	Cardiff	9	1
1897	Bramall Lane	4	0
1898	Wrexham	3	0
1899	Bristol	4	0
1900	Cardiff	1	1
1901	Newcastle	6	0
1902	Wrexham	0	0
1903	Portsmouth	2	1
1904	Wrexham	2	2
1905	Anfield	3	1
1906	Cardiff	1	0
1907	Fulham	1	1
1908	Wrexham	7	1
1909	Nottingham	2	0
1910	Cardiff	1	0
1911	Millwall	3	0

1912	Wrexham	2	0
1913	Bristol	4	3
1914	Cardiff	2	0
1920	Highbury	1	2
1921	Cardiff	0	0
1922	Anfield	1	0
1923	Cardiff	2	2
1924	Blackburn	1	2
1925	Swansea	2	1
1926	Selhurst Park	1	3
1927	Wrexham	3	3
1927	Burnley	1	2
1928	Swansea	3	2
1929	Stamford Bridge	6	0
1930	Wrexham	4	0
1931	Anfield	3	1
1932	Wrexham	0	0
1933	Newcastle	1	2
1934	Cardiff	4	0
1935	Wolverhampton	1	2
1936	Cardiff	1	2
1937	Middlesbrough	2	1
1938	Cardiff	2	4
1946	Maine Road	3	0
1947	Cardiff	3	0
1948	Villa Park	1	0
1949	Cardiff (WC)	4	1
1950	Sunderland	4	2
1951	Cardiff	1	1
1952	Wembley	5	2
1953	Cardiff (WC)	4	1
1954	Wembley	3	2
1955	Cardiff	1	2
1956	Wembley	3	1
1957	Cardiff	4	0
1958	Villa Park	2	2
1959	Cardiff	1	1
1960	Wembley	5	1
1961	Cardiff	1	1
1962	Wembley	4	0
1963	Cardiff	4	0
1964	Wembley	2	1
1965	Cardiff	0	0
1966	Wembley (EC)	5	1
1967	Cardiff (EC)	3	0
1969	Wembley	2	1
1970	Cardiff	1	1
1971	Wembley	0	0
1972	Cardiff	3	0
1972	Cardiff (WC)	1	0
1973	Wembley (WC)	1	1
1973	Wembley	3	0
1974	Cardiff	2	0
1975	Wembley	2	2
1976	Wrexham	2	1
1976	Cardiff	1	0
1977	Wembley	0	1
1978	Cardiff	3	1
1979	Wembley	0	0
1980	Wrexham	1	4
1981	Wembley	0	0
1982	Cardiff	1	0
1983	Wembley	2	1
1984	Wrexham	0	1
2004	Old Trafford (WC)	2	0
2005	Cardiff (WC)	1	0
2011	Cardiff (EC)	2	0
2011	Wembley (EC)	1	0
2016	Lens (EC)	2	1

ENGLAND v N IRELAND

Played 98; England won 75; Ireland 7; drawn 16 Goals: England 323, Ireland 81

		E	*I*
1882	Belfast	13	0
1883	Aigburth, Liverpool	7	0
1884	Belfast	8	1
1885	Whalley Range	4	0
1886	Belfast	6	1
1887	Bramall Lane	7	0
1888	Belfast	5	1
1889	Goodison Park	6	1
1890	Belfast	9	1
1891	Wolverhampton	6	1
1892	Belfast	2	0
1893	Perry Barr	6	1
1894	Belfast	2	2
1895	Derby	9	0
1896	Belfast	2	0
1897	Nottingham	6	0
1898	Belfast	3	2
1899	Sunderland	13	2
1900	Dublin	2	0
1901	Southampton	3	0
1902	Belfast	1	0
1903	Wolverhampton	4	0
1904	Belfast	3	1
1905	Middlesbrough	1	1
1906	Belfast	5	0
1907	Goodison Park	1	0
1908	Belfast	3	1
1909	Bradford PA	4	0
1910	Belfast	1	1
1911	Derby	2	1
1912	Dublin	6	1
1913	Belfast	1	2
1914	Middlesbrough	0	3
1919	Belfast	1	1
1920	Sunderland	2	0
1921	Belfast	1	1
1922	West Bromwich	2	0
1923	Belfast	1	2
1924	Goodison Park	3	1
1925	Belfast	0	0
1926	Anfield	3	3
1927	Belfast	0	2
1928	Goodison Park	2	1
1929	Belfast	3	0
1930	Bramall Lane	5	1
1931	Belfast	6	2
1932	Blackpool	1	0
1933	Belfast	3	0
1935	Goodison Park	2	1

1935	Belfast	3	1
1936	Stoke	3	1
1937	Belfast	5	1
1938	Old Trafford	7	0
1946	Belfast	7	2
1947	Goodison Park	2	2
1948	Belfast	6	2
1949	Maine Road (WC)	9	2
1950	Belfast	4	1
1951	Villa Park	2	0
1952	Belfast	2	2
1953	Goodison Park (WC)	3	1
1954	Belfast	2	0
1955	Wembley	3	0
1956	Belfast	1	1
1957	Wembley	2	3
1958	Belfast	3	3
1959	Wembley	2	1
1960	Belfast	5	2
1961	Wembley	1	1
1962	Belfast	3	1
1963	Wembley	8	3
1964	Belfast	4	3
1965	Wembley	2	1
1966	Belfast (EC)	2	0
1967	Wembley (EC)	2	0
1969	Belfast	3	1
1970	Wembley	3	1
1971	Belfast	1	0
1972	Wembley	0	1
1973	*Goodison Park	2	1
1974	Wembley	1	0
1975	Belfast	0	0
1976	Wembley	4	0
1977	Belfast	2	1
1978	Wembley	1	0
1979	Wembley (EC)	4	0
1979	Belfast	2	0
1979	Belfast (EC)	5	1
1980	Wembley	1	1
1982	Wembley	4	0
1983	Belfast	0	0
1984	Wembley	1	0
1985	Belfast (WC)	1	0
1985	Wembley (WC)	0	0
1986	Wembley (EC)	3	0
1987	Belfast (EC)	2	0
2005	Old Trafford (WC)	4	0
2005	Belfast (WC)	0	1

(*Switched from Belfast because of political situation)

SCOTLAND v WALES

Played 107; Scotland won 61; Wales 23; drawn 23; Goals: Scotland 243, Wales 124

		S	*W*
1876	Glasgow	4	0
1877	Wrexham	2	0
1878	Glasgow	9	0
1879	Wrexham	3	0
1880	Glasgow	5	1
1881	Wrexham	5	1
1882	Glasgow	5	0
1883	Wrexham	3	0
1884	Glasgow	4	1
1885	Wrexham	8	1
1886	Glasgow	4	1
1887	Wrexham	2	0
1888	Edinburgh	5	1
1889	Wrexham	0	0
1890	Paisley	5	0
1891	Wrexham	4	3
1892	Edinburgh	6	1
1893	Wrexham	8	0
1894	Kilmarnock	5	2
1895	Wrexham	2	2
1896	Dundee	4	0
1897	Wrexham	2	2
1898	Motherwell	5	2
1899	Wrexham	6	0
1900	Aberdeen	5	2
1901	Wrexham	1	1
1902	Greenock	5	1
1903	Cardiff	1	0
1904	Dundee	1	1
1905	Wrexham	1	3
1906	Edinburgh	0	2
1907	Wrexham	0	1
1908	Dundee	2	1
1909	Wrexham	2	3
1910	Kilmarnock	1	0
1911	Cardiff	2	2
1912	Tynecastle	1	0
1913	Wrexham	0	0
1914	Glasgow	0	0
1920	Cardiff	1	1
1921	Aberdeen	2	1
1922	Wrexham	1	2
1923	Paisley	2	0
1924	Cardiff	0	2
1925	Tynecastle	3	1
1926	Cardiff	3	0
1927	Glasgow	3	0
1928	Wrexham	2	2
1929	Glasgow	4	2
1930	Cardiff	4	2
1931	Glasgow	1	1
1932	Wrexham	3	2
1933	Edinburgh	2	5
1934	Cardiff	2	3
1935	Aberdeen	3	2
1936	Cardiff	1	1
1937	Dundee	1	2
1938	Cardiff	1	2
1939	Edinburgh	3	2
1946	Wrexham	1	3
1947	Glasgow	1	2
1948	Cardiff (WC)	3	1
1949	Glasgow	2	0
1950	Cardiff	3	1
1951	Glasgow	0	1
1952	Cardiff (WC)	2	1
1953	Glasgow	3	3
1954	Cardiff	1	0
1955	Glasgow	2	0

1956	Cardiff	2	2
1957	Glasgow	1	1
1958	Cardiff	3	0
1959	Glasgow	1	1
1960	Cardiff	0	2
1961	Glasgow	2	0
1962	Cardiff	3	2
1963	Glasgow	2	1
1964	Cardiff	2	3
1965	Glasgow (EC)	4	1
1966	Cardiff (EC)	1	1
1967	Glasgow	3	2
1969	Wrexham	5	3
1970	Glasgow	0	0
1971	Cardiff	0	0
1972	Glasgow	1	0
1973	Wrexham	2	0
1974	Glasgow	2	0
1975	Cardiff	2	2
1976	Glasgow	3	1
1977	Glasgow (WC)	1	0
1977	Wrexham	0	0
1977	Anfield (WC)	2	0
1978	Glasgow	1	1
1979	Cardiff	0	3
1980	Glasgow	1	0
1981	Swansea	0	2
1982	Glasgow	1	0
1983	Cardiff	2	0
1984	Glasgow	2	1
1985	Glasgow (WC)	0	1
1985	Cardiff (WC)	1	1
1997	Kilmarnock	0	1
2004	Cardiff	0	4
2009	Cardiff	0	3
2011	Dublin (CC)	3	1
2012	Cardiff (WC)	1	2
2013	Glasgow (WC	1	2

SCOTLAND v NORTHERN IRELAND

Played 96; Scotland won 64; Northern Ireland 15; drawn 17; Goals: Scotland 258, Northern Ireland 80

		S	*I*
1884	Belfast	5	0
1885	Glasgow	8	2
1886	Belfast	7	2
1887	Belfast	4	1
1888	Belfast	10	2
1889	Glasgow	7	0
1890	Belfast	4	1
1891	Glasgow	2	1
1892	Belfast	3	2
1893	Glasgow	6	1
1894	Belfast	2	1
1895	Glasgow	3	1
1896	Belfast	3	3
1897	Glasgow	5	1
1898	Belfast	3	0
1899	Glasgow	9	1
1900	Belfast	3	0
1901	Glasgow	11	0
1902	Belfast	5	1
1902	Belfast	3	0
1903	Glasgow	0	2
1904	Dublin	1	1
1905	Glasgow	4	0
1906	Dublin	1	0
1907	Glasgow	3	0
1908	Dublin	5	0
1909	Glasgow	5	0
1910	Belfast	0	1
1911	Glasgow	2	0
1912	Belfast	4	1
1913	Dublin	2	1
1914	Belfast	1	1
1920	Glasgow	3	0
1921	Belfast	2	0
1922	Glasgow	2	1
1923	Belfast	1	0
1924	Glasgow	2	0
1925	Belfast	3	0
1926	Glasgow	4	0
1927	Belfast	2	0
1928	Glasgow	0	1
1929	Belfast	7	3
1930	Glasgow	3	1
1931	Belfast	0	0
1932	Glasgow	3	1
1933	Belfast	4	0
1934	Glasgow	1	2
1935	Belfast	1	2
1936	Edinburgh	2	1
1937	Belfast	3	1
1938	Aberdeen	1	1
1939	Belfast	2	0
1946	Glasgow	0	0
1947	Belfast	0	2
1948	Glasgow	3	2
1949	Belfast	8	2
1950	Glasgow	6	1
1951	Belfast	3	0
1952	Glasgow	1	1
1953	Belfast	3	1
1954	Glasgow	2	2
1955	Belfast	1	2
1956	Glasgow	1	0
1957	Belfast	1	1
1958	Glasgow	2	2
1959	Belfast	4	0
1960	Glasgow	5	1
1961	Belfast	6	1
1962	Glasgow	5	1
1963	Belfast	1	2
1964	Glasgow	3	2
1965	Belfast	2	3
1966	Glasgow	2	1
1967	Belfast	0	1
1969	Glasgow	1	1
1970	Belfast	1	0
1971	Glasgow	0	1
1972	Glasgow	2	0
1973	Glasgow	1	2

1974	Glasgow	0	1
1975	Glasgow	3	0
1976	Glasgow	3	0
1977	Glasgow	3	0
1978	Glasgow	1	1
1979	Glasgow	1	0
1980	Belfast	0	1
1981	Glasgow (WC)	1	1
1981	Glasgow	2	0
1981	Belfast (WC)	0	0
1982	Belfast	1	1
1983	Glasgow	0	0
1984	Belfast	0	2
1992	Glasgow	1	0
2008	Glasgow	0	0
2011	Dublin (CC)	3	0
2015	Glasgow	1	0

WALES v NORTHERN IRELAND

Played 97; Wales won 45; Northern Ireland won 27; drawn 25; Goals: Wales 191 Northern Ireland 132

		W	*I*
1882	Wrexham	7	1
1883	Belfast	1	1
1884	Wrexham	6	0
1885	Belfast	8	2
1886	Wrexham	5	0
1887	Belfast	1	4
1888	Wrexham	11	0
1889	Belfast	3	1
1890	Shrewsbury	5	2
1891	Belfast	2	7
1892	Bangor	1	1
1893	Belfast	3	4
1894	Swansea	4	1
1895	Belfast	2	2
1896	Wrexham	6	1
1897	Belfast	3	4
1898	Llandudno	0	1
1899	Belfast	0	1
1900	Llandudno	2	0
1901	Belfast	1	0
1902	Cardiff	0	3
1903	Belfast	0	2
1904	Bangor	0	1
1905	Belfast	2	2
1906	Wrexham	4	4
1907	Belfast	3	2
1908	Aberdare	0	1
1909	Belfast	3	2
1910	Wrexham	4	1
1911	Belfast	2	1
1912	Cardiff	2	3
1913	Belfast	1	0
1914	Wrexham	1	2
1920	Belfast	2	2
1921	Swansea	2	1
1922	Belfast	1	1
1923	Wrexham	0	3
1924	Belfast	1	0
1925	Wrexham	0	0
1926	Belfast	0	3
1927	Cardiff	2	2
1928	Belfast	2	1
1929	Wrexham	2	2
1930	Belfast	0	7
1931	Wrexham	3	2
1932	Belfast	0	4
1933	Wrexham	4	1
1934	Belfast	1	1
1935	Wrexham	3	1
1936	Belfast	2	3
1937	Wrexham	4	1
1938	Belfast	0	1
1939	Wrexham	3	1
1947	Belfast	1	2
1948	Wrexham	2	0
1949	Belfast	2	0
1950	Wrexham (WC)	0	0
1951	Belfast	2	1
1952	Swansea	3	0
1953	Belfast	3	2
1954	Wrexham (WC)	1	2
1955	Belfast	3	2
1956	Cardiff	1	1
1957	Belfast	0	0
1958	Cardiff	1	1
1959	Belfast	1	4
1960	Wrexham	3	2
1961	Belfast	5	1
1962	Cardiff	4	0
1963	Belfast	4	1
1964	Swansea	2	3
1965	Belfast	5	0
1966	Cardiff	1	4
1967	Belfast (EC)	0	0
1968	Wrexham (EC)	2	0
1969	Belfast	0	0
1970	Swansea	1	0
1971	Belfast	0	1
1972	Wrexham	0	0
1973	*Goodison Park	0	1
1974	Wrexham	1	0
1975	Belfast	0	1
1976	Swansea	1	0
1977	Belfast	1	1
1978	Wrexham	1	0
1979	Belfast	1	1
1980	Cardiff	0	1
1982	Wrexham	3	0
1983	Belfast	1	0
1984	Swansea	1	1
2004	Cardiff (WC)	2	2
2005	Belfast (WC)	3	2
2007	Belfast	0	0
2008	Glasgow	0	0
2011	Dublin (CC)	2	0
2016	Cardiff	1	1
2016	Paris (EC)	1	0

(*Switched from Belfast because of political situation in N Ireland)

WORLD CUP 2018 – QUALIFYING

England and Scotland will resume rivalry in the new season in qualifying for the 2018 World Cup in Russia. They have been paired in Group F and both managers welcomed the prospect of two high-profile matches. 'The games will excite the public and get people in the mass media excited too,' said England's Roy Hodgson when the draw was made before his side's Euro 2016 failure, after which he stepped down from the job. 'It's a good draw all round.' Scotland's Gordon Strachan said: 'Just as the sun came up in Glasgow, we heard we will play England. I can see why the fans are celebrating. It's a fantastic fixture.' The teams last met in November, 2014 when England won a friendly 3-1 at Celtic Park, Wayne Rooney scoring twice. Their last competitive fixture was in the play-off round for a place in Euro 2000 when England won 2-1 on aggregate. Two goals by Paul Scholes gave them a 2-0 victory at Hampden and they went through despite losing the return 1-0 at Wembley to a Don Hutchinson goal. This time, the games will have added spice, with Scotland the only one of the British Isles teams not to have qualified for Euro 2016. The first leg is at Wembley on November 11, 2016 and the second at Hampden on June 10, 2017. Other countries in this group are Lithuania, Malta, Slovakia and Slovenia. Wales and the Republic of Ireland were also drawn in the same group, as they were in qualification for Euro 2008. Then, Stephen Ireland scored the only goal of the first match in Dublin and the second ended 2-2 in Cardiff. Neither qualified. Northern Ireland were drawn against defending champions Germany and the Czech Republic. The nine group winners go through to the finals, with the best eight-runners-up contesting two-leg play-offs for four further places.

EUROPEAN QUALIFYING GROUPS

Group A: Holland, France, Sweden, Bulgaria, Belarus, Luxembourg
Group B: Portugal, Switzerland, Hungary, Faroe Islands, Latvia, Andorra
Group C: Germany, Czech Republic, **Northern Ireland**, Norway, Azerbaijan, San Marino
Group D: **Wales**, Austria, Serbia, **Republic of Ireland**, Moldova, Georgia
Group E: Romania, Denmark, Poland, Montenegro, Armenia, Kazakhstan
Group F: **England**, Lithuania, Malta, **Scotland**, Slovakia, Slovenia
Group G: Spain, Italy, Albania, Israel, Macedonia, Liechtenstein
Group H: Belgium, Bosnia-Herzegovina, Greece, Estonia, Cyprus
Group I: Croatia, Iceland, Ukraine, Turkey, Finland

SOUTH AMERICAN QUALIFYING (to date)

	P	W	D	L	F	A	Pts
Uruguay	6	4	1	1	12	4	13
Ecuador	6	4	1	1	12	7	13
Argentina	6	3	2	1	6	4	11
Chile	6	3	1	2	12	10	10
Colombia	6	3	1	2	9	8	10
Brazil	6	2	3	1	11	8	9
Paraguay	6	2	3	1	7	6	9
Peru	6	1	1	4	6	12	4
Bolivia	6	1	0	5	7	13	3
Venezuela	6	0	1	5	7	17	10

WORLD CUP SUMMARIES 1930–2014

1930 – URUGUAY

WINNERS: Uruguay RUNNERS-UP: Argentina THIRD: USA FOURTH: Yugoslavia
Other countries taking part: Belgium, Bolivia, Brazil, Chile, France, Mexico, Paraguay, Peru, Romania. **Total entries:** 13
Venue: All matches played in Montevideo
Top scorer: Stabile (Argentina) 8 goals
Final (30/7/30): **Uruguay 4** (Dorado 12, Cea 55, Iriarte 64, Castro 89) **Argentina 2** (Peucelle 29, Stabile 35). **Att:** 90,000
Uruguay: Ballesteros; Nasazzi (capt), Mascheroni, Andrade, Fernandez, Gestido, Dorado, Scarone, Castro, Cea, Iriarte
Argentina: Botasso; Della Torre, Paternoster, J Evaristo, Monti, Suarez, Peucelle, Varallo, Stabile, Ferreira (capt), M Evaristo
Referee: Langenus (Belgium). **Half-time:** 1-2

1934 – ITALY

WINNERS: Italy RUNNERS-UP: Czechoslovakia THIRD: Germany FOURTH: Austria
Other countries in finals: Argentina, Belgium, Brazil, Egypt, France, Holland, Hungary, Romania, Spain, Sweden, Switzerland, USA. **Total entries:** 29 (16 qualifiers)
Venues: Bologna, Florence, Genoa, Milan, Naples, Rome, Trieste, Turin
Top scorers: Conen (Germany), Nejedly (Czechoslovakia), Schiavio (Italy), each 4 goals. **Final** (Rome, 10/6/34): **Italy 2** (Orsi 82, Schiavio 97) **Czechoslovakia 1** (Puc 70) after extra-time. **Att:** 50,000
Italy: Combi (capt); Monzeglio, Allemandi, Ferraris, Monti, Bertolini, Guaita, Meazza, Schiavio, Ferrari, Orsi
Czechoslovakia: Planicka (capt); Zenisek, Ctyroky, Kostalek, Cambal, Krcil, Junek, Svoboda, Sobotka, Nejedly, Puc
Referee: Eklind (Sweden). **Half-time:** 0-0 (90 mins: 1-1)

1938 – FRANCE

WINNERS: Italy RUNNERS-UP: Hungary THIRD: Brazil FOURTH: Sweden
Other countries in finals: Belgium, Cuba, Czechoslovakia, Dutch East Indies, France, Germany, Holland, Norway, Poland, Romania, Switzerland. **Total entries:** 25 (15 qualifiers)
Venues: Antibes, Bordeaux, Le Havre, Lille, Marseille, Paris, Reims, Strasbourg, Toulouse
Top scorer: Leonidas (Brazil) 8 goals
Final (Paris, 19/6/38): **Italy 4** (Colaussi 6, 36, Piola 15, 81) **Hungary 2** (Titkos 7, Sarosi 65). **Att:** 45,000
Italy: Olivieri; Foni, Rava, Serantoni, Andreolo, Locatelli, Biavati, Meazza (capt), Piola, Ferrari, Colaussi
Hungary: Szabo; Polgar, Biro, Szalay, Szucs, Lazar, Sas, Vincze, Sarosi (capt), Szengeller, Titkos
Referee: Capdeville (France). **Half-time:** 3-1

1950 – BRAZIL

WINNERS: Uruguay RUNNERS-UP: Brazil THIRD: Sweden FOURTH: Spain
Other countries in finals: Bolivia, Chile, England, Italy, Mexico, Paraguay, Switzerland, USA, Yugoslavia. **Total entries:** 29 (13 qualifiers)
Venues: Belo Horizonte, Curitiba, Porto Alegre, Recife, Rio de Janeiro, Sao Paulo
Top scorer: Ademir (Brazil) 9 goals
Deciding Match (Rio de Janeiro, 16/7/50): **Uruguay 2** (Schiaffino 64, Ghiggia 79) **Brazil 1** (Friaca 47). **Att:** 199,850
(For the only time, the World Cup was decided on a final pool system, in which the winners of the four qualifying groups met in a six-match series So, unlike previous and subsequent

tournaments, there was no official final as such, but Uruguay v Brazil was the deciding match in the final pool)
Uruguay: Maspoli; Gonzales, Tejera, Gambetta, Varela (capt), Andrade, Ghiggia, Perez, Miguez, Schiaffino, Moran
Brazil: Barbosa; Augusto (capt), Juvenal, Bauer, Danilo, Bigode, Friaca, Zizinho, Ademir, Jair, Chico
Referee: Reader (England). **Half-time:** 0-0

1954 – SWITZERLAND

WINNERS: West Germany RUNNERS-UP: Hungary THIRD: Austria FOURTH: Uruguay
Other countries in finals: Belgium, Brazil, Czechoslovakia, England, France, Italy, Korea, Mexico, Scotland, Switzerland, Turkey, Yugoslavia. **Total entries:** 35 (16 qualifiers)
Venues: Basle, Berne, Geneva, Lausanne, Lugano, Zurich
Top scorer: Kocsis (Hungary) 11 goals
Final (Berne, 4/7/54): **West Germany 3** (Morlock 12, Rahn 17, 84) **Hungary 2** (Puskas 4, Czibor 9). **Att:** 60,000
West Germany: Turek; Posipal, Kohlmeyer, Eckel, Liebrich, Mai, Rahn, Morlock, O Walter, F Walter (capt), Schaefer
Hungary: Grosics; Buzansky, Lantos, Bozsik, Lorant, Zakarias, Czibor, Kocsis, Hidegkuti, Puskas (capt), J Toth
Referee: Ling (England). **Half-time:** 2-2

1958 – SWEDEN

WINNERS: Brazil RUNNERS-UP: Sweden THIRD: France FOURTH: West Germany
Other countries in finals: Argentina, Austria, Czechoslovakia, England, Hungary, Mexico, Northern Ireland, Paraguay, Scotland, Soviet Union, Wales, Yugoslavia. **Total entries:** 47 (16 qualifiers)
Venues: Boras, Eskilstuna, Gothenburg, Halmstad, Helsingborgs, Malmo, Norrkoping, Orebro, Sandviken, Stockholm, Vasteras
Top scorer: Fontaine (France) 13 goals
Final (Stockholm, 29/6/58): **Brazil 5** (Vava 10, 32, Pele 55, 88, Zagalo 76) **Sweden 2** (Liedholm 4, Simonsson 83). **Att:** 49,737
Brazil: Gilmar; D Santos, N Santos, Zito, Bellini (capt), Orlando, Garrincha, Didi, Vava, Pele, Zagalo
Sweden: Svensson; Bergmark, Axbom, Boerjesson, Gustavsson, Parling, Hamrin, Gren, Simonsson, Liedholm (capt), Skoglund
Referee: Guigue (France). **Half-time:** 2-1

1962 – CHILE

WINNERS: Brazil RUNNERS-UP: Czechoslovakia THIRD: Chile FOURTH: Yugoslavia
Other countries in finals: Argentina, Bulgaria, Colombia, England, Hungary, Italy, Mexico, Soviet Union, Spain, Switzerland, Uruguay, West Germany. **Total entries:** 53 (16 qualifiers)
Venues: Arica, Rancagua, Santiago, Vina del Mar
Top scorer: Jerkovic (Yugoslavia) 5 goals
Final (Santiago, 17/6/62): **Brazil 3** (Amarildo 17, Zito 69, Vava 77) **Czechoslovakia 1** (Masopust 16). **Att:** 68,679
Brazil: Gilmar; D Santos, Mauro (capt), Zozimo, N Santos, Zito, Didi, Garrincha, Vava, Amarildo, Zagalo
Czechoslovakia: Schroiff; Tichy, Novak, Pluskal, Popluhar, Masopust (capt), Pospichal, Scherer, Kvasnak, Kadraba, Jelinek
Referee: Latychev (Soviet Union). **Half-time:** 1-1

1966 – ENGLAND

WINNERS: England RUNNERS-UP: West Germany THIRD: Portugal FOURTH: USSR
Other countries in finals: Argentina, Brazil, Bulgaria, Chile, France, Hungary, Italy, Mexico, North Korea, Spain, Switzerland, Uruguay. **Total entries:** 53 (16 qualifiers)

Venues: Birmingham (Villa Park), Liverpool (Goodison Park), London (Wembley and White City), Manchester (Old Trafford), Middlesbrough (Ayresome Park), Sheffield (Hillsborough), Sunderland (Roker Park)
Top scorer: Eusebio (Portugal) 9 goals
Final (Wembley, 30/7/66): **England 4** (Hurst 19, 100, 120, Peters 78) **West Germany 2** (Haller 13, Weber 89) after extra-time. **Att:** 93,802
England: Banks; Cohen, Wilson, Stiles, J Charlton, Moore (capt), Ball, Hurst, Hunt, R Charlton, Peters
West Germany: Tilkowski; Hottges, Schnellinger, Beckenbauer, Schulz, Weber, Haller, Held, Seeler (capt), Overath, Emmerich
Referee: Dienst (Switzerland). **Half-time:** 1-1 (90 mins: 2-2)

1970 – MEXICO

WINNERS: Brazil RUNNERS-UP: Italy THIRD: West Germany FOURTH: Uruguay
Other countries in finals: Belgium, Bulgaria, Czechoslovakia, El Salvador, England, Israel, Mexico, Morocco, Peru, Romania, Soviet Union, Sweden. **Total entries:** 68 (16 qualifiers)
Venues: Guadalajara, Leon, Mexico City, Puebla, Toluca
Top scorer: Muller (West Germany) 10 goals
Final (Mexico City, 21/6/70): **Brazil** 4 (Pele 18, Gerson 66, Jairzinho 71, Carlos Alberto 87) **Italy** 1 (Boninsegna 38). **Att:** 107,412
Brazil: Felix; Carlos Alberto (capt), Brito, Piazza, Everaldo, Clodoaldo, Gerson, Jairzinho, Tostao, Pele, Rivelino
Italy: Albertosi; Burgnich, Facchetti (capt), Cera, Rosato, Bertini (Juliano 72), Domenghini, De Sisti, Mazzola, Boninsegna (Rivera 84), Riva
Referee: Glockner (East Germany). **Half-time:** 1-1

1974 – WEST GERMANY

WINNERS: West Germany RUNNERS-UP: Holland THIRD: Poland FOURTH: Brazil
Other countries in finals: Argentina, Australia, Bulgaria, Chile, East Germany, Haiti, Italy, Scotland, Sweden, Uruguay, Yugoslavia, Zaire. **Total entries:** 98 (16 qualifiers)
Venues: Berlin, Dortmund, Dusseldorf, Frankfurt, Gelsenkirchen, Hamburg, Hanover, Munich, Stuttgart
Top scorer: Lato (Poland) 7 goals
Final (Munich, 7/7/74): **West Germany** 2 (Breitner 25 pen, Muller 43) **Holland** 1 (Neeskens 2 pen). **Att:** 77,833
West Germany: Maier; Vogts, Schwarzenbeck, Beckenbauer (capt), Breitner, Bonhof, Hoeness, Overath, Grabowski, Muller, Holzenbein
Holland: Jongbloed; Suurbier, Rijsbergen (De Jong 69), Haan, Krol, Jansen, Van Hanegem, Neeskens, Rep, Cruyff (capt), Rensenbrink (R Van der Kerkhof 46)
Referee: Taylor (England). **Half-time:** 2-1

1978 – ARGENTINA

WINNERS: Argentina RUNNERS-UP: Holland THIRD: Brazil FOURTH: Italy
Other countries in finals: Austria, France, Hungary, Iran, Mexico, Peru, Poland, Scotland, Spain, Sweden, Tunisia, West Germany. **Total entries:** 102 (16 qualifiers)
Venues: Buenos Aires, Cordoba, Mar del Plata, Mendoza, Rosario
Top scorer: Kempes (Argentina) 6 goals
Final (Buenos Aires, 25/6/78): **Argentina** 3 (Kempes 38, 104, Bertoni 115) **Holland** 1 (Nanninga 82) after extra-time. **Att:** 77,000
Argentina: Fillol; Passarella (capt), Olguin, Galvan, Tarantini, Ardiles (Larrosa 66), Gallego, Ortiz (Houseman 74), Bertoni, Luque, Kempes
Holland: Jongbloed; Krol (capt), Poortvliet, Brandts, Jansen (Suurbier 73), Haan, Neeskens, W Van der Kerkhof, Rep (Nanninga 58), R Van der Kerkhof, Rensenbrink
Referee: Gonella (Italy). **Half-time:** 1-0 (90 mins: 1-1)

1982 – SPAIN

WINNERS: Italy RUNNERS-UP: West Germany THIRD: Poland FOURTH: France
Other countries in finals: Algeria, Argentina, Austria, Belgium, Brazil, Cameroon, Chile, Czechoslovakia, El Salvador, England, Honduras, Hungary, Kuwait, New Zealand, Northern Ireland, Peru, Scotland, Soviet Union, Spain, Yugoslavia. **Total entries:** 109 (24 qualifiers)
Venues: Alicante, Barcelona, Bilbao, Coruna, Elche, Gijon, Madrid, Malaga, Oviedo, Seville, Valencia, Valladolid, Vigo, Zaragoza
Top scorer: Rossi (Italy) 6 goals
Final (Madrid, 11/7/82): **Italy** 3 (Rossi 57, Tardelli 69, Altobelli 81) **West Germany** 1 (Breitner 84). **Att:** 90,089
Italy: Zoff (capt); Bergomi, Scirea, Collovati, Cabrini, Oriali, Gentile, Tardelli, Conti, Rossi, Graziani (Altobelli 18 – Causio 88)
West Germany: Schumacher; Kaltz, Stielike, K-H Forster, B Forster, Dremmler (Hrubesch 63), Breitner, Briegel, Rummenigge (capt) (Muller 70), Fischer, Littbarski
Referee: Coelho (Brazil). **Half-time:** 0-0

1986 – MEXICO

WINNERS: Argentina RUNNERS-UP: West Germany THIRD: France FOURTH: Belgium
Other countries in finals: Algeria, Brazil, Bulgaria, Canada, Denmark, England, Hungary, Iraq, Italy, Mexico, Morocco, Northern Ireland, Paraguay, Poland, Portugal, Scotland, South Korea, Soviet Union, Spain, Uruguay. **Total entries:** 118 (24 qualifiers)
Venues: Guadalajara, Irapuato, Leon, Mexico City, Monterrey, Nezahualcoyotl, Puebla, Queretaro, Toluca
Top scorer: Lineker (England) 6 goals
Final (Mexico City, 29/6/86): **Argentina** 3 (Brown 23, Valdano 56, Burruchaga 85) **West Germany** 2 (Rummenigge 74, Voller 82). **Att:** 115,026
Argentina: Pumpido; Cuciuffo, Brown, Ruggeri, Olarticoechea, Batista, Giusti, Maradona (capt), Burruchaga (Trobbiani 89), Enrique, Valdano
West Germany: Schumacher; Berthold, K-H Forster, Jakobs, Brehme, Briegel, Eder, Matthaus, Magath (Hoeness 62), Allofs (Voller 45), Rummenigge (capt)
Referee: Filho (Brazil). **Half-time:** 1-0

1990 – ITALY

WINNERS: West Germany RUNNERS-UP: Argentina THIRD: Italy FOURTH: England
Other countries in finals: Austria, Belgium, Brazil, Cameroon, Colombia, Costa Rica, Czechoslovakia, Egypt, Holland, Republic of Ireland, Romania, Scotland, Spain, South Korea, Soviet Union, Sweden, United Arab Emirates, USA, Uruguay, Yugoslavia. **Total entries:** 103 (24 qualifiers)
Venues: Bari, Bologna, Cagliari, Florence, Genoa, Milan, Naples, Palermo, Rome, Turin, Udine, Verona
Top scorer: Schillaci (Italy) 6 goals
Final (Rome, 8/7/90): **Argentina** 0 **West Germany** 1 (Brehme 85 pen). **Att:** 73,603
Argentina: Goycochea; Ruggeri (Monzon 45), Simon, Serrizuela, Lorenzo, Basualdo, Troglio, Burruchaga (Calderon 53), Sensini, Maradona (capt), Dezotti **Sent-off**: Monzon (65), Dezotti (86) – first players ever to be sent off in World Cup Final
West Germany: Illgner; Berthold (Reuter 75), Buchwald, Augenthaler, Kohler, Brehme, Matthaus (capt), Littbarski, Hassler, Klinsmann, Voller
Referee: Codesal (Mexico). **Half-time:** 0-0

1994 – USA

WINNERS: Brazil RUNNERS-UP: Italy THIRD: Sweden FOURTH: Bulgaria
Other countries in finals: Argentina, Belgium, Bolivia, Cameroon, Colombia, Germany, Greece, Holland, Mexico, Morocco, Nigeria, Norway, Republic of Ireland, Romania, Russia, Saudi Arabia, South Korea, Spain, Switzerland, USA. **Total entries:** 144 (24 qualifiers)

Venues: Boston, Chicago, Dallas, Detroit, Los Angeles, New York City, Orlando, San Francisco, Washington
Top scorers: Salenko (Russia), Stoichkov (Bulgaria), each 6 goals
Final (Los Angeles, 17/7/94): **Brazil** 0 **Italy** 0 after extra-time; Brazil won 3-2 on pens
Att: 94,194
Brazil: Taffarel; Jorginho (Cafu 21), Aldair, Marcio Santos, Branco, Mazinho, Mauro Silva, Dunga (capt), Zinho (Viola 105), Romario, Bebeto
Italy: Pagliuca; Mussi (Apolloni 35), Baresi (capt), Maldini, Benarrivo, Berti, Albertini, D Baggio (Evani 95), Donadoni, R Baggio, Massaro
Referee: Puhl (Hungary)
Shoot-out: Baresi missed, Marco Santos saved, Albertini 1-0, Romario 1-1, Evani 2-1, Branco 2-2, Massaro saved, Dunga 2-3, R Baggio missed

1998 – FRANCE

WINNERS: France RUNNERS-UP: Brazil THIRD: Croatia FOURTH: Holland
Other countries in finals: Argentina, Austria, Belgium, Bulgaria, Cameroon, Chile, Colombia, Denmark, England, Germany, Iran, Italy, Jamaica, Japan, Mexico, Morocco, Nigeria, Norway, Paraguay, Romania, Saudi Arabia, Scotland, South Africa, South Korea, Spain, Tunisia, USA, Yugoslavia. **Total entries:** 172 (32 qualifiers)
Venues: Bordeaux, Lens, Lyon, Marseille, Montpellier, Nantes, Paris (St Denis, Parc des Princes), Saint-Etienne, Toulouse
Top scorer: Davor Suker (Croatia) 6 goals
Final (Paris St Denis, 12/7/98): **Brazil** 0 **France** 3 (Zidane 27, 45, Petit 90). **Att:** 75,000
Brazil: Taffarel; Cafu, Junior Baiano, Aldair, Roberto Carlos; Dunga (capt), Leonardo (Denilson 46), Cesar Sampaio (Edmundo 74), Rivaldo; Bebeto, Ronaldo
France: Barthez; Thuram, Leboeuf, Desailly, Lizarazu; Karembeu (Boghossian 56), Deschamps (capt), Petit, Zidane, Djorkaeff (Viera 75); Guivarc'h (Dugarry 66) **Sent-off**: Desailly (68)
Referee: Belqola (Morocco). **Half-time:** 0-2

2002 – JAPAN/SOUTH KOREA

WINNERS: Brazil RUNNERS-UP: Germany THIRD: Turkey FOURTH: South Korea
Other countries in finals: Argentina, Belgium, Cameroon, China, Costa Rica, Croatia, Denmark, Ecuador, England, France, Italy, Japan, Mexico, Nigeria, Paraguay, Poland, Portugal, Republic of Ireland, Russia, Saudi Arabia, Senegal, Slovenia, South Africa, Spain, Sweden, Tunisia, USA, Uruguay. **Total entries:** 195 (32 qualifiers)
Venues: Japan – Ibaraki, Kobe, Miyagi, Niigata, Oita, Osaka, Saitama, Sapporo, Shizuoka, Yokohama. **South Korea** – Daegu, Daejeon, Gwangju, Incheon, Jeonju, Busan, Seogwipo, Seoul, Suwon Ulsan
Top scorer: Ronaldo (Brazil) 8 goals
Final (Yokohama, 30/6/02): **Germany** 0, **Brazil** 2 (Ronaldo 67, 79). **Att:** 69,029
Germany: Kahn (capt), Linke, Ramelow, Metzelder, Frings, Jeremies (Asamoah 77), Hamann, Schneider, Bode (Zeige 84), Klose (Bierhoff 74), Neuville
Brazil: Marcos, Lucio, Edmilson, Roque Junior, Cafu (capt) Kleberson, Gilberto Silva, Roberto Carlos, Ronaldinho (Juninho 85), Rivaldo, Ronaldo (Denilson 90)
Referee: Collina (Italy). **Half-time:** 0-0

2006 – GERMANY

WINNERS: Italy RUNNERS-UP: France THIRD: Germany FOURTH: Portugal
Other countries in finals: Angola, Argentina, Australia, Brazil, Costa Rica, Croatia, Czech Republic, Ecuador, England, Ghana, Holland, Iran, Ivory Coast, Japan, Mexico, Paraguay, Poland, Saudi Arabia, Serbia & Montenegro, South Korea, Spain, Sweden, Switzerland, Trinidad & Tobago, Togo, Tunisia, Ukraine, USA. **Total entries:** 198 (32 qualifiers)
Venues: Berlin, Cologne, Dortmund, Frankfurt, Gelsenkirchen, Hamburg, Hanover, Kaiserslautern, Leipzig, Munich, Nuremberg, Stuttgart

op scorer: Klose (Germany) 5 goals
inal (Berlin, 9/7/06): **Italy** 1 (Materazzi 19) **France** 1 (Zidane 7 pen) after extra-time: Italy von 5-3 on pens. **Att:** 69,000
taly: Buffon; Zambrotta, Cannavaro (capt), Materazzi, Grosso, Perrotta (De Rossi 61), Pirlo, attuso, Camoranesi (Del Piero 86), Totti (Iaquinta 61), Toni
rance: Barthez; Sagnol, Thuram, Gallas, Abidal, Makelele, Vieira (Diarra 56), Ribery Trezeguet 100), Malouda, Zidane (capt), Henry (Wiltord 107) **Sent-off**: Zidane (110)
eferee: Elizondo (Argentina). **Half-time:** 1-1 90 mins: 1-1
hoot-out: Pirlo 1-0, Wiltord 1-1, Materazzi 2-1, Trezeguet missed, De Rossi 3-1, Abidal 3-2, el Piero 4-2, Sagnol 4-3, Grosso 5-3

2010 – SOUTH AFRICA

VINNERS: Spain RUNNERS-UP: Holland THIRD: Germany FOURTH: Uruguay
)ther countries in finals: Algeria, Argentina, Australia, Brazil, Cameroon, Chile, Denmark, ngland, France, Ghana, Greece, Honduras, Italy, Ivory Coast, Japan, Mexico, New Zealand, ligeria, North Korea, Paraguay, Portugal, Serbia, Slovakia, Slovenia, South Africa, South orea, Switzerland, USA. **Total entries**: 204 (32 qualifiers)
enues: Bloemfontein, Cape Town, Durban, Johannesburg (Ellis Park), Johannesburg (Soccer ity), Nelspruit, Polokwane, Port Elizabeth, Pretoria, Rustenburg
op scorers: Forlan (Uruguay), Muller (Germany), Sneijder (Holland), Villa (Spain) 5 goals
inal (Johannesburg, Soccer City, 11/7/10): **Holland** 0 **Spain** 1 (Iniesta 116) after extra-ime; **Att:** 84,490
Iolland: Stekelenburg; Van der Wiel, Heitinga, Mathijsen, Van Bronckhorst (capt) (Braafheid 05), Van Bommel, De Jong (Van der Vaart 99), Robben, Sneijder, Kuyt (Elia 71), Van ersie. **Sent off:** Heitinga (109)
pain: Casillas (capt); Sergio Ramos, Puyol, Piquet, Capdevila, Busquets, Xabi Alonso Fabregas 87), Iniesta, Xavi, Pedro (Jesus Navas 60), Villa (Torres 106)
eferee: Webb (England). **Half-time:** 0-0

2014 – BRAZIL

VINNERS: Germany RUNNERS-UP: Argentina THIRD: Holland FOURTH: Brazil
)ther countries in finals: Algeria, Argentina, Australia, Belgium, Bosnia-Herzegovina, Brazil, ameroon, Chile, Colombia, Costa Rica, Croatia, Ecuador, England, France, Germany, Ghana, ireece, Holland, Honduras, Iran, Italy, Ivory Coast, Japan, Mexico, Nigeria, Portugal, Russia, outh Korea, Spain, Switzerland, Uruguay, USA. **Total entries:** 204 (32 qualifiers)
enues: Belo Horizonte, Brasilia, Cuiaba, Curitiba, Fortaleza, Manaus, Natal, Porto Alegre, ecife, Rio de Janeiro, Salvador, Sao Paulo
op scorer: Rodriguez (Colombia) 6 goals
inal (Rio de Janeiro, 13/7/14): **Germany** 1 (Gotze 113) **Argentina** 0 after extra-time; **Att:** 74,738
iermany: Neuer; Lahm (capt), Boateng, Hummels, Howedes, Kramer (Schurrle 32), chweinsteiger, Muller, Kroos, Ozil (Mertesacker 120), Klose (Gotze 88)
rgentina: Romero; Zabaleta, Demichelis, Garay, Rojo, Biglia, Mascherano, Perez (Gago 86), Aessi (capt), Lavezzi (Aguero 46), Higuain (Palacio 78)
eferee: Rizzoli (Italy). **Half-time:** 0-0

BRITISH AND IRISH UNDER-21 INTERNATIONALS 2015–16

EUROPEAN CHAMPIONSHIP 2017 – QUALIFYING

LUXEMBOURG 1 WALES 3
Group 5: Esch (323); September 5, 2015

Wales: O'Brien (Manchester City), Yorwerth (Ipswich), Wright (Huddersfield), John (Cardiff), Jones (Everton), O'Sullivan (Cardiff), Evans (Wolves), Sheehan (Swansea) (Thompson, Norwich 82), Burns (Bristol City) (Charles, Huddersfield 82), Harrison (Bristol Rov) (Wilson, Liverpool 60), Hedges (Swansea). **Booked**: Yorwerth
Scorers – Luxembourg: Sinani (90). **Wales**: Burns (35, 72), Wilson (63). **Half-time**: 0-1

NORTHERN IRELAND 1 SCOTLAND 2
Group 3: Mourneview Park, Lurgan (338); September 5, 2015

Northern Ireland: Brennan (Kilmarnock), McLaughlin (Liverpool), Conlan (Burnley) (Sharpe, Notts Co 74), Donnelly (Fulham), Sendles-White (Hamilton), Dummigan (Burnley), Johnson (Stevenage), Gorman (Stevenage), McCartan (Accrington) (Maloney, Middlesbrough 61), Duffy (Celtic) (McDaid, Leeds 87), Kennedy (Charlton). **Booked**: Kennedy, Gorman, Donnelly. **Sent off**: Gorman (59)
Scotland: Hamilton (Hearts), Findlay (Celtic), Paterson (Hearts), Souttar (Dundee Utd), McGhee (Hearts), Fraser (Bournemouth) (King, Hearts 85), Gauld (Sporting), McGinn (Hibernian), McFadzean (Sheffield Utd), Christie (Celtic) (Nicholson, Hearts 81), Cummings (Hibernian) (Shankland, Aberdeen 75). **Booked**: Souttar, McFadzean, McGhee
Scorers – Northern Ireland: Kennedy (7). **Scotland**: Christie (33), Fraser (61). **Half-time**: 1-1

NORWAY 0 ENGLAND 1
Group 9: Drammen (3,750); September 7, 2015

England: Pickford (Sunderland), Gomez (Liverpool), Chambers (Arsenal), Dier (Tottenham), Targett (Southampton), Ward-Prowse (Southampton), Loftus-Cheek (Chelsea) (Forster-Caskey, Brighton 70), Alli (Tottenham) (Chalobah, Chelsea 46), Ibe (Liverpool), Redmond (Norwich), Woodrow (Fulham). **Booked**: Ward-Prowse, Chalobah
Scorer – England: Ward-Prowse (45 pen). **Half-time**: 0-1

ICELAND 1 NORTHERN IRELAND 1
Group 3: Reykjavik (552); September 8, 2015

Northern Ireland: Brennan (Kilmarnock), McLaughlin (Liverpool) (McCartan, Accrington 82), Donnelly (Fulham), Singleton (Glenavon), Dummigan (Burnley), Sharpe (Notts Co), Johnson (Stevenage), McKnight (Shrewsbury), Maloney (Middlesbrough), Duffy (Celtic), Kennedy (Charlton). **Booked**: Johnson, McLaughlin
Scorers – Iceland: Prandarson (39). **Northern Ireland**: Johnson (2). **Half-time**: 1-1

ANDORRA 0 REPUBLIC OF IRELAND 2
Group 2: La Vella (650); September 8, 2015

Republic of Ireland: Rogers (Aberdeen), B Lenihan (Hull), D Lenihan (Blackburn), Hoban (Watford), Connors (Dagenham), Rea (Brighton) (Long, Reading 87), Cullen (West Ham), Browne (Preston), Grego-Cox (QPR) (Maguire, Dundalk 85), O'Dowda (Oxford) (Connolly, Ipswich 85), Kavanagh (Fulham). **Booked**: Rea, Grego-Cox, Connors
Scorers – Republic of Ireland: Hoban (13), Cullen (21). **Half-time**: 0-2

DENMARK 0 WALES 0
Group 5: Aalborg (1,854); October 9, 2015

Wales: O'Brien (Manchester City), Yorwerth (Ipswich), Lockyer (Bristol Rov), John (Cardiff) (J Evans, Fulham 73), Jones (Everton), O'Sullivan (Cardiff) (Thompson, Norwich 87), L Evans

Wolves), Sheehan (Swansea), Wilson (Liverpool) (Charles, Huddersfield 70), Harrison (Bristol ov), Hedges (Swansea)

REPUBLIC OF IRELAND 3 LITHUANIA 0
Group 2: Sports Centre, Waterford (1,520); October 9, 2015

epublic of Ireland: Rogers (Aberdeen), Long (Reading), Connors (Dagenham), Rea (Brighton) Griffin, Reading 79), D Lenihan (Blackburn), Browne (Preston) (Charsley, Everton 82), 'Dowda (Oxford), Cullen (West Ham), Wilkinson (Bolton) (Connolly, Ipswich 65), Byrne Manchester City), Kavanagh (Fulham) **Booked**: Browne

corers – Republic of Ireland: O'Dowda (27), Wilkinson (30), Browne (77). **Half-time**: 2-0

SCOTLAND 1 FRANCE 2
Group 3: Pittodrie, Aberdeen (3,025); October 10, 2015

cotland: Hamilton (Hearts), Paterson (Hearts), Kingsley (Swansea), Findlay (Celtic), McGhee Hearts), McGinn (Hibernian), Slater (Kilmarnock) (Shankland, Aberdeen 58), Nicholson Hearts) (King, Hearts 68), Gauld (Sporting), Christie (Celtic), Cummings (Hibernian) McManus, Fleetwood 78). **Booked**: Christie, Kingsley. **Sent off**: Gauld (74)

corers – Scotland: King (90). **France**: Findlay (12 og), Tolisso (53). **Half-time**: 0-1

ENGLAND 3 KAZAKHSTAN 0
Group 9: Ricoh Stadium, Coventry (15,165); October 13, 2015

ngland: Pickford (Sunderland), Gomez (Liverpool) (Iorfa, Wolves 81), Chambers (Arsenal), ier (Tottenham), Targett (Southampton), Ward-Prowse (Southampton), Baker (Chelsea), edmond (Norwich), Loftus-Cheek (Chelsea) (Chalobah, Chelsea 84), Ibe (Liverpool) (Watmore, underland), Akpom (Arsenal)

corers – England: Loftus-Cheek (52), Redmond (69), Akpom (90). **Half-time**: 0-0

SCOTLAND 0 ICELAND 0
Group 3: Pittodrie, Aberdeen (1,935); October 13, 2015

cotland: Hamilton (Hearts), Paterson (Hearts), Kingsley (Swansea), Hyam (Reading), McGhee Hearts), McGinn (Hibernian), Fulton (Swansea) (Love, Manchester Utd 75), Nicholson Hearts), Christie (Celtic), King (Hearts) (McManus, Fleetwood 83), Cummings (Hibernian) Shankland, Aberdeen 69). **Booked**: Fulton, Love, Paterson

NORTHERN IRELAND 1 MACEDONIA 2
Group 3: Mourneview Park, Lurgan (160); October 13, 2015

Northern Ireland: Brennan (Kilmarnock), Dummigan (Burnley), Sharpe (Notts Co), Donnelly Fulham), Doherty (Watford), McKnight (Shrewsbury), Whyte (Crusaders) (Maloney, Middlesbrough 86), Singleton (Glenavon) (McCartan (Accrington), Kennedy (Charlton) (McDaid, eeds 88), Camps (Rochdale), Duffy (Celtic). **Booked**: Camps, Dummigan, Doherty

corers – Northern Ireland: Doherty (43). **Macedonia**: Bardhi (46), Markoski (85). **Half-time**: 1-0

ITALY 1 REPUBLIC OF IRELAND 0
Group 2: Vicenza (5,000); October 13, 2015

Republic of Ireland: Rogers (Aberdeen), Long (Reading), Connors (Dagenham), D Lenihan Blackburn), Rea (Brighton), Browne (Preston), O'Dowda (Oxford), Cullen (West Ham), Wilkinson (Bolton), Byrne (Manchester City) (Maguire, Dundalk 86), Kavanagh (Fulham) Connolly, Ipswich 86). **Booked**: Connors

corer – Italy: Paragini (66). **Half-time**: 0-0

BOSNIA-HERZEGOVINA 0 ENGLAND 0
Group 9: Sarajevo (400); November 12, 2015

England: Pickford (Sunderland), Iorfa (Wolves), Chambers (Arsenal), Stephens (Southampton), argett (Southampton), Chalobah (Chelsea), Ward-Prowse (Southampton), Baker (Chelsea), Solanke (Chelsea) (Woodrow, Fulham 88), Loftus-Cheek (Chelsea) (Forster-Caskey, Brighton 5), Akpom (Arsenal) (Watmore, Sunderland 70). **Booked**: Chalobah, Stephens, Chambers.

ent off: Stephens (72)

FRANCE 1 NORTHERN IRELAND 0

Group 3: Guingamp (9,242); November 12, 2015

Northern Ireland: Brennan (Kilmarnock), McLaughlin (Liverpool) (McCartan, Accrington 74), Conlan (Burnley), McCullough (Doncaster), Dummigan (Burnley), Doherty (Watford), McKnight (Shrewsbury), Maloney (Middlesbrough), Duffy (Celtic), Kennedy (Charlton) (McDaid, Leeds 87), Whyte (Crusaders) (Stewart, Swindon 67). **Booked**: McLaughlin, Maloney, Kennedy

Scorer – France: Crivelli (82). **Half-time**: 0-0

SCOTLAND 2 UKRAINE 2

Group 3: Paisley Stadium (2,148); November 13, 2015

Scotland: Hamilton (Hearts), Paterson (Hearts) (McFadzean, Sheffield Utd 46), Robertson (Hull), McGhee (Hearts), Hyam (Reading), McGinn (Hibernian), McKay (Rangers) (McBurnie, Swansea 74), Henderson (Celtic), Love (Manchester Utd) (Slater, Kilmarnock) 46), King (Hearts), Cummings (Hibernian). **Booked**: McGhee, Paterson, Love, McGinn. **Sent off**: Hyam (90)

Scorers – Scotland: Cummings (31), Paterson (37). **Ukraine**: Khlyobas (27), Syatok (83). **Half-time**: 2-1

WALES 2 ARMENIA 1

Group 5: Book People Stadium, Bangor (362); November 13, 2015

Wales: O'Brien (Manchester City), Shephard (Swansea), John (Cardiff), Yorweth (Ipswich), Lockyer (Bristol Rov), O'Sullivan (Cardiff) (Charles, Huddersfield 69), Evans (Wolves), Sheehan (Swansea), Burns (Bristol City) (Jones, Swansea 89), Wilson (Liverpool), Harrison (Bristol Rov) (Hedges, Swansea 60). **Booked**: Sheehan

Scorers – Wales: Harrison (9 pen), Wilson (90). **Armenia**: Malakyan (59). **Half-time**: 1-0

LITHUANIA 3 REPUBLIC OF IRELAND 1

Group 2: Vilnius (653); November 13, 2015

Republic of Ireland: Rogers (Aberdeen), Long (Reading), Griffin (Reading), Connors (Dagenham) (Grego-Cox, QPR 18), D Lenihan (Blackburn), Browne (Preston), O'Dowda (Oxford), Cullen (West Ham), Wilkinson (Bolton) (Maguire, Dundalk 81), Byrne (Manchester City) (Connolly, Ipswich 65), Kavanagh (Fulham) **Booked**: D Lenihan, Browne. **Sent off**: Kavanagh (89)

Scorers – Lithuania: Spalvis (22), Stankevicius (45), Kazlauskas (73). **Republic of Ireland**: Wilkinson (44). **Half-time**: 2-1

ENGLAND 3 SWITZERLAND 1

Group 9: Amex Stadium, Brighton (12,003); November 16, 2015

England: Pickford (Sunderland), Iorfa (Wolves), Chambers (Arsenal), Chalobah (Chelsea), Targett (Southampton), Ward-Prowse (Southampton), Baker (Chelsea), March (Brighton) (Akpom, Arsenal 58), Loftus-Cheek (Chelsea) (Watmore, Sunderland 75), Swift (Chelsea), Solanke (Chelsea) (Forster-Caskey, Brighton 86). **Booked**: Chalobah

Scorers – England: Ward-Prowse (82 pen), Watmore (85), Akpom (90). **Switzerland**: Tarashaj (45). **Half-time**: 0-1

WALES 1 ROMANIA 1

Group 5: Racecourse Ground, Wrexham (642); November 17, 2015

Wales: O'Brien (Manchester City), Shephard (Swansea), John (Cardiff), Yorweth (Ipswich), Lockyer (Bristol Rov), O'Sullivan (Cardiff) (Harrison, Bristol Rov 71), Evans (Wolves), Sheehan (Swansea), Burns (Bristol City), Hedges (Swansea) (Saunders, Crewe 87), Wilson (Liverpool) (Charles, Huddersfield 46). **Booked**: O'Sullivan, Burns

Scorers – Wales: Burns (14). **Romania**: Nedelcearu (2). **Half-time**: 1-1

NORTHERN IRELAND 1 UKRAINE 2

Group 3: Mourneview Park, Lurgan (113); November 17, 2015

Northern Ireland: Brennan (Kilmarnock), Conlan (Burnley), McCullough (Doncaster), Dummigan (Burnley), Doherty (Watford), McKnight (Shrewsbury), Maloney (Middlesbrough), McCartan (Accrington), Duffy (Celtic) (Cooper, Glenavon 78), Whyte (Crusaders) (Stewart, Swindon 78),

McDaid (Leeds) (McDonagh, Sheffield Utd 83)
Scorers – Northern Ireland: McCartan (53). **Ukraine**: Kovalenko (64, 73). **Half-time**: 0-0

FRANCE 2 SCOTLAND 0
Group 3: Angers (6,669); March 24, 2016

Scotland: Hamilton (Hearts), Kingsley (Swansea), Souttar (Hearts), McGhee (Hearts), Love (Manchester Utd), Slater (Kilmarnock), Gauld (Sporting), Nicholson (Hearts) (McKay, Rangers 70), Henderson (Celtic) (Christie , Celtic 78), King (Hearts), Cummings (Hibernian) (McBurnie, Swansea 83). **Booked**: Gauld
Scorer – France: Haller (69, 74). **Half-time**: 0-0

REPUBLIC OF IRELAND 1 ITALY 4
Group 2: Sports Centre, Waterford (1,632): March 24, 2016

Republic of Ireland: Rogers (Aberdeen), B Lenihan (Hull), Connors (Dagenham), Rea (Brighton), Keown (Reading), D Lenihan (Blackburn), Charsley (Everton) (Miele, Shamrock 72), O'Connor (Cork) (Hoare, St Patrick's 72), Wilkinson (Bolton), Byrne (Manchester City) (Maguire, Cork 84), O'Dowda (Oxford). **Booked**: Rea, D Lenihan, Charsley
Scorers – Republic of Ireland: Mandragora (16 og). **Italy**: Benassi (28), Rosseti (36), Romagnola (58), D Lenihan (82 og). **Half-time**: 1-2

BULGARIA 0 WALES 0
Group 5: Stara Zagora (1,560); March 25, 2016

Wales: O'Brien (Manchester City), Jones (Everton), John (Cardiff) (J Evans, Fulham 53), Sheehan (Swansea), Yorweth (Ipswich), Lockyer (Bristol Rov), Hedges (Swansea), L Evans (Wolves), Burns (Bristol City), O'Sullivan (Cardiff), Harrison (Bristol Rov) (Charles, Huddersfield 65). **Booked**: Hedges

SWITZERLAND 1 ENGLAND 1
Group 9: Thun (2,589); March 26, 2016

England: Pickford (Sunderland), Iorfa (Wolves), Chambers (Arsenal), Hause (Wolves), Targett (Southampton), Ward-Prowse (Southampton), Baker (Chelsea), Gray (Leicester), Loftus-Cheek (Chelsea) (Grimes, Swansea 69), Swift (Chelsea) (Ibe, Liverpool 27), Akpom (Arsenal) (Solanke, Chelsea 86). **Booked**: Ibe, Baker. **Sent off**: Ibe (90)
Scorers – Switzerland: Kamberi (76). **England**: Akpom (47). **Half-time**: 0-0

SLOVENIA 3 REPUBLIC OF IRELAND 1
Group 2: Koper (2,000); March 28, 2016

Republic of Ireland: Lawlor (Manchester City), Long (Reading), Hoare (St Patrick's), Keown (Reading), D Lenihan (Blackburn), Griffin (Reading) (Connolly, Bray 61), Dimaio (Chesterfield), Wilkinson (Bolton) (Maguire, Cork 39), Byrne (Manchester City), O'Dowda (Oxford) (Barrett, Reading 75), Connors (Dagenham). **Booked**: Connors, Connolly, D Lenihan
Scorers – Slovenia: Krajnc (14), Bajde (55 pen), Zajc (72). **Republic of Ireland**: O'Dowda (65). **Half-time**: 1-0

SCOTLAND 3 NORTHERN IRELAND 1
Group 3: Paisley Stadium (1,065); March 29, 2016

Scotland: Hamilton (Hearts), Love (Manchester Utd), McGhee (Hearts), Souttar (Hearts), Kingsley (Swansea), Nicholson (Hearts) (McBurnie, Swansea 53), Storie (Aberdeen) Gauld (Sporting), McKay (Rangers) (Polworth, Inverness 89), Christie (Celtic), Cummings (Hibernian) (Henderson, Celtic 82). **Booked**: Love
Northern Ireland: Brennan (Kilmarnock), McLaughlin (Liverpool), Conlan (Burnley), Donnelly (Fulham), Dummigan (Burnley), Johnson (Stevenage), Gorman (Stevenage), Maloney (Middlesbrough), McCartan (Accrington) (McDaid, Leeds 84), Duffy (Celtic) (Cooper, Glenavon 79), Kennedy (Charlton) (Sendles-White, Hamilton 69)
Scorers – Scotland: McBurnie (58), Cummings (64, 78). **Northern Ireland**: McCartan (13). **Half-time**: 0-1

ROMANIA 2 WALES 1

Group 5: Medias (1,722); March 29, 2016

Wales: O'Brien (Manchester City), Jones (Everton), J Evans (Fulham), Sheehan (Swansea), Yorweth (Ipswich), Lockyer (Bristol Rov), Hedges (Swansea), L Evans (Wolves), Burns (Bristol City), O'Sullivan (Cardiff), Harrison (Bristol Rov). **Booked**: Harrison, Lockyer, L Evans
Scorers – Romania: Hodorogea (37), Ionita (58). **Wales**: Charles (90). **Half-time**: 1-0

QUALIFYING TABLES

(Nine group winners qualify. Four best runners-up play-off for two further places. Hosts Poland qualify automatically for finals which have been expanded from eight to 12 teams)

GROUP 1

	P	W	D	L	F	A	Pts
Czech Rep	7	5	2	0	21	7	17
Montenegro	7	3	3	1	10	8	12
Belgium	6	4	0	2	9	4	12
Malta	7	1	2	4	3	15	5
Latvia	6	1	2	3	3	9	5
Moldova	7	1	1	5	3	11	4

GROUP 2

	P	W	D	L	F	A	Pts
Italy	7	6	1	0	13	2	19
Slovenia	7	5	0	2	17	5	15
Serbia	6	4	1	1	17	3	13
Rep of Ireland	7	3	0	4	9	11	9
Andora	8	1	0	7	1	22	3
Lithuania	7	1	0	6	3	17	3

GROUP 3

	P	W	D	L	F	A	Pts
France	7	4	2	1	12	7	14
Iceland	6	3	3	0	8	3	12
Macedonia	6	2	3	1	6	7	9
Scotland	6	2	2	2	8	8	8
Ukraine	5	1	1	3	4	7	4
N Ireland	6	0	1	5	5	11	1

GROUP 4

	P	W	D	L	F	A	Pts
Portugal	6	6	0	0	23	1	18
Albania	8	3	3	2	10	14	12
Israel	6	3	2	1	9	4	11
Hungary	7	2	2	3	11	10	8
Greece	6	2	1	3	8	7	7
Liechtenstein	7	0	0	7	0	25	0

GROUP 5

	P	W	D	L	F	A	Pts
Denmark	6	5	1	0	10	1	16
Romania	7	4	1	2	10	9	13
Wales	7	3	3	1	10	6	12
Bulgaria	7	3	2	2	8	4	11
Luxembourg	6	0	2	4	2	9	2
Armenia	7	0	1	6	5	16	1

GROUP 6

	P	W	D	L	F	A	Pts
Croatia	7	6	0	1	19	4	18
Sweden	5	4	1	0	12	1	13
Spain	6	4	1	1	16	8	13
Georgia	7	3	0	4	12	12	9
Estonia	7	1	1	5	3	17	4
San Marino	8	0	1	7	1	21	1

GROUP 7

	P	W	D	L	F	A	Pts
Germany	7	7	0	0	26	4	21
Austria	6	5	0	1	18	7	15
Finland	5	3	0	2	6	6	9
Azerbaijan	8	2	1	5	7	18	7
Russia	6	1	1	4	7	13	4
Faroe Is	6	0	0	6	1	17	0

GROUP 8

	P	W	D	L	F	A	Pts
Slovakia	5	4	0	1	14	4	12
Holland	5	3	0	2	9	7	9
Belarus	5	2	1	2	4	5	7
Turkey	4	2	0	2	5	6	6
Cyprus	5	0	1	4	2	12	1

GROUP 9

	P	W	D	L	F	A	Pts
England	5	3	2	0	8	2	11
Switzerland	5	2	2	1	7	6	8
Norway	4	2	1	1	5	3	7
Kazakhstan	5	1	1	3	3	7	4
Bos-Herz	5	0	2	3	2	7	2

TOULON TOURNAMENT

GROUP B

ENGLAND 1 PORTUGAL 0
Toulon; May 19, 2016

England: Pickford (Sunderland), Iorfa (Wolves), Chambers (Arsenal), Hause (Wolves), Chilwell (Leicester), Chalobah (Chelsea), Ward-Prowse (Southampton), Loftus-Cheek (Chelsea) (Grealish, Aston Villa 72), Baker (Chelsea) (Grimes, Swansea 80) Watmore (Sunderland) (Woodrow, Fulham 58), Palmer (Chelsea) (Redmond, Norwich 58. **Booked**: Chalobah, Woodrow
Scorer – England: Baker (60). **Half-time**: 0-0

ENGLAND 7 GUINEA 1
Aubagne; May 23, 2016

England: Gunn (Manchester City), Stephens (Southampton), Holding (Bolton), Hause (Wolves) (Chambers, Arsenal 54), Targett (Southampton), Ward-Prowse (Southampton) (Chalobah, Chelsea 41), Swift (Chelsea), Grimes (Swansea), Grealish (Aston Villa) (Watmore, Sunderland 60), Redmond (Norwich) (Palmer, Chelsea 54), Woodrow (Fulham)
Scorers – England: Grealish (7, 40), Ward-Prowse (30 pen), Redmond (34), Makadji (50 og), Woodrow (58, 73). **Guinea**: Diallo (1). **Half-time**: 4-1

ENGLAND 4 PARAGUAY 0
Six-Four-Les-Plages; May 25, 2016

England: Pickford (Sunderland), Iorfa (Wolves), Chambers (Arsenal), Hause (Wolves), Chilwell (Leicester) (Targett, Southampton 39), Chalobah (Chelsea), Ward-Prowse (Southampton), Baker (Chelsea), Loftus-Cheek (Chelsea) (Swift, Chelsea 71), Redmond (Norwich) (Palmer, Chelsea 68), Watmore (Sunderland) (Grealish, Aston Villa 62). **Booked**: Hause, Chalobah, Swift

Scorers – England: Baker (33), Loftus-Cheek (45, 59), Redmond (65). **Half-time**: 2-0

ENGLAND 1 JAPAN 0
Toulon; May 27, 2016

England: Gunn (Manchester City), Stephens (Southampton), Holding (Bolton), Chambers (Arsenal) (Hause, Wolves 54), Targett (Southampton) (Iorfa, Wolves 41), Swift (Chelsea), Grimes (Swansea), Baker (Chelsea) (Loftus-Cheek, Chelsea 41), Grealish (Aston Villa), Palmer (Chelsea), Woodrow (Fulham). **Booked**: Chambers

Scorers – England: Baker (15 pen). **Half-time**: 1-0

FINAL TABLE

	P	W	D	L	F	A	Pts
England	4	4	0	0	13	1	12
Portugal	4	3	0	1	6	1	9
Paraguay	4	2	0	2	5	9	6
Japan	4	1	0	3	3	5	3
Guinea	4	0	0	4	3	14	0

GROUP A

	P	W	D	L	F	A	Pts
France	4	4	0	0	8	2	12
Czech Rep	4	2	1	1	3	3	7
Mali	4	1	1	2	7	7	4
Mexico	4	1	1	2	6	8	4
Bulgaria	4	0	1	3	1	5	1

FINAL

ENGLAND 2 FRANCE 1
Avignon; May 29, 2016

England: Pickford (Sunderland), Iorfa (Wolves), Chambers (Arsenal), Hause (Wolves), Targett (Southampton) (Stephens, Southampton 80), Chalobah (Chelsea), Ward-Prowse (Southampton), Baker (Chelsea), Loftus-Cheek (Chelsea), Redmond (Norwich), Watmore (Sunderland) (Swift, Chelsea 65). **Booked**: Loftus-Cheek, Swift

Scorers – England: Baker (8), Loftus-Cheek (38). **France**: Diallo (78). **Half-time**: 2-0

INTERNATIONAL FRIENDLIES

ENGLAND 1 USA 0
Deepdale, Preston (10,192); September 3, 2015

England: Pickford (Sunderland) (Gunn, Manchester City 61), Gomez (Liverpool) (Stephens, Southampton 61), Chambers (Arsenal), Dier (Tottenham) (Hause, Wolves 61), Targett (Southampton) (Iorfa, Wolves 61), Ward-Prowse (Southampton) (Chalobah, Chelsea 61), Loftus-Cheek (Chelsea), Alli (Tottenham) (Forster-Caskey, Brighton 61), Ibe (Liverpool) (Watmore, Sunderland 61), Redmond (Norwich) (March, Brighton 61), Woodrow (Fulham) (Wilson, Manchester Utd 61)

Scorer – England: Wilson (72). **Half-time**: 0-0

TRANSFER TRAIL

Player	From	To	Date	£
Gareth Bale	Tottenham	Real Madrid	8/13	85,300,000
Cristiano Ronaldo	Manchester Utd	Real Madrid	7/09	80,000,000
Luis Suarez	Liverpool	Barcelona	7/14	75,000,000
Angel di Maria	Real Madrid	Manchester Utd	8/14	59,700,000
Kevin De Bruyne	Wolfsburg	Manchester City	8/15	52,000,000
Fernando Torres	Liverpool	Chelsea	1/11	50,000,000
Raheem Sterling	Liverpool	Manchester City	7/15	49,000,000
Angel di Maria	Manchester Utd	Paris SG	8/15	44,300,000
Mesut Ozil	Real Madrid	Arsenal	9/13	42,400,000
David Luiz	Chelsea	Paris SG	6/14	40,000,000
Sergio Aguero	Atletico Madrid	Manchester City	7/11	38,500,000
Juan Mata	Chelsea	Manchester Utd	1/14	37,100,000
Anthony Martial	Monaco	Manchester Utd	9/15	36,000,000
Andy Carroll	Newcastle	Liverpool	1/11	35,000,000
Cesc Fabregas	Arsenal	Barcelona	8/11	35,000,000
Alexis Sanchez	Barcelona	Arsenal	7/14	35,000,000
Sadio Mane	Southampton	Liverpool	6/16	34,000,000
Michy Batshuayi	Marseille	Chelsea	7/16	33,000,000
Robinho	Real Madrid	Manchester City	9/08	32,500,000
Christian Benteke	Aston Villa	Liverpool	7/15	32,500,000
Eden Hazard	Lille	Chelsea	6/12	32,000,000
Diego Costa	Atletico Madrid	Chelsea	7/14	32,000,000
N'Golo Kante	Leicester	Chelsea	7/16	32,000,000
Eliaquim Mangala	Porto	Manchester City	8/14	31,900,000
Dimitar Berbatov	Tottenham	Manchester Utd	9/08	30,750,000
Andriy Shevchenko	AC Milan	Chelsea	5/06	30,800,000
Xabi Alonso	Liverpool	Real Madrid	8/09	30,000,000
Fernandinho	Shakhtar Donetsk	Manchester City	6/13	30,000,000
Willian	Anzhi Makhachkala	Chelsea	8/13	30,000,000
Erik Lamela	Roma	Tottenham	8/13	30,000,000
Luke Shaw	Southampton	Manchester Utd	6/14	30,000,000
Eric Bailly	Villarreal	Manchester Utd	6/16	30,000,000
Rio Ferdinand	Leeds	Manchester Utd	7/02	29,100,000
Ander Herrara	Athletic Bilbao	Manchester Utd	6/14	28,800,000
Nicolas Otamendi	Valencia	Manchester City	8/15	28,500,000
Juan Sebastian Veron	Lazio	Manchester Utd	7/01	28,100,000
Romelu Lukaku	Chelsea	Everton	7/14	28,000,000
Yaya Toure	Barcelona	Manchester City	7/10	28,000,000
Wilfried Bony	Swansea	Manchester City	1/15	28,000,000
Roberto Firmino	Hoffenheim	Liverpool	6/15	28,000,000
Marouane Fellaini	Everton	Manchester Utd	9/13	27,500,000
Wayne Rooney	Everton	Manchester Utd	8/04	27,000,000
Edin Dzeko	Wolfsburg	Manchester City	1/11	27,000,000
Luka Modric	Tottenham	Real Madrid	8/12	27,000,000
Cesc Fabregas	Barcelona	Chelsea	6/14	27,000,000
Roberto Soldado	Valencia	Tottenham	8/13	26,000,000
Henrikh Mkhitaryan	Borussua Dortmund	Manchester Utd	7/16	26,000,000
Marc Overmars	Arsenal	Barcelona	7/00	25,000,000
Carlos Tevez	Manchester Utd	Manchester City	7/09	25,000,000
Emmanuel Adebayor	Arsenal	Manchester City	7/09	25,000,000
Samir Nasri	Arsenal	Manchester City	8/11	25,000,000
Oscar	Internacional	Chelsea	7/12	25,000,000
Adam Lallana	Southampton	Liverpool	7/14	25,000,000
Memphis Depay	PSV Eindhoven	Manchester Utd	6/15	25,000,000

Morgan Schneiderlin	Southampton	Manchester Utd	7/15	25,000,000
Ramires	Chelsea	Jiangsu Suning	2/16	25,000,000
Arjen Robben	Chelsea	Real Madrid	8/07	24,500,000
Michael Essien	Lyon	Chelsea	8/05	24,400,000
David Silva	Valencia	Manchester City	7/10	24,000,000
James Milner	Aston Villa	Manchester City	8/10	24,000,000
Mario Balotelli	Inter Milan	Manchester City	8/10	24,000,000
Robin van Persie	Arsenal	Manchester Utd	8/12	24,000,000
Juan Mata	Valencia	Chelsea	8/11	23,500,000
David Beckham	Manchester Utd	Real Madrid	7/03	23,300,000
Juan Cuadrado	Fiorentina	Chelsea	2/15	23,300,000
Didier Drogba	Marseille	Chelsea	7/04	23,200,000
Andre Schurrle	Chelsea	Wolfsburg	2/15	23,000,000
Luis Suarez	Ajax	Liverpool	1/11	22,700,000
Nicolas Anelka	Arsenal	Real Madrid	8/99	22,300,000
Fernando Torres	Atletico Madrid	Liverpool	7/07	22,000,000
Joloen Lescott	Everton	Manchester City	8/09	22,000,000
Stevan Jovetic	Fiorentina	Manchester City	7/13	22,000,000
Son Heung-min	Bayer Leverkusen	Tottenham	8/15	21,900,000
Baba Rahman	Augsburg	Chelsea	8/15	21,700,000
David Luiz	Benfica	Chelsea	1/11	21,300,000
Shaun Wright-Phillips	Manchester City	Chelsea	7/05	21,000,000
Nemanja Matic	Benfica	Chelsea	01/14	21,000,000
Pedro	Barcelona	Chelsea	8/15	21,000,000
Ilkay Gundogan	Borussia Dortmund	Manchester City	6/16	21,000,000
Lassana Diarra	Portsmouth	Real Madrid	12/08	20,000,000
Alberto Aquilani	Roma	Liverpool	8/09	20,000,000
Stewart Downing	Aston Villa	Liverpool	7/11	20,000,000
Lazar Markovic	Benfica	Liverpool	7/14	20,000,000
Dejan Lovren	Southampton	Liverpool	7/14	20,000,000
Ricardo Carvalho	Porto	Chelsea	7/04	19,850,000
Mario Balotelli	Manchester City	AC Milan	1/13	19,500,000
Ruud van Nistelrooy	PSV Eindhoven	Manchester Utd	4/01	19,000,000
Robbie Keane	Tottenham	Liverpool	7/08	19,000,000
Michael Carrick	Tottenham	Manchester Utd	8/06	18,600,000
Javier Mascherano	Media Sports	Liverpool	2/08	18,600,000
Giannelli Imbula	Porto	Stoke	2/11	18,300,000
Rio Ferdinand	West Ham	Leeds	11/00	18,000,000
Anderson	Porto	Manchester Utd	7/07	18,000,000
Jo	CSKA Moscow	Manchester City	6/08	18,000,000
Yuri Zhirkov	CSKA Moscow	Chelsea	7/09	18,000,000
Ramires	Benfica	Chelsea	8/10	18,000,000
Darren Bent	Sunderland	Aston Villa	1/11	18,000,000
Romelu Lukaku	Anderlecht	Chelsea	8/11	18,000,000
Andre Schurrle	Bayer Leverkusen	Chelsea	6/13	18,000,000
Mamadou Sakho	Paris SG	Liverpool	9/13	18,000,000
David De Gea	Atletico Madrid	Manchester Utd	6/11	17,800,000
Roque Santa Cruz	Blackburn	Manchester City	6/09	17,500,000
Jose Reyes	Sevilla	Arsenal	1/04	17,400,000
Javier Mascherano	Liverpool	Barcelona	8/10	17,250,000
Damien Duff	Blackburn	Chelsea	7/03	17,000,000
Owen Hargreaves	Bayern Munich	Manchester Utd	6/07	17,000,000
Glen Johnson	Portsmouth	Liverpool	6/09	17,000,000
Paulinho	Corinthians	Tottenham	7/13	17,000,000
Andrey Arshavin	Zenit St Petersburg	Arsenal	2/09	16,900,000
Hernan Crespo	Inter Milan	Chelsea	8/03	16,800,000
Claude Makelele	Real Madrid	Chelsea	9/03	16,600,000

Luka Modric	Dinamo Zagreb	Tottenham	6/08	16,600,000
Darren Bent	Charlton	Tottenham	6/07	16,500,000
Phil Jones	Blackburn	Manchester Utd	6/11	16,500,000
Santi Cazorla	Malaga	Arsenal	8/12	16,500,000
Jose Bosingwa	Porto	Chelsea	6/08	16,200,000
Michael Owen	Real Madrid	Newcastle	8/05	16,000,000
Thierry Henry	Arsenal	Barcelona	6/07	16,000,000
Aleksandar Kolarov	Lazio	Manchester City	7/10	16,000,000
Robinho	Manchester City	AC Milan	8/10	16,000,000
Jordan Henderson	Sunderland	Liverpool	6/11	16,000,000
Ashley Young	Aston Villa	Manchester Utd	6/11	16,000,000
Calum Chambers	Southampton	Arsenal	7/14	16,000,000
Mario Balotelli	AC Milan	Liverpool	8/14	16,000,000
Danny Welbeck	Manchester Utd	Arsenal	8/14	16,000,000
Adrian Mutu	Parma	Chelsea	8/03	15,800,000
Samir Nasri	Marseille	Arsenal	7/08	15,800,000
Javi Garcia	Benfica	Manchester City	8/12	15,800,000
Jermain Defoe	Portsmouth	Tottenham	1/09	15,750,000

BRITISH RECORD TRANSFERS FROM FIRST £1,000 DEAL

Player	From	To	Date	£
Alf Common	Sunderland	Middlesbrough	2/1905	1,000
Syd Puddefoot	West Ham	Falkirk	2/22	5,000
Warney Cresswell	South Shields	Sunderland	3/22	5,500
Bob Kelly	Burnley	Sunderland	12/25	6,500
David Jack	Bolton	Arsenal	10/28	10,890
Bryn Jones	Wolves	Arsenal	8/38	14,500
Billy Steel	Morton	Derby	9/47	15,000
Tommy Lawton	Chelsea	Notts Co	11/47	20,000
Len Shackleton	Newcastle	Sunderland	2/48	20,500
Johnny Morris	Manchester Utd	Derby	2/49	24,000
Eddie Quigley	Sheffield Wed	Preston	12/49	26,500
Trevor Ford	Aston Villa	Sunderland	10/50	30,000
Jackie Sewell	Notts Co	Sheffield Wed	3/51	34,500
Eddie Firmani	Charlton	Sampdoria	7/55	35,000
John Charles	Leeds	Juventus	4/57	65,000
Denis Law	Manchester City	Torino	6/61	100,000
Denis Law	Torino	Manchester Utd	7/62	115,000
Allan Clarke	Fulham	Leicester	6/68	150,000
Allan Clarke	Leicester	Leeds	6/69	165,000
Martin Peters	West Ham	Tottenham	3/70	200,000
Alan Ball	Everton	Arsenal	12/71	220,000
David Nish	Leicester	Derby	8/72	250,000
Bob Latchford	Birmingham	Everton	2/74	350,000
Graeme Souness	Middlesbrough	Liverpool	1/78	352,000
Kevin Keegan	Liverpool	Hamburg	6/77	500,000
David Mills	Middlesbrough	WBA	1/79	516,000
Trevor Francis	Birmingham	Nottm Forest	2/79	1,180,000
Steve Daley	Wolves	Manchester City	9/79	1,450,000
Andy Gray	Aston Villa	Wolves	9/79	1,469,000
Bryan Robson	WBA	Manchester Utd	10/81	1,500,000
Ray Wilkins	Manchester Utd	AC Milan	5/84	1,500,000
Mark Hughes	Manchester Utd	Barcelona	5/86	2,300,000
Ian Rush	Liverpool	Juventus	6/87	3,200,000
Chris Waddle	Tottenham	Marseille	7/89	4,250,000
David Platt	Aston Villa	Bari	7/91	5,500,000
Paul Gascoigne	Tottenham	Lazio	6/92	5,500,000

Andy Cole	Newcastle	Manchester Utd	1/95	7,000,000
Dennis Bergkamp	Inter Milan	Arsenal	6/95	7,500,000
Stan Collymore	Nottm Forest	Liverpool	6/95	8,500,000
Alan Shearer	Blackburn	Newcastle	7/96	15,000,000
Nicolas Anelka	Arsenal	Real Madrid	8/99	22,500,000
Juan Sebastian Veron	Lazio	Manchester Utd	7/01	28,100,000
Rio Ferdinand	Leeds	Manchester Utd	7/02	29,100,000
Andriy Shevchenko	AC Milan	Chelsea	5/06	30,800,000
Robinho	Real Madrid	Manchester City	9/08	32,500,000
Cristiano Ronaldo	Manchester Utd	Real Madrid	7/09	80,000,000
Gareth Bale	Tottenham	Real Madrid	9/13	85,300,000

• World's first £1m transfer: GuiseppeSavoldi, Bologna to Napoli, July 1975

TOP FOREIGN SIGNINGS

Player	From	To	Date	£
Zlatan Ibrahimovic	Inter Milan	Barcelona	7/09	60,300,000
James Rodriguez	Monaco	Real Madrid	7/14	60,000,000
Kaka	AC Milan	Real Madrid	6/08	56,000,000
Edinson Cavani	Napoli	Paris SG	7/13	53,000,000
Radamel Falcao	Atletico Madrid	Monaco	6/13	51,000,000
Neymar	Santos	Barcelona	6/13	48,600,000
Zinedine Zidane	Juventus	Real Madrid	7/01	47,200,000
James Rodriguez	Porto	Monaco	5/13	38,500,000
Alex Teixeira	Shekhtar Donetsk	Jiangsu Suning	2/16	38,400,000
Luis Figo	Barcelona	Real Madrid	7/00	37,200,000
Javier Pastore	Palermo	Paris SG	8/11	36,600,000
Karim Benzema	Lyon	Real Madrid	7/09	35,800,000
Hernan Crespo	Parma	Lazio	7/00	35,000,000
Radamel Falcao	Porto	Atletico Madrid	8/11	34,700,000
Gonzalo Higuain	Real Madrid	Napoli	7/13	34,500,000
David Villa	Valencia	Barcelona	5/10	34,000,000
Thiago Silva	AC Milan	Paris SG	7/12	34,000,000
Lucas Moura	Sao Paulo	Paris SG	1/13	34,000,000
Asier Illarramendi	Real Sociedad	Real Madrid	7/13	34,000,000
Ronaldo	Inter Milan	Real Madrid	8/02	33,000,000
Gianluigi Buffon	Parma	Juventus	7/01	32,600,000
Axel Witsel	Benfica	Zenit St Petersburg	8/12	32,500,000
Hulk	Porto	Zenit St Petersburg	8/12	32,000,000
Javi Martinez	Athletic Bilbao	Bayern Munich	8/12	31,600,000
Mario Gotze	Borussia Dortmund	Bayern Munich	6/13	31,500,000
Christian Vieri	Lazio	Inter Milan	6/99	31,000,000
Jackson Martinez	Atletico Madrid	Guangzhou Evergrande	2/16	31,000,000
Alessandro Nesta	Lazio	AC Milan	8/02	30,200,000

WORLD'S MOST EXPENSIVE TEENAGER

£36m: Anthony Martial, 19, Monaco to Manchester Utd, Aug 2015

WORLD RECORD FOR 16-YEAR-OLD

£12m: Theo Walcott, Southampton to Arsenal, Jan 2006

RECORD FEE BETWEEN SCOTTISH CLUBS

£4.4m: Scott Brown, Hibernian to Celtic, May 2007

RECORD NON-LEAGUE FEE

£1m: Jamie Vardy, Fleetwood to Leicester, May 2012

RECORD FEE BETWEEN NON-LEAGUE CLUBS

£275,000: Richard Brodie, York to Crawley, Aug 2010

MILESTONES OF SOCCER

1848: First code of rules compiled at Cambridge University.
1857: Sheffield FC, world's oldest football club, formed.
1862: Notts Co (oldest League club) formed.
1863: Football Association founded – their first rules of game agreed.
1871: FA Cup introduced.
1872: First official International: Scotland 0 England 0. Corner-kick introduced.
1873: Scottish FA formed; Scottish Cup introduced.
1874: Shinguards introduced.
1875: Crossbar introduced (replacing tape).
1876: FA of Wales formed.
1877: Welsh Cup introduced.
1878: Referee's whistle first used.
1880: Irish FA founded; Irish Cup introduced.
1883: Two-handed throw-in introduced.
1885: Record first-class score (Arbroath 36 Bon Accord 0 – Scottish Cup). Professionalism legalised.
1886: International Board formed.
1887: Record FA Cup score (Preston 26 Hyde 0).
1888: Football League founded by William McGregor. First matches on Sept 8.
1889 Preston win Cup and League (first club to complete Double).
1890: Scottish League and Irish League formed.
1891: Goal-nets introduced. Penalty-kick introduced.
1892: Inter-League games began. Football League Second Division formed.
1893: FA Amateur Cup launched.
1894: Southern League formed.
1895: FA Cup stolen from Birmingham shop window – never recovered.
1897: First Players' Union formed. Aston Villa win Cup and League.
1898: Promotion and relegation introduced.
1901: Maximum wage rule in force (£4 a week). Tottenham first professional club to take FA Cup south. First six-figure attendance (110,802) at FA Cup Final.
1902: Ibrox Park disaster (25 killed). Welsh League formed.
1904: FIFA founded (7 member countries).
1905: First £1,000 transfer (Alf Common, Sunderland to Middlesbrough).
1907: Players' Union revived.
1908: Transfer fee limit (£350) fixed in January and withdrawn in April.
1911: New FA Cup trophy – in use to 1991. Transfer deadline introduced.
1914: King George V first reigning monarch to attend FA Cup Final.
1916: Entertainment Tax introduced.
1919: League extended to 44 clubs.
1920: Third Division (South) formed.
1921: Third Division (North) formed.
1922: Scottish League (Div II) introduced.
1923: Beginning of football pools. First Wembley Cup Final.
1924: First International at Wembley (England 1 Scotland 1). Rule change allows goals to be scored direct from corner-kicks.
1925: New offside law.
1926: Huddersfield complete first League Championship hat-trick.
1927: First League match broadcast (radio): Arsenal v Sheffield United. First radio broadcast of Cup Final (winners Cardiff City). Charles Clegg, president of FA, becomes first knight of football.
1928: First £10,000 transfer – David Jack (Bolton to Arsenal). WR ('Dixie') Dean (Everton) creates League record – 60 goals in season. Britain withdraws from FIFA

1930: Uruguay first winners of World Cup.
1931: WBA win Cup and promotion.
1933: Players numbered for first time in Cup Final (1-22).
1934: Sir Frederick Wall retires as FA secretary; successor Stanley Rous. Death of Herbert Chapman (Arsenal manager).
1935: Arsenal equal Huddersfield's Championship hat-trick record. Official two-referee trials.
1936: Joe Payne's 10-goal League record (Luton 12 Bristol Rov 0).
1937: British record attendance: 149,547 at Scotland v England match.
1938: First live TV transmission of FA Cup Final. Football League 50th Jubilee. New pitch marking – arc on edge of penalty-area. Laws of Game re-drafted by Stanley Rous. Arsenal pay record £14,500 fee for Bryn Jones (Wolves).
1939: Compulsory numbering of players in Football League. First six-figure attendance for League match (Rangers v Celtic 118,567). All normal competitions suspended for duration of Second World War.
1945: Scottish League Cup introduced.
1946: British associations rejoin FIFA. Bolton disaster (33 killed) during FA Cup tie with Stoke. Walter Winterbottom appointed England's first director of coaching.
1947: Great Britain beat Rest of Europe 6-1 at Hampden Park, Glasgow. First £20,000 transfer – Tommy Lawton, Chelsea to Notts Co
1949: Stanley Rous, secretary FA, knighted. England's first home defeat outside British Champ. (0-2 v Eire).
1950: Football League extended from 88 to 92 clubs. World record crowd (203,500) at World Cup Final, Brazil v Uruguay, in Rio. Scotland's first home defeat by foreign team (0-1 v Austria).
1951: White ball comes into official use.
1952: Newcastle first club to win FA Cup at Wembley in successive seasons.
1953: England's first Wembley defeat by foreign opponents (3-6 v Hungary).
1954: Hungary beat England 7-1 in Budapest.
1955: First FA Cup match under floodlights (prelim round replay): Kidderminster v Brierley Hill Alliance.
1956: First FA Cup ties under floodlights in competition proper. First League match by floodlight (Portsmouth v Newcastle). Real Madrid win the first European Cup.
1957: Last full Football League programme on Christmas Day. Entertainment Tax withdrawn.
1958: Manchester United air crash at Munich. League re-structured into four divisions.
1960: Record transfer fee: £55,000 for Denis Law (Huddersfield to Manchester City). Wolves win Cup, miss Double and Championship hat-trick by one goal. For fifth time in ten years FA Cup Final team reduced to ten men by injury. FA recognise Sunday football. Football League Cup launched.
1961: Tottenham complete the first Championship–FA Cup double this century. Maximum wage (£20 a week) abolished in High Court challenge by George Eastham. First British £100-a-week wage paid (by Fulham to Johnny Haynes). First £100,000 British transfer – Denis Law, Manchester City to Torino. Sir Stanley Rous elected president of FIFA
1962: Manchester United raise record British transfer fee to £115,000 for Denis Law.
1963: FA Centenary. Season extended to end of May due to severe winter. First pools panel. English "retain and transfer" system ruled illegal in High Court test case.
1964: Rangers' second great hat-trick – Scottish Cup, League Cup and League. Football League and Scottish League guaranteed £500,000 a year in new fixtures copyright agreement with Pools. First televised 'Match of the Day' (BBC2): Liverpool 3 Arsenal 2.
1965: Bribes scandal – ten players jailed (and banned for life by FA) for match-fixing 1960–63. Stanley Matthews knighted in farewell season. Arthur Rowley (Shrewsbury) retires with record of 434 League goals. Substitutes allowed for injured players in Football League matches (one per team).
1966: England win World Cup (Wembley).

1967: Alf Ramsey, England manager, knighted; OBE for captain Bobby Moore. Celtic become first British team to win European Cup. First substitutes allowed in FA Cup Final (Tottenham v Chelsea) but not used. Football League permit loan transfers (two per club).

1968: First FA Cup Final televised live in colour (BBC2 – WBA v Everton). Manchester United first English club to win European Cup.

1970: FIFA/UEFA approve penalty shoot-out in deadlocked ties.

1971: Arsenal win League Championship and FA Cup.

1973: Football League introduce 3-up, 3-down promotion/relegation between Divisions 1, 2 and 3 and 4-up, 4-down between Divisions 3 and 4.

1974: First FA Cup ties played on Sunday. League football played on Sunday for first time. Last FA Amateur Cup Final. Joao Havelange (Brazil) succeeds Sir Stanley Rous as FIFA president.

1975: Scottish Premier Division introduced.

1976: Football League introduce goal difference (replacing goal average) and red/yellow cards.

1977: Liverpool achieve the double of League Championship and European Cup. Don Revie defects to United Arab Emirates when England manager – successor Ron Greenwood.

1978: Freedom of contract for players accepted by Football League. PFA lifts ban on foreign players in English football. Football League introduce Transfer Tribunal. Viv Anderson (Nottm Forest) first black player to win a full England cap. Willie Johnston (Scotland) sent home from World Cup Finals in Argentina after failing dope test.

1979: First all-British £500,000 transfer – David Mills, Middlesbrough to WBA. First British million pound transfer (Trevor Francis – Birmingham to Nottm Forest). Andy Gray moves from Aston Villa to Wolves for a record £1,469,000 fee.

1981: Tottenham win 100th FA Cup Final. Liverpool first British side to win European Cup three times. Three points for a win introduced by Football League. QPR install Football League's first artificial pitch. Death of Bill Shankly, manager–legend of Liverpool 1959–74. Record British transfer – Bryan Robson (WBA to Manchester United), £1,500,000.

1982: Aston Villa become sixth consecutive English winners of European Cup. Tottenham retain FA Cup – first club to do so since Tottenham 1961 and 1962. Football League Cup becomes the (sponsored) Milk Cup.

1983: Liverpool complete League Championship–Milk Cup double for second year running. Manager Bob Paisley retires. Aberdeen first club to do Cup-Winners' Cup and domestic Cup double. Football League clubs vote to keep own match receipts. Football League sponsored by Canon, Japanese camera and business equipment manufacturers – 3-year agreement starting 1983–4. Football League agree two-year contract for live TV coverage of ten matches per season (5 Friday night, BBC, 5 Sunday afternoon, ITV).

1984: One FA Cup tie in rounds 3, 4, 5 and 6 shown live on TV (Friday or Sunday). Aberdeen take Scottish Cup for third successive season, win Scottish Championship, too. Tottenham win UEFA Cup on penalty shoot-out. Liverpool win European Cup on penalty shoot-out to complete unique treble with Milk Cup and League title (as well as Championship hat-trick). N Ireland win the final British Championship. France win European Championship – their first honour. FA National Soccer School opens at Lilleshall. Britain's biggest score this century: Stirling Alb 20 Selkirk 0 (Scottish Cup).

1985: Bradford City fire disaster – 56 killed. First £1m receipts from match in Britain (FA Cup Final). Kevin Moran (Manchester United) first player to be sent off in FA Cup Final. Celtic win 100th Scottish FA Cup Final. European Cup Final horror (Liverpool v Juventus, riot in Brussels) 39 die. UEFA ban all English clubs indefinitely from European competitions. No TV coverage at start of League season – first time since 1963 (resumption delayed until January 1986). Sept: first ground-sharing in League history – Charlton Athletic move from The Valley to Selhurst Park (Crystal Palace).

1986: Liverpool complete League and Cup double in player-manager Kenny Dalglish's first season in charge. Swindon (4th Div Champions) set League points record (102). League approve reduction of First Division to 20 clubs by 1988. Everton chairman Philip Carter elected president of Football League. Death of Sir Stanley Rous (91). 100th edition of News of the World Football Annual. League Cup sponsored for next three years by Littlewoods (£2m). Football League voting majority (for rule changes) reduced from three-quarters to two-thirds. Wales move HQ from Wrexham to Cardiff after 110 years. Two substitutes in FA Cup and League (Littlewoods) Cup. Two-season League/TV deal (£6.2m):- BBC and ITV each show seven live League matches per season, League Cup semi-finals and Final. Football League sponsored by Today newspaper. Luton first club to ban all visiting supporters; as sequel are themselves banned from League Cup. Oldham and Preston install artificial pitches, making four in Football League (following QPR and Luton).

1987: League introduce play-off matches to decide final promotion/relegation places in all divisions. Re-election abolished – bottom club in Div 4 replaced by winners of GM Vauxhall Conference. Two substitutes approved for Football League 1987–8. Red and yellow disciplinary cards (scrapped 1981) re-introduced by League and FA Football League sponsored by Barclays. First Div reduced to 21 clubs.

1988: Football League Centenary. First Division reduced to 20 clubs.

1989: Soccer gets £74m TV deal: £44m over 4 years, ITV; £30m over 5 years, BBC/BSB. But it costs Philip Carter the League Presidency. Ted Croker retires as FA chief executive; successor Graham Kelly, from Football League. Hillsborough disaster: 95 die at FA Cup semi-final (Liverpool v Nottm Forest). Arsenal win closest-ever Championship with last kick. Peter Shilton sets England record with 109 caps.

1990: Nottm Forest win last Littlewoods Cup Final. Both FA Cup semi-finals played on Sunday and televised live. Play-off finals move to Wembley; Swindon win place in Div 1, then relegated back to Div 2 (breach of financial regulations) – Sunderland promoted instead. England reach World Cup semi-final in Italy and win FIFA Fair Play Award. Peter Shilton retires as England goalkeeper with 125 caps (world record). Graham Taylor (Aston Villa) succeeds Bobby Robson as England manager. International Board amend offside law (player 'level' no longer offside). FIFA make "professional foul" a sending-off offence. English clubs back in Europe (Manchester United and Aston Villa) after 5-year exile.

1991: First FA Cup semi-final at Wembley (Tottenham 3 Arsenal 1). Bert Millichip (FA chairman) and Philip Carter (Everton chairman) knighted. End of artificial pitches in Div 1 (Luton, Oldham). Scottish League reverts to 12-12-14 format (as in 1987–8). Penalty shoot-out introduced to decide FA Cup ties level after one replay.

1992: FA launch Premier League (22 clubs). Football League reduced to three divisions (71 clubs). Record TV-sport deal: BSkyB/BBC to pay £304m for 5-year coverage of Premier League. ITV do £40m, 4-year deal with Football League. Channel 4 show Italian football live (Sundays). FIFA approve new back-pass rule (goalkeeper must not handle ball kicked to him by team-mate). New League of Wales formed. Record all-British transfer, £3.3m: Alan Shearer (Southampton to Blackburn). Charlton return to The Valley after 7-year absence.

1993: Barclays end 6-year sponsorship of Football League. For first time both FA Cup semi-finals at Wembley (Sat, Sun). Arsenal first club to complete League Cup/FA Cup double. Rangers pull off Scotland's domestic treble for fifth time. FA in record British sports sponsorship deal (£12m over 4 years) with brewers Bass for FA Carling Premiership, from Aug. Brian Clough retires after 18 years as Nottm Forest manager; as does Jim McLean (21 years manager of Dundee Utd). Football League agree 3-year, £3m sponsorship with Endsleigh Insurance. Premier League introduce squad numbers with players' names on shirts. Record British transfer: Duncan Ferguson, Dundee Utd to Rangers (£4m). Record English-club signing: Roy Keane, Nottm Forest to Manchester United (£3.75m). Graham Taylor resigns as England manager after World Cup exit (Nov). Death of Bobby Moore (51), England World Cup winning captain 1966.

1994: Death of Sir Matt Busby. Terry Venables appointed England coach. Manchester United complete the Double. Last artificial pitch in English football goes – Preston revert to grass, summer 1994. Bobby Charlton knighted. Scottish League format changes to four divisions of ten clubs. Record British transfer: Chris Sutton, Norwich to Blackburn (£5m).

FA announce first sponsorship of FA Cup – Littlewoods Pools (4-year, £14m deal, plus £6m for Charity Shield). Death of Billy Wright.

1995: New record British transfer: Andy Cole, Newcastle to Manchester United (£7m). First England match abandoned through crowd trouble (v Republic of Ireland, Dublin). Blackburn Champions for first time since 1914. Premiership reduced to 20 clubs. British transfer record broken again: Stan Collymore, Nottm Forest to Liverpool (£8.5m). Starting season 1995–6, teams allowed to use 3 substitutes per match, not necessarily including a goalkeeper. European Court of Justice upholds Bosman ruling, barring transfer fees for players out of contract and removing limit on number of foreign players clubs can field.

1996: Death of Bob Paisley (77), ex-Liverpool, most successful manager in English Football. FA appoint Chelsea manager Glenn Hoddle to succeed Terry Venables as England coach after Euro 96. Manchester United first English club to achieve Double twice (and in 3 seasons). Football League completes £125m, 5-year TV deal with BSkyB starting 1996–7. England stage European Championship, reach semi-finals, lose on pens to tournament winners Germany. Keith Wiseman succeeds Sir Bert Millichip as FA Chairman. Linesmen become known as 'referees' assistants'. Alan Shearer football's first £15m player (Blackburn to Newcastle). Nigeria first African country to win Olympic soccer. Nationwide Building Society sponsor Football League in initial 3-year deal worth £5.25m Peter Shilton first player to make 1000 League appearances.

1997: Howard Wilkinson appointed English football's first technical director. England's first home defeat in World Cup (0-1 v Italy). Ruud Gullit (Chelsea) first foreign coach to win FA Cup. Rangers equal Celtic's record of 9 successive League titles. Manchester United win Premier League for fourth time in 5 seasons. New record World Cup score: Iran 17, Maldives 0 (qualifying round). Season 1997–8 starts Premiership's record £36m, 4-year sponsorship extension with brewers Bass (Carling).

1998: In French manager Arsene Wenger's second season at Highbury, Arsenal become second English club to complete the Double twice. Chelsea also win two trophies under new player-manager Gianluca Vialli (Coca-Cola Cup, Cup Winners' Cup). In breakaway from Scottish League, top ten clubs form new Premiership under SFA, starting season 1998–9. Football League celebrates its 100th season, 1998–9. New FA Cup sponsors – French insurance giants AXA (25m, 4-year deal). League Cup becomes Worthington Cup in £23m, 5-year contract with brewers Bass. Nationwide Building Society's sponsorship of Football League extended to season 2000–1.

1999: FA buy Wembley Stadium (£103m) for £320m, plan rebuilding (Aug 2000–March 2003) as new national stadium (Lottery Sports fund contributes £110m) Scotland's new Premier League takes 3-week mid-season break in January. Sky screen Oxford Utd v Sunderland (Div 1) as first pay-per-view match on TV. FA sack England coach Glenn Hoddle; Fulham's Kevin Keegan replaces him at £1m a year until 2003. Sir Alf Ramsey, England's World Cup-winning manager, dies aged 79. With effect 1999, FA Cup Final to be decided on day (via penalties, if necessary). Hampden Park re-opens for Scottish Cup Final after £63m refit. Alex Ferguson knighted after Manchester United complete Premiership, FA Cup, European Cup treble. Starting season 1999–2000, UEFA increase Champions League from 24 to 32 clubs. End of Cup-Winners' Cup (merged into 121-club UEFA Cup). FA allow holders Manchester United to withdraw from FA Cup to participate in FIFA's inaugural World Club Championship in Brazil in January. Chelsea first British club to field an all-foreign line-up – at Southampton (Prem). FA vote in favour of streamlined 14-man board of directors to replace its 92-member council.

2000: Scot Adam Crozier takes over as FA chief executive. Wales move to Cardiff's £125m Millennium Stadium (v Finland). Brent Council approve plans for new £475m Wembley Stadium (completion target spring 2003); demolition of old stadium to begin after England v Germany (World Cup qual.). Fulham Ladies become Britain's first female professional team. FA Premiership and Nationwide League to introduce (season 2000–01) rule whereby referees advance free-kick by 10 yards and caution player who shows dissent, delays kick or fails to retreat 10 yards. Scottish football increased to 42 League clubs in 2000–01 (12 in Premier League and 3 divisions of ten; Peterhead and Elgin elected from Highland League). France win European Championship – first time a major international tournament has been jointly hosted (Holland/ Belgium). England's £10m bid to stage 2006 World Cup fails; vote goes to Germany. England manager Kevin Keegan resigns after 1-0 World Cup defeat by Germany in Wembley's last International. Lazio's Swedish coach Sven-Goran Eriksson agrees to become England head coach.

2001: Scottish Premier League experiment with split into two 5-game mini leagues (6 clubs in each) after 33 matches completed. New transfer system agreed by FIFA/UEFA is ratified. Barclaycard begin £48m, 3-year sponsorship of the Premiership, and Nationwide's contract with the Football League is extended by a further 3 years (£12m). ITV, after winning auction against BBC's Match of the Day, begin £183m, 3-season contract for highlights of Premiership matches; BSkyB's live coverage (66 matches per season) for next 3 years will cost £1.1bn. BBC and BSkyB pay £400m (3-year contract) for live coverage of FA Cup and England home matches. ITV and Ondigital pay £315m to screen Nationwide League and Worthington Cup matches. In new charter for referees, top men can earn up to £60,000 a season in Premiership. Real Madrid break world transfer record, buying Zinedine Zidane from Juventus for £47.2m. FA introduce prize money, round by round, in FA Cup.

2002: Scotland appoint their first foreign manager, Germany's former national coach Bertie Vogts replacing Craig Brown. Collapse of ITV Digital deal, with Football League owed £178m, threatens lower-division clubs. Arsenal complete Premiership/FA Cup Double for second time in 5 seasons, third time in all. Newcastle manager Bobby Robson knighted in Queen's Jubilee Honours. New record British transfer and world record for defender, £29.1m Rio Ferdinand (Leeds to Manchester United). Transfer window introduced to British football. FA Charity Shield renamed FA Community Shield. After 2-year delay, demolition of Wembley Stadium begins. October: Adam Crozier, FA chief executive, resigns.

2003: FA Cup draw (from 4th Round) reverts to Monday lunchtime. Scottish Premier League decide to end mid-winter shut-down. Mark Palios appointed FA chief executive. For first time, two Football League clubs demoted (replaced by two from Conference). Ban lifted on loan transfers between Premiership clubs. July: David Beckham becomes record British export (Manchester United to Real Madrid, £23.3m). Biggest takeover in British football history – Russian oil magnate Roman Abramovich buys control of Chelsea for £150m Wimbledon leave rented home at Selhurst Park, become England's first franchised club in 68-mile move to Milton Keynes.

2004: Arsenal first club to win Premiership with unbeaten record and only the third in English football history to stay undefeated through League season. Trevor Brooking knighted in Queen's Birthday Honours. Wimbledon change name to Milton Keynes Dons. Greece beat hosts Portugal to win European Championship as biggest outsiders (80-1 at start) ever to succeed in major international tournament. New contracts – Premiership in £57m deal with Barclays, seasons 2004–07. Coca-Cola replace Nationwide as Football League sponsors (£15m over 3 years), rebranding Div 1 as Football League Championship, with 2nd and 3rd Divisions, becoming Leagues 1 and 2. All-time League record of 49 unbeaten Premiership matches set by Arsenal. Under new League rule, Wrexham forfeit 10 points for going into administration.

2005: Brian Barwick, controller of ITV Sport, becomes FA chief executive. Foreign managers take all major trophies for English clubs: Chelsea, in Centenary year, win Premiership (record 95 points) and League Cup in Jose Mourinho's first season; Arsene Wenger's Arsenal win FA Cup in Final's first penalty shoot-out; under new manager Rafael Benitez, Liverpool lift European Cup on penalties after trailing 0-3 in Champions League Final. Wigan, a League club only since 1978, promoted to Premiership. In new record British-club take-over, American tycoon Malcolm Glazer buys Manchester United for £790m Tributes are paid world-wide to George Best, who dies aged 59.

2006: Steve Staunton succeeds Brian Kerr as Republic of Ireland manager. Chelsea post record losses of £140m. Sven-Goran Eriksson agrees a settlement to step down as England coach. Steve McClaren replaces him. The Premier League announce a new 3-year TV deal worth £1.7 billion under which Sky lose their monopoly of coverage. Chelsea smash the British transfer record, paying £30.8m for Andriy Shevchenko. Clydesdale Bank replace Bank of Scotland as sponsor of the SPL.

2007: Michel Platini becomes the new president of UEFA. Walter Smith resigns as Scotland manager to return to Rangers and is replaced by Alex McLeish. The new £800m Wembley Stadium is finally completed. The BBC and Sky lose TV rights for England's home matches and FA Cup ties to ITV and Setanta. World Cup-winner Alan Ball dies aged 61. Lawrie Sanchez resigns as Northern Ireland manager to take over at Fulham. Nigel Worthington succeeds him. Lord Stevens names five clubs in his final report into alleged transfer irregularities. Steve McClaren is sacked after England fail to qualify for the European Championship Finals and is replaced by Fabio Capello. The Republic of Ireland's Steve Staunton also goes. Scotland's Alex McLeish resigns to become Birmingham manager.

2008: The Republic of Ireland follow England's lead in appointing an Italian coach – Giovanni Trapattoni. George Burley leaves Southampton to become Scotland manager. Manchester United beat Chelsea in the first all-English Champions League Final. Manchester City smash the British transfer record when signing Robinho from Real Madrid for £32.5m.

2009: Sky secure the rights to five of the six Premier League packages from 2010–13 with a bid of £1.6bn. Reading's David Beckham breaks Bobby Moore's record number of caps for an England outfield player with his 109th appearance. A British league record for not conceding a goal ends on 1,311 minutes for Manchester United's Edwin van der Sar. AC Milan's Kaka moves to Real Madrid for a world record fee of £56m. Nine days later, Manchester United agree to sell Cristiano Ronaldo to Real for £80m. Sir Bobby Robson dies aged 76 after a long battle with cancer. Shay Given and Kevin Kilbane win their 100th caps for the Republic of Ireland. The Premier League vote for clubs to have eight home-grown players in their squads. George Burley is sacked as Scotland manager and replaced by Craig Levein.

2010: npower succeed Coca-Cola as sponsors of the Football League. Portsmouth become the first Premier League club to go into administration. Chelsea achieve the club's first League and FA Cup double. Lord Triesman resigns as chairman of the FA and of England's 2018 World Cup bid. John Toshack resigns as Wales manager and is replaced by former captain Gary Speed. England are humiliated in the vote for the 2018 World Cup which goes to Russia, with the 2022 tournament awarded to Qatar.

2011: Seven club managers are sacked in a week. The transfer record between Britsh clubs is broken twice in a day, with Liverpool buying Newcastle's Andy Carroll for £35m and selling Fernando Torres to Chelsea for £50m. Vauxhall replace Nationwide as sponsors of England and the other home nations. John Terry is restored as England captain. Football League clubs vote to reduce the number of substitutes from seven to five. Nigel Worthington steps down as Northern Ireland manager and is succeeded by Michael O'Neill. Sir Alex Ferguson completes 25 years as Manchester United manager. Manchester City post record annual losses of nearly £195m. Huddersfield set a Football League record of 43 successive unbeaten league games. Football mourns Gary Speed after the Wales manager is found dead at his home.

2012: Chris Coleman is appointed the new Wales manager. Fabio Capello resigns as manager after John Terry is stripped of the England captaincy for the second time. Roy Hodgson takes over. Rangers are forced into liquidation by crippling debts and a newly-formed club are demoted from the Scottish Premier League to Division Three. Manchester City become champions for the first time since 1968 after the tightest finish to a Premier League season. Chelsea win a penalty shoot-out against Bayern Munich in the Champions League Final. Capital One replace Carling as League Cup sponsors. Steven Gerrard (England) and Damien Duff (Republic of Ireland) win their 100th caps. The FA's new £120m National Football Centre at Burton upon Trent is opened. Scotland manager Craig Levein is sacked.

2013: Gordon Strachan is appointed Scotland manager. FIFA and the Premier League announce the introduction of goal-line technology. Energy company npower end their sponsorship of the Football League and are succeeded by Sky Bet. Sir Alex Ferguson announces he is retiring after 26 years as Manchester United manager. Wigan become the first club to lift the FA Cup and be relegated in the same season. Chelsea win the Europa League. Ashley Cole and Frank Lampard win their 100th England caps. Robbie Keane becomes the most capped player in the British Isles on his 126th appearance for the Republic of Ireland. Scottish Football League clubs agree to merge with the Scottish Premier League. Greg Dyke succeeds David Bernstein as FA chairman. Real Madrid sign Tottenham's Gareth Bale for a world record £85.3m. Giovanni Trapatonni is replaced as Republic of Ireland manager by Martin O'Neill.

2014: Sir Tom Finney, one of the finest British players of all-time, dies aged 91. England experience their worst-ever World Cup, finishing bottom the group with a single point. Germany deliver one of the most remarkable scorelines in World Cup history – 7-1 against Brazil in the semi-finals. Manchester United announce a world-record kit sponsorship with adidas worth £750m. United break the incoming British transfer record by paying £59.7m for Real Madrid's Angel di Maria, part of a record £835m spending by Premier League clubs in the summer transfer window. England's Wayne Rooney and the Republic of Ireland's John O'Shea win their 100th caps.

2015: The Premier League sell live TV rights for 2016-19 to Sky and BT for a record £5.13bn. Bournemouth, a club on the brink of folding in 2008, win promotion to the Premier League. FIFA president Sepp Blatter resigns as a bribery and corruption scandal engulfs the world governing body. Blatter and suspended UEFA president Michel Platini are banned for eight years, reduced on appeal to six years.

2016: An inquest jury rules that the 96 Liverpool fans who died in the Hillsborough disaster of 1989 were unlawfully killed. Leicester, 5,000-1 outsiders become Premier League champions in one of the game's biggest-ever surprises. Aaron Hughes wins his 100th cap for Northern Ireland. FA Cup quarter-final replays are scrapped.

THE THINGS THEY SAY ...

'It's been a sensational 24 hours' – **Russell Martin**, Norwich captain, after returning home overnight from the team's Merseyside hotel for the birth of his third child, flying back to play at Anfield and scoring his team's equaliser in a 1-1 draw with Liverpool.

'That was crazy – unbelievable' – **Robert Lewandowski**, Bayern Munich striker, after coming off the bench to score five goals in nine second-half minutes against Wolfsburg in the Bundesliga.

'These young players are our future. If we handle them like horses then we get horses' – **Jurgen Klopp**, Liverpool manager, after his midfielder Jordan Rossiter played three times in six days for the England under-19 side.

'It's unbelievable how football can play with your emotions' – **Eddie Howe**, Bournemouth manager, after his side went 3-2 behind against Everton in the 95th minute, then equalised in the eighth minute of stoppage-time.

'Every time we try to get the headlines, Leicester just keep kicking us in the pants' – **Alan Pardew**, Crystal Palace manager, after his side's run of success was overshadowed by Leicester's remarkable run.

THE MAN WHO CHANGED THE FACE OF FOOTBALL

By Albert Sewell

The greatest innovator in the game's history, Jimmy Hill changed the face of football beyond everyone's imagination. As chairman of the Professional Footballers' Association, he successfully fought for the abolishment of the maximum wage in 1961, opening the way for today's stars to be paid millions. Jimmy, himself, never earned more than £20 a week as a player. His next big campaign led to the introduction in 1981 of three points for a win, instead of two, as the means to make the game more attractive. At first widely opposed, it was eventually accepted by FIFA and now operates worldwide.

James William Thomas Hill was born in Balham, south London. His father was a milkman-turned-baker. The Boys' Brigade bugler became a stockbroker's clerk on leaving school, but National Service in the Army led to his career in football. Playing in Services matches, he was spotted and signed as an amateur by Reading manager Ted Drake. On demob, he joined Brentford in 1949 and in 1952 moved to First Division Fulham, where, as an industrious inside-forward, he made 276 League appearances and scored 41 goals (five of them in one match away to Doncaster).

Retiring as a player in 1961, Hill moved into management with Coventry and in six years took them from being a struggling Third Division club to the top tier. He turned their out-of-date Highfield Road home into England's first all-seater stadium to combat hooliganism which threatened the game. He introduced the Sky Blue train to take supporters to away games. They sang a song written by him – and Coventry became the country's most successful club.

Then came a major change of direction as he took his endless enthusiasm and bearded chin into the media at top level – with BBC's *Match of the Day,* ITV's *Big Match* and as head of sport with *London Weekend.* There was to be one more notable appearance on the field. When a linesman pulled a muscle, and with no replacement on hand, the live Arsenal-Liverpool match on *London Weekend* faced being abandoned. The appeal went out on Highbury's public address system: 'Is there a qualified linesman in the house?' Jimmy, whose CV included a referee's badge, responded instantly, stepping down from the directors' box to pick up the flag.

He served three clubs as chairman – Coventry, Charlton, then back to his first love Fulham. His direct involvement with football ended as a chat-show host on *Sky.* Honours included the PFA's Special Award, the Football League's Merit Award and an OBE for unrivalled services to the game. As BBC TV's football statistician for 37 seasons (1968-2005), I was privileged to work with Jimmy on all but a few of his 600 appearances on *Match of the Day.* He spent the last three years of his life in care near his home in West Sussex. On December 19, 2015, football's most fertile mind was overtaken by Alzheimer's. He was 87.

THE THINGS THEY SAY ...

'Jimmy was a football man through and through. He did extraordinary things for which quite a few players, myself included, might be quite grateful for' – **Gary Lineker,** *Match of the Day* presenter and former England striker.

'He was original and revolutionary, an instigator, an innovator, an inspiration' – **John Motson,** BBC commentator.

"He had a sharp incisive mind and excellent communication skills. He was also a true and loyal friend and great fun' – **Des Lynam,** who also worked alongside Hill at the BBC.

FINAL WHISTLE – OBITUARIES 2015–16

JULY 2015

BRIAN HALL, 68, was an instant Liverpool hero, his first goal for the club securing victory over Everton in the 1971 FA Cup semi-final. They lost the final 2-1 to Arsenal, but he returned to Wembley three years later to play a leading role in a 3-0 victory over Newcastle. The university graduate also won two League Championships and two UEFA Cup medals – Liverpool beating Borussia Monchengladbach in 1973 and Bruges in 1976. Hall was nicknamed 'Little Bamber', with fellow graduate and midfielder Steve Heighway known as 'Big Bamber' after the University Challenge television host Bamber Gascoigne. Hall made 224 appearances before finishing his career at Plymouth and Burnley. He later returned to Anfield in a public relations role.

FRED ELSE, 82, made more than 600 club appearances, played for England B and was regarded by many as one of the best uncapped goalkeepers of his era. He started at Preston, where Tom Finney was among his team-mates, moved to Blackburn for a £17,000 fee in 1961, then served Barrow, where he also had a spell as manager.

AUGUST 2015

GRAHAM LEGGAT, 81, held the record for the fastest hat-trick in English top-flight football for more than half a century. It came in three minutes in Fulham's 10-1 win over Ipswich on Boxing Day 1963, a feat which stood until Southampton's Sadio Mane netted three in two minutes and 56 seconds against Aston Villa in the Premier League in May, 2015. Leggat scored 134 goals in 280 appearances for the club, including eight hat-tricks. The right-winger was also a prolific marksman for his previous side, Aberdeen, with five hat-tricks among his 92 goals in 152 appearances. He helped them become champions for the first time in 1955 and scored the winner in the following season's League Cup Final against St Mirren (2-1). While at the two clubs he won 18 Scotland caps, scored eight times and played against Yugoslavia and Paraguay in the 1958 World Cup Finals in Sweden. After leaving Fulham, he had spells with Birmingham and Rotherham and was briefly a coach at Aston Villa.

SANDY KENNON, 81, joined Norwich from Huddersfield in February 1959 and the following month was helping extend their giant-killing run in the FA Cup. The South African-born goalkeeper made his debut when replacing the injured Ken Nethercott for a 3-2 victory over Sheffield United in a sixth round replay. He then played in a 1-1 semi-final draw with Luton at White Hart Lane and in the replay at St Andrew's which his new side lost 1-0. The following season, Kennon missed only one match as Norwich won promotion from the Third Division and was an ever-present as they won the League Cup in 1962, defeating Rochdale 4-0 in the two-leg final. He made 255 appearances for the club, later served Colchester and also played Minor Counties cricket for Norfolk.

SAMMY COX, 91, won three League titles, three Scottish Cups and a League Cup with Rangers. The full-back, who operated at wing-half, played every game but one in the 1948–49 season when the club made history by finishing a point ahead of Dundee and lifting the two cups with 4-1 and 2-0 victories in finals against Clyde and Raith respectively. For good measure, he was outstanding as Scotland defeated England 3-1 at Wembley in the Home International Championship. Cox made 370 appearances for Rangers, having started his career as an amateur with Queen's Park, Third Lanark and Dundee, He also played for East Fife.

DANNY HEGAN, 72, was an influential figure in Ipswich's Second Division title win in 1968 when they finished a point ahead of Queens Park Rangers. The inside-forward made 207 appearances for the club after moving from Sunderland, then went on to win seven Northern Ireland caps while playing for West Bromwich Albion and Wolves. During his time at Molineux, he played in both legs of the first UEFA Cup Final which Wolves lost 3-2 on aggregate to Tottenham in 1972. Hegan finished his career back at Sunderland.

CHRIS MARUSTIK, 54, was part of John Toshack's Swansea team who won promotion in 1979 and 1981 to reach the First Division. He came through the club's youth system and made his senior debut at 17 in a League Cup tie against Tottenham. The full-back, capped six times by Wales, joined Cardiff in 1985, had spells with Barry and the old Newport County, then played in Australia for five years.

TONY MILLINGTON, 72, won 21 Wales caps between 1962–71. The flamboyant goalkeeper, who loved entertaining crowds, played his club football with West Bromwich Albion, Crystal Palace, Peterborough and Swansea, helping the Welsh club win promotion from Division Four in the 1969–70 season. His career ended while playing for Glenavon in 1975 when a car accident confined him to a wheelchair. Later, he became a disability officer at Wrexham FC.

TOMMY LOWRY, 69, played a record 482 games for Crewe. The right-back joined the club in 1966 after making a single appearance for Liverpool under Bill Shankly and remained at Gresty Road until retiring in 1977. He helped win promotion from Division Four in the 1967–68 season and had a testimonial match in 1976 which featured England World Cup winners Gordon Banks and Nobby Stiles.

FRANK MARSHALL, 86, captained Scunthorpe to the Third Division North title in 1958 and to a shock 3-1 FA Cup fourth round victory over Newcastle at St James' Park. The wing-half was previously with Rotherham and finished his career at Doncaster, where he also had spells as caretaker manager and coach. Marshall served Mansfield as assistant manager, then coached teams in Sweden.

GEORGE MERCHANT, 89, was a Scottish Cup winner with Falkirk in 1957. They beat Kilmarnock 2-1 after extra-time in the replayed final, following a 1-1 draw, with Merchant heading their first goal. The inside-forward previously played for Dundee.

NEVILLE NEVILLE, 65, led the campaign to keep Bury solvent when they faced a financial crisis. The father of former Manchester United and England defenders Gary and Phil Neville became a club ambassador and after his death Bury name their main stand after him. He collapsed in Australia, where he was travelling with daughter Tracey, the England netball head coach.

SEPTEMBER 2015

RON SPRINGETT, 80, played in all four England matches at the 1962 World Cup in Chile – group games against Hungary, Argentina and Bulgaria and the 3-1 quarter-final defeat by the eventual champions Brazil. He was part of the squad for the tournament in England in 1966, but by then Gordon Banks had taken over the No 1 goalkeeping spot. It was not until more than 40 years later that an FA campaign resulted in winners' medals for those who did not play in the final against West Germany. Springett, who won 33 caps, made 384 appearances for Sheffield Wednesday, helping the club return to the top flight as Division Two champions in 1959. He played in the 1966 FA Cup Final when Wednesday lost a 2-0 lead and were beaten 3-2 by Everton. He rejoined his first club, Queens Park Rangers, in 1967 as part of a unique swap deal which took brother, and fellow goalkeeper, Peter to Hillsborough.

RALPH MILNE, 54, was part of the successful Dundee United side of the 1980s. He scored the first goal in a 2-1 victory over city rivals Dundee to seal the club's first and only League Championship in 1983 when they finished a point ahead of both Celtic and Aberdeen. The Scottish Under-21 winger played in three finals – Scottish Cup defeats by Rangers, in a replay, and Celtic and a League Cup defeat by Rangers. Milne, who remains the club's leading scorer in Europe, made 286 appearances for the club before spells with Charlton and Bristol City. A £175,000 fee then took him to Manchester United – a move which was not a success.

TOMMY THOMPSON, 86, was one of the few players who had Tom Finney and Stanley Matthews as teammates for club and country. He forged a productive partnership with Finney at Preston, who finished runners-up to Wolves for the League Championship in 1958 after scoring 100 goals. Thompson scored 34 of them, a club record in the top flight. The inside-forward netted 128 in six seasons at Deepdale, at an average of more than one every two games, before helping to kick-start Stoke's resurgence alongside Matthews. He also played for Newcastle, Aston Villa and Barrow and won two England caps. One of them was against Scotland in the

Home Championship in 1957 when he lined up alongside Finney and Matthews in a 2-1 victory at Wembley.

PAT DUNNE, 72, started his career at Everton in 1960, won league and cup honours with Irish club Shamrock Rovers, then joined Manchester United. The goalkeeper was a League Championship winner under Matt Busby in his first season at Old Trafford, United having a superior goal average after finishing level on points with Leeds in 1965. Dunne was Plymouth's Player of the Year in his first season there, returned for eight more years at Shamrock and later became player-manager for Thurles and Shelbourne. He won five Republic of Ireland caps.

MALCOLM GRAHAM, 81, scored the goals which clinched Leyton Orient's place in the top flight for the first and only time. The inside-forward, who formed a productive attacking partnership with Dave Dunmore, netted twice in a 2-0 win over Bury on the final day of the 1961–62 season which earned the runners-up spot behind Liverpool in Division Two. Graham joined Orient from Bristol City, went on to play for Queens Park Rangers, then returned to Barnsley, where he started his career.

BARRIE MEYER, 83, had an outstanding sporting career as an inside-forward for five clubs, a county cricketer and a Test umpire. He scored 60 goals in 139 league games for Bristol Rovers, along with one in a 4-0 victory over Manchester United in the third round of the FA Cup at Eastville in 1956. Meyer also played for Bristol City, Plymouth, Newport and Hereford. He then concentrated on keeping wicket for Gloucestershire, making more than 400 first-class appearances. After retiring, he stood in 26 Tests – including the famous Ashes match at Headingley in 1981 – and two World Cup Finals at Lord's.

BOB LEDGER, 77, began his career with Huddersfield, scoring for the first time in their remarkable 7-6 defeat by Charlton in 1957 when his side surrendered a 5-1 lead. The winger made 222 league appearances for Oldham and was an ever-present in their Division Four promotion-winning side of the 1962–63 season. He then helped Mansfield reach the sixth round of the FA Cup in 1969 when they scored a 3-0 victory over a West Ham side including World Cup winners Bobby Moore, Martin Peters and Geoff Hurst. After that, he played for Barrow.

JOE WILSON, 78, started and finished his league career with Workington, making 347 appearances spread over 11 years at the club. In between, he played for Nottingham Forest and helped Wolves regain a place in the top flight when they finished runners-up to Coventry in the 1966–67 season. He also had a spell with Newport.

KEN HORNE, 89, joined Brentford from Blackpool in 1950 and spent 11 years at the club. He made 239 appearances at full-back or wing-half and shared a benefit match with three other players in 1956 against a team which included former Blackpool team-mate Stanley Matthews. Horne finished his career with Southern League Dover, then helped Brentford reform their youth side.

MICHAEL O'FLANAGAN, 92, was the Republic of Ireland's oldest surviving international. The Bohemians centre-forward gained one cap, against England in 1946. He also played rugby for Ireland. Brother Kevin was a dual international, too, having played his club football with Arsenal. They were the only Irish brothers to be capped at both sports.

MARTIN COLFER, won two Republic of Ireland caps, against Belgium and Norway, in 1950–51. He had seven seasons with Shelbourne, winning a League of Ireland medal in 1953 and playing in two losing FAI Cup Final teams.

OCTOBER 2015

HOWARD KENDALL, 69, achieved legendary status at Everton by delivering unprecedented success to the club in the first of three spells as manager between 1981–87. They were twice champions, beating Liverpool into second place each time, defeated Watford 2-0 in the FA Cup Final and overcame Rapid Vienna 3-1 in the European Cup-winners' Cup Final. He also won two Manager of the Year awards. Kendall, who was previously in charge of Blackburn, left Goodison Park for Athletic Bilbao, came back to England to take charge of Manchester City, then returned to Merseyside in 1990. This time there was no magic touch and he moved on again, first to Notts County, then Sheffield United, before completing a managerial career spanning 866 games back at Everton in 1998. Kendall also won the League title with the club as a player in 1970, forming a 'Holy Trinity' midfield partnership with Alan Ball and Colin Harvey. He had started out at Preston, becoming the youngest player to feature in a Wembley FA Cup Final (2-3 v West Ham in 1964) at the age of 17 years and 345 days. He also served Birmingham, Stoke and Blackburn in a playing career of 721 games.

JOHNNY PATON, 92, was Chelsea's oldest surviving player. The outside-left, who started his career at Celtic, had one season at Stamford Bridge – 1946–47. It was the first after the Second World War, during which he guested for Arsenal, Crystal Palace, Millwall, Manchester City and Leeds. After leaving Chelsea, Paton served Brentford and Watford. He later had a brief spell as Watford manager.

RON GREENER, 81, joined Darlington from Newcastle and made a club-record 515 appearances between 1955–1967. They included a notable FA Cup fourth round tie against Chelsea in 1958 when his team drew 3-3 at Stamford Bridge and won the replay 4-1. Another red-letter day came two years later when a record crowd of 21,000 packed the Feethams Ground for a League Cup third round match against Wolves, who won it 2-1. The centre-half was also a key figure in the club's promotion from Division Four in the 1965–66 season.

MATT WATSON, 79, helped Kilmarnock become Scottish champions for the first and only time. On a dramatic final day of the 1964–65 season, they overtook Hearts by winning 2-0 at Tynecastle to win the title on goal average. The left-back, who made 440 appearances for the club, appeared in three losing finals – against Rangers in the Scottish Cup and Rangers and Hearts in the League Cup. He also played for Queen of the South.

JOHNNY HAMILTON, 66, won league and cup honours during five seasons with Rangers. The midfielder helped them become champions in the 1975–76 season and played in the 3-1 Scottish Cup Final victory over Hearts. Two seasons later, he was in the side that defeated Celtic 2-1 in the League Cup Final. Hamilton joined the club from Hibernian and was later with Millwall and St Johnstone.

BOBBY BRAITHWAITE, 78, was a Northern Ireland international winger who won ten caps. Nicknamed 'Gento' after the Real Madrid player Francisco Gento, he helped Linfield complete a clean sweep of seven domestic trophies in the 1961–62 season. Braithwaite then gave up his shipyard job to go full-time with Middlesbrough, where injury contributed to him not fulfilling his potential. He later played for and managed Durban and Bloemfontein in South Africa.

JOE WARK, 67, was regarded as one of Motherwell's best-ever players. The one-club man spent 16 years there and made a record 539 appearances. Ironically, the full-back spent 87 minutes of his 1968 debut in a friendly against Tranmere in goal, following an injury to Keith McCrae.

PETER PRICE, 83, scored a record 213 goals in 251 appearances for Ayr United. They came in seven seasons at the club, with the 1957–58 and 1958–59 campaigns bringing 105 in league and cup. The centre-forward, who netted five in an 8-1 win over East Stirling in 1955, also played for St Mirren, Darlington, Raith and Albion Rovers.

NOVEMBER 2015

GERRY BYRNE, 77, won major club and international honours during a 12-year career with Liverpool. The left-back was one of the game's hard men, but was never sent off in 333 league and cup appearances during the Bill Shankly era at Anfield. Byrne will be remembered most for the 1965 FA Cup Final against Leeds when he broke his collarbone in a challenge with Bobby Collins after seven minutes. With no substitutes allowed in those days, he played on in pain for the remainder of the game, including 30 minutes of extra-time, and delivered the cross for Roger Hunt to score Liverpool's first goal in a 2-1 win – their first success in the competition. Byrne, who could also operate on the right side of defence, helped his side become Second Division champions in 1962 and shared their top division triumphs in 1964 and 1966 when finishing ahead of Manchester United and Leeds respective. He was also in the team beaten 2-1 by Borussia Dortmund in the 1966 European Cup-Winners Cup Final. Together with Hunt and Ian Callaghan, he was a member of England's World Cup-winning squad in that year and, along with the non-playing members, belatedly received a medal from FIFA in 2009. Byrne, who won two caps against Scotland and Norway, retired prematurely through injury in 1969 and joined Liverpool's coaching staff.

BOBBY CAMPBELL, 78, took over as manager from John Hollins towards the end of the 1987–88 season with Chelsea heading for relegation. He was unable to save them, but took the club straight back to the top flight as champions with a club-record 99 points. The season after that, Chelsea finished fifth – their highest position for 20 years – and beat Middlesbrough 1-0 to win the Full Members Cup, the competition organised in the wake of the post-Heysel ban on English clubs in Europe. He was replaced by Ian Porterfield after a disappointing 1990–91 campaign. Previously, Campbell managed Fulham, who had George Best and Bobby Moore in the side, and led Portsmouth to the Third Division title in 1983. He also coached Arsenal and Queens Park Rangers and had two spells in Kuwait. He had been an England youth international who played wing-half for Liverpool, Portsmouth and Aldershot.

MARTON FULOP, 32, was a Hungary international goalkeeper who spent eight years in English football between 2004–12. He died after a long illness. Fulop started his career with MTK Budapest, had a spell with Tottenham without making a first-team appearance, then played for Sunderland, Ipswich and West Bromwich Albion. He was also loaned out to Chesterfield, Coventry, Leicester, Stoke and then Manchester City. Fulop, who won 24 caps, last played for the Greek club Asteras Tripolis.

ARTHUR SHAW, 91, played at wing-half in Arsenal's successful side of the 1952–53 season when they finished level on 54 points with Preston and became champions on goal average. He spent seven years at Highbury after joining the club from Brentford and later served Watford.

DAVID SHAWCROSS, 74, spent seven years with Manchester City from 1958, making 47 first-team appearances. He went on to play for Stockport, Halifax, Altrincham and Macclesfield.

IAN DARGIE. 84, was a centre-half who joined Brentford from Tonbridge in 1952 and made 263 league appearances in ten years at the club. After retiring, he worked on the backroom staff at Crystal Palace and Charlton.

JACKIE MCGUGAN, 76, won a Scottish Cup winners' medal in 1959 with St Mirren, who defeated Aberdeen 3-1 in the final. The centre-half later played for Leeds, Tranmere, Ayr and Morton.

BROWN MCMASTER, 66, was president of the Scottish Football League between 2007–09. He had a 20-year association with Partick, twice serving as chairman, and later joined the Board at Stenhousemuir.

DECEMBER 2015

DON HOWE, 80, followed a distinguished playing career by becoming one of the country's most renowned and respected coaches. He served England in both capacities, winning 23 caps at right-back and featuring in all three group matches at the 1958 World Cup in Sweden. Howe then had key coaching roles under Ron Greenwood, Sir Bobby Robson when England reached the semi-finals of Italia 90, and Terry Venables when they made it to the last four of Euro 96. At club level, he made 379 appearances for West Bromwich Albion and had two years with Arsenal, following a £42,000 transfer, before a broken leg forced him to retire. After that, he was Bertie Mee's assistant when Arsenal won the 'Double' in 1971 and helped take the club to three more FA Cup Finals in successive years – 1978–1980 – alongside Terry Neill. He was also Bobby Gould's assistant when Wimbledon defeated Liverpool in the 1988 FA Cup Final. Howe, himself, had managerial spells, without the same success, at Albion, Arsenal, Queens Park Rangers, Coventry and the Turkish club Galatasaray.

ALAN HODGKINSON, 79, had a distinguished playing career for club and country, then became one of the game's first specialist goalkeeper coaches. At 5ft 9in he was relatively small for the position, but more than compensated with agility and positional sense. He joined Sheffield United from Worksop Town for a £250 fee in 1953 and remained at Bramall Lane until retiring in 1971, making 675 appearances and ranking second in United's all-time list to centre-half Joe Shaw (714). Hodgkinson won five international caps and was a non-playing member of the England squad for the World Cup of 1958 and 1962. In a wide-ranging coaching role, he worked with England's David Seaman, Scotland's Jim Leighton and Andy Goram, Neville Southall of Wales and nurtured Peter Schmeichel to prominence at Manchester United. He was awarded an MBE in 2008 for services to the game.

PAVEL SRNICEK, 47, became a big crowd favourite at St James' Park after joining Newcastle from Banik Ostrava in 1991. The goalkeeper helped them win promotion to the Premier League as First Division champions in 1993. He was also part of the side under Kevin Keegan that led the league by 12 points in January 1996 before fading and finishing four points behind Manchester United. He later played for Sheffield Wednesday, Portsmouth and West Ham, then returned in 2006 as cover for the injured Shay Given. Srnicek made 190 appearances in the two spells and played 49 times for the Czech Republic. He had been back to Newcastle promoting his book before suffering cardiac arrest while out running.

ROY SWINBOURNE, 86, was a prolific marksman for Wolves and a key figure in their first League Championship success. The centre-forward scored 24 goals in the 1953–54 season when they finished four points ahead of West Bromwich Albion in second place. The following season, he netted twice in arguably the most famous match in the club's history – a 3-2 win over the mighty Hungarian side Honved in a floodlit friendly, watched by a crowd of 60,000 at Molineux. Swinbourne, who started his career with Wolves' nursery club in Yorkshire, Wath Wanderers, scored 114 goals in 230 appearances before a knee injury forced him to retire in 1957.

MICK MCLAUGHLIN, 72, helped Hereford deliver one of the most famous giant-killing victories in the history of the FA Cup. The Southern League team held six-time winners Newcastle 2-2 in the third round at St James' Park and won the replay 2-1 at their Edgar Street ground. McLaughlin, a central defender, made 84 league appearances after signing from Newport County. He returned to the Welsh club to finish his career.

ARNOLD PERALTA, 26, signed a four-year contract with Rangers in June 2013 and made 20 appearances in their Scottish League One title season. It was cancelled by mutual agreement after 18 months and the Honduras international midfielder returned to his home country to join the Olimpia club. Peralta, who won 26 caps, died in a shooting incident in the town of La Ceiba.

STEVE GOHOURI, 34, joined Wigan from Borussia Monchengladbach and made 42 Premier League appearances between 2010–12. The Ivory Coast international defender also played in Israel, Switzerland, Liechtenstein and Greece. Gohouri, who won 12 caps, was reported missing after attending the Christmas party of his German club, Steinbach.

IAN BURNS, 76, played for his home-town club Aberdeen from 1957–66, making 192 appearances. He then had four years with Brechin before retiring.

WILLIE COBURN, 74, joined St Johnstone from junior football in 1962 and made 238 appearances in ten years at the Perth club. He also played for Forfar and Cowdenbeath.

JANUARY 2016

PETER BAKER, 84, was one of the defensive stalwarts of Tottenham's league and cup double triumph of the 1960–61 season. The right-back played every game but one as they finished eight points ahead of Sheffield Wednesday and went on to defeat Leicester 2-0 in the FA Cup Final. Baker returned to Wembley the following year for a 3-1 victory over Burnley and was a winner again as Tottenham became the first British side to enjoy European success by beating Atletico Madrid 5-1 in the 1963 Cup-Winners' Cup Final. He had made his debut for the club ten years earlier and completed 342 appearances before leaving to join Durban United in South Africa in 1965.

RAY POINTER, 79, was a prolific marksman whose goals helped Burnley become champions in the 1959–60 season. They finished a point ahead of Wolves and two clear of Tottenham, with Pointer netting 19 times. Two seasons later, he scored 25 as Burnley were runners-up to Ipswich and reached the FA Cup Final, losing 3-1 to Tottenham. In 270 appearances for the club, the centre-forward accumulated 133 goals. He was also on the mark in two of his three England appearances – against Luxembourg and Portugal. Pointer later played for Bury, Coventry and Portsmouth. After retiring, he returned to Turf Moor as youth team manager and coached at Bury.

JOHN ROBERTS, 69, played a part in Arsenal's double-winning triumph in the 1970–71 season. He made 18 appearances as Bertie Mee's side finished a point ahead of Leeds and defeated Liverpool 2-1 in the FA Cup Final. The centre-half, who did not feature in the Wembley success, joined the club from Northampton. He left Highbury after three years for Birmingham, helped Wrexham win the Third Division title and Welsh Cup, then played for Hull. Roberts won 22 caps with Wales and was part of the squad that reached the 1976 European Championship quarter-finals.

AMBROSE FOGARTY, 82, was a Republic of Ireland forward who won 11 caps. Ten of them came while playing for Sunderland, the club he joined in 1957 after spells with Bohemians and Glentoran. Fogarty then became the first international for Hartlepool, who paid a then record £10,000 fee for his services in 1963. After that, he returned to Ireland to become player-manager at Cork Hibernians and Cork Celtic, managed Drumcondra and Galway and had nearly 20 years at Athlone Town.

TOMMY BRYCELAND, 76, scored the first goal in St Mirren's 3-1 win over Aberdeen in the 1959 Scottish Cup Final, watched by a crowd of 108,000 at Hampden Park. The inside-forward also had a big moment in the FA Cup after joining Norwich – a 2-1 fourth round victory over Manchester United in 1967. Bryceland moved on to Oldham before returning to St Mirren as player and manager.

PERCY FREEMAN, 70, scored 23 goals in 35 appearances to help Lincoln become Fourth Division champions under Graham Taylor in the 1975–76 season. It was the centre-forward's second spell at the club, Taylor having previously sold him to Reading. Freeman, who had started his career with West Bromwich Albion as understudy to England's Jeff Astle, later moved into non-league football, playing for Boston and managing Stamford.

JOHN DOWIE, 60, was involved in Fulham's marathon run to the 1975 FA Cup Final. Including replays, they played 11 matches and the midfielder featured in eight, among them the semi-final replay victory over Birmingham. But he missed out on the 2-0 Wembley defeat by West Ham. Three years later, Dowie was in the Celtic side beaten 2-1 by Rangers in the Scottish League Cup Final. He also played for Doncaster and Clyde.

ERIC WEBSTER, 84, had five separate spells as manager of Stockport in the 1980s – four as caretaker and one on a permanent basis. During that time, he helped the club survive by selling players and unearthing new talent. The highlight was holding Liverpool to a goalless draw in the League Cup, then taking the second leg to extra-time at Anfield before losing it 2-0. After 16 years at Edgeley Park, Webster was awarded a testimonial against Manchester City, for whom he made his one Football League appearance as a player.

TOMMY O'HARA, 63, was one of the first British players to sample professional football in the United States. After spells with Celtic and Queen of the South, the midfielder joined Washington Diplomats in the NASL in 1978 and made 120 appearances for the club. O'Hara lined up alongside Johan Cruyff, former Celtic manager Wim Jansen and Bobby Stokes, scorer of Southampton's winner against Manchester United in the 1976 FA Cup Final. He then played for Jacksonville in 1981 before returning to Scotland to serve Motherwell, Falkirk and Partick.

STUART COWDEN, 90, was the oldest surviving Stoke player. The half-back made 50 appearances during and just after the Second World War. He went on play 374 games for non-league Witton Albion before a knee injury ended his career during the 1954–55 season.

DAVID THOMSON, 77, scored the opening goal in Dunfermline's first Scottish Cup triumph. Managed by Jock Stein, they defeated Celtic 2-0 in a replay after the teams' first meeting in 1961 ended goalless. Thomson, a forward, was sold to Leicester for a then club-record £8,000 and later played for Queen of the South and Berwick.

FEBRUARY 2016

FREDDIE GOODWIN, 82, was one of Matt Busby's Manchester United 'Babes' who made his first-team breakthrough as the club rebuilt after the 1958 Munich Air Disaster which claimed the lives of eight players. Goodwin, who was not selected for the ill-fated trip to play Red Star Belgrade in the European Cup, helped United reached the FA Cup Final that season and was in the team beaten 2-0 by Bolton at Wembley. Previously, he had been a member of their title-winning squads of 1956 and 1957. The wing-half spent six years at Old Trafford and also played first-class cricket for Lancashire over two summers, making 11 appearances as a fast bowler with a best analysis of 5-35 against Middlesex at Lord's. He went on to captain Leeds, before a broken leg cut short his playing career in 1964 and took him into management at Scunthorpe, where he gave a senior debut to future England goalkeeper Ray Clemence. Goodwin later managed Brighton, then led Birmingham into the old First Division, having given Trevor Francis his first chance at the club. He also coached in America, with New York Generals and Minnesota Kicks.

GRAHAM MOORE, 74 made a dream debut for Wales against England in a Home International match in 1959. He headed a last-minute equaliser at Ninian Park, in front of an all-time record crowd of 62,634, and went on win 21 caps. Later that season, the winner against Aston Villa confirmed Cardiff's promotion to the top division and his performances brought him the Welsh Sports Personality of the Year award. He then helped Chelsea gain promotion after a record £35,000 move to Stamford Bridge. Moore also played for Manchester United, Northampton, Charlton and Doncaster, making more than 400 Football League appearances in a 17-year career.

RONNIE BLACKMAN, 90, became Reading's all-time leading marksman – after a £10 transfer. Manager Ted Drake brought him to the club in 1947, initially as a part-timer, from Gosport Borough, who also received the promise of a friendly match. The centre-forward netted 39 goals in the 1951–52 season when Reading totalled 112 – another club record – to finish runners-up in the Third Division South. Blackman, the last living member of that squad, went on to accumulate 158 goals in 218 league appearances, 96 of them headers, and twice scored five times in a game, against Brighton and Southend. He left Elm Park in 1955 to join Nottingham Forest and also played for Ipswich.

JOHNNY MILLER, 65, joined Norwich from Ipswich during the 1974–75 season and a few weeks later returned to Portman Road to knock his home-town club out of the League Cup with two goals in a fifth round replay. Norwich went on to reach the final and the right-winger played in a 1-0 defeat by Aston Villa at Wembley. He also helped them return to the old First Division that season, making 14 league appearances. Miller then played in Mansfield's Third Division title-winning team of 1976–77 and later served Port Vale.

PHIL GARTSIDE, 63, became Bolton's chairman in 1999 and supervised the most successful period in the club's recent history. They gained promotion to the Premier League, qualified for the UEFA Cup for the first time and signed top players Jay-Jay Okocha, Youri Djorkaeff and Nicolas Anelka. His last years were in sharp contrast. Bolton were relegated in 2012, incurred debts of nearly £200m and he stepped aside from his duties because of ill health in November, 2015 with their Championship status under threat. Gartside also served on the FA Board, FA Council and as a non-executive director of Wembley Stadium.

DAVID SLOAN, 74, joined Oxford United from Scunthorpe in February, 1968 and in the last game of that season scored the winning goal against Southport to seal the Third Division title for his new club. He also became the first Oxford player to win a full international cap, for Northern Ireland against Israel, and won a second one against Spain. The right-winger finished his career with Walsall.

HARRY GLASGOW, 76, captained Clyde's part-timers during their notable 1966–67 season when they finished third behind Celtic and Rangers in the Scottish First Division. The full-back, made nearly 300 appearances after joining the club from Falkirk. He later played for, and managed, Stenhousemuir.

MARK FARREN, 33, had spells with Tranmere and Huddersfield as a teenager before becoming one of the best strikers in the League of Ireland. He became Derry City's record scorer with 114 goals in 209 appearances, was part of the FAI Cup-winning side of 2006 and 2012 and helped them become First Division champions in 2010. Farren, who died of cancer, also played for Finn Harps, Monaghan and Glenavon.

JACK MARRIOTT, 87, joined Sheffield Wednesday in 1947, spent seven years at Hillsborough and helped them gain promotion to the old First Division. The right-winger had a spell with Huddersfield, then returned to his first club, Scunthorrpe, where he was a key figure in their Third Division North title success and 3-1 FA Cup win over Newcastle at St James' Park, both in the 1957–58 season.

PAUL BANNON, 59, was a much-travelled forward who had spells with Nottingham Forest, Carlisle, Bristol Rovers, Breda in Holland and Salonika and Larissa in Greece. The Dublin-born striker-turned-defender joined Cork City in 1989 and scored the decisive goal in a 3-2 play-off victory over Shelbourne to give the club their first League of Ireland title in 1993. Bannon finished his career with Cobh Ramblers, then spent 17 years working for the FAI.

JIM MCFADZEAN, 77, played in two Scottish championship-winning teams. He was in the Hearts side that finished four points ahead of Kilmarnock in 1960. Five seasons later, the inside-forward helped Kilmarnock, his home-town club, win their only top division title on goal average from Hearts, both finishing on 50 points. McFadzean also played for St Mirren, Raith and Ayr.

BARRY HORSTEAD, 80, was a one-club player, making 364 appearances for Scunthorpe in 12 seasons at the Old Show Ground. He played every game in their Third Division North title-winning season of 1957–58, starting at full-back and switching to centre-half after eight games. Horstead was also in the side that recorded Scunthorpe's record home league win – 8-1 against Luton in 1965.

MARCH 2016

JOHAN CRUYFF, 68, changed the face of football as one of the world's finest players and through his work as a visionary coach. His influence stretched over a decade at Ajax. It continued at club level with Barcelona, impacted on the international stage with Holland and remains a force in the game today. Cruyff was a pioneer of Total Football, the style of play of continually interchanging roles. Initially, it brought six Dutch titles, the first in the 1965–66 season, and three successive European Cup triumphs, the first at Wembley against Panathinaikos in 1971, then in finals against Inter Milan and Juventus. After joining Barcelona for a then world record fee of £922,000, he won league and cup honours, along with two more European Player of the Year awards. There were two further titles in a second spell with Ajax and another with Feyenoord. In between, he also played for Levante, Los Angeles Aztecs and Washington Diplomats, making a total of 521 appearances and 293 goals. Cruyff was capped 48 times by Holland, scored 33 times and captained the 1974 World Cup side in West Germany. There, he first showcased the 'Cruyff turn' – a movement which involved dragging the ball back behind his standing leg with the other foot while turning through 180 degrees, then shimmying past an opponent. He won a penalty, awarded by English referee Jack Taylor, in the second minute of the final against the host country, who recovered to win 2-1. His subsequent coaching career delivered more trophies – the European Cup-winners' Cup with Ajax, followed by four successive La Liga titles for Barcelona, together with their first European Cup victory, against Sampdoria at Wembley in 1992. He died of lung cancer, having smoked from an early age.

JOHNNY KING, 77, was the most successful manager in Tranmere's history, taking the club from the Fourth Division to within sight of the Premier League. Between 1993–95, his side reached successive Division One play-off semi-finals, losing to Swindon, Leicester and Reading.

Previously, they had contested four Wembley finals in just over a year – winning and losing play-off finals against Bolton and Notts County respectively, defeating Bristol Rovers to win the Football League Trophy and losing to Birmingham in the same competition. They also reached the League Cup semi-finals in 1994. Those achievements, in his second spell in charge, led to the naming of a stand after him at Prenton Park and, later, a statue being unveiled at the ground. King captained Tranmere for seven years of his playing career, along with time spent at Everton, Bournemouth, Port Vale and Wigan. Between the two managerial stints at the club, he won the FA Trophy with Northwich in 1984 and led Welsh side Caernarfon into the third round of the FA Cup in 1987.

IAN BRITTON, 61, scored the goal which saved Burnley from dropping into non-league football. His header delivered a 2-1 win over Leyton Orient on the final day of the 1986–87 Fourth Division season when the club faced relegation to the Conference. They stayed up by a point, with Lincoln relegated. Britton previously spent ten years with Chelsea, making 289 appearances and helping them win promotion back to the top division in 1977. He also shared Dundee United's only major Scottish title success when they finished a point ahead of both Celtic and Aberdeen in 1983. The midfielder then had spells with Blackpool and Arbroath.

ALAN SPAVIN, 74, joined Preston in 1959, scored on his senior debut against Arsenal and went on to make 486 appearances for the club. He was in the side beaten 3-2 by West Ham in the 1964 FA Cup Final and captained the Third Division title-winning team of the 1970–71 season when they finished a point ahead of Fulham. The inside-forward left Deepdale in 1974 to sign for Washington Diplomats, returning three years later to play a handful of games before joining the coaching staff.

BILLY RITCHIE, 79, was part of the great Rangers team of the 1960s and an ever-present in their Treble-winning season of 1963–64. During a 12-year career at Ibrox, the goalkeeper won two League titles, four Scottish Cups and three League Cups. One of his finest performances came against Wolves in the second leg of a European Cup-Winners' Cup tie in 1961 at Molineux. It helped Rangers into the final, which they lost 4-1 on aggregate to Fiorentina. Ritchie, whose one Scottish cap came against Uruguay, left the club for Partick after making 369 appearances. He also played for Motherwell and Stranraer.

JACK MANSELL, 88, coached and managed in many parts of the world after a playing career with Brighton, Cardiff and Portsmouth from 1948–58, during which he also made two appearances at full-back for the England B team. Mansell started on Sheffield Wednesday's backroom staff and went on to manage Rotherham and Reading, Abroad, he coached in Holland, Israel, Bahrain, the United States and Turkey.

WALLY BRAGG, 86, was the last surviving member of the last Brentford team to play in the top flight of English football. That was in the 1946–47 season after he made his debut aged 17 – then the club's youngest-ever. After serving National Service and playing for the RAF, the centre-half returned to Griffin Park in 1952 and was there for another five years until a succession of injuries forced him to retire.

JIMMY TONER, 91, twice celebrated Scottish League Cup success with Dundee. His side defeated Rangers 3-2 in the 1951–52 season and 12 months later they overcame Kilmarnock 2-0 in the final. The inside-forward later played for Leeds, Motherwell and Forfar, before returning to Dens Park after a gap of 11 years to join the coaching staff. He died shortly after being inducted into Dundee's Hall of Fame.

DAVY WALSH, 92, won 20 caps for the Republic of Ireland thanks to his prolific scoring record with West Bromwich Albion and Aston Villa. The centre-forward netted 100 goals in 174 appearances for Albion after the War, then 40 in 114 games for Villa. He also played for Walsall, Limerick United, Shelbourne, Shamrock Rovers and Linfield. Walsh made his international debut against Portugal in 1946 and went on to score five times for the Republic.

JACK BOXLEY, 84, was a mainstay of Bristol City's Third Division South title-winning team of the 1954–55 season. The outside-left made 44 appearances and scored 11 goals as City finished nine points ahead of Leyton Orient. He also won promotion, from Division Four, with Coventry in 1959, before returning for a second spell at Ashton Gate.

APRIL 2016

CESARE MALDINI, 84, won four Serie A titles with AC Milan and was captain when they became the first Italian side to win the European Cup, beating Benfica 2-1 in the final at Wembley in 1963. He played 412 games for the club, became coach after retiring and was assistant to Enzo Bearzot when Italy won the World Cup in 1982. He led them to the last eight in 1998 and took Paraguay to the finals in 2002. Maldini's son Paolo, also a defender, made 902 appearances for Milan and 126 for Italy.

KEN WATERHOUSE, 85, played in the first League Cup Final in 1961. He was an inside-forward with Rotherham, who lost 3-2 on aggregate to Aston Villa when the competition started on a two-leg basis. Waterhouse joined the club from Preston, then had spells with Bristol City and Darlington. After his career was ended by a broken leg, he manager Morecambe.

GARRY JONES, 65, made 247 appearances and scored 55 goals for Bolton between 1968–78. High spot was a hat-trick in a 3-0 League Cup win over Manchester City in 1971, watched by a crowd of a crowd of more than 42,000 at Burnden Park. The striker played a key role in Bolton's Third Division title win in 1973 and was part of the side that narrowly missed promotion to the top division three seasons later when finishing fourth. He was also with Sheffield United, Blackpool, Hereford and Los Angeles Aztecs.

JOHN WAITE, 74, was an England schoolboy and youth international who played for Grimsby in 1961–62, making his debut while still a sixth-former at a local grammar school. The winger also played for Gainsborough and after retiring returned to Blundell Park to work in the club's commercial department.

MAY 2016

IAN GIBSON, 73, joined Coventry from Middlesbrough for a then record fee of £57,500 in 1966. Under Jimmy Hill, he helped them become Second Division champions in his first season, a 3-1 win over Wolves watched by a record crowd of more than 51,000 at Highfield Road effectively sealing the title. The inside-forward was also an influential figure in Coventry finishing sixth in the top division under Noel Cantwell in 1970 to qualify for Europe. Gibson, who had started his career with Accrington and Bradford Park Avenue, was then surprisingly sold to Cardiff and finished his career at Bournemouth.

GEORGE ROSS, 73, served Preston, on and off the field, for more than half a century. He played in the 1964 FA Cup Final, won 3-2 by West Ham, and was a key member of the Third Division title-winning side of 1971. The full-back, who started as a 15-year-old apprentice, made 441 appearances for the club, later playing for Southport and Washington Diplomats. He was chairman of Preston's former players' association for many years and worked in the Deepdale hospitality areas up to the time of his death.

BOBBY CARROLL, 77, scored Celtic's first goal in a Europe competition. The right-winger netted twice in a 4-2 defeat by holders Valencia in the first round of the Inter-Cities Fairs Cup – now the Europa League – in 1962. He spent six years at the club, then played for St Mirren, Dundee United, the Irish side Coleraine and Queen of the South.

JOHNNY COYLE, 83, achieved a notable treble for club and country. The centre-forward scored 43 goals for Dundee United in season 1955–56, which remains the club record. His overall tally was 112 in 132 matches. After joining Clyde, he netted the only goal of the 1958 Scottish Cup Final against Hibernian. That same year, Coyle won a place in Scotland's squad for the World Cup in Sweden, although he did not make an appearance.

ALAN LEWIS, 61, was a member of the England youth team who became European champions in 1972 and 1973. The left-back played for Derby, Peterborough, Sheffield Wednesday and Brighton before joining Reading, where he shared their Division Four title win in the 1978–79 season.

CHRIS MITCHELL, 27, won a Scottish Division Two and Challenge Cup double with Queen of the South in 2013. The Scotland Under-21 defender-midfielder had three seasons at the club before joining Clyde, where he made 18 appearances in the 2015–16 campaign before leaving for a new full-time job. Previously, he had spells with Falkirk, Ayr and Bradford.

FRED MIDDLETON, 85, was a wing-half who captained Lincoln after joining the club from Newcastle in 1954. He made 300 Football League appearances, along with 13 FA Cup ties, in nine years at Sincil Bank before playing non-league football.

ROBERT MCILVENNY, 89, was a 5ft 4in inside-forward who made up for a lack of inches with a quick elusive style of play. He had four years at Oldham from 1950 and went on to play for Bury, Southport and Barrow.

JOHN LUMSDEN, 55, joined Stoke from East Fife in 1979 and had three years at the Victoria Ground. The midfielder then played for Leytonstone and Ilford.

JUNE 2016

JOHNNY BROOKS, 84, scored on his first two appearances for England, against Wales and Yugoslavia in 1956. The inside-forward won one further cap while at Tottenham, for whom he played 179 matches and scored 51 goals. Brooks, who started his career with home-town team Reading, left White Hart Lane for Chelsea, helped Brentford win the Fourth Division title in 1963 and finished his professional career at Crystal Palace. His son Shaun had spells with Palace, Leyton Orient and Bournemouth.

BRYAN EDWARDS, 85, was a one-club player who signed for Bolton on his 17th birthday in 1947 and went on to make 518 appearances in an 18-year career. He missed the 1953 FA Cup Final against Blackpool through a combination of military service and a broken leg, but had a second chance five years later, setting up Nat Lofthouse for the first of his two goals in a 2-0 victory over Manchester United. The following season, the wing-half helped Bolton finish fourth in the old First Division. Edwards later managed Bradford City, held coaching positions at Blackpool, Preston and Plymouth and worked as a physio with Huddersfield and Leeds.

EAMONN DOLAN, 48, was Reading's academy manager who died after a long battle against cancer. He joined the club in 2004 and had a brief spell as caretaker-manager following Brian McDermott's dismissal in 2013. Previously, he managed Exeter and played for West Ham, Bristol City, Birmingham and Exeter. In his younger days, he played alongside twin brother Patrick for the Republic of Ireland's youth and under-21 international teams.

TONY BYRNE, 70, joined Southampton from Millwall in 1964 and spent a decade at the club, eventually breaking into the senior side after his career was interrupted by a broken leg. During that time, he helped them gain promotion to the old First Division, as runners-up to Manchester City in 1966, and played 14 times for the Republic of Ireland. Byrne, converted to left-back after starting out as a winger, featured in Hereford's Third Division title win of 1976 and finished his career at Newport.

ALEX GOVAN, 86, helped Plymouth become Third Division South champions in the 1951–52 season, then made his mark with Birmingham – on and off the field. They won the Division Two title, on goal average from Luton in 1955, and reached the FA Cup Final the following year, losing 3-1 to Manchester City. On the team bus during that run to Wembley, Govan introduced the Harry Lauder song,'Keep right on to the end of the road,' as the club's anthem. The left-winger went on to play for Portsmouth before seeing out his career back at Plymouth, who won the Third Division title in 1959.

HARRY GREGORY, 72, captained Charlton in the 1968–69 season when they finished third in the Second Division. The England youth international, an inside-forward, had five seasons at the club after joining from Leyton Orient. He then played for Aston Villa and Hereford.

NICKY JENNINGS, 70, was a diminutive winger who spent seven years with Portsmouth, making 227 appearances, scoring 50 goals and winning the club's Player of the Season award in 1970. He joined the club from Plymouth, went on to play for Aldershot and Exeter and had a summer in the United States with Dallas.

DAN MCCAFFREY, 86, was the first winner of the Irish soccer writers' Personality of the Year award after leading Drumcondra to the League of Ireland title in the 1960–61 season. McCaffrey, the league's top scorer with 29 goals, attended every subsequent presentation night until 2014. He also played for Derry, Sligo, Waterford, Cork Hibernians and Drogheda, as well as Yeovil when they were in the Southern League.

JULY 2016

JOHN O'ROURKE, 71, was a much-travelled centre-forward who scored important goals for clubs at both ends of the table. After joining Luton from Chelsea, he netted 22 in 23 appearances to save them from almost certain relegation to Division Four in 1964. O'Rourke scored 30 goals to help Middlesbrough win promotion from the Third Division three years later. Then the former England youth international moved to Ipswich for the final months of their Second Division championship-winning season. He went on to play for Coventry, Queens Park Rangers and Bournemouth, along with a spell in South Africa.

JIMMY FRIZZELL, 79, served Oldham as player and manager for 22 years. The full-back made 318 appearances after joining the club from Morton. He succeeded Jack Rowley in 1970 and won promotion from Division Four in his first season in charge. Three years later Oldham became Division Three champions. He became assistant manager to Billy McNeill at Manchester City in 1983 and moved up when McNeill took over at Aston Villa. It was a short-lived appointment, with Frizzell sacked after relegation from the top division in 1987. He later returned to Maine Road for a spell as chief scout.

JOHN MIDDLETON, 59, was an England youth and under-21 international goalkeeper who helped Nottingham Forest win promotion from Division Two in the 1976–77 season. He joined Derby in a deal which took Archie Gemmill to the City Ground, but had his career cut short by a shoulder injury which forced him to retire in 1980.

THE THINGS THEY SAY ...

'It is amazing we are mentioning him in the same breath' – **Claudio Ranieri**, Leicester manager, after Jamie Vardy scored in 11 successive Premier League matches to match the run Gabriel Batistuta achieved for Fiorentina when Ranieri was coach there.

'I want to give players the shot I had. There are some outstanding ones in non-league and they just need that chance' – **Jamie Vardy** launching his own academy.

'It's a temple of football. FA Cup wins are beautiful. We must be careful not to devalue the competition. Many people worldwide are focused on it' – **Gus Hiddink**, Chelsea's interim manager after his side's 5-1 victory over Manchester City.

A new contract, an Honours degree and now a match-clinching goal – we just have to keep his feet on the ground, eh' – **Sam Allardyce**, Sunderland manager, after Duncan Watmore's strike for 2-0 against Stoke.

'He spat his dummy out and threw his toys out of the pram last week. But he's a young player with lots of ability and it was good to see him get a hat-trick' – **Steve Bruce**, Hull manager, on Arsenal loanee Chuba Akpom's FA Cup treble against Bury after being left out of the side.

'Why is this difficult? People can trust me. I can multi-task, control both situations' – **Pep Guardiola**, Bayern Munich coach, asked how he can divide his thoughts between both clubs for the remainder of the season after being appointed Manchester City's new manager.

RECORDS SECTION

Compiled by Albert Sewell

INDEX

GOALSCORING

(†Football League pre-1992–93)

Highest: Arbroath 36 Bon Accord (Aberdeen) 0 in Scottish Cup 1, Sep 12, 1885. On same day, also in Scottish Cup 1, Dundee Harp beat Aberdeen Rov 35-0.

Internationals: France 0 England 15 in Paris, 1906 (Amateur); Ireland 0 England 13 in Belfast Feb 18, 1882 (record in UK); England 9 Scotland 3 at Wembley, Apr 15, 1961; Biggest England win at Wembley: 9-0 v Luxembourg (Euro Champ), Dec 15, 1982.

Other record wins: Scotland: 11-0 v Ireland (Glasgow, Feb 23, 1901); **Northern Ireland:** 7-0 v Wales (Belfast, Feb 1, 1930); **Wales:** 11-0 v Ireland (Wrexham, Mar 3, 1888); **Rep of Ireland:** 8-0 v Malta (Euro Champ, Dublin, Nov 16, 1983).

Record international defeats: England: 1-7 v Hungary (Budapest, May 23, 1954); **Scotland:** 3-9 v England (Wembley, Apr 15, 1961); **Ireland:** 0-13 v England (Belfast, Feb 18, 1882); **Wales:** 0-9 v Scotland (Glasgow, Mar 23, 1878); **Rep of Ireland:** 0-7 v Brazil (Uberlandia, May 27, 1982).

World Cup: Qualifying round – Australia 31 American Samoa 0, world record international score (Apr 11, 2001); Australia 22 Tonga 0 (Apr 9, 2001); Iran 19 Guam 0 (Nov 25, 2000); Maldives 0 Iran 17 (Jun 2, 1997). **Finals – highest scores:** Hungary 10 El Salvador 1 (Spain, Jun 15, 1982); Hungary 9 S Korea 0 (Switzerland, Jun 17, 1954); Yugoslavia 9 Zaire 0 (W Germany, Jun 18, 1974).

European Championship: Qualifying round – highest scorers: San Marino 0 Germany 13 (Serravalle, Sep 6, 2006). **Finals – highest score:** Holland 6 Yugoslavia 1 (quarter-final, Rotterdam, Jun 25, 2000).

Biggest England U-21 win: 9-0 v San Marino (Shrewsbury, Nov 19, 2013).

FA Cup: Preston 26 Hyde 0 1st round, Oct 15, 1887.

League Cup: West Ham 10 Bury 0 (2nd round, 2nd leg, Oct 25, 1983); Liverpool 10 Fulham 0 (2nd round, 1st leg, Sep 23, 1986). **Record aggregates:** Liverpool 13 Fulham 2 (10-0h, 3-2a), Sep 23, Oct 7, 1986; West Ham 12 Bury 1 (2-1a, 10-0h), Oct 4, 25, 1983; Liverpool 11 Exeter 0 (5-0h, 6-0a), Oct 7, 28, 1981.

League Cup – most goals in one match: 12 Reading 5 Arsenal 7 aet (4th round, Oct 30, 2012). Dagenham & Redbridge 6 Brentford 6 aet (Brentford won 4-2 on pens; 1st round, Aug 12, 2014

Premier League (beginning 1992–93): Manchester Utd 9 Ipswich 0, Mar 4, 1995. **Record away win:** Nottm Forest 1 Manchester Utd 8 Feb 6, 1999.

Highest aggregate scores in Premier League – 11: Portsmouth 7 Reading 4, Sep 29, 2007; **10:** Tottenham 6 Reading 4, Dec 29, 2007; Tottenham 9 Wigan 1, Nov 22, 2009; Manchester Utd 8 Arsenal 2, Aug 28, 2011; Arsenal 7 Newcastle 3, Dec 29, 2012; WBA 5 Manchester Utd 5, May 19, 2013.

†Football League (First Division): Aston Villa 12 Accrington 2, Mar 12, 1892; Tottenham 10 Everton 4, Oct 11, 1958 (highest Div 1 aggregate that century); WBA 12 Darwen 0, Apr 4, 1892; Nottm Forest 12 Leicester Fosse 0, Apr 21, 1909. **Record away win:** Newcastle 1 Sunderland 9, Dec 5,

1908; Cardiff 1 Wolves 9, Sep 3, 1955; Wolves 0 WBA 8, Dec 27, 1893.

New First Division (beginning 1992–93): Bolton 7 Swindon 0, Mar 8, 1997; Sunderland 7 Oxford Utd 0, Sep 19, 1998. **Record away win:** Stoke 0 Birmingham 7, Jan 10, 1998; Oxford Utd 0 Birmingham 7, Dec 12, 1998. **Record aggregate:** Grimsby 6 Burnley 5, Oct 29, 2002; Burnley 4 Watford 7, Apr 5, 2003.

Championship (beginning 2004–05): Birmingham 0 Bournemouth 8, Oct 25, 2014. **Record away win:** Birmingham 0 Bournemouth 8, Oct 25, 2014. **Record aggregate:** Leeds 4 Preston 6, Sep 29, 2010; Leeds 3 Nottm Forest 7, Mar 20, 2012.

†Second Division: Newcastle 13 Newport Co 0, Oct 5, 1946; Small Heath 12 Walsall Town Swifts 0, Dec 17, 1892; Darwen 12 Walsall 0, Dec 26, 1896; Woolwich Arsenal 12 Loughborough 0, Mar 12, 1900; Small Heath 12 Doncaster 0, Apr 11, 1903. **Record away win:** *Burslem Port Vale 0 Sheffield Utd 10, Dec 10, 1892. **Record aggregate:** Manchester City 11 Lincoln 3, Mar 23, 1895.

New Second Division (beginning 1992–93): Hartlepool 1 Plymouth Argyle 8, May 7, 1994; Hartlepool 8 Grimsby 1, Sep 12, 2003.

New League 1 (beginning 2004–05): MK Dons 7 Oldham 0, Dec 20, 2014. **Record aggregate:** Hartlepool 4 Wrexham 6, Mar 5, 2005; Wolves 6 Rotherham 4, Apr 18, 2014; Bristol City 8 Walsall 2, May 3, 2015.

†Third Division: Gillingham 10 Chesterfield 0, Sep 5, 1987; Tranmere 9 Accrington 0, Apr 18, 1959; Brentford 9 Wrexham 0, Oct 15, 1963. **Record away win:** Halifax 0 Fulham 8, Sep 16, 1969. **Record aggregate:** Doncaster 7 Reading 5, Sep 25, 1982.

New Third Division (beginning 1992–93): Barnet 1 Peterborough 9, Sep 5, 1998. **Record aggregate:** Hull 7 Swansea 4, Aug 30, 1997.

New League 2 (beginning 2004–05): Peterborough 7 Brentford 0, Nov 24, 2007 Shrewsbury 7 Gillingham 0, Sep 13, 2008; Crewe 7 Barnet 0, Aug 21, 2010; Crewe 8 Cheltenham 1, Apr 2, 2011; Cambridge 7 Morecambe 0, Apr 19, 2016.

Record away win: Boston 0 Grimsby 6, Feb 3, 2007; Macclesfield 0 Darlington 6, Aug 30, 2008; Lincoln 0 Rotherham 6, Mar 25, 2011. **Record aggregate:** Burton 5 Cheltenham 6, Mar 13, 2010; Accrington 7 Gillingham 4, Oct 2, 2010.

†Third Division (North): Stockport 13 Halifax 0 (still joint biggest win in Football League – see Div 2) Jan 6, 1934; Tranmere 13 Oldham 4, Dec 26, 1935. (17 is highest Football League aggregate score). **Record away win:** Accrington 0 Barnsley 9, Feb 3, 1934.

†Third Division (South): Luton 12 Bristol Rov 0, Apr 13, 1936; Bristol City 9 Gillingham 4, Jan 15, 1927; Gillingham 9 Exeter 4, Jan 7, 1951. **Record away win:** Northampton 0 Walsall 8, Apr 8, 1947.

†Fourth Division: Oldham 11 Southport 0, Dec 26, 1962. **Record away win:** Crewe 1 Rotherham 8, Sep 8, 1973. **Record aggregate:** Hartlepool 10 Barrow 1, Apr 4, 1959; Crystal Palace 9 Accrington 2, Aug 20, 1960; Wrexham 10 Hartlepool 1, Mar 3, 1962; Oldham 11 Southport 0, Dec 26, 1962; Torquay 8 Newport 3, Oct 19, 1963; Shrewsbury 7 Doncaster 4, Feb 1, 1975; Barnet 4 Crewe 7, Aug 17, 1991.

Scottish Premier – Highest aggregate: 12: Motherwell 6 Hibernian 6, May 5, 2010; **11:** Celtic 8 Hamilton 3, Jan 3, 1987; Motherwell 5 Aberdeen 6, Oct 20, 1999. **Other highest team scores:** Aberdeen 8 Motherwell 0 (Mar 26, 1979); Hamilton 0 Celtic 8 (Nov 5, 1988); Celtic 9 Aberdeen 0 (Nov 6, 2010).

Scottish League Div 1: Celtic 11 Dundee 0, Oct 26, 1895. **Record away win:** Hibs 11 *Airdrie 1, Oct 24, 1959.

Scottish League Div 2: Airdrieonians 15 Dundee Wanderers 1, Dec 1, 1894 (biggest win in history of League football in Britain).

Record modern Scottish League aggregate: 12 – Brechin 5 Cowdenbeath 7, Div 2, Jan 18, 2003.

Record British score since 1900: Stirling 20 Selkirk 0 (Scottish Cup 1, Dec 8, 1984). Winger Davie Thompson (7 goals) was one of 9 Stirling players to score.

LEAGUE GOALS – BEST IN SEASON (Before restructure in 1992)

Div		Goals	Games
1	WR (Dixie) Dean, Everton, 1927–28	60	39

2	George Camsell, Middlesbrough, 1926–27	59	37
3(S)	Joe Payne, Luton, 1936–37	55	39
3(N)	Ted Harston, Mansfield, 1936–37	55	41
3	Derek Reeves, Southampton, 1959–60	39	46
4	Terry Bly, Peterborough, 1960–61	52	46

(Since restructure in 1992)

Div		Goals	Games
1	Guy Whittingham, Portsmouth, 1992–93	42	46
2	Jimmy Quinn, Reading, 1993–94	35	46
3	Andy Morrell, Wrexham, 2002–03	34	45

Premier League – BEST IN SEASON

Andy Cole **34 goals** (Newcastle – 40 games, 1993–94); Alan Shearer **34 goals** (Blackburn – 42 games, 1994–95).

FOOTBALL LEAGUE – BEST MATCH HAULS

(Before restructure in 1992)

Div		Goals
1	Ted Drake (Arsenal), away to Aston Villa, Dec 14, 1935	**7**
	James Ross (Preston) v Stoke, Oct 6, 1888	**7**
2	*Neville (Tim) Coleman (Stoke) v Lincoln, Feb 23, 1957	**7**
	Tommy Briggs (Blackburn) v Bristol Rov, Feb 5, 1955	**7**
3(S)	Joe Payne (Luton) v Bristol Rov, Apr 13, 1936	**10**
3(N)	Robert ('Bunny') Bell (Tranmere) v Oldham, Dec 26, 1935 he also missed a penalty	**9**
3	Barrie Thomas (Scunthorpe) v Luton, Apr 24, 1965	**5**
	Keith East (Swindon) v Mansfield, Nov 20, 1965	**5**
	Steve Earle (Fulham) v Halifax, Sep 16, 1969	**5**
	Alf Wood (Shrewsbury) v Blackburn, Oct 2, 1971	**5**
	Tony Caldwell (Bolton) v Walsall, Sep 10, 1983	**5**
	Andy Jones (Port Vale) v Newport Co., May 4, 1987	**5**
4	Bert Lister (Oldham) v Southport, Dec 26, 1962	**6**

*Scored from the wing

(Since restructure in 1992)

Div Goals

1 **4** in match – John Durnin (Oxford Utd v Luton, 1992–93); Guy Whittingham (Portsmouth v Bristol Rov 1992–93); Craig Russell (Sunderland v Millwall, 1995–96); David Connolly (Wolves at Bristol City 1998–99); Darren Byfield (Rotherham at Millwall, 2002–03); David Connolly (Wimbledon at Bradford City, 2002–03); Marlon Harewood (Nottm Forest v Stoke, 2002–03); Michael Chopra (Watford at Burnley, 2002–03); Robert Earnshaw (Cardiff v Gillingham, 2003–04).

2 **5** in match – Paul Barnes (Burnley v Stockport, 1996–97); Robert Taylor (all 5, Gillingham at Burnley, 1998–99); Lee Jones (all 5, Wrexham v Cambridge Utd, 2001–02).

3 **5** in match – Tony Naylor (Crewe v Colchester, 1992–93); Steve Butler (Cambridge Utd v Exeter, 1993–4); Guiliano Grazioli (Peterborough at Barnet, 1998–99).

Champ **4** in match – Garath McCleary (Nottm Forest at Leeds 2011–12); Nikola Zigic (Birmingham at Leeds 2011–12; Craig Davies (Barnsley at Birmingham 2012–13; Ross McCormack (Leeds at Charlton 2013–14), Jesse Lingard (Birmingham v Sheffield Wed 2013–14); Odion Ighalo (Watford v Blackpool, 2014-15).

Lge 1 **4** in match – Jordan Rhodes (all 4, Huddersfield at Sheffield Wed, 2011–12)
5 in match – Juan Ugarte (Wrexham at Hartlepool, 2004–05); Jordan Rhodes (Huddersfield at Wycombe, 2011–12).

Last player to score 6 in English League match: Geoff Hurst (West Ham 8 Sunderland 0, Div 1 Oct 19,1968.

PREMIER LEAGUE – BEST MATCH HAULS

5 goals in match: Andy Cole (Manchester Utd v Ipswich, Mar 4, 1995); Alan Shearer (Newcastle v Sheffield Wed, Sep 19, 1999); Jermain Defoe (Tottenham v Wigan, Nov 22, 2009); Dimitar Berbatov (Manchester Utd v Blackburn, Nov 27, 2010), Sergio Aguero (Manchester City v Newcastle, Oct 3, 2015).

SCOTTISH LEAGUE

Div		Goals
Prem	Gary Hooper (Celtic) v Hearts, May 13, 2012	**5**
	Kris Boyd (Rangers) v Dundee Utd, Dec 30, 2009	**5**
	Kris Boyd (Kilmarnock) v Dundee Utd, Sep 25, 2004	**5**
	Kenny Miller (Rangers) v St Mirren, Nov 4, 2000	**5**
	Marco Negri (Rangers) v Dundee Utd, Aug. 23, 1997	**5**
	Paul Sturrock (Dundee Utd) v Morton, Nov 17, 1984	**5**
1	Jimmy McGrory (Celtic) v Dunfermline, Jan 14, 1928	**8**
1	Owen McNally (Arthurlie) v Armadale, Oct 1, 1927	**8**
2	Jim Dyet (King's Park) v Forfar, Jan 2, 1930 on his debut for the club	**8**
2	John Calder (Morton) v Raith, Apr 18, 1936	**8**
2	Norman Haywood (Raith) v Brechin, Aug. 20, 1937	**8**

SCOTTISH LEAGUE – BEST IN SEASON

Prem	Brian McClair (Celtic, 1986–87**) 35**	
	Henrik Larsson (Celtic, 2000–01)	**35**
1	William McFadyen (Motherwell, 1931–32)	**53**
2	*Jimmy Smith (Ayr, 1927–28 – 38 appearances)	**66**
	(*British record)	

CUP FOOTBALL

Scottish Cup: John Petrie (Arbroath) v Bon Accord, at Arbroath, 1st round, Sep 12, 1885	**13**
FA Cup: Ted MacDougall (Bournemouth) v Margate, 1st round, Nov 20,1971	**9**
FA Cup Final: Billy Townley (Blackburn) v Sheffield Wed, at Kennington Oval, 1890; Jimmy Logan (Notts Co) v Bolton, at Everton, 1894; Stan Mortensen (Blackpool) v Bolton, at Wembley, 1953	**3**
League Cup: Frank Bunn (Oldham) v Scarborough (3rd round), Oct 25, 1989	**6**
Scottish League Cup: Willie Penman (Raith) v Stirling, Sep 18, 1948	**6**

Scottish Cup: Most goals in match since war: 10 by **Gerry Baker** (St Mirren) in 15-0 win (1st round) v Glasgow Univ, Jan 30, 1960; 9 by his brother **Joe Baker** (Hibernian) in 15-1 win (2nd round) v Peebles, Feb 11, 1961.

AGGREGATE LEAGUE SCORING RECORDS

	Goals
*Arthur Rowley (1947–65, WBA, Fulham, Leicester, Shrewsbury)	**434**
†Jimmy McGrory (1922–38, Celtic, Clydebank)	**410**
Hughie Gallacher (1921–39, Airdrieonians, Newcastle, Chelsea, Derby, Notts Co, Grimsby, Gateshead)	**387**
William ('Dixie') Dean (1923–37, Tranmere, Everton, Notts Co)	**379**
Hugh Ferguson (1916–30, Motherwell, Cardiff, Dundee)	**362**
• Jimmy Greaves (1957–71, Chelsea, Tottenham, West Ham)	**357**
Steve Bloomer (1892–1914, Derby, Middlesbrough, Derby)	**352**
George Camsell (1923–39, Durham City, Middlesbrough)	**348**

Dave Halliday (1920–35, St Mirren, Dundee, Sunderland, Arsenal, Manchester City, Clapton Orient) **338**
John Aldridge (1979–98, Newport, Oxford Utd, Liverpool, Tranmere) **329**
Harry Bedford (1919–34), Nottm Forest, Blackpool, Derby, Newcastle, Sunderland, Bradford PA, Chesterfield **326**
John Atyeo (1951–66, Bristol City) **315**
Joe Smith (1908–29, Bolton, Stockport) **315**
Victor Watson (1920–36, West Ham, Southampton) **312**
Harry Johnson (1919–36, Sheffield Utd, Mansfield) **309**
Bob McPhail (1923–1939, Airdrie, Rangers) **306**
(***Rowley** scored 4 for WBA, 27 for Fulham, 251 for Leicester, 152 for Shrewsbury.
- **Greaves'** 357 is record top-division total (he also scored 9 League goals for AC Milan). **Aldridge** also scored 33 League goals for Real Sociedad. †**McGrory** scored 397 for Celtic, 13 for Clydebank).

Most League goals for one club: 349 – Dixie Dean (Everton 1925–37); **326 – George Camsell** (Middlesbrough 1925–39); **315 – John Atyeo** (Bristol City 1951–66); **306 – Vic Watson** (West Ham 1920–35); **291 – Steve Bloomer** (Derby 1892–1906, 1910–14); **259 – Arthur Chandler** (Leicester 1923–35); **255 – Nat Lofthouse** (Bolton 1946–61); **251 – Arthur Rowley** (Leicester 1950–58).

More than 500 goals: Jimmy McGrory (Celtic, Clydebank and Scotland) scored a total of **550** goals in his first-class career (1922–38).

More than 1,000 goals: Brazil's **Pele** is reputedly the game's all-time highest scorer with **1,283** goals in 1,365 matches (1956–77), but many of them were scored in friendlies for his club, Santos. He scored his 1,000th goal, a penalty, against Vasco da Gama in the Maracana Stadium, Rio, on Nov 19, 1969. • Pele (born Oct 23, 1940) played regularly for Santos from the age of 16. During his career, he was sent off only once. He played 95 'A' internationals for Brazil and in their World Cup-winning teams in 1958 and 1970. † Pele (Edson Arantes do Nascimento) was subsequently Brazil's Minister for Sport. He never played at Wembley, apart from being filmed there scoring a goal for a commercial. Aged 57, Pele received an 'honorary knighthood' (Knight Commander of the British Empire) from the Queen at Buckingham Palace on Dec 3, 1997.

Romario (retired Apr, 2008, aged 42) scored more than 1,000 goals for Vasco da Gama, Barcelona, PSV Eindhoven, Valencia and Brazil (56 in 73 internationals).

MOST LEAGUE GOALS IN SEASON: DEAN'S 60

WR ('Dixie') Dean, Everton centre-forward, created a League scoring record in 1927–28 with 60 in 39 First Division matches. He also scored three in FA Cup ties, and 19 in representative games, totalling 82 for the season.

George Camsell, of Middlesbrough, previously held the record with 59 goals in 37 Second Division matches in 1926–27, his total for the season being 75.

SHEARER'S RECORD 'FIRST'

Alan Shearer (Blackburn) is the only player to score more than 30 top-division goals in 3 successive seasons since the War: 31 in 1993–94, 34 in 1994–95, 31 in 1995–96.

Thierry Henry (Arsenal) is the first player to score more than 20 Premiership goals in five consecutive seasons (2002–06). **David Halliday** (Sunderland) topped 30 First Division goals in 4 consecutive seasons with totals of 38, 36, 36 and 49 from 1925–26 to 1928–29.

MOST GOALS IN A MATCH

Sep 12, 1885: John Petrie set the all-time British individual record for a first-class match when, in Arbroath's 36-0 win against Bon Accord (Scottish Cup 1), he scored **13.**

Apr 13, 1936: Joe Payne set the still-existing individual record on his debut as a centre-forward, for Luton v Bristol Rov (Div 3 South). In a 12-0 win he scored **10.**

ROWLEY'S ALL-TIME RECORD

Arthur Rowley is English football's top club scorer with a total of 464 goals for WBA, Fulham, Leicester and Shrewsbury (1947–65). There were 434 in the League, 26 FA Cup, 4 League Cup.

Jimmy Greaves is second with a total of 420 goals for Chelsea, AC Milan, Tottenham and West Ham, made up of 366 League, 35 FA Cup, 10 League Cup and 9 in Europe. He also scored nine goals for AC Milan.

John Aldridge retired as a player at the end of season 1997–98 with a career total of 329 League goals for Newport, Oxford Utd, Liverpool and Tranmere (1979–98). In all competitions for those clubs he scored 410 in 737 appearances. He also scored 45 in 63 games for Real Sociedad.

MOST GOALS IN INTERNATIONAL MATCHES

13 by **Archie Thompson** for Australia v American Samoa in World Cup (Oceania Group qualifier) at Coff's Harbour, New South Wales, Apr 11, 2001. Result: 31-0.

7 by **Stanley Harris** for England v France in Amateur International in Paris, Nov 1, 1906. Result: 15-0.

6 by **Nat Lofthouse** for Football League v Irish League, at Wolverhampton, Sep 24, 1952. Result: 7-1.

Joe Bambrick for Northern Ireland against Wales (7-0) in Belfast, Feb 1, 1930 – a record for a Home Nations International.

WC Jordan in Amateur International for England v France, at Park Royal, Mar 23, 1908. Result: 12-0.

Vivian Woodward for England v Holland in Amateur International, at Chelsea, Dec 11,1909. Result: 9-1.

5 by **Howard Vaughton** for England v Ireland (Belfast) Feb 18, 1882. Result: 13-0.

Steve Bloomer for England v Wales (Cardiff) Mar 16, 1896. Result: 9-1.

Hughie Gallacher for Scotland against Ireland (Belfast), Feb 23, 1929. Result: 7-3.

Willie Hall for England v Northern Ireland, at Old Trafford, Nov 16, 1938. Five in succession (first three in 3·5 mins – fastest international hat-trick). Result: 7-0.

Malcolm Macdonald for England v Cyprus (Wembley) Apr 16, 1975. Result: 5-0.

Hughie Gallacher for Scottish League against Irish League (Belfast) Nov 11, 1925. Result: 7-3.

Barney Battles for Scottish League against Irish League (Firhill Park, Glasgow) Oct 31, 1928. Result: 8-2.

Bobby Flavell for Scottish League against Irish League (Belfast) Apr 30, 1947. Result: 7-4.

Joe Bradford for Football League v Irish League (Everton) Sep 25, 1929. Result: 7-2.

Albert Stubbins for Football League v Irish League (Blackpool) Oct 18, 1950. Result: 6-3.

Brian Clough for Football League v Irish League (Belfast) Sep 23, 1959. Result: 5-0.

LAST ENGLAND PLAYER TO SCORE ...

3 goals: Jermain Defoe v Bulgaria (4-0), Euro Champ qual, Wembley, Sep 3, 2010.

4 goals: Ian Wright v San Marino (7-1), World Cup qual, Bologna, Nov 17, 1993.

5 goals: Malcolm Macdonald v Cyprus (5-0), Euro Champ qual, Wembley, Apr 16, 1975.

INTERNATIONAL TOP SHOTS

		Goals	Games
England	Wayne Rooney (2003–2016)	53	115
N Ireland	David Healy (2000–13)	36	95
Scotland	Denis Law (1958–74)	30	55
	Kenny Dalglish (1971–86)	30	102
Wales	Ian Rush (1980–96)	28	73
Rep of Ire	Robbie Keane (1998–2016)	67	145

ENGLAND'S TOP MARKSMEN

(As at start of season 2016–17)

	Goals	Games
Wayne Rooney (2003–16)	53	115
Bobby Charlton (1958–70)	49	106
Gary Lineker (1984–92)	48	80
Jimmy Greaves (1959–67)	44	57
Michael Owen (1998–2008)	40	89
Tom Finney (1946–58)	30	76
Nat Lofthouse (1950–58)	30	33
Alan Shearer (1992–2000)	30	63
Vivian Woodward (1903–11)	29	23
Frank Lampard (2003–14)	29	106
Steve Bloomer (1895–1907)	28	23
David Platt (1989–96)	27	62
Bryan Robson (1979–91)	26	90
Geoff Hurst (1966–72)	24	49
Stan Mortensen (1947–53)	23	25
Tommy Lawton (1938–48)	22	23
Peter Crouch (2005–11)	22	42
Mike Channon (1972–77)	21	46
Kevin Keegan (1972–82)	21	63

ROONEY'S ENGLAND RECORD

Wayne Rooney reached 50 international goals with a penalty against Switzerland at Wembley on September 8, 2015 to become England's record scorer, surpassing Bobby Charlton's mark. Charlton's record was set in 106 games, Rooney's tally in 107.

CONSECUTIVE GOALS FOR ENGLAND

Steve Bloomer scored in **10** consecutive appearances (19 goals) between Mar 1895 and Mar 1899.

Jimmy Greaves scored 11 goals in five consecutive matches from the start of season 1960–61.

Paul Mariner scored in five consecutive appearances (7 goals) between Nov 1981 and Jun 1982.

Wayne Rooney scored in five consecutive appearances (6 goals) between Oct 2012 and Mar 2013.

ENGLAND'S TOP FINAL SERIES MARKSMAN

Gary Lineker with 6 goals at 1986 World Cup in Mexico.

ENGLAND TOP SCORERS IN COMPETITIVE INTERNATIONALS

Michael Owen 26 goals in 53 matches; **Gary Lineker** 22 in 39; **Alan Shearer** 20 in 31.

MOST ENGLAND GOALS IN SEASON

13 – Jimmy Greaves (1960–61 in 9 matches); **12 – Dixie Dean** (1926–27 in 6 matches); **10 – Gary Lineker** (1990–91 in 10 matches); **10 – Wayne Rooney** – (2008–09 in 9 matches).

MOST ENGLAND HAT-TRICKS

Jimmy Greaves 6; **Gary Lineker** 5, **Bobby Charlton** 4, **Vivian Woodward** 4, **Stan Mortensen** 3.

MOST GOALS FOR ENGLAND U-21s

13 – Alan Shearer (11 apps) Francis Jeffers (13 apps).

GOLDEN GOAL DECIDERS

The Football League, in an experiment to avoid penalty shoot-outs, introduced a new golden goal system in the 1994–95 **Auto Windscreens Shield** to decide matches in the knock-out stages of the competition in which scores were level after 90 minutes. The first goal scored in overtime ended play.

Iain Dunn (Huddersfield) became the first player in British football to settle a match by this sudden-death method. His 107th-minute goal beat Lincoln 3-2 on Nov 30, 1994, and to mark his 'moment in history' he was presented with a golden football trophy.

The AWS Final of 1995 was decided when Paul Tait headed the only goal for Birmingham against Carlisle 13 minutes into overtime – the first time a match at Wembley had been decided by the 'golden goal' formula.

First major international tournament match to be decided by sudden death was the Final of the **1996 European Championship** at Wembley in which Germany beat Czech Rep 2-1 by **Oliver Bierhoff's** goal in the 95th minute.

In the **1998 World Cup Finals** (2nd round), host country France beat Paraguay 1-0 with **Laurent Blanc's** goal (114).

France won the **2000 European Championship** with golden goals in the semi-final, 2-1 v Portugal (Zinedine Zidane pen, 117), and in the Final, 2-1 v Italy (David Trezeguet, 103).

Galatasaray (Turkey) won the **European Super Cup** 2-1 against Real Madrid (Monaco, Aug 25, 2000) with a 103rd minute golden goal, a penalty.

Liverpool won the **UEFA Cup** 5-4 against Alaves with a 117th-min golden goal, an own goal, in the Final in Dortmund (May 19, 2001).

In the **2002 World Cup Finals**, 3 matches were decided by Golden Goals: in the 2nd round Senegal beat Sweden 2-1 (Henri Camara, 104) and South Korea beat Italy 2-1 (Ahn Jung-hwan, 117); in the quarter-final, Turkey beat Senegal 1-0 (Ilhan Mansiz, 94).

France won the 2003 **FIFA Confederations Cup Final** against Cameroon (Paris, Jun 29) with a 97th-minute golden goal by Thierry Henry.

Doncaster won promotion to Football League with a 110th-minute golden goal winner (3-2) in the Conference Play-off Final against Dagenham at Stoke (May 10, 2003).

Germany won the **Women's World Cup Final** 2-1 v Sweden (Los Angeles, Oct 12, 2003) with a 98th-minute golden goal.

GOLD TURNS TO SILVER

Starting with the 2003 Finals of the UEFA Cup and Champions League/European Cup, UEFA introduced a new rule by which a silver goal could decide the winners if the scores were level after 90 minutes.

Team leading after 15 minutes' extra time win match. If sides level, a second period of 15 minutes to be played. If still no winner, result to be decided by penalty shoot-out.

UEFA said the change was made because the golden goal put too much pressure on referees and prompted teams to play negative football.

Although both 2003 European Finals went to extra-time, neither was decided by a silver goal. The new rule applied in the 2004 European Championship Finals, and Greece won their semi-final against the Czech Republic in the 105th minute.

The **International Board** decided (Feb 28 2004) that the golden/silver goal rule was 'unfair' and that from July 1 competitive international matches level after extra-time would, when necessary, be settled on penalties.

PREMIER LEAGUE TOP SHOTS (1992–2016)

Alan Shearer	260	Robbie Keane	126
Wayne Rooney	193	Nicolas Anelka	125
Andy Cole	187	Dwight Yorke	123
Frank Lampard	177	Steven Gerrard	120
Thierry Henry	175	Ian Wright	113
Robbie Fowler	163	Dion Dublin	111
Michael Owen	150	Emile Heskey	111
Les Ferdinand	149	Ryan Giggs	109

Teddy Sheringham	146	Paul Scholes	107
Robin van Persie	144	Darren Bent	106
Jermain Defoe	143	Didier Drogba	104
Jimmy Floyd Hasselbaink	127	Matt Le Tissier	102

LEAGUE GOAL RECORDS

The highest goal-scoring aggregates in the Football League, Premier and Scottish League are as follows:

For

	Goals	*Games*	*Club*	*Season*
Prem	103	38	Chelsea	2009–10
Div 1	128	42	Aston Villa	1930–31
New Div 1	108	46	Manchester City	2001–02
New Champ	99	46	Reading	2005–06
Div 2	122	42	Middlesbrough	1926–27
New Div 2	89	46	Millwall	2000–01
New Lge 1	106	46	Peterborough	2010–11
Div 3(S)	127	42	Millwall	1927–28
Div 3(N)	128	42	Bradford City	1928–29
Div 3	111	46	QPR	1961–62
New Div 3	96	46	Luton	2001–02
New Lge 2	96	46	Notts Co	2009–10
Div 4	134	46	Peterborough	1960–61
Scot Prem	105	38	Celtic	2003–04
Scot L 1	132	34	Hearts	1957–58
Scot L 2	142	34	Raith Rov	1937–38
Scot L 3 (Modern)	130	36	Gretna	2004–05

Against

	Goals	*Games*	*Club*	*Season*
Prem	100	42	Swindon	1993–94
Div 1	125	42	Blackpool	1930–31
New Div 1	102	46	Stockport	2001–02
New Champ	86	46	Crewe	2004–05
Div 2	141	34	Darwen	1898–99
New Div 2	102	46	Chester	1992–93
New Lge 1	98	46	Stockport	2004–05
Div 3(S)	135	42	Merthyr T	1929–30
Div 3(N)	136	42	Nelson	1927–28
Div 3	123	46	Accrington Stanley	1959–60
New Div 3	113	46	Doncaster	1997–98
New Lge 2	96	46	Stockport	2010–11
Div 4	109	46	Hartlepool Utd	1959–60
Scot Prem	100	36	Morton	1984–85
Scot Prem	100	44	Morton	1987–88
Scot L 1	137	38	Leith A	1931–32
Scot L 2	146	38	Edinburgh City	1931–32
Scot L 3 (Modern)	118	36	East Stirling	2003–04

BEST DEFENSIVE RECORDS

**Denotes under old offside law*

Div	*Goals Agst*	*Games*	*Club*	*Season*
Prem	15	38	Chelsea	2004–05
1	16	42	Liverpool	1978–79
1	*15	22	Preston	1888–89

New Div 1	28	46	Sunderland	1998–99
New Champ	30	46	Preston	2005–06
2	18	28	Liverpool	1893–94
2	*22	34	Sheffield Wed	1899–1900
2	24	42	Birmingham	1947–48
2	24	42	Crystal Palace	1978–79
New Div 2	25	46	Wigan	2002–03
New Lge 1	32	46	Nottm Forest	2007–08
3(S)	*21	42	Southampton	1921–22
3(S)	30	42	Cardiff	1946–47
3(N)	*21	38	Stockport	1921–22
3(N)	21	46	Port Vale	1953–54
3	30	46	Middlesbrough	1986–87
New Div 3	20	46	Gillingham	1995–96
New Lge 2	31	46	Notts Co	2009–10
4	25	46	Lincoln	1980–81

SCOTTISH LEAGUE

Div	*Goals Agst*	*Games*	*Club*	*Season*
Prem	17	38	Celtic	2014–15
1	*12	22	Dundee	1902–03
1	*14	38	Celtic	1913–14
2	20	38	Morton	1966–67
2	*29	38	Clydebank	1922–23
2	29	36	East Fife	1995–96
New Div 3	21	36	Brechin	1995–96

TOP SCORERS (LEAGUE ONLY)

		Goals	*Div*
2015–16	Matt Taylor (Bristol Rov)	27	Lge 2
2014–15	Daryl Murphy (Ipswich)	27	Champ
2013–14	Luis Suarez (Liverpool)	31	Prem
2012–13	Tom Pope (Port Vale)	31	Lge 2
2011–12	Jordan Rhodes (Huddersfield)	36	Lge 1
2010–11	Clayton Donaldson (Crewe)	28	Lge 2
2009–10	Rickie Lambert (Southampton)	31	Lge 1
2008– 09	Simon Cox (Swindon)		
	Rickie Lambert (Bristol Rov)	29	Lge 1
2007–08	Cristiano Ronaldo (Manchester Utd)	31	Prem
2006–07	Billy Sharp (Scunthorpe)	30	Lge 1
2005–06	Thierry Henry (Arsenal)	27	Prem
2004–05	Stuart Elliott (Hull)	27	1
	Phil Jevons (Yeovil)	27	2
	Dean Windass (Bradford City)	27	1
2003–04	Thierry Henry (Arsenal)	30	Prem
2002–03	Andy Morrell (Wrexham)	34	3
2001–02	Shaun Goater (Manchester City)	28	1
	Bobby Zamora (Brighton)	28	2
2000–01	Bobby Zamora (Brighton)	28	3
1999–00	Kevin Phillips (Sunderland)	30	Prem
1998–99	Lee Hughes (WBA)	31	1
1997–98	Pierre van Hooijdonk (Nottm Forest)	29	1
	Kevin Phillips (Sunderland)	29	1
1996–97	Graeme Jones (Wigan)	31	3
1995–96	Alan Shearer (Blackburn)	31	Prem

1994–95	Alan Shearer (Blackburn)	34	Prem
1993–94	Jimmy Quinn (Reading)	35	2
1992–93	Guy Whittingham (Portsmouth)	42	1
1991–92	Ian Wright (Crystal Palace 5, Arsenal 24)	29	1
1990–91	Teddy Sheringham (Millwall)	33	2
1989–90	Mick Quinn (Newcastle)	32	2
1988–89	Steve Bull (Wolves)	37	3
1987–88	Steve Bull (Wolves)	34	4
1986–87	Clive Allen (Tottenham)	33	1
1985–86	Gary Lineker (Everton)	30	1
1984–85	Tommy Tynan (Plymouth Argyle)	31	3
	John Clayton (Tranmere)	31	4
1983–84	Trevor Senior (Reading)	36	4
1982–83	Luther Blissett (Watford)	27	1
1981–82	Keith Edwards (Hull 1, Sheffield Utd 35)	36	4
1980–81	Tony Kellow (Exeter)	25	3
1979–80	Clive Allen (Queens Park Rangers)	28	2
1978–79	Ross Jenkins (Watford)	29	3
1977–78	Steve Phillips (Brentford)	32	4
	Alan Curtis (Swansea City)	32	4
1976–77	Peter Ward (Brighton)	32	3
1975–76	Dixie McNeil (Hereford)	35	3
1974–75	Dixie McNeil (Hereford)	31	3
1973–74	Brian Yeo (Gillingham)	31	4
1972–73	Bryan (Pop) Robson (West Ham)	28	1
1971–72	Ted MacDougall (Bournemouth)	35	3
1970–71	Ted MacDougall (Bournemouth)	42	4
1969–70	Albert Kinsey (Wrexham)	27	4
1968–69	Jimmy Greaves (Tottenham)	27	1
1967–68	George Best (Manchester Utd)	28	1
	Ron Davies (Southampton)	28	1
1966–67	Ron Davies (Southampton)	37	1
1965–66	Kevin Hector (Bradford PA)	44	4
1964–65	Alick Jeffrey (Doncaster)	36	4
1963–64	Hugh McIlmoyle (Carlisle)	39	4
1962–63	Jimmy Greaves (Tottenham)	37	1
1961–62	Roger Hunt (Liverpool)	41	2
1960–61	Terry Bly (Peterborough)	52	4

100 LEAGUE GOALS IN SEASON

Manchester City, First Div Champions in 2001–02, scored 108 goals.

Bolton, First Div Champions in 1996–97, reached 100 goals, the first side to complete a century in League football since 103 by **Northampton** (Div 4 Champions) in 1986–87.

Last League Champions to reach 100 League goals: Chelsea (103 in 2009–10). Last century of goals in the top division: 111 by runners-up **Tottenham** in 1962–63.

Clubs to score a century of Premier League goals in season: **Chelsea** 103 in 2009–10, Manchester City (102) and Liverpool (101) in 2013–14.

Wolves topped 100 goals in four successive First Division seasons (1957–58, 1958–59, 1959–60, 1960–61).

In **1930–31,** the top three all scored a century of League goals: 1 Arsenal (127), 2 Aston Villa (128), 3 Sheffield Wed (102).

Latest team to score a century of League goals: Peterborough with 106 in 2010–11 (Lge 1).

100 GOALS AGAINST

Swindon, relegated with 100 goals against in 1993–94, were the first top-division club to concede a century of League goals since **Ipswich** (121) went down in 1964. Most goals conceded in the top division: 125 by **Blackpool** in 1930–31, but they avoided relegation.

MOST LEAGUE GOALS ON ONE DAY

A record of 209 goals in the four divisions of the Football League (43 matches) was set on **Jan 2, 1932:** 56 in Div 1, 53 in Div 2, 57 in Div 3 South and 43 in Div 3 North.

There were two 10-goal aggregates: Bradford City 9, Barnsley 1 in Div 2 and Coventry City 5, Fulham 5 in Div 3 South.

That total of 209 League goals on one day was equalled on **Feb 1, 1936** (44 matches): 46 in Div 1, 46 in Div 2, 49 in Div 3 South and 69 in Div 3 North. Two matches in the Northern Section produced 23 of the goals: Chester 12, York 0 and Crewe 5, Chesterfield 6.

MOST GOALS IN TOP DIV ON ONE DAY

This record has stood since **Dec 26, 1963,** when 66 goals were scored in the ten First Division matches played.

MOST PREMIER LEAGUE GOALS ON ONE DAY

47, in nine matches on **May 8, 1993** (last day of season). For the first time, all 20 clubs scored in the Premier League programme over the weekend of Nov 27-28, 2010.

FEWEST PREMIER LEAGUE GOALS IN ONE WEEK-END

10, in **10** matches on **Nov 24/25, 2001**.

FEWEST FIRST DIV GOALS ON ONE DAY

For full/near full programme: **Ten goals**, all by home clubs, in ten matches on Apr 28, 1923 (day of Wembley's first FA Cup Final).

SCORER OF LEAGUE'S FIRST GOAL

Kenny Davenport (2 mins) for Bolton v Derby, Sep 8, 1888.

VARDY'S RECORD

Jamie Vardy set a Premier League record by scoring in 11 consecutive matches for Leicester (Aug-Nov 2015). The all-time top division record of scoring in 12 successive games was set by **Jimmy Dunne** for Sheffield Utd in the old First Division in season 1931-32. **Stan Mortensen** scored in 15 successive matches for Blackpool (First Division) in season 1950-51, but that sequence included two injury breaks.

SCORERS FOR 7 PREMIER LEAGUE CLUBS

Craig Bellamy (Coventry, Newcastle, Blackburn, Liverpool, West Ham, Manchester City, Cardiff).

SCORERS FOR 6 PREMIER LEAGUE CLUBS

Les Ferdinand (QPR, Newcastle, Tottenham, West Ham, Leicester, Bolton); **Andy Cole** (Newcastle, Manchester Utd, Blackburn, Fulham, Manchester City, Portsmouth); **Marcus Bent** (Crystal Palace, Ipswich, Leicester, Everton, Charlton, Wigan); **Nick Barmby** (Tottenham, Middlesbrough, Everton, Liverpool, Leeds, Hull); **Peter Crouch** (Tottenham, Aston Villa, Southampton, Liverpool, Portsmouth, Stoke); **Robbie Keane** (Coventry, Leeds, Tottenham, Liverpool, West Ham, Aston Villa); **Nicolas Anelka** (Arsenal, Liverpool, Manchester City, Bolton, Chelsea, WBA); **Darren Bent** (Ipswich, Charlton, Tottenham, Sunderland, Aston Villa, Fulham).

SCORERS FOR 5 PREMIER LEAGUE CLUBS

Stan Collymore (Nottm Forest, Liverpool, Aston Villa, Leicester, Bradford); **Mark Hughes** (Manchester

Utd, Chelsea, Southampton, Everton, Blackburn); **Benito Carbone** (Sheffield Wed, Aston Villa, Bradford, Derby, Middlesbrough); **Ashley Ward** (Norwich, Derby, Barnsley, Blackburn Bradford); **Teddy Sheringham** (Nottm Forest, Tottenham, Manchester Utd, Portsmouth, West Ham); **Chris Sutton** (Norwich, Blackburn, Chelsea, Birmingham, Aston Villa).

SCORERS IN MOST CONSECUTIVE LEAGUE MATCHES

Arsenal broke the record by scoring in 55 successive Premiership fixtures: the last match in season 2000–01, then all 38 games in winning the title in 2001–02, and the first 16 in season 2002–03. The sequence ended with a 2-0 defeat away to Manchester Utd on December 7, 2002.

Chesterfield previously held the record, having scored in 46 consecutive matches in Div 3 (North), starting on Christmas Day, 1929 and ending on December 27, 1930.

SIX-OUT-OF-SIX HEADERS

When **Oxford Utd** beat Shrewsbury 6-0 (Div 2) on Apr 23, 1996, all six goals were headers.

ALL–ROUND MARKSMEN

Alan Cork scored in four divisions of the Football League and in the Premier League in his 18-season career with Wimbledon, Sheffield Utd and Fulham (1977–95).

Brett Ormerod scored in all four divisions (2, 1, Champ and Prem Lge) for Blackpool in two spells (1997–2002, 2008–11). **Grant Holt** (Sheffield Wed, Rochdale, Nottm Forest, Shrewsbury, Norwich) has scored in four Football League divisions and in the Premier League.

MOST CUP GOALS

FA Cup – most goals in one season: 20 by **Jimmy Ross** (Preston, runners-up 1887–88); 15 by **Alex (Sandy) Brown** (Tottenham, winners 1900–01).

Most FA Cup goals in individual careers: 49 by **Harry Cursham** (Notts Co 1877–89); 20th century: **44** by **Ian Rush** (39 for Liverpool, 4 for Chester, 1 for Newcastle 1979–98). **Denis Law** was the previous highest FA Cup scorer in the 20th century with 41 goals for Huddersfield Town, Manchester City and Manchester Utd (1957–74).

Most FA Cup Final goals by individual: 5 by **Ian Rush** for Liverpool (2 in 1986, 2 in 1989, 1 in 1992).

HOTTEST CUP HOT-SHOT

Geoff Hurst scored 21 cup goals in season 1965–66: 11 League Cup, 4 FA Cup and 2 Cup-Winners' Cup for West Ham, and 4 in the World Cup for England.

SCORERS IN EVERY ROUND

Twelve players have scored in every round of the FA Cup in one season, from opening to Final inclusive: **Archie Hunter** (Aston Villa, winners 1887); **Sandy Brown** (Tottenham, winners 1901); **Harry Hampton** (Aston Villa, winners 1905); **Harold Blackmore** (Bolton, winners 1929); **Ellis Rimmer** (Sheffield Wed, winners 1935); **Frank O'Donnell** (Preston, beaten 1937); **Stan Mortensen** (Blackpool, beaten 1948); **Jackie Milburn** (Newcastle, winners 1951); **Nat Lofthouse** (Bolton, beaten 1953); **Charlie Wayman** (Preston, beaten 1954); **Jeff Astle** (WBA, winners 1968); **Peter Osgood** (Chelsea, winners 1970).

Blackmore and the next seven completed their 'set' in the Final at Wembley; Osgood did so in the Final replay at Old Trafford.

Only player to score in every **Football League Cup** round possible in one season: **Tony Brown** for WBA, winners 1965–66, with 9 goals in 10 games (after bye in Round 1).

TEN IN A ROW

Dixie McNeill scored for Wrexham in ten successive FA Cup rounds (18 goals): 11 in Rounds 1-6, 1977–78; 3 in Rounds 3-4, 1978–79; 4 in Rounds 3-4, 1979–80.

Stan Mortensen (Blackpool) scored 25 goals in 16 FA Cup rounds out of 17 (1946–51).

TOP MATCH HAULS IN FA CUP

Ted MacDougall scored nine goals, a record for the competition proper, in the FA Cup first round on Nov 20, 1971, when Bournemouth beat Margate 11-0. On Nov 23, 1970 he had scored six in an 8-1 first round replay against Oxford City.

Other six-goal FA Cup scorers include **George Hilsdon** (Chelsea v Worksop, 9-1, 1907–08), **Ronnie Rooke** (Fulham v Bury, 6-0, 1938–39), **Harold Atkinson** (Tranmere v Ashington, 8-1, 1952–53), **George Best** (Manchester Utd v Northampton 1969–70, 8-2 away), **Duane Darby** (Hull v Whitby, 8-4, 1996–97).

Denis Law scored all six for Manchester City at Luton (6-2) in an FA Cup 4th round tie on Jan 28, 1961, but none of them counted – the match was abandoned (69 mins) because of a waterlogged pitch. He also scored City's goal when the match was played again, but they lost 3-1.

Tony Philliskirk scored **five** when Peterborough beat Kingstonian 9-1 in an FA Cup 1st round replay on Nov 25, 1992, but had them wiped from the records.

With the score at 3-0, the Kingstonian goalkeeper was concussed by a coin thrown from the crowd and unable to play on. The FA ordered the match to be replayed at Peterborough behind closed doors, and Kingstonian lost 1-0.

- Two players have scored **ten goals** in FA Cup preliminary round matches: **Chris Marron** for South Shields against Radcliffe in Sep 1947; **Paul Jackson** when Sheffield-based club Stocksbridge Park Steels beat Oldham Town 17-1 on Aug 31, 2002. He scored 5 in each half and all ten with his feet – goal times 6, 10, 22, 30, 34, 68, 73, 75, 79, 84 mins.

QUICKEST GOALS AND RAPID SCORING

A goal in **4 sec** was claimed by **Jim Fryatt,** for Bradford PA v Tranmere (Div 4, Apr 25, 1965), and by **Gerry Allen** for Whitstable v Danson (Kent League, Mar 3,1989). **Damian Mori** scored in **4 sec** for Adelaide v Sydney (Australian National League, December 6, 1995).

Goals after **6 sec – Albert Mundy** for Aldershot v Hartlepool, Oct 25, 1958; **Barrie Jones** for Notts Co v Torquay, Mar 31, 1962; **Keith Smith** for Crystal Palace v Derby, Dec 12, 1964.

9.6 sec by **John Hewitt** for Aberdeen at Motherwell, 3rd round, Jan 23, 1982 (fastest goal in Scottish Cup history).

Colin Cowperthwaite reputedly scored in **3.5 sec** for Barrow v Kettering (Alliance Premier League) on Dec 8, 1979, but the timing was unofficial.

Phil Starbuck for Huddersfield **3 sec** after entering the field as 54th min substitute at home to Wigan (Div 2) on Easter Monday, Apr 12, 1993. Corner was delayed, awaiting his arrival and he scored with a header.

Malcolm Macdonald after **5 sec** (officially timed) in Newcastle's 7-3 win in a pre-season friendly at St Johnstone on Jul 29, 1972.

World's fastest goal: 2.8 sec, direct from kick-off, Argentinian **Ricardo Olivera** for Rio Negro v Soriano (Uruguayan League), December 26, 1998.

Fastest international goal: 8.3 sec, Davide Gualtieri for San Marino v England (World Cup qual, Bologna, Nov 17, 1993).

Fastest England goals: 17 sec, Tommy Lawton v Portugal in Lisbon, May 25, 1947. **27 sec, Bryan Robson** v France in World Cup at Bilbao, Spain on Jun 16, 1982; **37 sec, Gareth Southgate** v South Africa in Durban, May 22, 2003; **30 sec, Jack Cock** v Ireland, Belfast, Oct 25, 1919; **30 sec, Bill Nicholson** v Portugal at Goodison Park, May 19, 1951. **38 sec, Bryan Robson** v Yugoslavia at Wembley, Dec 13, 1989; **42 sec, Gary Lineker** v Malaysia in Kuala Lumpur, Jun 12, 1991.

Fastest international goal by substitute: 5 sec, John Jensen for Denmark v Belgium (Euro Champ), Oct 12, 1994.

Fastest goal by England substitute: 10 sec, Teddy Sheringham v Greece (World Cup qualifier) at Old Trafford, Oct 6, 2001.

Fastest FA Cup goal: 4 sec, Gareth Morris (Ashton Utd) v Skelmersdale, 1st qual round, Sep 15, 2001.

Fastest FA Cup goal (comp proper): 9.7 sec, Jimmy Kebe for Reading v WBA, 5th Round, Feb 13, 2010.

Fastest FA Cup Final goal: 25 sec, Louis Saha for Everton v Chelsea at Wembley, May 30, 2009.

Fastest goal by substitute in FA Cup Final: 96 sec, Teddy Sheringham for Manchester Utd v Newcastle at Wembley, May 22, 1999.

Fastest League Cup Final goal: 45 sec, John Arne Riise for Liverpool v Chelsea, 2005.

Fastest goal on full League debut: 7.7 sec, Freddy Eastwood for Southend v Swansea (Lge 2), Oct 16, 2004. He went on to score hat-trick in 4-2 win.

Fastest goal in cup final: 4.07 sec, 14-year-old Owen Price for Ernest Bevin College, Tooting, beaten 3-1 by Barking Abbey in Heinz Ketchup Cup Final at Arsenal on May 18, 2000. Owen, on Tottenham's books, scored from inside his own half when the ball was played back to him from kick-off.

Fastest Premier League goals: 10 sec, Ledley King for Tottenham away to Bradford, Dec 9, 2000; **10.4 sec, Alan Shearer for** Newcastle v Manchester City, Jan 18, 2003: **11 sec, Mark Viduka** for Leeds v Charlton, Mar 17, 2001; **12.5 sec. James Beattie** for Southampton at Chelsea, Aug 28, 2004; **13 sec, Chris Sutton** for Blackburn at Everton, Apr 1, 1995; **13 sec, Dwight Yorke** for Aston Villa at Coventry, Sep 30, 1995; **13 sec Asmir Begovic** (goalkeeper) for Stoke v Southampton, Nov 2, 2013; **13 sec Jay Rodriguez** for Southampton at Chelsea, Dec 1, 2013.

Fastest top-division goal: 7 sec, Bobby Langton for Preston v Manchester City (Div 1), Aug 25, 1948.

Fastest goal in Champions League: 10 sec, Roy Makaay for Bayern Munich v Real Madrid (1st ko rd), Mar 7, 2007.

Fastest Premier League goal by substitute: 9 sec, Shaun Goater, Manchester City's equaliser away to Manchester Utd (1-1), Feb 9, 2003. In Dec, 2011, Wigan's **Ben Watson** was brought off the bench to take a penalty against Stoke and scored.

Fastest goal on Premier League debut: 36 sec, Thievy Bifouma on as sub for WBA away to Crystal Palace, Feb 8, 2014.

Fastest goal by goalkeeper in professional football: 13 sec, Asmir Begovic for Stoke v Southampton (Prem Lge), Nov 2, 2013.

Fastest goal in women's football: 7 sec, Angie Harriott for Launton v Thame (Southern League, Prem Div), season 1998–99.

Fastest hat-trick in League history: 2 min 20 sec, Bournemouth's 84th-minute substitute **James Hayter** in 6-0 home win v Wrexham (Div 2) on Feb 24, 2004 (goal times 86, 87, 88 mins).

Fastest First Division hat-tricks since war: Graham Leggat, 3 goals in 3 minutes (first half) when Fulham beat Ipswich 10-1 on Boxing Day, 1963; **Nigel Clough**, 3 goals in **4 minutes** (81, 82, 85 pen) when Nottm Forest beat QPR 4-0 on Dec 13, 1987.

Fastest Premier League hat-trick: 2 min 56 sec (13, 14, 16) by **Sadio Mane** in Southampton 6, Aston Villa 1 on May 16, 2015.

Fastest international hat-trick: 2 min 35 sec, Abdul Hamid Bassiouny for Egypt in 8-2 win over Namibia in Abdallah, Libya, (African World Cup qual), Jul 13, 2001.

Fastest international hat-trick in British matches: 3.5 min, Willie Hall for England v N Ireland at Old Trafford, Manchester, Nov 16, 1938. (Hall scored 5 in 7-0 win); **3min 30 sec, Arif Erdem** for Turkey v N Ireland, European Championship qualifier, at Windsor Park, Belfast, on Sep 4, 1999.

Fastest FA Cup hat-tricks: In 3 min, Billy Best for Southend v Brentford (2nd round, Dec 7, 1968); **2 min 20 sec, Andy Locke** for Nantwich v Droylsden (1st Qual round, Sep 9, 1995).

Fastest Scottish hat-trick: 2 min 30 sec, Ian St John for Motherwell away to Hibernian (Scottish League Cup), Aug 15, 1959.

Fastest hat-trick of headers: Dixie Dean's 5 goals in Everton's 7-2 win at home to Chelsea (Div 1) on Nov 14, 1931 included 3 headers between **5th** and **15th-min.**

Fastest all-time hat-trick: Reported at 1 min 50 sec, Eduardo Maglioni for Independiente against Gimnasia de la Plata in Argentina Div , Mar 18, 1973.

Scored first kick: Billy Foulkes (Newcastle) for Wales v England at Cardiff, Oct 20, 1951, in his first international match.

Preston scored six goals in **7 min** in record 26-0 FA Cup 1st round win v Hyde, Oct 15, 1887.

Notts Co scored six second-half goals in **12 min** (Tommy Lawton 3, Jackie Sewell 3) when beating Exeter 9-0 (Div 3 South) at Meadow Lane on Oct 16, 1948.

Arsenal scored six in **18 min** (71-89 mins) in 7-1 home win (Div 1) v Sheffield Wed, Feb 15, 1992.

Tranmere scored six in first **19 min** when beating Oldham 13-4 (Div 3 North), December 26, 1935.

Sunderland scored eight in **28 min** at Newcastle (9-1 Div 1), December 5, 1908. Newcastle went on to win the title.

Southend scored all seven goals in **29 min** in 7-0 win at home to Torquay (Leyland Daf Cup, Southern quarter-final), Feb 26, 1991. Score was 0-0 until 55th minute.

Plymouth scored five in first **18 min** in 7-0 home win v Chesterfield (Div 2), Jan 3, 2004.

Five in 20 min: Frank Keetley in Lincoln's 9-1 win over Halifax in Div 3 (North), Jan 16, 1932; **Brian Dear** for West Ham v WBA (6-1, Div 1) Apr 16, 1965. **Kevin Hector** for Bradford PA v Barnsley (7-2, Div 4), Nov 20, 1965.

Four in 5 min: John McIntyre for Blackburn v Everton (Div 1), Sep 16, 1922; **WG (Billy) Richardson** for WBA v West Ham (Div 1), Nov 7, 1931.

Three in 2·5 min: Jimmy Scarth for Gillingham v Leyton Orient (Div 3S), Nov 1, 1952.

Three in three minutes: Billy Lane for Watford v Clapton Orient (Div 3S), December 20, 1933; **Johnny Hartburn** for Leyton Orient v Shrewsbury (Div 3S), Jan 22, 1955; **Gary Roberts** for Brentford v Newport, (Freight Rover Trophy, South Final), May 17, 1985; **Gary Shaw** for Shrewsbury v Bradford City (Div 3), December 22, 1990.

Two in 9 sec: Jamie Bates with last kick of first half, **Jermaine McSporran** 9 sec into second half when Wycombe beat Peterborough 2-0 at home (Div 2) on Sep 23, 2000.

Premier League – fastest scoring: Four goals in 4 min 44 sec, Tottenham home to Southampton on Sunday, Feb 7, 1993.

Premiership – fast scoring away: When **Aston Villa** won 5-0 at Leicester (Jan 31, 2004), all goals scored in **18 second-half min** (50-68).

Four in 13 min by Premier League sub: Ole Gunnar Solskjaer for Manchester Utd away to Nottm Forest, Feb 6, 1999.

Five in 9 mins by substitute: Robert Lewandowski for Bayern Munich v Wolfsburg (5-1, Bundesliga), Sep 22, 2015.

FASTEST GOALS IN WORLD CUP FINAL SERIES

10.8 sec, Hakan Sukur for Turkey against South Korea in 3rd/4th-place match at Taegu, June 29, 2002; **15 sec, Vaclav Masek** for Czechoslovakia v Mexico (in Vina, Chile, 1962); **27 sec, Bryan Robson** for England v France (in Bilbao, Spain, 1982).

TOP MATCH SCORES SINCE WAR

By English clubs: 13-0 by Newcastle v Newport (Div 2, Oct 1946); 13-2 by Tottenham v Crewe (FA Cup 4th. Rd replay, Feb 1960); 13-0 by Chelsea v Jeunesse Hautcharage, Lux. (Cup-Winners' Cup 1st round, 2nd leg, Sep 1971).

By Scottish club: 20-0 by Stirling v Selkirk (E. of Scotland League) in Scottish Cup 1st round (Dec 1984). That is the highest score in British first-class football since Preston beat Hyde 26-0 in FA Cup, Oct 1887.

MOST GOALS IN CALENDAR YEAR

88 by **Lionel Messi** in 2012 (76 Barcelona, 12 Argentina).

PREMIER LEAGUE LONGEST-RANGE GOALS BY OUTFIELD PLAYERS

66 yards: Charlie Adam (Stoke at Chelsea, Apr 4, 2015)
64 yards: Xabi Alonso (Liverpool v Newcastle, Sep 20, 2006)
62 yards: Maynor Figueroa (Wigan at Stoke, Dec 12, 2009)
59 yards: David Beckham (Manchester Utd at Wimbledon, Aug 17, 1996)
55 yards: Wayne Rooney (Manchester Utd at West Ham, Mar 22, 2014)

GOALS BY GOALKEEPERS

(Long clearances unless stated)

Pat Jennings for Tottenham v Manchester Utd (goalkeeper Alex Stepney), Aug 12, 1967 (FA Charity Shield).

Peter Shilton for Leicester v Southampton (Campbell Forsyth), Oct 14, 1967 (Div 1).
Ray Cashley for Bristol City v Hull (Jeff Wealands), Sep 18, 1973 (Div 2).
Steve Sherwood for Watford v Coventry (Raddy Avramovic), Jan 14, 1984 (Div 1).
Steve Ogrizovic for Coventry v Sheffield Wed (Martin Hodge), Oct 25, 1986 (Div 1).
Andy Goram for Hibernian v Morton (David Wylie), May 7, 1988 (Scot Prem Div).
Andy McLean, on Irish League debut, for Cliftonville v Linfield (George Dunlop), Aug 20, 1988.
Alan Paterson for Glentoran v Linfield (George Dunlop), Nov 30, 1988 (Irish League Cup Final – only instance of goalkeeper scoring winner in a senior cup final in UK).
Ray Charles for East Fife v Stranraer (Bernard Duffy), Feb 28, 1990 (Scot Div 2).
Iain Hesford for Maidstone v Hereford (Tony Elliott), Nov 2, 1991 (Div 4).
Chris Mackenzie for Hereford v Barnet (Mark Taylor), Aug 12, 1995 (Div 3).
Peter Schmeichel for Manchester Utd v Rotor Volgograd, Sep 26, 1995 (header, UEFA Cup 1).
Mark Bosnich (Aston Villa) for Australia v Solomon Islands, Jun 11, 1997 (penalty in World Cup qual – 13-0).
Peter Keen for Carlisle away to Blackpool (goalkeeper John Kennedy), Oct 24, 2000 (Div 3).
Steve Mildenhall for Notts Co v Mansfield (Kevin Pilkington), Aug 21, 2001 (free-kick inside own half, League Cup 1).
Peter Schmeichel for Aston Villa v Everton (Paul Gerrard), Oct 20, 2001 (volley, first goalkeeper to score in Premiership).
Mart Poom for Sunderland v Derby (Andy Oakes), Sep 20, 2003 (header, Div 1).
Brad Friedel for Blackburn v Charlton (Dean Kiely), Feb 21, 2004 (shot, Prem).
Paul Robinson for Leeds v Swindon (Rhys Evans), Sep 24, 2003 (header, League Cup 2).
Andy Lonergan for Preston v Leicester (Kevin Pressman), Oct 2, 2004 (Champ).
Gavin Ward for Tranmere v Leyton Orient (Glenn Morris), Sep 2, 2006 (free-kick Lge 1).
Mark Crossley for Sheffield Wed v Southampton (Kelvin Davis), Dec 23, 2006 (header, Champ).
Paul Robinson for Tottenham v Watford (Ben Foster), Mar 17, 2007 (Prem).
Adam Federici for Reading v Cardiff (Peter Enckelman), Dec 28, 2008 (shot, Champ).
Chris Weale for Yeovil v Hereford (Peter Gulacsi), Apr 21, 2009 (header, Lge 1).
Scott Flinders for Hartlepool v Bournemouth (Shwan Jalal), Apr 30, 2011 (header, Lge 1).
Iain Turner for Preston v Notts Co (Stuart Nelson), Aug 27 2011 (shot, Lge 1).
Tim Howard for Everton v Bolton (Adam Bogdan), Jan 4, 2012 (Prem).
Asmir Begovic for Stoke v Southampton (Artur Boruc), Nov 2, 2013 (Prem).
Jesse Joronen for Stevenage v Wycombe (Matt Ingram), Oct 17, 2015 (Lge 2).
Barry Roche for Morecambe v Portsmouth (Ryan Fulton), Feb 2, 2016 (header, Lge 2).

MORE GOALKEEPING HEADLINES

Arthur Wilkie, sustained a hand injury in Reading's Div 3 match against Halifax on Aug 31, 1962, then played as a forward and scored twice in a 4-2 win.

Alex Stepney was Manchester Utd's joint top scorer for two months in season 1973–74 with two penalties.

Alan Fettis scored twice for Hull in 1994–95 Div 2 season, as a substitute in 3-1 home win over Oxford Utd (Dec 17) and, when selected outfield, with last-minute winner (2-1) against Blackpool on May 6.

Roger Freestone scored for Swansea with a penalty at Oxford Utd (Div 2, Apr 30, 1995) and twice from the spot the following season against Shrewsbury (Aug 12) and Chesterfield (Aug 26).

Jimmy Glass, on loan from Swindon, kept Carlisle in the Football League on May 8, 1999. With ten seconds of stoppage-time left, he went upfield for a corner and scored the winner against Plymouth that sent Scarborough down to the Conference instead.

Paul Smith, Nottm Forest goalkeeper, was allowed to run through Leicester's defence unchallenged and score direct from the kick-off of a Carling Cup second round second match on Sep 18, 2007. It replicated the 1-0 score by which Forest had led at half-time when the original match was abandoned after Leicester defender Clive Clarke suffered a heart attack. Leicester won the tie 3-2.

Tony Roberts (Dagenham), is the only known goalkeeper to score from open play in the FA Cup, his last-minute goal at Basingstoke in the fourth qualifying round on Oct 27, 2001 earning a 2-2 draw. Dagenham won the replay 3-0 and went on to reach the third round proper.

The only known instance in first-class football in Britain of a goalkeeper scoring direct from a goal-kick was in a First Division match at Roker Park on Apr 14, 1900. The kick by Manchester City's **Charlie Williams** was caught in a strong wind and Sunderland keeper J. E Doig fumbled the ball over his line.

Jose Luis Chilavert, Paraguay's international goalkeeper, scored a hat-trick of penalties when his club Velez Sarsfield beat Ferro Carril Oeste 6-1 in the Argentine League on Nov 28, 1999. In all, he scored 8 goals in 72 internationals. He also scored with a free-kick from just inside his own half for Velez Sarsfield against River Plate on Sep 20, 2000.

Most goals by a goalkeeper in a League season: 5 (all penalties) by **Arthur Birch** for Chesterfield (Div 3 North), 1923–24.

When Brazilian goalkeeper **Rogerio Ceni** (37) converted a free-kick for Sao Paulo's winner (2-1) v Corinthians in a championship match on Mar 27, 2011, it was his 100th goal (56 free-kicks, 44 pens) in a 20-season career.

OWN GOALS

Most by player in one season: 5 by **Robert Stuart** (Middlesbrough) in 1934–35.

Three in match by one team: Sheffield Wed's **Vince Kenny, Norman Curtis** and **Eddie Gannon** in 5-4 defeat at home to WBA (Div 1) on Dec 26, 1952; Rochdale's **George Underwood, Kenny Boyle** and **Danny Murphy** in 7-2 defeat at Carlisle (Div 3 North), Dec 25, 1954; Sunderland's **Stephen Wright** and **Michael Proctor** (2) at home to Charlton (1-3, Prem), Feb 1, 2003; Brighton's **Liam Bridcutt** (2) and **Lewis Dunk** in 6-1 FA Cup 5th rd defeat at Liverpool, Feb 19, 2012.; Sunderland's **Santiago Vergini, Liam Bridcutt** and **Patrick van Aanholt** in 8-0 defeat at Southampton (Prem), Oct 18, 2014.

Two in match by one player: Chris Nicholl (Aston Villa) scored all 4 goals in 2-2 draw away to Leicester (Div 1), Mar 20, 1976; **Jamie Carragher** (Liverpool) in first half at home to Manchester Utd (2-3) in Premiership, Sep 11, 1999; **Jim Goodwin** (Stockport) in 1-4 defeat away to Plymouth (Div 2), Sep 23, 2002; **Michael Proctor** (Sunderland) in 1-3 defeat at home to Charlton (Premiership), Feb 1, 2003. **Michael Duberry** (Oxford) scored two own goals against Hereford on Jan 21, 2012, then rescued a point for his side with a 90th minute equaliser. **Jonathan Walters** (Stoke) headed the first 2 Chelsea goals in their 4-0 Premier League win at the Britannia Stadium, Jan 12, 2013. He also missed a penalty.Newport's **Tom Naylor** conceded two own goals and gave away a penalty in a 3-2 defeat by Moreca\mbe on Sept 14, 2013.

Fastest own goals: 8 sec by **Pat Kruse** of Torquay, for Cambridge Utd (Div 4), Jan 3, 1977; in First Division, **16 sec** by **Steve Bould** (Arsenal) away to Sheffield Wed, Feb 17, 1990.

Late own-goal man: Frank Sinclair (Leicester) put through his own goal in the 90th minute of Premiership matches away to Arsenal (L1-2) and at home to Chelsea (2-2) in Aug 1999.

Half an own goal each: Chelsea's second goal in a 3-1 home win against Leicester on December 18, 1954 was uniquely recorded as 'shared own goal'. Leicester defenders **Stan Milburn** and **Jack Froggatt**, both lunging at the ball in an attempt to clear, connected simultaneously and sent it rocketing into the net.

Match of 149 own goals: When Adama, Champions of Malagasy (formerly Madagascar) won a League match 149-0 on Oct 31, 2002, all 149 were own goals scored by opponents Stade Olympique De L'Emryne. They repeatedly put the ball in their own net in protest at a refereeing decision.

MOST SCORERS IN MATCH

Liverpool set a Football League record with **eight** scorers when beating Crystal Palace 9-0 (Div 1) on Sep 12, 1989. Marksmen were: Steve Nicol (7 and 88 mins), Steve McMahon (16), Ian Rush (45), Gary Gillespie (56), Peter Beardsley (61), John Aldridge (67 pen), John Barnes (79), Glenn Hysen (82).

Fifteen years earlier, **Liverpool** had gone one better with **nine** different scorers when they achieved their record win, 11-0 at home to Stromsgodset (Norway) in the Cup-Winners' Cup 1st round, 1st leg on Sep 17, 1974.

Eight players scored for **Swansea** when they beat Sliema, Malta, 12-0 in the Cup-Winners' Cup 1st round, 1st leg on Sep 15, 1982.

Nine Stirling players scored in the 20-0 win against Selkirk in the Scottish Cup 1st Round on December 8, 1984.

Premier League record: **Seven Chelsea** scorers in 8-0 home win over Aston Villa, Dec 23, 2012. An eighth player missed a penalty.

LONG SCORING RUNS

Tom Phillipson scored in 13 consecutive matches for Wolves (Div 2) in season 1926–27, which is still an English League record. In the same season, **George Camsell** scored in 12 consecutive matches for Middlesbrough (Div 2). **Bill Prendergast** scored in 13 successive League and Cup appearances for Chester (Div 3 North) in season 1938–39.

Dixie Dean scored in 12 consecutive games (23 goals) for Everton in Div 2 in 1930–31.

Danish striker **Finn Dossing** scored in 15 consecutive matches (Scottish record) for Dundee Utd (Div 1) in 1964–65.

50-GOAL PLAYERS

With **52** goals for **Wolves** in 1987–78 (34 League, 12 Sherpa Van Trophy, 3 Littlewoods Cup, 3 FA Cup), **Steve Bull** became the first player to score 50 in a season for a League club since **Terry Bly** for Div 4 newcomers Peterborough in 1960–61. Bly's 54 comprised 52 League goals and 2 in the FA Cup, and included 7 hat-tricks, still a post-war League record. Bull was again the country's top scorer with 50 goals in season 1988–89: 37 League, 2 Littlewoods Cup and 11 Sherpa Van Trophy. Between Bly and Bull, the highest individual scoring total for a season was 49 by two players: **Ted MacDougall** (Bournemouth 1970–71, 42 League, 7 FA Cup) and **Clive Allen** (Tottenham 1986–87, 33 League, 12 Littlewoods Cup, 4 FA Cup).

HOT SHOTS

Jimmy Greaves was top Div 1 scorer (League goals) six times in 11 seasons: 32 for Chelsea (1958–59), 41 for Chelsea (1960–61) and, for Tottenham, 37 in 1962–63, 35 in 1963–64, 29 in 1964–65 (joint top) and 27 in 1968–69.

Brian Clough (Middlesbrough) was leading scorer in Div 2 in three successive seasons: 40 goals in 1957–58, 42 in 1958–59 and 39 in 1959–60.

John Hickton (Middlesbrough) was top Div 2 scorer three times in four seasons: 24 goals in 1967–68, 24 in 1969–70 and 25 in 1970–71.

MOST HAT-TRICKS

Nine by George Camsell (Middlesbrough) in Div 2, 1926–27, is the record for one season. Most League hat-tricks in career: 37 by **Dixie Dean** for Tranmere and Everton (1924–38).

Most top division hat-tricks in a season since last War: six by **Jimmy Greaves** for Chelsea (1960–61). **Alan Shearer** scored five hat-tricks for Blackburn in the Premier League, season 1995–96.

Frank Osborne (Tottenham) scored three consecutive hat-tricks in Div 1 in Oct–Nov 1925, against Liverpool, Leicester (away) and West Ham.

Tom Jennings (Leeds) scored hat-tricks in three successive Div 1 matches (Sep–Oct, 1926): 3 goals v Arsenal, 4 at Liverpool, 4 v Blackburn. Leeds were relegated that season.

Jack Balmer (Liverpool) scored his three hat-tricks in a 17-year career in successive Div 1 matches (Nov 1946): 3 v Portsmouth, 4 at Derby, 3 v Arsenal. No other Liverpool player scored during that 10-goal sequence by Balmer.

Gilbert Alsop scored hat-tricks in three successive matches for Walsall in Div 3 South in Apr 1939: 3 at Swindon, 3 v Bristol City and 4 v Swindon.

Alf Lythgoe scored hat-tricks in three successive games for Stockport (Div 3 North) in Mar 1934: 3 v Darlington, 3 at Southport and 4 v Wrexham.

TRIPLE HAT-TRICKS

There have been at least three **instances of 3 hat-tricks being scored for one team in a Football League match:**

Apr 21, 1909: Enoch West, Billy Hooper and **Alfred Spouncer** for Nottm Forest (12-0 v Leicester Fosse, Div 1).

Mar 3, 1962: Ron Barnes, Wyn Davies and **Roy Ambler** in Wrexham's 10-1 win against Hartlepool (Div 4).

Nov 7, 1987: Tony Adcock, Paul Stewart and **David White** for Manchester City in 10-1 win at home to Huddersfield (Div 2).

For the first time in the Premiership, **three** hat-tricks were completed on one day (Sep 23, 1995): **Tony Yeboah** for Leeds at Wimbledon; **Alan Shearer** for Blackburn v Coventry; **Robbie Fowler** with 4 goals for Liverpool v Bolton.

In the FA Cup, **Jack Carr, George Elliott** and **Walter Tinsley** each scored 3 in Middlesbrough's 9-3 first round win against Goole in Jan, 1915. **Les Allen** scored 5, **Bobby Smith** 4 and **Cliff Jones** 3 when Tottenham beat Crewe 13-2 in a fourth-round replay in Feb 1960.

HAT-TRICKS v THREE 'KEEPERS

When West Ham beat Newcastle 8-1 (Div 1) on Apr 21, 1986 **Alvin Martin** scored 3 goals against different goalkeepers: Martin Thomas injured a shoulder and was replaced, in turn, by outfield players Chris Hedworth and Peter Beardsley.

Jock Dodds of Lincoln had done the same against West Ham on Dec 18, 1948, scoring past Ernie Gregory, Tommy Moroney and George Dick in 4-3 win.

David Herd (Manchester Utd) scored against Sunderland's Jim Montgomery, Charlie Hurley and Johnny Parke in 5-0 First Division home win on Nov 26, 1966.

Brian Clark, of Bournemouth, scored against Rotherham's Jim McDonagh, Conal Gilbert and Michael Leng twice in 7-2 win (Div 3) on Oct 10, 1972.

On Oct 16, 1993 (Div 3) **Chris Pike** (Hereford) scored a hat-trick in 5-0 win over Colchester, who became the first team in league history to have two keepers sent off in the same game.

On Dec 18, 2004 (Lge 1), in 6-1 defeat at Hull, Tranmere used **John Achterberg** and **Russell Howarth,** both retired injured, and defender **Theo Whitmore.**

On Mar 9, 2008, Manchester Utd had three keepers in their 0-1 FA Cup quarter-final defeat by Portsmouth. **Tomasz Kuszczak** came on at half-time for **Edwin van der Sar** but was sent off when conceding a penalty. **Rio Ferdinand** went in goal and was beaten by Sulley Muntari's spot-kick.

Derby used three keepers in a 4-1 defeat at Reading (Mar 10, 2010, Champ). **Saul Deeney,** who took over when **Stephen Bywater** was injured, was sent off for a foul and **Robbie Savage** replaced him.

EIGHT-DAY HAT-TRICK TREBLE

Joe Bradford, of Birmingham, scored three hat-tricks in eight days in Sep 1929–30 v Newcastle (won 5-1) on the 21st, 5 for the Football League v Irish League (7-2) on the 25th, and 3 in his club's 5-7 defeat away to Blackburn on the 28th.

PREMIERSHIP DOUBLE HAT-TRICK

Robert Pires and **Jermaine Pennant** each scored 3 goals in Arsenal's 6-1 win at home to Southampton (May 7, 2003).

TON UP – BOTH ENDS

Manchester City are the only club to score and concede a century of League goals in the same season. When finishing fifth in the 1957–58 season, they scored 104 and gave away 100.

TOURNAMENT TOP SHOTS

Most individual goals in a World Cup Final series: 13 by **Just Fontaine** for France, in Sweden 1958. Most in European Championship Finals: 9 by **Michel Platini** for France, in France 1984.

MOST GOALS ON CLUB DEBUT

Jim Dyet scored eight in King's Park's 12-2 win against Forfar (Scottish Div 2, Jan 2, 1930). **Len Shackleton** scored six times in Newcastle's 13-0 win v Newport (Div 2, Oct 5, 1946) in the week he joined them from Bradford Park Avenue.

MOST GOALS ON LEAGUE DEBUT

Five by **George Hilsdon,** for Chelsea (9-2) v Glossop, Div 2, Sep 1, 1906. **Alan Shearer,** with three goals for Southampton (4-2) v Arsenal, Apr 9, 1988, became, at 17, the youngest player to score a First Division hat-trick on his full debut.

FOUR-GOAL SUBSTITUTE

James Collins (Swindon), sub from 60th minute, scored 4 in 5-0 home win v Portsmouth (Lge 1) on Jan 1, 2013.

CLEAN-SHEET RECORDS

On the way to promotion from Div 3 in season 1995–96, Gillingham's ever-present goalkeeper **Jim Stannard** set a clean-sheet record. In 46 matches. He achieved 29 shut-outs (17 at home, 12 away), beating the 28 by **Ray Clemence** for Liverpool (42 matches in Div 1, 1978–79) and the previous best in a 46-match programme of 28 by Port Vale (Div 3 North, 1953–54). In conceding only 20 League goals in 1995–96, Gillingham created a defensive record for the lower divisions.

Chris Woods, Rangers' England goalkeeper, set a British record in season 1986–87 by going 1,196 minutes without conceding a goal. The sequence began in the UEFA Cup match against Borussia Moenchengladbach on Nov 26, 1986 and ended when Rangers were sensationally beaten 1-0 at home by Hamilton in the Scottish Cup 3rd round on Jan 31, 1987 with a 70th-minute goal by **Adrian Sprott.** The previous British record of 1,156 minutes without a goal conceded was held by Aberdeen goalkeeper **Bobby Clark** (season 1970–01).

Manchester Utd set a new Premier League clean-sheet record of 1,333 minutes (including 14 successive match shut-outs) in season 2008–09 (Nov 15–Feb 21). **Edwin van der Sar's** personal British league record of 1,311 minutes without conceding ended when United won 2-1 at Newcastle on Mar 4, 2009.

Most clean sheets in season in top English division: **28** by **Liverpool** (42 matches) in 1978–79; **25** by **Chelsea** (38 matches) in 2004–05.

There have been three instances of clubs keeping 11 consecutive clean sheets in the Football League: **Millwall** (Div 3 South, 1925–26), **York** (Div 3, 1973–74) and **Reading** (Div 4, 1978–79). In his sequence, Reading goalkeeper **Steve Death** set the existing League shut-out record of 1,103 minutes.

Sasa Ilic remained unbeaten for over 14 hours with 9 successive shut-outs (7 in Div 1, 2 in play-offs) to equal a Charlton club record in Apr/May 1998. He had 12 clean sheets in 17 first team games after winning promotion from the reserves with 6 successive clean sheets.

Sebastiano Rossi kept a clean sheet in 8 successive away matches for AC Milan (Nov 1993–Apr 1994).

A world record of 1,275 minutes without conceding a goal was set in 1990–01 by **Abel Resino,** the Atletico Madrid goalkeeper. He was finally beaten by Sporting Gijon's Enrique in Atletico's 3-1 win on Mar 19, 1991.

In international football, the record is held by **Dino Zoff** with a shut-out for Italy (Sep 1972 to Jun 1974) lasting 1,142 minutes.

LOW SCORING

Fewest goals by any club in season in Football League: 18 by **Loughborough** (Div 2, 34 matches, 1899–1900); in 38 matches 20 by **Derby** (Prem Lge, 2007–08); in 42 matches, 24 by **Watford** (Div 2, 1971–72) and by **Stoke** (Div 1, 1984–85)); in 46-match programme, 27 by **Stockport** (Div 3, 1969–70).

Arsenal were the lowest Premier League scorers in its opening season (1992–93) with 40 goals in 42 matches, but won both domestic cup competitions. In subsequent seasons the lowest Premier League scorers were **Ipswich** (35) in 1993–94, **Crystal Palace** (34) in 1994–95, **Manchester City**

(33) in 1995–96 and **Leeds** (28) in 1996–97 until **Sunderland** set the Premiership's new fewest-goals record with only 21 in 2002–03. Then, in 2007–08, **Derby** scored just 20.

LONG TIME NO SCORE

The world international non-scoring record was set by **Northern Ireland** when they played 13 matches and 1,298 minutes without a goal. The sequence began against Poland on Feb 13, 2002 and ended 2 years and 5 days later when David Healy scored against Norway (1-4) in Belfast on Feb 18, 2004.

Longest non-scoring sequences in Football League: 11 matches by **Coventry** in 1919–20 (Div 2); 11 matches in 1992–93 (Div 2) by **Hartlepool,** who after beating Crystal Palace 1-0 in the FA Cup 3rd round on Jan 2, went 13 games and 2 months without scoring (11 League, 1 FA Cup, 1 Autoglass Trophy). The sequence ended after 1,227 blank minutes with a 1-1 draw at Blackpool (League) on Mar 6.

In the Premier League (Oct–Jan season 1994–95) **Crystal Palace** failed to score in nine consecutive matches.

The British non-scoring club record is held by **Stirling:** 14 consecutive matches (13 League, 1 Scottish Cup) and 1,292 minutes play, from Jan 31 1981 until Aug 8, 1981 (when they lost 4-1 to Falkirk in the League Cup).

In season 1971–72, **Mansfield** did not score in any of their first nine home games in Div 3. They were relegated on goal difference of minus two.

FA CUP CLEAN SHEETS

Most consecutive FA Cup matches without conceding a goal: 11 by **Bradford City.** The sequence spanned 8 rounds, from 3rd in 1910–11 to 4th. Round replay in 1911–12, and included winning the Cup in 1911.

GOALS THAT WERE WRONGLY GIVEN

Tottenham's last-minute winner at home to Huddersfield (Div 1) on Apr 2, 1952: Eddie Baily's corner-kick struck referee WR Barnes in the back, and the ball rebounded to Baily, who crossed for Len Duquemin to head into the net. Baily had infringed the Laws by playing the ball twice, but the result (1-0) stood. Those two points helped Spurs to finish Championship runners-up; Huddersfield were relegated.

The second goal (66 mins) in **Chelsea**'s 2-1 home win v Ipswich (Div 1) on Sep 26, 1970: Alan Hudson's shot hit the stanchion on the outside of goal and the ball rebounded on to the pitch. But instead of the goal-kick, referee Roy Capey gave a goal, on a linesman's confirmation. TV pictures proved otherwise. The Football League quoted from the Laws of the Game: 'The referee's decision on all matters is final.'

When **Watford's** John Eustace and **Reading's** Noel Hunt challenged for a 13th minute corner at Vicarage Road on Sep 20, 2008, the ball was clearly diverted wide. But referee Stuart Attwell signalled for a goal on the instruction on his assistant and it went down officially as a Eustace own goal. The Championship match ended 2-2.

Sunderland's 1-0 Premier League win over **Liverpool** on Oct 17, 2009 was decided by one of the most bizarre goals in football history when Darren Bent's shot struck a red beach ball thrown from the crowd and wrong-footed goalkeeper Jose Reina. Referee Mike Jones wrongly allowed it to stand. The Laws of the Game state: 'An outside agent interfering with play should result in play being stopped and restarted with a drop ball.'

Blackburn's 59th minute equaliser (2-2) in 3-3 draw away to Wigan (Prem) on Nov 19, 2011 was illegal. Morten Gamst Pedersen played the ball to himself from a corner and crossed for Junior Hoilett to net.

The Republic of Ireland were deprived of the chance of a World Cup place in the second leg of their play-off with France on Nov 18, 2009. They were leading 1-0 in Paris when Thierry Henry blatantly handled before setting up William Gallas to equalise in extra-time time and give his side a 2-1 aggregate victory. The FA of Ireland's call for a replay was rejected by FIFA.

• The most notorious goal in World Cup history was fisted in by Diego Maradona in **Argentina's** 2-1 quarter-final win over England in Mexico City on Jun 22, 1986.

ATTENDANCES

GREATEST WORLD CROWDS

World Cup, Maracana Stadium, Rio de Janeiro, Jul 16, 1950. Final match (Brazil v Uruguay) attendance 199,850; receipts £125,000.

Total attendance in three matches (including play-off) between Santos (Brazil) and AC Milan for the Inter-Continental Cup (World Club Championship) 1963, exceeded 375,000.

BRITISH RECORD CROWDS

Most to pay: 149,547, Scotland v England, at Hampden Park, Glasgow, Apr 17, 1937. This was the first all-ticket match in Scotland (receipts £24,000).

At Scottish FA Cup Final: 146,433, Celtic v Aberdeen, at Hampden Park, Apr 24, 1937. Estimated another 20,000 shut out.

For British club match (apart from a Cup Final): 143,470, Rangers v Hibernian, at Hampden Park, Mar 27, 1948 (Scottish Cup semi-final).

FA Cup Final: 126,047, Bolton v West Ham, Apr 28, 1923. Estimated 150,000 in ground at opening of Wembley Stadium.

New Wembley: 89,874, FA Cup Final, Cardiff v Portsmouth, May 17, 2008.

World Cup Qualifying ties: 120,000, Cameroon v Morocco, Yaounde, Nov 29, 1981; 107,580, Scotland v Poland, Hampden Park, Oct 13, 1965.

European Cup: 135,826, Celtic v Leeds (semi-final, 2nd leg) at Hampden Park, Apr 15, 1970.

European Cup Final: 127,621, Real Madrid v Eintracht Frankfurt, at Hampden Park, May 18, 1960.

European Cup-Winners' Cup Final: 100,000, West Ham v TSV Munich, at Wembley, May 19, 1965.

Scottish League: 118,567, Rangers v Celtic, Jan 2, 1939.

Scottish League Cup Final: 107,609, Celtic v Rangers, at Hampden Park, Oct 23, 1965.

Football League old format: First Div: 83,260, Manchester Utd v Arsenal, Jan 17, 1948 (at Maine Road); **Div 2** 70,302 Tottenham v Southampton, Feb 25, 1950; **Div 3S:** 51,621, Cardiff v Bristol City, Apr 7, 1947; **Div 3N:** 49,655, Hull v Rotherham, Dec 25, 1948; **Div 3:** 49,309, Sheffield Wed v Sheffield Utd, Dec 26, 1979; **Div 4:** 37,774, Crystal Palace v Millwall, Mar 31, 1961.

Premier League: 76,098, Manchester Utd v Blackburn, Mar 31, 2007.

Football League – New Div 1: 41,214, Sunderland v Stoke, Apr 25, 1998; **New Div2:** 32,471, Manchester City v York, May 8, 1999; **New Div 3:** 22,319, Hull v Hartlepool Utd, Dec 26, 2002. **New Champs:** 52,181, Newcastle v Ipswich, Apr 24, 2010; **New Lge 1:** 38,256, Leeds v Gillingham, May 3, 2008; **New Lge 2:** 17,250, MK Dons v Morecambe, May 3, 2008.

In English Provinces: 84,569, Manchester City v Stoke (FA Cup 6), Mar 3, 1934.

Record for Under-21 International: 55,700, England v Italy, first match at New Wembley, Mar 24, 2007.

Record for friendly match: 104,679, Rangers v Eintracht Frankfurt, at Hampden Park, Glasgow, Oct 17, 1961.

FA Youth Cup: 38,187, Arsenal v Manchester Utd, at Emirates Stadium, Mar 14, 2007.

Record Football League aggregate (season): 41,271,414 (1948–49) – 88 clubs.

Record Football League aggregate (single day): 1,269,934, December 27, 1949, previous day, 1,226,098.

Record average home League attendance for season: 75,691 by Manchester Utd in 2007–08.

Long-ago League attendance aggregates: 10,929,000 in 1906–07 (40 clubs); 28,132,933 in 1937–38 (88 clubs).

Last 1m crowd aggregate, League (single day): 1,007,200, December 27, 1971.

Record Amateur match attendance: 100,000 for FA Amateur Cup Final, Pegasus v Harwich & Parkeston at Wembley, Apr 11, 1953.

Record Cup-tie aggregate: 265,199, at two matches between Rangers and Morton, in Scottish Cup Final, 1947–48.

Abandoned match attendance records: In England – 63,480 at Newcastle v Swansea City FA Cup 3rd round, Jan 10, 1953, abandoned 8 mins (0-0), fog.

In Scotland: 94,596 at Scotland v Austria (4-1), Hampden Park, May 8, 1963. Referee Jim

Finney ended play (79 minutes) after Austria had two players sent off and one carried off.

Colchester's record crowd (19,072) was for the FA Cup 1st round tie v Reading on Nov 27, 1948, abandoned 35 minutes (0-0), fog.

SMALLEST CROWDS

Smallest League attendances: 450 Rochdale v Cambridge Utd (Div 3, Feb 5, 1974); 469, Thames v Luton (Div 3 South, December 6, 1930).

Only 13 people paid to watch Stockport v Leicester (Div 2, May 7, 1921) at Old Trafford, but up to 2,000 stayed behind after Manchester Utd v Derby earlier in the day. Stockport's ground was closed.

Lowest Premier League crowd: 3,039 for Wimbledon v Everton, Jan 26, 1993 (smallest top-division attendance since War).

Lowest Saturday post-war top-division crowd: 3,231 for Wimbledon v Luton, Sep 7, 1991 (Div 1).

Lowest Football League crowds, new format – Div 1: 849 for Wimbledon v Rotherham, (Div 1) Oct 29, 2002 (smallest attendance in top two divisions since War); 1,054 Wimbledon v Wigan (Div 1), Sep 13, 2003 in club's last home match when sharing Selhurst Park; **Div 2:** 1,077, Hartlepool Utd v Cardiff, Mar 22, 1994; **Div 3:** 739, Doncaster v Barnet, Mar 3, 1998.

Lowest top-division crowd at a major ground since the war: 4,554 for Arsenal v Leeds (May 5, 1966) – fixture clashed with live TV coverage of Cup-Winners' Cup Final (Liverpool v Borussia Dortmund).

Smallest League Cup attendances: 612, Halifax v Tranmere (1st round, 2nd leg) Sep 6, 2000; 664, Wimbledon v Rotherham (3rd round), Nov 5, 2002.

Smallest League Cup attendance at top-division ground: 1,987 for Wimbledon v Bolton (2nd Round, 2nd Leg) Oct 6, 1992.

Smallest Wembley crowds for England matches: 15,628 v Chile (Rous Cup, May 23, 1989 – affected by Tube strike); 20,038 v Colombia (Friendly, Sep 6, 1995); 21,432 v Czech. (Friendly, Apr 25, 1990); 21,142 v Japan (Umbro Cup, Jun 3, 1995); 23,600 v Wales (British Championship, Feb 23, 1983); 23,659 v Greece (Friendly, May 17, 1994); 23,951 v East Germany (Friendly, Sep 12, 1984); 24,000 v N Ireland (British Championship, Apr 4, 1984); 25,756 v Colombia (Rous Cup, May 24, 1988); 25,837 v Denmark (Friendly, Sep 14, 1988).

Smallest international modern crowds: 221 for Poland v N Ireland (4-1, friendly) at Limassol, Cyprus, on Feb 13, 2002. Played at neutral venue at Poland's World Cup training base. 265 (all from N Ireland) at their Euro Champ qual against Serbia in Belgrade on Mar 25, 2011. Serbia ordered by UEFA to play behind closed doors because of previous crowd trouble.

Smallest international modern crowds at home: N Ireland: 2,500 v Chile (Belfast, May 26, 1989 – clashed with ITV live screening of Liverpool v Arsenal Championship decider); Scotland: 7,843 v N Ireland (Hampden Park, May 6, 1969); Wales: 2,315 v N Ireland (Wrexham, May 27, 1982).

Smallest attendance for post-war England match: 2,378 v San Marino (World Cup) at Bologna (Nov 17, 1993). Tie clashed with Italy v Portugal (World Cup) shown live on Italian TV.

Lowest England attendance at New Wembley: 40,181 v Norway (friendly), Sep 3, 2014

Smallest paid attendance for British first-class match: 29 for Clydebank v East Stirling, CIS Scottish League Cup 1st round, Jul 31, 1999. Played at Morton's Cappielow Park ground, shared by Clydebank. Match clashed with the Tall Ships Race which attracted 200,000 to the area.

FA CUP CROWD RECORD (OUTSIDE FINAL)

The first FA Cup-tie shown on closed-circuit TV (5th round, Saturday, Mar 11, 1967, kick-off 7pm) drew a total of 105,000 spectators to Goodison Park and Anfield. At Goodison, 64,851 watched the match 'for real', while 40,149 saw the TV version on eight giant screens at Anfield. Everton beat Liverpool 1-0.

LOWEST SEMI-FINAL CROWD

The smallest FA Cup semi-final attendance since the War was 17,987 for the Manchester Utd–Crystal Palace replay at Villa Park on Apr 12, 1995. Palace supporters largely boycotted tie after a fan died in car-park clash outside pub in Walsall before first match.

Previous lowest: 25,963 for Wimbledon v Luton, at Tottenham on Apr 9, 1988.

Lowest quarter-final crowd since the war: 8,735 for Chesterfield v Wrexham on Mar 9, 1997.

Smallest FA Cup 3rd round attendances for matches between League clubs: 1,833 for Chester v Bournemouth (at Macclesfield) Jan 5, 1991; 1,966 for Aldershot v Oxford Utd, Jan 10, 1987.

PRE-WEMBLEY CUP FINAL CROWDS

AT CRYSTAL PALACE

1895	42,560	1902	48,036	1908	74,967
1896	48,036	Replay	33,050	1909	67,651
1897	65,891	1903	64,000	1910	76,980
1898	62,017	1904	61,734	1911	69,098
1899	73,833	1905	101,117	1912	54,434
1900	68,945	1906	75,609	1913	120,028
1901	110,802	1907	84,584	1914	72,778

AT OLD TRAFFORD

1915 50,000

AT STAMFORD BRIDGE

1920	50,018	1921	72,805	1922	53,000

England women's record crowd: 45,619 v Germany, 0-3 (Wembley, Nov 23, 2014) – Karen Carney's 100th cap.

INTERNATIONAL RECORDS

MOST APPEARANCES

Peter Shilton, England goalkeeper, then aged 40, retired from international football after the 1990 World Cup Finals with the European record number of caps – 125. Previous record (119) was set by **Pat Jennings,** Northern Ireland's goalkeeper from 1964–86, who retired on his 41st birthday during the 1986 World Cup in Mexico. Shilton's England career spanned 20 seasons from his debut against East Germany at Wembley on Nov 25, 1970.

Eight players have completed a century of appearances in full international matches for England. **Billy Wright** of Wolves, was the first, retiring in 1959 with a total of 105 caps. **Bobby Charlton,** of Manchester Utd, beat Wright's record in the World Cup match against West Germany in Leon, Mexico, in Jun 1970 and **Bobby Moore,** of West Ham, overtook Charlton's 106 caps against Italy in Turin, in Jun 1973. Moore played 108 times for England, a record that stood until **Shilton** reached 109 against Denmark in Copenhagen (Jun 7, 1989). In season 2008–09, **David Beckham** (LA Galaxy/AC Milan) overtook Moore as England's most-capped outfield player. In the vastly different selection processes of their eras, Moore played 108 full games for his country, whereas Beckham's total of 115 to the end of season 2009–10, included 58 part matches, 14 as substitute and 44 times substituted. **Steven Gerrard** won his 100th cap against Sweden in Stockholm on Nov 14, 2012 and **Ashley Cole** reached 100 appearances against Brazil at Wembley on Feb 6, 2013. **Frank Lampard** played his 100th game against Ukraine in Kiev (World Cup qual) on Sep 10, 2013.

Robbie Keane won his 126th Republic of Ireland cap, overtaking Shay Given's record, In a World Cup qualifier against the Faroe Islands on Jun 7, 2013. Keane scored all his team's three goals in a 3-0 win.

Kenny Dalglish became Scotland's first 100-cap international v Romania (Hampden Park, Mar 26, 1986).

World's most-capped player: Ahmed Hassan, 184 for Egypt (1995–2012).

Most-capped European player: Vitalijs Astafjevs, 167 for Latvia (1992–2010).

Most-capped European goalkeeper: Thomas Ravelli, 143 Internationals for Sweden (1981–97).

Gillian Coultard, (Doncaster Belles), England Women's captain, received a special presentation from Geoff Hurst to mark 100 caps when England beat Holland 1-0 at Upton Park on Oct 30, 1997. She made her international debut at 18 in May 1981, and retired at the end of season 1999–2000 with a record 119 caps (30 goals).

BRITAIN'S MOST-CAPPED PLAYERS

(As at start of season 2016–17)

England

Peter Shilton	125
David Beckham	115
Wayne Rooney	115
Steven Gerrard	114
Bobby Moore	108
Ashley Cole	107
Bobby Charlton	106
Frank Lampard	106
Billy Wright	105

Scotland

Kenny Dalglish	102
Jim Leighton	91
Alex McLeish	77
Paul McStay	76
Tommy Boyd	72

Wales

Neville Southall	92
Gary Speed	85
Craig Bellamy	78
Dean Saunders	75
Peter Nicholas	73
Ian Rush	73

Northern Ireland

Pat Jennings	119
Aaron Hughes	103
David Healy	95
Mal Donaghy	91
Sammy McIlroy	88
Maik Taylor	88

Republic of Ireland

Robbie Keane	145
Shay Given	134
John O'Shea	114
Kevin Kilbane	110
Steve Staunton	102
Damien Duff	100

ENGLAND'S MOST-CAPPED PLAYER (either gender)

Fara Williams (Liverpool midfielder) with 155 appearances for the England's women's team to end of season 2015–16.

MOST ENGLAND CAPS IN ROW

Most consecutive international appearances: 70 by **Billy Wright,** for England from Oct 1951 to May 1959. He played 105 of England's first 108 post-war matches.

England captains most times: Billy Wright and **Bobby Moore,** 90 each.

England captains – 4 in match (v Serbia & Montenegro at Leicester Jun 3, 2003): **Michael Owen** was captain for the first half and after the interval the armband passed to **Emile Heskey** (for 15 minutes), **Phil Neville** (26 minutes) and substitute **Jamie Carragher** (9 minutes, including time added).

MOST SUCCESSIVE ENGLAND WINS

10 (Jun 1908–Jun 1909. Modern: 8 (Oct 2005–Jun 2006).

ENGLAND'S LONGEST UNBEATEN RUN

19 matches (16 wins, 3 draws), Nov 1965–Nov 1966.

ENGLAND'S TALLEST

At **6ft 7in, Peter Crouch** became England's tallest-ever international when he made his debut against Colombia in New Jersey, USA on May 31, 2005.

MOST PLAYERS FROM ONE CLUB IN ENGLAND SIDES

Arsenal supplied seven men (a record) to the England team v Italy at Highbury on Nov 14, 1934. They were: Frank Moss, George Male, Eddie Hapgood, Wilf Copping, Ray Bowden, Ted Drake and Cliff Bastin. In addition, Arsenal's Tom Whittaker was England's trainer.

Since then until 2001, the most players from one club in an England team was six from **Liverpool** against Switzerland at Wembley in Sep 1977. The side also included a Liverpool old boy, Kevin Keegan (Hamburg).

Seven **Arsenal** men took part in the England – France (0-2) match at Wembley on Feb 10, 1999. Goalkeeper David Seaman and defenders Lee Dixon, Tony Adams and Martin Keown lined up for England. Nicolas Anelka (2 goals) and Emmanuel Petit started the match for France and Patrick Vieira replaced Anelka.

Manchester Utd equalled Arsenal's 1934 record by providing England with seven players in the World Cup qualifier away to Albania on Mar 28, 2001. Five started the match – David Beckham (captain), Gary Neville, Paul Scholes, Nicky Butt and Andy Cole – and two went on as substitutes: Wes Brown and Teddy Sheringham.

INTERNATIONAL SUBS RECORDS

Malta substituted all 11 players in their 1-2 home defeat against England on Jun 3, 2000. Six substitutes by England took the total replacements in the match to 17, then an international record.

Most substitutions in match by **England:** 11 in second half by Sven-Goran Eriksson against Holland at Tottenham on Aug 15, 2001; 11 against Italy at Leeds on Mar 27, 2002; Italy sent on 8 players from the bench – the total of 19 substitutions was then a record for an England match; 11 against Australia at Upton Park on Feb 12, 2003 (entire England team changed at half-time); 11 against Iceland at City of Manchester Stadium on Jun 5, 2004.

Forty three players, a record for an England match, were used in the international against Serbia & Montenegro at Leicester on Jun 3, 2003. England sent on 10 substitutes in the second half and their opponents changed all 11 players.

The **Republic of Ireland** sent on 12 second-half substitutes, using 23 players in all, when they beat Russia 2-0 in a friendly international in Dublin on Feb 13, 2002.

First England substitute: Wolves winger **Jimmy Mullen** replaced injured Jackie Milburn (15 mins) away to Belgium on May 18, 1950. He scored in a 4-1 win.

ENGLAND'S WORLD CUP-WINNERS

At Wembley, Jul 30, 1966, 4-2 v West Germany (2-2 after 90 mins), scorers Hurst 3, Peters. Team: Banks; Cohen, Wilson, Stiles, Jack Charlton, Moore (capt), Ball, Hurst, Bobby Charlton, Hunt, Peters. Manager **Alf Ramsey** fielded that same eleven in six successive matches (an England record): the World Cup quarter-final, semi-final and Final, and the first three games of the following season. England wore red shirts in the Final and The Queen presented the Cup to Bobby Moore. The players each received a £1,000 bonus, plus £60 World Cup Final appearance money, all less tax, and Ramsey a £6,000 bonus from the FA The match was shown live on TV (in black and white).

England's non-playing reserves – there were no substitutes – also received the £1,000 bonus, but no medals. That remained the case until FIFA finally decided that non-playing members and staff of World Cup-winning squads should be given replica medals. England's 'forgotten heroes' received theirs at a reception in Downing Street on June 10, 2009 and were later guests of honour at the World Cup qualifier against Andorra at Wembley. The 11 reserves were: Springett, Bonetti, Armfield, Byrne, Flowers, Hunter, Paine, Connelly, Callaghan, Greaves, Eastham.

BRAZIL'S RECORD RUN

Brazil hold the record for the longest unbeaten sequence in international football: 45 matches from 1993–97. The previous record of 31 was held by Hungary between Jun 1950 and Jul 1954.

ENGLAND MATCHES ABANDONED

May 17, 1953 v **Argentina** (Friendly, Buenos Aires) after 23 mins (0-0) – rain.

Oct 29, 1975 v **Czechoslovakia** (Euro Champ qual, Bratislava) after 17 mins (0-0) – fog. Played next day.

Feb 15, 1995 v **Rep of Ireland** (Friendly, Dublin) after 27 mins (1-0) – crowd disturbance.

ENGLAND POSTPONEMENTS

Nov 21, 1979 v **Bulgaria** (Euro Champ qual, Wembley, postponed for 24 hours – fog; Aug 10,

2011 v **Holland** (friendly), Wembley, postponed after rioting in London.

Oct 16, 2012 v **Poland** (World Cup qual, Warsaw) postponed to next day – pitch waterlogged.

The friendly against **Honduras** (Miami, Jun 7, 2014) was suspended midway through the first half for 44 minutes – thunderstorm.

ENGLAND UNDER COVER

England played indoors for the first time when they beat Argentina 1-0 in the World Cup at the Sapporo Dome, Japan, on Jun 7, 2002.

ALL-SEATED INTERNATIONALS

The first **all-seated crowd** (30,000) for a full international in Britain saw **Wales** and **West Germany** draw 0-0 at Cardiff Arms Park on May 31, 1989. The terraces were closed.

England's first all-seated international at Wembley was against Yugoslavia (2-1) on December 13, 1989 (attendance 34,796). The terracing behind the goals was closed for conversion to seating.

The first **full-house all-seated** international at Wembley was for England v Brazil (1-0) on Mar 28, 1990, when a capacity 80,000 crowd paid record British receipts of £1,200,000.

MOST NEW CAPS IN ENGLAND TEAM

6, by Sir Alf Ramsey (v Portugal, Apr 3, 1974) and **by Sven-Goran Eriksson** (v Australia, Feb 12, 2003; 5 at half-time when 11 changes made).

PLAYED FOR MORE THAN ONE COUNTRY

Multi-nationals in senior international football include: **Johnny Carey** (1938–53) – caps Rep of Ireland 29, N Ireland 7; **Ferenc Puskas** (1945–62) – caps Hungary 84, Spain 4; **Alfredo di Stefano** (1950–56) – caps Argentina 7, Spain 31; **Ladislav Kubala** (1948–58) – caps, Hungary 3, Czechoslovakia 11, Spain 19, only player to win full international honours with 3 countries. Kubala also played in a fourth international team, scoring twice for FIFA v England at Wembley in 1953. Eleven players, including **Carey**, appeared for both N Ireland and the Republic of Ireland in seasons directly after the last war.

Cecil Moore, capped by N Ireland in 1949 when with Glentoran, played for USA v England in 1953.

Hawley Edwards played for England v Scotland in 1874 and for Wales v Scotland in 1876.

Jack Reynolds (Distillery and WBA) played for both Ireland (5 times) and England (8) in the 1890s.

Bobby Evans (Sheffield Utd) had played 10 times for Wales when capped for England, in 1910–11. He was born in Chester of Welsh parents.

In recent years, several players have represented USSR and one or other of the breakaway republics. The same applies to Yugoslavia and its component states. **Josip Weber** played for Croatia in 1992 and made a 5-goal debut for Belgium in 1994.

THREE-GENERATION INTERNATIONAL FAMILY

When Bournemouth striker **Warren Feeney** was capped away to Liechtenstein on Mar 27, 2002, he became the third generation of his family to play for Northern Ireland. He followed in the footsteps of his grandfather James (capped twice in 1950) and father Warren snr. (1 in 1976).

FATHERS & SONS CAPPED BY ENGLAND

George Eastham senior (pre-war) and **George Eastham junior; Brian Clough** and **Nigel Clough; Frank Lampard snr** and **Frank Lampard jnr; Mark Chamberlain** and **Alex Oxlade-Chamberlain.**

FATHER & SON SAME-DAY CAPS

Iceland made father-and-son international history when they beat Estonia 3-0 in Tallin on Apr 24, 1996. **Arnor Gudjohnsen** (35) started the match and was replaced (62 mins) by his 17-year-old son **Eidur.**

LONGEST UNBEATEN START TO ENGLAND CAREER

Steven Gerrard, 21 matches (W16, D5) 2000–03.

SUCCESSIVE ENGLAND HAT-TRICKS

The last player to score a hat-trick in consecutive England matches was **Dixie Dean** on the summer tour in May 1927, against Belgium (9-1) and Luxembourg (5-2).

SCORED ON ENGLAND DEBUT

Marcus Rashford, against Australia on May 27, 2016, joined a list which includes **Stanley Matthews, Tom Finney, Jimmy Greaves, Bobby Charlton, Alan Shearer** and **Rickie Lambert**.

MOST GOALS BY PLAYER v ENGLAND

4 by **Zlatan Ibrahimovic** (Sweden 4 England 2, Stockholm, Nov 14, 2012).

POST-WAR HAT-TRICKS v ENGLAND

Nov 25, 1953, **Nandor Hidegkuti** (England 3, Hungary 6, Wembley); May 11, 1958, **Aleksandar Petakovic** (Yugoslavia 5, England 0, Belgrade); May 17, 1959, **Juan Seminario** (Peru 4, England 1, Lima); Jun 15, 1988, **Marco van Basten** (Holland 3, England 1, European Championship, Dusseldorf). Six other players scored hat-tricks against England (1878–1930).

NO-SAVE GOALKEEPERS

Chris Woods did not have one save to make when England beat San Marino 6-0 (World Cup) at Wembley on Feb 17, 1993. He touched the ball only six times.

Gordon Banks had a similar no-save experience when England beat Malta 5-0 (European Championship) at Wembley on May 12, 1971. Malta did not force a goal-kick or corner, and the four times Banks touched the ball were all from back passes.

Robert Green was also idle in the 6-0 World Cup qualifying win over Andorra at Wembley on Jun 10, 2009.

Joe Hart was untroubled in England's 5-0 win over San Marino in a World Cup qualifier at Wembley on Oct 12, 2012.

WORLD/EURO MEMBERS

FIFA has 209 member countries, **UEFA** 53

NEW FIFA PRESIDENT

The 18-year reign of FIFA president **Sepp Blatter** ended in December 2015 amid widespread allegations of corruption. He was replaced in February 2016 by Gianni Infantino, a 45-year-old Swiss-Italian lawyer, who was previously general secretary of UEFA. Under new rules, he will serve four years.

FIFA WORLD YOUTH CUP (UNDER-20)

Finals: 1977 (Tunis) Soviet Union 2 Mexico 2 (Soviet won 9-8 on pens.); **1979** (Tokyo) Argentina 3 Soviet Union 1; **1981** (Sydney) W Germany 4 Qatar 0; **1983** (Mexico City) Brazil 1 Argentina 0; **1985** (Moscow) Brazil 1 Spain 0; **1987** (Santiago) Yugoslavia 1 W Germany 1 (Yugoslavia won 5-4 on pens.); **1989** (Riyadh) Portugal 2 Nigeria 0; **1991** (Lisbon) Portugal 0 Brazil 0 (Portugal won 4-2 on pens.); **1993** (Sydney) Brazil 2 Ghana 1; **1995** (Qatar) Argentina 2 Brazil 0; **1997** (Kuala Lumpur) Argentina 2 Uruguay 1; **1999** (Lagos) Spain 4 Japan 0; **2001** (Buenos Aires) Argentina 3 Ghana 0; **2003** (Dubai) Brazil 1 Spain 0; **2005** (Utrecht) Argentina 2 Nigeria 1; **2007** (Toronto) Argentina 2 Czech Republic 1; **2009** (Cairo) Ghana 0 Brazil 0 (aet, Ghana won 4-3 on pens); **2011** (Bogota) Brazil 3 Portugal 2 (aet); **2013** (Istanbul) France 0 Uruguay 0 (aet, France won 4-1 on pens), **2015** (Auckland) Serbia 2 Brazil 1 (aet).

FAMOUS CLUB FEATS

Chelsea were Premiership winners in 2004–05, their centenary season with the highest points total (95) ever recorded by England Champions. They set these other records: Most Premiership wins in season (29); most clean sheets (25) and fewest goals conceded (15) in top-division history. They also won the League Cup in 2005.

Arsenal created an all-time English League record sequence of 49 unbeaten Premiership matches (W36, D13), spanning 3 seasons, from May 7, 2003 until losing 2-0 away to Manchester Utd on Oct 24, 2004. It included all 38 games in season 2003–04.

The Double: There have been 11 instances of a club winning the Football League/Premier League title and the FA Cup in the same season. **Manchester Utd** and **Arsenal** have each done so three times: **Preston** 1888–89; **Aston Villa** 1896–97; **Tottenham** 1960–61; **Arsenal** 1970–71, 1997–98, 2001–02; **Liverpool** 1985–86; **Manchester Utd** 1993–94, 1995–96, 1998–99; **Chelsea** 2009–10.

The Treble: Liverpool were the first English club to win three major competitions in one season when in 1983–84, Joe Fagan's first season as manager, they were League Champions, League Cup winners and European Cup winners.

Sir Alex Ferguson's **Manchester Utd** achieved an even more prestigious treble in 1998–99, completing the domestic double of Premiership and FA Cup and then winning the European Cup. In season 2008–09, they completed another major triple success – Premier League, Carling Cup and World Club Cup.

Liverpool completed a unique treble by an English club with three cup successes under Gerard Houllier in season 2000–01: the League Cup, FA Cup and UEFA Cup.

Liverpool the first English club to win five major trophies in one calendar year (Feb– Aug 2001): League Cup, FA Cup, UEFA Cup, Charity Shield, UEFA Super Cup.

As Champions in season 2001–02, **Arsenal** set a Premiership record by winning the last 13 matches. They were the first top-division club since Preston in the League's inaugural season (1888–89) to maintain an unbeaten away record.

(See Scottish section for treble feats by Rangers and Celtic).

Record Home Runs: Liverpool went 85 competitive first-team games unbeaten at home between losing 2-3 to Birmingham on Jan 21, 1978 and 1-2 to Leicester on Jan 31, 1981. They comprised 63 in the League, 9 League Cup, 7 in European competition and 6 FA Cup.

Chelsea hold the record unbeaten home League sequence of 86 matches (W62, D24) between losing 1-2 to Arsenal, Feb 21, 2004, and 0-1 to Liverpool, Oct 26, 2008.

Third to First: Charlton, in 1936, became the first club to advance from the Third to First Division in successive seasons. **Queens Park Rangers** were the second club to achieve the feat in 1968, and **Oxford Utd** did it in 1984 and 1985 as Champions of each division. Subsequently, **Derby** (1987), **Middlesbrough** (1988), **Sheffield Utd** (1990) and **Notts Co** (1991) climbed from Third Division to First in consecutive seasons.

Watford won successive promotions from the modern Second Division to the Premier League in 1997–98, 1998–99. **Manchester City** equalled the feat in 1998–99, 1999–2000. **Norwich** climbed from League 1 to the Premier League in seasons 2009–10, 2010–11. **Southampton** did the same in 2010–11 and 2011–12.

Fourth to First: Northampton , in 1965 became the first club to rise from the Fourth to the First Division. **Swansea** climbed from the Fourth Division to the First (three promotions in four seasons), 1977–78 to 1980–81. **Wimbledon** repeated the feat, 1982–83 to 1985–86 **Watford** did it in five seasons, 1977–8 to 1981–82. **Carlisle** climbed from Fourth Division to First, 1964–74.

Non-League to First: When **Wimbledon** finished third in the Second Division in 1986, they completed the phenomenal rise from non-League football (Southern League) to the First Division in nine years. Two years later they won the FA Cup.

Tottenham, in 1960–61, not only carried off the First Division Championship and the FA Cup for the first time that century but set up other records by opening with 11 successive wins, registering most First Division wins (31), most away wins in the League's history (16), and equalling Arsenal's First Division records of 66 points and 33 away points. They already held the Second Division record of 70 points (1919–20).

Arsenal, in 1993, became the first club to win both English domestic cup competitions (FA Cup and League Cup) in the same season. **Liverpool** repeated the feat in 2001. **Chelsea** did it in 2007.

Chelsea achieved the FA Cup/Champions League double in May 2012.

Preston, in season 1888–89, won the first League Championship without losing a match and the FA Cup without having a goal scored against them. Only other English clubs to remain unbeaten through a League season were **Liverpool** (Div 2 Champions in 1893–94) and **Arsenal** (Premiership Champions 2003–04).

Bury, in 1903, also won the FA Cup without conceding a goal.

Everton won Div 2, Div 1 and the FA Cup in successive seasons, 1930–31, 1931–32, 1932–33.

Wolves won the League Championship in 1958 and 1959 and the FA Cup in 1960.

Liverpool won the title in 1964, the FA Cup in 1965 and the title again in 1966. In 1978 they became the first British club to win the European Cup in successive seasons. Nottm Forest repeated the feat in 1979 and 1980.

Liverpool won the League Championship six times in eight seasons (1976–83) under **Bob Paisley's** management.

Sir Alex Ferguson's **Manchester Utd** won the Premier League in 13 of its 21 seasons (1992–2013). They were runners-up five times and third three times.

Most Premiership wins in season: 29 by Chelsea in 2004–05, 2005–06.

Biggest points-winning margin by League Champions: 18 by **Manchester Utd** (1999–2000).

Leicester, champions of England for first time, won Premier League, season 2015-16, by 10 points.

FA CUP/PROMOTION DOUBLE

WBA are the only club to achieve this feat in the same season (1930-31).

COVENTRY UNIQUE

Coventry are the only club to have played in the Premier League, all four previous divisions of the Football League, in both sections (North and South) of the old Third Division and in the modern Championship.

FAMOUS UPS & DOWNS

Sunderland: Relegated in 1958 after maintaining First Division status since their election to the Football League in 1890. They dropped into Division 3 for the first time in 1987.

Aston Villa: Relegated with Preston to the Third Division in 1970.

Arsenal up: When the League was extended in 1919, Woolwich Arsenal (sixth in Division Two in 1914–15, last season before the war) were elected to Division One. Arsenal have been in the top division ever since.

Tottenham down: At that same meeting in 1919 Chelsea (due for relegation) retained their place in Division One but the bottom club (Tottenham) had to go down to Division Two.

Preston and **Burnley down:** Preston, the first League Champions in season 1888–89, dropped into the Fourth Division in 1985. So did Burnley, also among the League's original members in 1888. In 1986, Preston had to apply for re-election.

Wolves' fall: Wolves, another of the Football League's original members, completed the fall from First Division to Fourth in successive seasons (1984–85–86).

Lincoln out: Lincoln became the first club to suffer automatic demotion from the Football League when they finished bottom of Div 4, on goal difference, in season 1986–87. They were replaced by Scarborough, champions of the GM Vauxhall Conference. Lincoln regained their place a year later.

Swindon up and down: In the 1990 play-offs, Swindon won promotion to the First Division for the first time, but remained in the Second Division because of financial irregularities.

MOST CHAMPIONSHIP WINS

Manchester Utd have been champions of England a record 20 times (7 Football League, 13 Premier League).

LONGEST CURRENT MEMBERS OF TOP DIVISION

Arsenal (since 1919), **Everton** (1954), **Liverpool** (1962), **Manchester Utd** (1975).

CHAMPIONS: FEWEST PLAYERS

Liverpool used only **14** players (five ever-present) when they won the League Championship in season 1965–66. **Aston Villa** also called on no more than 14 players to win the title in 1980–81, with seven ever-present.

UNBEATEN CHAMPIONS

Only two clubs have become Champions of England with an unbeaten record: **Preston** as the Football League's first winners in 1888–89 (22 matches) and **Arsenal**, Premiership winners in 2003–04 (38 matches).

LEAGUE HAT-TRICKS

Huddersfield created a record in 1924–25–26 by winning the League Championship three years in succession.

Arsenal equalled this hat-trick in 1933–34–35, **Liverpool** in 1982–83–84 and **Manchester Utd** in 1999–2000–01. Sir Alex Ferguson's side became the first to complete two hat-tricks (2007–08–09).

'SUPER DOUBLE' WINNERS

Since the War, there have been three instances of players appearing in and then managing FA Cup and Championship-winning teams:

Joe Mercer: Player in Arsenal Championship teams 1948, 1953 and in their 1950 FA Cup side; manager of Manchester City when they won Championship 1968, FA Cup 1969.

Kenny Dalglish: Player in Liverpool Championship-winning teams 1979, 1980, 1982, 1983, 1984, player-manager 1986, 1988, 1990: player-manager when Liverpool won FA Cup (to complete Double) 1986; manager of Blackburn, Champions 1995.

George Graham: Played in Arsenal's Double-winning team in 1971, and as manager took them to Championship success in 1989 and 1991 and the FA Cup – League Cup double in 1993.

ORIGINAL TWELVE

The original 12 members of the Football League (formed in 1888) were: **Accrington, Aston Villa, Blackburn, Bolton, Burnley, Derby, Everton, Notts Co, Preston, Stoke, WBA** and **Wolves.**

Results on the opening day (Sep 8, 1888): Bolton 3, Derby 6; Everton 2, Accrington 1; Preston 5, Burnley 2; Stoke 0, WBA 2; Wolves 1, Aston Villa 1. Preston had the biggest first-day crowd: 6,000. Blackburn and Notts Co did not play that day. They kicked off a week later (Sep 15) – Blackburn 5, Accrington 5; Everton 2, Notts Co 1.

Accrington FC resigned from the league in 1893 and later folded. A new club, Accrington Stanley, were members of the league from 1921 until 1962 when financial problems forced their demise. The current Accrington Stanley were formed in 1968 and gained league status in 2007.

FASTEST CLIMBS

Three promotions in four seasons by two clubs – **Swansea City**: 1978 third in Div 4; 1979 third in Div 3; 1981 third in Div 2; **Wimbledon:** 1983 Champions of Div 4; 1984 second in Div 3; 1986 third in Div 2.

MERSEYSIDE RECORD

Liverpool is the only city to have staged top-division football – through Everton and/or Liverpool – **in every season** since League football began in 1888.

EARLIEST PROMOTIONS TO TOP DIVISION POST-WAR

Mar 23, 1974, **Middlesbrough;** Mar 25, 2006, **Reading.**

EARLIEST RELEGATIONS POST-WAR

From top division: **QPR** went down from the old First Division on Mar 29, 1969; **Derby** went down from the Premier League on Mar 29, 2008, with 6 matches still to play. From modern First Division: **Stockport** on Mar 16, 2002, with 7 matches still to play; **Wimbledon** on Apr 6, 2004, with 7 matches to play.

LEAGUE RECORDS

CHAMPIONS OF ENGLAND 1888–2016

Football League and Premier league

Manchester Utd 20, Liverpool 18, Arsenal 13, Everton 9, Aston Villa 7, Sunderland 6, Chelsea 5, Manchester City 4, Newcastle 4, Sheffield Wed 4, Blackburn 3, Huddersfield 3, Leeds 3, Wolves 3, Burnley 2, Derby 2, Portsmouth 2, Preston 2, Tottenham 2, Ipswich 1, Leicester 1, Nottm Forest 1, Sheffield Utd 1, WBA 1

DOUBLE CHAMPIONS

Nine men have played in and managed League Championship-winning teams:

Ted Drake Player – Arsenal 1934, 1935, 1938. Manager – Chelsea 1955.

Bill Nicholson Player – Tottenham 1951. Manager – Tottenham 1961.

Alf Ramsey Player – Tottenham 1951. Manager – Ipswich 1962.

Joe Mercer Player – Everton 1939, Arsenal 1948, 1953. Manager – Manchester City 1968.

Dave Mackay Player – Tottenham 1961. Manager – Derby 1975.

Bob Paisley Player – Liverpool 1947. Manager – Liverpool 1976, 1977, 1979, 1980, 1982, 1983.

Howard Kendall Player – Everton 1970. Manager – Everton 1985, 1987.

Kenny Dalglish Player – Liverpool 1979, 1980, 1982, 1983, 1984. Player-manager – Liverpool 1986, 1988, 1990. Manager – Blackburn 1995.

George Graham Player – Arsenal 1971. Manager – Arsenal 1989, 1991.

CANTONA'S FOUR-TIMER

Eric Cantona played in four successive Championship-winning teams: Marseille 1990–01, Leeds 1991–92, Manchester Utd 1992–93 and 1993–94.

ARRIVALS AND DEPARTURES

The following are the Football League arrivals and departures since 1923:

Year	In	Out
1923	Doncaster New Brighton	Stalybridge Celtic
1927	Torquay	Aberdare Athletic
1928	Carlisle	Durham
1929	York	Ashington
1930	Thames	Merthyr Tydfil
1931	Mansfield Chester	Newport Co Nelson
1932	Aldershot Newport Co	Thames Wigan Borough
1938	Ipswich	Gillingham
1950	Colchester, Gillingham Scunthorpe, Shrewsbury	

1951	Workington	New Brighton
1960	Peterborough	Gateshead
1962	Oxford Utd	Accrington (resigned)
1970	Cambridge Utd	Bradford PA
1972	Hereford	Barrow
1977	Wimbledon	Workington
1978	Wigan	Southport
1987	Scarborough	Lincoln
1988	Lincoln	Newport Co
1989	Maidstone	Darlington
1990	Darlington	Colchester
1991	Barnet	
1992	Colchester	Aldershot, Maidstone (resigned)
1993	Wycombe	Halifax
1997	Macclesfield	Hereford
1998	Halifax	Doncaster
1999	Cheltenham	Scarborough
2000	Kidderminster	Chester
2001	Rushden	Barnet
2002	Boston	Halifax
2003	Yeovil, Doncaster	Exeter, Shrewsbury
2004	Chester, Shrewsbury	Carlisle, York
2005	Barnet, Carlisle	Kidderminster, Cambridge Utd
2006	Accrington, Hereford	Oxford Utd, Rushden & Diamonds
2007	Dagenham, Morecambe	Torquay, Boston
2008	Aldershot, Exeter	Wrexham, Mansfield
2009	Burton, Torquay	Chester, Luton
2010	Stevenage, Oxford Utd	Grimsby, Darlington
2011	Crawley, AFC Wimbledon	Lincoln, Stockport
2012	Fleetwood, York	Hereford, Macclesfield
2013	Mansfield, Newport	Barnet, Aldershot
2014	Luton, Cambridge Utd	Bristol Rov, Torquay
2015	Barnet, Bristol Rov	Cheltenham, Tranmere
2016	Cheltenham, Grimsby	Dagenham & Redbridge, York

Leeds City were expelled from Div 2 in Oct, 1919; Port Vale took over their fixtures.

EXTENSIONS TO FOOTBALL LEAGUE

Clubs	**Season**	**Clubs**	**Season**
12 to 14	1891–92	44 to 66†	1920–21
14 to 28*	1892–93	66 to 86†	1921–22
28 to 31	1893–94	86 to 88	1923–24
31 to 32	1894–95	88 to 92	1950–51
32 to 36	1898–99	92 to 93	1991–92
36 to 40	1905–06	(Reverted to 92 when Aldershot closed, Mar 1992)	

*Second Division formed. † Third Division (South) formed from Southern League clubs.

†Third Division (North) formed.

Football League reduced to 70 clubs and three divisions on the formation of the FA Premier League in 1992; increased to 72 season 1994–95, when Premier League reduced to 20 clubs.

RECORD RUNS

Arsenal hold the record unbeaten sequence in the English League – 49 Premiership matches (36 wins, 13 draws) from May 7, 2003 until Oct 24, 2004 when beaten 2-0 away to Manchester Utd. The record previously belonged to **Nottm Forest** – 42 First Division matches (21 wins, 21 draws) from Nov 19, 1977 until beaten 2-0 at Liverpool on December 9, 1978.

Huddersfield set a new Football League record of 43 League 1 matches unbeaten from Jan 1, 2011 until Nov 28, 2011 when losing 2-0 at Charlton.

Best debuts: Ipswich won the First Division at their first attempt in 1961–62.

Peterborough in their first season in the Football League (1960–01) not only won the Fourth Division but set the all-time scoring record for the League of 134 goals. **Hereford** were promoted from the Fourth Division in their first League season, 1972–73.

Wycombe were promoted from the Third Division (via the play-offs) in their first League season, 1993–94. **Stevenage** were promoted from League 2 (via the play-offs) in their first League season, 2010–11. **Crawley** gained automatic promotion in their first season in 2011–12.

Record winning sequence in a season: 14 consecutive League victories (all in Second Division): **Manchester Utd** 1904–05, **Bristol City** 1905–06 and **Preston** 1950–51.

Best winning start to League season: 13 successive victories in Div 3 by **Reading,** season 1985–86.

Best starts in 'old' First Division: 11 consecutive victories by **Tottenham** in 1960–61; 10 by **Manchester Utd in** 1985–86. In 'new' First Division, 11 consecutive wins by **Newcastle** in 1992–93 and by **Fulham** in 2000–01.

Longest unbeaten sequence (all competitions): 40 by **Nottm Forest,** Mar–December 1978. It comprised 21 wins, 19 draws (in 29 League matches, 6 League Cup, 4 European Cup, 1 Charity Shield).

Longest unbeaten starts to League season: 38 matches (26 wins, 12 draws) in **Arsenal's** undefeated Premiership season, 2003–04; 29 matches – **Leeds,** Div 1 1973–74 (19 wins, 10 draws); **Liverpool**, Div 1 1987–88 (22 wins, 7 draws).

Most consecutive League matches unbeaten in a season: 38 **Arsenal** Premiership season 2003–04 (see above); 33 **Reading** (25 wins, 8 draws) 2005–06.

Longest winning sequence in Div 1: 13 matches by **Tottenham** – last two of season 1959–60, first 11 of 1960–61.

Longest winning one-season sequences in League Championship: 13 matches by **Preston,** 1891–92; **Sunderland,** also 1891–92; **Arsenal** 2001–02.

Longest unbeaten home League sequence in top division: 86 matches (62 wins, 24 draws) by **Chelsea** (Mar 2004–Oct 2008).

League's longest winning sequence with clean sheets: 9 matches by **Stockport** (Lge 2, 2006–07 season).

Premier League – best starts to season: Arsenal, 38 games, 2003–04; **Manchester City,** 14 games, 2011–12.

Best winning start to Premiership season: 9 consecutive victories by **Chelsea** in 2005–06.

Premier League – most consecutive wins (two seasons): 14 by **Arsenal,** Feb–Aug, 2002. Single season: 13 by **Arsenal** (Feb–May, 2002).

Premier League – most consecutive home wins: 20 by **Manchester City** (last 5 season 2010–11, first 15 season 2011–12).

Most consecutive away League wins in top flight: 11 by **Chelsea** (3 at end 2007–08 season, 8 in 2008–09).

Premier League – longest unbeaten away run: 27 matches (W17, D10) by **Arsenal** (Apr 5, 2003–Sep 25, 2004).

Record home-win sequences: Bradford Park Avenue won 25 successive home games in Div 3 North – the last 18 in 1926–27 and the first 7 the following season. Longest run of home wins in the top division is 21 by **Liverpool** – the last 9 of 1971–72 and the first 12 of 1972–73.

British record for successive League wins: 25 by **Celtic** (Scottish Premier League), 2003–04.

WORST SEQUENCES

Derby experienced the longest run without a win in League history in season 2007–08 – 32 games from Sep 22 to the end of the campaign (25 lost, 7 drawn). They finished bottom by a 24-pt margin. The sequence increased to 36 matches (28 lost, 8 drawn) at the start of the following season.

Cambridge Utd had the previous worst of 31 in 1983–84 (21 lost, 10 drawn). They were bottom of Div 2.

Worst losing start to a League season : 12 consecutive defeats by **Manchester Utd** (Div 1), 1930–31.

Worst Premier League start: QPR 16 matches without win (7 draws, 9 defeats), 2012–13.

Premier League – most consecutive defeats: 20 **Sunderland** last 15 matches, 2002–03, first five matches 2005–06.

Longest non-winning start to League season: 25 matches (4 draws, 21 defeats) by **Newport,** Div 4. Worst no-win League starts since then: 16 matches by **Burnley** (9 draws, 7 defeats in Div 2, 1979–80); 16 by **Hull** (10 draws, 6 defeats in Div 2, 1989–90); 16 by **Sheffield Utd** (4 draws, 12 defeats in Div 1, 1990–91).

Most League defeats in season: 34 by **Doncaster** (Div 3) 1997–98.

Fewest League wins in season: 1 by **Loughborough** (Div 2, season 1899–1900). They lost 27, drew 6, goals 18-100 and dropped out of the League. (See also Scottish section). 1 by **Derby** (Prem Lge, 2007–08). They lost 29, drew 8, goals 20-89.

Most consecutive League defeats in season: 18 by **Darwen** (Div 1, 1898–99); 17 by **Rochdale** (Div 3 North, 1931–32).

Fewest home League wins in season: 1 by **Loughborough** (Div 2, 1899–1900), **Notts Co** (Div 1, 1904–05), **Woolwich Arsenal** (Div 1, 1912–13), **Blackpool** (Div 1, 1966–67), **Rochdale** (Div 3, 1973–74), **Sunderland** (Prem Lge, 2005–06); **Derby** (Prem Lge, 2007–08).

Most home League defeats in season: 18 by **Cambridge Utd** (Div 3, 1984–85).

Away League defeats record: 24 in row by **Crewe** (Div 2) – all 15 in 1894–95 followed by 9 in 1895–96; by **Nelson** (Div 3 North) – 3 in Apr 1930 followed by all 21 in season 1930–31. They then dropped out of the League.

Biggest defeat in Champions' season: During **Newcastle's** title-winning season in 1908–09, they were beaten 9-1 at home by Sunderland on December 5.

WORST START BY EVENTUAL CHAMPIONS

Sunderland took only 2 points from their first 7 matches in season 1912–13 (2 draws, 5 defeats). They won 25 of the remaining 31 games to clinch their fifth League title.

DISMAL DERBY

Derby were relegated in season 2007–08 as the worst-ever team in the Premier League: fewest wins (1), fewest points (11); fewest goals (20), first club to go down in March (29th).

UNBEATEN LEAGUE SEASON

Only three clubs have completed an English League season unbeaten: **Preston** (22 matches in 1888–89, the League's first season), **Liverpool** (28 matches in Div 2, 1893–94) and **Arsenal** (38 matches in Premiership, 2003–04).

100 PER CENT HOME RECORDS

Six clubs have won every home League match in a season: **Sunderland** (13 matches)' in 1891–92 and four teams in the old Second Division: **Liverpool** (14) in 1893–94, **Bury** (15) in 1894–95, **Sheffield Wed** (17) in 1899–1900 and **Small Heath,** subsequently **Birmingham** (17) in 1902–03. The last club to do it, **Brentford,** won all 21 home games in Div 3 South in 1929–30. **Rotherham** just failed to equal that record in 1946–47. They won their first 20 home matches in Div 3 North, then drew the last 3-3 v Rochdale.

BEST HOME LEAGUE RECORDS IN TOP FLIGHT

Sunderland, 1891–92 (P13, W13); **Newcastle,** 1906–07 (P19, W18, D1); **Chelsea,** 2005–06 (P19, W18, D1); **Manchester Utd,** 2010–11 (P19, W18, D1); **Manchester City,** 2011–12 (P19, W18, D1).

MOST CONSECUTIVE CLEAN SHEETS

Premier League – 14: **Manchester Utd** (2008–09); **Football League** – 11: **Millwall** (Div 3 South 1925–26); **York** (Div 3 1973–74); **Reading** (Div 4, 1978–79).

WORST HOME RUNS

Most consecutive home League defeats: 14 **Rochdale** (Div 3 North) seasons 1931–32 and 1932–33; 10 **Birmingham** (Div 1) 1985–86; 9 **Darwen** (Div 2) 1897–98; 9 **Watford** (Div 2) 1971–72.

Between Nov 1958 and Oct 1959 **Portsmouth** drew 2 and lost 14 out of 16 consecutive home games.

West Ham did not win in the Premiership at Upton Park in season 2002–03 until the 13th home match on Jan 29.

MOST AWAY WINS IN SEASON

Doncaster won 18 of their 21 away League fixtures when winning Div 3 North in 1946–47.

AWAY WINS RECORD

Most consecutive away League wins: 11 **Chelsea** (Prem Lge) – 8 at start of 2008–09 after ending previous season with 3.

100 PER CENT HOME WINS ON ONE DAY

Div 1 – All 11 home teams won on Feb 13, 1926 and on Dec 10, 1955. **Div 2** – All 12 home teams won on Nov 26, 1988. **Div 3**, all 12 home teams won in the week-end programme of Oct 18–19, 1968.

NO HOME WINS IN DIV ON ONE DAY

Div 1 – 8 away wins, 3 draws in 11 matches on Sep 6, 1986. **Div 2** – 7 away wins, 4 draws in 11 matches on Dec 26, 1987. **Premier League** – 6 away wins, 5 draws in 11 matches on Dec 26, 1994.

The week-end **Premiership** programme on Dec 7–8–9, 1996 produced no home win in the ten games (4 aways, 6 draws). There was again no home victory (3 away wins, 7 draws) in the week-end **Premiership** fixtures on Sep 23–24, 2000.

MOST DRAWS IN A SEASON (FOOTBALL LEAGUE)

23 by **Norwich** (Div 1, 1978–79), **Exeter** (Div 4, 1986–87). **Cardiff** and **Hartlepool** (both Div 3, 1997–98). **Norwich** played 42 matches, the others 46.

MOST DRAWS IN PREMIER LEAGUE SEASON

18 (in 42 matches) by **Manchester City** (1993–94), **Sheffield Utd** (1993–94), **Southampton** (1994–95).

MOST DRAWS IN ONE DIV ON ONE DAY

On Sep 18, 1948 **nine** out of 11 First Division matches were drawn.

MOST DRAWS IN PREMIER DIV PROGRAMME

Over the week-ends of December 2–3–4, 1995, and Sep 23–24, 2000, **seven** out of the ten matches finished level.

FEWEST DRAWS IN SEASON

In 46 matches: 3 by **Reading** (Div 3 South, 1951–52); **Bradford Park Avenue** (Div 3 North, 1956–57); **Tranmere** (Div 4, 1984–85); **Southend** (Div 3, 2002–03); in 42 matches: 2 by **Reading** (Div 3 South, 1935–36); **Stockport** (Div 3 North, 1946–47); in 38 matches: 2 by **Sunderland** (Div 1, 1908–09).

HIGHEST-SCORING DRAWS IN LEAGUE

Leicester 6, **Arsenal** 6 (Div 1 Apr 21, 1930); **Charlton** 6, **Middlesbrough** 6 (Div 2. Oct 22, 1960)

Latest **6-6** draw in first-class football was between **Tranmere** and **Newcastle** in the Zenith Data

Systems Cup 1st round on Oct 1, 1991. The score went from 3-3 at 90 minutes to 6-6 after extra time, and Tranmere won 3-2 on penalties. In Scotland: **Queen of the South** 6, **Falkirk** 6 (Div 1, Sep 20, 1947).

Most recent **5-5** draws in top division: **Southampton** v **Coventry** (Div 1, May 4, 1982); **QPR** v **Newcastle** (Div 1, Sep 22, 1984); **WBA** v **Manchester Utd** (Prem Lge, May 19, 2013).

DRAWS RECORDS

Most consecutive drawn matches in Football League: 8 by **Torquay** (Div 3, 1969–70), **Middlesbrough** (Div 2, 1970–71), **Peterborough** (Div 4, 1971–72), **Birmingham** (Div 3 (1990–91), **Southampton** (Champ, 2005–06), **Chesterfield** (Lge 1, 2005–06), **Swansea** (Champ, 2008–09).

Longest sequence of draws by the same score: six 1-1 results by **QPR** in season 1957–58. **Tranmere** became the first club to play **five consecutive 0-0 League draws**, in season 1997–98.

IDENTICAL RECORDS

There is only **one instance** of two clubs in one division finishing a season with identical records. In 1907–08, **Blackburn** and **Woolwich Arsenal** were bracketed equal 14th in the First Division with these figures: P38, W12, D12, L14, Goals 51-63, Pts. 36.

The total of **1195 goals** scored in the Premier League in season 1993–94 was repeated in 1994–95.

DEAD LEVEL

Millwall's record in Division Two in season 1973–74 was P42, W14, D14, L14, F51, A51, Pts 42.

CHAMPIONS OF ALL DIVISIONS

Wolves, Burnley and **Preston** are the only clubs to have won titles in the old Divisions 1, 2, 3 and 4. Wolves also won the Third Division North and the new Championship.

POINTS DEDUCTIONS

2000–01: Chesterfield 9 for breach of transfer regulations and falsifying gate receipts.

2002–03: Boston 4 for contractual irregularities.

2004–05: Wrexham, Cambridge Utd 10 for administration.

2005–06: Rotherham 10 for administration.

2006–07: Leeds, Boston 10 for administration; **Bury** 1 for unregistered player.

2007–08: Leeds 15 over insolvency rules; **Bournemouth, Luton, Rotherham** 10 for administration.

2008–09: Luton 20 for failing Insolvency rules, 10 over payments to agents; **Bournemouth, Rotherham** 17 for breaking administration rules; **Southampton, Stockport** 10 for administration – **Southampton** with effect from season 2009–10 **Crystal Palace** 1 for ineligible player.

2009–10: Portsmouth 9, **Crystal Palace** 10 for administration; **Hartlepool** 3 for ineligible player.

2010–11: Plymouth 10 for administration; **Hereford** 3, **Torquay** 1, each for ineligible player

2011–12: Portsmouth and **Port Vale** both 10 for administration – Portsmouth from following season.

2013–14: Coventry 10 for administration; **AFC Wimbledon** 3 for ineligible player.

2014–15: Rotherham 3 for ineligible player.

2015–16: Bury 3 for ineligible player.

Among previous points penalties imposed:

Nov 1990: Arsenal 2, **Manchester Utd** 1 following mass players' brawl at Old Trafford.

Dec 1996: Brighton 2 for pitch invasions by fans.

Jan 1997: Middlesbrough 3 for refusing to play Premiership match at Blackburn because of injuries and illness.

Jun 1994: Tottenham 12 (reduced to 6) and banned from following season's FA Cup for making illegal payments to players. On appeal, points deduction annulled and club re-instated in Cup.

NIGHTMARE STARTS

Most goals conceded by a goalkeeper on League debut: 13 by **Steve Milton** when Halifax lost 13-0 at Stockport (Div 3 North) on Jan 6, 1934.

Post-war: 11 by Crewe's new goalkeeper **Dennis Murray** (Div 3 North) on Sep 29, 1951, when Lincoln won 11-1.

RELEGATION ODD SPOTS

None of the Barclays Premiership relegation places in season 2004–05 were decided until the last day (Sunday, May 15). **WBA** (bottom at kick-off) survived with a 2-0 home win against Portsmouth, and the three relegated clubs were **Southampton** (1-2 v Manchester Utd), **Norwich** (0-6 at Fulham) and **Crystal Palace** (2-2 at Charlton).

In season 1937–38, **Manchester City** were the highest-scoring team in the First Division with 80 goals (3 more than Champions Arsenal), but they finished in 21st place and were relegated – a year after winning the title. They scored more goals than they conceded (77).

That season produced the **closest relegation battle** in top-division history, with only 4 points spanning the bottom 11 clubs in Div 1. **WBA** went down with **Manchester City**.

Twelve years earlier, in 1925–26, City went down to Division 2 despite totalling 89 goals – still the most scored in any division by a relegated team. Manchester City also scored 31 FA Cup goals that season, but lost the Final 1-0 to Bolton Wanderers.

Cardiff were relegated from Div 1 in season 1928–29, despite conceding fewest goals in the division (59). They also scored fewest (43).

On their way to relegation from the First Division in season 1984–85, **Stoke** twice lost ten matches in a row.

RELEGATION TREBLES

Two Football League clubs have been relegated three seasons in succession. **Bristol City** fell from First Division to Fourth in 1980–81–82 and **Wolves** did the same in 1984–85–86.

OLDEST CLUBS

Oldest Association Football Club is **Sheffield FC** (formed in 1857). The oldest Football League clubs are **Notts Co,** 1862; **Nottm Forest,** 1865; and **Sheffield Wed,** 1866.

FOUR DIVISIONS

In **May, 1957**, the Football League decided to re-group the two sections of the Third Division into Third and Fourth Divisions in **season 1958–59**.

The Football League was reduced to three divisions on the formation of the Premier League in **1992**.

In season 2004–05, under new sponsors Coca-Cola, the titles of First, Second and Third Divisions were changed to League Championship, League One and League Two.

THREE UP – THREE DOWN

The Football League annual general meeting of Jun 1973 agreed to adopt the promotion and relegation system of three up and three down.

The **new system** came into effect in **season 1973–74** and applied only to the first three divisions; four clubs were still relegated from the Third and four promoted from the Fourth.

It was the first change in the promotion and relegation system for the top two divisions in 81 years.

MOST LEAGUE APPEARANCES

Players with more than 700 English League apps (as at end of season 2012–13)

1005 Peter Shilton 1966–97 (286 Leicester, 110 Stoke, 202 Nottm Forest, 188 Southampton, 175 Derby, 34 Plymouth Argyle, 1 Bolton, 9 Leyton Orient).

931 Tony Ford 1975–2002 (423 Grimsby, 9 Sunderland, 112 Stoke, 114 WBA, 5 Bradford City, 76 Scunthorpe, 103 Mansfield, 89 Rochdale).

840 Graham Alexander 1991–2012 (159 Scunthorpe, 152 Luton, 372 Preston, 157 Burnley)
824 Terry Paine 1956–77 (713 Southampton, 111 Hereford).
795 Tommy Hutchison 1968–91 (165 Blackpool, 314 Coventry City, 46 Manchester City, 92 Burnley, 178 Swansea). In addition, 68 Scottish League apps for Alloa 1965–68, giving career League app total of 863.
790 Neil Redfearn 1982–2004 (35 Bolton, 100 Lincoln, 46 Doncaster, 57 Crystal Palace, 24 Watford, 62 Oldham, 292 Barnsley, 30 Charlton, 17 Bradford City, 22 Wigan, 42 Halifax, 54 Boston, 9 Rochdale).
782 Robbie James 1973–94 (484 Swansea, 48 Stoke, 87 QPR, 23 Leicester, 89 Bradford City, 51 Cardiff).
777 Alan Oakes 1959–84 (565 Manchester City, 211 Chester, 1 Port Vale).
773 Dave Beasant 1980–2003 (340 Wimbledon, 20 Newcastle, 6 Grimsby, 4 Wolves, 133 Chelsea, 88 Southampton, 139 Nottm F, 27 Portsmouth, 16 Brighton).
770 John Trollope 1960–80 (all for Swindon, record total for one club).
769 David James 1990–2012 (89 Watford, 214 Liverpool, 67 Aston Villa, 91 West Ham, 93 Manchester City, 134 Portsmouth, 81 Bristol City).
764 Jimmy Dickinson 1946–65 (all for Portsmouth).
761 Roy Sproson 1950–72 (all for Port Vale).
760 Mick Tait 1974–97 (64 Oxford Utd, 106 Carlisle, 33 Hull, 240 Portsmouth, 99 Reading, 79 Darlington, 139 Hartlepool Utd).
758 Billy Bonds 1964–88 (95 Charlton, 663 West Ham).
758 Ray Clemence 1966–88 (48 Scunthorpe, 470 Liverpool, 240 Tottenham).
757 Pat Jennings 1963–86 (48 Watford, 472 Tottenham, 237 Arsenal).
757 Frank Worthington 1966–88 (171 Huddersfield Town, 210 Leicester, 84 Bolton, 75 Birmingham, 32 Leeds, 19 Sunderland, 34 Southampton, 31 Brighton, 59 Tranmere, 23 Preston, 19 Stockport).
755 Wayne Allison 1986–2008 (84 Halifax, 7 Watford, 195 Bristol City, 103 Swindon, 76 Huddersfield, 102 Tranmere, 73 Sheffield Utd, 115 Chesterfield).
749 Ernie Moss 1968–88 (469 Chesterfield, 35 Peterborough, 57 Mansfield, 74 Port Vale, 11 Lincoln, 44 Doncaster, 26 Stockport, 23 Scarborough, 10 Rochdale).
746 Les Chapman 1966–88 (263 Oldham, 133 Huddersfield Town, 70 Stockport, 139 Bradford City, 88 Rochdale, 53 Preston).
744 Asa Hartford 1967–90 (214 WBA, 260 Manchester City, 3 Nottm Forest, 81 Everton, 28 Norwich, 81 Bolton, 45 Stockport, 7 Oldham, 25 Shrewsbury).
743 Alan Ball 1963–84 (146 Blackpool, 208 Everton, 177 Arsenal, 195 Southampton, 17 Bristol Rov).
743 John Hollins 1963–84 (465 Chelsea, 151 QPR, 127 Arsenal).
743 Phil Parkes 1968–91 (52 Walsall, 344 QPR, 344 West Ham, 3 Ipswich).
737 Steve Bruce 1979–99 (205 Gillingham, 141 Norwich, 309 Manchester Utd 72 Birmingham, 10 Sheffield Utd).
734 Teddy Sheringham 1983–2007 (220 Millwall, 5 Aldershot, 42 Nottm Forest, 104 Manchester Utd, 236 Tottenham, 32 Portsmouth, 76 West Ham, 19 Colchester)
732 Mick Mills 1966–88 (591 Ipswich, 103 Southampton, 38 Stoke).
731 Ian Callaghan 1959–81 (640 Liverpool, 76 Swansea, 15 Crewe).
731 David Seaman 1982–2003 (91 Peterborough, 75 Birmingham, 141 QPR, 405 Arsenal, 19 Manchester City).
725 Steve Perryman 1969–90 (655 Tottenham, 17 Oxford Utd, 53 Brentford).
722 Martin Peters 1961–81 (302 West Ham, 189 Tottenham, 207 Norwich, 24 Sheffield Utd).
718 Mike Channon 1966–86 (511 Southampton, 72 Manchester City, 4 Newcastle, 9 Bristol Rov, 88 Norwich, 34 Portsmouth).
716 Ron Harris 1961–83 (655 Chelsea, 61 Brentford).
716 Mike Summerbee 1959–79 (218 Swindon, 357 Manchester City, 51 Burnley, 3 Blackpool, 87 Stockport).

714 Glenn Cockerill 1976–98 (186 Lincoln, 26 Swindon, 62 Sheffield Utd, 387 Southampton, 90 Leyton Orient, 40 Fulham, 23 Brentford).

705 Keith Curle 1981–2003 (32 Bristol Rov, 16 Torquay, 121 Bristol City, 40 Reading, 93 Wimbledon, 171 Manchester City, 150 Wolves, 57 Sheffield Utd, 11 Barnsley, 14 Mansfield.

705 Phil Neal 1968–89 (186 Northampton, 455 Liverpool, 64 Bolton).

705 John Wile 1968–86 (205 Peterborough, 500 WBA).

701 Neville Southall 1980–2000 (39 Bury, 578 Everton, 9 Port Vale, 9 Southend, 12 Stoke, 53 Torquay, 1 Bradford City).

- **Stanley Matthews** made 701 League apps 1932–65 (322 Stoke, 379 Blackpool), incl. 3 for Stoke at start of 1939–40 before season abandoned (war).
- Goalkeeper **John Burridge** made a total of 771 League appearances in a 28-season career in English and Scottish football (1968–96). He played 691 games for 15 English clubs (Workington, Blackpool, Aston Villa, Southend, Crystal Palace, QPR, Wolves, Derby, Sheffield Utd, Southampton, Newcastle, Scarborough, Lincoln, Manchester City and Darlington) and 80 for 5 Scottish clubs (Hibernian, Aberdeen, Dumbarton, Falkirk and Queen of the South).

LONGEST LEAGUE APPEARANCE SEQUENCE

Harold Bell, centre-half of Tranmere, was ever-present for the first nine post-war seasons (1946–55), achieving a League record of 401 consecutive matches. Counting FA Cup and other games, his run of successive appearances totalled 459.

The longest League sequence since Bell's was 394 appearances by goalkeeper **Dave Beasant** for Wimbledon, Newcastle and Chelsea. His nine-year run began on Aug 29, 1981 and was ended by a broken finger sustained in Chelsea's League Cup-tie against Portsmouth on Oct 31, 1990. Beasant's 394 consecutive League games comprised 304 for Wimbledon (1981–88), 20 for Newcastle (1988–89) and 70 for Chelsea (1989–90).

Phil Neal made 366 consecutive First Division appearances for Liverpool between December 1974 and Sep 1983, a remarkable sequence for an outfield player in top-division football.

MOST CONSECUTIVE PREMIER LEAGUE APPEARANCES

310 by goalkeeper **Brad Friedel** (152 Blackburn, 114 Aston Villa, 44 Tottenham, May 2004–Oct 2012). He played in 8 **ever-present seasons** (2004–12, Blackburn 4, Villa 3, Tottenham 1).

EVER-PRESENT DEFENCE

The **entire defence** of **Huddersfield** played in all 42 Second Division matches in season 1952–53, namely, Bill Wheeler (goal), Ron Staniforth and Laurie Kelly (full-backs), Bill McGarry, Don McEvoy and Len Quested (half-backs). In addition, Vic Metcalfe played in all 42 League matches at outside-left.

FIRST SUBSTITUTE USED IN LEAGUE

Keith Peacock (Charlton), away to Bolton (Div 2) on Aug 21, 1965.

FROM PROMOTION TO CHAMPIONS

Clubs who have become Champions of England a year after winning promotion: **Liverpool** 1905, 1906; **Everton** 1931, 1932; **Tottenham** 1950, 1951; **Ipswich** 1961, 1962; **Nottm Forest** 1977, 1978. The first four were placed top in both seasons: Forest finished third and first.

PREMIERSHIP'S FIRST MULTI-NATIONAL LINE-UP

Chelsea made history on December 26, 1999 when starting their Premiership match at Southampton without a single British player in the side.

Fulham's Unique XI: In the Worthington Cup 3rd round at home to Bury on Nov 6, 2002, Fulham fielded 11 players of 11 different nationalities. Ten were full Internationals, with Lee Clark an England U–21 cap.

On Feb 14, 2005 **Arsenal** became the first English club to select an all-foreign match squad when Arsene Wenger named 16 non-British players at home to Crystal Palace (Premiership).

Fifteen nations were represented at Fratton Park on Dec 30, 2009 (Portsmouth 1 Arsenal 4) when, for the first time in Premier League history, not one Englishman started the match. The line-up comprised seven Frenchmen, two Algerians and one from each of 13 other countries.

Players from 22 nationalities (subs included) were involved in the Blackburn–WBA match at Ewood Park on Jan 23, 2011.

PREMIER LEAGUE'S FIRST ALL-ENGLAND LINE-UP

On Feb 27, 1999 **Aston Villa** (at home to Coventry) fielded the first all-English line up seen in the Premier League (starting 11 plus 3 subs).

ENTIRE HOME-GROWN TEAM

Crewe Alexandra's starting 11 in the 2-0 home win against Walsall (Lge 1) on Apr 27, 2013 all graduated from the club's academy.

THREE-NATION CHAMPIONS

David Beckham won a title in four countries: with Manchester Utd six times (1996–97–99–2000–01–03), Real Madrid (2007), LA Galaxy (2011 and Paris St Germain (2013).

Trevor Steven earned eight Championship medals in three countries: two with Everton (1985, 1987); five with Rangers (1990, 1991, 1993, 1994, 1995) and one with Marseille in 1992.

LEEDS NO WIN AWAY

Leeds, in 1992–93, provided the first instance of a club failing to win an away League match as reigning Champions.

PIONEERS IN 1888 AND 1992

Three clubs among the twelve who formed the Football League in 1888 were also founder members of the Premier League: **Aston Villa, Blackburn** and **Everton.**

CHAMPIONS (MODERN) WITH TWO CLUBS – PLAYERS

Francis Lee (Manchester City 1968, Derby 1975); **Ray Kennedy** (Arsenal 1971, Liverpool 1979, 1980, 1982); **Archie Gemmill** (Derby 1972, 1975, Nottm Forest 1978); **John McGovern** (Derby 1972, Nottm Forest 1978) **Larry Lloyd** (Liverpool 1973, Nottm Forest 1978); **Peter Withe** (Nottm Forest 1978, Aston Villa 1981); **John Lukic** (Arsenal 1989, Leeds 1992); **Kevin Richardson** (Everton 1985, Arsenal 1989); **Eric Cantona (**Leeds 1992, Manchester Utd 1993, 1994, 1996, 1997); **David Batty** (Leeds 1992, Blackburn 1995), **Bobby Mimms** (Everton 1987, Blackburn 1995), **Henning Berg** (Blackburn 1995, Manchester Utd 1999, 2000); **Nicolas Anelka** (Arsenal 1998, Chelsea 2010); **Ashley Cole** (Arsenal 2002, 2004, Chelsea 2010); **Gael Clichy** (Arsenal 2004, Manchester City 2012); **Kolo Toure** (Arsenal 2004, Manchester City 2012); **Carlos Tevez** (Manchester Utd 2008, 2009, Manchester City 2012).

TITLE TURNABOUTS

In Jan 1996, **Newcastle** led the Premier League by 13 points. They finished runners-up to Manchester Utd.

At Christmas 1997, **Arsenal** were 13 points behind leaders Manchester Utd and still 11 points behind at the beginning of Mar 1998. But a run of 10 wins took the title to Highbury.

On Mar 2, 2003, **Arsenal,** with 9 games left, went 8 points clear of Manchester Utd, who had a match in hand. United won the Championship by 5 points.

In Mar 2002, **Wolves** were in second (automatic promotion) place in Nationwide Div 1, 11 points ahead of WBA, who had 2 games in hand. They were overtaken by Albion on the run-in, finished third, then failed in the play-offs. A year later they won promotion to the Premiership via the play-offs.

CLUB CLOSURES

Four clubs have left the Football League in mid-season: **Leeds City** (expelled Oct 1919); **Wigan Borough** (Oct 1931, debts of £20,000); **Accrington Stanley** (Mar 1962, debts £62,000); **Aldershot** (Mar 1992, debts £1.2m). **Maidstone,** with debts of £650,000, closed Aug 1992, on the eve of the season.

FOUR-DIVISION MEN

In season 1986–87, goalkeeper **Eric Nixon,** became the first player to appear in **all four divisions** of the Football League **in one season**. He served two clubs in Div 1: Manchester City (5 League games) and Southampton (4); in Div 2 Bradford City (3); in Div 3 Carlisle (16); and in Div 4 Wolves (16). Total appearances: 44.

Harvey McCreadie, a teenage forward, played in four divisions over two seasons inside a calendar year – from Accrington (Div 3) to Luton (Div 1) in Jan 1960, to Div 2 with Luton later that season and to Wrexham (Div 4) in Nov.

Tony Cottee played in all four divisions in season 2000–01, for Leicester (Premiership), Norwich (Div 1), Barnet (Div 3, player-manager) and Millwall (Div 2).

FATHERS AND SONS

When player-manager **Ian** (39) and **Gary** (18) **Bowyer** appeared together in the **Hereford** side at Scunthorpe (Div 4, Apr 21, 1990), they provided the first instance of father and son playing in the same team in a Football League match for 39 years. Ian played as substitute, and Gary scored Hereford's injury-time equaliser in a 3-3 draw.

Alec (39) and **David** (17) **Herd** were among previous father-and-son duos in league football – for Stockport, 2-0 winners at Hartlepool (Div 3 North) on May 5, 1951.

When Preston won 2-1 at Bury in Div 3 on Jan 13, 1990, the opposing goalkeepers were brothers: **Alan Kelly** (21) for Preston and **Gary** (23) for Bury. Their father, **Alan** (who kept goal for Preston in the 1964 FA Cup Final and won 47 Rep of Ireland caps) flew from America to watch the sons he taught to keep goal line up on opposite sides.

Other examples: **Bill Dodgin Snr** (manager, Bristol Rov) faced son **Bill Jnr** (manager of Fulham) four times between 1969 and 1971. On Apr 16, 2013 (Lge 1), Oldham, under **Lee Johnson,** won 1-0 at home to Yeovil, managed by his father **Gary.**

George Eastham Snr (manager) and son **George Eastham Jnr** were inside-forward partners for Ards in the Irish League in season 1954–55.

FATHER AND SON REFEREE PLAY-OFF FINALS

Father and son refereed two of the 2009 Play-off Finals. **Clive Oliver**, 46, took charge of Shrewsbury v Gillingham (Lge 2) and **Michael Oliver,** 26, refereed Millwall v Scunthorpe (Lge 1) the following day.

FATHER AND SON BOTH CHAMPIONS

John Aston snr won a Championship medal with Manchester Utd in 1952 and **John Aston jnr** did so with the club in 1967. **Ian Wright** won the Premier League title with Arsenal in 1998 and **Shaun Wright-Phillips** won with Chelsea in 2006.

FATHER AND SON RIVAL MANAGERS

When **Bill Dodgin snr** took Bristol Rov to Fulham for an FA Cup 1st Round tie in Nov 1971, the opposing manager was his son, **Bill jnr.** Rovers won 2-1. Oldham's new manager, **Lee Johnson**, faced his father **Gary's** Yeovil in a Lge 1 match in April, 2013. Oldham won 1-0.

FATHER AND SON ON OPPOSITE SIDES

It happened for the first time in FA Cup history (1st Qual Round on Sep 14, 1996) when 21-year-old **Nick Scaife** (Bishop Auckland) faced his father **Bobby** (41), who played for Pickering. Both were in midfield. Home side Bishops won 3-1.

THREE BROTHERS IN SAME SIDE

Southampton provided the first instance for 65 years of three brothers appearing together in a Div 1 side when **Danny Wallace** (24) and his 19-year-old twin brothers **Rodney** and **Ray** played against Sheffield Wed on Oct 22, 1988. In all, they made 25 appearances together for Southampton until Sep 1989.

A previous instance in Div 1 was provided by the Middlesbrough trio, **William, John** and **George Carr** with 24 League appearances together from Jan 1920 to Oct 1923.

The **Tonner** brothers, **Sam, James** and **Jack,** played together in 13 Second Division matches for Clapton Orient in season 1919–20.

Brothers **David, Donald** and **Robert Jack** played together in Plymouth's League side in 1920.

TWIN TEAM-MATES (see also Wallace twins above)

Twin brothers **David** and **Peter Jackson** played together for three League clubs (Wrexham, Bradford City and Tranmere) from 1954–62. The **Morgan** twins, **Ian** and **Roger**, played regularly in the QPR forward line from 1964–68. WBA's **Adam** and **James Chambers,** 18, were the first twins to represent England (v Cameroon in World Youth Championship, Apr 1999). They first played together in Albion's senior team, aged 19, in the League Cup 2nd. Round against Derby in Sep 2000. Brazilian identical twins **Rafael** and **Fabio Da Silva** (18) made first team debuts at full-back for Manchester Utd in season 2008– 09. Swedish twins **Martin** and **Marcus Olsson** played together for Blackburn in season 2011–12. **Josh** and **Jacob Murphy**, 19, played for Norwich in season 2013–2014.

SIR TOM DOES THE HONOURS

Sir Tom Finney, England and Preston legend, opened the Football League's new headquarters on their return to Preston on Feb 23, 1999. Preston had been the League's original base for 70 years before the move to Lytham St Annes in 1959.

SHORTENED MATCHES

The 0-0 score in the **Bradford City v Lincoln** Third Division fixture on May 11, 1985, abandoned through fire after 40 minutes, was subsequently confirmed as a result. It is the shortest officially- completed League match on record, and was the fourth of only five instances in Football League history of the score of an unfinished match being allowed to stand.

The other occasions: **Middlesbrough 4, Oldham 1** (Div 1, Apr 3, 1915), abandoned after 55 minutes when Oldham defender Billy Cook refused to leave the field after being sent off; **Barrow 7, Gillingham 0** (Div 4, Oct 9, 1961), abandoned after 75 minutes because of bad light, the match having started late because of Gillingham's delayed arrival.

A crucial **Manchester** derby (Div 1) was abandoned after 85 minutes, and the result stood, on Apr 27, 1974, when a pitch invasion at Old Trafford followed the only goal, scored for City by Denis Law, which relegated United, Law's former club.

The only instance of a first-class match in England being abandoned **'through shortage of players'** occurred in the First Division at Bramall Lane on Mar 16, 2002. Referee Eddie Wolstenholme halted play after 82 minutes because **Sheffield Utd** were reduced to 6 players against **WBA.** They had had 3 men sent off (goalkeeper and 2 substitutes), and with all 3 substitutes used and 2 players injured, were left with fewer than the required minimum of 7 on the field. Promotion contenders WBA were leading 3-0, and the League ordered the result to stand.

The last 60 seconds of **Birmingham v Stoke** (Div 3, 1-1, on Feb 29, 1992) were played behind locked doors. The ground had been cleared after a pitch invasion.

A First Division fixture, **Sheffield Wed v Aston Villa** (Nov 26, 1898), was abandoned through bad light after 79 mins with Wednesday leading 3-1. The Football League ruled that the match should be completed, and the remaining 10.5 minutes were played four months later (Mar 13, 1899), when Wednesday added another goal to make the result 4-1.

FA CUP RECORDS

(See also Goalscoring section)

CHIEF WINNERS

12 Arsenal, Manchester Utd, **8** Tottenham; **7** Aston Villa, Chelsea, Liverpool; **6** Blackburn, Newcastle.

Three times in succession: The Wanderers (1876–77–78) and Blackburn (1884–85–86).

Trophy handed back: The FA Cup became the Wanderers' absolute property in 1878, but they handed it back to the Association on condition that it was not to be won outright by any club.

In successive years by professional clubs: Blackburn (1890 and 1891); Newcastle (1951 and 1952); Tottenham (1961 and 1962); Tottenham (1981 and 1982); Arsenal (2002 and 2003); Chelsea (2009–10).

Record Final-tie score: Bury 6, Derby 0 (1903).

Most FA Cup Final wins at Wembley: Manchester Utd 10, Arsenal 9, Chelsea 6, Tottenham 6, Liverpool 5, Newcastle 5.

SECOND DIVISION WINNERS

Notts Co (1894), **Wolves** (1908), **Barnsley** (1912), **WBA** (1931), **Sunderland** (1973), **Southampton** (1976), **West Ham** (1980). When **Tottenham** won the Cup in 1901 they were a Southern League club.

'OUTSIDE' SEMI-FINALISTS

Sheffield Utd, in 2014, became the ninth team from outside the top two divisions to reach the semi-finals, following **Millwall** (1937), **Port Vale** (1954), **York** (1955), **Norwich** (1959), **Crystal Palace** (1976), **Plymouth** (1984), **Chesterfield** (1997) and **Wycombe** (2001). None reached the Final.

FOURTH DIVISION QUARTER-FINALISTS

Oxford Utd (1964), **Colchester** (1971), **Bradford City** (1976), **Cambridge Utd** (1990).

FOURTH ROUND – NO REPLAYS

No replays were necessary in the 16 fourth round ties in January 2008 (7 home wins, 9 away). This had not happened for 51 years, since 8 home and 8 away wins in season 1956–57.

FIVE TROPHIES

The trophy which Arsenal won in 2014 was the fifth in FA Cup history. These were its predecessors:

1872–95: First Cup stolen from shop in Birmingham while held by Aston Villa. Never seen again.

1910: Second trophy presented to Lord Kinnaird on completing 21 years as FA president.

1911–91: Third trophy used until replaced ('battered and fragile') after 80 years' service.

1992–2013 Fourth FA Cup lasted 21 years – now retained at FA headquarters at Wembley Stadium.

Traditionally, the Cup stays with the holders until returned to the FA in March.

FINALISTS RELEGATED

Six clubs have reached the FA Cup Final and been relegated. The first five all lost at Wembley – **Manchester City** 1926, **Leicester** 1969, **Brighton** 1983, **Middlesbrough** 1997 and **Portsmouth** 2010. **Wigan,** Cup winners for the first time in 2013, were relegated from the Premier League three days later.

FA CUP – TOP SHOCKS

(2016 = season 2015–16; rounds shown in brackets; R = replay)

1922 (1)	Everton	0	Crystal Palace	6
1933 (3)	Walsall	2	Arsenal	0

1939 (F)	Portsmouth	4	Wolves	1
1948 (3)	Arsenal	0	Bradford PA	1
1948 (3)	Colchester	1	Huddersfield	0
1949 (4)	Yeovil	2	Sunderland	1
1954 (4)	Arsenal	1	Norwich	2
1955 (5)	York	2	Tottenham	1
1957 (4)	Wolves	0	Bournemouth	1
1957 (5)	Bournemouth	3	Tottenham	1
1958 (4)	Newcastle	1	Scunthorpe	3
1959 (3)	Norwich	3	Manchester Utd	0
1959 (3)	Worcester	2	Liverpool	1
1961 (3)	Chelsea	1	Crewe	2
1964 (3)	Newcastle	1	Bedford	2
1965 (4)	Peterborough	2	Arsenal	1
1971 (5)	Colchester	3	Leeds	2
1972 (3)	Hereford	2	Newcastle	1R
1973 (F)	Sunderland	1	Leeds	0
1975 (3)	Burnley	0	Wimbledon	1
1976 (F)	Southampton	1	Manchester Utd	0
1978 (F)	Ipswich	1	Arsenal	0
1980 (3)	Chelsea	0	Wigan	1
1980 (3)	Halifax	1	Manchester City	0
1980 (F)	West Ham	1	Arsenal	0
1981 (4)	Exeter	4	Newcastle	0R
1984 (3)	Bournemouth	2	Manchester Utd	0
1985 (4)	York	1	Arsenal	0
1986 (3)	Birmingham	1	Altrincham	2
1988 (F)	Wimbledon	1	Liverpool	0
1989 (3)	Sutton	2	Coventry	1
1991 (3)	WBA	2	Woking	4
1992 (3)	Wrexham	2	Arsenal	1
1994 (3)	Liverpool	0	Bristol City	1R
1994 (3)	Birmingham	1	Kidderminster	2
1997 (5)	Chesterfield	1	Nottm Forest	0
2001 (4)	Everton	0	Tranmere	3
2003 (3)	Shrewsbury	2	Everton	1
2005 (3)	Oldham	1	Manchester City	0
2008 (6)	Barnsley	1	Chelsea	0
2009 (2)	Histon	1	Leeds	0
2010 (4)	Liverpool	1	Reading	2R
2011 (3)	Stevenage	3	Newcastle	1
2012 (3)	Macclesfield	2	Cardiff	1
2013 (4)	Norwich	0	Luton	1
2013 (4)	Oldham	3	Liverpool	2
2013 (F)	Wigan	1	Manchester City	0
2014 (3)	Rochdale	2	Leeds	0
2015 (4)	Chelsea	2	Bradford City	4
2015 (5)	Bradford City	2	Sunderland	0
2016 (3)	Oxford	3	Swansea	2

YEOVIL TOP GIANT-KILLERS

Yeovil's victories over Colchester and Blackpool in season 2000–01 gave them a total of 20 FA Cup wins against League opponents. They set another non-League record by reaching the third round 13 times.

This was Yeovil's triumphant (non-League) Cup record against League clubs: 1924–25 Bournemouth 3-2; 1934–35 Crystal Palace 3-0, Exeter 4-1; 1938–39 Brighton 2-1; 1948–49 Bury 3-1, Sunderland 2-1; 1958–59 Southend 1-0; 1960–61 Walsall 1-0; 1963–64 Southend 1-0, Crystal Palace 3-1; 1970–71 Bournemouth 1-0; 1972–73 Brentford 2-1; 1987–88 Cambridge Utd 1-0; 1991–92 Walsall 1-0; 1992–93 Torquay 5-2, Hereford 2-1; 1993–94 Fulham 1-0; 1998–99 Northampton 2-0; 2000–01 Colchester 5-1, Blackpool 1-0.

NON-LEAGUE BEST

Since League football began in 1888, three non-League clubs have reached the FA Cup Final. **Sheffield Wed** (Football Alliance) were runners-up in 1890, as were **Southampton** (Southern League) in 1900 and 1902. **Tottenham** won the Cup as a Southern League team in 1901.

Otherwise, the furthest progress by non-League clubs has been to the 5th round on 7 occasions: **Colchester** 1948, **Yeovil** 1949, **Blyth** 1978, **Telford** 1985, **Kidderminster** 1994, **Crawley** 2011, **Luton** 2013.

Greatest number of non-League sides to reach the **3rd round** is **8** in 2009: **Barrow, Blyth, Eastwood, Forest Green, Histon, Kettering, Kidderminster** and **Torquay.**

Most to reach **Round 4: 3** in 1957 (**Rhyl, New Brighton, Peterborough**) and 1975 (**Leatherhead, Stafford** and **Wimbledon).**

Five non-League clubs reaching **round 3** in 2001 was a Conference record. They were **Chester, Yeovil, Dagenham, Morecambe** and **Kingstonian**.

In season 2002–03, **Team Bath** became the first University-based side to reach the FA Cup 1st Round since **Oxford University** (Finalists in 1880).

NON-LEAGUE 'LAST TIMES'

Last time no non-League club reached round 3: 1951. Last time only one did so: 1969 (**Kettering**).

TOP-DIVISION SCALPS

Victories in FA Cup by non-League clubs over top-division teams since 1900 include: 1900–01 (Final, replay): **Tottenham** 3 Sheffield Utd 1 (Tottenham then in Southern League); 1919–20 **Cardiff** 2, Oldham 0; Sheffield Wed 0, **Darlington** 2; 1923–24 **Corinthians** 1, Blackburn 0; 1947–48 **Colchester** 1, Huddersfield 0; 1948–9 **Yeovil** 2, Sunderland 1; 1971–72 **Hereford** 2, Newcastle 1; 1974–75 Burnley 0, **Wimbledon** 1; 1985–86 Birmingham 1, **Altrincham** 2; 1988–89 **Sutton** 2, Coventry 1; 2012–13 Norwich 0, **Luton** 1.

MOST WINNING MEDALS

Ashley Cole has won the trophy seven times, with (Arsenal 2002–03–05) and Chelsea (2007–09–10–12). **The Hon Arthur Kinnaird** (The Wanderers and Old Etonians), **Charles Wollaston** (The Wanderers) and **Jimmy Forrest** (Blackburn) each earned five winners' medals. Kinnaird, later president of the FA, played in nine of the first 12 FA Cup Finals, and was on the winning side three times for The Wanderers, in 1873 (captain), 1877, 1878 (captain), and twice as captain of Old Etonians (1879, 1882).

MANAGERS' MEDALS BACKDATED

In 2010, the FA agreed to award Cup Final medals to all living managers who took their teams to the Final before 1996 (when medals were first given to Wembley team bosses). Lawrie McMenemy had campaigned for the award since Southampton's victory in 1976.

MOST WINNERS' MEDALS AT WEMBLEY

4 – Mark Hughes (3 for Manchester Utd, 1 for Chelsea), **Petr Cech, Frank Lampard, John Terry, Didier Drogba, Ashley Cole** (all Chelsea).

3 – Dick Pym (3 clean sheets in Finals), **Bob Haworth, Jimmy Seddon, Harry Nuttall, Billy Butler** (all Bolton); **David Jack** (2 Bolton, 1 Arsenal); **Bob Cowell, Jack Milburn, Bobby Mitchell** (all Newcastle); **Dave Mackay** (Tottenham); **Frank Stapleton** (1 Arsenal, 2 Manchester Utd); **Bryan Robson (**3 times winning captain), **Arthur Albiston, Gary Pallister** (all Manchester Utd); **Bruce Grobbelaar, Steve Nicol, Ian Rush** (all Liverpool); **Roy Keane, Peter Schmeichel, Ryan Giggs**

(all Manchester Utd); **Dennis Wise** (1 Wimbledon, 2 Chelsea).

Arsenal's **David Seaman** and **Ray Parlour** have each earned 4 winners' medals (2 at Wembley, 2 at Cardiff) as have Manchester Utd's **Roy Keane** and **Ryan Giggs** (3 at Wembley, 1 at Cardiff).

MOST WEMBLEY FINALS

Nine players appeared in five FA Cup Finals at Wembley, replays excluded:

- **Joe Hulme** (Arsenal: 1927 lost, 1930 won, 1932 lost, 1936 won; Huddersfield: 1938 lost).
- **Johnny Giles** (Manchester Utd: 1963 won; Leeds: 1965 lost, 1970 drew at Wembley, lost replay at Old Trafford, 1972 won, 1973 lost).
- **Pat Rice** (all for Arsenal: 1971 won, 1972 lost, 1978 lost, 1979 won, 1980 lost).
- **Frank Stapleton** (Arsenal: 1978 lost, 1979 won, 1980 lost; Manchester Utd; 1983 won, 1985 won).
- **Ray Clemence** (Liverpool: 1971 lost, 1974 won, 1977 lost; Tottenham: 1982 won, 1987 lost).
- **Mark Hughes** (Manchester Utd: 1985 won, 1990 won, 1994 won, 1995 lost; Chelsea: 1997 won).
- **John Barnes** (Watford: 1984 lost; Liverpool: 1988 lost, 1989 won, 1996 lost; Newcastle: 1998 sub, lost): – first player to lose Wembley FA Cup Finals with three different clubs.
- **Roy Keane** (Nottm Forest: 1991 lost; Manchester Utd: 1994 won, 1995 lost, 1996 won, 1999 won).
- **Ryan Giggs** (Manchester Utd: 1994 won, 1995 lost, 1996 won, 1999 won, 2007 lost).
- Clemence, Hughes and Stapleton also played in a replay, making six actual FA Cup Final appearances for each of them.
- **Glenn Hoddle** also made six appearances at Wembley: 5 for Tottenham (incl. 2 replays), in 1981 won, 1982 won and 1987 lost, and 1 for Chelsea as sub in 1994 lost.
- **Paul Bracewell** played in four FA Cup Finals without being on the winning side – for Everton 1985, 1986, 1989, Sunderland 1992.

MOST WEMBLEY/CARDIFF FINAL APPEARANCES

8 by **Ashley Cole** (Arsenal: 2001 lost; 2002 won; 2003 won; 2005 won; Chelsea: 2007 won; 2009 won; 2010 won, 2012 won).

7 by **Roy Keane** (Nottm Forest: 1991 lost; Manchester Utd: 1994 won; 1995 lost; 1996 won; 1999 won; 2004 won; 2005 lost).

7 by **Ryan Giggs** (Manchester Utd): 1994 won; 1995 lost; 1996 won; 1999 won; 2004 won; 2005 lost; 2007 lost.

6 by **Paul Scholes** (Manchester Utd): 1995 lost; 1996 won; 1999 won; 2004 won; 2005 lost; 2007 lost.

5 by **David Seaman** and **Ray Parlour** (Arsenal): 1993 won; 1998 won; 2001 lost; 2002 won; 2003 won; **Dennis Wise** (Wimbledon 1988 won; Chelsea 1994 lost; 1997 won; 2000 won; Millwall 2004 lost); Patrick Vieira (Arsenal): 1998 won; 2001 lost; 2002 won; 2005 won; (Manchester City) 2011 won.

BIGGEST FA CUP SCORE AT WEMBLEY

5-0 by Stoke v Bolton (semi-final, Apr 17, 2011.

WINNING GOALKEEPER-CAPTAINS

1988 **Dave Beasant** (Wimbledon); 2003 **David Seaman** (Arsenal).

MOST WINNING MANAGERS

6 Arsene Wenger (Arsenal) 1998, 2002, 2003, 2005, 20014, 2015; **5 Sir Alex Ferguson** (Manchester Utd 1990, 1994, 1996, 1999, 2004).

PLAYER-MANAGERS IN FINAL

Kenny Dalglish (Liverpool, 1986); **Glenn Hoddle** (Chelsea, 1994); **Dennis Wise** (Millwall, 2004).

DEBUTS IN FINAL

Alan Davies (Manchester Utd v Brighton, 1983); **Chris Baird** (Southampton v Arsenal, 2003); **Curtis Weston** (Millwall sub v Manchester Utd, 2004).

SEMI-FINALS AT WEMBLEY

1991 Tottenham 3 Arsenal 1; **1993** Sheffield Wed 2 Sheffield Utd 1, Arsenal 1 Tottenham 0; **1994** Chelsea 2 Luton 0, Manchester Utd 1 Oldham 1; **2000** Aston Villa beat Bolton 4-1 on pens (after 0-0), Chelsea 2 Newcastle 1; **2008** Portsmouth 1 WBA 0, Cardiff 1 Barnsley 0; **2009** Chelsea 2 Arsenal 1, Everton beat Manchester Utd 4-2 on pens (after 0-0); **2010** Chelsea 3 Aston Villa 0, Portsmouth 2 Tottenham 0; **2011** Manchester City 1 Manchester Utd 0, Stoke 5 Bolton 0; **2012** Liverpool 2 Everton 1, Chelsea 5 Tottenham 1; **2013** Wigan 2 Millwall 0, Manchester City 2 Chelsea 1; **2014** Arsenal beat Wigan 4-2 on pens (after 1-1), Hull 5 Sheffield Utd 3; **2015** Arsenal 2 Reading 1, Aston Villa 2 Liverpool 1; **2016** Manchester Utd 2 Everton 1, Crystal Palace 2 Watford 1

CHELSEA'S FA CUP MILESTONES

Their victory over Liverpool in the 2012 Final set the following records:

Captain **John Terry** first player to lift the trophy four times for one club; **Didier Drogba** first to score in four Finals; **Ashley Cole** first to earn seven winner's medals (Arsenal 3, Chelsea 4); **Roberto Di Matteo** first to score for and manage the same winning club (player for Chelsea 1997, 2000, interim manager 2012).

Chelsea's four triumphs in six seasons (2007–12) the best winning sequence since Wanderers won five of the first seven competitions (1872–78) and Blackburn won five out of eight (1884–91).

FIRST ENTRANTS (1871–72)

Barnes, Civil Service, Crystal Palace, Clapham Rov, Donnington School (Spalding), Hampstead Heathens, Harrow Chequers, Hitchin, Maidenhead, Marlow, Queen's Park (Glasgow), Reigate Priory, Royal Engineers, Upton Park and Wanderers. Total 15.

LAST ALL-ENGLISH WINNERS

Manchester City, in 1969, were the last club to win the final with a team of all English players.

FA CUP FIRSTS

Out of country: Cardiff, by defeating Arsenal 1-0 in the 1927 Final at Wembley, became the first and only club to take the FA Cup out of England.

All-English Winning XI: First club to win the FA Cup with all-English XI: Blackburn Olympic in 1883. Others since: WBA in 1888 and 1931, Bolton (1958), Manchester City (1969), West Ham (1964 and 1975).

Non-English Winning XI: Liverpool in 1986 (Mark Lawrenson, born Preston, was a Rep of Ireland player).

Won both Cups: Old Carthusians won the FA Cup in 1881 and the FA Amateur Cup in 1894 and 1897. **Wimbledon** won Amateur Cup in 1963, FA Cup in 1988.

MOST GAMES NEEDED TO WIN

Barnsley played a record 12 matches (20 hours' football) to win the FA Cup in season 1911–12. All six replays (one in round 1, three in round 4 and one in each of semi-final and Final) were brought about by goalless draws.

Arsenal played 11 FA Cup games when winning the trophy in 1979. Five of them were in the 3rd round against Sheffield Wed.

LONGEST TIES

6 matches: (11 hours): Alvechurch v Oxford City (4th qual round, 1971–72). Alvechurch won 1-0.

5 matches: (9 hours, 22 mins – record for competition proper): Stoke v Bury (3rd round, 1954–55). Stoke won 3-2.

5 matches: Chelsea v Burnley (4th round, 1955–56). Chelsea won 2-0.

5 matches: Hull v Darlington (2nd round, 1960–61). Hull won 3-0.

5 matches: Arsenal v Sheffield Wed (3rd round, 1978–79). Arsenal won 2-0.

Other marathons (qualifying comp, all 5 matches, 9 hours): Barrow v Gillingham (last qual round, 1924–25) – winners Barrow; Leyton v Ilford (3rd qual round, 1924–25) – winners Leyton; Falmouth v Bideford (3rd qual round, 1973–74) – winners Bideford.

End of Cup Final replays: The FA decided that, with effect from 1999, there would be no Cup Final replays. In the event of a draw after extra-time, the match would be decided on penalties. This happened for the first time in 2005, when Arsenal beat Manchester Utd 5-4 on penalties after a 0-0 draw. A year later, Liverpool beat West Ham 3-1 on penalties after a 3-3 draw.

FA Cup marathons ended in season 1991–92, when the penalty shoot-out was introduced to decide ties still level after one replay and extra-time.

In 1932–33 **Brighton** (Div 3 South) played 11 FA Cup games, including replays, and scored 43 goals, without getting past round 5. They forgot to claim exemption and had to play from 1st qual round.

LONGEST ROUND

The longest round in FA Cup history was the **3rd round** in **1962–63**. It took 66 days to complete, lasting from Jan 5 to Mar 11, and included 261 postponements because of bad weather.

LONGEST UNBEATEN RUN

23 matches by Blackburn In winning the Cup in three consecutive years (1884–05–06), they won 21 ties (one in a replay), and their first Cup defeat in four seasons was in a first round replay of the next competition.

RE-STAGED TIES

Sixth round, Mar 9, 1974: Newcastle 4, Nottm Forest 3. Match declared void by FA and ordered to be replayed following a pitch invasion after Newcastle had a player sent off. Forest claimed the hold-up caused the game to change its pattern. The tie went to two further matches at Goodison Park (0-0, then 1-0 to Newcastle).

Third round, Jan 5, 1985: Burton 1, Leicester 6 (at Derby). Burton goalkeeper Paul Evans was hit on the head by a missile thrown from the crowd and continued in a daze. The FA ordered the tie to be played again, behind closed doors at Coventry (Leicester won 1-0).

First round replay, Nov 25, 1992: Peterborough 9 (Tony Philliskirk 5), Kingstonian 1. Match expunged from records because, at 3-0 after 57 mins, Kingstonian were reduced to ten men when goalkeeper Adrian Blake was concussed by a 50 pence coin thrown from the crowd. The tie was re-staged on the same ground behind closed doors (Peterborough won 1-0).

Fifth round: Within an hour of holders Arsenal beating Sheffield Utd 2-1 at Highbury on Feb 13, 1999, the FA took the unprecedented step of declaring the match void because an unwritten rule of sportsmanship had been broken. With United's Lee Morris lying injured, their goalkeeper Alan Kelly kicked the ball into touch. Play resumed with Arsenal's Ray Parlour throwing it in the direction of Kelly, but Nwankwo Kanu took possession and centred for Marc Overmars to score the 'winning' goal. After four minutes of protests by manager Steve Bruce and his players, referee Peter Jones confirmed the goal. Both managers absolved Kanu of cheating but Arsenal's Arsene Wenger offered to replay the match. With the FA immediately approving, it was re-staged at Highbury ten days later (ticket prices halved) and Arsenal again won 2-1.

PRIZE FUND

The makeover of the FA Cup competition took off in 2001–02 with the introduction of round-by-round prize-money.

FA CUP FOLLIES

1999–2000 The FA broke with tradition by deciding the 3rd round be moved from its regular Jan date and staged before Christmas. Criticism was strong, gates poor and the 3rd round in 2000–01 reverted to the New Year. By allowing the holders Manchester Utd to withdraw from the 1999–2000 competition in order to play in FIFA's inaugural World Club Championship in Brazil in Jan, the FA were left with an odd number of clubs in the 3rd round. Their solution was a 'lucky losers' draw among clubs knocked out in round 2. Darlington, beaten at Gillingham, won it to re-enter the competition, then lost 2-1 away to Aston Villa.

HAT-TRICKS IN FINAL

There have been three in the history of the competition: **Billy Townley** (Blackburn, 1890), **Jimmy Logan** (Notts Co, 1894) and **Stan Mortensen** (Blackpool, 1953).

MOST APPEARANCES

88 by **Ian Callaghan** (79 for Liverpool, 7 for Swansea City, 2 for Crewe); **87** by **John Barnes** (31 for Watford, **51** for Liverpool, 5 for Newcastle); **86** by **Stanley Matthews** (37 for Stoke, 49 for Blackpool); **84** by **Bobby Charlton** (80 for Manchester Utd, 4 for Preston); **84** by **Pat Jennings** (3 for Watford, 43 for Tottenham, 38 for Arsenal); **84** by **Peter Shilton** for seven clubs (30 for Leicester, 7 for Stoke, **18** for Nottm Forest, 17 for Southampton, 10 for Derby, 1 for Plymouth Argyle, 1 for Leyton Orient); **82** by **David Seaman** (5 for Peterborough, 5 for Birmingham, 17 for QPR, 54 for Arsenal, 1 for Manchester City).

THREE-CLUB FINALISTS

Five players have appeared in the FA Cup Final for three clubs: **Harold Halse** for Manchester Utd (1909), Aston Villa (1913) and Chelsea (1915); **Ernie Taylor** for Newcastle (1951), Blackpool (1953) and Manchester Utd (1958); **John Barnes** for Watford (1984), Liverpool (1988, 1989, 1996) and Newcastle (1998); **Dennis Wise** for Wimbledon (1988), Chelsea (1994, 1997, 2000), Millwall (2004); **David James** for Liverpool (1996), Aston Villa (2000) and Portsmouth (2008, 2010).

CUP MAN WITH TWO CLUBS IN SAME SEASON

Stan Crowther, who played for Aston Villa against Manchester Utd in the 1957 FA Cup Final, appeared for both Villa and United in the 1957–58 competition. United signed him directly after the Munich air crash and, in the circumstances, he was given dispensation to play for them in the Cup, including the Final.

CAPTAIN'S CUP DOUBLE

Martin Buchan is the only player to have captained Scottish and English FA Cup-winning teams – Aberdeen in 1970 and Manchester Utd in 1977.

MEDALS BEFORE AND AFTER

Two players appeared in FA Cup Final teams before and after the Second World War: **Raich Carter** was twice a winner (Sunderland 1937, Derby 1946) and **Willie Fagan** twice on the losing side (Preston 1937, Liverpool 1950).

DELANEY'S COLLECTION

Scotland winger **Jimmy Delaney** uniquely earned Scottish, English, Northern Ireland and Republic of Ireland Cup medals. He was a winner with Celtic (1937), Manchester Utd (1948) and Derry City (1954) and a runner-up with Cork City (1956).

STARS WHO MISSED OUT

Internationals who never won an FA Cup winner's medal include: Tommy Lawton, Tom Finney, Johnny Haynes, Gordon Banks, George Best, Terry Butcher, Peter Shilton, Martin Peters, Nobby Stiles, Alan Ball, Malcolm Macdonald, Alan Shearer, Matthew Le Tissier, Stuart Pearce, Des Walker, Phil Neal, Ledley King.

CUP WINNERS AT NO COST

Not one member of **Bolton**'s 1958 FA Cup-winning team cost the club a transfer fee. Each joined the club for a £10 signing-on fee.

11-NATIONS LINE-UP

Liverpool fielded a team of 11 different nationalities in the FA Cup 3rd round at Yeovil on Jan 4, 2004.

HIGH-SCORING SEMI-FINALS

The **record team score** in FA Cup semi-finals is **6**: 1891–92 WBA 6, Nottm Forest 2; 1907–08 Newcastle 6, Fulham 0; 1933–34 Manchester City 6, Aston Villa 1.

Most goals in semi-finals (aggregate): 17 in 1892 (4 matches) and 1899 (5 matches). In modern times: 15 in 1958 (3 matches, including Manchester Utd 5, Fulham 3 – highest-scoring semi-final since last war); 16 in 1989–90 (Crystal Palace 4, Liverpool 3; Manchester Utd v Oldham 3-3, 2-1. All **16 goals** in those three matches were scored by **different players**.

Stoke's win against Bolton at Wembley in 2011 was the first 5-0 semi-final result since Wolves beat Grimsby at Old Trafford in 1939. In 2014, Hull defeated Sheffield Utd 5-3.

Last hat-trick in an FA Cup semi-final was scored by **Alex Dawson** for Manchester Utd in 5-3 replay win against Fulham at Highbury in 1958.

SEMI-FINAL VENUES

Villa Park has staged more such matches (55 including replays) than any other ground. Next is Hillsborough (33).

ONE IN A HUNDRED

The 2008 semi-finals included only one top-division club, Portsmouth, for the first time in 100 years – since Newcastle in 1908.

FOUR SPECIAL AWAYS

For the only time in FA Cup history, **all four quarter-finals** in season 1986–87 were won by the away team.

DRAWS RECORD

In season 1985–86, **seven** of the eight 5th round ties went to replays – a record for that stage of the competition.

SHOCK FOR TOP CLUBS

The fourth round on Jan 24, 2015 produced an astonishing set of home defeats for leading clubs. The top three in the Premier League, Chelsea, Manchester City and Southampton were all knocked out and sixth-place Tottenham also lost at home. Odds against this happening were put at 3825-1.

LUCK OF THE DRAW

In the FA Cup on Jan 11, 1947, eight of **London**'s ten Football League clubs involved in the 3rd round were drawn at home (including Chelsea v Arsenal). Only Crystal Palace played outside the capital (at Newcastle).

In the 3rd round in Jan 1992, Charlton were the only London club drawn at home (against Barnet), but the venue of the Farnborough v West Ham tie was reversed on police instruction. So Upton Park staged Cup ties on successive days, with West Ham at home on the Saturday and Charlton (who shared the ground) on Sunday.

Arsenal were drawn away in every round on the way to reaching the Finals of 1971 and 1972. **Manchester Utd** won the Cup in 1990 without playing once at home.

The 1999 finalists, **Manchester Utd** and **Newcastle,** were both drawn at home every time in Rounds 3–6.

On their way to the semi-finals of both domestic Cup competitions in season 2002–03, **Sheffield**

Utd were drawn at home ten times out of ten and won all ten matches – six in the League's Worthington Cup and four in the FA Cup.

On their way to winning the Cup in 2014, **Arsenal** did not play once outside London. Home draws in rounds 3, 4, 5 and 6 were followed by the semi-final at Wembley.

ALL TOP-DIVISION VICTIMS

The only instance of an FA Cup-winning club meeting top-division opponents in every round was provided by Manchester Utd in 1947–48. They beat Aston Villa, Liverpool, Charlton, Preston, then Derby in the semi-final and Blackpool in the Final.

In contrast, these clubs have reached the Final without playing top-division opponents on the way: West Ham (1923), Bolton (1926), Blackpool (1948), Bolton (1953), Millwall (2004).

WON CUP WITHOUT CONCEDING GOAL

1873 **The Wanderers** (1 match; as holders, exempt until Final); 1889 **Preston** (5 matches); 1903 **Bury** (5 matches). In 1966 **Everton** reached Final without conceding a goal (7 matches), then beat Sheffield Wed 3-2 at Wembley.

HOME ADVANTAGE

For the first time in FA Cup history, all eight ties in the 1992–93 5th round were won (no replays) by the **clubs drawn at home.** Only other instance of eight home wins at the last 16 stage was in 1889–90, in what was then the 2nd round.

NORTH-EAST WIPE-OUT

For the first time in 54 years, since the 4th round in Jan, 1957, the North-East's 'big three' were knocked out on the same date, Jan 8, 2011 (3rd round). All lost to lower-division opponents – **Newcastle** 3-1 at Stevenage, **Sunderland** 2-1 at home to Notts County and **Middlesbrough** 2-1 at Burton.

FEWEST TOP-DIVISION CLUBS IN LAST 16 (5th ROUND)

5 in 1958; **6** in 1927, 1970, 1982; **7** in 1994, 2003; **8** in 2002, 2004.

SIXTH-ROUND ELITE

For the first time in FA Cup 6th round history, dating from 1926 when the format of the competition changed, all **eight quarter-finalists** in 1995–96 were from the top division.

SEMI-FINAL – DOUBLE DERBIES

There have been three instances of both FA Cup semi-finals in the same year being local derbies: **1950** Liverpool beat Everton 2-0 (Maine Road), Arsenal beat Chelsea 1-0 after 2-2 draw (both at Tottenham); **1993** Arsenal beat Tottenham 1-0 (Wembley), Sheffield Wed beat Sheffield Utd 2-1 (Wembley); **2012** Liverpool beat Everton 2-1 (Wembley), Chelsea beat Tottenham 5-1 (Wembley).

TOP CLUB DISTINCTION

Since the Football League began in 1888, there has never been an FA Cup Final in which **neither club** represented the top division.

CLUBS THROWN OUT

Bury expelled (Dec 2006) for fielding an ineligible player in 3-1 2nd rd replay win at Chester. **Droylsden** expelled for fielding a suspended player in 2-1 2nd rd replay win at home to Chesterfield (Dec 2008).

SPURS OUT – AND IN

Tottenham were banned, pre-season, from the 1994–95 competition because of financial irregularities, but were re-admitted on appeal and reached the semi-finals.

FATHER & SON FA CUP WINNERS

Peter Boyle (Sheffield Utd 1899, 1902) and **Tommy Boyle** (Sheffield Utd 1925); **Harry Johnson Snr** (Sheffield Utd 1899, 1902) and **Harry Johnson Jnr** (Sheffield Utd 1925); **Jimmy Dunn Snr** (Everton 1933) and **Jimmy Dunn Jnr** (Wolves 1949); **Alec Herd** (Manchester City 1934) and **David Herd** (Manchester Utd 1963); **Frank Lampard Snr** (West Ham 1975, 1980) and **Frank Lampard Jnr** (Chelsea 2007, 2009, 2010, 2012).

BROTHERS IN FA CUP FINAL TEAMS (modern times)

1950 **Denis and Leslie Compton** (Arsenal); 1952 **George and Ted Robledo** (Newcastle); 1967 **Ron and Allan Harris** (Chelsea); 1977 **Jimmy and Brian Greenhoff** (Manchester Utd); 1996 and 1999 **Gary and Phil Neville** (Manchester Utd).

FA CUP SPONSORS

Littlewoods Pools became the first sponsors of the FA Cup in season 1994–95 in a £14m, 4-year deal. French insurance giants **AXA** took over (season 1998–99) in a sponsorship worth £25m over 4 years. German energy company **E.ON** agreed a 4-year deal worth £32m from season 2006–07 and extended it for a year to 2011. American beer company **Budweiser** began a three-year sponsorship worth £24m in season 2011–12. The **Emirates** airline became the first title sponsor (2015-18) in a reported £30m deal with the FA.

FIRST GOALKEEPER-SUBSTITUTE IN FINAL

Paul Jones (Southampton), who replaced injured Antti Niemi against Arsenal in 2003.

LEAGUE CUP RECORDS

(See also Goalscoring section)

Highest scores: West Ham 10-0 v Bury (2nd round, 2nd leg 1983–84; agg 12-1); Liverpool 10-0 v Fulham (2nd round, 1st leg 1986–87; agg 13-2).

Most League Cup goals (career): 49 Geoff Hurst (43 West Ham, 6 Stoke, 1960–75); 49 Ian Rush (48 Liverpool, 1 Newcastle, 1981–98).

Highest scorer (season): 12 Clive Allen (Tottenham 1986–87 in 9 apps).

Most goals in match: 6 Frank Bunn (Oldham v Scarborough, 3rd round, 1989–90).

Most winners' medals: 5 Ian Rush (Liverpool).

Most appearances in Final: 6 Kenny Dalglish (Liverpool 1978–87), Ian Rush (Liverpool 1981–95). Emile Heskey (Leicester 1997, 1999, 2000), Liverpool (2001, 2003), Aston Villa (2010)

Biggest Final win: Swansea City 5 Bradford City 0 (2013).

League Cup sponsors: Milk Cup 1981–86, Littlewoods Cup 1987–90, Rumbelows Cup 1991–92, Coca-Cola Cup 1993–98. Worthington Cup 1999–2003, Carling Cup 2003–12; Capital One Cup from season 2012–16.

Up for the cup, then down: In 2011, Birmingham became only the second club to win a major trophy (the Carling Cup) and be relegated from the top division. It previously happened to Norwich in 1985 when they went down from the old First Division after winning the Milk Cup.

Liverpool's League Cup records: Winners a record 8 times. **Ian Rush** only player to win 5 times. Rush also first to play in 8 winning teams in Cup Finals **at Wembley**, all with Liverpool (FA Cup 1986–89–92; League Cup 1981–82–83–84–95).

Britain's first under-cover Cup Final: Worthington Cup Final between Blackburn and Tottenham at Cardiff's Millennium Stadium on Sunday, Feb 24, 2002. With rain forecast, the retractable roof was closed on the morning of the match.

Record penalty shoot-out: Liverpool beat Middlesbrough 14-13 (3rd round, Sep 23, 2014) after 2-2.

DISCIPLINE

SENDINGS-OFF

Season 2003–04 set an **all-time record** of 504 players sent off in English domestic football competitions. There were 58 in the Premiership, 390 Nationwide League, 28 FA Cup (excluding non-League dismissals), 22 League Cup, 2 in Nationwide play-offs, 4 in LDV Vans Trophy.

Most sendings-off in Premier League programme (10 matches): 9 (8 Sat, 1 Sun, Oct 31–Nov 1, 2009).

The 58 Premiership red cards was 13 fewer than the record English **top-division** total of 71 in 2002–03. **Bolton** were the only club in the English divisions without a player sent off in any first-team competition that season.

Worst day for dismissals in English football was Boxing Day, 2007, with **20 red cards** (5 Premier League and 15 Coca-Cola League). Three players, Chelsea's Ashley Cole and Ricardo Carvalho and Aston Villa's Zat Knight were sent off in a 4-4 draw at Stamford Bridge. Luton had three men dismissed in their game at Bristol Rov, but still managed a 1-1 draw.

Previous worst day was Dec 13, 2003, with **19 red cards** (2 Premiership and the 17 Nationwide League).

In the entire first season of post-war League football (1946–47) only 12 players were sent off, followed by 14 in 1949–50, and the total League dismissals for the first nine seasons after the War was 104.

The worst pre-War total was 28 in each of seasons 1921–22 and 1922–23.

ENGLAND SENDINGS-OFF

In a total of 15 England dismissals, David Beckham and Wayne Rooney have been red-carded twice. Beckham and Steven Gerrard are the only England captains to be sent off and Robert Green the only goalkeeper.

Jun 5, 1968	**Alan Mullery**	v Yugoslavia (Florence, Euro Champ)
Jun 6, 1973	**Alan Ball**	v Poland (Chorzow, World Cup qual)
Jun 12, 1977	**Trevor Cherry**	v Argentina (Buenos Aires, friendly)
Jun 6, 1986	**Ray Wilkins**	v Morocco (Monterrey, World Cup Finals)
Jun 30, 1998	**David Beckham**	v Argentina (St Etienne, World Cup Finals)
Sep 5, 1998	**Paul Ince**	v Sweden (Stockholm, Euro Champ qual)
Jun 5, 1999	**Paul Scholes**	v Sweden (Wembley, Euro Champ qual)
Sep 8, 1999	**David Batty**	v Poland (Warsaw, Euro Champ qual)
Oct 16, 2002	**Alan Smith**	v Macedonia (Southampton, Euro Champ qual)
Oct 8, 2005	**David Beckham**	v Austria (Old Trafford, World Cup qual)
Jul 1, 2006	**Wayne Rooney**	v Portugal (Gelsenkirchen, World Cup Finals)
Oct 10, 2009	**Robert Green**	v Ukraine (Dnipropetrovsk, World Cup qual)
Oct 7, 2011	**Wayne Rooney**	v Montenegro (Podgorica, Euro Champ qual)
Sep 11, 2012	**Steven Gerrard**	v Ukraine (Wembley, World Cup qual)
Jun 4, 2014	**Raheem Sterling**	v Ecuador (Miami, friendly)

Other countries: Most recent sendings-off of players representing other Home Countries:
N Ireland – Chris Baird (European Champ qual v Hungary, Belfast, Sep 7, 2015).
Scotland – Charlie Mulgrew (European Champ qual v Germany, Dortmund, Sep 7, 2014).
Wales – Andy King (European Champ qual v Cyprus, Cardiff, Oct 13, 2014).
Rep of Ireland – Shane Duffy (European Champ v France, Lyon, June 26, 2016).
England dismissals at other levels:

U-23: Stan Anderson (v Bulgaria, Sofia, May 19, 1957); **Alan Ball** (v Austria, Vienna, Jun 2, 1965); **Kevin Keegan** (v E Germany, Magdeburg, Jun 1, 1972); **Steve Perryman** (v Portugal, Lisbon, Nov 19, 1974).

U-21: Sammy Lee (v Hungary, Keszthely, Jun 5, 1981); **Mark Hateley** (v Scotland, Hampden Park, Apr 19, 1982); **Paul Elliott** (v Denmark, Maine Road, Manchester, Mar 26, 1986); **Tony**

Cottee (v W Germany, Ludenscheid, Sep 8, 1987); **Julian Dicks** (v Mexico, Toulon, France, Jun 12, 1988); **Jason Dodd** (v Mexico, Toulon, May 29, 1991; 3 Mexico players also sent off in that match); **Matthew Jackson** (v France, Toulon, May 28, 1992); **Robbie Fowler** (v Austria, Kafkenberg, Oct 11, 1994); **Alan Thompson** (v Portugal, Oporto, Sep 2, 1995); **Terry Cooke** (v Portugal, Toulon, May 30, 1996); **Ben Thatcher** (v Italy, Rieti, Oct 10, 1997); **John Curtis** (v Greece, Heraklion, Nov 13, 1997); **Jody Morris** (v Luxembourg, Grevenmacher, Oct 13, 1998); **Stephen Wright** (v Germany, Derby, Oct 6, 2000); **Alan Smith** (v Finland, Valkeakoski, Oct 10, 2000); **Luke Young** and **John Terry** (v Greece, Athens, Jun 5, 2001); **Shola Ameobi** (v Portugal, Rio Maior, Mar 28, 2003); **Jermaine Pennant** (v Croatia, Upton Park, Aug 19, 2003); **Glen Johnson** (v Turkey, Istanbul, Oct 10, 2003); **Nigel Reo-Coker** (v Azerbaijan, Baku, Oct 12, 2004); **Glen Johnson** (v Spain, Henares, Nov 16, 2004); **Steven Taylor** (v Germany, Leverkusen, Oct 10, 2006); **Tom Huddlestone** (v Serbia & Montenegro, Nijmegen, Jun 17, 2007); **Tom Huddlestone** (v Wales, Villa Park, Oct 14, 2008); **Michael Mancienne** (v Finland, Halmstad, Jun 15, 2009); **Fraizer Campbell** (v Sweden, Gothenburg, Jun 26, 2009); **Ben Mee** (v Italy, Empoli, Feb 8, 2011); **Danny Rose** (v Serbia, Krusevac, Oct 16, 2012); **Andre Wisdom** (v Finland, Tampere, Sep 9, 2013); **Jack Stephens** (v Bosnia-Herz, Sarajevo, Nov 12, 2015; **Jordon Ibe** (vSwitzerland, Thun, Mar 26, 2016.

England 'B' (1): **Neil Webb** (v Algeria, Algiers, Dec 11, 1990).

MOST DISMISSALS IN INTERNATIONAL MATCHES

19 (10 Chile, 9 Uruguay), Jun 25, 1975; **6** (2 Mexico, 4 Argentina), 1956; **6** (5 Ecuador, 1 Uruguay), Jan 4, 1977 (4 Ecuadorians sent off in 78th min, match abandoned, 1-1); **5** (Holland 3, Brazil 2), Jun 6, 1999 in Goianio, Brazil.

INTERNATIONAL STOPPED THROUGH DEPLETED SIDE

Portugal v Angola (5-1), friendly international in Lisbon on Nov 14, 2001, abandoned (68 mins) because Angola were down to 6 players (4 sent off, 1 carried off, no substitutes left).

MOST 'CARDS' IN WORLD CUP FINALS MATCH

20 in Portugal v Holland quarter-final, Nuremberg, Jun 25, 2006 (9 yellow, 2 red, Portugal; 7 yellow, 2 red, Holland).

FIVE OFF IN ONE MATCH

For the first time since League football began in 1888, five players were sent off in one match (two Chesterfield, three Plymouth) in Div 2 at Saltergate on **Feb 22, 1997.** Four were dismissed (two from each side) in a goalmouth brawl in the last minute. Five were sent off on Dec 2, 1997 (4 Bristol Rov, 1 Wigan) in Div 2 match at Wigan, four in the 45th minute. The third instance occurred at Exeter on **Nov 23, 2002** in Div 3 (three Exeter, two Cambridge United) all in the last minute. On **Mar 27, 2012** (Lge 2) three Bradford players and two from Crawley were shown red cards in the dressing rooms after a brawl at the final whistle at Valley Parade.

Matches with **four** Football League club players being sent off in one match:

Jan 8, 1955: Crewe v Bradford City (Div 3 North), two players from each side.

Dec 13, 1986: Sheffield Utd (1 player) v Portsmouth (3) in Div 2.

Aug 18, 1987: Port Vale v Northampton (Littlewoods Cup 1st Round, 1st Leg), two players from each side.

Dec 12, 1987: Brentford v Mansfield (Div 3), two players from each side.

Sep 6, 1992: First instance in British first-class football of four players from one side being sent off in one match. Hereford's seven survivors, away to Northampton (Div 3), held out for a 1-1 draw.

Mar 1, 1977: Norwich v Huddersfield (Div 1), two from each side.

Oct 4, 1977: Shrewsbury (1 player), Rotherham (3) in Div 3.

Aug 22, 1998: Gillingham v Bristol Rov (Div 2), two from each side, all after injury-time brawl.

Mar 16, 2001: Bristol City v Millwall (Div 2), two from each side.

Aug 17, 2002: Lincoln (1 player), Carlisle (3) in Div 3.

Aug 26, 2002: Wycombe v QPR (Div 2), two from each side.
Nov 1, 2005: Burnley (1 player) v Millwall (3) in Championship.
Nov 24, 2007: Swindon v Bristol Rov (Lge 1), two from each side.
Mar 4, 2008: Hull v Burnley (Champ) two from each side.

Four Stranraer players were sent off away to Airdrie (Scottish Div 1) on Dec 3, 1994, and that Scottish record was equalled when four Hearts men were ordered off away to Rangers (Prem Div) on Sep 14, 1996. Albion had four players sent off (3 in last 8 mins) away to Queen's Park (Scottish Div 3) on Aug 23, 1997.

In the **Island Games** in Guernsey (Jul 2003), five players (all from Rhodes) were sent off against Guernsey for violent conduct and the match was abandoned by referee Wendy Toms.

Most dismissals one team, one match: Five players of America Tres Rios in first ten minutes after disputed goal by opponents Itaperuna in Brazilian cup match in Rio de Janeiro on Nov 23, 1991. Tie then abandoned and awarded to Itaperuna.

Eight dismissals in one match: Four on each side in South American Super Cup quarter-final (Gremio, Brazil v Penarol, Uruguay) in Oct 1993.

Five dismissals in one season – Dave Caldwell (2 with Chesterfield, 3 with Torquay) in 1987–88.

First instance of four dismissals in Scottish match: three Rangers players (all English – Terry Hurlock, Mark Walters, Mark Hateley) and Celtic's Peter Grant in Scottish Cup quarter-final at Parkhead on Mar 17, 1991 (Celtic won 2-0).

Four players (3 Hamilton, 1 Airdrie) were sent off in Scottish Div 1 match on Oct 30, 1993.

Four players (3 Ayr, 1 Stranraer) were sent off in Scottish Div 1 match on Aug 27, 1994.

In Scottish Cup first round replays on Dec 16, 1996, there were two instances of three players of one side sent off: Albion Rov (away to Forfar) and Huntly (away to Clyde).

FASTEST SENDINGS-OFF

World record – 10 sec: Giuseppe Lorenzo (Bologna) for striking opponent in Italian League match v Parma, Dec 9, 1990. Goalkeeper **Preston Edwards** (Ebbsfleet) for bringing down opponent and conceding penalty in Blue Square Premier League South match v Farnborough, Feb 5, 2011.

World record (non-professional) – 3 sec: David Pratt (Chippenham) at Bashley (British Gas Southern Premier League, Dec 27, 2008).

Domestic – 13 sec: Kevin Pressman (Sheffield Wed goalkeeper at Wolves, Div 1, Sunday, Aug 14, 2000); **15 sec: Simon Rea** (Peterborough at Cardiff, Div 2, Nov 2, 2002). **19 sec: Mark Smith** (Crewe goalkeeper at Darlington, Div 3, Mar 12, 1994). **Premier League – 72 sec: Tim Flowers** (Blackburn goalkeeper v Leeds Utd, Feb 1, 1995).

In World Cup – 55 sec: Jose Batista (Uruguay v Scotland at Neza, Mexico, Jun 13, 1986).

In European competition – 90 sec: Sergei Dirkach (Dynamo Moscow v Ghent UEFA Cup 3rd round, 2nd leg, Dec 11, 1991).

Fastest FA Cup dismissal – 52 sec: Ian Culverhouse (Swindon defender, deliberate hand-ball on goal-line, away to Everton, 3rd Round, Sunday Jan 5, 1997).

Fastest League Cup dismissal – 33 sec: Jason Crowe (Arsenal substitute v Birmingham, 3rd Round, Oct 14, 1997). Also fastest sending off on debut.

Fastest Sending-off of substitute – 0 sec: Walter Boyd (Swansea City) for striking opponent before ball in play after he went on (83 mins) at home to Darlington, Div 3, Nov 23, 1999. **15 secs: Keith Gillespie** (Sheffield Utd) for striking an opponent at Reading (Premiership), Jan 20, 2007. **90 sec: Andreas Johansson** (Wigan), without kicking a ball, for shirt-pulling (penalty) away to Arsenal (Premiership), May 7, 2006.

MOST SENDINGS-OFF IN CAREER

21 **Willie Johnston** , 1964–82 (Rangers 7, WBA 6, Vancouver Whitecaps 4, Hearts 3, Scotland 1)
21 **Roy McDonough**, 1980–95 (13 in Football League – Birmingham, Walsall, Chelsea, Colchester, Southend, Exeter, Cambridge Utd plus 8 non-league)
13 **Steve Walsh** (Wigan, Leicester, Norwich, Coventry)
13 **Martin Keown** (Arsenal, Aston Villa, Everton)
13 **Alan Smith** (Leeds, Manchester Utd, Newcastle, England U–21, England)
12 **Dennis Wise** (Wimbledon, Chelsea, Leicester, Millwall)

12 **Vinnie Jones** (Wimbledon, Leeds, Sheffield Utd, Chelsea, QPR)
12 **Mark Dennis** (Birmingham, Southampton, QPR)
12 **Roy Keane** (Manchester Utd, Rep of Ireland)
10 **Patrick Vieira** (Arsenal)
10 **Paul Scholes** (Manchester Utd, England)

Most Premier League sendings-off: Patrick Vieira 9, Duncan Ferguson 8, Richard Dunne 8, Vinnie Jones 7, Roy Keane 7, Alan Smith 7. Lee Cattermole 7.

● **Carlton Palmer** holds the unique record of having been sent off with each of his five Premiership clubs: Sheffield Wed, Leeds, Southampton, Nottm Forest and Coventry.

FA CUP FINAL SENDINGS-OFF

Kevin Moran (Manchester Utd) v Everton, Wembley, 1985; **Jose Antonio Reyes** (Arsenal) v Manchester Utd, Cardiff, 2005; **Pablo Zabaleta** (Manchester City) v Wigan, Wembley 2013; **Chris Smalling** (Manchester Utd) v Crystal Palace , Wembley, 2016.

WEMBLEY SENDINGS-OFF

Aug 1948 **Branko Stankovic** (Yugoslavia) v Sweden, Olympic Games
Jul 1966 **Antonio Rattin** (Argentina captain) v England, World cup quarter-final
Aug 1974 **Billy Bremner** (Leeds) and **Kevin Keegan** (Liverpool), Charity Shield
Mar 1977 **Gilbert Dresch** (Luxembourg) v England, World Cup
May 1985 **Kevin Moran** (Manchester Utd) v Everton, FA Cup Final
Apr 1993 **Lee Dixon** (Arsenal) v Tottenham, FA Cup semi-final
May 1993 **Peter Swan** (Port Vale) v WBA, Div 2 Play-off Final
Mar 1994 **Andrei Kanchelskis** (Manchester Utd) v Aston Villa, League Cup Final
May 1994 **Mike Wallace, Chris Beaumont** (Stockport) v Burnley, Div 2 Play-off Final
Jun 1995 **Tetsuji Hashiratani** (Japan) v England, Umbro Cup
May 1997 **Brian Statham** (Brentford) v Crewe, Div 2 Play-off Final
Apr 1998 **Capucho** (Portugal) v England, friendly
Nov 1998 **Ray Parlour** (Arsenal) and **Tony Vareilles** (Lens), Champions League
Mar 1999 **Justin Edinburgh** (Tottenham) v Leicester, League Cup Final
Jun 1999 **Paul Scholes** (England) v Sweden, European Championship qual
Feb 2000 **Clint Hill** (Tranmere) v Leicester, League Cup Final
Apr 2000 **Mark Delaney** (Aston Villa) v Bolton, FA Cup semi-final
May 2000 **Kevin Sharp** (Wigan) v Gillingham, Div 2 Play-off Final
Aug 2000 **Roy Keane** (Manchester Utd captain) v Chelsea, Charity Shield
May 2007 **Marc Tierney** (Shrewsbury) v Bristol Rov, Lge 2 Play-off Final
May 2007 **Matt Gill** (Exeter) v Morecambe, Conf Play-off Final
May 2009 **Jamie Ward** (Sheffield Utd) and **Lee Hendrie** (Sheffield Utd) v Burnley, Champ Play-off Final (Hendrie after final whistle)
May 2009 **Phil Bolland** (Cambridge Utd) v Torquay, Blue Square Prem Lge Play-off Final
May 2010 **Robin Hulbert** (Barrow) and **David Bridges** (Stevenage), FA Trophy Final
Apr 2011 **Paul Scholes** (Manchester Utd) v Manchester City, FA Cup semi-final
Apr 2011 **Toumani Diagouraga** (Brentford) v Carlisle, Johnstone's Paint Trophy Final
Sep 2012 **Steven Gerrard** (England) v Ukraine, World Cup qual
Feb 2013 **Matt Duke** (Bradford) v Swansea, League Cup Final
May 2013 **Pablo Zabaleta** (Manchester City) v Wigan, FA Cup Final
Mar 2014 **Joe Newell** (Peterborough) v Chesterfield, Johnstone's Paint Trophy Final
May 2014 **Gary O'Neil** (QPR) v Derby, Champ Play-off Final
May 2016 **Chris Smalling** (Manchester Utd) v Crystal Palace, FA Cup Final

WEMBLEY'S SUSPENDED CAPTAINS

Suspension prevented four **club captains** playing at Wembley in modern finals, in successive years. Three were in FA Cup Finals – **Glenn Roeder** (QPR, 1982), **Steve Foster** (Brighton, 1983), **Wilf Rostron** (Watford, 1984). Sunderland's **Shaun Elliott** was banned from the 1985 Milk Cup

Final. Roeder was banned from QPR's 1982 Cup Final replay against Tottenham, and Foster was ruled out of the first match in Brighton's 1983 Final against Manchester Utd.

RED CARD FOR KICKING BALL-BOY

Chelsea's **Eden Hazard** was sent off (80 mins) in the League Cup semi-final, second leg at Swansea on Jan 23, 2013 for kicking a 17-year-old ball-boy who refused to hand over the ball that had gone out of play. The FA suspended Hazard for three matches.

BOOKINGS RECORDS

Most players of one Football League club booked in one match is **TEN** – members of the Mansfield team away to Crystal Palace in FA Cup third round, Jan 1963. Most yellow cards for one team in Premier League match – **9** for Tottenham away to Chelsea, May 2, 2016.

Fastest bookings – 3 seconds after kick-off, **Vinnie Jones** (Chelsea, home to Sheffield Utd, FA Cup fifth round, Feb 15, 1992); 5 seconds after kick-off: **Vinnie Jones** (Sheffield Utd, away to Manchester City, Div 1, Jan 19, 1991). He was sent-off (54 mins) for second bookable offence.

FIGHTING TEAM-MATES

Charlton's **Mike Flanagan** and **Derek Hales** were sent off for fighting each other five minutes from end of FA Cup 3rd round tie at home to Southern League Maidstone on Jan 9, 1979.

Bradford City's **Andy Myers** and **Stuart McCall** had a fight during the 1-6 Premiership defeat at Leeds on Sunday, May 13, 2001.

On Sep 28, 1994 the Scottish FA suspended Hearts players **Graeme Hogg** and **Craig Levein** for ten matches for fighting each other in a pre-season 'friendly' v Raith.

Blackburn's England players **Graeme Le Saux** and **David Batty** clashed away to Spartak Moscow (Champions League) on Nov 22, 1995. Neither was sent off.

Newcastle United's England Internationals **Lee Bowyer** and **Kieron Dyer** were sent off for fighting each other at home to Aston Villa (Premiership on Apr 2, 2005).

Arsenal's **Emmanuel Adebayor** and **Nicklas Bendtner** clashed during the 5-1 Carling Cup semi-final 2nd leg defeat at Tottenham on Jan 22, 2008. Neither was sent off; each fined by their club.

Stoke's **Richardo Fuller** was sent off for slapping his captain, Andy Griffin, at West Ham in the Premier League on Dec 28, 2008.

FOOTBALL'S FIRST BETTING SCANDAL

A Football League investigation into the First Division match which ended Manchester Utd 2, Liverpool 0 at Old Trafford on Good Friday, Apr 2, 1915 proved that the result had been 'squared' by certain players betting on the outcome. Four members of each team were suspended for life, but some of the bans were lifted when League football resumed in 1919 in recognition of the players' war service.

PLAYERS JAILED

Ten professional footballers found guilty of conspiracy to fraud by 'fixing' matches for betting purposes were given prison sentences at Nottingham Assizes on Jan 26, 1965.

Jimmy Gauld (Mansfield), described as the central figure, was given four years. Among the others sentenced, **Tony Kay** (Sheffield Wed, Everton & England), **Peter Swan** (Sheffield Wed & England) and **David 'Bronco' Layne** (Sheffield Wed) were suspended from football for life by the FA.

DRUGS BANS

Abel Xavier (Middlesbrough) was the first Premiership player found to have taken a performance-enchancing drug. He was banned by UEFA for 18 months in Nov 2005 after testing positive for an anabolic steroid. The ban was reduced to a year in Jul 2006 by the Court of Arbitration for Sport. **Paddy Kenny** (Sheffield Utd goalkeeper) was suspended by an FA commission for 9 months from July, 2009 for failing a drugs test the previous May. Kolo Toure (Manchester City) received a 6-month ban in May 2011 for a doping offence. It was backdated to Mar 2.

LONG SUSPENSIONS

The longest suspension (8 months) in modern times for a player in British football was imposed on two Manchester Utd players. First was **Eric Cantona** following his attack on a spectator as he left the pitch after being sent off at Crystal Palace (Prem League) on Jan 25, 1995. The club immediately suspended him to the end of the season and fined him 2 weeks' wages (est £20,000). Then, on a disrepute charge, the FA fined him £10,000 (Feb 1995) and extended the ban to Sep 30 (which FIFA confirmed as world-wide). A subsequent 2-weeks' jail sentence on Cantona for assault was altered, on appeal, to 120 hours' community service, which took the form of coaching schoolboys in the Manchester area.

On **Dec 19, 2003** an FA Commission, held at Bolton, suspended **Rio Ferdinand** from football for 8 months (plus £50,000 fine) for failing to take a random drug test at the club's training ground on Sep 23. The ban operated from Jan 12, 2004.

Aug 1974: Kevin Keegan (Liverpool) and **Billy Bremner** (Leeds) both suspended for 10 matches and fined £500 after being sent off in FA Charity Shield at Wembley.

Jan 1988: Mark Dennis (QPR) given 8-match ban after 11th sending-off of his career.

Oct 1988: Paul Davis (Arsenal) banned for 9 matches for breaking the jaw of Southampton's Glenn Cockerill.

Oct 1998: Paolo Di Canio (Sheff Wed) banned for 11 matches and fined £10,000 for pushing referee Paul Alcock after being sent off at home to Arsenal (Prem), Sep 26.

Mar 2005: David Prutton (Southampton) banned for 10 matches (plus 1 for red card) and fined £6,000 by FA for shoving referee Alan Wiley when sent off at home to Arsenal (Prem), Feb 26.

Aug 2006: Ben Thatcher (Manchester City) banned for 8 matches for elbowing Pedro Mendes (Portsmouth).

Sep 2008: Joey Barton (Newcastle) banned for 12 matches (6 suspended) and fined £25,000 by FA for training ground assault on former Manchester City team-mate Ousmane Dabo.

May 2012: Joey Barton (QPR) suspended for 12 matches and fined £75,000 for violent conduct when sent off against Manchester City on final day of Premier League season.

Mar 2014: Joss Labadie (Torquay) banned for 10 matches and fined £2,000 for biting Chesterfield's Ollie Banks (Lge 2) on Feb 15, 2014.

Seven-month ban: Frank Barson, 37-year-old Watford centre-half, sent off at home to Fulham (Div 3 South) on Sep 29, 1928, was suspended by the FA for the remainder of the season.

Twelve-month ban: Oldham full-back **Billy Cook** was given a 12-month suspension for refusing to leave the field when sent off at Middlesbrough (Div 1), on Apr 3, 1915. The referee abandoned the match with 35 minutes still to play, and the score (4-1 to Middlesbrough) was ordered to stand.

Long Scottish bans: Sep 1954: Willie Woodburn, Rangers and Scotland centre-half, suspended for rest of career after fifth sending-off in 6 years.

Billy McLafferty, Stenhousemuir striker, was banned (Apr 14) for 8 and a half months, to Jan 1, 1993, and fined £250 for failing to appear at a disciplinary hearing after being sent off against Arbroath on Feb 1.

Twelve-match ban: On May 12, 1994 Scottish FA suspended Rangers forward **Duncan Ferguson** for 12 matches for violent conduct v Raith on Apr 16. On Oct 11, 1995, Ferguson (then with Everton) sent to jail for 3 months for the assault (served 44 days); Feb 1, 1996 Scottish judge quashed 7 matches that remained of SFA ban on Ferguson.

On Sep 29, 2001 the SFA imposed a **17-match suspension** on Forfar's former Scottish international **Dave Bowman** for persistent foul and abusive language when sent off against Stranraer on Sep 22. As his misconduct continued, he was shown **5 red cards** by the referee.

On Apr 3, 2009, captain **Barry Ferguson** and goalkeeper **Allan McGregor** were banned for life from playing for Scotland for gestures towards photographers while on the bench for a World Cup qualifier against Iceland.

On Dec 20, 2011 Liverpool and Uruguay striker **Luis Suarez** was given an 8-match ban and fined £40,000 by the FA for making 'racially offensive comments' to Patrice Evra of Manchester Utd (Prem Lge, Oct 15).

On Apr 25, 2013 **Luis Suarez** was given a 10-match suspension by the FA for 'violent conduct' –

biting Chelsea defender Branislav Ivanovic, Prem Lge, Apr 21. The Liverpool player was also fined £200,000 by Liverpool. His ban covered the last 4 games of that season and the first 6 of 2013–14. On Jun 26, 2014, Suarez, while still a Liverpool player, received the most severe punishment in World Cup history – a four-month ban from 'all football activities' and £66,000 fine from FIFA for biting Giorgio Chiellini during Uruguay's group game against Italy.

TOP FINES

Clubs: £49,000,000 (World record) Manchester City: May 2014 for breaking UEFA Financial Fair Play rules **(£32,600,000** suspended subject to City meeting certain conditions over two seasons). **£7.6m** Bournemouth: May 2016, for breaking Financial Fair Play rules; **£5,500,000** West Ham: Apr 2007, for breaches of regulations involving 'dishonesty and deceit' over Argentine signings Carlos Tevez and Javier Mascherano; **£1,500,000** (increased from original £600,000) Tottenham: Dec 1994, financial irregularities; £875,000 QPR: May 2011 for breaching rules when signing Argentine Alejandro Faurlin; **£375,000** (reduced to £290,000 on appeal) Chelsea: May 2016, players brawl v Tottenham; **£300,000** (reduced to £75,000 on appeal) Chelsea: Jun 2005, illegal approach to Arsenal's Ashley Cole; **£225,000** (reduced to £175,000 on appeal) Tottenham: May 2016, players brawl v Chelsea; **£200,000** Aston Villa: May 2015 for fans' pitch invasion after FA Cup quarter-final v WBA; **£175,000** Arsenal: Oct 2003, players' brawl v Manchester Utd; **£150,000** Leeds: Mar 2000, players' brawl v Tottenham; **£150,000** Tottenham: Mar 2000, players brawl v Leeds; **£145,000** Hull: Feb 2015, breaching Financial Fair Play rules; **£115,000** West Ham: Aug 2009, crowd misconduct at Carling Cup; v Millwall; **£105,000** Chelsea: Jan 1991, irregular payments; **£100,000** Boston Utd: Jul 2002, contract irregularities; **£100,000** Arsenal and Chelsea: Mar 2007 for mass brawl after Carling Cup Final; **£100,000** (including suspended fine) Blackburn: Aug 2007, poor disciplinary record; **£100,000** Sunderland: May 2014, breaching agents' regulations; **£100,000** Reading: Aug 2015, pitch invasion, FA Cup tie v Bradford (reduced to £40,000 on appeal); **£90,000** Brighton: Feb 2015, breaching rules on agents; **£71,000** West Ham: Feb 2015 for playing Diafra Sakho in FA Cup 4th round tie against Bristol City after declaring him unfit for Senegal's Africa Cup of Nations squad; **£65,000** Chelsea: Jan 2016, players brawl v WBA; **£62,000** Macclesfield: Dec 2005, funding of a stand at club's ground.

Players: £220,000 (plus 4-match ban) John Terry (Chelsea): Sep 2012, racially abusing Anton Ferdinand (QPR); **£150,000** Roy Keane (Manchester Utd): Oct 2002, disrepute offence over autobiography; **£100,000** (reduced to £75,000 on appeal) Ashley Cole (Arsenal): Jun 2005, illegal approach by Chelsea; **£90,000** Ashley Cole (Chelsea): Oct 2012, offensive Tweet against FA; **£80,000 (plus 5-match ban)** Nicolas Anelka (WBA): Feb 2014, celebrating goal at West Ham with racially-offensive 'quenelle' gesture; **£75,000 (plus 12-match ban)** Joey Barton (QPR): May 2012, violent conduct v Manchester City; **£60,000 (plus 3-match ban)** John Obi Mikel (Chelsea): Dec 2012, abusing referee Mark Clattenburg after Prem Lge v Manchester Utd); **£60,000** Dexter Blackstock (Nottm Forest): May 2014, breaching betting rules; **£50,000** Cameron Jerome (Stoke): Aug 2013, breaching FA betting rules; **£50,000** Benoit Assou-Ekotto (Tottenham): Sep 2014, publicly backing Nicolas Anelka's controversial 'quenelle' gesture; **£45,000** Patrick Vieira (Arsenal): Oct 1999, tunnel incidents v West Ham; **£45,000** Rio Ferdinand (Manchester Utd): Aug 2012, improper comments about Ashley Cole on Twitter; **£40,000** Lauren (Arsenal): Oct 2003, players' fracas v Manchester Utd; **£40,000 (plus 8-match ban)** Luis Suarez (Liverpool): Dec 2011, racially abusing Patrice Evra (Manchester Utd); **£40,000 (plus 3-match ban)** Dani Osvaldo (Southampton): Jan 2014, violent conduct, touchline Newcastle.

*In eight seasons with Arsenal (1996–2004) **Patrick Vieira** was fined a total of £122,000 by the FA for disciplinary offences.

Managers: £200,000 (reduced to £75,000 on appeal) Jose Mourinho (Chelsea): Jun 2005, illegal approach to Arsenal's Ashley Cole; **£60,000 (plus 7-match ban)** Alan Pardew (Newcastle): head-butting Hull player David Meyler (also fined £100,000 by club); **£50,000** Jose Mourinho (Chelsea): Oct 2015, accusing referees of bias; **£40,000 (plus 1 match stadium ban)** Jose Mourinho (Chelsea): Nov 2015, abusive behaviour towards referee Jon Moss v West Ham, **£33,000 (plus 3-match Euro ban)** Arsene Wenger (Arsenal): Mar 2012, criticising referee after Champions League defeat by AC Milan; **£30,000** Sir Alex Ferguson (Manchester Utd): Mar 2011 criticising referee Martin Atkinson v Chelsea; **£30,000 (plus 6-match ban ((plus 6-match ban reduced to 4 on appeal)**; Rui Faria (Chelsea assistant): May 2014, confronting match officials v Sunderland.

- Jonathan Barnett, Ashley Cole's agent was fined **£100,000** in Sep 2006 for his role in the 'tapping up' affair involving the player and Chelsea.
- Gillingham and club chairman Paul Scally each fined £75,000 in Jul 2015 for 'racial victimisation' towards player Mark McCammon. Club fine reduced to £50,000 on appeal.
- Leyton Orient owner Francesco Becchetti fined £40,000 and given six-match stadium ban in Jan 2016 for violent conduct towards assistant manager Andy Hessenthaler.

***£68,000** FA: May 2003, pitch invasions and racist chanting by fans during England v Turkey, Sunderland.

£50,000 FA: Dec 2014, for Wigan owner-chairman Dave Whelan, plus six-week ban from all football activity, for remarks about Jewish and Chinese people in newspaper interview.

MANAGERS

INTERNATIONAL RECORDS

(As at start of season 2016–17)

	P	W	D	L	F	A
Gordon Strachan (Scotland – appointed Jan 2013)	29	15	5	9	43	28
Chris Coleman (Wales – appointed Jan 2012)	37	15	7	15	39	47
Michael O'Neill (Northern Ireland – appointed Oct 2011)	39	11	13	15	37	47
Martin O'Neill (Republic of Ireland) – appointed Nov 2013)	30	11	11	8	43	30

ENGLAND MANAGERS

		P	W	D	L
1946–62	**Walter Winterbottom**	139	78	33	28
1963–74	**Sir Alf Ramsey**	113	69	27	17
1974	**Joe Mercer**, caretaker	7	3	3	1
1974–77	**Don Revie**	29	14	8	7
1977–82	**Ron Greenwood**	55	33	12	10
1982–90	**Bobby Robson**	95	47	30	18
1990–93	**Graham Taylor**	38	18	13	7
1994–96	**Terry Venables**	23	11	11	1
1996–99	**Glenn Hoddle**	28	17	6	5
1999	**Howard Wilkinson**, caretaker	1	0	0	1
1999–2000	**Kevin Keegan**	18	7	7	4
2000	**Howard Wilkinson**, caretaker	1	0	1	0
2000	**Peter Taylor**, caretaker	1	0	0	1
2001–06	**Sven–Goran Eriksson**	67	40	17	10
2006–07	**Steve McClaren**	18	9	4	5
2007–12	**Fabio Capello**	42	28	8	6
2012–16	**Roy Hodgson**	56	33	15	8

INTERNATIONAL MANAGER CHANGES

England: Walter Winterbottom 1946–62 (initially coach); **Alf Ramsey** (Feb 1963–May 1974); **Joe Mercer** (caretaker May 1974); **Don Revie** (Jul 1974–Jul 1977); **Ron Greenwood** (Aug 1977–Jul 1982); **Bobby Robson** (Jul 1982–Jul 1990); **Graham Taylor** (Jul 1990–Nov 1993); **Terry Venables**, coach (Jan 1994–Jun 1996); **Glenn Hoddle**, coach (Jun 1996–Feb 1999); **Howard Wilkinson** (caretaker Feb 1999); **Kevin Keegan coach** (Feb 1999–Oct 2000); **Howard Wilkinson** (caretaker Oct 2000); **Peter Taylor** (caretaker Nov 2000); **Sven–Goran Eriksson** (Jan 2001–Aug 2006); **Steve McClaren** (Aug 2006–Nov 2007); **Fabio Capello** (Dec 2007–Feb 2012); **Roy Hodgson** (May 2012– Jun 2016).

Scotland (modern): Bobby Brown (Feb 1967–Jul 1971); **Tommy Docherty** (Sep 1971–Dec 1972); **Willie Ormond** (Jan 1973–May 1977); **Ally MacLeod** (May 1977–Sep 1978); **Jock Stein** (Oct 1978–Sep 1985); **Alex Ferguson** (caretaker Oct 1985–Jun 1986); **Andy Roxburgh**, coach (Jul 1986–Sep 1993); **Craig Brown** (Sep 1993–Oct 2001); **Berti Vogts** (Feb 2002–Oct 2004); **Walter Smith** (Dec 2004–Jan 2007); **Alex McLeish** (Jan 2007–Nov 2007); **George Burley** (Jan 2008–Nov 2009); **Craig Levein** (Dec 2009–Nov 2012); **Billy Stark** (caretaker Nov–Dec 2012); **Gordon Strachan** (since Jan 2013).

Northern Ireland (modern): Peter Doherty (1951–62); **Bertie Peacock** (1962–67); **Billy Bingham** (1967–Aug 1971); **Terry Neill** (Aug 1971–Mar 1975); **Dave Clements** (player-manager Mar 1975–1976); **Danny Blanchflower** (Jun 1976–Nov 1979); **Billy Bingham** (Feb 1980–Nov 1993); **Bryan Hamilton** Feb 1994–Feb 1998); **Lawrie McMenemy** (Feb 1998–Nov 1999); **Sammy McIlroy** (Jan 2000–Oct 2003); **Lawrie Sanchez** (Jan 2004–May 2007); **Nigel Worthington** (May 2007–Oct 2011); **Michael O'Neill** (since Oct 2011).

Wales (modern): Mike Smith (Jul 1974–Dec 1979); **Mike England** (Mar 1980–Feb 1988); **David Williams** (caretaker Mar 1988); **Terry Yorath** (Apr 1988–Nov 1993); **John Toshack** (Mar 1994, one match); **Mike Smith** (Mar 1994–Jun 1995); **Bobby Gould** (Aug 1995–Jun 1999); **Mark Hughes** (Aug 1999 – Oct 2004); **John Toshack** (Nov 2004–Sep 2010); Brian Flynn (caretaker Sep–Dec 2010); **Gary Speed** (Dec 2010–Nov 2011); **Chris Coleman** (since Jan 2012).

Republic of Ireland (modern): Liam Tuohy (Sep 1971–Nov 1972); **Johnny Giles** (Oct 1973–Apr 1980, initially player–manager); **Eoin Hand** (Jun 1980–Nov 1985); **Jack Charlton** (Feb 1986–Dec 1995); **Mick McCarthy** (Feb 1996–Oct 2002); **Brian Kerr** (Jan 2003–Oct 2005); **Steve Staunton** (Jan 2006–Oct 2007); **Giovanni Trapattoni** (May 2008–Sep 2013); **Martin O'Neill** (since Nov 2013).

WORLD CUP-WINNING MANAGERS

1930 Uruguay (Alberto Suppici); 1934 and 1938 Italy (Vittorio Pozzo); 1950 Uruguay (Juan Lopez Fontana); 1954 West Germany (Sepp Herberger); 1958 Brazil (Vicente Feola); 1962 Brazil (Aymore Moreira); 1966 England (Sir Alf Ramsey); 1970 Brazil (Mario Zagallo); 1974 West Germany (Helmut Schon); 1978 Argentina (Cesar Luis Menotti); 1982 Italy (Enzo Bearzot); 1986 Argentina (Carlos Bilardo); 1990 West Germany (Franz Beckenbauer); 1994 Brazil (Carlos Alberto Parreira); 1998 France (Aimee Etienne Jacquet); 2002 Brazil (Luiz Felipe Scolari); 2006 Italy (Marcello Lippi); 2010 Spain (Vicente Del Bosque); 2014 Germany (Joachim Low).

Each of the 20 winning teams had a manager/coach of that country's nationality.

YOUNGEST LEAGUE MANAGERS

Ivor Broadis, 23, appointed player-manager of Carlisle, Aug 1946; **Chris Brass**, 27, appointed player-manager of York, Jun 2003; **Terry Neill**, 28, appointed player manager of Hull, Jun 1970; **Graham Taylor**, 28, appointed manager of Lincoln, Dec 1972.

LONGEST-SERVING LEAGUE MANAGERS – ONE CLUB

Fred Everiss, secretary–manager of WBA for 46 years (1902–48); **George Ramsay**, secretary–manager of Aston Villa for 42 years (1884–1926); **John Addenbrooke**, Wolves, for 37 years (1885–1922). Since last war: **Sir Alex Ferguson** at Manchester Utd for 27 seasons (1986–2013); **Sir Matt Busby**, in charge of Manchester Utd for 25 seasons (1945–69, 1970–71; **Dario Gradi** at Crewe for 26 years (1983–2007, 2009–11); **Jimmy Seed** at Charlton for 23 years (1933–56); **Brian Clough** at Nottm Forest for 18 years (1975–93); **Arsene Wenger** at Arsenal for 18 years (1996-to-date).

LAST ENGLISH MANAGER TO WIN CHAMPIONSHIP

Howard Wilkinson (Leeds), season 1991–92.

1,000-TIME MANAGERS

Only six have managed in more than **1,000 English League games**: Alec Stock, Brian Clough, Jim Smith, Graham Taylor, Dario Gradi and Sir Alex Ferguson.

Sir Matt Busby, Dave Bassett, Lennie Lawrence, Alan Buckley, Denis Smith, Joe Royle, Ron Atkinson, Brian Horton, Neil Warnock, Harry Redknapp, Graham Turner, Steve Coppell, Roy Hodgson, Arsene Wenger, Len Ashurst, Lawrie McMenemy, Sir Bobby Robson and Danny Wilson have each managed more than **1,000 matches in all first class competitions**.

SHORT-TERM MANAGERS

Departed		
3 days	Bill Lambton (Scunthorpe)	Apr 1959
7 days	Tim Ward (Exeter)	Mar 1953
7 days	Kevin Cullis (Swansea City)	Feb 1996
8 days	Billy McKinlay (Watford)	Oct 2014
10 days	Dave Cowling (Doncaster)	Oct 1997
10 days	Peter Cormack (Cowdenbeath)	Dec 2000
13 days	Johnny Cochrane (Reading)	Apr 1939
13 days	Micky Adams (Swansea City)	Oct 1997
16 days	Jimmy McIlroy (Bolton)	Nov 1970
19 days	Martin Allen (Barnet)	Apr 2011
20 days	Paul Went (Leyton Orient)	Oct 1981
27 days	Malcolm Crosby (Oxford Utd)	Jan 1998
27 days	Oscar Garcia (Watford)	Sep 2014
28 days	Tommy Docherty (QPR)	Dec 1968
28 days	Paul Hart (QPR)	Jan 2010
32 days	Steve Coppell (Manchester City)	Nov 1996
32 days	Darko Milanic (Leeds)	Oct 2014
34 days	Niall Quinn (Sunderland)	Aug 2006
36 days	Steve Claridge (Millwall)	Jul 2005
39 days	Paul Gascoigne (Kettering)	Dec 2005
40 days	Alex McLeish (Nottm Forest)	Feb 2013
41 days	Steve Wicks (Lincoln)	Oct 1995
41 days	Les Reed (Charlton)	Dec 2006
43 days	Mauro Milanese (Leyton Orient)	Dec 2014
44 days	Brian Clough (Leeds)	Sep 1974
44 days	Jock Stein (Leeds)	Oct 1978
45 days	Paul Murray (Hartlepool)	Dec 2014
48 days	John Toshack (Wales)	Mar 1994
48 days	David Platt (Sampdoria coach)	Feb 1999
49 days	Brian Little (Wolves)	Oct 1986
49 days	Terry Fenwick (Northampton)	Feb 2003
57 days	Henning Berg (Blackburn)	Dec 2012
61 days	Bill McGarry (Wolves)	Nov 1985

- In May 1984, Crystal Palace named **Dave Bassett** as manager, but he changed his mind four days later, without signing the contract, and returned to Wimbledon.
- In May 2007, **Leroy Rosenior** was reportedly appointed manager of Torquay after relegation and sacked ten minutes later when the club came under new ownership.
- **Brian Laws** lost his job at Scunthorpe on Mar 25, 2004 and was reinstated three weeks later
- In an angry outburst after a play-off defeat in May 1992, Barnet chairman Stan Flashman sacked manager **Barry Fry** and re-instated him a day later.

EARLY-SEASON MANAGER SACKINGS

2012: Andy Thorn (Coventry) 8 days; John Sheridan (Chesterfield) 10 days; **2011:** Jim Jefferies (Hearts) 9 days; **2010** Kevin Blackwell (Sheffield Utd) 8 days; **2009** Bryan Gunn (Norwich) 6 days; **2007:** Neil McDonald (Carlisle) 2 days; Martin Allen (Leicester) 18 days; **2004** Paul Sturrock (Southampton) 9 days; **2004:** Sir Bobby Robson (Newcastle) 16 days; **2003** Glenn Roeder (West Ham) 15 days; **2000:** Alan Buckley (Grimsby) 10 days; **1997:** Kerry

Dixon (Doncaster) 12 days; **1996:** Sammy Chung (Doncaster) on morning of season's opening League match; **1996:** Alan Ball (Manchester City) 12 days; **1994:** Kenny Hibbitt (Walsall) and Kenny Swain (Wigan) 20 days; **1993:** Peter Reid (Manchester City) 12 days; **1991:** Don Mackay (Blackburn) 14 days; **1989:** Mick Jones (Peterborough) 12 days; **1980:** Bill McGarry (Newcastle) 13 days; **1979:** Dennis Butler (Port Vale) 12 days; **1977:** George Petchey (Leyton O) 13 days; **1977:** Willie Bell (Birmingham) 16 days; **1971:** Len Richley (Darlington) 12 days.

BRUCE'S FOUR-TIMER

Steve Bruce is the only manager to win four promotions to the Premier League – with Birmingham in 2002 and 2007 and with Hull in 2013 and 2016.

RECORD START FOR MANAGER

Russ Wilcox, appointed by Scunthorpe in Nov 2013, remained unbeaten in his first 28 league matches (14 won, 14 drawn) and took the club to promotion from League Two. It was the most successful start to a managerial career In English football, beating the record of 23 unbeaten games by Preston's William Sudell in 1889.

RECORD TOP DIVISION START

Arsenal were unbeaten in 17 league matches from the start of season 1947-48 under new manager **Tom Whittaker.**

SACKED, REINSTATED, FINISHED

Brian McDermott was sacked as Leeds manager on Jan 31, 2014. The following day, he was reinstated. At the end of the season, with the club under new ownership, he left by 'mutual consent.'

CARETAKER SUPREME

As Chelsea's season collapsed, Andre Villas-Boas was sacked in March 2012 after eight months as manager, 2012. Roberto Di Matteo was appointed caretaker and by the season's end his team had won the FA Cup and the Champions League.

MANAGER DOUBLES

Four managers have won the League Championship with different clubs: **Tom Watson**, secretary–manager with Sunderland (1892–93–95) and **Liverpool** (1901); **Herbert Chapman** with Huddersfield (1923–24, 1924–25) and Arsenal (1930–31, 1932–33); **Brian Clough** with Derby (1971–72) and Nottm Forest (1977–78); **Kenny Dalglish** with Liverpool (1985–86, 1987–88, 1989–90) and Blackburn (1994–95).

Managers to win the FA Cup with different clubs: **Billy Walker** (Sheffield Wed 1935, Nottm Forest 1959); **Herbert Chapman** (Huddersfield 1922, Arsenal 1930).

Kenny Dalglish (Liverpool) and **George Graham** (Arsenal) completed the Championship/FA Cup double as both player and manager with a single club. **Joe Mercer** won the title as a player with Everton, the title twice and FA Cup as a player with Arsenal and both competitions as manager of Manchester City.

CHAIRMAN–MANAGER

On Dec 20, 1988, after two years on the board, Dundee Utd manager **Jim McLean** was elected chairman, too. McLean, Scotland's longest–serving manager (appointed on Nov 24, 1971), resigned at end of season 1992–93 (remained chairman).

Ron Noades was chairman-manager of Brentford from Jul 1998–Mar 2001. **John Reames** did both jobs at Lincoln from Nov 1998–Apr 2000)

Niall Quinn did both jobs for five weeks in 2006 before appointing Roy Keane as manager of Sunderland.

TOP DIVISION PLAYER–MANAGERS

Les Allen (QPR 1968–69); **Johnny Giles** (WBA 1976–77); **Howard Kendall** (Everton 1981–82);

Kenny Dalglish (Liverpool, 1985–90); **Trevor Francis** (QPR, 1988–89); **Terry Butcher** (Coventry 1990–91), **Peter Reid** (Manchester City, 1990–93), **Trevor Francis** (Sheffield Wed, 1991–94) **Glenn Hoddle**, (Chelsea, 1993–95), **Bryan Robson** (Middlesbrough, 1994–97), **Ray Wilkins** (QPR, 1994–96), **Ruud Gullit** (Chelsea, 1996–98), **Gianluca Vialli** (Chelsea, 1998–2000).

FIRST FOREIGN MANAGER IN ENGLISH LEAGUE

Uruguayan **Danny Bergara** (Rochdale 1988–89).

COACHING KINGS OF EUROPE

Five coaches have won the European Cup/Champions League with two different clubs: **Erns Happel** with Feyenoord (1970) and Hamburg (1983); **Ottmar Hitzfeld** with Borussi Dortmund (1997) and Bayern Munich (2001); **Jose Mourinho** with Porto (2004) and Inte Milan (2010); **Jupp Heynckes** with Real Madrid (1998) and Bayern Munich (2013); **Carlo Ancelotti** with AC Milan (2003, 2007) and Real Madrid (2014).

FOREIGN TRIUMPH

Former Dutch star **Ruud Gullit** became the first foreign manager to win a major Englis competition when Chelsea took the FA Cup in 1997.

Arsene Wenger and **Gerard Houllier** became the first foreign managers to receive recognitio when they were awarded honorary OBEs in the Queen's Birthday Honours in Jun 2003 'fo their contribution to English football and Franco–British relations'.

MANAGERS OF POST-WAR CHAMPIONS (*Double winners)

1947 George Kay (Liverpool); **1948** Tom Whittaker (Arsenal); **1949** Bob Jackson (Portsmouth).

1950 Bob Jackson (Portsmouth); **1951** Arthur Rowe (Tottenham); **1952** Matt Busby (Mancheste Utd); **1953** Tom Whittaker (Arsenal); **1954** Stan Cullis (Wolves); **1955** Ted Drake (Chelsea) **1956** Matt Busby (Manchester Utd); **1957** Matt Busby (Manchester Utd); **1958** Stan Cullis (Wolves); **1959** Stan Cullis (Wolves).

1960 Harry Potts (Burnley); **1961** *Bill Nicholson (Tottenham); **1962** Alf Ramsey (Ipswich) **1963** Harry Catterick (Everton); **1964** Bill Shankly (Liverpool); **1965** Matt Busby (Mancheste Utd); **1966** Bill Shankly (Liverpool); **1967** Matt Busby (Manchester Utd); **1968** Joe Merce (Manchester City); **1969** Don Revie (Leeds).

1970 Harry Catterick (Everton); **1971** *Bertie Mee (Arsenal); **1972** Brian Clough (Derby); **1973** Bill Shankly (Liverpool); **1974** Don Revie (Leeds); **1975** Dave Mackay (Derby); **1976** Bob Paisley (Liverpool); **1977** Bob Paisley (Liverpool); **1978** Brian Clough (Nottm Forest); **1979** Bob Paisley (Liverpool).

1980 Bob Paisley (Liverpool); **1981** Ron Saunders (Aston Villa); **1982** Bob Paisley (Liverpool) **1983** Bob Paisley (Liverpool); **1984** Joe Fagan (Liverpool); **1985** Howard Kendall (Everton) **1986** *Kenny Dalglish (Liverpool – player/manager); **1987** Howard Kendall (Everton); **1988** Kenny Dalglish (Liverpool – player/manager); **1989** George Graham (Arsenal).

1990 Kenny Dalglish (Liverpool); **1991** George Graham (Arsenal); **1992** Howard Wilkinson (Leeds); **1993** Alex Ferguson (Manchester Utd); **1994** *Alex Ferguson (Manchester Utd), **1995** Kenny Dalglish (Blackburn); **1996** *Alex Ferguson (Manchester Utd); **1997** Alex Ferguson (Manchester Utd); **1998** *Arsene Wenger (Arsenal); **1999** *Alex Ferguson (Manchester Utd).

2000 Sir Alex Ferguson (Manchester Utd); **2001** Sir Alex Ferguson (Manchester Utd); **2002** *Arsene Wenger (Arsenal); **2003** Sir Alex Ferguson (Manchester Utd); **2004** Arsene Wenger (Arsenal); **2005** Jose Mourinho (Chelsea); **2006** Jose Mourinho (Chelsea); **2007** Sir Alex Ferguson (Manchester Utd); **2008** Sir Alex Ferguson (Manchester Utd); **2009** Sir Alex Ferguson (Manchester Utd); **2010** *Carlo Ancelotti (Chelsea); **2011** Sir Alex Ferguson (Manchester Utd); **2012** Roberto Mancini (Manchester City); **2013** Sir Alex Ferguson (Manchester Utd); **2014** Manuel Pellegrini (Manchester City); **2015** Jose Mourinho (Chelsea) **2016** Claudio Ranieri (Leicester)

WORLD NO 1 MANAGER

When **Sir Alex Ferguson**, 71, retired in May 2013, he ended the most successful managerial career in the game's history. He took Manchester United to a total of 38 prizes – 13 Premier League titles, 5 FA Cup triumphs, 4 League Cups, 10 Charity/Community Shields (1 shared), 2 Champions League wins, 1 Cup-Winners' Cup, 1 FIFA Club World Cup, 1 Inter-Continental Cup and 1 UEFA Super Cup. Having played centre-forward for Rangers, the Glaswegian managed 3 Scottish clubs, East Stirling, St Mirren and then Aberdeen, where he broke the Celtic/Rangers duopoly with 9 successes: 3 League Championships, 4 Scottish Cups, 1 League Cup and 1 UEFA Cup. Appointed at Old Trafford in November 1986, when replacing Ron Atkinson, he did not win a prize there until his fourth season (FA Cup 1990), but thereafter the club's trophy cabinet glittered with silverware. His total of 1,500 matches in charge ended with a 5-5 draw away to West Bromwich Albion. The longest-serving manager in the club's history, he constructed 4 triumphant teams. Sir Alex was knighted in 1999 and in 2012 he received the FIFA award for services to football. On retirement from management, he became a director and club ambassador. United maintained the dynasty of long-serving Scottish managers (Sir Matt Busby for 24 seasons) by appointing David Moyes, who had been in charge at Everton for 11 years.

MANAGERS' EURO TREBLES

Two managers have won the European Cup/Champions League three times. **Bob Paisley** did it with Liverpool (1977,78, 81).

Carlo Ancelotti's successes were with AC Milan in 2003 and 2007 and with Real Madrid in 2014.

WINNER MOURINHO

In winning the Premier League and League Cup in 2015, Jose Mourinho embellished his reputation as Chelsea's most successful manager. Those achievements took his total of honours in two spells at the club to 8: 3 Premier League, 3 League Cup, 1 FA Cup, 1 Community Shield. Joining from Portuguese champions Porto, Mourinho was initially with Chelsea from June 2004 to September 2007. He then successfulty coached Inter Milan and Real Madrid before returning to Stamford Bridge in June 2013. His Premier League triumph in 2015 was his eighth title In 11 years in four countries (England 3, Portugal 2, Italy 2, Spain 1). He starts season 2015–16 with the remarkable six-season Chelsea home record of only one loss in 98 Premier League matches (W76, D21, goals 207-48). That one defeat was by 2-1 against Sunderland on April 19, 2014.

WENGER'S CUP AGAIN

Holder's Arsenal's win against Aston Villa in the 2015 Final was a record 12th success for them in the FA Cup and a sixth triumph in the competition for manager Arsene Wenger, equalling the record of George Ramsay for Villa (1887-1920). With his sixth victory in seven Finals, Wenger made history as the first manager to win the Cup in successive seasons twice (previously in 2002 and 2003).

RECORD MANAGER FEE

Chelsea paid Porto a record £13.25m compensation when they appointed **Andre Villas-Boas** as manager in June 2011. He lasted less than nine months at Stamford Bridge.

FATHER AND SON MANAGERS WITH SAME CLUB

Fulham: Bill Dodgin Snr 1949–53; Bill Dodgin Jnr 1968–72. **Brentford:** Bill Dodgin Snr 1953–57; Bill Dodgin Jnr 1976–80. **Bournemouth:** John Bond 1970–73; Kevin Bond 2006–08. **Derby:** Brian Clough 1967–73; Nigel Clough 2009.

SIR BOBBY'S HAT-TRICK

Sir Bobby Robson, born and brought up in County Durham, achieved a unique hat-trick when he received the Freedom of Durham in Dec 2008. He had already been awarded the Freedom of Ipswich and Newcastle. He died in July 2009 and had an express loco named after him on the East Coast to London line.

MANAGERS WITH MOST FA CUP SUCCESSES

6 Arsene Wenger (Arsenal), **George Ramsay** (Aston Villa); **5 Sir Alex Ferguson** (Manchester Utd); **3 Charles Foweraker** (Bolton), **John Nicholson** (Sheffield Utd), **Bill Nicholson** (Tottenham).

RELEGATION 'DOUBLES'

Managers associated with two clubs relegated in same season: **John Bond** in 1985–86 (Swansea City and Birmingham); **Ron Saunders** in 1985–86 (WBA – and their reserve team – and Birmingham); **Bob Stokoe** in 1986–87 (Carlisle and Sunderland); **Billy McNeill** in 1986–87 (Manchester City and Aston Villa); **Dave Bassett** in 1987–88 (Watford and Sheffield Utd); **Mick Mills** in 1989–90 (Stoke and Colchester); **Gary Johnson** in 2014-15 (Yeovil and Cheltenham)

THREE FA CUP DEFEATS IN ONE SEASON

Manager **Michael Appleton** suffered three FA Cup defeats in season 2012-13, with Portsmouth (v Notts Co, 1st rd); Blackpool (v Fulham, 3rd rd); Blackburn (v Millwall, 6th rd).

WEMBLEY STADIUM

NEW WEMBLEY

A new era for English football began in March 2007 with the completion of the new national stadium. The 90,000-seater arena was hailed as one of the world's finest – but came at a price. Costs soared, the project fell well behind schedule and disputes involving the FA, builders Multiplex and the Government were rife. The old stadium, opened in 1923, cost £750,000. The new one, originally priced at £326m in 2000, ended up at around £800m. The first international after completion was an Under-21 match between England and Italy. The FA Cup Final returned to its spiritual home after being staged at the Millennium Stadium in Cardiff for six seasons. Then, England's senior team were back for a friendly against Brazil.

DROGBA'S WEMBLEY RECORD

Didier Drogba's FA Cup goal for Chelsea against Liverpool in May 2012 meant that he had scored in all his 8 competitive appearances for the club at Wembley. (7 wins, 1 defeat). They came in: 2007 FA Cup Final (1-0 v Manchester Utd); 2008 League Cup Final (1-2 v Tottenham); 2009 FA Cup semi-final (2-1 v Arsenal); 2009 FA Cup Final (2-1 v Everton); 2010 FA Cup semi-final (3-0 v Aston Villa); 2010 FA Cup Final (1-0 v Portsmouth); 2012 FA Cup semi-final (5-1 v Tottenham); 2012 FA Cup Final (2-1 v Liverpool).

INVASION DAY

Memorable scenes were witnessed at the first **FA Cup Final at Wembley**, Apr 28, 1923, between **Bolton** and **West Ham**. An accurate return of the attendance could not be made owing to thousands breaking in, but there were probably more than 200,000 spectators present. The match was delayed for 40 minutes by the crowd invading the pitch. Official attendance was 126,047. Gate receipts totalled £27,776. The two clubs and the FA each received £6,365 and the FA refunded £2,797 to ticket-holders who were unable to get to their seats. Cup Final admission has since been by ticket only.

REDUCED CAPACITY

Capacity of the all-seated Wembley Stadium was 78,000. The last 100,000 attendance was for the 1985 FA Cup Final between Manchester Utd and Everton. Crowd record for New Wembley: 89,874 for 2008 FA Cup Final (Portsmouth v Cardiff).

WEMBLEY'S FIRST UNDER LIGHTS

Nov 30, 1955 (England 4, Spain 1), when the floodlights were switched on after 73 minutes (afternoon match played in damp, foggy conditions).

First Wembley international played throughout under lights: England 8, N Ireland 3 on evening of Nov 20, 1963 (att: 55,000).

MOST WEMBLEY APPEARANCES

59 by **Tony Adams** (35 England, 24 Arsenal); 57 by **Peter Shilton** (52 England, 3 Nottm Forest, 1 Leicester, 1 Football League X1).

WEMBLEY HAT-TRICKS

Three players have scored hat-tricks in major finals at Wembley: **Stan Mortensen** for Blackpool v Bolton (FA Cup Final, 1953), **Geoff Hurst** for England v West Germany (World Cup Final, 1966) and **David Speedie** for Chelsea v Manchester City (Full Members Cup, 1985).

ENGLAND'S WEMBLEY DEFEATS

England have lost 25 matches to foreign opponents at Wembley:

Nov 1953	3-6 v Hungary	**Jun 1995**	1-3 v Brazil
Oct 1959	2-3 v Sweden	**Feb 1997**	0-1 v Italy
Oct 1965	2-3 v Austria	**Feb 1998**	0-2 v Chile
Apr 1972	1-3 v W Germany	**Feb 1999**	0-2 v France
Nov 1973	0-1 v Italy	**Oct 2000**	0-1 v Germany
Feb 1977	0-2 v Holland	**Aug 2007**	1-2 v Germany
Mar 1981	1-2 v Spain	**Nov 2007**	2-3 v Croatia
May 1981	0-1 v Brazil	**Nov 2010**	1-2 v France
Oct 1982	1-2 v W Germany	**Feb 2012**	2-3 v Holland
Sep 1983	0-1 v Denmark	**Nov 2013**	0-2 v Chile
Jun 1984	0-2 v Russia	**Nov 2013**	0-1 v Germany
May 1990	1-2 v Uruguay	**Mar 2016**	1-2 v Holland
Sep 1991	0-1 v Germany		

A further defeat came in **Euro 96**. After drawing the semi-final with Germany 1-1, England went out 6-5 on penalties.

FASTEST GOALS AT WEMBLEY

In first-class matches: **25 sec** by **Louis Saha** for Everton in 2009 FA Cup Final against Chelsea; **38 sec** by **Bryan Robson** for England's against Yugoslavia in 1989; **42 sec** by **Roberto Di Matteo** for Chelsea in 1997 FA Cup Final v Middlesbrough; **44 sec** by **Bryan Robson** for England v Northern Ireland in 1982.

Fastest goal in **any** match at Wembley: **20 sec** by **Maurice Cox** for Cambridge University against Oxford in 1979.

FOUR WEMBLEY HEADERS

When **Wimbledon** beat Sutton 4-2 in the FA Amateur Cup Final at Wembley on May 4, 1963, Irish centre-forward **Eddie Reynolds** headed all four goals.

WEMBLEY ONE-SEASON DOUBLES

In 1989, **Nottm Forest** became the first club to win two Wembley Finals in the same season (Littlewoods Cup and Simod Cup).

In 1993, **Arsenal** made history there as the first club to win the League (Coca-Cola) Cup and the FA Cup in the same season. They beat Sheffield Wed 2-1 in both finals.

In 2012, **York** won twice at Wembley in nine days at the end of the season, beating Newport 2-0 in the FA Trophy Final and Luton 2-1 in the Conference Play-off Final to return to the Football League.

SUDDEN-DEATH DECIDERS

First Wembley Final decided on sudden death (first goal scored in overtime): Apr 23, 1995 – **Birmingham** beat Carlisle (1-0, Paul Tait 103 mins) to win Auto Windscreens Shield.

First instance of a golden goal deciding a major international tournament was at Wembley on Jun 30, 1996, when **Germany** beat the Czech Republic 2-1 in the European Championship Final with Oliver Bierhoff's goal in the 95th minute.

WEMBLEY'S MOST ONE-SIDED FINAL (in major domestic cups)

Swansea 5 **Bradford City** 0 (League Cup, Feb 24, 2013).

FOOTBALL TRAGEDIES

DAYS OF TRAGEDY – CLUBS

Season 1988–89 brought the worst disaster in the history of British sport, with the death of 96 Liverpool supporters (200 injured) at the **FA Cup semi-final** against Nottm Forest at **Hillsborough, Sheffield,** on Saturday, Apr 15. The tragedy built up in the minutes preceding kick-off, when thousands surged into the ground at the Leppings Lane end. Many were crushed in the tunnel between entrance and terracing, but most of the victims were trapped inside the perimeter fencing behind the goal. The match was abandoned without score after six minutes' play. The dead included seven women and girls, two teenage sisters and two teenage brothers. The youngest victim was a boy of ten, the oldest 67-year-old Gerard Baron, whose brother Kevin played for Liverpool in the 1950 Cup Final. (*Total became 96 in Mar 1993, when Tony Bland died after being in a coma for nearly four years). A two-year inquest at Warrington ended on April 26, 2016 with the verdict that the 96 were 'unlawfully killed.' It cleared Liverpool fans of any blame and ruled that South Yorkshire Police and South Yorkshire Ambulance Service 'caused or contributed' to the loss of life.

The two worst disasters in one season in British soccer history occurred at the end of 1984–85. On May 11, the last Saturday of the League season, 56 people (two of them visiting supporters) were burned to death – and more than 200 taken to hospital – when fire destroyed the main stand at the **Bradford City–Lincoln** match at Valley Parade.

The wooden, 77-year-old stand was full for City's last fixture before which, amid scenes of celebration, the club had been presented with the Third Division Championship trophy. The fire broke out just before half-time and, within five minutes, the entire stand was engulfed.

Heysel Tragedy

Eighteen days later, on May 29, at the European Cup Final between **Liverpool** and **Juventus** at the Heysel Stadium, Brussels, 39 spectators (31 of them Italian) were crushed or trampled to death and 437 injured. The disaster occurred an hour before the scheduled kick-off when Liverpool supporters charged a Juventus section of the crowd at one end of the stadium, and a retaining wall collapsed. The sequel was a 5-year ban by UEFA on English clubs generally in European competition, with a 6-year ban on Liverpool.

On May 26 1985 ten people were trampled to death and 29 seriously injured in a crowd panic on the way into the **Olympic Stadium, Mexico City** for the Mexican Cup Final between local clubs National University and America.

More than 100 people died and 300 were injured in a football disaster at **Nepal's national stadium** in Katmandu in Mar 1988. There was a stampede when a violent hailstorm broke over the capital. Spectators rushed for cover, but the stadium exits were locked, and hundreds were trampled in the crush.

In South Africa, on Jan 13 1991 40 black fans were trampled to death (50 injured) as they tried to escape from fighting that broke out at a match in the gold-mining town of Orkney, 80 miles from Johannesburg. The friendly, between top teams **Kaiser Chiefs** and **Orlando Pirates**, attracted a packed crowd of 20,000. Violence erupted after the referee allowed Kaiser Chiefs a disputed second-half goal to lead 1-0.

Disaster struck at the French Cup semi-final (May 5, 1992), with the death of 15 spectators and 1,300 injured when a temporary metal stand collapsed in the Corsican town of Bastia. The tie between Second Division **Bastia** and French Champions **Marseille** was cancelled. Monaco, who won the other semi-final, were allowed to compete in the next season's Cup-Winners' Cup.

A total of 318 died and 500 were seriously injured when the crowd rioted over a disallowed goal at the National Stadium in Lima, Peru, on May 24, 1964. **Peru** and **Argentina** were competing to play in the Olympic Games in Tokyo.

That remained **sport's heaviest death** toll until Oct 20, 1982, when (it was revealed only in Jul 1989) 340 Soviet fans were killed in Moscow's Lenin Stadium at the UEFA Cup second round first leg match between **Moscow Spartak** and **Haarlem** (Holland). They were crushed on an open stairway when a last-minute Spartak goal sent departing spectators surging back into the ground.

Among other crowd disasters abroad: Jun, 1968 – 74 died in Argentina. Panic broke out at the end of a goalless match between River Plate and Boca Juniors at Nunez, Buenos Aires, when Boca supporters threw lighted newspaper torches on to fans in the tiers below.

Feb 1974 – 49 killed in **Egypt** in crush of fans clamouring to see Zamalek play Dukla Prague.

Sep 1971 – 44 died in **Turkey**, when fighting among spectators over a disallowed goal (Kayseri v Siwas) led to a platform collapsing.

The then worst disaster in the history of British football, in terms of loss of life, occurred at Glasgow Rangers' ground at **Ibrox Park**, Jan 2 1971. Sixty-six people were trampled to death (100 injured) as they tumbled down Stairway 13 just before the end of the **Rangers v Celtic** New Year's match. That disaster led to the 1975 Safety of Sports Grounds legislation.

The Ibrox tragedy eclipsed even the Bolton disaster in which 33 were killed and about 500 injured when a wall and crowd barriers collapsed near a corner-flag at the **Bolton v Stoke** FA Cup sixth round tie on Mar 9 1946. The match was completed after half an hour's stoppage.

In a previous crowd disaster at **Ibrox** on Apr 5, 1902, part of the terracing collapsed during the Scotland v England international and 25 people were killed. The match, held up for 20 minutes, ended 1-1, but was never counted as an official international.

Eight leading players and three officials of **Manchester Utd** and eight newspaper representatives were among the 23 who perished in the air crash at **Munich** on Feb 6, 1958, during take-off following a European Cup-tie in Belgrade. The players were Roger Byrne, Geoffrey Bent, Eddie Colman, Duncan Edwards, Mark Jones, David Pegg, Tommy Taylor and Liam Whelan, and the officials were Walter Crickmer (secretary), Tom Curry (trainer) and Herbert Whalley (coach). The newspaper representatives were Alf Clarke, Don Davies, George Follows, Tom Jackson, Archie Ledbrooke, Henry Rose, Eric Thompson and Frank Swift (former England goalkeeper of Manchester City).

On May 14, 1949, the entire team of Italian Champions **Torino**, 8 of them Internationals, were killed when the aircraft taking them home from a match against Benfica in Lisbon crashed at Superga, near Turin. The total death toll of 28 included all the club's reserve players, the manager, trainer and coach.

On Feb 8, 1981, 24 spectators died and more than 100 were injured at a match in **Greece**. They were trampled as thousands of the 40,000 crowd tried to rush out of the stadium at Piraeus after Olympiacos beat AEK Athens 6-0.

On Nov 17, 1982, 24 people (12 of them children) were killed and 250 injured when fans stampeded at the end of a match at the Pascual Guerrero stadium in **Cali, Colombia**. Drunken spectators hurled fire crackers and broken bottles from the higher stands on to people below and started a rush to the exits.

On Dec 9, 1987, the 18-strong team squad of **Alianza Lima**, one of Peru's top clubs, were wiped out, together with 8 officials and several youth players, when a military aircraft taking them home from Puccalpa crashed into the sea off Ventillana, ten miles from Lima. The only survivor among 43 on board was a member of the crew.

On Apr 28, 1993, 18 members of **Zambia's international squad** and 5 ZFA officials died when the aircraft carrying them to a World Cup qualifying tie against Senegal crashed into the Atlantic soon after take-off from Libreville, Gabon.

On Oct 16 1996, 81 fans were crushed to death and 147 seriously injured in the '**Guatemala Disaster**' at the World Cup qualifier against Costa Rica in Mateo Flores stadium. The tragedy happened an hour before kick-off, allegedly caused by ticket forgery and overcrowding – 60,000 were reported in the 45,000-capacity ground – and safety problems related to perimeter fencing.

On Jul 9, 1996, 8 people died, 39 injured in riot after derby match between **Libya's two top clubs** in Tripoli. Al-Ahli had beaten Al-Ittihad 1-0 by a controversial goal.

On Apr 6, 1997, 5 spectators were crushed to death at **Nigeria's national stadium** in Lagos after the 2-1 World Cup qualifying victory over Guinea. Only two of five gates were reported open as the 40,000 crowd tried to leave the ground.

It was reported from the **Congo** (Oct 29, 1998) that a bolt of lightning struck a village match, killing all 11 members of the home team Benatshadi, but leaving the opposing players from Basangana unscathed. It was believed the surviving team wore better-insulated boots.

On Jan 10, 1999, eight fans died and 13 were injured in a stampede at **Egypt's Alexandria Stadium**. Some 25,000 spectators had pushed into the ground. Despite the tragedy, the cup-tie between Al-Ittihad and Al-Koroum was completed.

Three people suffocated and several were seriously injured when thousands of fans forced their way into **Liberia's national stadium** in Monrovia at a goalless World Cup qualifying match against Chad on Apr 23, 2000. The stadium (capacity 33,000) was reported 'heavily overcrowded'.

On Jul 9, 2000, 12 spectators died from crush injuries when police fired tear gas into the 50,000 crowd after South Africa scored their second goal in a World Cup group qualifier against Zimbabwe in **Harare**. A stampede broke out as fans scrambled to leave the national stadium. Players of both teams lay face down on the pitch as fumes swept over them. FIFA launched an investigation and decided that the result would stand, with South Africa leading 2-0 at the time of the 84th-minute abandonment.

On Apr 11, 2001, at one of the biggest matches of the South African season, 43 died and 155 were injured in a crush at **Ellis Park, Johannesburg**. After tearing down a fence, thousands of fans surged into a stadium already packed to its 60,000 capacity for the Premiership derby between top Soweto teams Kaizer Chiefs and Orlando Pirates. The match was abandoned at 1-1 after 33 minutes. In Jan 1991, 40 died in a crowd crush at a friendly between the same clubs at Orkney, 80 miles from Johannesburg.

On Apr 29, 2001, seven people were trampled to death and 51 injured when a riot broke out at a match between two of Congo's biggest clubs, Lupopo and Mazembe at **Lubumbashi**, southern Congo.

On May 6, 2001, two spectators were killed in Iran and hundreds were injured when a glass fibre roof collapsed at the over-crowded Mottaqi Stadium at Sari for the match between Pirouzi and Shemshak Noshahr.

On May 9, 2001, in Africa's worst football disaster, 123 died and 93 were injured in a stampede at the national stadium in **Accra, Ghana**. Home team Hearts of Oak were leading 2-1 against Asante Kotoko five minutes from time, when Asanti fans started hurling bottles on to the pitch. Police fired tear gas into the stands, and the crowd panicked in a rush for the exits, which were locked. It took the death toll at three big matches in Africa in Apr/May to 173.

On Aug 12, 2001, two players were killed by lightning and ten severely burned at a **Guatemala** Third Division match between Deportivo Culquimulilla and Pueblo Nuevo Vinas.

On Nov 1, 2002, two players died from injuries after lightning struck Deportivo Cali's training ground in **Colombia**.

On Mar 12 2004, five people were killed and more than 100 injured when spectators stampeded shortly before the Syrian Championship fixture between Al-Jihad and Al-Fatwa in **Qameshli**, Northern Syria. The match was cancelled.

On Oct 10, 2004, three spectators died in a crush at the African Zone World Cup qualifier between **Guinea** and **Morocco** (1-1) at Conakry, Guinea.

On Mar 25, 2005, five were killed as 100,000 left the Azadi Stadium, **Tehran**, after Iran's World Cup qualifying win (2-1) against Japan.

On Jun 2, 2007, 12 spectators were killed and 46 injured in a crush at the Chillabombwe Stadium, **Zambia**, after an African Nations Cup qualifier against Congo.

On Mar 29, 2009, 19 people died and 139 were injured after a wall collapsed at the Ivory Coast stadium in **Abidjan** before a World Cup qualifier against Malawi. The match went ahead, Ivory Coast winning 5-0 with two goals from Chelsea's Didier Drogba. The tragedy meant that, in 13 years, crowd disasters at club and internationals at ten different grounds across Africa had claimed the lives of 283 people.

On Jan 8, 2010, terrorists at **Cabinda**, Angola machine-gunned the Togo team buses travelling to the Africa Cup of Nations. They killed a driver, an assistant coach and a media officer and injured several players. The team were ordered by their Government to withdraw from the tournament.

On Oct 23, 2010, seven fans were trampled to death when thousands tried to force their way into the Nyayo National Stadium in **Nairobi** at a Kenya Premier League match between the Gor Mahia and AFC Leopards clubs.

On Feb 1, 2012, 74 died and nearly 250 were injured in a crowd riot at the end of the Al-Masry v Al-Ahly match in **Port Said** – the worst disaster in Egyptian sport.

DAYS OF TRAGEDY – PERSONAL

Sam Wynne, Bury right-back, collapsed five minutes before half-time in the First Division match away to Sheffield Utd on Apr 30, 1927, and died in the dressing-room.

John Thomson, Celtic and Scotland goalkeeper, sustained a fractured skull when diving at an opponent's feet in the Rangers v Celtic League match on Sep 5, 1931, and died the same evening.

Sim Raleigh (Gillingham), injured in a clash of heads at home to Brighton (Div 3 South) on Dec 1, 1934, continued to play but collapsed in second half and died in hospital the same night.

James Thorpe, Sunderland goalkeeper, was injured during the First Division match at home to Chelsea on Feb 1, 1936 and died in a diabetic coma three days later.

Derek Dooley, Sheffield Wed centre-forward and top scorer in 1951–52 in the Football League with 46 goals in 30 matches, broke a leg in the League match at Preston on Feb 14, 1953, and, after complications set in, had to lose the limb by amputation.

John White, Tottenham's Scottish international forward, was killed by lightning on a golf course at Enfield, North London in Jul, 1964.

Tony Allden, Highgate centre-half, was struck by lightning during an Amateur Cup quarter-final with Enfield on Feb 25, 1967. He died the following day. Four other players were also struck but recovered.

Roy Harper died while refereeing the York v Halifax (Div 4) match on May 5, 1969.

Jim Finn collapsed and died from a heart attack while refereeing Exeter v Stockport (Div 4) on Sep 16, 1972.

Scotland manager **Jock Stein**, 62, collapsed and died at the end of the Wales-Scotland World Cup qualifying match (1-1) at Ninian Park, Cardiff on Sep 10, 1985.

David Longhurst, York forward, died after being carried off two minutes before half-time in the Fourth Division fixture at home to Lincoln on Sep 8, 1990. The match was abandoned (0-0). The inquest revealed that Longhurst suffered from a rare heart condition.

Mike North collapsed while refereeing Southend v Mansfield (Div 3) on Apr 16, 2001 and died shortly afterwards. The match was abandoned and re-staged on May 8, with the receipts donated to his family.

Marc-Vivien Foe, on his 63rd appearance in Cameroon's midfield, collapsed unchallenged in the centre circle after 72 minutes of the FIFA Confederations Cup semi-final against Colombia in Lyon, France, on Jun 26, 2003, and despite the efforts of the stadium medical staff he could not be revived. He had been on loan to Manchester City from Olympique Lyonnais in season 2002–03, and poignantly scored the club's last goal at Maine Road.

Paul Sykes, Folkestone Invicta (Ryman League) striker, died on the pitch during the Kent Senior Cup semi-final against Margate on Apr 12, 2005. He collapsed after an innocuous off-the-ball incident.

Craig Gowans, Falkirk apprentice, was killed at the club's training ground on Jul 8, 2005 when he came into contact with power lines.

Peter Wilson, Mansfield goalkeeping coach, died of a heart attack after collapsing during the warm-up of the League Two game away to Shrewsbury on Nov 19, 2005.

Matt Gadsby, Hinckley defender, collapsed and died while playing in a Conference North match at Harrogate on Sep 9, 2006.

Phil O'Donnell, 35-year-old Motherwell captain and Scotland midfield player, collapsed when about to be substituted near the end of the SPL home game against Dundee Utd on Dec 29, 2007 and died shortly afterwards in hospital.

GREAT SERVICE

'For services to Association Football', **Stanley Matthews** (Stoke, Blackpool and England), already a CBE, became the first professional footballer to receive a knighthood. This was bestowed in 1965, his last season. Before he retired and five days after his 50th birthday, he played for Stoke to set a record as the oldest First Division footballer (v Fulham, Feb 6, 1965).

Over a brilliant span of 33 years, he played in 886 first-class matches, including 54 full Internationals (plus 31 in war time), 701 League games (including 3 at start of season 1939–40, which was abandoned on the outbreak of war) and 86 FA Cup-ties, and scored 95 goals. He was never booked in his career.

Sir Stanley died on Feb 23, 2000, three weeks after his 85th birthday. His ashes were buried under the centre circle of Stoke's Britannia Stadium. After spending a number of years in Toronto, he made his home back in the Potteries in 1989, having previously returned to his home town, Hanley in Oct, 1987 to unveil a life-size bronze statue of himself. The inscription reads: 'Sir Stanley Matthews, CBE. Born Hanley, 1 Feb 1915.

His name is symbolic of the beauty of the game, his fame timeless and international, his sportsmanship and modesty universally acclaimed. A magical player, of the people, for the people.' On his home-coming in 1989, Sir Stanley was made President of Stoke, the club he joined as a boy of 15 and served as a player for 20 years between 1931 and 1965, on either side of his spell with Blackpool.

In Jul 1992 FIFA honoured him with their 'Gold merit award' for outstanding services to the game.

Former England goalkeeper **Peter Shilton** has made more first-class appearances (1,387) than any other footballer in British history. He played his 1,000th. League game in Leyton Orient's 2-0 home win against Brighton on Dec 22, 1996 and made 9 appearances for Orient in his final season. He retired from international football after the 1990 World Cup in Italy with 125 caps, then a world record. Shilton kept a record 60 clean sheets for England.

Shilton's career spanned 32 seasons, 20 of them on the international stage. He made his League debut for Leicester in May 1966, two months before England won the World Cup.

His 1,387 first-class appearances comprise a record 1,005 in the Football League, 125 Internationals, 102 League Cup, 86 FA Cup, 13 for England U-23s, 4 for the Football League and 52 other matches (European Cup, UEFA Cup, World Club Championship, Charity Shield, European Super Cup, Full Members' Cup, Play-offs, Screen Sports Super Cup, Anglo-Italian Cup, Texaco Cup, Simod Cup, Zenith Data Systems Cup and Autoglass Trophy).

Shilton appeared 57 times at Wembley, 52 for England, 2 League Cup Finals, 1 FA Cup Final, 1 Charity Shield match, and 1 for the Football League. He passed a century of League appearances with each of his first five clubs: Leicester (286), Stoke (110), Nottm Forest (202), Southampton (188) and Derby (175) and subsequently played for Plymouth, Bolton and Leyton Orient.

He was awarded the MBE and OBE for services to football. At the Football League Awards ceremony in March 2013, he received the League's Contribution award.

Six other British footballers have made more than 1,000 first-class appearances:

Ray Clemence, formerly with Tottenham, Liverpool and England, retired through injury in season 1987–88 after a goalkeeping career of 1,119 matches starting in 1965–66.

Clemence played 50 times for his first club, Scunthorpe; 665 for Liverpool; 337 for Tottenham; his 67 representative games included 61 England caps.

A third great British goalkeeper, **Pat Jennings**, ended his career (1963–86) with a total of 1,098 first-class matches for Watford, Tottenham, Arsenal and N Ireland. They were made up of 757 in the Football League, 119 full Internationals, 84 FA Cup appearances, 72 League/Milk Cup, 55 European club matches, 2 Charity Shield, 3 Other Internationals, 1 Under-23 cap, 2 Texaco Cup, 2 Anglo-Italian Cup and 1 Super Cup. Jennings played his 119th and final international on his 41st birthday, Jun 12, 1986, against Brazil in Guadalajara in the Mexico World Cup.

Yet another outstanding 'keeper, **David Seaman**, passed the 1,000 appearances milestone for clubs and country in season 2002–03, reaching 1,004 when aged 39, he captained Arsenal to FA Cup triumph against Southampton.

With Arsenal, Seaman won 3 Championship medals, the FA Cup 4 times, the Double twice, the League Cup and Cup-Winners' Cup once each. After 13 seasons at Highbury, he joined Manchester City (Jun 2003) on a free transfer. He played 26 matches for City before a shoulder injury forced his retirement in Jan 2004, aged 40.

Seaman's 22-season career composed 1,046 first-class matches: 955 club apps (Peterborough 106, Birmingham 84, QPR 175, Arsenal 564, Manchester City 26); 75 senior caps for England, 6 'B' caps and 10 at U-21 level.

Defender **Graeme Armstrong**, 42-year-old commercial manager for an Edinburgh whisky company and part-time assistant-manager and captain of Scottish Third Division club Stenhousemuir, made the 1000th first team appearance of his career in the Scottish Cup 3rd Round against Rangers at Ibrox on Jan 23, 1999. He was presented with the Man of the Match award before kick-off.

Against East Stirling on Boxing Day, he had played his 864th League game, breaking the British record for an outfield player set by another Scot, Tommy Hutchison, with Alloa, Blackpool, Coventry, Manchester City, Burnley and Swansea City.

Armstrong's 24-year career, spent in the lower divisions of the Scottish League, began as a 1-match trialist with Meadowbank Thistle in 1975 and continued via Stirling Albion, Berwick Rangers, Meadowbank and, from 1992, Stenhousemuir.

Tony Ford became the first English outfield player to reach 1000 senior appearances in Rochdale's 1-0 win at Carlisle (Auto Windscreens Shield) on Mar 7, 2000. Grimsby-born, he began his 26-season midfield career with Grimsby and played for 7 other League clubs: Sunderland (loan), Stoke, WBA, Bradford City (loan), Scunthorpe, Mansfield and Rochdale. He retired, aged 42, in 2001 with a career record of 1072 appearances (121 goals) and his total of 931 League games is exceeded only by Peter Shilton's 1005.

On Apr 16, 2011, **Graham Alexander** reached 1,000 appearances when he came on as a sub for Burnley at home to Swansea. Alexander, 40, ended a 22-year career with the equaliser for Preston against Charlton (2-2, Lge 1) on Apr 28, 2012 – his 1,023rd appearance. He also played for Luton and Scunthorpe and was capped 40 times by Scotland.

GIGGS RECORD COLLECTION

Ryan Giggs (Manchester Utd) has collected the most individual honours in English football with a total of 34 prizes. They comprise: 13 Premier League titles, 4 FA Cups, 3 League Cups, 2 European Cups, 1 UEFA Super Cup, 1 Inter-Continental Cup, 1 World Club Cup, 9 Charity Shields/ Community Shields. One-club man Giggs played 24 seasons for United, making a record 963 appearances. He won 64 Wales caps and on retiring as a player, aged 40, in May 2014, became the club's assistant manager. He ended a 29-year association with the club in June 2016.

KNIGHTS OF SOCCER

Players, managers and administrators who have been honoured for their services to football: **Charles Clegg** (1927), **Stanley Rous** (1949), **Stanley Matthews** (1965), **Alf Ramsey** (1967), **Matt Busby** (1968), **Walter Winterbottom** (1978) **Bert Millichip** (1991), **Bobby Charlton** (1994), **Tom Finney** (1998), **Geoff Hurst** (1998), **Alex Ferguson** (1999), **Bobby Robson** (2002), **Trevor Brooking** (2004), **Dave Richards** (2006), **Doug Ellis** (2011).

- On Nov 6, 2014, **Karren Brady**, vice-chairman of West Ham, was elevated to the Lords as Karren, Baroness Brady, OBE, of Knightsbridge, life peer

PENALTIES

The **penalty-kick** was introduced to the game, following a proposal to the Irish FA in 1890 by William McCrum, son of the High Sheriff for Co Omagh, and approved by the International Football Board on Jun 2, 1891.

First penalty scored in a first-class match in England was by John Heath, for Wolves v Accrington Stanley (5-0 in Div 1, Sep 14, 1891).

The greatest influence of the penalty has come since the 1970s, with the introduction of the shoot-out to settle deadlocked ties in various competitions.

Manchester Utd were the first club to win a competitive match in British football via a shoot-out (4-3 away to Hull, Watney Cup semi-final, Aug 5, 1970); in that penalty contest, George Best was the first player to score, Denis Law the first to miss.

The shoot-out was adopted by FIFA and UEFA the same year (1970).

In season 1991–92, penalty shoot-outs were introduced to decide FA Cup ties still level after one replay and extra time.

Wembley saw its first penalty contest in the 1974 Charity Shield. Since then many major matches across the world have been settled in this way, including:

1976 **European Championship Final (Belgrade):** Czechoslovakia beat West Germany 5-3 (after 2-2)
1980 **Cup-Winners' Cup Final (Brussels):** Valencia beat Arsenal 5-4 (after 0-0)
1984 **European Cup Final (Rome):** Liverpool beat Roma 4-2 (after 1-1)
1984 **UEFA Cup Final:** Tottenham (home) beat Anderlecht 4-3 (2-2 agg)
1986 **European Cup Final (Seville):** Steaua Bucharest beat Barcelona 2-0 (after 0-0).
1987 **Freight Rover Trophy Final (Wembley):** Mansfield beat Bristol City 5-4 (after 1-1)
1987 **Scottish League Cup Final (Hampden Park):** Rangers beat Aberdeen 5-3 (after 3-3)
1988 **European Cup Final (Stuttgart):** PSV Eindhoven beat Benfica 6-5 (after 0-0)
1988 **UEFA Cup Final:** Bayer Leverkusen (home) beat Espanyol 3-2 after 3-3 (0-3a, 3-0h)
1990 **Scottish Cup Final (Hampden Park):** Aberdeen beat Celtic 9-8 (after 0-0)
1991 **European Cup Final (Bari):** Red Star Belgrade beat Marseille 5-3 (after 0-0)
1991 **Div 4 Play-off Final (Wembley):** Torquay beat Blackpool 5-4 (after 2-2)
1992 **Div 4 Play-off Final (Wembley):** Blackpool beat Scunthorpe 4-3 (after 1-1)
1993 **Div 3 Play-off Final(Wembley):** York beat Crewe 5-3 (after 1-1)
1994 **Autoglass Trophy Final (Wembley):** Swansea City beat Huddersfield 3-1 (after 1-1)
1994 **World Cup Final (Los Angeles):** Brazil beat Italy 3-2 (after 0-0)
1994 **Scottish League Cup Final (Ibrox Park):** Raith beat Celtic 6-5 (after 2-2)
1995 **Copa America Final (Montevideo):** Uruguay beat Brazil 5-3 (after 1-1)
1996 **European Cup Final (Rome):** Juventus beat Ajax 4-2 (after 1-1)
1996 **European U-21 Champ Final (Barcelona):** Italy beat Spain 4-2 (after 1-1)
1997 **Auto Windscreens Shield Final (Wembley):** Carlisle beat Colchester 4-3 (after 0-0)
1997 **UEFA Cup Final:** FC Schalke beat Inter Milan 4-1 (after 1-1 agg)
1998 **Div 1 Play-off Final (Wembley):** Charlton beat Sunderland 7-6 (after 4-4)
1999 **Div 2 Play-off Final (Wembley):** Manchester City beat Gillingham 3-1 (after 2-2)
1999 **Women's World Cup Final (Pasedena):** USA beat China 5-4 (after 0-0)
2000 **African Nations Cup Final (Lagos):** Cameroon beat Nigeria 4-3 (after 0-0)
2000 **UEFA Cup Final (Copenhagen):** Galatasaray beat Arsenal 4-1 (after 0-0)
2000 **Olympic Final (Sydney):** Cameroon beat Spain 5-3 (after 2-2)
2001 **League Cup Final (Millennium Stadium):** Liverpool beat Birmingham 5-4 (after 1-1)
2001 **Champions League Final (Milan):** Bayern Munich beat Valencia 5-4 (after 1-1)
2002 **Euro U-21 Champ Final (Basle):** Czech Republic beat France 3-1 (after 0-0)
2002 **Div 1 Play-off Final (Millennium Stadium):** Birmingham beat Norwich 4-2 (after 1-1)
2003 **Champions League Final (Old Trafford):** AC Milan beat Juventus 3-2 (after 0-0)
2004 **Div 3 Play-off Final (Millennium Stadium):** Huddersfield beat Mansfield 4-1 (after 0-0)
2004 **Copa America Final (Lima):** Brazil beat Argentina 4-2 (after 2-2)
2005 **FA Cup Final (Millennium Stadium):** Arsenal beat Manchester Utd 5-4 (after 0-0)
2005 **Champions League Final (Istanbul):** Liverpool beat AC Milan 3-2 (after 3-3)
2006 **African Cup of Nations Final (Cairo):** Egypt beat Ivory Coast 4-2 (after 0-0)
2006 **FA Cup Final (Millennium Stadium):** Liverpool beat West Ham 3-1 (after 3-3)
2006 **Scottish Cup Final (Hampden Park):** Hearts beat Gretna 4-2 (after 1-1)
2006 **Lge 1 Play-off Final (Millennium Stadium):** Barnsley beat Swansea City 4-3 (after 2-2)
2006 **World Cup Final (Berlin):** Italy beat France 5-3 (after 1-1)

2007 **UEFA Cup Final (Hampden Park):** Sevilla beat Espanyol 3-1 (after 2-2)
2008 **Champions League Final (Moscow):** Manchester Utd beat Chelsea 6-5 (after 1-1)
2008 **Scottish League Cup Final (Hampden Park):** Rangers beat Dundee Utd 3-2 (after 2-2)
2009 **League Cup Final (Wembley):** Manchester Utd beat Tottenham 4-1 (after 0-0)
2011 **Women's World Cup Final (Frankfurt):** Japan beat USA 3-1 (after 2-2)
2012 **League Cup Final (Wembley):** Liverpool beat Cardiff 3-2 (after 2-2)
2012 **Champions League Final (Munich):** Chelsea beat Bayern Munich 4-3 (after 1-1)
2012 **Lge 1 Play-off Final (Wembley):** Huddersfield beat Sheffield Utd 8-7 (after 0-0)
2012 **Africa Cup of Nations Final (Gabon):** Zambia beat Ivory Coast 8-7 (after 0-0)
2013 **FA Trophy Final (Wembley):** Wrexham beat Grimsby 4-1 (after 1-1)
2013 **European Super Cup (Prague):** Bayern Munich beat Chelsea 5-4 (after 2-2)
2014 **Scottish League Cup Final (Celtic Park):** Aberdeen beat Inverness 4-2 (after 0-0)
2014 **Lge 1 Play-off Final (Wembley):** Rotherheam beat Leyton Orient 4-3 (after 2-2)
2014 **Europa Lge Final (Turin):** Sevilla beat Benfica 4-2 (after 0-0)
2015 **Africa Cup of Nations Final (Equ Guinea):** Ivory Coast beat Ghana 9-8 (after 0-0)
2015 **Conference Play-off Final (Wembley):** Bristol Rov beat Grimsby 5-3 (after 1-1)
2015 **Lge 2 Play-off Final (Wembley):** Southend beat Wycombe 7-6 (after 1-1)
2015 **FA Trophy Final (Wembley)** North Ferriby beat Wrexham 5-4 (after3-3)
2015 **Euro U-21 Champ Final (Prague):** Sweden beat Portugal 4-3 (after 0-0)
2015 **Copa America Final (Santiago):** Chile beat Argentina 4-1 (after 0-0)
2016 **League Cup Final (Wembley):** Manchester City beat Liverpool 3-1 (after 1-1)
2016 **Champions League Final (Milan):** Real Madrid beat Atletico Madrid 5-3 (after 1-1)

In South America in 1992, in a 26-shot competition, **Newell's Old Boys** beat America 11-10 in the Copa Libertadores.

Longest-recorded penalty contest in first-class matches was in Argentina in 1988 – from 44 shots, **Argentinos Juniors** beat Racing Club 20-19. Genclerbirligi beat Galatasaray 17-16 in a Turkish Cup-tie in 1996. Only one penalty was missed.

Highest-scoring shoot-outs in international football: **North Korea** beat Hong Kong 11-10 (after 3-3 draw) in an Asian Cup match in 1975; and **Ivory Coast** beat Ghana 11-10 (after 0-0 draw) in African Nations Cup Final, 1992.

Most penalties needed to settle an adult game in Britain: **44** in Norfolk Primary Cup 4th round replay, Dec 2000. Aston Village side **Freethorpe** beat Foulsham 20-19 (5 kicks missed). All 22 players took 2 penalties each, watched by a crowd of 20. The sides had drawn 2-2, 4-4 in a tie of 51 goals.

Penalty that took 24 days: That was how long elapsed between the award and the taking of a penalty in an Argentine Second Division match between **Atalanta** and Defensores in 2003. A riot ended the original match with 5 minutes left. The game resumed behind closed doors with the penalty that caused the abandonment. Lucas Ferreiro scored it to give Atalanta a 1-0 win.

INTERNATIONAL PENALTIES, MISSED

Four penalties out of five were missed when **Colombia** beat Argentina 3-0 in a Copa America group tie in Paraguay in Jul 1999. Martin Palmermo missed three for Argentina and Colombia's Hamilton Ricard had one spot-kick saved.

In the European Championship semi-final against Italy in Amsterdam on Jun 29, 2000, **Holland** missed five penalties – two in normal time, three in the penalty contest which Italy won 3-1 (after 0-0). Dutch captain Frank de Boer missed twice from the spot.

ENGLAND'S SHOOT-OUT RECORD

England have been beaten in seven out of nine penalty shoot-outs in major tournaments:
1990 (World Cup semi-final, Turin) 3-4 v West Germany after 1-1.
1996 (Euro Champ quarter-final, Wembley) 4-2 v Spain after 0-0.
1996 (Euro Champ semi-final, Wembley) 5-6 v Germany after 1-1.
1998 (World Cup 2nd round., St Etienne) 3-4 v Argentina after 2-2.
2004 (Euro Champ quarter-final, Lisbon) 5-6 v Portugal after 2-2.
2006 (World Cup quarter-final, Gelsenkirchen) 1-3 v Portugal after 0-0.

2007 (Euro U-21 Champ semi-final, Heerenveen) 12-13 v Holland after 1-1.
2009 (Euro U-21 Champ semi-final, Gothenburg) 5-4 v Sweden after 3-3.
2012 (Euro Champ quarter-final, Kiev) 2-4 v Italy after 0-0.

FA CUP SHOOT-OUTS

First penalty contest in the FA Cup took place in 1972. In the days of the play-off for third place, the match was delayed until the eve of the following season when losing semi-finalists Birmingham and Stoke met at St Andrew's on Aug 5. The score was 0-0 and Birmingham won 4-3 on penalties.

Highest-scoring: Preliminary round replay (Aug 30, 2005): Tunbridge Wells beat Littlehampton 16-15 after 40 spot-kicks (9 missed).

Competition proper: Scunthorpe beat Worcester 14-13 in 2nd round replay (Dec 17, 2014) after 1-1 (32 kicks).

Shoot-out abandoned: The FA Cup 1st round replay between Oxford City and Wycombe at Wycombe on Nov 9, 1999 was abandoned (1-1) after extra-time. As the penalty shoot-out was about to begin, a fire broke out under a stand. Wycombe won the second replay 1-0 at Oxford Utd's ground.

First FA Cup Final to be decided by shoot-out was in 2005 (May 21), when Arsenal beat Manchester Utd 5-4 on penalties at Cardiff's Millennium Stadium (0-0 after extra time). A year later (May 13) Liverpool beat West Ham 3-1 (3-3 after extra-time).

MARATHON SHOOT-OUT BETWEEN LEAGUE CLUBS

Highest recorded score in shoot-out between league clubs: Dagenham & Redbridge 14-13 against Leyton Orient (after 1-1) in Johnstone's Paint Trophy southern section on Sep 7, 2011

SHOOT-OUT RECORD WINNERS AND LOSERS

When **Bradford** beat Arsenal 3-2 on penalties in a League Cup fifth round tie, it was the club's ninth successive shoot-out victory in FA Cup, League Cup and Johnstone's Paint Trophy ties between Oct 2009 and Dec 2012.

Tottenham's 4-1 spot-kick failure against Basel in the last 16 of the Europa League was their seventh successive defeat in shoot-outs from Mar 1996 to Apr 2013 (FA Cup, League Cup, UEFA Cup, Europa League)

MISSED CUP FINAL PENALTIES

John Aldridge (Liverpool) became the first player to miss a penalty in an FA Cup Final at Wembley when Dave Beasant saved his shot in 1988 to help Wimbledon to a shock 1-0 win. Seven penalties before had been scored in the Final at Wembley.

Previously, **Charlie Wallace**, of Aston Villa, had failed from the spot in the 1913 Final against Sunderland at Crystal Palace, which his team won 1-0

Gary Lineker (Tottenham) had his penalty saved by Nottm Forest's Mark Crossley in the 1991 FA Cup Final.

For the first time, two spot-kicks were missed in an FA Cup Final. In 2010, Petr Cech saved from Portsmouth's **Kevin-Prince Boateng** while Chelsea's **Frank Lampard** put his kick wide.

Another miss at Wembley was by Arsenal's **Nigel Winterburn**, Luton's Andy Dibble saving his spot-kick in the 1988 Littlewoods Cup Final, when a goal would have put Arsenal 3-1 ahead. Instead, they lost 3-2.

Winterburn was the third player to fail with a League Cup Final penalty at Wembley, following **Ray Graydon** (Aston Villa) against Norwich in 1975 and **Clive Walker** (Sunderland), who shot wide in the 1985 Milk Cup Final, also against Norwich who won 1-0. Graydon had his penalty saved by Kevin Keelan, but scored from the rebound and won the cup for Aston Villa (1-0).

Derby's Martin Taylor saved a penalty from **Eligio Nicolini** in the Anglo-Italian Cup Final at Wembley on Mar 27, 1993, but Cremonese won 3-1.

LEAGUE PENALTIES RECORD

Most penalties in Football League match: Five – 4 to Crystal Palace (3 missed), 1 to Brighton (scored) in Div 2 match at Selhurst Park on Mar 27 (Easter Monday), 1989. Crystal Palace won 2-1. Three of the penalties were awarded in a 5-minute spell. The match also produced 5 bookings and a sending-off. Other teams missing 3 penalties in a match: Burnley v Grimsby (Div 2), Feb 13, 1909; Manchester City v Newcastle (Div 1), Jan 17, 1912.

HOTTEST MODERN SPOT-SHOTS

Matthew Le Tissier ended his career in season 2001–02 with the distinction of having netted 48 out of 49 first-team penalties for Southampton. He scored the last 27 after his only miss when Nottm Forest keeper Mark Crossley saved in a Premier League match at The Dell on Mar 24, 1993.

Graham Alexander scored 78 out of 84 penalties in a 22-year career (Scunthorpe, Luton, Preston twice and Burnley) which ended in 2012.

SPOT-KICK HAT-TRICKS

Right-back **Joe Willetts** scored three penalties when Hartlepool beat Darlington 6-1 (Div 3N) on Good Friday 1951.

Danish international **Jan Molby**'s only hat-trick in English football, for Liverpool in a 3-1 win at home to Coventry (Littlewoods Cup, 4th round replay, Nov 26, 1986) comprised three goals from the penalty spot.

It was the first such hat-trick in a major match for two years – since **Andy Blair** scored three penalties for Sheffield Wed against Luton (Milk Cup 4th round, Nov 20 1984).

Portsmouth's **Kevin Dillon** scored a penalty hat-trick in the Full Members Cup (2nd round) at home to Millwall (3-2) on Nov 4, 1986.

Alan Slough scored a hat-trick of penalties in an away game, but was on the losing side, when Peterborough were beaten 4-3 at Chester (Div 3, Apr 29, 1978).

Penalty hat-tricks in **international football: Dimitris Saravakos** (in 9 mins) for Greece v Egypt in 1990. He scored 5 goals in match. **Henrik Larsson**, among his 4 goals in Sweden's 6-0 home win v Moldova in World Cup qualifying match, Jun 6, 2001.

MOST PENALTY GOALS (LEAGUE) IN SEASON

13 out of 13 by **Francis Lee** for Manchester City (Div 1) in 1971–72. His goal total for the season was 33. In season 1988–89, **Graham Roberts** scored 12 League penalties for Second Division Champions Chelsea. In season 2004–05, **Andrew Johnson** scored 11 Premiership penalties for Crystal Palace, who were relegated.

PENALTY-SAVE SEQUENCES

Ipswich goalkeeper **Paul Cooper** saved eight of the ten penalties he faced in 1979–80. **Roy Brown** (Notts Co) saved six in a row in season 1972–73.

Andy Lomas, goalkeeper for Chesham (Diadora League) claimed a record eighth **consecutive** penalty saves – three at the end of season 1991–92 and five in 1992–93.

Mark Bosnich (Aston Villa) saved five in two consecutive matches in 1993–94: three in Coca-Cola Cup semi-final penalty shoot-out v Tranmere (Feb 26), then two in Premiership at Tottenham (Mar 2).

MISSED PENALTIES SEQUENCE

Against Wolves in Div 2 on Sep 28, 1991, **Southend** missed their seventh successive penalty (five of them the previous season).

SCOTTISH RECORDS

(See also under 'Goals' & 'Discipline')

RANGERS' MANY RECORDS

Rangers' record-breaking feats include:

League Champions: 54 times (once joint holders) – world record.

Winning every match in Scottish League (18 games, 1898–99 season).

Major hat-tricks: Rangers have completed the domestic treble (League Championship, League Cup and Scottish FA Cup) a record seven times (1948–49, 1963–64, 1975–76, 1977–78, 1992–93, 1998–99, 2002–03).

League & Cup double: 17 times.

Nine successive Championships (1989–97). Four men played in all nine sides: Richard Gough, Ally McCoist, Ian Ferguson and Ian Durrant.

115 major trophies: Championships 54, Scottish Cup 33, League Cup 27, Cup-Winners' Cup 1.

CELTIC'S GRAND SLAM

Celtic's record in 1966–67 was the most successful by a British club in one season. They won the **Scottish League,** the **Scottish Cup,** the **Scottish League Cup** and became the first British club to win the **European Cup**. They also won the **Glasgow Cup**.

Celtic have three times achieved the Scottish treble (League Championship, League Cup and FA Cup), in 1966–67, 1968–69 and 2000–01 (in Martin O'Neill's first season as their manager). They became Scottish Champions for 2000–01 with a 1-0 home win against St Mirren on Apr 7 – the earliest the title had been clinched for 26 years, since Rangers' triumph on Mar 29, 1975. They have been champions 47 times.

They have won the Scottish Cup 36 times, and have completed the League and Cup double 15 times.

Celtic won nine consecutive Scottish League titles (1966–74) under Jock Stein.

They set a **British record** of 25 consecutive League wins in season 2003–04 (Aug 15 to Mar 14). They were unbeaten for 77 matches (all competitions) at Celtic Park from Aug 22, 2001, to Apr 21, 2004. They have won the Scottish Championship 46 times.

UNBEATEN SCOTTISH CHAMPIONS

Celtic and **Rangers** have each won the Scottish Championship with an unbeaten record: Celtic in 1897–98 (P18, W15, D3), Rangers in 1898–99 (P18, W18).

FORSTER'S SHUT-OUT RECORD

Celtic goalkeeper **Fraser Forster** set a record in Scottish top-flight football by not conceding a goal for 1,256 consecutive minutes in season 2013–14.

TRIO OF TOP CLUBS MISSING

Three of Scotland's leading clubs were missing from the 2014-15 Premiership season. With **Hearts** finishing bottom and **Rangers** still working their way back through the divisions after being demoted, they were joined in the second tier by **Hibernian,** who lost the play-off final on penalties to Hamilton.

SCOTTISH CUP HAT-TRICKS

Aberdeen's feat of winning the Scottish FA Cup in 1982–83–84 made them only the third club to achieve that particular hat-trick. **Queen's Park** did it twice (1874–75–76 and 1880–81–82), and **Rangers** have won the Scottish Cup three years in succession on three occasions: 1934–35–36, 1948–49–50 and 1962–63–64.

SCOTTISH CUP FINAL DISMISSALS

Five players have been sent off in the Scottish FA Cup Final: **Jock Buchanan** (Rangers v Kilmarnock, 1929); **Roy Aitken** (Celtic v Aberdeen, 1984); **Walter Kidd** (Hearts captain v Aberdeen, 1986); **Paul Hartley** (Hearts v Gretna, 2006); **Pa Kujabi** (Hibernian v Hearts, 2012).

HIGHEST-SCORING SHOOT-OUT

In Scottish football's highest-scoring penalty shoot-out, **Stirling Albion** beat junior club Hurlford 13-12 after 28 spot-kicks in a third round replay. The tie, on Nov 8, 2014, had ended 2-2 after extra-time.

RECORD SEQUENCES

Celtic hold Britain's League record of 62 matches undefeated, from Nov 13, 1915 to Apr 21, 1917, when Kilmarnock won 2-0 at Parkhead. They won 49, drew 13 (111 points) and scored 126 goals to 26.

Greenock Morton in 1963–64 accumulated 67 points out of 72 and scored 135 goals.

Queen's Park did not have a goal scored against them during the first seven seasons of their existence (1867–74, before the Scottish League was formed).

EARLIEST PROMOTIONS IN SCOTLAND

Dundee promoted from Div 2, Feb 1, 1947; **Greenock Morton** promoted from Div 2, Mar 2, 1964; **Gretna** promoted from Div 3, Mar 5, 2005; **Hearts** promoted from Championship, Mar 21, 2015.

WORST HOME SEQUENCE

After gaining promotion to Div 1 in 1992, **Cowdenbeath** went a record 38 consecutive home League matches without a win. They ended the sequence (drew 8, lost 30) when beating Arbroath 1-0 on Apr 2, 1994, watched by a crowd of 225.

ALLY'S RECORDS

Ally McCoist became the first player to complete 200 goals in the Premier Division when he scored Rangers' winner (2-1) at Falkirk on Dec 12, 1992. His first was against Celtic in Sep 1983, and he reached 100 against Dundee on Boxing Day 1987.

When McCoist scored twice at home to Hibernian (4-3) on Dec 7, 1996, he became Scotland's record post-war League marksman, beating Gordon Wallace's 264.

Originally with St Johnstone (1978–81), he spent two seasons with Sunderland (1981–83), then joined Rangers for £200,000 in Jun 1983.

In 15 seasons at Ibrox, he scored 355 goals for Rangers (250 League), and helped them win 10 Championships (9 in succession), 3 Scottish Cups and earned a record 9 League Cup winner's medals. He won the European Golden Boot in consecutive seasons (1991–92, 1992–93).

His 9 Premier League goals in three seasons for Kilmarnock gave him a career total of 281 Scottish League goals when he retired at the end of 2000–01. McCoist succeeded Walter Smith as manager of Rangers in May 2011.

SCOTLAND'S MOST SUCCESSFUL MANAGER

Bill Struth, 30 trophies for Rangers, 1920–54 (18 Championships, 10 Scottish Cups, 2 League Cups.

SMITH'S IBROX HONOURS

Walter Smith, who retired in May, 2011, won a total of 21 trophies in two spells as Rangers manager (10 League titles, 5 Scottish Cups, 6 League Cups).

RANGERS PUNISHED

In April 2012, **Rangers** (in administration) were fined £160,000 by the Scottish FA and given a 12-month transfer ban on charges relating to their finances. The ban was later overturned in court. The club had debts estimated at around £135m and on June 12, 2012 were forced into liquidation. A new company emerged, but Rangers were voted out of the Scottish Premier League and demoted to Division Three for the start of the 2012-13 season. They returned to the top division in 2016 via three promotions in four seasons.

FIVE IN A MATCH

Paul Sturrock set an individual scoring record for the Scottish Premier Division with 5 goals in Dundee Utd's 7-0 win at home to Morton on Nov 17, 1984. **Marco Negri** equalled the feat with all 5 when Rangers beat Dundee Utd 5-1 at Ibrox (Premier Division) on Aug 23, 1997, and **Kenny Miller** scored 5 in Rangers' 7-1 win at home to St Mirren on Nov 4, 2000. **Kris**

Boyd scored all Kilmarnock's goals in a 5-2 SPL win at home to Dundee Utd on Sep 25, 2004. **Boyd** scored another 5 when Rangers beat Dundee Utd 7-1 on Dec 30, 2009. That took his total of SPL goals to a record 160. **Gary Hooper** netted all Celtic's goals in 5-0 SPL win against Hearts on May 13, 2012

NEGRI'S TEN-TIMER

Marco Negri scored in Rangers' first ten League matches (23 goals) in season 1997–98, a Premier Division record. The previous best was 8 by **Ally MacLeod** for Hibernian in 1978.

DOUBLE SCOTTISH FINAL

Rangers v Celtic drew **129,643** and **120,073** people to the Scottish Cup Final and replay at Hampden Park, Glasgow, in 1963. Receipts for the two matches totalled £50,500.

MOST SCOTTISH CHAMPIONSHIP MEDALS

13 by **Sandy Archibald** (Rangers, 1918–34). Post-war record: 10 by **Bobby Lennox** (Celtic, 1966–79).

Alan Morton won **nine** Scottish Championship medals with Rangers in 1921–23–24–25–27–28–29–30–31. **Ally McCoist** played in the Rangers side that won nine successive League titles (1989–97).

Between 1927 and 1939 **Bob McPhail** helped Rangers win nine Championships, finish second twice and third once. He scored 236 League goals but was never top scorer in a single season.

TOP SCOTTISH LEAGUE SCORERS IN SEASON

Raith Rovers (Div 2) 142 goals in 1937–38; **Morton** (Div 2) 135 goals in 1963–64; **Hearts** (Div 1) 132 goals in 1957–58; **Falkirk** (Div 2) 132 goals in 1935–36; **Gretna** (Div 3) 130 goals in 2004–05.

SCOTTISH CUP – NO DECISION

The **Scottish FA** withheld their Cup and medals in 1908–09 after Rangers and Celtic played two drawn games in the Final. Spectators rioted.

FEWEST LEAGUE WINS IN SEASON

In modern times: 1 win by **Ayr** (34 matches, Div 1, 1966–67); **Forfar** (38 matches, Div 2, 1973–74); **Clydebank** (36 matches, Div 1, 1999–2000).

Vale of Leven provided the only instance of a British team failing to win a single match in a league season (Div 1, 18 games,1891–92).

HAMPDEN'S £63M REDEVELOPMENT

On completion of redevelopment costing £63m **Hampden Park**, home of Scottish football and the oldest first-class stadium in the world, was re-opened full scale for the Rangers-Celtic Cup Final on May 29, 1999.

Work on the 'new Hampden' (capacity 52,000) began in 1992. The North and East stands were restructured (£12m); a new South stand and improved West stand cost £51m. The Millennium Commission contributed £23m and the Lottery Sports Fund provided a grant of £3.75m.

FIRST FOR INVERNESS

Inverness Caledonian Thistle won the Scottish Cup for the Highlands for the first time when beating Falkirk 2-1 in the Final on May 30, 2015.

DEMISE OF AIRDRIE AND CLYDEBANK

In May 2002, First Division **Airdrieonians**, formed in 1878, went out of business. They had debts of £3m. Their place in the Scottish League was taken by **Gretna**, from the English Unibond League, who were voted into Div 3. Second Division **Clydebank** folded in Jul 2002 and were taken over by the new **Airdrie United** club.

FASTEST GOAL IN SPL

12.4 sec by **Anthony Stokes** for Hibernian in 4-1 home defeat by Rangers, Dec 27, 2009.

YOUNGEST SCORER IN SPL

Fraser Fyvie, aged 16 years and 306 days, for Aberdeen v Hearts (3-0) on Jan 27, 2010.

12 GOALS SHARED

There was a record aggregate score for the SPL on May 5, 2010, when **Motherwell** came from 6-2 down to draw 6-6 with **Hibernian**.

25-POINT DEDUCTION

Dundee were deducted 25 points by the Scottish Football League in November 2010 for going into administration for the second time. It left the club on minus 11 points, but they still managed to finish in mid-table in Division One.

GREAT SCOTS

In Feb 1988, the Scottish FA launched a national **Hall of Fame**, initially comprising the first 11 Scots to make 50 international appearances, to be joined by all future players to reach that number of caps. Each member receives a gold medal, invitation for life at all Scotland's home matches, and has his portrait hung at Scottish FA headquarters in Glasgow.

MORE CLUBS IN 2000

The **Scottish Premier League** increased from 10 to 12 clubs in season 2000–01. The **Scottish Football League** admitted two new clubs – Peterhead and Elgin City from the Highland League – to provide three divisions of 10 in 2000–01.

FIRST FOR EDINBURGH CITY

In May 2016, **Edinburgh City** became the first club to be promoted to Scottish League Two through the pyramid system with a 2-1 aggregate play-off aggregate win over East Stirling, whose 61 years in senior football came to an end.

NOTABLE SCOTTISH 'FIRSTS'

- The father of League football was a Scot, **William McGregor**, a draper in Birmingham. The 12-club Football League kicked off in Sep 1888, and McGregor was its first president.
- **Hibernian** were the first British club to play in the European Cup, by invitation. They reached the semi-final when it began in 1955–56.
- **Celtic** were Britain's first winners of the European Cup, in 1967.
- Scotland's First Division became the **Premier Division** in season 1975–76.
- Football's **first international** was staged at the West of Scotland cricket ground, Partick, on Nov 30, 1872: Scotland 0, England 0.
- Scotland introduced its **League Cup** in 1945–46, the first season after the war. It was another 15 years before the Football League Cup was launched.
- Scotland pioneered the use in British football of **two subs** per team in League and Cup matches.
- The world's **record football score** belongs to Scotland: Arbroath 36, Bon Accord 0 (Scottish Cup 1st rd) on Sep 12, 1885.
- The Scottish FA introduced the penalty **shoot-out** to their Cup Final in 1990.
- On Jan 22, 1994 all six matches in the **Scottish Premier Division** ended as draws.
- Scotland's new Premier League introduced a **3-week shut-down** in Jan 1999 – first instance of British football adopting the winter break system that operates in a number of European countries. The SPL ended its New Year closure after 2003.
- **Rangers** made history at home to St Johnstone (Premier League, 0-0, Mar 4, 2000) when fielding a team entirely without Scottish players.

John Fleck, aged 16 years, 274 days, became the youngest player in a Scottish FA Cup Final when he came on as a substitute for Rangers in their 3-2 win over Queen of the South at Hampden Park on May 24, 2008

SCOTTISH CUP SHOCK RESULTS

1885–86	(1)	Arbroath 36 Bon Accord 0
1921–22	(F)	Morton 1 Rangers 0
1937–38	(F)	East Fife 4 Kilmarnock 2 (replay, after 1-1)
1960–61	(F)	Dunfermline 2 Celtic 0 (replay, after 0-0)
1966–67	(1)	Berwick 1 Rangers 0
1979–80	(3)	Hamilton 2 Keith 3
1984–85	(1)	Stirling 20 Selkirk 0
1984–85	(3)	Inverness 3 Kilmarnock 0
1986–87	(3)	Rangers 0 Hamilton 1
1994–95	(4)	Stenhousemuir 2 Aberdeen 0
1998–99	(3)	Aberdeen 0 Livingston 1
1999–2000	(3)	Celtic 1 Inverness 3
2003–04	(5)	Inverness 1 Celtic 0
2005–06	(3)	Clyde 2 Celtic 1
2008–09	(6)	St Mirren 1 Celtic 0
2009–10	(SF)	Ross Co 2 Celtic 0
2013–14	(4)	Albion 1 Motherwell 0

Scottish League (Coca-Cola) Cup Final

1994–95 Raith 2, Celtic 2 (Raith won 6-5 on pens)

MISCELLANEOUS

NATIONAL ASSOCIATIONS FORMED

FA	**1863**
FA of Wales	**1876**
Scottish FA	**1873**
Irish FA	**1904**
Federation of International Football Associations (FIFA)	**1904**

NATIONAL & INTERNATIONAL COMPETITIONS LAUNCHED

FA Cup	**1871**
Welsh Cup	**1877**
Scottish Cup	**1873**
Irish Cup	**1880**
Football League	**1888**
Premier League	**1992**
Scottish League	**1890**
Scottish Premier League	**1998**
Scottish League Cup	**1945**
Football League Cup	**1960**
Home International Championship	**1883–84**
World Cup	**1930**
European Championship	**1958**
European Cup	**1955**
Fairs/UEFA Cup	**1955**
Cup-Winners' Cup	**1960**
European Champions League	**1992**
Olympic Games Tournament, at Shepherd's Bush	**1908**

INNOVATIONS

Size of Ball: Fixed in **1872**.

Shinguards: Introduced and registered by Sam Weller Widdowson (Nottm Forest & England) in **1874**.

Referee's whistle: First used on Nottm Forest's ground in **1878**.

Professionalism: Legalised in England in the summer of **1885** as a result of agitation by Lancashire clubs.

Goal-nets: Invented and patented in **1890** by Mr JA Brodie of Liverpool. They were first used in the North v South match in Jan, **1891**.

Referees and linesmen: Replaced umpires and referees in Jan, **1891**.

Penalty-kick: Introduced at Irish FA's request in the season **1891–92**. The penalty law ordering the goalkeeper to remain on the goal-line came into force in Sep, **1905**, and the order to stand on his goal-line until the ball is kicked arrived in **1929–30**.

White ball: First came into official use in **1951**.

Floodlighting: First FA Cup-tie (replay), Kidderminster Harriers v Brierley Hill Alliance, **1955**. First Football League match: Portsmouth v Newcastle (Div 1), **1956**.

Heated pitch to beat frost tried by Everton at Goodison Park in **1958**.

First soccer closed-circuit TV: At Coventry ground in Oct **1965** (10,000 fans saw their team win at Cardiff, 120 miles away).

Substitutes (one per team) were first allowed in Football League matches at the start of season **1965–66**. Three substitutes (one a goalkeeper) allowed, two of which could be used, in Premier League matches, **1992–93**. The Football League introduced three substitutes for **1993–94**.

Three points for a win: Introduced by the Football League in **1981–82**, by FIFA in World Cup games in **1994**, and by the Scottish League in the same year.

Offside law amended, player 'level' no longer offside, and 'professional foul' made sending-off offence, **1990**.

Penalty shoot-outs introduced to decide FA Cup ties level after one replay and extra time, **1991–92**.

New back-pass rule: goalkeeper must not handle ball kicked to him by team-mate, **1992**.

Linesmen became 'referees' assistants', **1998**.

Goalkeepers not to hold ball longer than 6 seconds, **2000**.

Free-kicks advanced by ten yards against opponents failing to retreat, **2000**. This experimental rule in England was scrapped in 2005).

YOUNGEST AND OLDEST

Youngest Caps

Harry Wilson (Wales v Belgium, Oct 15, 2013)	**16 years 207 days**
Norman Whiteside (N Ireland v Yugoslavia, Jun 17, 1982)	**17 years 41 days**
Theo Walcott (England v Hungary, May 30, 2006)	**17 years 75 days**
Johnny Lambie (Scotland v Ireland, Mar 20, 1886)	**17 years 92 days**
Jimmy Holmes (Rep of Ireland v Austria, May 30, 1971)	**17 years 200 days**

Youngest England scorer: Wayne Rooney (17 years, 317 days) v Macedonia, Skopje, Sep 6, 2003.

Youngest scorer on England debut: Marcus Rashford (18 years, 208 days) v Australia, Sunderland, May 27, 2016.

Youngest England hat-trick scorer: Theo Walcott (19 years, 178 days) v Croatia, Zagreb, Sep 10, 2008.

Youngest England captains: Bobby Moore (v Czech., Bratislava, May 29, 1963), 22 years, 47 days; Michael Owen (v Paraguay, Anfield, Apr 17, 2002), 22 years, 117 days.

Youngest England goalkeeper: Jack Butland (19 years, 158 days) v Italy, Bern, Aug 15, 2012

Youngest England players to reach 50 caps: Michael Owen (23 years, 6 months) v Slovakia at Middlesbrough, Jun 11, 2003; Bobby Moore (25 years, 7 months) v Wales at Wembley, Nov 16, 1966.

Youngest player in World Cup Final: Pele (Brazil) aged 17 years, 237 days v Sweden in

Stockholm, Jun 12, 1958.

Youngest player to appear in World Cup Finals: Norman Whiteside (N Ireland v Yugoslavia in Spain – Jun 17, 1982, age 17 years and 42 days.

Youngest First Division player: Derek Forster (Sunderland goalkeeper v Leicester, Aug 22, 1964) aged 15 years, 185 days.

Youngest First Division scorer: At 16 years and 57 days, schoolboy Jason Dozzell (substitute after 30 minutes for Ipswich at home to Coventry on Feb 4, 1984). Ipswich won 3-1 and Dozzell scored their third goal.

Youngest Premier League player: Matthew Briggs (Fulham sub at Middlesbrough, May 13, 2007) aged 16 years and 65 days.

Youngest Premier League scorer: James Vaughan (Everton, home to Crystal Palace, Apr 10, 2005), 16 years, 271 days.

Youngest Premier League captain: Lee Cattermole (Middlesbrough away to Fulham, May 7, 2006) aged 18 years, 47 days.

Youngest player sent off in Premier League: Wayne Rooney (Everton, away to Birmingham, Dec 26, 2002) aged 17 years, 59 days.

Youngest First Division hat-trick scorer: Alan Shearer, aged 17 years, 240 days, in Southampton's 4-2 home win v Arsenal (Apr 9, 1988) on his full debut. Previously, Jimmy Greaves (17 years, 309 days) with 4 goals for Chelsea at home to Portsmouth (7-4), Christmas Day, 1957.

Youngest to complete 100 Football League goals: Jimmy Greaves (20 years, 261 days) when he did so for Chelsea v Manchester City, Nov 19, 1960.

Youngest players in Football League: Reuben Noble-Lazarus (Barnsley 84th minute sub at Ipswich, Sep 30, 2008, Champ) aged 15 years, 45 days; Mason Bennett (Derby at Middlesbrough, Champ, Oct 22, 2011) aged 15 years, 99 days; Albert Geldard (Bradford PA v Millwall, Div 2, Sep 16, 1929) aged 15 years, 158 days; Ken Roberts (Wrexham v Bradford Park Avenue, Div 3 North, Sep 1, 1951) also 15 years, 158 days.

Youngest Football League scorer: Ronnie Dix (for Bristol Rov v Norwich, Div 3 South, Mar 3, 1928) aged 15 years, 180 days.

Youngest player in Scottish League: Goalkeeper Ronnie Simpson (Queens Park) aged 15 in 1946.

Youngest player in FA Cup: Andy Awford, Worcester City's England Schoolboy defender, aged 15 years, 88 days when he substituted in second half away to Boreham Wood (3rd qual round) on Oct 10, 1987.

Youngest player in FA Cup proper: Luke Freeman, Gillingham substitute striker (15 years, 233 days) away to Barnet in 1st round, Nov 10, 2007.

Youngest FA Cup scorer: Sean Cato (16 years, 25 days), second half sub in Barrow Town's 7-2 win away to Rothwell Town (prelim rd), Sep 3, 2011.

Youngest Wembley Cup Final captain: Barry Venison (Sunderland v Norwich, Milk Cup Final, Mar 24, 1985 – replacing suspended captain Shaun Elliott) – aged 20 years, 220 days.

Youngest FA Cup-winning captain: Bobby Moore (West Ham, 1964, v Preston), aged 23 years, 20 days.

Youngest FA Cup Final captain: David Nish aged 21 years and 212 days old when he captained Leicester against Manchester City at Wembley on Apr 26, 1969.

Youngest FA Cup Final player: Curtis Weston (Millwall sub last 3 mins v Manchester Utd, 2004) aged 17 years, 119 days.

Youngest FA Cup Final scorer: Norman Whiteside (Manchester Utd v Brighton, 1983 replay, Wembley), aged 18 years, 19 days.

Youngest FA Cup Final managers: Stan Cullis, Wolves (32) v Leicester, 1949; Steve Coppell, Crystal Palace (34) v Manchester Utd, 1990; Ruud Gullit, Chelsea (34) v Middlesbrough, 1997.

Youngest player in Football League Cup: Chris Coward (Stockport) sub v Sheffield Wed, 2nd Round, Aug 23, 2005, aged 16 years and 31 days.

Youngest Wembley scorer: Norman Whiteside (Manchester Utd v Liverpool, Milk Cup Final, Mar 26, 1983) aged 17 years, 324 days.

Youngest Wembley Cup Final goalkeeper: Chris Woods (18 years, 125 days) for Nottm Forest v Liverpool, League Cup Final on Mar 18, 1978.

Youngest Wembley FA Cup Final goalkeeper: Peter Shilton (19 years, 219 days) for Leicester v Manchester City, Apr 26, 1969.

Youngest senior international at Wembley: Salomon Olembe (sub for Cameroon v England, Nov 15, 1997), aged 16 years, 342 days.

Youngest winning manager at Wembley: Stan Cullis, aged 32 years, 187 days, as manager of Wolves, FA Cup winners on April 30 1949.

Youngest scorer in full international: Mohamed Kallon (Sierra Leone v Congo, African Nations Cup, Apr 22, 1995), reported as aged 15 years, 192 days.

Youngest English scorer in Champions League: Alex Oxlade-Chamberlain (Arsenal v Olympiacos, Sep 28, 2011) aged 18 years 1 month, 13 days

Youngest player sent off in World Cup Final series: Rigobert Song (Cameroon v Brazil, in USA, Jun 1994) aged 17 years, 358 days.

Youngest FA Cup Final referee: Kevin Howley, of Middlesbrough, aged 35 when in charge of Wolves v Blackburn, 1960.

Youngest player in England U-23 team: Duncan Edwards (v Italy, Bologna, Jan 20, 1954), aged 17 years, 112 days.

Youngest player in England U-21 team: Theo Walcott (v Moldova, Ipswich, Aug 15, 2006), aged 17 years, 152 days.

Youngest player in Scotland U-21 team: Christian Dailly (v Romania, Hampden Park, Sep 11, 1990), aged 16 years, 330 days.

Youngest player in senior football: Cameron Campbell Buchanan, Scottish-born outside right, aged 14 years, 57 days when he played for Wolves v WBA in War-time League match, Sep 26, 1942.

Youngest player in peace-time senior match: Eamon Collins (Blackpool v Kilmarnock, Anglo-Scottish Cup quarter-final 1st leg, Sep 9, 1980) aged 14 years, 323 days.

World's youngest player in top division match: Centre-forward Fernando Rafael Garcia, aged 13, played for 23 minutes for Peruvian club Juan Aurich in 3-1 win against Estudiantes on May 19, 2001.

Oldest player to appear in Football League: New Brighton manager Neil McBain (51 years, 120 days) as emergency goalkeeper away to Hartlepool (Div 3 North, Mar 15, 1947).

Other oldest post-war League players: Sir Stanley Matthews (Stoke, 1965, 50 years, 5 days); Peter Shilton (Leyton Orient 1997, 47 years, 126 days); Kevin Poole (Burton, 2010, 46 years, 291 days); Dave Beasant (Brighton 2003, 44 years, 46 days); Alf Wood (Coventry, 1958, 43 years, 199 days); Tommy Hutchison (Swansea City, 1991, 43 years, 172 days).

Oldest Football League debutant: Andy Cunningham, for Newcastle at Leicester (Div 1) on Feb 2, 1929, aged 38 years, 2 days.

Oldest post-war debut in English League: Defender David Donaldson (35 years, 7 months, 23 days) for Wimbledon on entry to Football League (Div 4) away to Halifax, Aug 20, 1977.

Oldest player to appear in First Division: Sir Stanley Matthews (Stoke v Fulham, Feb 6, 1965), aged 50 years, 5 days – on that his last League appearance, the only 50-year-old ever to play in the top division.

Oldest players in Premier League: Goalkeepers John Burridge (Manchester City v QPR, May 14, 1995), 43 years, 5 months, 11 days; Alec Chamberlain (Watford v Newcastle, May 13, 2007) 42 years, 11 months, 23 days; Steve Ogrizovic (Coventry v Sheffield Wed, May 6, 2000), 42 years, 7 months, 24 days; Brad Friedel (Tottenham v Newcastle, Nov 10, 2013) 42 years, 4 months, 22 days; Neville Southall (Bradford City v Leeds, Mar 12, 2000), 41 years, 5 months, 26 days. Outfield: Teddy Sheringham (West Ham v Manchester City, Dec 30, 2006), 40 years, 8 months, 28 days; Ryan Giggs (Manchester Utd v Hull, May 6, 2014), 40 years, 5 months, 7 days; Gordon Strachan (Coventry City v Derby, May 3, 1997), 40 years, 2 months, 24 days.

Oldest player for British professional club: John Ryan (owner-chairman of Conference club Doncaster, played as substitute for last minute in 4-2 win at Hereford on Apr 26, 2003), aged 52 years, 11 months, 3 weeks.

Oldest FA Cup Final player: Walter (Billy) Hampson (Newcastle v Aston Villa on Apr 26, 1924), aged 41 years, 257 days.

Oldest captain and goalkeeper in FA Cup Final: David James (Portsmouth v Chelsea, May 15, 2010) aged 39 years, 287 days.

Oldest FA Cup Final scorers: Bert Turner (Charlton v Derby, Apr 27, 1946) aged 36 years, 312 days. Scored for both sides. Teddy Sheringham (West Ham v Liverpool, May 13, 2006) aged 40 years, 41 days. Scored in penalty shoot-out.

Oldest FA Cup-winning team: Arsenal 1950 (average age 31 years, 2 months). Eight of the players were over 30, with the three oldest centre-half Leslie Compton 37, and skipper Joe Mercer and goalkeeper George Swindin, both 35.

Oldest World Cup-winning captain: Dino Zoff, Italy's goalkeeper v W Germany in 1982 Final, aged 40 years, 92 days.

Oldest player capped by England: Stanley Matthews (v Denmark, Copenhagen, May 15, 1957), aged 42 years, 103 days.

Oldest England scorer: Stanley Matthews (v N Ireland, Belfast, Oct 6, 1956), aged 41 years, 248 days.

Oldest British international player: Billy Meredith (Wales v England at Highbury, Mar 15, 1920), aged 45 years, 229 days.

Oldest 'new caps': Goalkeeper Alexander Morten, aged 41 years, 113 days when earning his only England Cap against Scotland on Mar 8, 1873; Arsenal centre-half Leslie Compton, at 38 years, 64 days when he made his England debut in 4-2 win against Wales at Sunderland on Nov 15, 1950. **For Scotland:** Goalkeeper Ronnie Simpson (Celtic) at 36 years, 186 days v England at Wembley, Apr 15, 1967.

Oldest scorer in Wembley Final: Chris Swailes, 45, for Morpeth in 4-1 win over Hereford (FA Vase), May 22, 2016.

Longest Football League career: This spanned 32 years and 10 months, by Stanley Matthews (Stoke, Blackpool, Stoke) from Mar 19, 1932 until Feb 6, 1965.

Shortest FA Cup-winning captain: 5ft 4in – Bobby Kerr (Sunderland v Leeds, 1973).

SHIRT NUMBERING

Numbering players in Football League matches was made compulsory in 1939. Players wore numbered shirts (1-22) in the FA Cup Final as an experiment in 1933 (Everton 1-11 v Manchester City 12-22).

Squad numbers for players were introduced by the Premier League at the start of season 1993–94. They were optional in the Football League until made compulsory in 1999–2000.

Names on shirts: For first time, players wore names as well as numbers on shirts in League Cup and FA Cup Finals, 1993.

SUBSTITUTES

In **1965**, the Football League, by 39 votes to 10, agreed that **one substitute** be allowed for an injured player at any time during a League match. First substitute used in Football League: Keith Peacock (Charlton), away to Bolton in Div 2, Aug 21, 1965.

Two substitutes per team were approved for the League (Littlewoods) Cup and FA Cup in season 1986–87 and two were permitted in the Football League for the first time in 1987–88.

Three substitutes (one a goalkeeper), two of which could be used, introduced by the Premier League for 1992–93. The Football League followed suit for 1993–94.

Three substitutes (one a goalkeeper) were allowed at the World Cup Finals for the first time at US '94.

Three substitutes (any position) introduced by Premier League and Football League in 1995–96.

Five named substitutes (three of which could be used) introduced in Premier League in 1996–97, in FA Cup in 1997–98, League Cup in 1998–99 and Football League in 1999–2000.

Seven named substitutes for Premier League, FA Cup and League Cup in 2008–09. Still only three to be used. Football League adopted this rule for 2009–10, reverted to five in 2011–12 and went back to seven for the 2012–13 season.

First substitute to score in FA Cup Final: Eddie Kelly (Arsenal v Liverpool, 1971). The **first recorded use** of a substitute was in 1889 (Wales v Scotland at Wrexham on Apr 15) when Sam Gillam arrived late – although he was a Wrexham player – and Allen Pugh (Rhostellyn) was allowed to keep goal until he turned up. The match ended 0-0.

When **Dickie Roose**, the Welsh goalkeeper, was injured against England at Wrexham, Mar 16, 1908, **Dai Davies** (Bolton) was allowed to take his place as substitute. Thus Wales used 12 players. England won 7-1.

END OF WAGE LIMIT

Freedom from the maximum wage system – in force since the formation of the Football League in 1888 – was secured by the Professional Footballers' Association in 1961. About this time Italian clubs renewed overtures for the transfer of British stars and Fulham's **Johnny Haynes** became the first British player to earn £100 a week.

THE BOSMAN RULING

On Dec 15, 1995 the **European Court of Justice** ruled that clubs had no right to transfer fees for out-of-contract players, and the outcome of the 'Bosman case' irrevocably changed football's player-club relationship. It began in 1990, when the contract of 26-year-old **Jean-Marc Bosman**, a midfield player with FC Liege, Belgium, expired. French club Dunkirk wanted him but were unwilling to pay the £500,000 transfer fee, so Bosman was compelled to remain with Liege. He responded with a lawsuit against his club and UEFA on the grounds of 'restriction of trade', and after five years at various court levels the European Court of Justice ruled not only in favour of Bosman but of all professional footballers.

The end of restrictive labour practices revolutionised the system. It led to a proliferation of transfers, rocketed the salaries of elite players who, backed by an increasing army of agents, found themselves in a vastly improved bargaining position as they moved from team to team, league to league, nation to nation. Removing the limit on the number of foreigners clubs could field brought an increasing ratio of such signings, not least in England and Scotland.

Bosman's one-man stand opened the way for footballers to become millionaires, but ended his own career. All he received for his legal conflict was 16 million Belgian francs (£312,000) in compensation, a testimonial of poor reward and martyrdom as the man who did most to change the face of football.

By 2011, he was living on Belgian state benefits, saying: 'I have made the world of football rich and shifted the power from clubs to players. Now I find myself with nothing.'

INTERNATIONAL SHOCK RESULTS

1950 USA 1 England 0 (World Cup).
1953 England 3 Hungary 6 (friendly).
1954 Hungary 7 England 1 (friendly)
1966 North Korea 1 Italy 0 (World Cup).
1982 Spain 0, Northern Ireland 1; Algeria 2, West Germany 1 (World Cup).
1990 Cameroon 1 Argentina 0; Scotland 0 Costa Rica 1; Sweden 1 Costa Rica 2 (World Cup).
1990 Faroe Islands 1 Austria 0 (European Champ qual).
1992 Denmark 2 Germany 0 (European Champ Final).
1993 USA 2 England 0 (US Cup tournament).
1993 Argentina 0 Colombia 5 (World Cup qual).
1993 France 2 Israel 3 (World Cup qual).
1994 Bulgaria 2 Germany 1 (World Cup).
1994 Moldova 3 Wales 2; Georgia 5 Wales 0 (European Champ qual).
1995 Belarus 1 Holland 0 (European Champ qual).
1996 Nigeria 4 Brazil 3 (Olympics).
1998 USA 1 Brazil 0 (Concacaf Gold Cup).
1998 Croatia 3 Germany 0 (World Cup).
2000 Scotland 0 Australia 2 (friendly).
2001 Australia 1 France 0; Australia 1, Brazil 0 (Confederations Cup).
2001 Honduras 2 Brazil 0 (Copa America).
2001 Germany 1 England 5 (World Cup qual).

2002 France 0 Senegal 1; South Korea 2 Italy 1 (World Cup).
2003: England 1 Australia 3 (friendly)
2004: Portugal 0 Greece 1 (European Champ Final).
2005: Northern Ireland 1 England 0 (World Cup qual).
2014: Holland 5 Spain 1 (World Cup).
2014: Brazil 1 Germany 7 (World Cup).
2016 England 1 Iceland 2 (European Champ)

GREAT RECOVERIES – DOMESTIC FOOTBALL

On Dec 21, 1957, **Charlton** were losing 5-1 against Huddersfield (Div 2) at The Valley with only 28 minutes left, and from the 15th minute, had been reduced to ten men by injury, but they won 7-6, with left-winger Johnny Summers scoring five goals. **Huddersfield** (managed by Bill Shankly) remain the only team to score six times in a League match and lose. On Boxing Day, 1927 in Div 3 South, **Northampton** won 6-5 at home to Luton after being 1-5 down at half-time.

Season 2010–11 produced a Premier League record for **Newcastle**, who came from 4-0 down at home to Arsenal to draw 4-4. Previous instance of a team retrieving a four-goal deficit in the top division to draw was in 1984 when Newcastle trailed at QPR in a game which ended 5-5.

In the 2012-13 League Cup, **Arsenal** were 0-4 down in a fourth round tie at Reading, levelled at 4-4 and went on to win 7-5 in extra-time.

MATCHES OFF

Worst day for postponements: Feb 9, 1963, when 57 League fixtures in England and Scotland were frozen off. Only 7 Football League matches took place, and the entire Scottish programme was wiped out.

Other weather-hit days:

Jan 12, 1963 and Feb 2, 1963 – on both those Saturdays, only 4 out of 44 Football League matches were played.

Jan 1, 1979 – 43 out of 46 Football League fixtures postponed.

Jan 17, 1987 – 37 of 45 scheduled Football League fixtures postponed; only 2 Scottish matches survived.

Feb 8–9, 1991 – only 4 of the week-end's 44 Barclays League matches survived the freeze-up (4 of the postponements were on Friday night). In addition, 11 Scottish League matches were off.

Jan 27, 1996 – 44 Cup and League matches in England and Scotland were frozen off.

On the weekend of Jan 9, 10, 11, 2010, 46 League and Cup matches in England and Scotland were victims of the weather. On the weekend of Dec 18-21, 2010, 49 matches were frozen off in England and Scotland.

Fewest matches left on one day by postponements was during the Second World War – Feb 3, 1940 when, because of snow, ice and fog only one out of 56 regional league fixtures took place. It resulted Plymouth Argyle 10, Bristol City 3.

The Scottish Cup second round tie between Inverness Thistle and Falkirk in season 1978–79 was **postponed 29 times** because of snow and ice. First put off on Jan 6, it was eventually played on Feb 22. Falkirk won 4-0.

Pools Panel's busiest days: Jan 17, 1987 and Feb 9, 1991 – on both dates they gave their verdict on 48 postponed coupon matches.

FEWEST 'GAMES OFF'

Season 1947–48 was the best since the war for English League fixtures being played to schedule. Only six were postponed.

LONGEST SEASON

The latest that League football has been played in a season was **Jun 7, 1947** (six weeks after the FA Cup Final). The season was extended because of mass postponements caused by bad weather in mid-winter.

The latest the FA Cup competition has been completed was in season 2014–15 when Arsenal beat Aston Villa 4-0 in the Final on May 30, kick-off 5.30pm

Worst winter hold-up was in season 1962–63. The Big Freeze began on Boxing Day and lasted until Mar, with nearly 500 first-class matches postponed. The FA Cup 3rd round was the longest on record – it began with only three out of 32 ties playable on Jan 5 and ended 66 days and 261 postponements later on Mar 11. The Lincoln–Coventry tie was put off 15 times. The Pools Panel was launched that winter, on Jan 26, 1963.

HOTTEST DAYS

The Nationwide League kicked off season 2003–04 on Aug 9 with pitch temperatures of 102 degrees recorded at Luton v Rushden and Bradford v Norwich. On the following day, there was a pitch temperature of 100 degrees for the Community Shield match between Manchester Utd and Arsenal at Cardiff's Millennium Stadium. Wembley's pitch-side thermometer registered 107 degrees for the 2009 Chelsea–Everton FA Cup Final.

FOOTBALL LEAGUE NAME CHANGE

From the start of the 2016-17 season, the Football League was renamed the English Football League, as part of a corporate and competition rebranding.

FOOTBALL ASSOCIATION SECRETARIES/CHIEF EXECUTIVES

1863–66 Ebenezer Morley; 1866–68 **Robert Willis**; 1868–70 **RG Graham**; 1870–95 **Charles Alcock** (paid from 1887); 1895–1934 **Sir Frederick Wall**; 1934–62 **Sir Stanley Rous**; 1962–73 **Denis Follows**; 1973–89 **Ted Croker** (latterly chief executive); 1989–99 **Graham Kelly** (chief executive); 2000–02 **Adam Crozier** (chief executive); 2003–04 **Mark Palios** (chief executive); 2005–08: **Brian Barwick** (chief executive); 2009–10 **Ian Watmore** (chief executive); 2010-15 **Alex Horne** (chief executive); 2015 **Martin Glenn** (chief executive).

FOOTBALL'S SPONSORS

Football League: Canon 1983–86; Today Newspaper 1986–87; Barclays 1987–93; Endsleigh Insurance 1993–96; Nationwide Building Society 1996–2004; Coca-Cola 2004–10; npower 2010–14; Sky Bet from 2014.

League Cup: Milk Cup 1982–86; Littlewoods 1987–90; Rumbelows 1991–92; Coca-Cola 1993–98; Worthington 1998–2003; Carling 2003–12; Capital One 2012–16.

Premier League: Carling 1993–2001; Barclaycard 2001–04; Barclays from 2004.

FA Cup: Littlewoods 1994–98; AXA 1998–2002; E.ON 2006–11; Budweiser 2011–15; Emirates (title sponsor) from 2015.

NEW HOMES FOR CLUBS

Newly-constructed League grounds in England since the war: 1946 Hull (Boothferry Park); 1950 Port Vale (Vale Park); 1955 Southend (Roots Hall); 1988 Scunthorpe (Glanford Park); 1990 Walsall (Bescot Stadium); 1990 Wycombe (Adams Park); 1992 Chester (Deva Stadium); 1993 Millwall (New Den); 1994 Huddersfield (McAlpine Stadium); 1994 Northampton (Sixfields Stadium); 1995 Middlesbrough (Riverside Stadium); 1997 Bolton (Reebok Stadium); 1997 Derby (Pride Park); 1997 Stoke (Britannia Stadium); 1997 Sunderland (Stadium of Light); 1998 Reading (Madejski Stadium); 1999 Wigan (JJB Stadium); 2001 Southampton (St Mary's Stadium); 2001 Oxford Utd (Kassam Stadium); 2002 Leicester (Walkers Stadium); 2002 Hull (Kingston Communications Stadium); 2003 Manchester City (City of Manchester Stadium); 2003 Darlington (New Stadium); 2005 Coventry (Ricoh Arena); Swansea (Stadium of Swansea, Morfa); 2006 Arsenal (Emirates Stadium); 2007 Milton Keynes Dons (Stadium: MK); Shrewsbury (New Meadow); 2008 Colchester (Community Stadium); 2009 Cardiff City Stadium; 2010 Chesterfield (b2net Stadium), Morecambe (Globe Arena); 2011 Brighton (American Express Stadium); 2012 Rotherham (New York Stadium).

Bolton now Macron Stadium; Chesterfield now Proact Stadium; Derby now iPro Stadium; Huddersfield now John Smith's Stadium; Leicester now King Power Stadium; Manchester City now Etihad Stadium; Shrewsbury now Greenhous Meadow Stadium; Stoke now bet365 Stadium; Swansea now Liberty Stadium; Walsall now Banks's Stadium; Wigan now DW Stadium; 2016 West Ham (Olympic Stadium).

NATIONAL FOOTBALL CENTRE

The FA's new £120m centre at St George's Park, Burton upon Trent, was opened on Oct 9, 20012 by the Duke of Cambridge, president of the FA. The site covers 330 acres, has 12 full-size pitches (5 with undersoil heating and floodlighting). There are 5 gyms, a 90-seat lecture theatre, a hydrotherapy unit with swimming pool for the treatment of injuries and two hotels. It is the base for England teams, men and women, at all levels.

GROUND-SHARING

Manchester Utd played their home matches at **Manchester City's** Maine Road ground for 8 years after Old Trafford was bomb-damaged in Aug 1941. **Crystal Palace** and **Charlton** shared Selhurst Park (1985–91); **Bristol Rov** and **Bath City** (Twerton Park, Bath, 1986–96); **Partick Thistle** and **Clyde** (Firhill Park, Glasgow, 1986–91; in seasons 1990–01, 1991–92 **Chester** shared **Macclesfield**'s ground (Moss Rose).

Crystal Palace and **Wimbledon** shared Selhurst Park, from season 1991–92, when **Charlton** (tenants) moved to rent Upton Park from **West Ham**, until 2003 when Wimbledon relocated to Milton Keynes. **Clyde** moved to Douglas Park, **Hamilton Academical's** home, in 1991–92. **Stirling Albion** shared **Stenhousemuir**'s ground, Ochilview Park, in 1992–93. In 1993–94, **Clyde** shared **Partick**'s home until moving to Cumbernauld. In 1994–95, **Celtic s**hared Hampden Park with **Queen's Park** (while Celtic Park was redeveloped); **Hamilton** shared **Partick**'s ground. **Airdrie** shared **Clyde**'s Broadwood Stadium. **Bristol Rov** left **Bath City**'s ground at the start of season 1996–97, sharing Bristol Rugby Club's Memorial Ground. **Clydebank** shared **Dumbarton**'s Boghead Park from 1996–97 until renting **Greenock Morton**'s Cappielow Park in season 1999–2000. **Brighton** shared **Gillingham**'s ground in seasons 1997–98, 1998–99. **Fulham** shared **QPR**'s home at Loftus Road in seasons 2002–03, 2003–04, returning to Craven Cottage in Aug 2004. **Coventry** played home fixtures at Northampton in season 2013–14, returning to their own ground, the Ricoh Arena, in Sept 2014.

Inverness Caledonian Thistle moved to share **Aberdeen**'s Pittodrie Stadium in 2004–05 after being promoted to the SPL; **Gretna's** home matches on arrival in the SPL in 2007–08 were held at Motherwell and Livingston.

ARTIFICIAL TURF

QPR were the first British club to install an artificial pitch, in 1981. They were followed by **Luton** in 1985, and **Oldham** and **Preston** in **1986**. QPR reverted to grass in 1988, as did Luton and promoted Oldham in season 1991–92 (when artificial pitches were banned in Div 1). **Preston** were the last Football League club playing 'on plastic' in 1993–94, and their Deepdale ground was restored to grass for the start of 1994–95.

Stirling were the **first Scottish club** to play on plastic, in season 1987–88.

DOUBLE RUNNERS-UP

There have been nine instances of clubs finishing runner-up in **both the League Championship** and **FA Cup** in the same season: 1928 Huddersfield; 1932 Arsenal; 1939 Wolves; 1962 Burnley; 1965 and 1970 Leeds; 1986 Everton; 1995 Manchester Utd; 2001 Arsenal.

CORNER-KICK RECORDS

Not a single corner-kick was recorded when **Newcastle** drew 0-0 at home to **Portsmouth** (Div 1) on Dec 5, 1931.

The record for **most corners** in a match for one side is believed to be **Sheffield Utd's 28** to **West Ham's 1** in Div 2 at Bramall Lane on Oct 14, 1989. For all their pressure, Sheffield Utd lost 2-0.

Nottm Forest led **Southampton** 22-2 on corners (Premier League, Nov 28, 1992) but lost the match 1-2.

Tommy Higginson (Brentford, 1960s) once passed back to his own goalkeeper from a corner kick.

When **Wigan** won 4-0 at home to Cardiff (Div 2) on Feb 16, 2002, all four goals were headed in from corners taken by N Ireland international **Peter Kennedy**.

Steve Staunton (Rep of Ireland) is believed to be the only player to score direct from a corner in **two** Internationals.

In the 2012 Champions League Final, **Bayern Munich** forced 20 corners without scoring, while **Chelsea** scored from their only one.

SACKED AT HALF-TIME

Leyton Orient sacked **Terry Howard** on his 397th appearance for the club – at half-time in a Second Division home defeat against Blackpool (Feb 7, 1995) for 'an unacceptable performance'. He was fined two weeks' wages, given a free transfer and moved to Wycombe.

Bobby Gould resigned as **Peterborough**'s head coach at half-time in their 1-0 defeat in the LDV Vans Trophy 1st round at Bristol City on Sep 29, 2004.

Harald Schumacher, former Germany goalkeeper, was sacked as Fortuna Koln coach when they were two down at half-time against Waldhof Mannheim (Dec 15, 1999). They lost 5-1.

MOST GAMES BY 'KEEPER FOR ONE CLUB

Alan Knight made 683 League appearances for Portsmouth, over 23 seasons (1978–2000), a record for a goalkeeper at one club. The previous holder was Peter Bonetti with 600 League games for Chelsea (20 seasons, 1960–79).

PLAYED TWO GAMES ON SAME DAY

Jack Kelsey played full-length matches for both club and country on Wednesday Nov 26, 1958. In the afternoon he kept goal for Wales in a 2-2 draw against England at Villa Park, and he then drove to Highbury to help Arsenal win 3-1 in a prestigious floodlit friendly against Juventus.

On the same day, winger **Danny Clapton** played for England (against Wales and Kelsey) and then in part of Arsenal's match against Juventus.

On Nov 11, 1987, **Mark Hughes** played for Wales against Czechoslovakia (European Championship) in Prague, then flew to Munich and went on as substitute that night in a winning Bayern Munich team, to whom he was on loan from Barcelona.

On Feb 16, 1993 goalkeeper **Scott Howie** played in Scotland's 3-0 U-21 win v Malta at Tannadice Park, Dundee (ko 1.30pm) and the same evening played in Clyde's 2-1 home win v Queen of South (Div 2).

Ryman League **Hornchurch**, faced by end-of-season fixture congestion, played **two matches** on the same night (May 1, 2001). They lost 2-1 at home to Ware and drew 2-2 at Clapton.

RECORD LOSS

Manchester City made a record loss of £194.9m in the 2010–11 financial year.

FIRST 'MATCH OF THE DAY'

BBC TV (recorded highlights): Liverpool 3, Arsenal 2 on Aug 22, 1964. **First complete match to be televised:** Arsenal 3, Everton 2 on Aug 29, 1936. **First League match televised in colour:** Liverpool 2, West Ham 0 on Nov 15, 1969.

'MATCH OF THE DAY' – BIGGEST SCORES

Football League: Tottenham 9, Bristol Rov 0 (Div 2, 1977–78). **Premier League:** Nottm Forest 1, Manchester Utd 8 (1998–99); Portsmouth 7 Reading 4 (2007–08).

FIRST COMMENTARY ON RADIO

Arsenal 1 Sheffield Utd 1 (Div 1) broadcast on BBC, Jan 22, 1927.

OLYMPIC FOOTBALL WINNERS

1908 Great Britain (in London); **1912** Great Britain (Stockholm); **1920** Belgium (Antwerp); **1924** Uruguay (Paris); **1928** Uruguay (Amsterdam); **1932** No soccer in Los Angeles Olympics; **1936** Italy (Berlin); **1948** Sweden (London); **1952** Hungary (Helsinki); **1956** USSR (Melbourne); **1960** Yugoslavia (Rome); **1964** Hungary (Tokyo); **1968** Hungary (Mexico City); **1972** Poland (Munich); **1976** E Germany (Montreal); **1980** Czechoslovakia (Moscow); **1984** France (Los Angeles); **1988** USSR (Seoul); **1992** Spain (Barcelona); **1996** Nigeria (Atlanta); **2000**

Cameroon (Sydney); **2004** Argentina (Athens); **2008** Argentina (Beijing); **2012** Mexico (Wembley)

Highest scorer in Final tournament: Ferenc Bene (Hungary) 12 goals, 1964.

Record crowd for Olympic Soccer Final: 108,800 (France v Brazil, Los Angeles 1984).

MOST AMATEUR CUP WINS

Bishop Auckland set the FA Amateur Cup record with 10 wins, and in 1957 became the only club to carry off the trophy in three successive seasons. The competition was discontinued after the Final on Apr 20, 1974. (Bishop's Stortford 4, Ilford 1, at Wembley).

FOOTBALL FOUNDATION

This was formed (May 2000) to replace the **Football Trust**, which had been in existence since 1975 as an initiative of the Pools companies to provide financial support at all levels, from schools football to safety and ground improvement work throughout the game.

SEVEN-FIGURE TESTIMONIALS

The first was **Sir Alex Ferguson**'s at Old Trafford on Oct 11, 1999, when a full-house of 54,842 saw a Rest of the World team beat Manchester Utd 4-2. United's manager pledged that a large percentage of the estimated £1m receipts would go to charity.

Estimated receipts of £1m and over came from testimonials for **Denis Irwin** (Manchester Utd) against Manchester City at Old Trafford on Aug 16, 2000 (45,158); **Tom Boyd** (Celtic) against Manchester Utd at Celtic Park on May 15, 2001 (57,000) and **Ryan Giggs** (Manchester Utd) against Celtic on Aug 1, 2001 (66,967).

Tony Adams' second testimonial (1-1 v Celtic on May 13, 2002) two nights after Arsenal completed the Double, was watched by 38,021 spectators at Highbury. Of £1m receipts, he donated £500,000 to Sporting Chance, the charity that helps sportsmen/women with drink, drug, gambling problems.

Sunderland and a Republic of Ireland XI drew 0-0 in front of 35,702 at the Stadium of Light on May 14, 2002. The beneficiary, **Niall Quinn**, donated his testimonial proceeds, estimated at £1m, to children's hospitals in Sunderland and Dublin, and to homeless children in Africa and Asia.

A record testimonial crowd of 69,591 for **Roy Keane** at Old Trafford on May 9, 2006 netted more than £2m for charities in Dublin, Cork and Manchester. Manchester Utd beat Celtic 1-0, with Keane playing for both teams.

Alan Shearer's testimonial on May 11, 2006, watched by a crowd of 52,275 at St James' Park, raised more than £1m. The club's record scorer, in his farewell match, came off the bench in stoppage time to score the penalty that gave Newcastle a 3-2 win over Celtic. Total proceeds from his testimonial events, £1.64m, were donated to 14 charities in the north-east.

Ole Gunnar Solskjaer, who retired after 12 years as a Manchester Utd player, had a crowd of 68,868, for his testimonial on Aug 2, 2008 (United 1 Espanyol 0). He donated the estimated receipts of £2m to charity, including the opening of a dozen schools In Africa.

Liverpool's **Jamie Carragher** had his testimonial against Everton (4-1) on Sep 4, 2010. It was watched by a crowd of 35,631 and raised an estimated £1m for his foundation, which supports community projects on Merseyside.

Gary Neville donated receipts of around £1m from his testimonial against Juventus (2-1) in front of 42,000 on May 24, 2011, to charities and building a Supporters' Centre near Old Trafford.

Paul Scholes had a crowd of 75,000 for his testimonial, Manchester United against New York Cosmos, on Aug 5, 2011. Receipts were £1.5m.

Steven Gerrard, Liverpool captain, donated £500,000 from his testimonial to the local Alder Hey Children's Hospital after a match against Olympiacos was watched by a crowd of 44,362 on Aug 3, 2013. Gerrard chose the Greek champions because he scored a special goal against them in the season Liverpool won the 2005 Champions League.

WHAT IT USED TO COST

Minimum admission to League football was one shilling in 1939 After the war, it was increased to 1s 3d in 1946; 1s 6d in 1951; 1s 9d in 1952; 2s in 1955; 2s 6d; in 1960; 4s in 1965; 5s in 1968; 6s in 1970; and 8s (40p) in 1972 After that, the fixed minimum charge was dropped.

Wembley's first Cup Final programme in 1923 cost three pence (1¼p in today's money). The programme for the 'farewell' FA Cup Final in May, 2000 was priced £10.

FA Cup Final ticket prices in 2011 reached record levels – £115, £85, £65 and £45.

WHAT THEY USED TO EARN

In the 1930s, First Division players were on £8 a week (£6 in close season) plus bonuses of £2 win, £1 draw. The maximum wage went up to £12 when football resumed post-war in 1946 and had reached £20 by the time the limit was abolished in 1961.

EUROPEAN TROPHY WINNERS

European Cup/Champions League: 11 Real Madrid; **7** AC Milan; **5** Liverpool, Barcelona, Bayern Munich; **4** Ajax; **3** Inter Milan, Manchester Utd; **2** Benfica, Juventus, Nottm Forest, Porto; **1** Aston Villa, Borussia Dortmund, Celtic, Chelsea, Feyenoord, Hamburg, Marseille, PSV Eindhoven, Red Star Belgrade, Steaua Bucharest

Cup-Winners' Cup: 4 Barcelona; **2** Anderlecht, Chelsea, Dynamo Kiev, AC Milan; **1** Aberdeen, Ajax, Arsenal, Atletico Madrid, Bayern Munich, Borussia Dortmund, Dynamo Tbilisi, Everton, Fiorentina, Hamburg, Juventus, Lazio, Magdeburg, Manchester City, Manchester Utd, Mechelen, Paris St Germain, Parma, Rangers, Real Zaragoza, Sampdoria, Slovan Bratislava, Sporting Lisbon, Tottenham, Valencia, Werder Bremen, West Ham.

UEFA Cup: 3 Barcelona, Inter Milan, Juventus, Liverpool, Valencia; **2** Borussia Moenchengladbach, Feyenoord, Gothenburg, Leeds, Parma, Real Madrid, Sevilla, Tottenham; **1** Anderlecht, Ajax, Arsenal, Bayer Leverkusen, Bayern Munich, CSKA Moscow, Dynamo Zagreb, Eintracht Frankfurt, Ferencvaros, Galatasaray, Ipswich, Napoli, Newcastle, Porto, PSV Eindhoven, Real Zaragoza, Roma, Schalke, Shakhtar Donetsk, Zenit St Petersburg.

Europa League: 3 Sevilla; **2** Atletico Madrid, **1** Chelsea, Porto.

- The Champions League was introduced into the European Cup in 1992–93 to counter the threat of a European Super League. The UEFA Cup became the Europa League, with a new format, in season 2009–10.

BRITAIN'S 34 TROPHIES IN EUROPE

Euro Cup/Champs Lge (13)
1967 Celtic
1968 Manchester Utd
1977 Liverpool
1978 Liverpool
1979 Nottm Forest
1980 Nottm Forest
1981 Liverpool
1982 Aston Villa
1984 Liverpool
1999 Manchester Utd
2005 Liverpool
2008 Manchester Utd

Cup-Winners' Cup (10)
1963 Tottenham
1965 West Ham
1970 Manchester City
1971 Chelsea
1972 Rangers
1983 Aberdeen
1985 Everton
1991 Manchester Utd
1994 Arsenal
1998 Chelsea

Fairs/UEFA Cup/Europa Lge (11)
1968 Leeds
1969 Newcastle
1970 Arsenal
1971 Leeds
1972 Tottenham
1973 Liverpool
1976 Liverpool
1981 Ipswich
1984 Tottenham
2001 Liverpool
2012 Chelsea
2013 Chelsea

ENGLAND'S EUROPEAN RECORD

Manchester Utd, Chelsea, Arsenal and Liverpool all reached the Champions League quarter-finals in season 2007–08 – the first time one country had provided four of the last eight. For the first time, England supplied both finalists in 2008 (Manchester Utd and Chelsea) and have provided three semi-finalists in 2007–08–09).

END OF CUP-WINNERS' CUP

The **European Cup-Winners' Cup**, inaugurated in 1960–61, terminated with the 1999 Final. The competition merged into a revamped **UEFA Cup**.

From its inception in 1955, the **European Cup** comprised only championship-winning clubs until 1998–99, when selected runners-up were introduced. Further expansion came in 1999–2000 with the inclusion of clubs finishing third in certain leagues and fourth in 2002.

EUROPEAN CLUB COMPETITIONS – SCORING RECORDS

European Cup – record aggregate: 18-0 by Benfica v Dudelange (Lux) (8-0a, 10-0h), prelim rd, 1965–66.

Record single-match score: 11-0 by Dinamo Bucharest v Crusaders (rd 1, 2nd leg, 1973-74 (agg 12-0).

Champions League – record single-match score: Liverpool 8-0 v Besiktas, Group A qual (Nov 6, 2007).

Highest match aggregate: 13 – Bayern Munich 12 Sporting Lisbon 1 (5-0 away, 7-1 at home, 1st ko rd, 2008–09)

Cup-Winners' Cup – *record aggregate: 21-0 by Chelsea v Jeunesse Hautcharage (Lux) (8-0a, 13-0h), 1st rd, 1971–72.

Record single-match score: 16-1 by Sporting Lisbon v Apoel Nicosia, 2nd round, 1st leg, 1963–64 (aggregate was 18-1).

UEFA Cup (prev Fairs Cup) – *Record aggregate: 21-0 by Feyenoord v US Rumelange (Lux) (9-0h, 12-0a), 1st round, 1972–73.

Record single-match score: 14-0 by Ajax Amsterdam v Red Boys (Lux) 1st rd, 2nd leg, 1984–85 (aggregate also 14-0).

Record British score in Europe: 13-0 by **Chelsea** at home to Jeunesse Hautcharage (Lux) in Cup-Winners' Cup 1st round, 2nd leg, 1971–72. Chelsea's overall 21-0 win in that tie is highest aggregate by British club in Europe.

Individual scoring record for European tie (over two legs): 10 goals (6 home, 4 away) by **Kiril Milanov** for Levski Spartak in 19-3 agg win Cup-Winners' Cup 1st round v Lahden Reipas, 1976–77. Next highest: **8 goals** by **Jose Altafini** for AC Milan v US Luxembourg (European Cup, prelim round, 1962–63, agg 14-0) and by **Peter Osgood** for Chelsea v Jeunesse Hautcharage (Cup-Winners' Cup, 1st round 1971–72, agg 21-0). Altafini and Osgood each scored 5 goals at home, 3 away.

Individual single-match scoring record in European competition: **6** by **Mascarenhas** for Sporting Lisbon in 16-1 Cup-Winner's Cup 2nd round, 1st leg win v Apoel, 1963–64; and by **Lothar Emmerich** for Borussia Dortmund in 8-0 CWC 1st round, 2nd leg win v Floriana 1965–66; and by **Kiril Milanov** for Levski Spartak in 12-2 CWC 1st round, 1st leg win v Lahden Reipas, 1976–77.

Most goals in single European campaign: 15 by **Jurgen Klinsmann** for Bayern Munich (UEFA Cup 1995–96).

Most goals by British player in European competition: 30 by **Peter Lorimer** (Leeds, in 9 campaigns).

Most individual goals in Champions League match: 5 by **Lionel Messi** (Barcelona) in 7-1 win at home to Bayer Leverkusen in round of 16 second leg, 2011–12.

Most European Cup goals by individual player: 49 by **Alfredo di Stefano** in 58 apps for Real Madrid (1955–64).

(*Joint record European aggregate)

First European treble: Clarence Seedorf became the first player to win the European Cup with three clubs: Ajax in 1995, Real Madrid in 1998 and AC Milan in 2003.

EUROPEAN FOOTBALL – BIG RECOVERIES

In the most astonishing Final in the history of the European Cup/Champions League, **Liverpool** became the first club to win it from a 3-0 deficit when they beat AC Milan 3-2 on penalties after a 3-3 draw in Istanbul on May 25, 2005. Liverpool's fifth triumph in the competition meant that they would keep the trophy.

The following season, **Middlesbrough** twice recovered from three-goal aggregate deficits in the **UEFA Cup**, beating Basel 4-3 in the quarter finals and Steaua Bucharest by the same scoreline in the semi-finals. In 2010, **Fulham** beat Juventus 5-4 after trailing 1-4 on aggregate in the second leg of their Europa League, Round of 16 match at Craven Cottage.

Two Scottish clubs have won a European tie from a 3-goal, first leg deficit: **Kilmarnock** 0-3, 5-1 v Eintracht Frankfurt (Fairs Cup 1st round, 1964–65); **Hibernian** 1-4, 5-0 v Napoli (Fairs Cup 2nd Round, 1967–68).

English clubs have three times gone out of the **UEFA Cup** after leading 3-0 from the first leg: 1975–76 (2nd Rd) **Ipswich** lost 3-4 on agg to Bruges; 1976–77 (quarter-final) **QPR** lost on penalties to AEK Athens after 3-3 agg; 1977–78 (3rd round) **Ipswich** lost on penalties to Barcelona after 3-3 agg.

On Oct 16, 2012, Sweden recovered from 0-4 down to draw 4-4 with Germany (World Cup qual) in Berlin.

- In the **1966 World Cup quarter-final** (Jul 23) at Goodison Park, North Korea led Portugal 3-0, but Eusebio scored 4 times to give **Portugal** a 5-3 win.

HEAVIEST ENGLISH-CLUB DEFEATS IN EUROPE

(Single-leg scores)

European Cup: Artmedia Bratislava 5, **Celtic** 0 (2nd qual round), Jul 2005 (agg 5-4); Ajax 5, **Liverpool** 1 (2nd round), Dec 1966 (agg 7-3); Real Madrid 5, **Derby** 1 (2nd round), Nov 1975 (agg 6-5).

Cup-Winners' Cup: Sporting Lisbon 5, **Manchester Utd** 0 (quarter-final), Mar 1964 (agg 6-4).

Fairs/UEFA Cup: Bayern Munich 6, **Coventry** 1 (2nd round), Oct 1970 (agg 7-3). **Combined London** team lost 6-0 (agg 8-2) in first Fairs Cup Final in 1958. Barcelona 5, **Chelsea** 0 in Fairs Cup semi-final play-off, 1966, in Barcelona (after 2-2 agg).

SHOCK ENGLISH CLUB DEFEATS

1968–69 (Eur Cup, 1st round): **Manchester City** beaten by Fenerbahce, 1-2 agg.
1971–72 (CWC, 2nd round): **Chelsea** beaten by Atvidaberg on away goals.
1993–94 (Eur Cup, 2nd round): **Manchester Utd** beaten by Galatasaray on away goals.
1994–95 (UEFA Cup, 1st round): **Blackburn** beaten by Trelleborgs, 2-3 agg.
2000–01 (UEFA Cup, 1st round): **Chelsea** beaten by St Gallen, Switz 1-2 agg.

PFA FAIR PLAY AWARD (Bobby Moore Trophy from 1993)

1988	Liverpool	2002	Crewe
1989	Liverpool	2003	Crewe
1990	Liverpool	2004	Crewe
1991	Nottm Forest	2005	Crewe
1992	Portsmouth	2006	Crewe
1993	Norwich	2007	Crewe
1994	Crewe	2008	Crewe
1995	Crewe	2009	Stockport
1996	Crewe	2010	Rochdale
1997	Crewe	2011	Rochdale
1998	Cambridge Utd	2012	Chesterfield
1999	Grimsby	2013	Crewe
2000	Crewe	2014	Exeter
2001	Hull	2015	Exeter

RECORD MEDAL SALES

At Sotherby's in London on Nov 11, 2014, the FA Cup winner's medal which **Sir Stanley Matthews** earned with Blackpool in 1953 was sold for £220,000 – the most expensive medal in British sporting history. At the same auction, **Ray Wilson's** 1966 World Cup winner's medal fetched £136,000, while **Jimmy Greaves**, who was left out of the winning England team, received £44,000 for the medal the FA belatedly awarded him in 2009

West Ham bought (Jun 2000) the late **Bobby Moore**'s collection of medals and trophies for £1.8m at Christie's auction. It was put up for sale by his first wife Tina and included his World Cup-winner's medal.

A No. 6 duplicate red shirt made for England captain **Bobby Moore** for the 1966 World Cup Final fetched £44,000 at an auction at Wolves' ground in Sep, 1999. Moore kept the shirt he wore in that Final and gave the replica to England physio Harold Shepherdson.

Sir Geoff Hurst's 1966 World Cup-winning shirt fetched a record £91,750 at Christie's in Sep, 2000. His World Cup Final cap fetched £37,600 and his Man of the Match trophy £18,800. Proceeds totalling £274,410 from the 129 lots went to Hurst's three daughters and charities of his choice, including the Bobby Moore Imperial Cancer Research Fund.

In Aug, 2001, Sir Geoff sold his World Cup-winner's medal to his former club West Ham Utd (for their museum) at a reported £150,000.

'The **Billy Wright** Collection' – caps, medals and other memorabilia from his illustrious career – fetched over £100,000 at Christie's in Nov, 1996.

At the sale in Oct 1993, trophies, caps and medals earned by **Ray Kennedy**, former England, Arsenal and Liverpool player, fetched a then record total of £88,407. Kennedy, suffering from Parkinson's Disease, received £73,000 after commission. The PFA paid £31,080 for a total of 60 lots – including a record £16,000 for his 1977 European Cup winner's medal – to be exhibited at their Manchester museum. An anonymous English collector paid £17,000 for the medal and plaque commemorating Kennedy's part in the Arsenal Double in 1971.

Previous record for one player's medals, shirts etc collection: £30,000 (**Bill Foulkes**, Manchester Utd in 1992). The sale of **Dixie Dean**'s medals etc in 1991 realised £28,000.

In Mar, 2001, **Gordon Banks**' 1966 World Cup-winner's medal fetched a new record £124,750. TV's Nick Hancock, a Stoke fan, paid £23,500 for **Sir Stanley Matthews's** 1953 FA Cup-winner's medal. He also bought one of Matthews's England caps for £3,525 and paid £2,350 for a Stoke Div 2 Championship medal (1963).

Dave Mackay's 1961 League Championship and FA Cup winner's medals sold for £18,000 at Sotherby's. Tottenham bought them for their museum.

A selection of England World Cup-winning manager **Sir Alf Ramsey**'s memorabilia – England caps, championship medals with Ipswich etc. – fetched more than £80,000 at Christie's. They were offered for sale by his family, and his former clubs Tottenham and Ipswich were among the buyers.

Ray Wilson's 1966 England World Cup-winning shirt fetched £80,750. Also in Mar, 2002, the No. 10 shirt worn by **Pele** in Brazil's World Cup triumph in 1970 was sold for a record £157,750 at Christies. It went to an anonymous telephone bidder.

In Oct, 2003, **George Best**'s European Footballer of the Year (1968) trophy was sold to an anonymous British bidder for £167,250 at Bonham's. It was the then most expensive item of sporting memorabilia ever auctioned in Britain.

England captain **Bobby Moore**'s 1970 World Cup shirt, which he swapped with Pele after Brazil's 1-0 win in Mexico, was sold for £60,000 at Christie's in Mar, 2004.

Sep, 2004: England shirt worn by tearful **Paul Gascoigne** in 1990 World Cup semi-final v Germany sold at Christie's for £28,680. At same auction, shirt worn by Brazil's **Pele** in 1958 World Cup Final in Sweden sold for £70,505.

May, 2005: The **second FA Cup** (which was presented to winning teams from 1896 to 1909) was bought for £420,000 at Christie's by Birmingham chairman David Gold, a world record for an item of football memorabilia. It was presented to the National Football Museum, Preston. At the same auction, the World Cup-winner's medal earned by England's **Alan Ball** in 1966 was sold for £164,800.

Oct, 2005: At auction at Bonham's, the medals and other memorabilia of Hungary and Real Madrid legend **Ferenc Puskas** were sold for £85,000 to help pay for hospital treatment.

Nov, 2006: A ball used in the 2006 World Cup Final and signed by the winning **Italy** team was sold for £1.2m (a world record for football memorabilia) at a charity auction in Qatar. It was bought by the Qatar Sports Academy.

Feb, 2010: A pair of boots worn by **Sir Stanley Matthews** in the 1953 FA Cup Final was sold at Bonham's for £38,400.

Oct, 2010: Trophies and memorabilia belonging to **George Best** were sold at Bonham's for £193,440. His 1968 European Cup winner's medal fetched £156,000.

Oct–Nov 2010: **Nobby Stiles** sold his 1966 World Cup winner's medal at an Edinburgh auction for a record £188,200. His old club, Manchester Utd, also paid £48,300 for his 1968 European Cup medal to go to the club's museum at Old Trafford. In London, the shirt worn by Stiles in the 1966 World Cup Final went for £75,000. A total of 45 items netted £424,438. **George Cohen** and **Martin Peters** had previously sold their medals from 1966.

Oct 2011: **Terry Paine** (who did not play in the Final) sold his 1966 World Cup medal for £27,500 at auction.

Mar 2013: **Norman Hunter** (Leeds and England) sold his honours' collection on line for nearly £100,000

Nov 2013: A collection of **Nat Lofthouse's** career memorabilia was sold at auction for £100,000. Bolton Council paid £75,000 for items including his 1958 FA Cup winner's medal to go on show at the local museum.

LONGEST UNBEATEN CUP RUN

Liverpool established the longest unbeaten Cup sequence by a Football League club: 25 successive rounds in the League/Milk Cup between semi-final defeat by Nottm Forest (1-2 agg) in 1980 and defeat at Tottenham (0-1) in the third round on Oct 31, 1984. During this period Liverpool won the tournament in four successive seasons, a feat no other Football League club has achieved in any competition.

BIG HALF-TIME SCORES

Tottenham 10, Crewe 1 (FA Cup 4th round replay, Feb 3, 1960; result 13-2); Tranmere 8, Oldham 1 (Div 3N., Dec 26, 1935; result 13-4); **Chester City 8, York 0** (Div 3N., Feb 1, 1936; result 12-0; believed to be record half-time scores in League football).

Nine goals were scored in the first half – **Burnley 4, Watford 5** in Div 1 on Apr 5, 2003. Result: 4-7.

Stirling Albion led Selkirk 15-0 at half-time (result 20-0) in the Scottish Cup 1st round, Dec 8, 1984.

World record half-time score: **16-0** when **Australia** beat **American Samoa** 31-0 (another world record) in the World Cup Oceania qualifying group at Coff's Harbour, New South Wales, on Apr 11 2001.

- On Mar 4 1933 **Coventry** beat QPR (Div 3 South) 7-0, having led by that score at half-time. This repeated the half-time situation in Bristol City's 7-0 win over Grimsby on Dec 26, 1914.

TOP SECOND-HALF TEAM

Most goals scored by a team in one half of a League match is **11. Stockport** led Halifax 2-0 at half-time in Div 3 North on Jan 6 1934 and won 13-0.

FIVE NOT ENOUGH

Last team to score **5** in League match and lose: **Burton**, beaten 6-5 by Cheltenham (Lge 2, Mar 13, 2010).

LONG SERVICE WITH ONE CLUB

Bill Nicholson, OBE, was associated with Tottenham for 67 years – as a wing-half (1938–55), then the club's most successful manager (1958–74) with 8 major prizes, subsequently chief advisor and scout. He became club president, and an honorary freeman of the borough, had an executive suite named after him at the club, and the stretch of roadway from Tottenham High Road to the main gates has the nameplate Bill Nicholson Way. He died, aged 85, in Oct 2004.

Ted Bates, the Grand Old Man of Southampton with 66 years of unbroken service to the club, was awarded the Freedom of the City in Apr, 2001. He joined Saints as an inside-forward from Norwich in 1937, made 260 peace-time appearances for the club, became reserve-team trainer in 1953 and manager at The Dell for 18 years (1955–73), taking Southampton into the top division in 1966. He was subsequently chief executive, director and club president. He died in Oct 2003, aged 85.

Bob Paisley was associated with Liverpool for 57 years from 1939, when he joined them from Bishop Auckland, until he died in Feb 1996. He served as player, trainer, coach, assistant-manager, manager, director and vice-president. He was Liverpool's most successful manager, winning 13 major trophies for the club (1974–83).

Dario Gradi, MBE, stepped down after completing 24 seasons and more than 1,000 matches as manager of Crewe (appointed Jun 1983). Never a League player, he previously managed Wimbledon and Crystal Palace. At Crewe, his policy of finding and grooming young talent has earned the club more than £20m in transfer fees. He stayed with Crewe as technical director, and twice took charge of team affairs again following the departure of the managers who succeeded him, Steve Holland and Gudjon Thordarson.

Ronnie Moran, who joined Liverpool in as a player 1952, retired from the Anfield coaching staff in season 1998–99.

Ernie Gregory served West Ham for 52 years as goalkeeper and coach. He joined them as boy of 14 from school in 1935, retired in May 1987.

Ryan Giggs played 24 seasons for Manchester Utd (1990-2014), then became assistant manager under Louis van Gaal.

Ted Sagar, Everton goalkeeper, 23 years at Goodison Park (1929–52, but only 16 League seasons because of war).

Alan Knight, goalkeeper, played 23 seasons (1977–2000) for his only club, Portsmouth.

Sam Bartram was recognised as one of the finest goalkeepers never to play for England, apart from unofficial wartime games. He was with Charlton from 1934–56

Jack Charlton, England World Cup winner, served Leeds from 1952–73.

Roy Sproson, defender, played 21 League seasons for his only club, Port Vale (1950–71).

TIGHT AT HOME

Fewest home goals conceded in League season (modern times): 4 by **Liverpool** (Div 1, 1978–9); 4 by **Manchester Utd** (Premier League, 1994–95) – both in 21 matches.

VARSITY MATCH

First played in 1873, this is the game's second oldest contest (after the FA Cup). Played 132, Oxford 51 wins, Cambridge 49 wins, Draws 32. Goals: Oxford 208, Cambridge 205. Latest result: Oxford 2 Cambridge 0 (Mar 27, 2016, at Fulham.

TRANSFER WINDOW

This was introduced to Britain in Sep 2002 via FIFA regulations to bring uniformity across Europe (the rule previously applied in a number of other countries).

The transfer of contracted players is restricted to two periods: Jun 1–Aug 31 and Jan 1–31).

On appeal, Football League clubs continued to sign/sell players (excluding deals with Premiership clubs).

PROGRAMME PIONEERS

Chelsea pioneered football's magazine-style programme by introducing a 16-page issue for the First Division match against Portsmouth on Christnmas Day 1948. It cost sixpence (2.5p). A penny programme from the 1909 FA Cup Final fetched £23,500 at a London auction in May, 2012.

WORLD'S OLDEST FOOTBALL ANNUAL

Now in its 130th edition, this publication begawn as the 16-page Athletic News Football Supplement & Club Directory in 1887. From the long-established Athletic News, it became the Sunday Chronicle Annual in 1946, the Empire News in 1956, the News of the World & Empire News in 1961 and the News of the World Annual from 1965 until becoming the Nationwide Annual in 2008.

PREMIER LEAGUE CLUB DETAILS AND SQUADS 2016–17

(at time of going to press)

ARSENAL

Ground: Emirates Stadium, Highbury, London, N5 IBU
Telephone: 0207 619 5000. **Club nickname**: Gunners
Capacity: 60,260. **Colours**: Red and white. **Main sponsor**: Emirates
Record transfer fee: £42.4m to Real Madrid for Mesut Ozil, Sep 2013
Record fee received: £35m from Barcelona for Cesc Fabregas, Aug 2011
Record attendance: Highbury: 73,295 v Sunderland (Div 1) Mar 9, 1935. Wembley: 73,707 v Lens (Champ Lge) Nov 1998. Emirates Stadium: 60,161 v Manchester Utd (Prem Lge) Nov 3, 2007
League Championship: Winners 1930–31, 1932–33, 1933–34, 1934–35, 1937–38, 1947–48, 1952–53, 1970–71, 1988–89, 1990–91, 1997–98, 2001–02, 2003–04
FA Cup: Winners 1930, 1936, 1950, 1971, 1979, 1993, 1998, 2002, 2003, 2005, 2014, 2015
League Cup: Winners 1987, 1993
European competitions: Winners Fairs Cup 1969–70; Cup-Winners' Cup 1993–94
Finishing positions in Premier League: 1992–93 10th, 1993–94 4th, 1994–95 12th, 1995–96 5th, 1996–97 3rd, 1997–98 1st, 1998–99 2nd, 1999–2000 2nd, 2000–01 2nd, 2001–02 1st, 2002–03 2nd, 2003–04 1st, 2004–05 2nd, 2005–06 4th, 2006–07 4th, 2007–08 3rd, 2008–09 4th, 2009–10 3rd, 2010–11 4th, 2011–12 3rd, 2012–13 4th, 2013–14 4th, 2014–15 3rd, 2015–16 2nd
Biggest win: 12-0 v Loughborough (Div 2) Mar 12, 1900
Biggest defeat: 0-8 v Loughborough (Div 2) Dec 12, 1896
Highest League scorer in a season: Ted Drake 42 (1934–35)
Most League goals in aggregate: Thierry Henry 175 (1999–2007) (2012)
Longest unbeaten League sequence: 49 matches (2003–04)
Longest sequence without a League win: 23 matches (1912–13)
Most capped player: Thierry Henry (France) 81

Name	Height ft in	Previous club	Birthplace	Birthdate
Goalkeepers				
Cech, Petr	6.5	Chelsea	Plzen, Cz	20.05.82
Martinez, Damian	6.4	Independiente	Mar del Plata, Arg	02.09.92
Ospina, David	6.0	Nice	Medellin, Col	31.08.88
Szczesny, Wojciech	6.5	–	Warsaw, Pol	18.04.90
Defenders				
Bellerin, Hector	5.10	Barcelona	Barcelona, Sp	19.03.95
Chambers, Calum	6.0	Southampton	Petersfield	20.01.95
Debuchy, Mathieu	5.10	Newcastle	Fretin, Fr	28.07.85
Gabriel Paulista	6.2	Villarreal	Sao Paulo, Br	26.11.90
Gibbs, Kieran	5.10	–	Lambeth	26.09.89
Jenkinson, Carl	6.1	Charlton	Harlow	08.02.92
Koscielny, Laurent	6.1	Lorient	Tulle, Fr	10.09.85
Mertesacker, Per	6.6	Werder Bremen	Hannover, Ger	29.09.84
Monreal, Nacho	5.10	Malaga	Pamplona, Sp	26.02.86
Midfielders				
Bielik, Krystian	6.2	Legia Warsaw	Konin, Pol	04.01.98
Cazorla, Santi	5.6	Malaga	Llanera, Sp	13.12.84
Coquelin, Francis	5.10	–	Laval, Fr	13.05.91

Elneny, Mohamed	5.11	Basle	El-Mahalla, Egy	11.07.92
Oxlade-Chamberlain, Alex	5.11	Southampton	Portsmouth	15.08.93
Ozil, Mesut	5.11	Real Madrid	Gelsenkirchen, Ger	15.10.88
Rosicky, Tomas	5.10	Borussia Dortmund	Prague, Cz	04.10.80
Ramsey, Aaron	5.11	Cardiff	Caerphilly	26.12.90
Wilshere, Jack	5.8	–	Stevenage	01.01.92
Xhaka, Granit	6.1	Borussia M'gladbach	Basle, Swi	27.09.92
Zelalem, Gedion	5.11	Hertha Berlin	Berlin	26.01.97
Forwards				
Akpom, Chuba	6.0	Southend	Canning Town	09.10.95
Campbell, Joel	5.10	Saprissa	San Jose, CRica	26.06.92
Giroud, Olivier	6.4	Montpellier	Chambery, Fr	30.09.86
Gnabry, Serge	5.9	Stuttgart	Stuttgart, Ger	14.07.95
Sanchez, Alexis	5.7	Barcelona	Tocopilla, Chil	19.12.88
Sanogo, Yaya	6.4	Auxerre	Massy, Fr	27.01.93
Walcott, Theo	5.8	Southampton	Newbury	16.03.89
Welbeck, Danny	5.10	Manchester Utd	Manchester	26.11.90

BOURNEMOUTH

Ground: Vitality Stadium, Dean Court, Bournemouth BH7 7AF
Telephone: 0344 576 1910. **Club nickname**: Cherries
Capacity: 11,464. **Colours**: Red and black. **Main sponsor**: Mansion Group
Record transfer fee: £15m to Liverpool for Jordon Ibe, Jul 2016
Record fee received: £3m from Norwich for Lewis Grabban, Jun 2014
Record attendance: 28,799 v Manchester Utd (FA Cup 6) Mar 2, 1957
FA Cup: Sixth round 1957
League Cup: Fifth round 2014
Finishing position in Premier League: 2015–16 16th
Biggest win: 8-0 v Birmingham (Champ) Oct 15, 2014. Also: 11-0 v Margate (FA Cup 1) Nov 20, 1971
Biggest defeat: 0-9 v Lincoln (Div 3) Dec 18, 1982
Highest League scorer in a season: Ted MacDougall 42 (1970–71)
Most League goals in aggregate: Ron Eyre 202 (1924–33)
Longest unbeaten League sequence: 18 (1982)
Longest sequence without a League win: 14 (1974)
Most capped player: Gerry Peyton (Republic of Ireland) 7

Goalkeepers				
Allsop, Ryan	6.3	Leyton Orient	Birmingham	17.06.92
Boruc, Artur	6.4	Southampton	Siedice, Pol	20.02.80
Federici, Adam	6.2	Reading	Nowra, Aus	31.01.85
Defenders				
Ake, Nathan	5.11	Chelsea (loan)	The Hague, Hol	18.02.95
Cargill, Baily	6.2	–	Winchester	05.07.95
Cook, Steve	6.1	Brighton	Hastings	19.04.91
Francis, Simon	6.0	Charlton	Nottingham	16.02.85
Mings, Tyrone	6.3	Ipswich	Bath	13.03.93
Smith, Adam	5.11	Tottenham	Leystonstone	29.04.91
Wiggins, Rhoys	5.9	Sheffield Wed	Hillingdon	04.11.87
Midfielders				
Arter, Harry	5.9	Woking	Eltham	28.12.89
Cook, Lewis	5.9	Leeds	Leeds	28.03.97
Daniels, Charlie	5.10	Leyton Orient	Harlow	07.09.86
Gosling, Dan	5.10	Newcastle	Brixham	02.02.90

Gradel, Max	5.10	St Etienne	Abidjan, Iv C	30.11.87
Hyndman, Emerson	5.8	Fulham	Dallas, US	09.04.96
Ibe, Jordon	5.7	Liverpool	Bermondsey	08.12.95
MacDonald, Shaun	6.1	Swansea	Swansea	17.06.88
Mousset, Lys	6.0	Le Havre	Montivilliers, Fr	08.12.96
O'Kane, Eunan	5.8	Torquay	Derry	10.07.90
Pugh, Marc	5.11	Hereford	Bacup	02.04.87
Stanislas, Junior	6.0	Burnley	Eltham	26.11.89
Surman, Andrew	5.11	Norwich	Johannesburg, SA	20.08.86
Forwards				
Afobe, Benik	6.0	Wolves	Waltham Forest	12.02.93
Grabban, Lewis	6.0	Norwich	Croydon	12.01.88
King, Josh	5.11	Blackburn	Oslo, Nor	15.01.92
Rantie, Tokelo	5.9	Malmo	Parys, SA	08.09.90
Wilson, Callum	5.11	Coventry	Coventry	27.02.92

BURNLEY

Ground: Turf Moor, Harry Potts Way, Burnlety BB10 4BX
Telephone: 0871 221 1882. **Club nickname**: Clarets
Capacity: 21,401. **Colours**: Claret and blue. **Main sponsor**: Dafabet
Record transfer fee: £6m to Brentford for Andre Gray, Aug 2015
Record fee received: £6.5m from Wolves for Steven Fletcher, Jun 2010
Record attendance: 54,775 v Huddersfield (FA Cup 3) Feb 23, 1924
League Championship: Winners 1920–21, 1959–60
FA Cup: Winners 1914
League Cup: Semi-finals 1961, 1969, 1983, 2009
European competitions: European Cup quarter-finals 1960–61
Finishing position in Premier League: 2014–15 19th
Biggest win: 9-0 v Darwen (Div 1) Jan 9, 1892, v Crystal Palace (FA Cup 2) Feb 10, 1909, v New Brighton (FA Cup 4) Jan 26, 1957, v Penrith (FA Cup 1) Nov 17, 1984
Biggest defeat: 0-10 v Aston Villa (Div 1) Aug 29, 1925, v Sheffield Utd (Div 1) Jan 19, 1929
Highest League scorer in a season: George Beel 35 (1927–28
Highest League scorer in aggregate: George Beel 178 (1923–32
Longest unbeaten League sequence: 30 matches (1920–21)
Longest sequence without a League win: 24 matches (1979)
Most capped player: Jimmy McIlroy (Northern Ireland) 51

Goalkeepers				
Heaton, Tom	6.1	Bristol City	Chester	15.04.86
Robinson, Paul	6.4	Blackburn	Beverley	15.10.79
Defenders				
Anderson, Tom	6.4	–	Burnley	02.09.93
Darikwa, Tendayi	6.2	Chesterfield	Nottingham	13.12.91
Dummigan, Cameron	5.11	Cliftonville	Lurgan	02.06.96
Keane, Michael	5.10	Manchester Utd	Stockport	11.01.93
Lafferty, Danny	6.1	Derry	Derry	01.04.89
Long, Kevin	6.2	Cork	Cork, Ire	18.08.90
Lowton, Matthew	5.11	Aston Villa	Chesterfield	09.06.89
Mee, Ben	5.11	Manchester City	Sale	23.09.89
Ward, Stephen	5.11	Wolves	Dublin, Ire	20.08.85
Midfielders				
Arfield, Scott	5.10	Huddersfield	Livingston	01.11.88
Boyd, George	5.10	Hull	Chatham	02.10.85
Jones, David	5.10	Wigan	Southport	04.11.84

Kightly, Michael	5.11	Stoke	Basildon	24.01.86
Marney, Dean	5.11	Hull	Barking	31.01.84
Tarkowski, James	6.1	Brentford	Manchester	19.11.92
Ulvestad, Fredrik	6.0	Aalesund	Aalesund, Nor	17.06.92
Forwards				
Barnes, Ashley	6.0	Brighton	Bath	31.10.89
Gray, Andre	5.10	Brentford	Wolverhampton	26.06.91
Hennings, Rouwen	5.11	Karlsruhe	Bad Oldesloe, Ger	28.08.87
Jutkiewicz, Lukas	6.1	Middlesbrough	Southampton	20.03.89
Long, Chris	5.7	Everton	Huyton	25.02.95
Vokes, Sam	5.11	Wolves	Lymington	21.10.89

CHELSEA

Ground: Stamford Bridge Stadium, London SW6 1HS
Telephone: 0871 984 1905. **Club nickname**: Blues
Capacity: 41,798. **Colours**: Blue. **Main sponsor**: Yokohama Rubber
Record transfer fee: £50m to Liverpool for Fernando Torres, Jan 2011
Record fee received: £40m from Paris SG for David Luiz, Jun 2014
Record attendance: 82,905 v Arsenal (Div 1) Oct 12, 1935
League Championship: Winners 1954–55, 2004–05, 2005–06, 2009–10, 2014–15
FA Cup: Winners 1970, 1997, 2000, 2007, 2009, 2010, 2012
League Cup: Winners 1965, 1998, 2005, 2007, 2015
European competitions: Winners Champions League 2011–12; Cup-Winners' Cup 1970–71, 1997–98; Europa League 2012–13; European Super Cup 1998
Finishing positions in Premier League: 1992–93 11th, 1993–94 14th, 1994–95 11th, 1995–96 11th, 1996–97 6th, 1997–98 4th, 1998–99 3rd, 1999–2000 5th, 2000–01 6th, 2001–02 6th, 2002–03 4th, 2003–04 2nd, 2004–05 1st, 2005–06 1st, 2006–07 2nd, 2007–08 2nd, 2008–09 3rd, 2009–10 1st, 2010–11 2nd, 2011–12 6th, 2012–13 3rd, 2013–14 3rd, 2014–15 1st, 2015–16 10th
Biggest win: 8-0 v Aston Villa (Prem Lge) Dec 23, 2012. Also: 13-0 v Jeunesse Hautcharage, (Cup-Winners' Cup 1) Sep 29, 1971
Biggest defeat: 1-8 v Wolves (Div 1) Sep 26, 1953; 0-7 v Leeds (Div 1) Oct 7, 1967, v Nottm Forest (Div 1) Apr 20, 1991
Highest League scorer in a season: Jimmy Greaves 41 (1960–61)
Most League goals in aggregate: Bobby Tambling 164 (1958–70)
Longest unbeaten League sequence: 40 matches (2004–05)
Longest sequence without a League win: 21 matches (1987–88)
Most capped player: Frank Lampard (England) 104

Goalkeepers				
Begovic, Asmir	6.5	Stoke	Trebinje, Bos	20.06.87
Blackman, Jamal	6.6	–	Croydon	27.10.93
Courtois, Thibaut	6.6	Genk	Bree, Bel	11.05.92
Defenders				
Azpilicueta, Cesar	5.10	Marseille	Pamplona, Sp	28.08.89
Cahill, Gary	6.2	Bolton	Sheffield	19.12.85
Christensen, Andreas	6.2	Brondby	Lillerod, Den	10.04.96
Djilobodji, Papy	6.4	Nantes	Kaolack, Sen	01.12.88
Hector, Michael	6.4	Reading	East Ham	19.07.92
Ivanovic, Branislav	6.2	Lokomotive Moscow	Mitrovica, Serb	22.02.84
Miazga, Matt	6.4	New York Bulls	Clifton, US	19.07.95
Rahman, Baba	5.11	Augsburg	Tamale, Gha	02.07.94
Terry, John	6.1	–	Barking	07.12.80
Zouma, Kurt	6.3	St Etienne	Lyon, Fr	27.10.94

Midfielders

Cuadrado, Juan	5.10	Fiorentina	Necocli, Col	26.05.88
Chalobah, Nathaniel	6.1	–	Freetown, SLeone	12.12.94
Fabregas, Cesc	5.11	Barcelona	Arenys de Mar, Sp	04.05.87
Hazard, Eden	5.8	Lille	La Louviere, Bel	07.01.91
Kante, N'Golo	5.7	Leicester	Paris, Fr	29.03.91
Loftus-Cheek, Ruben	6.3	–	Lewisham	23.01.96
Matic, Nemanja	6.4	Benfica	Sabac, Serb	01.08.88
Mikel, John Obi	6.2	Lyn Oslo	Plato State, Nig	22.04.87
Oscar	5.10	Internacional	Americana, Br	09.09.91
Pedro	5.6	Barcelona	Santa Cruz, Ten	28.07.87
Willian	5.9	Anzhi Makhachkala	Ribeirao Pires, Br	09.08.88
Forwards				
Bamford, Patrick	6.1	Nottm Forest	Grantham	05.09.93
Batshuayi, Michy	6.0	Marseille	Brussels, Bel	02.10.93
Diego Costa	6.2	Atletico Madrid	Lagarto, Br	07.10.88
Kenedy	6.0	Fluminense	Santa Rita, Br	08.02.96
Moses, Victor	5.10	Wigan	Lagos, Nig	12.12.90
Remy, Loic	6.1	QPR	Rilleux, Fr	02.01.87

CRYSTAL PALACE

Ground: Selhurst Park, Whitehorse Lane, London SE25, 6PU
Telephone: 0208 768 6000. **Club nickname**: Eagles
Capacity: 25,456. **Colours**: Red and blue. **Main sponsor**: Mansion
Record transfer fee: £10m to Paris St-Germain for Yohan Cabaye, Jul 2015
Record fee received: £15m from Manchester Utd for Wilfried Zaha, Jan 2013
Record attendance: 51,482 v Burnley (Div 2), May 11, 1979
League Championship: 3rd 1990–91
FA Cup: Runners-up 1990, 2016
League Cup: Semi-finals 1993, 1995, 2001, 2012
Finishing positions in Premier League: 1992–93 20th, 1994–95 19th, 1997–98 20th, 2004–05 18th, 2013–14 11th, 2014–15 10th, 2015–16 15th
Biggest win: 9-0 v Barrow (Div 4) Oct 10, 1959
Biggest defeat: 0-9 v Liverpool (Div 1) Sep 12, 1989. Also: 0-9 v Burnley (FA Cup 2 rep) Feb 10, 1909
Highest League scorer in a season: Peter Simpson 46 (1930–31)
Most League goals in aggregate: Peter Simpson 153 (1930–36)
Longest unbeaten League sequence: 18 matches (1969)
Longest sequence with a League win: 20 matches (1962)
Most capped player: Mile Jedinak (Australia) 37

Goalkeepers

Hennessey, Wayne	6.5	Wolves	Bangor, Wal	24.01.87
Mandana, Steve	6.1	Marseille	Kinshasa, DR Cong	28.03.85
McCarthy, Alex	6.4	QPR	Guildford	03.12.89
Speroni, Julian	6.1	Dundee	Buenos Aires, Arg	18.05.79
Defenders				
Dann, Scott	6.2	Blackburn	Liverpool	14.02.87
Delaney, Damien	6.2	Ipswich	Cork, Ire	29.07.81
Fryers, Zeki	6.0	Tottenham	Manchester	09.09.92
Kelly, Martin	6.3	Liverpool	Whiston	27.04.90
Souare, Pape	5.10	Lille	Mbao, Sen	06.06.90
Tomkins, James	6.3	West Ham	Basildon	29.03.89
Ward, Joel	6.2	Portsmouth	Portsmouth	29.10.89

Midfielders

Bolasie, Yannick	6.2	Bristol City	Kinshasa, DR Cong	24.05.89
Cabaye, Yohan	5.9	Paris SG	Tourcoing, Fr	14.01.86
Jedinak, Mile	6.3	Genclerbirligi	Sydney, Aus	03.08.84
Kaikai, Sullay	6.0	–	Southwark	26.08.95
Ledley, Joe	6.0	Celtic	Cardiff	23.01.87
Lee Chung-Yong	5.11	Bolton	Seoul, S Kor	02.07.88
McArthur, James	5.7	Wigan	Glasgow	07.10.87
Mutch, Jordon	5.9	QPR	Birmingham	02.12.91
Puncheon, Jason	5.8	Southampton	Croydon	26.06.86
Sako, Bakary	5.11	Wolves	Ivry-sur-Seine, Fr	26.04.88
Townsend, Andros	6.0	Newcastle	Leytonstone	16.07.91
Williams, Jonathan	5.7	–	Pembury	09.10.93
Zaha, Wilfried	5.10	Manchester Utd	Abidjan, Iv C	10.11.92

Forwards

Appiah, Kwesi	5.11	Margate	Thamesmead	12.08.90
Campbell, Fraizer	5.11	Cardiff	Huddersfield	13.09.87
Wickham, Connor	6.3	Sunderland	Colchester	31.03.93

EVERTON

Ground: Goodison Park, Liverpool L4 4EL
Telephone: 0151 556 1878. **Club nickname**: Toffees
Capacity: 39,571. **Colours**: Blue and white. **Main sponsor**: Chang
Record transfer fee: £28m to Chelsea for Romelu Lukaku, Jul 2014
Record fee received: £27m from Manchester Utd for Wayne Rooney, Aug 2004
Record attendance: 78,299 v Liverpool (Div 1) Sep 18, 1948
League Championship: Winners 1890–91, 1914–15, 1927–28, 1931–31, 1938–39, 1962–63, 1969–70, 1984–85, 1986–87
FA Cup: Winners 1906, 1933, 1966, 1984, 1995
League Cup: Runners-up 1977, 1984
European competitions: Winners Cup-Winners' Cup 1984–85
Finishing positions in Premier League: 1992–93 13th, 1993–94 17th, 1994–95 15th, 1995–96 6th 1996–97 15th 1997–98 17th 1998–99 14th, 1999–2000 13th, 2000–01 16th, 2001–02 15th, 2002–03 7th, 2003–04 17th, 2004–05 4th, 2005–06 11th, 2006–07 6th, 2007–08 5th, 2008–09 5th, 2009–10 8th, 20010–11 7th, 2011–12 7th, 2012–13 6th 2013–14 5th, 2014–15 11th, 2015–16 11th
Biggest win: 9-1 v Manchester City (Div 1) Sep 3, 1906, v Plymouth (Div 2) Dec 27, 1930. Also: 11-2 v Derby (FA Cup 1) Jan 18, 1890
Biggest defeat: 0-7 v Portsmouth (Div 1) Sep 10, 1949, v Arsenal (Prem Lge) May 11, 2005
Highest League scorer in a season: Ralph 'Dixie' Dean 60 (1927–28)
Most League goals in aggregate: Ralph 'Dixie' Dean 349 (1925–37)
Longest unbeaten League sequence: 20 matches (1978)
Longest sequence without a League win: 14 matches (1937)
Most capped player: Neville Southall (Wales) 92

Goalkeepers

Robles, Joel	6.5	Atletico Madrid	Getafe, Sp	17.06.90
Stekelenburg, Maarten	6.6	Fulham	Haarlem, Hol	22.09.82

Defenders

Baines, Leighton	5.7	Wigan	Liverpool	11.12.84
Browning, Tyias	5.11	–	Liverpool	27.05.94
Coleman, Seamus	5.10	Sligo	Donegal, Ire	11.10.88
Funes Mori, Ramiro	6.1	River Plate	Mendoza, Arg	01.07.91
Galloway, Brendan	6.2	MK Dons	Harare, Zimb	17.03.96

Garbutt, Luke	5.10	Leeds	Harrogate	21.05.93
Holgate, Mason	5.11	Barnsley	Doncaster	22.10.96
Jagielka, Phil	5.11	Sheffield Utd	Manchester	17.08.82
Pennington, Matthew	6.1	–	Warrington	06.10.94
Stones, John	5.10	Barnsley	Barnsley	28.05.94
Midfielders				
Barkley, Ross	6.2	–	Liverpool	05.12.93
Barry, Gareth	6.0	Manchester City	Hastings	23.02.81
Besic, Muhamed	5.10	Ferencvaros	Berlin, Ger	10.09.92
Cleverley, Tom	5.10	Manchester Utd	Basingstoke	12.08.89
Deulofeu, Gerard	5.10	Barcelona	Riudarenes, Sp	13.03.94
Dowell, Kieran	5.10	–	Ormskirk	10.10.97
Gibson, Darron	5.9	Manchester Utd	Derry	25.10.87
Lennon, Aaron	5.5	Tottenham	Leeds	16.04.87
McCarthy, James	5.11	Wigan	Glasgow	12.11.90
McGeady, Aiden	5.11	Spartak Moscow	Paisley	04.04.86
Mirallas, Kevin	6.0	Olympiacos	Liege, Bel	05.10.87
Niasse, Oumar	6.1	Lokomotiv Moscow	Oukam, Sen	18.04.90
Oviedo, Bryan	5.8	Copenhagen	Ciudad, C Rica	18.02.90
Forwards				
Henen, David	6.1	Olympiacos	Libramont, Bel	19.04.96
Kone, Arouna	5.11	Wigan	Anyama Iv C	11.11.83
Lukaku, Romelu	6.3	Chelsea	Antwerp, Bel	13.05.93
McAleny, Conor	5.10	–	Liverpool	12.08.92
Rodriguez, Leandro	5.11	River Plate (Uruguay)	Montevideo, Uru	19.11.92

HULL CITY

Ground: Kingston Communications Stadium, Anlaby Road, Hull, HU3 6HU
Telephone: 01482 504 600. **Club nickname:** Tigers
Capacity: 25,586. **Colours**: Amber and black. **Main sponsor:** Flamingo Land
Record transfer fee: £10m to Palermo for Abel Hernandez, Sep 2014
Record fee received: £12m from Southampton for Shane Long, Aug 2014
Record attendance: Boothferry Park: 55,019 v Manchester Utd (FA Cup 6) Feb 26, 1949. KC Stadium: 25,030 v Liverpool (Prem Lge) May 9, 2010. Also: 25,280 (England U21 v Holland) Feb 17, 2004
League Championship: 16th 2013–14
FA Cup: Runners-up 2014
League Cup: 4th rd 1974, 1976, 1978
Finishing positions in Premier League: 2008–09 17th, 2009–10 19th, 2013–14 16th, 2014–15 18th
Biggest win: 11-1 v Carlisle (Div 3 N) Jan 14, 1939
Biggest defeat: 0-8 v Wolves (Div 2) Nov 4, 1911
Highest League scorer in a season: Bill McNaughton 39 (1932–33)
Most League gols in aggregate: Chris Chilton 195 (1960–71)
Longest unbeaten League sequence: 15 matches (1983)
Longest sequence without a League win: 27 matches (1989)
Most capped player: Theodore Whitmore (Jamaica) 28

Goalkeepers				
Jakupovic, Eldin	6.3	Aris	Sarajevo, Bos	02.10.84
Kuciak, Dusan	6.4	Legia Warsaw	Zilina, Slovak	21.05.85
McGregor, Allan	6.0	Besiktas	Edinburgh	31.01.82
Defenders				
Bruce, Alex	5.11	Leeds	Norwich	28.09.84

Davies, Curtis	6.2	Birmingham	Waltham Forest	15.03.85
Dawson, Michael	6.2	Tottenham	Northallerton	18.11.83
Lenihan, Brian	5.10	Cork	Cork	08.06.94
Maguire, Harry	6.2	Sheffield Utd	Sheffield	05.03.93
Odubajo, Moses	5.10	Brentford	Greenwich	28.07.93
Robertson, Andrew	5.10	Dundee Utd	Glasgow	11.03.94
Midfielders				
Clucas, Sam	5.10	Chesterfield	Lincoln	25.09.90
Diame, Mohamed	6.1	West Ham	Creteil, Fr	14.06.87
Elmohamady, Ahmed	5.11	Sunderland	Basyoun, Egy	09.09.87
Huddlestone, Tom	6.1	Tottenham	Nottingham	28.12.86
Livermore, Jake	6.2	Tottenham	Enfield	14.11.89
Maloney, Shaun	5.7	Chicago Fire	Miri, Malay	24.01.83
Meyler, David	6.2	Sunderland	Cork, Ire	29.05.89
Snodgrass, Robert	6.0	Norwich	Glasgow	07.09.87
Forwards				
Diomande, Adama	5.11	Stabaek	Oslo, Nor	14.02.90
Hernandez, Abel	6.1	Palermo	Pando, Uru	08.08.90

LEICESTER CITY

Ground: King Power Stadium, Filbert Way, Leicester, LE2 7FL
Telephone: 0844 815 5000. **Club nickname**: Foxes
Capacity: 32,312. **Colours**: Blue and white. **Main sponsor**: King Power
Record transfer fee: £16.6m to CSKA Moscow for Ahmed Musa, Jul 2016
Record fee received: £11m from Liverpool for Emile Heskey, Mar 2000
Record attendance: Filbert Street: 47,298 v. Tottenham (FA Cup 5) Feb 18, 1928; King Power Stadium: 32,148 v Newcastle (Prem Lge) Dec 26, 2003. Also: 32,188 v Real Madrid (friendly) Jul 30, 2011
League Championship: Winners 2015–16
FA Cup: Runners-up 1949, 1961, 1963, 1969
League Cup: Winners 1964, 1997, 2000
European competitions: Cup-Winners' Cup rd 1 1961–62; UEFA Cup rd 1 1997–98, 2000–01
Finishing positions in Premier League: 1994–95 21st, 1996–97 9th, 1997–98 10th, 1998–99 10th, 1999–2000 8th, 2000–01 13th, 2001–02 20th, 2003–04 18th, 2014–15 14th, 2015–16 1st
Biggest win: 10-0 v Portsmouth (Div 1) Oct 20, 1928. Also: 13-0 v Notts Olympic (FA Cup) Oct 13, 1894
Biggest defeat (while Leicester Fosse): 0-12 v Nottm Forest (Div 1) Apr 21, 1909
Highest League scorer in a season: Arthur Rowley 44 (1956–57)
Most League goals in aggregate: Arthur Chandler 259 (1923–35)
Longest unbeaten League sequence: 23 matches (2008–09)
Longest sequence without a League win: 19 matches (1975)
Most capped player: John O'Neill (Northern Ireland) 39

Goalkeepers				
Hamer, Ben	6.4	Charlton	Taunton	20.11.87
Schmeichel, Kasper	6.0	Leeds	Copenhagen, Den	05.11.86
Zieler, Ron-Robert	6.2	Hannover	Cologne, Ger	12.02.89
Defenders				
Benalouane, Yohan	6.2	Atalatna	Bagnols-sur-Ceze, Fr	28.03.87
Chilwell, Ben	5.10	–	Milton Keynes	21.12.96
De Laet, Ritchie	6.1	Manchester Utd	Antwerp, Bel	28.11.88
Fuchs, Christian	6.1	Schalke	Neunkirchen, Aut	07.04.86
Hernandez, Luis	6.0	Sporting Gijon	Madrid, Sp	14.04.89

Huth, Robert	6.3	Stoke	Berlin, Ger	18.08.84
Morgan, Wes	5.11	Nottm Forest	Nottingham	21.01.84
Moore, Liam	6.1	–	Leicester	31.01.93
Schlupp, Jeffrey	5.8	–	Hamburg, Ger	23.12.92
Simpson, Danny	6.0	QPR	Salford	04.01.87
Wesilewski, Marcin	6.1	Anderlecht	Krakow, Pol	09.06.80
Midfielders				
Albrighton, Mark	6.1	Aston Villa	Tamworth	18.11.89
Amartey, Daniel	6.0	Copenhagen	Ghana	01.12.94
Drinkwater, Danny	5.10	Manchester Utd	Manchester	05.03.90
Gray, Demarai	5.10	Birmingham	Birmingham	28.06.96
Inler, Gokhan	6.0	Napoli	Olten, Switz	27.06.84
James, Matty	5.10	Manchester Utd	Bacup	22.07.91
King, Andy	6.0	–	Maidenhead	29.10.88
Mahrez, Riyad	5.11	Le Havre	Sarcelles, Fr	21.02.91
Mendy, Nampalys	5.6	Nice	La Seyne, Fr	23.06.92
Musa, Ahmed	5.7	CSKA Moscow	Jos, Nig	14.10.92
Forwards				
Lawrence, Tom	5.10	Manchester Utd	Wrexham	13.01.94
Okazaki, Shinji	5.9	Mainz	Takarazuka, Jap	16.04.86
Ulloa, Leonardo	6.2	Brighton	General Roca, Arg	26.07.86
Vardy, Jamie	5.10	Fleetwood	Sheffield	11.01.87

LIVERPOOL

Ground: Anfield, Liverpool L4 OTH
Telephone: 0151 263 2361. **Club nickname**: Reds or Pool
Capacity: 54,000 (approx) **Colours**: Red. **Main sponsor**: Standard Chartered
Record transfer fee: £35m to Newcastle for Andy Carroll, Jan 2011
Record fee received: £75m from Barcelona for Luis Suarez, Jul 2014
Record attendance: 61,905 v Wolves, (FA Cup 4), Feb 2, 1952
League Championship: Winners 1900–01, 1905–06, 1921–22, 1922–23, 1946–47, 1963–64, 1965–66, 1972–73, 1975–76, 1976–77, 1978–79, 1979–80, 1981–82, 1982–83, 1983–84, 1985–86, 1987–88, 1989–90
FA Cup: Winners 1965, 1974, 1986, 1989, 1992, 2001, 2006
League Cup: Winners 1981, 1982, 1983, 1984, 1995, 2001, 2003, 2012
European competitions: Winners European Cup/Champions League 1976–77, 1977–78, 1980–81, 1983–84, 2004–05; UEFA Cup 1972–73, 1975–76, 2000–01; European Super Cup 1977, 2001, 2005
Finishing positions in Premier League: 1992–93 6th, 1993–94 8th, 1994–95 4th, 1995–96 3rd, 1996–97 4th, 1997–98 3rd, 1998–99 7th, 1999–2000 4th, 2000–01 3rd, 2001–02 2nd, 2002–03 5th, 2003–04 4th, 2004–05 5th, 2005–06 3rd, 2006–07 3rd, 2007–08 4th, 2008–09 2nd, 2009–10 7th, 2010–11 6th, 2011–12 8th, 2012–13 7th, 2013–14 2nd, 2014–15 6th, 2015–16 8th
Biggest win: 10-1 v Rotherham (Div 2) Feb 18, 1896. Also: 11-0 v Stromsgodset (Cup-Winners' Cup 1) Sep 17, 1974
Biggest defeat: 1-9 v Birmingham (Div 2) Dec 11, 1954
Highest League scorer in a season: Roger Hunt 41 (1961–62)
Most League goals in aggregate: Roger Hunt 245 (1959–69)
Longest unbeaten League sequence: 31 matches (1987–88))
Longest sequence without a League win: 14 matches (1953–54))
Most capped player: Steven Gerrard (England) 114

Goalkeepers				
Bogdan, Adam	6.4	Stoke	Budapest, Hun	27.09.87
Karius, Loris	6.3	Mainz	Biberach, Ger	22.06.93

Mignolet, Simon	6.4	Sunderland	Sint-Truiden, Bel	06.08.88
Defenders				
Clyne, Nathaniel	5.9	Southampton	Stockwell	05.04.91
Flanagan, Jon	5.11	–	Liverpool	01.01.93
Gomez, Joe	6.1	Charlton	Catford	23.05.97
Ilori, Tiago	6.3	Sporting	London	26.02.93
Lovren, Dejan	6.2	Southampton	Zenica, Bos	05.07.89
Matip, Joel	6.5	Schalke	Bochum, Ger	08.08.91
Moreno, Alberto	5.7	Sevilla	Seville, Sp	05.07.92
Sakho, Mamadou	6.2	Paris SG	Paris, Fr	13.02.90
Smith, Brad	5.10	–	Penrith, Aus	09.04.94
Wisdom, Andre	6.1	–	Leeds	09.05.93
Midfielders				
Allen, Joe	5.7	Swansea	Carmarthen	14.03.90
Brannagan, Cameron	5.11	–	Manchester	09.05.96
Coutinho, Philippe	5.8	Inter Milan	Rio de Janeiro, Br	12.06.92
Emre Can	6.1	Bayer Leverkusen	Frankfurt, Ger	12.01.94
Grujic, Marko	6.3	Red Star Belgrade	Belgrade, Serb	13.04.96
Henderson, Jordan	5.10	Sunderland	Sunderland	17.06.90
Lallana, Adam	5.10	Southampton	Bournemouth	10.05.88
Lucas Leiva	5.10	Gremio	Dourados, Br	09.01.87
Markovic, Lazar	5.9	Benfica	Cacak, Serb	02.03.94
Milner, James	5.11	Manchester City	Leeds	04.01.86
Ojo, Sheyi	5.10	–	Hemel Hempstead	19.06.97
Stewart, Kevin	5.7	Tottenham	Enfield	07.09.93
Forwards				
Benteke, Christian	6.3	Aston Villa	Kinshasa, DR Cong	03.12.90
Firmino, Roberto	6.0	Hoffenheim	Maceio, Br	02.10.91
Ings, Danny	5.10	Burnley	Winchester	16.03.92
Mane, Sadio	5.9	Southampton	Sedhiou, Sen	10.04.92
Origi, Divock	6.1	Lille	Ostend, Bel	18.04.95
Sturridge, Daniel	6.2	Chelsea	Birmingham	01.09.89

MANCHESTER CITY

Ground: Etihad Stadium, Etihad Campus, Manchester M11 3FF
Telephone: 0161 444 1894. **Club nickname**: City
Capacity: 55,097. **Colours**: Sky blue and white. **Main sponsor**: Etihad
Record transfer fee: £54m to Wolfsburg for Kevin De Bruyne, Aug 2015
Record fee received: £23.8m from Valencia for Alvaro Negredo, Jul 2015
Record attendance: Maine Road: 84,569 v Stoke (FA Cup 6) Mar 3, 1934 (British record for any game outside London or Glasgow). Etihad Stadium: 54,693 v Leicester (Prem Lge) February 6, 2016
League Championship: Winners 1936–37, 1967–68, 2011–12, 2013–14
FA Cup: Winners 1904, 1934, 1956, 1969, 2011
League Cup: Winners 1970, 1976, 2014, 2016
European competitions: Winners Cup-Winners' Cup 1969–70
Finishing positions in Premier League: 1992–93 9th, 1993–94 16th, 1994–95 17th, 1995–96 18th, 2000–01: 18th, 2002–03 9th, 2003–04 16th, 2004–05 8th, 2005–06 15th, 2006–07 14th, 2007–08 9th, 2008–09 10th, 2009–10 5th, 2010–11 3rd, 2011–12 1st, 2012–13 2nd, 2013–14 1st, 2014–15 2nd, 2015–16 4th
Biggest win: 10-1 Huddersfield (Div 2) Nov 7, 1987. Also: 10-1 v Swindon (FA Cup 4) Jan 29, 1930
Biggest defeat: 1-9 v Everton (Div 1) Sep 3, 1906
Highest League scorer in a season: Tommy Johnson 38 (1928–29)
Most League goals in aggregate: Tommy Johnson, 158 (1919–30)

Longest unbeaten League sequence: 22 matches (1946–47)
Longest sequence without a League win: 17 matches (1979–80)
Most capped player: Joe Hart (England) 63

Goalkeepers				
Caballero, Willy	6.1	Malaga	Santa Elena, Arg	28.09.81
Hart, Joe	6.3	Shrewsbury	Shrewsbury	19.04.87
Defenders				
Clichy, Gael	5.11	Arsenal	Paris, Fr	26.07.85
Kompany, Vincent	6.4	Hamburg	Uccle, Bel	10.04.86
Kolarov, Aleksandar	6.2	Lazio	Belgrade, Serb	10.11.85
Mangala, Eliaquim	6.2	Porto	Colombes, Fr	13.02.91
Otamendi, Nicolas	6.0	Valencia	Buenos Aires, Arg	12.02.88
Sagna, Bacary	5.9	Arsenal	Sens, Fr	14.02.83
Zabaleta, Pablo	5.10	Espanyol	Buenos Aires, Arg	16.01.85
Midfielders				
De Bruyne, Kevin	5.11	Wolfsburg	Drongen, Bel	28.06.91
Delph, Fabian	5.9	Aston Villa	Bradford	21.11.89
Fernandinho	5.10	Shakhtar Donetsk	Londrina, Br	04.05.85
Fernando	6.0	Porto	Alto Paraiso, Br	25.07.87
Gundogan, Ilkay	5.11	Borussia Dortmund	Gelsenkirchen, Ger	24.10.90
Jesus Navas	5.8	Sevilla	Los Palacios, Sp	21.11.85
Nasri, Samir	5.10	Arsenal	Marseille, Fr	26.06.87
Silva, David	5.7	Valencia	Arguineguin, Sp	08.01.86
Sterling, Raheem	5.7	Liverpool	Kingston, Jam	08.12.94
Toure, Yaya	6.3	Barcelona	Bouake, Iv C	13.05.83
Zinchenko, Oleksandr	5.10	FC Ufa	Radomyshi, Ukr	15.12.96
Zuculini, Bruno	5.10	Racing Club	Belen, Arg	02.04.93
Forwards				
Aguero, Sergio	5.8	Atletico Madrid	Quilmes, Arg	02.06.88
Bony, Wilfried	6.0	Swansea	Bingerville, Iv C	10.12.88
Iheanacho, Kelechi	6.2	–	Owerri, Nig	03.10.96
Nolito	5.9	Celta Vigo	Sanlucar, Sp	15.10.86
Unal, Enes	6.1	Bursaspor	Osmangazi, Tur	10.05.97

MANCHESTER UNITED

Ground: Old Trafford Stadium, Sir Matt Busby Way, Manchester, M16 ORA
Telephone: 0161 868 8000. **Club nickname**: Red Devils
Capacity: 75,653. **Colours**: Red and white. **Main sponsor**: Chevrolet
Record transfer fee: £59.7m to Real Madrid for Angel di Maria, Aug 2014
Record fee received: £80m from Real Madrid for Cristiano Ronaldo, Jun 2009
Record attendance: 75,811 v Blackburn (Prem Lge), Mar 31, 2007. Also: 76,962 Wolves v Grimsby (FA Cup semi-final) Mar 25, 1939. Crowd of 83,260 saw Manchester Utd v Arsenal (Div 1) Jan 17, 1948 at Maine Road – Old Trafford out of action through bomb damage
League Championship: Winners 1907–08, 1910–11, 1951–52, 1955–56, 1956–7, 1964–65, 1966–67, 1992–93, 1993–94, 1995–96, 1996–97, 1998–99, 1999–2000, 2000–01, 2002–03, 2006–07, 2007–08, 2008–09, 2010–11, 2012–13
FA Cup: Winners 1909, 1948, 1963, 1977, 1983, 1985, 1990, 1994, 1996, 1999, 2004, 2016
League Cup: Winners 1992, 2006, 2009
European competitions: Winners European Cup/Champions League 1967–68, 1998–99, 2007–08; Cup-Winners' Cup 1990–91; European Super Cup 1991
World Club Cup: Winners 2008
Finishing positions in Premier League: 1992–93 1st, 1993–94 1st, 1994–95 2nd, 1995–96 1st, 1996–97 1st, 1997–98 2nd, 1998–99 1st, 1999–2000 1st, 2000–01 1st, 2001–02

3rd, 2002–03 1st, 2003–04 3rd, 2004–05 3rd, 2005–06 2nd, 2006–07 1st, 2007–08 1st, 2000–09 1st, 2009–10 2nd, 2010–11 1st, 2011–12 2nd, 2012–13 1st, 2013–14 7th, 2014–15 4th, 2015–16 5th

Biggest win: As Newton Heath: 10-1 v Wolves (Div 1) Oct 15, 1892. As Manchester Utd: 9-0 v Ipswich (Prem Lge), Mar 4, 1995. Also: 10-0 v Anderlecht (European Cup prelim rd) Sep 26, 1956

Biggest defeat: 0-7v Blackburn (Div 1) Apr 10, 1926, v Aston Villa (Div 1) Dec 27, 1930, v Wolves (Div 2) 26 Dec, 1931

Highest League scorer in a season: Dennis Viollet 32 (1959–60)

Most League goals in aggregate: Bobby Charlton 199 (1956–73)

Longest unbeaten League sequence: 29 matches (1998–99)

Longest sequence without a League win: 16 matches (1930)

Most capped player: Bobby Charlton (England) 106

Goalkeepers				
De Gea, David	6.4	Atletico Madrid	Madrid, Sp	07.11.90
Johnstone, Sam	6.3	–	Preston	25.03.93
Romero, Sergio	6.4	Sampdoria	Bernardo, Arg	22.02.87
Defenders				
Bailly, Eric	6.1	Villarreal	Bingerville, Iv C	12.04.94
Blackett, Tyler	6.1	–	Manchester	02.04.94
Borthwick-Jackson, Cameron	6.2	–	Manchester	02.02.97
Darmian, Matteo	6.0	Torino	Legnano, It	02.12.89
Fosu-Mensah, Tim	6.3	–	Amsterdam, Hol	02.01.98
Jones, Phil	5.11	Blackburn	Blackburn	21.02.92
McNair, Paddy	6.0	–	Ballyclare	27.04.95
Rojo, Marcos	6.2	Sporting Lisbon	La Plata, Arg	20.03.90
Shaw, Luke	6.1	Southampton	Kingston	12.07.95
Smalling, Chris	6.1	Fulham	Greenwich	22.11.89
Midfielders				
Blind, Daley	5.11	Ajax	Amsterdam, Hol	09.03.90
Carrick, Michael	6.0	Tottenham	Wallsend	28.07.81
Depay, Memphis	5.10	PSV Eindhoven	Moordrecht, Hol	13.02.94
Fellaini, Marouane	6.4	Everton	Etterbeek, Bel	22.11.87
Herrera, Ander	6.0	Athletic Bilbao	Bilbao, Sp	14.08.89
Januzaj, Adnan	5.11	Anderlecht	Brussels, Bel	05.02.95
Mata, Juan	5.7	Chelsea	Burgos, Sp	28.04.88
Mkhitaryan, Henrikh	5.10	Borussia Dortmund	Yerevan, Arm	21.01.89
Schneiderlin, Morgan	5.11	Southampton	Zellwiller, Fr	08.11.89
Schweinsteiger, Bastian	6.0	Bayern Munich	Kolbermoor, Ger	01.08.84
Valencia, Antonio	5.10	Wigan	Lago Agrio, Ec	04.08.85
Young, Ashley	5.10	Aston Villa	Stevenage	09.07.85
Forwards				
Ibrahimovic, Zlatan	6.5	Paris SG	Malmo, Swe	03.10.81
Keane, Will	6.2	–	Stockport	11.01.93
Lingard, Jesse	6.2	–	Warrington	15.12.92
Martial, Anthony	5.11	Monaco	Massy, Fr	05.12.95
Rashford, Marcus	6.0	–	Wythensawe	31.10.97
Rooney, Wayne	5.10	Everton	Liverpool	24.10.85
Wilson, James	6.1	–	Biddulph	01.12.95

MIDDLESBROUGH

Ground: Riverside Stadium, Middlesbrough, TS3 6RS

Telephone: 0844 499 6789. **Club nickname**: Boro

Capacity: 34,998. **Colours**: Red. **Main sponsor**: Ramsdens
Record attendance: Ayresome Park: 53,596 v Newcastle (Div 1) Dec 27, 1949; Riverside Stadium: 35,000 (England v Slovakia) Jun 11, 2003. Club: 34,836 v Norwich (Prem Lge) Dec 28, 2004
Record transfer fee: £12.8m to Heerenveen for Afonso Alves, Jan 2008
Record fee received: £12m from Atletico Madrid for Juninho, Jul 1997 and from Aston Villa for Stewart Downing Jul 2009
League Championship: 3rd 1913–14
FA Cup: Runners-up 1997
League Cup: Winners 2004
European competitions: UEFA Cup Final, 2005–06
Finishing positions in Premier League: 1992–93 21st, 1995–96 12th, 1996–97 19th, 1998–99 9th, 1999–2000 12th, 2000–01 14th, 2001–02 12th, 2002–03 11th, 2003–04 11th, 2004–05 7th, 2005–06 14th, 2006–07 12th, 2007–08 13th, 2008–09 19th
Biggest win: 9-0 v Brighton (Div 2) Aug 23, 1958
Biggest defeat: 0-9 v Blackburn (Div 2) Nov 6, 1954
Highest League scorer in a season: George Camsell 59 (1926–27)
Most League goals in aggregate: George Camsell 326 (1925–39)
Longest unbeaten League sequence: 24 matches (1973–74)
Longest sequence with a League win: 19 matches (1981–82)
Most capped player: Mark Schwarzer (Australia) 51

Goalkeepers				
Konstantopoulos, Dimitrios	6.5	AEK Athens	Thessaloniki, Gre	29.11.79
Mejias, Tomas	6.5	Real Madrid	Madrid, Sp	30.01.89
Valdes, Victor	6.0	Manchester Utd	L'Hospitalet, Sp	14.01.82
Defenders				
Ayala, Daniel	6.3	Norwich	El Saucejo, Sp	07.11.90
Baptiste, Alex	5.11	Bolton	Sutton-in-Ashfield	31.01.86
Barragan, Antonio	6.1	Valencia	Pontedueme, Sp	12.06.87
Espinosa, Bernardo	6.3	Sporting Gijon	Cali, Col	11.07.89
Friend, George	6.0	Doncaster	Barnstaple	19.10.87
Fry, Dael	6.0	–	Middlesbrough	30.08.97
Gibson, Ben	6.1	–	Nunthorpe	15.01.93
Husband, James	5.11	Doncaster	Leeds	03.01.94
McGhee, Jordan	6.2	Hearts (loan)	East Kilbride	24.07.96
Midfielders				
Adomah, Albert	6.1	Bristol City	Lambeth	13.12.87
Carayol, Mustapha	5.10	Bristol Rov	Banjul, Gam	10.06.89
Clayton, Adam	5.9	Huddersfield	Manchester	14.01.89
De Pena, Carlos	5.10	Nacional	Montevideo, Uru	11.03.92
De Roon, Marten	6.1	Atalanta	Zwijndrecht, Hol	29.03.91
De Sart, Julien	6.2	Standard Liege	Waremme, Bel	23.12.94
Downing, Stewart	6.0	West Ham	Middlesbrough	02.07.84
Fischer, Viktor	5.11	Ajax	Aarhus, Den	09.06.94
Forshaw, Adam	6.1	Wigan	Liverpool	08.10.91
Leadbitter, Grant	5.9	Ipswich	Chester-le-Street	07.01.86
Morris, Bryn	6.0	–	Hartlepool	25.04.96
Nsue, Emilio	6.0	Mallorca	Palma, Sp	30.09.89
Reach, Adam	6.1	–	Gateshead	03.02.93
Forwards				
Nugent, David	5.11	Leicester	Liverpool	02.05.85
Rhodes, Jordan	6.1	Blackburn	Oldham	05.02.90
Stuani, Cristhian	6.1	Espanyol	Tala, Uru	12.10.86

SOUTHAMPTON

Ground: St Mary's Stadium, Britannia Road, Southampton, SO14 5FP
Telephone: 0845 688 9448. **Club nickname**: Saints
Capacity: 32,505. **Colours**: Red and white. **Main sponsor**: Virgin Media
Record transfer fee: £14.6m to Roma for Dani Osvaldo, Aug 2013
Record fee received: £34m from Liverpool for Sadio Mane, Jun 2016
Record attendance: The Dell: 31,044 v Manchester Utd (Div 1) Oct 8, 1969. St Mary's: 32,363 v Coventry (Champ) Apr 28, 2012
League Championship: Runners-up 1983–84
FA Cup: Winners 1976
League Cup: Runners-up 1979
European competitions: Fairs Cup rd 3 1969–70; Cup-Winners' Cup rd 3 1976–77
Finishing positions in Premier League: 1992–93 18th, 1993–94 18th, 1994–5 10th, 1995–96 17th, 1996–97 16th, 1997–98 12th, 1998–99 17th, 1999–200 15th, 2000–01 10th, 2001–02 11th, 2002–03 8th, 2003–04 12th, 2004–05 20th, 2012–13 14th, 2013–14 8th 2014–15 7th, 2015–16 6th,
Biggest win: 8-0 v Northampton (Div 3S) Dec 24, 1921, v Sunderland (Prem Lge) Oct 18, 2014
Biggest defeat: 0-8 v Tottenham (Div 2) Mar 28, 1936, v Everton (Div 1) Nov 20, 1971
Highest League scorer in a season: Derek Reeves 39 (1959–60)
Most League goals in aggregate: Mick Channon 185 (1966–82)
Longest unbeaten League sequence: 19 matches (1921)
Longest unbeaten League sequence: 20 matches (1969)
Most capped player: Peter Shilton (England) 49

Goalkeepers				
Forster, Fraser	6.7	Celtic	Hexham	17.03.88
Gazzaniga, Paulo	6.5	Gillingham	Murphy, Arg	02.01.92
Defenders				
Bertrand, Ryan	5.10	Chelsea	Southwark	05.08.89
Fonte, Jose	6.2	Crystal Palace	Penafiel, Por	22.12.83
Gardos, Florin	6.4	Steaua Bucharest	Satu Mare, Rom	29.10.88
Martina, Cuco	6.1	Twente	Rotterdam, Hol	25.09.89
Soares, Cedric	5.8	Sporting Lisbon	Singen, Ger	31.08.91
Stephens, Jack	6.1	Plymouth	Torpoint	27.01.94
Targett, Matt	6.0	–	Eastleigh	18.09.95
Turnbull, Jordan	6.1	–	Trowbridge	30.10.94
Van Dijk, Virgil	6.4	Celtic	Breda, Hol	08.07.91
Yoshida, Maya	6.2	Venlo	Nagasaki, Jap	24.08.88
Midfielders				
Clasie, Jordy	5.7	Feyenoord	Haarlem, Hol	27.06.91
Davis, Steven	5.8	Rangers	Ballymena	01.01.85
Gape, Dominic	5.11	–	Burton Bradstock	09.09.94
Hojbjerg, Pierre-Emile	6.1	Bayern Munich	Copenhagen, Den	05.08.95
Isgrove, Lloyd	5.10	–	Yeovil	12.01.93
McQueen, Sam	5.11	–	Southampton	06.02.95
Redmond, Nathan	5.8	Norwich	Birmingham	06.03.94
Reed, Harrison	5.7	–	Worthing	27.01.95
Romeu, Oriol	6.0	Chelsea	Ulldecona, Sp	24.09.91
Tadic, Dusan	5.11	Twente	Backa Topola, Serb	20.11.88
Ward-Prowse, James	5.8	–	Portsmouth	01.11.94
Forwards				
Austin, Charlie	6.2	QPR	Hungerford	05.07.89
Gallagher, Sam	6.4	–	Crediton	15.09.95
Long, Shane	5.10	Hull	Gortnahoe, Ire	22.01.87

Rodriguez, Jay	6.1	Burnley	Burnley	29.07.89
Seager, Ryan	5.9	–	Yeovil	05.02.96

STOKE CITY

Ground: bet365 Stadium, Stanley Matthews Way, Stoke-on-Trent ST4 7EG
Telephone: 01782 367598. **Club nickname**: Potters
Capacity: 27,902. **Colours**: Red and white. **Main sponsor**: bet365
Record transfer fee: £18.3m to Porto for Giannelli Imbula, Feb 2016
Record fee received: £8m from Chelsea for Asmir Begoic, Jul 2015
Record attendance: Victoria Ground: 51,380 v Arsenal (Div 1) Mar 29, 1937. Britannia Stadium: 28,218 v Everton (FA Cup 3) Jan 5, 2002
League Championship: 4th 1935–36, 1946–47
FA Cup: Runners-up 2011
League Cup: Winners 1972
European competitions: Europa League rd of 32 2011–12
Finishing positions in Premier League: 2008–09 12th, 2009–10 11th, 2010–11 1, 2015–16 3th, 2011–12 14th, 2012–13 13th, 2013–14 9th, 2014–15 9th, 2015–16 9th
Biggest win: 10-3 v WBA (Div 1) Feb 4, 1937
Biggest defeat: 0-10 v Preston (Div 1) Sep 14, 1889
Highest League scorer in a season: Freddie Steele 33 (1936–37)
Most League goals in aggregate: Freddie Steele 142 (1934–49)
Longest unbeaten League sequence: 25 matches (1992–93)
Longest sequence without a League win: 17 matches (1989)
Most capped player: Glenn Whelan (Republic of Ireland) 73

Goalkeepers				
Butland, Jack	6.4	Birmingham	Bristol	10.03.93
Given, Shay	6.2	Aston Villa	Lifford, Ire	20.04.76
Haugaard, Jakob	6.6	Midtjylland	Sundby, Den	01.05.92
Defenders				
Bardsley, Phil	5.11	Sunderland	Salford	28.06.85
Cameron, Geoff	6.3	Houston	Attleboro, US	11.07.85
Johnson, Glen	6.0	Liverpool	Greenwich	23.08.84
Muniesa, Marc	5.11	Barcelona	Lloret de Mar, Sp	27.03.92
Pieters, Erik	6.1	PSV Eindhoven	Tiel, Hol	07.08.88
Shawcross, Ryan	6.3	Manchester Utd	Chester	04.10.87
Teixeira, Dionatan	6.4	Banska Bystrica	Londrina, Br	24.07.92
Wilson, Marc	6.2	Portsmouth	Belfast	17.08.87
Wollscheid, Philipp	6.4	Bayer Leverkusen	Wadern, Ger	06.03.89
Midfielders				
Adam, Charlie	6.1	Liverpool	Dundee	10.12.85
Afellay, Ibrahim	5.11	Barcelona	Utrecht, Hol	02.04.86
El Ouriachi, Moha	5.10	Barcelona	Nador, Mor	13.01.96
Imbula, Giannelli	6.1	Porto	Vilvoorde, Bel	12.09.92
Ireland, Stephen	5.8	Aston Villa	Cork, Ire	22.08.86
Shaqiri, Xherdan	5.7	Inter Milan	Gjilan, Kos	10.10.91
Whelan, Glenn	5.10	Sheffield Wed	Dublin, Ire	13.01.84
Forwards				
Arnautovic, Marko	6.4	Werder Bremen	Vienna, Aut	19.04.89
Biram Diouf, Mame	6.1	Hannover	Dakar, Sen	16.12.87
Crouch, Peter	6.7	Tottenham	Macclesfield	30.01.81
Joselu	6.3	Hannover	Stuttgart, Ger	27.03.90
Krkic, Bojan	5.7	Barcelona	Linyola, Sp	28.08.90
Walters, Jon	6.0	Ipswich	Birkenhead	20.09.83

SUNDERLAND

Ground: Stadium of Light, Sunderland SR5 1SU
Telephone: 0871 911 1200. **Club nickname**: Black Cats
Capacity: 48,707. **Colours**: Red and white. **Main sponsor**: Dafabet
Record transfer fee: £13m to Rennes for Asamoah Gyan, Aug 2010
Record fee received: £18m from Aston Villa for Darren Bent, Jan 2011
Record attendance: Roker Park: 75,118 v Derby (FA Cup 6 rep) Mar 8, 1933. Stadium of Light: 48,353 v Liverpool (Prem Lge) Apr 13, 2002
League Championship: Winners 1891–92, 1892–93, 1894–95, 1901–02, 1912–13, 1935–36
FA Cup: Winners 1937, 1973
League Cup: Runners-up 1985
European competitions: Cup-Winners' Cup rd 2 1973–74
Finishing positions in Premier League: 1996–97 18th, 1999–2000 7th, 2000–01 7th, 2001–02 17th, 2002–03 20th, 2005–06 20th, 2007–08 15th, 2008–09 16th, 2009–10 13th, 2010–11 10th, 2011–12 13th, 2012–13 17th, 2013–14 14th, 2014–15 16th, 2015–16 17th
Biggest win: 9-1 v Newcastle (Div 1) Dec 5, 1908. Also: 11-1 v Fairfield (FA Cup 1) Feb 2, 1895
Biggest defeat: 0-8 v Sheffield Wed (Div 1) Dec 26, 1911, v West Ham (Div 1) Oct 19, 1968, v Watford (Div 1) Sep 25, 1982, v Southampton (Prem Lge) Oct 18, 2014
Highest League scorer in a season: Dave Halliday 43 (1928–29)
Most League goals in aggregate: Charlie Buchan 209 (1911–25)
Longest unbeaten League sequence: 19 matches (1998–99)
Longest sequence without a League win: 22 matches (2003–04)
Most capped player: Charlie Hurley (Republic of Ireland) 38

Goalkeepers				
Mannone, Vito	6.3	Arsenal	Desio, It	02.03.88
Pickford, Jordan	6.1	–	Washington, Co Dur	07.03.94
Defenders				
Coates, Sebastian	6.5	Liverpool	Montevideo, Uru	07.10.90
Jones, Billy	5.11	WBA	Shrewsbury	24.03.87
Kaboul, Younes	6.3	Tottenham	St Julien, Fr	04.01.86
Kirchhoff, Jan	6.5	Bayern Munich	Frankfurt, Ger	01.10.90
Kone, Lamine	6.3	Lorient	Paris, Fr	01.02.88
Matthews, Adam	5.10	Celtic	Swansea	13.01.92
O'Shea, John	6.3	Manchester Utd	Waterford, Ire	30.04.81
Van Aanholt, Patrick	5.9	Chelsea	Hertogenbosch, Hol	29.08.90
Vergini, Santiago	6.3	Estudiantes	Maximo Paz, Arg	03.08.88
Midfielders				
Bridcutt, Liam	5.9	Brighton	Reading	08.05.89
Buckley, Will	6.0	Brighton	Oldham	12.08.88
Cattermole, Lee	5.10	Wigan	Stockton	21.03.88
Giaccherini, Emanuele	5.8	Juventus	Bibbiena, It	05.05.85
Gomez, Jordi	5.10	Wigan	Barcelona, Sp	24.05.85
Khazri, Wahbi	6.0	Bordeaux	Ajaccio, Fr	08.02.91
Larsson, Sebastian	5.10	Birmingham	Eskiltuna, Swe	06.06.85
Lens, Jeremain	5.10	Dynamo Kiev	Amsterdam, Hol	24.11.87
Mavrias, Charis	5.10	Panathinaikos	Zakynthos, Gre	21.02.94
Rodwell, Jack	6.1	Manchester City	Birkdale	17.09.89
Forwards				
Borini, Fabio	5.11	Liverpool	Bentivoglio, It	29.03.91
Defoe, Jermain	5.8	Toronto	Beckton	07.10.82
Watmore, Duncan	5.9	Altrincham	Cheadle Hulme	08.03.94

SWANSEA CITY

Ground: Liberty Stadium, Morfa, Swansea SA1 2FA
Telephone: 01792 616600. **Club nickname**: Swans
Capacity: 20,972. **Colours**: White. **Main sponsor**: GWFX
Record transfer fee: £12m to Vitesse Arnhem for Wilfried Bony, Jan 2015
Record fee received: £28m from Manchester City for Wilfried Bony, Aug 2012
Record attendance: Vetch Field: 32,796 v Arsenal (FA Cup 4) Feb 17, 1968. Liberty Stadium: 20,972 v Liverpool (Prem Lge) May 1, 2016
League Championship: 6th 1981–82
FA Cup: Semi-finals 1926, 1964
League Cup: Winners 2013
Finishing positions in Premier League: 2011–12 11th, 2012–13 9th, 2013–14 12th, 2014–15 8th, 2015–16 12th
European competitions: Cup-Winners' Cup rd 2 1982–83; Europa Lge rd of 32 2013–14
Biggest win: 8-0 v Hartlepool (Div 4) Apr 1, 1978. Also: 12-0 v Sliema (Cup-Winners' Cup rd 1, 1st leg), Sep 15, 1982
Biggest defeat: 0-8 v Liverpool (FA Cup 3) Jan 9, 1990, 0-8 v Monaco (Cup-Winners' Cup rd 1, 2nd leg) Oct 1, 1991
Highest League scorer in a season: Cyril Pearce 35 (1931–32)
Most League goals in aggregate: Ivor Allchuch 166 (1949–58, 1965–68)
Longest unbeaten League sequence: 19 matches (1970–71)
Longest sequence without a League win: 15 matches (1989)
Most capped player: Ashley Williams (Wales) 64

Goalkeepers				
Fabianski, Lukasz	6.3	Arsenal	Kostrzyn, Pol	18.04.85
Nordfeldt, Kristoffer	6.3	Heerenveen	Stockholm, Swe	23.06.89
Tremmel, Gerhard	6.3	Salzburg	Munich, Ger	16.11.78
Defenders				
Amat, Jordi	6.1	Espanyol	Canet de Mar, Sp	21.03.92
Fernandez, Federico	6.3	Napoli	Tres Algarrobos, Arg	21.02.89
Kingsley, Stephen	5.10	Falkirk	Stirling	23.07.94
Naughton, Kyle	5.10	Tottenham	Sheffield	11.11.88
Reid Tyler	5.11	Manchester Utd	Luton	02.09.97
Rangel, Angel	5.11	Terrassa	Tortosa, Sp	28.10.82
Taylor, Neil	5.9	Wrexham	St Asaph	07.02.89
Van der Hoorn, Mike	6.3	Ajax	Almere, Hol	15.10.92
Williams, Ashley	6.0	Stockport	Wolverhampton	23.08.84
Midfielders				
Britton, Leon	5.5	Sheffield Utd	Merton	16.09.82
Cork, Jack	6.1	Southampton	Carshalton	25.06.89
Dyer, Nathan	5.10	Southampton	Trowbridge	29.11.87
Fer, Leroy	6.2	QPR	Zoetermeer, Hol	05.01.90
Fulton, Jay	5.10	Falkirk	Bolton	04.04.94
Gorre, Kenji	5.10	Manchester Utd	Spijkenisse, Hol	29.09.94
Ki Sung-Yueng	6.2	Celtic	Gwangju, S Kor	24.01.89
King, Adam	5.11	Hearts	Edinburgh	11.10.95
Montero, Jefferson	5.7	Morelia	Babahoyo, Ec	01.09.89
Routledge, Wayne	5.7	Newcastle	Sidcup	07.01.85
Sigurdsson, Gylfi	6.1	Tottenham	Hafnarfjordur, Ice	08.09.89
Forwards				
Ayew, Andre	5.10	Marseille	Seclin, Fr	17.12.89
Barrow, Modou	5.10	Ostersunds	Gambia	13.10.92
Emnes, Marvin	5.11	Middlesbrough	Rotterdam, Hol	27.05.88

Gomis, Bafetimbi	6.0	Lyon	La Seyne, Fr	06.08.85
McBurnie, Oliver	6.2	Bradford	Leeds	04.06.96

TOTTENHAM HOTSPUR

Ground: White Hart Lane, Tottenham, London N17 OAP
Telephone: 0844 499 5000. **Club nickname**: Spurs
Capacity: 36,284. **Colours**: White. **Main sponsor**: AIA
Record transfer fee: £30m to Roma for Erik Lamela, Aug 2013
Record fee received: £85.3m from Real Madrid for Gareth Bale, Aug 2013
Record attendance: 75,038 v Sunderland (FA Cup 6) Mar 5, 1938
League Championship: Winners 1950–51, 1960–61
FA Cup: Winners 1901, 1921, 1961, 1962, 1967, 1981, 1982, 1991
League Cup: Winners 1971, 1973, 1999, 2008
European competitions: Winners Cup-Winners' Cup 1962–63; UEFA Cup 1971–72, 1983–84
Finishing positions in Premier League: 1992–93 8th, 1993–94 15th, 1994–95 7th, 1995–96 8th, 1996–97 10th, 1997–98 14th, 1998–99 11th, 1999–2000 10th, 2000–01 12th, 2001–02 9th, 2002–03 10th, 2003–04 14th, 2004–05 9th, 2005–06 5th, 2006–07 5th, 2007–08 11th, 2008–09 8th, 2009–10 4th, 2010–11 5th, 2011–12 4th, 2012–13 5th, 2013–14 6th, 2014–15 5th, 2015–16 3rd
Biggest win: 9-0 v Bristol Rov (Div 2) Oct 22, 1977. Also: 13-2 v Crewe (FA Cup 4 replay) Feb 3, 1960
Biggest defeat: 0-7 v Liverpool (Div 1) Sep 2, 1979. Also: 0-8 v Cologne (Inter Toto Cup) Jul 22, 1995
Highest League scorer in a season: Jimmy Greaves 37 (1962–63)
Most League goals in aggregate: Jimmy Greaves 220 (1961–70)
Longest unbeaten League sequence: 22 matches (1949)
Longest sequence without a League win: 16 matches (1934–35)
Most capped player: Pat Jennings (Northern Ireland) 74

Goalkeepers				
Lloris, Hugo	6.2	Lyon	Nice, Fr	26.12.86
Vorm, Michel	6.0	Swansea	Nieuwegein, Hol	20.10.83
Defenders				
Alderweireld, Toby	6.2	Atletico Madrid	Antwerp, Bel	02.03.89
Davies, Ben	5.6	Swansea	Neath	24.04.93
Dier, Eric	6.2	Sporting Lisbon	Cheltenham	15.01.94
Fazio, Federico	6.5	Sevilla	Buenos Aires, Arg	17.03.87
Rose, Danny	5.8	Leeds	Doncaster	02.07.90
Trippier, Kieran	5.10	Burnley	Bury	19.09.90
Vertonghen, Jan	6.2	Ajax	Sint-Niklaas, Bel	24.04.87
Walker, Kyle	5.10	Sheffield Utd	Sheffield	28.05.90
Wimmer, Kevin	6.2	Cologne	Wels, Aut	15.11.92
Yedlin, DeAndre	5.9	Seattle	Seattle, US	09.07.93
Midfielders				
Alli, Dele	6.1	MK Dons	Milton Keynes	11.04.96
Bentaleb, Nabil	6.2	–	Lille, Fr	24.11.94
Carroll, Tom	5.10	–	Watford	28.05.92
Chadli, Nacer	6.2	Twente	Liege, Bel	02.08.89
Dembele, Mousa	6.1	Fulham	Wilrijk, Bel	16.07.87
Eriksen, Christian	5.10	Ajax	Middelfart, Den	14.02.92
Lamela, Erik	6.0	Roma	Buenos Aires, Arg	04.03.92
Mason, Ryan	5.9	–	Enfield	13.06.91
Wanyama, Victor	6.2	Southampton	Nairobi, Ken	25.06.91

Forwards

Janssen, Vincent	5.11	Alkmaar	Heesch, Hol	15.06.94
Kane, Harry	6.2	–	Walthamstow	28.07.93
Son Heung-Min	6.1	Bayer Leverkusen	Chuncheon, S Kor	08.07.92

WATFORD

Ground: Vicarage Road Stadium, Vicarage Road, Watford WD18 OER
Telephone: 01923 496000. **Club nickname**: Hornets
Capacity: 21,500. **Colours**: Yellow and black. **Main sponsor**: 138.com
Record transfer fee: £12.5m to Granada for Isaac Success, Jul 2016
Record fee received: £9.65m from Aston Villa for Ashley Young, Jan 2007
Record attendance: 34,099 v Manchester Utd (FA Cup 4 rep) Feb 3, 1969
League Championship: Runners-up 1982–83
FA Cup: Runners-up 1984
League Cup: Semi-finals 1979, 2005
European competitions: UEFA Cup rd 3 1983–84
Finishing positions in Premier League: 1999–2000 20th, 2006–07 20th, 2015–16 13th
Biggest win: 8-0 v Sunderland (Div 1) Sep 25, 1982. Also: 10-1 v Lowestoft (FA Cup 1) Nov 27, 1926
Biggest defeat: 0-10 v Wolves (FA Cup 1 replay) Jan 24, 1912
Highest League scorer in a season: Cliff Holton 42 (1959–60)
Most League goals in aggregate: Luther Blissett 148 (1976–83, 1984–88, 1991–92)
Longest unbeaten League sequence: 22 matches (1996–97)
Longest sequence without a League win: 19 matches (1971–72)
Most capped players: John Barnes (England) 31, Kenny Jackett (Wales) 31

Goalkeepers				
Arlauskis, Giedrius	6.4	Steaua Bucharest	Telsiai, Lith	01.12.87
Gomes, Heurelho	6.2	PSV Eindhoven	Joao Pinheiro, Br	15.12.81
Pantilimon, Costel	6.8	Sunderland	Bacau, Rom	01.02.87
Defenders				
Angella, Gabriele	6.3	Udinese	Florence, It	28.04.89
Britos, Miguel	6.2	Napoli	Maldonado, Uru	17.07.85
Cathcart, Craig	6.2	Blackpool	Belfast	06.02.89
Guedioura, Adlene	6.0	Crystal Palace	La Roche, Fr	12.11.85
Hoban, Tommie	6.2	–	Waltham Forest	24.01.94
Kabasele, Christian	6.1	Genk	Lubumbashi, DR Cong	24.02.91
Layun, Miguel	5.10	Granada	Cordoba, Mex	25.06.88
Nyom, Allan	6.2	Udinese	Neuilly-sur-Seine, Fr	10.05.88
Paredes, Juan Carlos	5.9	Granada	Esmeraldas, Ec	08.07.87
Prodl, Sebastian	6.4	Werder Bremen	Graz, Aut	21.06.87
Pudil, Daniel	6.1	Granada	Prague, Cz	27.09.85
Midfielders				
Abdi, Almen	5.11	Udinese	Prizren, Kos	21.10.86
Amrabat, Nordin	5.11	Malaga	Naarden, Hol	31.03.87
Anya, Ikechi	5.7	Granada	Glasgow	03.01.88
Behrami, Valon	6.1	Hamburg	Mitrovica, Kos	19.04.85
Berghuis, Steven	6.0	Alkmaar	Apeldoorn, Hol	19.12.91
Capoue, Etienne	6.2	Tottenham	Niort, Fr	11.07.88
Doucoure, Abdoulaye	6.0	Rennes	Meulan, Fr	01.01.93
Jurado, Jose Manuel	5.8	Spartak Moscow	Sanlucar, Sp	29.06.86
Suarez, Mario	6.2	Fiorentina	Alcobendas, Sp	24.02.87
Watson, Ben	5.10	Wigan	Camberwell	09.07.85
Forwards				
Deeney, Troy	6.0	Walsall	Birmingham	29.06.88

Ighalo, Odion	6.2	Udinese	Lagos, Nig	16.06.89
Oulare, Obbi	6.5	Club Bruges	Waregem, Bel	08.01.96
Penaranda, Adalberto	6.0	Udinese	El Vigia, Ven	31.05.97
Sinclair, Jerome	6.0	Liverpool	Birmingham	20.09.96
Success, Isaac	6.0	Granada	Benin City, Nig	07.01.96
Vydra, Matej	5.11	Udinese	Chotebor, Cz	01.05.92

WEST BROMWICH ALBION

Ground: The Hawthorns, Halfords Lane, West Bromwich B71 4LF
Telephone: 0871 271 1100. **Club nickname**: Baggies
Capacity: 26,850. **Colours**: Blue and white. **Main sponsor**: TLCBET
Record transfer fee: £12m to Zenit St Petersburg for Salomon Rondon, Aug 2015
Record fee received: £8.5m from Aston Villa for Curtis Davies, Jul 2008
Record attendance: 64,815 v Arsenal (FA Cup 6) Mar 6, 1937
League Championship: Winners 1919–20
FA Cup: Winners 1888, 1892, 1931, 1954, 1968
League Cup: Winners 1966
European competitions: Cup-Winners' Cup quarter-finals 1968–69; UEFA Cup quarter-finals 1978–79
Finishing positions in Premier League: 2002–03 19th, 2004–5 17th, 2005–6 19th; 2008–09 20th, 2010–11 11th, 2011–12 10th, 2012–13 8th, 2013–14 17th, 2014–15 13th, 2015–16 14th
Biggest win: 12-0 v Darwen (Div 1) Apr 4, 1892
Biggest defeat: 3-10 v Stoke (Div 1) Feb 4, 1937
Highest League scorer in a season: William Richardson 39 (1935–36)
Most League goals in aggregate: Tony Brown 218 (1963–79)
Longest unbeaten League sequence: 17 matches (1957)
Longest sequence without a League win: 14 matches (1995)
Most capped player: Chris Brunt (Northern Ireland) 44

Goalkeepers				
Foster, Ben	6.2	Birmingham	Leamington	03.04.83
Myhill, Boaz	6.3	Hull	Modesto, US	09.11.82
Defenders				
Chester, James	5.10	Hull	Warrington	23.01.89
Dawson, Craig	6.2	Rochdale	Rochdale	06.05.90
Evans, Jonny	6.2	Manchester Utd	Belfast	02.01.88
Gamboa, Cristian	5.10	Rosenborg	Liberia, C Rica	26.01.87
McAuley, Gareth	6.3	Ipswich	Larne	05.12.79
Olsson, Jonas	6.4	Nijmegen	Landskrona, Swe	10.03.83
Pocognoli, Sebastien	6.0	Hannover	Liege, Bel	01.08.87
Midfielders				
Brunt, Chris	6.1	Sheffield Wed	Belfast	14.12.84
Fletcher, Darren	6.0	Manchester Utd	Edinburgh	01.02.84
Gardner, Craig	5.10	Sunderland	Solihull	25.11.86
McClean, James	5.11	Wigan	Derry	22.04.89
Morrison, James	5.10	Middlesbrough	Darlington	25.05.86
Phillips, Matt	6.0	QPR	Aylesbury	13.03.91
Yacob, Claudio	5.11	Racing Club	Carcarana, Arg	18.07.87
Forwards				
Berahino, Saido	5.10	–	Bujumbura, Bur	04.08.93
Lambert, Rickie	6.2	Liverpool	Liverpool	16.02.82
McManaman, Callum	5.11	Wigan	Knowsley	25.04.91
Nabi, Adil	5.8	–	Birmingham	28.02.94
Rondon, Salomon	6.2	Zenit St Petersburg	Caracas, Ven	16.09.89

WEST HAM UNITED

Ground: Olympic Stadium, Queen Elizabeth Olympic Park, London E20 2ST
Telephone: TBC. **Club nickname**: Hammers
Capacity: 60,000. **Colours**: Claret and blue. **Main sponsor**: Betway
Record transfer fee: £15m to Liverpool for Andy Carroll, Jul 2013
Record fee received: £18m from Leeds for Rio Ferdinand, Nov 2000
Record attendance: Upton Park: 43,322 v Tottenham (Div 1) Oct 17, 1970
League Championship: 3rd 1985–86
FA Cup: Winners 1964, 1975, 1980
League Cup: Runners-up 1966, 1981
European competitions: Winners Cup-Winners' Cup 1964–65
Finishing positions in Premier League: 1993–94 13th, 1994–95 14th, 1995–96 10th, 1996–97 14th, 1997–98 8th, 1998–99 5th, 1999–2000 9th, 2000–01 15th, 2001–02 7th, 2002–03 18th, 2005–06 9th, 2006–07 15th, 2007–08 10th, 2008–09: 9th, 2009 10 17th, 2010–11 20th, 2012–13 10th, 2013–14 13th, 2014–15 12th, 2015–16 7th
Biggest win: 8-0 v Rotherham (Div 2) Mar 8, 1958, v Sunderland (Div 1) Oct 19, 1968. Also: 10-0 v Bury (League Cup 2) Oct 25, 1983
Biggest defeat: 0-7 v Barnsley (Div 2) Sep 1, 1919, v Everton (Div 1) Oct 22, 1927, v Sheffield Wed (Div 1) Nov 28, 1959
Highest League scorer in a season: Vic Watson 42 (1929–30)
Most League goals in aggregate: Vic Watson 298 (1920–35)
Longest unbeaten League sequence: 27 matches (1980–81)
Longest sequence without a League win: 17 matches (1976)
Most capped player: Bobby Moore (England) 108

Goalkeepers				
Adrian	6.3	Real Betis	Seville, Sp	03.01.87
Randolph, Darren	6.1	Birmingham	Bray, Ire	12.05.87
Defenders				
Byram, Sam	5.11	Leeds	Thurrock	16.09.93
Burke, Reece	6.2	–	Newham	02.09.96
Collins, James	6.2	Aston Villa	Newport	23.08.83
Cresswell, Aaron	5.7	Ipswich	Liverpool	15.12.89
Henry, Doneil	6.2	Apollon Limassol	Brampton, Can	20.04.93
Ogbonna, Angelo	6.3	Juventus	Cassino, It	23.05.88
Reid, Winston	6.3	Midtjylland	Auckland, NZ	03.07.88
Tore, Gokhan	5.10	Besiktas (loan)	Cologne, Ger	20.01.92
Midfielders				
Antonio, Michail	5.11	Nottm Forest	Wandsworth	28.03.90
Feghouli, Sofiane	5.10	Valencia	Levallois Perret, Fr	26.12.89
Kouyate, Cheikhou	6.4	Anderlecht	Dakar, Sen	21.12.89
Lanzini, Manuel	5.6	Al Jazira	Ituzaingo, Arg	15.02.93
Noble, Mark	5.11	–	West Ham	08.05.87
Nordveit, Havard	6.2	Borussia M'gladbach	Vats, Nor	21.06.90
Obiang, Pedro	6.1	Sampdoria	Alcala, Sp	27.03.92
Oxford, Reece	6.3	–	Edmonton	16.12.98
Payet, Dimitri	5.9	Marseille	St-Pierre, Reunion, Fr	29.03.87
Poyet, Diego	5.11	Charlton	Zaragoza, Sp	08.04.95
Forwards				
Carroll, Andy	6.3	Liverpool	Gateshead	06.01.89
Fletcher, Ashley	6.1	Manchester Utd	Keighley	02.10.95
Sakho, Diafra	6.1	Metz	Guediawaye, Sen	24.12.89
Valencia, Enner	5.11	Pachuca	Esmeraldas, Ec	04.11.89

FOOTBALL LEAGUE PLAYING STAFFS 2016–17

(At time of going to press)

CHAMPIONSHIP

ASTON VILLA

Ground: Villa Park, Trinity Road, Birmingham, B6 6HE
Telephone: 0800 612 0970. **Club nickname**: Villans
Colours: Claret and blue. **Capacity**: 42,785
Record attendance: 76,588 v Derby (FA Cup 6) Mar 2, 1946

Goalkeepers				
Bunn, Mark	6.0	Norwich	Southgate	16.11.84
Gollini, Pierluigi	6.2	Hellas Verona	Bologna, It	18.03.95
Guzan, Brad	6.4	Chivas	Evergreen Park, US	09.09.84
Steer, Jed	6.3	Norwich	Norwich	23.09.92
Defenders				
Amavi, Jordan	5.9	Nice	Toulon, Fr	09.03.94
Baker, Nathan	6.3	–	Worcester	23.04.91
Cissokho, Aly	5.11	Valencia	Blois, Fr	15.09.87
Clark, Ciaran	6.2	–	Harrow	26.09.89
Elphick, Tommy	5.11	Bournemouth	Brighton	07.09.87
Hutton, Alan	6.1	Tottenham	Glasgow	30.11.84
Lescott, Joleon	6.2	WBA	Birmingham	16.08.82
Okore, Jores	6.0	Nordsjaelland	Abidjan Iv C	11.08.92
Richards, Micah	5.11	Manchester City	Birmingham	24.06.88
Midfielders				
Bacuna, Leandro	6.2	Groningen	Groningen, Hol	21.08.91
Gil, Charles	5.7	Valencia	Valencia, Sp	22.11.92
Grealish, Jack	5.9	–	Solihull	10.09.95
Gueye, Idrissa	5.9	Lille	Dakar, Sen	26.09.89
Sanchez, Carlos	6.0	Elche	Quibdo, Col	06.02.86
Sinclair, Scott	5.10	Manchester City	Bath	25.03.89
Traore, Adama	5.10	Barcelona	L'Hospitalet, Sp	25.01.96
Tshibola, Aaron	6.3	Reading	Newham	02.01.95
Veretout, Jordan	5.10	Nantes	Ancenis, Fr	01.03.93
Westwood, Ashley	5.8	Crewe	Nantwich	01.04.90
Forwards				
Agbonlahor, Gabriel	5.11	–	Birmingham	13.10.86
Ayew, Jordan	6.0	Lorient	Marseille, Fr	11.09.91
Gestede, Rudy	6.4	Blackburn	Nancy, Fr	10.10.88
Kozak, Libor	6.4	Lazio	Opava, Cz	30.05.89

BARNSLEY

Ground: Oakwell Stadium, Barnsley S71 1ET
Telephone: 01226 211211. **Club nickname**: Tykes
Colours: Red and white. **Capacity**: 23,009
Record attendance: 40,255 v Stoke (FA Cup 5) Feb 15, 1936

Goalkeepers				
Davies, Adam	6.1	Sheffield Wed	Rinteln, Ger	17.07.92

Townsend, Nick	5.11	Birmingham	Solihull	01.11.94
Defenders				
Bree, James	5.10	–	Wakefield	11.10.97
Cowgill, Jack	6.1	–	Wakefield	08.01.97
Mawson, Alfie	6.2	Brentford	Hillingdon	19.01.94
Nyatanga, Lewin	6.2	Bristol City	Burton	18.08.88
Roberts, Marc	6.0	Halifax	Wakefield	26.07.90
White, Aidy	5.9	Rotherham	Otley	10.10.91
Yiadom, Andy	5.11	Barnet	Holloway	09.12.91
Midfielders				
Bailey, James	6.0	Derby	Bollington	18.09.88
Hammill, Adam	5.10	Huddersfield	Liverpool	25.01.88
Hourihane, Conor	6.0	Plymouth	Cork, Ire	02.02.91
Moncur, George	5.9	Colchester	Swindon	18.08.93
Scowen, Josh	5.10	Wycombe	Enfield	28.03.93
Watkins, Marley	6.1	Inverness	Lewisham	17.10.90
Williams, Ryan		Fulham	Perth, Aus	28.10.93
Forwards				
Bradshaw, Tom	5.10	Walsall	Shrewsbury	27.07.92
Jackson, Kayden	–	Wrexham	Bradford	22.02.94
Lee, Elliot	5.11	West Ham	Durham	16.12.94
Payne, Stefan	5.10	Dover	Lambeth	10.08.91
Phenix, Mike	5.10	Telford	Manchester	15.03.89
Tuton, Shaun	6.1	Halifax	Sheffield	03.12.91
Winnall, Sam	5.11	Scunthorpe	Wolverhampton	19.01.91

BIRMINGHAM CITY

Ground: St Andrew's, Birmingham B9 4NH
Telephone: 0844 557 1875. **Club nickname**: Blues
Colours: Blue and white. **Capacity**: 30,016
Record attendance: 66,844 v Everton (FA Cup 5) Feb 11, 1939

Goalkeepers				
Kuszczak, Tomasz	6.3	Wolves	Krosno, Pol	20.03.82
Legzdins, Adam	6.0	Leyton Orient	Penkridge	28.11.86
Trueman, Connal	6.1	–	Birmingham	26.03.96
Defenders				
Caddis, Paul	5.7	Swindon	Irvine	19.04.88
Grounds, Jonathan	6.1	Oldham	Thornaby	02.02.88
Morrison, Michael	6.1	Charlton	Bury St Edmunds	03.03.88
Robinson, Paul	5.9	Bolton	Watford	14.12.78
Shotton, Ryan	6.3	Derby	Stoke	30.09.88
Spector, Jonathan	6.1	West Ham	Arlington Heights, US	03.01.86
Midfielders				
Adams, Charlee	5.11	–	Redbridge	16.02.95
Arthur, Koby	5.8	–	Kumasi, Gh	31.01.96
Brown, Reece	5.9	–	Dudley	03.03.96
Cotterill, David	5.9	Doncaster	Cardiff	04.12.87
Davis, David	5.8	Wolves	Smethwick	20.02.91
Gleeson, Stephen	6.2	MK Dons	Dublin, Ire	03.08.88
Kieftenbeld, Maikel	5.10	Groningen	Dalfsen, Hol	26.06.90
Maghoma, Jacques	5.11	Sheffield Wed	Lubumbashi, DR Cong	23.10.87
Shinnie, Andrew	5.11	Inverness	Aberdeen	17.07.89
Solomon-Otabor, Viv	5.9	–	London	02.01.96

Tesche, Robert	5.11	Nottm Forest	Wismar, Ger	27.05.87
Forwards				
Brock-Madsen, Nicolai	6.4	Randers	Randers, Den	09.01.93
Donaldson, Clayton	6.1	Brentford	Bradford	07.02.84
Fabbrini, Diego	6.0	Watford	Pisa, It	31.07.90

BLACKBURN ROVERS

Ground: Ewood Park, Blackburn BB2 4JF
Telephone: 0871 702 1875. **Club nickname**: Rovers
Colours: Blue and white. **Capacity**: 31,367
Record attendance: 62,522 v Bolton (FA Cup 6) Mar 2, 1929

Goalkeepers				
Raya, David	6.0	Cornella	Barcelona, Sp	15.09.95
Steele, Jason	6.2	Middlesbrough	Newton Aycliffe	18.08.90
Defenders				
Duffy, Shane	6.4	Everton	Derry	01.01.92
Hanley, Grant	6.2	–	Dumfries	20.11.91
Hendrie, Stephen	5.10	West Ham (loan)	Glasgow	08.01.95
Henley, Adam	5.10	–	Knoxville, US	14.06.94
Nyambe, Ryan	6.0	–	Katima Mulilo, Nam	04.12.97
Ward, Elliott	6.1	Bournemouth	Harrow	19.01.85
Midfielders				
Akpan, Hope	6.0	Reading	Liverpool	14.08.91
Bennett, Elliott	5.9	Norwich	Telford	18.12.88
Byrne, Jack	5.9	Manchester City (loan)	Dublin, Ire	24.04.96
Conway, Craig	5.8	Cardiff	Irvine	02.05.85
Evans, Corry	5.11	Hull	Belfast	30.07.90
Feeney, Liam	6.0	Bolton	Hammersmith	28.04.86
Guthrie, Danny	5.9	Reading	Shrewsbury	18.04.87
Lowe, Jason	6.0	–	Wigan	02.09.91
Lenihan, Darragh	5.10	Belvedere	Dublin	16.03.94
Mahoney, Connor	5.9	Accrington	Blackburn	12.02.97
Marshall, Ben	6.0	Leicester	Salford	29.09.91
O'Sullivan, John	5.11	–	Dublin, Ire	18.09.93
Forwards				
Graham, Danny	6.1	Sunderland	Gateshead	12.08.85
Stokes, Anthony	6.1	Celtic	Dublin, Ire	25.07.88

BRENTFORD

Ground: Griffin Park, Braemar Road, Brentford TW8 0NT
Telephone: 0845 345 6442. **Club nickname**: Bees
Colours: Red, white and black. **Capacity**: 12,763
Record attendance: 38,678 v Leicester (FA Cup 6) Feb 26, 1949

Goalkeepers				
Bentley, Daniel	6.2	Southend	Basildon	13.07.93
Bonham, Jack	6.3	Watford	Stevenage	14.09.93
Button, David	6.3	Charlton	Stevenage	27.02.89
Defenders				
Barbet, Yoann	6.2	Chamois	Libourne, Fr	10.05.93
Bjelland, Andreas	6.2	Twente	Vedbaek, Den	11.07.88
Clarke, Josh	5.8	–	Walthamstow	05.07.94

Colin, Maxime	5.11	Anderlecht	Arras, Fr	15.11.91
Dean, Harlee	5.10	Southampton	Basingstoke	26.07.91
Egan, John	6.2	Gillingham	Cork, Ire	20.10.92
Yennaris, Nico	5.9	Arsenal	Leytonstone	24.05.93
Midfielders				
Gogia, Akaki	5.10	Hallescher	Rustavi, Geor	18.01.92
Judge, Alan	6.0	Blackburn	Dublin, Ire	11.11.88
Kerschbaumer, Konstantin	5.11	Admira Wacker	Tulln Donau, Aut	01.07.92
MacLeod, Lewis	5.9	Rangers	Wishaw	16.06.94
McCormack, Alan	5.8	Swindon	Dublin, Ire	10.01.84
McEachran, Josh	5.10	Chelsea	Oxford	01.03.93
Saunders, Sam	5.11	Dagenham	Greenwich	29.08.83
Sawyers, Romaine	5.9	Walsall	Birmingham	02.11.91
Woods, Ryan	5.8	Shrewsbury	Norton Canes	13.12.93
Forwards				
Hofmann, Philipp	6.4	Kaiserslautern	Arnsberg, Ger	30.03.93
Hogan, Scott	5.11	Rochdale	Salford	13.04.92
Vibe, Lasse	6.0	Gothenburg	Aarhus, Den	22.02.87

BRIGHTON AND HOVE ALBION

Ground: American Express Stadium, Village Way, Brighton BN1 9BL
Telephone: 01273 878288. **Club nickname**: Seagulls
Colours: Blue and white. **Capacity**: 30,500
Record attendance: Goldstone Ground: 36,747 v Fulham (Div 2) Dec 27, 1958; Withdean Stadium: 8,729 v Manchester City (Carling Cup 2) Sep 23, 2008; Amex Stadium: 30,292 v Derby (Champ) May 2, 2016

Goalkeepers				
Maenpaa, Niki	6.3	Venlo	Espoo, Fin	23.01.85
Stockdale, David	6.3	Fulham	Leeds	28.09.85
Defenders				
Bong, Gaetan	6.2	Wigan	Sakbayeme, Cam	25.04.88
Bruno	5.11	Valencia	El Masnou, Sp	01.10.80
Dunk, Lewis	6.4	–	Brighton	21.11.91
Goldson, Conor	6.3	Shrewsbury	Wolverhampton	18.12.92
Hall, Ben	6.1	Motherwell	Enniskillen	16.01.97
Hunemeier, Uwe	6.2	Paderborn	Rietberg, Ger	09.01.86
Rosenior, Liam	5.10	Hull	Wandsworth	09.07.84
Midfielders				
Forster-Caskey, Jake	5.10	–	Southend	25.04.94
Holla, Danny	6.0	Den Haag	Almere, Hol	31.12.87
Hornby-Forbes, Tyler	5.11	Fleetwood	Preston	08.03.96
Ince, Rohan	6.3	Chelsea	Whitechapel	08.11.92
Kayal, Beram	5.10	Celtic	Jadeidi, Isr	02.05.88
Knockaert, Anthony	5.8	Standard Liege	Roubaix, Fr	20.11.91
LuaLua, Kazenga	5.11	Newcastle	Kinshasa, DR Cong	10.12.90
March, Solly	5.11	–	Eastbourne	20.07.94
Sidwell, Steve	5.10	Stoke	Wandsworth	14.12.82
Stephens, Dale	5.7	Charlton	Bolton	12.06.89
Towell, Richie	5.8	Dundalk	Dublin, Ire	17.07.91
Forwards				
Akindayini, Daniel	6.0	Tottenham	Plaistow	25.10.95
Baldock, Sam	5.8	Bristol City	Bedford	15.03.89
Hambo, Vahid	6.4	Inter Turku	Helsinki, Fin	03.02.95

Harper, Jack	6.1	Real Madrid	Malaga, Sp	28.02.96
Hemed, Tomer	6.0	Almeria	Kiryat Tivon, Isr	02.05.87
Manu, Elvis	5.8	Feyenoord	Dordrecht, Hol	13.08.93
Murphy, Jamie	5.10	Sheffield Utd	Glasgow	28.08.89
Murray, Glenn	6.1	Bournemouth (loan)	Maryport	25.09.83
O'Grady, Chris	6.1	Barnsley	Nottingham	25.01.86
Skalak, Jiri	5.9	`Mlada Boleslav	Pardubice, Cz	12.03.92

BRISTOL CITY

Ground: Ashton Gate, Bristol BS3 2EJ
Telephone: 0871 222 6666. **Club nickname**: Robins
Colours: Red and white. **Capacity**: 16,500 (appox)
Record attendance: 43,335 v Preston (FA Cup 5) Feb 16, 1935

Goalkeepers				
Fielding, Frank	6.0	Derby	Blackburn	04.04.88
O'Donnell, Richard	6.2	Wigan	Sheffield	12.09.88
Defenders				
Ayling, Luke	6.1	Yeovil	Lambeth	25.08.91
Flint, Aden	6.2	Swindon	Pinxton	11.07.89
Little, Mark	6.1	Peterborough	Worcester	20.08.88
Magnusson, Hordur	6.3	Juventus	Reykjavik, Ice	11.02.93
O'Dowda, Callum	5.11	Oxford	Oxford	23.04.95
Williams, Derrick	6.2	Aston Villa	Waterford, Ire	17.01.93
Midfielders				
Brownhill, Josh	5.10	Preston	Warrington	19.12.95
Bryan, Joe	5.7	–	Bristol	17.09.93
Freeman, Luke	5.10	Stevenage	Dartford	22.03.92
Golbourne, Scott	5.9	Wolves	Bristol	29.02.88
O'Neil, Gary	5.8	Norwich	Beckenham	18.05.83
Pack, Marlon	6.2	Cheltenham	Portsmouth	25.03.91
Reid, Bobby	5.7	–	Bristol	02.02.93
Smith, Korey	6.0	Oldham	Hatfield	31.01.91
Forwards				
Agard, Kieran	5.10	Rotherham	Newham	10.10.89
Kodjia, Jonathan	6.2	Angers	St Denis, Fr	22.10.89
Tomlin, Lee	5.11	Bournemouth	Leicester	12.01.89
Wilbrahan, Aaron	6.3	Crystal Palace	Knutsford	21.10.79

BURTON ALBION

Ground: Pirelli Stadium, Princess Way, Burton upon Trent DE13 AR
Telephone: 01283 565938. **Club nickname**: Brewers
Colours: Yellow and black. **Capacity**: 6,912
Record attendance: 6,192 v Oxford Utd (Blue Square Prem Lge) Apr 17, 2009

Goalkeepers				
Bywater, Stephen	6.3	Kerala	Oldham	07.06.81
McLaughlin, Jon	6.2	Bradford	Edinburgh	09.09.87
Defenders				
Edwards, Phil	5.9	Rochdale	Bootle	08.11.85
Flanagan, Tom	6.2	MK Dons	Hammersmith	17.01.92
Maynard, Kelvin	5.11	Royal Antwerp	Paramaribo, Sur	29.05.87
McFadzean, Kyle	6.1	MK Dons	Sheffield	28.02.87

Turner, Ben	6.4	Cardiff	Birmingham	21.08.88
Midfielders				
Butcher, Calum	6.0	Dundee Utd	Rochford	26.02.91
Harness, Marcus	6.0	–	Coventry	01.08.94
Irvine, Jackson	6.2	Ross Co	Melbourne, Aus	07.03.93
McCrory, Damien	6.2	Dagenham	Croom, Ire	23.02.90
Mousinho, John	6.1	Preston	Isleworth	30.04.86
Naylor, Tom	6.0	Derby	Sutton-in-Ashfield	28.06.91
Palmer, Matt	5.10	–	Derby	01.08.93
Reilly, Callum	6.1	Birmingham	Warrington	03.10.93
Forwards				
Akins, Lucas	6.0	Stevenage	Huddersfield	25.02.89
Beavon, Stuart	5.10	Preston	Reading	05.05.84

CARDIFF CITY

Ground: Cardiff City Stadium, Leckwith Road, Cardiff CF11 8AZ
Telephone: 0845 365 1115. **Club nickname**: Bluebirds
Colours:Red and black. **Capacity**: 33,300
Record attendance: Ninian Park: 62,634 Wales v England, Oct 17, 1959; Club: 57,893 v Arsenal (Div 1) Apr 22, 1953, Cardiff City Stadium: 33,280 (Wales v Belgium) Jun 12, 2015. Club: 28,680 v Derby (Champ) Apr 2, 2016

Goalkeepers				
Marshall, David	6.3	Norwich	Glasgow	05.03.85
Moore, Simon	6.3	Brentford	Sandown	19.05.90
Defenders				
Ajayi, Semi	6.4	Arsenal	Crayford	09.11.93
Connolly, Matthew	6.2	QPR	Barnet	24.09.87
Fabio	5.6	Manchester Utd	Petropolis, Br	09.07.90
John, Declan	5.10	–	Merthyr Tydfil	30.06.95
Malone, Scott	6.2	Millwall	Rowley Regis	25.03.91
Manga, Bruno	6.1	Lorient	Libreville, Gab	16.07.88
Morrison, Sean	6.1	Reading	Plymouth	08.01.91
Peltier, Lee	5.11	Huddersfield	Liverpool	11.12.86
Midfielders				
Adeyemi, Tom	6.1	Birmingham	Norwich	24.10.91
Dikgacoi, Kagisho	5.11	Crystal Palace	Brandfort, SA	24.11.84
Gunnarsson, Aron	5.11	Coventry	Akureyri, Ice	22.04.89
Harris, Kadeem	5.9	Wycombe	Westminster	08.06.93
Kennedy, Matthew	5.9	Everton	Dundonald	01.11.94
Noone, Craig	6.3	Brighton	Fazakerly	17.11.87
O'Keefe, Stuart	5.8	Crystal Palace	Norwich	04.03.91
Pilkington, Anthony	6.0	Norwich	Blackburn	06.06.88
Ralls, Joe	6.0	–	Aldershot	13.10.93
Whittingham, Peter	5.10	Aston Villa	Nuneaton	08.09.84
Forwards				
Immers, Lex	6.2	Feyenoord	The Hague, Hol	08.06.86
Le Fondre, Adam	5.9	Reading	Stockport	02.12.86
Macheda, Federico	6.0	Manchester Utd	Rome, It	22.08.91
Saadi, Idriss	5.10	Clermont	Valence, Fr	08.02.92
Zohore, Kenneth	6.3	Kortrijk	Copenhagen, Den	31.01.94

DERBY COUNTY

Ground: iPro Stadium, Pride Park, Derby DE24 8XL
Telephone: 0871 472 1884. **Club nickname**: Rams
Colours: White and black. **Capacity**: 33,597
Record attendance: Baseball Ground: 41,826 v Tottenham (Div 1) Sep 20, 1969; iPro Stadium: 33,597 (England v Mexico) May 25, 2011; Club: 33,475 v Rangers (Ted McMinn testimonial) May 1, 2006

Goalkeepers				
Carson, Scott	6.3	Wigan	Whitehaven	03.09.85
Grant, Lee	6.2	Burnley	Hemel Hempstead	27.01.83
Mitchell, Jonathan	6.2	Newcastle	Hartlepool	24.11.94
Roos, Kelle	6.5	Nuneaton	Rijkevoort, Hol	31.05.92
Defenders				
Baird, Chris	5.11	WBA	Rasharkin	25.02.82
Buxton, Jake	5.11	Burton	Sutton-in-Ashfield	04.03.85
Christie, Cyrus	6.2	Coventry	Coventry	30.09.92
Forsyth, Craig	6.0	Watford	Carnoustie	24.02.89
Hanson, Jamie	6.3	–	Burton upon Trent	10.11.95
Keogh, Richard	6.2	Coventry	Harlow	11.08.86
Lowe, Max	5.9	–	Birmingham	11.05.97
Olsson, Markus	6.0	Blackburn	Gavle, Swe	17.05.88
Pearce, Alex	6.2	Reading	Wallingford	09.11.88
Shackell, Jason	6.4	Burnley	Stevenage	27.09.83
Midfielders				
Bryson, Craig	5.8	Kilmarnock	Rutherglen	06.11.86
Butterfield, Jacob	5.11	Huddersfield	Bradford	10.06.90
Hendrick, Jeff	6.1	–	Dublin, Ire	31.01.92
Hughes, Will	6.1	–	Weybridge	07.04.95
Ince, Thomas	5.10	Hull	Stockport	30.01.92
Johnson, Bradley	5.10	Norwich	Hackney	28.04.87
Thorne, George	6.2	WBA	Chatham	04.01.93
Forwards				
Bent, Darren	5.11	Aston Villa	Wandsworth	06.02.84
Blackman, Nick	6.1	Reading	Whitefield	11.11.89
Camara, Abdoul	5.10	Angers	Mamou, Guin	20.02.90
Martin, Chris	5.10	Norwich	Beccles	04.11.88
Russell, Johnny	5.10	Dundee Utd	Glasgow	08.04.90
Weimann, Andreas	6.2	Aston Villa	Vienna, Aut	05.08.91

FULHAM

Ground: Craven Cottage, Stevenage Road, London SW6 6HH
Telephone: 0870 442 1222. **Club nickname**: Cottagers
Colours: White and black. **Capacity**: 25,678
Record attendance: 49,335 v Millwall (Div 2) Oct 8, 1938

Goalkeepers				
Bettinelli, Marcus	6.4	–	Camberwell	24.05.92
Joronen, Jesse	6.5	–	Helsinki, Fin	21.03.93
Defenders				
Amorebieta, Fernando	6.4	Athletic Bilbao	Cantaura, Ven	29.03.85
Bodurov, Nikolay	5.11	Litex Lovech	Blagoevgrad, Bul	03.05.86
Burgess, Cameron	6.4	–	Aberdeen	21.10.95

Fredericks, Ryan	5.8	Bristol City	Potters Bar	10.10.92
Grimmer, Jack	6.1	Aberdeen	Aberdeen	25.01.94
Kavanagh, Sean	5.9	Belvedere	Dublin, Ire	24.01.94
Madl, Michael	6.0	Sturm Graz	Judenburg, Aut	21.03.88
Odoi, Denis	5.10	Lokeren	Leuven, Bel	27.05.88
Ream, Tim	6.1	Bolton	St Louis, US	05.10.87
Richards, Jazz	6.1	Swansea	Swansea	12.04.91
Stearman, Richard	6.2	Wolves	Wolverhampton	19.08.87
Midfielders				
Cairney, Tom	6.0	Blackburn	Nottingham	20.01.91
Christensen, Lasse	5.10	Midjtylland	Esbjerg, Den	15.08.94
Mattila, Sakari	6.1	Aalesunds	Tampere, Fin	14.07.89
Parker, Scott	5.7	Tottenham	Lambeth	13.10.80
Pringle, Ben	5.9	Rotherham	Newcastle	25.07.89
Tunnicliffe, Ryan	6.0	Manchester Utd	Heywood	30.12.92
Forwards				
Aluko, Sone	5.8	Hull	Hounslow	19.12.89
McCormack, Ross	5.10	Leeds	Glasgow	18.08.86
Smith, Matt	6.6	Leeds	Birmingham	07.06.89
Williams, George	5.8	MK Dons	Milton Keynes	07.09.95
Woodrow, Cauley	6.1	Luton	Hemel Hempstead	02.12.94

HUDDERSFIELD TOWN

Ground: John Smith's Stadium, Huddersfield HD1 6PX
Telephone: 0870 444 4677. **Club nickname**: Terriers
Colours: Blue and white. **Capacity**: 24,500
Record attendance: Leeds Road: 67,037 v Arsenal (FA Cup 6) Feb 27, 1932; John Smith's Stadium: 23,678 v Liverpool (FA Cup 3) Dec 12, 1999

Goalkeepers				
Coleman, Joel	6.4	Oldham	Bolton	26.09.95
Murphy, Joe	6.2	Coventry	Dublin, Ire	21.08.81
Ward, Danny	6.3	Liverpool (loan)	Wrexham	22.06.93
Defenders				
Cranie, Martin	6.0	Barnsley	Yeovil	23.09.86
Davidson, Jason	5.11	WBA	Melbourne, Ais	29.06.91
Hefele, Michael	6.3	Dynamo Dresden	Pfaffenhofen, Ger	01.09.90
Hudson, Mark	6.3	Cardiff	Guildford	30.03.82
Lowe, Chris	5.8	Kaiserslautern	Plauen, Ger	16.04.89
Schindler, Christopher	6.2	1860 Munich	Munich, Ger	29.04.90
Smith, Tommy	6.1	Manchester City	Warrington	14.04.92
Stankovic, Jon Gorenc	6.3	Borussia Dortmund	Ljubljana, Sloven	14.01.96
Midfielders				
Billing, Philip	6.4	–	Esbjerg, Den	11.06.96
Dempsey, Kyle	5.10	Carlisle	Whitehaven	17.09.95
Hogg, Jonathan	5.7	Watford	Middlesbrough	06.12.88
Lolley, Joe	5.10	Kidderminster	Redditch	25.08.92
Mooy, Aaron	5.11	Manchester City (loan)	Sydney, Aus	15.09.90
Paurevic, Ivan	6.4	FC Ufa	Essen, Ger	01.07.91
Payne, Jack	5.6	Southend	Tower Hamlets	25.10.94
Scannell, Sean	5.9	Crystal Palace	Croydon	21.03.89
Whitehead, Dean	5.11	Middlesbrough	Abingdon	12.01.82
Forwards				
Bojaj, Florent	6.0	–	Kosovo	13.04.96

Bunn, Harry	5.9	Manchester City	Oldham	21.11.92
Kachunga, Elias	5.10	Ingolstadt (loan)	Haan, Ger	22.04.92
Palmer, Kasey	5.10	Chelsea (loan)	London	09.11.96
Van La Parra, Rajiv	5.11	Wolves	Rotterdam, Hol	04.06.91
Wells, Nahki	5.7	Bradford	Bermuda	01.06.90

IPSWICH TOWN

Ground: Portman Road, Ipswich IP1 2DA
Telephone: 01473 400500. **Club nickname**: Blues/Town
Colours: Blue and white. **Capacity**: 30,300
Record attendance: 38,010 v Leeds (FA Cup 6) Mar 8, 1975

Goalkeepers				
Bialkowski, Bartosz	6.0	Notts Co	Braniewo, Pol	06.07.87
Gerken, Dean	6.2	Bristol City	Southend	04.08.85
Defenders				
Berra, Christophe	6.1	Wolves	Edinburgh	31.01.85
Chambers, Luke	5.11	Nottm Forest	Kettering	29.08.85
Emmanuel, Josh	5.11	–	London	18.08.97
Kenlock, Myles	6.1	–	Croydon	29.11.96
Knudsen, Jonas	6.1	Esbjerg	Esbjerg, Den	16.09.92
Smith, Tommy	6.1	–	Macclesfield	31.03.90
Webster, Adam	6.3	Portsmouth	Chichester	04.01.95
Midfielders				
Bru, Kevin	6.0	Levski Sofia	Paris, Fr	12.12.88
Bishop, Teddy	5.11	–	Cambridge	15.07.96
Digby, Paul	6.3	Barnsley	Sheffield	02.02.95
Dozzell, Andre	5.10	–	Ipswich	02.05.99
Coke, Giles	6.0	Sheffield Wed	Westminster	03.06.86
Douglas, Jonathan	5.11	Brentford	Monaghan, Ire	22.11.81
Hyam, Luke	5.10	–	Ipswich	24.10.91
McDonnell, Adam	5.9	Shelbourne	Dublin, Ire	14.05.97
Skuse, Cole	5.9	Bristol City	Bristol	29.03.86
Forwards				
McGoldrick, David	6.1	Nottm Forest	Nottingham	29.11.87
Murphy, Daryl	6.2	Celtic	Waterford, Ire	15.03.83
Pitman, Brett	6.0	Bournemouth	St Helier, Jer	03.01.88
Sears, Freddie	5.10	Colchester	Hornchurch	27.11.89

LEEDS UNITED

Ground: Elland Road, Leeds LS11 OES
Telephone: 0871 334 1919. **Club nickname**: Whites
Colours: White. **Capacity**: 37,900
Record attendance: 57,892 v Sunderland (FA Cup 5 rep) Mar 15, 1967

Goalkeepers				
Green, Robert	6.3	QPR	Chertsey	18.01.80
Peacock-Farrell, Bailey	6.2	–	Darlington	29.10.96
Silvestri, Marco	6.3	Chievo	Castelnovo, It	02.03.91
Turnbull, Ross	6.4	Barnsley	Bishop Auckland	04.01.85
Defenders				
Bartley, Kyle	6.4	Swansea (loan)	Stockport	22.05.91
Bamba, Sol	6.3	Palermo	Ivry-sur-Seine, Fr	13.01.85
Bellusci, Giuseppe	6.1	Catania	Trebisacce, It	21.08.89

Berardi, Gaetano	5.11	Sampdoria	Sorengo, Swi	21.08.88
Cooper, Liam	6.0	Chesterfield	Hull	30.08.91
Coyle, Lewie	5.8	–	Hull	15.10.95
McKay, Paul	6.2	Doncaster	Glasgow	19.11.96
Taylor, Charlie	5.9	–	York	18.09.93
Midfielders				
Bianchi, Tommaso	6.0	Sassuolo	Piombino, It	01.11.88
Botaka, Jordan	6.0	Excelsior	Kinshasa, DR Cong	24.06.93
Dallas, Stuart	6.0	Brentford	Cookstown	19.04.91
Diagouraga, Toumani	6.3	Brentford	Paris, Fr	09.06.87
Grimes, Matt	5.10	Swansea (loan)	Exeter	15.07.95
Mowatt, Alex	5.10	–	Doncaster	13.02.95
Murphy, Luke	6.2	Crewe	Alsager	21.10.89
Roofe, Kemar	5.10	Oxford	Walsall	06.01.93
Sacko, Hadi	6.0	Sporting Lisbon (loan)	Corbeil, Fr	24.03.94
Vieira, Ronaldo	5.11	–	Bissau, Guin	20.07.98
Forwards				
Antonsson, Marcus	6.1	Kalmar	Sweden	08.05.91
Doukara, Souleymane	6.1	Catania	Meudon, Fr	29.09.91
McKay, Jack	6.2	Doncaster	Glasgow	19.11.96
Wood, Chris	6.3	Leicester	Auckland, NZ	07.12.91

NEWCASTLE UNITED

Ground: St James' Park, Newcastle-upon-Tyne, NE1 4ST
Telephone: 0844 372 1892. **Club nickname:** Magpies
Colours: Black and white. Capacity: 52,401.
Record attendance: 68,386 v Chelsea (Div 1) Sep 3, 1930

Goalkeepers				
Darlow, Karl	6.1	Nottm Forest	Northampton	08.10.90
Elliot, Rob	6.3	Charlton	Chatham	30.04.86
Krul, Tim	6.3	Den Haag	Den Haag, Hol	03.04.88
Sels, Matz	6.2	Gent	Lint, Bel	26.02.92
Defenders				
Dummett, Paul	6.0	–	Newcastle	26.09.91
Findlay, Stuart	6.3	Celtic	Rutherglen	14.09.95
Gamez, Jesus	6.0	Atletico Madrid	Fuengirola, Sp	10.04.85
Hayden, Isaac	6.1	Arsenal	Chelmsford	22.03.95
Janmaat, Daryl	6.1	Feyenoord	Leidschendam, Hol	22.07.89
Haidara, Massadio	5.10	Nancy	Trappes, Fr	02.12.92
Lascelles, Jamaal	6.2	Nottm Forest	Derby	11.11.93
Mbabu, Kevin	6.0	Servette	Chene-Bougeries, Swi	19.04.95
Mbemba, Chancel	6.0	Anderlecht	Kinshasa, DR Cong	08.08.94
Midfielders				
Aarons, Rolando	5.9	Bristol City	Kingston, Jam	16.11.95
Ameobi, Sammy	6.4	–	Newcastle	01.05.92
Anita, Vurnon	5.6	Ajax	Willemstad, Cur	04.04.89
Bigirimana, Gael	5.10	Coventry	Bujumbura, Bur	22.10.93
Colback, Jack	5.10	Sunderland	Killingworth	24.10.89
De Jong, Siem	6.1	Ajax	Aigle, Swi	28.01.89
Ritchie, Matt	5.8	Bournemouth	Gosport	10.09.89
Shelvey, Jonjo	6.0	Swansea	Romford	27.02.92
Sissoko, Moussa	6.2	Toulouse	Paris, Fr	16.08.89
Thauvin, Florian	5.10	Marseille	Orleans. Fr	26.01.93

Tiote, Cheick	5.11	Twente	Yamoussoukro, Iv C	21.06.86
Vuckic, Haris	6.2	Domzale	Ljubljana, Sloven	21.08.92
Wijnaldum, Georginio	5.9	PSV Eindhoven	Rotterdam, Hol	11.11.90
Forwards				
Armstrong, Alan	5.8	–	Newcastle	10.02.97
Ayoze Perez	5.11	Tenerife	Santa Cruz, Ten	23.07.93
Gayle, Dwight	5.10	Crystal Palace	Walthamstow	20.10.90
Gouffran, Yoan	5.10	Bordeaux	Villeneuve Georges, Fr	25.05.86
Mitrovic, Aleksandar	6.3	Anderlecht	Smederevo, Serb	16.09.94
Riviere, Emmanuel	6.0	Monaco	La Lamentin, Mart	03.03.90

NORWICH CITY

Ground: Carrow Road, Norwich NR1 1JE
Telephone: 01603 760760. **Club nickname**: Canaries
Colours: Yellow and green. Capacity: 27,220
Record attendance: 43,984 v Leicester City (FA Cup 6), Mar 30, 1963

Goalkeepers				
Kean, Jake	6.4	Blackburn	Derby	04.02.91
Rudd, Declan	6.3	–	Diss	16.01.91
Ruddy, John	6.4	Everton	St Ives, Cam	24.10.86
Defenders				
Bassong, Sebastien	6.2	Tottenham	Paris, Fr	09.07.86
Bennett, Ryan	6.2	Peterborough	Orsett	06.03.90
Klose, Timm	6.4	Wolfsburg	Frankfurt, Ger	09.05.88
Martin, Russell	6.0	Peterborough	Brighton	04.01.86
Olsson, Martin	5.10	Blackburn	Gavle, Swe	17.05.88
Pinto, Ivo	6.1	Dinamo Zagreb	Lourosa, Por	07.01.90
Toffolo, Harry	6.0	–	Welwyn Garden City	19.08.95
Turner, Michael	6.4	Sunderland	Lewisham	09.11.83
Whittaker, Steven	6.1	Rangers	Edinburgh	16.06.84
Midfielders				
Andreu, Tony	5.10	Hamilton	Cagnes-sur-Mer, Fr	22.05.88
Brady, Robbie	5.10	Hull	Dublin, Ire	14.01.92
Canos, Sergi	5.9	Liverpool	Nules, Sp	02.02.97
Dorrans, Graham	5.9	WBA	Glasgow	05.05.87
Hoolahan, Wes	5.7	Blackpool	Dublin, Ire	10.08.83
Howson, Jonathan	5.11	Norwich	Leeds	21.05.88
Maddison, James	5.10	Coventry	Coventry	23.11.96
McGrandles, Conor	6.0	Falkirk	Falkirk	24.09.95
Mulumbu, Youssouf	5.10	WBA	Kinshasa, DR Cong	25.01.87
Odjidja-Ofoe, Vadis	6.1	Club Bruges	Ghent, Bel	21.02.89
Tettey, Alexander	5.11	Rennes	Accra, Gh	04.04.86
Thompson, Louis	5.11	Swindon	Bristol	19.12.94
Forwards				
Jerome, Cameron	6.1	Stoke	Huddersfield	14.08.86
Lafferty, Kyle	6.4	Palermo	Enniskillen	16.09.87
Murphy, Jacob	5.10	–	Wembley	24.02.95
Murphy, Josh	5.9	–	Wembley	24.02.95
Naismith, Steven	5.10	Everton	Irvine	14.09.86

NOTTINGHAM FOREST

Ground: City Ground, Pavilion Road, Nottingham NG2 5FJ
Telephone: 0115 982 4444. **Club nickname**: Forest

Colours: Red and white. **Capacity**: 30,576
Record attendance: 49,946 v Manchester Utd (Div 1) Oct 28, 1967

Goalkeepers				
De Vries, Dorus	6.0	Wolves	Beverwijk, Hol	29.12.80
Evtimov, Dimitar	6.3	Etropole	Shumen, Bul	07.09.93
Defenders				
Fox, Danny	6.0	Southampton	Winsford	29.05.86
Hobbs, Jack	6.3	Hull	Portsmouth	18.08.88
Lam, Thomas	6.2	Zwolle	Amsterdam, Hol	18.12.93
Lichaj, Eric	5.10	Aston Villa	Illinois, US	17.11.88
Mancienne, Michael	6.0	Hamburg	Feltham	08.01.88
Mills, Matt	6.3	Bolton	Swindon	14.07.86
Pinillos, Dani	6.0	Cordoba	Logrono, Sp	22.10.92
Midfielders				
Cohen, Chris	5.11	Yeovil	Norwich	05.03.87
Grant, Jorge	5.9	–	Banbury	19.12.94
Lansbury, Henri	6.0	Arsenal	Enfield	12.10.90
Osborn, Ben	5.10	–	Derby	05.08.94
Vaughan, David	5.7	Sunderland	Rhuddlan	18.02.83
Forwards				
Assombalonga, Britt	5.10	Peterborough	Kinshasa, DR Cong	06.12.92
Blackstock, Dexter	6.2	Nottm Forest	Oxford	20.05.86
Fryatt, Matt	5.10	Hull	Nuneaton	05.03.86
Paterson, Jamie	5.9	Walsall	Coventry	20.12.91
Vellios, Apostolos	6.4	Iraklis	Thessaloniki, Gre	08.01.92
Walker, Tyler	5.10	–	Nottingham	07.10.96
Ward, Jamie	5.5	Derby	Birmingham	12.05.86

PRESTON NORTH END

Ground: Deepdale, Sir Tom Finney Way, Preston PR1 6RU
Telephone: 0844 856 1964. **Club nickname**: Lilywhites
Colours: White and navy. **Capacity**: 23,408
Record attendance: 42,684 v Arsenal (Div 1) Apr 23, 1938

Goalkeepers				
Lindegaard, Anders	6.4	WBA	Odense, Den	13.04.84
Maxwell, Chris	6.2	Fleetwood	St Asaph	30.07.90
Defenders				
Clarke, Tom	5.11	Huddersfield	Halifax	21.12.87
Cunningham, Greg	6.0	Bristol City	Carnmore, Ire	31.01.91
Davies, Ben	5.11	–	Barrow	11.08.95
Huntington, Paul	6.2	Yeovil	Carlisle	17.09.87
Smith, Clive	5.10	Manchester City	–	12.12.97
Spurr, Tommy	6.1	Blackburn	Leeds	30.09.87
Woods, Calum	5.11	Huddersfield	Liverpool	05.02.87
Wright, Bailey	5.10	VIS	Melbourne, Aus	28.07.92
Midfielders				
Browne, Alan	5.8	Cork	Cork, Ire	15.04.95
Grimshaw, Liam	5.10	Manchester Utd	Burnley	02.02.95
Humphrey, Chris	5.9	Motherwell	St Catherine, Jam	19.09.87
Johnson, Daniel	5.8	Aston Villa	Kingston, Jam	08.10.92
Pearson, Ben	5.5	Manchester Utd	Oldham	04.01.95
Welsh, John	6.0	Tranmere	Liverpool	10.01.84

Forwards

Beckford, Jermaine	6.2	Bolton	Ealing	09.12.83
Doyle, Eoin	6.0	Cardiff	Dublin, Ire	12.03.88
Gallagher, Paul	6.0	Leicester	Glasgow	09.08.84
Garner, Joe	5.10	Watford	Blackburn	12.04.88
Hugill, Jordan	6.0	Port Vale	Middlesbrough	04.06.92
Makienok, Simon	6.7	Palermo, (loan)	Naestved, Den	21.11.90
May, Stevie	5.10	Sheffield Wed	Perth, Scot	03.11.92
Robinson, Callum	5.10	Aston Villa	Northampton	02.02.95

QUEENS PARK RANGERS

Ground: Loftus Road Stadium, South Africa Road, London W12 7PA
Telephone:0208 743 0262. **Club nickname**:Hoops
Colours: Blue and white. **Capcity**: 18,360
Record attendance: 35,353 v Leeds (Div 1) 27 Apr, 1974

Goalkeepers				
Ingram, Matt	6.3	Wycombe	High Wycombe	18.12.93
Smithies, Alex	6.3	Huddersfield	Huddersfield	05.03.90
Defenders				
Bidwell, Jake	6.0	Brentford	Southport	21.03.93
Caulker, Steven	6.3	Cardiff	Feltham	29.12.91
Hall, Grant	6.4	Tottenham	Brighton	29.10.91
Lynch, Joel	6.1	Huddersfield	Eastbourne	03.10.87
Kpekawa, Cole	6.3	–	Blackpool	20.05.96
Onuoha, Nedum	6.2	Manchester City	Warri, Nig	12.11.86
Perch, James	6.0	Wigan	Mansfield	28.09.85
Robinson, Jack	5.7	Liverpool	Warrington	01.09.93
Midfielders				
Borysiuk, Ariel	5.10	Legia Warsaw	Biala Podlaska, Pol	28.07.91
Chery, Tjaronn	5.7	Groningen	The Hague, Hol	04.06.88
Cousins, Jordan	5.10	Charlton	Greenwich	06.03.94
Doughty, Michael	6.1	–	Westminster	20.11.92
Gladwin, Ben	6.3	Swindon	Reading	08.06.92
Henry, Karl	6.0	Wolves	Wolverhampton	26.11.82
Luongo, Massimo	5.10	Swindon	Sydney, Aus	25.09.92
Petrasso, Michael	5.6	–	Toronto, Canm	09.07.95
Sandro	6.2	Tottenham	Riachinho, Br	15.03.89
Tozser, Daniel	6.2	Parma	Szolnok, Hun	12.05.85
Forwards				
El Khayati, Abdenasser	6.1	Burton	Rotterdam, Hol	07.02.89
Emmanuel-Thomas, Jay	6.3	Bristol City	Forest Gate	27.12.90
Grego-Cox, Reece	5.7	–	Hammersmith	12.11.96
Mackie, Jamie	5.8	Nottm Forest	Dorking	22.09.85
Polter, Sebastian	6.4	Mainz	Wilhelmshaven, Ger	01.04.91
Washington, Conor	5.10	Peterborough	Chatham	18.05.92

READING

Ground: Madejski Stadium, Junction 11 M4, Reading RG2 OFL
Telephone: 0118 968 1100. **Club nickname**: Royals
Colours: Blue and white. **Capacity**: 24,200
Record attendance: Elm Park: 33,042 v Brentford (FA Cup 5) Feb 19, 1927; Madejski Stadium: 24,184 v Everton (Prem Lge) Nov 17, 2012

Goalkeepers				
Al Habsi, Ali	6.4	Wigan	Al-Mudhaibi, Om	30.12.81
Bond, Jonathan	6.3	Watford	Hemel Hempstead	19.05.93
Jaakkola, Anssi	6.5	Ajax Cape Town	Kemi, Fin	13.03.87
Defenders				
Cooper, Jake	6.4	–	Bracknell	03.02.95
Gravenberch, Danzell	6.1	Dordrecht	Amsterdam, Hol	13.02.94
Griffin, Shane	5.11	–	Cork, Ire	08.09.94
Gunter, Chris	5.11	Nottm Forest	Newport	21.07.89
Keown, Niall	6.0	–	Oxford	05.04.95
McShane, Paul	6.0	Hull	Kilpedder, Ire	06.01.86
Long, Sean	5.10	Cherry Orchard	Dublin, Ire	02.05.95
Obita, Jordan	5.11	–	Oxford	08.12.93
Midfielders				
Barrett, Josh	5.8	–	Oxford	21.06.98
Beerens, Roy	5.9	Hertha Berlin	Bladel, Hol	22.12.87
Evans, George	6.1	Manchester City	Cheadle	13.12.94
Fosu, Tarique	5.8	–	Wandsworth	05.11.95
Hurtado, Paolo	5.10	Pacos de Ferreira	Callao, Per	27.07.90
McCleary, Garath	5.11	Nottm Forest	Bromley	15.05.87
Norwood, Oliver	5.11	Huddersfield	Burnley	12.04.91
Quinn, Stephen	5.6	Hull	Dublin, Ire	04.04.86
Swift, John	6.0	Chelsea	Portsmouth	23.06.95
Van den Berg, Joey	6.1	Heerenveen	Nijeveen, Hol	13.02.86
Williams, Danny	6.0	Hoffenheim	Karlsruhe, Ger	08.03.89
Forwards				
Kermorgant, Yann	6.1	Bournemouth	Vannes, Fr	08.11.81
Mendes, Joseph	6.1	Le Havre	Evreux, Fr	30.03.91
Rakels, Deniss	5.11	Cracovia	Jekabpils, Lat	20.08.92
Samuel, Dominic	6.0	–	Southwark	01.04.94

ROTHERHAM UNITED

Ground: New York Stadium, New York Way, Rotherham S60 1AH
Telephone: 08444 140733. **Club nickname**: Millers
Colours: Red and white. **Capacity**: 12,021
Record attendance: Millmoor: 25,170 v Sheffield Wed (Div 2) Jan 26, 1952 and v Sheffield Wed (Div 2) Dec 13, 1952; **Don Valley Stadium**: 7,082 v Aldershot (Lge 2 play-off semi-final, 2nd leg) May 19, 2010; **New York Stadium**: 11,758 v Sheffield Utd (Lge 1) Sep 7, 2013

Goalkeepers				
Camp, Lee	6.1	Bournemouth	Derby	22.08.84
Defenders				
Belaid, Aymen	6.2	Levski Sofia	Paris, Fr	02.01.89
Broadfoot, Kirk	6.3	Blackpool	Irvine	08.08.84
Halford, Greg	6.4	Nottm Forest	Chelmsford	08.12.84
Kelly, Stephen	6.1	Reading	Dublin, Ire	06.09.83
Mattock, Joe	6.0	Sheffield Wed	Leicester	15.05.90
Thorpe, Tom	6.2	Manchester Utd	Manchester	13.01.93
Wood, Richard	6.3	Charlton	Ossett	05.07.85
Midfielders				
Dawson, Chris	5.7	Leeds	Dewsbury	02.09.94
Forde, Anthony	5.9	Walsall	Ballingarry, Ire	16.11.93
Frecklington, Lee	5.8	Peterborough	Lincoln	08.09.85
Newell, Joe	5.11	Peterborough	Tamworth	15.03.93

Smallwood, Richard	5.11	Middlesbrough	Redcar	29.12.90
Ward, Danny	5.11	Huddersfield	Bradford	09.12.90
Forwards				
Clarke-Harris, Jonson	6.0	Oldham	Leicester	20.07.94

SHEFFIELD WEDNESDAY

Ground: Hillsborough, Sheffield, S6 1SW
Telephone: 0871 995 1867. **Club nickname**: Owls
Colours: Blue and white. **Capacity**: 39,814
Record attendance: 72,841 v Manchester City (FA Cup 5) Feb 17, 1934

Goalkeepers				
Dawson, Cameron	6.0	Sheffield Utd	Sheffield	07.07.95
Price, Lewis	6.3	Crystal Palace	Bournemouth	19.07.84
Westwood, Keiren	6.1	Sunderland	Manchester	23.10.84
Defenders				
Helan, Jeremy	5.11	Manchester City	Clichy, Fr	09.05.92
Hunt, Jack	5.9	Crystal Palace	Rothwell	06.12.90
Lachman, Darryl	6.3	Twente	Zaanstad, Hol	11.11.89
Lees, Tom	6.1	Leeds	Warwick	18.11.90
Loovens, Glenn	6.2	Zaragoza	Doetinchem, Hol	22.10.83
Vermijl, Marnick	5.11	Manchester Utd	Peer, Bel	13.01.92
Midfielders				
Bannan, Barry	5.11	Crystal Palace	Airdrie	01.12.89
Filipe Melo	6.2	Moreirenses	Santa Maria, Port	03.11.89
Hutchinson, Sam	6.0	Chelsea	Windsor	03.08.89
Lee, Kieran	6.1	Oldham	Tameside	22.06.88
McGugan, Lewis	5.10	Watford	Long Eaton	25.10.88
Palmer, Liam	6.2	–	Worksop	19.09.91
Semedo, Jose	6.0	Charlton	Setubal, Por	11.01.85
Sougou, Modou	5.10	Marseille	Fissel, Sen	18.12.84
Wallace, Ross	5.6	Burnley	Dundee	23.05.85
Forwards				
Bus, Sergiu	5.11	CSKA Sofia	Cluj-Napoca, Rom	02.11.92
Fletcher, Steven	6.1	Sunderland	Shrewsbury	26.03.87
Forestieri, Fernando	5.8	Watford	Rosario, Arg	15.01.90
Hooper, Gary	5.9	Norwich	Loughton	26.01.88
Joao, Lucas	6.4	Nacional	Angola	04.09.93
Lavery, Caolan	5.11	Ipswich	Alberta, Can	22.10.92
Matias, Marco	5.10	Nacional	Barreiro, Por	10.05.89
Nuhiu, Atdhe	6.6	Rapid Vienna	Prishtina, Kos	29.07.89

WIGAN ATHLETIC

Ground: DW Stadium, Robin Park, Wigan WN5 OUZ
Telephone: 01942 774000. **Club nickname**: Latics
Colours: Blue and white. **Capacity**: 25,023
Record attendance: Springfield Park: 27,526 v Hereford (FA Cup 2) Dec 12, 1953; DW Stadium: 25,133 v Manchester Utd (Prem Lge) May 11, 2008

Goalkeepers				
Jaaskelainen, Jussi	6.3	West Ham	Mikkeli, Fin	19.04.75
Nicholls, Lee	6.3	–	Huyton	05.10.92
Defenders				
Burn, Dan	6.7	Fulham	Blyth	09.05.92

Daniels, Donervon	6.1	WBA	Montserrat	24.11.93
James, Reece	5.6	Manchester Utd	Bacup	07.11.93
Kellett, Andy	5.8	Bolton	Bolton	10.11.93
Knoyle, Kyle	5,8	West Ham (loan)	Newham	24.09.96
Morgan, Craig	6.0	Rotherham	Flint	16.06.85
Pearce, Jason	5.11	Leeds	Hillingdon	06.12.87
Taylor, Andrew	5.10	Cardiff	Hartlepool	01.08.86
Warnock, Stephen	5.10	Derby	Ormskirk	12.12.81
Midfielders				
Chow, Tim	5.11	–	Wigan	18.01.94
Colclough, Ryan	6.0	Crewe	Burslem	27.12.94
Gilbey, Alex	6.0	Colchester	Dagenham	09.12.94
Huws, Emyr	5.10	Manchester City	Llanelli	30.09.93
Jacobs, Michael	5.9	Wolves	Rothwell	04.11.91
Morsy, Sam	5.9	Chesterfield	Wolverhampton	10.09.91
Odelusi, Sanmi	6.0	Bolton	Dagenham	11.06.93
Perkins, David	5.6	Blackpool	Heysham	21.06.82
Powell, Nick	6.0	Manchester Utd	Crewe	23.03.94
Power, Max	5.11	Tranmere	Birkenhead	27.07.93
Whitehead, Danny	5.10	Macclesfield	Trafford	23.10.93
Forwards				
Davies, Craig	6.2	Bolton	Burton	09.01.86
Grigg, Will	5.11	Brentford	Solihull	03.07.91
McKay, Billy	5.9	Inverness	Corby	22.10.88
Wildschut, Yanic	6.2	Middlesbrough	Amsterdam, Hol	01.11.91

WOLVERHAMPTON WANDERERS

Ground: Molineux Stadium, Waterloo Road, Wolverhampton WV1 4QR
Telephone: 0871 222 2220. **Club nickname**: Wolves
Colours: Gold and black. **Capacity**: 31,700
Record attendance: 61,315 v Liverpool (FA Cup 5) Feb 11, 1939

Goalkeepers				
Ikeme, Carl	6.2	–	Sutton Coldfield	08.06.86
Lonergan, Andy	6.3	Fulham	Preston	19.10.83
Defenders				
Batth, Danny	6.3	–	Brierley Hill	21.09.90
Byrne, Nathan	5.11	Swindon	St Albans	05.06.92
Deslandes, Sylvain	6.1	Caen	Kouoptamo, Cam	25.04.97
Doherty, Matt	5.11	–	Dublin, Ire	16.01.92
Ebanks-Landell, Ethan	6.2	–	Smethwick	12.12.92
Hause, Kortney	6.3	Wycombe	Goodmayes	16.07.95
Iorfa, Dominic	6.2	–	Southend	08.07.95
Williamson, Mike	6.4	Newcastle	Stoke	08.11.83
Midfielders				
Coady, Conor	6.1	Huddersfield	St Helens	25.02.93
Edwards, David	5.11	Luton	Pontesbury	03.02.85
Evans, Lee	6.1	Newport	Newport	24.07.94
Graham, Jordan	6.0	Aston Villa	Coventry	05.03.95
Henry, James	6.1	Millwall	Reading	10.06.89
Hunte, Connor	5.10	Sutton	London	12.09.96
McDonald, Kevin	6.2	Sheffield Utd	Carnoustie	04.11.88
Price, Jack	5.7	–	Shrewsbury	19.12.92
Randall, Will	5.11	Swindon	Swindon	02.05.97

Saville, George	5.9	Chelsea	Camberley	01.06.93
Wallace, Jed	5.10	Portsmouth	Reading	26.03.94
Zyro, Michal	6.2	Legia Warsaw	Warsaw, Pol	20.09.92
Forwards				
Enobakhare, Bright	6.0	–	Nigeria	08.02.98
Collins, Aaron	6.0	Newport	Newport	27.05.97
Dicko, Nouha	5.8	Wigan	Paris, Fr	14.05.92
Mason, Joe	5.10	Cardiff	Plymouth	13.05.91

LEAGUE ONE

AFC WIMBLEDON

Ground: Cherry Red Records Stadium, Kingston Road, Kingston upon Thames KT1 3PB
Telephone: 0208 547 3528. **Club nickname**: Dons
Colours: Blue. **Capacity**: 4,850
Record attendance: 4,749 v Exeter (Lge 2) Apr 23, 2013

Goalkeepers				
Clarke, Ryan	6.3	Northampton	Bristol	30.04.82
McDonnell, Joe	5.11	Basingstoke	Basingstoke	19.05.94
Shea, James	5.11	Harrow	Islington	16.06.91
Defenders				
Charles, Darius	6.1	Burton	Ealing	10.12.87
Fuller, Barry	5.10	Barnet	Ashford, Kent	25.09.84
Meades, Jon	6.1	Oxford	Cardiff	02.03.92
Nightingale, Will	6.1	–	Wandsworth	02.08.95
Robinson, Paul	6.1	Portsmouth	Barnet	07.01.82
Sweeney, Ryan	6.1	–	Kingston upon Thames	15.04.97
Midfielders				
Barcham, Andy	5.10	Portsmouth	Basildon	16.12.86
Beere, Tom	5.11	–	Southwark	27.11.95
Bulman, Dannie	5.8	Crawley	Ashford, Sur	24.01.79
Fitzpatrick, Dave	5.10	QPR	Surbiton	10.08.94
Francomb, George	6.0	Norwich	Hackney	08.09.91
Gallagher, Dan	6.1	–	Epsom	20.06.97
Kaja, Egli	5.10	Kingstonian	Albania	26.07.97
Parrett, Dean	5.9	Stevenage	Hampstead	16.11.91
Reeves, Jake	5.7	Swindon	Greenwich	30.05.93
Whelpdale, Chris	6.0	Stevenage	Harold Wood	27.01.87
Forwards				
Elliott, Tom	6.4	Cambridge	Leeds	09.11.90
Oakley, George	6.2	–	Wandsworth	18.11.95
Poleon, Dominic	6.2	Oldham	Newham	07.09.93
Taylor, Lyle	6.2	Scunthorpe	Greenwich	29.03.90

BOLTON WANDERERS

Ground: Macron Stadium, Burnden Way, Lostock, Bolton BL6 6JW
Telephone: 0844 871 2932. **Club nickname**: Trotters
Colours: White and navy. **Capacity**: 28,723
Record attendance: Burnden Park: 69,912 v Manchester City (FA Cup 5) Feb 18, 1933; Macron Stadium: 28,353 v Leicester (Prem Lge) Dec 28, 2003

Goalkeepers				
Amos, Ben	6.2	Manchester Utd	Macclesfield	10.04.90
Fitzsimons, Ross	6.1	Crystal Palace	Hammersmith	28.05.94
Howard, Mark	6.1	Sheffield Utd	Southwark	21.09.86
Defenders				
Beevers, Mark	6.4	Millwall	Barnsley	21.11.89
Casado, Jose Manuel	5.8	Almeria	Coria del Rio, Sp	09.08.86
Dervite, Dorian	6.3	Charlton	Lille, Fr	25.07.88
Moxey, Dean	5.11	Crystal Palace	Exeter	14.01.86
Osede, Derik	6.0	Real Madrid	Madrid, Sp	21.02.93
Taylor, Quade	6.3	Crystal Palace	Tooting	11.12.92
Midfielders				
Davies, Mark	5.11	Wolves	Wolverhampton	18.02.88
Holden, Stuart	5.10	Houston	Aberdeen	01.08.85
Medo, Mohamed	5.9	Partizan Belgrade	Bo, SLeone	16.11.87
Pratley, Darren	6.0	Swansea	Barking	22.04.85
Spearing, Jay	5.7	Liverpool	Wallasey	25.11.88
Trotter, Liam	6.2	Millwall	Ipswich	24.08.88
Twardzik, Filip	6.1	Celtic	Trinec, Cz	10.02.93
Vela, Josh	5.11	–	Salford	14.12.93
Wilson, Lawrie	5.10	Charlton	Collier Row	11.09.87
Forwards				
Clayton, Max	5.9	Crewe	Crewe	09.08.94
Clough, Zach	5.8	–	Manchester	08.03.95
Madine, Gary	6.3	Sheffield Wed	Gateshead	24.08.90
Proctor, Jamie	6.2	Bradford	Preston	25.03.92
Woolery, Kaiyne	5.10	Tamworth	Hackney	11.01.95

BRADFORD CITY

Ground: Coral Windows Stadium, Valley Parade, Bradford BD8 7DY
Telephone: 01274 773355. **Club nickname**: Bantams
Colours: Yellow and claret. **Capacity**: 25,136
Record attendance: 39,146 v Burnley (FA Cup 4) Mar 11, 1911

Goalkeepers				
Doyle, Colin	6.5	Blackpool	Cork, Ire	12.08.85
Defenders				
Clarke, Nathan	6.2	Leyton Orient	Halifax	30.11.83
Darby, Stephen	5.9	Liverpool	Liverpool	06.10.88
Knight-Percival, Nat	6.0	Shrewsbury	Cambridge	31.03.87
McArdle, Rory	6.1	Aberdeen	Sheffield	01.05.87
McMahon, Tony	5.10	Blackpool	Bishop Auckland	24.03.86
Meredith, James	6.1	York	Albury, Aus	04.04.88
Midfielders				
Anderson, Paul	5.9	Ipswich	Leicester	23.07.88
Dieng, Timothee	6.2	Oldham	Grenoble, Fr	09.04.92
Law, Nicky	5.10	Rangers	Plymouth	29.03.88
Marshall, Mark	5.7	Port Vale	Manchester, Jam	05.05.87
Morais, Filipe	5.9	Stevenage	Benavente, Por	21.11.85
Forwards				
Clarke, Billy	5.9	Crawley	Cork, Ire	13.12.87
Hanson, James	6.4	Guiseley	Bradford	09.11.87
Hiwula, Jordy	5.10	Huddersfield (loan)	Manchester	21.09.94

BRISTOL ROVERS

Ground: Memorial Stadium, Filton Avenue, Horfield, Bristol BS7 OBF
Telephone: 0117 909 6648. **Club nickname**: Pirates
Colours: Blue and white. **Capacity**: 12,011
Record attendance: Eastville: 38,472 v Preston (FA Cup 4) Jan 30, 1960. Memorial Stadium: 12,011 v WBA (FA Cup 6) Mar 9, 2008

Goalkeepers				
Mildenhall, Steve	6.4	Millwall	Swindon	13.05.78
Puddy, Will	6.1	Salisbury	Salisbury	04.10.87
Defenders				
Broom, Ryan	5.10	–	Newport	04.09.96
Brown, Lee	6.0	QPR	Farnborough	10.08.90
Clarke, James	6.0	Woking	Aylesbury	17.11.89
Hartley, Peter	6.2	Plymouth	Hartlepool	03.04.88
Leadbitter, Daniel	6.0	Hereford	Newcastle	24.06.91
Lockyer, Tom	6.1	–	Cardiff	03.12.94
McChrystal, Mark	6.1	Tranmere	Derry	26.06.84
Midfielders				
Clarke, Ollie	5.11	–	Bristol	29.06.92
Gosling, Jake	5.9	Exeter	Newquay	11.08.93
James, Luke	6.0	Peterborough (loan)	Amble	04.11.94
Lawrence, Liam	5.11	Shrewsbury	Retford	14.12.81
Lines, Chris	6.2	Port Vale	Bristol	30.11.85
Mansell, Lee	5.9	Torquay	Gloucester	23.09.82
Montano, Cristian	5.11	America de Cali	Cali, Col	11.12.91
Sinclair, Stuart	5.8	Salisbury	Houghton Conquest	09.11.87
Thomas, Dominic	6.1	Charlton	London	23.11.95
Forwards				
Bodin, Billy	5.11	Northampton	Swindon	24.03.92
Easter, Jermaine	5.9	Millwall	Cardiff	15.01.82
Gaffney, Rory	6.0	Cambridge Utd	Tuam, Ire	23.10.89
Harrison, Ellis	5.11	–	Newport	29.01.94
Lucas, Jamie	6.2	–	Pontypridd	06.12.95
Moore, Byron	6.0	Port Vale	Stoke	24.08.88
Taylor, Matt	5.9	Forest Green	–	30.03.90

BURY

Ground: J D Stadium, Gigg Lane, Bury BL9 9HR
Telephone: 08445 790009. **Club nickname**: Shakers
Colours: White and blue. **Capacity**: 11,640
Record attendance: 35,000 v Bolton (FA Cup 3) Jan 9, 1960

Goalkeepers				
Kirkland, Chris	6.6	Preston	Barwell	02.05.81
Ruddy, Jack	6.5	Real Murcia	Glasgow	27.12.97
Williams, Ben	6.0	Bradford	Manchester	27.08.82
Defenders				
Cameron, Nathan	6.2	Coventry	Birmingham	21.11.91
Clarke, Peter	6.0	Blackpool	Southport	03.01.82
Jones, Craig	5.8	New Saints	Chester	20.03.87
Kay, Antony	5.11	MK Dons	Barnsley	21.10.82
Leigh, Greg	5.11	Bradford	Manchester	30.09.94

Maher, Niall	5.10	Bolton	Manchester	31.07.95
Midfielders				
Burgess, Scott	5.10	–	Warrington	27.06.96
Etuhu, Kelvin	6.1	Barnsley	Kano, Nig	30.05.88
Ismail, Zeli	5.9	Wolves	Kukes, Alb	12.12.93
Mayor, Danny	6.0	Sheffield Wed	Leyland	18.10.90
Mellis, Jacob	5.11	Blackpool	Nottingham	08.01.91
Pugh, Danny	6.0	Coventry	Cheadle Hulme	19.10.82
Soares, Tom	6.0	Stoke	Reading	10.07.86
Tutte, Andrew	5.9	Rochdale	Liverpool	21.09.90
Forwards				
Clark, Nicky	5.9	Rangers	Bellshill	03.06.91
Clarke, Leon	6.2	Wolves	Wolverhampton	10.02.85
Dudley, Anthony	5.10	–	Manchester	03.01.96
Hope, Haliam	5.11	Everton	Manchester	17.03.94
Pope, Tom	6.3	Port Vale	Stoke	27.08.85

CHARLTON ATHLETIC

Ground: The Valley, Floyd Road, London SE7 8BL
Telephone: 0208 333 4000. **Club nickname**: Addicks
Colours: Red and white. **Capacity**: 27,111
Record attendance: 75,031 v Aston Villa (FA Cup 5) Feb 12, 1938

Goalkeepers				
Dmitrovic, Marko	6.4	Ujpest	Subotica, Serb	24.01.92
Henderson, Stephen	6.3	West Ham	Dublin, Ire	02.05.88
Pope, Nick	6.3	Bury Town	Cambridge	19.04.92
Defenders				
Bauer, Patrick	6.4	Maritimo	Backnang, Ger	28.10.92
Bergdich, Zakarya	5.9	Valladolid	Compiegne, Fr	07.01.89
Fox, Morgan	6.1	–	Chelmsford	21.09.93
Holmes-Dennis, Tarique	5.9	–	Farnborough	31.10.95
Johnson, Roger	6.3	Pune City	Ashford, Surr	28.04.83
Lennon, Harry	6.3	–	Romford	16.12.94
Sarr, Naby	6.5	Sporting Lisbon	Marseille, Fr	13.08.93
Solly, Chris	5.8	–	Rochester	20.01.90
Teixeira, Jorge	6.2	Standard Liege	Lisbon, Port	27.08.86
Midfielders				
Ba, El Hadji	6.0	Sunderland	Paris, Fr	05.03.93
Ceballos, Cristian	5.8	Tottenham	Barcelona, Sp	03.12.92
Diarra, Alou	6.3	West Ham	Villepinte, Fr	15.07.81
Gudmundsson, Johann Berg	6.1	Alkmaar	Reykjavik, Ice	27.10.90
Harriott, Callum	5.5	–	Norbury	04.03.94
Jackson, Johnnie	6.1	Notts Co	Camden	15.08.82
Kashi, Ahmed	5.10	Metz	Aubervilliers, Fr	18.11.88
Forwards				
Ahearne-Grant, Karlan	6.0	–	Greenwich	19.12.97
Ajose, Nicky	5.10	Swindon	Bury	07.10.91
Holmes, Ricky	6.2	Northampton	Uxbridge	19.06.87
Lookman, Ademola	5.9	–	Wandsworth	20.10.97
Novak, Lee	6.0	Birmingham	Newcastle	28.09,88
Watt, Tony	6.0	Standard Liege	Coatbridge	29.12.93

CHESTERFIELD

Ground: Proact Stadium, Whittington Moor, Chesterfield S41 8NZ
Telephone: 01246 209765. **Club nickname**: Spireites
Colours: Blue and white. **Capacity**: 10,400
Record attendance: Saltergate: 30,561 v Tottenham (FA Cup 5) Feb 12, 1938; Proact Stadium: 10,089 v Rotherham (Lge 2) Mar 18, 2011

Goalkeepers				
Lee, Tommy	6.2	Macclesfield	Keighley	03.01.86
Defenders				
Evatt, Ian	6.3	Blackpool	Coventry	19.11.81
Hird Sam	6.0	Doncaster	Doncaster	07.09.87
Humphreys, Richie	5.11	Hartlepool	Sheffield	30.11.77
Jones, Daniel	6.2	Port Vale	Wordsley	23.12.86
McGinn, Paul	5/8	Dundee	Glasgow	22.10.90
O'Neil, Liam	5.11	WBA	Cambridge	31.07.93
Raglan, Charlie	6.0	FC United	Wythenshawe	28.04.93
Midfielders				
Angel Martinez	5.9	Millwall	Girona, Sp	19.01.86
Ariyibi, Gregory	6.0	Leeds	Virginia, US	18.01.95
Banks, Ollie	6.3	FC United	Rotherham	21.09.92
Dimaio, Connor	5.10	Sheffield Utd	Chesterfield	28.01.96
Donohue, Dion	5.10	Sutton Coldield	Anglesey	26.08.93
Gardner, Dan	6.1	Halifax	Gorton	05.04.90
Liddle, Gary	6.1	Bradford	Middlesbrough	15.06.86
Nolan, Jon	5.10	Grimsby	Huyton	22.04.92
O'Shea, Jay	6.0	MK Dons	Dublin, Ire	10.08.88
Forwards				
Beesley, Jake	6.1	–	Sheffield	02.12.96
Dennis, Kristian	5.11	Stockport	Manchester	12.03.90
Ebanks-Blake, Sylvan	5.8	Preston	Cambridge	29.03.86
Evans, Ched	6.0	Sheffield Utd	St Asaph	28.12.88
Mitchell, Reece	5.9	Chelsea	Westminster	19.09.95
Simons, Rai	6.0	Ilkeston	Hamilton, Berm	11.01.96

COVENTRY CITY

Ground: Ricoh Arena, Phoenix Way, Coventry CV6 6GE.
Telephone: 02476 992326. **Club nickname**: Sky Blues
Colours: Sky blue. **Capacity**: 32,500
Record attendance: Highfield Road: 51,455 v Wolves (Div 2) Apr 29, 1967; Ricoh Arena: 31,407 v Chelsea (FA Cup 6), Mar 7, 2009

Goalkeepers				
Burge, Lee	5.11	–	Hereford	09.01.93
Charles-Cook, Reice	6.1	Bury	Lewisham	08.04.94
Defenders				
Harries, Cian	6.1	–	Birmingham	01.04.97
Haynes, Ryan	5.7	–	Northampton	27.09.95
Kelly-Evans, Dion	5.10	–	Coventry	21.09.96
Ricketts, Sam	6.1	Wolves	Aylesbury	11.10.81
Stokes, Chris	6.1	Forest Green	Trowbridge	08.03.91
Vincelot, Romain	5.10	Leyton Orient	Poitiers, Fr	29.10.85
Willis, Jordan	5.11	–	Coventry	24.08.94

Midfielders

Finch, Jack	6.1	–	Southam	06.08.96
Gadzhev, Vladimir	5.10	Levski Sofia	Pazardzhik, Bul	18.07.87
Jones, Jodi	5.10	Dagenham	Bow	22.10.97
Lameiras, Ruben	5.9	Tottenham	Lisbon, Port	22.12.94
Lawton, Ivor	5.11	–	Coventry	05.09.95
Rose, Andy	6.2	Seattle	Melbourne, Aus	13.02.90
Stevenson, Ben	6.0	–	Leicester	23.03.97
Forwards				
Thomas, Kwame	5.10	Derby	Nottingham	28.09.95
Sordell, Marvin	5.10	Colchester	Harrow	17.02.91
Spence, Kyle	5.6	–	Croydon	14.01.97
Thomas, George	5.8	–	Leicester	24.03.97
Tudgay, Marcus	5.10	Nottm Forest	Shoreham	03.02.83

FLEETWOOD TOWN

Ground: Highbury Stadium, Park Avenue, Fleetwod FY7 6TX
Telephone: 01253 775080. **Club nickname**: Fishermen
Colours: Red and white. **Capacity**: 5,311
Record attendance: 5,194 v York (Lge 2 play-off semi-final, 2nd leg) May 16, 2014

Goalkeepers				
Cairns, Alex	6.0	Rotherham	Doncaster	04.01.93
Neal, Chris	6.2	Port Vale	St Albans	23.10.85
Defenders				
Bell, Amari'i	5.11	Birmingham	Burton	05.05.94
Bolger, Cian	6.4	Southend	Cellbridge, Ire	12.03.92
Davis, Joe	6.3	Leicester	Burnley	10.11.93
Duckworth, Michael	5.11	Hartlepool	Rinteln, Ger	28.04.92
Eastham, Ashley	6.3	Rochdale	Preston	22.03.91
McLaughlin, Conor	6.0	Preston	Belfast	26.07.91
Nilsson, Marcus	6.4	Kalmar	Rydeback, Swe	26.02.88
Nirennold, Victor	6.0	Nova Univ	Rennes, Fr	
Pond, Nathan	6.2	Lancaster	Preston	05.01.85
Midfielders				
Grant, Thomas	5.8	Falkirk	Aberdeen	31.05.95
Haughton, Nick	5.10	–	Manchester	20.09.94
Jonsson, Eggert	6.2	Vestsjaelland	Reykjavik, Ice	18.08.88
Kip, Ricardo	5.7	Almere City	Zoetermeer, Hol	15.03.92
Ryan, Jimmy	5.10	Chesterfield	Maghull	06.09.88
Forwards				
Ball, David	6.0	Peterborough	Whitefield	14.12.89
Cole, Devante	6.1	Bradford	Alderley Edge	10.05.95
Grant, Bobby	5.11	Blackpool	Litherland	01.07.90
Holloway, Aaron	6.2	Wycombe	Cardiff	01.02.93
Hunter, Ashley	5.10	Ilkeston	Derby	29.09.95
Sowerby, Jack	5.9	–	Preston	23.03.95

GILLINGHAM

Ground: Priestfield Stadium, Redfern Avenue, Gillingham ME7 4DD
Telephone: 01634 300000. **Club nickname**: Gills
Colours: Blue and white. **Capacity**: 11,582
Record attendance: 23,002 v QPR. (FA Cup 3) Jan 10, 1948

Goalkeepers

Nelson, Stuart	6.1	Notts Co	Stroud	17.09.81
Defenders				
Garmston, Bradley	5.11	WBA	Chorley	18.01.94
Jackson, Ryan	5.9	Newport	Streatham	31.07.90
Morris, Aaron	6.0	Wimbledon	Rumney	30.12.89
Midfielders				
Byrne, Mark	5.9	Newport	Dublin, Ire	09.11.88
Dack, Bradley	5.8	–	Greenwich	31.12.93
Ehmer, Max	6.2	QPR	Frankfurt, Ger	03.02.92
Hessenthaler, Jake	5.10	–	Gravesend	20.04.90
Knott, Billy	5.8	Bradford	Canvey Island	28.11.92
Martin, Lee	5.10	Millwall	Taunton	09.02.87
Osadebe, Emmanuel	6.2	Tottenham	Dundalk, Ire	01.10.96
Wagstaff, Scott	5.9	Bristol City	Maidstone	31.03.90
Wright, Josh	6.0	Leyton Orient	Bethnal Green	06.11.89
Forwards				
Donnelly, Rory	6.2	Swansea	Belfast	18.02.92
McDonald, Cody	6.0	Coventry	Witham	30.05.86
Norris, Luke	6.1	Brentford	Stevenage	03.06.93
Quigley, Joe	6.4	Bournemouth (loan)	Hayes	10.12.96

MILLWALL

Ground: The Den, Zampa Road, London SE16 3LN
Telephone: 0207 232 1222. **Club nickname:** Lions
Colours: Blue. **Capacity**: 20,146
Record attendance: The Den: 48,672 v Derby (FA Cup 5) Feb 20, 1937; New Den: 20,093 v Arsenal (FA Cup 3) Jan 10, 1994

Goalkeepers

Archer, Jordan	6.3	Tottenham	Walthamstow	12.04.93
Forde, David	6.2	Cardiff	Galway, Ire	20.12.79
King, Tom	6.1	Crystal Palace	Plymouth	09.03.95
Defenders				
Craig, Tony	6.0	Brentford	Greenwich	20.04.85
Cummings, Shaun	6.0	Reading	Hammersmith	28.02.89
Hutchinson, Shaun	6.2	Fulham	Newcastle	23.11.90
Mbulu, Christian	6.4	Brentwood	–	06.08.96
Nelson, Sid	6.1	–	Lewisham	01.01.96
Romeo, Mahlon	5.10	Gillingham	Westminster	19.09.95
Webster, Byron	6.4	Yeovil	Leeds	31.03.87
Midfielders				
Abdou, Nadjim	5.10	Plymouth	Martigues, Fr	13.07.84
Ferguson, Shane	5.11	Newcastle	Derry	12.07.91
Martin, Joe	6.0	Gillingham	Dagenham	29.11.88
Philpot, Jamie	5.11	–	Tunbridge Wells	02.10.96
Thompson, Ben	5.10	–	Sidcup	03.10.95
Twardek, Kris	6.2	–	Ottawa, Can	08.03.97
Williams, Shaun	6.0	MK Dons	Dublin, Ire	19.09.86
Worrall, David	6.0	Southend	Manchester	12.06.90
Wylde, Gregg	5.10	Plymouth	Kirkintilloch	23.03.91
Forwards				
Gregory, Lee	6.2	Halifax	Sheffield	26.08.88
Morison, Steve	6.2	Leeds	Enfield	29.08.83

O'Brien, Aiden	5.8	–	Islington	04.10.93
Oyedinma, Fred	6.1	–	Plumstead	24.11.96
Pavey, Alfie	5.11	Maidstone	Southwark	02.10.95

MILTON KEYNES DONS

Ground: stadiummk, Stadium Way West, Milton Keynes MK1 1ST
Telephone: 01908 622922. **Club nickname**: Dons
Colours: White. **Capacity**: 30,500
Record attendance: 28,127 v Chelsea (FA Cup 4) Jan 31, 2016

Goalkeepers				
Burns, Charlie	6.2	–	Croydon	27.05.95
Martin, David	6.2	Liverpool	Romford	22.01.86
Defenders				
Baldock, George	5.9	–	Buckingham	09.03.93
Downing, Paul	6.1	Walsall	Taunton	26.10.91
Hickford, Harry	6.0	–	Milton Keynes	23.06.95
Lewington, Dean	5.11	Wimbledon	Kingston	18.05.84
Walsh, Joe	5.11	Crawley	Cardiff	13.05.92
Williams, George	5.9	Barnsley	Hillingdon	14.04.93
Midfielders				
Carruthers, Samir	5.8	Aston Villa	Islington	04.04.93
Potter, Darren	5.10	Sheffield Wed	Liverpool	21.12.84
Powell, Daniel	6.2	–	Luton	12.03.91
Rasulo, Giorgio	5.10	–	Banbury	23.01.97
Reeves, Ben	5.10	Southampton	Verwood	19.11.91
Upson, Ed	5.10	Milwall	Bury St Edmunds	21.11.89
Forwards				
Bowditch, Dean	5.11	Yeovil	Bishop's Stortford	15.06.86
Church, Simon	6.0	Charlton	High Wycombe	10.12.88
Hitchcock, Tom	5.11	QPR	Hemel Hempstead	01.10.92

NORTHAMPTON TOWN

Ground: Sixfields Stadium, Upton Way, Northampton NN5 5QA
Telephone: 01604 683700. **Club nickname**: Cobblers
Colours: Claret and white. **Capacity**: 7,750
Record attendance: County Ground: 24,523 v Fulham (Div 1) Apr 23, 1966; Sixfields Stadium: 7,664 v Luton (Lge 2) Apr 30, 2016

Goalkeepers				
Cornell, David	6.0	Oldham	Swansea	28.03.91
Smith, Adam	5.11	Leicester	Sunderland	23.01.92
Defenders				
Buchanan, David	5.9	Preston	Rochdale	06.05.86
Cresswell, Ryan	6.2	Fleetwood	Rotherham	22.12.87
Diamond, Zander	6.2	Burton	Alexandria, Sco	03.12.85
Hanley, Raheem	5.8	Swansea	Blackburn	24.03.94
McDonald, Rod	6.3	Telford	Crewe	11.04.92
Moloney, Brendan	5.10	Yeovil	Beaufort, Ire	18.01.89
Phillips, Aaron	5.8	Coventry	Warwick	20.11.93
Zakuani, Gabriel	6.1	Peterborough	Kinshasa, DR Cong	31.05.86
Midfielders				
Byrom, Joel	6.0	Preston	Oswaldtwistle	14.09.86
D'Ath, Lawson	5.9	Reading	Witney	24.12.92

McCourt, Jak	5.10	Barnsley	Liverpool	06.07.95
McWilliams, Shaun	5.11	–	Northampton	14.08.98
O'Toole, John-Joe	6.2	Bristol Rov	Harrow	30.09.88
Potter, Alfie	5.7	Wimbledon	Islington	09.01.89
Taylor, Jason	6.1	Cheltenham	Ashton-under-Lyne	28.01.87
Forwards				
Hoskins, Sam	5.8	Yeovil	Dorchester	04.02.93
Revell, Alex	6.3	MK Dons	Cambridge	07.07.83
Richards, Marc	5.11	Chesterfield	Wolverhampton	08.07.82

OLDHAM ATHLETIC

Ground: SportsDirect Park, Oldham OL1 2PA
Telephone: 0161 624 4972. **Club nickname**: Latics
Colours: Blue and white. **Capacity**: 13,500
Record attendance: 47,761 v Sheffield Wed (FA Cup 4) Jan 25, 1930

Goalkeepers				
Kettings, Chris	6.4	Crystal Palace	Glasgow	25.10.92
Ripley, Connor	6.3	Middlesbrough (loan)	Middlesbrough	13.02.93
Defenders				
Brown, Connor	5.9	Sheffield Utd	Sheffield	22.08.92
Edmundson, George	6.1	–	Wythenshawe	15.08.97
Gerrard, Anthony	6.2	Shrewsbury	Liverpool	06.02.86
Reckord, Jamie	5.10	Ross Co	Wolverhampton	09.03.92
Wilson, Brian	5.10	Colchester	Manchester	09.05.83
Midfielders				
Byrnes, Danny	5.9	–	Ashton-under-Lyne	17.01.97
Croft, Lee	5.11	St Johnstone	Wigan	21.06.85
Flynn, Ryan	5.7	Sheffield Utd	Edinburgh	04.09.88
Klok, Marc	5.10	Cherno More	Amsterdam, Hol	20.04.93
Law, Josh	5.11	Motherwell	Nottingham	19.08.89
Tuohy, Jack	5.10	–	Oldham	06.09.96
Winchester, Carl	6.0	Linfield	Belfast	12.04.93
Woodland, Luke	6.0	Bradford PA	Abu Dhabi	21.07.95
Forwards				
Cassidy, Jake	6.2	Wolves	Glan Conwy	09.02.93
Erwin, Lee	6.2	Leeds (loan)	Bellshill	19.03.94
Mckay, Billy	5.9	Wigan (loan)	Corby	22.10.88
Murphy, Rhys	6.1	Dagenham	Shoreham	06.11.90

OXFORD UNITED

Ground: Kassam Stadium, Grenoble Road, Oxford OX4 4XP
Telephone: 01865 337500. **Club nickname**: U's
Colours: Yellow. **Capacity**: 12,500
Record attendance: Manor Ground: 22,750 v Preston (FA Cup 6) Feb 29, 1964; Kassam Stadium: 12,243 v Leyton Orient (Lge 2) May 6, 2006

Goalkeepers				
Buchel, Benjamin	6.1	Bournemouth	Ruggell, Liech	04.07.89
Crocombe, Max	6.4	Buckingham	Auckland, NZ	12.08.93
Eastwood, Simon	6.2	Blackburn	Luton	26.06.89
Slocombe, Sam	6.0	Scunthorpe	Scunthorpe	05.06.88
Defenders				
Cundy, Robbie	6.2	–	Oxford	30.05.97

Dunkley, Chey	6.2	Kiddeminster	Wolverhampton	13.02.92
Long, Sam	5.10	–	Oxford	16.01.95
Lundstram, John	5.11	Everton	Liverpool	18.02.94
Martin, Aaron	6.1	Coventry	Newport IOW	29.09.89
Nelson, Curtis	6.0	Plymouth	Newcastle-under-Lyme	21.05.93
Ribeiro, Christian	6.0	Exeter	Neath	14.12.89
Skarz, Joe	6.0	Rotherham	Huddersfield	13.07.89
Midfielders				
Ashby, Josh	5.11	–	Oxford	03.05.96
Crowley, Dan	5.7	Arsenal (loan)	Coventry	03.08.97
MacDonald, Alex	5.7	Burton	Chester	14.04.90
Roofe, Kemar	5.10	WBA	Walsall	06.01.93
Rothwell, Joe	6.1	Manchester Utd	Manchester	11.01.95
Ruffels, Josh	5.10	Coventry	Oxford	23.10.93
Sercombe, Liam	5.10	Exeter	Exeter	25.04.90
Forwards				
Maguire, Chris	5.8	Rotherham	Bellshill	16.01.89
Roberts, James	5.11	Wycombe	Stoke Mandeville	21.06.96
Taylor, Ryan	6.2	Portsmouth	Rotherham	04.05.88
Thomas, Wes	5.11	Birmingham	Barking	23.01.87

PETERBOROUGH UNITED

Ground: Abax Stadium, London Road, Peterborough PE2 8AL
Telephone: 01733 563947. **Club nickname**: Posh
Colours: Blue and white. **Capacity**: 14,319
Record attendance: 30,096 v Swansea (FA Cup 5) Feb 20, 1965

Goalkeepers				
Alnwick, Ben	6.2	Leyton Orient	Prudhoe	01.01.87
Henry, Dion	5.11	–	Ipswich	12.09.97
Defenders				
Baldwin, Jack	6.1	Hartlepool	Barking	30.06.93
Hughes, Andrew	5.11	Newport	Cardiff	05.06.92
Ntlhe, Kgosi	5.9	–	Pretoria, SA	21.02.94
Santos, Ricardo	6.5	Thurrock	Almada, Port	18.06.95
Smith, Michael	5.11	Bristol Rov	Ballyclare	04.09.88
Tafazolli, Ryan	6.5	Mansfield	Sutton	28.09.91
White, Hayden	6.1	Bolton	Greenwich	15.04.95
Midfielders				
Anderson, Harry	5.7	Crawley	–	09.01.97
Anderson, Jermaine	5.11	–	Camden	16.05.96
Beautyman, Harry	5.10	Welling	Newham	01.04.92
Bostwick, Michael	6.1	Stevenage	Greenwich	17.05.88
Da Silva-Lopes, Leon	5.7	–	Lisbon, Por	30.11.98
Edwards, Gwion	5.9	Crawley	Lampeter	01.03.93
Forrester Chris	5.11	St Patrick's	Dublin, Ire	17.12.92
Inman, Brad	5.9	Crewe	Adelaide, Aus	10.12.91
Maddison, Marcus	5.11	Gateshead	Durham	26.09.93
Payne, Jack	5.9	Gillingham	Gravesend	05.12.91
Taylor, Jon	5.11	Shrewsbury	Liverpool	20.07.92
Forwards				
Angol, Lee	6.2	Luton	Sutton	04.08.94
Coulthirst, Shaquile	5.11	Tottenham	Hackney	02.11.94
Gormley, Joe	6.0	Cliftonville	Belfast	26.11.90

Nabi, Adil	5.8	WBA	Birmingham	28.02.94
Nichols, Tom	5.10	Exeter	Taunton	28.08.93
Nicholson, Jordan	5.10	Histon	Godmanchester	29.09.93
Stevens, Matty	5.11	Barnet	Surrey	12.02.98
Taylor, Paul	5.11	Ipswich	Liverpool	04.10.87
Williams, Aaron	5.10	Nuneaton	Sandwell	21.10.93

PORT VALE

Ground: Vale Park, Hamil Road, Burslem, Stoke-on-Trent ST6 1AW
Telephone: 01782 655800. **Club nickname**: Valiants
Colours: Black and white. **Capacity**: 18,947
Record attendance: 49,768 v Aston Villa (FA Cup 5) Feb 20, 1960

Goalkeepers				
Alnwick, Jak	6.2	Newcastle	Hexham	17.06.93
Johnson, Sam	6.6	Stoke	Newcastle-under-Lyme	01.12.92
Defenders				
Kiko	6.0	Setubal	Alcacer, Por	20.01.93
Knops, Kjell	6.0	Maastricht	Wijlre, Hol	21.07.87
Mac-Intisch, Calvin	6.0	Cambuur	Amsterdam, Hol	09.08.89
Purkiss, Ben	6.2	Walsall	Sheffield	01.04.84
Smith, Nathan	6.0	–	Madeley	03.04.96
Streete, Remie	6.2	Newcastle	South Shields	02.11.94
Yates, Adam	5.10	Morecambe	Stoke	28.05.83
Midfielders				
Andoh, Enoch	5.7	Limassol	Kumasi, Gh	01.01.93
Birchall, Chris	5.9	Columbus	Stafford	05.05.84
Brown, Michael	5.10	Leeds	Hartlepool	25.01.77
De Freitas, Anthony	5.11	Monaco	Lyon, Fr	10.05.94
Foley, Sam	6.0	Yeovil	Upton-on-Severn	17.10.86
Grant, Anthony	5.10	Crewe	Lambeth	04.06.87
Kelly, Sam	5.10	Norwich	Huntingdon	21.10.93
Lloyd, Ryan	5.10	–	Newcastle-under-Lyme	01.02.94
Mbamba, Christopher	6.0	Hamarkameratene	Harare, Zim	30.04.92
Pereira, Quentin	5.9	Epernay Champagne	Reims, Fr	21.04.92
Tavares, Paulo	5.11	Setubal	Massarelos, Por	09.12.85
Thomas, Jerome	5.11	Rotherham	Wembley	23.03.83
Forwards				
Cicilia, Rigino	6.5	Roda JC	Willemstad, Cur	23.09.94
Forrester, Anton	6.0	Blackburn	Liverpool	11.02.94
Hooper JJ	6.1	Havant	Greenwich	09.10.93
Saleiro, Carlos	6.1	Oriental	Lisbon, Por	25.02.86

ROCHDALE

Ground: Spotland, Wilbutts Lane, Rochdale OL11 5DS
Telephone: 01706 644648. **Club nickname**: Dale
Colours: Blue and black. **Capacity**: 10,249
Record attendance: 24,231 v Notts Co (FA Cup 2) Dec 10, 1949

Goalkeepers				
Collis, Steve	6.3	Macclesfield	Harrow	18.03.81
Lillis, Josh	6.0	Scunthorpe	Derby	24.06.87
Defenders				
Canavan, Niall	6.3	Scunthorpe	Leeds	11.04.91

McGahey, Harrison	6.1	Sheffield Utd	Preston	26.09.95
McNulty, Jim	6.0	Bury	Liverpool	13.02,.85
Rafferty, Joe	6.0	Liverpool	Liverpool	06.10.93
Tanser, Scott	6.0	–	Blackpool	23.10.94
Midfielders				
Allen, Jamie	5.11	–	Rochdale	29.01.95
Barry-Murphy, Brian	6.0	Bury	Cork, Ire	27.07.78
Camps, Callum	5.11	–	Stockport	14.03.96
Cannon, Andy	5.9	–	Tameside	14.03.96
Lund, Matthew	6.0	Stoke	Manchester	21.11.90
Mendez-Laing, Nathaniel	5.10	Peterborough	Birmingham	15.04.92
Rathbone, Oliver	5.11	Manchester Utd	Blackburn	10.10.96
Vincenti, Peter	6.2	Aldershot	St Peter, Jer	07.07.86
Forwards				
Andrew, Calvin	6.2	York	Luton	19.12.86
Bunney, Joe	5.10	–	Northwich	26.09.93
Henderson, Ian	5.10	Colchester	Thetford	24.01.85
Hooper, James	5.10	–	Wythenshawe	10.02.97
McDermott, Donal	5.10	Dundalk	Dublin, Ire	19.10.89

SCUNTHORPE UNITED

Ground: Glanford Park, Doncaster Road, Scunthorpe DN15 8TD
Telephone: 0871 221 1899. **Club nickname**: Iron
Colours: Claret and blue. **Capacity**: 9,183
Record attendance: Old Show Ground: 23,935 v Portsmouth (FA Cup 4) Jan 30, 1954; Glanford Park: 8,921 v Newcastle (Champ) Oct 20, 2009

Goalkeepers				
Anyon, Joe	6.2	Shrewsbury	Lytham St Annes	29.12.86
Daniels, Luke	6.4	WBA	Bolton	05.01.88
Defenders				
Clarke, Jordan	6.0	Coventry	Coventry	19.11.91
Dyche, Jack	5.9	–	Leeds	11.10.97
Goode, Charlie	6.5	Hendon	Watford	03.08.95
King, Jack	6.0	Preston	Oxford	20.08.85
Laird, Scott	5.9	Preston	Taunton	15.05.88
Mirfin, David	6.1	Watford	Sheffield	18.04.85
Townsend, Conor	5.6	Hull	Hessle	04.03.93
Wallace, Murray	6.2	Huddersfield	Glasgow	10.01.93
Wiseman, Scott	6.0	Preston	Hull	13.12.85
Midfielders				
Bishop, Neal	6.0	Blackpool	Stockton	07.08.81
Dawson, Stephen	5.6	Rochdale	Dublin, Ire	04.12.85
Mantom, Sam	5.9	Walsall	Stourbridge	20.02.92
Morris, Josh	5.10	Bradford	Preston	30.09.91
Ness, Jamie	6.1	Stoke	Irvine	02.03.91
Sutton, Levi	5.11	–	Scunthorpe	24.03.96
Forwards				
Adelakun, Hakeeb	6.0	–	Hackney	11.06.96
Hopper, Tom	6.1	Leicester	Boston	14.12.93
Madden, Paddy	6.0	Yeovil	Dublin, Ire	04.03.90
Van Veen, Kevin	6.0	FC Oss	Eindhovern, Hol	01.06.91
Williams, Luke	6.1	Middlesbrough	Middlesbrough	11.06.93
Wootton, Kyle	6.2	–	Epworth	11.10.96

SHEFFIELD UNITED

Ground: Bramall Lane, Sheffield S2 4SU
Telephone: 0871 995 1899. **Club nickname**: Blades
Colours: Red and white. **Capacity**: 32,702
Record attendance: 68,287 v Leeds (FA Cup 5) Feb 15, 1936

Goalkeepers				
Long, George	6.4	–	Sheffield	05.11.93
Willis, George	5.11	–	Rotherham	30.07.95
Defenders				
Basham, Chris	5.11	Blackpool	Hebburn	18.02.88
Brayford, John	5.8	Cardiff	Stoke	29.12.87
Freeman, Kieron	6.1	Derby	Bestwood	21.03.92
Hussey, Chris	6.0	Bury	Hammersmith	02.01.89
O'Connell, Jack	6.3	Brentford	Liverpool	29.03.94
Wilson, James	6.2	Oldham	Chepstow	26.02.89
Wright, Jake	5.11	Oxford	Keighley	11.03.86
Midfielders				
Coutts, Paul	6.1	Derby	Aberdeen	22.07.88
Done, Matt	5.10	Rochdale	Oswestry	22.07.88
Duffy, Mark	5.9	Birmingham	Liverpool	07.10.85
Fleck, John	5.7	Coventry	Glasgow	24.08.91
Hammond, Dean	6,0	Leicester	Hastings	07.03.83
Reed, Louis	5.8	–	Barnsley	25.07.97
Scougall, Stefan	5.7	Livingston	Edinburgh	07.12.92
Wallace, Keiran	6.1	Ilkeston	Nottingham	26.01.95
Wallace, James	6.0	Tranmere	Fazackerley	19.12.91
Woolford, Martyn	6.0	Millwall	Pontefract	13.10.85
Whiteman, Ben	6.0	–	Rochdale	17.06.96
Forwards				
Adams, Che	5.10	Ilkeston	Leicester	13.07.96
McNulty, Marc	5.10	Livingston	Edinburgh	14.09.92
Sharp, Billy	5.9	Leeds	Sheffield	05.02.86

SHREWSBURY TOWN

Ground: Greenhous Meadow Stadium, Oteley Road, Shrewsbury SY2 6ST
Telephone: 01743 289177. **Club nickname**: Shrews
Colours: Blue and yellow. **Capacity**: 9,875
Record attendance: Gay Meadow: 18,917 v Walsall (Div 3) Apr 26, 1961; Greenhous Meadow: 10,210 v Chelsea (Lge Cup 4) Oct 28, 2014

Goalkeepers				
Halstead, Mark	6.3	Blackpool	Blackpool	01.01.90
Leutwiler, Jayson	6.4	Middlesbrough	Switzerland	25.04.89
Defenders				
Brown, Junior	5.9	Mansfield	Crewe	07.05.89
El-Abd, Adam	6.0	Bristol City	Brighton	11.09.84
Lancashire, Olly	6.1	Rochdale	Basingstoke	13.12.88
McGivern, Ryan	6.2	Port Vale	Newry	08.01.90
Riley, Joe	6.0	Bury	Salford	13.10.91
Sadler, Mat	5.11	Rotherham	Birmingham	26.02.85
Smith, Dominic	6.0	–	Shrewsbury	09.02.96
Midfielders				
Black, Ian	5.8	Rangers	Edinburgh	14.03.85

Deegan, Gary	5.9	Southend	Dublin, Ire	28.09.87
O'Brien, Jim	6.0	Coventry	Vale of Leven	28.09.87
Ogogo, Abu	5.10	Dagenham	Epsom	03.11.89
Sarcevic, Antoni	6.0	Fleetwood	Manchester	13.03.92
Wellens, Richie	5.9	Doncaster	Manchester	26.03.80
Wesolowski, James	5.9	Oldham	Sydney, Aus	25.08.87
Whalley, Shaun	5.9	Luton	Whiston	07.08.87
Forwards				
Anderson, Kaiman	6.1	–	Shrewsbury	15.08.95
Barnett, Tyrone	6.3	Peterborough	Stevenage	28.10.85
Dodds, Louis	5.10	Port Vale	Sheffield	08.10.86
Jones, Ethan	5.11	–	Dudley	04.04.98
Leitch-Smith AJ	5.11	Port Vale	Crewe	06.03.90
Mangan, Andrew	5.10	Tranmere	Liverpool	30.08.86

SOUTHEND UNITED

Ground: Roots Hall, Victoria Avenue, Southend SS2 6NQ
Telephone: 01702 304050. **Club nickname**: Shrimpers
Colours: Blue and white. **Capacity**: 12,392
Record attendance: 31,090 v Liverpool (FA Cup 3) Jan 10, 1979

Goalkeepers				
Oxley, Mark	6.2	Hibernian	Sheffield	28.09.90
Smith, Ted	6.1	–	Benfleet	18.01.96
Defenders				
Barrett, Adam	5.10	Gillingham	Dagenham	29.11.79
Coker, Ben	5.11	Colchester	Cambridge	01.07.90
Demetriou, Jason	5.11	Walsall	Newham	18.11.87
Leonard, Ryan	6.1	Plymouth	Plymouth	24.05.92
O'Neill, Luke	6.0	Burnley	Slough	20.08.91
Thompson, Adam	6.2	Watford	Harlow	28.09.92
White, John	6.0	Colchester	Colchester	25.07.86
Midfielders				
Atkinson, Will	5.10	Bradford	Beverley	14.10.88
McGlashan, Jermaine	5.7	Gillingham	Croydon	14.04.88
McLaughlin, Stephen	5.10	Nottm Forest	Donegal, Ire	14.06.90
Timlin, Michael	5.8	Swindon	Lambeth	19.03.85
Wordsworth, Anthony	6.1	Ipswich	Camden	03.01.89
Forwards				
Mooney, David	6.2	Leyton Orient	Dublin, Ire	30.10.84
Williams, Jason	5.10	–	Islington	28.09.95

SWINDON TOWN

Ground: County Ground, County Road, Swindon SN1 2ED
Telephone: 0871 423 6433. **Club nickname**: Robins
Colours: Red and white. **Capacity**: 15,728
Record attendance: 32,000 v Arsenal (FA Cup 3) Jan 15, 1972

Goalkeepers				
Belford, Tyrell	6.0	Liverpool	Nuneaton	06.05.94
Vigouroux, Lawrence	6.4	Liverpool	Camden	19.11.93
Defenders				
Bradley, Barry	6.0	Brighton	Hastings	13.02.95

Brophy, James	5.11	Edgware	London	25.07.94
Ormonde-Ottewill, Brandon	5.9	Arsenal	–	21.12.95
Rossi Branco, Raphael	6.3	Whitehawk	Campinas, Br	25.07.90
Sendles-White, Jamie	6.2	Hamilton	Kingston upon Thames	10.04.94
Thompson, Nathan	5.10	–	Chester	22.04.91
Midfielders				
Goddard, John	5.10	Woking	Sandhurst	02.06.93
Iandolo, Ellis	5.10	–	Chatham	22.08.97
Kasim, Yaser	5.11	Brighton	Baghdad, Irq	16.05.91
Thomas, Conor	6.1	Coventry	Coventry	29.10.93
Rodgers, Anton	5.8	Oldham	Reading	26.01.93
Stewart, Jordan	5.9	Glentoran	Belfast	31.03.95
Forwards				
Hylton, Jermaine	5.10	Redditch	Birmingham	28.06.93
Obika, Jonathan	6.0	Tottenham	Enfield	12.09.90

WALSALL

Ground: Banks's Stadium, Bescot Crescent, Walsall WS1 4SA
Telephone: 01922 622791. **Club nickname**: Saddlers
Colours: Red and white. **Capacity**: 11,300
Record attendance: Fellows Park: 25,453 v Newcastle (Div 2) Aug 29, 1961; Banks's Stadium: 11,049 v Rotherham (Div 1) May 10, 2004

Goalkeepers				
Etheridge, Neil	6.3	Charlton	Enfield	07.02.90
MacGillivray, Craig	6.2	Harrogate	Harrogate	12.01.93
Roberts, Liam	6.0	–	Walsall	24.11.94
Defenders				
Edwards, Joe	5.9	Colchester	Gloucester	31.10.90
Henry, Rico	5.8	–	Birmingham	08.07.97
McCarthy, Jason	6.1	Southampton (loan)	Southampton	07.11.95
O'Connor, James	5.10	Derby	Birmingham	20.11.84
Preston, Matt	6.0	–	Birmingham	16.03.95
Vassell, Theo	6.1	Oldham	Stoke	02.01.97
Midfielders				
Chambers, Adam	5.10	Leyton Orient	Sandwell	20.11.80
Cuvelier, Florent	6.0	Sheffield Utd	Brussels, Bel	12.09.92
Dobson, George	6.1	West Ham (loan)	Harold Wood	15.11.97
Flanagan, Reece	5.11	–	Birmingham	19.10.94
Kinsella, Liam	5.9	–	Colchester	23.02.96
Morris, Kieron	5.10	–	Hereford	03.06.94
Moussa, Franck	5.8	Southend	Brussels, Bel	24.07.89
Oztumer, Erhun	5.3	Peterborough	Greenwich	29.05.91
Sangha, Jordon	5.11	–	West Bromwich	04.01.98
Forwards				
Bakayoko, Amadou	6.3	–	Sierra Leone	01.01.96

LEAGUE TWO

ACCRINGTON STANLEY

Ground: Wham Stadium, Livingstone Road, Accrington BB5 5BX
Telephone: 0871 434 1968. **Club nickname**: Stanley
Colours: Red and white. **Capacity**: 5,057
Record attendance: 4,368 v Colchester (FA Cup 3) Jan 3, 2004

Goalkeepers				
Chapman, Aaron	6.8	Chesterfield	Rotherham	29.05.90
Parish, Elliot	6.2	Colchester	Towcester	20.05.90
Defenders				
Beckles, Omar	6.3	Aldershot	Kettering	19.10.91
Buxton, Adam	6.1	Wigan	Liverpool	12.05.92
Conneely, Seamus	6.1	Sligo	Lambeth	09.07.88
Davies, Tom	5.11	Fleetwood	Warrington	18.04.92
Hughes, Mark	6.3	Stevenage	Kirkby	09.12.86
Pearson, Matty	6.3	Halifax	Keighley	03.08.93
Shaw, Frazer	5.9	Leyton Orient	Newham	23.12.94
Midfielders				
Boco, Romuald	5.10	Portsmouth	Bernay, Fr	08.07.85
Hery, Bastien	5.9	Carlisle	Chantereine, Fr	23.03.92
Hewitt, Steven	5.7	Burnley	Manchester	05.12.93
McConville, Sean	5.11	Chester	Burscough	06.03.89
Forwards				
Gornell, Terry	5.11	Cheltenham	Liverpool	16.12.89
Hazeldine, Max	5.10	–	Stockport	13.02.97
Kee, Billy	5.9	Scunthorpe	Leicester	01.12.90
McCartan, Shay	5.10	Burnley	Newry	18.05.94

BARNET

Ground:The Hive, Camrose Avenue, London HA8 6AG
Telephone: 0208 381 3800. **Club nickname:** Bees
Colours: Gold and black. **Capacity**: 5,233
Record attendance:Underderhill:11,026 v Wycombe (FA Amateur Cup 4) Feb 23, 1952. The Hive: 5,233 v Gateshead (Conf) Apr 25, 2015

Goalkeepers				
Stack, Graham	6.2	Hibernian	Hampstead	26.09.81
Stephens, Jamie	6.1	Newport	Wotton-under-Edge	24.08.93
Defenders				
Dembele, Bira	6.3	Stevenage	Villepinte, Fr	22.03.88
Hoyte, Gavin	5.11	Gillingham	Leytonstone	06.06.90
Johnson, Elliot	5.10	Norwich	Edgware	17.08.94
Muggleton, Sam	5.11	Gillingham	Melton Mowbray	17.11.95
Nelson, Michael	6.2	Cambridge Utd	Bishop Auckland	23.03.80
N'Gala, Bondz	6.0	Portsmouth	Newham	03.10.89
Pearson, James	6.1	Leicester	Sheffield	19.01.93
Sesay, Alie	6.0	Leicester	Enfield	25.07.93
Midfielders				
Champion, Tom	6.3	Cambridge Utd	Barnet	15.05.86
Gambin, Luke	5.7	–	Sutton	16.03.93

Togwell, Sam	5.10	Chesterfield	Maidenhead	14.10.84
Vilhete, Mauro	5.9	–	Rio de Mauro, Por	10.05.93
Weston, Curtis	5.11	Gillingham	Greenwich	24.01.87
Forwards				
Akinde, John	6.2	Alfreton	Gravesend	08.07.89
Gash, Michael	5.10	Kidderminster	Cambridge	03.09.86
Nicholls, Alex	5.10	Exeter	Stourbridge	09.12.87
Tomlinson, Ben	5.11	Lincoln	Dinnington	31.10.89

BLACKPOOL

Ground: Bloomfield Road, Blackpool FY1 6JJ
Telephone: 0871 622 1953. **Club nickname**: Seasiders
Colours: Tangerine and white. **Capacity**: 16,750
Record attendance: 38,098 v Wolves (Div 1) Sep 17, 1955

Goalkeepers				
Letheren, Kyle	6.2	Dundee	Llanelli	26.12.87
Defenders				
Aimson, Will	5.10	Hull	Christchurch	01.01.94
Aldred, Tom	6.2	Accrington	Bolton	11.09.90
Higham, Luke	6.1	–	Blackpool	21.10.96
McAlister, Jim	5.11	Dundee	Rothesay	02.11.85
Mellor, Kelvin	6.2	Plymouth	Crewe	25.01.91
Robertson, Clark	6.2	Aberdeen	Aberdeen	05.09.93
Taylor, Andy	5.11	Walsall	Blackburn	14.03.86
Midfielders				
Cameron, Henry	5.10	–	Lytham St Annes	28.06.97
Daniel, Colin	5.11	Port Vale	Nottingham	15.02.88
Herron, John	5.10	Celtic	Coatbridge	01.02.94
Norris, David	5.7	Yeovil	Stamford	22.02.81
Potts, Brad	6.2	Carlisle	Hexham	07.03.94
Yeates, Mark	5.9	Oldham	Tallaght, Ire	11.01.85
Forwards				
Cullen, Mark	5.9	Luton	Stakeford	21.04.92
Matt, Jamille	6.2	Fleetwood	Walsall	02.12.90
Osayi-Samuel, Bright	5.9	–	Nigeria	01.02.97
Philliskirk, Danny	5.10	Oldham	Oldham	10.04.91
Redshaw, Jack	5.7	Morecambe	Salford	20.11.90
Vassell, Kyle	6.0	Peterborough	Milton Keynes	07.02.93

CAMBRIDGE UNITED

Ground: Costings Abbey Stadium, Newmarket Road, Cambridge CB5 8LN
Telephone: 01223 566500. **Club nickname**: U's
Colours: Yellow and black. **Capacity**: 9,617
Record attendance: 14,000 v Chelsea (friendly) May 1, 1970

Goalkeepers				
Gregory, David	6.1	Crystal Palace	Croydon	01.10.94
Norris, Will	6.5	Royston	Watford	12.08.93
Defenders				
Coulson, Josh	6.3	–	Cambridge	28.01.89
Legge, Leon	6.1	Gillingham	Hastings	28.04.85
Omozusi, Elliot	5.11	Leyton Orient	Hackney	15.12.88

Roberts, Mark	6.1	Stevenage	Northwich	16.10.83
Taylor, Greg	6.1	Luton	Bedford	15.01.90
Midfielders				
Berry, Luke	5.9	Barnsley	Cambridge	12.07.92
Dunne James	5.11	Portsmouth	Farnborough	18.09.89
Dunk, Harrison	6.0	Bromley	London	25.10.90
Elito, Medy	6.0	Newport	Kinshasa, DR Cong	20.03.90
Hughes, Jeff	6.0	Fleetwood	Larne	29.05.85
Keane, Keith	5.9	Preston	Luton	20.11.86
Mingoia, Piero	5.7	Accrington	Enfield	20.10.91
Newton, Conor	5.11	Rotherham	Whickham	17.10.91
Forwards				
Carr, Danny	5.11	Huddersfield	Lambeth	30.11.93
Corr, Barry	6.3	Southend	Newcastle, NI	02.04.85
Maris, George	5.11	Barnsley	Sheffield	06.03.96
Pigott, Joe	6.1	Charlton	Maidstone	24.11.93
Williamson, Ben	5.11	Gillingham	Lambeth	25.12.88

CARLISLE UNITED

Ground: Brunton Park, Warwick Road, Carlisle CA1 1LL
Telephone: 01228 526237. **Club nickname**: Cumbrians
Colours: Blue and white. **Capacity**: 18,202
Record attendance: 27,500 v Birmingham City (FA Cup 3) Jan 5, 1957, v Middlesbrough (FA Cup 5) Jan 7, 1970

Goalkeepers				
Gillespie, Mark	6.0	–	Newcastle	27.03.92
Defenders				
Atkinson, David	5.10	Middlesbrough	Shildon	27.04.93
Brisley, Shaun	6.2	Peterborough	Macclesfield	06.05.90
Ellis, Mark	6.2	Shrewsbury	Plymouth	30.09.88
Grainger, Danny	5.10	Dunfermline	Penrith	28.07.86
McQueen, Alexander	6.2	Tottenham	London	24.03.95
Miller, Tom	5.11	Lincoln	Ely	29.06.90
Raynes, Michael	6.3	Mansfield	Manchester	15.10.87
Midfielders				
Adams, Nicky	5.10	Northampton	Bolton	16.10.86
Devitt, Jamie	5.10	Morecambe	Dublin, Ire	06.07.90
Jones, Mike	6.0	Oldham	Birkenhead	15.08.87
Joyce, Luke	5.11	Accrington	Bolton	09.07.87
Kennedy, Jason	6.1	Bradford	Roseworth	11.09.86
Lambe, Reggie	5.8	Mansfield	Hamilton, Berm	04.02.91
McKee, Joe	5.11	Morton	Glasgoow	31.10.92
Penn, Russell	6.0	York	Wordsley	08.11.85
Forwards				
Ibehre, Jabo	6.2	Colchester	Islington	28.01.83
Miller, Shaun	5.8	Morecambe	Alsager	25.09.87
Wyke, Charlie	5.11	Middlesbrough	Middlesbrough	06.12.92

CHELTENHAM TOWN

Ground: Abbey Business Stadium, Whaddon Road, Cheltnham GL52 5NA
Telephone: 01242 573558
Colours: Red and black. **Capacity**: 7,066
Record attendance: 8,326 v Reading (FA Cup 1) Nov 17, 1956

Goalkeepers				
Kitscha, Calum	6.4	Swindon	Edmonton	06.04.93
Defenders				
Barthram, Jack	5.8	Swindon	Newham	13.10.93
Downes, Aaron	6.1	Torquay	15.05.85	
Jennings, James	5.10	Forest Green	Manchester	02.09.87
O'Shaughnessy, Daniel	6.2	Brentford	Riihimaki, Fin	14.09.94
Parslow, Daniel	5.11	York	Rhymney Valley	11./09.85
Midfielders				
Dayton, James	5.8	Oldham	Enfield	12.12.88
Hall, Asa	6.1	Shrewsbury	Sandwell	29.11.86
Munns, Jack	5.6	Charlton	Dagenham	18.03.93
Pell, Harry	6.4	Eastleigh	Tilbury	21.10.91
Rowe, James	5.11	Tranmere	Oxford	21.10.91
Storer, Kyle	5.11	Wrexham	Nuneaton	30.04.87
Waters, Buill	5.9	Crewe	Epsom	15.10.94
Forwards				
Holman, Dan	5.11	Colchester	Northampton	05.06.90
Morgan-Smith, Amari	6.0	–	–	03.04.86
Wright, Danny	6.2	Kidderminster	Southampton	10.,09.84

COLCHESTER UNITED

Ground: Weston Homes Community Stadium, United Way, Colchester CO4 5HE
Telephone: 01206 755100. **Club nickname**: U's
Colours: Blue and white. **Capacity**: 10,105
Record attendance: Layer Road:19,072 v Reading (FA Cup 1) Nov 27, 1948; Community Stadium: 10,064 v Norwich (Lge 1) Jan 16, 2010

Goalkeepers				
Bransgrove, James	6.4	Brentford	Harlow	12.05.95
Walker, Sam	6.6	Chelsea	Gravesend	02.10.91
Defenders				
Briggs, Matthew	6.2	Millwall	Wandsworth	09.03.91
Brindley, Richard	5.11	Rotherham	Norwich	05.05.93
Eastman, Tom	6.3	Ipswich	Colchester	21.10.91
Elokobi, George	6.0	Oldham	Mamfe, Cam	31.01.86
Harney, Jamie	6.0	West Ham	Plumbridge	04.03.96
Kent, Frankie	6.2	–	Romford	21.11.95
O'Donoghue, Michael	5.11	Leyton Orient	Islington	18.01.96
Prosser, Luke	6.3	Southend	Enfield	28.05.88
Vincent-Young, Kane	5.11	Tottenham	Camden	15.03.96
Wynter, Alex	6.1	Crystal Palace	Croydon	16.09.93
Midfielders				
Curtis, Jack	5.7	–	–	11.09.95
Garvan, Owen	6.0	Crystal Palace	Dublin, Ire	29.01.88
Loft, Doug	6.0	Gillingham	Maidstone	25.12.86
Senior, Courtney	5.9	Brentford	Croydon	30.06.97
Slater, Craig	5.10	Kilmarnock	Glasgow	26.04.94
Szmodics, Sammie	5.7	–	Colchester	24.09.95
Wright, Drey	5.9	–	Greenwich	30.04.95
Forwards				
Bonne, Macauley	5.11	Ipswich	Ipswich	26.10.95
Dickenson, Brennan	6.0	Gillingham	Ferndown	26.02.93
Johnstone, Denny	6.2	Birmingham	Dumfries	09.01.95
Porter, Chris	6.1	Sheffield Utd	Wigan	12.12.83

CRAWLEY TOWN

Ground: Checkatrade Stadium, Winfield Way, Crawley RH11 9RX
Telephone: 01293 410000. **Club nickname:** Reds
Colours: Red. **Capacity:** 5,996
Record attendance: 5,880 v Reading (FA Cup 3) Jan 5, 2013

Goalkeepers				
Mersin, Yusuf	6.4	Kasimpasa	Greenwich	23.09.94
Morris, Glenn	6.0	Gillingham,	Woolwich	20.12.83
Defenders				
Connolly, Mark	6.1	Kilmarnock	Monaghan, Ire	16.12.91
McNerney, Joe	6.4	Woking	–	24.01.90
Oyebanjo, Lanre	6.1	York	Hackney	27.04.90
Yorwerth, Josh	6.0	Ipswich	Bridgend	28.02.95
Midfielders				
Arthur, Chris	5.10	Woking	Enfield	25.01.90
Banton, Jason	5.11	Notts Co	Tottenham	15.12.92
Bawling, Bobson	5.10	Watford	Islington	21.09.95
Boldewijn, Enzio	6.1	Almere City	Almere, Hol	17.11.92
Payne, Josh	6.0	Eastleigh	Basingstoke	25.11.90
Smith, Jimmy	6.1	Stevenage	Newham	07.01.87
Walton, Simon	6.1	Stevenage	Sherburn	13.09.87
Young, Lewis	5.9	Bury	Stevenage	27.09.89
Forwards				
Collins, James	6.2	Shrewsbury	Coventry	01.12.90
Harrold, Matt	6.1	Bristol Rov	Leyton	25.07.84

CREWE ALEXANDRA

Ground: Alexandra Stadium, Gresty Road, Crewe CW2 6EB
Telephone: 01270 213014. **Club nickname:** Railwaymen
Colours: Red and white. **Capacity:** 10,066
Record attendance: 20,000 v Tottenham (FA Cup 4) Jan 30, 1960

Goalkeepers				
Garratt, Ben	6.1	–	Shrewsbury	25.04.93
Richards, David	6.0	Bristol City	Abergavenny	31.12.93
Defenders				
Bakayogo, Zoumana	5.9	Leicester	Paris, Fr	11.08.86
Davis, Harry	6.2	–	Burnley	24.09.91
Guthrie, Jon	5.10	–	Devizes	29.07.92
Ng, Perry	5.11	–	Liverpool	27.04.96
Nugent, Ben	6.5	Cardiff	Street	28.11.93
Ray, George	6.0	–	Warrington	13.10.93
Midfielders				
Ainley, Callum	5.8	–	Middlewich	02.11.97
Bingham. Billy	5.11	Dagenham	Greenwich	15.07.90
Cooper, George	5.9	–	Warrington	02.11.96
Finney, Oliver	5.9	–	Stoke	15.12.97
Jones, James	5.9	–	Winsford	01.02.96
Kirk, Charlie	5.7	–	Winsford	24.12.97
Turton, Oliver	5.11	–	Manchester	06.12.92
Wintle, Ryan	5.6	Alsager	Newcastle-under-Lyme	13.06.97
Forwards				
Dagnall, Chris	5.8	Hibernian	Liverpool	15.04.86

Lowe, Ryan	5.11	Bury	Liverpool	18.09.78
Saunders, Callum	5.10	–	Istanbul, Tur	26.09.95
Udoh, Daniel	6.1	Ilkeston	Lagos, Nig	30.08.96

DONCASTER ROVERS

Ground: Keepmoat Stadium, Stadium Way, Doncaster DN4 5JW
Telephone: 01302 764664. **Club nickname**: Rovers
Colours: Red and white. **Capacity**: 15,231
Record attendance: Belle Vue: 37,149 v Hull (Div 3 N) Oct 2, 1948; Keepmoat Stadium: 15,001 v Leeds (Lge 1) Apr 1, 2008

Goalkeepers				
Etheridge, Ross	6.2	Accrington	–	04.09.94
Marosi, Marko	6.3	Wigan	Slovakia	23.10.93
Defenders				
Alcock, Craig	5.8	Sheffield Utd	Truro	08.12.87
Baudry, Mathieu	6.2	Leyton Orient	Le Havre, Fr	24.02.88
Butler, Andy	6.0	Sheffield Utd	Doncaster	04.11.83
Calder, Riccardo	6.0	Aston Villa	Birmingham	26.01.96
Evina, Cedric	5.9	Charlton	Cameroon	16.11.91
Garrett, Tyler	6.0	Bolton	Lincoln	26.10.96
Lund, Mitchell	6.1	–	Leeds	27.08.96
McCullough, Luke	6.1	Manchester Utd	Portadown	15.02.94
Wright, Joe	6.4	Huddersfield	Monk Fryston	26.02.95
Midfielders				
Blair, Matty	5.10	Mansfield	Warwick	30.11.87
Coppinger, James	5.7	Exeter	Middlesbrough	10.01.81
Keegan, Paul	5.7	Bohemians	Dublin, Ire	05.07.84
McSheffrey, Gary	5.8	Scunthorpe	Coventry	13.08.72
Middleton, Harry	5.11	–	Doncaster	12.04.95
Rowe, Tommy	5.11	Wolves	Manchester	01.05.89
Forwards				
Mandeville, Liam	5.11	–	Lincoln	17.02.97
Marquis, John	6.1	Millwall	Lewisham	16.05.92
Williams, Andy	5.10	Swindon	Hereford	14.08.86

EXETER CITY

Ground: St James Park, Stadium Way, Exeter EX4 6PX
Telephone: 01392 411243. **Club nickname**: Grecians
Colours: Red and white. **Capacity**: 8,830
Record attendance: 20,984 v Sunderland (FA Cup 6 replay) Mar 4, 1931

Goalkeepers				
Olejnik, Bobby	6.0	Peterborough	Vienna, Aut	26.11.86
Pym, Christy	5.11	–	Exeter	24.04.95
Defenders				
Archibald-Henville, Troy	6.2	Carlisle	Newham	04.11.88
Brown, Troy	6.1	Cheltenham	Croydon	17.09.90
Butterfield, Danny	5.9	Carlisle	Boston	21.11.79
McAllister, Jamie	5.10	Kerala	Glasgow	26.04.78
Moore-Taylor, Jordan	5.10	–	Exeter	21.01.94
Riley-Lowe, Connor	5.10	–	Paignton	10.01.96
Tillson, Jordan	6.0	Bristol Rov	Bath	05.03.93

Woodman, Craig	5.9	Brentford	Tiverton	22.12.82
Midfielders				
Davies, Arron	5.9	Northampton	Cardiff	22.06.84
Harley, Ryan	5.9	Swindon	Bristol	22.01.85
Holmes, Lee	5.9	Preston	Mansfield	02.04.87
James, Lloyd	5.11	Leyton Orient	Bristol	16.02.88
McCready, Tom	6.0	Morecambe	Chester	07.06.91
Taylor, Jake	5.10	Reading	Ascot	01.12.91
Wheeler, David	5.11	Staines	Brighton	04.10.90
Forwards				
Grant, Joel	6.0	Yeovil	Acton	26.08.87
McAlinden, Liam	6.1	Wolves	Cannock	26.09.93
Reid, Jamie	5.11	–	Torquay	12.07.94
Simpson, Robbie	6.1	Cambridge	Poole	15.03.85
Watkins, Ollie	5.10	–	Torbay	30.12.95

GRIMSBY TOWN

Ground: Blundell Park, Cleethorpes DN35 7PY
Telephone:01472 605050
Colours: Black and white: **Capacity**: 9,052
Record attendance: 31,651 v Wolves (FA Cup 5) 20 February, 1937

Goalkeepers				
McKeown, James	6.1	Peterborough	Birmingham	24.07.89
Warrington, Andy	6.3	Buxton	Sheffield	10.06.76
Defenders				
Andrew, Danny	5.11	Fleetwood	Holbeach	23.12.90
Boyce, Andrew	6.2	Scunthorpe	Doncaster	05.11.89
Gowling, Josh	6.3	Kidderminster	Coventry	29.11.83
Jones, Dan	6.0	Hartlepool	Bishop Auckland	14.12.94
Pearson, Shaun	6.0	Boston	York	28.04.89
Midfielders				
Berrett, James	5.10	York	Halifax	13.01.89
Bolarinwa, Tom	5.11	Sutton	Greenwich	21.01.90
Browne, Rhys	5.9	Aldershot	Romford	16.11.95
Chambers, Ashley	5.10	Dagenham	Leicester	01.03.90
Clifton, Harryy	5.11	–	Grimsby	12.06.98
Davies, Ben	5.7	Portsmouth	Birmingham	27.05.81
Disley, Craig	5.11	Shrewsbury	Worksop	24.08.81
McAllister, Sean	5.8	Scunthorpe	Bolton	15.08.87
Summerfield, Luke	6.0	York	Ivybridge	06.12.87
Venney, Josh	5.5	–	Grimsby	09.02.97
Vose, Dominic	5.8	Scunthorpe (loan)	Lambeth	23.11.93
Forwards				
Bogle, Omar	6.3	Solihull	Birmingham	26.07.92

HARTLEPOOL UNITED

Ground: Victoria Park, Clarence Road, Hartlepool TS24 8BZ
Telephone: 01429 272584. **Club nickname**: Pool
Colours: Blue and white. **Capacity**: 7,833
Record attendance: 17,426 v Manchester Utd (FA Cup 3) Jan 5, 1957

Goalkeepers				
Bartlett, Adam	6.0	Gateshead	Newcastle	27.02.86

Carson, Trevor	6.0	Cheltenham	Killyleagh	05.03.88
Defenders				
Bates, Matthew	5.10	Bradford	Stockton	10.12.86
Carroll, Jake	6.0	Huddersfield	Dublin, Ire	11.08.91
Green, Kieran	5.9	–	Stockton-on-Tees	30.06.97
Jones, Rob	6.7	Doncaster	Stockton-on-Tees	03.11.79
Magnay, Carl	6.1	Grimsby	Birtley	20.01.89
Nearney, Josh	5.11	–	Newcastle	07.09.95
Nsiala, Aristote	6.4	Grimsby	Kinshasa, DR Cong	25.03.92
Pollock, Ben	6.1	Newcastle	Bolton	06.01.98
Midfielders				
Blackford, Jack	5.10	–	Hartlepool	13.05.98
Deverdics, Nicky	5.11	Dover	Newcastle	24.11.87
Featherstone, Nicky	5.9	Harrogate	Goole	22.09.88
Hawkins, Lewis	5.10	–	Hartlepool	15.06.93
Laurent, Josh	6.2	Brentford	Leystonstone	06.05.95
Richards, Jordan	5.9	–	Sunderland	25.04.93
Smith, Connor	6.1	–	Stockton	14.10.96
Thomas, Nathan	5.10	Mansfield	Ingleby Barwick	27.09.94
Walker, Brad	6.1	–	Billingham	25.04.96
Woods, Michael	5.8	Harrogate	York	06.04.90
Forwards				
Alessandra, Lewis	5.10	Rochdale	Heywood	08.02.89
Amond, Padraig	5.11	Grimsby	Carlow, Ire	15.04.88
Bingham, Rakish	6.0	Mansfield	Newham	25.10.93
Oates, Rhys	6.2	Barnsley	Pontefract	04.12.94
Orrell, Jake	5.4	Chesterfield	Sunderland	17.07.97
Paynter, Billy	6.0	Carlisle	Liverpool	13.07.84

LEYTON ORIENT

Ground: Matchroom Stadium, Brisbane Road, London E10 5NE
Telephone: 0871 310 1881. **Club nickname**: O's
Colours: Red. **Capacity**: 9,271
Record attendance: 34,345 v West Ham (FA Cup 4) Jan 25, 1964

Goalkeepers				
Cisak, Alex	6.4	Burnley	Krakow, Pol	19.05.89
Grainger, Charlie	6.2	–	Enfield	31.07.96
Defenders				
Clohessy, Sean	5.11	Colchester	Croydon	12.12.86
Doherty, Josh	5.11	Watford	Newtonards	15.03.96
Dunne, Alan	5.10	Millwall	Dublin, Ire	23.08.82
Erichot, Yvan	6.2	Sint-Truiden	Chambray-les-Tours, Fr	25.03.90
Hunt, Nicky	6.1	Mansfield	Westhoughton	03.09.83
Kennedy, Callum	6.1	Wimbledon	Chertsey	09.11.89
Parkes, Tom	6.3	Bristol Rov	Mansfield	15.01.92
Midfielders				
Atangana, Nigel	6.2	Portsmouth	Corbeil-Essonnes, Fr	09.09.89
Cox, Dean	5.4	Brighton	Haywards Heath	12.08.87
Kashket, Scott	5.9	Wingate	Chigwell	25.02.96
Kelly, Liam	5.10	Oldham	Milton Keynes	10.02.90
Moore, Sammy	5.8	Wimbledon	Deal	07.09.87
Moncur, Freddy	5.9	–	Harlow	08.09.96
Semedo, Sandro	5.9	Colchester	Portugal	03.12.96

Weir, Robbie	5.9	Burton	Belfast	09.12.88
Forwards				
Adeboyejo, Victor	6.1	–	Ibadara, Nig	12.01.98
Bowery, Jordan	6.1	Oxford	Nottingham	02.07.91
Gnanduillet, Armand	6.3	Chesterfield	Angers, Fr	13.02.92
Massey, Gavin	5.10	Colchester	Watford	14.10.92
McCallum, Paul	6.3	West Ham	Streatham	28.07.93
Palmer, Ollie	6.2	Mansfield	Epsom	21.01.92
Simpson, Jay	5.11	Buriram	Enfield	01.12.88

LUTON TOWN

Ground: Kenilworth Stadium, Maple Road, Luton LU4 8AW
Telephone: 01582 411622. **Club nickname**: Hatters
Colours: Orange and black. **Capacity**: 10,226
Record attendance: 30,069 v Blackpool (FA Cup 6) Mar 4, 1959

Goalkeepers				
Walton Christian	6.0	Brighton (loan)	Wadebridge	09.11.95
Defenders				
Cuthbert, Scott	6.2	Leyton Orient	Alexandria, Sco	15.06.87
Mullins, Johnny	5.11	Oxford	Hampstead	06.11.85
Musonda, Frankie	6.0	–	Bedford	12.12.97
O'Donnell, Stephen	6.0	Partick	Aberdeen	11.05.92
Potts, Dan	5.8	West Ham	Romford	13.04.94
Rea, Glen	6.1	Brighton	Brighton	03.09.94
Sheehan, Alan	5.11	Bradford	Athlone, Ire	14.09.86
Midfielders				
Doyle, Nathan	5.11	Bradford	Derby	12.01.87
Green, Danny	6.0	MK Dons	Harlow	09.07.88
Lee, Olly	6.0	Birmingham	Hornchurch	11.07.91
McGeehan, Cameron	5.11	Norwich	Kingston	06.04.95
Ruddock, Pelly	5.9	West Ham	Hendon	17.07.93
Smith, Jonathan	6.3	York	Preston	17.10.86
Forwards				
Banton, Zane	5.6	–	Stevenage	06.09.96
Cook, Jordan	5.9	Walsall	Sunderland	20.03.90
Hylton, Danny	6.0	Oxford	Camden	25.02.89
Mackail-Smith, Craig	5.10	Brighton	Watford	25.02.84
Marriott, Jack	5.9	Ipswich	Beverley	09.09.84
McQuoid, Josh	5.10	Bournemouth	Southampton	15.12.89

MANSFIELD TOWN

Ground: One Call Stadium, Quarry Lane, Mansfield NG18 5DA
Telephone: 01623 482482. **Club nickname**: Stags
Colours: Amber and blue. **Capacity**: 10,000
Record attendance: 24,467 v Nottm Forest (FA Cup 3) Jan 10, 1953

Goalkeepers				
Jensen, Brian	6.1	Crawley	Copenhagen, Den	08.06.75
Shearer, Scott	6.3	Crewe	Glasgow	15.02.81
Defenders				
Bennett, Rhys	6.3	Rochdale	Manchester	01.09.91
Benning, Malvind	5.10	Walsall	Sandwell	02.11.93

Collins, Lee	5.11	Northampton	Telford	28.09.88
Pearce, Krystian	6.2	Torquay	Birmingham	05.01.90
Shires, Corbin	6.3	Hallam	Sheffield	31.12.97
Taft, George	6.3	Burton	Leicester	29.07.93
Midfielders				
Baxendale, James	5.8	Walsall	Thorne	16.09.92
Chapman, Adam	5.10	Newport	Doncaster	29.11.89
Clements, Chris	5.9	Hednesford	Birmingham	06.02.90
Hakeem, Zayn	5.10	Nottm Forest	–	15.02.99
Hamilton CJ	5.7	Sheffield Utd	Harrow	23.03.95
Hurst, Kevan	5.11	Southend	Chesterfield	27.08.85
McGuire, Jamie	5.7	Fleetwood	Birkenhead	13.11.83
Rose, Mitchell	5.9	Rotherham	Doncaster	04.07.94
Thomas, Jack	5.9	–	Sutton-in-Ashfield	03.06.96
Forwards				
Green, Matt	6.0	Birmingham	Bath	02.01.87
Hemmings, Ashley	5.8	Dagenham	Wolverhampton	03.03.91
Hoban, Pat	5.11	Oxford	Galway, Ire	28.07.91
Rose, Danny	5.10	Bury	Barnsley	10.12.93
Yussuf, Adi	6.1	Oxford City	Zanzibar, Tanz	20.02.92

MORECAMBE

Ground: Globe Arena, Christie Way, Westgate, Morecambe LA4 4TB
Telephone: 01524 411797. **Club nickname**: Shrimps
Colours: Red and white. **Capacity**: 6,476
Record attendance: Christie Park: 9,234 v Weymouth (FA Cup 3) Jan 6, 1962. Globe Arena: 5,003 v Burnley (League Cup 2) Aug 24, 2010

Goalkeepers				
Roche, Barry	6.4	Chesterfield	Dublin, Ire	06.04.82
Defenders				
Conlan, Luke	5.11	Burnley	Portaferry	31.10.94
Edwards, Ryan	5.11	Blackburn	Liverpool	07.10.93
McGowan, Aaron	5.9	–	Kirkby	24.07.96
Molyneux, Lee	6.1	Tranmere	Huyton	24.02.89
Murphy, Peter	6.0	Wycombe	Liverpool	13.02.90
Wakefield, Liam	5.10	Accrington	Doncaster	09.04.94
Winnard, Dean	5.9	Accrington	Wigan	20.08.89
Midfielders				
Ellison, Kevin	6.0	Rotherham	Liverpool	23.02.79
Fleming, Andy	5.11	Wrexham	Liverpool	05.10.87
Kenyon, Alex	6.0	Stockport	Euxton	17.07.92
Wildig, Aaron	5.9	Shrewsbury	Hereford	15.04.92
Forwards				
Barkhuizen, Tom	5.11	Blackpool	Blackpool	04.07.93
Mullin, Paul	5.10	Huddersfield	Liverpool	06.11.94
Turner, Rhys	5.11	Oldham	Preston	22.07.95

NEWPORT COUNTY

Ground: Rodney Parade, Newport NP19 OUU
Telephone: 01633 670690. **Club nickname**: Exiles
Colours: Amber and black. **Capacity**: 7,012
Record attendance: Somerton Park: 24,268 v Cardiff (Div 3S) Oct 16, 1937. Rodney Parade: 6,615 v Grimsby (Conf play-off semi-finals 2nd leg) Apr 28, 2013

Goalkeepers				
Bittner, James	6.1	Plymouth	Devizes	02.02.82
Day, Joe	6.0	Peterborough	Brighton	13.08.90
Defenders				
Bamford, Lewis	5.10	–	Newport	23.11.97
Barnum-Bobb, Jazzi	5.11	Cardiff	Enfield	15.09.95
Bennett, Scott	5.10	Notts Co	Newquay	30.11.90
Butler, Dan	5.9	Torquay	Cowes	26.08.94
Jones, Darren	6.1	Forest Green	Newport	28.08.83
Parselle, Kieran	6.0	–	Bristol	01.12.96
Randall, Mark	6.0	Barnet	Milton Keynes	28.09.89
Turley, Jamie	6.1	Eastleigh	Reading	07.04.90
Midfielders				
Compton, Jack	5.11	Yeovil	Torquay	02.09.88
Jones, Dafydd	5.7	–	Abergavenny	05.06.98
Labadie, Joss	6.3	Dagenham	Croydon	30.08.90
Myrie-Williams, Jennison	6.0	Sligo	Lambeth	17.05.88
Rigg, Sean	5.9	Wimbledon	Bristol	01.10.88
Tozer, Ben	6.1	Yeovil	Plymouth	01.03.90
Forwards				
John-Lewis, Lenell	5.10	Grimsby	Hammersmith	17.05.89
Owen-Evans, Tom	5.11	–	Bristol	18.03.97

NOTTS COUNTY

Ground: Meadow Lane, Nottingham NG2 3HJ
Telephone: 0115 952 9000. **Club nickname**: Magpies
Colours: White and black. **Capacity**: 20,300
Record attendance: 47,310 v York (FA Cup 6) Mar 12, 1955

Goalkeepers				
Collin, Adam	6.1	Rotherham	Carlisle	09.12.84
Loach, Scott	6.2	Rotherham	Nottingham	14.10.79
Defenders				
Amevor, Mawouna	6.3	Go Ahead	Rotterdam, Hol	16.12.91
Audel, Thierry	6.2	Macclesfield	Nice, Fr	15.01.87
Dickinson, Carl	6.1	Port Vale	Swadlincote	31.03.8
Duffy, Richard	5.11	Port Vale	Swansea	30.08.85
Hewitt, Elliott	5.11	Ipswich	Bodelwyddan	30.05.94
Hollis, Haydn	6.4	–	Selston	14.10.92
Sharpe, Rhys	5.10	Derby	Nottingham	17.10.94
Tootle, Matt	5.9	Shrewsbury	Knowsley	11.10.90
Midfielders				
Aborah, Stanley	5.7	Ferencvaros	Kumasi, Gh	23.06.87
Milsom, Rob	5.10	Rotherham	Redhill	02.01.87
O'Connor, Michael	6.1	Port Vale	Belfast	06.10.87
Rodman, Alex	6.2	Newport	Sutton Coldfield	15.12.87
Smith, Alan	5.10	MK Dons	Rothwell	28.10.80
Snijders, Genaro	5.7	FC Oss	Amsterdam, Hol	29.07.89
Thompson, Curtis	5.7	–	Nottingham	02.09.93
Forwards				
Burke, Graham	5.11	Aston Villa	Dublin, Ire	21.09.93
Campbell, Adam	5.9	Newcastle	North Shields	01.01.95
Forte, Jonathan	6.0	Oldham	Sheffield	25.07.86
McLeod, Izale	6.0	Crawley	Birmingham	15.10.84

Murray, Ronan	5.8	Ipswich	Mayo, Ire	12.09.91
Stead, Jon	6.3	Huddersfield	Huddersfield	07.04.83

PLYMOUTH ARGYLE

Ground: Home Park, Plymouth PL2 3DQ
Telephone: 01752 562561. **Club nickname**: Pilgrims
Colours: Green and white. **Capacity**: 16,906
Record attendance: 43,596 v Aston Villa (Div 2) Oct 10, 1936

Goalkeepers				
Dorel, Vincent	6.3	Le Poire	Rennes	21.03.92
McCormick, Luke	6.0	Oxford	Coventry	15.08.83
Defenders				
Bradley, Sonny	6.4	Crawley	Hull	13.09.91
Bulvitis, Nauris	6.3	Spartaks Jurmala	Riga, Lat	15.03.87
Miller, Gary	6.0	Partick	Glasgow	15.04.87
Osborne, Karleigh	6.2	Bristol City	Southall	19.03.88
Purrington, Ben	5.9	–	Exeter	05.05.96
Songo'o, Yann	6.2	Blackburn	Yaounde, Cam	19.11.91
Sawyer, Gary	6.0	Leyton Orient	Bideford	05.07.85
Threlkeld, Oscar	6.0	Bolton	Bolton	15.12.94
Midfielders				
Carey, Graham	6.0	Ross Co	Dublin, Ire	02.05.89
Donaldson, Ryan	5.9	Cambridge	Newcastle	01.05.91
Smith, Connor	5.11	Wimbledon	Mullingar, Ire	18.02.93
Forwards				
Brunt, Ryan	6.1	Bristol Rov	Birmingham	26.05.93
Goodwillie, David	5.10	Aberdeen	Stirling	28.03.89
Harvey, Tyler	6.1	–	Plymouth	29.06.95
Jervis, Jake	6.3	Ross Co	Birmingham	17.09.91
Rooney, Louis	6.0	–	Plymouth	28.09.96
Slew, Jordan	6.3	Chesterfield	Sheffield	07.09.92
Spencer, Jimmy	6.1	Cambridge	Leeds	13.12.91

PORTSMOUTH

Ground: Fratton Park, Frogmore Road, Portsmouth, PO4 8RA
Telephone: 0239 273 1204. **Club nickname**: Pompey
Colours: Blue and white. **Capacity**: 20,700
Record attendance: 51,385 v Derby (FA Cup 6) Feb 26, 1949

Goalkeepers				
Jones, Paul	6.3	Crawley	Maidstone	28.06.86
Defenders				
Burgess. Christian	6.5	Peterborough	Barking	07.10.91
Clarke, Matt	5.11	Ipswich	Ipswich	22.09.96
Haunstrup, Brandon	5.8	–	Waterlooville	26.10.96
Stevens, Enda	6.0	Aston Villa	Dublin, Ire	09.07.90
Whatmough, Jack	6.0	–	Gosport	19.08.96
Midfielders				
Baker, Carl	6.2	MK Dons	Whiston	26.12.82
Barton, Adam	5.11	Coventry	Blackburn	07.01.91
Bennett, Kyle	5.5	Doncaster	Telford	09.09.90
Evans, Gareth	6.0	Fleetwood	Macclesfield	26.04.88

Close, Ben	5.9	–	Portsmouth	08.08.96
Doyle, Michael	5.10	Sheffield Utd	Dublin, Ire	08.07.81
Naismith, Kal	6.1	Accrington	Glasgow	18.02.92
Roberts, Gary	5.10	Chesterfield	Chester	18.03.84
Rose, Danny	5.8	Northampton	Bristol	21.02.88
Talbot, Drew	5.10	Chesterfield	Barnsley	19.07.86
Tollitt, Ben	6.0	Skelmersdale	Liverpool	30.11.94
Forwards				
Chaplin, Conor	5.10	–	Worthing	16.02.97
Lalkovic, Milan	5.10	Walsall	Kosice, Slovak	09.12.92
Main, Curtis	5.10	Doncaster	South Shields	20.06.92
McGurk, Adam	5.10	Burton	St Helier	24.01.89
Smith, Michael	6.4	Swindon	Wallsend	17.10.91

STEVENAGE

Ground: Lamex Stadium, Broadhall Way, Stevenage SG2 8RH
Telephone: 01438 223223. **Club nickname**: Boro
Colours: White and red. **Capacity**: 6,920
Record attendance: 8,040 v Newcastle (FA Cup 4) January 25, 1998

Goalkeepers				
Day, Chris	6.2	Millwall	Walthamstow	28.07.75
Jones, Jamie	6.2	Preston	Kirkby	18.02.89
Defenders				
Fox, Andrew	5.11	Peterborough	Swavesey	15.01.93
Franks, Fraser	6.0	Luton	Hammersmith	22.11.90
Henry, Ronnie	5.11	Luton	Hemel Hempstead	02.01.84
Johnson, Ryan	6.2	–	Birmingham	02.10.96
Wells, Dean	6.1	Braintree	Isleworth	25.05.85
Wilkinson, Luke	6.2	Luton	Wells	02.12.91
Midfielders				
Casey, George	6.0	–	Enfield	08.09.97
Conlon, Tom	5.9	Peterborough	Stoke	03.02.96
Gorman, Dale	5.11	–	Letterkenny, Ire	28.06.96
Lee, Charlie	5.11	Gillingham	Whitechapel	05.01.87
Pett, Tom	5.8	Wealdstone	Hatfield	03.12.91
Schumacher, Steven	6.0	Fleetwood	Liverpool	30.04.84
Tonge, Michael	6.0	Leeds	Manchester	07.04.83
Forwards				
Godden, Matt	6.1	Ebbsfleet	Canterbury	29.07.91
Hyde, Jake	6.1	York	Maidenhead	01.07.90
Kennedy, Ben	5.10	–	Northern Ireland	12.01.97
Liburd, Rowan	6.3	Reading	Croydon	28.08.92

WYCOMBE WANDERERS

Ground: Adams Park, Hillbottom Road, High Wycombe HP12 4HJ
Telephone: 01494 472100. **Club nickname**: Chairboys
Colours: Light and dark blue. **Capacity**: 10,300
Record attendance: 10,000 v Chelsea (friendly) July 13, 2005

Goalkeepers				
Defenders				
Harriman, Michael	5.6	QPR	Chichester	23.10.92
Jacobson, Joe	5.11	Shrewsbury	Cardiff	17.11.86

Jombati, Sido	6.1	Cheltenham	Lisbon, Por	20.08.87
Pierre, Aaron	6.1	Brentford	Souhall	17.02.93
Rowe, Danny	6.2	Rotherham	Middlesbrough	24.10.95
Stewart, Anthony	6.0	Crewe	Lambeth	18.09.92
Midfielders				
Bean, Marcus	5.11	Colchester	Hammersmith	02.11.84
Bloomfield, Matt	5.8	Ipswich	Felixstowe	08.02.84
Cowan-Hall, Paris	5.8	Millwall (loan)	Hillingdon	05.10.90
McGinn, Stephen	5.10	Dundee	Glasgow	02.12.88
O'Nien, Luke	5.9	Watford	Hemel Hempstead	21.11.94
Wood, Sam	6.0	Brentford	Bexley	09.08.86
Forwards				
Akinfenwa, Adebayo	6.0	Wimbledon	Islington	10.05.82
Hayes, Paul	6.0	Scunthorpe	Dagenham	20.09.83
Southwell, Dayle	5.11	Boston	Grimsby	20.10.93
Thompson, Garry	5.11	Notts Co	Kendal	24.11.80
Weston, Myles	5.11	Southend	Lewisham	12.03.88

YEOVIL TOWN

Ground: Huish Park, Lufton Way, Yeovil BA22 8YF
Telephone: 01935 423662. **Club nickname**: Glovers
Colours: Green and white. **Capacity**: 9,665
Record attendance: 9,527 v Leeds (Lge 1) Apr 25, 2008

Goalkeepers				
Krysiak, Artur	6.4	Exeter	Lodz, Pol	11.08.89
Maddison, Jonny	6.1	Leicester	Chester-le-Street	04.09.94
Defenders				
Dickson, Ryan	5.10	Crawley	Saltash	14.12.86
Lacey, Alex	6.0	Luton	Milton Keynes	31.05.93
Shephard, Liam	5.10	Swansea (loan)	Pentre	22.11.94
Smith, Nathan	6.0	Chesterfield	Enfield	11.01.87
Sowunmi, Omar	6.6	Ipswich	Colchester	07.11.95
Ward, Darren	6.3	Swindon	Kenton	13.09.78
Midfielders				
Bassett, Ollie	5.8	–	Packington	06.03.98
Dawson, Kevin	5.11	Shelbourne	Dublin, Ire	30.06.90
Dolan, Matt	5.9	Bradford	Hartlepool	11.02.93
Khan, Otis	5.9	Barnsley	Ashton-under-Lyne	05.09.95
Forwards				
Bird, Ryan	6.4	Cambridge	Slough	15.11.87
Eaves, Tom	6.4	Bolton	Liverpool	14.01.92
Zoko, Francois	6.0	Blackpool	Daloa, Iv C	13.09.83

SCOTTISH PREMIERSHIP SQUADS 2016–17

(at time of going to press)

ABERDEEN

Ground: Pittodrie Stadium, Pittodrie Street, Aberdeen AB24 5QH. **Capacity**: 22,199. **Telephone**: 01224 650400. **Manager**: Derek McInnes. **Colours**: Red and white. **Nickname**: Dons

Goalkeepers: Neal Alexander, Aaron Lennox, Joe Lewis, Danny Rogers

Defenders: Andrew Considine, Daniel Harvie, Shaleum Logan, Scott McKenna, Callum Morris, Anthony O'Connor, Mark Reynolds, Graeme Shinnie, Ash Taylor

Midfielders: Jonny Hayes, Ryan Jack, Niall McGinn, Kenny McLean, Peter Pawlett, Frank Ross, Craig Storie

Forwards: Wes Burns (loan), Joe Nuttall, Adam Rooney, Lawrence Shankland, Cameron Smith, Miles Storey, Jayden Stockley, Scott Wright

CELTIC

Ground: Celtic Park, Glasgow G40 3RE. **Capacity**: 60,832. **Telephone**: 0871 226 1888. **Manager**: Brendan Rodgers. **Colours**: Green and white. **Nickname**: Bhoys

Goalkeepers: Logan Bailly, Craig Gordon, Leonardo Fasan

Defenders: Efe Ambrose, Dedryck Boyata, Darnell Fisher, Emilio Izaguirre, Saidy Janko, Mikael Lustig, Charlie Mulgrew, Eoghan O'Connell, Tony Ralston, Jozo Simunovic, Erik Sviatchenko, Kieran Tierney

Midfielders: Kristoffer Ajer, Scott Allan, Stuart Armstrong, Nir Biton, Scott Brown, Kris Commons, Ryan Christie, James Forrest, Liam Henderson, Stefan Johansen, Callum McGregor, Gary Mackay-Steven, Tom Rogic, Joe Thomson

Forwards: Jack Aitchison, Nadir Ciftci, Moussa Dembele, Leigh Griffiths, Aidan Nesbitt, Patrick Roberts (loan)

DUNDEE

Ground: Dens Park, Sandeman Street, Dundee DD3 7JY. **Capacity**: 11,850. **Telephone**: 01382. 889966. **Manager**: Paul Hartley. **Colours**: Blue and white. **Nickname**: Dark Blues

Goalkeepers: Scott Bain, Kyle Gourlay, David Mitchell

Defenders: Matty Allan, Andrew Black, Sam, Dryden, Julen Etxabeguren, Kostadin Gadzhalov, Kevin Holt, Cammy Kerr, Darren O'Dea, Mark O'Hara, James McPake

Midfielders: Calvin Colquhoun, Jesse Curran, Gary Harkins, Nicky Low, Paul McGowan, Nick Ross, James Vincent, Danny Williams

Forwards: Kane Hemmings, Rory Loy, Josh Skelly, Greg Stewart, Yordi Teijsse, Craig Wighton

HAMILTON ACADEMICAL

Ground: New Douglas Park, Hamilton ML3 OFT. **Capacity**: 6,000. **Telephone**: 01698 368652. **Manager**: Martin Canning. **Colours**: Red and white. **Nickname**: Accies

Goalkeepers: Alan Martin, Michael McGovern

Defenders: Jack Breslin, Martin Canning, Michael Devlin, Antons Kurakins, Lucas, Jordan McGregor, Scott McMann, Jesus Garcia Tena

Midfielders: Steven Boyd, Ali Crawford, Greg Docherty, Grant Gillespie, Doug Imrie, Gramoz Kurtaj, Darren Lyon, Louis Longridge, Danny Redmond, Ryan Tierney, Craig Watson

Forwards: Eamonn Brophy, Ross Cunningham, Alex D'Acol, Darian MacKinnon

HEART OF MIDLOTHIAN

Ground: Tynecastle Stadium, McLeod Street Edinburgh EH11 2NL. **Capacity**: 18,008. **Telephone**: 0871 663 1874. **Manager**: Robbie Neilson. **Colours**: Maroon and white. **Nickname**:

Jam Tarts
Goalkeepers: Paul Gallacher, Jack Hamilton, Viktor Noring
Defenders: Juwon Oshaniway, Alim Ozturk, Callum Paterson, Faycal Rherras, Igor Rossi, Liam Smith, John Souttar
Midfielders: Angus Beith, Prince Buaben, Arnaud Djoum, Don Cowie, Billy King, Perry Kitchen, Russell McLean, Callumn Morrison, Sam Nicholson, Jamie Walker
Forwards: Robbie Buchanan, Juanma Delgado, Soufian Robbie Muirhead, Alistair Roy, Conor Sammon, Nikolay Todorov, Dario Zanatta

INVERNESS CALEDONIAN THISTLE

Ground: Tulloch Caledonian Stadium, Stadium Road, Inverness IV1 1FF. **Capacity**: 7,711. **Telephone**: 01463 222880. **Manager**: Richie Foran. **Colours**: Blue and red. **Nickname**: Caley Thistle
Goalkeepers: Ryan Esson, Owain Fon Williams, Cameron Mackay
Defenders: Kevin McNaughton, Josh Meekings, David Raven, Carl Tremarco, Gary Warren
Midfielders: Jason Brown, Aaron Doran, Ross Draper, Lewis Horner, Billy King (loan), Jake Mulraney, Liam Polworth, Greg Tansey, Iain Vigurs
Forwards: Scott Boden, Alex Fisher, Alasdair Sutherland

KILMARNOCK

Ground: Rugby Park, Kilmarnock KA 1 2DP. **Capacity**: 18,128. **Telephone**: 01563 545300. **Manager**: Lee Clark. **Colours**: Blue and white. **Nickname**: Killie
Goalkeepers: Jamie MacDonald, Devlin MacKay, Oliver Davies (loan)
Defenders: Miles Addison, William Boyle (loan), Jonathan Burn (loan), Jamie Coburn, Steven Smith, Mark Waddington (loan), Johua Webb
Midfielders: Gary Dicker, Adam Frizzell, Jordan Jones, Callum McFadzean, Martin Smith, Greg Taylor
Forwards: Flo Bojaj, Kris Boyd, Souleymane Coulibaly, Greg Kiltie, Josh Magennis, Rory McKenzie

MOTHERWELL

Ground: Fir Park, Firpark Street, Motherwell ML1 2QN. **Capacity**: 13,742. **Telephone**: 01698 333333. **Manager**: Mark McGhee. **Colours**: Claret and amber. **Nickname**: Well
Goalkeepers: Dean Brill, Peter Morrison, Craig Samson
Defenders: Joe Chalmers, David Ferguson, Steven Hammell, Ben Heneghan, Kieran Kennedy, Louis Laing, Adam Livingstone, Barry Maguire, Stephen McManus, Jack McMillan, Josh Stachini, Richard Tait, Luke Watt
Midfielders: Lionel Ainsworth, Jordan Armstrong, Chris Cadden, Jake Hastie, Marvin Johnson, Keith Lasley, Ross MacLean, Josh Moore, Dom Thomas, David Turnbull
Forwards: Jacob Blyth, Dylan Falconer, Dylan Mackin, Scott McDonald, Craig Moore, Louis Moult, James Scott, Ryan Watters

PARTICK THISTLE

Ground: Firhill Stadium, Firhill Road, Glasgow G20 7BA. **Capacity**: 13,079. **Telephone**: 0141 579 1971. **Manager**: Alan Archibald. **Colours**: Yellow, red and black. **Nickname**: Jags
Goalkeepers: Tomas Cerny, Ryan Scully
Defenders: Callum Booth, Mustapha Dumbuya, Daniel Devine, Ziggy Gordon, Lee Hodson, Liam Lindsay, Michael McMullin, James Penrice, David Syme
Midfielders: David Amoo, Stuart Bannigan, Ryan Edwards, Chris Erskine, Gary Fraser, Steve Lawless, Declan McDaid, Abdul Osman, Sean Welsh, David Wilson
Forwards: Ade Azeez, Kris Doolan, Christie Elliott, Kevin Nisbet, Mathias Pogba

RANGERS

Ground: Ibrox Park, Edmison Drive, Glasgow G51 2XD. **Capacity**: 50,411
Telephone: 0871 702 1972. **Manager**: Mark Warburton. **Colours**: Blue. **Nickname**: Gers
Goalkeepers: Wes Foderingham, Matt Gilks, Rob McCrorie
Defenders: Matt Crooks, Clint Hill, Lee Hodson, Rob Kiernan, Ross McCrorie, James Tavernier, Lee Wallace, Danny Wilson
Midfielders: Joey Barton, Matt Crooks, Harry Forrester, Andy Halliday, Jason Holt, Niko Kranjcar, Jordan Rossiter,Jordan Thompson, Tom Walsh
Forwards: Ryan Hardie, Barrie McKay, Kenny Miller, Michael O'Halloran, Martin Waghorn, Josh Windass

ROSS COUNTY

Ground: Global Energy Stadium, Victoria Park, Jubilee Road, Dingwall IV15 9QZ. **Capacity**: 6,541. **Telephone**: 01349 860860. **Manager**: Jim McIntyre. **Colours**: Blue. **Nickname**: Staggies
Goalkeepers: Scott Fox, Aaron McCarey
Defenders: Scott Boyd, Erik Cikos, Andrew Davies, Richard Foster, Marcus Fraser, Jay McEveley, Paul Quinn, Chris Robertson, Christopher Routis, Kenny van der Weg
Midfielders: Tony Dingwall, Jonathan Franks, Ian McShane, Martin Woods
Forwards: Liam Boyce, Craig Curran, Michael Gardyne, Brian Graham, Kyle Macleod, Alex Schalk

ST JOHNSTONE

Ground: McDiarmid Park, Crieff Road, Perth PH1 2SJ. **Capacity**: 10,673. **Telephone**: 01738 459090. **Manager**: Tommy Wright. **Colours**: Blue and white. **Nickname**: Saints
Goalkeepers: Zander Clark, Mark Hurst, Alan Mannus
Defenders: Steven Anderson, Brian Easton, Liam Gordon, Dave MacKay, Brad McKay, Tom Scobbie, Joe Shaughnessy, Keith Watson
Midfielders: Blair Alston, Liam Craig, Murray Davidson, Greg Hurst, Eoghan McCawl, Chris Millar, Paul Paton, Danny Swanson, Craig Thomson, David Wotherspoon
Forwards: Michael Coulson, Graham Cummins, Ally Gilchrist, George Hunter, Chris Kane, Steven MacLean, Connor McLaren

ENGLISH FIXTURES 2016–2017

Premier League and Football League

Friday, 5 August

Championship

Fulham v Newcastle

Saturday, 6 August

Championship

Birmingham v Cardiff
Blackburn v Norwich
Bristol City v Wigan
Derby v Brighton
Huddersfield v Brentford
Ipswich v Barnsley
Nottm Forest v Burton
Reading v Preston
Rotherham v Wolves

League One

Bolton v Sheff Utd
Bradford v Port Vale
Bury v Charlton
Millwall v Oldham
Northampton v Fleetwood
Oxford v Chesterfield
Rochdale v Peterborough
Scunthorpe v Bristol Rov
Shrewsbury v MK Dons
Southend v Gillingham
Swindon v Coventry
Walsall v AFC Wimbledon

League Two

Accrington v Doncaster
Blackpool v Exeter
Cambridge v Barnet
Cheltenham v Leyton Orient
Crawley v Wycombe
Grimsby v Morecambe
Hartlepool v Colchester
Newport v Mansfield
Plymouth v Luton
Portsmouth v Carlisle
Stevenage v Crewe
Yeovil v Notts Co

Sunday, 7 August

Championship

QPR v Leeds
Sheff Wed v Aston Villa

Friday, 12 August

Championship

Brighton v Nottm Forest

Saturday, 13 August

Premier League

Burnley v Swansea
C Palace v WBA
Everton v Tottenham
Hull v Leicester
Man City v Sunderland
Middlesbrough v Stoke
Southampton v Watford

Championship

Aston Villa v Rotherham
Barnsley v Derby
Brentford v Ipswich
Burton v Bristol City
Leeds v Birmingham
Newcastle v Huddersfield
Norwich v Sheff Wed
Preston v Fulham
Wigan v Blackburn
Wolves v Reading

League One

AFC Wimbledon v Bolton
Charlton v Northampton
Chesterfield v Swindon
Coventry v Shrewsbury
Fleetwood v Scunthorpe
Gillingham v Bury
MK Dons v Millwall
Oldham v Walsall
Peterborough v Bradford
Port Vale v Southend
Sheff Utd v Rochdale

League Two

Barnet v Accrington
Carlisle v Plymouth
Colchester v Cambridge
Crewe v Portsmouth
Doncaster v Crawley
Exeter v Hartlepool
Leyton Orient v Newport
Luton v Yeovil
Mansfield v Cheltenham
Morecambe v Blackpool
Notts Co v Stevenage
Wycombe v Grimsby

Sunday, 14 August

Premier League

Arsenal v Liverpool
Bournemouth v Man Utd

Championship

Cardiff v QPR

League One

Bristol Rov v Oxford

Monday, 15 August

Premier League

Chelsea v West Ham

Tuesday, 16 August

Championship

Aston Villa v Huddersfield
Brentford v Nottm Forest
Brighton v Rotherham
Burton v Sheff Wed
Leeds v Fulham
Norwich v Bristol City
Preston v Derby
Wigan v Birmingham
Wolves v Ipswich

League One

AFC Wimbledon v Scunthorpe
Charlton v Shrewsbury
Chesterfield v Walsall
Coventry v Bury
Gillingham v Swindon
MK Dons v Bradford
Oldham v Northampton
Peterborough v Millwall
Port Vale v Rochdale
Sheff Utd v Southend

League Two

Barnet v Blackpool
Carlisle v Cheltenham
Colchester v Grimsby
Crewe v Hartlepool
Doncaster v Cambridge
Exeter v Crawley
Leyton Orient v Stevenage
Luton v Newport
Mansfield v Yeovil
Morecambe v Portsmouth
Notts Co v Plymouth
Wycombe v Accrington

Wednesday, 17 August

Championship
Barnsley v QPR
Cardiff v Blackburn
Newcastle v Reading

League One
Bristol Rov v Bolton
Fleetwood v Oxford

Friday, 19 August

Premier League
Man Utd v Southampton

Saturday, 20 August

Premier League
Burnley v Liverpool
Leicester v Arsenal
Stoke v Man City
Swansea v Hull
Tottenham v C Palace
Watford v Chelsea
WBA v Everton

Championship
Birmingham v Wolves
Blackburn v Burton
Bristol City v Newcastle
Derby v Aston Villa
Fulham v Cardiff
Huddersfield v Barnsley
Nottm Forest v Wigan
QPR v Preston
Reading v Brighton
Rotherham v Brentford
Sheff Wed v Leeds

League One
Bolton v Fleetwood
Bradford v Coventry
Bury v Oldham
Millwall v Sheff Utd
Northampton v AFC Wimbledon
Oxford v Peterborough
Rochdale v MK Dons
Scunthorpe v Gillingham
Shrewsbury v Chesterfield
Southend v Bristol Rov
Swindon v Port Vale
Walsall v Charlton

League Two
Accrington v Exeter
Blackpool v Wycombe
Cambridge v Carlisle
Cheltenham v Doncaster
Crawley v Barnet
Grimsby v Leyton Orient
Hartlepool v Notts Co
Newport v Crewe
Plymouth v Mansfield
Portsmouth v Colchester
Stevenage v Luton
Yeovil v Morecambe

Sunday, 21 August

Premier League
Sunderland v Middlesbrough
West Ham v Bournemouth

Championship
Ipswich v Norwich

Friday, 26 August

Championship
Burton v Derby

Saturday, 27 August

Premier League
Chelsea v Burnley
C Palace v Bournemouth
Everton v Stoke
Hull v Man Utd
Leicester v Swansea
Southampton v Sunderland
Tottenham v Liverpool
Watford v Arsenal

Championship
Barnsley v Rotherham
Birmingham v Norwich
Blackburn v Fulham
Brentford v Sheff Wed
Bristol City v Aston Villa
Cardiff v Reading
Huddersfield v Wolves
Ipswich v Preston
Newcastle v Brighton
Nottm Forest v Leeds
Wigan v QPR

League One
Bradford v Oldham
Charlton v Bolton
Chesterfield v Millwall
Coventry v Northampton
MK Dons v Peterborough
Port Vale v Scunthorpe
Rochdale v AFC Wimbledon
Sheff Utd v Oxford
Shrewsbury v Gillingham
Southend v Fleetwood
Swindon v Bristol Rov
Walsall v Bury

League Two
Accrington v Morecambe
Barnet v Carlisle
Blackpool v Plymouth
Cambridge v Luton
Cheltenham v Crewe
Crawley v Notts Co
Doncaster v Yeovil
Exeter v Portsmouth
Grimsby v Stevenage
Hartlepool v Newport
Leyton Orient v Mansfield
Wycombe v Colchester

Sunday, 28 August

Premier League
Man City v West Ham
WBA v Middlesbrough

Saturday, 3 September

League One
AFC Wimbledon v Chesterfield
Bolton v Southend
Bristol Rov v Walsall
Bury v Port Vale
Fleetwood v Coventry
Millwall v Bradford
Oldham v Shrewsbury
Oxford v Rochdale
Peterborough v Swindon
Scunthorpe v Charlton

League Two
Carlisle v Accrington
Colchester v Exeter
Crewe v Doncaster
Luton v Wycombe
Mansfield v Cambridge
Morecambe v Leyton Orient
Newport v Barnet
Notts Co v Grimsby
Plymouth v Cheltenham
Portsmouth v Crawley
Stevenage v Hartlepool
Yeovil v Blackpool

Sunday, 4 September
League One
Gillingham v Sheffield Utd
Northampton v MK Dons

Friday, 9 September
Championship
Reading v Ipswich

Saturday, 10 September
Premier League
Arsenal v Southampton
Bournemouth v WBA
Burnley v Hull
Liverpool v Leicester
Man Utd v Man City
Middlesbrough v C Palace
Stoke v Tottenham
West Ham v Watford

Championship
Brighton v Brentford
Derby v Newcastle
Fulham v Birmingham
Leeds v Huddersfield
Norwich v Cardiff
Preston v Barnsley
QPR v Blackburn
Rotherham v Bristol City
Sheff Wed v Wigan
Wolves v Burton

League One
AFC Wimbledon v Sheff Utd
Bolton v MK Dons
Bristol Rov v Rochdale
Bury v Shrewsbury
Fleetwood v Charlton
Gillingham v Bradford
Millwall v Coventry
Northampton v Walsall
Oldham v Chesterfield
Oxford v Swindon
Peterborough v Port Vale
Scunthorpe v Southend

League Two
Carlisle v Leyton Orient
Colchester v Blackpool
Crewe v Exeter
Luton v Grimsby
Mansfield v Barnet
Morecambe v Doncaster
Newport v Cheltenham
Notts Co v Accrington
Plymouth v Cambridge
Portsmouth v Wycombe
Stevenage v Crawley
Yeovil v Hartlepool

Sunday, 11 September
Premier League
Swansea v Chelsea

Championship
Aston Villa v Nottm Forest

Monday, 12 September
Premier League
Sunderland v Everton

Tuesday, 13 September
Championship
Brighton v Huddersfield
Derby v Ipswich
Fulham v Burton
Leeds v Blackburn
Norwich v Wigan
Preston v Cardiff
QPR v Newcastle
Sheff Wed v Bristol City
Wolves v Barnsley
Reading v Birmingham

Wednesday, 14 September
Championship
Aston Villa v Brentford
Rotherham v Nottm Forest

Friday, 16 September
Prenier League
Chelsea v Liverpool

Saturday, 17 September
Premier League
Everton v Middlesbrough
Hull v Arsenal
Leicester v Burnley
Man City v Bournemouth
Southampton v Swansea
WBA v West Ham

Championship
Barnsley v Reading
Birmingham v Sheff Wed
Blackburn v Rotherham
Brentford v Preston
Bristol City v Derby
Burton v Brighton
Cardiff v Leeds
Huddersfield v QPR
Ipswich v Aston Villa
Newcastle v Wolves
Nottm Forest v Norwich
Wigan v Fulham

League One
Bradford v Bristol Rov
Charlton v AFC Wimbledon
Chesterfield v Northampton
Coventry v Oldham
MK Dons v Oxford
Port Vale v Gillingham
Rochdale v Fleetwood
Sheff Utd v Peterborough
Shrewsbury v Scunthorpe
Southend v Millwall
Swindon v Bury
Walsall v Bolton

League Two
Accrington v Portsmouth
Barnet v Colchester
Blackpool v Carlisle
Cambridge v Morecambe
Cheltenham v Notts Co
Crawley v Luton
Doncaster v Newport
Exeter v Plymouth
Grimsby v Crewe
Hartlepool v Mansfield
Leyton Orient v Yeovil
Wycombe v Stevenage

Sunday, 18 September
Premier League
C Palace v Stoke
Tottenham v Sunderland
Watford v Man Utd

Friday, 23 September
Championship
Preston v Wigan

Saturday, 24 September
Premier League
Arsenal v Chelsea
Bournemouth v Everton
Liverpool v Hull
Man Utd v Leicester

Middlesbrough v Tottenham
Stoke v WBA
Sunderland v C Palace
Swansea v Man City

Championship
Aston Villa v Newcastle
Brighton v Barnsley
Derby v Blackburn
Fulham v Bristol City
Leeds v Ipswich
Norwich v Burton
QPR v Birmingham
Reading v Huddersfield
Rotherham v Cardiff
Sheff Wed v Nottm Forest
Wolves v Brentford

League One
AFC Wimbledon v Shrewsbury
Bolton v Bradford
Bristol Rov v Port Vale
Bury v Chesterfield
Fleetwood v MK Dons
Gillingham v Coventry
Millwall v Rochdale
Northampton v Southend
Oldham v Swindon
Oxford v Charlton
Peterborough v Walsall
Scunthorpe v Sheff Utd

League Two
Carlisle v Wycombe
Colchester v Accrington
Crewe v Blackpool
Luton v Doncaster
Mansfield v Grimsby
Morecambe v Crawley
Newport v Cambridge
Notts Co v Leyton Orient
Plymouth v Hartlepool
Portsmouth v Barnet
Stevenage v Exeter
Yeovil v Cheltenham

Sunday, 25 September

Premier League
West Ham v Southampton

Monday, 26 September

Premier League
Burnley v Watford

Tuesday, 27 September

Championship
Barnsley v Aston Villa
Birmingham v Preston
Blackburn v Sheff Wed
Brentford v Reading
Bristol City v Leeds
Burton v QPR
Cardiff v Derby
Huddersfield v Rotherham
Ipswich v Brighton
Nottm Forest v Fulham
Wigan v Wolves

League One
Bradford v Fleetwood
Charlton v Oldham
Chesterfield v Gillingham
MK Dons v Bury
Port Vale v Millwall
Rochdale v Bolton
Sheff Utd v Bristol Rov
Shrewsbury v Peterborough
Southend v Oxford
Swindon v Northampton
Walsall v Scunthorpe

League Two
Accrington v Mansfield
Barnet v Morecambe
Blackpool v Portsmouth
Cambridge v Yeovil
Cheltenham v Stevenage
Crawley v Colchester
Doncaster v Carlisle
Exeter v Notts Co
Grimsby v Newport
Hartlepool v Luton
Leyton Orient v Plymouth
Wycombe v Crewe

Wednesday, 28 September

Championship
Newcastle v Norwich

League One
Coventry v AFC Wimbledon

Saturday, 1 October

Premier League
Burnley v Arsenal
Hull v Chelsea
Everton v C Palace
Leicester v Southampton
Man Utd v Stoke
Tottenham v Man City
Sunderland v WBA
Swansea v Liverpool
Watford v Bournemouth
West Ham v Middlesbrough

Championship
Birmingham v Blackburn
Brentford v Wigan
Bristol City v Nottm Forest
Burton v Cardiff
Fulham v QPR
Ipswich v Huddersfield
Leeds v Barnsley
Preston v Aston Villa
Reading v Derby
Rotherham v Newcastle
Sheff Wed v Brighton
Wolves v Norwich

League One
AFC Wimbledon v Gillingham
Bolton v Oxford
Bury v Scunthorpe
Charlton v Rochdale
Chesterfield v Bradford
Fleetwood v Sheff Utd
Northampton v Bristol Rov
Oldham v MK Dons
Port Vale v Coventry
Shrewsbury v Swindon
Southend v Peterborough
Walsall v Millwall

League Two
Barnet v Leyton Orient
Cambridge v Accrington
Carlisle v Colchester
Cheltenham v Luton
Crawley v Blackpool
Crewe v Mansfield
Grimsby v Hartlepool
Newport v Stevenage
Notts Co v Morecambe
Plymouth v Yeovil
Portsmouth v Doncaster
Wycombe v Exeter

Saturday, 8 October

League One
Bradford v Shrewsbury
Bristol Rov v Fleetwood
Coventry v Chesterfield

Gillingham v Oldham
Millwall v Charlton
MK Dons v Port Vale
Oxford v AFC Wimbledon
Peterborough v Bury
Rochdale v Southend
Scunthorpe v Northampton
Sheff Utd v Walsall
Swindon v Bolton

League Two
Accrington v Cheltenham
Blackpool v Cambridge
Colchester v Newport
Doncaster v Barnet
Exeter v Grimsby
Hartlepool v Crawley
Leyton Orient v Portsmouth
Luton v Crewe
Mansfield v Notts Co
Morecambe v Carlisle
Stevenage v Plymouth
Yeovil v Wycombe

Friday, 14 October
Championship
Nottm Forest v Birmingham

Saturday, 15 October
Premier League
Arsenal v Swansea
Bournemouth v Hull
Chelsea v Leicester
C Palace v West Ham
Liverpool v Man Utd
Man City v Everton
Middlesbrough v Watford
Southampton v Burnley
Stoke v Sunderland
WBA v Tottenham

Championship
Aston Villa v Wolves
Barnsley v Fulham
Blackburn v Ipswich
Brighton v Preston
Cardiff v Bristol City
Derby v Leeds
Huddersfield v Sheff Wed
Newcastle v Brentford
Norwich v Rotherham
QPR v Reading
Wigan v Burton

League One
AFC Wimbledon v Swindon
Bolton v Oldham
Bristol Rov v Gillingham
Charlton v Coventry
Fleetwood v Peterborough
Northampton v Millwall
Oxford v Bradford
Rochdale v Bury
Scunthorpe v MK Dons
Sheff Utd v Port Vale
Southend v Chesterfield
Walsall v Shrewsbury

League Two
Accrington v Blackpool
Barnet v Exeter
Cambridge v Grimsby
Carlisle v Hartlepool
Cheltenham v Crawley
Doncaster v Colchester
Leyton Orient v Luton
Mansfield v Wycombe
Morecambe v Stevenage
Notts Co v Crewe
Plymouth v Portsmouth
Yeovil v Newport

Tuesday, 18 October
Championship
Barnsley v Newcastle
Birmingham v Rotherham
Blackburn v Nottm Forest
Brighton v Wolves
Cardiff v Sheff Wed
Derby v Brentford
Fulham v Norwich
Ipswich v Burton
Leeds v Wigan
Preston v Huddersfield
QPR v Bristol City
Reading v Aston Villa

League One
Bradford v Southend
Bury v AFC Wimbledon
Chesterfield v Fleetwood
Coventry v Oxford
Gillingham v Walsall
Millwall v Bolton
MK Dons v Bristol Rov
Oldham v Scunthorpe
Peterborough v Northampton
Port Vale v Charlton
Shrewsbury v Sheff Utd
Swindon v Rochdale

Saturday, 22 October
Premier League
Arsenal v Middlesbrough
Bournemouth v Tottenham
Burnley v Everton
Chelsea v Man Utd
Hull v Stoke
Leicester v C Palace
Liverpool v WBA
Man City v Southampton
Swansea v Watford
West Ham v Sunderland

Championship
Aston Villa v Fulham
Brentford v Barnsley
Bristol City v Blackburn
Burton v Birmingham
Huddersfield v Derby
Newcastle v Ipswich
Norwich v Preston
Nottm Forest v Cardiff
Rotherham v Reading
Sheff Wed v QPR
Wigan v Brighton
Wolves v Leeds

League One
Bradford v Sheff Utd
Bury v Bolton
Chesterfield v Scunthorpe
Coventry v Rochdale
Gillingham v Charlton
Millwall v Fleetwood
MK Dons v Southend
Oldham v Bristol Rov
Peterborough v AFC Wimbledon
Port Vale v Oxford
Shrewsbury v Northampton
Swindon v Walsall

League Two
Blackpool v Doncaster
Colchester v Morecambe
Crawley v Accrington
Crewe v Yeovil
Exeter v Cambridge
Grimsby v Cheltenham
Hartlepool v Leyton Orient
Luton v Mansfield

Newport v Plymouth
Portsmouth v Notts Co
Stevenage v Carlisle
Wycombe v Barnet

Saturday, 29 October

Premier League
C Palace v Liverpool
Everton v West Ham
Man Utd v Burnley
Middlesbrough v Bournemouth
Southampton v Chelsea
Sunderland v Arsenal
Stoke v Swansea
Tottenham v Leicester
Watford v Hull
WBA v Man City

Championship
Barnsley v Bristol City
Blackburn v Wolves
Brighton v Norwich
Cardiff v Wigan
Derby v Sheff Wed
Fulham v Huddersfield
Ipswich v Rotherham
Leeds v Burton
Preston v Newcastle
QPR v Brentford
Reading v Nottm Forest

League One
AFC Wimbledon v Bradford
Bolton v Port Vale
Bristol Rov v Peterborough
Charlton v Chesterfield
Fleetwood v Gillingham
Northampton v Bury
Oxford v Millwall
Rochdale v Oldham
Scunthorpe v Swindon
Sheff Utd v MK Dons
Southend v Shrewsbury
Walsall v Coventry

League Two
Accrington v Newport
Barnet v Hartlepool
Cambridge v Portsmouth
Carlisle v Crawley
Cheltenham v Blackpool
Doncaster v Wycombe
Leyton Orient v Crewe
Mansfield v Stevenage
Morecambe v Exeter
Notts Co v Luton
Plymouth v Colchester
Yeovil v Grimsby

Sunday, 30 October

Championship
Birmingham v Aston Villa

Saturday, 5 November

Premier League
Arsenal v Tottenham
Bournemouth v Sunderland
Burnley v C Palace
Chelsea v Everton
Hull v Southampton
Leicester v WBA
Liverpool v Watford
Man City v Middlesbrough
Swansea v Man Utd
West Ham v Stoke

Championship
Aston Villa v Blackburn
Brentford v Fulham
Bristol City v Brighton
Burton v Barnsley
Huddersfield v Birmingham
Newcastle v Cardiff
Norwich v Leeds
Nottm Forest v QPR
Rotherham v Preston
Sheff Wed v Ipswich
Wigan v Reading
Wolves v Derby

Saturday, 12 November

League One
Bradford v Rochdale
Bury v Southend
Chesterfield v Sheff Utd
Coventry v Scunthorpe
Gillingham v Northampton
Millwall v Bristol Rov
MK Dons v Walsall
Oldham v AFC Wimbledon
Peterborough v Bolton
Port Vale v Fleetwood
Shrewsbury v Oxford
Swindon v Charlton

League Two
Blackpool v Notts Co
Colchester v Leyton Orient
Crawley v Cambridge
Crewe v Plymouth
Exeter v Doncaster
Grimsby v Barnet
Hartlepool v Cheltenham
Luton v Accrington
Newport v Carlisle
Portsmouth v Mansfield
Stevenage v Yeovil
Wycombe v Morecambe

Saturday, 19 November

Premier League
C Palace v Man City
Everton v Swansea
Man Utd v Arsenal
Middlesbrough v Chelsea
Southampton v Liverpool
Stoke v Bournemouth
Sunderland v Hull
Tottenham v West Ham
Watford v Leicester
WBA v Burnley

Championship
Barnsley v Wigan
Birmingham v Bristol City
Blackburn v Brentford
Brighton v Aston Villa
Cardiff v Huddersfield
Derby v Rotherham
Fulham v Sheff Wed
Ipswich v Nottm Forest
Leeds v Newcastle
Preston v Wolves
QPR v Norwich
Reading v Burton

League One
AFC Wimbledon v Bury
Bolton v Millwall
Bristol Rov v MK Dons
Charlton v Port Vale
Fleetwood v Chesterfield
Northampton v Peterborough
Oxford v Coventry
Rochdale v Swindon
Scunthorpe v Oldham
Sheff Utd v Shrewsbury
Southend v Bradford
Walsall v Gillingham

League Two
Accrington v Stevenage

Barnet v Crewe
Cambridge v Wycombe
Carlisle v Exeter
Cheltenham v Portsmouth
Doncaster v Hartlepool
Leyton Orient v Blackpool
Mansfield v Crawley
Morecambe v Luton
Notts Co v Newport
Plymouth v Grimsby
Yeovil v Colchester

Tuesday, 22 November

League One

Bradford v Northampton
Bristol Rov v Charlton
Fleetwood v Shrewsbury
Millwall v AFC Wimbledon
MK Dons v Chesterfield
Oxford v Gillingham
Peterborough v Scunthorpe
Port Vale v Oldham
Rochdale v Walsall
Sheff Utd v Bury
Southend v Swindon
Bolton v Coventry

League Two

Cheltenham v Colchester
Crewe v Morecambe
Grimsby v Carlisle
Hartlepool v Accrington
Leyton Orient v Exeter
Luton v Portsmouth
Mansfield v Blackpool
Newport v Wycombe
Notts Co v Cambridge
Plymouth v Barnet
Stevenage v Doncaster
Yeovil v Crawley

Saturday, 26 November

Premier League

Arsenal v Bournemouth
Burnley v Man City
Chelsea v Tottenham
Hull v WBA
Leicester v Middlesbrough
Liverpool v Sunderland
Man Utd v West Ham
Southampton v Everton
Swansea v C Palace
Watford v Stoke

Championship

Aston Villa v Cardiff
Barnsley v Nottm Forest
Brentford v Birmingham
Brighton v Fulham
Derby v Norwich
Huddersfield v Wigan
Ipswich v QPR
Newcastle v Blackburn
Preston v Burton
Reading v Bristol City
Rotherham v Leeds
Wolves v Sheff Wed

League One

AFC Wimbledon v Fleetwood
Bury v Millwall
Charlton v Sheff Utd
Chesterfield v Bristol Rov
Coventry v MK Dons
Gillingham v Rochdale
Northampton v Bolton
Oldham v Peterborough
Scunthorpe v Oxford
Shrewsbury v Port Vale
Swindon v Bradford
Walsall v Southend

League Two

Accrington v Yeovil
Barnet v Notts Co
Blackpool v Newport
Cambridge v Cheltenham
Carlisle v Mansfield
Colchester v Crewe
Crawley v Grimsby
Doncaster v Leyton Orient
Exeter v Luton
Morecambe v Plymouth
Portsmouth v Stevenage
Wycombe v Hartlepool

Saturday, 3 December

Premier League

Bournemouth v Liverpool
C Palace v Southampton
Everton v Man Utd
Man City v Chelsea
Middlesbrough v Hull
Stoke v Burnley
Sunderland v Leicester
Tottenham v Swansea
WBA v Watford
West Ham v Arsenal

Championship

Birmingham v Barnsley
Blackburn v Huddersfield
Bristol City v Ipswich
Burton v Rotherham
Cardiff v Brighton
Fulham v Reading
Leeds v Aston Villa
Norwich v Brentford
Nottm Forest v Newcastle
QPR v Wolves
Sheff Wed v Preston
Wigan v Derby

Saturday, 10 December

Premier League

Arsenal v Stoke
Burnley v Bournemouth
Chelsea v WBA
Hull v C Palace
Leicester v Man City
Liverpool v West Ham
Man Utd v Tottenham
Southampton v Middlesbrough
Swansea v Sunderland
Watford v Everton

Championship

Aston Villa v Wigan
Barnsley v Norwich
Brentford v Burton
Brighton v Leeds
Derby v Nottm Forest
Huddersfield v Bristol City
Ipswich v Cardiff
Newcastle v Birmingham
Preston v Blackburn
Reading v Sheff Wed
Rotherham v QPR
Wolves v Fulham

League One

Bolton v Gillingham
Bradford v Charlton
Bristol Rov v Bury
Fleetwood v Walsall
Millwall v Shrewsbury
MK Dons v AFC Wimbledon
Oxford v Oldham
Peterborough v Chesterfield
Port Vale v Northampton
Rochdale v Scunthorpe
Sheff Utd v Swindon
Southend v Coventry

League Two
Cheltenham v Exeter
Crewe v Crawley
Grimsby v Portsmouth
Hartlepool v Cambridge
Leyton Orient v Accrington
Luton v Carlisle
Mansfield v Colchester
Newport v Morecambe
Notts Co v Wycombe
Plymouth v Doncaster
Stevenage v Blackpool
Yeovil v Barnet

Tuesday, 13 December

Premier League
Bournemouth v Leicester
C Palace v Man Utd
Middlesbrough v Liverpool
Sunderland v Chelsea
WBA v Swansea
West Ham v Burnley

Championship
Birmingham v Ipswich
Blackburn v Brighton
Bristol City v Brentford
Burton v Huddersfield
Cardiff v Wolves
Fulham v Rotherham
Leeds v Reading
Norwich v Aston Villa
Nottm Forest v Preston
QPR v Derby
Sheff Wed v Barnsley
Wigan v Newcastle

Wednesday, 14 December

Premier League
Everton v Arsenal
Man City v Watford
Stoke v Southampton
Tottenham v Hull

Saturday, 17 December

Premier League
Bournemouth v Southampton
C Palace v Chelsea
Everton v Liverpool
Man City v Arsenal
Middlesbrough v Swansea
Stoke v Leicester
Sunderland v Watford
Tottenham v Burnley
WBA v Man Utd
West Ham v Hull

Championship
Birmingham v Brighton
Blackburn v Reading
Bristol City v Preston
Burton v Newcastle
Cardiff v Barnsley
Fulham v Derby
Leeds v Brentford
Norwich v Huddersfield
Nottm Forest v Wolves
QPR v Aston Villa
Sheff Wed v Rotherham
Wigan v Ipswich

League One
AFC Wimbledon v Port Vale
Bury v Oxford
Charlton v Peterborough
Chesterfield v Bolton
Coventry v Sheff Utd
Gillingham v MK Dons
Northampton v Rochdale
Oldham v Southend
Scunthorpe v Millwall
Shrewsbury v Bristol Rov
Swindon v Fleetwood
Walsall v Bradford

League Two
Accrington v Plymouth
Barnet v Stevenage
Blackpool v Luton
Cambridge v Crewe
Carlisle v Yeovil
Colchester v Notts Co
Crawley v Newport
Doncaster v Grimsby
Exeter v Mansfield
Morecambe v Cheltenham
Portsmouth v Hartlepool
Wycombe v Leyton Orient

Monday, 26 December

Premier League
Arsenal v WBA
Burnley v Middlesbrough
Chelsea v Bournemouth
Hull v Man City
Leicester v Everton
Man Utd v Sunderland
Southampton v Tottenham
Swansea v West Ham
Liverpool v Stoke
Watford v C Palace

Championship
Aston Villa v Burton
Barnsley v Blackburn
Brentford v Cardiff
Brighton v QPR
Derby v Birmingham
Huddersfield v Nottm Forest
Ipswich v Fulham
Newcastle v Sheff Wed
Preston v Leeds
Reading v Norwich
Rotherham v Wigan
Wolves v Bristol City

League One
Bolton v Shrewsbury
Bradford v Scunthorpe
Bristol Rov v Coventry
Fleetwood v Bury
Millwall v Swindon
MK Dons v Charlton
Oxford v Northampton
Peterborough v Gillingham
Port Vale v Walsall
Rochdale v Chesterfield
Sheff Utd v Oldham
Southend v AFC Wimbledon

League Two
Cheltenham v Barnet
Crewe v Carlisle
Grimsby v Accrington
Hartlepool v Blackpool
Leyton Orient v Crawley
Luton v Colchester
Mansfield v Morecambe
Newport v Portsmouth
Notts Co v Doncaster
Plymouth v Wycombe
Stevenage v Cambridge
Yeovil v Exeter

Friday, 30 December

Championship
Brighton v Cardiff
Ipswich v Bristol City
Reading v Fulham

League One
MK Dons v Swindon

League Two
Cheltenham v Wycombe
Hartlepool v Morecambe

Saturday, 31 December

Premier League
Arsenal v C Palace
Burnley v Sunderland
Chelsea v Stoke
Hull v Everton
Leicester v West Ham
Liverpool v Man City
Man Utd v Middlesbrough
Southampton v WBA
Swansea v Bournemouth
Watford v Tottenham

Championship
Aston Villa v Leeds
Barnsley v Birmingham
Brentford v Norwich
Derby v Wigan
Huddersfield v Blackburn
Newcastle v Nottm Forest
Preston v Sheff Wed
Rotherham v Burton
Wolves v QPR

League One
Bolton v Scunthorpe
Bradford v Bury
Bristol Rov v AFC Wimbledon
Fleetwood v Oldham
Millwall v Gillingham
Oxford v Walsall
Peterborough v Coventry
Port Vale v Chesterfield
Rochdale v Shrewsbury
Sheff Utd v Northampton
Southend v Charlton

League Two
Crewe v Accrington
Grimsby v Blackpool
Luton v Barnet
Mansfield v Doncaster
Newport v Exeter
Notts Co v Carlisle
Plymouth v Crawley
Stevenage v Colchester
Yeovil v Portsmouth

Monday, 2 January

Premier League
Bournemouth v Arsenal
C Palace v Swansea
Everton v Southampton
Man City v Burnley
Middlesbrough v Leicester
Stoke v Watford
Sunderland v Liverpool
Tottenham v Chelsea
WBA v Hull
West Ham v Man Utd

Championship
Birmingham v Brentford
Blackburn v Newcastle
Bristol City v Reading
Burton v Preston
Cardiff v Aston Villa
Fulham v Brighton
Leeds v Rotherham
Norwich v Derby
Nottm Forest v Barnsley
QPR v Ipswich
Sheff Wed v Wolves
Wigan v Huddersfield

League One
AFC Wimbledon v Millwall
Bury v Sheff Utd
Charlton v Bristol Rov
Chesterfield v MK Dons
Coventry v Bolton
Gillingham v Oxford
Northampton v Bradford
Oldham v Port Vale
Scunthorpe v Peterborough
Shrewsbury v Fleetwood
Swindon v Southend
Walsall v Rochdale

League Two
Accrington v Hartlepool
Barnet v Plymouth
Blackpool v Mansfield
Cambridge v Notts Co
Carlisle v Grimsby
Colchester v Cheltenham
Crawley v Yeovil
Doncaster v Stevenage
Exeter v Leyton Orient
Morecambe v Crewe
Portsmouth v Luton
Wycombe v Newport

Saturday, 7 January

League One
Bradford v Chesterfield
Bristol Rov v Northampton
Coventry v Port Vale
Gillingham v AFC Wimbledon
Millwall v Walsall
MK Dons v Oldham
Oxford v Bolton
Peterborough v Southend
Rochdale v Charlton
Scunthorpe v Bury
Sheff Utd v Fleetwood
Swindon v Shrewsbury

League Two
Accrington v Cambridge
Blackpool v Crawley
Colchester v Carlisle
Doncaster v Portsmouth
Exeter v Wycombe
Hartlepool v Grimsby
Leyton Orient v Barnet
Luton v Cheltenham
Mansfield v Crewe
Morecambe v Notts Co
Stevenage v Newport
Yeovil v Plymouth

Saturday, 14 January

Premier League
Burnley v Southampton
Everton v Man City
Hull v Bournemouth
Leicester v Chelsea
Man Utd v Liverpool
Sunderland v Stoke
Swansea v Arsenal
Tottenham v WBA
Watford v Middlesbrough
West Ham v C Palace

Championship
Birmingham v Nottm Forest
Brentford v Newcastle
Bristol City v Cardiff
Burton v Wigan
Fulham v Barnsley
Ipswich v Blackburn
Leeds v Derby
Preston v Brighton
Reading v QPR
Rotherham v Norwich
Sheff Wed v Huddersfield
Wolves v Aston Villa

League One
AFC Wimbledon v Oxford
Bolton v Swindon
Bury v Peterborough
Charlton v Millwall
Chesterfield v Coventry
Fleetwood v Bristol Rov
Northampton v Scunthorpe
Oldham v Gillingham
Port Vale v MK Dons
Shrewsbury v Bradford
Southend v Rochdale
Walsall v Sheff Utd

League Two
Barnet v Doncaster
Cambridge v Blackpool
Carlisle v Morecambe
Cheltenham v Accrington
Crawley v Hartlepool
Crewe v Luton
Grimsby v Exeter
Newport v Colchester
Notts Co v Mansfield
Plymouth v Stevenage
Portsmouth v Leyton Orient
Wycombe v Yeovil

Friday, 20 January

League One
Port Vale v Bury

Saturday, 21 January

Premier League
Arsenal v Burnley
Bournemouth v Watford
Chelsea v Hull
C Palace v Everton
Liverpool v Swansea
Man City v Tottenham
Middlesbrough v West Ham
Southampton v Leicester
Stoke v Man Utd
WBA v Sunderland

Championship
Aston Villa v Preston
Barnsley v Leeds
Blackburn v Birmingham
Brighton v Sheff Wed
Cardiff v Burton
Derby v Reading
Huddersfield v Ipswich
Newcastle v Rotherham
Norwich v Wolves
Nottm Forest v Bristol City
QPR v Fulham
Wigan v Brentford

League One
Bradford v Millwall
Charlton v Scunthorpe
Chesterfield v AFC Wimbledon
Coventry v Fleetwood
MK Dons v Northampton
Rochdale v Oxford
Sheff Utd v Gillingham
Shrewsbury v Oldham
Southend v Bolton
Swindon v Peterborough
Walsall v Bristol Rov

League Two
Accrington v Carlisle
Barnet v Newport
Blackpool v Yeovil
Cambridge v Mansfield
Cheltenham v Plymouth
Crawley v Portsmouth
Doncaster v Crewe
Exeter v Colchester
Grimsby v Notts Co
Hartlepool v Stevenage
Leyton Orient v Morecambe
Wycombe v Luton

Saturday, 28 January

Championship
Aston Villa v Bristol City
Brighton v Newcastle
Derby v Burton
Fulham v Blackburn
Leeds v Nottm Forest
Norwich v Birmingham
Preston v Ipswich
QPR v Wigan
Reading v Cardiff
Rotherham v Barnsley
Sheff Wed v Brentford
Wolves v Huddersfield

League One
AFC Wimbledon v Rochdale
Bolton v Charlton
Bristol Rov v Swindon
Bury v Walsall
Fleetwood v Southend
Gillingham v Shrewsbury
Millwall v Chesterfield
Northampton v Coventry
Oldham v Bradford
Oxford v Sheff Utd
Peterborough v MK Dons
Scunthorpe v Port Vale

League Two
Carlisle v Barnet
Colchester v Wycombe
Crewe v Cheltenham
Luton v Cambridge
Mansfield v Leyton Orient
Morecambe v Accrington
Newport v Hartlepool
Notts Co v Crawley
Plymouth v Blackpool
Portsmouth v Exeter
Stevenage v Grimsby
Yeovil v Doncaster

Tuesday, 31 January

Premier League
Arsenal v Watford
Bournemouth v C Palace
Burnley v Leicester
Man Utd v Hull
Middlesbrough v WBA
Sunderland v Tottenham
Swansea v Southampton
West Ham v Man City

Championship
Barnsley v Wolves
Birmingham v Reading
Brentford v Aston Villa
Bristol City v Sheff Wed
Burton v Fulham
Cardiff v Preston
Huddersfield v Brighton
Ipswich v Derby
Nottm Forest v Rotherham
Wigan v Norwich

Wednesday, 1 February

Premier League
Liverpool v Chelsea
Stoke v Everton

Championship
Blackburn v Leeds
Newcastle v QPR

Saturday, 4 February

Premier League

Chelsea v Arsenal
C Palace v Sunderland
Everton v Bournemouth
Hull v Liverpool
Leicester v Man Utd
Man City v Swansea
Southampton v West Ham
Tottenham v Middlesbrough
Watford v Burnley
WBA v Stoke

Championship

Barnsley v Preston
Birmingham v Fulham
Blackburn v QPR
Brentford v Brighton
Bristol City v Rotherham
Burton v Wolves
Cardiff v Norwich
Huddersfield v Leeds
Ipswich v Reading
Newcastle v Derby
Nottm Forest v Aston Villa
Wigan v Sheff Wed

League One

Bradford v Gillingham
Charlton v Fleetwood
Chesterfield v Oldham
Coventry v Millwall
MK Dons v Bolton
Port Vale v Peterborough
Rochdale v Bristol Rov
Sheff Utd v AFC Wimbledon
Shrewsbury v Bury
Southend v Scunthorpe
Walsall v Northampton

League Two

Accrington v Notts Co
Barnet v Mansfield
Blackpool v Colchester
Cambridge v Plymouth
Cheltenham v Newport
Crawley v Stevenage
Doncaster v Morecambe
Exeter v Crewe
Grimsby v Luton
Hartlepool v Yeovil
Leyton Orient v Carlisle
Wycombe v Portsmouth

Sunday, 5 February

League One

Swindon v Oxford

Saturday, 11 February

Premier League

Arsenal v Hull
Bournemouth v Man City
Burnley v Chelsea
Liverpool v Tottenham
Man Utd v Watford
Middlesbrough v Everton
Stoke v C Palace
Sunderland v Southampton
Swansea v Leicester
West Ham v WBA

Championship

Aston Villa v Ipswich
Brighton v Burton
Derby v Bristol City
Fulham v Wigan
Leeds v Cardiff
Norwich v Nottm Forest
Preston v Brentford
QPR v Huddersfield
Reading v Barnsley
Rotherham v Blackburn
Sheff Wed v Birmingham
Wolves v Newcastle

League One

AFC Wimbledon v Charlton
Bolton v Walsall
Bristol Rov v Bradford
Bury v Swindon
Fleetwood v Rochdale
Gillingham v Port Vale
Millwall v Southend
Northampton v Chesterfield
Oldham v Coventry
Oxford v MK Dons
Peterborough v Sheff Utd
Scunthorpe v Shrewsbury

League Two

Carlisle v Blackpool
Colchester v Barnet
Crewe v Grimsby
Luton v Crawley
Mansfield v Hartlepool
Morecambe v Cambridge
Newport v Doncaster
Notts Co v Cheltenham
Plymouth v Exeter
Portsmouth v Accrington
Stevenage v Wycombe
Yeovil v Leyton Orient

Tuesday, 14 February

Championship

Aston Villa v Barnsley
Brighton v Ipswich
Derby v Cardiff
Fulham v Nottm Forest
Leeds v Bristol City
Norwich v Newcastle
Preston v Birmingham
QPR v Burton
Rotherham v Huddersfield
Sheff Wed v Blackburn
Wolves v Wigan
Reading v Brentford

League One

AFC Wimbledon v Coventry
Bristol Rov v Sheff Utd
Bury v MK Dons
Fleetwood v Bradford
Gillingham v Chesterfield
Millwall v Port Vale
Northampton v Swindon
Oldham v Charlton
Oxford v Southend
Peterborough v Shrewsbury
Scunthorpe v Walsall
Bolton v Rochdale

League Two

Carlisle v Doncaster
Colchester v Crawley
Crewe v Wycombe
Luton v Hartlepool
Mansfield v Accrington
Morecambe v Barnet
Newport v Grimsby
Notts Co v Exeter
Plymouth v Leyton Orient
Portsmouth v Blackpool
Stevenage v Cheltenham
Yeovil v Cambridge

Saturday, 18 February

Championship

Barnsley v Brighton
Birmingham v QPR
Blackburn v Derby
Brentford v Wolves

Bristol City v Fulham
Burton v Norwich
Cardiff v Rotherham
Huddersfield v Reading
Ipswich v Leeds
Newcastle v Aston Villa
Nottm Forest v Sheff Wed
Wigan v Preston

League One
Bradford v Bolton
Charlton v Oxford
Chesterfield v Bury
Coventry v Gillingham
MK Dons v Fleetwood
Port Vale v Bristol Rov
Rochdale v Millwall
Sheff Utd v Scunthorpe
Shrewsbury v AFC Wimbledon
Southend v Northampton
Swindon v Oldham
Walsall v Peterborough

League Two
Accrington v Colchester
Barnet v Portsmouth
Blackpool v Crewe
Cambridge v Newport
Cheltenham v Yeovil
Crawley v Morecambe
Doncaster v Luton
Exeter v Stevenage
Grimsby v Mansfield
Hartlepool v Plymouth
Leyton Orient v Notts Co
Wycombe v Carlisle

Friday, 24 February

Championship
Burton v Blackburn

Saturday, 25 February

Premier League
Chelsea v Swansea
C Palace v Middlesbrough
Everton v Sunderland
Hull v Burnley
Leicester v Liverpool
Man City v Man Utd
Southampton v Arsenal
Tottenham v Stoke
Watford v West Ham
WBA v Bournemouth

Championship
Aston Villa v Derby
Barnsley v Huddersfield
Brentford v Rotherham
Brighton v Reading
Cardiff v Fulham
Leeds v Sheff Wed
Newcastle v Bristol City
Preston v QPR
Wigan v Nottm Forest
Wolves v Birmingham

League One
AFC Wimbledon v Walsall
Bristol Rov v Scunthorpe
Charlton v Bury
Chesterfield v Oxford
Coventry v Swindon
Fleetwood v Northampton
Gillingham v Southend
MK Dons v Shrewsbury
Oldham v Millwall
Peterborough v Rochdale
Port Vale v Bradford
Sheff Utd v Bolton

League Two
Barnet v Cambridge
Carlisle v Portsmouth
Colchester v Hartlepool
Crewe v Stevenage
Doncaster v Accrington
Exeter v Blackpool
Leyton Orient v Cheltenham
Luton v Plymouth
Mansfield v Newport
Morecambe v Grimsby
Notts Co v Yeovil
Wycombe v Crawley

Sunday, 26 February

Championship
Norwich v Ipswich

Tuesday, 28 February

League One
Bradford v MK Dons
Bury v Coventry
Millwall v Peterborough
Northampton v Oldham
Oxford v Fleetwood
Rochdale v Port Vale
Scunthorpe v AFC Wimbledon
Shrewsbury v Charlton
Southend v Sheff Utd
Swindon v Gillingham
Walsall v Chesterfield
Bolton v Bristol Rov

League Two
Accrington v Wycombe
Blackpool v Barnet
Cambridge v Doncaster
Cheltenham v Carlisle
Crawley v Exeter
Grimsby v Colchester
Hartlepool v Crewe
Newport v Luton
Plymouth v Notts Co
Portsmouth v Morecambe
Stevenage v Leyton Orient
Yeovil v Mansfield

Saturday, 4 March

Premier League
Leicester v Hull
Liverpool v Arsenal
Man Utd v Bournemouth
Stoke v Middlesbrough
Sunderland v Man City
Swansea v Burnley
Tottenham v Everton
Watford v Southampton
West Ham v Chelsea
WBA v C Palace

Championship
Birmingham v Leeds
Blackburn v Wigan
Bristol City v Burton
Derby v Barnsley
Fulham v Preston
Huddersfield v Newcastle
Ipswich v Brentford
Nottm Forest v Brighton
QPR v Cardiff
Reading v Wolves
Rotherham v Aston Villa
Sheff Wed v Norwich

League One
Bolton v AFC Wimbledon
Bradford v Peterborough
Bury v Gillingham
Millwall v MK Dons
Northampton v Charlton
Oxford v Bristol Rov
Rochdale v Sheff Utd

Scunthorpe v Fleetwood
Shrewsbury v Coventry
Southend v Port Vale
Swindon v Chesterfield
Walsall v Oldham

League Two
Accrington v Barnet
Blackpool v Morecambe
Cambridge v Colchester
Cheltenham v Mansfield
Crawley v Doncaster
Grimsby v Wycombe
Hartlepool v Exeter
Newport v Leyton Orient
Plymouth v Carlisle
Portsmouth v Crewe
Stevenage v Notts Co
Yeovil v Luton

Tuesday, 7 March

Championship
Birmingham v Wigan
Blackburn v Cardiff
Bristol City v Norwich
Derby v Preston
Fulham v Leeds
Huddersfield v Aston Villa
Ipswich v Wolves
Nottm Forest v Brentford
QPR v Barnsley
Rotherham v Brighton
Sheff Wed v Burton
Reading v Newcastle

Saturday, 11 March

Premier League
Arsenal v Leicester
Bournemouth v West Ham
Chelsea v Watford
C Palace v Tottenham
Everton v WBA
Hull v Swansea
Liverpool v Burnley
Man City v Stoke
Middlesbrough v Sunderland
Southampton v Man Utd

Championship
Aston Villa v Sheff Wed
Barnsley v Ipswich
Brentford v Huddersfield
Brighton v Derby
Burton v Nottm Forest
Cardiff v Birmingham
Leeds v QPR
Newcastle v Fulham
Norwich v Blackburn
Preston v Reading
Wigan v Bristol City
Wolves v Rotherham

League One
AFC Wimbledon v Northampton
Bristol Rov v Southend
Charlton v Walsall
Chesterfield v Shrewsbury
Coventry v Bradford
Fleetwood v Bolton
Gillingham v Scunthorpe
MK Dons v Rochdale
Oldham v Bury
Peterborough v Oxford
Port Vale v Swindon
Sheff Utd v Millwall

League Two
Barnet v Crawley
Carlisle v Cambridge
Colchester v Portsmouth
Crewe v Newport
Doncaster v Cheltenham
Exeter v Accrington
Leyton Orient v Grimsby
Luton v Stevenage
Mansfield v Plymouth
Morecambe v Yeovil
Notts Co v Hartlepool
Wycombe v Blackpool

Tuesday, 14 March

League One
AFC Wimbledon v MK Dons
Bury v Bristol Rov
Charlton v Bradford
Chesterfield v Peterborough
Coventry v Southend
Gillingham v Bolton
Northampton v Port Vale
Oldham v Oxford
Scunthorpe v Rochdale
Shrewsbury v Millwall
Swindon v Sheff Utd
Walsall v Fleetwood

League Two
Accrington v Leyton Orient
Barnet v Yeovil
Blackpool v Stevenage
Cambridge v Hartlepool
Carlisle v Luton
Colchester v Mansfield
Crawley v Crewe
Doncaster v Notts Co
Exeter v Cheltenham
Morecambe v Newport
Portsmouth v Grimsby
Wycombe v Plymouth

Friday, 17 March

Championship
Sheffield Wed v Reading

Saturday, 18 March

Premier League
Bournemouth v Swansea
C Palace v Watford
Everton v Hull
Man City v Liverpool
Middlesbrough v Man Utd
Stoke v Chelsea
Sunderland v Burnley
Tottenham v Southampton
WBA v Arsenal
West Ham v Leicester

Championship
Birmingham v Newcastle
Blackburn v Preston
Bristol City v Huddersfield
Burton v Brentford
Cardiff v Ipswich
Fulham v Wolves
Leeds v Brighton
Norwich v Barnsley
Nottm Forest v Derby
QPR v Rotherham
Wigan v Aston Villa

League One
Bolton v Northampton
Bradford v Swindon
Bristol Rov v Chesterfield
Fleetwood v AFC Wimbledon
Millwall v Bury
MK Dons v Coventry
Oxford v Scunthorpe
Peterborough v Oldham
Port Vale v Shrewsbury
Rochdale v Gillingham
Sheff Utd v Charlton
Southend v Walsall

League Two
Cheltenham v Cambridge
Crewe v Colchester
Grimsby v Crawley
Hartlepool v Wycombe
Leyton Orient v Doncaster
Luton v Exeter
Mansfield v Carlisle
Newport v Blackpool
Plymouth v Morecambe
Stevenage v Portsmouth
Yeovil v Accrington

Sunday, 19 March
League Two
Notts Co v Barnet

Saturday, 25 March
League One
AFC Wimbledon v Southend
Bury v Fleetwood
Charlton v MK Dons
Chesterfield v Rochdale
Coventry v Bristol Rov
Gillingham v Peterborough
Northampton v Oxford
Oldham v Sheff Utd
Scunthorpe v Bradford
Shrewsbury v Bolton
Swindon v Millwall
Walsall v Port Vale

League Two
Accrington v Grimsby
Barnet v Cheltenham
Blackpool v Hartlepool
Cambridge v Stevenage
Carlisle v Crewe
Colchester v Luton
Crawley v Leyton Orient
Doncaster v Plymouth
Exeter v Yeovil
Morecambe v Mansfield
Portsmouth v Newport
Wycombe v Notts Co

Saturday, 1 April
Premier League
Arsenal v Man City
Burnley v Tottenham
Chelsea v C Palace
Hull v West Ham
Leicester v Stoke
Liverpool v Everton
Man Utd v WBA
Southampton v Bournemouth
Swansea v Middlesbrough
Watford v Sunderland

Championship
Aston Villa v Norwich
Barnsley v Sheff Wed
Brentford v Bristol City
Brighton v Blackburn
Derby v QPR
Huddersfield v Burton
Ipswich v Birmingham
Newcastle v Wigan
Preston v Nottm Forest
Reading v Leeds
Rotherham v Fulham
Wolves v Cardiff

League One
Bolton v Chesterfield
Bradford v Walsall
Bristol Rov v Shrewsbury
Fleetwood v Swindon
Millwall v Scunthorpe
MK Dons v Gillingham
Oxford v Bury
Peterborough v Charlton
Port Vale v AFC Wimbledon
Rochdale v Northampton
Sheff Utd v Coventry
Southend v Oldham

League Two
Cheltenham v Morecambe
Crewe v Cambridge
Grimsby v Doncaster
Hartlepool v Portsmouth
Leyton Orient v Wycombe
Luton v Blackpool
Mansfield v Exeter
Newport v Crawley
Notts Co v Colchester
Plymouth v Accrington
Stevenage v Barnet
Yeovil v Carlisle

Tuesday, 4 April
Premier League
Arsenal v West Ham
Burnley v Stoke
Hull v Middlesbrough
Leicester v Sunderland
Man Utd v Everton
Swansea v Tottenham
Watford v WBA

Championship
Aston Villa v QPR
Barnsley v Cardiff
Brentford v Leeds
Brighton v Birmingham
Derby v Fulham
Huddersfield v Norwich
Ipswich v Wigan
Preston v Bristol City
Rotherham v Sheff Wed
Wolves v Nottm Forest
Reading v Blackburn

Wednesday, 5 April
Premier League
Chelsea v Man City
Liverpool v Bournemouth
Southampton v C Palace

Championship
Newcastle v Burton

Saturday, 8 April
Premier League
Bournemouth v Chelsea
C Palace v Arsenal
Everton v Leicester
Man City v Hull
Middlesbrough v Burnley
Stoke v Liverpool
Sunderland v Man Utd
Tottenham v Watford
WBA v Southampton
West Ham v Swansea

Championship
Birmingham v Derby
Blackburn v Barnsley
Bristol City v Wolves
Burton v Aston Villa
Cardiff v Brentford
Fulham v Ipswich
Leeds v Preston
Norwich v Reading
Nottm Forest v Huddersfield
QPR v Brighton
Sheff Wed v Newcastle
Wigan v Rotherham

League One
AFC Wimbledon v Bristol Rov

Bury v Bradford
Charlton v Southend
Chesterfield v Port Vale
Coventry v Peterborough
Gillingham v Millwall
Northampton v Sheff Utd
Oldham v Fleetwood
Scunthorpe v Bolton
Shrewsbury v Rochdale
Swindon v MK Dons
Walsall v Oxford

League Two
Accrington v Crewe
Barnet v Luton
Blackpool v Grimsby
Cambridge v Leyton Orient
Carlisle v Notts Co
Colchester v Stevenage
Crawley v Plymouth
Doncaster v Mansfield
Exeter v Newport
Morecambe v Hartlepool
Portsmouth v Yeovil
Wycombe v Cheltenham

Friday, 14 April

Championship
Brentford v Derby
Burton v Ipswich
Huddersfield v Preston
Norwich v Fulham
Nottm Forest v Blackburn
Rotherham v Birmingham
Sheffield Wed v Cardiff
Wolves v Brighton

League One
Bradford v Oxford
Coventry v Charlton
Gillingham v Bristol Rov
Millwall v Northampton
MK Dons v Scunthorpe
Peterborough v Fleetwood
Port Vale v Sheffield Utd
Shrewsbury v Walsall
Swindon v Wimbledon

League Two
Blackpool v Accrington
Colchester v Doncaster
Crawley v Cheltenham
Crewe v Notts Co
Exeter v Barnet
Hartlepool v Carlisle
Luton v Carlisle
Portsmouth v Plymouth
Stevenage v Morecambe
Wycombe v Mansfield

Saturday, 15 April

Premier League
C Palace v Leicester
Everton v Burnley
Man Utd v Chelsea
Middlesbrough v Arsenal
Southampton v Man City
Stoke v Hull
Sunderland v West Ham
Tottenham v Bournemouth
Watford v Swansea
WBA v Liverpool

Championship
Aston Villa v Reading
Bristol City v QPR
Newcastle v Leeds
Wigan v Barnsley

League One
Bury v Rochdale
Chesterfield v Southend
Oldham v Bolton

League Two
Grimsby v Cambridge
Newport v Yeovil

Monday, 17 April

Championship
Barnsley v Brentford
Birmingham v Burton
Blackburn v Bristol City
Brighton v Wigan
Cardiff v Nottm Forest
Derby v Huddersfield
Fulham v Aston Villa
Ipswich v Newcastle
Leeds v Wolves
Preston v Norwich
QPR v Sheff Wed
Reading v Rotherham

League One
AFC Wimbledon v Peterborough
Bristol Rov v Oldham
Charlton v Gillingham
Fleetwood v Millwall
Northampton v Shrewsbury
Oxford v Port Vale
Rochdale v Coventry
Scunthorpe v Chesterfield
Sheff Utd v Bradford
Southend v MK Dons
Walsall v Swindon

League Two
Accrington v Crawley
Barnet v Wycombe
Cambridge v Exeter
Carlisle v Stevenage
Cheltenham v Grimsby
Doncaster v Blackpool
Leyton Orient v Hartlepool
Mansfield v Luton
Morecambe v Colchester
Notts Co v Portsmouth
Plymouth v Newport
Yeovil v Crewe

Tuesday, 18 April

League One
Bolton v Bury

Saturday, 22 April

Premier League
Arsenal v Sunderland
Bournemouth v Middlesbrough
Burnley v Man Utd
Hull v Watford
Leicester v Tottenham
Liverpool v C Palace
Man City v WBA
Swansea v Stoke
West Ham v Everton

Championship
Brentford v QPR
Bristol City v Barnsley
Burton v Leeds
Huddersfield v Fulham
Newcastle v Preston
Norwich v Brighton
Nottm Forest v Reading
Rotherham v Ipswich
Sheff Wed v Derby
Wigan v Cardiff
Wolves v Blackburn

League One
Bradford v AFC Wimbledon
Bury v Northampton
Chesterfield v Charlton

Coventry v Walsall
Gillingham v Fleetwood
Millwall v Oxford
MK Dons v Sheff Utd
Oldham v Rochdale
Peterborough v Bristol Rov
Port Vale v Bolton
Shrewsbury v Southend
Swindon v Scunthorpe

League Two
Blackpool v Cheltenham
Colchester v Plymouth
Crawley v Carlisle
Crewe v Leyton Orient
Exeter v Morecambe
Grimsby v Yeovil
Hartlepool v Barnet
Luton v Notts Co
Newport v Accrington
Portsmouth v Cambridge
Stevenage v Mansfield
Wycombe v Doncaster

Sunday, 23 April
Championship
Aston Villa v Birmingham

Saturday, 29 April
Premier League
C Palace v Burnley
Everton v Chelsea
Man Utd v Swansea
Middlesbrough v Man City
Southampton v Hull
Stoke v West Ham
Sunderland v Bournemouth
Tottenham v Arsenal
Watford v Liverpool
WBA v Leicester

Championship
Barnsley v Burton
Birmingham v Huddersfield
Blackburn v Aston Villa
Brighton v Bristol City
Cardiff v Newcastle
Derby v Wolves
Fulham v Brentford
Ipswich v Sheff Wed
Leeds v Norwich
Preston v Rotherham
QPR v Nottm Forest
Reading v Wigan

League Two
Accrington v Luton
Barnet v Grimsby
Cambridge v Crawley
Carlisle v Newport
Cheltenham v Hartlepool
Doncaster v Exeter
Leyton Orient v Colchester
Mansfield v Portsmouth
Morecambe v Wycombe
Notts Co v Blackpool
Plymouth v Crewe
Yeovil v Stevenage

Sunday, 30 April
League One
AFC Wimbledon v Oldham
Bolton v Peterborough
Bristol Rov v Millwall
Charlton v Swindon
Fleetwood v Port Vale
Northampton v Gillingham
Oxford v Shrewsbury
Rochdale v Bradford
Scunthorpe v Coventry
Sheff Utd v Chesterfield
Southend v Bury
Walsall v MK Dons

Saturday, 6 May
Premier League
Arsenal v Man Utd
Bournemouth v Stoke
Burnley v WBA
Chelsea v Middlesbrough
Hull v Sunderland
Leicester v Watford
Liverpool v Southampton
Man City v C Palace
Swansea v Everton
West Ham v Tottenham

League Two
Blackpool v Leyton Orient
Colchester v Yeovil
Crawley v Mansfield
Crewe v Barnet
Exeter v Carlisle
Grimsby v Plymouth
Hartlepool v Doncaster
Luton v Morecambe
Newport v Notts Co
Portsmouth v Cheltenham
Stevenage v Accrington
Wycombe v Cambridge

Sunday, 7 May
Championship
Aston Villa v Brighton
Brentford v Blackburn
Bristol City v Birmingham
Burton v Reading
Huddersfield v Cardiff
Newcastle v Barnsley
Norwich v QPR
Nottm Forest v Ipswich
Rotherham v Derby
Sheff Wed v Fulham
Wigan v Leeds
Wolves v Preston

Saturday, 13 May
Premier League
Bournemouth v Burnley
C Palace v Hull
Everton v Watford
Man City v Leicester
Middlesbrough v Southampton
Stoke v Arsenal
Sunderland v Swansea
Tottenham v Man Utd
WBA v Chelsea
West Ham v Liverpool

Sunday, 21 May
Premier League
Arsenal v Everton
Burnley v West Ham
Chelsea v Sunderland
Hull v Tottenham
Southampton v Stoke
Man Utd v C Palace
Liverpool v Middlesbrough
Leicester v Bournemouth
Swansea v WBA
Watford v Man City

SCOTTISH FIXTURES 2016–2017

Premiership, Championship, League One and League Two

Saturday, 6 August

Premiership

Kilmarnock v Motherwell
Partick v Inverness
Rangers v Hamilton
Ross Co v Dundee

Championship

Ayr v Raith
Dundee Utd v Queen of South
Dunfermline v Dumbarton
Falkirk v Hibernian
St Mirren v Morton

League One

Alloa v Peterhead
Brechin v Stenhousemuir
East Fife v Albion
Livingston v Stranraer
Queen's Park v Airdrieonians

League Two

Annan v Stirling
Arbroath v Berwick
Clyde v Montrose
Cowdenbeath v Elgin
Edinburgh v Forfar

Sunday, 7 August

Premiership

Hearts v Celtic
St Johnstone v Aberdeen

Saturday, 13 August

Premiership

Aberdeen v Hearts
Dundee v Rangers
Hamilton v Kilmarnock
Inverness v Ross Co
Motherwell v St Johnstone

Championship

Dumbarton v Dundee Utd
Hibernian v Dunfermline
Morton v Falkirk
Queen of South v Ayr
Raith v St Mirren

League One

Airdrieonians v Livingston
Albion v Brechin
Peterhead v East Fife
Stenhousemuir v Queen's Park
Stranraer v Alloa

League Two

Berwick v Annan
Elgin v Edinburgh
Forfar v Cowdenbeath
Montrose v Arbroath
Stirling v Clyde

Friday, 19 August

Premiership

Dundee v Hamilton

Saturday, 20 August

Premiership

Aberdeen v Partick
Hearts v Inverness
Rangers v Motherwell
Ross Co v Kilmarnock
St Johnstone v Celtic

Championship

Dundee Utd v Ayr
Morton v Dumbarton
Queen of South v Falkirk
Raith v Dunfermline
St Mirren v Hibernian

League One

Airdrieonians v Stranraer
Alloa v East Fife
Brechin v Queen's Park
Livingston v Stenhousemuir
Peterhead v Albion

League Two

Annan v Clyde
Berwick v Forfar
Cowdenbeath v Edinburgh
Elgin v Arbroath
Stirling v Montrose

Saturday, 27 August

Premiership

Celtic v Aberdeen
Hamilton v Ross Co
Inverness v St Johnstone
Kilmarnock v Rangers
Motherwell v Dundee
Partick v Hearts

Championship

Ayr v St Mirren
Dundee Utd v Raith
Dunfermline v Queen of South
Falkirk v Dumbarton
Hibernian v Morton

League One

Albion v Alloa
East Fife v Brechin
Queen's Park v Livingston
Stenhousemuir v Airdrieonians
Stranraer v Peterhead

League Two

Arbroath v Stirling
Clyde v Cowdenbeath
Edinburgh v Berwick
Forfar v Elgin
Montrose v Annan

Saturday, 10 September

Premiership

Aberdeen v Inverness
Celtic v Rangers
Dundee v Kilmarnock
Hearts v Hamilton
Partick v St Johnstone
Ross Co v Motherwell

Championship

Ayr v Morton
Dumbarton v Hibernian
Dunfermline v Dundee Utd
Raith v Falkirk
St Mirren v Queen of South

League One

Albion v Stenhousemuir
Alloa v Livingston
Brechin v Airdrieonians
East Fife v Stranraer
Peterhead v Queen's Park

League Two

Annan v Forfar
Berwick v Elgin
Clyde v Arbroath
Montrose v Cowdenbeath
Stirling v Edinburgh

Saturday, 17 September

Premiership
Dundee v Aberdeen
Inverness v Celtic
Kilmarnock v Partick
Motherwell v Hamilton
Rangers v Ross Co
St Johnstone v Hearts

Championship
Dumbarton v St Mirren
Falkirk v Dundee Utd
Hibernian v Ayr
Morton v Dunfermline
Queen of South v Raith

League One
Airdrieonians v East Fife
Livingston v Brechin
Queen's Park v Alloa
Stenhousemuir v Peterhead
Stranraer v Albion

League Two
Arbroath v Annan
Cowdenbeath v Berwick
Edinburgh v Montrose
Elgin v Clyde
Forfar v Stirling

Saturday, 24 September

Premiership
Aberdeen v Rangers
Celtic v Kilmarnock
Hamilton v St Johnstone
Hearts v Ross Co
Inverness v Dundee
Partick v Motherwell

Championship
Dundee Utd v Morton
Dunfermline v St Mirren
Falkirk v Ayr
Queen of South v Hibernian
Raith v Dumbarton

League One
Airdrieonians v Albion
Brechin v Peterhead
East Fife v Livingston
Queen's Park v Stranraer
Stenhousemuir v Alloa

League Two
Annan v Edinburgh
Arbroath v Cowdenbeath
Clyde v Forfar
Montrose v Berwick
Stirling v Elgin

Saturday, 1 October

Premiership
Dundee v Celtic
Hamilton v Inverness
Kilmarnock v Aberdeen
Motherwell v Hearts
Rangers v Partick
Ross Co v St Johnstone

Championship
Ayr v Dunfermline
Dumbarton v Queen of South
Hibernian v Dundee Utd
Morton v Raith
St Mirren v Falkirk

League One
Albion v Queen's Park
Alloa v Airdrieonians
East Fife v Stenhousemuir
Peterhead v Livingston
Stranraer v Brechin

League Two
Berwick v Clyde
Cowdenbeath v Stirling
Edinburgh v Arbroath
Elgin v Annan
Forfar v Montrose

Saturday, 15 October

Premiership
Aberdeen v Ross Co
Celtic v Motherwell
Hearts v Dundee
Inverness v Rangers
Partick v Hamilton
St Johnstone v Kilmarnock

Championship
Dumbarton v Ayr
Falkirk v Dunfermline
Queen of South v Morton
Raith v Hibernian
St Mirren v Dundee Utd

League One
Airdrieonians v Peterhead
Brechin v Alloa
Livingston v Albion
Queen's Park v East Fife
Stenhousemuir v Stranraer

League Two
Arbroath v Forfar
Cowdenbeath v Annan
Edinburgh v Clyde
Montrose v Elgin
Stirling v Berwick

Saturday, 22 October

Premiership
Aberdeen v Motherwell
Celtic v Hamilton
Hearts v Rangers
Inverness v Kilmarnock
Partick v Ross Co
St Johnstone v Dundee

Championship
Ayr v Queen of South
Dundee Utd v Dumbarton
Dunfermline v Hibernian
Falkirk v Raith
Morton v St Mirren

League One
Airdrieonians v Queen's Park
Albion v Peterhead
Livingston v Alloa
Stenhousemuir v Brechin
Stranraer v East Fife

Wednesday, 26 October

Premiership
Dundee v Partick
Hamilton v Aberdeen
Kilmarnock v Hearts
Motherwell v Inverness
Rangers v St Johnstone
Ross Co v Celtic

Saturday, 29 October

Premiership
Aberdeen v Celtic
Hamilton v Dundee
Inverness v Hearts
Motherwell v Ross Co
Rangers v Kilmarnock
St Johnstone v Partick

Championship
Dumbarton v Dunfermline
Dundee Utd v Falkirk
Hibernian v St Mirren
Morton v Ayr
Raith v Queen of South

League One
Alloa v Albion
Brechin v Livingston
East Fife v Airdrieonians
Peterhead v Stranraer
Queen's Park v Stenhousemuir

League Two
Annan v Montrose
Berwick v Arbroath
Clyde v Stirling
Elgin v Cowdenbeath
Forfar v Edinburgh

Saturday, 5 November

Premiership
Celtic v Inverness
Dundee v Motherwell
Hearts v St Johnstone
Kilmarnock v Hamilton
Partick v Aberdeen
Ross Co v Rangers

Championship
Ayr v Hibernian
Dunfermline v Raith
Falkirk v Morton
Queen of South v Dundee Utd
St Mirren v Dumbarton

League One
Albion v Airdrieonians
Alloa v Stenhousemuir
Livingston v East Fife
Peterhead v Brechin
Stranraer v Queen's Park

League Two
Annan v Arbroath
Berwick v Cowdenbeath
Clyde v Elgin
Montrose v Edinburgh
Stirling v Forfar

Saturday, 12 November

Championship
Dumbarton v Morton
Dundee Utd v Dunfermline
Hibernian v Falkirk
Queen of South v St Mirren
Raith v Ayr

League One
Airdrieonians v Brechin
Albion v Stranraer
East Fife v Alloa
Queen's Park v Peterhead
Stenhousemuir v Livingston

League Two
Arbroath v Clyde
Cowdenbeath v Montrose
Edinburgh v Annan
Elgin v Stirling
Forfar v Berwick

Saturday, 19 November

Premiership
Hamilton v Hearts
Inverness v Aberdeen
Kilmarnock v Celtic
Motherwell v Partick
Rangers v Dundee
St Johnstone v Ross Co

Championship
Ayr v Falkirk
Dumbarton v Raith
Hibernian v Queen of South
Morton v Dundee Utd
St Mirren v Dunfermline

League One
Airdrieonians v Alloa
Brechin v Albion
East Fife v Queen's Park
Livingston v Peterhead
Stranraer v Stenhousemuir

League Two
Annan v Elgin
Clyde v Berwick
Edinburgh v Cowdenbeath
Montrose v Forfar
Stirling v Arbroath

Saturday, 26 November

Premiership
Aberdeen v Kilmarnock
Celtic v St Johnstone
Dundee v Inverness
Hearts v Motherwell
Partick v Rangers
Ross Co v Hamilton

Saturday, 3rd December

Premiership
Hamilton v Partick
Kilmarnock v Dundee
Motherwell v Celtic
Rangers v Aberdeen
Ross Co v Hearts
St Johnstone v Inverness

Championship
Dundee Utd v Hibernian
Dunfermline v Ayr
Falkirk v St Mirren
Queen of South v Dumbarton
Raith v Morton

League One
Albion v Livingston
Alloa v Stranraer
Peterhead v Airdrieonians
Queen's Park v Brechin
Stenhousemuir v East Fife

League Two
Arbroath v Edinburgh
Berwick v Stirling
Cowdenbeath v Clyde
Elgin v Montrose
Forfar v Annan

Saturday, 10 December

Premiership
Aberdeen v St Johnstone
Dundee v Ross Co
Inverness v Hamilton
Motherwell v Kilmarnock
Partick v Celtic
Rangers v Hearts

Championship
Ayr v Dundee Utd
Dunfermline v Morton
Falkirk v Queen of South
Hibernian v Dumbarton
St Mirren v Raith

League One
Airdrieonians v Stenhousemuir
Brechin v East Fife
Peterhead v Alloa

Queen's Park v Albion
Stranraer v Livingston

League Two
Annan v Cowdenbeath
Edinburgh v Stirling
Elgin v Berwick
Forfar v Arbroath
Montrose v Clyde

Saturday, 17 December

Premiership
Celtic v Dundee
Hamilton v Rangers
Hearts v Partick
Kilmarnock v Inverness
Ross Co v Aberdeen
St Johnstone v Motherwell

Championship
Dumbarton v Falkirk
Morton v Hibernian
Queen of South v Dunfermline
Raith v Dundee Utd
St Mirren v Ayr

League One
Alloa v Queen's Park
Brechin v Stranraer
East Fife v Peterhead
Livingston v Airdrieonians
Stenhousemuir v Albion

League Two
Arbroath v Elgin
Berwick v Montrose
Clyde v Edinburgh
Cowdenbeath v Forfar
Stirling v Annan

Saturday, 24 December

Premiership
Dundee v Hearts
Hamilton v Celtic
Kilmarnock v St Johnstone
Motherwell v Aberdeen
Rangers v Inverness
Ross Co v Partick

Championship
Ayr v Dumbarton
Dundee Utd v St Mirren
Dunfermline v Falkirk
Hibernian v Raith
Morton v Queen of South

League One
Albion v East Fife
Alloa v Brechin
Livingston v Queen's Park
Stranraer v Airdrieonians

League Two
Annan v Berwick
Cowdenbeath v Arbroath
Edinburgh v Elgin
Montrose v Stirling

Monday, 26 December

League One
Peterhead v Stenhousemuir

League Two
Forfar v Clyde

Wednesday, 28 December

Premiership
Aberdeen v Hamilton
Celtic v Ross Co
Hearts v Kilmarnock
Inverness v Motherwell
Partick v Dundee
St Johnstone v Rangers

Saturday, 31 December

Premiership
Dundee v St Johnstone
Hamilton v Motherwell
Hearts v Aberdeen
Partick v Kilmarnock
Rangers v Celtic
Ross Co v Inverness

Championship
Dumbarton v Dundee Utd
Falkirk v Hibernian
Queen of South v Ayr
Raith v Dunfermline
St Mirren v Morton

League One
East Fife v Livingston
Queen's Park v Stranraer
Stenhousemuir v Alloa

League Two
Berwick v Edinburgh
Clyde v Annan
Stirling v Cowdenbeath

Monday, 2 January

League One
Airdrieonians v Albion
Brechin v Peterhead

League Two
Arbroath v Montrose
Elgin v Forfar

Saturday, 7 January

Championship
Ayr v Dunfermline
Hibernian v Dundee Utd
Morton v Dumbarton
Raith v Falkirk
St Mirren v Queen of South

League One
Albion v Brechin
East Fife v Stenhousemuir
Peterhead v Livingston
Queen's Park v Airdrieonians
Stranraer v Alloa

League Two
Annan v Forfar
Cowdenbeath v Berwick
Edinburgh v Arbroath
Montrose v Elgin
Stirling v Clyde

Saturday, 14 January

Championship
Dumbarton v Hibernian
Dundee Utd v Queen of South
Dunfermline v St Mirren
Falkirk v Ayr
Morton v Raith

League One
Airdrieonians v East Fife
Alloa v Peterhead
Brechin v Queen's Park
Livingston v Albion
Stenhousemuir v Stranraer

League Two
Arbroath v Berwick
Clyde v Montrose
Cowdenbeath v Edinburgh
Elgin v Annan
Forfar v Stirling

Saturday, 21 January

League Two
Arbroath v Annan
Berwick v Clyde
Edinburgh v Forfar
Montrose v Cowdenbeath
Stirling v Elgin

Saturday, 28 January

Premiership
Aberdeen v Dundee
Celtic v Hearts
Inverness v Partick
Kilmarnock v Ross Co
Motherwell v Rangers
St Johnstone v Hamilton

Championship
Ayr v Morton
Dunfermline v Dundee Utd
Queen of South v Hibernian
Raith v Dumbarton
St Mirren v Falkirk

League One
Albion v Alloa
East Fife v Stranraer
Livingston v Brechin
Peterhead v Queen's Park
Stenhousemuir v Airdrieonians

League Two
Annan v Stirling
Clyde v Arbroath
Elgin v Edinburgh
Forfar v Cowdenbeath
Montrose v Berwick

Wednesday, 1 February

Premiership
Celtic v Aberdeen
Dundee v Kilmarnock
Hamilton v Inverness
Hearts v Rangers
Partick v St Johnstone
Ross Co v Motherwell

Saturday, 4 February

Premiership
Aberdeen v Partick
Hamilton v Kilmarnock
Inverness v Dundee
Motherwell v Hearts
Rangers v Ross Co
St Johnstone v Celtic

Championship
Dumbarton v St Mirren
Dundee Utd v Raith
Falkirk v Dunfermline
Hibernian v Ayr
Queen of South v Morton

League One
Airdrieonians v Peterhead
Alloa v Livingston
Brechin v Stenhousemuir
Queen's Park v East Fife
Stranraer v Albion

League Two
Arbroath v Forfar
Berwick v Annan
Cowdenbeath v Elgin
Edinburgh v Clyde
Stirling v Montrose

Saturday, 11 February

League One
Alloa v East Fife
Brechin v Airdrieonians
Livingston v Stranraer
Peterhead v Albion
Stenhousemuir v Queen's Park

League Two
Annan v Edinburgh
Clyde v Cowdenbeath
Forfar v Elgin
Montrose v Arbroath
Stirling v Berwick

Saturday, 18 February

Premiership
Celtic v Motherwell
Dundee v Rangers
Hearts v Inverness
Kilmarnock v Aberdeen
Partick v Hamilton
Ross Co v St Johnstone

Championship
Dumbarton v Ayr
Dunfermline v Queen of South
Morton v Falkirk
Raith v Hibernian
St Mirren v Dundee Utd

League One
Airdrieonians v Livingston
Albion v Stenhousemuir
East Fife v Brechin
Queen's Park v Alloa
Stranraer v Peterhead

League Two
Arbroath v Stirling
Berwick v Forfar
Cowdenbeath v Annan
Edinburgh v Montrose
Elgin v Clyde

Saturday, 25 February

Premiership
Aberdeen v Ross Co
Celtic v Hamilton
Inverness v Rangers
Motherwell v Dundee
Partick v Hearts
St Johnstone v Kilmarnock

Championship
Ayr v St Mirren
Dundee Utd v Morton
Falkirk v Dumbarton
Hibernian v Dunfermline
Queen of South v Raith

League One
Albion v Queen's Park
Alloa v Airdrieonians
Livingston v Stenhousemuir
Peterhead v East Fife
Stranraer v Brechin

League Two
Annan v Clyde
Arbroath v Cowdenbeath
Berwick v Elgin
Forfar v Montrose
Stirling v Edinburgh

Wednesday, 1 March

Premiership
Dundee v Partick
Hamilton v Aberdeen
Hearts v Ross Co
Inverness v Celtic
Kilmarnock v Motherwell
Rangers v St Johnstone

Championship
Ayr v Raith
Dumbarton v Queen of South

Falkirk v Dundee Utd
Morton v Dunfermline
St Mirren v Hibernian

Saturday, 4 March

Championship
Dundee Utd v Ayr
Dunfermline v Dumbarton
Hibernian v Morton
Queen of South v Falkirk
Raith v St Mirren

League One
Airdrieonians v Stranraer
Brechin v Alloa
East Fife v Albion
Queen's Park v Livingston
Stenhousemuir v Peterhead

League Two
Clyde v Forfar
Cowdenbeath v Stirling
Edinburgh v Berwick
Elgin v Arbroath
Montrose v Annan

Saturday, 11 March

Premiership
Aberdeen v Motherwell
Celtic v Rangers
Hearts v Hamilton
Partick v Inverness
Ross Co v Kilmarnock
St Johnstone v Dundee

Championship
Ayr v Falkirk
Dumbarton v Raith
Dundee Utd v Hibernian
Morton v Queen of South
St Mirren v Dunfermline

League One
Albion v Airdrieonians
Alloa v Stenhousemuir
Livingston v East Fife
Peterhead v Brechin
Stranraer v Queen's Park

League Two
Annan v Elgin
Arbroath v Clyde
Berwick v Cowdenbeath
Forfar v Edinburgh
Montrose v Stirling

Saturday, 18 March

Premiership
Aberdeen v Hearts
Dundee v Celtic
Inverness v Ross Co
Kilmarnock v Partick
Motherwell v St Johnstone
Rangers v Hamilton

Championship
Dunfermline v Ayr
Falkirk v Morton
Hibernian v Dumbarton
Queen of South v St Mirren
Raith v Dundee Utd

League One
Airdrieonians v Stenhousemuir
Albion v Peterhead
East Fife v Alloa
Queen's Park v Brechin
Stranraer v Livingston

League Two
Berwick v Arbroath
Clyde v Edinburgh
Cowdenbeath v Montrose
Elgin v Forfar
Stirling v Annan

Saturday, 25 March

Championship
Ayr v Dumbarton
Dundee Utd v Dunfermline
Hibernian v Falkirk
Morton v St Mirren
Raith v Queen of South

League One
Alloa v Queen's Park
Brechin v East Fife
Livingston v Airdrieonians
Peterhead v Stranraer
Stenhousemuir v Albion

League Two
Annan v Cowdenbeath
Arbroath v Montrose
Clyde v Stirling
Edinburgh v Elgin
Forfar v Berwick

Saturday, 1 April

Premiership
Dundee v Aberdeen
Hamilton v St Johnstone
Hearts v Celtic
Inverness v Kilmarnock
Partick v Ross Co
Rangers v Motherwell

Championship
Dumbarton v Morton
Dunfermline v Hibernian
Falkirk v Raith
Queen of South v Dundee Utd
St Mirren v Ayr

League One
Alloa v Albion
Brechin v Livingston
East Fife v Queen's Park
Peterhead v Airdrieonians
Stranraer v Stenhousemuir

League Two
Annan v Arbroath
Cowdenbeath v Clyde
Elgin v Berwick
Montrose v Edinburgh
Stirling v Forfar

Wednesday, 5 April

Premiership
Aberdeen v Inverness
Celtic v Partick
Kilmarnock v Rangers
Motherwell v Hamilton
Ross Co v Dundee
St Johnstone v Hearts

Saturday, 8 April

Premiership
Aberdeen v Rangers
Celtic v Kilmarnock
Hamilton v Ross Co
Hearts v Dundee
Inverness v St Johnstone
Partick v Motherwell

Championship
Ayr v Queen of South
Dundee Utd v Falkirk
Dunfermline v Raith
Morton v Hibernian
St Mirren v Dumbarton

League One
Airdrieonians v Brechin
Albion v Stranraer
Livingston v Alloa
Queen's Park v Peterhead
Stenhousemuir v East Fife

League Two
Berwick v Stirling
Clyde v Annan
Edinburgh v Cowdenbeath
Elgin v Montrose
Forfar v Arbroath

Saturday, 15 April

Premiership
Dundee v Hamilton
Kilmarnock v Hearts
Motherwell v Inverness
Rangers v Partick
Ross Co v Celtic
St Johnstone v Aberdeen

Championship
Ayr v Dundee Utd
Dumbarton v Dunfermline
Falkirk v St Mirren
Hibernian v Queen of South
Raith v Morton

League One
Alloa v Brechin
East Fife v Peterhead
Queen's Park v Albion
Stenhousemuir v Livingston
Stranraer v Airdrieonians

League Two
Annan v Berwick
Arbroath v Edinburgh
Clyde v Elgin
Montrose v Forfar
Stirling v Cowdenbeath

Saturday, 22 April

Championship
Dundee Utd v St Mirren
Dunfermline v Falkirk
Hibernian v Raith
Morton v Ayr
Queen of South v Dumbarton

League One
Airdrieonians v Alloa
Albion v East Fife
Brechin v Stranraer
Livingston v Queen's Park
Peterhead v Stenhousemuir

League Two
Berwick v Montrose
Cowdenbeath v Arbroath
Edinburgh v Annan
Elgin v Stirling
Forfar v Clyde

Saturday, 29 April

Championship
Ayr v Hibernian
Dundee Utd v Dumbarton
Dunfermline v Morton
Falkirk v Queen of South
St Mirren v Raith

League One
Alloa v Stranraer
Brechin v Albion
East Fife v Airdrieonians
Livingston v Peterhead
Queen's Park v Stenhousemuir

League Two
Annan v Montrose
Arbroath v Elgin
Clyde v Berwick
Cowdenbeath v Forfar
Edinburgh v Stirling

Saturday, 6 May

Championship
Dumbarton v Falkirk
Hibernian v St Mirren
Morton v Dundee Utd
Queen of South v Dunfermline
Raith v Ayr

League One
Airdrieonians v Queen's Park
Albion v Livingston
Peterhead v Alloa
Stenhousemuir v Brechin
Stranraer v East Fife

League Two
Berwick v Edinburgh
Elgin v Cowdenbeath
Forfar v Annan
Montrose v Clyde
Stirling v Arbroath

NATIONAL LEAGUE FIXTURES 2016–2017

Premiership

Saturday, 6 August

Barrow v Aldershot
Boreham Wood v Forest Green
Bromley v Tranmere
Dag & Red v Southport
Eastleigh v Guiseley
Gateshead v Chester
Macclesfield v Torquay
Maidstone v York
North Ferriby v Braintree
Sutton v Solihull
Woking v Lincoln
Wrexham v Dover

Tuesday, 9 August

Aldershot v Maidstone
Braintree v Eastleigh
Chester v Dag & Red
Dover v Boreham Wood
Forest Green v Sutton
Guiseley v Wrexham
Lincoln v North Ferriby
Solihull v Woking
Southport v Gateshead
Torquay v Bromley
Tranmere v Barrow
York v Macclesfield

Saturday, 13 August

Aldershot v Wrexham
Braintree v Macclesfield
Chester v Maidstone
Dover v North Ferriby
Forest Green v Gateshead
Guiseley v Dag & Red
Lincoln v Sutton
Solihull v Bromley
Southport v Woking
Torquay v Barrow
Tranmere v Eastleigh
York v Boreham Wood

Tuesday, 16 August
Barrow v Chester
Boreham Wood v Tranmere
Bromley v Aldershot
Dag & Red v Lincoln
Eastleigh v Dover
Gateshead v York
Macclesfield v Southport
Maidstone v Braintree
North Ferriby v Guiseley
Sutton v Torquay
Woking v Forest Green
Wrexham v Solihull

Saturday, 20 August
Boreham Wood v Chester
Braintree v Aldershot
Bromley v Gateshead
Dover v Barrow
Forest Green v York
Lincoln v Southport
North Ferriby v Torquay
Solihull v Guiseley
Sutton v Macclesfield
Tranmere v Maidstone
Woking v Dag & Red
Wrexham v Eastleigh

Saturday, 27 August
Aldershot v North Ferriby
Barrow v Braintree
Chester v Sutton
Dag & Red v Wrexham
Eastleigh v Solihull
Gateshead v Boreham Wood
Guiseley v Bromley
Macclesfield v Lincoln
Maidstone v Forest Green
Southport v Tranmere
Torquay v Dover
York v Woking

Monday, 29 August
Boreham Wood v Maidstone
Braintree v Torquay
Bromley v Eastleigh
Dover v Aldershot
Forest Green v Southport
Lincoln v Gateshead
North Ferriby v Barrow
Solihull v Macclesfield
Sutton v Dag & Red
Tranmere v Guiseley
Woking v Chester
Wrexham v York

Saturday, 3 September
Aldershot v Tranmere
Barrow v Bromley
Chester v Forest Green
Dag & Red v Boreham Wood
Eastleigh v North Ferriby
Gateshead v Sutton
Guiseley v Braintree
Macclesfield v Woking
Maidstone v Wrexham
Southport v Dover
Torquay v Lincoln
York v Solihull

Saturday, 10 September
Aldershot v Chester
Barrow v Boreham Wood
Braintree v Gateshead
Bromley v Macclesfield
Dover v Forest Green
Eastleigh v Southport
Guiseley v Woking
North Ferriby v Maidstone
Solihull v Dag & Red
Torquay v York
Tranmere v Lincoln
Wrexham v Sutton

Tuesday, 13 September
Boreham Wood v Aldershot
Chester v Guiseley
Dag & Red v Dover
Forest Green v Eastleigh
Gateshead v North Ferriby
Lincoln v Solihull
Macclesfield v Wrexham
Maidstone v Bromley
Southport v Barrow
Sutton v Braintree
Woking v Torquay
York v Tranmere

Saturday, 17 September
Boreham Wood v Torquay
Chester v Braintree
Dag & Red v North Ferriby
Forest Green v Bromley
Gateshead v Solihull
Lincoln v Barrow
Macclesfield v Eastleigh
Maidstone v Guiseley
Southport v Aldershot
Sutton v Tranmere
Woking v Wrexham
York v Dover

Saturday, 24 September
Aldershot v Gateshead
Barrow v York
Braintree v Forest Green
Bromley v Dag & Red
Dover v Lincoln
Eastleigh v Sutton
Guiseley v Macclesfield
North Ferriby v Southport
Solihull v Boreham Wood
Torquay v Maidstone
Tranmere v Woking
Wrexham v Chester

Saturday, 1 October
Boreham Wood v Wrexham
Chester v Dover
Dag & Red v Tranmere
Forest Green v Barrow
Gateshead v Torquay
Lincoln v Braintree
Macclesfield v North Ferriby
Maidstone v Solihull
Southport v Bromley
Sutton v Guiseley
Woking v Eastleigh
York v Aldershot

Tuesday, 4 October
Aldershot v Forest Green
Barrow v Macclesfield
Braintree v Boreham Wood
Bromley v Woking
Dover v Sutton
Eastleigh v Maidstone
Guiseley v York
North Ferriby v Chester
Solihull v Southport
Torquay v Dag & Red
Tranmere v Gateshead
Wrexham v Lincoln

Saturday, 8 October
Aldershot v Solihull
Barrow v Maidstone
Braintree v York
Bromley v Lincoln
Chester v Torquay
Eastleigh v Dag & Red

Gateshead v Dover
Guiseley v Southport
Macclesfield v Boreham Wood
North Ferriby v Forest Green
Sutton v Woking
Tranmere v Wrexham

Saturday, 22nd October
Boreham Wood v North Ferriby
Dag & Red v Macclesfield
Dover v Braintree
Forest Green v Guiseley
Lincoln v Eastleigh
Maidstone v Gateshead
Solihull v Tranmere
Southport v Sutton
Torquay v Aldershot
Woking v Barrow
Wrexham v Bromley
York v Chester

Tuesday, 25 October
Bromley v Dover
Dag & Red v Aldershot
Eastleigh v Torquay
Guiseley v Gateshead
Lincoln v Boreham Wood
Macclesfield v Chester
Solihull v Forest Green
Southport v York
Sutton v Maidstone
Tranmere v North Ferriby
Woking v Braintree
Wrexham v Barrow

Saturday, 29 October
Aldershot v Guiseley
Barrow v Eastleigh
Boreham Wood v Woking
Braintree v Solihull
Chester v Lincoln
Dover v Tranmere
Forest Green v Dag & Red
Gateshead v Wrexham
Maidstone v Macclesfield
North Ferriby v Bromley
Torquay v Southport
York v Sutton

Saturday, 12 November
Bromley v Boreham Wood
Dag & Red v Gateshead
Eastleigh v York
Guiseley v Torquay
Lincoln v Aldershot
Macclesfield v Forest Green
Solihull v Dover
Southport v Maidstone
Sutton v Barrow
Tranmere v Chester
Woking v North Ferriby
Wrexham v Braintree

Saturday, 19 November
Aldershot v Macclesfield
Barrow v Solihull
Boreham Wood v Southport
Braintree v Tranmere
Chester v Bromley
Dover v Guiseley
Forest Green v Lincoln
Gateshead v Eastleigh
Maidstone v Woking
North Ferriby v Sutton
Torquay v Wrexham
York v Dag & Red

Tuesday, 22nd November
Aldershot v Eastleigh
Barrow v Guiseley
Boreham Wood v Sutton
Braintree v Bromley
Chester v Southport
Dover v Woking
Forest Green v Tranmere
Gateshead v Macclesfield
Maidstone v Dag & Red
North Ferriby v Wrexham
Torquay v Solihull
York v Lincoln

Saturday, 26 November
Bromley v York
Dag & Red v Barrow
Eastleigh v Chester
Guiseley v Boreham Wood
Lincoln v Maidstone
Macclesfield v Dover
Solihull v North Ferriby
Southport v Braintree
Sutton v Aldershot
Tranmere v Torquay
Woking v Gateshead
Wrexham v Forest Green

Tuesday, 29 November
Boreham Wood v Braintree
Chester v North Ferriby
Dag & Red v Torquay
Forest Green v Aldershot
Gateshead v Tranmere
Lincoln v Wrexham
Macclesfield v Barrow
Maidstone v Eastleigh
Southport v Solihull
Sutton v Dover
Woking v Bromley
York v Guiseley

Saturday, 3 December
Aldershot v Boreham Wood
Barrow v Southport
Braintree v Sutton
Bromley v Maidstone
Dover v Dag & Red
Eastleigh v Forest Green
Guiseley v Chester
North Ferriby v Gateshead
Solihull v Lincoln
Torquay v Woking
Tranmere v York
Wrexham v Macclesfield

Saturday, 17 December
Boreham Wood v Barrow
Chester v Aldershot
Dag & Red v Solihull
Forest Green v Dover
Gateshead v Braintree
Lincoln v Tranmere
Macclesfield v Bromley
Maidstone v North Ferriby
Southport v Eastleigh
Sutton v Wrexham
Woking v Guiseley
York v Torquay

Monday, 26 December
Aldershot v Woking
Barrow v Gateshead
Braintree v Dag & Red
Bromley v Sutton
Dover v Maidstone
Eastleigh v Boreham Wood
Guiseley v Lincoln
North Ferriby v York
Solihull v Chester
Torquay v Forest Green
Tranmere v Macclesfield
Wrexham v Southport

Sunday 1 January
Boreham Wood v Eastleigh
Chester v Solihull
Dag & Red v Braintree
Forest Green v Torquay
Gateshead v Barrow
Lincoln v Guiseley
Macclesfield v Tranmere
Maidstone v Dover
Southport v Wrexham
Sutton v Bromley
Woking v Aldershot
York v North Ferriby

Saturday, 7 January
Aldershot v Southport
Barrow v Lincoln
Braintree v Chester
Bromley v Forest Green
Dover v York
Eastleigh v Macclesfield
Guiseley v Maidstone
North Ferriby v Dag & Red
Solihull v Gateshead
Torquay v Boreham Wood
Tranmere v Sutton
Wrexham v Woking

Saturday, 21 January
Boreham Wood v Solihull
Chester v Wrexham
Dag & Red v Bromley
Forest Green v Braintree
Gateshead v Aldershot
Lincoln v Dover
Macclesfield v Guiseley
Maidstone v Torquay
Southport v North Ferriby
Sutton v Eastleigh
Woking v Tranmere
York v Barrow

Saturday, 28 January
Aldershot v York
Barrow v Forest Green
Braintree v Lincoln
Bromley v Southport
Dover v Chester
Eastleigh v Woking
Guiseley v Sutton
North Ferriby v Macclesfield
Solihull v Maidstone
Torquay v Gateshead
Tranmere v Dag & Red
Wrexham v Boreham Wood

Saturday, 4 February
Barrow v Tranmere
Boreham Wood v Dover
Bromley v Torquay
Dag & Red v Chester
Eastleigh v Braintree
Gateshead v Southport
Macclesfield v York
Maidstone v Aldershot
North Ferriby v Lincoln
Sutton v Forest Green
Woking v Solihull
Wrexham v Guiseley

Saturday, 11 February
Aldershot v Barrow
Braintree v North Ferriby
Chester v Gateshead
Dover v Wrexham
Forest Green v Boreham Wood
Guiseley v Eastleigh
Lincoln v Woking
Solihull v Sutton
Southport v Dag & Red
Torquay v Macclesfield
Tranmere v Bromley
York v Maidstone

Saturday, 18 February
Barrow v Torquay
Boreham Wood v York
Bromley v Solihull
Dag & Red v Guiseley
Eastleigh v Tranmere
Gateshead v Forest Green
Macclesfield v Braintree
Maidstone v Chester
North Ferriby v Dover
Sutton v Lincoln
Woking v Southport
Wrexham v Aldershot

Saturday, 25 February
Aldershot v Bromley
Braintree v Maidstone
Chester v Barrow
Dover v Eastleigh
Forest Green v Woking
Guiseley v North Ferriby
Lincoln v Dag & Red
Solihull v Wrexham
Southport v Macclesfield
Torquay v Sutton
Tranmere v Boreham Wood
York v Gateshead

Tuesday, 28 February
Bromley v Braintree
Dag & Red v Maidstone
Eastleigh v Aldershot
Guiseley v Barrow
Lincoln v York
Macclesfield v Gateshead
Solihull v Torquay
Southport v Chester
Sutton v Boreham Wood
Tranmere v Forest Green
Woking v Dover
Wrexham v North Ferriby

Saturday, 4 March
Aldershot v Lincoln
Barrow v Sutton
Boreham Wood v Bromley
Braintree v Wrexham
Chester v Tranmere
Dover v Solihull
Forest Green v Macclesfield
Gateshead v Dag & Red
Maidstone v Southport
North Ferriby v Woking
Torquay v Guiseley
York v Eastleigh

Saturday, 11 March
Bromley v North Ferriby
Dag & Red v Forest Green
Eastleigh v Barrow
Guiseley v Aldershot
Lincoln v Chester
Macclesfield v Maidstone
Solihull v Braintree
Southport v Torquay
Sutton v York
Tranmere v Dover
Woking v Boreham Wood
Wrexham v Gateshead

Saturday, 18 March
Aldershot v Sutton
Barrow v Dag & Red
Boreham Wood v Guiseley
Braintree v Southport
Chester v Eastleigh

Dover v Macclesfield
Forest Green v Wrexham
Gateshead v Woking
Maidstone v Lincoln
North Ferriby v Solihull
Torquay v Tranmere
York v Bromley

Tuesday, 21 March
Aldershot v Dag & Red
Barrow v Wrexham
Boreham Wood v Lincoln
Braintree v Woking
Chester v Macclesfield
Dover v Bromley
Forest Green v Solihull
Gateshead v Guiseley
Maidstone v Sutton
North Ferriby v Tranmere
Torquay v Eastleigh
York v Southport

Saturday, 25 March
Bromley v Chester
Dag & Red v York
Eastleigh v Gateshead
Guiseley v Dover
Lincoln v Forest Green
Macclesfield v Aldershot
Solihull v Barrow
Southport v Boreham Wood
Sutton v North Ferriby
Tranmere v Braintree
Woking v Maidstone
Wrexham v Torquay

Saturday, 1 April
Boreham Wood v Macclesfield
Dag & Red v Eastleigh
Dover v Gateshead
Forest Green v North Ferriby
Lincoln v Bromley
Maidstone v Barrow
Solihull v Aldershot
Southport v Guiseley
Torquay v Chester
Woking v Sutton
Wrexham v Tranmere
York v Braintree

Saturday, 8 April
Aldershot v Torquay
Barrow v Woking
Braintree v Dover
Bromley v Wrexham
Chester v York
Eastleigh v Lincoln
Gateshead v Maidstone
Guiseley v Forest Green
Macclesfield v Dag & Red
North Ferriby v Boreham Wood
Sutton v Southport
Tranmere v Solihull

Friday, 14 April
Boreham Wood v Dag & Red
Braintree v Guiseley
Bromley v Barrow
Dover v Southport
Forest Green v Chester
Lincoln v Torquay
North Ferriby v Eastleigh
Solihull v York
Sutton v Gateshead
Tranmere v Aldershot
Woking v Macclesfield
Wrexham v Maidstone

Monday, 17 April
Aldershot v Dover
Barrow v North Ferriby
Chester v Woking
Dag & Red v Sutton
Eastleigh v Bromley
Gateshead v Lincoln
Guiseley v Tranmere
Macclesfield v Solihull
Maidstone v Boreham Wood
Southport v Forest Green
Torquay v Braintree
York v Wrexham

Saturday, 22nd April
Boreham Wood v Gateshead
Braintree v Barrow
Bromley v Guiseley
Dover v Torquay
Forest Green v Maidstone
Lincoln v Macclesfield
North Ferriby v Aldershot
Solihull v Eastleigh
Sutton v Chester
Tranmere v Southport
Woking v York
Wrexham v Dag & Red

Saturday, 29 April
Aldershot v Braintree
Barrow v Dover
Chester v Boreham Wood
Dag & Red v Woking
Eastleigh v Wrexham
Gateshead v Bromley
Guiseley v Solihull
Macclesfield v Sutton
Maidstone v Tranmere
Southport v Lincoln
Torquay v North Ferriby
York v Forest Green